Dear Jim,
I had to take this sociology course as part of my program requirements, and I honestly thought (and was told by others who took it) that it was a boring, easy class, that anybody can pass.....how misleading this was! **I loved this course more than all other courses I have taken in the past.**

Cindy Gasparino/LPN/FF/EMT and soon to be RN
GATEWAY TECHNICAL COLLEGE

Greetings Mr. Henslin,
I just want you to know I scored a 95% on my first Sociology exam. Being out of school for thirty years and learning so well is such a great feeling.

Happy Trails,
Ella Lipchik
COMMUNITY COLLEGE OF ALLEGHENY COUNTY

Dear Professor Henslin,
I am emailing you because this was one of the best textbooks I have ever read. Seriously! It was very interesting and fabulously written. I enjoyed the personal perspective you gave throughout the book and the way you encourage us to "use our sociological imagination." Your book has taught me to slow down and really listen to what other people are saying (or not saying), and to look at all aspects of their life—not just their current situation.

Thank you for writing such a wonderful book! Take care!
Danielle Thompson
CAPE COD COMMUNITY COLLEGE

Hi Mr. Henslin,
I am currently taking Introduction to Sociology and **I must tell you, your book rocks!!!!**
It is the most fun I have ever had reading any textbook in my life!
Sincerely,
Kim B.
GREENVILLE TECHNICAL COLLEGE

Professor Henslin,
It is fascinating reading and the best, most organized textbook that I have ever purchased. I commend you on the excellent writing and I find myself sharing a lot of what I have read with my husband and other family members. **If there was a Pulitzer for textbook writing, you would definitely win, hands down.**
Thanks so much!

Sincerely,
Wendy Betts
SEMINOLE COMMUNITY COLLEGE

Mr. Henslin,
I just want to take the time to write and say how much I have enjoyed your book. Not only is it very simple to understand, it is also very interesting. **I was reluctant to take the class but through the text, I enjoy the class so much more.**

Sincerely,
Julissa Rodriguez
THE UNIVERSITY OF TEXAS, PAN AMERICAN

Hello Dr. Henslin,
I found myself in some of these pages, and learned to be more open-minded.
I will not forget this class or its teachings.

Thanks again,
Jesus Fuentes
VALENCIA COMMUNITY COLLEGE

SOCIOLOGY

A Down-to-Earth Approach

Edition 10

James M. Henslin

Southern Illinois University, Edwardsville

Allyn & Bacon

Boston   Columbus   Indianapolis   New York   San Francisco   Upper Saddle River
Amsterdam   Cape Town   Dubai   London   Madrid   Milan   Munich   Paris   Montreal   Toronto
Delhi   Mexico City   São Paulo   Sydney   Hong Kong   Seoul   Singapore   Taipei   Tokyo

Executive Editor: Jeff Lasser
Senior Development Editor: Leah R. Strauss
Series Editorial Assistant: Lauren Macey
Executive Marketing Manager: Kelly May
Marketing Assistant: Elaine Almquist
Editorial Production and Composition Service: The Book Company/Nesbitt Graphics, Inc.
Manufacturing Buyer: Debbie Rossi
Interior Design: Nesbitt Graphics, Inc.
Photo Researcher: Katherine S. Cebik
Cover Designer: Kristina Mose-Libon

Credits appear on pages PC1-2, which constitutes an extension of the copyright page.

Library of Congress Cataloging-in-Publication Data
Henslin, James M.
  Sociology : a down-to-earth approach / James M. Henslin. — 10th ed.
    p. cm.
  Includes bibliographical references and index.
  ISBN 978-0-205-68862-3 (hbk)
  1. Sociology. I. Title.
  HM586.H45 2009
  301—dc22
                        2009028886

10 9 8 7 6 5 4 3 2 1 CIN 13 12 11 10 09

Allyn & Bacon
is an imprint of

www.pearsonhighered.com

ISBN-10: 0-205-68862-4
ISBN-13: 978-0-205-68862-3

To my fellow sociologists, who do such creative research on social life and who communicate the sociological imagination to generations of students.

With my sincere admiration and appreciation,

Jim Henslin

What's New?

Because sociology is about social life and we live in a changing global society, an introductory sociology text must reflect the national and global changes that engulf us, as well as new sociological research. In this revision of *Sociology: A Down-to-Earth Approach,* there are over 60 new suggested readings, 350 new references, 300 new instructional photos, and 115 updated illustrations. Here are some of the new topics, illustrations, tables, and boxed features.

CHAPTER 1

Topic: Suicide patterns are so consistent that we can predict the number of whites and African Americans who will commit suicide this year—and the ways they will do so

Illustration: A collage of The Forgotten Sociologists (includes photos of Frances Perkins, Alice Paul, and eight other early female sociologists)

CHAPTER 3

Topic: A new stage in the life course: The transitional older years

Cultural Diversity box: Women Becoming Men: The Sworn Virgins

CHAPTER 4

Down-to-Earth Sociology box: Looks: The Last Frontier for Socially Acceptable Discrimination?

CHAPTER 5

Topics:
Computer-assisted self-interviewing
Case studies added to research methods

Down-to-Earth Sociology box: Gang Leader for a Day: Adventures of a Rogue Sociologist

CHAPTER 6

Topic: Replication of Milgram's obedience to authority experiments

Down-to-Earth Sociology box: The Power of Cascades: When Errors Escalate

Sociology and the New Technology box: Avatar Fantasy Life: The Fading Line of Reality

CHAPTER 7

Down-to-Earth Sociology box: Group Pranking: Escaping the Boredom of Bureaucracy?

CHAPTER 8

Topics:
Citigroup as a career criminal
On death row, those most likely to be executed are African Americans and Latinos who killed whites

Down-to-Earth Sociology box: Shaming: Making a Comeback?

Illustration: Figure 8.5 Who Gets Executed? Gender Bias in Capital Punishment

CHAPTER 9

Topics:
Wealth of the global superclass
Cracks in the global banking system

Illustration: Figure 9.5: The Distribution of the Earth's Wealth

CHAPTER 10

Topics:
Status symbols of the rich, such as $35,000 bottles of champagne
Percentage of the poor made up of each racial–ethnic group (added to Figure 10.6)

CHAPTER 11

Topic: Rwanda, the first country in the world to elect more women than men to its national legislature

Mass Media in Social Life box: Women in Iran: The Times Are Changing, Ever So Slowly

Down-to-Earth Sociology box: Women and Smoking: Let's Count the Reasons

Down-to-Earth Sociology box: Where Are the Cheerleaders? (Male, That Is)

Down-to-Earth Sociology box: Affirmative Action for Men?

CHAPTER 12

Photo essay: Ethnic work: Explorations in Cultural Identity

Topics:
Institutional discrimination: How the subprime debacle hit African Americans and Latinos
Techno Patriots

Table: Table 12.1: Race–Ethnicity and Mother/Child Deaths

CHAPTER 13

Topic: Tuti Yusupova, claiming age 128, perhaps the world's oldest living person

Down-to-Earth Sociology box: Do You Want to Live in a Nursing Home?

CHAPTER 14

Topics:
The global economic crisis
Concentration of power and the global superclass
Transcreation (products designed originally for one culture are modified to match the preferences of another culture)
Global corporate dominance: The decline of the United States and the rise of China
Bankruptcy of General Motors
Estimates of illegal immigrants incorporated into Table 14.2

Illustration: Figure 14.1: Changes in the Medium of Exchange

Cultural Diversity Around the World box: When Capitalism Fails: Consequences for All of Us

CHAPTER 15

Topic: How "handlers" in U.S. politics bypass limits to political contributions

Down-to-Earth Sociology boxes:
How Can "Good" People Torture Others?
Who Are the Suicide Terrorists? Testing Your Stereotypes

Table: Election 2008 data incorporated into Tables 15.1 and 15.2

CHAPTER 16

Topics:

The emerging equality in U.S. marriages (research by Morin and Cohn)

Ideal family size since the 1930s

The chances of divorce increase if a couple's first-born child is a girl

The "widowhood effect"

Proposition 8 in California

Illustrations:

Figure 16.1: Who Makes the Decisions at Home?

Figure 16.4: The Number of Children Americans Think Are Ideal

Sociology and the New Technology box: Rent-a-Womb: "How Much for Your Uterus?"

CHAPTER 17

Topics:

Japan's low birth rate is leading to easier admission to college

Cheating (reporting fake data) by high school administrators and how to solve this problem

Using avatars in distance learning

CHAPTER 18

Opening vignette: Based on the Texas raid on Yearning for Zion Ranch

Through the Author's Lens: Holy Week in Spain

Topic: The pope launched his own YouTube channel

CHAPTER 19

Topics:

Ghostwriting medical research

Harvard medical students protesting their professors' ties with drug companies

Nicotine deaths increasing in China

The future of medicine

The Veterans' Administration is using down-and-out veterans to test drugs.

Thinking Critically section: How Will Your Lifestyle Affect Your Health?

Sociology and the New Technology Box: Making Virtual House Calls: Visiting Your Doctor Online

CHAPTER 20

Topics:

Biofuels as a threat to the world food supply

New research indicating that gentrification draws middle-class minorities to the neighborhood and improves their incomes

The end of "white flight"

Critique of Gans's typology of urban dwellers

Change in immigration because of the economic crisis

Illustrations:

Figure 20.8: Country of Origin of Unauthorized Immigrants to the United States

Figure 20.11: The 20 Largest Cities in the World

Table: Table 20.3: Urbanization and Industrial Development

CHAPTER 21

Topic: The assassination of George Tiller, doctor who did late term abortions

CHAPTER 22

Opening vignette about the international market in body parts

Topics:

Russia's threat of a nuclear attack on Poland

China's identity cards that include reproductive history to enforce its "one child" policy

China now emits more carbon dioxide than does the United States

Sociology and the New Technology box: From Electronic Toy to Political Weapon: Twittering in the Digital Age

Brief Contents

Contents

PART I The Sociological Perspective

CHAPTER 3
Socialization   62

CHAPTER 4
Social Structure and Social Interaction 94

Through the Author's Lens

When a Tornado Strikes
Social Organization Following a Natural Disaster

As I was watching television on March 20, 2003, I heard a report that a tornado had hit Camilla, Georgia. "Like a big lawn mower," the report said, it had cut a path of destruction through this little town. In its fury, the tornado had left behind six dead and about 200 injured. (pages 120–121)

CHAPTER 5
How Sociologists Do Research 124

PART II Social Groups and Social Control

CHAPTER 6
Societies to Social Networks   146

CHAPTER 7
Bureaucracy and Formal Organizations   172

CHAPTER 8
Deviance and Social Control   196

PART III Social Inequality

CHAPTER 9
Global Stratification   228

Through the Author's Lens

The Dump People
Working and Living and Playing in the City Dump
of Phnom Penh, Cambodia

I went to Phnom Penh, the capital of Cambodia, to inspect orphanages, to see how well the children were being cared for. While there, I was told about people who live in the city dump. *Live* there? I could hardly believe my ears. I knew that people made their living by picking scraps from the city dump, but I didn't know they actually lived among the garbage. This I had to see for myself. (pages 250–251)

CHAPTER 10
Social Class in the United States   260

CHAPTER 11
Sex and Gender   292

Through the Author's Lens

Work and Gender
Women at work in India

Traveling through India was both a pleasure and an eye-opening experience. The country is incredibly diverse, the people friendly, and the land culturally rich. For this photo essay, wherever I went—whether city, village, or countryside—I took photos of women at work. (pages 304–305)

CHAPTER 12
Race and Ethnicity   328

CHAPTER 13
The Elderly   366

PART IV Social Institutions

CHAPTER 14
The Economy 396

Through the Author's Lens

Small Town USA
Struggling to Survive

All across the nation, small towns are struggling to survive. Parents and town officials are concerned because so few young adults remain in their home town. There is little to keep them there, and when they graduate from high school, most move to the city. With young people leaving and old ones dying, the small towns are shriveling. I took most of these photos in the South. (pages 412–413)

CHAPTER 17
Education 496

CHAPTER 18
Religion 522

Through the Author's Lens

Holy Week in Spain

Taking these photos of Holy Week being observed in Spain—in Malaga, a capital city, and Almuñecar, a small town in Granada—was both enjoyable and a challenge. The rituals here, like those of religious groups everywhere, are designed to evoke memories, create awe, inspire reverence, and stimulate social solidarity. (pages 532–533)

CHAPTER 19
Medicine and Health   556

PART V Social Change

CHAPTER 20
Population and Urbanization 590

CHAPTER 21
Collective Behavior and Social Movements 624

Through the Author's Lens

A Walk Through El Tiro in Medellin, Colombia

One of the most significant changes in our time is the global rush of poor, rural people to the cities of the Least Industrialized Nations. Some of these settlements are dangerous. I was fortunate to be escorted by an insider through this section of Medellin, Colombia. (pages 606–607)

CHAPTER 22
Social Change and the Environment   650

Special Features

Down-to-Earth Sociology
Who Are the Suicide Terrorists?
Testing Your Stereotypes

What does a suicide bomber look like? Iraqi police arrested this girl, who was wearing an explosives vest.

We carry a lot of untested ideas around in our heads, and we use those ideas to make sense out of our experiences. When something hap-

Cultural Diversity in the United States
Unanticipated Public Sociology:
Studying Job Discrimination

Cultural Diversity around the World
Women Becoming Men: The Sworn Virgins

MASS MEDIA In SOCIAL LIFE
School Shootings: Exploring a Myth

The media sprinkle their reports of school shootings with such dramatic phrases as "alarming proportions," "outbreak of violence," and "out of control." They give us the impression that wackos walk our hallways, ready to spray our schools with gunfire. Parents used to consider schools safe havens, but no longer. Those naïve thoughts have been shattered by the bullets that have ripped

Thinking CRITICALLY

SOCIOLOGY and the NEW TECHNOLOGY

From Electronic Toy to Political Weapon: Twittering in the Digital Age

Why would anyone want to Twitter? Do you really want to know the up-to-the-minute and by-the-minute blow-by-blow detailed activities and thoughts of your friends? All those instantaneous, brief messages (up to 140 characters, like

Guide to Social Maps

To the Student...
from the Author

WELCOME TO SOCIOLOGY! I've loved sociology since I was in my teens, and I hope you enjoy it, too. Sociology is fascinating because it is about human behavior, and many of us find that it holds the key to understanding social life.

If you like to watch people and try to figure out why they do what they do, you will like sociology. Sociology pries open the doors of society so you can see what goes on behind them. *Sociology: A Down-to-Earth Approach* stresses how profoundly our society and the groups to which we belong influence us. Social class, for example, sets us on a particular path in life. For some, the path leads to more education, more interesting jobs, higher income, and better health, but for others it leads to dropping out of school, dead-end jobs, poverty, and even a higher risk of illness and disease. These paths are so significant that they affect our chances of making it to our first birthday, as well as of getting in trouble with the police. They even influence our satisfaction in marriage, the number of children we will have—and whether or not we will read this book in the first place.

When I took my first course in sociology, I was "hooked." Seeing how marvelously my life had been affected by these larger social influences opened my eyes to a new world, one that has been fascinating to explore. I hope that you will have this experience, too.

From how people become homeless to how they become presidents, from why people commit suicide to why women are discriminated against in every society around the world—all are part of sociology. This breadth, in fact, is what makes sociology so intriguing. We can place the sociological lens on broad features of society, such as social class, gender, and race–ethnicity, and then immediately turn our focus on the smaller, more intimate level. If we look at two people interacting—whether quarreling or kissing—we see how these broad features of society are being played out in their lives.

We aren't born with instincts. Nor do we come into this world with preconceived notions of what life should be like. At birth, we have no concepts of race–ethnicity, gender, age, or social class. We have no idea, for example, that people "ought" to act in certain ways because they are male or female. Yet we all learn such things as we grow up in our society. Uncovering the "hows" and the "whys" of this process is also part of what makes sociology so fascinating.

One of sociology's many pleasures is that as we study life in groups (which can be taken as a definition of sociology), whether those groups are in some far-off part of the world or in some nearby corner of our own society, we gain new insights into who we are and how we got that way. As we see how *their* customs affect *them,* the effects of our own society on us become more visible.

This book, then, can be part of an intellectual adventure, for it can lead you to a new way of looking at your social world—and in the process, help you to better understand both society and yourself.

I wish you the very best in college—and in your career afterward. It is my sincere desire that *Sociology: A Down-to-Earth Approach* will contribute to that success.

James M. Henslin
Department of Sociology
Southern Illinois University, Edwardsville

P.S. I enjoy communicating with students, so feel free to comment on your experiences with this text. Because I travel a lot, it is best to reach me by e-mail: henslin@aol.com

To the Instructor...
from the Author

REMEMBER WHEN YOU FIRST GOT "HOOKED" on sociology, how the windows of perception opened as you began to see life-in-society through the sociological perspective? For most of us, this was an eye-opening experience. This text is designed to open those windows onto social life, so students can see clearly the vital effects of group membership on their lives. Although few students will get into what Peter Berger calls "the passion of sociology," we at least can provide them the opportunity.

To study sociology is to embark on a fascinating process of discovery. We can compare sociology to a huge jigsaw puzzle. Only gradually do we see how the intricate pieces fit together. As we begin to see these interconnections, our perspective changes as we shift our eyes from the many small, disjointed pieces to the whole that is being formed. Of all the endeavors we could have entered, we chose sociology because of the ways in which it joins the "pieces" of society together and the challenges it poses to "ordinary" thinking. To share with students this process of awareness and discovery called the sociological perspective is our privilege.

Chapter 2

Culture

Chapter 14

The Economy

As instructors of sociology, we have set ambitious goals for ourselves: to teach both social structure and social interaction and to introduce students to the sociological literature—both the classic theorists and contemporary research. As we accomplish this, we would also like to enliven the classroom, encourage critical thinking, and stimulate our students' sociological imagination. Although formidable, these goals are attainable, and this book is designed to help you reach them. Based on many years of frontline (classroom) experience, its subtitle, *A Down-to-Earth Approach*, was not proposed lightly. My goal is to share the fascination of sociology with students and thereby make your teaching more rewarding.

Over the years, I have found the introductory course especially enjoyable. It is singularly satisfying to see students' faces light up as they begin to see how separate pieces of their world fit together. It is a pleasure to watch them gain insight into how their social experiences give shape to even their innermost desires. This is precisely what this text is designed to do—to stimulate your students' sociological imagination so they can better perceive how the "pieces" of society fit together—and what this means for their own lives.

Filled with examples from around the world as well as from our own society, this text helps to make today's multicultural, global society come alive for students. From learning how the international elite carve up global markets to studying the intimacy of friendship and marriage, students can see how sociology is the key to explaining contemporary life—and their own place in it.

In short, this text is designed to make your teaching easier. There simply is no justification for students to have to wade through cumbersome approaches to sociology. I am firmly convinced that the introduction to sociology should be enjoyable and that the introductory textbook can be an essential tool in sharing the discovery of sociology with students.

THE ORGANIZATION OF THIS TEXT

The text is laid out in five parts. Part I focuses on the sociological perspective, which is introduced in the first chapter. We then look at how culture influences us (Chapter 2), examine socialization (Chapter 3), and compare macrosociology and microsociology (Chapter 4). After this, we look at how sociologists do research (Chapter 5). Placing research methods in the fifth chapter does not follow the usual sequence, but doing so allows students to first become immersed in the captivating findings of sociology—then, after their interest is awakened, they learn how sociologists gather their data. This works very well, but if you prefer the more traditional order, simply teach this chapter as the second chapter. No content will be affected.

Part II, which focuses on groups and social control, adds to the students' understanding of how far-reaching society's influence is—how group membership penetrates even their thinking, attitudes, and orientations to life. We first examine the different types of groups that have such profound influences on us and then look at the fascinating area of group dynamics (Chapter 6). We then examine the impact of bureaucracy and formal organizations (Chapter 7). After this, we focus on how groups "keep us in line" and sanction those who violate their norms (Chapter 8).

In Part III, we turn our focus on social inequality, examining how it pervades society and how it has an impact on our own lives. Because social stratification is so significant, I have written two chapters on this topic. The first (Chapter 9), with its global focus, presents an overview of the principles of stratification. The second (Chapter 10), with its emphasis on social class, focuses on stratification in U.S. society. After establishing this broader context of social stratification, we examine gender, the most global of the inequalities (Chapter 11). Then we focus on inequalities of race and ethnicity (Chapter 12) and those of age (Chapter 13).

Part IV helps students to become more aware of how social institutions encompass their lives. We first look at economy, the social institution that has become dominant in U.S. society (Chapter 14) and then at politics, our second overarching social institution (Chapter 15). We then place the focus on marriage and family (Chapter 16), and education (Chapter 17). After this, we look at the significance of religion (Chapter 18) and, finally, that of medicine (Chapter 19). One of the emphases in this part of the book is how our social institutions are changing and how their changes, in turn, have an impact on our own lives.

With its focus on broad social change, Part V provides an appropriate conclusion for the book. Here we examine why our world is changing so rapidly, as well as catch a glimpse of what is yet to come. We first analyze trends in population and urbanization, those sweeping forces that affect our lives so significantly but that ordinarily remain below our level of awareness (Chapter 20). Our focus on collective behavior and social movements (Chapter 21) and social change and the environment (Chapter 22) takes us to the "cutting edge" of the vital changes that engulf us all.

THEMES AND FEATURES

Six central themes run throughout this text: down-to-earth sociology, globalization, cultural diversity, critical thinking, the new technology, and the influence of the mass media on our lives. For each of these themes, except globalization, which is incorporated in several of the others, I have written a series of boxes. These boxed features are one of my favorite components of the book. They are especially useful for introducing the controversial topics that make sociology such a lively activity.

Let's look at these six themes.

Down-to-Earth Sociology

As many years of teaching have shown me, all too often textbooks are written to appeal to the adopters of texts rather than to the students who must learn from them. Therefore, a central concern in writing this book has been to present sociology in a way that not only facilitates understanding but also shares its excitement. During the course of writing other texts, I often have been told that my explanations and writing style are "down-to-earth," or accessible and inviting to students—so much so that I chose this phrase as the book's subtitle. The term is also featured in my introductory reader, *Down-to-Earth Sociology: Introductory Readings,* now in its 15th edition (New York: The Free Press, 2010).

This first theme is highlighted by a series of boxed features that explore sociological processes that underlie everyday life. The topics that we review in these *Down-to-Earth Sociology* boxes are highly diverse. Here are some of them.

- the experiences of W. E. B. Du Bois in studying U.S. race relations (Chapter 1)

- the relationship between heredity and environment (Chapter 3)

- how football can help us understand social structure (Chapter 4)

- beauty and success (Chapter 4)

- improper and fraudulent social research (Chapter 5)

- the power of cascades (Chapter 6)

- the McDonaldization of society (Chapter 7)

- serial killers (Chapter 8)

- the lifestyles of the super-rich (Chapter 10)

- cold-hearted surgeons and their women victims (Chapter 11)

- the taken-for-granted privileges attached to being white (Chapter 12)

- gender roles among the elderly (Chapter 13)

- women navigating male-dominated corporations (Chapter 14)

- the life of child soldiers (Chapter 15)

- how cohabitation means different things to people—and how this affects their chances of marriage (Chapter 16)

- homeschooling (Chapter 17)

- terrorism in the name of God (Chapter 18)

- the international black market in human body parts (Chapter 19)

- how tsunamis can help us to understand world population growth (Chapter 20)

- mass hysteria (Chapter 21)

- the coming Star Wars (Chapter 22)

This first theme is actually a hallmark of the text, as my goal is to make sociology "down to earth." To help students grasp the fascination of sociology, I continuously stress sociology's relevance to their lives. To reinforce this theme, I avoid unnecessary jargon and use concise explanations and clear and simple (but not reductive) language. I also use student-relevant examples to illustrate key concepts, and I base several of the chapters' opening vignettes on my own experiences in exploring social life. That this goal of sharing sociology's fascination is being reached is evident from the many comments I receive from instructors and students alike that the text helps make sociology "come alive."

Globalization

In the second theme, globalization, we explore the impact of global issues on our lives and on the lives of people around the world. All of us are feeling the effects of an increasingly powerful and encompassing global economy, one that intertwines the fates of nations. The globalization of capitalism influences the kinds of skills and knowledge we need, the types of work available to us—and whether work is available at all. Globalization also underlies the costs of the goods and services we consume and whether our country is at war or peace—or in some uncharted middle ground between the two. In addition to the strong emphasis on global issues that runs throughout this text, I have written a separate chapter on global stratification (Chapter 9). I have also featured global issues in the chapters on social institutions and the final chapters on social change: population, urbanization, social movements, and the environment.

What occurs in Russia, Germany, and China, as well as in much smaller nations such as Afghanistan and Iraq, has far-reaching consequences on our own lives. Consequently, in addition to the global focus that runs throughout the text, the next theme, cultural diversity, also has a strong global emphasis.

Cultural Diversity around the World and in the United States

The third theme, cultural diversity, has two primary emphases. The first is cultural diversity around the world. Gaining an understanding of how social life is "done" in other parts of the world often challenges our taken-for-granted assumptions about social life. At times, when we learn about other cultures, we gain an appreciation for the life of other peoples; at other times, we may be shocked or even disgusted at some aspect of another group's way of life (such as female circumcision) and come away with a renewed with of our own customs.

To highlight this first subtheme, I have written a series with boxes called **Cultural Diversity around the World.** Among the topics with this subtheme are

- food customs that shock people from different cultures (Chapter 2)
- where virgins become men (Chapter 3)
- where inmates can work outside of the prison—and have guns (Chapter 8)
- human sexuality in Mexico and Kenya (Chapter 8)
- selling brides in China (Chapter 11)

- female circumcision in Africa (Chapter 11)
- the life of child workers (Chapter 14)
- China's new capitalism (Chapter 14)
- the globalization of capitalism (Chapter 14)
- love and arranged marriage in India (Chapter 16)
- female infanticide in China and India (Chapter 20)
- the destruction of the rain forests and indigenous peoples of Brazil (Chapter 22)

In the second subtheme, **Cultural Diversity in the United States,** we examine groups that make up the fascinating array of people who form the U.S. population. The boxes I have written with this subtheme review such topics as

- the Hmong's culture shock when they arrived in the United States (Chapter 2)
- the controversy over the use of Spanish or English (Chapter 2)
- the terms that people choose to refer to their own race–ethnicity (Chapter 2)
- how the Amish resist social change (Chapter 4)
- the upward social mobility of African Americans (Chapter 10)

- affirmative action for men (Chapter 11)
- how Tiger Woods represents a changing racial–ethnic identity (Chapter 12)
- the author's travels with a Mexican who transports undocumented workers to the U.S. border (Chapter 12)
- Pentecostalism among Latino immigrants (Chapter 18)
- human heads, animal sacrifices, and religious freedom (Chapter 18)
- our shifting racial–ethnic mix (Chapter 20)

Seeing that there are so many ways of "doing" social life can remove some of our cultural smugness, making us more aware of how arbitrary our own customs are—and how our taken-for-granted ways of thinking are rooted in culture. The stimulating contexts of these contrasts can help students develop their sociological imagination. They encourage students to see connections among key sociological concepts such as culture, socialization, norms, race–ethnicity, gender, and social class. As your students' sociological imagination grows, they can attain a new perspective on their experiences in their own corners of life—and a better understanding of the social structure of U.S. society.

Critical Thinking

In our fourth theme, critical thinking, we focus on controversial social issues, inviting students to examine various sides of those issues. In these sections, titled **Thinking Critically,** I present objective, fair portrayals of positions and do not take a side—although occasionally I do play the "devil's advocate" in the questions that close each of the topics. Like the boxed features, these sections can enliven your classroom with a vibrant exchange of ideas. Among the issues addressed are

- whether rapists are sick (Chapter 5)

- our tendency to conform to evil authority, as uncovered by the Milgram experiments (Chapter 6)

- the three-strikes-and-you're-out laws (Chapter 8)

- bounties paid to kill homeless children in Brazil (Chapter 9)

- the welfare debate (Chapter 10)

- biology versus culture (Chapter 11)

- whether it is desirable to live as long as Methuselah (Chapter 13)

- medically assisted suicide (Chapter 19)

- abortion as a social movement (Chapter 21)

These *Thinking Critically* sections are based on controversial social issues that either affect the student's own life or focus on topics that have intrinsic interest for students. Because of their controversial nature, these sections stimulate both critical thinking and lively class discussions. These sections also provide provocative topics for in-class debates and small discussion groups, effective ways to enliven a class and present sociological ideas. In the Instructor's Manual, I describe the nuts and bolts of using samll groups in the classroom.

Sociology and the New Technology

The fifth theme, sociology and the new technology, explores an aspect of social life that has come to be central in our lives. We welcome these new technological tools, for they help us to be more efficient at performing our daily tasks, from making a living to communicating with others—whether those people are nearby or on the other side of the globe. The significance of our new technology, however, extends far beyond the tools and the ease and efficiency they bring to our lives. The new technology is better envisioned as a social revolution that will leave few aspects of our lives untouched. Its effects are so profound that it even changes the ways we view life.

This theme is introduced in Chapter 2, where technology is defined and presented as a major aspect of culture. The impact of technology is then discussed throughout the text. Examples include how technology is related to cultural change (Chapter 2), the control of workers (Chapter 7), the maintenance of global stratification (Chapter 9), social class (Chapter 10), and social inequality in early human history (Chapter 14). We also look at the impact of technology on dating (Chapter 16), education (Chapter 17), religion (Chapter 18), and medicine (Chapter 19). The final chapter (Chapter 22), "Social Change and the Environment," concludes the book with a focus on this theme.

To highlight this theme, I have written a series of boxes called **Sociology and the New Technology.** In these boxes, we explore how technology affects our lives as it changes society. We examine how technology

- blurs the distinction between reality and fantasy (Chapter 6)

- is used to avoid work ("cyberloafing") (Chapter 7)

- is changing the way people find mates (Chapter 16)

- is aiding—and complicating—reproduction (Chapter 16)

- is changing education through distance learning (Chapter 17)

- has created controversy about rationing medical care (Chapter 19)

- is creating a new form of intimacy (Chapter 22)

The Mass Media and Social Life

In the sixth theme, we stress how the mass media affect our behavior and permeate our thinking. We consider how the media penetrate our consciousness to such a degree that they even influence how we perceive our own bodies. As your students consider this theme, they may begin to grasp how the mass media shape their attitudes. If so, they will come to view the mass media in a different light, which should further stimulate their sociological imagination.

To make this theme more prominent for students, I have written a series of boxed features called **Mass Media in Social Life.** Among these are

- an analysis of why Native Americans like Westerns even though Indians are usually portrayed as victims (Chapter 2)

- the presentation of gender in computer games (Chapter 3)

- the worship of thinness—and how this affects our own body images (Chapter 4)

- the issue of censoring high-tech pornography (Chapter 8)

- the reemergence of slavery in today's world (Chapter 9)

- the slowly changing status of women in Iran (Chapter 11)

- the pros and cons of electronic voting (Chapter 15)

- God on the Net (Chapter 18)

New Topics and Boxes

Because sociology is about social life and we live in a rapidly changing global society, the topics of an introductory text must reflect the national and global changes that engulf us, as well as new sociological research. For a quick overview of the new topics and boxes in this edition, see *What's New* on page iv.

Visual Presentations of Sociology

Through the Author's Lens Using this format, students are able to look over my shoulder as I experience other cultures or explore aspects of this one. These *six* photo essays should expand your students' sociological imagination and open their minds to other ways of doing social life, as well as stimulate thought-provoking class discussion.

Holy Week in Spain is new to this edition. I was fortunate to be able to photograph processions in two cities, Malaga, a provincial capital, and Almuñecar, a smaller city of Granada. Spain has a Roman Catholic heritage so deep that the *La Asunción de María* (The Assumption of Mary) is a national holiday. City streets carry such names as (translated) Conception, Piety, Humility, Calvary, Crucifixion, The Blessed Virgin. In large and small towns throughout Spain, elaborate processions during Holy Week feature *tronos* that depict the biblical account of Jesus' suffering, death, and resurrection. As you will see in this photo essay, these events have a decidedly Spanish flavor.

I was also allowed to photograph the preparations for a procession, so this essay also includes some "behind-the-scenes" photos. During the processions, the participants walk slowly for one or two minutes; then because of the weight of the *tronos*, they rest for one or two minutes. This process repeats for about six hours. As you will see, some of the most interesting activities occur during the rest periods (Chapter 18).

When a Tornado Strikes: Social Organization Following a Natural Disaster When a tornado hit a small town just hours from where I lived, I photographed the aftermath of the disaster. The police let me in to view the neighborhood where the tornado had struck, destroying homes and killing several people. I was impressed by how quickly people were putting their lives back together, the topic of this photo essay (Chapter 4).

The Dump People of Phnom Penh, Cambodia Among the culture shocks I experienced in Cambodia was not to discover that people scavenge at Phnom Penh's huge city dump—this I knew about—but that they also live there. With the aid of an interpreter, I was able to interview these people, as well as photograph them as they went about their everyday lives. An entire community lives in the city dump, complete with restaurants amidst the smoke and piles of garbage. This photo essay reveals not just these people's activities but also their social organization (Chapter 9).

Work and Gender: Women at Work in India   As I traveled in India, I took photos of women at work in public places. The more I traveled in this country and the more photos I took, the more insight I gained into gender relations. Despite the general dominance of men in India, women's worlds are far from limited to family and home. Women are found at work throughout the society. What is even more remarkable is how vastly different "women's work" is in India than it is in the United States. This, too, is an intellectually provocative photo essay (Chapter 11).

Small Town USA: Struggling to Survive   To take the photos for this essay, I went off the beaten path. On a road trip from California to Florida, instead of following the interstates, I followed those "little black lines" on the map. They took me to out-of-the-way places that the national transportation system has bypassed. Many of these little towns are putting on a valiant face as they struggle to survive, but, as the photos show, the struggle is apparent, and, in some cases, so are the scars (Chapter 14).

A Walk Through El Tiro in Medellin, Colombia   One of the most significant social changes in the world is taking place in the Least Industrialized Nations. There, in the search for a better life, people are abandoning rural areas. Fleeing poverty, they are flocking to the cities, only to be greeted with more poverty. Some of these settlements of the new urban poor are dangerous. I was fortunate to be escorted by an insider through a section of Medellin, Colombia, that is controlled by gangs (Chapter 20).

Other Photo Essays   I am very pleased with the new photo essay on ethnic work in Chapter 12, as it helps student see that ethnicity doesn't "just happen." To help students better understand subcultures, I have retained the photo essay in Chapter 2. Because these photo essays consist of photos taken by others, they are not a part of the series, *Through the Author's Lens*. I think you will appreciate the understanding they can give your students.

Photo Collages   Because sociology lends itself so well to photographic illustrations, this text also includes photo collages. I am very pleased with the new one in Chapter 1 that features some of the many women who became sociologists in earlier generations, as these women have largely gone unacknowledged as sociologists. In Chapter 2, students can catch a glimpse of the fascinating variety that goes into the cultural relativity of beauty. The collage in Chapter 6 illustrates categories, aggregates, and primary and secondary groups, concepts that students sometimes wrestle to distinguish. The photo collage in Chapter 11 lets students see how differently gender is portrayed in different cultures.

Other Photos by the Author   Sprinkled throughout the text are photos that I took in Austria, Cambodia, India, and Latvia. These photos illustrate sociological principles and topics better than photos available from commercial sources. As an example, while in the United States, I received a report about a feral child who had been discovered living with monkeys and who had been taken to an orphanage in Cambodia. The possibility of photographing and interviewing that child was one of the reasons that I went to Cambodia. That particular photo is on page 64. Another of my favorites is on page 198.

Other Special Pedagogical Features

In addition to chapter summaries and reviews, key terms, and a comprehensive glossary, I have included several special features to aid students in learning sociology. **In Sum** sections help students review important points within the chapter before going on to new sections. I have also developed a series of **Social Maps,** which illustrate how social conditions vary by geography.

Chapter-Opening Vignettes These accounts feature down-to-earth illustrations of a major aspect of each chapter's content. Several of these are based on my research with the homeless, the time I spent with them on the streets and slept in their shelters (Chapters 1, 10, and 19). Others recount my travels in Africa (Chapters 2 and 11) and Mexico (Chapter 20). I also share my experiences when I spent a night with street people at DuPont Circle in Washington, D.C. (Chapter 4). For other vignettes, I use current and historical events (Chapters 5, 7, 9, 12, 17, 18, 21, and 22), composite accounts (Chapters 14 and 16), classical studies in the social sciences (Chapters 3, 8, and 13), and even scenes from novels (Chapters 6 and 15). Many students have told their instructors that they find these vignettes compelling, that they stimulate interest in the chapter.

Thinking Critically About the Chapters　I close each chapter with critical thinking questions. Each question focuses on a major feature of the chapter, asking students to reflect on and consider some issue. Many of the questions ask the students to apply sociological findings and principles to their own lives.

On Sources Sociological data are found in a wide variety of sources, and this text reflects that variety. Cited throughout this text are standard journals such as the *American Journal of Sociology, Social Problems, American Sociological Review,* and *Journal of Marriage and Family,* as well as more esoteric journals such as the *Bulletin of the History of Medicine, Chronobiology International,* and *Western Journal of Black Studies.* I have also drawn heavily from standard news sources, especially the *New York Times* and the *Wall Street Journal,* as well as more unusual sources such as *El País.* In addition, I cite unpublished papers by sociologists.

Acknowledgments

The gratifying response to earlier editions indicates that my efforts at making sociology down to earth have succeeded. The years that have gone into writing this text are a culmination of the many more years that preceded its writing—from graduate school to that equally demanding endeavor known as classroom teaching. No text, of course, comes solely from its author. Although I am responsible for the final words on the printed page, I have received excellent feedback from instructors who have taught from the first nine editions. I am especially grateful to

Reviewers of the First through Eighth Editions

Francis O. Adeola, *University of New Orleans*

Brian W. Agnitsch, *Marshalltown Community College*

Sandra L. Albrecht, *The University of Kansas*

Christina Alexander, *Linfield College*

Richard Alman, *Sierra College*

Gabriel C. Alvarez, *Duquesne University*

Kenneth Ambrose, *Marshall University*

Alberto Arroyo, *Baldwin–Wallace College*

Karren Baird-Olsen, *Kansas State University*

Rafael Balderrama, *University of Texas—Pan American*

Linda Barbera-Stein, *The University of Illinois*

Brenda Blackburn, *California State University. Fullerton*

Ronnie J. Booxbaum, *Greenfield Community College*

Cecil D. Bradfield, *James Madison University*

Karen Bradley, *Central Missouri State University*

Francis Broouer, *Worcester State College*

Valerie S. Brown, *Cuyahoga Community College*

Sandi Brunette-Hill, *Carrol College*

Richard Brunk, *Francis Marion University*

Karen Bullock, *Salem State College*

Allison R. Camelot, *California State University at Fullerton*

Paul Ciccantell, *Kansas State University*

John K. Cochran, *The University of Oklahoma*

James M. Cook, *Duke University*

Joan Cook-Zimmern, *College of Saint Mary*

Larry Curiel, *Cypress College*

Russell L. Curtis, *University of Houston*

John Darling, *University of Pittsburgh—Johnstown*

Ray Darville, *Stephen F. Austin State University*

Jim David, *Butler County Community College*

Nanette J. Davis, *Portland State University*

Vincent Davis, *Mt. Hood Community College*

Lynda Dodgen, *North Harris Community College*

Terry Dougherty, *Portland State University*

Marlese Durr, *Wright State University*

Helen R. Ebaugh, *University of Houston*

Obi N. Ebbe, *State University of New York—Brockport*

Cy Edwards, Chair, *Cypress Community College*

John Ehle, *Northern Virginia Community College*

Morten Ender, *U.S. Military Academy*

Rebecca Susan Fahrlander, *Bellevue University*

Louis J. Finkle, *Horry-Georgetown Technical College*

Nicole T. Flynn, *University of South Alabama*

Lorna E. Forster, *Clinton Community College*

David O. Friedrichs, *University of Scranton*

Bruce Friesen, *Kent State University—Stark*

Lada Gibson-Shreve, *Stark State College*

Norman Goodman, *State University of New York—Stony Brook*

Rosalind Gottfried, *San Joaquin Delta College*

G. Kathleen Grant, *The University of Findlay*

Bill Grisby, *University of Northern Colorado*

Ramon Guerra, *University of Texas—Pan American*

Remi Hajjar, *U.S. Military Academy*

Donald W. Hastings, *The University of Tennessee—Knoxville*

Lillian O. Holloman, *Prince George's Community College*

Michael Hoover, *Missouri Western State College*

Howard R. Housen, *Broward Community College*

James H. Huber, *Bloomsburg University*

Erwin Hummel, *Portland State University*

Charles E. Hurst, *The College of Wooster*

Nita Jackson, *Butler County Community College*

Jennifer A. Johnson, *Germanna Community College*

Kathleen R. Johnson, *Keene State College*

Tammy Jolley, *University of Arkansas Community College at Batesville*

David Jones, *Plymouth State College*

Arunas Juska, *East Carolina University*

Ali Kamali, *Missouri Western State College*

Irwin Kantor, *Middlesex County College*

Mark Kassop, *Bergen Community College*

Myles Kelleher, *Bucks County Community College*

Mary E. Kelly, *Central Missouri State University*

Alice Abel Kemp, *University of New Orleans*

Diana Kendall, *Austin Community College*

Gary Kiger, *Utah State University*

Gene W. Kilpatrick, *University of Maine—Presque Isle*

Jerome R. Koch, *Texas Tech University*

Joseph A. Kotarba, *University of Houston*

Michele Lee Kozimor-King, *Pennsylvania State University*

Darina Lepadatu, *Kennesaw State University*

Abraham Levine, *El Camino Community College*

Diane Levy, *The University of North Carolina, Wilmington*

Stephen Mabry, *Cedar Valley College*

David Maines, *Oakland University*

Ron Matson, *Wichita State University*

Armaund L. Mauss, *Washington State University*

Evelyn Mercer, *Southwest Baptist University*

Robert Meyer, *Arkansas State University*

Michael V. Miller, *University of Texas—San Antonio*

John Mitrano, *Central Connecticut State University*

W. Lawrence Neuman, *University of Wisconsin—Whitewater*

Charles Norman, *Indiana State University*

Patricia H. O'Brien, *Elgin Community College*

Robert Ostrow, *Wayne State*

Laura O'Toole, *University of Delaware*

Mike K. Pate, *Western Oklahoma State College*

Lawrence Peck, *Erie Community College*

Ruth Pigott, *University of Nebraska—Kearney*

Phil Piket, *Joliet Junior College*

Trevor Pinch, *Cornell University*

Daniel Polak, *Hudson Valley Community College*

James Pond, *Butler Community College*

Deedy Ramo, *Del Mar College*

Adrian Rapp, *North Harris Community College*

Ray Rich, *Community College of Southern Nevada*

Barbara Richardson, *Eastern Michigan University*

Salvador Rivera, *State University of New York—Cobleskill*

Howard Robboy, *Trenton State College*

Paulina X. Ruf, *University of Tampa*

Michael Samano, *Portland Community College*

Michael L. Sanow, *Community College of Baltimore County*

Mary C. Sengstock, *Wayne State University*

Walt Shirley, *Sinclair Community College*

Marc Silver, *Hofstra University*

Roberto E. Socas, *Essex County College*

Susan Sprecher, *Illinois State University*

Mariella Rose Squire, *University of Maine at Fort Kent*

Rachel Stehle, *Cuyahoga Community College*

Marios Stephanides, *University of Tampa*

Randolph G. Ston, *Oakland Community College*

Vickie Holland Taylor, *Danville Community College*

Maria Jose Tenuto, *College of Lake County*

Gary Tiederman, *Oregon State University*

Kathleen Tiemann, *University of North Dakota*

Judy Turchetta, *Johnson & Wales University*

Stephen L. Vassar, *Minnesota State University, Mankato*

William J. Wattendorf, *Adirondack Community College*

Jay Weinstein, *Eastern Michigan University*

Larry Weiss, *University of Alaska*

Douglas White, *Henry Ford Community College*

Stephen R. Wilson, *Temple University*

Anthony T. Woart, *Middlesex Community College*

Stuart Wright, *Lamar University*

Mary Lou Wylie, *James Madison University*

Diane Kholos Wysocki, *University of Nebraska—Kearney*

Stacey G. H. Yap, *Plymouth State College*

William Yoels, *University of Alabama Birmingham*

I couldn't ask for a more outstanding team than the one that I have the pleasure to work with at Allyn and Bacon. I want to thank Jeff Lasser, whose counsel I rely on; Judy Fiske, for constantly hovering over the many details—and for wholeheartedly supporting my many suggestions; Jenn Albanese, who has provided excellent research, tracking down both standard and esoteric leads; Joan Pendleton, whose copy editing and successful efforts in meeting a harried schedule I appreciate; Kate Cebik, for her creativity in photo research—and for her willingness to "keep on looking"; and Gary Kliewer, for coordinating the many separate tasks that must be integrated into a whole.

I do so appreciate this team. It is difficult to heap too much praise on such fine, capable, and creative people. Often going "beyond the call of duty" as we faced nonstop deadlines, their untiring efforts coalesced with mine to produce this text. Students, whom we constantly kept in mind as we prepared this edition, are the beneficiaries of this intricate teamwork.

Since this text is based on the contributions of many, I would count it a privilege if you would share with me your teaching experiences with this book, including suggestions for improving the text. Both positive and negative comments are welcome. It is in this way that I continue to learn.

I wish you the very best in your teaching. It is my sincere desire that *Sociology: A Down-to-Earth Approach* contributes to your classroom success.

Jim Henslin

James M. Henslin
Professor Emeritus
Department of Sociology
Southern Illinois University, Edwardsville

I welcome your correspondence. E-mail is the best way to reach me: henslin@aol.com

A Note from the Publisher
on the Supplements

INSTRUCTOR'S SUPPLEMENTS

Unless otherwise noted, instructor's supplements are available at no charge to adopters—in printed or duplicated formats, as well as electronically through Pearson Higher Education's Instructor's Resource Center (www.pearsonhighered.com/irc).

Instructor's Manual *Jessica Herrmeyer, Hawkeye Community College*

For each chapter in the text, the Instructor's Manual provides a list of key changes to the new edition, chapter summaries and outlines, learning objectives, key terms and people, classroom activities, discussion topics, recommended films, Web sites, and additional references. (0-205-68863-2)

Test Bank *Rochelle Zaranek, Macomb Community College*

The Test Bank contains approximately 150 questions per chapter in multiple-choice, true-false, short-answer, essay, vocabulary-matching, and open-book formats. Some questions challenge students to look beyond words and answer questions based on the text's figures, tables, and maps. All questions are labeled and scaled by cognitive level, using the categories in Bloom's Taxonomy: Knowledge, Comprehension, Application, Analysis, Synthesis, Evaluation. (www.pearsonhighered.com/irc) (0-205-69330-X)

MyTest Computerized Test Bank

The printed Test Bank is also available online through Pearson's computerized testing system, MyTest. This fully networkable test-generating program is available online. The user-friendly interface allows you to view, edit, and add questions, transfer questions to tests, and print tests in a variety of fonts. Search and sort features allow you to locate questions quickly and to arrange them in whatever order you prefer. The test bank can be accessed anywhere with a free MyTest user account. There is no need to download a program or a file to your computer. (0-205-69618-X)

PowerPoint Presentation *Dan Cavanaugh*

These PowerPoint slides, available online and created especially for the Tenth Edition, feature lecture outlines for every chapter and many of the tables, charts, and maps from the text. PowerPoint software is not required: A PowerPoint viewer is included. (0-205-69616-3)

Instructor's Resource CD

This CD contains electronic versions of all Instructor and Student Supplements in one convenient place. Print supplements are provided both in PDF format and as Word documents that can be edited. The CD includes the Instructor's Manual, Test Bank, PowerPoint Presentation, Study Guide, and Telecourse Faculty Guide. (0-205-72763-8)

Exploring Society Telecourse Faculty Guide *Shelly Dutchin, Western Wisconsin Technical College*

Pearson provides special assistance for instructors who use the video series from Dallas TeleLearning, *Exploring Society.* This manual coordinates reading and video assignments and correlates all test questions in our Test Bank with 22 half-hour video programs. For information about the *Exploring Society* Telecourse, contact Dallas TeleLearning directly (972-669-6650, http://telelearning.dcccd.edu). (www.pearsonhighered.com/irc) (0-205-79001-1)

InterWrite PRS (Personal Response System)

Assess your students' progress with the Personal Response System—an easy-to-use wireless polling system that enables you to pose questions, record results, and display those results instantly in your classroom. Designed by teachers, for teachers, PRS is easy to integrate into your lectures:

- Students use cell-phone-sized transmitters that they bring to class.
- You ask multiple-choice, numerical-answer, or matching questions during class; students simply click their answers into their transmitter.
- A classroom receiver (portable or mounted) connected to your computer tabulates all answers and displays them graphically in class.
- Results can be recorded for grading or attendance, or they can simply be used as a discussion point.

Our partnership with PRS allows us to offer student rebate cards bundled with any Pearson text. The rebate card is a direct value of $20.00 and can be redeemed with the purchase of a new PRS student transmitter. In addition, institutions that order 40 or more new textbook + rebate card bundles will receive the classroom receiver (a $250 value), software, and support at no additional cost. We also offer sets of questions for introductory sociology designed to be used with Personal Response Systems. Contact your Pearson Arts and Sciences representative or visit www.ablongman.com/prs for more information.

STUDENT SUPPLEMENTS

Life in Society: Readings to Accompany *Sociology: A Down-to-Earth Approach*, Fourth Edition *James M. Henslin*

This brief reader, revised for the Tenth Edition, contains one reading for each chapter of the text, chosen and introduced by James M. Henslin. The reader can be purchased separately at full price or packaged with this text for an additional $5 net to the bookstore. An instructor's manual for the reader is available electronically through the Pearson Higher Education Instructor's Resource Center. (0-205-78041-5)

Study Guide *Jessica Herrmeyer, Hawkeye Community College*

This study guide is designed to help students prepare for quizzes and exams. For each chapter in the text, the guide contains a chapter summary; a chapter outline; a list of key terms and people; a practice test with 30 multiple-choice, 20 true-false, 15 short-answer, 10 matching, and 5 essay questions; an answer key; and a set of PowerPoint lecture outlines. Available separately for student purchase. (0-205-69615-5)

ONLINE COURSE MANAGEMENT

MySocLab

MySocLab for *Sociology: A Down-to-Earth Approach,* Tenth Edition, is a state-of-the-art interactive and instructive solution for introductory sociology, designed to be used as a supplement to a traditional lecture course or to completely administer an online course. MySocLab provides access to a wealth of resources all geared to meet the individual teaching and learning needs of every instructor and every student. MySocLab is available at no additional cost to the student when a text is packaged with a *MySocLab Student Access Code Card.* (0-205-72776-X)

WebCT™ and Blackboard Test Banks

For colleges and universities with **WebCT™** and **Blackboard** licenses, we have converted the complete Test Bank into these popular course management platforms. Adopters can download the electronic file by logging in to our Instructor Resource Center. (www.pearsonhighered .com/irc) Blackboard (0-205-72762-X) WebCT (0-205-72761-1)

Exploring Society Telecourse
Study Guide *Shelly Dutchin, Western Wisconsin Technical College*

This student manual is included in MySocLab for *Sociology: A Down-to-Earth Approach*, Tenth Edition, and is written for students who are using *Sociology: A Down-to-Earth Approach* with the 22 video programs in the *Exploring Society* series from Dallas TeleLearning. Each section coordinates reading and video assignments and includes summaries, learning objectives, video outlines, lists of key terms and people, and student application projects. The Guide also provides a self-test section containing multiple-choice, true-false, fill-in, matching, and essay questions that correlate to the video programs as well as Henslin's text. (0-205-79000-3)

ADDITIONAL SUPPLEMENTS
Student Texts and Supplements

Data Analysis:

Doing Sociology with Student CHIP, Fifth Edition, Gregg Lee Carter, 0-205-77733-3

Hands-On Sociology, Third Edition, William Feigelman and Yih-Jin Young, 0-205-42846-0

Social Atlas of the United States, William Frey, Amy Beth Aronson, and John Paul Dewitt, 0-205-43917-9

Research and Writing:

The Sociology Student Writer's Manual, William A. Johnson, Jr., Richard P. Rettig, Greg M. Scott, Steve M. Garrison, 0-205-72345-4

MySearchLab, 0-205-69939-1

Sociology Writer's Guide, Linda L. Yellin, 0-205-58238-9

Applying Sociology:

Building Bridges: The Allyn & Bacon Student Guide to Service-Learning, Doris Hamner, 0-205-31974-2

Practicing Sociology in the Community: A Student's Guide, Phyllis A. Langton and Dianne A. Kammerer, 0-13-042019-0

Careers in Sociology, Richard W. Stephens, 0-205-27904-X

College and Society, Stephen Sweet, 0-205-30556-3

Think Twice! Sociology Looks at Current Issues, Second Edition, Lorne Tepperman and Jenny Blain, 0-13-099528-2

Study and Review:

Introduction to Sociology Study Card, 0-205-44608-6

Readers:

Empirical Approaches to Sociology: A Collection of Classic and Contemporary Readings, Fifth Edition, Gregg Lee Carter, 0-205-62809-5

The Meaning of Sociology: A Reader, Eighth Edition, Joel M. Charon and Lee Ga Vigalant, 0-13-813328-X

Sociological Classics: A Prentice Hall Pocket Reader, David Kauzlarich, 0-13-191806-0

The Spirit of Sociology, Second Edition, Ron Matson, 0-205-52464-8

Seeing Ourselves: Classic, Contemporary, and Cross-Cultural Readings in Sociology, Eighth Edition, John J. Macionis and Nijole V. Benokraitis, 0-205-73316-6

Crisis in American Institutions, Fourteenth Edition, Jerome H. Skolnick and Elliott Currie, 0-205-61064-1

Instructor Supplements

ABC News/Pearson Video Library for Introductory Sociology, Series 1, 0-13-228496-0

Exercises in Sociology: A Lab Manual for the Study of Social Behavior, Kelly F. McGeever and Charles E. Faupel, 0-13-94661-7

The Video Professor: Applying Lessons in Sociology to Classic and Modern Films, Anthony Zumpetta, 0-205-45624-3

About the Author

JIM HENSLIN, who was born in Minnesota, graduated from high school and junior college in California and from college in Indiana. Awarded scholarships, he earned his master's and doctorate degrees in sociology at Washington University in St. Louis, Missouri. After this, he won a postdoctoral fellowship from the National Institute of Mental Health and spent a year studying how people adjust to the suicide of a family member. His primary interests in sociology are the sociology of everyday life, deviance, and international relations. Among his many books are *Down to Earth Sociology: Introductory Readings* (Free Press), now in its fifteenth edition, and *Social Problems* (Allyn and Bacon), now in its 9th edition. He has also published widely in sociology journals, including *Social Problems* and *American Journal of Sociology*.

While a graduate student, Jim taught at the University of Missouri at St. Louis. After completing his doctorate, he joined the faculty at Southern Illinois University, Edwardsville, where he is Professor Emeritus of Sociology. He says, "I've always found the introductory course enjoyable to teach. I love to see students' faces light up when they first glimpse the sociological perspective and begin to see how society has become an essential part of how they view the world."

Jim enjoys reading and fishing, and he also does a bit of kayaking and weight lifting. His two favorite activities are writing and traveling. He especially enjoys visiting and living in other cultures, for this brings him face to face with behaviors and ways of thinking that challenge his perspectives and "make sociological principles come alive." A special pleasure has been the preparation of the photo essays that appear in this text.

Jim moved to Latvia, an Eastern European country formerly dominated by the Soviet Union, where he observed firsthand how people struggle to adjust to capitalism. While there, he happened to be present at a historical event. See the two photos on page 656. He also interviewed aged political prisoners who had survived the Soviet gulag. He then moved to Spain, where he was able to observe how people adjust to a declining economy and the immigration of people from contrasting cultures. (Of course, for this he didn't need to leave the United States.) To better round out his cultural experiences, he is making plans for extended stays in India and South America, where he expects to do more photo essays to reflect their fascinating cultures. He is grateful to be able to live in such exciting social, technological, and geopolitical times—and to have access to portable broadband Internet while he pursues his sociological imagination.

Anita Henslin

The author at work—sometimes getting a little too close to "the action" (preparing the new "Through the Author's Lens" photo essay on pages 532–533.)

Chapter

1

The Sociological
Perspective

Bangladesh

E ven from the glow of the faded red-and-white exit sign, its faint light barely illuminating the upper bunk, I could see that the sheet was filthy. Resigned to another night of fitful sleep, I reluctantly crawled into bed. I kept my clothes on.

The next morning, I joined the long line of disheveled men leaning against the chain-link fence. Their faces were as downcast as their clothes were dirty. Not a glimmer of hope among them.

I was determined. "I will experience what they experience," I kept telling myself.

No one spoke as the line slowly inched forward.

When my turn came, I was handed a cup of coffee, a white plastic spoon, and a bowl of semiliquid that I couldn't identify. It didn't look like any food I had seen before. Nor did it taste like anything I had ever eaten.

My stomach fought the foul taste, every spoonful a battle. But I was determined. "I will experience what they experience," I kept telling myself. My stomach reluctantly gave in and accepted its morning nourishment.

The room was strangely silent. Hundreds of men were eating, each one immersed in his own private hell, his mind awash with disappointment, remorse, bitterness.

As I stared at the Styrofoam cup that held my coffee, grateful for at least this small pleasure, I noticed what looked like teeth marks. I shrugged off the thought, telling myself that my long weeks as a sociological observer of the homeless were finally getting to me. "It must be some sort of crease from handling," I concluded.

I joined the silent ranks of men turning in their bowls and cups. When I saw the man behind the counter swishing out Styrofoam cups in a washtub of murky water, I began to feel sick to my stomach. I knew then that the jagged marks on my cup really had come from another person's mouth.

How much longer did this research have to last? I felt a deep longing to return to my family—to a welcome world of clean sheets, healthy food, and "normal" conversations.

sociological perspective
understanding human behavior by placing it within its broader social context

society people who share a culture and a territory

social location the group memberships that people have because of their location in history and society

The Sociological Perspective

Why were these men so silent? Why did they receive such despicable treatment? What was I doing in that homeless shelter? After all, I hold a respectable, professional position, and I have a home and family.

Sociology offers a perspective, a view of the world. The *sociological perspective* (or imagination) opens a window onto unfamiliar worlds—and offers a fresh look at familiar ones. In this text, you will find yourself in the midst of Nazis in Germany and warriors in South America, as well as among people who live in a city dump. (If you want to jump ahead, you can see the photos I took of the people who live in a dump in Cambodia: pages 250–251.) You will also find yourself looking at your own world in a different light. As you view other worlds—or your own—the sociological perspective enables you to gain a new perception of social life. In fact, this is what many find appealing about sociology.

The sociological perspective has been a motivating force in my own life. Ever since I took my introductory course in sociology, I have been enchanted by the perspective that sociology offers. I have enjoyed both observing other groups and questioning my own assumptions about life. I sincerely hope the same happens to you.

Seeing the Broader Social Context

The **sociological perspective** stresses the social contexts in which people live. It examines how these contexts influence people's lives. At the center of the sociological perspective is the question of how groups influence people, especially how people are influenced by their **society**—a group of people who share a culture and a territory.

To find out why people do what they do, sociologists look at **social location,** the corners in life that people occupy because of where they are located in a society. Sociologists look at how jobs, income, education, gender, age, and race–ethnicity affect people's ideas and behavior. Consider, for example, how being identified with a group called *females* or with a group called *males* when you were growing up has shaped your ideas of who you are. Growing up as a female or a male has influenced not only how you feel about yourself but also your ideas of what you should attain in life and how you relate to others.

Sociologist C. Wright Mills (1959) put it this way: "The sociological imagination [perspective] enables us to grasp the connection between history and biography." By *history,* Mills meant that each society is located in a broad stream of events. This gives each society specific characteristics—such as its ideas about the proper roles of men and women. By *biography,* Mills referred to the specific experiences that give individuals their orientations to life. In short, people don't do what they do because they inherited some internal mechanism, such as instincts. Rather, *external* influences—our experiences—become part of our thinking and motivation. In short, the society in which we grow up, and our particular location in that society, lie at the center of what we do and how we think.

Examining the broad social context in which people live is essential to the *sociological perspective,* for this context shapes our beliefs and attitudes and sets guidelines for what we do. From this photo of a Yanomamö man blowing yokoana, a hallucinogenic powder, up his nose, you can see how distinctive those guidelines are for the Yanomamö Indians who live on the border of Brazil and Venezuela. How has this Yanomamö man been influenced by his group? How have groups influenced *your* views and behavior?

Consider a newborn baby. As you know, if we were to take the baby away from its U.S. parents and place it with the Yanomamö Indians in the jungles of South America, when the child began to speak, his or her words would not be in English. You also know that the child would not think like an American. The child would not grow up wanting credit cards, for example, or designer clothes, a car, a cell phone, an iPod, and the latest video game. He or she would take his or her place in Yanomamö society—perhaps as a food gatherer, a hunter, or a warrior—and would not even know about the world left behind at birth. And, whether male or female, the child would grow up assuming that it is natural to want many children, not debating whether to have one, two, or three children.

People around the globe take their particular views of the world for granted. Something inside us Americans tells us that hamburgers are delicious, small families desirable, and designer clothing attractive. Yet something inside some of the Sinai Desert Arab tribes tells them that warm, fresh camel's blood makes a fine drink and that everyone should have a large family and wear flowing robes (Murray 1935; McCabe and Ellis 1990). And that something certainly isn't an instinct. As sociologist Peter Berger (1963) phrased it, that "something" is *society within us.*

Although obvious, this point frequently eludes us. We often think and talk about people's behavior as though it were caused by their sex ("men are like that"), their race ("they are like that"), or some other factor transmitted by their genes. The sociological perspective helps us escape from this cramped, personal view by exposing the broader social context that underlies human behavior. It helps us see the links between what people do and the social settings that shape their behavior.

If you have been thinking along with me—and I hope you have—you should be thinking about how *your* social groups have shaped *your* ideas and desires. Over and over in this text, you will see that the way you look at the world is the result of your exposure to specific human groups. I think you will enjoy the process of self-discovery that sociology offers.

The Global Context—and the Local

As is evident to all of us—from the labels on our clothing that say Hong Kong, Brunei, or Macau, to the many other imported products that have become part of our daily lives—our world has become a global village. How life has changed! Our predecessors lived on isolated farms and in small towns. They grew their own food and made their own goods, buying some sugar, coffee, and a few other items that they couldn't produce. Beyond the borders of their communities lay a world they perceived only dimly.

And how slow communications used to be! In December 1814, the United States and Great Britain signed a peace treaty to end the War of 1812. Yet two weeks *later* their armies fought a major battle in New Orleans. The armed forces there had not heard that the war was over (Volti 1995).

Even though we can now pick up a telephone or use the Internet to communicate instantly with people anywhere on the planet, we continue to occupy our own little corners of life. Like those of our predecessors, our worlds, too, are marked by differences in family background, religion, job, gender, race–ethnicity, and social class. In these corners, we continue to learn distinctive ways of viewing the world.

One of the beautiful—and fascinating—aspects of sociology is that it enables us to analyze both parts of our current reality: the changes that incorporate us into a global network *and* our unique experiences in our smaller corners of life. In this text, we shall examine both of these vital aspects of our lives.

Sociology and the Other Sciences

Just as humans today have an intense desire to unravel the mysteries around them, so did people in ancient times. Their explanations were not based on observations alone, however, but were also mixed with magic and superstition.

To satisfy their basic curiosities about the world, humans gradually developed **science,** systematic methods to study the social and natural worlds and the knowledge obtained by those methods. *Sociology,* the study of society and human behavior, is one of these sciences.

A useful way of comparing these sciences—and of gaining a better understanding of sociology's place—is to divide them into the natural and the social sciences.

science the application of systematic methods to obtain knowledge and the knowledge obtained by those methods

The Natural Sciences

The **natural sciences** are the intellectual and academic disciplines that are designed to explain and predict the events in our natural environment. The natural sciences are divided into specialized fields of research according to subject matter, such as biology, geology, chemistry, and physics. These are further subdivided into even more highly specialized areas. Biology is divided into botany and zoology; geology into mineralogy and geomorphology; chemistry into its organic and inorganic branches; and physics into biophysics and quantum mechanics. Each area of investigation examines a particular "slice" of nature.

The Social Sciences

People have not limited themselves to investigating nature. To try to understand life, they have also developed fields of science that focus on the social world. The **social sciences** examine human relationships. Just as the natural sciences attempt to objectively understand the world of nature, the social sciences attempt to objectively understand the social world. Just as the world of nature contains ordered (or lawful) relationships that are not obvious but must be discovered through controlled observations, so the ordered relationships of the human or social world are not obvious and must be revealed by means of repeated observations.

   Like the natural sciences, the social sciences are divided into specialized fields based on their subject matter. These divisions are anthropology, economics, political science, psychology, and sociology. The social sciences are subdivided further into specialized fields. Thus, anthropology is divided into cultural and physical anthropology; economics has macro (large-scale) and micro (small-scale) specialties; political science has theoretical and applied branches; psychology may be clinical or experimental; and sociology has its quantitative and qualitative branches. Since our focus is sociology, let's contrast sociology with each of the other social sciences.

Anthropology.   Anthropology, which traditionally focuses on tribal peoples, is closely related to sociology. The chief concern of anthropologists is to understand *culture,* a people's total way of life. Culture includes a group's (1) *artifacts,* such as its tools, art, and weapons; (2) *structure,* the patterns that determine how its members interact with one another (such as positions of leadership); (3) *ideas and values,* the ways the group's beliefs affect its members' lives; and (4) *forms of communication,* especially language.

   Graduate students working on their doctorate in anthropology usually spend a period of time living with a tribal group. In their reports, they emphasize the group's family (kin) relationships. As there are no "undiscovered" groups left in the world, this focus on tribal groups is giving way to the study of groups in industrialized settings. When anthropologists study the same groups that sociologists do, they place greater emphasis on artifacts, authority (hierarchy), and language, especially kinship terms.

Economics.   Economics concentrates on a single social institution. Economists study the production and distribution of the material goods and services of a society. They want to know what goods are being produced, what they cost, and how those goods are distributed. Economists also are interested in the choices that determine production and consumption; for example, they study what motivates people to buy a certain item instead of another.

Political Science.   Political science focuses on politics and government. Political scientists examine how governments are formed, how they operate, and how they are related to other institutions of society. Political scientists are especially interested in how people attain ruling positions in their society, how they maintain those positions, and the consequences of their actions for the people they govern.

Psychology.   The focus of psychology is on processes that occur *within* the individual, inside what they call the "skin-bound organism." Experimental psychologists do research on intelligence, emotions, perception, memory, even dreams. Some study how personality is formed and the causes of mental illness. Clinical psychologists work as therapists,

natural sciences the intellectual and academic disciplines designed to comprehend, explain, and predict events in our natural environments

social sciences the intellectual and academic disciplines designed to understand the social world objectively by means of controlled and repeated observations

helping people resolve personal problems, such as recovering from abuse or addiction to drugs. Others work as counselors in school and work settings, where they give personality tests, intelligence tests, and vocational aptitude tests.

Sociology.   Sociology overlaps these other social sciences. Like anthropologists, sociologists also study culture; they, too, do research on group structure and belief systems, as well as on how people communicate with one another. Like economists, sociologists do research on how a society's goods and services are distributed, especially how that distribution results in inequality. Like political scientists, sociologists study how people govern one another, especially how those in power affect people's lives. And like psychologists, sociologists also study how people adjust to the difficulties of life.

With such similarities, what distinguishes sociology from the other social sciences? Unlike anthropologists, sociologists focus primarily on industrialized societies. Unlike economists and political scientists, sociologists do not concentrate on a single social institution. And unlike psychologists, sociologists stress factors *external* to the individual to determine what influences people and how they adjust to life. These differences might not be entirely clear, so let's go to the Down-to-Earth Sociology box below and, in an updated ancient tale, consider how members of different disciplines might perceive the same subject matter.

Down-to-Earth Sociology
An Updated Version of the Old Elephant Story

It is said that in the recent past, five wise men and women, all blindfolded, were led to an elephant and asked to explain what they "saw." The first, an anthropologist, tenderly touching the trunk and the tusks, broke into a grin and said, "This is really primitive. I feel very comfortable here. Concentrate on these."

The second, an economist, feeling the mouth, said, "This is what counts. What goes in here is distributed throughout the body. Concentrate your research on how it is distributed."

The third, a political scientist, feeling the gigantic ears, announced, "This is the power center. What goes in here controls the entire beast. Concentrate your studies here."

The fourth, a psychologist, stroking the top of the elephant's head, smiled contentedly and said, "This is the only thing that counts. All feeling and thinking take place inside here. To understand this beast, we'll study this part."

Then came the sociologist (of course!), who, after feeling the entire body, said, "You can't understand the beast by concentrating on only one part. Each is but part of the whole. The trunk and tusks, the mouth, the ears, the head—all are important. But so are the parts of the beast that you haven't mentioned. We must remove our blindfolds so we can see the larger picture. We have to see how

everything works together to form the entire animal."

Pausing for emphasis, the sociologist added, "And we also need to understand how this creature interacts with similar creatures. How does its life in groups influence its behavior?"

I wish I could conclude this tale by saying that the anthropologist, the economist, the political scientist, and the psychologist were dazzled on hearing the wisdom of the sociologist, and, amidst gasps of wonderment, they tore off their blindfolds, joined together, and began to examine the entire animal. But, alas and alack! On hearing this sage advice, the specialists stubbornly bound their blindfolds even tighter so they could concentrate all the more on their particular part. And if you listened very, very carefully, you could even hear them mutter, "Don't touch the tusks." "Stay away from the mouth—that's my area." "Take your hand off the ears." "The top of the head is mine—stay away from it."

The Goals of Science

The first goal of each science is to *explain* why something happens. The second goal is to make **generalizations,** that is, to go beyond the individual case and make statements that apply to a broader group or situation. For example, a sociologist wants to explain not only why Mary went to college or became an armed robber but also why people with her characteristics are more likely than others to go to college or to become armed robbers. To achieve generalizations, sociologists look for *patterns,* recurring characteristics or events. The third scientific goal is to *predict,* to specify in the light of current knowledge what will happen in the future.

To attain these goals, scientists do not rely on magic, superstition, or common beliefs, but, instead, they do systematic research. They explain exactly how they did their research so it can be reviewed by others. Secrecy, prejudice, and other biases go against the grain of science.

Sociologists and other scientists also move beyond **common sense**—the prevailing ideas in a society, the things that "everyone knows" are true. "Everyone" can be misguided today just as everyone was wrong when common sense dictated that the world was flat or that no human could ever walk on the moon. As sociologists do their research, their findings may confirm or contradict commonsense notions about social life. To test your own "common sense," take the "fun quiz" on the next page.

The Risks of Being a Sociologist.   Sometimes the explorations of sociologists take them into nooks and crannies that people would prefer remain unexplored. For example, a sociologist might study how people make decisions to commit a crime or to cheat on their spouses. Since sociologists want above all to understand social life, they don't cease their studies because people feel uncomfortable. Sociologists consider all realms of human life legitimate avenues to explore, and they do so, from the respectable to the downright disreputable.

As they examine how groups operate, sociologists sometimes face pressure to keep things secret. Every group, it seems, nourishes some ideal image that it presents to others. Because sociologists are interested in knowing what is *really* going on, they peer behind the scenes to get past those sugar-coated images (Berger 1963; 2007). This can threaten groups that are being studied, leading to pressure and conflict—all part of the adventure, and risk, of being a sociologist.

Origins of Sociology

Tradition Versus Science

Ancient peoples tried to figure out how social life works. They asked questions about why war exists, why some people become more powerful than others, and why some are rich but others are poor. However, they often based their answers on superstition, myth, or even the positions of the stars, and they did not *test* their assumptions.

Science, in contrast, requires theories that can be tested by research. Measured by this standard, sociology emerged about the middle of the 1800s, when social observers began to use scientific methods to test their ideas. Three main events set the stage for the challenge to tradition and the emergence of sociology.

The first was the social upheaval of the Industrial Revolution. As agriculture gave way to factory production, masses of people moved to cities in search of work. The city's greeting was harsh: miserable pay, long hours, and dangerous work. To help their family survive, even children worked in these miserable conditions, some of them chained to machines to keep them from running away. With their ties to the land broken and their world turned upside down, no longer could people count on tradition to provide the answers to the difficult questions of life.

The second was the social upheaval of revolution. The American and French revolutions swept away the existing social orders—and with them the answers they had provided.

generalization a statement that goes beyond the individual case and is applied to a broader group or situation

common sense those things that "everyone knows" are true

Down-to-Earth Sociology

Enjoying A Sociology Quiz—Sociological Findings Versus Common Sense

Some findings of sociology support commonsense understandings of social life, and others contradict them. Can you tell the difference? To enjoy this quiz, complete *all* the questions before turning the page to check your answers.

1. **True/False** More U.S. students are killed in school shootings now than ten or fifteen years ago.
2. **True/False** The earnings of U.S. women have just about caught up with those of U.S. men.
3. **True/False** With life so rushed and more women working for wages, today's parents spend less time with their children than previous generations did.
4. **True/False** It is more dangerous to walk near topless bars than fast-food restaurants.
5. **True/False** Most rapists are mentally ill.
6. **True/False** A large percentage of terrorists are mentally ill.
7. **True/False** Most people on welfare are lazy and looking for a handout. They could work if they wanted to.
8. **True/False** Compared with women, men make more eye contact in face-to-face conversations.
9. **True/False** Couples who lived together before marriage are usually more satisfied with their marriage than couples who did not live together before marriage.
10. **True/False** Because bicyclists are more likely to wear helmets now than a few years ago, their rate of head injuries has dropped.

Before this period, tradition had ruled. The reply to questions of "why" was "We do this because it has always been done this way." A new social order challenges traditional answers, stimulates original thinking, and brings new ideas. The ideas that emerged during this period challenged tradition even further. Especially powerful was the idea that individuals possess inalienable rights. This idea caught fire to such an extent that people were willing to die for it, forcing many traditional Western monarchies to give way to more democratic forms of government.

The third was the imperialism (empire building) of the time. The Europeans had conquered many parts of the world, and their new colonies stretched from Asia and Africa to North and South America. Exposed to radically different ways of life, they began to ask why cultures differ.

About this same time that people were finding traditional answers inadequate, **the scientific method**—using objective, systematic observations to test theories—was being tried out in chemistry and physics. The result was the uncovering of many secrets that had been concealed in nature. With traditional answers failing, the logical step was to apply the scientific method to questions about social life. The result was the birth of sociology.

Auguste Comte and Positivism

Applying the scientific method to the social world, a process known as **positivism,** apparently was first proposed by Auguste Comte (1798–1857). Reflecting on the upheavals of the French Revolution and on the changes he experienced when he moved to Paris from the small town in which he had grown up, Comte became interested in what holds society together. He began to ask what creates social order, instead of anarchy or chaos. And once society does become set on a particular course, what causes it to change, he wondered.

Comte decided that the scientific method was the key to answering such questions. Just as the scientific method had revealed the law of gravity, so, too, it would uncover the laws that underlie society. Comte called this new science **sociology**—"the study of society" (from the Greek *logos,* "study of," and the Latin *socius,* "companion," or "being with others"). The purpose of this new science, he said, would be not only to discover social principles but also to apply them to social reform. Comte developed a grandiose view: Sociologists would reform the entire society, making it a better place to live.

[the] scientific method the use of objective systematic observations to test theories

positivism the application of the scientific approach to the social world

sociology the scientific study of society and human behavior

Auguste Comte (1798–1857), who is credited as the founder of sociology, began to analyze the bases of the social order. Although he stressed that the scientific method should be applied to the study of society, he did not apply it himself.

Down-to-Earth Sociology

Sociological Findings Versus Common Sense—Answers to the Sociology Quiz

1. **False.** More students were shot to death at U.S. schools in the early 1990s than now (National School Safety Center 2009). See page 517.
2. **False.** Over the years, the wage gap has narrowed, but only slightly. On average, full-time working women earn about 72 percent of what full-time working men earn. This low figure is actually an improvement over earlier years. See Figures 11.7 and 11.8 on pages 317–318.
3. **False.** Today's parents actually spend more time with their children (Bianchi et al. 2006). To see how this could be, see page 467.
4. **False.** The crime rate outside fast-food restaurants is considerably higher. The likely reason for this is that topless bars hire private security and parking lot attendants (Linz et al. 2004).
5. **False.** Sociologists compared the psychological profiles of prisoners convicted of rape and prisoners convicted of other crimes. Their profiles were similar. Like robbery, rape is a learned behavior. See pages 143–144.
6. **False.** Extensive testing of Islamic terrorists shows that they actually tend to score more "normal" on psychological tests than most "normal" people. As a group, they are in better mental health than the rest of the population (Sageman 2008b:64).
7. **False.** Most people on welfare are children, elderly, sick, mentally or physically handicapped, or young mothers with few skills. Less than 2 percent fit the stereotype of an able-bodied man. See page 282.
8. **False.** Women make considerably more eye contact (Henley et al. 1985).
9. **False.** The opposite is true. Among other reasons, couples who cohabit before marriage are usually less committed to one another—and a key to marital success is a strong commitment (Dush et al. 2003; Osborne et al. 2007).
10. **False.** Bicyclists today are more likely to wear helmets, but their rate of head injuries is higher. Apparently, they take more risks because the helmets make them feel safer (Barnes 2001). (Unanticipated consequences of human action are studied by functionalists. See page 31.)

How to apply the scientific method to social life meant something quite different to Comte than it does to us. To him, it meant a kind of "armchair philosophy"—drawing conclusions from informal observations of social life. Comte did not do what we today call research, and his conclusions have been abandoned. Nevertheless, Comte's insistence that we must observe and classify human activities to uncover society's fundamental laws is well taken. Because he developed and coined the term *sociology,* Comte often is credited with being the founder of sociology.

Herbert Spencer and Social Darwinism

Herbert Spencer (1820–1903), who grew up in England, is sometimes called the second founder of sociology. Spencer disagreed sharply with Comte. He said that sociology should *not* guide social reform. Societies go through a natural evolution, he said, evolving from lower ("barbarian") to higher ("civilized") forms. This natural process improves societies. As generations pass, the most capable and intelligent ("the fittest") members of a society survive, while the less capable die out. The fittest members will produce a more advanced society—unless misguided do-gooders get in the way and help the less fit (the lower classes) survive.

Spencer called this principle *the survival of the fittest.* Although Spencer coined this phrase, it usually is attributed to his contemporary, Charles Darwin, who proposed that organisms evolve over time as they adapt to their environment. Where Darwin refers to the evolution of organisms, Spencer refers to the evolution of societies. Because Darwin is better known, Spencer's idea is called *social Darwinism.* (If fame had gone the other way, we might be speaking of "biological Spencerism.")

Herbert Spencer (1820–1903), sometimes called the second founder of sociology, coined the term "survival of the fittest." Spencer thought that helping the poor was wrong, that this merely helped the "less fit" survive.

Spencer's idea that it was wrong to help the poor offended many. Many wealthy businessmen of the time, however, liked the concept of the survival of the fittest: They saw themselves as "the fittest"—and therefore superior. I'm sure that Spencer's views also helped some of them avoid feeling guilty for living like royalty while people around them went hungry.

Like Comte, Spencer did armchair philosophy instead of conducting scientific studies. His ideas about society became popular, and he was sought after as a speaker in both England and the United States. Eventually social Darwinism was discredited, and few today remember Spencer.

Karl Marx and Class Conflict

Karl Marx (1818–1883) not only influenced sociology but also left his mark on world history. Marx's influence has been so great that even the *Wall Street Journal,* that staunch advocate of capitalism, has called him one of the three greatest modern thinkers (the other two being Sigmund Freud and Albert Einstein).

Like Comte, Marx thought that people should try to change society. His proposal for change was radical: revolution. This got him thrown out of Germany, and he settled in England. Marx believed that the engine of human history is **class conflict.** Society is made up of two social classes, he said, and they are natural enemies: the **bourgeoisie** (boo-shwa-ZEE) (the *capitalists,* those who own the capital, land, factories, and machines) and the **proletariat** (the exploited workers, who do not own the means of production). Eventually, the workers will unite and break their chains of bondage. The revolution will be bloody, but it will usher in a classless society, one free of exploitation. People will work according to their abilities and receive goods and services according to their needs (Marx and Engels 1848/1967).

Marxism is not the same as communism. Although Marx proposed revolution as the way for workers to gain control of society, he did not develop the political system called *communism.* This is a later application of his ideas. Marx himself felt disgusted when he heard debates about his insights into social life. After listening to some of the positions attributed to him, he shook his head and said, "I am not a Marxist" (Dobriner 1969b:222; Gitlin 1997:89).

Unlike Comte and Spencer, Marx did not think of himself as a sociologist—and with his reputation for communism and revolution, many sociologists wish that no one else did either. Marx spent years studying in the library of the British Museum in London, where he wrote widely on history, philosophy, economics, and political science. Because of his insights into the relationship between the social classes, Marx is generally recognized as a significant early sociologist. He introduced *conflict theory,* one of today's major perspectives in sociology. Later in this book, we will examine this perspective in detail.

Karl Marx (1818–1883) believed that the roots of human misery lay in class conflict, the exploitation of workers by those who own the means of production. Social change, in the form of the overthrow of the capitalists by the workers (*proletariat*), was inevitable from Marx's perspective. Although Marx did not consider himself a sociologist, his ideas have influenced many sociologists, particularly conflict theorists.

class conflict Marx's term for the struggle between capitalists and workers

bourgeoisie Marx's term for capitalists, those who own the means of production

proletariat Marx's term for the exploited class, the mass of workers who do not own the means of production

The French Revolution of 1789 not only overthrew the aristocracy but also upset the entire social order. This extensive change removed the past as a sure guide to the present. The events of this period stimulated Auguste Comte to analyze how societies change. His writings are often taken as the origin of sociology. This painting shows a crowd of women marching to Versailles to capture the royal family.

The French sociologist **Emile Durkheim** (1858–1917) contributed many important concepts to sociology. His comparison of the suicide rates of several counties revealed an underlying social factor: People are more likely to commit suicide if their ties to others in their communities are weak. Durkheim's identification of the key role of *social integration* in social life remains central to sociology today.

social integration the degree to which members of a group or a society feel united by shared values and other social bonds; also known as social cohesion

Emile Durkheim and Social Integration

The primary professional goal of Emile Durkheim (1858–1917) was to get sociology recognized as a separate academic discipline (Coser 1977). Until Durkheim's time, sociology was viewed as part of history and economics. Durkheim, who grew up in eastern France and was educated in both Germany and France, achieved his goal in 1887 when the University of Bordeaux awarded him the world's first academic appointment in sociology.

Durkheim's second goal was to show how social forces affect people's behavior. To accomplish this, he conducted rigorous research. Comparing the suicide rates of several European countries, Durkheim (1897/1966) found that each country has a different suicide rate—and that these rates remain about the same year after year. He also found that different groups within a country have different suicide rates and that these, too, remain stable from year to year. His data showed that Protestants, males, and the unmarried kill themselves at a higher rate than do Catholics or Jews, females, and the married. From these observations, Durkheim concluded that suicide is not what it appears—simply a matter of individuals here and there deciding to take their lives for personal reasons. Instead, *social factors underlie suicide,* which is why a group's rate remains fairly constant year after year.

Durkheim identified **social integration,** the degree to which people are tied to their social group, as a key social factor in suicide. He concluded that people who have weaker social ties are more likely to commit suicide. This, he said, explains why Protestants, males, and the unmarried have higher suicide rates. This is how it works: Protestantism encourages greater freedom of thought and action; males are more independent than females; and the unmarried lack the ties and responsibilities that come with marriage. In other words, members of these groups have fewer of the social bonds that keep people from committing suicide. In Durkheim's term, they have less social integration.

Although strong social ties help protect people from suicide, Durkheim noted that in some instances strong bonds encourage suicide. An example is people who, torn apart by grief, kill themselves after their spouse dies. Their own feelings are so integrated with those of their spouse that they prefer death rather than life without the one who gave it meaning.

Despite the many years that have passed since Durkheim did his research, the principle he uncovered still applies: People who are less socially integrated have higher rates of suicide. Even today, those same groups that Durkheim identified—Protestants, males, and the unmarried—are more likely to kill themselves.

Here is the principle that was central in Durkheim's research: *Human behavior cannot be understood only in terms of the individual; we must always examine the social forces that affect people's lives.* Suicide, for example, appears to be such an intensely individual act that psychologists should study it, not sociologists. As Durkheim stressed, however, if we

Durkheim believed that modern societies produce feelings of isolation, much of which comes from the division of labor. In contrast, members of traditional societies, who work alongside family and neighbors and participate in similar activities, experience a high degree of *social integration*. The photo on the right shows Miao women in China harvesting spring tea.

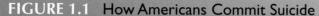

FIGURE 1.1   How Americans Commit Suicide

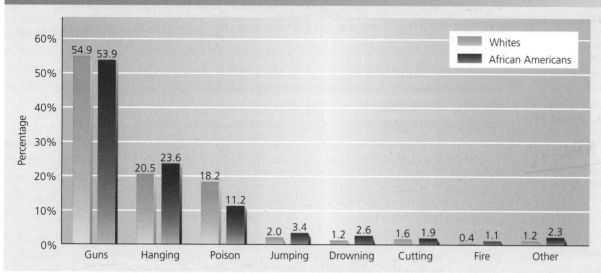

Note: These totals are the mean of years 2001–2005. ("Mean" is explained on page 130.)
Source: By the author. Based on Centers for Disease Control and Prevention 2007c, and earlier years.

look at human behavior only in reference to the individual, we miss its *social* basis. For another glimpse of what Durkheim meant, look at Figure 1.1, which shows the methods by which African Americans and whites commit suicide. I'm sure you'll be struck by how similar their methods are. It might surprise you that the patterns are so consistent that we can predict, with high accuracy, that 29,000 whites and 2,000 African Americans will commit suicide this year. The patterns are so detailed and precise that we can also predict that of the 29,000 whites about 15,500 will use guns to kill themselves, and that of the 2,000 African Americans 60 to 70 will jump to their deaths. Since these patterns recur year after year, they indicate something far beyond individuals. They reflect conditions in society, such as the popularity and accessibility of guns. They also reflect conditions that we don't understand. I am hoping that one day this textbook will pique a student's interest enough to investigate such matters.

Max Weber and the Protestant Ethic

Max Weber (Mahx VAY-ber) (1864–1920), a German sociologist and a contemporary of Durkheim's, also held professorships in the new academic discipline of sociology. Like Durkheim and Marx, Weber is one of the most influential of all sociologists, and you will come across his writings and theories in later chapters. Let's consider an issue Weber raised that remains controversial today.

Religion and the Origin of Capitalism.   Weber disagreed with Marx's claim that economics is the central force in social change. That role, he said, belongs to religion. Weber (1904/1958) theorized that the Roman Catholic belief system encouraged followers to hold on to traditional ways of life, while the Protestant belief system encouraged its members to embrace change. Roman Catholics were taught that because they were church members they were on the road to heaven, but Protestants, those of the Calvinist tradition, were told that they wouldn't know if they were saved until Judgment Day. Uncomfortable with this, they began to look for "signs" that they were in God's will. They concluded that financial success was the blessing that indicated that God was on their side. To bring about this "sign" and receive spiritual comfort, they began to live frugal lives, saving their money and investing it in order to make even more. This, said Weber, brought about the birth of capitalism.

Weber called this self-denying approach to life the *Protestant ethic*. He termed the readiness to invest capital in order to make more money the *spirit of capitalism*. To test

Max Weber (1864–1920) was another early sociologist who left a profound impression on sociology. He used cross-cultural and historical materials to trace the causes of social change and to determine how social groups affect people's orientations to life.

value free the view that a sociologist's personal values or biases should not influence social research

values the standards by which people define what is desirable or undesirable, good or bad, beautiful or ugly

objectivity value neutrality in research

replication the repetition of a study in order to test its findings

his theory, Weber compared the extent of capitalism in Roman Catholic and Protestant countries. In line with his theory, he found that capitalism was more likely to flourish in Protestant countries. Weber's conclusion that religion was the key factor in the rise of capitalism was controversial when he made it, and it continues to be debated today (Wade 2007). We'll explore these ideas in more detail in Chapter 7.

Values in Sociological Research

Weber raised another issue that remains controversial among sociologists. He said that sociology should be **value free.** By this, he meant that a sociologist's **values**—beliefs about what is good or desirable in life and the way the world ought to be—should not affect his or her research. Weber wanted **objectivity,** value neutrality, to be the hallmark of social research. If values influence research, he said, sociological findings will be biased.

That bias has no place in research is not a matter of debate. All sociologists agree that no one should distort data to make them fit preconceived ideas or personal values. It is equally clear, however, that because sociologists—like everyone else—are members of a particular society at a given point in history, they, too, are infused with values of all sorts. These values inevitably play a role in the topics we choose to research. For example, values are part of the reason that one sociologist chooses to do research on the Mafia, while another turns a sociological eye on kindergarten students.

Because values can lead to unintended distortions in how we interpret our findings, sociologists stress the need of **replication,** repeating a study in order to compare the new results with the original findings. If an individual's values have distorted research findings, replication by other sociologists should uncover the bias and correct it.

Despite this consensus, however, values remain a hotly debated topic in sociology (Burawoy 2007; Piven 2007). As summarized in Figure 1.2, the disagreement centers on the proper purposes and uses of sociology. Regarding its *purpose,* some sociologists take the position that their goal should be simply to advance understanding of social life. They should gather data on any topic in which they are interested and then use the best theory available to interpret their findings. Others are convinced that sociologists have the responsibility to investigate the social arrangements that harm people—the causes of poverty, crime, racism, war, and other forms of human exploitation.

Then there is the disagreement over the *uses* of sociology. Those who say that sociology's purpose is to understand human behavior take the position that there is no specific use for the knowledge gained by social research. This knowledge belongs to both the scientific community and the world, and it can be used by anyone for any purpose. In contrast, those who say that sociologists should focus on investigating harmful social conditions take the position that sociological knowledge should be used to alleviate human suffering and improve society. Some also say that sociologists should spearhead social reform.

Although this debate is more complicated than the argument summarized here—few sociologists take such one-sided views—this sketch does identify its major issues. Here is how sociologist John Galliher (1991) expresses today's majority position:

FIGURE 1.2   The Debate over Values in Sociological Research

The Purposes of Social Research

To understand human behavior   *versus*   To investigate harmful social arrangements

The Uses of Social Research

Can be used by anyone for any purpose   *versus*   Should be used to reform society

Source: By the author.

> **Some argue that social scientists, unlike politicians and religious leaders, should merely attempt to describe and explain the events of the world but should never make value judgments based on those observations. Yet a value-free and nonjudgmental social science has no place in a world that has experienced the Holocaust, in a world having had slavery, in a world with the ever-present threat of rape and other sexual assault, in a world with frequent, unpunished crimes in high places, including the production of products known**

by their manufacturers to cause death and injury as has been true of asbestos products and continues to be true of the cigarette industry, and in a world dying from environmental pollution by these same large multinational corporations.

Verstehen and Social Facts

Weber and *Verstehen*

Weber also stressed that to understand human behavior, we should use **Verstehen** (vare-shtay-in) (a German word meaning "to understand"). Perhaps the best translation of this term is "to grasp by insight." By emphasizing *Verstehen,* Weber meant that the best interpreter of human behavior is someone who "has been there," someone who can understand the feelings and motivations of the people being studied. In short, we must pay attention to what are called **subjective meanings**—how people interpret their situation in life, how they view what they are doing and what is happening to them.

To better understand this term, let's return to the homeless in our opening vignette. As in the photo below, why were the men so silent? Why were they so unlike the noisy, sometimes boisterous college students who swarm dorms and cafeterias?

Verstehen can help explain this. When I interviewed men in the shelters (and, in other settings, homeless women), they revealed their despair. Because you know—at least on some level—what the human emotion of despair is, you can apply your understanding to their situation. You know that people in despair feel a sense of hopelessness. The future looks bleak, hardly worth plodding toward. Consequently, why is it worth talking about? Who wants to hear another hard-luck story?

By applying *Verstehen*—your understanding of what it means to be human and to face some situation in life—you gain insight into other people's behavior. In this case, you can understand these men's silence, their lack of communication in the shelter.

Durkheim and Social Facts

In contrast to Weber's emphasis on *Verstehen* and subjective meanings, Durkheim stressed what he called **social facts.** By this term, he meant the patterns of behavior that characterize a social group. Examples of social facts in the United States include June being the most popular month for weddings, suicide rates being higher among the elderly, and more births occurring on Tuesdays than on any other day of the week.

Durkheim said that we must use social facts to interpret social facts. In other words, each pattern reflects some condition of society. People all over the country don't just coincidentally decide to do similar things, whether that is to get married or to commit suicide. If this were the case, in some years, middle-aged people would be the most likely to kill themselves, in other years, young people, and so on. *Patterns that hold true year after year indicate that as thousands and even millions of people make their individual decisions, they are responding to conditions in their society.* It is the job of the sociologist, then, to uncover social facts and to explain them through other social facts. To see how this works, let's look at how the social facts I mentioned—weddings, suicide, and births—are explained by other social facts.

Verstehen a German word used by Weber that is perhaps best understood as "to have insight into someone's situation"

subjective meanings the meanings that people give their own behavior

social facts Durkheim's term for a group's patterns of behavior

Granted their deprivation, it is not surprising that the homeless are not brimming with optimism. This scene at a homeless shelter in New York City is typical, reminiscent of the many meals I ate in soup kitchens with men like this.

How Social Facts and *Verstehen* Fit Together

Social facts and *Verstehen* go hand in hand. As a member of U.S. society, you know how June weddings are related to the end of the school year and how this month, now locked in tradition, common sentiment, and advertising, carries its own momentum. As for suicide among the elderly (see Chapter 13), you probably already have a sense of the greater despair that many older Americans feel.

But do you know why more Americans are born on Tuesday than on any other day of the week? One would expect Tuesday to be no more common than any other day, and that is how it used to be. But no longer (Martin et al. 2007). To understand this change, we need a combination of social facts and *Verstehen.* Four social facts are relevant: First, technology has made the hospital a dominating force in the U.S. medical system. Second, medical technology has made births by cesarean section safer. Third, as discussed in Chapter 19 (page 564), doctors have replaced midwives in the delivery of babies. Fourth, medicine in the United States is a business, with profit a major goal. These four social facts have coalesced to make an operation that used to be a last resort for emergencies so routine that 30 percent of all U.S. babies are now delivered in this manner (Martin et al 2007).

If we add *Verstehen* to these social facts, we gain insight that goes far beyond the cold statistics. We can understand that most mothers-to-be prefer to give birth in a hospital and that, under the influence of physicians at an emotionally charged moment, alternatives appear quite slim. We can also understand that physicians schedule births for a time that is most convenient for them. Tuesday is the day that fits their schedules the best.

Sociology in North America

Transplanted to U.S. soil, sociology first took root at the University of Kansas in 1890, at the University of Chicago in 1892, and at Atlanta University (then an all-black school) in 1897. From there, sociology spread rapidly throughout North America, jumping from four instructors offering courses in 1880 to 225 instructors and 59 sociology departments just 20 years later (Lengermann and Niebrugge 2007).

Some universities were slow to adopt sociology. Not until 1922 did McGill University become Canada's first department of sociology. Harvard University did not open its sociology department until 1930, and it took until the 1950s for the University of California at Berkeley to do so.

The University of Chicago initially dominated North American sociology. Albion Small (1854–1926), who founded this department, also launched the *American Journal of Sociology* and was its editor from 1895 to 1925. Members of this sociology faculty whose ideas continue to influence today's sociologists include Robert E. Park (1864–1944), Ernest Burgess (1886–1966), and George Herbert Mead (1863–1931). Mead developed the symbolic interactionist perspective, which we will examine later.

Sexism at the Time: Women in Early Sociology

As you may have noticed, all the sociologists we have discussed are men. In the 1800s, sex roles were rigid, with women assigned the roles of wife and mother. In the classic German phrase, women were expected to devote themselves to the four K's: *Kirche, Küchen, Kinder, und Kleider* (church, cooking, children, and clothes). Trying to break out of this mold meant risking severe disapproval.

Few people, male or female, attained any education beyond basic reading and writing and a little math. Higher education, for the rare few who received it, was reserved primarily for men. Of the handful of women who did pursue higher education, some became prominent in early sociology. Marion Talbot, for example, was an associate editor of the *American Journal of Sociology* for thirty years, from its founding in 1895 to 1925. The influence of some early female sociologists went far beyond sociology. Grace Abbott became chief of the U.S. government's Children's Bureau, and Frances Perkins was the first woman to hold a cabinet position, serving twelve years as Secretary of Labor under President Franklin Roosevelt. On the next page are photos of some of these early sociologists.

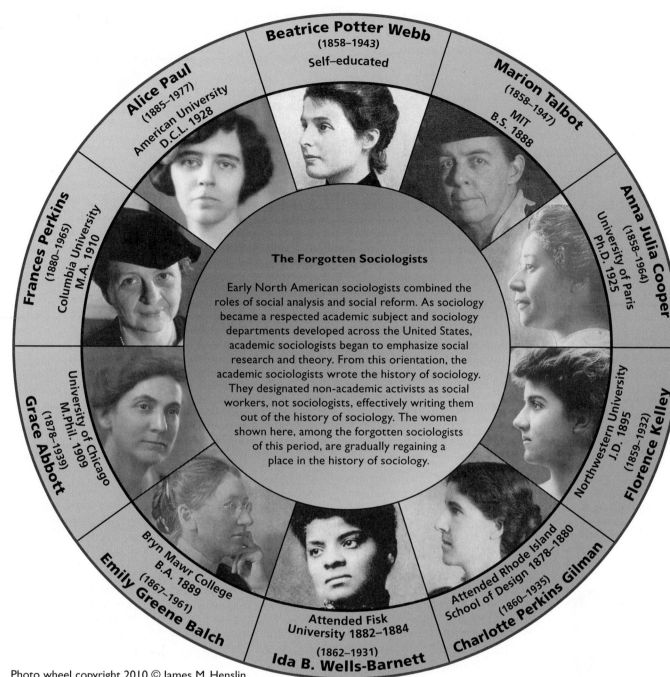

The Forgotten Sociologists

Early North American sociologists combined the roles of social analysis and social reform. As sociology became a respected academic subject and sociology departments developed across the United States, academic sociologists began to emphasize social research and theory. From this orientation, the academic sociologists wrote the history of sociology. They designated non-academic activists as social workers, not sociologists, effectively writing them out of the history of sociology. The women shown here, among the forgotten sociologists of this period, are gradually regaining a place in the history of sociology.

Beatrice Potter Webb (1858–1943) Self-educated

Marion Talbot (1858–1947) MIT B.S. 1888

Anna Julia Cooper (1858–1964) University of Paris Ph.D. 1925

Florence Kelley (1859–1932) Northwestern University J.D. 1895

Charlotte Perkins Gilman (1860–1935) Attended Rhode Island School of Design 1878–1880

Ida B. Wells-Barnett (1862–1931) Attended Fisk University 1882–1884

Emily Greene Balch (1867–1961) Bryn Mawr College B.A. 1889

Grace Abbott (1878–1939) University of Chicago M.Phil. 1909

Frances Perkins (1880–1965) Columbia University M.A. 1910

Alice Paul (1885–1977) American University D.C.L. 1928

Photo wheel copyright 2010 © James M. Henslin

Many early female sociologists wrote extensively. Their writings—and matching social activism—were directed almost exclusively at social reform, such as ways to improve the working conditions of poorly paid workers, the integration of immigrants into society, and the anti-lynching movement. As sociology developed in North America, a prolonged debate ensued about the proper purpose of sociology. You are already familiar with this tension: Should the purpose of sociology be social reform or objective analysis? This debate on advocacy versus objectivity was won by men who held university positions, men who feared that advocacy for social causes would jeopardize the reputation of sociology—and their own university positions. It was these men who wrote the history of sociology. Distancing themselves from the social reformers, they ignored the early female sociologists when they recounted the development of sociology (Lengermann and Niebrugge 2007). Now that women have regained their voice in sociology—and have begun to rewrite its history—early female sociologists are slowly being acknowledged.

Harriet Martineau (1802–1876) provides a classic example of how the contributions of early female sociologists were ignored. Although Martineau was from England, she is included here because she did extensive analyses of U.S. social customs. Sexism was so pervasive that when Martineau first began to analyze social life, she would hide her writing beneath her sewing when visitors arrived, for writing was "masculine" and sewing "feminine" (Gilman 1911/1971:88). Despite her extensive and acclaimed research on social life in both Great Britain and the United States, until recently Martineau was known primarily for translating Comte's ideas into English. The Down-to-Earth Sociology box on the next page features Martineau's research on the United States.

Racism at the Time: W. E. B. Du Bois

Not only was sexism assumed to be normal during this early period of sociology, but so was racism, which made life difficult for African American professionals such as W. E. B. Du Bois (1868–1963). After earning a bachelor's degree from Fisk University, Du Bois became the first African American to earn a doctorate at Harvard. He then studied at the University of Berlin, where he attended lectures by Max Weber. After teaching Greek and Latin at Wilberforce University, in 1897 Du Bois moved to Atlanta University to teach sociology and do research. He remained there for most of his career (Du Bois 1935/1992).

It is difficult to grasp how racist society was at this time. As Du Bois passed a butcher shop in Georgia one day, he saw the fingers of a lynching victim displayed in the window (Aptheker 1990). When Du Bois went to national meetings of the American Sociological Society, restaurants and hotels would not allow him to eat or room with the white sociologists. How times have changed. Today, sociologists would not only boycott such establishments, but also refuse to hold meetings in that state. At that time, however, racism, like sexism, prevailed throughout society, rendering it mostly invisible to white sociologists. Du Bois eventually became such an outspoken critic of racism that the U.S. State Department, fearing he would criticize the United States, refused to issue him a passport (Du Bois 1968).

Each year between 1896 and 1914, Du Bois published a book on relations between African Americans and whites. Not content to collect and interpret objective data, Du Bois, along with Jane Addams and others from Hull-House (see below), was one of the founders of the National Association for the Advancement of Colored People (NAACP) (Deegan 1988). Continuing to battle racism both as a sociologist and as a journalist, Du Bois eventually embraced revolutionary Marxism. At age 93, dismayed that so little improvement had been made in race relations, he moved to Ghana, where he is buried (Stark 1989).

Until recently, Du Bois' work was neglected by sociologists. As a personal example, during my entire graduate program at Washington University, the faculty never mentioned him. Today, however, sociologists are rediscovering Du Bois, reading and discussing his research. Of his almost 2,000 writings, *The Philadelphia Negro* (1899/1967) stands out. In this analysis, Du Bois pointed out that some successful African Americans were breaking their ties with other African Americans in order to win acceptance by whites. This, he said, weakened the African American community by depriving it of their influence. Taken from a 1903 book by Du Bois, the Down-to-Earth Sociology box on page 20 provides a picture of race relations following the Civil War.

Jane Addams: Sociologist and Social Reformer

Of the many early sociologists who combined the role of sociologist with that of social reformer, none was as successful as Jane Addams (1860–1935), who was a member of the American Sociological Society from its founding in 1895. Like Harriet Martineau, Addams, too, came from a background of wealth and privilege. She attended the Women's Medical College of Philadelphia, but dropped out because of illness (Addams 1910/1981). On a trip to Europe, Addams saw the work being done to help London's poor. The memory wouldn't leave her, she said, and she decided to work for social justice.

In 1889, Addams co-founded Hull-House with Ellen Gates Starr. Located in Chicago's notorious slums, Hull-House was open to people who needed refuge—to immigrants,

W(illiam) **E**(dward) **B**(urghardt) **Du Bois** (1868–1963) spent his lifetime studying relations between African Americans and whites. Like many early North Americans sociologists, Du Bois combined the role of academic sociologist with that of social reformer. He was also the editor of *Crisis*, an influential journal of the time.

Jane Addams (1860–1935) a recipient of the Nobel Prize for Peace, worked on behalf of poor immigrants. With Ellen G. Starr, she founded Hull-House, a center to help immigrants in Chicago. She was also a leader in women's rights (women's suffrage), as well as the peace movement of World War I.

Down-to-Earth Sociology
Harriet Martineau and U.S. Customs: Listening to an Early Feminist

The breadth of Martineau's research is striking. In 1834, two or three decades before Durkheim and Weber were born, Martineau began a two-year study of U.S. customs. Traveling by foot, horseback, stagecoach, and steamboat, she visited twenty of the then twenty-four states. She observed and interviewed Americans, from those who lived in poverty to Andrew Jackson, then the President of the United States, with whom she had dinner (Lengermann and Niebrugge 2007). She spoke with both slaveholders and abolitionists. She also visited prisons and attended sessions of the U.S. Supreme Court. To summarize her research, in 1837 she published *Society in America,* from which these excerpts are taken.

Concerning women not being allowed to vote

One of the fundamental principles announced in the Declaration of Independence is that governments derive their just powers from the consent of the governed. How can the political condition of women be reconciled with this?

Governments in the United States have power to tax women who hold property . . . to fine, imprison, and execute them for certain offences. Whence do these governments derive their powers? They are not "just," as they are not derived from the consent of the women thus governed. . . .

The democratic principle condemns all this as wrong; and requires the equal political representation of all rational beings. Children, idiots, and criminals . . . are the only fair exceptions. . . .

Interested in social reform, Harriet Martineau (1802–1876) turned to sociology, where she discovered the writing of Comte. She became on advocate for the abolition of slavery, traveled widely, and wrote extensive analyses of social life.

Concerning the education of women

The intellect of woman is confined by an unjustifiable restriction. . . . As women have none of the objects in life for which an enlarged education is considered requisite, the education is not given. . . . [S]ome things [are] taught which . . . serve to fill up time . . . to improve conversation, and to make women something like companions to their husbands, and able to teach their children somewhat. . . . There is rarely or never a . . . promotion of clear intellectual activity. . . . [A]s long as women are excluded from the objects for which men are trained . . . intellectual activity is dangerous: or, as the phrase is, unfit. Accordingly marriage is the only object left open to woman.

Concerning sex and, slavery, and relations between white women and men in the South

[White American women] are all married young . . . and there is ever present an unfortunate servile class of their own sex [female slaves] to serve the purposes of licentiousness [as sexual objects for white slaveholders]. . . . [When most] men carry secrets which their wives must be the last to know . . . there is an end to all wholesome confidence and sympathy, and woman sinks to be the ornament of her husband's house, the domestic manager of his establishment, instead of being his all-sufficient friend. . . . I have seen, with heart-sorrow, the kind politeness, the gallantry, so insufficient to the loving heart, with which the wives of the south are treated by their husbands. . . . I know the tone of conversation which is adopted towards women; different in its topics and its style from that which any man would dream of offering to any other man. I have heard the boast of chivalrous consideration in which women are held throughout their woman's paradise; and seen something of the anguish of crushed pride, of the conflict of bitter feelings with which such boasts have been listened to by those whose aspirations teach them the hollowness of the system. . . .

---

the sick, the aged, the poor. Sociologists from the nearby University of Chicago were frequent visitors at Hull-House. With her piercing insights into the exploitation of workers and the adjustment of immigrants to city life, Addams strove to bridge the gap between the powerful and the powerless. She co-founded the American Civil Liberties Union and campaigned for the eight-hour work day and for laws against child labor. She wrote books on poverty, democracy, and peace. Adams' writings and efforts at social reform were so outstanding that in 1931, she was a co-winner of the Nobel Prize for Peace. She and Emily Greene Balch are the only sociologists to have won this coveted award.

Talcott Parsons and C. Wright Mills: Contrasting Views

Like Du Bois and Addams, many early North American sociologists saw society, or parts of it, as corrupt and in need of reform. During the 1920s and 1930s, for example, Robert Park and Ernest Burgess (1921) not only studied crime, drug addiction, juvenile

Down-to-Earth Sociology
W. E. B. Du Bois: The Souls of Black Folk

Du Bois wrote more like an accomplished novelist than a sociologist. The following excerpts are from pages 66–68 of *The Souls of Black Folk* (1903). In this book, Du Bois analyzes changes that occurred in the social and economic conditions of African Americans during the thirty years following the Civil War.

For two summers, while he was a student at Fisk, Du Bois taught in a segregated school housed in a log hut "way back in the hills" of rural Tennessee. The following excerpts help us understand conditions at that time.

In the 1800s, most people were so poor that they expended their life energies on just getting enough food, fuel, and clothing to survive. The average person died before reaching age 40. Formal education beyond the first several grades was a luxury. This photo depicts the conditions of the people Du Bois worked with.

It was a hot morning late in July when the school opened. I trembled when I heard the patter of little feet down the dusty road, and saw the growing row of dark solemn faces and bright eager eyes facing me. . . . There they sat, nearly thirty of them, on the rough benches, their faces shading from a pale cream to deep brown, the little feet bare and swinging, the eyes full of expectation, with here and there a twinkle of mischief, and the hands grasping Webster's blue-black spelling-book. I loved my school, and the fine faith the children had in the wisdom of their teacher was truly marvelous. We read and spelled together, wrote a little, picked flowers, sang, and listened to stories of the world beyond the hill. . . .

On Friday nights I often went home with some of the children,—sometimes to Doc Burke's farm. He was a great, loud, thin Black, ever working, and trying to buy these seventy-five acres of hill and dale where he lived; but people said that he would surely fail and the "white folks would get it all." His wife was a magnificent Amazon, with saffron face and shiny hair, uncorseted and barefooted, and the children were strong and barefooted. They lived in a one-and-a-half-room cabin in the hollow of the farm near the spring. . . .

Often, to keep the peace, I must go where life was less lovely; for instance, "Tildy's mother was incorrigibly dirty, Reuben's larder was limited seriously, and herds of untamed insects wandered over the Eddingses' beds. Best of all I loved to go to Josie's, and sit on the porch, eating peaches, while the mother bustled and talked: how Josie had bought the sewing-machine; how Josie worked at service in winter, but that four dollars a month was "mighty little" wages; how Josie longed to go away to school, but that it "looked liked" they never could get far enough ahead to let her; how the crops failed and the well

was yet unfinished; and, finally, how mean some of the white folks were.

For two summers I lived in this little world. . . . I have called my tiny community a world, and so its isolation made it; and yet there was among us but a half-awakened common consciousness, sprung from common joy and grief, at burial, birth, or wedding; from common hardship in poverty, poor land, and low wages, and, above all, from the sight of the Veil* that hung between us and Opportunity. All this caused us to think some thoughts together; but these, when ripe for speech, were spoken in various languages. Those whose eyes twenty-five and more years had seen "the glory of the coming of the Lord," saw in every present hindrance or help a dark fatalism bound to bring all things right in His own good time. The mass of those to whom slavery was a dim recollection of childhood found the world a puzzling thing: it asked little of them, and they answered with little, and yet it ridiculed their offering. Such a paradox they could not understand, and therefore sank into listless indifference, or shiftlessness, or reckless bravado.

---

*"The Veil" is shorthand for the Veil of Race, referring to how race colors all human relations. Du Bois' hope, as he put it, was that "sometime, somewhere, men will judge men by their souls and not by their skins" (p. 261).

delinquency, and prostitution but also offered suggestions for how to alleviate these social problems. As the emphasis shifted from social reform to objective analyses, the abstract models of society developed by sociologist Talcott Parsons (1902–1979) influenced a generation of sociologists. These models of how the parts of society work together harmoniously did nothing to stimulate social activism.

Another sociologist, C. Wright Mills (1916–1962), deplored such theoretical abstractions. Trying to push the pendulum the other way, he urged sociologists to get back to social reform. In his writings, he warned that the nation faced an imminent threat to freedom—the coalescing of interests of a *power elite*, the top leaders of business, politics, and the military. The precedent-shaking 1960s and 1970s that followed Mills' death sparked interest in social activism among a new generation of sociologists.

C. Wright Mills (1916–1962) was a controversial figure in sociology because of his analysis of the role of the power elite in U.S. society. Today, his analysis is taken for granted by many sociologists and members of the public.

The Continuing Tension and Applied Sociology

As we have seen, two apparently contradictory aims—analyzing society versus working toward its reform—have run through North American sociology since its founding. This tension is still with us. As we saw in Figure 1.2 on page 14, some sociologists see their proper role as analyzing some aspect of society and publishing their findings in books and sociology journals. This is called **basic** (or **pure**) **sociology.** Others argue that basic sociology is not enough, that sociologists have an obligation to use their expertise to try to help reform society, especially to help bring justice to the poor and oppressed.

As Figure 1.3 below shows, somewhere between these extremes lies **applied sociology,** using sociology to solve problems. Applied sociology is not new, for as we've seen, sociologists founded the NAACP. The vision that accompanies today's applied sociology, however, seems considerably less comprehensive. Earlier sociologists saw sociology as a way to reform broad swaths of society. Today's applied sociologists generally lack such a broad vision, but as illustrated in the Down-to-Earth Sociology box on the next page, their application of sociology is wide-ranging. Some work for business firms to solve problems in the workplace, while others investigate social problems such as pornography, rape, pollution, or the spread of AIDS. A new application of sociology is determining ways to disrupt terrorist groups (Sageman 2008).

basic (or **pure**) **sociology** sociological research for the purpose of making discoveries about life in human groups, not for making changes in those groups

applied sociology the use of sociology to solve problems—from the micro level of family relationships to the macro level of global pollution

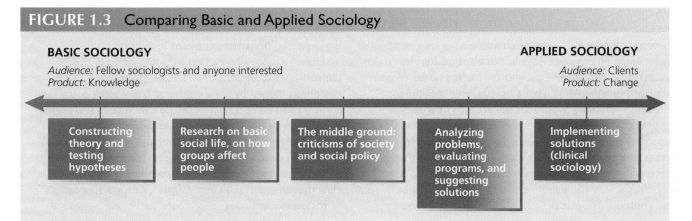

FIGURE 1.3   Comparing Basic and Applied Sociology

BASIC SOCIOLOGY
Audience: Fellow sociologists and anyone interested
Product: Knowledge

APPLIED SOCIOLOGY
Audience: Clients
Product: Change

| Constructing theory and testing hypotheses | Research on basic social life, on how groups affect people | The middle ground: criticisms of society and social policy | Analyzing problems, evaluating programs, and suggesting solutions | Implementing solutions (clinical sociology) |

Source: By the author. Based on DeMartini 1982.

Although applied sociology pleases many sociologists, it frustrates both those who want the emphasis to be on social reform and those who want it to be on objective analysis. Those who favor social reform point out that the application of sociology in some specific setting is far from an attempt to rebuild society. Those who want sociology's emphasis to be the discovery of objective knowledge say that when sociology is applied, it is no longer sociology. If, for example, sociologists use sociological principles to help teenagers escape from pimps, they say, what makes it sociology?

This contemporary debate on the purpose and use of sociology, with roots that go back a century or more, is likely to continue for another generation. At this point, let's consider how theory fits into sociology.

Down-to-Earth Sociology
Careers in Sociology: What Applied Sociologists Do

Most sociologists teach in colleges and universities, sharing sociological knowledge with students, as your instructor is doing with you in this course. Applied sociologists, in contrast, work in a wide variety of areas—from counseling children to studying how diseases are transmitted. To give you an idea of this variety, let's look over the shoulders of four applied sociologists.

Leslie Green, who does marketing research at Vanderveer Group in Philadelphia, Pennsylvania, earned her bachelor's degree in sociology at Shippensburg University. She helps to develop strategies to get doctors to prescribe particular drugs. She sets up the meetings, locates moderators for the discussion groups, and arranges payments to the physicians who participate in the research. "My training in sociology," she says, "helps me in 'people skills.' It helps me to understand the needs of different groups, and to interact with them."

Stanley Capela, whose master's degree is from Fordham University, works as an applied sociologist at HeartShare Human Services in New York City. He evaluates how children's programs—such as ones that focus on housing, AIDS, group homes, and preschool education—actually work, compared with how they are supposed to work. He spots problems and suggests solutions. One of his assignments was to find out why it was taking so long to get children adopted, even though there was a long list of eager adoptive parents. Capela pinpointed how the paperwork got bogged down as it was routed through the system and suggested ways to improve the flow of paperwork.

Laurie Banks, who received her master's degree in sociology from Fordham University, analyzes statistics for the New York City Health Department. As she examined death certificates, she noticed that a Polish neighborhood had a high rate of stomach cancer. She

As detailed in this box, applied sociology *takes many forms. Some applied sociologists focus their efforts on improving social conditions of the poor. A rare few turn to revolutionary activities. This photo taken in Santiago, Chile, of social activists who espouse violence on behalf of farm workers in South America includes a sociologist.*

alerted the Centers for Disease Control and Prevention, which conducted interviews in the neighborhood. Scientists from the CDC traced the cause to eating large amounts of sausage. In another case, Banks compared birth certificates with school records. She found that problems at birth—low birth weight, lack of prenatal care, and birth complications—were linked to low reading skills and behavior problems in school.

Daniel Knapp, who earned a doctorate from the University of Oregon, applied sociology by going to the city dump. Moved by the idea that urban wastes could be recycled and reused, he first tested this idea by scavenging in a small way—at the city dump at Berkeley, California. After starting a company called Urban Ore, Knapp (2005) did research on how to recycle urban wastes and worked to change waste disposal laws. As a founder of the recycling movement in the United States, Knapp's application of sociology continues to influence us all.

From just these few examples, you can catch a glimpse of the variety of work that applied sociologists do. Some work for corporations, some are employed by government and private agencies, and others run their own businesses. You can also see that you don't need a doctorate in order to work as an applied sociologist.

Sociologist W. E. B. Du Bois analyzed segregation in U.S. society, which changed only slowly. From being relegated to the back of the bus in the 1950s to being elected president of the United States 50 years later, African Americans have made a remarkable journey. Shown here is a Jim Crow sign being removed from a bus in North Carolina in 1956.

Theoretical Perspectives in Sociology

Facts never interpret themselves. To make sense out of life, we use our common sense. That is, to understand our experiences (our "facts"), we place them into a framework of more-or-less related ideas. Sociologists do this, too, but they place their observations into a conceptual framework called a theory. A **theory** is a general statement about how some parts of the world fit together and how they work. It is an explanation of how two or more "facts" are related to one another.

Sociologists use three major theories: symbolic interactionism, functional analysis, and conflict theory. Let's look at each theory, first examining its main elements and then applying it to the U.S. divorce rate, to see why it is so high. As we do this, you will see how each theory, or perspective, provides a distinct interpretation of social life.

Symbolic Interactionism

The central idea of **symbolic interactionism** is that *symbols*—things to which we attach meaning—are the key to understanding how we view the world and communicate with one another. As discussed on pages 68–69, Charles Horton Cooley (1864–1929) and George Herbert Mead (1863–1931) developed this perspective in sociology. Let's look at the main elements of this theory.

Symbols in Everyday Life.   Without symbols, our social life would be no more sophisticated than that of animals. For example, without symbols we would have no aunts or uncles, employers or teachers—or even brothers and sisters. I know that this sounds strange, but it is symbols that define our relationships. There would still be reproduction, of course, but no symbols to tell us how we are related to whom. We would not know to whom we owe respect and obligations, or from whom we can expect privileges—the essence of human relationships.

Look at it like this: If you think of someone as your aunt or uncle, you behave one way, but if you think of that person as a boyfriend or girlfriend, you behave quite differently. It is the symbol that tells you how you are related to others—and how you should act toward them.

theory a statement about how some parts of the world fit together and how they work; an explanation of how two or more facts are related to one another

symbolic interactionism a theoretical perspective in which society is viewed as composed of symbols that people use to establish meaning, develop their views of the world, and communicate with one another

George Herbert Mead
(1863–1931) is one of the founders of symbolic interactionism, a major theoretical perspective in sociology. He taught at the University of Chicago, where his lectures were popular. Although he wrote little, after his death students compiled his lectures into an influential book, *Mind, Self, and Society*.

Let's make this a little less abstract. Consider this example:

Suppose that you have fallen head over heels in love. Finally, after what seems forever, it is the night before your wedding. As you are contemplating tomorrow's bliss, your mother comes to you in tears. Sobbing, she tells you that she had a child before she married your father, a child that she gave up for adoption. Breaking down, she says that she has just discovered that the person you are going to marry is this child.

You can see how the symbol will change overnight—and your behavior, too!

It is not only relationships that depend on symbols to exist, but even society itself. Without symbols, we could not coordinate our actions with those of others. We could not make plans for a future day, time, and place. Unable to specify times, materials, sizes, or goals, we could not build bridges and highways. Without symbols, there would be no movies or musical instruments. We would have no hospitals, no government, no religion. The class you are taking could not exist—nor could this book. On the positive side, there would be no war.

In Sum: Symbolic interactionists analyze how social life depends on the ways we define ourselves and others. They study face-to-face interaction, examining how people make sense out of life and their place in it. Symbolic interactionists point out that even the *self* is a symbol, for it consists of the ideas we have about who we are. We'll get more into this later.

Applying Symbolic Interactionism.   Look at Figure 1.4, which shows U.S. marriages and divorces over time. Let's see how symbolic interactionists would use changing symbols to explain this figure. For background, you should understand that marriage used to be a *life-long commitment*. A hundred years ago (and less) getting divorced was viewed as immoral, a flagrant disregard for public opinion, and the abandonment of adult responsibilities. Let's see what changed.

The meaning of marriage: By the 1930s, young people were coming to view marriage in a different way, a change that was reported by sociologists of the time. In 1933, William Ogburn observed that they were placing more emphasis on the personality of potential mates. Then in 1945, Ernest Burgess and Harvey Locke noted that people were expecting

FIGURE 1.4   U.S. Marriage, U.S. Divorce

Source: By the author. Based on *Statistical Abstract of the United States* 1998: Table 92 and 2009: Tables 77, 123; earlier editions for earlier years. The broken lines indicate the author's estimates.

more affection, understanding, and compatibility in marriage. In addition, less and less people saw marriage as a lifelong commitment based on duty and obligation. As they began to view marriage as an arrangement that was based on attraction and feelings of intimacy, it became one that could be broken when feelings changed.

The meaning of divorce: As divorce became more common, its meaning changed. Rather than being a symbol of failure, divorce came to indicate freedom and new beginnings. Removing the stigma from divorce shattered a strong barrier that had prevented husbands and wives from breaking up.

Changed guidelines: Related symbols also changed—and none of these changes strengthened marriage. For example, traditional marriage had firm guidelines, and newly-weds knew what each was supposed to do regarding work, home, and children. In contrast, today's guidelines are vague, and couples must figure out how to divide up responsibilities. This can be a struggle, even a source of conflict, and many flounder. Although couples find it a relief not to have to conform to what they consider to be burdensome notions, those traditional expectations (or symbols) did provide a structure that made marriages last. Changing symbols weakened this structure, making marriage more fragile and divorce more common.

The meaning of parenthood: Ideas of parenthood and childhood also used to be quite different. Parents had little responsibility for their children beyond providing food, clothing, shelter, and moral guidance. And they needed to do this for only a short time, because children began to contribute to the support of the family early in life. Among many people, parenthood is still like this. In Colombia, for example, children of the poor often are expected to support themselves by the age of 8 or 10. In industrial societies, however, we assume that children are vulnerable beings who must depend on their parents for financial and emotional support for many years—often until they are well into their 20s. That this is not the case in many cultures often comes as a surprise to Americans, who assume that their own situation is some sort of worldwide, natural arrangement. The greater responsibilities that we assign to parenthood place heavy burdens on today's couples and, with them, more strain on marriage.

The meaning of love: And we can't overlook the love symbol. As surprising as it may sound, to have love as the main reason for marriage is to weaken marriage. In some depth of our being, we expect "true love" to deliver constant emotional highs. This expectation sets people up for crushed hopes, as dissatisfactions in marriage are inevitable. When they come, spouses tend to blame one another for failing to deliver the expected satisfaction.

In Sum: Symbolic interactionists look at how changing ideas (or symbols) of love, marriage, relationships, parenthood, and divorce put pressure on married couples. No single change is *the* cause of our divorce rate, but, taken together, these changes provide a strong push toward divorce.

Functional Analysis

The central idea of **functional analysis** is that society is a whole unit, made up of inter-related parts that work together. Functional analysis (also known as *functionalism* and *structural functionalism*) is rooted in the origins of sociology. Auguste Comte and Herbert Spencer viewed society as a kind of living organism. Just as a person or animal has organs that function together, they wrote, so does society. And like an organism, if society is to function smoothly, its parts must work together in harmony.

Emile Durkheim also viewed society as being composed of many parts, each with its own function. When all the parts of society fulfill their functions, society is in a "normal" state. If they do not fulfill their functions, society is in an "abnormal" or "pathological" state. To understand society, then, functionalists say that we need to look at both *structure* (how the parts of a society fit together to make the whole) and *function* (what each part does, how it contributes to society).

> **functional analysis** a theoretical framework in which society is viewed as composed of various parts, each with a function that, when fulfilled, contributes to society's equilibrium; also known as *functionalism* and *structural functionalism*

Robert K. Merton (1910–2003), who spent most of his academic career at Columbia University, was a major proponent of functionalism, one of the main theoretical perspectives in sociology.

Robert Merton and Functionalism.   Robert Merton (1910–2003) dismissed the organic analogy, but he did maintain the essence of functionalism—the image of society as a whole composed of parts that work together. Merton used the term *functions* to refer to the beneficial consequences of people's actions: Functions help keep a group (society, social system) in balance. In contrast, *dysfunctions* are consequences that harm a society: They undermine a system's equilibrium.

Functions can be either manifest or latent. If an action is *intended* to help some part of a system, it is a *manifest function.* For example, suppose that government officials become concerned about our low rate of childbirth. Congress offers a $10,000 bonus for every child born to a married couple. The intention, or manifest function, of the bonus is to increase childbearing within the family unit. Merton pointed out that people's actions can also have *latent functions;* that is, they can have *unintended* consequences that help a system adjust. Let's suppose that the bonus works. As the birth rate jumps, so does the sale of diapers and baby furniture. Because the benefits to these businesses were not the intended consequences, they are latent functions of the bonus.

Of course, human actions can also hurt a system. Because such consequences usually are unintended, Merton called them *latent dysfunctions.* Let's assume that the government has failed to specify a "stopping point" with regard to its bonus system. To collect more bonuses, some people keep on having children. The more children they have, however, the more they need the next bonus to survive. Large families become common, and poverty increases. Welfare is reinstated, taxes jump, and the nation erupts in protest. Because these results were not intended and because they harmed the social system, they would be latent dysfunctions of the bonus program.

In Sum: From the perspective of functional analysis, society is a functioning unit, with each part related to the whole. Whenever we examine a smaller part, we need to look for its functions and dysfunctions to see how it is related to the larger unit. This basic approach can be applied to any social group, whether an entire society, a college, or even a group as small as a family.

Applying Functional Analysis.   Now let's apply functional analysis to the U.S. divorce rate. Functionalists stress that industrialization and urbanization undermined the traditional functions of the family. For example, before industrialization, the family formed an economic team. On the farm where most people lived, each family member had jobs or "chores" to do. The wife was in charge not only of household tasks but also of raising small animals, such as chickens. Milking cows, collecting eggs, and churning butter were also her responsibility—as were cooking, baking, canning, sewing, darning, washing, and cleaning. The daughters helped her. The husband was responsible for caring for large animals, such as horses and cattle, for planting and harvesting, and for maintaining buildings and tools. The sons helped him. Together, they formed an economic unit in which each depended on the others for survival.

This certainly doesn't sound like life today!

Other functions also bound family members to one another: educating the children, teaching them religion, providing home-based recreation, and caring for the sick and elderly. To further see how sharply family functions have changed, look at this example from the 1800s:

> When Phil became sick, he was nursed by Ann, his wife. She cooked for him, fed him, changed the bed linens, bathed him, read to him from the Bible, and gave him his medicine. (She did this in addition to doing the housework and taking care of their six children.) Phil was also surrounded by the children, who shouldered some of his chores while he was sick. When Phil died, the male neighbors and relatives made the casket while Ann, her mother, and female friends washed and dressed the body. Phil was then "laid out" in the front parlor (the formal living room), where friends, neighbors, and relatives paid their last respects. From there, friends moved his body to the church for the final message and then to the grave they themselves had dug.

In Sum: When the family loses functions, it becomes more fragile, and an increase in divorce is inevitable. Economic production is an excellent example of how the family has

Sociologists who use the *functionalist perspective* stress how industrialization and urbanization undermined the traditional *functions* of the family. Before industrialization, members of the family worked together as an economic unit, as in this painting of Italian farm life by Francesco Bassano (1549–1592). As production moved away from the home, it took with it first the father and, more recently, the mother. One consequence is a major dysfunction, the weakening of family ties.

lost functions. No longer is making a living a cooperative, home-based effort, with husband and wife depending on one another for their interlocking contributions to a mutual endeavor. Husbands and wives today earn individual paychecks and increasingly function as separate components in an impersonal, multinational, and even global system. The fewer functions that family members share, the fewer are their "ties that bind"—and these ties are what help husbands and wives get through the problems they inevitably experience.

Conflict Theory

Conflict theory provides a third perspective on social life. Unlike the functionalists, who view society as a harmonious whole, with its parts working together, conflict theorists stress that society is composed of groups that are competing with one another for scarce resources. Although the surface may show alliances or cooperation, scratch that surface and you will find a struggle for power.

Karl Marx and Conflict Theory.   Karl Marx, the founder of conflict theory, witnessed the Industrial Revolution that transformed Europe. He saw that peasants who had left the land to seek work in cities had to work for wages that barely provided enough to eat. Things were so bad that the average worker died at age 30, the average wealthy person at age 50 (Edgerton 1992:87). Shocked by this suffering and exploitation, Marx began to analyze society and history. As he did so, he developed **conflict theory.** He concluded that the key to human history is *class conflict.* In each society, some small group controls the means of production and exploits those who are not in control. In industrialized societies, the struggle is between the *bourgeoisie*, the small group of capitalists who own the means to produce wealth, and the *proletariat,* the mass of workers who are exploited by the bourgeoisie. The capitalists also control the legal and political system: If the workers rebel, the capitalists call on the power of the state to subdue them.

When Marx made his observations, capitalism was in its infancy and workers were at the mercy of their employers. Workers had none of what we take for granted today—minimum wages, eight-hour days, coffee breaks, five-day work weeks, paid vacations

conflict theory a theoretical framework in which society is viewed as composed of groups that are competing for scarce resources

and holidays, medical benefits, sick leave, unemployment compensation, Social Security, and, for union workers, the right to strike. Marx's analysis reminds us that these benefits came not from generous hearts, but by workers forcing concessions from their employers.

Conflict Theory Today.   Many sociologists extend conflict theory beyond the relationship of capitalists and workers. They examine how opposing interests permeate every layer of society—whether that be a small group, an organization, a community, or the entire society. For example, when police, teachers, and parents try to enforce conformity, this creates resentment and resistance. It is the same when a teenager tries to "change the rules" to gain more independence. There is, then, a constant struggle throughout society to determine who has authority or influence and how far that dominance goes (Turner 1978; Leeson 2006; Piven 2008).

Sociologist Lewis Coser (1913–2003) pointed out that conflict is most likely to develop among people who are in close relationships. These people have worked out ways to distribute power and privilege, responsibilities and rewards. Any change in this arrangement can lead to hurt feelings, resentment, and conflict. Even in intimate relationships, then, people are in a constant balancing act, with conflict lying uneasily just beneath the surface.

Feminists and Conflict Theory.   Just as Marx examined conflict between capitalists and workers, many feminists analyze conflict between men and women. A primary focus is the historical, contemporary, and global inequalities of men and women—and how the traditional dominance by men can be overcome to bring about equality of the sexes. Feminists are not united by the conflict perspective, however. They tackle a variety of topics and use whatever theory applies. (Feminism is discussed in Chapter 11.)

Applying Conflict Theory.   To explain why the U.S. divorce rate is high, conflict theorists focus on how men's and women's relationships have changed. For millennia, men dominated women. Women had few alternatives other than to accept their exploitation. Then industrialization ushered in a new world, one in which women could meet their basic survival needs outside of marriage. Industrialization also fostered a culture in which females participate in social worlds beyond the home. With this new ability to refuse to bear burdens that earlier generations accepted as inevitable, today's women are likely to dissolve a marriage that becomes intolerable—or even unsatisfactory.

In Sum: The dominance of men over women was once considered natural and right. As women gained education and earnings, however, they first questioned and then rejected this assumption. As wives strove for more power and grew less inclined to put up with relationships that they defined as unfair, the divorce rate increased. From the conflict perspective, then, our high divorce rate does not mean that marriage has weakened, but, rather, that women are making headway in their historical struggle with men.

Levels of Analysis: Macro and Micro

macro-level analysis an examination of large-scale patterns of society

micro-level analysis an examination of small-scale patterns of society

social interaction what people do when they are in one another's presence

nonverbal interaction communication without words through gestures, use of space, silence, and so on

A major difference between these three theoretical perspectives is their level of analysis. Functionalists and conflict theorists focus on the **macro level;** that is, they examine large-scale patterns of society. In contrast, symbolic interactionists usually focus on the **micro level,** on **social interaction**—what people do when they are in one another's presence. These levels are summarized in Table 1.1 on the next page.

To make this distinction between micro and macro levels clearer, let's return to the example of the homeless, with which we opened this chapter. To study homeless people, symbolic interactionists would focus on the micro level. They would analyze what homeless people do when they are in shelters and on the streets. They would also analyze their communications, both their talk and their **nonverbal interaction** (gestures, silence, use of space, and so on). The observations I made at the beginning of this chapter about the silence in the homeless shelter, for example, would be of interest to symbolic interactionists.

TABLE 1.1　Three Theoretical Perspectives in Sociology

Perspective	Usual Level of Analysis	Focus of Analysis	Key Terms	Applying the Perspective to the U.S. Divorce Rate
Symbolic Interactionism	Microsociological: examines small-scale patterns of social interaction	Face-to-face interaction, how people use symbols to create social life	Symbols Interaction Meanings Definitions	Industrialization and urbanization changed marital roles and led to a redefinition of love, marriage, children, and divorce.
Functional Analysis (also called functionalism and structural functionalism)	Macrosociological: examines large-scale patterns of society	Relationships among the parts of society; how these parts are functional (have beneficial consequences) or dysfunctional (have negative consequences)	Structure Functions (manifest and latent) Dysfunctions Equilibrium	As social change erodes the traditional functions of the family, family ties weaken, and the divorce rate increases.
Conflict Theory	Macrosociological: examines large-scale patterns of society	The struggle for scarce resources by groups in a society; how the elites use their power to control the weaker groups	Inequality Power Conflict Competition Exploitation	When men control economic life, the divorce rate is low because women find few alternatives to a bad marriage. The high divorce rate reflects a shift in the balance of power between men and women.

This micro level, however, would not interest functionalists and conflict theorists. They would focus instead on the macro level. Functionalists would examine how changes in the parts of society have increased homelessness. They might look at how changes in the family (fewer children, more divorce) and economic conditions (inflation, fewer unskilled jobs, loss of jobs to workers overseas) cause homelessness among people who are unable to find jobs and who have no family to fall back on. For their part, conflict theorists would stress the struggle between social classes. They would be especially interested in how decisions by international elites on global production and trade affect the local job market, and along with it unemployment and homelessness.

Putting the Theoretical Perspectives Together

Which theoretical perspective should we use to study human behavior? Which level of analysis is the correct one? As you have seen, these three perspectives produce contrasting pictures of social life. In the case of divorce, these interpretations are quite different from the commonsense understanding that two people are simply "incompatible." *Because each theory focuses on different features of social life, each provides a distinct interpretation. Consequently, we need to use all three theoretical lenses to analyze human behavior. By combining the contributions of each, we gain a more comprehensive picture of social life.*

Trends Shaping the Future of Sociology

Two major trends indicate changing directions in sociology. Let's look again at the relationship of sociology to social reform, and then at globalization.

Sociology Full Circle: Reform Versus Research

Three Stages in Sociology.　As you have seen, a tension between social reform and social analysis runs through the history of sociology. To better understand this tension, we can divide sociology into three time periods (Lazarsfeld and Reitz 1989). During the *first* phase, which lasted until the 1920s, the primary purpose of research was to improve society. During the *second* phase, from the 1920s until World War II, the initial concern with improving society switched to developing abstract knowledge. We are now in a *third* phase, which began around the end of World War II, in which sociologists are increasingly seeking ways to apply their research findings. Many sociology departments offer courses in applied sociology, with some offering internships in applied sociology at both the graduate and undergraduate levels.

Diversity of Orientations.   I want to stress that sociology is filled with diverse opinions. Sociologists do not move in lockstep toward a single goal. To divide sociology into three separate phases overlooks as much as it reveals. Even during the first phase, Durkheim and Weber did research for the purpose of gaining academic respectability for sociology. Similarly, during the second phase, many sociologists who wanted to reform society chafed at the emphasis on understanding. And today, many sociologists want the emphasis to remain on basic sociology. Some do not even acknowledge that applied sociology is "real" sociology. They say that it is actually social work or psychology masquerading as sociology.

Each particular period, however, does have basic emphases, and this division of sociology into three phases pinpoints major trends. The tension that has run through sociology—between gaining knowledge and applying knowledge—will continue. During this current phase, the pendulum is swinging toward applying sociological knowledge.

Public Sociology.   The American Sociological Association (ASA) is promoting **public sociology.** By this term, the ASA refers to sociology being used for the public good. One goal of public sociology is to have politicians and policy makers use the sociological perspective as they decide social policy. In the Cultural Diversity box on the next page, you can see that basic research can also lead to public sociology.

Globalization

A second major trend, globalization, is also leaving its mark on sociology. **Globalization** is the breaking down of national boundaries because of advances in communications, trade, and travel. Because the United States dominates sociology and we U.S. sociologists tend to concentrate on events and relationships that occur in our own country, most of our findings are based on U.S. samples. Globalization is destined to broaden our horizons, directing us to a greater consideration of global issues. This, in turn, is likely to motivate us to try more vigorously to identify universal principles.

Application of Globalization to This Text.   You and I are living at a great historical moment, something that isn't always easy to do. We are personally experiencing globalization, one of the most significant events in all of world history. This process is shaping our lives, our hopes, and our future—sometimes even twisting them. As globalization shrinks the globe, that is, as people around the world become more interconnected within the same global village, our own welfare is increasingly tied to that of people in other nations. From time to time in the following pages, we will also explore how the **globalization of capitalism**—capitalism becoming the world's dominant economic system—is also having profound effects on our lives. Your will also confront the developing *new world order,* which, if it can shave off its rough edges, also appears destined to play a significant role in your future.

To help broaden your horizons, in the following chapters you will visit many cultures around the world, looking at what life is like for the people who live in those cultures. Seeing how *their* society affects their behavior and orientations to life helps us to understand how *our* society influences what we do and how we feel about life. This, of course, takes us to one of the main goals of this book.

public sociology sociology being used for the public good; especially the sociological perspective (of how things are related to one another) guiding politicians and policy makers

globalization the extensive interconnections among nations due to the expansion of capitalism

globalization of capitalism capitalism (investing to make profits within a rational system) becoming the globe's dominant economic system

Cultural Diversity in the United States

Unanticipated Public Sociology: Studying Job Discrimination

Basic sociology—research aimed at learning more about some behavior—can turn into public sociology. Here is what happened to Devah Pager, a graduate student at the University of Wisconsin in Madison, who was doing volunteer work in a homeless shelter. Some of the men told her how hard it was to find work if they had had been in prison. Were the men exaggerating? she wondered. To find out what difference a prison record makes in getting a job, she sent pairs of college men to apply for 350 entry-level jobs in Milwaukee. One team was African American, and one was white. Pager prepared identical résumés for the teams, but with one difference: On each team, one of the men said he had served 18 months in prison for possession of cocaine.

Figure 1.5 shows the difference that the prison record made. Men without a prison record were two or three times as likely to be called back.

But Pager came up with another significant finding. Look at the difference that race–ethnicity made. White men with a prison record were more likely to be offered a job than African American men who had a clean record!

Sociological research often remains in obscure journals, read by only a few specialists. But Pager's findings got around, turning basic research into public sociology. Someone told President George W. Bush about the research, and he announced in his State of the Union

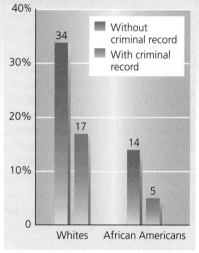

FIGURE 1.5   Call-Back Rates by Race–Ethnicity and Criminal Record

Source: Courtesy of Devah Pager.

speech that he wanted Congress to fund a $300 million program to provide mentoring and other support to help former prisoners get jobs (Kroeger 2004).

As you can see, sometimes only a thin line separates basic and public sociology.

For Your Consideration

What findings would you expect if women had been included in this study?

SUMMARY *and* REVIEW

The Sociological Perspective

What is the sociological perspective?

The **sociological perspective** stresses that people's social experiences—the groups to which they belong and their experiences within these groups—underlie their behavior. C. Wright Mills referred to this as the intersection of biography (the individual) and history (social factors that influence the individual). Pp. 4–5.

Sociology and the Other Sciences

What is science, and where does sociology fit in?

Science is the application of systematic methods to obtain knowledge and the knowledge obtained by those methods. The sciences are divided into the **natural sciences,** which seek to explain and predict events in the natural environment, and the **social sciences,** which seek to understand the social world objectively by means of controlled and repeated observations. **Sociology** is the scientific study of society and human behavior. Pp. 5–8.

Origins of Sociology

When did sociology first appear as a separate discipline?

Sociology emerged as a separate discipline in the mid-1800s in western Europe, during the onset of the Industrial Revolution. Industrialization affected all aspects of human existence—where people lived, the nature of their work, their relationships, and how they viewed life. Early sociologists who focused on these social changes include Auguste Comte, Herbert Spencer, Karl Marx, Emile Durkheim, Max Weber, Harriet Martineau, and W. E. B. Du Bois. P. 8–14.

Values in Sociological Research

Should the purpose of social research be only to advance human understanding or also to reform society?

Sociologists agree that research should be objective, that is, that the researcher's **values** and beliefs should not influence conclusions. But sociologists do not agree on the uses and purposes of social research. Some say that its purpose should be only to advance understanding of human behavior; others, that its goal should be to reform harmful social arrangements. Pp. 14–15.

Verstehen and Social Facts

How do sociologists use Verstehen *and social facts to study human behavior?*

According to Weber, to understand why people act as they do, sociologists must try to put themselves in their shoes. He used the German verb ***Verstehen,*** "to grasp by insight," to describe this essentially subjective approach. Although not denying the importance of *Verstehen,* Emile Durkheim emphasized the importance of uncovering **social facts,** social conditions that influence how people behave. Contemporary sociologists use both approaches to understand human behavior. Pp. 15–16.

Sociology in North America

When were the first academic departments of sociology established in the United States?

The earliest departments of sociology were established in the late 1800s at the universities of Kansas, Chicago, and Atlanta. In sociology's early years, the contributions of women and minorities were largely ignored. P. 16.

What was the position of women and minorities in early sociology?

Sociology developed during a historical period of deep sexism and racism. The few women, such as Harriet Martineau, and minorities, such as W. E. B. Du Bois, who received the education necessary to become sociologists felt the sting of discrimination. Pp. 16–21.

What is the difference between basic (or pure) and applied sociology?

Basic (or **pure**) **sociology** is sociological research whose purpose is to make discoveries. In contrast, **applied sociology** is the use of sociology to solve problems. Pp. 21–23.

Theoretical Perspectives in Sociology

What is a theory?

A **theory** is a general statement about how facts are related to one another. A theory provides a conceptual framework for interpreting facts. Pp. 23.

What are sociology's major theoretical perspectives?

Sociologists use three primary theoretical frameworks to interpret social life. **Symbolic interactionists** examine how people use symbols to develop and share their views of the world. Symbolic interactionists usually focus on the **micro level**—on small-scale, face-to-face interaction. **Functionalists,** in contrast, focus on the **macro level**—on large-scale patterns of society. They stress that a social system is made up of interrelated parts. When working properly, each part fulfills a function that contributes to the system's stability. **Conflict theorists** also focus on large-scale patterns of society. They stress that society is composed of competing groups that struggle for scarce resources.

With each perspective focusing on select features of social life and each providing a unique interpretation, no single theory is adequate. The combined insights of all three perspectives yield a more comprehensive picture of social life. Pp. 23–29.

Trends Shaping the Future of Sociology

What trends are likely to have an impact on sociology?

Sociology has gone through three phases: The first was an emphasis on reforming society; the second had its focus on basic sociology; the third, today's phase, is taking us closer to our roots of applying sociology to social change. **Public sociology** is the most recent example of this change. A second major trend, **globalization,** is likely to broaden sociological horizons, refocusing research and theory away from its concentration on U.S. society. Pp. 29–31.

THINKING CRITICALLY *ABOUT* Chapter 1

1. Do you think that sociologists should try to reform society or to study it dispassionately?

2. Of the three theoretical perspectives, which one would you prefer to use if you were a sociologist? Why?

3. Considering the macro- and micro-level approaches in sociology, which one do you think better explains social life? Why?

ADDITIONAL RESOURCES

What can you find in MySocLab? mysoclab www.mysoclab.com

- Complete Ebook
- Practice Tests and Video and Audio activities
- Mapping and Data Analysis exercises

- Sociology in the News
- Classic Readings in Sociology
- Research and Writing advice

Where Can I Read More on This Topic?

Suggested readings for this chapter are listed at the back of this book.

2

Culture

Kenya

I had never felt heat like this before. This was northern Africa, and I wondered what it must be like closer to the equator. Sweat poured off me as the temperature climbed past 110 degrees Fahrenheit.

As we were herded into the building—which had no air conditioning—hundreds of people lunged toward the counter at the rear of the structure. With body crushed against body, we waited as the uniformed officials behind the windows leisurely examined each passport. At times like this, I wondered what I was doing in Africa.

> Everyone stared.
> No matter
> where I went,
> they stared.

When I first arrived in Morocco, I found the sights that greeted me exotic—not unlike the scenes in *Casablanca, Raiders of the Lost Ark,* and other movies. The men, women, and even the children really did wear those white robes that reached down to their feet. What was especially striking was that the women were almost totally covered. Despite the heat, they wore not only full-length gowns but also head coverings that reached down over their foreheads and veils that covered their faces from the nose down. You could see nothing but their eyes—and every eye seemed the same shade of brown.

And how short everyone was! The Arab women looked to be, on average, 5 feet, and the men only about three or four inches taller. As the only blue-eyed, blond, 6-foot-plus person around, and the only one who was wearing jeans and a pullover shirt, in a world of white-robed short people I stood out like a creature from another planet. Everyone stared. No matter where I went, they stared. Wherever I looked, I found brown eyes watching me intently. Even staring back at those many dark brown eyes had no effect. It was so different from home, where, if you caught someone staring at you, that person would look embarrassed and immediately glance away.

And lines? The concept apparently didn't even exist. Buying a ticket for a bus or train meant pushing and shoving toward the ticket man (always a man—no women were visible in any public position), who took the money from whichever outstretched hand he decided on.

And germs? That notion didn't seem to exist here either. Flies swarmed over the food in the restaurants and the unwrapped loaves of bread in the stores. Shopkeepers would considerately shoo off the flies before handing me a loaf. They also offered home delivery. I watched a bread vendor deliver a loaf to a woman who was standing on a second-floor balcony. She first threw her money to the bread vendor, and he then threw the unwrapped bread up to her. Only, his throw was off. The bread bounced off the wrought-iron

35

balcony railing and landed in the street, which was filled with people, wandering dogs, and the ever-present urinating and defecating donkeys. The vendor simply picked up the unwrapped loaf and threw it again. This certainly wasn't his day, for he missed again. But he made it on his third attempt. The woman smiled as she turned back into her apartment, apparently to prepare the noon meal for her family.

As I left Morocco, I entered a crowded passport-check building on the Algerian border. With no air conditioning, the oppressive heat—about 115° was made all the worse as body crushed body. As people pushed to get to the front, tempers began to flare. When a fight broke out, a little man in uniform appeared, shouting and knocking people aside as he forced his way to a little wooden box nailed to the floor. Climbing onto this makeshift platform, he shouted at the crowd, his arms flailing about him. The people fell silent. But just as soon as the man left, the shouting and shoving began again.

The situation had become unbearable. His body pressed against mine, the man behind me decided that this was a good time to take a nap. Determining that I made a good support, he placed his arm against my back and leaned his head against his arm. Sweat streamed down my back at the point where his arm and head touched me.

Finally, I realized that I had to abandon U.S. customs. So I pushed my way forward, forcing my frame into every square inch of vacant space that I could create. At the counter, I shouted in English. The official looked up at the sound of this strange tongue, and I thrust my long arms over the heads of three people, shoving my passport into his hand.

What Is Culture?

What is culture? The concept is sometimes easier to grasp by description than by definition. For example, suppose you meet a young woman from India who has just arrived in the United States. That her culture is different from yours is immediately evident. You first see it in her clothing, jewelry, makeup, and hairstyle. Next you hear it in her speech. It then becomes apparent by her gestures. Later, you might hear her express unfamiliar beliefs about relationships or what is valuable in life. All of these characteristics are indicative of **culture**—the language, beliefs, values, norms, behaviors, and even material objects that are passed from one generation to the next.

In northern Africa, I was surrounded by a culture quite different from mine. It was evident in everything I saw and heard. The **material culture**—such things as jewelry, art, buildings, weapons, machines, and even eating utensils, hairstyles, and clothing— provided a sharp contrast to what I was used to seeing. There is nothing inherently "natural" about material culture. That is, it is no more natural (or unnatural) to wear gowns on the street than it is to wear jeans.

I also found myself immersed in an unfamiliar **nonmaterial culture,** that is, a group's ways of thinking (its beliefs, values, and other assumptions about the world) and doing (its common **patterns** of behavior, including language, gestures, and other forms of interaction). North African assumptions that it is acceptable to stare at others in public and to push people aside to buy tickets are examples of nonmaterial culture. So are U.S. assumptions that it is wrong to do either of these things. Like material culture, neither custom is "right." People simply become comfortable with the customs they learn during childhood, and—as when I visited northern Africa—uncomfortable when their basic assumptions about life are challenged.

Culture and Taken-for-Granted Orientations to Life

To develop a sociological imagination, it is essential to understand how culture affects people's lives. If we meet someone from a different culture, the encounter may make us aware of culture's pervasive influence on all aspects of a person's life. Attaining the same level of

culture the language, beliefs, values, norms, behaviors, and even material objects that characterize a group and are passed from one generation to the next

material culture the material objects that distinguish a group of people, such as their art, buildings, weapons, utensils, machines, hairstyles, clothing, and jewelry

nonmaterial culture (also called symbolic culture) a group's ways of thinking (including its beliefs, values, and other assumptions about the world) and doing (its common patterns of behavior, including language and other forms of interaction)

patterns recurring characteristics or events

awareness regarding our own culture, however, is quite another matter. We usually take *our* speech, *our* gestures, *our* beliefs, and *our* customs for granted. We assume that they are "normal" or "natural," and we almost always follow them without question. As anthropologist Ralph Linton (1936) said, "The last thing a fish would ever notice would be water." So also with people: Except in unusual circumstances, most characteristics of our own culture remain imperceptible to us.

Yet culture's significance is profound; it touches almost every aspect of who and what we are. We came into this life without a language; without values and morality; with no ideas about religion, war, money, love, use of space, and so on. We possessed none of these fundamental orientations that are so essential in determining the type of people we become. Yet by this point in our lives, we all have acquired them—and take them for granted. Sociologists call this *culture within us.* These learned and shared ways of believing and of doing (another definition of culture) penetrate our beings at an early age and quickly become part of our taken-for-granted assumptions about what normal behavior is. *Culture becomes the lens through which we perceive and evaluate what is going on around us.* Seldom do we question these assumptions, for, like water to a fish, the lens through which we view life remains largely beyond our perception.

The rare instances in which these assumptions are challenged, however, can be upsetting. Although as a sociologist I should be able to look at my own culture "from the outside," my trip to Africa quickly revealed how fully I had internalized my culture. My upbringing in Western culture had given me assumptions about aspects of social life that had become rooted deeply in my being—appropriate eye contact, proper hygiene, and the use of space. But in this part of Africa these assumptions were useless in helping me navigate everyday life. No longer could I count on people to stare only surreptitiously, to take precautions against invisible microbes, or to stand in line in an orderly fashion, one behind the other.

As you can tell from the opening vignette, I found these unfamiliar behaviors upsetting, for they violated my basic expectations of "the way people *ought* to be"—and I did not even realize how firmly I held these expectations until they were challenged so abruptly. When my nonmaterial culture failed me—when it no longer enabled me to make sense out of the world—I experienced a disorientation known as **culture shock.** In the case of buying tickets, the fact that I was several inches taller than most Moroccans and thus able to outreach others helped me to adjust partially to their different ways of doing things. But I never did get used to the idea that pushing ahead of others was "right," and I always felt guilty when I used my size to receive preferential treatment.

Culture shock is a two-way street, of course. You can imagine what cultural shock people from a tribal society would experience if they were thrust into the United States. This actually happened, as the Cultural Diversity box on the next page describes.

An important consequence of culture within us is **ethnocentrism,** a tendency to use our own group's ways of doing things as a yardstick for judging others. All of us learn that the ways of our own group are good, right, and even superior to other ways of life. As sociologist William Sumner (1906), who developed this concept, said, "One's own group is the center of everything, and all others are scaled and rated with reference to it." Ethnocentrism has both positive and negative consequences. On the positive side, it creates in-group loyalties. On the negative side, ethnocentrism can lead to discrimination against people whose ways differ from ours.

The many ways in which culture affects our lives fascinate sociologists. In this chapter, we'll examine how profoundly culture influences everything we are and do. This will serve as a basis from which you can start to analyze your own assumptions of reality. I should give you a warning at this point: You might develop a changed perspective on social life and your role in it. If so, life will never look the same.

In Sum: To avoid losing track of the ideas under discussion, let's pause for a moment to summarize and, in some instances, clarify the principles we have covered.

> **1.** There is nothing "natural" about material culture. Arabs wear gowns on the street and feel that it is natural to do so. Americans do the same with jeans.

culture shock the disorientation that people experience when they come in contact with a fundamentally different culture and can no longer depend on their taken-for-granted assumptions about life

ethnocentrism the use of one's own culture as a yardstick for judging the ways of other individuals or societies, generally leading to a negative evaluation of their values, norms, and behaviors

Cultural Diversity in the United States

Culture Shock: The Arrival of the Hmong

Imagine that you were a member of a small tribal group in the mountains of Laos. Village life and the clan were all you knew. There were no schools, and you learned everything you needed to know from your relatives. U.S. agents recruited the men of your village to fight communists, and they gained a reputation as fierce fighters. When the U.S. forces were defeated in Vietnam, your people were moved to the United States so they wouldn't be killed in reprisal.

Here is what happened. Keep in mind that you had never seen a television or a newspaper and that you had never gone to school. Your entire world had been the village.

They put you in a big house with wings. It flew.

They gave you strange food on a tray. The Sani-Wipes were hard to chew.

Children make the fastest adjustment to a new culture, although they remain caught between the old and new ones.

After the trip, you were placed in a house. This was an adventure. You had never seen locks before, as no one locked up anything in the village. Most of the village homes didn't even have doors, much less locks.

You found the bathroom perplexing. At first, you tried to wash rice in the bowl of water, which seemed to be provided for this purpose. But when you pressed the handle, the water and rice disappeared. After you learned what the toilet was for, you found it difficult not to slip off the little white round thing when you stood on it. In the village, you didn't need a toilet seat when you squatted in a field to defecate.

When you threw water on the electric stove to put out the burner, it sparked and smoked. You became afraid to use the stove because it might explode.

And no one liked it when you tried to plant a vegetable garden in the park.

Your new world was so different that, to help you adjust, the settlement agency told you (Fadiman 1997):

1. To send mail, you must use stamps.
2. The door of the refrigerator must be shut.
3. Do not stand or squat on the toilet since it may break.
4. Always ask before picking your neighbor's flowers, fruit, or vegetables.
5. In colder areas you must wear shoes, socks, and appropriate outerwear. Otherwise, you may become ill.
6. Always use a handkerchief or a tissue to blow your nose in public places or inside a public building.
7. Picking your nose or ears in public is frowned upon in the United States.
8. Never urinate in the street. This creates a smell that is offensive to Americans. They also believe that it causes disease.

To help the Hmong assimilate, U.S. officials dispersed them across the nation. This, they felt, would help them to adjust to the dominant culture and prevent a Hmong subculture from developing. The dispersal brought feelings of isolation to the clan- and village-based Hmong. As soon as they had a chance, the Hmong moved from these towns scattered across the country to the same areas, the major one being in California's Central Valley. Here they renewed village relationships and helped one another adjust to the society they had never desired to join.

For Your Consideration

Do you think you would have reacted differently if you had been a displaced Hmong? Why did the Hmong need one another more than their U.S. neighbors to adjust to their new life? What cultural shock do you think a U.S.-born 19-year-old Hmong would experience if his or her parents decided to return to Laos?

2. There is nothing "natural" about nonmaterial culture. It is just as arbitrary to stand in line as to push and shove.
3. Culture penetrates deeply into our thinking, becoming a taken-for-granted lens through which we see the world and obtain our perception of reality.
4. Culture provides implicit instructions that tell us what we ought to do and how we ought to think. It provides a fundamental basis for our decision making.

5. Culture also provides a "moral imperative"; that is, the culture that we internalize becomes the "right" way of doing things. (I, for example, believed deeply that it was wrong to push and shove to get ahead of others.)

6. Coming into contact with a radically different culture challenges our basic assumptions of life. (I experienced culture shock when I discovered that my deeply ingrained cultural ideas about hygiene and the use of personal space no longer applied.)

7. Although the particulars of culture differ from one group of people to another, culture itself is universal. That is, all people have culture, for a society cannot exist without developing shared, learned ways of dealing with the challenges of life.

8. All people are ethnocentric, which has both positive and negative consequences.

cultural relativism not judging a culture but trying to understand it on its own terms

Practicing Cultural Relativism

To counter our tendency to use our own culture as the standard by which we judge other cultures, we can practice **cultural relativism;** that is, we can try to understand a culture on its own terms. This means looking at how the elements of a culture fit together, without judging those elements as superior or inferior to our own way of life.

With our own culture embedded so deeply within us, however, practicing cultural relativism can challenge our orientations to life. For example, most U.S. citizens appear to have strong feelings against raising bulls for the purpose of stabbing them to death in front of crowds that shout "Olé!" According to cultural relativism, however, bullfighting must be viewed from the perspective of the culture in which it takes place—*its* history, *its* folklore, *its* ideas of bravery, and *its* ideas of sex roles.

You may still regard bullfighting as wrong, of course, if your culture, which is deeply ingrained in you, has no history of bullfighting. We all possess culturally specific ideas about cruelty to animals, ideas that have evolved slowly and match other elements of our culture. In the United States, for example, practices that once were common in some areas—cock fighting, dog fighting, bear–dog fighting, and so on—have been gradually eliminated.

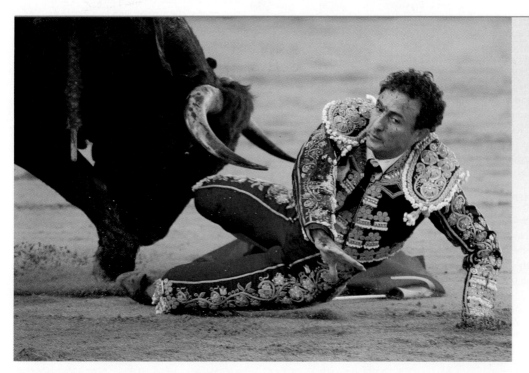

Many Americans perceive bullfighting as a cruel activity that should be illegal everywhere. To most Spaniards, bullfighting is a sport that pits matador and bull in a unifying image of power, courage, and glory. *Cultural relativism* requires that we suspend our own perspectives in order to grasp the perspectives of others, something easier described than attained.

None of us can be entirely successful at practicing cultural relativism. Look at the Cultural Diversity box below. My best guess is that you will evaluate these "strange" foods through the lens of your own culture. Applying cultural relativism, however, is an attempt to refocus that lens so we can appreciate other ways of life rather than simply asserting "Our way is right." Look at the photos on the next page. As you view them, try to appreciate the cultural differences in standards of beauty.

Although cultural relativism helps us to avoid cultural smugness, this view has come under attack. In a provocative book, *Sick Societies* (1992), anthropologist Robert Edgerton suggests that we develop a scale for evaluating cultures on their "quality of life," much as we do for U.S. cities. He also asks why we should consider cultures that practice female circumcision, gang rape, or wife beating, or cultures that sell little girls into prostitution, as

Cultural Diversity around the World

The World

You Are What You Eat? An Exploration in Cultural Relativity

Here is a chance to test your ethnocentrism and ability to practice cultural relativity. You probably know that the French like to eat snails and that in some Asian cultures chubby dogs and cats are considered a delicacy ("Ah, lightly browned with a little doggy sauce!"). But did you know that cod sperm is a delicacy in Japan (Raisfeld and Patronite 2006)? That flies, scorpions, crickets, and beetles are on the menu of restaurants in parts of Thailand (Gampbell 2006)?

Marston Bates (1967), a zoologist, noted this ethnocentric reaction to food:

I remember once, in the llanos of Colombia, sharing a dish of toasted ants at a remote farmhouse. . . . My host and I fell into conversation about the general question of what people eat or do not eat, and I remarked that in my country people eat the legs of frogs.

The very thought of this filled my ant-eating friends with horror; it was as though I had mentioned some repulsive sex habit.

Then there is the experience of a friend, Dusty Friedman, who told me:

When traveling in Sudan, I ate some interesting things that I wouldn't likely eat now that I'm back in our society. Raw baby camel's liver with chopped herbs was a delicacy. So was camel's milk cheese patties that had been cured in dry camel's dung.

You might be able to see yourself eating frog legs and toasted ants, beetles, even flies. (Or maybe not.) Perhaps

What some consider food, even delicacies, can turn the stomachs of others. These little critters were for sale in a market in Laos.

you could even stomach cod sperm and raw camel liver, maybe even dogs and cats, but here's another test of your ethnocentrism and cultural relativity. Maxine Kingston (1975), an English professor whose parents grew up in China, wrote:

"Do you know what people in [the Nantou region of] China eat when they have the money?" my mother began. "They buy into a monkey feast. The eaters sit around a thick wood table with a hole in the middle. Boys bring in the monkey at the end of a pole. Its neck is in a collar at the end of the pole, and it is screaming. Its hands are tied behind it. They clamp the monkey into the table; the whole table fits like another collar around its neck. Using a surgeon's saw, the cooks cut a clean line in a circle at the top of its head. To loosen the bone, they tap with a tiny hammer and wedge here and there with a silver pick. Then an old woman reaches out her hand to the monkey's face and up to its scalp, where she tufts some hairs and lifts off the lid of the skull. The eaters spoon out the brains."

For Your Consideration

What is your opinion about eating toasted ants? Beetles? Flies? Fried frog legs? Cod sperm? About eating puppies and kittens? About eating brains scooped out of a living monkey?

If you were reared in U.S. society, more than likely you think that eating frog legs is okay; eating ants or beetles is disgusting; and eating flies, cod sperm, dogs, cats, and monkey brains is downright repugnant. How would you apply the concepts of ethnocentrism and cultural relativism to your perceptions of these customs?

Ecuador

New Guinea

Thailand

China

Cameroon

Tibet

Kenya

United States

Standards of Beauty

Standards of beauty vary so greatly from one culture to another that what one group finds attractive, another may not. Yet, in its *ethnocentrism,* each group thinks that its standards are the best—that the appearance reflects what beauty "really" is.

As indicated by these photos, around the world men and women aspire to their group's norms of physical attractiveness. To make themselves appealing to others, they try to make their appearance reflect those standards.

symbolic culture another term for nonmaterial culture

symbol something to which people attach meanings and then use to communicate with others

gestures the ways in which people use their bodies to communicate with one another

morally equivalent to those that do not. Cultural values that result in exploitation, he says, are inferior to those that enhance people's lives.

Edgerton's sharp questions and incisive examples bring us to a topic that comes up repeatedly in this text: the disagreements that arise among scholars as they confront contrasting views of reality. It is such questioning of assumptions that keeps sociology interesting.

Components of Symbolic Culture

Sociologists sometimes refer to nonmaterial culture as **symbolic culture,** because its central component is the set of symbols that people use. A **symbol** is something to which people attach meaning and that they then use to communicate with one another. Symbols include gestures, language, values, norms, sanctions, folkways, and mores. Let's look at each of these components of symbolic culture.

Gestures

Gestures, movements of the body to communicate with others, are shorthand ways to convey messages without using words. Although people in every culture of the world use gestures, a gesture's meaning may change completely from one culture to another. North Americans, for example, communicate a succinct message by raising the middle finger in a short, upward stabbing motion. I wish to stress "North Americans," for this gesture does not convey the same message in most parts of the world.

I was surprised to find that this particular gesture was not universal, having internalized it to such an extent that I thought everyone knew what it meant. When I was comparing gestures with friends in Mexico, however, this gesture drew a blank look from them. After I explained its intended meaning, they laughed and showed me their rudest gesture—placing the hand under the armpit and moving the upper arm up and down. To me, they simply looked as if they were imitating monkeys, but to them the gesture meant "Your mother is a whore"—the worst possible insult in that culture.

With the current political, military, and cultural dominance of the United States, "giving the finger" is becoming well known in other cultures. Following the September 11, 2001, terrorist attack, the United States began to photograph and fingerprint foreign visitors. Feeling insulted, Brazil retaliated by doing the same to U.S. visitors. Angry at this, a U.S. pilot raised his middle finger while being photographed. Having become aware of the meaning of this gesture, Brazilian police arrested him. To gain his release, the pilot had to pay a fine of $13,000 ("Brazil Arrests" 2004).

Gestures not only facilitate communication but also, because they differ around the world, can lead to misunderstanding, embarrassment, or worse. One time in Mexico, for example, I raised my hand to a certain height to indicate how tall a child was. My hosts began to laugh. It turned out that Mexicans use three hand gestures to indicate height: one for people, a second for animals, and yet another for plants. They were amused because I had ignorantly used the plant gesture to indicate the child's height. (See Figure 2.1.)

To get along in another culture, then, it is important to learn the gestures of that culture. If you don't, you will fail to achieve the simplicity of communication that gestures allow and you may overlook or misunderstand much of what is happening, run the risk of appearing foolish, and possibly offend people. In some cultures, for example, you would provoke deep offense if you were to offer food or a gift with your left hand, because the left hand is reserved for dirty tasks, such as wiping after going to the toilet. Left-handed Americans visiting Arabs, please note!

Suppose for a moment that you are visiting southern Italy. After eating one of the best meals in your life, you are so pleased that when you catch the waiter's eye, you smile broadly and use the standard U.S. "A-OK" gesture of putting your thumb and forefinger together and making a large "**O.**" The

Although most *gestures* are learned, and therefore vary from culture to culture, some gestures that represent fundamental emotions such as sadness, anger, and fear appear to be inborn. This crying child whom I photographed in India differs little from a crying child in China—or the United States or anywhere else on the globe. In a few years, however, this child will demonstrate a variety of gestures highly specific to his Hindu culture.

FIGURE 2.1 Gestures to Indicate Height, Southern Mexico

waiter looks horrified, and you are struck speechless when the manager asks you to leave. What have you done? Nothing on purpose, of course, but in that culture this gesture refers to a lower part of the human body that is not mentioned in polite company (Ekman et al. 1984).

Is it really true that there are no universal gestures? There is some disagreement on this point. Some anthropologists claim that no gesture is universal. They point out that even nodding the head up and down to indicate "yes" is not universal, because in some parts of the world, such areas of Turkey, nodding the head up and down means "no" (Ekman et al. 1984). However, ethologists, researchers who study biological bases of behavior, claim that expressions of anger, pouting, fear, and sadness are built into our biological makeup and are universal (Eibl-Eibesfeldt 1970:404; Horwitz and Wakefield 2007). They point out that even infants who are born blind and deaf, who have had no chance to *learn* these gestures, express themselves in the same way.

Although this matter is not yet settled, we can note that gestures tend to vary remarkably around the world. It is also significant that certain gestures can elicit emotions; some gestures are so closely associated with emotional messages that the gestures themselves summon up emotions. For example, my introduction to Mexican gestures took place at a dinner table. It was evident that my husband-and-wife hosts were trying to hide their embarrassment at using their culture's obscene gesture at their dinner table. And I felt the same way—not about *their* gesture, of course, which meant nothing to me—but about the one I was teaching them.

Language

The primary way in which people communicate with one another is through **language**—symbols that can be combined in an infinite number of ways for the purpose of communicating abstract thought. Each word is actually a symbol, a sound to which we have attached some particular meaning. Although all human groups have language, there is nothing universal about the meanings given to particular sounds. Like gestures, in different cultures the same sound may mean something entirely different—or may have no meaning at all. In German, for example, *gift* means "poison," so if you give a box of chocolates to a non-English-speaking German and say, "Gift, Eat" . . .

Because *language allows culture to exist,* its significance for human life is difficult to overstate. Consider the following effects of language.

Language Allows Human Experience to Be Cumulative. By means of language, we pass ideas, knowledge, and even attitudes on to the next generation. This allows others to build on experiences in which they may never directly participate. As a result, humans are able to modify their behavior in light of what earlier generations have learned. This takes us to the central sociological significance of language: *Language allows culture to develop by freeing people to move beyond their immediate experiences.*

language a system of symbols that can be combined in an infinite number of ways and can represent not only objects but also abstract thought

Without language, human culture would be little more advanced than that of the lower primates. If we communicated by grunts and gestures, we would be limited to a short time span—to events now taking place, those that have just taken place, or those that will take place immediately—a sort of slightly extended present. You can grunt and gesture, for example, that you want a drink of water, but in the absence of language how could you share ideas concerning past or future events? There would be little or no way to communicate to others what event you had in mind, much less the greater complexities that humans communicate—ideas and feelings about events.

Language Provides a Social or Shared Past.   Without language, our memories would be extremely limited, for we associate experiences with words and then use words to recall the experience. Such memories as would exist in the absence of language would be highly individualized, for only rarely and incompletely could we communicate them to others, much less discuss them and agree on something. By attaching words to an event, however, and then using those words to recall it, we are able to discuss the event. As we talk about past events, we develop shared understandings about what those events mean. In short, through talk, people develop a shared past.

Language Provides a Social or Shared Future.   Language also extends our time horizons forward. Because language enables us to agree on times, dates, and places, it allows us to plan activities with one another. Think about it for a moment. Without language, how could you ever plan future events? How could you possibly communicate goals, times, and plans? Whatever planning could exist would be limited to rudimentary communications, perhaps to an agreement to meet at a certain place when the sun is in a certain position. But think of the difficulty, perhaps the impossibility, of conveying just a slight change in this simple arrangement, such as "I can't make it tomorrow, but my neighbor can take my place, if that's all right with you."

Language Allows Shared Perspectives.   Our ability to speak, then, provides us a social (or shared) past and future. This is vital for humanity. It is a watershed that distinguishes us from animals. But speech does much more than this. When we talk with one another, we are exchanging ideas about events; that is, we are sharing perspectives. Our words are the embodiment of our experiences, distilled into a readily exchangeable form, one that

Language is the basis of human culture around the world. The past decade has seen major developments in communication—the ease and speed with which we can "speak" to people across the globe. This development is destined to have vital effects on culture.

is mutually understandable to people who have learned that language. *Talking about events allows us to arrive at the shared understandings that form the basis of social life.* Not sharing a language while living alongside one another, however, invites miscommunication and suspicion. This risk, which comes with a diverse society, is discussed in the Cultural Diversity box below.

Language Allows Shared, Goal-Directed Behavior.   Common understandings enable us to establish a *purpose* for getting together. Let's suppose you want to go on a picnic. You use speech not only to plan the picnic but also to decide on reasons for having the picnic—which may be anything from "because it's a nice day and it shouldn't be wasted studying" to "because it's my birthday." Language permits you to blend individual activities into an integrated sequence. In other words, through discussion you decide where you will go; who will drive; who will bring the hamburgers, the potato chips, the soda; where you will meet; and so on. Only because of language can you participate in such a common yet complex event as a picnic—or build roads and bridges or attend college classes.

In Sum: The sociological significance of language is that it takes us beyond the world of apes and allows culture to develop. Language frees us from the present, actually giving us

Cultural Diversity in the United States

Miami—Continuing Controversy over Language

Immigration from Cuba and other Spanish-speaking countries has been so vast that most residents of Miami are Latinos. Half of Miami's 385,000 residents have trouble speaking English. Only *one-fourth* of Miamians speak English at home. Many English-only speakers are leaving Miami, saying that not being able to speak Spanish is a handicap to getting work. "They should learn Spanish," some reply. As Pedro Falcon, an immigrant from Nicaragua, said, "Miami is the capital of Latin America. The population speaks Spanish."

As the English-speakers see it, this pinpoints the problem: Miami is in the United States, not in Latin America.

Controversy over immigrants and language isn't new. The millions of Germans who moved to the United States in the 1800s brought their language with them. Not only did they hold their religious services in German, but they also opened private schools in which the teachers taught in German, published German-language newspapers, and spoke German at home, in the stores, and in the taverns.

Mural from Miami.

Some of their English-speaking neighbors didn't like this a bit. "Why don't those Germans assimilate?" they wondered. "Just whose side would they fight on if we had a war?"

This question was answered, of course, with the participation of German Americans in two world wars. It was even a general descended from German immigrants (Eisenhower) who led the armed forces that defeated Hitler.

But what happened to all this German language? The first generation of immigrants spoke German almost exclusively. The second generation assimilated, speaking English at home, but also speaking German when they visited their parents. For the most part, the third generation knew German only as "that language" that their grandparents spoke.

The same thing is happening with the Latino immigrants. Spanish is being kept alive longer, however, because Mexico borders the United States, and there is constant traffic between the countries. The continuing migration from Mexico and other Spanish-speaking countries also feeds the language.

If Germany bordered the United States, there would still be a lot of German spoken here.

Sources: Based on Sharp 1992; Usdansky 1992; Kent and Lalasz 2007; Salomon 2008.

a social past and a social future. That is, language gives us the capacity to share understandings about the past and to develop shared perceptions about the future. Language also allows us to establish underlying purposes for our activities. In short, *language is the basis of culture.*

Language and Perception: The Sapir-Whorf Hypothesis. In the 1930s, two anthropologists, Edward Sapir and Benjamin Whorf, became intrigued when they noticed that the Hopi Indians of the southwestern United States had no words to distinguish among the past, the present, and the future. English, in contrast—as well as French, Spanish, Swahili, and other languages—distinguishes carefully among these three time frames. From this observation, Sapir and Whorf began to think that words might be more than labels that people attach to things. *Eventually, they concluded that language has embedded within it ways of looking at the world.* In other words, language not only expresses our thoughts and perceptions but also shapes the way we think and perceive. When we learn a language, we learn not only words but also ways of thinking and perceiving (Sapir 1949; Whorf 1956).

The **Sapir-Whorf hypothesis** reverses common sense: It indicates that rather than objects and events forcing themselves onto our consciousness, it is our language that determines our consciousness, and hence our perception of objects and events. For English speakers, the term *nuts* combines almonds, walnuts, and pecans in such a way that we see them as belonging together. Spanish has no such overarching, combining word, so native Spanish speakers don't see such a connection. Sociologist Eviatar Zerubavel (1991) points out that his native language, Hebrew, does not have separate words for jam and jelly. Both go by the same term, and only when Zerubavel learned English could he "see" this difference, which is "obvious" to native English speakers. Similarly, if you learn to classify students as Jocks, Goths, Stoners, Skaters, Band Geeks, and Preps, you will perceive students in an entirely different way from someone who does not know these classifications.

Although Sapir and Whorf's observation that the Hopi do not have tenses was inaccurate (Edgerton 1992:27), they did stumble onto a major truth about social life. Learning a language means not only learning words but also acquiring the perceptions embedded in that language. In other words, language both reflects and shapes our cultural experiences (Drivonikou et al. 2007). The racial–ethnic terms that our culture provides, for example, influence how we see both ourselves and others, a point that is discussed in the Cultural Diversity box on the next page.

Values, Norms, and Sanctions

To learn a culture is to learn people's **values,** their ideas of what is desirable in life. When we uncover people's values, we learn a great deal about them, for values are the standards by which people define what is good and bad, beautiful and ugly. Values underlie our preferences, guide our choices, and indicate what we hold worthwhile in life.

Every group develops expectations concerning the right way to reflect its values. Sociologists use the term **norms** to describe those expectations (or rules of behavior) that develop out of a group's values. The term **sanctions** refers to the reactions people receive for following or breaking norms. A **positive sanction** expresses approval for following a norm, and a **negative sanction** reflects disapproval for breaking a norm. Positive sanctions can be material, such as a prize, a trophy, or money, but in everyday life they usually consist of hugs, smiles, a pat on the back, or even handshakes and "high fives." Negative sanctions can also be material—being fined in court is one example—but negative sanctions, too, are more likely to be symbolic: harsh words, or gestures such as frowns, stares, clenched jaws, or raised fists. Getting a raise at work is a positive sanction, indicating that you have followed the norms clustering around work values. Getting fired, however, is a negative sanction, indicating that you have violated these norms. The North American finger gesture discussed earlier is, of course, a negative sanction.

Sapir-Whorf hypothesis Edward Sapir and Benjamin Whorf's hypothesis that language creates ways of thinking and perceiving

values the standards by which people define what is desirable or undesirable, good or bad, beautiful or ugly

norms expectations, or rules of behavior, that reflect and enforce behavior

sanctions either expressions of approval given to people for upholding norms or expressions of disapproval for violating them

positive sanction a reward or positive reaction for following norms, ranging from a smile to a material reward

negative sanction an expression of disapproval for breaking a norm, ranging from a mild, informal reaction such as a frown to a formal reaction such as a prison sentence or an execution

Cultural Diversity in the United States

Race and Language: Searching for Self-Labels

The groups that dominate society often determine the names that are used to refer to racial–ethnic groups. If those names become associated with oppression, they take on negative meanings. For example, the terms *Negro* and *colored people* came to be associated with submissiveness and low status. To overcome these meanings, those referred to by these terms began to identify themselves as *black* or *African American*. They infused these new terms with respect—a basic source of self-esteem that they felt the old terms denied them.

In a twist, African Americans—and to a lesser extent Latinos, Asian Americans, and Native Americans—have changed the rejected term *colored people* to *people of color*. Those who embrace this modified term are imbuing it with meanings that offer an identity of respect. The term also has political meanings. It indicates bonds that cross racial–ethnic lines, mutual ties, and a sense of identity rooted in historical oppression.

There is *always* disagreement about racial–ethnic terms, and this one is no exception. Although most rejected the term *colored people*, some found in it a sense of respect and claimed it for themselves. The acronym

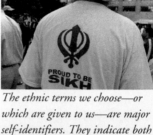

The ethnic terms we choose—or which are given to us—are major self-identifiers. They indicate both membership in some group and a separation from other groups.

NAACP, for example, stands for the National Association for the Advancement of Colored People. The new term, *people of color*, arouses similar feelings. Some individuals whom this term would include claim that it is inappropriate. They point out that this new label still makes color the primary identifier of people. They stress that humans transcend race–ethnicity, that what we have in common as human beings goes much deeper than what you see on the surface. They stress that we should avoid terms that focus on differences in the pigmentation of our skin.

The language of self-reference in a society that is so conscious of skin color is an ongoing issue. As long as our society continues to emphasize such superficial differences, the search for adequate terms is not likely to ever be "finished." In this quest for terms that strike the right chord, the term *people of color* may become a historical footnote. If it does, it will be replaced by another term that indicates a changing self-identification in a changing historical context.

For Your Consideration

What terms do you use to refer to your race–ethnicity? What "bad" terms do you know that others have used to refer to your race–ethnicity? What is the difference in meaning between the terms you use and the "bad" terms? Where does that meaning come from?

Because people can find norms stifling, some cultures relieve the pressure through *moral holidays,* specified times when people are allowed to break norms. Moral holidays such as Mardi Gras often center on getting rowdy. Some activities for which people would otherwise be arrested are permitted—and expected—including public drunkenness and some nudity. The norms are never completely dropped, however—just loosened a bit. Go too far, and the police step in.

Some societies have *moral holiday places,* locations where norms are expected to be broken. Red light districts of our cities are examples. There, prostitutes are allowed to work the streets, bothered only when political pressure builds to "clean up" the area. If these same prostitutes attempt to solicit customers in adjacent areas, however, they are promptly arrested. Each year, the hometown of the team that wins the Super Bowl becomes a moral holiday place—for one night.

One of the more interesting examples is "Party Cove" at Lake of the Ozarks in Missouri, a fairly straightlaced area of the country. During the summer, hundreds of boaters—those operating cabin cruisers to jet skis—moor their vessels together in a highly publicized cove, where many get drunk, take off their clothes, and dance on the

Many societies relax their norms during specified occasions. At these times, known as *moral holidays*, behavior that is ordinarily not permitted is allowed. Shown here at Mardi Gras in New Orleans is a woman showing her breasts to get beads dropped to her from the balcony. When a *moral holiday* is over, the usual enforcement of rules follows.

boats. In one of the more humorous incidents, boaters complained that a nude woman was riding a jet ski outside of the cove. The water patrol investigated but refused to arrest the woman because she was within the law—she had sprayed shaving cream on certain parts of her body. The Missouri Water Patrol has even given a green light to Party Cove, announcing in the local newspaper that officers will not enter this cove, supposedly because "there is so much traffic that they might not be able to get out in time to handle an emergency elsewhere."

Folkways and Mores

Norms that are not strictly enforced are called **folkways.** We expect people to comply with folkways, but we are likely to shrug our shoulders and not make a big deal about it if they don't. If someone insists on passing you on the right side of the sidewalk, for example, you are unlikely to take corrective action, although if the sidewalk is crowded and you must move out of the way, you might give the person a dirty look.

Other norms, however, are taken much more seriously. We think of them as essential to our core values, and we insist on conformity. These are called **mores** (MORE-rays). A person who steals, rapes, or kills has violated some of society's most important mores. As sociologist Ian Robertson (1987:62) put it,

A man who walks down a street wearing nothing on the upper half of his body is violating a folkway; a man who walks down the street wearing nothing on the lower half of his body is violating one of our most important mores, the requirement that people cover their genitals and buttocks in public.

It should also be noted that one group's folkways may be another group's mores. Although a man walking down the street with the upper half of his body uncovered is deviating from a folkway, a woman doing the same thing is violating the mores. In addition, the folkways and mores of a subculture (discussed in the next section) may be the opposite of mainstream culture. For example, to walk down the sidewalk in a nudist camp with the entire body uncovered would conform to that subculture's folkways.

A **taboo** refers to a norm so strongly ingrained that even the thought of its violation is greeted with revulsion. Eating human flesh and parents having sex with their children are examples of such behaviors. When someone breaks a taboo, the individual is usually

The violation of *mores* is a serious matter. In this case, it is serious enough that the security at a football match in Edmonton, Alberta (Canada) have swung into action to protect the public from seeing a "disgraceful" sight, at least one so designated by this group.

judged unfit to live in the same society as others. The sanctions are severe and may include prison, banishment, or death.

Many Cultural Worlds

Subcultures

Groups of people who focus on some activity or who occupy some small corner in life tend to develop specialized ways to communicate with one another. To outsiders, their talk, even if it is in English, can seem like a foreign language. Here is one of my favorite quotes by a politician:

> There are things we know that we know. There are known unknowns; that is to say, there are things that we now know we don't know. But there are also unknown unknowns; there are things we do not know we don't know. (Donald Rumsfeld, quoted in Dickey and Barry 2006:38)

Whatever Rumsfeld, the former secretary of defense under George W. Bush, meant by his statement probably will remain a known unknown. (Or would it be an unknown known?)

We have a similar problem with communication in the subculture of sociology. Try to figure out what this means:

> The self-interested and self-sufficient individual remains the ideal, in which the centering of rational choice and a capacity for transcendence both occludes group-based harms of systemic oppression and conceals the complicity of individuals in the perpetuation of systemic injustices. (Reay et al. 2008:239)

People who specialize in an occupation—from cabbies to politicians—tend to develop a **subculture,** *a world within the larger world of the dominant culture.* Subcultures are not limited to occupations, for they include any corner in life in which people's experiences lead them to have distinctive ways of looking at the world. Even if we cannot understand the quotation from Donald Rumsfeld, it makes us aware that politicians don't view life in quite the same way most of us do.

U.S. society contains *thousands* of subcultures. Some are as broad as the way of life we associate with teenagers, others as narrow as those we associate with body builders—or with politicians. Some U.S. ethnic groups also form subcultures: Their values, norms, and foods set them apart. So might their religion, music, language, and clothing. Even sociologists form a subculture. As you are learning, they also use a unique language in their efforts to understand the world.

For a visual depiction of subcultures, see the photo essay on the next two pages.

Countercultures

Consider this quote from another subculture:

> If everyone applying for welfare had to supply a doctor's certificate of sterilization, if everyone who had committed a felony were sterilized, if anyone who had mental illness to any degree were sterilized—then our economy could easily take care of these people for the rest of their lives, giving them a decent living standard—but getting them out of the way. That way there would be no children abused, no surplus population, and, after a while, no pollution. . . .
>
> Now let's talk about stupidity. The level of intellect in this country is going down, generation after generation. The average IQ is always 100 because that is the accepted average. However, the kid with a 100 IQ today would have tested out at 70 when I was a lad. You get the concept . . . the marching morons. . . .
>
> When the . . . present world system collapses, it'll be good people like you who will be shooting people in the streets to feed their families. (Zellner 1995:58, 65)

Welcome to the world of the survivalists, where the message is much clearer than that of politicians—and much more disturbing.

folkways norms that are not strictly enforced

mores norms that are strictly enforced because they are thought essential to core values or to the well-being of the group

taboo a norm so strong that it brings extreme sanctions and even revulsion if someone violates it

subculture the values and related behaviors of a group that distinguish its members from the larger culture; a world within a world

Looking at Subcultures

ubcultures can form around any interest or activity. Each subculture has its own values and norms that its members share, giving them a common identity. Each also has special terms that pinpoint the group's corner of life and that its members use to communicate with one another. Some of us belong to several subcultures.

As you can see from these photos, most subcultures are compatible with the values and norms of the mainstream culture. They represent specialized interests around which its members have chosen to build tiny worlds. Some subcultures, however, conflict with the mainstream culture. Sociologists give the name *counterculture* to subcultures whose values (such as those of outlaw motorcyclists) or activities and goals (such as those of terrorists) are opposed to the mainstream culture. Countercultures, however, are exceptional, and few of us belong to them.

Membership in this subculture is not easily awarded. Not only must high-steel ironworkers prove that they are able to work at great heights but also that they fit into the group socially. Newcomers are tested by members of the group, and they must demonstrate that they can take joking without offense.

Specialized values and interests are two of the characteristics that mark subcultures. What values and interests distinguish the modeling subculture?

The cabbies' subculture, centering on their occupational activities and interests, is also broken into smaller subcultures that reflect their experiences of race-ethnicity.

Even subcultures can have subcultures. The rodeo subculture is a subculture of "western" subculture. The values that unite its members are reflected in their speech, clothing, and specialized activities, such as the one shown here.

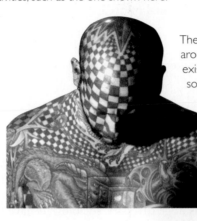

The subculture that centers around tattooing previously existed on the fringes of society, with seamen and circus folk its main participants. It now has entered mainstream society, but not to this extreme.

Why is professional dancing a subculture and not a counterculture?

Each subculture provides its members with values and distinctive ways of viewing the world. What values and perceptions do you think are common among body builders?

What values, interests, language, and activities do you think characterize participants in flat-track women's roller derby leagues?

Why would someone decorate himself like this and use such an outrageous prop? Among the many reasons, one is to show solidarity with the football subculture.

The values and norms of most subcultures blend in with mainstream society. In some cases, however, as with these survivalists, some of the group's values and norms place it at odds with the dominant culture. Sociologists use the term **counterculture** to refer to such groups. To better see this distinction, consider motorcycle enthusiasts and motorcycle gangs. Motorcycle enthusiasts—who emphasize personal freedom and speed *and* affirm cultural values of success through work or education—are members of a subculture. In contrast, the Hell's Angels, Pagans, and Bandidos not only stress freedom and speed but also value dirtiness and contempt toward women, work, and education. This makes them a counterculture.

Countercultures do not have to be negative, however. Back in the 1800s, the Mormons were a counterculture that challenged the dominant culture's core value of monogamy.

An assault on core values is always met with resistance. To affirm their own values, members of the mainstream culture may ridicule, isolate, or even attack members of the counterculture. The Mormons, for example, were driven out of several states before they finally settled in Utah, which was then a wilderness. Even there, the federal government would not let them practice *polygyny* (one man having more than one wife), and Utah's statehood was made conditional on its acceptance of monogamy (Anderson 1942/1966; Williams 2007).

Values in U.S. Society

An Overview of U.S. Values

As you know, the United States is a **pluralistic society,** made up of many different groups. The United States has numerous religious and racial–ethnic groups, as well as countless interest groups that focus on activities as divergent as hunting deer and geese and collecting Barbie dolls. Within this huge diversity, sociologists have tried to identify the underlying core values that are shared by most of the groups that make up U.S. society. Here are ten that sociologist Robin Williams (1965) identified:

1. *Achievement and success.* Americans praise personal achievement, especially outdoing others. This value includes getting ahead at work and school, and attaining wealth, power, and prestige.
2. *Individualism.* Americans cherish the ideal that an individual can rise from the bottom of society to its very top. If someone fails to "get ahead," Americans generally find fault with that individual rather than with the social system for placing roadblocks in his or her path.
3. *Hard work.* Americans expect people to work hard to achieve financial success and material comfort.
4. *Efficiency and practicality.* Americans award high marks for getting things done efficiently. Even in everyday life, Americans consider it important to do things fast, and they seek ways to increase efficiency.
5. *Science and technology.* Americans have a passion for applied science, for using science to control nature—to tame rivers and harness winds—and to develop new technology, from iPods to Segways.
6. *Material comfort.* Americans expect a high level of material comfort. This includes not only good nutrition, medical care, and housing but also late-model cars and recreational playthings—from iPhones to motor homes.
7. *Freedom.* This core value pervades U.S. life. It underscored the American Revolution, and Americans pride themselves on their personal freedom. The Mass Media in Social Life box on the next page highlights an interesting study on how this core value applies to Native Americans.
8. *Democracy.* By this term, Americans refer to majority rule, to the right of everyone to express an opinion, and to representative government.
9. *Equality.* It is impossible to understand Americans without being aware of the central role that the value of equality plays in their lives. Equality of opportunity (part

counterculture a group whose values, beliefs, norms, and related behaviors place its members in opposition to the broader culture

pluralistic society a society made up of many different groups, with contrasting values and orientations to life

MASS MEDIA In SOCIAL LIFE

Why Do Native Americans Like Westerns?

Although Western movies go through a cycle of popularity, their themes are a mainstay of Hollywood. It is easy to see why Anglos might like Westerns. In the standard western format, it is they who tame the wilderness while defending themselves from the attacks of cruel, savage Indians intent on their destruction. But why would Indians like Westerns?

Sociologist JoEllen Shively, a Chippewa who grew up on Indian reservations in Montana and North Dakota, observed that Western themes are so popular that Native Americans bring bags of paperbacks into taverns to trade with one another. They even call each other "cowboy."

Intrigued, Shively decided to investigate the matter by showing a Western movie to adult Native Americans and Anglos in a reservation town. She matched the groups on education, age, income, and percentage of unemployment. To select the movie, Shively (1991, 1992) previewed more than seventy Westerns. She chose a John Wayne movie, *The Searchers*, because it not only focuses on conflict between Indians and cowboys but also shows the cowboys defeating the Indians. After the movie, the viewers filled out questionnaires, and Shively interviewed them.

She found something surprising: *All* Native Americans and Anglos identified with the cowboys; *none* identified with the Indians. Anglos and Native Americans, however, identified with the cowboys in different ways. Each

Although John Wayne often portrayed an Anglo who kills Indians, Wayne is popular among Indian men. These men tend to identify with the cowboys, who reflect their values of bravery, autonomy, and toughness.

projected a different fantasy onto the story. Anglos saw the movie as an accurate portrayal of the Old West and a justification of their own status in society. Native Americans, in contrast, saw it as embodying a free, natural way of life. In fact, Native Americans said that they were the "real cowboys." They said, "Westerns relate to the way I wish I could live"; "He's not tied down to an eight-to-five job, day after day"; "He's his own man."

Shively adds,

"What appears to make westerns meaningful to Indians is the fantasy of being free and independent like the cowboy. . . . Indians . . . find a fantasy in the cowboy story in which the important parts of their ways of life triumph and are morally good, validating their own cultural group in the context of a dramatically satisfying story.

To express their real identity—a combination of marginality on the one hand with a set of values which are about the land, autonomy, and being free—they [use] a cultural vehicle written for Anglos about Anglos, but it is one in which Indians invest a distinctive set of meanings that speak to their own experience, which they can read in a manner that affirms a way of life they value, or a fantasy they hold to."

In other words, it is not race–ethnicity, but values, that are the central issue in how Indians identify with Westerns. As Shively says, Native Americans make cowboys "honorary Indians," for the cowboys express their values of bravery, autonomy, and toughness.

For Your Consideration

If a Native American film industry were to produce Westerns that portrayed Native Americans with the same values that the Anglo movie industry projects onto cowboys, whom do you think that Native Americans would identify with? Why?

---

of the ideal culture discussed later) has significantly influenced U.S. history and continues to mark relations among the groups that make up U.S. society.

10. *Group superiority.* Although it contradicts the values of freedom, democracy, and equality, Americans regard some groups more highly than others and have done so throughout their history. The denial of the vote to women, the slaughter of Native Americans, and the enslavement of Africans are a few examples of how the groups considered superior have denied equality and freedom to others.

In an earlier publication, I updated Williams' analysis by adding these three values.

11. *Education.* Americans are expected to go as far in school as their abilities and finances allow. Over the years, the definition of an "adequate" education has

changed, and today a college education is considered an appropriate goal for most Americans. Those who have an opportunity for higher education and do not take it are sometimes viewed as doing something "wrong"—not merely as making a bad choice, but as somehow being involved in an immoral act.

12. *Religiosity.* There is a feeling that "every true American ought to be religious." This does not mean that everyone is expected to join a church, synagogue, or mosque, but that everyone ought to acknowledge a belief in a Supreme Being and follow some set of matching precepts. This value is so pervasive that Americans stamp "In God We Trust" on their money and declare in their national pledge of allegiance that they are "one nation under God."

13. *Romantic love.* Americans feel that the only proper basis for marriage is romantic love. Songs, literature, mass media, and "folk beliefs" all stress this value. Americans grow misty-eyed at the theme that "love conquers all."

Value Clusters

As you can see, values are not independent units; some cluster together to form a larger whole. In the **value cluster** that surrounds success, for example, we find hard work, education, material comfort, and individualism bound up together. Americans are expected to go far in school, to work hard afterward, and then to attain a high level of material comfort, which, in turn, demonstrates success. Success is attributed to the individual's efforts; lack of success is blamed on his or her faults.

Value Contradictions

You probably were surprised to see group superiority on the list of dominant American values. This is an example of what I mentioned in Chapter 1, how sociology upsets people and creates resistance. Few people want to bring something like this into the open. It violates today's *ideal* culture, a concept we discuss on the next page. But this is what sociologists do—they look beyond the façade to penetrate what is really going on. And when you look at our history, there is no doubt that group superiority has been a dominant value. It still is, but values change, and this one is diminishing.

Value contradictions, then, are part of culture. Not all values are wrapped in neat packages, and you can see how group superiority contradicts freedom, democracy, and equality. There simply cannot be full expression of freedom, democracy, and equality along with racism and sexism. Something has to give. One way in which Americans in the past sidestepped this contradiction was to say that freedom, democracy, and equality applied only to some groups. The contradiction was bound to surface over time, however, and so it did with the Civil War and the women's liberation movement. *It is precisely at the point of value contradictions, then, that one can see a major force for social change in a society.*

Emerging Values

A value cluster of four interrelated core values—leisure, self-fulfillment, physical fitness, and youthfulness—is emerging in the United States. So is a fifth core value—concern for the environment.

1. *Leisure.* The emergence of leisure as a value is reflected in a huge recreation industry—from computer games, boats, vacation homes, and spa retreats to sports arenas, home theaters, adventure vacations, and luxury cruises.

The many groups that comprise the United States contribute to its culture. With their growing numbers, Latinos are making greater impact on U.S. art, entertainment, music, and literature. This is also true of other areas of everyday life, such as customized vehicles. These "tricked out" cars at a lowrider show in San Diego, California, feature bumping hydraulics and ornate paint.

2. *Self-fulfillment.* This value is reflected in the "human potential" movement, which emphasizes becoming "all you can be," and in magazine articles, books, and talk shows that focus on "self-help," "relating," and "personal development."

3. *Physical fitness.* Physical fitness is not a new U.S. value, but a greater emphasis on it is moving it into this emerging cluster. You can see this trend in the publicity given to nutrition, organic foods, weight, and diet; the growing number of joggers, cyclists, and backpackers; and the countless health clubs and physical fitness centers.

4. *Youthfulness.* Valuing youth and disparaging old age are also not new, but some analysts note a sense of urgency about today's emphasis on youthfulness. They attribute this to the huge number of aging baby boomers, who, aghast at the physical changes that accompany their advancing years, attempt to deny or at least postpone their biological fate. One physician even claims that "aging is not a normal life event, but a disease" (Cowley 1996). As you age, you will be bombarded with techniques for maintaining and enhancing a youthful appearance—from cosmetic surgery to exotic creams and Botox injections.

Values don't "just happen." They are related to conditions of society, and this emerging value cluster is a response to fundamental change. Earlier generations of Americans were focused on forging a nation and fighting for economic survival. Today, millions of Americans are freed from long hours of work, and millions retire from work at an age when they anticipate decades of life ahead of them. This value cluster centers on helping people to maintain their health and vigor during their younger years and enabling them to enjoy their years of retirement.

5. *Concern for the environment.* During most of U.S. history, the environment was viewed as something to be exploited—a wilderness to be settled, forests to be cleared for farm land and lumber, rivers and lakes to be fished, and animals to be hunted. One result was the near extinction of the bison and the extinction in 1915 of the passenger pigeon, a species of bird previously so numerous that its annual migration would darken the skies for days. Today, Americans have developed a genuine and apparently long-term concern for the environment.

Again, values don't "just happen," and this emerging value of environmental concern is related to the current stage of U.S. economic development: People act on environmental concerns only after they have met their basic needs. At this point in their development, for example, the world's poor nations have a difficult time "affording" this value.

Values, both those held by individuals and those that represent a nation or people, can undergo deep shifts. It is difficult for many of us to grasp the pride with which earlier Americans destroyed trees that took thousands of years to grow, are located only on one tiny speck of the globe, and that we today consider part of the nation's and world's heritage. But this is a value statement, representing current views. The pride expressed on these woodcutters' faces represents another set of values entirely.

Culture Wars: When Values Clash

Challenges in core values are met with strong resistance by the people who hold them dear. They see change as a threat to their way of life, an undermining of both their present and their future. Efforts to change gender roles, for example, arouse intense controversy, as do same-sex marriages. Alarmed at such onslaughts against their values, traditionalists fiercely defend historical family relationships and the gender roles they grew up with. *Culture wars*—a highly exaggerated term—refers to the clash in values between traditionalists and those advocating change. Compared with the violence directed against the Mormons, today's culture clashes are mild.

Values as Distorting Lenses

Values and their supporting beliefs are lenses through which we see the world. The view they produce is often of what life *ought* to be like, not what it is. For example, Americans value individualism so highly that they tend to see almost everyone as free and equal in pursuing the goal of success. This value blinds them to the significance of circumstances that keep people from achieving success. The dire consequences of family poverty, parents' low education, and dead-end jobs tend to drop from sight. Instead, Americans see the unsuccessful as not putting out enough effort. And they "know" they are right, for the mass media dangles before their eyes enticing stories of individuals who have succeeded despite the greatest of handicaps.

"Ideal" Versus "Real" Culture

Many of the norms that surround cultural values are followed only partially. Differences always exist between a group's ideals and what its members actually do. Consequently, sociologists use the term **ideal culture** to refer to the values, norms, and goals that a group considers ideal, worth aiming for. Success, for example, is part of ideal culture. Americans glorify academic progress, hard work, and the display of material goods as signs of individual achievement. What people actually do, however, usually falls short of the cultural ideal. Compared with their abilities, for example, most people don't work as hard as they could or go as far as they could in school. Sociologists call the norms and values that people actually follow **real culture.**

Cultural Universals

With the amazing variety of human cultures around the world, are there any **cultural universals**—values, norms, or other cultural traits that are found everywhere?

To answer this question, anthropologist George Murdock (1945) combed through the data that anthropologists had gathered on hundreds of groups around the world. He compared their customs concerning courtship, marriage, funerals, games, laws, music, myths, incest taboos, and even toilet training. He found that these activities are present in all cultures, but *the specific customs differ from one group to another.* There is no universal form of the family, no universal way of toilet training children, nor a universal way of disposing of the dead.

Incest is a remarkable example. Groups even differ on their view of what incest is. The Mundugumors of New Guinea extend the incest taboo so far that for each man, *seven* of every eight women are ineligible marriage partners (Mead 1935/1950). Other groups go in the opposite direction and allow some men to marry their own daughters (La Barre 1954). Some groups even *require* that brothers and sisters marry one another, although only in certain circumstances (Beals and Hoijer 1965). The Burundi of Africa even insist that a son have sex with his mother—but only to remove a certain curse (Albert 1963). Such sexual relations, so surprising to us, are limited to special people (royalty) or to extraordinary situations (such as when a lion hunter faces a dangerous hunt). No society permits generalized incest for its members.

ideal culture a people's ideal values and norms; the goals held out for them

real culture the norms and values that people actually follow

cultural universal a value, norm, or other cultural trait that is found in every group

In Sum: Although there are universal human activities (singing, playing games, story-telling, preparing food, marrying, child rearing, disposing of the dead, and so on), there is no universally accepted way of doing any of them. Humans have no biological imperative that results in one particular form of behavior throughout the world. As indicated in the following Thinking Critically section, although a few sociologists take the position that genes significantly influence human behavior, almost all sociologists reject this view.

ThinkingCRITICALLY

Are We Prisoners of Our Genes? Sociobiology and Human Behavior

A controversial view of human behavior, called **sociobiology** (also known as neo-Darwinism and evolutionary psychology), provides a sharp contrast to the perspective of this chapter, that human behavior is primarily due to culture. Sociobiologists (evolutionary psychologists, evolutionary anthropologists) believe that because of natural selection, biology is the basic cause of human behavior.

Charles Darwin (1859), who, as we saw in Chapter 1, adopted Spencer's idea of natural selection, pointed out that the genes of a species—the units that contain the individual's traits—are not distributed evenly among the offspring. The characteristics that some members inherit make it easier for them to survive their environment, increasing the likelihood that they will pass their genetic traits to the next generation. Over thousands of generations, the genetic traits that aid survival become common in a species, while those that do not aid survival become less common or even disappear. Natural selection explains not only the physical characteristics of animals but also their behavior, for over countless generations, instincts emerged.

Edward Wilson (1975), an insect specialist, set off an uproar when he claimed that human behavior is also the result of natural selection. Human behavior, he said, is no different from the behavior of cats, dogs, rats, bees, or mosquitoes—it has been bred into *Homo sapiens* through evolutionary principles. Wilson went on to claim that competition and cooperation, envy and altruism—even religion, slavery, genocide, and war and peace—can be explained by sociobiology. He provocatively added that because human behavior can be explained in terms of genetic programming, sociobiology will eventually absorb sociology, as well as anthropology and psychology.

Obviously, most sociologists disagree with Wilson's position. Not only is it a direct attack on our discipline but it also bypasses the essence of what sociologists focus on: humans developing their own cultures, their own unique ways of life. Sociologists do not deny that biology underlies human behavior—at least not in the sense that it takes a highly developed brain to develop human culture and abstract thought and that there would be no speech if humans had no tongue or larynx.

But most sociologists find it difficult to believe that anyone would claim that genetic programming causes human behavior. Pigs act like pigs because they don't have a cerebral cortex, and instincts control their behavior. So it is for spiders, elephants, and so on (Howe et al. 1992). We humans, in contrast, possess a self and engage in abstract thought. We discuss the reasons that underlie what we do. We develop purposes and goals. We immerse ourselves in a world of symbols that allow us to consider, reflect, and make reasoned choices.

This controversy has turned into much more than simply an academic debate among scientists. Homosexuals, for example, have a personal interest in its outcome. If homosexuality is a lifestyle *choice,* then those who consider that lifestyle to be immoral will try to use this as a basis to exclude homosexuals from full social participation. If, however, homosexuality has a genetic base, then choice as a reason for social exclusion is eliminated. Sociologist

sociobiology a framework of thought that views human behavior as the result of natural selection and considers biological factors to be the fundamental cause of human behavior

technology in its narrow sense, tools; its broader sense includes the skills or procedures necessary to make and use those tools

new technology the emerging technologies of an era that have a significant impact on social life

Peter Conrad (1997) expressed the dominant sociological position when he pointed out that not all homosexuals have Xq28, the so-called gay gene, and that some people who have this gene are not homosexual. This gene, then, does not determine behavior. Instead, we must look for *social* causes (Bearman and Bruckner 2002). That there are social causes is not a basis for excluding anyone from anything.

In short, sociobiologists and sociologists stand on opposite sides, the one looking at human behavior as determined by genetics, the other looking at human behavior as determined by social learning, by experiences in the human group. Sociologists point out that if we humans were prisoners of our genes, we would not have developed such fascinatingly different ways of life around the world; instead, we would live in a monoculture of some sort.

Technology in the Global Village

The New Technology

The gestures, language, values, folkways, and mores that we have discussed—all are part of symbolic (nonmaterial) culture. Culture, as you recall, also has a material aspect: a group's *things,* from its houses to its toys. Central to a group's material culture is its technology. In its simplest sense, **technology** can be equated with tools. In a broader sense, technology also includes the skills or procedures necessary to make and use those tools.

We can use the term **new technology** to refer to an emerging technology that has a significant impact on social life. People develop minor technologies all the time. Most are slight modifications of existing technologies. Occasionally, however, they develop a technology that makes a major impact on human life. It is primarily to these innovations that the term *new technology* refers. Five hundred years ago, the new technology was the printing press. For us, the new technology consists of computers, satellites, and the Internet.

The sociological significance of technology goes far beyond the tool itself. *Technology sets the framework for a group's nonmaterial culture.* If a group's technology changes, so do the ways people's think and how they relate to one another. An example is gender relations. Through the centuries and throughout the world, it has been the custom (nonmaterial culture) for men to dominate women. Today's global communications (material culture) make this custom more difficult to maintain. For example, when Arab women watch Western television, they observe a freedom in gender relations that is unknown to them.

The use of new forms of communication by people who not long ago were cut off from events in the rest of the world is bound to change their *nonmaterial culture.* How do you think computers are changing this man's thinking and views of the world?

As these women use e-mail and telephones to talk to one another about what they have seen, they both convey and create discontent, as well as feelings of sisterhood. These communications motivate some of them to agitate for social change.

In today's world, the long-accepted idea that it is proper to withhold rights on the basis of someone's sex can no longer be sustained. What usually lies beyond our awareness in this revolutionary change is the role of the new technology, which joins the world's nations into a global communications network.

Cultural Lag and Cultural Change

About three generations ago, sociologist William Ogburn (1922/1938) coined the term **cultural lag.** By this, Ogburn meant that not all parts of a culture change at the same pace. When one part of a culture changes, other parts lag behind.

Ogburn pointed out that *a group's material culture usually changes first, with the nonmaterial culture lagging behind.* This leaves the nonmaterial (or symbolic) culture playing a game of catch-up. For example, when we get sick, we can type our symptoms into a computer and get an immediate diagnosis and a recommended course of treatment. In some tests, computer programs outperform physicians. Yet our customs have not caught up with our technology, and we continue to visit the doctor's office.

Sometimes nonmaterial culture never does catch up. We can rigorously hold onto some outmoded form—one that once was needed, but that long ago was bypassed by technology. Have you ever wondered why our "school year" is nine months long, and why we take summers off? For most of us, this is "just the way it's always been," and we have never questioned it. But there is more to this custom than meets the eye. In the late 1800s, when universal schooling came about, the school year matched the technology of the time. Most parents were farmers, and for survival they needed their children's help at the crucial times of planting and harvesting. Today, generations later, when few people farm and there is no need for the "school year" to be so short, we still live with this cultural lag.

Technology and Cultural Leveling

For most of human history, communication was limited and travel slow. Consequently, in their relative isolation, human groups developed highly distinctive ways of life as they responded to the particular situations they faced. The unique characteristics they developed that distinguished one culture from another tended to change little over time. The Tasmanians, who live on a remote island off the coast of Australia, provide an extreme example. For thousands of years, they had no contact with other people. They were so isolated that they did not even know how to make clothing or fire (Edgerton 1992).

Except in such rare instances, humans have always had *some* contact with other groups. During these contacts, people learned from one another, adopting things they found desirable. In this process, called **cultural diffusion,** groups are most open to changes in their technology or material culture. They usually are eager, for example, to adopt superior weapons and tools. In remote jungles in South America one can find metal cooking pots, steel axes, and even bits of clothing spun in mills in South Carolina. Although the direction of cultural diffusion today is primarily from the West to other parts of the world, cultural diffusion is not a one-way street—as bagels, woks, hammocks, and sushi in the United States attest.

With today's travel and communications, cultural diffusion is occurring rapidly. Air travel has made it possible to journey around the globe in a matter of hours. In the not-so-distant past, a trip from the United States to Africa was so unusual that only a few

LITERATURE

" JUST THINK OF IT AS IF YOU'RE READING A LONG TEXT-MESSAGE."

© Dave Carpenter/www.CartoonStock.com

Technological advances are now so rapid that there can be cultural gaps between generations.

cultural lag Ogburn's term for human behavior lagging behind technological innovations

cultural diffusion the spread of cultural traits from one group to another; includes both material and nonmaterial cultural traits

This Barbie doll, sold in Japan, is dressed in a stage costume of a Japanese singer. As objects diffuse from one culture to another, they are modified to meet the tastes of the adoptive culture. In this instance, the modification has been done intentionally as part of the globalization of capitalism.

adventurous people made it, and newspapers would herald their feat. Today, hundreds of thousands make the trip each year.

The changes in communication are no less vast. Communication used to be limited to face-to-face speech, written messages that were passed from hand to hand, and visual signals such as smoke or light that was reflected from mirrors. Despite newspapers and even the telegraph, people in some parts of the United States did not hear that the Civil War had ended until weeks and even months after it was over. Today's electronic communications transmit messages across the globe in a matter of seconds, and we learn almost instantaneously what is happening on the other side of the world. During the Iraq War, reporters traveled with U.S. soldiers, and for the first time in history, the public was able to view live video reports of battles as they took place and of people as they died.

Travel and communication bridge time and space to such an extent that there is almost no "other side of the world" anymore. One result is **cultural leveling,** a process in which cultures become similar to one another. The globalization of capitalism brings with it both technology and Western culture. Japan, for example, has adopted not only capitalism but also Western forms of dress and music, transforming it into a blend of Western and Eastern cultures.

cultural leveling the process by which cultures become similar to one another; refers especially to the process by which Western culture is being exported and diffused into other nations

Cultural leveling is apparent to any traveler. The Golden Arches of McDonald's welcome visitors to Tokyo, Paris, London, Madrid, Moscow, Hong Kong, and Beijing. When I visited a jungle village in India—no electricity, no running water, and so remote that the only entrance was by a footpath—I saw a young man sporting a cap with the Nike emblem.

Although the bridging of geography, time, and culture by electronic signals and the exportation of Western icons do not in and of themselves mark the end of traditional cultures, the inevitable result is some degree of *cultural leveling*. We are producing a blander, less distinctive way of life—U.S. culture with French, Japanese, and Brazilian accents, so to speak. Although the "cultural accent" remains, something vital is lost forever.

SUMMARY and REVIEW

What Is Culture?

All human groups possess **culture**—language, beliefs, values, norms, and material objects that are passed from one generation to the next. **Material culture** consists of objects (art, buildings, clothing, weapons, tools). **Nonmaterial** (or **symbolic**) **culture** is a group's ways of thinking and its patterns of behavior. **Ideal culture** is a group's ideal values, norms, and goals. **Real culture** is people's actual behavior, which often falls short of their cultural ideals. Pp. 36–42.

What are cultural relativism and ethnocentrism?

People are **ethnocentric;** that is, they use their own culture as a yardstick for judging the ways of others. In contrast, those who embrace **cultural relativism** try to understand other cultures on those cultures' own terms. Pp. 39–40.

Components of Symbolic Culture

What are the components of nonmaterial culture?

The central component is **symbols,** anything to which people attach meaning and that they use to communicate with others. Universally, the symbols of nonmaterial culture are **gestures, language, values, norms, sanctions, folkways,** and **mores.** Pp. 42–43.

Why is language so significant to culture?

Language allows human experience to be goal-directed, cooperative, and cumulative. It also lets humans move beyond the present and share a past, future, and other common perspectives. According to the **Sapir-Whorf hypothesis,** language even shapes our thoughts and perceptions. Pp. 43–46.

How do values, norms, sanctions, folkways, and mores reflect culture?

All groups have **values,** standards by which they define what is desirable or undesirable, and **norms,** rules or expectations about behavior. Groups use **positive sanctions** to show approval of those who follow their norms and **negative sanctions** to show disapproval of those who do not. Norms that are not strictly enforced are called **folkways,** while **mores** are norms to which groups demand conformity because they reflect core values. Pp. 46–49.

Many Cultural Worlds

How do subcultures and countercultures differ?

A **subculture** is a group whose values and related behaviors distinguish its members from the general culture. A **counterculture** holds some values that stand in opposition to those of the dominant culture. Pp. 49–52.

Values in U.S. Society

What are some core U.S. values?

Although the United States is a **pluralistic society,** made up of many groups, each with its own set of values, certain values dominate: achievement and success, individualism, hard work, efficiency and practicality, science and technology, material comfort, freedom, democracy, equality, group superiority, education, religiosity, and romantic love. Some values cluster together (**value clusters**) to form a larger whole. **Value contradictions** (such as equality, sexism, and racism) indicate areas of tension, which are likely points of social change. Leisure, self-fulfillment, physical fitness, youthfulness, and concern for the environment are emerging core values. Core values do not change without opposition. Pp. 52–56.

Cultural Universals

Do cultural universals exist?

Cultural universals are values, norms, or other cultural traits that are found in all cultures. Although all human groups have customs concerning cooking, childbirth, funerals, and so on, because these customs differ from one culture to another, there are no cultural universals. Pp. 56–58.

Technology in the Global Village

How is technology changing culture?

William Ogburn coined the term **cultural lag** to describe how a group's nonmaterial culture lags behind its changing technology. With today's technological advances in travel and communications, **cultural diffusion** is occurring rapidly. This leads to **cultural leveling,** groups becoming similar as they adopt items from other cultures. Much of the richness of the world's diverse cultures is being lost in the process. Pp. 58–60.

THINKING CRITICALLY *ABOUT* Chapter 2

1. Do you favor ethnocentrism or cultural relativism? Explain your position.

2. Do you think that the language change in Miami, Florida (discussed on page 45), indicates the future of the United States? Why or why not?

3. Are you a member of any subcultures? Which one(s)? Why do you think that your group is a subculture? What is your group's relationship to the mainstream culture?

ADDITIONAL RESOURCES

What can you find in MySocLab? mysoclab www.mysoclab.com

- Complete Ebook
- Practice Tests and Video and Audio activities
- Mapping and Data Analysis exercises

- Sociology in the News
- Classic Readings in Sociology
- Research and Writing advice

Where Can I Read More on This Topic?

Suggested readings for this chapter are listed at the back of this book.

chapter

3

Socialization

The old man was horrified when he found out. Life never had been good since his daughter lost her hearing when she was just 2 years old. She couldn't even talk—just fluttered her hands around trying to tell him things.

Over the years, he had gotten used to that. But now . . . he shuddered at the thought of her being pregnant. No one would be willing to marry her; he knew that. And the neighbors, their tongues would never stop wagging. Everywhere he went, he could hear people talking behind his back.

Her behavior toward strangers, especially men, was almost that of a wild animal, manifesting much fear and hostility.

If only his wife were still alive, maybe she could come up with something. What should he do? He couldn't just kick his daughter out into the street.

After the baby was born, the old man tried to shake his feelings, but they wouldn't let loose. Isabelle was a pretty name, but every time he looked at the baby he felt sick to his stomach.

He hated doing it, but there was no way out. His daughter and her baby would have to live in the attic.

Unfortunately, this is a true story. Isabelle was discovered in Ohio in 1938 when she was about 6 ½ years old, living in a dark room with her deaf-mute mother. Isabelle couldn't talk, but she did use gestures to communicate with her mother. An inadequate diet and lack of sunshine had given Isabelle a disease called rickets.

> [Her legs] were so bowed that as she stood erect the soles of her shoes came nearly flat together, and she got about with a skittering gait. Her behavior toward strangers, especially men, was almost that of a wild animal, manifesting much fear and hostility. In lieu of speech she made only a strange croaking sound. (Davis 1940/2007:156–157)

When the newspapers reported this case, sociologist Kingsley Davis decided to find out what had happened to Isabelle after her discovery. We'll come back to that later, but first let's use the case of Isabelle to gain insight into human nature.

Florida

63

social environment the entire human environment, including direct contact with others

feral children children assumed to have been raised by animals, in the wilderness, isolated from humans

Society Makes Us Human

"What do you mean, society makes us human?" is probably what you are asking. "That sounds ridiculous. I was born a human." The meaning of this statement will become more apparent as we get into the chapter. Let's start by considering what is human about human nature. How much of a person's characteristics comes from "nature" (heredity) and how much from "nurture" (the **social environment,** contact with others)? Experts are trying to answer the nature–nurture question by studying identical twins who were separated at birth and reared in different environments, such as those discussed in the Down-to-Earth Sociology box on the next page. Another way is to examine children who have had little human contact. Let's consider such children.

Feral Children

> The naked child was found in the forest, walking on all fours, eating grass and lapping water from the river. When he saw a small animal, he pounced on it. Growling, he ripped at it with his teeth. Tearing chunks from the body, he chewed them ravenously.

This is an apt description of reports that have come in over the centuries. Supposedly, these **feral** (wild) **children** could not speak; they bit, scratched, growled, and walked on all fours. They drank by lapping water, ate grass, tore ravenously at raw meat, and showed insensitivity to pain and cold. Why am I even mentioning stories that sound so exaggerated?

It is because of what happened in 1798. In that year, such a child was found in the forests of Aveyron, France. "The wild boy of Aveyron," as he became known, would have been written off as another folk myth, except that French scientists took the child to a laboratory and studied him. Like the feral children in the earlier informal reports, this child, too, gave no indication of feeling the cold. Most startling, though, the boy would growl when he saw a small animal, pounce on it, and devour it uncooked. Even today, the scientists' detailed reports make fascinating reading (Itard 1962).

Ever since I read Itard's account of this boy, I've been fascinated by the seemingly fantastic possibility that animals could rear human children. In 2002, I received a report from a contact in Cambodia that a feral child had been found in the jungles. When I had the opportunity the following year to visit the child and interview his caregivers, I grabbed it. The boy's photo is to the left. If we were untouched by society, would we be like feral children? By nature, would our behavior be like that of wild animals? That is the sociological question. Unable to study feral children, sociologists have studied isolated children, like Isabelle in our opening vignette. Let's see what we can learn from them.

One of the reasons I went to Cambodia was to interview a feral child—the boy shown here—who supposedly had been raised by monkeys. When I arrived at the remote location where the boy was living, I was disappointed to find that the story was only partially true. During its reign of terror, the Khmer Rouge had shot and killed the boy's parents, leaving him, at about the age of two, abandoned on an island. Some months later, villagers found him in the care of monkeys. They shot the female monkey who was carrying the boy. Not quite a feral child—but the closest I'll ever come to one.

Isolated Children

What can isolated children tell us about human nature? We can first conclude that humans have no natural language, for Isabelle and others like her are unable to speak.

But maybe Isabelle was mentally impaired. Perhaps she simply was unable to progress through the usual stages of development. It certainly looked that way—she scored practically zero on her first intelligence test. But after a few months of language training, Isabelle was able to speak in short sentences. In just a year, she could write a few words, do simple addition, and retell stories after hearing them. Seven months later, she had a vocabulary of almost 2,000 words. In just two years, Isabelle reached the intellectual level that is normal for her age. She then went on to school, where she was "bright, cheerful, energetic . . . and participated in all school activities as normally as other children" (Davis 1940/2007:157–158).

Down-to-Earth Sociology

Heredity or Environment?
The Case of Jack and Oskar, Identical Twins

Identical twins are identical in their genetic heritage. They are born when one fertilized egg divides to produce two embryos. If heredity determines personality—or attitudes, temperament, skills, and intelligence—then identical twins should be identical not only in their looks but also in these characteristics.

The fascinating case of Jack and Oskar helps us unravel this mystery. From their experience, we can see the far-reaching effects of the environment—how social experiences override biology.

Jack Yufe and Oskar Stohr are identical twins. Born in 1932 to a Roman Catholic mother and a Jewish father, they were separated as babies after their parents divorced. Jack was reared in Trinidad by his father. There, he learned loyalty to Jews and hatred of Hitler and the Nazis. After the war, Jack and his father moved to Israel. When he was 17, Jack joined a kibbutz and later served in the Israeli army.

Oskar's upbringing was a mirror image of Jack's. Oskar was reared in Czechoslovakia by his mother's mother, who was a strict Catholic. When Oskar was a toddler, Hitler annexed this area of Czechoslovakia, and Oskar learned to love Hitler and to hate Jews. He joined the Hitler Youth (a sort of Boy Scout organization, except that this one was designed to instill the "virtues" of patriotism, loyalty, obedience—and hatred).

In 1954, the two brothers met. It was a short meeting, and Jack had been warned not to tell Oskar that they were Jews. Twenty-five years later, in 1979, when they were 47 years old, social scientists at the University of Minnesota brought them together again. These researchers figured that because Jack and Oskar had the same genes, any differences they showed would have to be the result of their environment—their different social experiences.

Not only did Jack and Oskar hold different attitudes toward the war, Hitler, and Jews, but their basic orientations to life were also different. In their politics, Jack was liberal, while Oskar was more conservative. Jack was a workaholic, while Oskar enjoyed leisure. And, as you can predict, Jack was proud of being a Jew. Oskar, who by this time knew that he was a Jew, wouldn't even mention it.

The question of the relative influence of heredity and the environment in human behavior has fascinated and plagued researchers. To try to answer this question, researchers have studied identical twins. In this photo, what behaviors can you see that are clearly due to the environment? Any that are due to biology?

That would seem to settle the matter. But there were other things. As children, Jack and Oskar had both excelled at sports but had difficulty with math. They also had the same rate of speech, and both liked sweet liqueur and spicy foods. Strangely, both flushed the toilet both before and after using it, and they both enjoyed startling people by sneezing in crowded elevators.

For Your Consideration

Heredity or environment? How much influence does each have? The question is not yet settled, but at this point it seems fair to conclude that the *limits* of certain physical and mental abilities are established by heredity (such as ability at sports and aptitude for mathematics), while attitudes are the result of the environment. Basic temperament, though, seems to be inherited. Although the answer is still fuzzy, we can put it this way: For some parts of life, the blueprint is drawn by heredity; but even here the environment can redraw those lines. For other parts, the individual is a blank slate, and it is up to the environment to determine what is written on that slate.

Sources: Based on Begley 1979; Chen 1979; Wright 1995; Segal and Hershberger 2005; De Moor et al. 2007.

As discussed in the previous chapter, language is the key to human development. Without language, people have no mechanism for developing thought and communicating their experiences. Unlike animals, humans have no instincts that take the place of language. If an individual lacks language, he or she lives in a world of internal silence, without shared ideas, lacking connections to others.

Without language, there can be no culture—no shared way of life—and culture is the key to what people become. Each of us possesses a biological heritage, but this heritage does not determine specific behaviors, attitudes, or values. It is our culture that superimposes the specifics of what we become onto our biological heritage.

Institutionalized Children

Other than language, what else is required for a child to develop into what we consider a healthy, balanced, intelligent human being? We find part of the answer in an intriguing experiment from the 1930s. Back then, orphanages were common because parents were more likely than now to die before their children were grown. Children reared in orphanages tended to have low IQs. "Common sense" (which we noted in Chapter 1 is unreliable) made it obvious that their low intelligence was because of poor brains ("They're just born that way"). But two psychologists, H. M. Skeels and H. B. Dye (1939), began to suspect a social cause.

Skeels (1966) provides this account of a "good" orphanage in Iowa, one where he and Dye were consultants:

> Until about six months, they were cared for in the infant nursery. The babies were kept in standard hospital cribs that often had protective sheeting on the sides, thus effectively limiting visual stimulation; no toys or other objects were hung in the infants' line of vision. Human interactions were limited to busy nurses who, with the speed born of practice and necessity, changed diapers or bedding, bathed and medicated the infants, and fed them efficiently with propped bottles.

Perhaps, thought Skeels and Dye, the problem was the absence of stimulating social interaction, not the children's brains. To test their controversial idea, they selected thirteen infants who were so mentally slow that no one wanted to adopt them. They placed them in an institution for mentally retarded women. They assigned each infant, then about 19 months old, to a separate ward of women ranging in mental age from 5 to 12 and in chronological age from 18 to 50. The women were pleased with this. They enjoyed taking care of the infants' physical needs—diapering, feeding, and so on. And they also loved to play with the children. They cuddled them and showered them with attention. They even competed to see which ward would have "its baby" walking or talking first. In each ward, one woman became particularly attached to the child and figuratively adopted him or her:

> As a consequence, an intense one-to-one adult–child relationship developed, which was supplemented by the less intense but frequent interactions with the other adults in the environment. Each child had some one person with whom he [or she] was identified and who was particularly interested in him [or her] and his [or her] achievements. (Skeels 1966)

The researchers left a control group of twelve infants at the orphanage. These infants received the usual care. They also had low IQs, but they were considered somewhat higher in

Infants in this orphanage in Siem Reap, Cambodia, are drugged and hung in these mesh baskets for up to ten hours a day. The staff of the orphanage pockets most of the money contributed by Westerners for the children's care. The treatment of these children is likely to affect their ability to reason and to function as adults.

intelligence than the thirteen in the experimental group. Two and a half years later, Skeels and Dye tested all the children's intelligence. Their findings are startling: Those cared for by the women in the institution gained an average of 28 IQ points while those who remained in the orphanage lost 30 points.

What happened after these children were grown? Did these initial differences matter? Twenty-one years later, Skeels and Dye did a follow-up study. The twelve in the control group, those who had remained in the orphanage, averaged less than a third-grade education. Four still lived in state institutions, and the others held low-level jobs. Only two had married. The thirteen in the experimental group, those cared for by the institutionalized women, had an average education of twelve grades (about normal for that period). Five had completed one or more years of college. One had even gone to graduate school. Eleven had married. All thirteen were self-supporting or were homemakers (Skeels 1966). Apparently, "high intelligence" depends on early, close relations with other humans.

A recent experiment in India confirms this early research. Many of India's orphanages are like those that Skeels and Dye studied—dismal places where unattended children lie in bed all day. When experimenters added stimulating play and interaction to the children's activities, the children's motor skills improved and their IQs increased (Taneja et al. 2002). The longer that children lack stimulating interaction, though, the more difficulty they have intellectually (Meese 2005).

Let's consider Genie, a 13-year-old girl who had been locked in a small room and tied to a chair since she was 20 months old:

Apparently Genie's father (70 years old when Genie was discovered in 1970) hated children. He probably had caused the death of two of Genie's siblings. Her 50-year-old mother was partially blind and frightened of her husband. Genie could not speak, did not know how to chew, was unable to stand upright, and could not straighten her hands and legs. On intelligence tests, she scored at the level of a 1-year-old. After intensive training, Genie learned to walk and to say simple sentences (although they were garbled). Genie's language remained primitive as she grew up. She would take anyone's property if it appealed to her, and she went to the bathroom wherever she wanted. At the age of 21, she was sent to a home for adults who cannot live alone. (Pines 1981)

Like humans, monkeys need interaction to thrive. Those raised in isolation are unable to interact with others. In this photograph, we see one of the monkeys described in the text. Purposefully frightened by the experimenter, the monkey has taken refuge in the soft terrycloth draped over an artificial "mother."

In Sum: From Genie's pathetic story and from the research on institutionalized children, we can conclude that the basic human traits of intelligence and the ability to establish close bonds with others depend on early interaction with other humans. In addition, there seems to be a period prior to age 13 in which children must learn language and experience human bonding if they are to develop normal intelligence and the ability to be sociable and follow social norms.

Deprived Animals

Finally, let's consider animals that have been deprived of normal interaction. In a series of experiments with rhesus monkeys, psychologists Harry and Margaret Harlow demonstrated the importance of early learning. The Harlows (1962) raised baby monkeys in isolation. They gave each monkey two artificial mothers. One "mother" was only a wire frame with a wooden head, but it did have a nipple from which the baby could nurse. The frame of the other "mother," which had no bottle, was covered with soft terrycloth. To obtain food, the baby monkeys nursed at the wire frame.

When the Harlows (1965) frightened the baby monkeys with a mechanical bear or dog, the babies did not run to the wire frame "mother." Instead, as shown in the photo on the previous page, they would cling pathetically to their terrycloth "mother." The Harlows concluded that infant–mother bonding is not the result of feeding but, rather, of what they termed "intimate physical contact." To most of us, this phrase means cuddling.

The monkeys raised in isolation could not adjust to monkey life. Placed with other monkeys when they were grown, they didn't know how to participate in "monkey interaction"— to play and to engage in pretend fights—and the other monkeys rejected them. They didn't even know how to have sexual intercourse, despite futile attempts to do so. The experimenters designed a special device, which allowed some females to become pregnant. Their isolation, however, made them "ineffective, inadequate, and brutal mothers." They "struck their babies, kicked them, or crushed the babies against the cage floor."

In one of their many experiments, the Harlows isolated baby monkeys for different lengths of time and then put them in with the other monkeys. Monkeys that had been isolated for shorter periods (about three months) were able to adjust to normal monkey life. They learned to play and engage in pretend fights. Those isolated for six months or more, however, couldn't make the adjustment, and the other monkeys rejected them. In other words, the longer the period of isolation, the more difficult its effects are to overcome. In addition, there seems to be a critical learning stage: If that stage is missed, it may be impossible to compensate for what has been lost. This may have been the case with Genie.

Because humans are not monkeys, we must be careful about extrapolating from animal studies to human behavior. The Harlow experiments, however, support what we know about children who are reared in isolation.

In Sum: Babies do not develop "naturally" into social adults. If children are reared in isolation, their bodies grow, but they become little more than big animals. Without the concepts that language provides, they can't grasp relationships between people (the "connections" we call brother, sister, parent, friend, teacher, and so on). And without warm, friendly interactions, they can't bond with others. They don't become "friendly" or cooperate with others. In short, it is through human contact that people learn to be members of the human community. This process by which we learn the ways of society (or of particular groups), called **socialization,** is what sociologists have in mind when they say "Society makes us human."

Further keys to understanding how society makes us human are our self-concept, ability to "take the role of others," reasoning, morality, and emotions. Let's look at how we develop these capacities.

Socialization into the Self and Mind

When you were born, you had no ideas. You didn't know that you were a son or daughter. You didn't even know that you were a he or she. How did you develop a **self,** your image of who you are? How did you develop your ability to reason? Let's find out.

Cooley and the Looking-Glass Self

About a hundred years ago, Charles Horton Cooley (1864–1929), a symbolic interactionist who taught at the University of Michigan, concluded that the self is part of how *society* makes us human. He said that *our sense of self develops from interaction with others.* To describe the process by which this unique aspect of "humanness" develops, Cooley (1902) coined the term **looking-glass self.** He summarized this idea in the following couplet:

> Each to each a looking-glass
> Reflects the other that doth pass.

The looking-glass self contains three elements:

1. *We imagine how we appear to those around us.* For example, we may think that others perceive us as witty or dull.

---

socialization the process by which people learn the characteristics of their group—the knowledge, skills, attitudes, values, norms, and actions thought appropriate for them

self the unique human capacity of being able to see ourselves "from the outside"; the views we internalize of how others see us

looking-glass self a term coined by Charles Horton Cooley to refer to the process by which our self develops through internalizing others' reactions to us

taking the role of the other putting oneself in someone else's shoes; understanding how someone else feels and thinks and thus anticipating how that person will act

significant other an individual who significantly influences someone else's life

generalized other the norms, values, attitudes, and expectations of people "in general"; the child's ability to take the role of the generalized other is a significant step in the development of a self

2. *We interpret others' reactions.* We come to conclusions about how others evaluate us. Do they like us for being witty? Do they dislike us for being dull?

3. *We develop a self-concept.* How we interpret others' reactions to us frames our feelings and ideas about ourselves. A favorable reflection in this *social mirror* leads to a positive self-concept; a negative reflection leads to a negative self-concept.

Note that the development of the self does *not* depend on accurate evaluations. Even if we grossly misinterpret how others think about us, those misjudgments become part of our self-concept. Note also that *although the self-concept begins in childhood, its development is an ongoing, lifelong process.* During our everyday lives, we monitor how others react to us. As we do so, we continually modify the self. The self, then, is never a finished product—it is always in process, even into our old age.

Mead and Role Taking

Another symbolic interactionist, George Herbert Mead (1863–1931), who taught at the University of Chicago, pointed out how important play is as we develop a self. As we play with others, we learn to **take the role of the other.** That is, we learn to put ourselves in someone else's shoes—to understand how someone else feels and thinks and to anticipate how that person will act.

This doesn't happen overnight. We develop this ability over a period of years (Mead 1934; Denzin 2007). Psychologist John Flavel (1968) asked 8- and 14-year-olds to explain a board game to children who were blindfolded and to others who were not. The 14-year-olds gave more detailed instructions to those who were blindfolded, but the 8-year-olds gave the same instructions to everyone. The younger children could not yet take the role of the other, while the older children could.

As we develop this ability, at first we can take only the role of **significant others,** individuals who significantly influence our lives, such as parents or siblings. By assuming their roles during play, such as dressing up in our parents' clothing, we cultivate the ability to put ourselves in the place of significant others.

As our self gradually develops, we internalize the expectations of more and more people. Our ability to take the role of others eventually extends to being able to take the role of "the group as a whole." Mead used the term **generalized other** to refer to our perception of how people in general think of us.

Taking the role of others is essential if we are to become cooperative members of human groups—whether they be our family, friends, or co-workers. This ability allows us to modify our behavior by anticipating how others will react—something Genie never learned.

As Figure 3.1 illustrates, we go through three stages as we learn to take the role of the other:

1. *Imitation.* Under the age of 3, we can only mimic others. We do not yet have a sense of self separate from others, and we can only imitate people's gestures and words. (This stage is actually not role taking, but it prepares us for it.)

2. *Play.* During the second stage, from the ages of about 3 to 6, we pretend to take the roles of specific people. We might pretend that we are a firefighter, a wrestler, a nurse, Supergirl, Spiderman, a princess, and so on. We also like costumes at this stage and enjoy dressing up in our parents' clothing, or tying a towel around our neck to "become" Superman or Wonder Woman.

3. *Team Games.* This third stage, organized play, or team games, begins roughly when we enter school. The

FIGURE 3.1 How We Learn to Take the Role of the Other: Mead's Three Stages

Stage 1: Imitation
Children under age 3
No sense of self
Imitate others

Stage 2: Play
Ages 3 to 6
Play "pretend" others
  (princess, Spiderman, etc.)

Stage 3: Team Games
After about age 6 or 7
Team games
  ("organized play")
Learn to take multiple roles

To help his students understand the term *generalized other,* Mead used baseball as an illustration. Why are team sports and organized games excellent examples to use in explaining this concept?

Mead analyzed *taking the role of the other* as an essential part of learning to be a full-fledged member of society. At first, we are able to take the role only of *significant others*, as this child is doing. Later we develop the capacity to take the role of the *generalized other*, which is essential not only for cooperation but also for the control of antisocial desires.

significance for the self is that to play these games we must be able to take multiple roles. One of Mead's favorite examples was that of a baseball game, in which each player must be able to take the role of all the other players. To play baseball, it isn't enough that we know our own role; we also must be able to anticipate what everyone else on the field will do when the ball is hit or thrown.

Mead also said there were two parts of the self, the "I" and the "me." The "*I*" is *the self as subject,* the active, spontaneous, creative part of the self. In contrast, the "*me*" is *the self as object.* It is made up of attitudes we internalize from our interactions with others. Mead chose these pronouns because in English "I" is the active agent, as in "I shoved him," while "me" is the object of action, as in "He shoved me." Mead stressed that we are not passive in the socialization process. We are not like robots, with programmed software shoved into us. Rather, our "I" is active. It evaluates the reactions of others and organizes them into a unified whole. Mead added that the "I" even monitors the "me," fine-tuning our ideas and attitudes to help us better meet what others expect of us.

In Sum: In studying the details, you don't want to miss the main point, which some find startling: *Both our self and our mind are social products.* Mead stressed that we cannot think without symbols. But where do these symbols come from? Only from society, which gives us our symbols by giving us language. If society did not provide the symbols, we would not be able to think and so would not possess a self-concept or that entity we call the mind. The self and mind, then, like language, are products of society.

Piaget and the Development of Reasoning

Shown here is Jean Piaget with one of the children he studied in his analysis of the development of human reasoning.

The development of the mind—specifically, how we learn to reason—was studied in detail by Jean Piaget (1896–1980). This Swiss psychologist noticed that when young children take intelligence tests, they often give similar wrong answers. This set him to thinking that the children might be using some consistent, but incorrect, reasoning. It might even indicate that children go through some natural process as they learn how to reason.

Stimulated by such an intriguing possibility, Piaget set up a laboratory where he could give children of different ages problems to solve (Piaget 1950, 1954; Flavel et al. 2002). After years of testing, Piaget concluded that children do go through a natural process as they develop their ability to reason. This process has four stages. (If you mentally substitute "reasoning skills" for the term *operational* as we review these stages, Piaget's findings will be easier to understand.)

1. **The sensorimotor stage** (from birth to about age 2) During this stage, our understanding is limited to direct contact—sucking, touching, listening, looking. We aren't able to "think." During the first part of this stage, we do not even know that our bodies are separate from the environment. Indeed, we have yet to discover that we have toes. Neither can we recognize cause and effect. That is, we do not know that our actions cause something to happen.

2. **The preoperational stage** (from about age 2 to age 7) During this stage, we *develop the ability to use symbols.* However, we do not yet understand common concepts such as size, speed, or causation. Although we are learning to count, we do not really understand what

numbers mean. Nor do we yet have the ability to take the role of the other. Piaget asked preoperational children to describe a clay model of a mountain range. They did just fine. But when he asked them to describe how the mountain range looked from where another child was sitting, they couldn't do it. They could only repeat what they saw from their view.

3. **The concrete operational stage** (from the age of about 7 to 12) Our reasoning abilities are more developed, but they remain *concrete*. We can now understand numbers, size, causation, and speed, and we are able to take the role of the other. We can even play team games. Unless we have concrete examples, however, we are unable to talk about concepts such as truth, honesty, or justice. We can explain why Jane's answer was a lie, but we cannot describe what truth itself is.

4. **The formal operational stage** (after the age of about 12) We now are capable of abstract thinking. We can talk about concepts, come to conclusions based on general principles, and use rules to solve abstract problems. During this stage, we are likely to become young philosophers (Kagan 1984). If we were shown a photo of a slave during our concrete operational stage, we might have said, "That's wrong!" Now at the formal operational stage we are likely to add, "If our county was founded on equality, how could anyone own slaves?"

Global Aspects of the Self and Reasoning

Cooley's conclusions about the looking-glass self appear to be true for everyone around the world. So do Mead's conclusions about role taking and the mind and self as social products, although researchers are finding that the self may develop earlier than Mead indicated. The stages of reasoning that Piaget identified probably also occur worldwide, although researchers have found that the stages are not as distinct as Piaget concluded and the ages at which individuals enter the stages differ from one person to another (Flavel et al. 2002). Even during the sensorimotor stage, for example, children show early signs of reasoning, which may indicate an innate ability that is wired into the brain. Although Piaget's theory is being refined, his contribution remains: *A basic structure underlies the way we develop reasoning, and children all over the world begin with the concrete and move to the abstract.* Interestingly, some people seem to get stuck in the concreteness of the third stage and never reach the fourth stage of abstract thinking (Kohlberg and Gilligan 1971; Suizzo 2000). College, for example, nurtures the fourth stage, and people with this experience apparently have more ability for abstract thought. Social experiences, then, can modify these stages.

Learning Personality, Morality, and Emotions

Our personality, morality, and emotions are vital aspects of who we are. Let's look at how we learn these essential aspects of our being.

Freud and the Development of Personality

Along with the development of the mind and the self comes the development of the personality. Sigmund Freud (1856–1939) developed a theory of the origin of personality that has had a major impact on Western thought. Freud, a physician in Vienna in the early 1900s, founded *psychoanalysis,* a technique for treating emotional problems through long-term exploration of the subconscious mind. Let's look at his theory.

Freud believed that personality consists of three elements. Each child is born with the first element, an **id,** Freud's term for inborn drives that cause us to seek self-gratification. The id of the newborn is evident in its cries of hunger or pain. The pleasure-seeking id operates throughout life. It demands the immediate fulfillment of basic needs: food, safety, attention, sex, and so on.

id Freud's term for our inborn basic drives

Sigmund Freud in 1932 in Hochroterd, Austria. Although Freud was one of the most influential theorists of the 20th century, most of his ideas have been discarded.

The id's drive for immediate gratification, however, runs into a roadblock: primarily the needs of other people, especially those of the parents. To adapt to these constraints, a second component of the personality emerges, which Freud called the ego. The **ego** is the balancing force between the id and the demands of society that suppress it. The ego also serves to balance the id and the **superego,** the third component of the personality, more commonly called the *conscience.*

The superego represents *culture within us,* the norms and values we have internalized from our social groups. As the *moral* component of the personality, the superego provokes feelings of guilt or shame when we break social rules, or pride and self-satisfaction when we follow them.

According to Freud, when the id gets out of hand, we follow our desires for pleasure and break society's norms. When the superego gets out of hand, we become overly rigid in following those norms and end up wearing a straitjacket of rules that inhibit our lives. The ego, the balancing force, tries to prevent either the superego or the id from dominating. In the emotionally healthy individual, the ego succeeds in balancing these conflicting demands of the id and the superego. In the maladjusted individual, the ego fails to control the conflict between the id and the superego. Either the id or the superego dominates this person, leading to internal confusion and problem behaviors.

Sociological Evaluation.　Sociologists appreciate Freud's emphasis on socialization—his assertion that the social group into which we are born transmits norms and values that restrain our biological drives. Sociologists, however, object to the view that inborn and subconscious motivations are the primary reasons for human behavior. *This denies the central principle of sociology:* that factors such as social class (income, education, and occupation) and people's roles in groups underlie their behavior (Epstein 1988; Bush and Simmons 1990).

Feminist sociologists have been especially critical of Freud. Although what I just summarized applies to both females and males, Freud assumed that what is "male" is "normal." He even referred to females as inferior, castrated males (Chodorow 1990; Gerhard 2000). It is obvious that sociologists need to continue to research how we develop personality.

Kohlberg, Gilligan, and the Development of Morality

If you have observed young children, you know that they want immediate gratification and show little or no concern for others. ("Mine!" a 2-year-old will shout, as she grabs a toy from another child.) Yet, at a later age this same child will become considerate of others and try to be fair in her play. How does this change happen?

Kohlberg's Theory.　Psychologist Lawrence Kohlberg (1975, 1984, 1986; Reed 2008) concluded that we go through a sequence of stages as we develop morality. Building on Piaget's work, he found that children start in the *amoral stage* I just described. For them, there is no right or wrong, just personal needs to be satisfied. From about ages 7 to 10, children are in what Kohlberg called a *preconventional stage.* They have learned rules, and they follow them to stay out of trouble. They view right and wrong as what pleases or displeases their parents, friends, and teachers. Their concern is to avoid punishment. At

ego Freud's term for a balancing force between the id and the demands of society

superego Freud's term for the conscience; the internalized norms and values of our social groups

moment just some of the factors that influence how you act: the expectations of friends and parents, of neighbors and teachers; classroom norms and college rules; city, state, and federal laws. For example, if in a moment of intense frustration, or out of a devilish desire to shock people, you wanted to tear off your clothes and run naked down the street, what would stop you?

The answer is your socialization—*society within you.* Your experiences in society have resulted in a self that thinks along certain lines and feels particular emotions. This helps to keep you in line. Thoughts such as "Would I get kicked out of school?" and "What would my friends (parents) think if they found out?" represent an awareness of the self in relationship to others. So does the desire to avoid feelings of shame and embarrassment. Your *social mirror,* then—the result of your being socialized into a self and emotions—sets up effective controls over your behavior. In fact, socialization into self and emotions is so effective that some people feel embarrassed just thinking about running naked in public!

In Sum: Socialization is essential for our development as human beings. From interaction with others, we learn how to think, reason, and feel. The net result is the shaping of our behavior—including our thinking and emotions—according to cultural standards. This is what sociologists mean when they refer to "*society within us.*"

Socialization into Gender

Learning the Gender Map

For a child, society is uncharted territory. A major signpost on society's map is **gender,** the attitudes and behaviors that are expected of us because we are a male or a female. In learning the gender map (called **gender socialization**), we are nudged into different lanes in life—into contrasting attitudes and behaviors. We take direction so well that, as adults, most of us act, think, and even feel according to this gender map, our culture's guidelines to what is appropriate for our sex.

The significance of gender is emphasized throughout this book, and we focus specifically on gender in Chapter 11. For now, though, let's briefly consider some of the "gender messages" that we get from our family and the mass media.

Gender Messages in the Family

Our parents are the first significant others who show us how to follow the gender map. Sometimes they do so consciously, perhaps by bringing into play pink and blue, colors that have no meaning in themselves but that are now associated with gender. Our parents' own gender orientations have become embedded so firmly that they do most of this teaching without being aware of what they are doing.

This is illustrated in a classic study by psychologists Susan Goldberg and Michael Lewis (1969), whose results have been confirmed by other researchers (Fagot et al. 1985; Connors 1996; Clearfield and Nelson 2006).

> Goldberg and Lewis asked mothers to bring their 6-month-old infants into their laboratory, supposedly to observe the infants' development. Covertly, however, they also observed the mothers. They found that the mothers kept their daughters closer to them. They also touched their daughters more and spoke to them more frequently than they did to their sons.
>
> By the time the children were 13 months old, the girls stayed closer to their mothers during play, and they returned to their mothers sooner and more often than the boys did. When Goldberg and Lewis set up a barrier to separate the children from their mothers, who were holding toys, the girls were more likely to cry and motion for help; the boys, to try to climb over the barrier.

Goldberg and Lewis concluded that mothers subconsciously reward daughters for being passive and dependent, and sons for being active and independent.

gender the behaviors and attitudes that a society considers proper for its males and females; masculinity or femininity

gender socialization the ways in which society sets children on different paths in life *because* they are male or female

The *gender roles* that we learn during childhood become part of our basic orientations to life. Although we refine these roles as we grow older, they remain built around the framework established during childhood.

Frank and Ernest

SOON WE'LL GIVE UP DOLLS AND HOPSCOTCH---BUT THEY'LL BE INTO FOOTBALL FOREVER.

www.cartoonistgroup.com

Our gender lessons continue throughout childhood. On the basis of our sex, we are given different kinds of toys. Boys are more likely to get guns and "action figures" that destroy enemies. Girls are more likely to get dolls and jewelry. Some parents try to choose "gender neutral" toys, but kids know what is popular, and they feel left out if they don't have what the other kids have. The significance of toys in gender socialization can be summarized this way: Almost all parents would be upset if someone gave their son Barbie dolls.

Parents also subtly encourage boys to participate in more rough-and-tumble play. They expect their sons to get dirtier and to be more defiant, their daughters to be daintier and more compliant (Gilman 1911/1971; Henslin 2007). In large part, they get what they expect. Such experiences in socialization lie at the heart of the sociological explanation of male–female differences. For a fascinating account of how socialization trumps biology, read the Cultural Diversity box on the next page.

Gender Messages from Peers

Sociologists stress how this sorting process that begins in the family is reinforced as the child is exposed to other aspects of society. Of those other influences, one of the most powerful is the **peer group,** individuals of roughly the same age who are linked by common interests. Examples of peer groups are friends, classmates, and "the kids in the neighborhood."

peer group a group of individuals of roughly the same age who are linked by common interests

The family is one of the primary ways that we learn gender. Shown here is a woman in South Africa. What gender messages do you think her daughter is learning?

Cultural Diversity around the World

Women Becoming Men: The Sworn Virgins

"I will become a man," said Pashe. "I will do it."

The decision was final. Taking a pair of scissors, she soon had her long, black curls lying at her feet. She took off her dress—never to wear one again in her life—and put on her father's baggy trousers. She armed herself with her father's rifle. She would need it.

Going before the village elders, she swore to never marry, to never have children, and to never have sex.

Pashe had become a sworn virgin—and a man.

There was no turning back. The penalty for violating the oath was death.

Pashke Ndocaj, shown here in Thethi, Albania, became a sworn virgin after the death of her father and brothers.

In Albania, where Pashe Keqi lives, and in parts of Bosnia and Serbia, it is the custom for some women to become men. They are neither transsexuals nor lesbians. Nor do they have a sex-change operation, something unknown in those parts.

The custom is a practical matter, a way to support the family. In these traditional societies, women must stay home and take care of the children and household. They can go hardly anywhere except to the market and mosque. Women depend on men for survival.

And when there is no man? That is the problem.

Pashe's father was killed in a blood feud. In these traditional groups, when the family patriarch (male head) dies and there are no male heirs, how are the women to survive? In the fifteenth century, people in this area hit upon a solution: One of the women takes an oath of lifelong virginity and takes over the man's role. She then becomes a social he, wears male clothing, carries a gun, owns property, and moves freely throughout the society.

She drinks in the tavern with the men. She sits with the men at weddings. She prays with the men at the mosque.

When a man wants to marry a girl of the family, she is the one who approves or disapproves of the suitor.

In short, the woman really becomes a man. Actually, a social man, sociologists would add. Her biology does not change, but her gender does. Pashe had become the man of the house, a status she occupied her entire life.

Taking this position at the age of 11—she is in her 70s now—also made Pashe responsible for avenging her father's murder. But when his killer was released from prison, her 15-year-old nephew (she is his uncle) rushed in and did the deed instead.

Sworn virgins walk like men, they talk like men, they hunt with the men, and they take up manly occupations. They become shepherds, security guards, truck drivers, and political leaders. Those around them know that they are women, but in all ways they treat them as men. When they talk to women, the women recoil in shyness.

The sworn virgins of Albania are a fascinating cultural contradiction: In the midst of a highly traditional group, one built around male superiority that severely limits women, we find both the belief and practice that a biological woman can do the work of a man and function in all of a man's social roles. The sole exception is marriage.

Under a communist dictator until 1985, with travel restricted by law and custom, mountainous northern Albania had been cut off from the rest of the world. Now there is a democratic government, and the region is connected to the rest of the world by better roads, telephones, and even television. As modern life trickles into these villages, few women want to become men. "Why should we?" they ask. "Now we have freedom. We can go to the city and work and support our families."

For Your Consideration

How do the sworn virgins of Albania help to explain what gender is? Apply functionalism: How was the custom and practice of sworn virgins functional for this society? Apply symbolic interactionism: How do symbols underlie and maintain women becoming men in this society? Apply conflict theory: How do power relations between men and women underlie this practice?

Based on Zumbrun 2007; Bilefsky 2008; Smith 2008.

As you grew up, you saw girls and boys teach one another what it means to be a female or a male. You might not have recognized what was happening, however, so let's eavesdrop on a conversation between two eighth-grade girls studied by sociologist Donna Eder (2007).

CINDY: The only thing that makes her look anything is all the makeup . . .
PENNY: She had a picture, and she's standing like this. (Poses with one hand on her hip and one by her head)
CINDY: Her face is probably this skinny, but it looks that big 'cause of all the makeup she has on it.
PENNY: She's ugly, ugly, ugly.

Do you see how these girls were giving gender lessons? They were reinforcing images of appearance and behavior that they thought were appropriate for females. Boys, too, reinforce cultural expectations of gender. Sociologist Melissa Milkie (1994), who studied junior high school boys, found that much of their talk centered on movies and TV programs. Of the many images they saw, the boys would single out those associated with sex and violence. They would amuse one another by repeating lines, acting out parts, and joking and laughing at what they had seen.

If you know boys in their early teens, you've probably seen a lot of behavior like this. You may have been amused, or even have shaken your head in disapproval. But did you peer beneath the surface? Milkie did. What is really going on? The boys, she concluded, were using media images to develop their identity as males. They had gotten the message: "Real" males are obsessed with sex and violence. Not to joke and laugh about murder and promiscuous sex would have marked a boy as a "weenie," a label to be avoided at all costs.

Gender Messages in the Mass Media

As you can see with the boys Milkie studied, a major guide to the gender map is the **mass media,** forms of communication that are directed to large audiences. Let's look further at how media images reinforce **gender roles,** the behaviors and attitudes considered appropriate for our sex.

Advertising.   The advertising assault of stereotypical images begins early. The average U.S. child watches about 25,000 commercials a year (Gantz et al. 2007). In these commercials, girls are more likely to be shown as cooperative and boys as aggressive (Larson 2001). Girls are also more likely to be portrayed as giggly and less capable at tasks (Browne 1998).

The gender messages continue in advertising directed at adults. I'm sure you have you noticed the many ads that portray men as dominant and rugged and women as sexy and submissive. *Your mind and internal images* are the target of this assault of stereotypical, culturally molded images—from cowboys who roam the wide-open spaces to scantily clad women, whose physical assets couldn't possibly be real. Although the purpose is to sell products—from booze and bras to cigarettes and cellphones—the ads also give lessons in gender. Through images both overt and exaggerated and subtle and below our awareness, they help teach what is expected of us as men and women in our culture.

Television.   Television reinforces stereotypes of the sexes. On prime-time television, male characters outnumber female characters. Male characters are also more likely to be portrayed in higher-status positions (Glascock 2001). Sports news also maintains traditional stereotypes. Sociologists who studied the content of televised sports news in Los Angeles found that female athletes receive less coverage and are sometimes trivialized (Messner et al. 2003). Male newscasters often focus on humorous events in women's sports or turn the female athlete into a sexual object. Newscasters even manage to emphasize breasts and bras and to engage in locker-room humor.

Stereotype-breaking characters, in contrast, are a sign of changing times. In comedies, women are more verbally aggressive than men (Glascock 2001). The powers of the teenager *Buffy, The Vampire Slayer,* were remarkable. On *Alias,* Sydney Bristow exhibited extraordinary strength. In cartoons, Kim Possible divides her time between cheerleading practice and saving the world from evil, while, also with tongue in cheek, the Powerpuff

mass media forms of communication, such as radio, newspapers, television, and blogs that are directed to mass audiences

gender role the behaviors and attitudes expected of people because they are female or male

Girls are touted as "the most elite kindergarten crime-fighting force ever assembled." This new gender portrayal continues in a variety of programs, such as *Totally Spies*.

The gender messages on these programs are mixed. Girls are powerful, but they have to be skinny and gorgeous and wear the latest fashions. Such messages present a dilemma for girls, for this model continuously thrust before them is almost impossible to replicate in real life.

Video Games.   The movement, color, virtual dangers, unexpected dilemmas, and ability to control the action make video games highly appealing. High school and college students, especially men, find them a seductive way of escaping from the demands of life. The first members of the "Nintendo Generation," now in their thirties, are still playing video games—with babies on their laps.

Sociologists have begun to study how video games portray the sexes, but we still know little about their influence on the players' ideas of gender (Dietz 2000; Berger 2002). Women, often portrayed with exaggerated breasts and buttocks, are now more likely to be main characters than they were just a few years ago (Jansz and Martis 2007). Because these games are on the cutting edge of society, they sometimes also reflect cutting-edge changes in sex roles, the topic of the Mass Media in Social Life box on the next page.

Anime.   *Anime* is a Japanese cartoon form. Because anime crosses boundaries of video games, television, movies, and books (comic), we shall consider it as a separate category. As shown below, one of the most recognizable features of anime is the big-eyed little girls and the fighting little boys. Japanese parents are concerned about anime's antisocial heroes and its depiction of violence, but to keep peace they reluctantly buy anime for their children (Khattak 2007). In the United States, violence is often part of the mass media aimed at children—so with its cute characters, anime is unlikely to bother parents. Anime's depiction of active, dominant little boys and submissive little girls leads to the question, of course, of what gender lessons it is giving children.

In Sum: "Male" and "female" are such powerful symbols that learning them forces us to interpret the world in terms of gender. As children learn their society's symbols of gender, they learn that different behaviors and attitudes are expected of boys and girls. First transmitted by the family, these gender messages are reinforced by other social institutions. As they become integrated into our views of the world, gender messages form a picture of "how" males and females "are." Because gender serves as a primary basis for **social inequality**—giving privileges and obligations to one group of people while denying them to another—gender images are especially important in our socialization.

social inequality a social condition in which privileges and obligations are given to some but denied to others

Anime is increasing in popularity—cartoons and comics aimed at children and pornography targeted to adults. Its gender messages, especially those directed to children, are yet to be explored.

MASS MEDIA In SOCIAL LIFE

Lara Croft, Tomb Raider: Changing Images of Women in the Mass Media

With digital advances, video games have crossed the line from what are usually thought of as games to something that more closely resembles interactive movies. Costing an average of $10 million to produce and another $10 million to market, some video games have intricate subplots and use celebrity voices for the characters (Nussenbaum 2004). Some introduce new songs by major rock groups (Levine 2008). Sociologically, what is significant is the *content* of video games. They expose gamers not only to action but also to ideas and images. Just as in other forms of the mass media, the gender images of video games communicate powerful messages.

Amidst the traditional portrayals of women as passive and subordinate, a new image has broken through. As exaggerated as it is, this new image reflects a fundamental change in gender relations. Lara Croft, an adventure-seeking archeologist and star of *Tomb Raider* and its many sequels, is the essence of the new gender image. Lara is smart, strong, and able to utterly vanquish foes. With both guns blazing, she is the cowboy of the twenty-first century, the term *cowboy* being purposefully chosen, as Lara breaks stereotypical gender roles and dominates what previously was the domain of men. She was the first female protagonist in a field of muscle-rippling, gun-toting macho caricatures (Taylor 1999).

Yet the old remains powerfully encapsulated in the new. As the photos on this page make evident, Lara is a fantasy girl for young men of the digital generation. No matter her foe, no matter her predicament, Lara oozes sex. Her form-fitting outfits, which flatter her voluptuous figure, reflect the mental images of the men who fashioned this digital character.

The mass media not only reflect gender stereotypes but they also play a role in changing them. Sometimes they do both simultaneously. The images of Lara Croft not only reflect women's changing role in society, but also, by exaggerating the change, they mold new stereotypes.

Lara has caught young men's fancy to such an extent that they have bombarded corporate headquarters with questions about her personal life. Lara is the star of two movies and a comic book. There is also a Lara Croft action figure.

For Your Consideration

A sociologist who reviewed this text said, "It seems that for women to be defined as equal, we have to become symbolic males—warriors with breasts." Why is gender change mostly one-way—females adopting traditional male characteristics? To see why men get to keep their gender roles, these two questions should help: Who is moving into the traditional territory of the other? Do people prefer to imitate power or weakness?

Finally, consider just how far stereotypes have actually been left behind. One reward for beating time trials is to be able to see Lara wearing a bikini.

Agents of Socialization

agents of socialization individuals or groups that affect our self-concept, attitudes, behaviors, or other orientations toward life

Individuals and groups that influence our orientations to life—our self-concept, emotions, attitudes, and behavior—are called **agents of socialization.** We have already considered how three of these agents—the family, our peers, and the mass media—influence our ideas of gender. Now we'll look more closely at how agents of socialization prepare us in other ways to take our place in society. We shall first consider the family, then the neighborhood, religion, day care, school and peers, and the workplace.

This photo captures an extreme form of family socialization. The father seems to be more emotionally involved in the goal—and in more pain—than his daughter, as he pushes her toward the finish line in the Teen Tours of America Kid's Triathlon.

The Family

The first group to have a major impact on us is our family. Our experiences in the family are so intense that their influence is lifelong. These experiences establish our initial motivations, values, and beliefs. In the family, we receive our basic sense of self, ideas about who we are and what we deserve out of life. It is here that we begin to think of ourselves as strong or weak, smart or dumb, good-looking or ugly—or somewhere in between. And as already noted, the lifelong process of defining ourselves as female or male also begins in the family.

The Family and Social Class.   Social class makes a huge difference in how parents socialize their children. Sociologist Melvin Kohn (1959, 1963, 1976, 1977; Kohn et al. 1986) found that working-class parents are mainly concerned that their children stay out of trouble. For discipline, they tend to use physical punishment. Middle-class parents, in contrast, focus more on developing their children's curiosity, self-expression, and self-control. They are more likely to reason with their children than to use physical punishment.

But why such differences? As a sociologist, Kohn knew that the answer was life experiences of some sort. He found that answer in the world of work. Blue-collar workers are usually told exactly what to do. Since they expect their children's lives to be like theirs, they stress obedience. Middle-class parents, in contrast, have work that requires more initiative, and they socialize their children into the qualities they find valuable.

Kohn wanted to know why some working-class parents act more like middle-class parents, and vice versa. As he probed further, he found the key—the parents' type of job. Some middle-class workers, such as office workers, are supervised closely. It turned out that they follow the working-class pattern and emphasize conformity. And some blue-collar workers, such as those who do home repairs, have a good deal of freedom. These workers follow the middle-class model in rearing their children (Pearlin and Kohn 1966; Kohn and Schooler 1969).

Social class also makes a difference in the ideas that parents have of how children develop, ideas that have fascinating consequences for children's play (Lareau 2002).

Working-class parents think of children as similar to wild flowers—they develop naturally. Since the child's development will take care of itself, they see parenting primarily as providing food, shelter, and comfort. They set limits on their children's play ("Don't go near the railroad tracks") and let them play as they wish. Middle-class parents, in contrast, think of children as more like tender house plants—to develop correctly, they need a lot of guidance. With this orientation, they try to structure their children's play to help them develop knowledge and social skills. They may want them to play baseball, for example, not for the enjoyment of the sport, but to help them learn how to be team players.

The Neighborhood

As all parents know, some neighborhoods are better than others for their children. Parents try to move to those neighborhoods—if they can afford them. Their commonsense evaluations are borne out by sociological research. Children from poor neighborhoods are more likely to get in trouble with the law, to become pregnant, to drop out of school, and even to have worse mental health in later life (Brooks-Gunn et al. 1997; Sampson et al. 2001; Wheaton and Clarke 2003; Yonas et al. 2006).

Sociologists have also found that the residents of more affluent neighborhoods keep a closer eye on the children than do the residents of poor neighborhoods (Sampson et al. 1999). The basic reason is that the more affluent neighborhoods have fewer families in transition, so the adults are more likely to know the local children and their parents. This better equips them to help keep the children safe and out of trouble.

Religion

How important is religion in your life? You could be among the two-thirds of Americans who belong to a local congregation, but what if you are among the other third (Gallup Poll 2007b)? Why would religion be significant for you? To see the influence of religion, we can't look only at people who are religious. Even in the extreme—people who wouldn't be caught dead near a church, synagogue, or mosque—religion plays a powerful role. Perhaps this is the most significant aspect of religion: Religious ideas so pervade U.S. society that they provide the foundation of morality for both the religious and the nonreligious.

For many Americans, the influence of religion is more direct. This is especially true for the two of every five Americans who report that during a typical week they attend a religious service (Gallup Poll 2007). Through their participation in congregational life, they learn doctrine, values, and morality, but the effects on their lives are not limited to these obvious factors. For example, people who participate in religious services learn not only beliefs about the hereafter but also ideas about what kinds of clothing, speech, and manners are appropriate for formal occasions. Life in congregations also provides a sense of identity for its participants, giving them a feeling of belonging. It also helps to integrate immigrants into their new society, offers an avenue of social mobility for the poor, provides social contacts for jobs, and in the case of African American churches, has been a powerful influence in social change.

Day Care

It is rare for social science research to make national news, but occasionally it does. This is what happened when researchers published their findings on 1,200 kindergarten children they had studied since they were a month old. They observed the children multiple times both at home and at day care. They also videotaped and made detailed notes on the children's interaction with their mothers (National Institute of Child Health and Human Development 1999; Guensburg 2001). What caught the media's attention? Children who spend more time in day care have weaker bonds with their mothers and are less affectionate to them. They are also less cooperative with others and more likely to fight and to be "mean." By the time they get to kindergarten, they are more likely to talk back to teachers and to disrupt the classroom. This holds true regardless of the quality of the day care, the family's social class, or whether the child is a girl or a boy (Belsky 2006). On the positive side, the children also scored higher on language tests.

Are we producing a generation of "smart but mean" children? This is not an unreasonable question, since the study was designed well and an even larger study of children in England has come up with similar findings (Belsky 2006). Some point out that the differences between children who spend a lot of time in day care and those who spend less time are slight. Others stress that with 5 million children in day care (*Statistical Abstract* 2009:Table 559), slight differences can be significant for society. The researchers are following these children as they continue in school. The most recent report on the children, when they were in the 6th grade, indicates that these patterns are continuing (Belsky et al. 2007).

The School

Part of the **manifest function,** or *intended* purpose, of formal education is to teach knowledge and skills, such as reading, writing, and arithmetic. The teaching of such skills is certainly part of socialization, but so are the schools' **latent functions,** their *unintended* consequences that help the social system. Let's look at this less visible aspect of education.

At home, children learn attitudes and values that match their family's situation in life. At school, they learn a broader perspective that helps prepare them to take a role in the world beyond the family. At home, a child may have been the almost exclusive focus of doting parents, but in school, the child learns *universality*—that the same rules apply to everyone, regardless of who their parents are or how special they may be at home. The Cultural Diversity box on the next page explores how these new values and ways of looking at the world sometimes even replace those the child learns at home.

Schools are one of the primary *agents of socialization*. One of their chief functions is to sort young people into the adult roles thought appropriate for them, and to teach them the attitudes and skills that match these roles. What sorts of attitudes, motivations, goals, and adult roles do you think this child is learning?

Sociologists have also identified a *hidden curriculum* in our schools. This term refers to values that, although not explicitly taught, are part of a school's "cultural message." For example, the stories and examples that are used to teach math and English may bring with them lessons in patriotism, democracy, justice, and honesty. There is also a *corridor curriculum,* what students teach one another outside the classroom. Unfortunately, the corridor curriculum seems to emphasize racism, sexism, illicit ways to make money, and coolness (Hemmings 1999). You can determine for yourself which of these is functional and which is dysfunctional.

Conflict theorists point out that social class separates children into different educational worlds. Children born to wealthy parents go to private schools, where they learn skills and values that match their higher position. Children born to middle- and lower-class parents go to public schools, which further refine the separate worlds of social class. Middle-class children learn that good jobs, even the professions, beckon, while children from blue-collar families learn that not many of "their kind" will become professionals or leaders. This is one of the many reasons that children from blue-collar families are less likely to take college prep courses or to go to college. In short, schools around the world reflect and reinforce their nation's social class, economic, and political systems. We will return to this topic in Chapter 17.

manifest functions the intended beneficial consequences of people's actions

latent functions unintended beneficial consequences of people's actions

Peer Groups

As a child's experiences with agents of socialization broaden, the influence of the family decreases. Entry into school marks only one of many steps in this transfer of allegiance.

Cultural Diversity in the United States

Immigrants and Their Children: Caught Between Two Worlds

It is a struggle to adapt to a new culture, for its behaviors and ways of thinking may be at odds with the ones already learned. This can lead to inner turmoil. One way to handle the conflict is to cut ties with your first culture. Doing so, however, can create a sense of loss, one that is perhaps recognized only later in life.

Richard Rodriguez, a literature professor and essayist, was born to working-class Mexican immigrants. Wanting their son to be successful in their adopted land, his parents named him Richard instead of Ricardo. While his English–Spanish hybrid name indicates the parents' aspirations for their son, it was also an omen of the conflict that Richard would experience.

Like other children of Mexican immigrants, Richard first spoke Spanish—a rich mother tongue that introduced him to the world. Until the age of 5, when he began school, Richard knew only fifty words in English. He describes what happened when he began school:

> The change came gradually but early. When I was beginning grade school, I noted to myself the fact that the classroom environment was so different in its styles and assumptions from my own family environment that survival would essentially entail a choice between both worlds. When I became a student, I was literally "remade"; neither I nor my teachers considered anything I had known before as relevant. I had to forget most of what my culture had provided, because to remember it was a disadvantage. The past and its cultural values became detachable, like a piece of clothing grown heavy on a warm day and finally put away.

As happened to millions of immigrants before him, whose parents spoke German, Polish, Italian, and so on, learning English eroded family and class ties and ate away at his ethnic roots. For Rodriguez, language and education were not simply devices that eased the transition to the dominant culture. They also slashed at the roots that had given him life.

To face conflicting cultures is to confront a fork in the road. Some turn one way and withdraw from the new culture—a clue that helps to explain why so many Latinos drop out of U.S. schools. Others go in the opposite direction. Cutting ties with their family and cultural roots, they wholeheartedly adopt the new culture.

Rodriguez took the second road. He excelled in his new language—so much, in fact, that he graduated from Stanford University and then became a graduate student in English at the University of California at Berkeley. He was even awarded a Fulbright fellowship to study English Renaissance literature at the University of London.

But the past shadowed Rodriguez. Prospective employers were impressed with his knowledge of Renaissance literature. At job interviews, however, they would skip over the Renaissance training and ask him if he would teach the Mexican novel and be an adviser to Latino students. Rodriguez was also haunted by the image of his grandmother, the warmth of the culture he had left behind, and the language and thought to which he had become a stranger.

Richard Rodriguez represents millions of immigrants—not just those of Latino origin but those from other cultures, too—who want to be a part of life in the United States without betraying their past. They fear that to integrate into U.S. culture is to lose their roots. They are caught between two cultures, each beckoning, each offering rich rewards.

For Your Consideration

I saw this conflict firsthand with my father, who did not learn English until after the seventh grade (his last in school). German was left behind, but broken English and awkward expressions remained for a lifetime. Then, too, there were the lingering emotional connections to old ways, as well as the suspicions, haughtiness, and slights of more assimilated Americans. He longed for security by grasping the past, but at the same time, he wanted to succeed in the everyday reality of the new culture. Have you seen similar conflicts?

Sources: Based on Richard Rodriguez 1975, 1982, 1990, 1991, 1995.

Gradeschool boys and girls often separate themselves by gender, as in this playground in Schenectady, New York. The socialization that occurs during self-segregation by gender is a topic of study by sociologists.

One of the most significant aspects of education is that it exposes children to peer groups that help them resist the efforts of parents and schools to socialize them.

When sociologists Patricia and Peter Adler (1998) observed children at two elementary schools in Colorado, they saw how children separate themselves by sex and develop separate gender worlds. The norms that made boys popular were athletic ability, coolness, and toughness. For girls, popularity was based on family background, physical appearance (clothing and use of makeup), and the ability to attract popular boys. In this children's subculture, academic achievement pulled in opposite directions: For boys, high grades lowered their popularity, but for girls, good grades increased their standing among peers.

You know from your own experience how compelling peer groups are. It is almost impossible to go against a peer group, whose cardinal rule seems to be "conformity or rejection." Anyone who doesn't do what the others want becomes an "outsider," a "nonmember," an "outcast." For preteens and teens just learning their way around in the world, it is not surprising that the peer group rules.

As a result, the standards of our peer groups tend to dominate our lives. If your peers, for example, listen to rap, Nortec, death metal, rock and roll, country, or gospel, it is almost inevitable that you also prefer that kind of music. In high school, if your friends take math courses, you probably do, too (Crosnoe et al. 2008). It is the same for clothing styles and dating standards. Peer influences also extend to behaviors that violate social norms. If your peers are college-bound and upwardly striving, that is most likely what you will be; but if they use drugs, cheat, and steal, you are likely to do so, too.

The Workplace

Another agent of socialization that comes into play somewhat later in life is the workplace. Those initial jobs that we take in high school and college are much more than just a way to earn a few dollars. From the people we rub shoulders with at work, we learn not only a set of skills but also perspectives on the world.

Most of us eventually become committed to some particular line of work, often after trying out many jobs. This may involve **anticipatory socialization,** learning to play a role before entering it. Anticipatory socialization is a sort of mental rehearsal for some future activity. We may talk to people who work in a particular career, read novels about that type of work, or take a summer internship in that field. Such activities allow us to

anticipatory socialization the process of learning in advance an anticipated future role or status

gradually identify with the role, to become aware of what would be expected of us. Sometimes this helps people avoid committing themselves to an unrewarding career, as with some of my students who tried student teaching, found that they couldn't stand it, and then moved on to other fields more to their liking.

An intriguing aspect of work as a socializing agent is that the more you participate in a line of work, the more the work becomes a part of your self-concept. Eventually you come to think of yourself so much in terms of the job that if someone asks you to describe yourself, you are likely to include the job in your self-description. You might say, "I'm a teacher," "I'm a nurse," or "I'm a sociologist."

Resocialization

What does a woman who has just become a nun have in common with a man who has just divorced? The answer is that they both are undergoing **resocialization;** that is, they are learning new norms, values, attitudes, and behaviors to match their new situation in life. In its most common form, resocialization occurs each time we learn something contrary to our previous experiences. A new boss who insists on a different way of doing things is resocializing you. Most resocialization is mild—only a slight modification of things we have already learned.

Resocialization can also be intense. People who join Alcoholics Anonymous (AA), for example, are surrounded by reformed drinkers who affirm the destructive effects of excessive drinking. Some students experience an intense period of resocialization when they leave high school and start college—especially during those initially scary days before they find companions, start to fit in, and feel comfortable. The experiences of people who join a cult or begin psychotherapy are even more profound, for they learn views that conflict with their earlier socialization. If these ideas "take," not only does the individual's behavior change but he or she also learns a fundamentally different way of looking at life.

Total Institutions

Relatively few of us experience the powerful agent of socialization that sociologist Erving Goffman (1961) called the **total institution.** He coined this term to refer to a place in which people are cut off from the rest of society and where they come under almost total control of the officials who are in charge. Boot camp, prisons, concentration camps, convents, some religious cults, and some military schools, such as West Point, are total institutions.

A person entering a total institution is greeted with a **degradation ceremony** (Garfinkel 1956), an attempt to remake the self by stripping away the individual's current identity and stamping a new one in its place. This unwelcome greeting may involve fingerprinting, photographing, or shaving the head. Newcomers may be ordered to strip, undergo an examination (often in a humiliating, semipublic setting), and then put on a uniform that designates their new status. Officials also take away the individual's *personal identity kit,* items such as jewelry, hairstyles, clothing, and other body decorations used to express individuality.

Total institutions are isolated from the public. The bars, walls, gates, and guards not only keep the inmates in but also keep outsiders out. Staff members supervise the day-to-day lives of the residents. Eating, sleeping, showering, recreation—all are standardized. Inmates learn that their previous statuses—student, worker, spouse, parent—mean nothing. The only thing that counts is their current status.

No one leaves a total institution unscathed, for the experience brands an indelible mark on the individual's self and colors the way he or she sees the world. Boot camp, as described in the Down-to-Earth Sociology box on the next page, is brutal but swift. Prison, in contrast, is brutal and prolonged. Neither recruit nor prisoner, however, has difficulty in knowing that the institution has had profound effects on attitudes and orientations to life.

resocialization the process of learning new norms, values, attitudes, and behaviors

total institution a place that is almost totally controlled by those who run it, in which people are cut off from the rest of society and the society is mostly cut off from them

degradation ceremony a term coined by Harold Garfinkel to refer to a ritual whose goal is to strip away someone's position (social status); in doing so, a new social and self-identity is stamped on the individual

Down-to-Earth Sociology
Boot Camp as a Total Institution

A recruit with drill sergeants

The bus arrives at Parris Island, South Carolina, at 3 A.M. The early hour is no accident. The recruits are groggy, confused. Up to a few hours ago, the young men were ordinary civilians. Now, as a sergeant sneeringly calls them "maggots," their heads are buzzed (25 seconds per recruit), and they are quickly thrust into the harsh world of Marine boot camp.

Buzzing the boys' hair is just the first step in stripping away their identity so that the Marines can stamp a new one in its place. The uniform serves the same purpose. There is a ban on using the first person "I." Even a simple request must be made in precise Marine style or it will not be acknowledged. ("Sir, Recruit Jones requests permission to make a head call, Sir.")

Every intense moment of the next eleven weeks reminds the recruits, men and women, that they are joining a subculture of self-discipline. Here pleasure is suspect and sacrifice is good. As they learn the Marine way of talking, walking, and thinking, they are denied the diversions they once took for granted: television, cigarettes, cars, candy, soft drinks, video games, music, alcohol, drugs, and sex.

Lessons are taught with fierce intensity. When Sgt. Carey checks brass belt buckles, Recruit Robert Shelton nervously blurts, "I don't have one." Sgt. Carey's face grows red as his neck cords bulge. "I?" he says, his face just inches from the recruit. With spittle flying from his mouth, he screams, " 'I' is gone!"

"Nobody's an individual" is the lesson that is driven home again and again. "You are a team, a Marine. Not a civilian. Not black or white, not Hispanic or Indian or some hyphenated American—but a Marine. You will live like a Marine, fight like a Marine, and, if necessary, die like a Marine."

Each day begins before dawn with close-order formations. The rest of the day is filled with training in hand-to-hand combat, marching, running, calisthenics, Marine history, and—always—following orders.

"An M-16 can blow someone's head off at 500 meters," Sgt. Norman says. "That's beautiful, isn't it?"

"Yes, sir!" shout the platoon's fifty-nine voices.

"Pick your nose!" Simultaneously fifty-nine index fingers shoot into nostrils.

The pressure to conform is intense. Those who are sent packing for insubordination or suicidal tendencies are mocked in cadence during drills. ("Hope you like the sights you see/Parris Island casualty.") As lights go out at 9 P.M., the exhausted recruits perform the day's last task: The entire platoon, in unison, chants the virtues of the Marines.

Recruits are constantly scrutinized. Subpar performance is not accepted, whether it be a dirty rifle or a loose thread on a uniform. The underperformer is shouted at, derided, humiliated. The group suffers for the individual. If one recruit is slow, the entire platoon is punished.

The system works.

One of the new Marines (until graduation, they are recruits, not Marines) says, "I feel like I've joined a new society or religion."

He has.

For Your Consideration
Of what significance is the recruits' degradation ceremony? Why are recruits not allowed video games, cigarettes, or calls home? Why are the Marines so unfair as to punish an entire platoon for the failure of an individual? Use concepts in this chapter to explain why the system works.

Sources: Based on Garfinkel 1956; Goffman 1961; Ricks 1995; Dyer 2007.

Socialization Through the Life Course

You are at a particular stage in your life now, and college is a good part of it. You know that you have more stages ahead of you as you go through life. These stages, from birth to death, are called the **life course** (Elder 1975; 1999). The sociological significance of the life course is twofold. First, as you pass through a stage, it affects your behavior and orientations. You simply don't think about life in the same way when you are 30, are

life course the stages of our life as we go from birth to death

In contemporary Western societies such as the United States, children are viewed as innocent and in need of protection from adult responsibilities such as work and self-support. Ideas of childhood vary historically and cross-culturally. From paintings, such as this 1559 Italian painting by Sofonisba Anguissola (1532–1625), "The Artist's Family," some historians conclude that Europeans once viewed children as miniature adults who assumed adult roles early in life.

married, and have a baby and a mortgage, as you do when you are 18 or 20, single, and in college. (Actually, you don't even see life the same way as a freshman and as a senior.) Second, your life course differs by social location. Your social class, race–ethnicity, and gender, for example, map out distinctive worlds of experience. This means that the typical life course differs for males and females, the rich and the poor, and so on. To emphasize this major sociological point, in the sketch that follows I will stress the *historical* setting of people's lives. Because of your particular social location, your own life course may differ from this sketch, which is a composite of stages that others have suggested (Levinson 1978; Carr et al. 1995; Quadagno 2007).

Childhood (from birth to about age 12)

Consider how different your childhood would have been if you had grown up in another historical era. Historian Philippe Ariès (1965) noticed that in European paintings from about A.D. 1000 to 1800 children were always dressed in adult clothing. If they were not depicted stiffly posed, as in a family portrait, they were shown doing adult activities.

From this, Ariès drew a conclusion that sparked a debate among historians: He said that during this era in Europe, childhood was not regarded as a special time of life. He said that adults viewed children as miniature adults and put them to work at an early age. At the age of 7, for example, a boy might leave home for good to learn to be a jeweler or a stonecutter. A girl, in contrast, stayed home until she married, but by the age of 7 she assumed her share of the household tasks. Historians do not deny that these were the customs of that time, but some say that Ariès' conclusion is ridiculous. They say that other evidence of that period indicates that childhood was viewed as a special time of life (Orme 2002).

Having children work like adults did not disappear with the Middle Ages. It is still common in the Least Industrialized Nations today, where children work in many occupations—from blacksmiths to waiters. They are most visible as street peddlers, hawking everything from shoelaces to chewing gum and candy. The photo on the upper left of page 251 not only illustrates different activities, but also reflects a view of children remarkably different from the one common in the Most Industrialized Nations.

Child rearing, too, was remarkably different. Three hundred years ago, parents and teachers considered it their moral duty to *terrorize* children to keep them in line. They would lock children in dark closets, frighten them with bedtime stories of death and hellfire, and force them to witness gruesome events. Consider this:

> A common moral lesson involved taking children to visit the gibbet [an upraised post on which executed bodies were left hanging], where they were forced to inspect the rotting corpses as an example of what happens to bad children when they grow up. Whole classes were taken out of school to witness hangings, and parents would often whip their children afterwards to make them remember what they had seen. (DeMause 1975)

Industrialization transformed the way we perceive children. When children had the leisure to go to school and postponed taking on adult roles, parents and officials came to think of them as tender and innocent, as needing more care, comfort, and protection. Such attitudes of dependency grew, and today we view children as needing gentle guidance if they are to develop emotionally, intellectually, morally, even physically. We take our

transitional adulthood
a term that refers to a period following high school when young adults have not yet taken on the responsibilities ordinarily associated with adulthood; also called *adultolescence*

view for granted—after all, it is only "common sense." Yet, as you can see, our view is not "natural." It is, instead, rooted in geography, history, and economic development.

In Sum: Childhood is more than biology. Everyone's childhood occurs at some point in history and is embedded in particular social locations, especially social class and gender. *These social factors are as vital as our biology, for they determine what our childhood will be like.* Although a child's *biological* characteristics (such as being small and dependent) are universal, the child's *social* experiences (the kind of life the child lives) are not. Because of this, sociologists say that childhood varies from culture to culture.

Adolescence (ages 13–17)

It might seem strange to you, but adolescence is a *social invention,* not a "natural" age division. In earlier centuries, people simply moved from childhood to young adulthood, with no stopover in between. The Industrial Revolution allowed adolescence to be invented. It brought such an abundance of material surpluses that for the first time in history people in their teens were not needed in the labor force. At the same time, education became more important for achieving success. As these two forces in industrialized societies converged, they created a gap between childhood and adulthood. The term *adolescence* was coined to indicate this new stage in life (Hall 1904), one that has become renowned for inner turmoil.

To mark the passage of children into adulthood, tribal societies hold *initiation rites.* This grounds their self-identity. They know how they fit in the society. In the industrialized world, however, adolescents must "find" themselves, grappling with the dilemma of "I am neither a child nor an adult. Who am I?" As they attempt to carve out an identity that is distinct from both the "younger" world being left behind and the "older" world that is still out of reach, adolescents develop their own subcultures, with distinctive clothing, hairstyles, language, gestures, and music. We usually fail to realize that contemporary society, not biology, created this period of inner turmoil that we call *adolescence.*

Transitional Adulthood (ages 18–29)

If society invented adolescence, can it also invent other periods of life? As Figure 3.2 illustrates, this is actually happening now. Postindustrial societies are adding another period of extended youth to the life course, which sociologists call **transitional adulthood** (also known as *adultolescence*). After high school, millions of young adults postpone adult responsibilities by going to college. They are mostly freed from the control of their parents, yet they don't have to support themselves. After college, many live at home, so they can live cheaply while they establish themselves in a career—and, of course, continue to "find themselves." During this time, people are "neither psychological adolescents nor sociological adults" (Keniston 1971). At some point during this period of extended youth, young adults ease into adult responsibilities. They take a full-time job, become serious about a career, engage in courtship rituals, get married—and go into debt.

In many societies, manhood is not bestowed upon males simply because they reach a certain age. Manhood, rather, signifies a standing in the community that must be achieved. Shown here is an initiation ceremony in Indonesia, where boys, to lay claim to the status of manhood, must jump over this barrier.

FIGURE 3.2 Transitional Adulthood: A New Stage in the Life Course

Who has completed the transition?

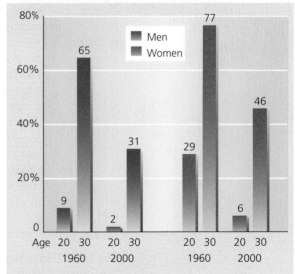

The data show the percentage who have completed the transition to adulthood, as measured by leaving home, finishing school, getting married, having a child, and being financially independent.

Source: Furstenberg, et al. 2004.

The Middle Years (ages 30–65)

The Early Middle Years (ages 30–49). During their early middle years, most people are more sure of themselves and of their goals in life. As with any point in the life course, however, the self can receive severe jolts. Common in this period are divorce and losing jobs. It may take years for the self to stabilize after such ruptures.

The early middle years pose a special challenge for many U.S. women, who have been given the message, especially by the media, that they can "have it all." They can be superworkers, superwives, and supermoms—all rolled into one. Reality, however, hits them in the face: too little time, too many demands, even too little sleep. Something has to give, and attempts to resolve this dilemma are anything but easy.

The Later Middle Years (ages 50–65). During the later middle years, health issues and mortality begin to loom large as people feel their bodies change, especially if they watch their parents become frail, fall ill, and die. The consequence is a fundamental reorientation in thinking—*from time since birth to time left to live* (Neugarten 1976). With this changed orientation, people attempt to evaluate the past and come to terms with what lies ahead. They compare what they have accomplished with what they had hoped to achieve. Many people also find themselves caring not only for their own children but also for their aging parents. Because of this double burden, which is often crushing, people in the later middle years sometimes are called the "sandwich generation."

Life during this stage isn't stressful for everyone. Many find late middle age to be the most comfortable period of their lives. They enjoy job security and a standard of living higher than ever before; they have a bigger house (one that may even be paid for), drive newer cars, and take longer and more exotic vacations. The children are grown, the self is firmly planted, and fewer upheavals are likely to occur.

As they anticipate the next stage of life, however, most people do not like what they see.

The Older Years (about age 65 on)

The Transitional Older Years. In agricultural societies, when most people died early, old age was thought to begin at around age 40. As industrialization brought improved nutrition, medicine, and public health, allowing more people to live longer, the beginning of "old age" gradually stretched out. People who are in good health today are coming to experience their 60s not as old age, but as an extension of their middle years. This change is so recent that a *new stage of life* seems to be evolving, the period between retirement (averaging about 63) and old age—which people are increasingly coming to see as beginning around age 75 ("Schwab Study . . . " 2008). We can call this stage the *transitional older years.*

Researchers are focusing more on this transitional stage of life. They have found that social isolation harms both the body and brain, that people who are more integrated into social networks stay mentally sharper (Ertel et al. 2008). With improved heath, two-thirds of the men and two-fifths of the women between their late 60s and age 75 continue to be sexually active (Lindau et al. 2007). Not only are people in this stage of life having more sex, but they also are enjoying it more (Beckman et al. 2008).

Because we have a self and can reason abstractly, we can contemplate death. In our early years, we regard death as a vague notion, a remote possibility. As people see their parents and friends die and observe their own bodies no longer functioning as before, however, the thought of death becomes less abstract. Increasingly during this stage in the life course, people feel that "time is closing in" on them.

The Later Older Years. As with the preceding periods of life, except the first one, there is no precise beginning point to this last stage. For some, the 75th birthday may mark entry into this period of life. For others, that marker may be the 80th or even the 85th birthday. For most, this stage is marked by growing frailty and illness; for all who reach this stage, it is ended by death. For some, the physical decline is slow, and a rare few manage to see their 100th birthday mentally alert and in good physical health.

The Sociological Significance of the Life Course

The sociological significance of the life course is that it does not merely represent biology, things that naturally occur to all of us as we add years to our lives. Rather, *social* factors influence our life course. As you just saw, *when* you live makes a huge difference in the course that your life takes. And with today's rapid social change, the difference in historical time does not have to be vast. Being born just ten years earlier or later may mean that you experience war or peace, an expanding economy or a depression—factors that vitally affect what happens to you not just during childhood but throughout your life.

Your *social location,* such as social class, gender, and race–ethnicity, is also highly significant. Your experience of society's events will be similar to that of people who share your social location, but different from that of people who do not. If you are poor, for example, you likely will feel older sooner than most wealthy people for whom life is less demanding. Individual factors—such as your health or marrying early or entering college late—may throw your life course "out of sequence."

For all these reasons, this sketch of the life course may not adequately reflect your own past, present, and future. As sociologist C. Wright Mills (1959) would say, because employers are beating a path to your door, or failing to do so, you are more inclined to marry, to buy a house, and to start a family—or to postpone these life course events. In short, changing times change lives, steering the life course into different directions.

This January 1937 photo from Sneedville, Tennessee, shows Eunice Johns, age 9, and her husband, Charlie Johns, age 22. The groom gave his wife a doll as a wedding gift. The new husband and wife planned to build a cabin, and, as Charlie Johns phrased it, "go to housekeepin'." This couple illustrates the cultural relativity of life stages, which we sometimes mistake as fixed. It also is interesting from a symbolic interactionist perspective—that of changing definitions.

The marriage lasted. The couple had 7 children, 5 boys and 2 girls. Charlie died in 1997 at age 83, and Eunice in 2006 at age 78. The two were buried in the Johns Family Cemetery.

Are We Prisoners of Socialization?

From our discussion of socialization, you might conclude that sociologists think of people as robots: The socialization goes in, and the behavior comes out. People cannot help what they do, think, or feel, for everything is simply a result of their exposure to socializing agents.

Sociologists do *not* think of people in this way. Although socialization is powerful, and affects all of us profoundly, we have a self. Established in childhood and continually modified by later experience, our self is dynamic. Our self is not a sponge that passively absorbs influences from the environment but, rather, a vigorous, essential part of our being that allows us to act on our environment.

It is precisely because people are not robots that their behavior is so hard to predict. The countless reactions of others merge in each of us. As the self develops, we each internalize or "put together" these innumerable reactions, producing a unique whole called the *individual.* Each of us uses our mind to reason and to make choices in life.

In this way, *each of us is actively involved in the construction of the self.* Although our experiences in the family lay down our fundamental orientations to life, we are not doomed to keep those orientations if we do not like them. We can purposely expose ourselves to other groups and ideas. Those experiences, in turn, will have their own effects on our self. In short, although socialization is powerful, we can change even the self within the limitations of the framework laid down by our social locations. And that self—along with the options available within society—is the key to our behavior.

By the Numbers: *Then and Now*

Percentage of men who complete the transition to adulthood by age 30
1960 **65%** | NOW **31%**

Percentage of women who complete the transition to adulthood by age 30
1960 **77%** | NOW **46%**

About when does old age begin?
40 PREINDUSTRIAL TIMES | **75** NOW (IN TRANSITION)

SUMMARY *and* REVIEW

Society Makes Us Human

How much of our human characteristics come from "nature" (heredity) and how much from "nurture" (the social environment)?

Observations of isolated, institutionalized, and **feral children** help to answer the nature–nurture question, as do experiments with monkeys that were raised in isolation. Language and intimate social interaction—aspects of "nurture"—are essential to the development of what we consider to be human characteristics. Pp. 64–68.

Socialization into the Self and Mind

How do we acquire a self?

Humans are born with the *capacity* to develop a **self,** but the self must be socially constructed; that is, its contents depend on social interaction. According to Charles Horton Cooley's concept of the **looking-glass self,** our self develops as we internalize others' reactions to us. George Herbert Mead identified the ability to **take the role of the other** as essential to the development of the self. Mead concluded that even the mind is a social product. Pp. 68–70.

How do children develop reasoning skills?

Jean Piaget identified four stages that children go through as they develop the ability to reason: (1) *sensorimotor,* in which understanding is limited to sensory stimuli such as touch and sight; (2) *preoperational,* the ability to use symbols; (3) *concrete operational,* in which reasoning ability is more complex but not yet capable of complex abstractions; and (4) *formal operational,* or abstract thinking. Pp. 70–71.

Learning Personality, Morality, and Emotions

How do sociologists evaluate Freud's psychoanalytic theory of personality development?

Sigmund Freud viewed personality development as the result of our **id** (inborn, self-centered desires) clashing with the demands of society. The **ego** develops to balance the id and the **superego,** the conscience. Sociologists, in contrast, do not examine inborn or subconscious motivations, but, instead, consider how *social* factors—social class, gender, religion, education, and so forth—underlie personality. Pp. 71–72.

How do people develop morality?

Children are born without morality. Lawrence Kohlberg identified four stages children go through as they learn morality: amoral, preconventional, conventional, and postconventional. As they make moral decisions, both men and women use personal relationships and abstract principles. Pp. 72–73.

How does socialization influence emotions?

Socialization influences not only *how we express our emotions* but also *what emotions we feel.* Socialization into emotions is one of the means by which society produces conformity. Pp. 73–75.

Socialization into Gender

How does gender socialization affect our sense of self?

Gender socialization—sorting males and females into different roles—is a primary means of controlling human behavior. Children receive messages about gender even in infancy. A society's ideals of sex-linked behaviors are reinforced by its social institutions. Pp. 75–80.

Agents of Socialization

What are the main agents of socialization?

The **agents of socialization** include the family, neighborhood, religion, day care, school, **peer groups,** the **mass media,** and the workplace. Each has its particular influences in socializing us into becoming full-fledged members of society. Pp. 80–86.

Resocialization

What is resocialization?

Resocialization is the process of learning new norms, values, attitudes, and behavior. Most resocialization is voluntary, but some, as with residents of **total institutions,** is involuntary. Pp. 86–87.

Socialization Through the Life Course

Does socialization end when we enter adulthood?

Socialization occurs throughout the life course. In industrialized societies, the **life course** can be divided into childhood, adolescence, young adulthood, the middle years, and the older years. The West is adding a new stage, **transitional adulthood.** Life course patterns vary by geography, history, gender, race–ethnicity, and social class, as well as by individual experiences such as health and age at marriage. Pp. 87–91.

Are We Prisoners of Socialization?

Although socialization is powerful, we are not merely the sum of our socialization experiences. Just as socialization influences human behavior, so humans act on their environment and influence even their self-concept. P. 91.

THINKING CRITICALLY *ABOUT* Chapter 3

1. What two agents of socialization have influenced you the most? Can you pinpoint their influence on your attitudes, beliefs, values, or other orientations to life?

2. Summarize your views of the "proper" relationships of women and men. What in your socialization has led you to have these views?

3. What is your location in the life course? How does the text's summary of that location match your experiences? Explain the similarities and differences.

ADDITIONAL RESOURCES

What can you find in MySocLab? mysoclab www.mysoclab.com

- Complete Ebook
- Practice Tests and Video and Audio activities
- Mapping and Data Analysis exercises

- Sociology in the News
- Classic Readings in Sociology
- Research and Writing advice

Where Can I Read More on This Topic?

Suggested readings for this chapter are listed at the back of this book.

Social Structure and Social Interaction

Japan

My curiosity had gotten the better of me. When the sociology convention finished, I climbed aboard the first city bus that came along. I didn't know where the bus was going, and I didn't know where I would spend the night.

"Maybe I overdid it this time," I thought, as the bus began winding down streets I had never seen before. Actually, this was my first visit to Washington, D.C., so everything was unfamiliar to me.

Suddenly one of the men jumped up, smashed the empty bottle against the sidewalk, and . . .

I had no destination, no plans, not even a map. I carried no billfold, just a driver's license shoved into my jeans for emergency identification, some pocket change, and a $10 bill tucked into my sock. My goal was simple: If I saw something interesting, I would get off the bus and check it out.

"Nothing but the usual things," I mused, as we passed row after row of apartment buildings and stores. I could see myself riding buses the entire night. Then something caught my eye. Nothing spectacular—just groups of people clustered around a large circular area where several streets intersected.

I climbed off the bus and made my way to what turned out to be Dupont Circle. I took a seat on a sidewalk bench and began to observe what was going on around me. As the scene came into focus, I noticed several streetcorner men drinking and joking with one another. One of the men broke from his companions and sat down next to me. As we talked, I mostly listened.

As night fell, the men said that they wanted to get another bottle of wine. I contributed. They counted their money and asked if I wanted to go with them.

Although I felt my stomach churning—a combination of hesitation and fear—I heard a confident "Sure!" come out of my mouth. As we left the circle, the three men began to cut through an alley. "Oh, no," I thought. "This isn't what I had in mind."

I had but a split second to make a decision. I found myself continuing to walk with the men, but holding back half a step so that none of the three was behind me. As we walked, they passed around the remnants of their bottle. When my turn came, I didn't know what to do. I shuddered to think about the diseases lurking within that bottle. I made another quick decision. In the semidarkness I faked it, letting only my thumb and forefinger touch my lips and nothing enter my mouth.

When we returned to Dupont Circle, we sat on the benches, and the men passed around their new bottle of Thunderbird.

I couldn't fake it in the light, so I passed, pointing at my stomach to indicate that I was having digestive problems.

Suddenly one of the men jumped up, smashed the emptied bottle against the sidewalk, and thrust the jagged neck outward in a menacing gesture. He glared straight ahead at another bench, where he had spotted someone with whom he had some sort of unfinished business. As the other men told him to cool it, I moved slightly to one side of the group—ready to flee, just in case.

Levels of Sociological Analysis

On this sociological adventure, I almost got in over my head. Fortunately, it turned out all right. The man's "enemy" didn't look our way, the man put the broken bottle next to the bench "just in case he needed it," and my intriguing introduction to a life that up until then I had only read about continued until dawn.

Sociologists Elliot Liebow (1967/1999), Mitchell Duneier (2001), and Elijah Anderson (1978, 1990, 2006) have written fascinating accounts about men like my companions from that evening. Although streetcorner men may appear to be disorganized—simply coming and going as they please and doing whatever feels good at the moment—sociologists have analyzed how, like us, these men are influenced by the norms and beliefs of our society. This will become more apparent as we examine the two levels of analysis that sociologists use.

Macrosociology and Microsociology

The first level, **macrosociology,** focuses on broad features of society. Conflict theorists and functionalists use this approach to analyze such things as social class and how groups are related to one another. If they were to analyze streetcorner men, for example, they would stress that these men are located at the bottom of the U.S. social class system. Their low status means that many opportunities are closed to them: The men have few job skills, little education, hardly anything to offer an employer. As "able-bodied" men, however, they are not eligible for welfare—even for a two-year limit—so they hustle to survive. As a consequence, they spend their lives on the streets.

In the second level, **microsociology,** the focus is on **social interaction,** what people do when they come together. Sociologists who use this approach are likely to analyze the men's rules, or "codes," for getting along; their survival strategies ("hustles"); how they divide up money, wine, or whatever other resources they have; their relationships with girlfriends, family, and friends; where they spend their time and what they do there; their language; their pecking order; and so on. Microsociology is the primary focus of symbolic interactionists.

Because each approach has a different focus, macrosociology and microsociology yield distinctive perspectives, and both are needed to gain a fuller understanding of social life. We cannot adequately understand streetcorner men, for example, without using *macrosociology.* It is essential that we place the men within the broad context of how groups in U.S. society are related to one another—for, as is true for ourselves, the social class of these men helps to shape their attitudes and behavior. Nor can we adequately understand these men without *microsociology,* for their everyday situations also form a significant part of their lives—as they do for all of us.

Let's look in more detail at how these two approaches in sociology work together to help us understand social life. As we examine them more closely, you may find yourself feeling more comfortable with one approach than the other. This is what happens with sociologists. For reasons that include personal background and professional training, sociologists find themselves more comfortable with one approach and tend to use it in their research. Both approaches, however, are necessary to understand life in society.

macrosociology analysis of social life that focuses on broad features of society, such as social class and the relationships of groups to one another; usually used by functionalists and conflict theorists

microsociology analysis of social life that focuses on social interaction; typically used by symbolic interactionists

social interaction what people do when they are in one another's presence

Sociologists use both macro and micro levels of analysis to study social life. Those who use *macrosociology* to analyze the homeless—or any human behavior—focus on broad aspects of society, such as the economy and social classes. Sociologists who use the *microsociological approach* analyze how people interact with one another. This photo illustrates *social structure*—the disparities between power and powerlessness are amply evident. It also illustrates the micro level—the isolation of this man.

The Macrosociological Perspective: Social Structure

Why did the street people in our opening vignette act as they did, staying up all night drinking wine, prepared to use a lethal weapon? Why don't *we* act like this? Social structure helps us answer such questions.

The Sociological Significance of Social Structure

To better understand human behavior, we need to understand *social structure,* the framework of society that was already laid out before you were born. **Social structure** refers to the typical patterns of a group, such as its usual relationships between men and women or students and teachers. *The sociological significance of social structure is that it guides our behavior.*

Because this term may seem vague, let's consider how you experience social structure in your own life. As I write this, I do not know your race–ethnicity. I do not know your religion. I do not know whether you are young or old, tall or short, male or female. I do not know whether you were reared on a farm, in the suburbs, or in the inner city. I do not know whether you went to a public high school or to an exclusive prep school. But I do know that you are in college. And this, alone, tells me a great deal about you.

From this one piece of information, I can assume that the social structure of your college is now shaping what you do. For example, let's suppose that today you felt euphoric over some great news. I can be fairly certain (not absolutely, mind you, but relatively confident) that when you entered the classroom, social structure overrode your mood. That is, instead of shouting at the top of your lungs and joyously throwing this book into the air, you entered the classroom in a fairly subdued manner and took your seat.

The same social structure influences your instructor, even if he or she, on the one hand, is facing a divorce or has a child dying of cancer or, on the other, has just been awarded a promotion or a million-dollar grant. Your instructor may feel like either retreating into seclusion or celebrating wildly, but most likely he or she will conduct class in the usual manner. In short, social structure tends to override personal feelings and desires.

Just as social structure influences you and your instructor, so it also establishes limits for street people. They, too, find themselves in a specific location in the U.S. social structure—although it is quite different from yours or your instructor's. Consequently, they are

social structure the framework (or typical patterns) that surrounds us, consisting of the relationships of people and groups to one another, which gives direction to and sets limits on behavior

social class according to Weber, a large group of people who rank close to one another in property power, and prestige; according to Marx, one of two groups: capitalists who own the means of production or workers who sell their labor

status the position that someone occupies in a social group

status set all the statuses or positions that an individual occupies

affected in different ways. Nothing about their social location leads them to take notes or to lecture. Their behaviors, however, are as logical an outcome of where they find themselves in the social structure as are your own. In their position in the social structure, it is just as "natural" to drink wine all night as it is for you to stay up studying all night for a crucial examination. It is just as "natural" for you to nod and say, "Excuse me," when you enter a crowded classroom late and have to claim a desk on which someone has already placed books as it is for them to break off the neck of a wine bottle and glare at an enemy. To better understand social structure, read the Down-to-Earth Sociology box on the next page.

In short, people learn their behaviors and attitudes because of their location in the social structure (whether they be privileged, deprived, or in between), and they act accordingly. This is as true of street people as it is of us. *The differences in behavior and attitudes are due not to biology (race-ethnicity, sex, or any other supposed genetic factors), but to people's location in the social structure.* Switch places with street people and watch your behaviors and attitudes change!

Because social structure so crucially affects who we are and what we are like, let's look more closely at its major components: culture, social class, social status, roles, groups, and social institutions.

Culture

In Chapter 2, we considered culture's far-reaching effects on our lives. At this point, let's simply summarize its main impact. Sociologists use the term *culture* to refer to a group's language, beliefs, values, behaviors, and even gestures. Culture also includes the material objects that a group uses. Culture is the broadest framework that determines what kind of people we become. If we are reared in Chinese, Arab, or U.S. culture, we will grow up to be like most Chinese, Arabs, or Americans. On the outside, we will look and act like them; and on the inside, we will think and feel like them.

Social Class

To understand people, we must examine the social locations that they hold in life. Especially significant is *social class,* which is based on income, education, and occupational prestige.

Large numbers of people who have similar amounts of income and education and who work at jobs that are roughly comparable in prestige make up a **social class.** It is hard to overemphasize this aspect of social structure, for our social class influences not only our behaviors but even our ideas and attitudes. We have this in common, then, with the street people described in the opening vignette: We both are influenced by our location in the social class structure. Theirs may be a considerably less privileged position, but it has no less influence on their lives. Social class is so significant that we shall spend an entire chapter (Chapter 10) on this topic.

Social Status

When you hear the word *status,* you are likely to think of prestige. These two words are welded together in people's minds. As you saw in the box on football, however, sociologists use **status** in a different way—to refer to the *position* that someone occupies. That position may carry a great deal of prestige, as in the case of a judge or an astronaut, or it may bring little prestige, as in the case of a convenience store clerk or a waitress at the local truck stop. The status may also be looked down on, as in the case of a streetcorner man, an ex-convict, or a thief.

All of us occupy several positions at the same time. You may simultaneously be a son or daughter, a worker, a date, and a student. Sociologists use the term **status set** to refer to all the statuses or positions that you occupy. Obviously your status set changes as your particular statuses change. For example, if you graduate from college and take a full-time job, get married, buy a home, have children, and so on, your status set changes to include the positions of worker, spouse, homeowner, and parent.

Social class is one of the most significant factors in social life. Fundamental to what we become, it affects our orientations to life. Can you see how this photo illustrates this point?

Down-to-Earth Sociology
College Football as Social Structure

To gain a better idea of what *social structure* is, think of college football (Dobriner 1969a). You probably know the various positions on the team: center, guards, tackles, ends, quarterback, running backs, and the like. Each is a *status;* that is, each is a social position. For each of the statuses shown in Figure 4.1, there is a *role;* that is, each of these positions has certain expectations attached to it. The center is expected to snap the ball, the quarterback to pass it, the guards to block, the tackles to tackle or block, the ends to receive passes, and so on. Those role expectations guide each player's actions; that is, the players try to do what their particular role requires.

Let's suppose that football is your favorite sport and you never miss a home game at your college. Let's also suppose that you graduate, get a great job, and move across the country. Five years later, you return to your campus for a nostalgic visit. The climax of your visit is the biggest football game of the season. When you get to the game, you might be surprised to see a different coach, but you are not surprised that each playing position is occupied by people you don't know, for all the players you knew have graduated, and their places have been filled by others.

This scenario mirrors *social structure,* the framework around which a group exists. In football, that framework consists of the coaching staff and the eleven playing positions. The game does not depend on any particular individual, but, rather, on *social statuses,* the positions that the individuals occupy. When someone leaves a position, the game can go on because someone else takes over that position or status and plays the role. The game will continue even though not a single individual remains

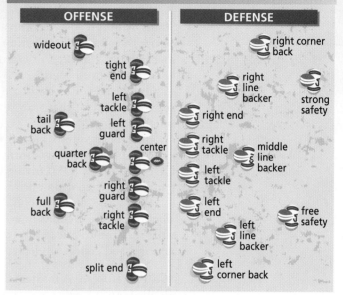

FIGURE 4.1   Team Positions (Statuses) in Football

from one period of time to the next. Notre Dame's football team endures today even though Knute Rockne, the Gipper, and his teammates are long dead.

Even though you may not play football, you do live your life within a clearly established social structure. The statuses that you occupy and the roles you play were already in place before you were born. You take your particular positions in life, others do the same, and society goes about its business. Although the specifics change with time, the game—whether of life or of football—goes on.

For Your Consideration
How does social structure influence your life? To answer this question, you can begin by analyzing your social statuses.

Like other aspects of social structure, statuses are part of our basic framework of living in society. The example I gave of students and teachers who come to class and do what others expect of them despite their particular circumstances and moods illustrates how statuses affect our actions—and those of the people around us. Our statuses—whether daughter or son, teacher or student—serve as guides for our behavior.

Ascribed and Achieved Statuses. An **ascribed status** is involuntary. You do not ask for it, nor can you choose it. At birth, you inherit ascribed statuses such as your race–ethnicity, sex, and the social class of your parents, as well as your statuses as female or male, daughter or son, niece or nephew. Others, such as teenager and senior citizen, are related to the life course discussed in Chapter 3, and are given to you later in life.

Achieved statuses, in contrast, are voluntary. These you earn or accomplish. As a result of your efforts you become a student, a friend, a spouse, a lawyer, or a member of the

ascribed status a position an individual either inherits at birth or receives involuntarily later in life

achieved status a position that is earned, accomplished, or involves at least some effort or activity on the individual's part

status symbols items used to identify a status

master status a status that cuts across the other statuses that an individual occupies

clergy. Or, for lack of effort (or for efforts that others fail to appreciate), you become a school dropout, a former friend, an ex-spouse, a debarred lawyer, or a defrocked member of the clergy. In other words, achieved statuses can be either positive or negative; both college president and bank robber are achieved statuses.

Each status provides guidelines for how we are to act and feel. Like other aspects of social structure, statuses set limits on what we can and cannot do. Because social statuses are an essential part of the social structure, all human groups have them.

Status Symbols.　People who are pleased with their social status often want others to recognize their particular position. To elicit this recognition, they use **status symbols,** signs that identify a status. For example, people wear wedding rings to announce their marital status; uniforms, guns, and badges to proclaim that they are police officers (and not so subtly to let you know that their status gives them authority over you); and "backward" collars to declare that they are Lutheran ministers or Roman Catholic or Episcopal priests.

Some social statuses are negative and so, therefore, are their status symbols. The scarlet letter in Nathaniel Hawthorne's book by the same title is one example. Another is the CONVICTED DUI (Driving Under the Influence) bumper sticker that some U.S. courts require convicted drunk drivers to display if they wish to avoid a jail sentence.

All of us use status symbols. We use them to announce our statuses to others and to help smooth our interactions in everyday life. Can you identify your own status symbols and what they communicate? For example, how does your clothing announce your statuses of sex, age, and college student?

Master Statuses.　A **master status** cuts across your other statuses. Some master statuses are ascribed. An example is your sex. Whatever you do, people perceive you as a male or as a female. If you are working your way through college by flipping burgers, people see you not only as a burger flipper and a student but also as a *male* or *female* burger flipper and a *male* or *female* college student. Other master statuses are race–ethnicity and age.

Some master statuses are achieved. If you become very, very wealthy (and it doesn't matter whether your wealth comes from a successful invention or from winning the lottery—it is still *achieved* as far as sociologists are concerned), your wealth is likely to become a master status. For example, people might say, "She is a very rich burger flipper"—or, more likely, "She's very rich, and she used to flip burgers!"

Master Statuses are those that overshadow our other statuses. Shown here is Stephen Hawking, who is severely disabled by Lou Gehrig's disease. For some, his *master status* is that of a person with disabilities. Because Hawking is one of the greatest physicists who has ever lived, however, his outstanding achievements have given him another *master status,* that of a world-class physicist in the ranking of Einstein.

Similarly, people who become disfigured find, to their dismay, that their condition becomes a master status. For example, a person whose face is scarred from severe burns will be viewed through this unwelcome master status regardless of occupation or accomplishments. In the same way, people who are confined to wheelchairs can attest to how their wheelchair overrides all their other statuses and influences others' perceptions of everything they do.

Although our statuses usually fit together fairly well, some people have a contradiction or mismatch between their statuses. This is known as **status inconsistency** (or discrepancy). A 14-year-old college student is an example. So is a 40-year-old married woman who is dating a 19-year-old college sophomore.

These examples reveal an essential aspect of social statuses: Like other components of social structure, they come with built-in *norms* (that is, expectations) that guide our behavior. When statuses mesh well, as they usually do, we know what to expect of people. This helps social interaction to unfold smoothly. Status inconsistency, however, upsets our expectations. In the preceding examples, how are you supposed to act? Are you supposed to treat the 14-year-old as you would a young teenager, or as you would your college classmate? Do you react to the married woman as you would to the mother of your friend, or as you would to a classmate's date?

Roles

All the world's a stage
And all the men and women merely players.
They have their exits and their entrances;
And one man in his time plays many parts . . .

(William Shakespeare, *As You Like It,* Act II, Scene 7)

Like Shakespeare, sociologists see roles as essential to social life. When you were born, **roles**—the behaviors, obligations, and privileges attached to a status—were already set up for you. Society was waiting with outstretched arms to teach you how it expected you to act as a boy or a girl. And whether you were born poor, rich, or somewhere in between, that, too, attached certain behaviors, obligations, and privileges to your statuses.

The difference between role and status is that you *occupy* a status, but you *play* a role (Linton 1936). For example, being a son or daughter is your status, but your expectations of receiving food and shelter from your parents—as well as their expectations that you show respect to them—are part of your role. Or, again, your status is student, but your role is to attend class, take notes, do homework, and take tests.

Roles are like a fence. They allow us a certain amount of freedom, but for most of us that freedom doesn't go very far. Suppose that a woman decides that she is not going to wear dresses—or a man that he will not wear suits and ties—regardless of what anyone says. In most situations, they'll stick to their decision. When a formal occasion comes along, however, such as a family wedding or a funeral, they are likely to cave in to norms that they find overwhelming. Almost all of us follow the guidelines for what is "appropriate" for our roles. Few of us are bothered by such constraints, for our **socialization** is thorough, and we usually *want* to do what our roles indicate is appropriate.

The sociological significance of roles is that they lay out what is expected of people. As individuals throughout society perform their roles, those many roles mesh together to form this thing called *society.* As Shakespeare put it, people's roles provide "their exits and their entrances" on the stage of life. In short, roles are remarkably effective at keeping people in line—telling them when they should "enter" and when they should "exit," as well as what to do in between.

Groups

A **group** consists of people who interact with one another and who feel that the values, interests and norms they have in common are important. The groups to which we belong—just like social class, statuses, and roles—are powerful forces in our lives. By belonging to a group, we assume an obligation to affirm the group's values, interests, and norms. To remain a member in good standing, we need to show that we share those characteristics. This means that *when we belong to a group we yield to others the right to judge our behavior—*even though we don't like it!

status inconsistency ranking high on some dimensions of social class and low on others, also called *status discrepancy*

role the behaviors, obligations, and privileges attached to a status

socialization the process by which people learn the characteristics of their group—the knowledge, skills, attitudes, values, norms, and actions thought appropriate for them

group people who have something in common and who believe that what they have in common is significant; also called a *social group*

social institution the organized, usual, or standard ways by which society meets its basic needs

Although this principle holds true for all groups, some groups wield influence over only small segments of our behavior. For example, if you belong to a stamp collector's club, the group's influence may center on your display of knowledge about stamps and perhaps your fairness in trading them. Other groups, in contrast, such as the family, control many aspects of our behavior. When parents say to their 15-year-old daughter, "As long as you are living under our roof, you had better be home by midnight," they show their expectation that their daughter, as a member of the family, will conform to their ideas about many aspects of life, including their views on curfew. They are saying that as long as the daughter wants to remain a member of the family in good standing, her behavior must conform to their expectations.

In Chapters 6 and 7, we will examine groups in detail. For now, let's look at the next component of social structure, social institutions.

Social Institutions

At first glance, the term *social institution* may seem cold and abstract—with little relevance to your life. In fact, however, **social institutions**—the standard or usual ways that a society meets its basic needs—vitally affect your life. They not only shape your behavior but even color your thoughts. How can this be?

The first step in understanding how this can be is to look at Figure 4.2 on the next page. Look at what social institutions are: the family, religion, education, economics, medicine, politics, law, science, the military, and the mass media. By weaving the fabric of society, the social institutions set the context for your behavior and orientations to life. Note that each institution satisfies a basic need and has its own groups, statuses, values, and norms. Social institutions are so significant that an entire part of this book, Part IV, focuses on them.

The Sociological Significance of Social Institutions

To understand social institutions is to realize how profoundly social structure affects your life. Much of the influence of social institutions lies beyond your ordinary awareness. For example, because of our economic institution, it is common to work eight hours a day for five days every week. There is nothing normal or natural about this pattern, however. This rhythm is only an arbitrary arrangement for dividing work and leisure. Yet this one aspect of a single social institution has far-reaching effects. Not only does it dictate how people divide up their days, but it also lays out a structure for our interaction with family and friends and for how we meet our personal needs.

Each of the other social institutions also has far-reaching effects on our lives. Social institutions are so significant that if they were different, our orientations to the social world, even to life itself, would be different. Let's consider just the mass media.

The mass media are a major influence in contemporary life. Until 1436, when Johann Gutenberg invented movable type, printing was a slow process, and printed materials were expensive. Today, printed materials are common and often cheap. "Cheap" has a double meaning, with its second meaning illustrated in this photo.

An Example: The Mass Media.   Far beyond serving simply as sources of information, the mass media influence our attitudes toward social issues, the ways that we view other people, and even our self-concept. Because the media significantly shape public opinion, all governments attempt to influence them. Totalitarian governments try to control them.

The mass media are relatively new in human history, owing their origins to the invention of the printing press in the 1400s. This invention had profound consequences on all social institutions. The printing of the Bible altered religion, for instance, while the publication of political broadsides and newspapers altered politics. From these beginnings, a series of inventions—from radio and movies to television and the microchip—has made the media an increasingly powerful force.

One of the most significant questions we can ask about this social institution is, Who controls it? That control, which in totalitarian countries is obvious, is much less visible in democratic nations. Functionalists might conclude that the media in a democratic nation represent the varied interests of the many groups that make up that nation. Conflict theorists,

FIGURE 4.2 Social Institutions in Industrial and Postindustrial Societies

Social Institution	Basic Needs	Some Groups or Organizations	Some Statuses	Some Values	Some Norms
Family	Regulate reproduction, socialize and protect children	Relatives, kinship groups	Daughter, son, father, mother, brother, sister, aunt, uncle, grandparent	Sexual fidelity, providing for your family, keeping a clean house, respect for parents	Have only as many children as you can afford, be faithful to your spouse
Religion	Concerns about life after death, the meaning of suffering and loss; desire to connect with the Creator	Congregation, synagogue, mosque, denomination, charity, clergy associations	Priest, minister, rabbi, imam, worshipper, teacher, disciple, missionary, prophet, convert	Reading and adhering to holy texts such as the Bible, the Torah, and the Koran; honoring God	Attend worship services, contribute money, follow the teachings
Education	Transmit knowledge and skills across generations	School, college, student senate, sports team, PTA, teachers' union	Teacher, student, dean, principal, football player, cheerleader	Academic honesty, good grades, being "cool"	Do homework, prepare lectures, don't snitch on classmates
Economy	Produce and distribute goods and services	Credit unions, banks, credit card companies, buying clubs	Worker, boss, buyer, seller, creditor, debtor, advertiser	Making money, paying bills on time, producing efficiently	Maximize profits, "the customer is always right," work hard
Medicine	Heal the sick and injured, care for the dying	AMA, hospitals, pharmacies, HMOs, insurance companies	Doctor, nurse, patient, pharmacist, medical insurer	Hippocratic oath, staying in good health, following doctor's orders	Don't exploit patients, give best medical care available
Politics	Allocate power, determine authority, prevent chaos	Political party, congress, parliament, monarchy	President, senator, lobbyist, voter, candidate, spin doctor	Majority rule, the right to vote as a privilege and a sacred trust	One vote per person, be informed about candidates
Law	Maintain social order, enforce norms	Police, courts, prisons	Judge, police officer, lawyer, defendant, prison guard	Trial by one's peers, innocence until proven guilty	Give true testimony, follow the rules of evidence
Science	Master the environment	Local, state, regional, national, and international associations	Scientist, researcher, technician, administrator, journal editor	Unbiased research, open dissemination of research findings, originality	Follow scientific method, be objective, disclose findings, don't plagiarize
Military	Protection from enemies, enforce national interests	Army, navy, air force, marines, coast guard, national guard	Soldier, recruit, enlisted person, officer, veteran, prisoner, spy	To die for one's country is an honor, obedience unto death	Follow orders, be ready to go to war, sacrifice for your buddies
Mass Media	Disseminate information, report events, mold public opinion	TV networks, radio stations, publishers, association of bloggers	Journalist, newscaster, author, editor, publisher, blogger	Timeliness, accuracy, freedom of the press	Be accurate, fair, timely, and profitable

in contrast, see the matter quite differently: The mass media—at least a country's most influential newspapers and television stations—represent the interests of the political elite. They give coverage to mildly dissenting opinions, but they stand solidly behind the government. The most obvious example is the positive treatment that the media give to the inauguration of a president.

Since the mass media are so influential in our lives today, the answer to this question of who controls the media is of more than passing interest. This matter is vital to our understanding of contemporary society.

Comparing Functionalist and Conflict Perspectives

Just as the functionalist and conflict perspectives of the mass media differ, so do their views of the nature of social institutions. Let's compare these views.

The Functionalist Perspective.   Because the first priority is to survive, all societies establish customary ways to meet their basic needs. As a result, no society is without social institutions. In tribal societies, some social institutions are less visible because the group meets its basic social needs in more informal ways. A society may be too small to have people specialize in education, for example, but it will have established ways of teaching skills and ideas to the young. It may be too small to have a military, but it will have some mechanism of self-defense.

What are society's basic needs? Functionalists identify five *functional requisites* (basic needs) that each society must meet if it is to survive (Aberle et al. 1950; Mack and Bradford 1979).

1. *Replacing members.* Obviously, if a society does not replace its members, it cannot continue to exist. With reproduction fundamental to a society's existence, and the need to protect infants and children universal, all groups have developed some version of the family. The family gives the newcomer to society a sense of belonging by providing a *lineage,* an account of how he or she is related to others. The family also functions to control people's sex drive and to maintain orderly reproduction.

2. *Socializing new members.* Each baby must be taught what it means to be a member of the group into which it is born. To accomplish this, each human group develops devices to ensure that its newcomers learn the group's basic expectations. As the primary "bearer of culture," the family is essential to this process, but other social institutions, such as religion and education, also help meet this basic need.

3. *Producing and distributing goods and services.* Every society must produce and distribute basic resources, from food and clothing to shelter and education. Consequently, every society establishes an *economic* institution, a means of producing goods and services along with routine ways of distributing them.

4. *Preserving order.* Societies face two threats of disorder: one internal, the potential for chaos, and the other external, the possibility of attack. To protect themselves from internal threat, they develop ways to police themselves, ranging from informal means such as gossip to formal means such as armed groups. To defend themselves against external conquest, they develop a means of defense, some form of the military.

5. *Providing a sense of purpose.* Every society must get people to yield self-interest in favor of the needs of the group. To convince people to sacrifice personal gains, societies instill a sense of purpose. Human groups develop many ways to implant such beliefs, but a primary one is religion, which attempts to answer questions about ultimate meaning. Actually, all of a society's institutions are involved in meeting this functional requisite; the family provides one set of answers about the sense of purpose, the school another, and so on.

The Conflict Perspective.   Although conflict theorists agree that social institutions were designed originally to meet basic survival needs, they do not view social institutions as working harmoniously for the common good. On the contrary, conflict theorists stress that powerful groups control our society's institutions, manipulating them in order to maintain

Functionalist theorists have identified *functional requisites* for the survival of society. One, providing a sense of purpose, is often met through religious groups. To most people, snake handling, as in this church service in Sand Mountain, Alabama, is nonsensical. From a functional perspective, however, it makes a great deal of sense. Can you identify its sociological meanings?

their own privileged position of wealth and power (Useem 1984; Domhoff 1999a, b, 2006, 2007).

Conflict theorists point out that a fairly small group of people has garnered the lion's share of our nation's wealth. Members of this elite group sit on the boards of our major corporations and our most prestigious universities. They make strategic campaign contributions to influence (or control) our lawmakers, and it is they who are behind the nation's major decisions: to go to war or to refrain from war; to increase or to decrease taxes; to raise or to lower interest rates; and to pass laws that favor or impede moving capital, technology, and jobs out of the country.

Feminist sociologists (both women and men) have used conflict theory to gain a better understanding of how social institutions affect gender relations. Their basic insight is that gender is also an element of social structure, not simply a characteristic of individuals. In other words, throughout the world, social institutions divide males and females into separate groups, each with unequal access to society's resources.

In Sum: Functionalists view social institutions as working together to meet universal human needs, but conflict theorists regard social institutions as having a single primary purpose—to preserve the social order. For them, this means safeguarding the wealthy and powerful in their positions of privilege.

Changes in Social Structure

As you can see, this enveloping system that we call social structure powerfully affects our lives. This means that as social structure changes, so, too, do our orientations to life. Our culture is not static. It is continuously evolving as it responds to changing values, to new technology, and to contact with cultures around the world. As our culture changes, so do we. Similarly, as our economy responds to globalization, it either opens or closes opportunities, changing our lives, sometimes brutally so. New groups such as the Department of Homeland Security come into being, wielding extraordinary power over us. In short, the corner in life that we occupy, though small and seemingly private, is not closed off; rather, it is pushed and pulled and stretched in different directions as our social structure changes.

What Holds Society Together?

With its many, often conflicting, groups and its extensive social change, how can a society manage to hold together? Let's examine two answers that sociologists have proposed.

Mechanical and Organic Solidarity.   Sociologist Emile Durkheim (1893/1933) was interested in how societies manage to have **social integration**—their members being united by shared values and other social bonds. For smaller groups, he found the answer in what he called **mechanical solidarity.** By this term, Durkheim meant that people who perform similar tasks develop a shared consciousness. Think of a farming community in which everyone is involved in planting, cultivating, and harvesting. Members of this group have so much in common that they know how almost everyone else in the community feels about life. Societies with mechanical solidarity tolerate little diversity in behavior, thinking, or attitudes, for their unity depends on agreement in these matters.

As societies get larger, they develop different kinds of work, a specialized **division of labor.** Some people mine gold, others sell it, while still others turn it into jewelry. Such a division of labor disperses people into different interest groups where they develop different ideas about life. No longer do they depend on one another to have similar ideas and behaviors. Rather, they depend on one another for the specific work that each person contributes to the whole group. Durkheim called this new form of solidarity based on interdependence **organic solidarity.**

To see why Durkheim used the term *organic solidarity,* think about how you depend on your teacher to guide you through this introductory course in sociology. At the same time, without students your teacher would be without a job. You and your teacher are *like two organs in the same body.* (The "body" in this case is the college or university.) Although each of you performs different tasks, you depend on one another. This creates a form of unity.

social integration the degree to which members of a group or a society feel united by shared values and other social bonds; also known as social cohesion

mechanical solidarity Durkheim's term for the unity (a shared consciousness) that people feel as a result of performing the same or similar tasks

division of labor the splitting of a group's or a society's tasks into specialties

organic solidarity Durkheim's term for the interdependence that results from the division of labor; people depending on others to fulfill their jobs

The warm, more intimate relationships of *Gemeinschaft* society are apparent in the photo taken during *Oktoberfest* in Munich, Germany. The more impersonal relationships of *Gesellschaft* society are evident in this Internet cafe, where, customers are ignoring one another.

As you can see, organic solidarity produced a new basis for social integration—not a sharing of views because of planting and harvesting crops together and marrying into one another's families—but participation in separate activities that together contribute to the welfare of the group. As a result, our society can tolerate a wide diversity of orientations to life and still manage to work as a whole. Both past and present societies are based on social solidarity, but, as Durkheim pointed out, the types of solidarity differ remarkably.

Gemeinschaft* and *Gesellschaft*.**   Ferdinand Tönnies (1887/1988) also analyzed this fundamental shift in relationships. He used the term ***Gemeinschaft (Guh-MINE-shoft), or "intimate community," to describe village life, the type of society in which everyone knows everyone else. He noted that in the society that was emerging, the personal ties, kinship connections, and lifelong friendships that marked village life were being crowded out by short-term relationships, individual accomplishments, and self-interest. Tönnies called this new type of society ***Gesellschaft*** (Guh-ZELL-shoft), or "impersonal association." He did not mean that we no longer have intimate ties to family and friends but, rather, that our lives no longer center on them. Few of us take jobs in a family business, for example, and contracts replace handshakes. Much of our time is spent with strangers and short-term acquaintances.

How Relevant Are These Concepts Today?   I know that *Gemeinschaft, Gesellschaft,* and *mechanical* and *organic solidarity* are strange terms and that Durkheim's and Tönnies' observations must seem like a dead issue. The concern these sociologists expressed, however—that their world was changing from a community in which people were united by close ties and shared ideas and feelings to an anonymous association built around impersonal, short-term contacts—is still very real. In large part, this same concern explains the rise of Islamic fundamentalism (Volti 1995). Islamic leaders fear that Western values will uproot their traditional culture, that cold rationality will replace the warm, informal, personal relationships among families and clans. They fear, rightly so, that this will also change their views on life and morality. Although the terms may sound strange, even obscure, you can see that the ideas remain a vital part of today's world.

In Sum: Whether the terms are *Gemeinschaft* and *Gesellschaft* or *mechanical solidarity* and *organic solidarity,* they indicate that as societies change, so do people's orientations to life. *The sociological point is that social structure sets the context for what we do, feel, and think, and ultimately, then, for the kind of people we become.* As you read the Cultural Diversity box on the next page which describes one of the few remaining *Gemeinschaft* societies in the United States, think of how fundamentally different your life would be if you had been reared in an Amish family.

Gemeinschaft a type of society in which life is intimate; a community in which everyone knows everyone else and people share a sense of togetherness

Gesellschaft a type of society that is dominated by impersonal relationships, individual accomplishments, and self-interest

Cultural Diversity in the United States

The Amish: *Gemeinschaft* Community in a *Gesellschaft* Society

One of the best examples of a *Gemeinschaft* community in the United States is the Old Order Amish, followers of a sect that broke away from the Swiss-German Mennonite church in the 1600s and settled in Pennsylvania around 1727. Most of today's 225,000 Old Order Amish live in just three states—Pennsylvania, Ohio, and Indiana—but in the search for cheaper farmland, they have moved to Arkansas, Colorado, Kentucky, Maine, Mississippi, Missouri, Nebraska, and West Virginia. About 10 percent live in Lancaster County, Pennsylvania. The Amish, who believe that birth control is wrong, have doubled in population in less than two decades.

Because Amish farmers use horses instead of tractors, most of their farms are one hundred acres or less. To the five million tourists who pass through Lancaster County each year, the rolling green pastures, white farmhouses, simple barns, horse-drawn buggies, and clotheslines hung with somber-colored garments convey a sense of peace and innocence reminiscent of another era. Although just sixty-five miles from Philadelphia, "Amish country" is a world away.

Amish life is based on separation from the world—an idea taken from Christ's Sermon on the Mount—and obedience to the church's teachings and leaders. This rejection of worldly concerns, writes sociologist Donald Kraybill in *The Riddle of Amish Culture* (2002), "provides the foundation of such Amish values as humility, faithfulness, thrift, tradition, communal goals, joy of work, a slow-paced life, and trust in divine providence."

The *Gemeinschaft* of village life that has been largely lost to industrialization remains a vibrant part of Amish life. The Amish make their decisions in weekly meetings, where, by consensus, they follow a set of rules, or *Ordnung,* to guide their behavior. Religion and discipline are the glue that holds the Amish together. Brotherly love and the welfare of the community are paramount values. In times of birth, sickness, and death, neighbors pitch in with the chores. In these ways, they maintain the bonds of intimate community.

The Amish are bound by other ties, including language (a dialect of German known as Pennsylvania Dutch), plain clothing—often black, whose style has remained unchanged for almost 300 years—and church-sponsored schools. Nearly all Amish marry, and divorce is forbidden. The family is a vital ingredient in Amish life; all major events take place in the home, including weddings, births, funerals, and church services. Amish children attend church schools, but only until the age of 13. (In 1972, the Supreme Court ruled that Amish parents had the right to take their children out of school after the eighth grade.) To go to school beyond the eighth grade would expose them to values and "worldly concerns" that would drive a wedge between the children and their community. The Amish believe that violence is bad, even personal self-defense, and they register as conscientious objectors during times of war. They pay no Social Security, and they receive no government benefits.

The Amish cannot resist all change, of course. Instead, they try to adapt to change in ways that will least disrupt their core values. A special threat has come from urban sprawl, which has driven up the price of farmland. Unable to afford farms, about half of Amish men now work at jobs other than farming. Most work in farm-related businesses or in woodcrafts. They go to great lengths to avoid leaving the home. The Amish believe that when a husband works away from home, all aspects of life change—from the marital relationship to the care of the children—certainly an astute sociological insight. They also believe that if a man receives a paycheck, he will think that his work is of more value than his wife's. Because intimate, or *Gemeinschaft,* society is essential to maintain the Amish way of life, concerns are growing about the men who have begun to work for non-Amish businesses. They are being exposed to the outside world, and some are even using modern technology such as cell phones and computers at work.

Despite living in the midst of a highly materialistic and secular culture, the Amish are retaining their way of life. Perhaps the most poignant illustration of how the Amish differ from the dominant culture is this: When in 2006 a non-Amish man shot several Amish girls at a one-room school, the Amish community established charitable funds not only for the families of the dead children but also for the family of the killer.

For Your Consideration

Identify some of your *specific* ideas, attitudes, and behaviors that would be different if you had been reared in an Amish family. What do you like and dislike about Amish life? Why?

Sources: Aeppel 1996; Kephart and Zellner 2001; Kraybill 2002; Johnson-Weiner 2007; Scolforo 2008; Rifkin 2009.

The Microsociological Perspective: Social Interaction in Everyday Life

As you have seen, macrosociologists examine the broad features of society. Microsociologists, in contrast, examine narrower slices of social life. Their primary focus is *face-to-face interaction*—what people do when they are in one another's presence.

Symbolic Interaction

Symbolic interactionists are especially interested in the symbols people use. They want to know how people look at things and how this, in turn, affects their behavior and orientations to life. As you can see from the Down-to-Earth Sociology box below, jokes can be loaded with significant symbols. Of the many areas of social life symbolic interactionists study, let's look at stereotypes, personal space, eye contact, smiling, and body language.

Down-to-Earth Sociology
Looks: The Last Frontier for Socially Acceptable Discrimination?

A birthday card showing a close-up of an elderly person with sagging skin and missing teeth—asking to be kissed.

A college guy wearing a T-shirt that says, "Freshman girls. Get 'em while they're skinny."

A bumper sticker that reads: "BEER: Helping ugly people have sex since 1862."

A license plate holder that reads: "No Fat Chicks."*

Just harmless jokes, right? They show a sense of humor and might bring a few chuckles.

People used to joke openly about Jews, Poles, African Americans, the Irish, Asian Americans, people with disabilities, homosexuals, and women—among the long list of targets that used to be socially acceptable objects of public humor. We've all heard these jokes. "There was this black guy . . . this Chinese chick . . . this Jew . . . this Polish guy . . . this blonde . . . who walked into a . . ." With today's ethics, such jokes usually inhabit a subterranean area of our society.

Men still tell jokes about women—if no women are around. Whites tell jokes about blacks—if no blacks are present. Blacks tell jokes about whites—if no whites are within earshot. Except in a close circle of old friends, the jokes are told cautiously, as both the teller and the hearer know they aren't politically correct. But jokes about—and discrimination against—people who are fat, old, or ugly—these are still considered OK.

How can I say that?

Take a look at the greeting cards in your local grocery store. You won't find cards that are anti-Semitic or that depict people of color in demeaning but humorous situations. But you will find cards about people who are considered ugly, fat, or old.

"Looksism"—the last socially acceptable area of discrimination? Probably an overstatement. Gender is still a fair target, for you will find cards about women, even some depicting men's helplessness in the kitchen.

If the incipient movement to raise our sensitivities is successful, your children won't be able to fathom how you could have lived in a society that tolerated such humor.

For Your Consideration
Why do you think the ethics of joke telling have changed? Are we getting too sensitive?

*All examples from Berry 2007.

Stereotypes in Everyday Life.   You are familiar with how first impressions set the tone for interaction. When you first meet someone, you cannot help but notice certain features, especially the person's sex, race–ethnicity, age, and clothing. Despite your best intentions, your assumptions about these characteristics shape your first impressions. They also affect how you act toward that person—and, in turn, how that person acts toward you. These fascinating aspects of our social interaction are discussed in the Down-to-Earth Sociology box on the next page.

Personal Space.   We all surround ourselves with a "personal bubble" that we go to great lengths to protect. We open the bubble to intimates—to our friends, children, and parents—but we're careful to keep most people out of this space. In a crowded hallway between classes, we might walk with our books clasped in front of us (a strategy often chosen by females). When we stand in line, we make certain there is enough space so that we don't touch the person in front of us and aren't touched by the person behind us.

At times, we extend our personal space. In the library, for example, you might place your coat on the chair next to you—claiming that space for yourself even though you aren't using it. If you want to really extend your space, you might even spread books in front of the other chairs, keeping the whole table to yourself by giving the impression that others have just stepped away.

The amount of space that people prefer varies from one culture to another. South Americans, for example, like to be closer when they speak to others than do people reared in the United States. Anthropologist Edward Hall (1959; Hall and Hall 2007) recounts a conversation with a man from South America who had attended one of his lectures.

> He came to the front of the class at the end of the lecture. . . . We started out facing each other, and as he talked I became dimly aware that he was standing a little too close and that I was beginning to back up. Fortunately I was able to suppress my first impulse and remain stationary because there was nothing to communicate aggression in his behavior except the conversational distance. . . .
>
> By experimenting I was able to observe that as I moved away slightly, there was an associated shift in the pattern of interaction. He had more trouble expressing himself. If I shifted to where I felt comfortable (about twenty-one inches), he looked somewhat puzzled and hurt, almost as though he were saying, "Why is he acting that way? Here I am doing everything I can to talk to him in a friendly manner and he suddenly withdraws. Have I done anything wrong? Said something I shouldn't?" Having ascertained that distance had a direct effect on his conversation, I stood my ground, letting him set the distance.

As you can see, despite Hall's extensive knowledge of other cultures, he still felt uncomfortable in this conversation. He first interpreted the invasion of his personal space as

How people use space as they interact is studied by sociologists who have a microsociological focus. What do you see in common in these two photos?

Down-to-Earth Sociology
Beauty May Be Only Skin Deep, But Its Effects Go On Forever: Stereotypes in Everyday Life

Mark Snyder, a psychologist, wondered whether **stereotypes**—our assumptions of what people are like—might be self-fulfilling. He came up with an ingenious way to test this idea. He (1993) gave college men a Polaroid snapshot of a woman (supposedly taken just moments before) and told them that he would introduce them to her after they talked with her on the telephone. Actually, the photographs—showing either a pretty or a homely woman—had been prepared before the experiment began. The photo was *not* of the woman the men would talk to.

Stereotypes came into play immediately. As Snyder gave each man the photograph, he asked him what he thought the woman would be like. The men who saw the photograph of the attractive woman said that they expected to meet a poised, humorous, outgoing woman. The men who had been given a photo of the unattractive woman described her as awkward, serious, and unsociable.

The men's stereotypes influenced the way they spoke to the women on the telephone, who did *not* know about the photographs. The men who had seen the photograph of a pretty woman were warm, friendly, and humorous. This, in turn, affected the women they spoke to, for they responded in a warm, friendly, outgoing manner. And the men who had seen the photograph of a homely woman? On the phone, they were cold, reserved, and humorless, and the women they spoke to became cool, reserved, and humorless. Keep in mind that the women

did not know that their looks had been evaluated—and that the photographs were not even of them. In short, stereotypes tend to produce behaviors that match the stereotype. This principle is illustrated in Figure 4.3.

Beauty might be only skin deep, but it has real consequences (Katz 2007). Not only do pretty people get a pass in a lot of situations, but they also are likely to make more money. For example, advertising agencies with better-looking executives have higher revenues (Bosman et al. 1997; Pfann et al. 2000). Apparently, people are more willing to hire individuals whom they perceive as good-looking.

For Your Consideration

Stereotypes have no single, inevitable effect. They are not magical. People can resist stereotypes and change outcomes. However, these studies do illustrate that stereotypes deeply influence how we react to one another.

Instead of beauty, consider gender and race–ethnicity. How do they affect those who do the stereotyping and those who are stereotyped?

Physical attractiveness underlies much of our social interaction in everyday life. The experiment reviewed in this box illustrates how college men modified their interactions on the basis of attractiveness. How do you think women would modify their interactions if they were to meet the two men in these photographs? How about men? Would they change their interactions in the same way?

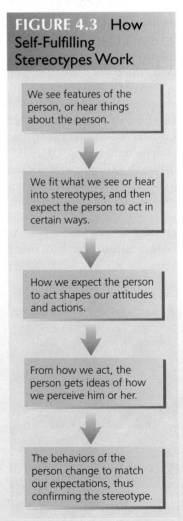

FIGURE 4.3   How Self-Fulfilling Stereotypes Work

We see features of the person, or hear things about the person.

↓

We fit what we see or hear into stereotypes, and then expect the person to act in certain ways.

↓

How we expect the person to act shapes our attitudes and actions.

↓

From how we act, the person gets ideas of how we perceive him or her.

↓

The behaviors of the person change to match our expectations, thus confirming the stereotype.

possible aggression, for people get close (and jut out their chins and chests) when they are hostile. But when he realized that this was not the case, Hall resisted his impulse to move.

After Hall (1969; Hall and Hall 2007) analyzed situations like this, he observed that North Americans use four different "distance zones."

1. *Intimate distance.* This is the zone that the South American unwittingly invaded. It extends to about 18 inches from our bodies. We reserve this space for comforting, protecting, hugging, intimate touching, and lovemaking.
2. *Personal distance.* This zone extends from 18 inches to 4 feet. We reserve it for friends and acquaintances and ordinary conversations. This is the zone in which Hall would have preferred speaking with the South American.
3. *Social distance.* This zone, extending out from us about 4 to 12 feet, marks impersonal or formal relationships. We use this zone for such things as job interviews.
4. *Public distance.* This zone, extending beyond 12 feet, marks even more formal relationships. It is used to separate dignitaries and public speakers from the general public.

Eye contact is a fascinating aspect of everyday life. We use fleeting eye contact for most of our interactions, such as those with clerks or people we pass in the hall between classes. Just as we reserve our close personal space for intimates, so, too, we reserve soft, lingering eye contact for them.

Eye Contact.   One way that we protect our personal bubble is by controlling eye contact. Letting someone gaze into our eyes—unless the person is an eye doctor—can be taken as a sign that we are attracted to that person, even as an invitation to intimacy. Wanting to become "the friendliest store in town," a chain of supermarkets in Illinois ordered its checkout clerks to make direct eye contact with each customer. Female clerks complained that male customers were taking their eye contact the wrong way, as an invitation to intimacy. Management said they were exaggerating. The clerks' reply was, "We know the kind of looks we're getting back from men," and they refused to make direct eye contact with them.

Smiling.   In the United States, we take it for granted that clerks will smile as they wait on us. But it isn't this way in all cultures. Apparently, Germans aren't used to smiling clerks, and when Wal-Mart expanded into Germany, it brought its American ways with it. The company ordered its German clerks to smile at their customers. They did—and the customers complained. The German customers interpreted the smiles as flirting (Samor et al. 2006).

Applied Body Language.   While we are still little children, we learn to interpret **body language,** the ways people use their bodies to give messages to others. This skill in interpreting facial expressions, posture, and gestures is essential for getting us through everyday life. Without it—as is the case for people with Asperger's syndrome—we wouldn't know how to react to others. It would even be difficult to know whether someone were serious or joking. This common and essential skill for traversing everyday life is now becoming one of the government's tools in its fight against terrorism. Because many of our body messages lie beneath our consciousness, airport personnel and interrogators are being trained to look for telltale facial signs—from a quick downturn of the mouth to rapid blinking—that might indicate nervousness or lying (Davis et al. 2002).

This is an interesting twist for an area of sociology that had been entirely theoretical. Let's now turn to dramaturgy, a special area of symbolic interactionism.

Dramaturgy: The Presentation of Self in Everyday Life

It was their big day, two years in the making. Jennifer Mackey wore a white wedding gown adorned with an 11-foot train and 24,000 seed pearls that she and her mother had sewn onto the dress. Next to her at the altar in Lexington, Kentucky, stood her intended, Jeffrey Degler, in black tie. They said their vows, then turned to gaze for a moment at the four hundred guests.

stereotype assumptions of what people are like, whether true or false

body language the ways in which people use their bodies to give messages to others

dramaturgy an approach, pioneered by Erving Goffman, in which social life is analyzed in terms of drama or the stage; also called *dramaturgical analysis*

impression management people's efforts to control the impressions that others receive of them

front stage places where we give performances

back stage places where people rest from their performances, discuss their presentations, and plan future performances

role performance the ways in which someone performs a role within the limits that the role provides; showing a particular "style" or "personality"

> That's when groomsman Daniel Mackey collapsed. As the shocked organist struggled to play Mendelssohn's "Wedding March," Mr. Mackey's unconscious body was dragged away, his feet striking—loudly—every step of the altar stairs.
>
> "I couldn't believe he would die at my wedding," the bride said. (Hughes 1990)

Sociologist Erving Goffman (1922–1982) added a new twist to microsociology when he recast the theatrical term **dramaturgy** into a sociological term. Goffman used the term to mean that social life is like a drama or a stage play: Birth ushers us onto the stage of everyday life, and our socialization consists of learning to perform on that stage. The self that we studied in the previous chapter lies at the center of our performances. We have ideas of how we want others to think of us, and we use our roles in everyday life to communicate those ideas. Goffman called these efforts to manage the impressions that others receive of us **impression management.**

Stages.   Everyday life, said Goffman, involves playing our assigned roles. We have **front stages** on which to perform them, as did Jennifer and Jeffrey. (By the way, Daniel Mackey didn't really die—he had just fainted.) But we don't have to look at weddings to find front stages. Everyday life is filled with them. Where your teacher lectures is a front stage. And if you wait until your parents are in a good mood to tell them some bad news, you are using a front stage. In fact, you spend most of your time on front stages, for a front stage is wherever you deliver your lines. We also have **back stages,** places where we can retreat and let our hair down. When you close the bathroom or bedroom door for privacy, for example, you are entering a back stage.

The same setting can serve as both a back and a front stage. For example, when you get into your car and look over your hair in the mirror or check your makeup, you are using the car as a back stage. But when you wave at friends or if you give that familiar gesture to someone who has just cut in front of you in traffic, you are using your car as a front stage.

Role Performance, Conflict, and Strain.   Everyday life brings with it many roles. As discussed earlier, the same person may be a student, a teenager, a shopper, a worker, and a date, as well as a daughter or a son. Although a role lays down the basic outline for a performance, it also allows a great deal of flexibility. The particular emphasis or interpretation that we give a role, our "style," is known as **role performance.** Consider your role as son or daughter. You may play the role of ideal daughter or son—being respectful, coming home at the hours your parents set, and so forth. Or this description may not even come close to your particular role performance.

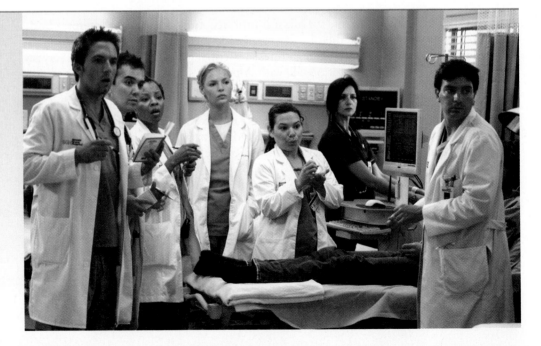

In *dramaturgy,* a specialty within sociology, social life is viewed as similar to the theater. In our everyday lives, we all are actors. Like those in the cast of *Grey's Anatomy,* we, too, perform roles, use props, and deliver lines to fellow actors—who, in turn, do the same.

Ordinarily, our statuses are separated sufficiently that we find minimal conflict between them. Occasionally, however, what is expected of us in one status (our role) is incompatible with what is expected of us in another status. This problem, known as **role conflict,** is illustrated in Figure 4.4, in which family, friendship, student, and work roles come crashing together. Usually, however, we manage to avoid role conflict by segregating our statuses, although doing so can require an intense juggling act.

Sometimes the *same* status contains incompatible roles, a conflict known as **role strain.** Suppose that you are exceptionally well prepared for a particular class assignment. Although the instructor asks an unusually difficult question, you find yourself knowing the answer when no one else does. If you want to raise your hand, yet don't want to make your fellow students look bad, you will experience role strain. As illustrated in Figure 4.4, the difference between role conflict and role strain is that role conflict is conflict *between roles,* while role strain is conflict *within* a role.

Sign-Vehicles. To communicate information about the self, we use three types of **sign-vehicles:** the social setting, our appearance, and our manner. The *social setting* is the place where the action unfolds. This is where the curtain goes up on your performance, where you find yourself on stage playing parts and delivering lines. A social setting might be an office, dorm, living room, church, gym, or bar. It is wherever you interact with others. Your social setting includes *scenery,* the furnishings you use to communicate messages, such as desks, blackboards, scoreboards, couches, and so on.

The second sign-vehicle is *appearance,* or how we look when we play our roles. Appearance includes *props,* which are like scenery except that they decorate the person rather than the setting. The teacher has books, lecture notes, and chalk, while the football player wears a costume called a uniform. Although few of us carry around a football, we all use makeup, hairstyles, and clothing to communicate messages about ourselves. Props and other aspects of appearance give us cues that help us navigate everyday life: By letting us know what to expect from others, props tell us how we should react. Think of the messages that props communicate. Some people use clothing to say they are college students, others to say they are older adults. Some use clothing to say they are clergy, others to say they are prostitutes. Similarly, people choose brands of cigarettes, liquor, and automobiles to convey messages about the self.

role conflict conflicts that someone feels *between* roles because the expectations attached to one role are incompatible with the expectations of another role

role strain conflicts that someone feels *within* a role

sign-vehicle a term used by Goffman to refer to how people use social setting, appearance, and manner to communicate information about the self

---

FIGURE 4.4 Role Strain and Role Conflict

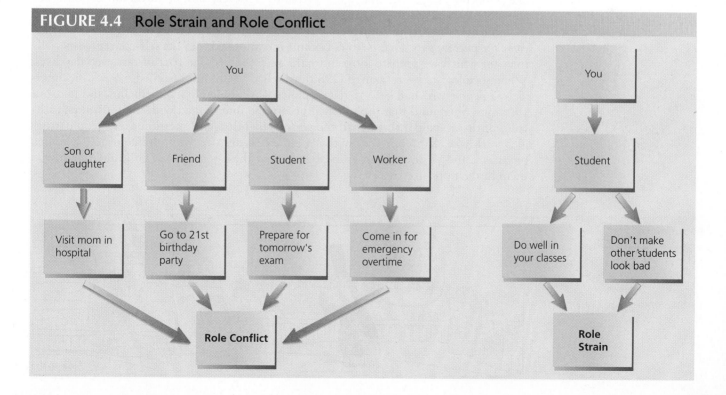

teamwork the collaboration of two or more people to manage impressions jointly

face-saving behavior techniques used to salvage a performance (interaction) that is going sour

Our body is an especially important sign-vehicle, its shape proclaiming messages about the self. The messages that are attached to various shapes change over time, but, as explored in the Mass Media box on the next page, thinness currently screams desirability.

The third sign-vehicle is *manner*, the attitudes we show as we play our roles. We use manner to communicate information about our feelings and moods. If we show anger or indifference, sincerity or good humor, for example, we indicate to others what they can expect of us as we play our roles.

Teamwork.   Being a good role player brings positive recognition from others, something we all covet. To accomplish this, we use **teamwork**—two or more people working together to help a performance come off as planned. If you laugh at your boss's jokes, even though you don't find them funny, you are doing teamwork to help your boss give a good performance.

If a performance doesn't come off quite right, the team might try to save it by using **face-saving behavior.**

> Suppose your teacher is about to make an important point. Suppose also that her lecturing has been outstanding and the class is hanging on every word. Just as she pauses for emphasis, her stomach lets out a loud growl. She might then use a face-saving technique by remarking, "I was so busy preparing for class that I didn't get breakfast this morning."

It is more likely, however, that both the teacher and class will simply ignore the sound, giving the impression that no one heard a thing—a face-saving technique called *studied nonobservance*. This allows the teacher to make the point or, as Goffman would say, it allows the performance to go on.

Becoming the Roles We Play

> Have you ever noticed how some clothing simply doesn't "feel" right for certain occasions? Have you ever changed your mind about something you were wearing and decided to change your clothing? Or maybe you just switched shirts or added a necklace?

What you were doing was fine-tuning the impressions you wanted to make. Ordinarily, we are not this aware that we're working on impressions. We become so used to the roles we play in everyday life that we tend to think we are "just doing" things, not that we are like actors on a stage who manage impressions. Yet every time we dress for school, or for any other activity, we are preparing for impression management.

Some new roles are uncomfortable at first, but after we get used to them *we tend to become the roles we play.* That is, roles become incorporated into the self-concept, especially roles for which we prepare long and hard and that become part of our everyday lives. When sociologist Helen Ebaugh (1988), who had been a nun, studied *role exit,* she interviewed people who had left marriages, police work, the military, medicine, and religious vocations. She found that the role had become so intertwined with the individual's self-concept that leaving it threatened the person's identity. The question these people struggled with was "Who am I, now that I am not a nun (or wife, police officer, colonel, physician, and so on)?" Even years after leaving these roles, many continue to perform them in their dreams.

Both individuals and organizations do *impression management,* trying to communicate messages about the self (or organization) that best meets their goals. At times, these efforts fail.

MASS MEDIA In SOCIAL LIFE

You Can't Be Thin Enough: Body Images and the Mass Media

When you stand before a mirror, do you like what you see? To make your body more attractive, do you watch your weight or work out? You have ideas about what you should look like. Where did you get them?

TV and magazine ads keep pounding home the message that our bodies aren't good enough, that we've got to improve them. The way to improve them, of course, is to buy the advertised products: hair extensions, padded bras, diet programs, anti-aging products, and exercise equipment. Muscular hulks show off machines that magically produce "six-pack abs" and incredible biceps—in just a few minutes a day. Female movie stars go through tough workouts without even breaking into a sweat. Women and men get the feeling that attractive members of the opposite sex will flock to them if they purchase that wonder-working workout machine.

Although we try to shrug off such messages, knowing that they are designed to sell products, the messages penetrate our thinking and feelings, helping to shape ideal images of how we "ought" to look. Those models so attractively clothed and coiffed as they walk down the runway, could they be any thinner? For women, the message is clear: You can't be thin enough. The men's message is also clear: You can't be muscular enough.

With impossibly shaped models at *Victoria's Secret* and skinny models showing off the latest fashions in *Vogue* and *Seventeen*, half of U.S. adolescent girls feel fat and count calories (Grabe et al. 2008). Some teens even call the plastic surgeon. Anxious lest their child violate peer ideals and trail behind in her race for popularity, parents foot the bill. Some parents pay $25,000 just to give their daughters a flatter tummy (Gross 1998).

The thinness craze has moved to the East, where glossy magazines feature skinny models. Not limited by our rules, advertisers in Japan and China push a soap that supposedly "sucks up fat through the skin's pores" (Marshall 1995). What a dream product! After all, even though our TV models smile as they go through their paces, those exercise machines do look like a lot of hard work.

And attractiveness does pay off. U.S. economists studied physical attractiveness and earnings. The result? "Good-looking" men and women earn the most, "average-looking" men and women earn more than "plain" people, and the "ugly" earn the least (Hamermesh and

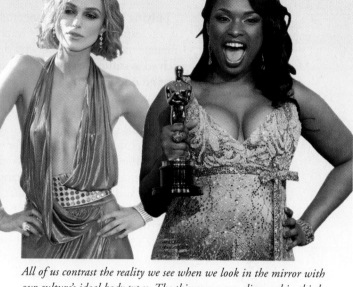

All of us contrast the reality we see when we look in the mirror with our culture's ideal body types. The thinness craze, discussed in this box, encourages some people to extremes, as with Keira Knightley. It also makes it difficult for larger people to have positive self-images. Overcoming this difficulty, Jennifer Hudson is in the forefront of promoting an alternative image.

Biddle 1994). In Europe, too, the more attractive workers earn more (Brunello and D'Hombres 2007). Then there is that potent cash advantage that "attractive" women have: They attract and marry higher-earning men (Kanazawa and Kovar 2004).

More popularity *and* more money? Maybe you can't be thin enough after all. Maybe those exercise machines are a good investment. If only we could catch up with the Japanese and develop a soap that would suck the fat right out of our pores. You can practically hear the jingle now.

For Your Consideration

What image do you have of your body? How do cultural expectations of "ideal" bodies underlie your image? Can you recall any advertisements or television programs that have affected your body image?

Most advertising and television programs that focus on weight are directed at women. Women are more likely than men to be dissatisfied with their bodies and to have eating disorders (Honeycutt 1995; Hill 2006). Do you think that the targeting of women in advertising creates these attitudes and behaviors? Or do you think that these attitudes and behaviors would exist even if there were no such ads? Why?

ethnomethodology the study of how people use background assumptions to make sense out of life

background assumption a deeply embedded common understanding of how the world operates and of how people ought to act

A statement by one of my respondents illustrates how roles become part of the person and linger even after the individual leaves them:

> After I left the ministry, I felt like a fish out of water. Wearing that backward collar had become a part of me. It was especially strange on Sunday mornings when I'd listen to someone else give the sermon. I knew that I should be up there preaching. I felt as though I had left God.

Applying Impression Management.   I can just hear someone say, "Impression management is interesting, but is it really important?" In fact, it is so significant that the right impression management can make a vital difference in your career. To be promoted, you must be perceived as someone who *should* be promoted. You must appear dominant. You certainly cannot go unnoticed. But how you manage this impression is crucial. If a female executive tries to appear dominant by wearing loud clothing, using garish makeup, and cursing, this will get her noticed—but it will not put her on the path to promotion. How, then, can she exhibit dominance in the right way? To help women walk this fine line between femininity and dominance, career counselors advise women on fine details of impression management. Here are four things they recommend—clothing that doesn't wrinkle, makeup that doesn't have to be reapplied during the day, placing one's hands on the table during executive sessions, not in the lap, and carrying a purse that looks more like a briefcase (Needham 2006; Brinkley 2008).

Male or female, in your own life you will have to walk this thin line, finding the best way to manage impressions in order to further your career. Much success in the work world depends not on what you actually know but, instead, on your ability to give the impression that you know what you should know.

Ethnomethodology: Uncovering Background Assumptions

Certainly one of the strangest words in sociology is *ethnomethodology.* To better understand this term, consider the word's three basic components. *Ethno* means "folk" or "people"; *method* means how people do something; *ology* means "the study of." Putting them together, then, *ethno–method–ology* means "the study of how people do things." Specifically, **ethnomethodology** is the study of how people use commonsense understandings to make sense of life.

Let's suppose that during a routine office visit, your doctor remarks that your hair is rather long, then takes out a pair of scissors and starts to give you a haircut. You would feel strange about this, for your doctor would be violating **background assumptions**— your ideas about the way life is and the way things ought to work. These assumptions, which lie at the root of everyday life, are so deeply embedded in our consciousness that we are seldom aware of them, and most of us fulfill them unquestioningly. Thus, your doctor does not offer you a haircut, even if he or she is good at cutting hair and you need one!

The founder of ethnomethodology, sociologist Harold Garfinkel, conducted some exercises designed to reveal our background assumptions. Garfinkel (1967, 2002) asked his students to act as though they did not understand the basic rules of social life. Some tried to bargain with supermarket clerks; others would inch close to people and stare directly at them. They were met with surprise, bewilderment, even anger. In one exercise, Garfinkel asked students to act as though they were boarders in their own homes. They addressed their parents as "Mr." and "Mrs.," asked permission to use the bathroom, sat stiffly, were courteous, and spoke only when spoken to. As you can imagine, the other family members didn't know what to make of this (Garfinkel 1967):

All of us have *background assumptions,* deeply ingrained assumptions of how the world operates. How do you think the background assumptions of this Londoner differ from this Ecuadoran shaman, who is performing a healing ceremony to rid London of its evil spirits?

They vigorously sought to make the strange actions intelligible and to restore the situation to normal appearances. Reports (by the students) were filled with accounts of astonishment, bewilderment, shock, anxiety, embarrassment, and anger, and with charges by various family members that the student was mean, inconsiderate, selfish, nasty, or impolite. Family members demanded explanations: What's the matter? What's gotten into you? . . . Are you sick? . . . Are you out of your mind or are you just stupid?

In another exercise, Garfinkel asked students to take words and phrases literally. When a student asked his girlfriend what she meant when she said that she had a flat tire, she said:

What do you mean, "What do you mean?" A flat tire is a flat tire. That is what I meant. Nothing special. What a crazy question!

Another conversation went like this:

ACQUAINTANCE: How are you?
STUDENT: How am I in regard to what? My health, my finances, my schoolwork, my peace of mind, my . . . ?
ACQUAINTANCE: (red in the face): Look! I was just trying to be polite. Frankly, I don't give a damn how you are.

Students who are asked to break background assumptions can be highly creative. The young children of one of my students were surprised one morning when they came down for breakfast to find a sheet spread across the living room floor. On it were dishes, silverware, lit candles—and bowls of ice cream. They, too, wondered what was going on, but they dug eagerly into the ice cream before their mother could change her mind.

This is a risky assignment to give students, however, for breaking some background assumptions can make people suspicious. When a colleague of mine gave this assignment, a couple of his students began to wash dollar bills in a laundromat. By the time they put the bills in the dryer, the police had arrived.

In Sum: Ethnomethodologists explore *background assumptions,* the taken-for-granted ideas about the world that underlie our behavior. Most of these assumptions, or basic rules of social life, are unstated. We learn them as we learn our culture, and we violate them only with risk. Deeply embedded in our minds, they give us basic directions for living everyday life.

The Social Construction of Reality

On a visit to Morocco, in northern Africa, I decided to buy a watermelon. When I indicated to the street vendor that the knife he was going to use to cut the watermelon was dirty (encrusted with filth would be more apt), he was very obliging. He immediately bent down and began to swish the knife in a puddle on the street. I shuddered as I looked at the passing burros that were urinating and defecating as they went by. Quickly, I indicated by gesture that I preferred my melon uncut after all.

"If people define situations as real, they are real in their consequences," said sociologists W. I. and Dorothy S. Thomas in what has become known as *the definition of the situation,* or the **Thomas theorem.** For that vendor of watermelons, germs did not exist. For me, they did. And each of us acted according to our definition of the situation. My perception and behavior did not come from the fact that germs are real but, rather, from *my having grown up in a society that teaches they are real.* Microbes, of course, *objectively* exist, and whether or not germs are part of our thought world makes no difference as to whether we are infected by them. Our behavior, however, does not depend on the *objective* existence of something but, rather, on our *subjective interpretation,* on what sociologists call our *definition of reality.* In other words, it is not the reality of microbes that impresses itself on us, but society that impresses the reality of microbes on us.

Let's consider another example. Do you remember the identical twins, Oskar and Jack, who grew up so differently? As discussed on page 65, Jack was reared in Trinidad and learned to hate Hitler, while Oskar was reared in Germany and learned to love Hitler. As you can

Thomas theorem William I. and Dorothy S. Thomas' classic formulation of the definition of the situation: "If people define situations as real, they are real in their consequences."

**social construction of
reality** the use of background
assumptions and life experiences to define what is real

see, what Hitler meant to Oskar and Jack (and what he means to us) depends not on Hitler's acts, but, rather, on how we view his acts—that is, on our definition of the situation.

Sociologists call this the **social construction of reality.** Our society, or the social groups to which we belong, holds particular views of life. From our groups (the *social* part of this process), we learn ways of looking at life—whether that be our view of Hitler or Osama bin Laden (they're good, they're evil), germs (they exist, they don't exist), or *anything else in life.* In short, through our interaction with others, we *construct reality;* that is, we learn ways of interpreting our experiences in life.

Gynecological Examinations.   To better understand the social construction of reality, let's consider what I learned when I interviewed a gynecological nurse who had been present at about 14,000 vaginal examinations. I focused on *how doctors construct social reality in order to define this examination as nonsexual* (Henslin and Biggs 1971/2007). It became apparent that the pelvic examination unfolds much as a stage play does. I will use "he" to refer to the physician because only male physicians were part of this study. Perhaps the results would be different with women gynecologists.

> *Scene 1 (the patient as person)* In this scene, the doctor maintains eye contact with his patient, calls her by name, and discusses her problems in a professional manner. If he decides that a vaginal examination is necessary, he tells a nurse, "Pelvic in room 1." By this statement, he is announcing that a major change will occur in the next scene.

> *Scene 2 (from person to pelvic)* This scene is the depersonalizing stage. In line with the doctor's announcement, the patient begins the transition from a "person" to a "pelvic." The doctor leaves the room, and a female nurse enters to help the patient make the transition. The nurse prepares the "props" for the coming examination and answers any questions the woman might have.

What occurs at this point is essential for the social construction of reality, for *the doctor's absence removes even the suggestion of sexuality.* To undress in front of him could suggest either a striptease or intimacy, thus undermining the reality that the team is so carefully defining: that of nonsexuality.

The patient, too, wants to remove any hint of sexuality, and during this scene she may express concern about what to do with her panties. Some mutter to the nurse, "I don't want him to see these." Most women solve the problem by either slipping their panties under their other clothes or placing them in their purse.

> *Scene 3 (the person as pelvic)* This scene opens when the doctor enters the room. Before him is a woman lying on a table, her feet in stirrups, her knees tightly together, and her body covered by a drape sheet. The doctor seats himself on a low stool before the woman and says, "Let your knees fall apart" (rather than the sexually loaded "Spread your legs"), and begins the examination.

The drape sheet is crucial in this process of desexualization, for it *dissociates the pelvic area from the person:* Leaning forward and with the drape sheet above his head, the physician can see only the vagina, not the patient's face. Thus dissociated from the individual, the vagina is transformed dramaturgically into an object of analysis. If the doctor examines the patient's breasts, he also dissociates them from her person by examining them one at a time, with a towel covering the unexamined breast. Like the vagina, each breast becomes an isolated item dissociated from the person.

In this third scene, the patient cooperates in being an object, becoming, for all practical purposes, a pelvis to be examined. She withdraws eye contact from the doctor, and usually from the nurse, is likely to stare at the wall or at the ceiling, and avoids initiating conversation.

> *Scene 4 (from pelvic to person)* In this scene, the patient becomes "repersonalized." The doctor has left the examining room; the patient dresses and fixes her hair and makeup. Her reemergence as a person is indicated by such statements to the nurse as, "My dress isn't too wrinkled, is it?" showing a need for reassurance that the metamorphosis from "pelvic" back to "person" has been completed satisfactorily.

> *Scene 5 (the patient as person)* In this final scene, the patient is once again treated as a person rather than as an object. The doctor makes eye contact with her and addresses her by

name. She, too, makes eye contact with the doctor, and the usual middle-class interaction patterns are followed. She has been fully restored.

In Sum: To an outsider to our culture, the custom of women going to a male stranger for a vaginal examination might seem bizarre. But not to us. We learn that pelvic examinations are nonsexual. To sustain this definition requires teamwork—patients, doctors, and nurses working together to *socially construct reality*.

It is not just pelvic examinations or our views of microbes that make up our definitions of reality. Rather, *our behavior depends on how we define reality*. Our definitions (or constructions) provide the basis for what we do and how we feel about life. To understand human behavior, then, we must know how people define reality.

The Need for Both Macrosociology and Microsociology

As was noted earlier, both microsociology and macrosociology make vital contributions to our understanding of human behavior. Our understanding of social life would be vastly incomplete without one or the other. The photo essay on the next two pages should help to make clear why we need *both* perspectives.

To illustrate this point, let's consider two groups of high school boys studied by sociologist William Chambliss (1973/2007). Both groups attended Hanibal High School. In one group were eight middle-class boys who came from "good" families and were perceived by the community as "going somewhere." Chambliss calls this group the "Saints." The other group consisted of six lower-class boys who were seen as headed down a dead-end road. Chambliss calls this group the "Roughnecks."

Boys in both groups skipped school, got drunk, and did a lot of fighting and vandalism. The Saints were actually somewhat more delinquent, for they were truant more often and engaged in more vandalism. Yet the Saints had a good reputation, while the Roughnecks were seen by teachers, the police, and the general community as no good and headed for trouble.

The boys' reputations set them on distinct paths. Seven of the eight Saints went on to graduate from college. Three studied for advanced degrees: One finished law school and became active in state politics, one finished medical school, and one went on to earn a Ph.D. The four other college graduates entered managerial or executive training programs with large firms. After his parents divorced, one Saint failed to graduate from high school on time and had to repeat his senior year. Although this boy tried to go to college by attending night school, he never finished. He was unemployed the last time Chambliss saw him.

In contrast, only four of the Roughnecks finished high school. Two of these boys did exceptionally well in sports and were awarded athletic scholarships to college. They both graduated from college and became high school coaches. Of the two others who graduated from high school, one became a small-time gambler and the other disappeared "up north," where he was last reported to be driving a truck. The two who did not complete high school were convicted of separate murders and sent to prison.

To understand what happened to the Saints and the Roughnecks, we need to grasp *both* social structure and social interaction. Using *macrosociology*, we can place these boys within the larger framework of the U.S. social class system. This reveals how opportunities open or close to people depending on their social class and how people learn different goals as they grow up in different groups. We can then use *microsociology* to follow their everyday lives. We can see how the Saints manipulated their "good" reputations to skip classes and how their access to automobiles allowed them to protect those reputations by spreading their trouble-making around different communities. In contrast, the Roughnecks, who did not have cars, were highly visible. Their lawbreaking, which was limited to a small area, readily came to the attention of the community. Microsociology also reveals how their reputations opened doors of opportunity to the first group of boys while closing them to the other.

It is clear that we need both kinds of sociology, and both are stressed in the following chapters.

When a **Tornado Strikes:**

Social Organization Following a Natural Disaster

as I was watching television on March 20, **2003, I heard** a report that a tornado had hit Camilla, Georgia. "Like a big lawn mower," the report said, it had cut a path of destruction through this little town. In its fury, the tornado had left behind six dead and about 200 injured.

From sociological studies of natural disasters, I knew that immediately after the initial shock the survivors of natural disasters work together to try to restore order to their disrupted lives. I wanted to see this restructuring process firsthand. The next morning, I took off for Georgia.

These photos, taken the day after the tornado struck, tell the story of people in the midst of trying to put their lives back together. I was impressed at how little time people spent commiserating about their misfortune and how quickly they took practical steps to restore their lives.

As you look at these photos, try to determine why you need both microsociology and macrosociology to understand what occurs after a natural disaster.

After making sure that their loved ones are safe, one of the next steps people take is to recover their possessions. The cooperation that emerges among people, as documented in the sociological literature on natural disasters, is illustrated here.

© James M. Henslin, all photos

◀ The owners of this house invited me inside to see what the tornado had done to their home. In what had been her dining room, this woman is trying to salvage whatever she can from the rubble. She and her family survived by taking refuge in the bathroom. They had been there only five seconds, she said, when the tornado struck.

▲ In addition to the inquiring sociologist, television teams also were interviewing survivors and photographing the damage. This was the second time in just three years that a tornado had hit this neighborhood.

▲ No building or social institution escapes a tornado as it follows its path of destruction. Just the night before, members of this church had held evening worship service. After the tornado, someone mounted a U.S. flag on top of the cross, symbolic of the church members' patriotism and religiosity—and of their enduring hope.

▲ Personal relationships are essential in putting lives together. Consequently, reminders of these relationships are one of the main possessions that people attempt to salvage. This young man, having just recovered the family photo album, is eagerly reviewing the photos.

ormal organizations also help the survivors of natural
sters recover. In this neighborhood, I saw represen-
es of insurance companies, the police, the fire depart-
t, and an electrical co-op. The Salvation Army brought
ls to the neighborhood.

▲ For children, family photos are not as important as toys. This girl has managed to salvage a favorite toy, which will help anchor her to her previous life.

▲ Like electricity and gas, cable television is also restored as soon as possible.

SUMMARY *and* REVIEW

Levels of Sociological Analysis

What two levels of analysis do sociologists use?

Sociologists use macrosociological and microsociological levels of analysis. In **macrosociology,** the focus is placed on large-scale features of social life, while in **microsociology,** the focus is on **social interaction.** Functionalists and conflict theorists tend to use a macrosociological approach, while symbolic interactionists are more likely to use a microsociological approach. P. 96.

The Macrosociological Perspective: Social Structure

How does social structure influence our behavior?

The term **social structure** refers to the social envelope that surrounds us and establishes limits on our behavior. Social structure consists of culture, social class, social statuses, roles, groups, and social institutions. Our location in the social structure underlies our perceptions, attitudes, and behaviors.

Culture lays the broadest framework, while **social class** divides people according to income, education, and occupational prestige. Each of us receives **ascribed statuses** at birth; later we add **achieved statuses.** Our behaviors and orientations are further influenced by the **roles** we play, the **groups** to which we belong, and our experiences with social institutions. These components of society work together to help maintain social order. Pp. 97–102.

Social Institutions

What are social institutions?

Social institutions are the standard ways that a society develops to meet its basic needs. As summarized in Figure 4.2 (page 103), industrial and postindustrial societies have ten social institutions—the family, religion, education, economy, medicine, politics, law, science, the military, and the mass media. From the functionalist perspective, social institutions meet universal group needs, or *functional requisites.* Conflict theorists stress how society's elites use social institutions to maintain their privileged positions. Pp. 102–105.

What holds society together?

According to Emile Durkheim, in agricultural societies people are united by **mechanical solidarity** (having similar views and feelings). With industrialization comes **organic solidarity** (people depend on one another to do their more specialized jobs). Ferdinand Tönnies pointed out that the informal means of control in *Gemeinschaft* (small, intimate) societies are replaced by formal mechanisms in *Gesellschaft* (larger, more impersonal) societies. Pp. 105–107.

The Microsociological Perspective: Social Interaction in Everyday Life

What is the focus of symbolic interactionism?

In contrast to functionalists and conflict theorists, who as macrosociologists focus on the "big picture," symbolic interactionists tend to be microsociologists who focus on face-to-face social interaction. Symbolic interactionists analyze how people define their worlds, and how their definitions, in turn, influence their behavior. P. 108.

How do stereotypes affect social interaction?

Stereotypes are assumptions of what people are like. When we first meet people, we classify them according to our perceptions of their visible characteristics. Our ideas about those characteristics guide our behavior toward them. Our behavior, in turn, may influence them to behave in ways that reinforce our stereotypes. Pp. 109–110.

Do all human groups share a similar sense of personal space?

In examining how people use physical space, symbolic interactionists stress that we surround ourselves with a "personal bubble" that we carefully protect. People from different cultures use "personal bubbles" of varying sizes, so the answer to the question is no. Americans typically use four different "distance zones": intimate, personal, social, and public. Pp. 110–111.

What is dramaturgy?

Erving Goffman developed **dramaturgy** (or dramaturgical analysis), in which everyday life is analyzed in terms of the stage. At the core of this analysis is **impression management,** our attempts to control the impressions we make on others. For this, we use the **sign-vehicles** of setting, appearance, and manner. Our performances often call for **teamwork** and **face-saving behavior.** Pp. 111–116.

What is the social construction of reality?

The phrase **the social construction of reality** refers to how we construct our views of the world, which, in turn, underlie our actions. **Ethnomethodology** is the study of how people make sense of everyday life. Ethnomethodologists try to uncover **background assumptions,** our basic ideas about the way life is. Pp. 116–119.

The Need for Both Macrosociology and Microsociology

Why are both levels of analysis necessary?

Because each focuses on different aspects of the human experience, both microsociology and macrosociology are necessary for us to understand social life. P. 119.

THINKING CRITICALLY *ABOUT* Chapter 4

1. The major components of social structure are culture, social class, social status, roles, groups, and social institutions. Use social structure to explain why Native Americans have such a low rate of college graduation. (See Table 12.3 on page 352.)

2. Dramaturgy is a form of microsociology. Use dramaturgy to analyze a situation with which you are intimately familiar

(such as interaction with your family or friends or in one of your college classes).

3. To illustrate why we need both macrosociology and microsociology to understand social life, analyze the situation of a student getting kicked out of college.

ADDITIONAL RESOURCES

What can you find in MySocLab? mysoclab www.mysoclab.com

- Complete Ebook
- Practice Tests and Video and Audio activities
- Mapping and Data Analysis exercises

- Sociology in the News
- Classic Readings in Sociology
- Research and Writing advice

Where Can I Read More on This Topic?

Suggested readings for this chapter are listed at the back of this book.

chapter 5

How Sociologists
Do Research

South Korea

C indy Hudo, a 21-year-old mother of two in Charleston, South Carolina, who was charged with the murder of her husband, Buba, said:

I start in the car, and I get down the road, and I see Buba walking, and he's real mad. . . . I pull over, you know, and [I said] "I didn't know to pick you up. You know, I'm sorry." And he didn't even say nothing to me. He just started hitting on me. And that's all I wanted to do, was just get home, because I was just self-conscious. I don't want nobody to see him hitting me, because I didn't want him to look bad.

> "I don't want nobody to see him hitting me, because I didn't want him to look bad."

I had to go to work in a half-hour, because I was working a double-shift. And he told me I had forty minutes to get all my furniture out of the house and get my clothes and be out or he was going to throw them out. And I was sitting there, because I could talk him down. You know, because I didn't want to leave him. I just talked to him. I said, "Buba, I don't want to leave." I said, "This is my house." And then he told me . . . (unclear) . . . "my kids." And I said, "No, you're not taking my kids from me. That's too much." And so I said, "Just let me leave. Just let me take the kids. And, you know I'll go, and you know, I won't keep the kids from you or nothing like that." And he said, "I'm going to take them, and you're getting out."

[After they went inside their trailer, Buba threatened to shoot Cindy. He loaded a shotgun, pointed it at her, and said]: "The only way you're going to get out of this is if you kill me, and I'll—I'll kill you." [Buba gave me the shotgun and] turned around and walked right down the hall, because he knew I wouldn't do nothing. And I just sat there a minute. And I don't know what happened. I just, you know, I went to the bedroom, and I seen him laying there, and I just shot him. He moved. I shot him again because I thought he was going to get up again. . . .

I loved him too much. And I just wanted to help him.

Source: Transcript, ABC Television, *20/20,* October 18, 1979.

What Is a Valid Sociological Topic?

Sociologists do research on just about every area of human behavior. On the macro level, they study such broad matters as race relations (Schaefer 2008), the military (Caforio 2006), and multinational corporations (Kristensen and Morgan 2006). On the micro level, they study such individualistic matters as pelvic examinations (Henslin and Biggs 1971/2007), how people interact on street corners (Whyte 1989, 2001), and even shyness (Scott 2006). Sociologists study priests and prostitutes, cops and criminals, as well as all kinds of people in between. In fact, no human behavior is ineligible for sociological scrutiny—whether that behavior is routine or unusual, respectable or reprehensible.

What happened to Cindy and Buba, then, is also a valid topic of sociological research. But exactly *how* would you research spouse abuse? As we look at how sociologists do research, we shall try to answer this question.

Common Sense and the Need for Sociological Research

First, why do we need sociological research? Why can't we simply depend on common sense, on "what everyone knows"? As noted in Chapter 1 (page 8), commonsense ideas may or may not be true. Common sense, for example, tells us that spouse abuse has a significant impact on the lives of the people who are abused.

Although this particular idea is accurate, we need research to test commonsense ideas, because not all such ideas are true. After all, common sense also tells us that if a woman is abused, she will pack up and leave her husband. Research, however, shows that the reality of abuse is much more complicated than this. Some women do leave right away, some even after the first incident of abuse. For a variety of reasons, however, some women suffer abuse for years. The main reason is that they feel trapped and don't perceive any viable alternatives.

This brings us to the need for sociological research, for we may want to know why some women put up with abuse, while others don't. Or we may want to know something entirely different, such as why men are more likely to be the abusers. Or why some people abuse the people they say they love.

In order to answer a question, we need to move beyond guesswork and common sense. We want to *know* what is really going on. To find out, sociologists do research on about every aspect of social life. Let's look at how they do their research.

A Research Model

As shown in Figure 5.1 on the next page, scientific research follows eight basic steps. This is an ideal model, however, and in the real world of research some of these steps may run together. Some may even be omitted.

1. Selecting a Topic

The first step is to select a topic. What do you want to know more about? Many sociologists simply follow their curiosity, their drive to learn more about social life. They become interested in a particular topic and they pursue it, as I did in studying the homeless. Some sociologists choose a topic because funding is available for that topic, others because a social problem such as domestic violence is in the news and they want to help people better understand it—and perhaps to help solve it. Let's use spouse abuse as our example.

Because sociologists find all human behavior to be valid research topics, their research runs from the unusual to the routines of everyday life. Their studies range from broad scale social change, such as the globalization of capitalism, to smaller scale social interaction, such as people having fun.

2. Defining the Problem

The second step is to define the problem, to specify what you want to learn about the topic. My interest in the homeless increased until I wanted to learn about homelessness across the nation. Ordinarily, sociologists' interests are much more focused than this; they examine some specific aspect of the topic, such as how homeless people survive on the streets. In the case of spouse abuse, sociologists may want to know whether violent and nonviolent husbands have different work experiences. Or they may want to learn what can be done to reduce spouse abuse.

The topics that sociologists study are far-ranging. In fact, sociologists do research on any aspect of social life that interests them. The "problem" can be as earth shattering as trying to figure out why nations would ever contemplate nuclear war, as perplexing as understanding how "good" people can torture and kill (see Chapter 15), or as simple as wanting to find out why Native Americans like Westerns (see the Mass Media in Social Life box on page 53).

3. Reviewing the Literature

You must read what has been published on your topic. This helps you to narrow the problem, identify areas that are already known, and learn what areas need to be researched. Reviewing the literature may also help you to pinpoint the questions that you will ask. You might even find out that the problem has been answered already. You don't want to waste your time rediscovering what is already known.

4. Formulating a Hypothesis

The fourth step is to formulate a **hypothesis,** a statement of what you expect to find according to predictions from a theory. A hypothesis predicts a relationship between or among **variables,** factors that change, or vary, from one person or situation to another. For example, the statement "Men who are more socially isolated are more likely to abuse their wives than are men who are more socially integrated" is a hypothesis.

Your hypothesis will need **operational definitions**—that is, precise ways to measure the variables. In this example, you would need operational definitions for three variables: social isolation, social integration, and spouse abuse.

5. Choosing a Research Method

You then need to decide how you are going to collect your data. Sociologists use seven basic **research methods** (or *research designs*), which are outlined in the next section. You will want to choose the research method that will best answer your particular questions.

6. Collecting the Data

When you gather your data, you have to take care to assure their **validity;** that is, your operational definitions must measure what they are intended to measure. In this case, you must be certain that you really are measuring social isolation, social integration, and spouse abuse—and not something else. Spouse abuse, for example, seems to be obvious. Yet what some people consider to be abuse is not regarded as abuse by others. Which definition will you choose? In other words, you must state your operational definitions so precisely that no one has any question about what you are measuring.

You must also be sure that your data are reliable. **Reliability** means that if other researchers use your operational definitions, their findings will be consistent with yours. If

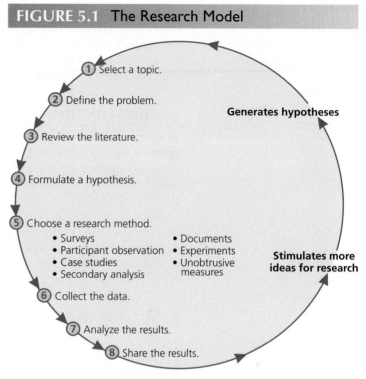

FIGURE 5.1   The Research Model

1. Select a topic.
2. Define the problem.
3. Review the literature.
4. Formulate a hypothesis.
5. Choose a research method.
   - Surveys
   - Participant observation
   - Case studies
   - Secondary analysis
   - Documents
   - Experiments
   - Unobtrusive measures
6. Collect the data.
7. Analyze the results.
8. Share the results.

Generates hypotheses

Stimulates more ideas for research

Source: Modification of Figure 2.2 of Schaeffer 1989.

hypothesis a statement of how variables are expected to be related to one another, often according to predictions from a theory

variable a factor thought to be significant for human behavior, which can vary (or change) from one case to another

operational definition the way in which a researcher measures a variable

research method (or research design) one of seven procedures that sociologists use to collect data: surveys, participant observation, case studies, secondary analysis, documents, experiments, and unobtrusive measures

validity the extent to which an operational definition measures what it is intended to measure

reliability the extent to which research produces consistent or dependable results

replication the repetition of a study in order to test its findings

survey the collection of data by having people answer a series of questions

your operational definitions are sloppy, husbands who have committed the same act of violence might be included in some research but excluded from other studies. You would end up with erratic results. If you show a 10 percent rate of spouse abuse, for example, but another researcher using the same operational definitions determines it to be 30 percent, the research is unreliable.

7. Analyzing the Results

You can choose from a variety of techniques to analyze the data you gather. If a hypothesis has been part of your research, now is when you will test it. (Some research, especially participant observation and case studies, has no hypothesis. You may know so little about the setting you are going to research that you cannot even specify the variables in advance.)

With today's software, in just seconds you can run tests on your data that used to take days or even weeks to perform. Two basic programs that sociologists and many undergraduates use are Microcase and the Statistical Package for the Social Sciences (SPSS). Some software, such as the Methodologist's Toolchest, provides advice about collecting data and even about ethical issues.

8. Sharing the Results

To wrap up your research, you will write a report to share your findings with the scientific community. You will review how you did your research, including your operational definitions. You will also show how your findings fit in with what has already been published on the topic and how they support or disagree with the theories that apply to your topic.

When research is published, usually in a scientific journal or a book, it "belongs" to the scientific community. Your findings will be available for **replication;** that is, others can repeat your study to see if they come up with similar results. As Table 5.1 on the next page illustrates, sociologists often summarize their findings in tables. As finding is added to finding, scientific knowledge builds.

Let's look in greater detail at the fifth step to see what research methods sociologists use.

THE FAR SIDE® By GARY LARSON

© 1984 FarWorks, Inc. All Rights Reserved/Dist. by Creators Syndicate

The Far Side® by Gary Larson © 1984 FarWorks, Inc. All Rights Reserved. The Far Side® and the Larson® signature are registered trademarks of FarWorks, Inc. Used with permission.

"Anthropologists! Anthropologists!"

A major concern of sociologists and other social scientists is that their research methods do not influence their findings. Respondents often change their behavior when they know they are being studied.

Research Methods

As we review the seven research methods (or *research designs*) that sociologists use, we will continue our example of spouse abuse. As you will see, the method you choose will depend on the questions you want to answer. So that you can have a yardstick for comparison, you will want to know what "average" is in your study. Table 5.2 on page 130 discusses ways to measure average.

Surveys

Let's suppose that you want to know how many wives are abused each year. Some husbands also are abused, of course, but let's assume that you are going to focus on wives. An appropriate method for this purpose would be the **survey,** in which you would ask individuals a series of questions. Before you begin your research, however, you must deal with practical matters that face all researchers. Let's look at these issues.

TABLE 5.1   How to Read a Table

Tables summarize information. Because sociological findings are often presented in tables, it is important to understand how to read them. Tables contain six elements: title, headnote, headings, columns, rows, and source. When you understand how these elements fit together, you know how to read a table.

1. The **title** states the topic. It is located at the top of the table. What is the title of this table? Please determine your answer before looking at the correct answer at the bottom of this page.

2. The **headnote** is not always included in a table. When it is, it is located just below the title. Its purpose is to give more detailed information about how the data were collected or how data are presented in the table. What are the first eight words of the headnote of this table?

3. The **headings** tell what kind of information is contained in the table. There are three headings in this table. What are they? In the second heading, what does *n* = 25 mean?

Comparing Violent and Nonviolent Husbands

Based on interviews with 150 husbands and wives in a Midwestern city who were getting a divorce.

Husband's Achievement and Job Satisfaction	Violent Husbands *n* = 25	Nonviolent Husbands *n* = 125
He started but failed to complete high school or college.	44%	27%
He is very dissatisfied with his job.	44%	18%
His income is a source of constant conflict.	84%	24%
He has less education than his wife.	56%	14%
His job has less prestige than his father-in-law's.	37%	28%

Source: Modification of Table 1 in O'Brien 1975.

4. The **columns** present information arranged vertically. What is the fourth number in the second column and the second number in the third column?

5. The **rows** present information arranged horizontally. In the fourth row, which husbands are more likely to have less education than their wives?

6. The **source** of a table, usually listed at the bottom, provides information on where the data in the table originated. Often, as in this instance, the information is specific enough for you to consult the original source. What is the source for this table?

Some tables are much more complicated than this one, but all follow the same basic pattern. To apply these concepts to a table with more information, see page 352.

ANSWERS
1. Comparing Violent and Nonviolent Husbands
2. Based on interviews with 150 husbands and wives
3. Husband's Achievement and Job Satisfaction, Violent Husbands, Nonviolent Husbands. The *n* is an abbreviation for number, and *n* = 25 means that 25 violent husbands were in the sample.
4. 56%, 18%
5. Violent Husbands
6. A 1975 article by O'Brien (listed in the References section of this text).

Selecting a Sample. Ideally, you might want to learn about all wives in the world. Obviously, your resources will not permit such research, and you will have to narrow your **population,** the target group that you are going to study.

Let's assume that your resources (money, assistants, time) allow you to investigate spouse abuse only on your campus. Let's also assume that your college enrollment is large, so you won't be able to survey all the married women who are enrolled. Now you must

population a target group to be studied

TABLE 5.2 Three Ways to Measure "Average"

The Mean	The Median	The Mode
The term *average* seems clear enough. As you learned in grade school, to find the average you add a group of numbers and then divide the total by the number of cases that you added. Assume that the following numbers represent men convicted of battering their wives:	To compute the second average, the *median*, first arrange the cases in order—either from the highest to the lowest or the lowest to the highest. That arrangement will produce the following distribution.	The third measure of average, the *mode*, is simply the cases that occur the most often. In this instance the mode is 57, which is way off the mark.

EXAMPLE (The Mean)

```
  321
  229
   57
  289
  136
   57
1,795
```

EXAMPLE (The Median)

```
   57      1,795
   57        321
  136        289
  229  or   229
  289        136
  321         57
1,795         57
```

EXAMPLE (The Mode)

```
   57
   57
  136
  229
  289
  321
1,795
```

The Mean	The Median	The Mode
The total is 2,884. Divided by 7 (the number of cases), the average is 412. Sociologists call this form of average the *mean*. The mean can be deceptive because it is strongly influenced by extreme scores, either low or high. Note that six of the seven cases are less than the mean. Two other ways to compute averages are the median and the mode.	Then look for the middle case, the one that falls halfway between the top and the bottom. That number is 229, for three numbers are lower and three numbers are higher. When there is an even number of cases, the median is the halfway mark between the two middle cases.	Because the mode is often deceptive, and only by chance comes close to either of the other two averages, sociologists seldom use it. In addition, not every distribution of cases has a mode. And if two or more numbers appear with the same frequency, you can have more than one mode.

sample the individuals intended to represent the population to be studied

random sample a sample in which everyone in the target population has the same chance of being included in the study

stratified random sample a sample from selected subgroups of the target population in which everyone in those subgroups has an equal chance of being included in the research

respondents people who respond to a survey, either in interviews or by self-administered questionnaires

questionnaires a list of questions to be asked of respondents

self-administered questionnaires questionnaires that respondents fill out

select a **sample,** individuals from among your target population. How you choose a sample is crucial, for your choice will affect the results of your research. For example, married women enrolled in introductory sociology and engineering courses might have quite different experiences. If so, surveying just one or the other would produce skewed results.

Because you want to generalize your findings to your entire campus, you need a sample that accurately represents the campus. How can you get a representative sample?

The best way is to use a **random sample.** This does *not* mean that you stand on some campus corner and ask questions of any woman who happens to walk by. *In a random sample, everyone in your population (the target group) has the same chance of being included in the study.* In this case, because your population is every married woman enrolled in your college, all married women—whether first-year or graduate students, full- or part-time—must have the same chance of being included in your sample.

How can you get a random sample? First, you need a list of all the married women enrolled in your college. Then you assign a number to each name on the list. Using a table of random numbers, you then determine which of these women will become part of your sample. (Tables of random numbers are available in statistics books and online, or they can be generated by a computer.)

A random sample will represent your study's population fairly—in this case, married women enrolled at your college. This means that you can generalize your findings to *all* the married women students on your campus, even if they were not included in your sample.

What if you want to know only about certain subgroups, such as freshmen and seniors? You could use a **stratified random sample.** You would need a list of the married women in the freshman and senior classes. Then, using random numbers, you would select a sample from each group. This would allow you to generalize to all the freshman and senior married women at your college, but you would not be able to draw any conclusions about the sophomores or juniors.

Asking Neutral Questions.   After you have decided on your population and sample, your next task is to make certain that your questions are neutral. Your questions must allow **respondents,** the people who answer your questions, to express their own opinions. Otherwise, you will end up with biased answers—which are worthless. For example, if you were to ask, "Don't you think that men who beat their wives should go to prison?" you would be tilting the answer toward agreement with a prison sentence. The *Doonesbury* cartoon below illustrates another blatant example of biased questions. For examples of flawed research, see the Down-to-Earth Sociology box on the next page.

Questionnaires and Interviews.   Even if you have a representative sample and ask neutral questions, you can still end up with biased findings. **Questionnaires,** the list of questions to be asked, can be administered in ways that are flawed. There are two basic techniques for administering questionnaires. The first is to ask the respondents to fill them out. These **self-administered questionnaires** allow a larger number of people to be sampled at a lower cost, but the researchers lose control of the data collection. They don't know the conditions under which people answered the questions. For example, others could have influenced their answers.

The second technique is the **interview.** Researchers ask people questions, often face to face, sometimes by telephone or e-mail. The advantage of this method is that the researchers can ask each question in the same way. The main disadvantage is that interviews are time-consuming, so researchers end up with fewer respondents. Interviews can also create **interviewer bias;** that is, the presence of interviewers can affect what people say. For example, instead of saying what they really feel, respondents might give "socially acceptable" answers. Although they may be willing to write their true opinions on an anonymous questionnaire, they won't tell them to another person. Some respondents even shape their answers to match what they think an interviewer wants to hear.

In some cases, **structured interviews** work best. This type of interview uses **closed-ended questions**—each question is followed by a list of possible answers. Structured interviews are faster to administer, and they make it easier to *code* (categorize) answers so

Sociologists usually cannot interview or observe every member of a group or participant in an event that they want to study. As explained in the text, to be able to generalize their findings, they select samples. Sociologists would have several ways to study this protest in San Francisco against U.S. foreign policy.

interview direct questioning of respondents

interviewer bias effects that interviewers have on respondents that lead to biased answers

structured interviews interviews that use closed-ended questions

closed-ended questions questions that are followed by a list of possible answers to be selected by the respondent

Improperly worded questions can steer respondents toward answers that are not their own, which produces invalid results.

Down-to-Earth Sociology
Loading the Dice: How *Not* to Do Research

The methods of science lend themselves to distortion, misrepresentation, and downright fraud. Consider these findings from surveys:

Americans overwhelmingly prefer Toyotas to Chryslers. Americans overwhelmingly prefer Chryslers to Toyotas.

Obviously, these opposite conclusions cannot both be true. In fact, both sets of findings are misrepresentations, even though the responses came from surveys conducted by so-called independent researchers. These researchers, however, are biased, not independent and objective.

It turns out that some consumer researchers load the dice. Hired by firms that have a vested interest in the outcome of the research, they deliver the results their clients are looking for (Armstrong 2007). Here are six ways to load the dice.

1. **Choose a biased sample.** If you want to "prove" that Americans prefer Chryslers over Toyotas, interview unemployed union workers who trace their job loss to Japanese imports. The answer is predictable. You'll get what you're looking for.

2. **Ask biased questions.** Even if you choose an unbiased sample, you can phrase questions in such a way that you direct people to the answer you're looking for. Suppose that you ask this question:

We are losing millions of jobs to workers overseas who work for just a few dollars a day. After losing their jobs, some Americans are even homeless and hungry. Do you prefer a car that gives jobs to Americans, or one that forces our workers to lose their homes?

This question is obviously designed to channel people's thinking toward a predetermined answer—quite contrary to the standards of scientific research. Look again at the Doonesbury cartoon on page 131.

3. **List biased choices.** Another way to load the dice is to use closed-ended questions that push people into the answers you want. Consider this finding:

U.S. college students overwhelmingly prefer Levis 501 to the jeans of any competitor.

Sound good? Before you rush out to buy Levis, note what these researchers did: In asking students which jeans would be the most popular in the coming year, their list of choices included no other jeans but Levis 501!

4. **Discard undesirable results.** Researchers can keep silent about results they find embarrassing, or they can continue to survey samples until they find one that matches what they are looking for. As has been stressed in this chapter, research must be objective if it is to be scientific. Obviously, none of the preceding results qualifies. The underlying problem with the research cited here—and with so many surveys bandied about in the media as fact—is that survey research has become big business. Simply put, the money offered by corporations has corrupted some researchers.

The beginning of the corruption is subtle. Paul Light, dean at the University of Minnesota, put it this way: "A funder will never come to an academic and say, 'I want you to produce finding X, and here's a million dollars to do it.' Rather, the subtext is that if the researchers produce the right finding, more work—and funding—will come their way."

The first four sources of bias are inexcusable, intentional fraud. The next two sources of bias reflect sloppiness, which is also inexcusable in science.

5. **Misunderstand the subjects' world.** This route can lead to errors every bit as great as those just cited. Even researchers who use an adequate sample and word their questions properly can end up with skewed results. They may, for example, fail to anticipate that people may be embarrassed to express an opinion that isn't "politically correct." For example, surveys show that 80 percent of Americans are environmentalists. Most Americans, however, are probably embarrassed to tell a stranger otherwise. Today, that would be like going against the flag, motherhood, and apple pie.

6. **Analyze the data incorrectly.** Even when researchers strive for objectivity, the sample is good, the wording is neutral, and the respondents answer the questions honestly, the results can still be skewed. The researchers may make a mistake in their calculations, such as entering incorrect data into computers. This, too, of course, is inexcusable in science.

Sources: Based on Crossen 1991; Goleman 1993; Barnes 1995; Resnik 2000; Hotz 2007.

they can be fed into a computer for analysis. As you can see from Table 5.3, the answers listed on a questionnaire might fail to include the respondent's opinions. Consequently, some researchers prefer **unstructured interviews.** Here the interviewer asks **open-ended questions,** which allow people to answer in their own words. Open-ended questions allow you to tap the full range of people's opinions, but they make it difficult to compare answers. For example, how would you compare the following answers to the question "Why do you think men abuse their wives?"

"They're sick."

"I think they must have had problems with their mother."

"We oughta string 'em up!"

TABLE 5.3 Closed and Open–Ended Questions	
A. Closed–Ended Question	**B. Open–Ended Question**
Which of the following best fits your idea of what should be done to someone who has been convicted of spouse abuse? 1. probation 2. jail time 3. community service 4. counseling 5. divorce 6. nothing—it's a family matter	What do you think should be done to someone who has been convicted of spouse abuse?

Establishing Rapport.   Research on spouse abuse brings up another significant issue. You may have been wondering if your survey would be worth anything even if you rigorously followed scientific procedures. Will women who have been abused really give honest answers to strangers?

If your method of interviewing consisted of walking up to women on the street and asking if their husbands had ever beaten them, there would be little basis for taking your findings seriously. Researchers have to establish **rapport** ("ruh-POUR"), a feeling of trust, with their respondents, especially when it comes to sensitive topics—those that elicit feelings of embarrassment, shame, or other deep emotions.

We know that once rapport is gained (often by first asking nonsensitive questions), victims will talk about personal, sensitive issues. A good example is rape. To go beyond police statistics, each year researchers interview a random sample of 100,000 Americans. They ask them whether they have been victims of burglary, robbery, or other crimes. After establishing rapport, the researchers ask about rape. They find that rape victims will talk about their experiences. The National Crime Victimization Survey shows that the actual incidence of rape is about 40 percent higher than the number reported to the police—and that attempted rapes are *nine* times higher than the official statistics (*Statistical Abstract* 2009:Tables 303, 304).

A new technique to gather data on sensitive areas, Computer-Assisted Self-Interviewing, overcomes lingering problems of distrust. In this technique, the interviewer gives a laptop computer to the respondent, then moves aside, while the individual enters his or her own answers into the computer. In some versions of this method, the respondent listens to the questions on a headphone and answers them on the computer screen. When the respondent clicks the "Submit" button, the interviewer has no idea how the respondent answered any question (Mosher et al. 2005).

Participant Observation (Fieldwork)

In the second method, **participant observation** (or **fieldwork),** the researcher *participates* in a research setting while *observing* what is happening in that setting. But how is it possible to study spouse abuse by participant observation? Obviously, this method does not mean that you would sit around and watch someone being abused. Spouse abuse, however, is a broad topic, and many questions about abuse cannot be answered adequately by any method other than participant observation.

Let's suppose that you are interested in learning how spouse abuse affects wives. You might want to know how the abuse has changed the wives' relationship with their husbands. How has it changed their hopes and dreams? Or their ideas about men? Certainly it has affected their self-concept as well. But how? Participant observation could provide insight into such questions.

For example, if your campus has a crisis intervention center, you might be able to observe victims of spouse abuse from the time they report the attack through their participation in counseling. With good rapport, you might even be able to spend time with them in other

unstructured interviews interviews that use open-ended questions

open-ended questions questions that respondents answer in their own words

rapport (ruh-POUR) a feeling of trust between researchers and the people they are studying

participant observation (or fieldwork) research in which the researcher participates in a research setting while observing what is happening in that setting

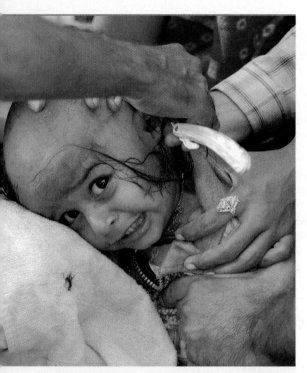

Participant observation, participating and observing in a research setting, is usually supplemented by interviewing, asking questions to better understand why people do what they do. In this instance, the sociologist would want to know what this hair removal ceremony in Gujarat, India, means to the child's family and to the community.

settings, observing further aspects of their lives. What they say and how they interact with others might help you to understand how the abuse has affected them. This, in turn, could give you insight into how to improve college counseling services.

Participant observers face two major dilemmas. The first is **generalizability,** the extent to which their findings apply to larger populations. Most participant observation studies are exploratory, documenting in detail the experiences of people in a particular setting. Although such research suggests that other people who face similar situations react in similar ways, we don't know how far the findings apply beyond their original setting. Participant observation, however, can stimulate hypotheses and theories that can be tested in other settings, using other research techniques. A second dilemma is the extent to which the participant observers should get involved in the lives of the people they are observing. Consider this as you read the Down-to-Earth Sociology box on the next page.

Case Studies

To do a **case study,** the researcher focuses on a single event, situation, or even individual. The purpose is to understand the dynamics of relationships, power, or even the thought processes that led to some particular event. Sociologist Ken Levi (2009), for example, wanted to study hit men. He would have loved to have had a large number of hit men to interview, but he had access to only one. He interviewed this man over and over again, giving us an understanding of how someone can kill others for money. Sociologist Kai Erikson (1978), who became intrigued with the bursting of a dam in West Virginia that killed several hundred people, focused on the events that led up to and followed this disaster. For spouse abuse, a case study would focus on a single wife and husband, exploring the couple's history and relationship.

As you can see, the case study reveals a lot of detail about some particular situation, but the question always remains: How much of this detail applies to other situations? This problem of generalizability, which plagues case studies, is the primary reason that few sociologists use this method.

Secondary Analysis

In **secondary analysis,** a fourth research method, researchers analyze data that others have collected. For example, if you were to analyze the original interviews from a study of women who had been abused by their husbands, you would be doing secondary analysis. Ordinarily, researchers prefer to gather their own data, but lack of resources, especially money, may make this impossible. In addition, existing data could contain a wealth of information that wasn't pertinent to the goals of the original researchers, which you can analyze for your own purposes.

Like the other methods, secondary analysis also poses its own problems. How can a researcher who did not carry out the initial study be sure that the data were gathered systematically and recorded accurately and that biases were avoided? This problem plagues researchers who do secondary analysis, especially if the original data were gathered by a team of researchers, not all of whom were equally qualified.

Documents

The fifth method that sociologists use is the study of **documents,** recorded sources. To investigate social life, sociologists examine such diverse documents as books, newspapers, diaries, bank records, police reports, immigration files, and records kept by organizations. The term *documents* is broad, and it also includes video and audio recordings.

To study spouse abuse, you might examine police reports and court records. These could reveal what percentage of complaints result in arrest and what proportion of the men arrested are charged, convicted, or put on probation. If these were your questions, police statistics would be valuable (Kingsnorth and MacIntosh 2007).

generalizability the extent to which the findings from one group (or sample) can be generalized or applied to other groups (or populations)

case study an analysis of a single event, situation, or individual

secondary analysis the analysis of data that have been collected by other researchers

documents in its narrow sense, written sources that provide data; in its extended sense, archival material of any sort, including photographs, movies, CDs, DVDs, and so on

Down-to-Earth Sociology

Gang Leader for a Day: Adventures of a Rogue Sociologist

Next to the University of Chicago is an area of poverty so dangerous that the professors warn students to avoid it. One of the graduate students in sociology, Sudhir Venkatesh, the son of immigrants from India, who was working on a research project with William Julius Wilson, decided to ignore the warning.

With clipboard in hand, Sudhir entered "the projects." Ignoring the glares of the young men standing around, he went into the lobby of a high-rise. Seeing a gaping hole where the elevator was supposed to be, he decided to climb the stairs, where he was almost overpowered by the smell of urine. After climbing five flights, Sudhir came upon some young men shooting craps in a dark hallway. One of them jumped up, grabbed Sudhir's clipboard, and demanded to know what he was doing there.

Sudhir blurted, "I'm a student at the university, doing a survey, and I'm looking for some families to interview."

One man took out a knife and began to twirl it. Another pulled out a gun, pointed it at Sudhir's head, and said, "I'll take him."

Then came a series of rapid-fire questions that Sudhir couldn't answer. He had no idea what they meant: "You flip right or left? Five or six? You run with the Kings, right?"

Grabbing Sudhir's bag, two of the men searched it. They could find only questionnaires, pen and paper, and a few sociology books. The man with the gun then told Sudhir to go ahead and ask him a question.

Sweating despite the cold, Sudhir read the first question on his survey, "How does it feel to be black and poor?" Then he read the multiple-choice answers: "Very bad, somewhat bad, neither bad nor good, somewhat good, very good."

As you might surmise, the man's answer was too obscenity laden to be printed here.

As the men deliberated Sudhir's fate ("If he's here and he don't get back, you know they're going to come looking for him"), a powerfully built man with a few glittery gold teeth and a sizable diamond earring appeared. The man, known as J.T., who, it turned out, directed the drug trade in the building, asked what was going on. When the younger men mentioned the questionnaire, J.T. said to ask *him* a question.

Amidst an eerie silence, Sudhir asked, "How does it feel to be black and poor?"

"I'm not black," came the reply.

"Well, then, how does it feel to be African American and poor?"

"I'm not African American either. I'm a nigger."

Sudhir was left speechless. Despite his naïveté, he knew better than to ask, "How does it feel to be a nigger and poor?"

As Sudhir stood with his mouth agape, J.T. added, "Niggers are the ones who live in this building. African Americans live in the suburbs. African Americans wear ties to work. Niggers can't find no work."

Not exactly the best start to a research project.

But this weird and frightening beginning turned into several years of fascinating research. Over time, J.T. guided Sudhir into a world that few outsiders ever see. Not only did Sudhir get to know drug dealers, crackheads, squatters, prostitutes, and pimps, but he also was present at beatings by drug crews, drive-by shootings done by rival gangs, and armed robberies by the police.

How Sudhir got out of his predicament in the stairwell, his immersion into a threatening underworld—the daily life for many people in "the projects"—and his moral dilemma at witnessing so many crimes are part of his fascinating experience in doing participant observation of the Black Kings.

Sudhir, who was reared in a middle-class suburb in California, even took over this Chicago gang for a day. This is one reason that he calls himself a rogue sociologist—the decisions he made that day were serious violations of law, felonies that could bring years in prison. There are other reasons, too: During the research, he kicked a man in the stomach, and he was present as the gang planned drive-by shootings.

Sudhir eventually completed his Ph.D., and he now teaches at Columbia University.

Based on Venkatesh 2008.

Sudhir Venkatesh, who now teaches at Columbia University, New York City.

But for other questions, those records would be useless. If you want to learn about the victims' social and emotional adjustment, for example, those records would tell you little. Other documents, however, might provide answers. For example, diaries kept by victims could yield insight into their reactions to abuse, showing how their attitudes and

The *research methods* that sociologists choose depend partially on the questions they want to answer. They might want to learn, for example, which forms of publicity are more effective in increasing awareness of spouse abuse as a social problem.

relationships change. If no diaries were available, you might ask victims to keep diaries. Perhaps the director of a crisis intervention center might ask clients to keep diaries for you—or get the victims' permission for you to examine records of their counseling sessions. To my knowledge, no sociologist has yet studied spouse abuse in this way.

Of course, I am presenting an ideal situation, a crisis intervention center that opens its arms to you. In actuality, the center might not cooperate at all. It might refuse to ask victims to keep diaries—or it might not even let you near its records. *Access,* then, is another problem that researchers face. Simply put, you can't study a topic unless you can gain access to it.

Experiments

Do you think there is a way to change a man who abuses his wife into a loving husband? No one has made this claim, but a lot of people say that abusers need therapy. Yet no one knows whether therapy really works. Because **experiments** are useful for determining cause and effect (discussed in Table 5.4 on the next page), let's suppose that you propose an experiment to a judge and she gives you access to men who have been arrested for spouse abuse. As in Figure 5.2 below, you would randomly divide the men into two groups. This helps to ensure that their individual characteristics (attitudes, number of arrests, severity of crimes, education, race–ethnicity, age, and so on) are distributed evenly between the groups. You then would arrange for the men in the **experimental group** to receive some form of therapy. The men in the **control group** would not get therapy.

experiment the use of *control* and *experimental groups* and *dependent* and *independent variables* to test causation

experimental group the group of subjects in an experiment who are exposed to the independent variable

control group the subjects in an experiment who are not exposed to the independent variable

FIGURE 5.2   The Experiment

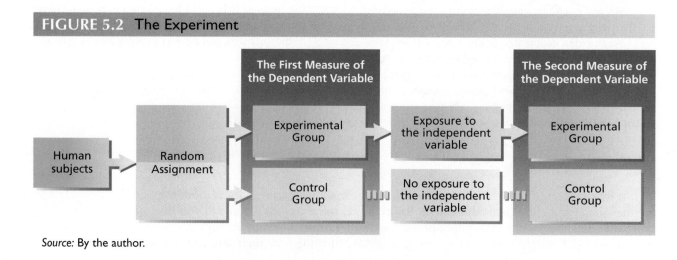

Source: By the author.

TABLE 5.4 Cause, Effect, and Spurious Correlations

Causation means that a change in one variable is caused by another variable. Three conditions are necessary for causation: correlation, temporal priority, and no spurious correlation. Let's apply each of these conditions to spouse abuse and alcohol abuse.

(1) The first necessary condition is *correlation*.

If two variables exist together, they are said to be correlated. If batterers get drunk, battering and alcohol abuse are correlated.

Spouse Abuse + Alcohol Abuse

People sometimes assume that correlation is causation. In this instance, they conclude that alcohol abuse causes spouse abuse.

Alcohol Abuse ⟶ Spouse Abuse

But *correlation never proves causation. Either* variable could be the cause of the other. Perhaps battering upsets men and they then get drunk.

Spouse Abuse ⟶ Alcohol Abuse

(2) The second necessary condition is *temporal priority*.

Temporal priority means that one thing happens before something else does. For a variable to be a cause (*the independent variable*), it must *precede* that which is changed (*the dependent variable*).

           precedes
Alcohol Abuse ⟶ Spouse Abuse

If the men had not drunk alcohol until after they beat their wives, obviously alcohol abuse could not be the cause of the spouse abuse. Although the necessity of temporal priority is obvious, in many studies this is not easy to determine.

(3) The third necessary condition is *no spurious correlation*.

This is the necessary condition that really makes things difficult. Even if we identify the correlation of getting drunk and spouse abuse and can determine temporal priority, we still don't know that alcohol abuse is the cause. We could have a *spurious correlation;* that is, the cause may be some underlying third variable. These are usually not easy to identify. Some sociologists think that male culture is that underlying third variable.

Male Culture ⟶ Spouse Abuse

Socialized into dominance, some men learn to view women as objects on which to take out their frustration. In fact, this underlying third variable could be a cause of both spouse abuse and alcohol abuse.

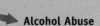

Male Culture ⟶ **Spouse Abuse** / **Alcohol Abuse**

But since only some men beat their wives, while all males are exposed to male culture, other variables must also be involved. Perhaps specific subcultures that promote violence and denigrate women lead to both spouse abuse and alcohol abuse.

Male Subculture ⟶ **Spouse Abuse** / **Alcohol Abuse**

If so, this does *not* mean that it is the only causal variable, for spouse abuse probably has many causes. Unlike the movement of amoebas or the action of heat on some object, human behavior is infinitely complicated. Especially important are people's *definitions of the situation*, including their views of right and wrong. To explain spouse abuse, then, we need to add such variables as the ways that men view violence and their ideas about the relative rights of women and men. It is precisely to help unravel such complicating factors in human behavior that we need the experimental method.

MORE ON CORRELATIONS

Correlation simply means that two or more variables are present together. The more often that these variables are found together, the stronger their relationship. To indicate their strength, sociologists use a number called a *correlation coefficient*. If two variables are always related, that is, they are always present together, they have what is called a *perfect positive correlation*. The number 1.0 represents this correlation coefficient. Nature has some 1.0's, such as the lack of water and the death of trees. 1.0's also apply to the human physical state, such as the absence of nutrients and the absence of life. But social life is much more complicated than physical conditions, and there are no 1.0's in human behavior.

Two variables can also have a *perfect negative correlation*. This means that when one variable is present, the other is always absent. The number –1.0 represents this correlation coefficient.

Positive correlations of 0.1, 0.2, and 0.3 mean that one variable is associated with another only 1 time out of 10, 2 times out of 10, and 3 times out of 10. In other words, in most instances the first variable is *not* associated with the second, indicating a weak relationship. A strong relationship may indicate causation, but not necessarily. Testing the relationship between variables is the goal of some sociological research.

independent variable a factor that causes a change in another variable, called the dependent variable

dependent variable a factor in an experiment that is changed by an independent variable

unobtrusive measures ways of observing people so they do not know they are being studied

Your **independent variable,** something that causes a change in another variable, would be therapy. Your **dependent variable,** the variable that might change, would be the men's behavior: whether they abuse women after they get out of jail. Unfortunately, your operational definition of the men's behavior will be sloppy: either reports from the wives or records indicating which men were rearrested for abuse. This is sloppy because some of the women will not report the abuse, and some of the men who abuse their wives will not be arrested. Yet it may be the best you can do.

Let's assume that you choose rearrest as your operational definition. If you find that the men who received therapy are *less* likely to be rearrested for abuse, you can attribute the difference to the therapy. If you find *no difference* in rearrest rates, you can conclude that the therapy was ineffective. If you find that the men who received the therapy have a *higher* rearrest rate, you can conclude that the therapy backfired.

Ideally, you would test different types of therapy. Perhaps only some types work. You might even want to test self-therapy by assigning articles, books, and videos.

Unobtrusive Measures

Researchers sometimes use **unobtrusive measures,** observing the behavior of people who are not aware that they are being studied. For example, social researchers studied the level of whisky consumption in a town that was legally "dry" by counting empty bottles in trashcans (Lee 2000). Researchers have also gone high-tech in their unobtrusive measures. To trace customers' paths through stores, they attach infrared surveillance devices to shopping carts. Grocery chains use these findings to place higher-profit items in more strategic locations (McCarthy 1993). Casino operators use chips that transmit radio frequencies, allowing them to track how much their high rollers are betting at every hand of poker or blackjack (Sanders 2005; Grossman 2007). Billboards read information embedded on a chip in your car key. As you drive by, the billboard displays *your* name with a personal message (Feder 2007). The same device can *collect* information as you drive by. Cameras in sidewalk billboards scan the facial features of people who pause to look at its advertising, reporting their sex, race, and how long they looked (Clifford 2008). The billboards, which raise ethical issues of invasion of privacy, are part of marketing, not sociological research.

It would be considered unethical to use most unobtrusive measures to research spouse abuse. You could, however, analyze 911 calls. Also, if there were a public forum held by abused or abusing spouses on the Internet, you could record and analyze the online conversations. Ethics in unobtrusive research are still a matter of dispute: To secretly record the behavior of people in public settings, such as a crowd, is generally considered acceptable, but to do so in private settings is not.

To prevent cheating by customers and personnel, casinos use *unobtrusive measures.* In the ceiling above this blackjack table are video cameras that record every action. Observors are also posted there.

Deciding Which Method to Use

How do sociologists choose among these methods? Four primary factors affect their decision. The first is *access to resources.* They may want to conduct a survey, for example, but if their finances won't permit this, they might analyze documents instead. The second is *access to subjects.* Even though they prefer face-to-face interviews, if the people who make up the sample live far away, researchers might mail them questionnaires or conduct a survey by telephone or e-mail. The third factor concerns the *purpose of the research.* Each method is better for answering certain types of questions. Participant observation, for example, is good at uncovering people's attitudes, while experiments are better at resolving questions of cause and effect. Fourth, *the researcher's background or training* comes into play. In graduate school, sociologists study many methods, but they are able to practice only some of them. After graduate school, sociologists who were trained in quantitative research methods, which emphasize measurement and statistics, are likely to use surveys. Sociologists who were trained in qualitative research methods, which emphasize observing and interpreting people's behavior, lean toward participant observation.

Controversy in Sociological Research

Sociologists sometimes find themselves in the hot seat because of their research. Some poke into private areas of life, which upsets people. Others investigate political matters, and their findings threaten those who have a stake in the situation. When researchers in Palestine asked refugees if they would be willing to accept compensation and not return to Israel if there were a peace settlement, most said they would take the buyout. When the head researcher released these findings, an enraged mob beat him and trashed his office (Bennet 2003). In the following Thinking Critically section, you can see how even such a straightforward task as counting the homeless can land sociologists in the midst of controversy.

Thinking CRITICALLY

Doing Controversial Research—Counting the Homeless

What could be less offensive than counting the homeless? As sometimes occurs, however, even basic research lands sociologists in the midst of controversy. This is what happened to sociologist Peter Rossi and his associates.

There was a dispute between advocates for the homeless and federal officials. The advocates claimed that 3 to 7 million Americans were homeless; the officials claimed that the total was about 250,000. Each side accused the other of gross distortion—the one to place pressure on Congress, the other to keep the public from knowing how bad the situation really was. But each side was only guessing.

Only an accurate count could clear up the picture. Peter Rossi and the National Opinion Research Center took on that job. They had no vested interest in supporting either side, only in answering this question honestly.

The challenge was immense. The *population* was evident—the U.S. homeless. A *survey* would be appropriate, but how do you survey a *sample* of the homeless? No one has a list of the homeless, and only some of the homeless stay at shelters. As for *validity,* to make certain that they were counting only people who were really homeless, the researchers needed a good *operational definition* of homelessness. To include people who weren't really homeless would destroy the study's *reliability.* The researchers wanted results that would be consistent if others were to *replicate,* or repeat, the study.

As an operational definition, the researchers used "literally homeless," people "who do not have access to a conventional dwelling and who would be homeless by any conceivable definition of the term." With funds limited, the researchers couldn't do a national count, but they could count the homeless in Chicago.

By using a *stratified random sample,* the researchers were able to *generalize* to the entire city. How could they do this since there is no list of the homeless? They did have a list of the city's shelters and a map of the city. A stratified random sample of the city's shelters gave them access to the homeless who sleep in the shelters. For the homeless who sleep in the streets, parks, and vacant buildings, they used a stratified random sample of the city's blocks.

Their findings? On an average night, 2,722 people are homeless in Chicago. Because people move in and out of homelessness, between 5,000 and 7,000 are homeless at

Research sometimes lands sociologists in the midst of controversy. As described here, the results of a study to determine how many homeless people there are in the United States displeased homeless advocates. Homelessness is currently growing at such a pace that many U.S. cities have set up "tent cities." Shown here is a tile worker in St. Petersburg, Florida, who lost his home and lives in a tent.

some point during the year. On warm nights, only two out of five sleep in the shelters, and even during Chicago's cold winters only three out of four do so. Seventy-five percent are men, 60 percent African Americans. One in four is a former mental patient, one in five a former prisoner. Projecting these findings to the United States yields a national total of about 350,000 homeless people.

This total elated government officials and stunned the homeless advocates. The advocates said that the number couldn't possibly be right, and they began to snipe at the researchers. This is one of the risks of doing research, for sociologists never know whose toes they will step on. The sniping made the researchers uncomfortable, and to let everyone know they weren't trying to minimize the problem, they stressed that these 350,000 Americans live desperate lives. They sleep in city streets, live in shelters, eat out of garbage cans, and suffer from severe health problems.

The controversy continues. With funding at stake for shelters and for treating mental problems and substance abuse, homeless advocates continue to insist that at least 2 million Americans are homeless. While the total is not in the millions, it has doubled recently to 672,000. As a sign of changing times, veterans, many of them emotionally disturbed, make up 15 percent of this total.

Sources: Based on Anderson 1986; Rossi et al. 1986; Rossi et al. 1987; Rossi 1989, 1991, 1999; Bialik 2006; Chan 2007; National Coalition for the Homeless 2008; Preston 2008.

Gender in Sociological Research

You know how significant gender is in your own life, how it affects your orientations and your attitudes. You also may be aware that gender opens and closes doors to you, a topic that we will explore in Chapter 11. Because gender is also a factor in social research, researchers must take steps to prevent it from biasing their findings. For example, sociologists Diana Scully and Joseph Marolla (1984, 2007) interviewed convicted rapists in prison. They were concerned that their gender might lead to *interviewer bias*—that the prisoners might shift their answers, sharing certain experiences or opinions with Marolla, but saying something else to Scully. To prevent gender bias, each researcher interviewed half the sample. Later in this chapter, we'll look at what they found out.

Gender certainly can be an impediment in research. In our imagined research on spouse abuse, for example, could a man even do participant observation of women who have been beaten by their husbands? Technically, the answer is yes. But because the women have been victimized by men, they might be less likely to share their experiences and feelings with men. If so, women would be better suited to conduct this research, more likely to achieve valid results. The supposition that these victims will be more open with women than with men, however, is just that—a supposition. Research alone will verify or refute this assumption.

Gender is significant in other ways, too. It is certainly a mistake to assume that what applies to one sex also applies to the other (Bird and Rieker 1999; Neuman 2006). Women's and men's lives differ significantly, and if we do research on just half of humanity, our research will be vastly incomplete. Today's huge numbers of women sociologists guarantee that women will not be ignored in social research. In the past, however, when almost all sociologists were men, women's experiences were neglected.

Gender issues can pop up in unexpected ways in sociological research. I vividly recall this incident in San Francisco.

The streets were getting dark, and I was still looking for homeless people. When I saw someone lying down, curled up in a doorway, I approached the individual. As I got close, I began my opening research line, "Hi, I'm Dr. Henslin from. . . . " The individual began to scream and started to thrash wildly. Startled by this sudden, high-pitched scream and by the rapid movements, I quickly backed away. When I later analyzed what had happened, I concluded that I had intruded into a woman's bedroom.

This incident also holds another lesson. Researchers do their best, but they make mistakes. Sometimes these mistakes are minor, and even humorous. The woman sleeping in the doorway wasn't frightened. It was only just getting dark, and there were many people on the street. She was just assertively marking her territory and letting me know in no uncertain terms that I was an intruder. If we make a mistake in research, we pick up and go on. As we do so, we take ethical considerations into account, which is the topic of our next section.

Ethics in Sociological Research

In addition to choosing an appropriate research method, we must also follow the ethics of sociology (American Sociological Association 1999). Research ethics require honesty, truth, and openness (sharing findings with the scientific community). Ethics clearly forbid the falsification of results. They also condemn plagiarism—that is, stealing someone else's work. Another ethical guideline states that research subjects should generally be informed that they are being studied and should never be harmed by the research. Ethics also require that sociologists protect the anonymity of those who provide information. Sometimes people reveal things that are intimate, potentially embarrassing, or otherwise harmful to themselves. Finally, although not all sociologists agree, it generally is considered unethical for researchers to misrepresent themselves.

Sociologists take their ethical standards seriously. To illustrate the extent to which they will go to protect their respondents, consider the research conducted by Mario Brajuha.

Protecting the Subjects: The Brajuha Research

Mario Brajuha, a graduate student at the State University of New York at Stony Brook, was doing participant observation of restaurant workers. He lost his job as a waiter when the restaurant where he was working burned down—a fire of "suspicious origin," as the police said. When detectives learned that Brajuha had taken field notes (Brajuha and Hallowell 1986), they asked to see them. Because he had promised to keep the information confidential, Brajuha refused to hand them over. When the district attorney subpoenaed the notes, Brajuha still refused. The district attorney then threatened to put Brajuha in jail. By this time, Brajuha's notes had become rather famous, and unsavory characters—perhaps those who had set the fire—also wanted to know what was in them. They, too, demanded to see them, accompanying their demands with threats of a different nature. Brajuha found himself between a rock and a hard place.

For two years, Brajuha refused to hand over his notes, even though he grew anxious and had to appear at several court hearings. Finally, the district attorney dropped the subpoena. When the two men under investigation for setting the fire died, the threats to Brajuha, his wife, and their children ended.

Misleading the Subjects: The Humphreys Research

Sociologists agree on the necessity to protect respondents, and they applaud the professional manner in which Brajuha handled himself. Although it is considered acceptable for sociologists to do covert participant observation (studying some situation without announcing that they are doing research), to deliberately misrepresent oneself is considered unethical. Let's look at the case of Laud Humphreys, whose research forced sociologists to rethink and refine their ethical stance.

Laud Humphreys, a classmate of mine at Washington University in St. Louis, was an Episcopal priest who decided to become a sociologist. For his Ph.D. dissertation, Humphreys (1971, 1975) studied social interaction in "tearooms," public restrooms where some men go for quick, anonymous oral sex with other men.

Humphreys found that some restrooms in Forest Park, just across from our campus, were tearooms. He began a participant observation study by hanging around these restrooms. He found that in addition to the two men having sex, a third man—called a "watch queen"—served as a lookout for police and other unwelcome strangers.

Ethics in social research are of vital concern to sociologists. As discussed in the text, sociologists may disagree on some of the issue's finer points, but none would approve of slipping LSD to unsuspecting subjects like these Marine recruits in basic training at Parris Island, South Carolina. This was done to U.S. soldiers in the 1960s under the guise of legitimate testing—just "to see what would happen."

Humphreys took on the role of watch queen, not only watching for strangers but also observing what the men did. He wrote field notes after the encounters.

Humphreys decided that he wanted to learn about the regular lives of these men. For example, what was the significance of the wedding rings that many of the men wore? He came up with an ingenious technique: Many of the men parked their cars near the tearooms, and Humphreys recorded their license plate numbers. A friend in the St. Louis police department gave Humphreys each man's address. About a year later, Humphreys arranged for these men to be included in a medical survey conducted by some of the sociologists on our faculty.

Disguising himself with a different hairstyle and clothing, Humphreys visited the men's homes. He interviewed the men, supposedly for the medical study. He found that they led conventional lives. They voted, mowed their lawns, and took their kids to Little League games. Many reported that their wives were not aroused sexually or were afraid of getting pregnant because their religion did not allow them to use birth control. Humphreys concluded that heterosexual men were also using the tearooms for a form of quick sex.

This study stirred controversy among sociologists and nonsociologists alike. Many sociologists criticized Humphreys, and a national columnist even wrote a scathing denunciation of "sociological snoopers" (Von Hoffman 1970). One of our professors even tried to get Humphreys' Ph.D. revoked. As the controversy heated up and a court case loomed, Humphreys feared that his list of respondents might be subpoenaed. He gave me the list to take from Missouri to Illinois, where I had begun teaching. When he called and asked me to destroy it, I burned the list in my backyard.

Was this research ethical? This question is not decided easily. Although many sociologists sided with Humphreys—and his book reporting the research won a highly acclaimed award—the criticisms continued. At first, Humphreys defended his position vigorously, but five years later, in a second edition of his book (1975), he stated that he should have identified himself as a researcher.

How Research and Theory Work Together

Research cannot stand alone. Nor can theory. As sociologist C. Wright Mills (1959) argued so forcefully, research without theory is simply a collection of unrelated "facts." But theory without research, Mills added, is abstract and empty—it can't represent the way life really is.

Research and theory, then, are both essential for sociology. Every theory must be tested, which requires research. And as sociologists do research, they often come up with surprising findings. Those findings must be explained, and for that we need theory. As sociologists study social life, then, they combine research and theory.

The Real World: When the Ideal Meets the Real

Although we can list the ideals of research, real-life situations often force sociologists to settle for something that falls short of the ideal. In the following Thinking Critically section, let's look at how two sociologists confronted the ideal and the real.

ThinkingCRITICALLY
Are Rapists Sick? A Close-Up View of Research

Two sociologists, Diana Scully and Joseph Marolla, whose research was mentioned earlier, were not satisfied with the typical explanation that rapists are "sick," psychologically disturbed, or different from other men. They developed the hypothesis that rape is like most human behavior—learned through interaction with others. That is, some men learn to think of rape as appropriate behavior.

To test this hypothesis, it would be best to interview a random sample of rapists. But this is impossible. There is no list of all rapists, so there is no way to give them all the same chance of being included in a sample. You can't even use prison populations to select a random sample, for many rapists have never been caught, some who were caught were found not guilty, and some who were found guilty were given probation. And as we know from DNA testing, some who were convicted of rape are innocent. Consequently, Scully and Marolla confronted the classic dilemma of sociologists—either to not do the research or to do it under less than ideal conditions.

They chose to do the research. When they had the opportunity to interview convicted rapists in prison, they jumped at it. They knew that whatever they learned would be more than we already knew. They sent out 3,500 letters to men serving time in seven prisons in Virginia, the state where they were teaching. About 25 percent of the prisoners agreed to be interviewed. They matched these men on the basis of age, education, race–ethnicity, severity of offense, and previous criminal record. This resulted in a sample of 98 prisoners who were convicted of rape and a control sample of 75 men convicted of other offenses.

As noted earlier, because the sex of the interviewer can bias research results, Scully and Marolla each interviewed half the sample. It took them 600 hours to gather information on the prisoners, including their psychological, criminal, and sexual history. To guard against lies, they checked what the individuals told them against their institutional records. They used twelve scales to measure the men's attitudes about women, rape, and themselves. In order to find out what circumstances the men defined as rape or when they viewed the victim as responsible, they also gave the men nine vignettes of forced sexual encounters and asked them to determine responsibility in each one.

Scully and Marolla discovered something that goes against common sense—that most rapists are not sick and that they are not overwhelmed by uncontrollable urges. The psychological histories of the rapists and the nonrapists were similar. These men rape for a variety of reasons: to "blow off steam" over problems they are having with others, to get sex, to feel powerful, and to hurt women (Monahan et al. 2005). Some rape spontaneously, while others plan their rapes. Some rape as a form of revenge, to get even with someone, not necessarily their victim. For some, rape is even a form of recreation, and they rape with friends on weekends.

Scully and Marolla also found support for what feminists had been pointing out for years, that power is a major element in rape. Here is what one man said:

> Rape gave me the power to do what I wanted to do without feeling I had to please a partner or respond to a partner. I felt in control, dominant. Rape was the ability to have sex without caring about the woman's response. I was totally dominant.

To discover that most rape is calculated behavior—that rapists are not "sick"; that a motivating force can be power, not passion; that the behavior stems from the criminal pursuit of pleasure, not from mental illness—is significant. It makes the sociological quest worthwhile.

In comparing their sample of rapists with their control group of nonrapists, Scully and Marolla also made another significant finding: The rapists are more likely to believe "rape myths." They are more likely to believe that women cause their own rape by the way they act and the clothes they wear, that a woman who charges rape has simply changed her mind after participating in consensual sex, and that most men accused of rape are innocent.

Connecting Research and Theory

Such findings go far beyond simply adding to our storehouse of "facts." As indicated in Figure 5.1 on page 127, research stimulates both the development of theory and the need for more research. Scully and Marolla suggest that rape myths act as neutralizers, that they allow "potential rapists to turn off social prohibitions against injuring others."

This hypothesis needs to be confirmed by other research. It also pinpoints the need to determine how such myths are transmitted. Which male subcultures perpetuate them? Do the mass media contribute to these myths? Do family, religion, and education create respect for females and help keep males from learning such myths? Or do they somehow contribute to these myths? If so, how?

Sociologists have begun to build on this path-breaking research, which was done, as usual, under less than ideal conditions. The resulting theorizing and research may provide the basis for making changes that reduce the incidence of rape in our society.

Sources: Marolla and Scully 1986; Scully 1990; Scully and Marolla 1984, 2007.

Sociology needs more of this type of research—imaginative and sometimes daring investigations conducted in an imperfect world under less than ideal conditions. This is really what sociology is all about. Sociologists study what people do—whether their behaviors are conforming or deviant, whether they please others or disgust them. No matter what behavior is studied, systematic research methods and the application of social theory take us beyond common sense. They allow us to penetrate surface realities so we can better understand human behavior—and, in the ideal case, make changes to help improve social life.

SUMMARY *and* REVIEW

What Is a Valid Sociological Topic?

Any human behavior is a valid sociological topic, even disreputable behavior. Spouse abuse is an example. Sociological research is based on the sociologist's interests, access to subjects, appropriate methods, and ethical considerations. P. 126.

Common Sense and the Need for Sociological Research

Why isn't common sense adequate?

Common sense doesn't provide reliable information. When subjected to scientific research, commonsense ideas often are found to be limited or false. P. 126.

A Research Model

What are the eight basic steps of sociological research?

(1) Selecting a topic, (2) Defining the problem, (3) Reviewing the literature, (4) Formulating a **hypothesis,** (5) Choosing a research method, (6) Collecting the data, (7) Analyzing the results, and (8) Sharing the results. These steps are explained in detail on Pp. 126–128.

Research Methods

How do sociologists gather data?

To collect data, sociologists use seven **research methods** (or research designs): **surveys, participant observation** (fieldwork), **case studies, secondary analysis, documents, experiments,** and **unobtrusive measures.** Pp. 128–138.

How do sociologists choose a research method?

Sociologists choose their research method based on questions to be answered, their access to potential subjects, the resources available, their training, and ethical considerations. P. 138.

Controversy in Sociological Research

Why is sociological research often controversial?

Some people get upset because sociologists do research on disreputable or illegal activities or on personal or intimate areas of life. Other people get upset when research findings go against their interests or biases. Pp. 139–140.

Gender in Sociological Research

What is the relationship between gender and research?

There are two aspects. First, findings based on samples of men do not necessarily apply to women and findings based on samples of women do not necessarily apply to men. Second, in some kinds of research, such as studying abused spouses, rape victims, and rapists, the gender of the researcher could affect findings. Pp. 140–141.

Ethics in Sociological Research

How important are ethics in sociological research?

Ethics are of fundamental concern to sociologists, who are committed to openness, honesty, truth, and protecting their subjects from harm. The Brajuha research on restau-rant workers and the Humphreys research on "tearooms" were cited to illustrate ethical issues that concern sociologists. Pp. 141–142.

How Research and Theory Work Together

What is the relationship between theory and research?

Theory and research depend on one another. Theory generates questions that need to be answered by research, and sociologists use theory to interpret the data they gather. Research, in turn, helps to generate theory: Findings that don't match what is expected can indicate a need to modify theory. Pp. 142–144.

THINKING CRITICALLY *ABOUT* Chapter 5

1. Should sociologists be allowed to do research on disreputable or disapproved behavior? On illegal behavior? Why or why not?

2. What factors make for *bad* sociological research? How can these be avoided?

3. What ethics govern sociological research?

4. Is it right (or ethical) for sociologists to not identity themselves when they do research? To misrepresent themselves? What if identifying themselves as researchers will destroy their access to a research setting or to informants?

ADDITIONAL RESOURCES

What can you find in MySocLab? mysoclab www.mysoclab.com

- Complete Ebook
- Practice Tests and Video and Audio activities
- Mapping and Data Analysis exercises

- Sociology in the News
- Classic Readings in Sociology
- Research and Writing advice

Where Can I Read More on This Topic?

Suggested readings for this chapter are listed at the back of this book.

Societies to Social Networks

Brazil

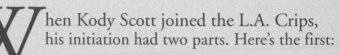

When Kody Scott joined the L.A. Crips, his initiation had two parts. Here's the first:

"How old is you now anyway?"

"Eleven, but I'll be twelve in November."

I never saw the blow to my head come from Huck. Bam! And I was on all fours. . . . Kicked in the stomach, I was on my back counting stars in the blackness. Grabbed by the collar, I was made to stand again. A solid blow to my chest exploded pain on the blank screen that had now become my mind. Bam! Another, then another. Blows rained on me from every direction. . . .

> "Kody, you got eight shots, you don't come back to the car unless they all are gone."

Up until this point not a word had been spoken. . . . Then I just started swinging, with no style or finesse, just anger and the instinct to survive. . . . [This] reflected my ability to represent the set [gang] in hand-to-hand combat. The blows stopped abruptly. . . . My ear was bleeding, and my neck and face were deep red. . . .

Scott's beating was followed immediately by the second part of his initiation. For this, he received the name *Monster,* which he carried proudly:

"Give Kody the pump" [12-gauge pump action shotgun] . . . Tray Ball spoke with the calm of a football coach. "Tonight we gonna rock they world." . . . Hand slaps were passed around the room. . . . "Kody, you got eight shots, you don't come back to the car unless they all are gone."

"Righteous," I said, eager to show my worth. . . .

Hanging close to buildings, houses, and bushes, we made our way, one after the other, to within spitting distance of the Bloods. . . . Huck and Fly stepped from the shadows simultaneously and were never noticed until it was too late. Boom! Boom! Heavy bodies hitting the ground, confusion, yells of dismay, running. . . . By my sixth shot I had advanced past the first fallen bodies and into the street in pursuit of those who had sought refuge behind cars and trees. . . .

Back in the shack we smoked more pot and drank more beer. I was the center of attention for my acts of aggression. . . .

Tray Ball said. "You got potential, 'cause' you eager to learn. Bangin' [being a gang member] ain't no part-time thang, it's full-time, it's a career. It's bein' down when ain't nobody else down with you. It's gettin' caught and not tellin'. Killin' and not caring, and dyin' without fear. It's love for your set and hate for the enemy. You hear what I'm sayin'?"

Kody adds this insightful remark:

Though never verbally stated, death was looked upon as a sort of reward, a badge of honor, especially if one died in some heroic capacity for the hood. . . . The supreme sacrifice was to "take a bullet for a homie" [fellow gang member]. The set functioned as a religion. Nothing held a light to the power of the set. If you died on the trigger you surely were smiled upon by the Crip God.

147

Excerpts from Scott 1994:8–13, 103.

group people who have something in common and who believe that what they have in common is significant; also called a *social group*

society people who share a culture and a territory

hunting and gathering society a human group that depends on hunting and gathering for its survival

shaman the healing specialist of a tribe who attempts to control the spirits thought to cause a disease or injury; commonly called a witch doctor

Could you be like Kody and shoot strangers in cold blood—just because others tell you to pull the trigger? Although none of us want to think that we could, don't bet on it. In this chapter, you are going to read some surprising things about **groups**—people who interact with one another and who think of themselves as belonging together. As we move into this topic, let's first look at the big picture, how societies have changed over time.

Societies and Their Transformation

The largest and most complex group that sociologists study is **society,** which consists of people who share a culture and a territory. Society, which surrounds us, sets the stage for our life experiences. *The sociological principle is that the type of society we live in is the fundamental reason for why we become who we are.* Not only does our society lay the broad framework for our behavior, but it also influences the ways we think and feel. Its effects are so significant that if you had grown up in a different society, you would be a different type of person.

To see how our society developed, look at Figure 6.1 on the next page. You can see that technology is the key to understanding the sweeping changes that produced our society. Let's review these broad changes. As we do, picture yourself as a member of each society. Consider how your life—even your thoughts and values—would be different as a member of these societies.

Hunting and Gathering Societies

The members of **hunting and gathering societies** have few social divisions and little inequality. As the name implies, in order to survive, these groups depend on hunting animals and gathering plants. In some groups, the men do the hunting, and the women the gathering. In others, both men and women (and children) gather plants, the men hunt large animals, and both men and women hunt small animals. The groups usually have a **shaman,** an individual thought to be able to influence spiritual forces, but shamans, too, must help obtain food. Although these groups give greater prestige to

As *society*—the largest and complex type of group—changes, so, too, do the groups, activities, and, ultimately, the type of people who form that society. This photo of a Norwegian competitor in the Beijing Olympics captures some of the changes occurring in Western societies. What social changes can you identify from this photo?

the men hunters, who supply most of the meat, the women gatherers contribute more food to the group, perhaps even four-fifths of their total food supply (Bernard 1992).

Because a region cannot support a large number of people who hunt animals and gather plants (group members do not plant—they only gather what is already there), hunting and gathering societies are small. They usually consist of only twenty-five to forty people. These groups are nomadic. As their food supply dwindles in one area, they move to another location. They place high value on sharing food, which is essential to their survival. Because of disease, drought, and pestilence, children have only about a fifty-fifty chance of surviving to adulthood (Lenski and Lenski 1987).

Of all societies, hunters and gatherers are the most egalitarian. Because what they hunt and gather is perishable, the people accumulate few personal possessions. Consequently, no one becomes wealthier than anyone else. There are no rulers, and most decisions are arrived at through discussion. Because their needs are basic and they do not work to store up material possessions, hunters and gatherers have the most leisure of all human groups (Sahlins 1972; Lorber 1994; Volti 1995).

As in the photo on the next page, all human groups were once hunters and gatherers. Until several hundred years ago, such societies were common, but only about 300 hunter-gatherer groups remain today (Stiles 2003). Their demise came when other groups moved into the territory on which they depended for food. The groups that remain include the pygmies of central Africa, the aborigines of Australia, and various groups in South America. As populations expand, these groups seem doomed to a similar fate, and it is likely that their way of life will soon disappear from the human scene (Lenski and Lenski 1987).

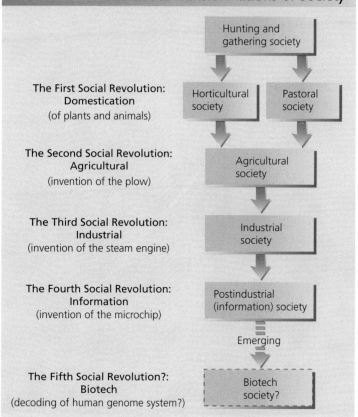

FIGURE 6.1 The Social Transformations of Society

Note: Not all the world's societies will go through the transformations shown in this figure. Whether any hunting and gathering societies will survive, however, remains to be seen. A few might, perhaps kept on "small reserves" that will be off limits to developers—but open to guided "ethnotours" at a hefty fee.

Source: By the author.

Pastoral and Horticultural Societies

About ten thousand years ago, some groups found that they could tame and breed some of the animals they hunted—primarily goats, sheep, cattle, and camels. Others discovered that they could cultivate plants. As a result, hunting and gathering societies branched into two directions, each with different means of acquiring food.

The key to understanding the first branching is the word *pasture;* **pastoral** (or herding) **societies** are based on the *pasturing of animals.* Pastoral societies developed in regions where low rainfall made it impractical to build life around growing crops. Groups that took this turn remained nomadic, for they followed their animals to fresh pasture. The key to understanding the second branching is the word *horticulture,* or plant cultivation. **Horticultural** (or gardening) **societies** are based on the *cultivation of plants by the use of hand tools.* Because they no longer had to abandon an area as the food supply gave out, these groups developed permanent settlements.

We can call the domestication of animals and plants the *first social revolution.* As shown in Figure 6.2 on page 151, it transformed society. Although the **domestication revolution** was gradual, occurring over thousands of years, it represented such a

pastoral society a society based on the pasturing of animals

horticultural society a society based on cultivating plants by the use of hand tools

domestication revolution the first social revolution, based on the domestication of plants and animals, which led to pastoral and horticultural societies

The simplest forms of societies are called *hunting and gathering societies*. Members of these societies have adapted well to their environments, and they have more leisure than the members of other societies. Not many hunting and gathering groups remain on earth. This man, who is spear fishing, is from the Turkana of Kenya.

fundamental break with the past that it changed human history. The more dependable food supply ushered in changes that touched almost every aspect of human life. Groups grew larger because the more dependable food supply supported more people. With more food available than was needed for survival, no longer was it necessary for everyone to work at providing food. As a result, a *division of labor* developed. Some people began to make jewelry, others tools, others weapons, and so on. This led to a surplus of objects, which, in turn, stimulated trade. As groups traded with one another, they began to accumulate objects they prized, such as gold, jewelry, and utensils.

Figure 6.2 illustrates how these changes led to *social inequality*. Some families (or clans) acquired more goods than others. This led to feuds and war, for groups now possessed animals, pastures, croplands, jewelry, and other material goods to fight about. War, in turn, opened the door to slavery, for people found it convenient to let captives do their drudge work. Social inequality remained limited, however, for the surplus itself was limited. As individuals passed their possessions on to their descendants, wealth grew more concentrated. So did power, and for the first time, some individuals became chiefs.

Note the pattern that runs through this transformation: the change *from fewer to more possessions and from greater to lesser equality*. Where people were located *within* the hierarchy of a society became vital for determining what happened to them in life.

Agricultural Societies

The invention of the plow about five or six thousand years ago once again changed social life forever. Compared with hoes and digging sticks, using animals to pull plows is immensely efficient. As the earth was plowed, more nutrients were returned to the soil, making the land more productive. The food surplus of the **agricultural revolution** was unlike anything ever seen in human history. It allowed even more people to engage in activities other than farming. In this new **agricultural society,** people developed cities and what is popularly known as "culture," activities such as philosophy, art, music, literature, and architecture. Accompanied by the inventions of the wheel, writing, and numbers, the changes were so profound that this period is sometimes referred to as "the dawn of civilization."

The social inequality of pastoral and horticultural societies turned out to be only a hint of what was to come. When some people managed to gain control of the growing surplus of resources in agricultural societies, *inequality became a fundamental feature of life in society*. To protect their expanding privileges and power, this elite surrounded itself with armed men. This small group even levied taxes on others, who now had become their "subjects." As conflict theorists point out, this concentration of resources and power—along with the oppression of people not in power—was the forerunner of the state.

No one knows exactly how it happened, but during this period females also became subject to males. Sociologist Elise Boulding (1976) theorizes that this change occurred because men were in charge of plowing and the cows. She suggests that when metals were

agricultural revolution the second social revolution, based on the invention of the plow, which led to agricultural societies

agricultural society a society based on large-scale agriculture

Industrial Revolution the third social revolution, occurring when machines powered by fuels replaced most animal and human power

industrial society a society based on the use of machines powered by fuels

developed, men took on the new job of attaching the metal as tips to the wooden plows and doing the plowing. As a result,

> the shift of the status of the woman farmer may have happened quite rapidly, once there were two male specializations relating to agriculture: plowing and the care of cattle. This situation left women with all the subsidiary tasks, including weeding and carrying water to the fields. The new fields were larger, so women had to work just as many hours as they did before, but now they worked at more secondary tasks. . . . This would contribute further to the erosion of the status of women.

This explanation, however, creates more questions than it answers. Why, for example, did men take over metal work and plowing? Why didn't women? It also does not account for why men control societies in which women are in charge of the cattle. In short, we are left in the dark as to why and how men became dominant, a reason likely to remain lost in human history.

Industrial Societies

The *third* social invention also turned society upside down. The **Industrial Revolution** began in Great Britain in 1765 when the steam engine was first used to run machinery. Before this, a few machines (such as windmills and water wheels) had been used to harness nature, but most machines depended on human and animal power. The resulting **industrial society** is defined by sociologist Herbert Blumer (1990) as one in which goods are produced by machines powered by fuels, instead of by the brute force of humans or animals.

The steam engine ushered in even more social inequality. This new technology was far more efficient than anything that preceded it. Just as its surplus was greater, so also were its effects on social life. The cities had a massive supply of desperate labor, people who had been thrown off the lands that their ancestors had farmed as tenants for centuries. Homeless, they faced the choice of stealing, starving, or being paid the equivalent of a loaf of bread for a day's work. Some of the men who first harnessed the steam engine and employed these desperate workers accumulated such wealth that their riches outran the imagination of royalty.

Workers had no legal right to unionize, not even the right to safe working conditions. If workers banded together to protest or to ask for higher wages, they were fired. If they returned to the factory, they were arrested for trespassing on private property. Strikes were illegal, and strikers were arrested—or beaten by the employer's private security force. During the early 1900s, some U.S. strikers were shot by private police and even by the National Guard. Against these odds, workers gradually won their fight for better working conditions.

As industrialization continued, bringing an abundance of goods, and as workers won what we call basic rights, a surprising change occurred—*the pattern of growing inequality was reversed.* Home ownership became common, as did the ownership of automobiles and an incredible variety of consumer goods. Today's typical worker enjoys a high standard of living in terms of health care, food, housing, material possessions, and access to libraries and education. On an even broader scale of growing equality came the abolition of slavery, the shift from monarchies to more representative political systems, greater rights for women and minorities, and the rights to a jury trial, to cross-examine witnesses, to vote, and to travel. A recent extension of these equalities is the right to set up your own Internet blog where you can bemoan life in your school or criticize the president.

Postindustrial (Information) Societies

If you were to choose one word to characterize our society, what would it be? Of the many candidates, the word *change* would have to rank high. The primary

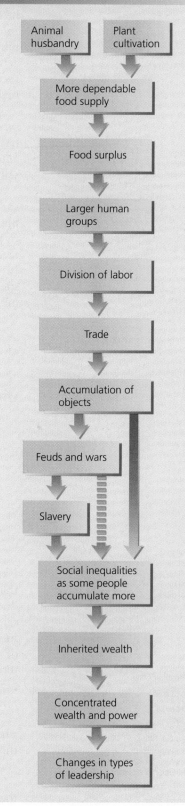

FIGURE 6.2 Consequences of Animal Domestication and Plant Cultivation

Animal husbandry / Plant cultivation → More dependable food supply → Food surplus → Larger human groups → Division of labor → Trade → Accumulation of objects → Feuds and wars → Slavery → Social inequalities as some people accumulate more → Inherited wealth → Concentrated wealth and power → Changes in types of leadership

Source: By the author.

source of the sweeping changes that are transforming our lives is the technology centering on the microchip. The change is so vast that sociologists say that a new type of society has emerged. They call it the **postindustrial** (or **information**) **society.**

What are the main characteristics of this new society? Unlike the industrial society, its hallmark is not turning raw materials into products. Rather, its basic component is *information.* Teachers pass knowledge on to students, while lawyers, physicians, bankers, pilots, and interior decorators sell their specialized knowledge of law, the body, money, aerodynamics, and color schemes to clients. Unlike the factory workers of an industrial society, these individuals don't *produce* anything. Rather, they transmit or apply information to provide services that others are willing to pay for.

The United States was the first country to have more than half of its workers in service industries such as banking, counseling, education, entertainment, government, health, insurance, law, mass media, research, and sales. Australia, Japan, New Zealand, and western Europe soon followed. This trend away from manufacturing and toward selling information and services shows no sign of letting up.

The changes are so profound that they have led to a *fourth social revolution.* The surface changes of this new technology are obvious. Our purchases are scanned and billed in some remote place. While we ride in cars, trucks, boats, and airplanes, we talk to people in distant cities or even on the other side of the globe. We examine the surface of Mars and probe other remote regions of space. We spend billions of dollars on Internet purchases. And because of this tiny device, millions of children (and adults) spend countless hours battling virtual video villains. Beyond such surface changes lie much more fundamental ones: The microchip is transforming relations among people. It is also uprooting our old perspectives and replacing them with new ones. In the Sociology and the New Technology box on the next page, we explore an extreme aspect of virtual reality.

Biotech Societies: Is a New Type of Society Emerging?

- Tobacco that fights cancer. ("Yes, smoke your way to health!")
- Corn that fights herpes and is a contraceptive. ("Corn flakes in the morning— and safe sex all day!")
- Goats whose milk contains spider silk (to make fishing lines and body armor) ("Got milk? The best bulletproofing.")
- Animals that are part human so they produce medicines for humans. ("Ah, those liver secretions. Good for what ails you.")
- No-Sneeze kitties—hypoallergenic cats at $4,000 each. (You can write your own jingle for this one.)

I know that such products sound like science fiction, but we *already* have the goats that make spider silk. Human genes have been inserted into animals so that they produce medicine (Elias 2001; Kristoff 2002; Osborne 2002). The no-sneeze cats are for sale—and there is a waiting list of allergic cat lovers (Rosenthal 2006). The changes in which we are immersed are so extensive that we may be entering another new type of society. In this new **biotech society,** the economy will center on applying and altering genetic structures—both plant and animal—to produce food, medicine, and materials.

If there is a new society—and this is not certain—when did it begin? There are no firm edges to new societies, for each new one overlaps the one it is replacing. The opening to a biotech society could have been 1953, when Francis Crick and James Watson identified the double-helix structure of DNA. Or perhaps historians will trace the date to the decoding of the human genome in 2001.

Whether the changes that are swirling around us are part of a new type of society is not the main point. The larger group called society always profoundly affects people's thinking and behavior. *The sociological significance of these changes, then, is that as society is transformed, it will sweep us along with it. The transformation will be so fundamental that it will change even the ways we think about the self and life.* With cloning and bioengineering, we

postindustrial (information) society a society based on information, services, and high technology, rather than on raw materials and manufacturing

biotech society a society whose economy increasingly centers on the application of genetics to produce medicine, food, and materials

SOCIOLOGY and the NEW TECHNOLOGY

Avatar Fantasy Life: The Blurring Lines of Reality

Dissatisfied with your current life? Would you like to become someone else? Maybe someone rich? Maybe someone with no responsibilities? You can. Join a world populated with virtual people and live out your fantasy.

For some, the appeal is strong. *Second Life,* one of several Internet sites that offer an alternative virtual reality, has exploded in popularity. Of its 8 million "residents," 450,000 spend twenty to forty hours a week in their second life.

To start your second life, you select your avatar, a kind of digital hand puppet, to be your persona in this virtual world. Your avatar comes in just a basic form, although you can control its movements just fine. But that bare body certainly won't do. You will want to clothe it. For this, you have your choice of outfits for every occasion. Although you buy them from other avatars in virtual stores, you have to spend real dollars. You might want some hair, too. For that, too, you'll have your choice of designers. And again, you'll spend real dollars. And you might want to have a sex organ. There is even a specialty store for that.

All equipped the way you want to be?

Then it is time to meet other avatars, the virtual personas of real-life people. In this virtual world, they buy property, open businesses, and interact with one another. They share stories, talk about their desires in life, and have drinks in virtual bars.

Avatars flirt, too. Some even date and marry.

For most people, this second life is just an interesting game. They come and go, as if playing *Tomb Raider* or *World of Warcraft* now and then. Some people, though, get so caught up in their virtual world that their real world shrinks in appeal, and they neglect friends and family. That is, they neglect their real friends and family, but remain attentive to their virtual friends and family. As the virtual replaces the real, the virtual becomes real and the real fades into nonreality.

Ric Hoogestraat in Phoenix, Arizona, loves his virtual life. He operates his avatar, Dutch—a macho motorcycle man, who is also filthy rich—from the time he gets up to the time he goes to bed. Dutch visits his several homes, where he can lounge on specially designed furniture. He pours his favorite drink and from his penthouse watches the sun setting over the ocean.

And here he also spends time with his wife, Tenaj. Dutch met Tenaj on *Second Life.* As courtships go, theirs went well. Their wedding was announced, of course, and about

A scene from Second Life. *Each image is an avatar, a real person's fantasy self.*

twenty avatar friends attended. They gave the newlyweds real congratulations, in a virtual sort of way.

Dutch and Tenaj have two dogs and pay the mortgage together. They love cuddling and intimate talks. Their love life is quite good, as avatars can have virtual sex.

But then there is Sue, whose last name is Hoogestraat, and Sue is not pleased. Sue is also Ric's wife, but this one is in real life. Sue feels neglected and doesn't like Ric spending so much time in his virtual world. She also doesn't appreciate Tenaj.

The whole thing has become more than a little irritating. "I'll try to talk to him or bring him a drink, and he'll be having sex with a cartoon," she says.

Tenaj, the avatar, also has a real life counterpart, Janet, who lives in Canada. Ric and Janet have never met—nor do they plan to meet. They haven't even talked on the phone as Ric and Janet—just a lot of sweet talking in their virtual world as Dutch and Tenaj.

For gamers, the virtual always overlaps the real to some extent, but for some the virtual overwhelms the real. Their satisfactions, which are quite real, come from living a fantasy life.

This is all quite new, but quite real.

For Your Consideration

How much time do you spend on computer games? Are you involved in any virtual reality? Do you think that Ric is cheating on Sue? Is this grounds for divorce? (One wife certainly thought so. She divorced her husband when she caught a glimpse of his avatar having sex with an avatar prostitute ["Second Life Affair . . ." 2008]). Other than the sexual aspect, is having a second life really any different from people's involvement in fantasy football? (Keep in mind the term *football widows.*)

Based on Alter 2007; Corbett 2009.

could even see changes in the human species. The Sociology and the New Technology box below examines implications of cloning.

In Sum: Each society sets boundaries around its members. By laying a framework of statuses, roles, groups, and social institutions, society establishes the prevailing behaviors and beliefs. It also determines the type and extent of social inequality. These factors, in turn, set the stage for relationships between men and women, racial–ethnic groups, the young and the elderly, the rich and the poor, and so on.

Society is not stagnant, and *you* are affected directly by the sweeping historical changes that transform it. On the obvious level, if you lived in a hunting and gathering society you would not be listening to your favorite music, watching TV, playing video games—or taking this course. On a deeper level, you would not feel the same about life, have the same beliefs, or hold your particular aspirations for the future. Actually, no aspect of your life would be the same. You would be locked into the attitudes and views that come with a hunting and gathering way of life.

SOCIOLOGY and the NEW TECHNOLOGY

"So, You Want to Be Yourself?" Cloning and the Future of Society

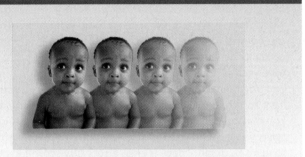

No type of society ends abruptly. The edges are fuzzy, as the old merges into the new. With time speeded up, our information society hasn't even matured, and it looks as though a biotech society is hard on its heels. Let's try to peer over the edge of today's society to glimpse the one that might be arriving. If it does, what will life be like? We could examine many issues, but since space is limited, let's consider just one: cloning. Since human embryos have been cloned, it seems inevitable that some group somewhere will complete the process. If cloning humans becomes routine—well, consider these two scenarios:

It turns out that you can't have children. You go to Cleto's Cloning Clinic, pay the standard fee, and clone either yourself or your spouse. Who is your child? Is that little boy or girl, in effect, either yourself or your spouse—as a child? Or instead of a daughter or son, even a sister or brother?

Or suppose that you love your mother dearly, and she is dying. With her permission, you decide to clone her. Who is the clone? Would you be rearing your own mother?

When we have genetic replicates, we will have to wrestle with new questions of human relationships: What is a clone's relationship to its "parents"? Indeed, what are "parents" and "children"?

Cloning also takes us to weighty ethical matters, ones that may involve the future of society. I'm sure you have heard people object that cloning is immoral.

But have you heard the opposite, that cloning should be our moral choice? Let's suppose that mass cloning becomes possible. Let's also assume that geneticists trace high creative ability, high intelligence, compassion, and a propensity for peace to specific genes—along with the ability to appreciate and create beautiful poetry, music, and architecture; to excel in mathematics, science, and other intellectual pursuits; even to be successful in love. Why, then, they argue, should we leave human reproduction to people who have inferior traits—genetic diseases, low IQs, perhaps even the propensity for crime and violence? They suggest that we select people with the finer characteristics to reproduce—and to clone.

For Your Consideration

Do you think that we have a moral obligation to try to build a society that is better for all—one without terrorism, war, violence, and greed? If so, do you think we also have the moral obligation to populate society with people who have the characteristics that would bring about such a society? Could this even be our evolutionary destiny?

Source: Based on Kaebnick 2000; McGee 2000; Bjerklie et al. 2001; Davis 2001; Weiss 2004; Regalado 2005.

Now that we have reviewed the major historical shifts in societies, let's turn to groups within society. Just how do they affect our lives?

Groups Within Society

Our society is huge, dominating, sometimes even threatening and oppressive. This can create a bewildering sense of not belonging. Sociologist Emile Durkheim (1893/1933) called this condition *anomie* (AN-uh-mee). He said that small groups help prevent anomie by standing as a buffer between the individual and the larger society. By providing intimate relationships, small groups give us a sense of belonging, something that we all need. Because smaller groups are essential for our well-being, let's look at them in detail.

Smaller groups, then, are vital for our well-being, but before we examine them in detail, we should distinguish some terms. Two terms sometimes confused with "group" are *aggregate* and *category*. An **aggregate** consists of individuals who temporarily share the same physical space but who do not see themselves as belonging together. Shoppers standing in a checkout line or drivers waiting at a red light are an aggregate. A **category** is simply a statistic. It consists of people who share similar characteristics, such as all college women who wear glasses or all men over 6 feet tall. Unlike group members, the individuals who make up a category don't think of themselves as belonging together, and they don't interact with one another. These concepts are illustrated in the photos on the next page.

Primary Groups

Our first group, the family, gives us our basic orientations to life. Later, among friends, we find more intimacy and an expanded sense of belonging. These groups are what sociologist Charles Cooley called **primary groups.** By providing intimate, face-to-face interaction, they give us an identity, a feeling of who we are. As Cooley (1909) put it,

> By primary groups I mean those characterized by intimate face-to-face association and cooperation. They are primary in several senses, but chiefly in that they are fundamental in forming the social nature and ideals of the individual.

Producing a Mirror Within.   Cooley called primary groups the "springs of life." By this, he meant that primary groups, such as family and friends, are essential to our emotional well-being. As humans, we have an intense need for face-to-face interaction that generates feelings of self-esteem. By offering a sense of belonging and a feeling of being appreciated—and sometimes even loved—primary groups are uniquely equipped to meet this basic need. From our opening vignette, you can see that gangs are also primary groups.

Primary groups are also significant because their values and attitudes become fused into our identity. We internalize their views, which then become the lenses through which we view life. Even when we are adults—no matter how far we move away from our childhood roots—early primary groups remain "inside" us. There, they continue to form part of the perspective from which we look out onto the world. Ultimately, then, it is difficult, if not impossible, for us to separate the self from our primary groups, for the self and our groups merge into a "we."

Secondary Groups

Compared with primary groups, **secondary groups** are larger, more anonymous, more formal, and more impersonal. Secondary groups are based on some common interest or activity, and their members are likely to interact on the basis of specific statuses, such as president, manager, worker, or student. Examples are a college class, the American Sociological

aggregate individuals who temporarily share the same physical space but who do not see themselves as belonging together

category people who have similar characteristics

primary group a group characterized by intimate, long-term, face-to-face association and cooperation

secondary group compared with a primary group, a larger, relatively temporary, more anonymous, formal, and impersonal group based on some interest or activity

Categories, Aggregates, Primary and Secondary Groups

Groups have a deep impact on our actions, views, orientations, even what we feel and think about life. Yet, as illustrated by these photos, not everything that appears to be a group is actually a group in the sociological sense.

▲ **Aggregates** are people who happen to be in the same place at the same time.

▲ The outstanding trait that these three people have in common does not make them a group, but a **category.**

◄ **Secondary groups** are larger and more anonymous, formal, and impersonal than primary groups. Why are the participants of a dog show an example of a secondary group?

▶ **Primary groups** such as the family play a key role in the development of the self. As a small group, the family also serves as a buffer from the often-threatening larger group known as society. The family has been of primary significance in forming the basic orientations of this couple, as it will be for their son.

Association, and the Democratic Party. Contemporary society could not function without secondary groups. They are part of the way we get our education, make our living, spend our money, and use our leisure time.

As necessary as secondary groups are for contemporary life, they often fail to satisfy our deep needs for intimate association. Consequently, *secondary groups tend to break down into primary groups.* At school and work, we form friendships. Our interaction with our friends is so important that we sometimes feel that if it weren't for them, school or work "would drive us crazy." The primary groups that we form within secondary groups, then, serve as a buffer between ourselves and the demands that secondary groups place on us.

in-groups groups toward which people feel loyalty

out-groups groups toward which people feel antagonism

In-Groups and Out-Groups

What groups do you identity with? Which groups in our society do you dislike? We all have **in-groups,** groups toward which we feel loyalty. And we all have **out-groups,** groups toward which we feel antagonism. For Monster Kody in our opening vignette, the Crips were an in-group, while the Bloods were an out-group. That the Crips—and we—make such a fundamental division of the world has far-reaching consequences for our lives.

Implications for a Socially Diverse Society: Shaping Perception and Morality.   You know how vital some of your groups are to you, the sense of belonging they give you. This can bring positive consequences for others, such as our tendency to excuse the faults of people we love and to encourage them to do better. Unfortunately, dividing the world into a "we" and "them" also leads to discrimination, hatred, and, as we saw in our opening vignette, even murder.

At the center of it all is how in-group membership shapes our perception of the world. Let's look at two examples. The first you see regularly, prejudice and discrimination on the basis of sex. As sociologist Robert Merton (1968) said, our favoritism creates a fascinating double standard. We tend to view the traits of our in-group as virtues, while we perceive those *same* traits as vices in out-groups. Men may perceive an aggressive man as assertive but an aggressive woman as pushy. They may think that a male employee who doesn't speak up "knows when to keep his mouth shut," while they consider a quiet woman as too timid to make it in the business world.

The "we" and "they" division of the world can lead to such twisted perception that harming others comes to be viewed as right. The Nazis provide one of the most startling examples. For them, the Jews were an out-group who symbolized an evil that should be eliminated. Many ordinary, "good" Germans shared this view and defended the Holocaust as "dirty work" that someone had to do (Hughes 1962/2005).

An example from way back then, you might say—and the world has moved on. But our inclination to divide the world into in-groups and out-groups has not moved on—nor has the twisting of perception that accompanies it. After the terrorist attacks of September 11, 2001, top U.S. officials came to view Arabs as sinister, bloodthirsty villains. They said that it was OK for interrogators to be "cruel, inhuman, and degrading" to prisoners" (Gonzales 2002). Inflicting pain, they said, was not torture unless it caused "death, organ failure, or permanent damage" (Johnston and Shane 2008). (For more on this, see the section on dehumanization in Chapter 15, pages 450–451.) Alan Dershowitz, a professor at Harvard Law School who usually takes very liberal views, went even further. He said that we should make torture legal so judges

"So long, Bill. This is my club. You can't come in."

How our participation in social groups shapes our self-concept is a focus of symbolic interactionists. In this process, knowing who we are *not* is as significant as knowing who we are.

can issue "torture warrants" (Schulz 2002). After 9/11, inflicting pain on prisoners became "dirty work" that someone had to do. Can you see the principle at work—and understand that in-group/out-group thinking can be so severe that even "good people" can torture and kill? And with a good conscience.

Economic downturns are especially perilous in this regard. The Nazis took power during a depression so severe that it was wiping out the middle classes. If such a depression were to occur in the United States, immigrants would be transformed from "nice people who for low wages will do jobs that Americans think are beneath them" to "sneaky people who steal jobs from friends and family." A national anti-immigration policy would follow, accompanied by a resurgence of hate groups such as the neo-Nazis, the Ku Klux Klan, and skinheads.

In short, to divide the world into in-groups and out-groups is a natural part of social life. But in addition to bringing functional consequences, it can also bring dysfunctional ones.

Reference Groups

Suppose you have just been offered a good job. It pays double what you hope to make even after you graduate from college. You have only two days to make up your mind. If you accept it, you will have to drop out of college. As you consider the matter, thoughts like this may go through your mind: "My friends will say I'm a fool if I don't take the job . . . but Dad and Mom will practically go crazy. They've made sacrifices for me, and they'll be crushed if I don't finish college. They've always said I've got to get my education first, that good jobs will always be there. . . . But, then, I'd like to see the look on the faces of those neighbors who said I'd never amount to much!"

Evaluating Ourselves.   This is an example of how people use **reference groups,** the groups we refer to when we evaluate ourselves. Your reference groups may include your family, neighbors, teachers, classmates, co-workers, and the Scouts or the members of a church, synagogue, or mosque. If you were like Monster Kody in our opening vignette, the "set" would be your main reference group. Even a group you don't belong to can be a reference group. For example, if you are thinking about going to graduate school, graduate students or members of the profession you want to join may form a reference group. You would consider their standards as you evaluate your grades or writing skills.

Reference groups exert tremendous influence over our lives. For example, if you want to become a corporate executive, you might start to dress more formally, try to improve your vocabulary, read the *Wall Street Journal,* and change your major to business or law. In contrast, if you want to become a rock musician, you might wear jewelry in several places where you have pierced your body, get elaborate tattoos, dress in ways your parents and many of your peers consider extreme, read *Rolling Stone,* drop out of college, and hang around clubs and rock groups.

Exposure to Contradictory Standards in a Socially Diverse Society. From these examples, you can see how we use reference groups to evaluate our behavior. When we see ourselves as measuring up to a reference group's standards, we feel no conflict. If our behavior—or even aspirations—does not match the group's standards, however, the mismatch can lead to inner turmoil. For example, wanting to become a corporate executive would create no inner turmoil for most of us. It would, however, for someone who had grown up in an Amish home. The Amish strongly disapprove of such aspirations for their children. They ban high school and college education, suits and ties, and corporate employment. Similarly, if you want to join the military and your parents are dedicated pacifists, you likely would feel deep conflict, because your parents would have quite different aspirations for you.

All of us have *reference groups*—the groups we use as standards to evaluate ourselves. How do you think the reference groups of these members of the KKK who are demonstrating in Jaspar, Texas, differ from those of the police officer who is protecting their right of free speech? Although the KKK and this police officer use different groups to evaluate their attitudes and behaviors, the process is the same.

Two chief characteristics of our society are social diversity and social mobility. This exposes us to standards and orientations that are inconsistent with those we learned during childhood. The "internal recordings" that play contradictory messages from different reference groups, then, are one price we pay for our social mobility.

Social Networks

Although we live in a huge and diverse society, we don't experience social life as a sea of nameless, strange faces. Instead, we interact within social networks. The term **social network** refers to people who are linked to one another. Your social network includes your family, friends, acquaintances, people at work and school, and even "friends of friends." Think of your social network as a spider's web. You are at the center, with lines extending outward, gradually encompassing more and more people.

If you are a member of a large group, you probably associate regularly with a few people within that group. In a sociology class I was teaching at a commuter campus, six women who didn't know one another ended up working together on a project. They got along well, and they began to sit together. Eventually they planned a Christmas party at one of their homes. This type of social network, the clusters within a group, or its internal factions, is called a **clique** (cleek).

The analysis of social networks has become part of applied sociology. One of its most surprising applications was the capture of Saddam Hussein.

> After U.S.-led forces took over Baghdad, Hussein was nowhere to be found. Rumors placed him all over the map, from neighboring countries to safe houses in Baghdad. To find him, U.S. intelligence officers began to apply network analysis. On a color-coded "people map," they placed Hussein's photo in a yellow circle, like a bull's-eye. They then drew links to people who were connected to Hussein, placing their photos closer to or farther from Hussein's photo on the basis of how close they were to Hussein (Schmitt 2003; Hougham 2005).
>
> The photos closest to Hussein represented an intimate and loyal group. These people were the most likely to know where Hussein was, but because of their close ties to him, they also were the least likely to reveal this information. Those who were pictured slightly farther away knew people in this more intimate group, so it was likely that some of them had information about Hussein's whereabouts. Because these people's social ties to Hussein were not as strong, they represented the weaker links that might be broken.
>
> The approach worked. Using software programs to sift through vast amounts of information gained from informants and electronic intercepts, the analysts drew the "people map" that pictured these social relationships. Identifying the weaker links led to the capture of Saddam Hussein.

social network the social ties radiating outward from the self that link people together

clique a cluster of people within a larger group who choose to interact with one another

We all use *reference groups* to evaluate our accomplishments, failures, values, and attitudes. We compare what we see in ourselves with what we perceive as normative in our reference groups. From these two photos, can you see how the *reference groups* and *social networks* of these youths are not likely to lead them to the same social destination?

The Small World Phenomenon.   Social scientists have wondered just how extensive the connections are among social networks. If you list everyone you know, each of those individuals lists everyone he or she knows, and you keep doing this, would almost everyone in the United States eventually be included on those lists?

It would be too cumbersome to test this hypothesis by drawing up such lists, but psychologist Stanley Milgram (1933–1984) came up with an interesting idea. In a classic study known as "the small world phenomenon," Milgram (1967) addressed a letter to "targets": the wife of a divinity student in Cambridge and a stockbroker in Boston. He sent the letter to "starters," who did not know these people. He asked them to send the letter to someone they knew on a first-name basis, someone they thought might know the "target." The recipients, in turn, were asked to mail the letter to someone they knew who might know the "target," and so on. The question was, Would the letters ever reach the "target"? If so, how long would the chain be?

Think of yourself as part of this study. What would you do if you were a "starter," but the "target" lived in a state in which you knew no one? You would send the letter to someone you know who might know someone in that state. This, Milgram reported, is just what happened. Although none of the senders knew the targets, the letters reached the designated individual in an average of just six jumps.

Milgram's study caught the public's fancy, leading to the phrase "six degrees of separation." This expression means that, on average, everyone in the United States is separated by just six individuals. Milgram's conclusions have become so popular that a game, "Six Degrees of Kevin Bacon," was built around it.

Is the Small World Phenomenon an Academic Myth?   Unfortunately, things are not this simple. There is a problem with Milgram's research, as psychologist Judith Kleinfeld (2002a, 2002b) discovered when she decided to replicate Milgram's study. When she went to the archives at Yale University Library to get more details, she found that Milgram had stacked the deck in favor of finding a small world. The "starters" came from mailing lists of people who were likely to have higher incomes and therefore were not representative of average people. In addition, one of the "targets" was a stockbroker, and that person's "starters" were investors in blue-chip stocks. Kleinfeld also found another discrepancy: On average, only 30 percent of the letters reached their "target." In one of Milgram's studies, the success rate was just 5 percent.

Since most letters did *not* reach their targets, even with the deck stacked in favor of success, we can draw the *opposite* conclusion from the one that Milgram reported: People who don't know one another are dramatically separated by social barriers. How great the barriers are is illustrated by another attempt to replicate Milgram's study, this one using e-mail. Only 384 of 24,000 chains reached their targets (Dodds et al. 2003).

As Kleinfeld says, "Rather than living in a small world, we may live in a world that looks like a bowl of lumpy oatmeal, with many small worlds loosely connected and perhaps some small worlds not connected at all." Somehow, I don't think that the phrase, "lumpy oatmeal phenomenon," will become standard, but the criticism of Milgram's research is valid.

Kleinfeld's revelations of the flaws in Milgram's research reinforce the need for replication, a topic discussed in the previous chapter. For our knowledge of social life, we cannot depend on single studies—there may be problems of generalizability on the one hand, or those of negligence or even fraud on the other. Replication by objective researchers is essential to build and advance solid social knowledge.

A New Group: Electronic Communities

In the 1990s, a new type of human group, the **electronic community,** made its appearance. People "meet" online to talk about almost any conceivable topic, from donkey racing and bird watching to sociology and quantum physics. Some online encounters in chat rooms, Facebook, LinkedIn, and Twitter meet our definition of *group*, people who interact with one another and who think of themselves as belonging together. They pride themselves on the distinctive nature of their interests and knowledge—factors that give them a common identity and bind them together. Although sociologists have begun to study these groups, the results are preliminary and tentative.

electronic community individuals who regularly interact with one another on the Internet and who think of themselves as belonging together

Group Dynamics

As you know from personal experience, the lively interaction *within* groups—who does what with whom—has profound consequences for how you adjust to life. Sociologists use the term **group dynamics** to refer to how groups influence us and how we affect groups. Let's consider how the size of a group makes a difference and then examine leadership, conformity, and decision making.

Before doing so, we should see how sociologists define the term *small group*. In a **small group,** there are few enough members that each one can interact directly with all the other members. Small groups can be either primary or secondary. A wife, husband, and children make up a primary small group, as do workers who take their breaks together, while bidders at an auction and students in a small introductory sociology class are secondary small groups. You might want to look again at the photos on page 156.

Effects of Group Size on Stability and Intimacy

Writing in the early 1900s, sociologist Georg Simmel (1858–1918) noted the significance of group size. He used the term **dyad** for the smallest possible group, which consists of two people. Dyads, which include marriages, love affairs, and close friendships, show two distinct qualities. First, they are the most intense or intimate of human groups. Because only two people are involved, the interaction is focused on them. Second, dyads tend to be unstable. Because dyads require that both members participate and be committed, it takes just one member to lose interest for the dyad to collapse. In larger groups, by contrast, even if one member withdraws, the group can continue, for its existence does not depend on any single member (Simmel 1950).

A **triad** is a group of three people. As Simmel noted, the addition of a third person fundamentally changes the group. With three people, interaction between the first two decreases. This can create strain. For example, with the birth of a child, hardly any aspect of a couple's relationship goes untouched. Attention focuses on the baby, and interaction between the husband and wife diminishes. Despite this, the marriage usually becomes stronger. Although the intensity of interaction is less in triads, they are inherently stronger and give greater stability to a relationship.

Yet, as Simmel noted, triads, too, are unstable. They tend to form **coalitions**—some group members aligning themselves against others. It is not uncommon for two

group dynamics the ways in which individuals affect groups and the ways in which groups influence individuals

small group a group small enough for everyone to interact directly with all the other members

dyad the smallest possible group, consisting of two persons

triad a group of three people

coalition the alignment of some members of a group against others

Japanese companies encourage their employees to think of themselves, not as individuals, but as members of a group. Similarity of appearance and activity help to fuse group identity and company loyalty. Why do you think there are two subgroups in this photo?

Group size has a significant influence on how people interact. When a group changes from a dyad (two people) to a triad (three people), the relationships among the participants undergo a shift. How do you think the birth of this child affected the relationship between the mother and father?

members of a triad to feel stronger bonds and to prefer one another. This leaves the third person feeling hurt and excluded. Another characteristic of triads is that they often produce an arbitrator or mediator, someone who tries to settle disagreements between the other two. In one-child families, you can often observe both of these characteristics of triads—coalitions and arbitration.

The general principle is this: *As a small group grows larger, it becomes more stable, but its intensity, or intimacy, decreases.* To see why, look at Figure 6.3 on the next page. As each new person comes into a group, the connections among people multiply. In a dyad, there is only 1 relationship; in a triad, there are 3; in a group of four, 6; in a group of five, 10. If we expand the group to six, we have 15 relationships, while a group of seven yields 21 relationships. If we continue adding members, we soon are unable to follow the connections: A group of eight has 28 possible relationships; a group of nine, 36 relationships; a group of ten, 45; and so on.

It is not only the number of relationships that makes larger groups more stable. As groups grow, they also tend to develop a more formal structure. For example, leaders emerge and more specialized roles come into play. This often results in such familiar offices as president, secretary, and treasurer. This structure provides a framework that helps the group survive over time.

Effects of Group Size on Attitudes and Behavior

Imagine that you are taking a team-taught course in social psychology and your professors have asked you to join a few students to discuss your adjustment to college life. When you arrive, they tell you that to make the discussion anonymous they want you to sit unseen in a booth. You will participate in the discussion over an intercom, talking when your microphone comes on. The professors say that they will not listen to the conversation, and they leave.

You find the format somewhat strange, to say the least, but you go along with it. You have not seen the other students in their booths, but when they talk about their experiences, you find yourself becoming wrapped up in the problems that they begin to share. One student even mentions how frightening it is to be away from home because of his history of epileptic seizures. Later, you hear this individual breathe heavily into the microphone. Then he stammers and cries for help. A crashing noise follows, and you imagine him lying helpless on the floor.

Nothing but an eerie silence follows. What do you do?

Your professors, John Darley and Bibb Latané (1968), staged the whole thing, but you don't know this. No one had a seizure. In fact, no one was even in the other booths. Everything, except your comments, was on tape.

Some participants were told that they would be discussing the topic with just one other student, others with two, others with three, four, and five. Darley and Latané found that all students who thought they were part of a dyad rushed out to help. If they thought they were part of a triad, only 80 percent went to help—and they were slower in leaving the booth. In six-person groups, only 60 percent went to see what was wrong—and they were even slower.

This experiment demonstrates how deeply group size influences our attitudes and behavior: It even affects our willingness to help one another. Students in the dyad knew that it was up to them to help the other student. The professor was gone, and if they didn't help there was no one else. In the larger groups, including the triad, students felt *a diffusion of responsibility:* Giving help was no more their responsibility than anyone else's.

You probably have observed the second consequence of group size firsthand. When a group is small, its members act informally, but as the group grows, the members lose their sense of intimacy and become more formal with one another. No longer can the members assume that the others are "insiders" in sympathy with what they say. Now they must take a "larger audience" into consideration, and instead of merely "talking," they begin to "address" the group. As their speech becomes more formal, their body language stiffens.

You probably have observed a third aspect of group dynamics, too. In the early stages of a party, when only a few people are present, almost everyone talks with everyone else. But as others arrive, the guests break into smaller groups. Some hosts, who want their guests to mix together, make a nuisance of themselves trying to achieve *their* idea of what a group should be like. The division into small groups is inevitable, however, for it follows the basic sociological principles that we have just reviewed. Because the addition of each person rapidly increases connections (in this case, "talk lines"), conversation becomes more difficult. The guests break into smaller groups in which they can look at each other directly and interact comfortably with one another.

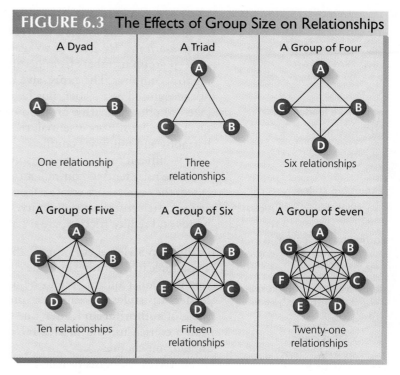

FIGURE 6.3 The Effects of Group Size on Relationships

A Dyad — One relationship

A Triad — Three relationships

A Group of Four — Six relationships

A Group of Five — Ten relationships

A Group of Six — Fifteen relationships

A Group of Seven — Twenty-one relationships

Leadership

All of us are influenced by leaders, so it is important to understand leadership. Let's look at how people become leaders, the types of leaders there are, and their different styles of leadership. Before we do this, though, it is important to clarify that leaders don't necessarily hold formal positions in a group. **Leaders** are people who influence the behaviors, opinions, or attitudes of others. Even a group of friends has leaders.

Who Becomes a Leader? Are leaders born with characteristics that propel them to the forefront of a group? No sociologist would agree with such an idea. In general, people who become leaders are perceived by group members as strongly representing their values or as able to lead a group out of a crisis (Trice and Beyer 1991). Leaders also tend to be more talkative and to express determination and self-confidence.

These findings may not be surprising, since such traits appear to be related to leadership. Researchers, however, have also discovered traits that seem to have no bearing on the ability to lead. For example, taller people and those who are judged better looking are more likely to become leaders (Stodgill 1974; Judge and Cable 2004). Some of the factors that go into our choice of leaders are quite subtle, as social psychologists Lloyd Howells and Selwyn Becker (1962) found in a simple experiment. They had groups of five people who did not know one another sit at a rectangular table. Three, of course, sat on one side, and two on the other. After discussing a topic for a set period of time, each group chose a leader. The findings are startling: Although only 40 percent of the people sat on the two-person side, 70 percent of the leaders emerged from that side. The explanation is that we tend to interact more with people facing us than with people to the side of us.

leader someone who influences other people

instrumental leader an individual who tries to keep the group moving toward its goals; also known as a *task-oriented leader*

expressive leader an individual who increases harmony and minimizes conflict in a group; also known as a *socioemotional leader*

leadership styles ways in which people express their leadership

authoritarian leader an individual who leads by giving orders

democratic leader an individual who leads by trying to reach a consensus

laissez-faire leader an individual who leads by being highly permissive

Types of Leaders. Groups have two types of leaders (Bales 1950, 1953; Cartwright and Zander 1968). The first is easy to recognize. This person, called an **instrumental leader** (or *task-oriented leader*), tries to keep the group moving toward its goals. These leaders try to keep group members from getting sidetracked, reminding them of what they are trying to accomplish. The **expressive leader** (or *socioemotional leader*), in contrast, usually is not recognized as a leader, but he or she certainly is one. This person is likely to crack jokes, to offer sympathy, or to do other things that help to lift the group's morale. Both types of leadership are essential: the one to keep the group on track, the other to increase harmony and minimize conflicts.

It is difficult for the same person to be both an instrumental and an expressive leader, for these roles tend to contradict one another. Because instrumental leaders are task oriented, they sometimes create friction as they prod the group to get on with the job. Their actions often cost them popularity. Expressive leaders, in contrast, who stimulate personal bonds and reduce friction, are usually more popular (Olmsted and Hare 1978).

Leadership Styles. Let's suppose that the president of your college has asked you to head a task force to determine how the college can improve race relations on campus. Although this position requires you to be an instrumental leader, you can adopt a number of **leadership styles,** or ways of expressing yourself as a leader. The three basic styles are those of **authoritarian leader,** one who gives orders; **democratic leader,** one who tries to gain a consensus; and **laissez-faire leader,** one who is highly permissive. Which style should you choose?

Social psychologists Ronald Lippitt and Ralph White (1958) carried out a classic study of these leadership styles. Boys who were matched for IQ, popularity, physical energy, and leadership were assigned to "craft clubs" made up of five boys each. The experimenters trained adult men in the three leadership styles. As the researchers peered through peepholes, taking notes and making movies, each adult rotated among the clubs, playing all three styles to control possible influences of their individual personalities.

The *authoritarian* leaders assigned tasks to the boys and told them what to do. They also praised or condemned the boys' work arbitrarily, giving no explanation for why they judged it good or bad. The *democratic* leaders discussed the project with the boys, outlining the steps that would help them reach their goals. They also suggested different approaches and let the boys work at their own pace. When they evaluated the project, they gave "facts" as the bases for their decisions. The *laissez-faire* leaders were passive. They gave the boys almost total freedom to do as they wished. They offered help when asked, but made few suggestions. They did not evaluate the boys' projects, either positively or negatively.

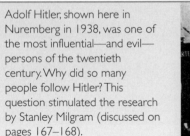
Adolf Hitler, shown here in Nuremberg in 1938, was one of the most influential—and evil—persons of the twentieth century. Why did so many people follow Hitler? This question stimulated the research by Stanley Milgram (discussed on pages 167–168).

The results? The boys who had authoritarian leaders grew dependent on their leader and showed a high degree of internal solidarity. They also became either aggressive or apathetic, with the aggressive boys growing hostile toward their leader. In contrast, the boys who had democratic leaders were friendlier and looked to one another for mutual approval. They did less scapegoating, and when the leader left the room they continued to work at a steadier pace. The boys with laissez-faire leaders asked more questions, but they made fewer decisions. They were notable for their lack of achievement. The researchers concluded that the democratic style of leadership works best. This conclusion, however, may be biased, as the researchers favored a democratic style of leadership in the first place (Olmsted and Hare 1978). Apparently, this same bias in studies of leadership continues (Cassel 1999).

You may have noticed that only boys and men were involved in this experiment. It is interesting to speculate how the results might differ if we were to repeat the experiment with all-girl groups and with mixed groups of girls and boys—and if we used both men and women as leaders. Perhaps you will become the sociologist to study such variations of this classic experiment.

Leadership Styles in Changing Situations.   Different situations require different styles of leadership. Suppose, for example, that you are leading a dozen backpackers in the mountains, and it is time to make dinner. A laissez-faire style would be appropriate if the backpackers had brought their own food, or perhaps a democratic style if everyone is expected to pitch in. Authoritarian leadership—you telling the hikers how to prepare their meals—would create resentment. This, in turn, would likely interfere with meeting the primary goal of the group, which in this case is to have a good time while enjoying nature.

Now assume the same group but a different situation: One of your party is lost, and a blizzard is on its way. This situation calls for you to exercise authority. To simply shrug your shoulders and say "You figure it out" would invite disaster—and probably a lawsuit.

The Power of Peer Pressure: The Asch Experiment

How influential are groups in our lives? To answer this, let's look first at *conformity* in the sense of going along with our peers. Our peers have no authority over us, only the influence that we allow.

Imagine again that you are taking a course in social psychology, this time with Dr. Solomon Asch. You have agreed to participate in an experiment. As you enter his laboratory, you see seven chairs, five of them already filled by other students. You are given the sixth. Soon the seventh person arrives. Dr. Asch stands at the front of the room next to a covered easel. He explains that he will first show a large card with a vertical line on it, then another card with three vertical lines. Each of you is to tell him which of the three lines matches the line on the first card (see Figure 6.4).

Dr. Asch then uncovers the first card with the single line and the comparison card with the three lines. The correct answer is easy, for two of the lines are obviously wrong, and one is exactly right. Each person, in order, states his or her answer aloud. You all answer correctly. The second trial is just as easy, and you begin to wonder why you are there.

Then on the third trial, something unexpected happens. Just as before, it is easy to tell which lines match. The first student, however, gives a wrong answer. The second gives the same incorrect answer. So do the third and the fourth. By now, you are wondering what is wrong. How will the person next to you answer? You can hardly believe it when he, too, gives the same wrong answer. Then it is your turn, and you give what you know is the right answer. The seventh person also gives the same wrong answer.

On the next trial, the same thing happens. You know that the choice of the other six is wrong. They are giving what to you are obviously wrong answers. You don't know what to think. Why aren't they seeing things the same way you are? Sometimes they do, but in twelve trials they don't. Something is seriously wrong, and you are no longer sure what to do.

When the eighteenth trial is finished, you heave a sigh of relief. The experiment is finally over, and you are ready to bolt for the door. Dr. Asch walks over to you with a big smile on his face and thanks you for participating in the experiment. He explains that you were the only real subject in the experiment! "The other six were stooges. I paid them to give those answers," he says. Now you feel real relief. Your eyes weren't playing tricks on you after all.

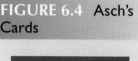

FIGURE 6.4   Asch's Cards

Card 1

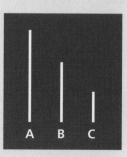

A   B   C

Card 2

The cards used by Solomon Asch in his classic experiment on group conformity

Source: Asch 1952:452–453.

What were the results? Asch (1952) tested fifty people. One-third (33 percent) gave in to the group half the time, providing what they knew to be wrong answers. Another two out of five (40 percent) gave wrong answers, but not as often. One out of four (25 percent) stuck to their guns and always gave the right answer. I don't know how I would do on this test (if I knew nothing about it in advance), but I like to think that I would be part of the 25 percent. You probably feel the same way about yourself. But why should we feel that we wouldn't be like *most* people?

The results are disturbing, and researchers are still replicating Asch's experiment (Bond 2005). In our "land of individualism," the group is so powerful that most people are willing to say things that they know are not true. And this was a group of strangers! How much more conformity can we expect when our group consists of friends, people we value highly and depend on for getting along in life? Again, maybe you will become the sociologist to run that variation of Asch's experiment, perhaps using female subjects.

But do Asch's experiments apply to everyday life, where no stooges are giving wrong answers on purpose? Read the following Down-to-Earth Sociology box to find out.

Down-to-Earth Sociology
The Power of Cascades: When Error Escalates

Cascades are eerily similar to Asch's experiments. In a *cascade,* someone unintentionally gives a wrong answer, others agree with it, and eventually that agreement turns the wrong answer into "truth." You might think that such things belong to the past, but cascades powerfully influence our attitudes, beliefs, and behavior today (Sunstein and Hastie 2008).

Cascades are especially common in medicine because few doctors do research. They get their ideas from others as a consensus emerges about some medical condition. Not long ago, for example, almost every doctor knew that tonsils were bad. A little problem in a child's throat, and the scalpel came tearing into the mouth. Everybody knew this was the right thing to do.

The same was true of fat and heart disease (Taubes 2007; Tierney 2007). In the 1950s, doctors began to treat a lot more patients with heart disease. What could have been causing this new epidemic? Ancel Keys, a medical researcher, became convinced that the cause was diet, that Americans were eating too much fat. He compared the diets and heart disease rates in the United States, Japan, and four other countries. His findings matched his theory—more fat and more heart disease.

When Dr. Keys became a member of a committee of the American Heart Association, he promoted his research, convincing the AHA to recommend a lower-fat diet to Americans. His findings were considered so important that Keys was featured on the cover of *Time* magazine, and in 1980 the U.S. government incorporated his ideas into its "food pyramid," which it promoted around the country. Soon experts and non-experts, doctors and

patients alike, "knew" that diets rich in fats led to heart attacks. This became such established knowledge that in 1988 the Surgeon General of the United States announced that ice cream had become a major health hazard.

There were two problems with the Keys research. First, and rather relevant, there was no new epidemic. Heart disease had become more common, certainly, but this was because people were living longer, giving them more years to come down with heart problems. Second, if Keys had analyzed all twenty-two countries for which there were data, not just four of them, he would have found no correlation between fat and heart disease.

Some researchers disagreed with what "everyone" had come to know to be fact, but it was difficult for them to speak out against such almost unanimous agreement. When they published contradictory findings, they tended to be ignored as exceptions. Some medical researchers didn't express their doubts because they didn't want to disagree with "everyone"—much like the victims of Asch's experiments.

We are taught the food pyramid in school. Does it represent fact, or is it the result of a cascade?

For Your Consideration
What else do we "know" that you think might be the result of cascades?

The Power of Authority: The Milgram Experiment

Let's look at the results of another experiment in the following Thinking Critically section.

Thinking CRITICALLY

If Hitler Asked You to Execute a Stranger, Would You?
The Milgram Experiment

Imagine that you are taking a course with Dr. Stanley Milgram (1963, 1965), a former student of Dr. Asch's. Assume that you do not know about the Asch experiment and have no reason to be wary. You arrive at the laboratory to participate in a study on punishment and learning. You and a second student draw lots for the roles of "teacher" and "learner." You are to be the teacher. When you see that the learner's chair has protruding electrodes, you are glad that you are the teacher. Dr. Milgram shows you the machine you will run. You see that one side of the control panel is marked "Mild Shock, 15 volts," while the center says "Intense Shock, 350 Volts," and the far right side reads "DANGER: SEVERE SHOCK."

"As the teacher, you will read aloud a pair of words," explains Dr. Milgram. "Then you will repeat the first word, and the learner will reply with the second word. If the learner can't remember the word, you press this lever on the shock generator. The shock will serve as punishment, and we can then determine if punishment improves memory." You nod, now very relieved that you haven't been designated the learner.

"Every time the learner makes an error, increase the punishment by 15 volts," instructs Dr. Milgram. Then, seeing the look on your face, he adds, "The shocks can be very painful, but they won't cause any permanent tissue damage." He pauses, and then says, "I want you to see." You then follow him to the "electric chair," and Dr. Milgram gives you a shock of 45 volts. "There. That wasn't too bad, was it?" "No," you mumble.

The experiment begins. You hope for the learner's sake that he is bright, but unfortunately he turns out to be rather dull. He gets some answers right, but you have to keep turning up the dial. Each turn makes you more and more uncomfortable. You find yourself hoping that the learner won't miss another answer. But he does. When he received the first

In the 1960s, social psychologists did highly creative but controversial experiments. This photo, taken during Stanley Milgram's experiment, should give you an idea of how convincing the experiment was to the "teacher."

shocks, he let out some moans and groans, but now he is screaming in agony. He even protests that he suffers from a heart condition.

How far do you turn that dial?

By now, you probably have guessed that there was no electricity attached to the electrodes and that the "learner" was a stooge who only pretended to feel pain. The purpose of the experiment was to find out at what point people refuse to participate. Does anyone actually turn the lever all the way to "DANGER: SEVERE SHOCK"?

Milgram wanted the answer because millions of ordinary people did nothing to stop the Nazi slaughter of Jews, gypsies, Slavs, homosexuals, people with disabilities, and others whom the Nazis designated as "inferior." The cooperation of so many ordinary people in the face of all this killing seemed bizarre, and Milgram wanted to see how ordinary, intelligent Americans might react in an analogous situation.

Milgram was upset by what he found. Many "teachers" broke into a sweat and protested that the experiment was inhuman and should be stopped. But when the experimenter calmly replied that the experiment must go on, this assurance from an "authority" ("scientist, white coat, university laboratory") was enough for most "teachers" to continue, even though the "learner" screamed in agony. Even "teachers" who were "reduced to twitching, stuttering wrecks" continued to follow orders.

Milgram varied the experiments. He used both men and women. In some experiments, he put the "teachers" and "learners" in the same room, so the "teacher" could see the suffering. In others, he put the "learners" in an adjacent room, and had them pound and kick the wall during the first shocks and then go silent. The results varied. When there was no verbal feedback from the "learner," 65 percent of the "teachers" pushed the lever all the way to 450 volts. Of those who could see the "learner," 40 percent turned the lever all the way. When Milgram added a second "teacher," a stooge who refused to go along with the experiment, only 5 percent of the "teachers" turned the lever all the way.

Milgram's research set off a stormy discussion about research ethics. Researchers agreed that to reduce subjects to "twitching, stuttering wrecks" was unethical, and almost all deception was banned. Universities began to require that subjects be informed of the nature and purpose of social research.

Although researchers were itching to replicate Milgram's research, it took almost 50 years before they found a way to satisfy committees that approve research. The findings: People today obey the experimenter at about the same rate people did in the 1960s (Burger 2007).

For Your Consideration

Taking into account how significant Milgram's findings are, do you think that the scientific community overreacted to these experiments? Should we allow such research? Consider both the Asch and Milgram experiments, and use symbolic interactionism, functionalism, and conflict theory to explain why groups have such influence over us.

Global Consequences of Group Dynamics: Groupthink

Suppose you are a member of the U.S. president's inner circle. It is midnight, and the president has just called an emergency meeting to deal with a terrorist attack. At first, several options are presented. Eventually, these are narrowed to only a couple of choices, and at some point, everyone seems to agree on what now appears to be "the only possible course of action." To express doubts at that juncture will bring you into conflict with all the other important people in the room. To criticize the proposed solution will mark you as not being a "team player." So you keep your mouth shut, with the result that each step commits you—and them—more and more to the "only" course of action.

From the Milgram and Asch experiments, we can see the power of authority and the influence of peers. Under some circumstances, as in this example, these factors can lead to

groupthink. Sociologist Irving Janis (1972, 1982) used this term to refer to the collective tunnel vision that group members sometimes develop. As they begin to think alike, they become convinced that there is only one "right" viewpoint and a single course of action to follow. They take any suggestion of alternatives as a sign of disloyalty. With their perspective narrowed and fully convinced that they are right, they may even put aside moral judgments and disregard risk (Hart 1991; Flippen 1999).

Groupthink can bring serious consequences. Consider the *Columbia* space shuttle disaster of 2003.

> **Foam broke loose during launch, and engineers were concerned that it might have damaged tiles on the nose cone. Because this would make reentry dangerous, they sent e-mails to NASA officials, warning them about the risk. One engineer even suggested that the crew do a "space walk" to examine the tiles (Vartabedian and Gold 2003). The team in charge of the Columbia shuttle, however, disregarded the warnings. Convinced that a piece of foam weighing less than two pounds could not seriously harm the shuttle, they refused to even consider the possibility (Wald and Schwartz 2003). The fiery results of their closed minds were transmitted around the globe.**

The consequences of groupthink can be even greater than this. In 1941, President Franklin D. Roosevelt and his chiefs of staff had evidence that the Japanese were preparing to attack Pearl Harbor. They simply refused to believe it and decided to continue naval operations as usual. The destruction of the U.S. naval fleet ushered the United States into World War II. In the war with Vietnam, U.S. officials had evidence of the strength and determination of the North Vietnamese military. They arrogantly threw such evidence aside, refusing to believe that "little, uneducated, barefoot people in pajamas" could defeat the U.S. military.

In each of these cases, options closed as officials committed themselves to a single course of action. Questioning the decisions would have indicated disloyalty and disregard for "team playing." No longer did those in power try to objectively weigh events as they happened; instead, they interpreted everything as supporting their one "correct" decision. They plunged ahead, unable to see alternative perspectives.

Groupthink knows few bounds. Consider what I mentioned earlier, when in the aftermath of 9/11 government officials defended torture as moral, "the lesser of two evils." Thought narrowed so greatly that the U.S. Justice Department ruled that the United States was not bound by the Geneva Convention that prohibits torture. Facing protests, the Justice Department backed down (Lewis 2005).

The U.S. military involvement in Iraq appears to be similar. Top leaders, convinced that they made the right decision to go to war and that they were finding success in building a new Iraqi society, continuously interpreted even disconfirming evidence as favorable. Opinions and debate that contradicted their mind-set were written off as signs of ignorance and disloyalty. Despite mounting casualties, negative public sentiment, and political opposition to the war, it was as though the president and his advisors had been blinded by groupthink.

Preventing Groupthink.   Groupthink is a danger for government leaders, who tend to surround themselves with an inner circle that closely reflects their own views. In "briefings," written summaries, and "talking points," this inner circle spoon feeds the leaders the information it has selected. The result is that top leaders, such as the president, become largely cut off from information that does not support their own opinions.

Perhaps the key to preventing the mental captivity and intellectual paralysis known as groupthink is the widest possible circulation—especially among a nation's top government officials—of research that has been conducted by social scientists independent of the government and information that media reporters have gathered freely. If this conclusion comes across as an unabashed plug for sociological research and the free exchange of ideas, it is. Giving free rein to diverse opinions can curb groupthink, which—if not prevented—can lead to the destruction of a society and, in today's world of nuclear, chemical, and biological weapons, the obliteration of Earth's inhabitants.

groupthink a narrowing of thought by a group of people, leading to the perception that there is only one correct answer, in which to even suggest alternatives becomes a sign of disloyalty

SUMMARY *and* REVIEW

Societies and Their Transformation

What is a group?

Sociologists use many definitions of groups, but, in general, **groups** consist of people who interact with one another and think of themselves as belonging together. **Societies** are the largest and most complex group that sociologists study. P. 148.

How is technology linked to the change from one type of society to another?

On their way to postindustrial society, humans passed through four types of societies. Each emerged from a social revolution that was linked to new technology. The **domestication revolution,** which brought the pasturing of animals and the cultivation of plants, transformed **hunting and gathering societies** into **pastoral** and **horticultural societies.** Then the invention of the plow ushered in the **agricultural society,** while the **Industrial Revolution,** brought about by machines that were powered by fuels, led to **industrial society.** The computer chip ushered in a new type of society called **postindustrial** (or **information**) **society.** Another new type of society, the **biotech society,** may be emerging. Pp. 148–154.

How is social inequality linked to the transformation of societies?

Social equality was greatest in hunting and gathering societies, but as societies changed social inequality grew. The root of the transition to social inequality was the accumulation of a food surplus, made possible through the domestication revolution. This surplus stimulated the division of labor, trade, the accumulation of material goods, the subordination of females by males, the emergence of leaders, and the development of the state. Pp. 150–151.

Groups Within Society

How do sociologists classify groups?

Sociologists divide groups into primary groups, secondary groups, in-groups, out-groups, reference groups, and networks. The cooperative, intimate, long-term, face-to-face relationships provided by **primary groups** are fundamental to our sense of self. **Secondary groups** are larger, relatively temporary, and more anonymous, formal, and impersonal than primary groups. **In-groups** provide members with a strong sense of identity and belonging. **Out-groups** also foster identity by showing in-group members what they are *not.* **Reference groups** are groups whose standards we refer to as we evaluate ourselves. **Social networks** consist of social ties that link people together. Developments in communications technology have given birth to a new type of group, the **electronic community.** Pp. 155–160.

Group Dynamics

How does a group's size affect its dynamics?

The term **group dynamics** refers to how individuals affect groups and how groups influence individuals. In a **small group,** everyone can interact directly with everyone else. As a group grows larger, its intensity decreases but its stability increases. A **dyad,** consisting of two people, is the most unstable of human groups, but it provides the most intense intimate relationships. The addition of a third person, forming a **triad,** fundamentally alters relationships. Triads are unstable, as **coalitions** (the alignment of some members of a group against others) tend to form. Pp. 161–163.

What characterizes a leader?

A **leader** is someone who influences others. **Instrumental leaders** try to keep a group moving toward its goals, even though this causes friction and they lose popularity. **Expressive leaders** focus on creating harmony and raising group morale. Both types are essential to the functioning of groups. Pp. 163–164.

What are three leadership styles?

Authoritarian leaders give orders, **democratic leaders** try to lead by consensus, and **laissez-faire leaders** are highly permissive. An authoritarian style appears to be more effective in emergency situations, a democratic style works best for most situations, and a laissez-faire style is usually ineffective. Pp. 164–165.

How do groups encourage conformity?

The Asch experiment was cited to illustrate the power of peer pressure, the Milgram experiment to illustrate the influence of authority. Both experiments demonstrate how easily we can succumb to **groupthink,** a kind of collective tunnel vision. Preventing groupthink requires the free circulation of diverse and opposing ideas. Pp. 165–169.

THINKING CRITICALLY *ABOUT* Chapter 6

1. How would your orientations to life (your ideas, attitudes, values, goals) be different if you had been reared in a hunting and gathering society? In an agricultural society?

2. Identify your in-groups and your out-groups. How have your in-groups influenced the way you see the world? And what influence have your out-groups had on you?

3. Asch's experiments illustrate the power of peer pressure. How has peer pressure operated in your life? Think about something that you did not want to do but did anyway because of peer pressure.

ADDITIONAL RESOURCES

What can you find in MySocLab? mysoclab www.mysoclab.com

- Complete Ebook
- Practice Tests and Video and Audio activities
- Mapping and Data Analysis exercises

- Sociology in the News
- Classic Readings in Sociology
- Research and Writing advice

Where Can I Read More on This Topic?

Suggested readings for this chapter are listed at the back of this book.

chapter 7

Bureaucracy and Formal
Organizations

New York City

I magine for a moment that you are a high school senior who has applied to Cornell University. It's a long shot, you know, since you aren't at the top of your class—but what the heck? It's worth the extra hour it takes to fill out the application—since you have everything you need from the applications you've already sent to your regional colleges.

Now imagine the unthinkable. Like betting on the 125-to-1 long shot at the racetrack, your horse comes in! You open the letter from Cornell, expecting to see a polite rejection. Instead, with hands shaking and tears of joy starting to cloud your eyes, you stare at the first words, scarcely grasping what you are seeing: "Greetings from Cornell, your future alma mater!" and, below this, "Cornell is pleased to welcome you to its incoming freshman class."

"Just too good to be true," you keep telling yourself, as you imagine yourself on the ivy-covered campus.

You don't know whether to laugh, scream, cry, or what. You shout to your parents, who come running in to see what the problem is. They, too, are flabbergasted. While your Dad and Mom are proudly saying that they knew you could do it, you are already dialing your friends.

The next day, you are the talk of your class at school. Hardly anyone can believe it, for you are just an average student. "They must be trying for diversity of ability," jealously mumbles someone (who just took a sociology course), whom you *used* to count as a friend.

"This is just too good to be true," you keep telling yourself, as you imagine yourself on the ivy-covered campus.

And it is.

The call from the solemn Cornell admissions counselor explains that they sent the wrong letter to 550 students. "We apologize for any confusion and distress this has caused," she says.

Confusion? How about shattered dreams?

—Based on Arenson 2003.

rationality using rules, efficiency, and practical results to determine human affairs

traditional society a society in which the past is thought to be the best guide for the present; characterizes tribal, peasant, and feudal societies

Some colleges admit thousands of students. To make the job manageable, they have broken the admissions process into several separate steps. Each step is an integrated part of the entire procedure. Computer programs have facilitated this process, but, as this event indicates, things don't always go as planned. In this case, a low-level bureaucrat at Cornell had mixed up the codes, releasing the wrong letter.

Despite their flaws, we need bureaucracies, and in this chapter we'll look at how society is organized to "get its job done." As you read this analysis, you may be able to trace the source of some of your frustrations to this social organization—as well as understand how your welfare depends on it.

The Rationalization of Society

In the previous chapter, we discussed how societies have undergone transformations so extensive that whole new types of societies have emerged. We also saw that we are now in the midst of one of those earth-shattering transformations. Underlying our information society (which may be merging into a biotech society) is an emphasis on **rationality,** the idea that efficiency and practical results should dominate human affairs. Let's examine how this approach to life—which today we take for granted—came about.

Why Did Society Make a Deep Shift in Human Relationships?

Until recently, people lived in **traditional societies.** Their way of life is so different from ours that I want you to take a moment to grasp what life in such a society is like. As Table 7.1 shows, personal relationships are the heart of this kind of society. Everything centers on deep obligation and responsibility. In producing goods, for example, what counts is not who is best at doing something, but people's relationships, which are often lifelong. Based

TABLE 7.1	Production in Traditional and Nontraditional Societies
Traditional Societies (Horticultural, Agricultural)	**Nontraditional Societies (Industrial, Postindustrial)**
PRODUCING GOODS	
1. Production is done by family members and same-sex groups (men's and women's groups).	1. Production is done by workers hired for the job.
2. Production takes place in the home or in fields and other areas adjacent to the home.	2. Production takes place in a centralized location. (Some decentralization is occurring in the information society.)
3. Tasks are assigned according to personal relationships (men, women, and children do specific tasks based on custom).	3. Tasks are assigned according to agreements and training.
4. The "how" of production is not evaluated; the attitude is "We want to keep doing it the way we've always done it."	4. The "how" of production is evaluated; the attitude is "How can we make this more efficient?"
RELATIONSHIPS IN PRODUCTION	
5. Relationships are based on history ("the way it's always been").	5. Relationships are based on contracts, which change as the situation changes.
6. Relationships are diffuse (vague, covering many areas of life).	6. Relationships are specific; contracts (even if not written) specify conditions.
7. Relationships are long-term, often lifelong.	7. Relationships are short-term, for the length of the contract.
EVALUATING WORKERS	
8. It is assumed that arrangements will continue indefinitely.	8. Arrangements are evaluated periodically, to decide whether to continue or to change them.
9. People are evaluated informally according to how they fulfill their traditional roles.	9. People are evaluated formally according to the "bottom line" (the organization's goals).

Note: This model is an ideal type. Rationality is never totally absent from any society, and no society (or organization) is based entirely on rationality. Even the most rational organizations (those that most carefully and even ruthlessly compute the "bottom line") have traditional components. To properly understand this table, consider these nine characteristics as being "more" or "less" present.

Source: The author.

To understand the sociological significance of this photo from Vietnam, compare what you see here with the list of characteristics of traditional societies in Table 7.1.

on origins that are lost in history, everyone has an established place in the society. A good part of socialization is learning one's place in the group, the obligations one has to others.

A second key aspect of traditional society is the idea that the past is the best guide for living life today. What exists is good because it has passed the test of time. Customs—and relationships based on them—have served people well, and they should be maintained. With the past prized and ruling the present, change is viewed with suspicion and comes about slowly, if at all.

The traditional orientation is a roadblock to industrialization. Because capitalism requires an entirely different approach to life, if a society is to industrialize, a deep shift must occur in how people think about relationships. As you can see from Table 7.1, in industrial societies production is based on impersonal, short-term contracts, not personal relationships. The primary concern is the "bottom line" (explicitly measured results), not who is being affected by hiring and firing and assigning tasks. Tradition ("This is the way we've always done it") must be replaced with *rationality* ("Let's find the most efficient way to do it").

This change to rationality is a fundamental divergence from all of human history. Because we live in a society in which rationality is part of our taken-for-granted assumptions for much of social life, such as how schools and businesses are run, it is difficult for us to grasp the depths of this historical shift. The following illustration may help.

Let's suppose that family relationships change from personal to rational. If this were to occur, a wife might say to her husband, "Each year, I'm going to do a progress report. I will evaluate how much you've contributed to the family budget, how much time you've put in on household tasks, and how you rank on this standardized list of sexual performance—and on that basis I'll keep or replace you."

I'm sure you'll agree that this would be such a fundamental change in human relationships that it would produce a new type of marriage and family. So it was with organizations as they made the change from tradition to rationality. The question, then, is what could have brought about such a profound change? How did people change from a traditional orientation to the **rationalization of society**—the widespread acceptance of rationality and the construction of social organizations built largely around this idea?

Marx: Capitalism Broke Tradition

An early sociologist, Karl Marx (1818–1883), was one of the first to note how tradition was giving way to rationality. As Marx analyzed this change, he concluded that capitalism was

[the] rationalization of society a widespread acceptance of *rationality* and social organizations that are built largely around this idea

breaking the bonds of tradition. As people who had money experimented with capitalism, they saw that it was more efficient. They were impressed that capitalism produced things they wanted in greater abundance and yielded high profits. This encouraged them to invest capital in manufacturing. As capitalism spread, traditional thinking receded. Gradually, the rationality of capitalism replaced the traditional approach to life. Marx's conclusion: The change to capitalism changed the way people thought about life.

Weber: Religion Broke Tradition

To sociologist Max Weber (1864–1920), this problem was as intriguing as an unsolved murder is to a detective. Weber wasn't satisfied with Marx's answer. He wanted to probe more deeply and find out what brought about capitalism. He found a clue when he noted that capitalism thrived only in certain parts of Europe. "There has to be a reason for this," he mused. As Weber pursued the matter, he noted that capitalism flourished in Protestant countries, while Roman Catholic countries held on to tradition and were relatively untouched by capitalism. "Somehow, then, religion holds the key," he thought.

But why did Roman Catholics cling to the past, while Protestants embraced change? Weber's solution to this puzzle has been the source of controversy ever since he first proposed it in his influential book *The Protestant Ethic and the Spirit of Capitalism* (1904–1905). Weber concluded that Roman Catholic doctrine emphasized the acceptance of present arrangements: "God wants you where you are. You owe allegiance to the Church, to your family, and to your king. Accept your lot in life and remain rooted." Weber argued that Protestant theology, in contrast, opened its followers to change. Weber was intimately familiar with Calvinism, his mother's religion. Calvinists (followers of the teachings of John Calvin, 1509–1564) believed that before birth, people are destined for either heaven or hell—and they do not know their destiny until after they die. Weber said that this teaching filled Calvinists with anxiety. Salvation became their chief concern—they wanted to know *now* where they were going after death.

To resolve their spiritual dilemma, Calvinists arrived at an ingenious solution: God surely did not want those chosen for heaven to be ignorant of their destiny. Therefore, those who were in God's favor would know it—they would receive a sign from God. But what sign? The answer, claimed Calvinists, would be found not in mystical, spiritual experiences, but in things that people could see and measure. The sign of God's approval was success: Those whom God had predestined for heaven would be blessed with visible success in this life.

This idea transformed the lives of Calvinists. It motivated them to work hard, and because Calvinists also believed that thrift is a virtue, their dedication to work led to an accumulation of money. They could not spend this money on themselves, however, for to purchase items beyond the basic necessities was considered sinful. **Capitalism,** the investment of capital in the hope of making profits, became an outlet for their excess money. The success of those investments, in turn, became another sign of God's approval. In this way, Calvinists transformed worldly success into a spiritual virtue. Other branches of Protestantism, although not in agreement with the notion of predestination, also adopted the creed of thrift and hard work. Weber's conclusion: A changed way of thinking (God will give a sign to the elect) among Protestants produced capitalism.

The Two Views Today.　Who is correct? Weber, who concluded that Protestantism produced rationality, which then paved the way for capitalism? Or Marx, who concluded that capitalism produced rationality? No analyst has yet reconciled these two opposing answers to the satisfaction of sociologists: The two views still remain side by side.

Formal Organizations and Bureaucracies

capitalism an economic system characterized by the private ownership of the means of production, the pursuit of profit, and market competition

Regardless of whether Marx or Weber was right about its cause, rationality brought a profound change in how work is organized. When work is rooted in personal relationships, a main purpose of business decisions is to maintain those relationships—for example, to make sure that all relatives and friends have jobs. As this new orientation began to permeate society, however, performing tasks efficiently and keeping an eye on the bottom line gradually replaced the traditional orientation. To meet these goals, new types of organizations emerged. Let's look at these organizations and how they affect our lives today.

Formal Organizations

It is not surprising that **formal organizations,** secondary groups designed to achieve explicit objectives, are rare in traditional societies. As you have seen, life there is organized around personal relationships. There were three exceptions in traditional societies, however, that foreshadowed the changes ushered in by industrialization. An outstanding example is the twelfth-century guilds of western Europe. Men who performed the same type of work organized to control their craft in a local area. They set prices and standards of workmanship (Bridgwater 1953; "Guilds" 2008). Much like modern unions, guilds also prevented outsiders (nonmembers of the guild) from working at their particular craft. Two other examples of early formal organizations are the army and the Roman Catholic Church, each with its hierarchical structure. Although they use different names for their ranks (commander-in-chief/pope, general/cardinal, private/priest, and so on), in each, senior ranks are in charge of junior ranks.

Formal organizations, however, used to be rare, but with rationality they have become a central feature of today's social life. Society has changed so extensively that most of us are even born within a formal organization. We are also educated in formal organizations, we spend our working lives in them, and we are even buried by them. The change is so extensive that we can't even think of modern society without referring to formal organizations. One of the main characteristics of formal organizations is that they tend to develop into bureaucracies. As we examine them, let's start there.

The Characteristics of Bureaucracies

What do the Russian army and the U.S. postal service have in common? Or the government of Mexico and your college? The sociological answer is that they all are *bureaucracies.* As Weber (1913/1947) pointed out, **bureaucracies** have

1. *Clear levels, with assignments flowing downward and accountability flowing upward.* Each level assigns responsibilities to the level beneath it, and each lower level is accountable to the level above it for fulfilling those assignments. Figure 7.1 on the next page shows the bureaucratic structure of a typical university.

formal organization a secondary group designed to achieve explicit objectives

bureaucracy a formal organization with a hierarchy of authority and a clear division of labor; emphasis on impersonality of positions and written rules, communications, and records

Today's armies, no matter what country they are from, are *bureaucracies.* They have a strict hierarchy of rank, division of labor, impersonality and replaceability (an emphasis on the office, not the person holding it), and they stress written records, rules, and communications—essential characteristics identified by Max Weber. Though its outward appearance may differ from Western standards, this army in India is no exception to this principle.

FIGURE 7.1 The Typical Bureaucratic Structure of a Medium-Sized University

This is a scaled-down version of a university's bureaucratic structure. The actual lines of a university are likely to be much more complicated than those depicted here. A large university may have a chancellor and several presidents under the chancellor, each president being responsible for a particular campus. Although in this figure extensions of authority are shown only for the Vice President for Administration and the College of Social Sciences, each of the other vice presidents and colleges has similar positions. If the figure were to be extended, departmental secretaries would be shown and, eventually, somewhere, even students.

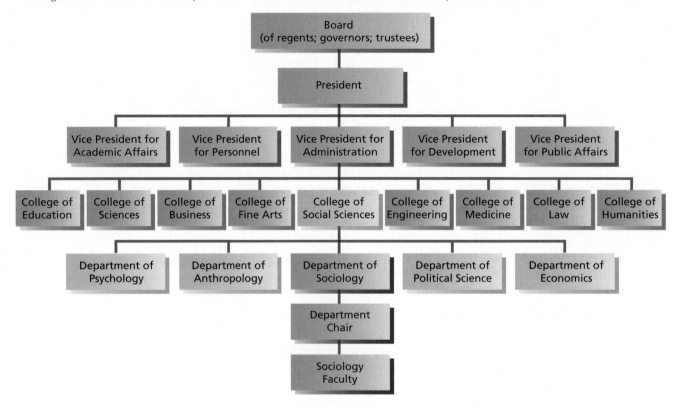

2. *A division of labor.* Each worker is assigned specific tasks, and the tasks of all the workers are coordinated to accomplish the purpose of the organization. In a college, for example, a teacher does not fix the heating system, the president does not approve class schedules, and a secretary does not evaluate textbooks. These tasks are distributed among people who have been trained to do them.

3. *Written rules.* In their attempt to become efficient, bureaucracies stress written procedures. In general, the longer a bureaucracy exists and the larger it grows, the more written rules it has. The rules of some bureaucracies cover just about every imaginable situation. In my university, for example, the rules are published in handbooks: separate ones for faculty, students, administrators, civil service workers, and perhaps others that I don't even know about.

4. *Written communications and records.* Records are kept for much of what occurs in a bureaucracy ("Be sure to CC all immediate supervisors."). Some workers must detail their activities in written reports. My university, for example, requires that each semester, faculty members compile a summary of the number of hours they spent performing specified activities. They must also submit an annual report listing what they accomplished in teaching, research, and service—all accompanied by copies of publications, evidence of service, and written teaching evaluations from each course. These materials go to committees that evaluate the performance of each faculty member.

5. *Impersonality and replaceability.* The office is important, not the individual who holds the office. Each worker is a replaceable unit. You work for the organization, not for the replaceable person who heads some post in the organization. When a professor retires, for example, someone else is appointed to take his or her place. This makes each person a small cog in a large machine.

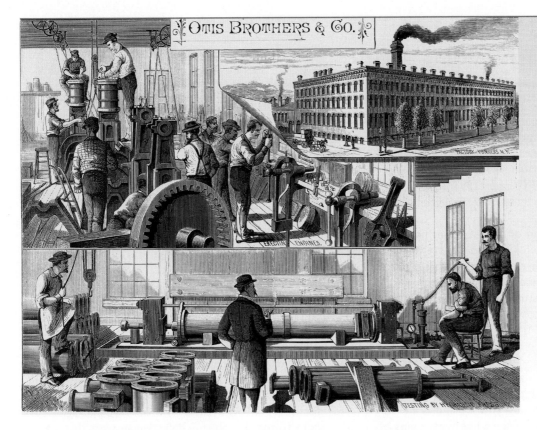

When society began to be rationalized, production of items was broken into its components, with individuals assigned only specific tasks. Shown in this 1875 wood engraving is the engine construction room at the Otis Brothers plant in New York City.

These five characteristics help bureaucracies reach their goals. They also allow them to grow and endure. One bureaucracy in the United States, the postal service, has become so large that 1 out of every 180 employed Americans works for it (*Statistical Abstract* 2009:Tables 581, 1085). If the head of a bureaucracy resigns, retires, or dies, the organization continues without skipping a beat, for unlike a "mom and pop" operation, its functioning does not depend on the individual who heads it. The expansion (some would say domination) of bureaucracies in contemporary society is illustrated by the Down-to-Earth Sociology box on the next page.

"Ideal" Versus "Real" Bureaucracy

Just as people often act differently from the way the norms say they should, so it is with bureaucracies. The characteristics of bureaucracies that Weber identified are *ideal types*; that is, they are a composite of characteristics based on many specific examples. Think of the judges at a dog show. They have a mental image of how each particular breed of dog should look and behave, and they judge each individual dog according to that mental image. Each dog will rank high on some of these characteristics and lower on others. In the same way, a particular organization will rank higher or lower on the traits of a bureaucracy, yet still qualify as a bureaucracy. Instead of labeling a particular organization as a "bureaucracy" or "not a bureaucracy," it probably makes more sense to consider the *extent* to which it is bureaucratized (Udy 1959; Hall 1963).

As with culture, then, a bureaucracy often differs from its ideal image. The actual lines of authority ("going through channels"), for example, may be different from those portrayed on organizational charts such as the one shown in Figure 7.1 on page 178. For example, suppose that before being promoted, the university president taught in the history department. As a result, friends from that department may have direct access to him or her. If they wish to provide "input" (ranging from opinions about how to solve problems to personal grievances or even gossip), these individuals might be able to skip their chairperson or even the dean of their college and go directly to the president.

Down-to-Earth Sociology
The McDonaldization of Society

McDonalds in Tokyo, Japan.

The McDonald's restaurants that are located across the United States—and, increasingly, the world—have a significance that goes far beyond the convenience of quick hamburgers, milk shakes, and salads. As sociologist George Ritzer (1993, 1998, 2001) says, our everyday lives are being "McDonaldized." Let's see what he means by this.

The McDonaldization of society does not refer just to the robotlike assembly of food. This term refers to the standardization of everyday life, a process that is transforming our lives. Want to do some shopping? Shopping malls offer one-stop shopping in controlled environments. Planning a trip? Travel agencies offer "package" tours. They will transport middle-class Americans to ten European capitals in fourteen days. All visitors experience the same hotels, restaurants, and other scheduled sites—and no one need fear meeting a "real" native. Want to keep up with events? *USA Today* spews out McNews—short, bland, non-analytical pieces that can be digested between gulps of the McShake or the McBurger.

Efficiency brings dependability. You can expect your burger and fries to taste the same whether you buy them in Los Angeles or Beijing. Although efficiency also lowers prices, it does come at a cost. Predictability washes away spontaneity, changing the quality of our lives. It produces a sameness, a bland version of what used to be unique experiences. In my own travels, for example, had I taken packaged tours I never would have had the eye-opening experiences that have added so much to my appreciation of human diversity. (Bus trips with chickens in Mexico, hitchhiking in Europe and Africa, sleeping on a granite table in a nunnery in Italy and in a cornfield in Algeria are just not part of tour agendas.)

For good or bad, our lives are being McDonaldized, and the predictability of packaged settings seems to be our social destiny. When education is rationalized, no longer will our children have to put up with real professors, who insist on discussing ideas endlessly, who never come to decisive answers, and who come saddled with idiosyncrasies. At some point, such an approach to education is going to be a bit of quaint history.

Our programmed education will eliminate the need for discussion of social issues—we will have packaged solutions to social problems, definitive answers that satisfy our need for closure. Computerized courses will teach the same answers to everyone—the approved, "politically correct" ways to think about social issues. Mass testing will ensure that students regurgitate the programmed responses.

Our coming prepackaged society will be efficient, of course. But it also means that we will be trapped in the "iron cage" of bureaucracy—just as Weber warned would happen.

For Your Consideration

What do you like and dislike about the standardization of society? What do you think about the author's comments on the future of our educational system?

Dysfunctions of Bureaucracies

Although in the long run no other form of social organization is more efficient, as Weber recognized, bureaucracies also have a dark side. Let's look at some of their dysfunctions.

Red Tape: A Rule Is a Rule.   Bureaucracies can be so bound by red tape that when officials apply their rules, the results can defy all logic. I came across an example so ridiculous that it can make your head swim—if you don't burst from laughing first.

> In Spain, the Civil Registry of Barcelona recorded the death of a woman named Maria Antonieta Calvo in 1992. Apparently, Maria's evil brother had reported her dead so he could collect the family inheritance.
>
> When Maria learned that she was supposedly dead, she told the Registry that she was very much alive. The bureaucrats at this agency looked at their records, shook their heads,

[the] McDonaldization of society the process by which ordinary aspects of life are rationalized and efficiency comes to rule them, including such things as food preparation

and insisted that she was dead. Maria then asked lawyers to represent her in court. They all refused—because no dead person can bring a case before a judge.

When Maria's boyfriend asked her to marry him, the couple ran into a serious obstacle: No man in Spain (or most other places) can marry a dead woman—so these bureaucrats said, "So sorry, but no license."

After years of continuing to insist that she was alive, Maria finally got a hearing in court. When the judges looked at Maria, they believed that she really was a living person, and they ordered the Civil Registry to declare her alive.

alienation Marx's term for workers' lack of connection to the product of their labor; caused by their being assigned repetitive tasks on a small part of a product, which leads to a sense of powerlessness and normlessness

The ending of this story gets even happier, for now that Maria was alive, she was able to marry her boyfriend. I don't know if the two lived happily ever after, but, after overcoming the bureaucrats, they at least had that chance ("Mujer 'resucita'" 2006).

Lack of Communication Between Units.   Each unit within a bureaucracy performs specialized tasks, which are designed to contribute to the organization's goals. At times, units fail to communicate with one another and end up working at cross-purposes. In Granada, Spain, for example, the local government was concerned about the run-down appearance of buildings along one of its main streets. Consequently, one unit of the government fixed the fronts of these buildings, repairing concrete and restoring decorations of iron and stone. The results were impressive, and the unit was proud of what it had accomplished. The only problem was that another unit of the government had slated these same buildings for demolition (Arías 1993). Because neither unit of this bureaucracy knew what the other was doing, one beautified the buildings while the other planned to turn them into a heap of rubble.

Bureaucratic Alienation.   Perceived in terms of roles, rules, and functions rather than as individuals, many workers begin to feel more like objects than people. Marx termed these reactions **alienation,** a result, he said, of workers being cut off from the finished product of their labor. He pointed out that before industrialization, workers used their own tools to produce an entire product, such as a chair or table. Now the capitalists own the tools (machinery, desks, computers) and assign each worker only a single step or two in the entire production process. Relegated to performing repetitive tasks that seem remote from the final product, workers no longer identify with

Some view bureaucracies as impediments to reaching goals. While bureaucracies can be slow and even stifling, most are highly functional in uniting people's efforts toward reaching goals and in maintaining social order.

Peter principle a tongue-in-cheek observation that the members of an organization are promoted for their accomplishments until they reach their level of incompetence; there they cease to be promoted, remaining at the level at which they can no longer do good work

what they produce. They come to feel estranged not only from the results of their labor but also from their work environment.

Resisting Alienation.   Because workers need to feel valued and want to have a sense of control over their work, they resist alienation. A major form of that resistance is forming primary groups at work. Workers band together in informal settings—at lunch, around desks, or for a drink after work. There, they give one another approval for jobs well done and express sympathy for the shared need to put up with cantankerous bosses, meaningless routines, and endless rules. In these contexts, they relate to one another not just as workers, but also as people who value one another. They flirt, laugh and tell jokes, and talk about their families and goals. Adding this multidimensionality to their work relationships maintains their sense of being individuals rather than mere cogs in a machine.

As in the photo below, workers often decorate their work areas with personal items. The sociological implication is that of workers who are striving to resist alienation. By staking a claim to individuality, the workers are rejecting an identity as machines that exist to perform functions. Since our lives and persons can be engulfed by bureaucracies, perhaps another form of escape is the new pranksterism discussed in the Down-to-Earth Sociology box on the next page.

The Alienated Bureaucrat.   Not all workers succeed in resisting alienation. Some become alienated and quit. Others became alienated but remain in the organization because they see no viable alternative, or they wait it out because they have "only so many years until retirement." They hate every minute of work, and it shows—in their attitudes toward clients, toward fellow workers, and toward bosses. The alienated bureaucrat does not take initiative, will not do anything for the organization beyond what is absolutely required, and uses company rules to justify doing as little as possible.

Despite poor attitude and performance, alienated workers often retain their jobs. Some keep their jobs because of seniority, while others threaten costly, time-consuming, and embarrassing legal action if anyone tries to fire them. Some alienated workers are shunted off into small bureaucratic corners, where they spend the day doing trivial tasks and have little chance of coming in contact with the public. This treatment, of course, only alienates them further.

Bureaucratic Incompetence.   In a tongue-in-cheek analysis of bureaucracies, Laurence Peter proposed what has become known as the **Peter principle:** Each employee of a bureaucracy

How is this worker at China's Google headquarters trying to avoid becoming a depersonalized unit in a bureaucratic-economic machine?

Down-to-Earth Sociology
Group Pranking: Escaping the Boredom of Bureaucracy?

It gets so boring sitting here all day. These silly cubicle walls seem to be closing in. The customer calls mix into an endless, blurry stream. The hours drag on. How much longer do I have to stare at that computer screen? Does the sun still shine? Is it raining outside? Does it really matter? The lighting and temperature in here are the same, winter or summer. Is this what I was born for? Did I go to college for five years to do this? Some day a robot will take over this job. Yeah, but for now I'm that robot.

The annual "No Pants Subway Ride" in New York City is intended to make people laugh and have a "New York experience." When asked, participants are supposed to respond with something such as, "I forgot my pants today."

Thoughts like these go through a lot of college graduates' minds as they sit at their desks doing mind-numbing work. Absorbed into the bureaucratic maze, wondering how they ever ended up where they are, they look into the future, starting to wonder when retirement—and freedom—will come. Then they realize they've been on the job only six months. It's enough to make a grown-up cry.

Escape! The weekends. Calling in sick and going to the beach. Video games. Office flirtations and sexual conquests. The annual vacation.

And then there is pranking, a form of silliness that provides a moment of connectedness with fellow pranksters and the pleasure of shocking onlookers. Organizing via the Internet, people perform the same harmless public joke, sharing a few laughs with one another.

- Dressed in identical outfits, fifteen pairs of twins march into a New York subway. Without saying a word, they mirror each other's actions.
- At a designated time, groups in Chicago, New York, San Francisco, and Toronto gather in public parks. Following the same MP3 instructions, they play Twister in unison.
- Eighty people dressed like Best Buy employees converge on a Best Buy store in Manhattan.
- One hundred eleven shirtless men enter an Abercrombie & Fitch store. They tell the clerks they

must be in the right place because they saw barechested men in the store's ads.
- In New York's Grand Central Station, 200 people walking in the crowd suddenly freeze. They remain motionless for five minutes, then unfreeze and nonchalantly go on their way.
- Nine hundred pantless men and women enter New York's subways. The cops don't seem to get the joke and arrest some.
- In Manhattan Beach, California, a crowd breaks into cheers as unsuspecting joggers and bicyclists cross an improvised finish line. The bewildered "contestants" are handed bottles of water and medals.

For Your Consideration
Just joking around? Nothing more than having a little fun? Or is something serious going on? Are people attempting to retrieve an identity or sense of community threatened by mass society? Could it be something like I suggested in the title of this box, a way of relieving the boredom of the bureaucracy? Is Internet-organized group pranking, perhaps, a new form of "urban art"? What do you think?

Based on Gamerman 2008.

---

is promoted to his or her *level of incompetence* (Peter and Hull 1969). People who perform well in a bureaucracy come to the attention of those higher up the chain of command and are promoted. If they continue to perform well, they are promoted again. This process continues *until* they are promoted to a level at which they can no longer handle the responsibilities well—their level of incompetence. There they hide behind the work of others, taking credit for the accomplishments of employees under their direction. In our opening vignette, the employee who sent the wrong mail has already reached his or her level of incompetence.

Although the Peter principle contains a grain of truth, if it were generally true, bureaucracies would be staffed by incompetents, and these organizations would fail. In reality,

goal displacement an organization replacing old goals with new ones; also known as *goal replacement*

bureaucracies are remarkably successful. Sociologists Peter Evans and James Rauch (1999) examined the government bureaucracies of thirty-five developing countries. They found that greater prosperity comes to the countries that have central bureaucracies and hire workers on the basis of merit.

Goal Displacement and the Perpetuation of Bureaucracies

Bureaucracies are so good at harnessing people's energies to reach specific goals that they have become a standard feature of our lives. Once in existence, however, bureaucracies tend to take on a life of their own. In a process called **goal displacement,** even after an organization achieves its goal and no longer has a reason to continue, continue it does.

A classic example is the March of Dimes, organized in the 1930s with the goal of fighting polio (Sills 1957). At that time, the origin of polio was a mystery. The public was alarmed and fearful, for overnight a healthy child could be stricken with this crippling disease. To raise money to find a cure, the March of Dimes placed posters of children on crutches near cash registers in almost every store in the United States. The organization raised money beyond its wildest dreams. When Dr. Jonas Salk developed a vaccine for polio in the 1950s, the threat of polio was wiped out almost overnight.

Did the staff that ran the March of Dimes hold a wild celebration and then quietly fold up their tents and slip away? Of course not. They had jobs to protect, so they targeted a new enemy—birth defects. But then in 2001 another ominous threat of success reared its ugly head. Researchers finished mapping the human genome system, a breakthrough that held the possibility of eliminating birth defects—and their jobs. Officials of the March of Dimes had to come up with something new—and something that would last this time. Their new slogan, "Stronger, healthier babies," is so vague that it should ensure the organization's existence forever: We are not likely to ever run out of the need for "stronger, healthier babies."

Then there is NATO (North Atlantic Treaty Organization), founded during the Cold War to prevent Russia from invading Western Europe. When the Cold War ended, removing the organization's purpose, the Western powers tried to find a reason to continue their organization. As with the March of Dimes, why waste a perfectly good bureaucracy? They found a new goal: to create "rapid response forces" to combat terrorism and "rogue nations" (Tyler 2002). To keep this bureaucracy going, they even allowed Russia to become a junior partner. Russia was pleased—until it felt threatened by NATO's expansion.

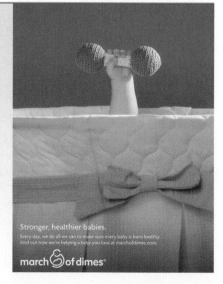

The March of Dimes was founded by President Franklin Roosevelt in the 1930s to fight polio. When a vaccine for polio was discovered in the 1950s, the organization did not declare victory and disband. Instead, its leaders kept the organization intact by creating new goals—fighting birth defects. Sociologists use the term *goal displacement* to refer to this process of adopting new goals.

Voluntary Associations

Although bureaucracies have become the dominant form of organization for large, task-oriented groups, even more common are voluntary associations. Let's examine their characteristics.

Back in the 1830s, Alexis de Tocqueville, a Frenchman, traveled across the United States, observing the customs of this new nation. His report, *Democracy in America* (1835/1966), was popular both in Europe and in the United States. It is still quoted for its insights into the American character. One of de Tocqueville's observations was that Americans joined a lot of **voluntary associations,** groups made up of volunteers who organize on the basis of some mutual interest.

Over the years, Americans have maintained this pattern. A visitor entering one of the thousands of small towns that dot the U.S. landscape is often greeted by a sign proclaiming some of the town's voluntary associations: Girl Scouts, Boy Scouts, Kiwanis, Lions, Elks, Eagles, Knights of Columbus, Chamber of Commerce, American Legion, Veterans of Foreign Wars, and perhaps a host of others. One type of voluntary association is so prevalent that a separate sign sometimes indicates which varieties are present in the town: Roman Catholic, Baptist, Lutheran, Methodist, Episcopalian, and so on. Not listed on these signs are many other voluntary associations, such as political parties, unions, health clubs, National Right to Life, National Organization for Women, Alcoholics Anonymous, Gamblers Anonymous, Association of Pinto Racers, and Citizens United For or Against This and That.

Americans love voluntary associations and use them to express a wide variety of interests. Some groups are local, consisting of only a few volunteers; others are national, with a paid professional staff. Some are temporary, organized to accomplish some specific task, such as arranging for Fourth of July fireworks. Others, such as the Scouts and political parties, are permanent—large, secondary organizations with clear lines of command—and they are also bureaucracies.

Functions of Voluntary Associations

Whatever their form, voluntary associations are numerous because they meet people's needs. People do not *have* to belong to these organizations. They join because they believe in "the cause" and obtain benefits from their participation. Functionalists have identified seven functions of voluntary associations.

1. They advance particular interests. For example, adults who are concerned about children's welfare volunteer for the Scouts because they think kids are better off joining this group than hanging out on the street. In short, voluntary associations get things done, whether that means organizing a neighborhood crime watch or informing people about the latest legislation on abortion.
2. They offer people an identity. Some even provide a sense of purpose in life. As ingroups, they give their members a feeling of belonging and, in many cases, a sense of doing something worthwhile. This function is so important for some individuals that their participation in voluntary associations becomes the center of their lives.
3. They help govern the nation and maintain social order. Obvious examples are groups that help "get out the vote" or assist the Red Cross in coping with disasters.

The first two functions apply to all voluntary associations. In a general sense, so does the third. Even though an organization does not focus on political action, it helps to incorporate individuals into society, which helps to maintain social order.

Sociologist David Sills (1968) identified four other functions, which apply only to some voluntary associations.

4. Some voluntary groups mediate between the government and the individual. For example, some groups provide a way for people to join forces to put pressure on lawmakers. Voluntary associations can even represent opposing sides of an issue, such as pro- and anti-immigration groups.

voluntary association a group made up of people who voluntarily organize on the basis of some mutual interest; also known as *voluntary memberships* and *voluntary organizations*

5. By providing training in organizational skills, some groups help people climb the occupational ladder.
6. Other groups help bring people into the political mainstream. The National Association for the Advancement of Colored People (NAACP) is an example of such a group.
7. Finally, some voluntary associations pave the way to social change. As they challenge established ways of doing things in society, boundaries start to give way. The actions of groups such as Greenpeace and Sea Shepherds, for example, are reshaping taken-for-granted definitions of "normal" when it comes to the environment.

Motivations for Joining

People have many motivations for joining voluntary associations. Some join because they hold strong convictions concerning the stated purpose of the organization, and they want to help fulfill the group's goals. Others join because membership helps them politically or professionally—or looks good on a college or job application. Some may even join because they have romantic interests in a group member.

With so many motivations for joining, and because the commitment of some members is fleeting, voluntary associations often have high turnover. Some people move in and out of groups almost as fast as they change clothes. Within each organization, however, is an *inner circle*—individuals who actively promote the group, who stand firmly behind the group's goals, and who are committed to maintaining the organization itself. If this inner circle loses its commitment, the group is likely to fold.

Let's look more closely at this inner circle.

The "Iron Law" of Oligarchy

A significant aspect of a voluntary association is that its key members, its inner circle, often grow distant from the regular members. They become convinced that only they can be trusted to make the group's important decisions. To see this principle at work, let's look at the Veterans of Foreign Wars (VFW).

Sociologists Elaine Fox and George Arquitt (1985) studied three local posts of the VFW, a national organization of former U.S. soldiers who have served in foreign wars. They found that although the leaders conceal their attitudes from the other members, the inner circle views the rank and file as a bunch of ignorant boozers. Because the leaders can't stand the thought that such people might represent them in the community and at national meetings, a curious situation arises. Although the VFW constitution makes rank-and-file members eligible for top leadership positions, they never become leaders. In fact, the inner circle is so effective in controlling these top positions that even before an election they can tell you who is going to win. "You need to meet Jim," the sociologists were told. "He's the next post commander after Sam does his time."

At first, the researchers found this puzzling. The election hadn't been held yet. As they investigated further, they found that leadership is actually determined behind the scenes. The current leaders appoint their favored people to chair the key committees. This spotlights their names and accomplishments, propelling the members to elect them. By appointing its own members to highly visible positions, then, the inner circle maintains control over the entire organization.

Like the VFW, most organizations are run by only a few of their members. Building on the term *oligarchy*, a system in which many are ruled by a few, sociologist Robert Michels (1876–1936) coined the term the **iron law of oligarchy** to refer to how organizations come to be dominated by a small, self-perpetuating elite (Michels 1911/1949). Most members of voluntary associations are passive, and an elite inner circle keeps itself in power by passing the leadership positions among its members.

What many find disturbing about the iron law of oligarchy is that people are excluded from leadership because they don't represent the inner circle's values—or, in some instances, their background. This is true even of organizations that are committed to democratic principles. For example, U.S. political parties—supposedly the backbone of the nation's representative government—are run by an inner circle that passes leadership positions from one elite member to another. This principle also applies to the U.S. Senate. With their

[the] iron law of oligarchy Robert Michels' term for the tendency of formal organizations to be dominated by a small, self-perpetuating elite

In a process called *the iron law of oligarchy*, a small, self-perpetuating elite tends to take control of formal organizations. The text explains that the leaders of the local VFW posts separate themselves from the rank and file members, such as those shown here in Sacramento, California.

statewide control of political machinery and access to free mailing, about 90 percent of U.S. senators who choose to run are reelected (*Statistical Abstract* 2006:Table 394).

The iron law of oligarchy is not without its limitations, of course. Members of the inner circle must remain attuned to the opinions of the rank-and-file members, regardless of their personal feelings. If the oligarchy gets too far out of line, it runs the risk of a grassroots rebellion that would throw the elite out of office. This threat often softens the iron law of oligarchy by making the leadership responsive to the membership. In addition, because not all organizations become captive to an elite, the iron law of oligarchy is not really iron; it is a strong tendency, not an inevitability.

Working for the Corporation

Since you are likely to end up working in a bureaucracy, let's look at how its characteristics might affect your career.

Self-Fulfilling Stereotypes in the "Hidden" Corporate Culture

As you might recall from Chapter 4, stereotypes can be self-fulfilling. That is, stereotypes can produce the very characteristics that they are built around. The example used there was of stereotypes of appearance and personality. *Self-fulfilling stereotypes* also operate in corporate life—and are so powerful that they can affect *your* career. Here's how they work.

Self-Fulfilling Stereotypes and Promotions. Corporate and department heads have ideas of "what it takes" to get ahead. Not surprisingly, since they themselves got ahead, they look for people who have characteristics similar to their own. They feed better information to workers who have these characteristics, bring them into stronger networks, and put them in "fast track" positions. With such advantages, these workers perform better and become more committed to the company. This, of course, confirms the boss's initial expectation or stereotype. But for workers who don't look or act like the corporate leaders, the opposite happens. Thinking of these people as less capable, the bosses give them fewer opportunities and challenges. When these workers see others get ahead and realize that they are working beneath their own abilities, they lose morale, become less committed to the company, and don't perform as well. This, of course, confirms the stereotypes the bosses had of them.

Sociologist Rosabeth Moss Kanter (1977, 1983), who has done research on U.S. corporations, says that self-fulfilling stereotypes are part of "hidden" corporate culture. By this, she means that such stereotypes and their powerful effects on workers remain hidden to *everyone,* even the bosses. What bosses and workers see is the surface: Workers who have superior performance and greater commitment to the company get promoted. To bosses and workers alike, this seems to be just the way it should be. Hidden below this surface, however, are the higher and lower expectations and the open and closed opportunities that produce the attitudes and the accomplishments—or the lack of them.

As corporations grapple with growing diversity, the stereotypes in the hidden corporate culture are likely to give way, although slowly and grudgingly. In the following Thinking Critically section, we'll consider diversity in the workplace.

ThinkingCRITICALLY
Managing Diversity in the Workplace

Times have changed. The San Jose, California, electronic phone book lists *ten* times more *Nguyens* than *Joneses* (Albanese 2007). More than half of U.S. workers are minorities, immigrants, and women. Diversity in the workplace is much more than skin color. Diversity includes age, ethnicity, gender, religion, sexual orientation, and social class.

In the past, the idea was for people to join the "melting pot," to give up their distinctive traits and become like the dominant group. With the successes of the civil rights and women's movements, people today are more likely to prize their distinctive traits. Realizing that assimilation (being absorbed into the dominant culture) is probably not the wave of the future, most large companies have "diversity training" (G. Johnson 2004; Hymowitz 2007). They hold lectures and workshops so that employees can learn to work with colleagues of diverse cultures and racial–ethnic backgrounds.

Coors Brewery is a prime example of this change. Coors went into a financial tailspin after one of the Coors brothers gave a racially charged speech in the 1980s. Today, Coors holds diversity workshops, sponsors gay dances, has paid for a corporate-wide mammography program, and has officially opposed an amendment to the Colorado constitution that would ban same-sex marriage. Coors has even sent a spokesperson to gay bars to promote its beer (Kim 2004). The company has also had rabbis certify its suds as kosher. All of this is quite a change.

The cultural and racial-ethnic diversity of today's work force has led to the need for diversity training, the topic of this Thinking Critically section. Shown here is an architectural team in San Francisco.

When Coors adopted the slogan "Coors cares," it did not mean that Coors cares about diversity. What Coors cares about is the same as other corporations, the bottom line. Blatant racism and sexism once made no difference to profitability. Today, they do. To promote profitability, companies must promote diversity—or at least pretend to. The sincerity of corporate leaders is not what's important; diversity in the workplace is.

Diversity training has the potential to build bridges, but it can backfire. Managers who are chosen to participate can resent it, thinking that it is punishment for some unmentioned insensitivity on their part (Sanchez and Medkik 2004). Some directors of these programs are so incompetent that they create antagonisms and reinforce stereotypes. For example, the leaders of a diversity training session at the U.S. Department of Transportation had women grope men as the men ran by. They encouraged blacks and whites to insult one another and to call each other names (Reibstein 1996). The intention may have been good (understanding the other through role reversal and getting hostilities "out in the open"), but the approach was moronic. Instead of healing, such behaviors wound and leave scars.

Pepsi provides a positive example of diversity training. Managers at Pepsi are given the assignment of sponsoring a group of employees who are unlike themselves. Men sponsor women, African Americans sponsor whites, and so on. The executives are expected to try to understand work from the perspective of the people they sponsor, to identify key talent, and to personally mentor at least three people in their group. Accountability is built in—the sponsors have to give updates to executives even higher up (Terhune 2005).

For Your Consideration

Do you think that corporations and government agencies should offer diversity training? If so, how can we develop diversity training that fosters mutual respect? Can you suggest practical ways to develop workplaces that are not divided by gender and race–ethnicity?

Humanizing the Corporate Culture

Bureaucracies have transformed society by harnessing people's energies to reach goals and monitoring progress toward those goals. Weber (1946) predicted that bureaucracies, because they were so efficient and had the capacity to replace themselves, would come to dominate social life. More than any other prediction in sociology, this one has withstood the test of time (Rothschild and Whitt 1986; Perrow 1991).

Attempts to Humanize the Work Setting

Bureaucracies appear likely to remain our dominant form of social organization, and like it or not, most of us are destined to spend our working lives in them. Many people have become concerned about the negative side of bureaucracies and would like to make them more humane. **Humanizing a work setting** means to organize work in such a way that it develops rather than impedes human potential. Humanized work settings have more flexible rules, are more open in decision making, distribute power more equally, and offer more uniform access to opportunities.

Can bureaucracies adapt to such a model? Contrary to some images, not all bureaucracies are unyielding, unwieldy monoliths. There is nothing in the nature of bureaucracies that makes them *inherently* insensitive to people's needs or that prevents them from fostering a corporate culture that maximizes human potential.

But what about the cost of such changes? The United States faces formidable economic competitors—Japan, Europe, South America, and now China and India. Humanizing corporate culture, however, can actually increase profits. Kanter (1983) compared forty-seven companies that were rigidly bureaucratic with competitors of the same size that were more flexible. Kanter found that the more flexible companies were more profitable—probably because their greater flexibility encouraged greater creativity, productivity, and company loyalty.

humanizing a work setting organizing a workplace in such a way that it develops rather than impedes human potential

Attempts to *humanize the work setting* are taking many forms. By allowing workers to bring pets to work, the employer not only aims to promote a happier work environment but also to lower health care costs.

In light of such findings, many corporations have experimented with humanizing their work settings. As we look at them, keep in mind that they are not motivated by some altruistic urge to make life better for their workers, but by the same motivation as always—the bottom line. It is in management's self-interest to make their company more competitive.

Work Teams.   Work teams are small groups of workers who try to develop solutions to problems in the workplace. Organizational gurus praise work teams and offer seminars (for hefty fees) on how to establish work teams. They point out that employees in work teams work harder, are absent less, are more productive, and react more quickly to threats posed by technological change and competitors' advances (Drucker 1992; Petty et al. 2008). In what is known as *worker empowerment,* some self-managed teams even replace bosses as the ones who control everything from setting schedules to hiring and firing (Lublin 1991; Vanderburg 2004).

The concepts we discussed in the last chapter help to explain such positive results. In small work groups, people form primary relationships, and their identities become intertwined with their group. This reduces alienation, as individuals are not lost in a bureaucratic maze. Instead, their individuality is appreciated, and their contributions are more readily acknowledged. The group's successes become the individual's successes—as do its failures. With more accountability within a system of personal ties, workers make more of an effort. Not all teams work together well, however, and researchers are trying to determine the factors that make teams succeed or fail (Borsch-Supan et al. 2007).

Corporate Child Care.   Some companies help to humanize the work setting by offering on-site child care facilities. This eases the strain on parents, for while at work they can keep in touch with a baby or toddler. They can observe the quality of care their child is receiving, and they can even spend time with their child during breaks and lunch hours. Mothers can nurse their children at the child care center or express milk in the "lactation room" (Kantor 2006).

In the face of steep global competition, including cheap labor in the Least Industrialized Nations, how can U.S. firms afford child care? Staring at such costs, most U.S. companies offer no child care at all. Surprisingly, however, corporate child care can reduce labor costs. Officers of the Union Bank of Monterey, California, grew concerned about the cost of their day care center, but they weren't sure what the cost actually was. To find out, they hired researchers, who looked beyond the salaries of day care workers, utilities, and such. They reported that the annual turnover of employees who used the center was just one-fourth that of employees who did not use it. Users of the center were also absent from work less, and they took shorter maternity leaves. The net cost? After subtracting the center's costs from these savings, the bank saved more than $200,000 (Solomon 1988).

Some corporations that don't offer on-site child care do offer *back-up care* for both children and dependent adults. This service helps employees avoid missing work even when they face emergencies, such as a sitter who can't make it. In some programs, the worker has the option of the caregiver coming to the home or of taking the one who needs care to a back-up care center.

As more women become managers and have a greater voice in policy, it is likely that more firms will offer care for children and dependent adults as part of a benefits package designed to attract and hold skilled workers.

Employee Stock Ownership Plans.   To increase their workers' loyalty and productivity, many companies let their employees buy the firm's stock either at a discount or as part of their salary. About 10 million U.S. workers own part of 11,000 companies. What are the results? Some studies show that these companies are more profitable than other firms (White 1991; Logue and Yates 2000). Other studies, in contrast, report that their profits are about the same, although their productivity may be higher (Blassi and Conte 1996). We need more definitive research on this matter.

It would seem obvious that if the employees own *all* or most of the company stock, problems between workers and management are eliminated. After all, the workers and owners are the same people. But this is not the case. The pilots of United Airlines, for example, who own the largest stake in their airline, staged a work slowdown during their

2001 contract negotiations, forcing the cancellation of thousands of flights. The machinists, who are also owners, followed suit. The machinists' union even threatened to strike. As passengers fled the airline, United racked up huge losses, and its stock plummeted (Zuckerman 2001). The irony is that the company's losses were the worker-owners' losses.

Profitability, not ownership, appears to be the key to reducing worker–management conflict. Unprofitable firms put more pressure on their employee-owners, while profitable companies are quicker to resolve problems.

The Conflict Perspective

Conflict theorists point out that the term *humanizing the work setting* is camouflage for what is really going on. Workers and owners walk different paths in life, and their basic relationship is always confrontational. Owners exploit workers to extract greater profits, and workers try to resist that exploitation. What employers call humanizing the work setting (or managing diversity) is just one of endless attempts to manipulate workers into co-operating in their own exploitation. Nice-sounding terms like *humanizing* are attempts to conceal the capitalists' goal of exploiting workers.

Fads in Corporate Culture

Business practices go through fads, and something that is hot one day may be cold the next. Twenty years ago, the rage was *quality circles,* workers and a manager or two who met regularly to try to improve the quality of both working conditions and the company's products. Because quality circles were used in Japan, U.S. managers embraced them, thinking they had discover ed the secret of Japanese success. At their height of popularity in 1983, tens of thousands of U.S. firms were using quality circles, and sixty consultants specialized in teaching them (Strang and Macy 2001). No longer. Quality circle has been shuffled into the garbage bin of history.

Sold on the team concept for problem-solving, however, corporations hop from one fad to another. "Cook-offs" are one of the latest. Going cleaver to cleaver, corporate teams slice, chop, and sauté against the clock (Hafner 2007). Professional chefs lend an aura of credibility by overseeing the cook-offs and judging the teams' culinary efforts. It seems safe to predict that, like quality circles and rope-climbing, these team-building exercises will soon pass—to be replaced by still another fad. The Dilbert cartoon picks up this point.

DILBERT: © Scott Adams/Dist. by United Feature Syndicate, Inc.

Despite the rationality that is essential to them, bureaucracies are also marked by non-rational elements. Fads that sweep businesses and universities are an example.

Technology and the Control of Workers

As mentioned in the last chapter, the microchip has revolutionized society. Among the changes it has ushered in is the greater ease of keeping tabs on people. Computers make it easier for governments to operate a police state by monitoring our every move. The Big Brother in Orwell's classic novel *1984* may turn out to be a master computer to which we all become servants.

We should know shortly. Computers now monitor millions of workers. In some workplaces, cameras even transmit workers' facial expressions for computer analysis (Neil 2008). These cameras, called "little brothers" (as compared with Orwell's "Big Brother"), are making their appearance in shopping malls, on street corners, and in our homes. As some analysts suggest, we seem to be moving toward a *maximum-security society* (Marx 1995). This seems an apt term. As with the workers in the Sociology and the New Technology box on the next page, few of us realize how extensively our actions are being monitored.

SOCIOLOGY and the NEW TECHNOLOGY

Cyberloafers and Cybersleuths: Surfing at Work

Few people work constantly at their jobs. Most of us take breaks and, at least once in a while, goof off. We meet fellow workers at the coffee machine, and we talk in the hallway. Much of this interaction is good for the company, for it bonds us to fellow workers and ties us to our jobs.

Our personal lives may even cross over into our workday. Some of us make personal calls from the office. Bosses know that we need to check in with our child's preschool or make arrangements for a babysitter. They expect such calls. Some even wink as we make a date or nod as we arrange to have our car worked on. And most bosses make personal calls of their own from time to time. It's the abuse that bothers bosses, and it's not surprising that they fire anyone who talks on the phone all day for personal reasons.

Using computers at work for personal purposes is called *cyberslacking*. Many workers trade stocks, download music, gamble, and play games. They read books, shop, exchange jokes, send personal e-mail, post messages in chat rooms, and visit porno sites. Some cyberslackers even operate their own businesses online—when they're not battling virtual enemies during "work."

To take an afternoon off without the boss knowing it, some use remote devices to make their computer switch screens and their printer spew out documents (Spencer 2003). It looks as though they just stepped away from their desk. Some download special audio recordings for their cell phone: Although they may be sitting on the beach when they call the office, their boss hears background sounds of a dentist's drill or of honking horns (Richtel 2004).

Some workers defend their cyberloafing. They argue, reasonably enough, that since their work invades their homes—forcing them to work evenings and weekends—employers should accommodate their personal lives. Some Web sites protect cyberloafers: They feature a panic button in case the boss pokes her head in your office. Click the button and a phony spreadsheet pops onto your screen.

Cyberslacking has given birth to the *cybersleuth,* investigators who use specialized software to recover every note employees have written and every Web site they have visited (Nusbaum 2003). They can bring up every file that employees have deleted, every word they've erased. What some workers don't know (and what some of us forget) is that "delete" does not mean erase. Hitting the delete button simply pushes the text into the background of our hard drive. With a few clicks, the cybersleuth, as if revealing invisible ink, exposes our "deleted" information, opening our hidden diary for anyone to read.

There is also cybersleuthing of employees' off-time behavior. For whatever reason, people get a kick out of posting photos of themselves drunk, naked, or doing obnoxious things (Stross 2007). The photos pose little risk when access is limited to a group of friends. But without tough access controls, the photos can end up in the boss's office—or, I should say, the former boss's office.

For Your Consideration

Do you think that cybersleuthing is an abuse of power? An invasion of privacy? Or do employers have a right to check on what their employees are doing with company computers on company time? Do you think employers have the right to check on what their employees are doing on their own time?

The Global Competition

Competition around the globe has heated up. Old organizations are passing into history, giving way to more efficient, bottom-line-oriented bureaucracies. In this fierce competition, each organization looks over its shoulder, fearful that another bureaucracy will discover a more efficient way to produce its product or sell its service, consigning it to the corporate has-beens. Countries do the same, even spying on one another to obtain competitive business secrets. The race may not always go to the swiftest, but organizations have to stay nimble if they are to survive. In the Cultural Diversity box with which we close this chapter, let's look at two of the main competitors in this global race to wealth and power.

Cultural Diversity around the World

Japanese and U.S. Corporations: Awkward Symbiosis

Do you know which of these statements is false?

The Japanese are more productive than Americans.
The living standard of Americans has fallen behind that of the Japanese.
Japanese workers enjoy lifetime job security.
The Japanese are paid less than Americans.

A while back, Japanese corporations seemed invincible. There was even talk that the United States had won World War II, but had lost the economic war. Impressed with Japan's success, Western corporations, including those from the United States, sent executives to Japan to study their companies. U.S. corporations then copied parts of that model.

Cracks in the facade soon appeared. Small at first, they grew, destroying some of Japan's major corporations. The change has been so extensive that all four of the statements above are false.

Unlike the corporations that surround us, Japanese companies had been built on personal relationships, on mutual obligations that transcend contracts. This had been their key to creating a fierce loyalty among production workers and executive staff. When workers were hired, they remained with a company for life. This corporate strength, however, turned out to be its Achilles heel. When Japan's economy went into a nosedive in the 1990s, companies did not lay off workers. Layoffs were not part of Japan's corporate culture; they signified disloyalty. As labor costs mounted while profits disappeared, companies sank in a sea of red ink.

After studying U.S. corporations to see why they were more efficient, Japan began to make tough adjustments.

Ford and Mazda have partnered with Changan Automobile of China to form Changan Ford Automobile Nanjing Company to manufacture cars in China.

Flying in the face of their traditions, Japanese companies began to lay off workers. Seeing its success in the United States, they also began to offer merit pay. Although layoffs and merit pay were standard U.S. practices, they had been unthinkable in Japan (Tokoro 2005). Today, a third of Japanese factory workers are temporary workers who are paid just two-thirds of regular workers' pay, have no job security, and can be dismissed without severance pay (Murphy and Inada 2008).

One of the biggest surprises was Ford's takeover of Mazda. When Mazda teetered on the edge of bankruptcy, its creditors decided that Ford knew more about building and marketing cars than Mazda and invited Ford to take a controlling interest in and manage the company. In true U.S. fashion, Ford laid off workers and renegotiated contracts with suppliers. With its work force slashed from 46,000 to 36,000, Mazda again became profitable. Similarly, when Sony's profits plummeted, an American who couldn't even speak Japanese became its CEO (Kane and Dvorak 2007).

In a continuing ironic twist of corporate evolution, the Japanese learned their lessons just as their U.S. mentors stumbled. Although Ford was able to turn Mazda to profitability, it failed to apply its own lessons to save itself from being swallowed in red ink. Under Ford's direction, Mazda turned in healthy profits, while Ford suffered its greatest losses since Henry Ford founded the company (Kageyama 2008). In a desperate bid to raise money to survive, in 2008 Ford sold much of its stake in Mazda. In the global economic shakeout that is rocking the world as I write this, we don't know what companies will survive—but we do know this: Those that survive, whether thriving or hanging on by their corporate fingernails, will be bureaucracies.

SUMMARY *and* REVIEW

The Rationalization of Society

How did the rationalization of society come about?

The term **rationalization of society** refers to a transformation in people's thinking and behaviors—one that shifts the focus from following time-honored ways to being efficient in producing results. Max Weber, who developed this term, traced this change to Protestant theology, which he said brought about capitalism. Karl Marx attributed rationalization to capitalism itself. Pp. 174–176.

Formal Organizations and Bureaucracies

What are formal organizations?

Formal organizations are secondary groups designed to achieve specific objectives. Their dominant form is the **bureaucracy,** which Weber said consists of a hierarchy, division of labor, written rules and communications, and impersonality and replaceability of positions—characteristics that make bureaucracies efficient and enduring. Pp. 176–180.

What dysfunctions are associated with bureaucracies?

The dysfunctions of bureaucracies include alienation, red tape, lack of communication between units, **goal displacement,** and incompetence (as seen in the **Peter principle**). In Weber's view, the impersonality of bureaucracies tends to produce **alienation** among workers—the feeling that no one cares about them and that they do not really fit in. Marx's view of alienation is somewhat different—workers do not identify with the product of their labor because they participate in only a small part of the production process. Pp. 181–185.

Voluntary Associations

What are the functions of voluntary associations?

Voluntary associations are groups made up of volunteers who organize on the basis of common interests. These associations promote mutual interests, provide a sense of identity and purpose, help to govern and maintain order, mediate between the government and the individual, give training in organizational skills, help provide access to political power, and pave the way for social change. Pp. 185–186.

What is "the iron law of oligarchy"?

Sociologist Robert Michels noted that formal organizations have a tendency to become controlled by an inner circle that limits leadership to its own members. The dominance of a formal organization by an elite that keeps itself in power is called **the iron law of oligarchy.** Pp. 186–187.

Working for the Corporation

How does the corporate culture affect workers?

Within corporate culture are values and stereotypes that are not readily visible. Often, **self-fulfilling stereotypes** are at work: People who match a corporation's hidden values tend to be put on career tracks that enhance their chance of success, while those who do not match those values are set on a course that minimizes their performance. Pp. 187–189.

Humanizing the Corporate Culture

What does it mean to humanize the work setting?

Humanizing a work setting means to organize it in a way that it develops rather than impedes human potential. Among the attempts to make bureaucracies more humane are work teams and corporate day care. Employee stock ownership plans give workers a greater stake in the outcomes of their work organizations, but they do not prevent worker–management conflict. Conflict theorists see attempts to humanize work as a way of manipulating workers. Pp. 189–191.

Technology and the Control of Workers

What is the maximum security society?

It is the use of computers and surveillance devices to monitor people, especially in the workplace. This technology is being extended to monitoring our everyday lives. Pp. 191–192.

The Global Competition

How do bureaucracies fit into the global competition?

Of the corporations now in global competition, only the most efficient will survive. That a corporation knows how to apply lessons in efficiency to others does not mean that it knows how to apply them to itself. P. 193.

THINKING CRITICALLY *ABOUT* Chapter 7

1. You are likely to work for a bureaucracy. How do you think that this will affect your orientations to life? How can you make the "hidden culture" work to your advantage?

2. Do you think the Peter principle is right? Why or why not?

3. Do you think U.S. corporations should have diversity training? Why or why not? If so, how should they go about it?

4. Why do you think the iron law of oligarchy is such a common feature of voluntary organizations?

ADDITIONAL RESOURCES

What can you find in MySocLab? mysoclab www.mysoclab.com

- Complete Ebook
- Practice Tests and Video and Audio activities
- Mapping and Data Analysis exercises

- Sociology in the News
- Classic Readings in Sociology
- Research and Writing advice

Where Can I Read More on This Topic?

Suggested readings for this chapter are listed at the back of this book.

8

Deviance and Social Control

South Dakota

I n just a few moments I was to meet my first Yanomamö, my first primitive man. What would it be like? . . . I looked up [from my canoe] and gasped when I saw a dozen burly, naked, filthy, hideous men staring at us down the shafts of their drawn arrows. Immense wads of green tobacco were stuck between their lower teeth and lips, making them look even more hideous, and strands of dark-green slime dripped or hung from their noses. We arrived at the village while the men were blowing a hallucinogenic drug up their noses. One of the side effects of the drug is a runny nose. The mucus is always saturated with the green powder, and the Indians usually let it run freely from their nostrils. . . . I just sat there holding my notebook, helpless and pathetic . . .

> They would "clean" their hands by spitting slimy tobacco juice into them.

The whole situation was depressing, and I wondered why I ever decided to switch from civil engineering to anthropology in the first place. . . . [Soon] I was covered with red pigment, the result of a dozen or so complete examinations. . . . These examinations capped an otherwise grim day. The Indians would blow their noses into their hands, flick as much of the mucus off that would separate in a snap of the wrist, wipe the residue into their hair, and then carefully examine my face, arms, legs, hair, and the contents of my pockets. I said [in their language], "Your hands are dirty"; my comments were met by the Indians in the following way: they would "clean" their hands by spitting a quantity of slimy tobacco juice into them, rub them together, and then proceed with the examination.

This is how Napoleon Chagnon describes the culture shock he felt when he met the Yanomamö tribe of the rain forests of Brazil. His ensuing months of fieldwork continued to bring surprise after surprise, and often Chagnon (1977) could hardly believe his eyes—or his nose.

deviance the violation of norms (or rules or expectations)

crime the violation of norms written into law

stigma "blemishes" that discredit a person's claim to a "normal" identity

If you were to list the deviant behaviors of the Yanomamö, what would you include? The way they appear naked in public? Use hallucinogenic drugs? Let mucus hang from their noses? Or the way they rub hands filled with mucus, spittle, and tobacco juice over a frightened stranger who doesn't dare to protest? Perhaps. But it isn't this simple, for as we shall see, deviance is relative.

What Is Deviance?

Sociologists use the term **deviance** to refer to any violation of norms, whether the infraction is as minor as driving over the speed limit, as serious as murder, or as humorous as Chagnon's encounter with the Yanomamö. This deceptively simple definition takes us to the heart of the sociological perspective on deviance, which sociologist Howard S. Becker (1966) described this way: *It is not the act itself, but the reactions to the act, that make something deviant.* What Chagnon saw disturbed him, but to the Yanomamö those same behaviors represented normal, everyday life. What was deviant to Chagnon was *conformist* to the Yanomamö. From their viewpoint, you *should* check out strangers the way they did—and nakedness is good, as are hallucinogenic drugs and letting mucus be "natural."

Chagnon's abrupt introduction to the Yanomamö allows us to see the *relativity of deviance,* a major point made by symbolic interactionists. Because different groups have different norms, *what is deviant to some is not deviant to others.* This principle holds both *within* a society and across cultures. Thus, acts that are acceptable in one culture—or in one group within a society—may be considered deviant in another culture or by another group within the same society. This idea is explored in the photo on this page, the one on page 200, and in the Cultural Diversity box on the next page.

This principle also applies to a specific form of deviance known as **crime,** the violation of rules that have been written into law. In the extreme, an act that is applauded by one group may be so despised by another group that it is punishable by death. Making a huge profit on business deals is one example. Americans who do this are admired. Like Donald Trump, Jack Welch, and Warren Buffet, they may even write books about their exploits. In China, however, until recently this same act was considered a crime called *profiteering.* Those found guilty were hanged in a public square as a lesson to all.

Unlike the general public, sociologists use the term *deviance* nonjudgmentally, to refer to any act to which people respond negatively. When sociologists use this term, it does not mean that they agree that an act is bad, just that people judge it negatively. To sociologists, then, *all* of us are deviants of one sort or another, for we all violate norms from time to time.

To be considered deviant, a person does not even have to *do* anything. Sociologist Erving Goffman (1963) used the term **stigma** to refer to characteristics that discredit people. These include violations of norms of ability (blindness, deafness, mental handicaps) and norms of appearance (a facial birthmark, a huge nose). They also include involuntary memberships, such as being a victim of AIDS or the brother of a rapist. The stigma can become a person's master status, defining him or her as deviant. Recall from Chapter 4 that a master status cuts across all other statuses that a person occupies.

How Norms Make Social Life Possible

No human group can exist without norms, for *norms make social life possible by making behavior predictable.* What would life be like if you could not predict what others would do? Imagine for a moment that you have gone to a store to purchase milk:

Suppose the clerk says, "I won't sell you any milk. We're overstocked with soda, and I'm not going to sell anyone milk until our soda inventory is reduced."

I took this photo on the outskirts of Hyderabad, India. Is this man deviant? If this were a U.S. street, he would be. But here? No houses have running water in his neighborhood, and the men, women, and children bathe at the neighborhood water pump. This man, then, would not be deviant in this culture. And yet, he is actually mugging for my camera, making the three bystanders laugh. Does this additional factor make this a scene of deviance?

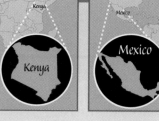

Cultural Diversity around the World

Human Sexuality in Cross-Cultural Perspective

Human sexuality illustrates how a group's *definition* of an act, not the act itself, determines whether it will be considered deviant. Let's look at some examples reported by anthropologist Robert Edgerton (1976).

Norms of sexual behavior vary so widely around the world that what is considered normal in one society may be considered deviant in another. In Kenya, a group called the Pokot place high emphasis on sexual pleasure, and they expect that both a husband and wife will reach orgasm. If a husband does not satisfy his wife, he is in trouble—especially if she thinks that his failure is because of adultery. If this is so, the wife and her female friends will sneak up on her husband when he is asleep. The women will tie him up, shout obscenities at him, beat him, and then urinate on him. Before releasing him, as a final gesture of their contempt they will slaughter and eat his favorite ox. The husband's hours of painful humiliation are intended to make him more dutiful concerning his wife's conjugal rights.

People can also become deviants for following their group's ideal norms instead of its real norms. As with

A Pokot married man Northern Kenya

many groups, the Zapotec Indians of Mexico profess that sexual relations should take place exclusively between husband and wife. Sexual affairs among the Zapotec are common, however, as the Zapotec also have a covert norm, an unspoken understanding, that married people will have affairs, but that they should be discreet about them. In one Zapotec community, the *only* person who did not have an extramarital affair was condemned by everyone in the village. The reason was not that she did not have an affair but that she told the other wives the names of the women their husbands were sleeping with. It is an interesting case, for if this virtuous woman had had an affair—and kept her mouth shut—she would not have become a deviant. Clearly, real norms can conflict with ideal norms—another illustration of the gap between ideal and real culture.

For Your Consideration

How do the behaviors of the Pokot wives and husbands mentioned here look from the perspective of U.S. norms? What are those U.S. norms? Did the Zapotec woman break norms of sexual behavior or of gossip and privacy? How does cultural relativity apply to the Pokot and Zapotec? (We discussed this concept in Chapter 2, pages 37–42.)

You don't like it, but you decide to buy a case of soda. At the checkout, the clerk says, "I hope you don't mind, but there's a $5 service charge on every fifteenth customer." You, of course, are the fifteenth.

Just as you start to leave, another clerk stops you and says, "We're not working any more. We decided to have a party." Suddenly a CD player begins to blast, and everyone in the store begins to dance. "Oh, good, you've brought the soda," says a different clerk, who takes your package and passes sodas all around.

Life is not like this, of course. You can depend on grocery clerks to sell you milk. You can also depend on paying the same price as everyone else and not being forced to attend a party in the store. Why can you depend on this? Because we are socialized to follow norms, to play the basic roles that society assigns to us.

Without norms, we would have social chaos. Norms lay out the basic guidelines for how we should play our roles and interact with others. In short, norms bring about **social order,** a group's customary social arrangements. Our lives are based on these arrangements, which is why deviance often is perceived as threatening: *Deviance undermines predictability, the foundation of social life.* Consequently, human groups develop a system of **social control**—formal and informal means of enforcing norms.

social order a group's usual and customary social arrangements, on which its members depend and on which they base their lives

social control a group's formal and informal means of enforcing its norms

Violating background assumptions is a common form of deviance. Although we have no explicit rule that says, "Do not put snakes through your nose," we all know that it exists (perhaps as a subcategory of "Don't do strange things in public"). Is this act also deviant for this man in Chennai, India?

Sanctions

As we discussed in Chapter 2, people do not enforce folkways strictly, but they become upset when people break mores (MO-rays). Expressions of disapproval of deviance, called **negative sanctions,** range from frowns and gossip for breaking folkways to imprisonment and capital punishment for breaking mores. In general, the more seriously the group takes a norm, the harsher the penalty for violating it. In contrast, **positive sanctions**—from smiles to formal awards—are used to reward people for conforming to norms. Getting a raise is a positive sanction; being fired is a negative sanction. Getting an *A* in intro to sociology is a positive sanction; getting an *F* is a negative one.

Most negative sanctions are informal. You might stare if you observe someone dressed in what you consider to be inappropriate clothing, or you might gossip if a married person you know spends the night with someone other than his or her spouse. Whether you consider the breaking of a norm merely an amusing matter that warrants no sanction or a serious infraction that does, however, depends on your perspective. Let's suppose that a woman appears at your college graduation in a bikini. You might stare, laugh, and nudge the person next to you, but if this is *your* mother, you are likely to feel that different sanctions are appropriate. Similarly, if it is *your* father who spends the night with an 18-year-old college freshman, you are likely to do more than gossip.

In Sum: In sociology, the term *deviance* refers to all violations of social rules, regardless of their seriousness. The term is neutral, not a judgment about the behavior. Deviance is relative, for what is deviant in one group may be conformist in another. Consequently, we must consider deviance from *within* a group's own framework, for it is their meanings that underlie their behavior.

Competing Explanations of Deviance: Sociobiology, Psychology, and Sociology

If social life is to exist, norms are essential. So why do people violate them? To better understand the reasons, it is useful to know how sociological explanations differ from biological and psychological ones.

Sociobiologists explain deviance by looking for answers *within* individuals. They assume that **genetic predispositions** lead people to such deviances as juvenile delinquency and crime (Lombroso 1911; Wilson and Herrnstein 1985; Goozen et al. 2007). Among their explanations were these three theories: (1) intelligence—low intelligence leads to crime; (2) the "XYY" theory—an extra Y chromosome in males leads to crime; and (3) body type—people with "squarish, muscular" bodies are more likely to commit **street crime**—acts such as mugging, rape, and burglary.

How have these theories held up? We should first note that most people who have these supposedly "causal" characteristics do not become criminals. Regarding intelligence, you already know that some criminals are very intelligent and that most people of low intelligence do not commit crimes. Regarding the extra Y chromosome, most men who commit crimes have the normal XY chromosome combination, and most men with the XYY combination do not become criminals. No women have this combination of genes, so this explanation can't even be applied to female criminals. Regarding body type, criminals exhibit the full range of body types, and most people with "squarish, muscular" bodies do not become street criminals.

Psychologists also focus on abnormalities *within* the individual. They examine what are called **personality disorders.** Their supposition is that deviating individuals have deviating personalities (Barnes 2001; Mayer 2007) and that subconscious motives drive people to deviance. No specific childhood experience, however, is invariably linked with deviance. For example, children who had "bad toilet training," "suffocating mothers," or

negative sanction an expression of disapproval for breaking a norm, ranging from a mild, informal reaction such as a frown to a formal reaction such as a prison sentence or an execution

positive sanction a reward or positive reaction for following norms, ranging from a smile to a material award

genetic predisposition inborn tendencies (for example, a tendency to commit deviant acts)

street crime crimes such as mugging, rape, and burglary

personality disorders the view that a personality disturbance of some sort causes an individual to violate social norms

In a changing society, the boundaries of what is considered deviance are constantly changing. After a mother was kicked off a Delta flight for nursing her child, mothers protested by staging a "nurse-in" at Delta ticket counters across the country.

"emotionally aloof fathers" may become embezzling bookkeepers—or good accountants. Just as college students, teachers, and police officers represent a variety of bad—and good—childhood experiences, so do deviants. Similarly, people with "suppressed anger" can become freeway snipers or military heroes—or anything else. In short, there is no inevitable outcome of any childhood experience. Deviance is not associated with any particular personality.

Sociologists, in contrast with both sociobiologists and psychologists, search for factors *outside* the individual. They look for social influences that "recruit" people to break norms. To account for why people commit crimes, for example, sociologists examine such external influences as socialization, membership in subcultures, and social class. *Social class,* a concept that we will discuss in depth in Chapter 10, refers to people's relative standing in terms of education, occupation, and especially income and wealth.

The point stressed earlier, that deviance is relative, leads sociologists to ask a crucial question: Why should we expect to find something constant within people to account for a behavior that is conforming in one society and deviant in another? To explain deviance, sociologists apply the three sociological perspectives—symbolic interactionism, functionalism, and conflict theory.

The Symbolic Interactionist Perspective

As we examine symbolic interactionism, it will become more evident why sociologists are not satisfied with explanations that are rooted in sociobiology or psychology. A basic principle of symbolic interactionism is that we are thinking beings who act according to our interpretations of situations. Let's consider how our membership in groups influences how we view life and, from there, our behavior.

Differential Association Theory

The Theory.   Going directly against the idea that biology or personality is the source of deviance, sociologists stress our experiences in groups (Deflem 2006; Chambliss 1973/2007). Consider an extreme: boys and girls who join street gangs and those who join the Scouts. Obviously, each will learn different attitudes and behaviors concerning deviance and conformity. Edwin Sutherland coined the term **differential association** to indicate this: From the *different* groups we *associate* with, we learn to deviate from or conform to society's norms (Sutherland 1924, 1947; Sutherland et al. 1992).

differential association
Edwin Sutherland's term to indicate that people who associate with some groups learn an "excess of definitions" of deviance, increasing the likelihood that they will become deviant

To experience a sense of belonging is a basic human need. Membership in groups, especially peer groups, is a primary way that people meet this need. Regardless of the orientation of the group—whether to conformity or deviance—the process is the same. These teens belong to DEFYIT (Drug-Free Youth in Town), an organization that promotes a drug-free lifestyle.

Sutherland's theory is more complicated than this, but he basically said that the different groups with which we associate (our "*differential* association") give us messages about conformity and deviance. We may receive mixed messages, but we end up with more of one than the other (an "excess of definitions," as Sutherland put it). The end result is an imbalance—attitudes that tilt us in one direction or another. Consequently, we learn to either conform or to deviate.

Families.   Since our family is so important for teaching us attitudes, it probably is obvious to you that the family makes a big difference in whether we learn deviance or conformity. Researchers have confirmed this informal observation. Of the many confirming studies, this one stands out: Of all prison inmates across the United States, about *half* have a father, mother, brother, sister, or spouse who has served time in prison (*Criminal Justice Statistics* 2003:Table 6.0011; Glaze and Maruschak 2008:Table 11). In short, families that are involved in crime tend to set their children on a lawbreaking path.

Friends, Neighborhoods, and Subcultures.   Most people don't know the term *differential association*, but they do know how it works. Most parents want to move out of "bad" neighborhoods because they know that if their kids have delinquent friends, they are likely to become delinquent, too. Sociological research also supports this common observation (Miller 1958; Chung and Steinberg 2006; Yonas et al. 2006). Some neighborhoods even develop a subculture of violence. In these places, even a teasing remark can mean instant death. If the neighbors feel that a victim deserved to be killed, they refuse to testify because "he got what was coming to him" (Kubrin and Weitzer 2003).

In some neighborhoods, killing is even considered an honorable act:

> Sociologist Ruth Horowitz (1983, 2005), who did participant observation in a lower-class Chicano neighborhood in Chicago, discovered how associating with people who have a certain concept of "honor" propels young men to deviance. The formula is simple. "A real man has honor. An insult is a threat to one's honor. Therefore, not to stand up to someone is to be less than a real man."
>
> Now suppose you are a young man growing up in this neighborhood. You likely would do a fair amount of fighting, for you would interpret many things as attacks on your honor. You might even carry a knife or a gun, for words and fists wouldn't always be sufficient. Along with members of your group, you would define fighting, knifing, and shooting quite differently from the way most people do.

Members of the Mafia also intertwine ideas of manliness with violence. For them, *to kill is a measure of their manhood.* Not all killings are accorded the same respect, however, for "the more awesome and potent the victim, the more worthy and meritorious the killer" (Arlacchi 1980). Some killings are done to enforce norms. A member of the Mafia who gives information to the police, for example, has violated *omertá* (the Mafia's vow of secrecy). This offense can never be tolerated, for it threatens the very existence of the group. Mafia killings further illustrate just how relative deviance is. Although killing is deviant to mainstream society, for members of the Mafia, *not* to kill after certain rules are broken—such as when someone "squeals" to the cops—is the deviant act.

Prison or Freedom?   As was mentioned in Chapter 3, an issue that comes up over and over again in sociology is whether we are prisoners of socialization. Symbolic interactionists stress that we are not mere pawns in the hands of others. We are not destined to think and act as our groups dictate. Rather, we *help to produce our own orientations to life.* By joining one group rather than another (differential association), for example, we help to shape the self. For instance, one college student may join a feminist group that is trying to change the treatment of women in college; another may associate with a group of women who shoplift on weekends. Their choice of groups points them in different directions. The one who joins the feminist group may develop an even greater interest in producing social change, while the one who associates with shoplifters may become even more oriented toward criminal activities.

Control Theory

Do you ever feel the urge to do something that you know you shouldn't, something that would get you in trouble if you did it? Most of us fight temptations to break society's norms. We find that we have to stifle things

The social control of deviance takes many forms. One of its most obvious is the use of the police to enforce norms. The man in the center of this photo taken in Naples, Italy, is Edoardo Contini, a mafia boss who was considered one of Italy's 30 most dangerous fugitives.

inside us—urges, hostilities, desires of various sorts. And most of the time, we manage to keep ourselves out of trouble. The basic question that control theory tries to answer is: With the desire to deviate so common, why don't we all just "bust loose"?

The Theory.   Sociologist Walter Reckless (1973), who developed **control theory,** stressed that two control systems work against our motivations to deviate. Our *inner controls* include our internalized morality—conscience, religious principles, ideas of right and wrong. Inner controls also include fears of punishment, feelings of integrity, and the desire to be a "good" person (Hirschi 1969; McShane and Williams 2007). Our *outer controls* consist of people—such as family, friends, and the police—who influence us not to deviate.

The stronger our bonds are with society, the more effective our inner controls are (Hirschi 1969). Bonds are based on *attachments* (our affection and respect for people who conform to mainstream norms), *commitments* (having a stake in society that you don't want to risk, such as a respected place in your family, a good standing at college, a good job), *involvements* (participating in approved activities), and *beliefs* (convictions that certain actions are morally wrong).

This theory can be summarized as *self*-control, says sociologist Travis Hirschi. The key to learning high self-control is socialization, especially in childhood. Parents help their children to develop self-control by supervising them and punishing their deviant acts (Gottfredson and Hirschi 1990; Hay and Forrest 2006). They sometimes use shame to keep their children in line. You probably had that forefinger shaken at you. I certainly recall it aimed at me. Do you think that more use of shaming, discussed in the Down-to-Earth Sociology box on the next page, could help increase people's internal controls?

Applying Control Theory

Suppose that some friends invite you to go to a nightclub with them. When you get there, you notice that everyone seems unusually happy—almost giddy. They seem to be euphoric in their animated conversations and dancing. Your friends tell you that almost everyone here has taken the drug Ecstasy, and they invite you to take some with them.

What do you do? Let's not explore the question of whether taking Ecstasy in this setting is a deviant or a conforming act. That is a separate issue. Instead, concentrate on the pushes and

control theory the idea that two control systems—inner controls and outer controls—work against our tendencies to deviate

Down-to-Earth Sociology
Shaming: Making a Comeback?

Shaming can be effective, especially when members of a primary group use it. In some small communities, where the individual's reputation was at stake, shaming was the centerpiece of the enforcement of norms. Violators were marked as deviant and held up for all the world to see. In Spain, where one's reputation with neighbors still matters, debt collectors, dressed in tuxedo and top hat, walk slowly to the front door. The sight shames debtors into paying (Catan 2008). In Nathaniel Hawthorne's *The Scarlet Letter*, town officials forced Hester Prynne to wear a scarlet A sewn on her dress. The A stood for *adulteress*. Wherever she went, Prynne had to wear this badge of shame, and the community expected her to wear it every day for the rest of her life.

As our society grew large and urban, its sense of community diminished, and shaming lost its effectiveness. Now shaming is starting to make a comeback. One Arizona sheriff makes the men in his jail wear striped prison uniforms—and pink underwear (Billeaud 2008). As in the photo on this page, they also wear pink while they work in chain gangs. Women prisoners, too, are put in chain gangs and forced to pick up street trash. Online shaming sites have also appeared. Captured on cell phone cameras are bad drivers, older men who leer at teenaged girls, and dog walkers who don't pick up their dog's poop (Saranow 2007). Some sites post photos of the offenders, as well as their addresses and phone numbers.

Sociologist Harold Garfinkel (1956) gave the name **degradation ceremony** to an extreme form of shaming. The individual is called to account before the group, witnesses denounce him or her, the offender is pronounced guilty, and steps are taken to strip the individual of his or her identity as a group member. In some courts martial, officers who are found guilty stand at attention before their peers while the insignia of rank are ripped from their uniforms. This procedure screams that the individual is no longer a member of the group. Although Hester Prynne was not banished from the group physically, she was banished morally; her degradation ceremony proclaimed her a *moral* outcast from the community. The scarlet A marked her as "not one" of them.

Although we don't use scarlet A's today, informal degradation ceremonies still occur. Consider what happened to this New York City police officer (Chivers 2001):

"If you drive and drink, you'll wear pink" is the slogan of a campaign to shame drunk drivers in Phoenix, Arizona. Shown here are convicted drunk drivers who will pick up trash while wearing pink.

Joseph Gray had been a police officer in New York City for fifteen years. As with some of his fellow officers, alcohol and sex helped relieve the pressures of police work. After spending one afternoon drinking in a topless bar, bleary-eyed, Gray plowed his car into a vehicle carrying a pregnant woman, her son, and her sister. All three died. Gray was accused of manslaughter and drunk driving.

The *New York Times* and New York television stations kept hammering this story to the public. Three weeks later, Gray resigned from the police force. As he left police headquarters after resigning, an angry crowd surrounded him. Gray hung his head in public disgrace as Victor Manuel Herrera, whose wife and son were killed in the crash, followed him, shouting, "You're a murderer!" (Gray was later convicted of drunk driving and manslaughter.)

For Your Consideration

1. How do you think law enforcement officials might use shaming to reduce law breaking?
2. How do you think school officials could use shaming?
3. Suppose that you were caught shoplifting at a store near where you live. Would you rather spend a week in jail with no one but your family knowing it (and no permanent record) or a week walking in front of the store you stole from wearing a placard that proclaims in bold red capital letters: I AM A THIEF! and in smaller letters says: "I am sorry for stealing from this store and causing you to have to pay higher prices"? Why?

pulls you would feel. The pushes toward taking the drug: your friends, the setting, and your curiosity. Then there are your inner controls—those inner voices of your conscience and your parents, perhaps of your teachers, as well as your fears of arrest and the dangers you've heard about illegal drugs. There are also the outer controls—perhaps the uniformed security guard looking in your direction.

So, what *did* you decide? Which was stronger: your inner and outer controls or the pushes and pulls toward taking the drug? It is you who can best weigh these forces, for they differ with each of us. This little example puts us at the center of what control theory is all about.

Labeling Theory

Suppose for one undesirable moment that you had the reputation as a "whore," a "pervert," or a "cheat." (Pick one.) What power such a reputation would have—both on how others would see you and on how you would see yourself. How about if you became known as "very intelligent," "truthful in everything," or "honest to the core"? (Choose one.) You can see that such a reputation would give people a different expectation of your character and behavior. This is what labeling theory focuses on, the significance of reputations, how they help set us on paths that propel us into deviance or that divert us away from it.

Degradation ceremonies, a form of shaming, are intended to humiliate norm violators and mark them as "not members" of the group. This photo was taken by the U.S. army in 1945 after U.S. troops liberated Cherbourg, France. Members of the French resistance shaved the heads of these women, who had "collaborated" (had sex with) the occupying Nazis. They then marched the shamed women down the streets of the city, while the public shouted insults and spat on them.

Rejecting Labels: How People Neutralize Deviance.   Not many of us want to be called "whores," "perverts," and so on. Most of us resist the negative labels that others try to pin on us. Some of us are so successful that even though we persist in deviance, we still consider ourselves conformists. For example, some people who beat up others and vandalize property consider themselves to be conforming members of society. How do they do it?

Sociologists Gresham Sykes and David Matza (1957/1988) studied boys like this. They found that the boys used five **techniques of neutralization** to deflect society's norms.

Denial of Responsibility Some boys said, "I'm not responsible for what happened because . . ." and then they were quite creative about the "becauses." Some said that what happened was an "accident." Other boys saw themselves as "victims" of society. What else could you expect? They were like billiard balls shot around the pool table of life.

Denial of Injury Another favorite explanation was "What I did wasn't wrong because no one got hurt." The boys would define vandalism as "mischief," gang fights as a "private quarrel," and stealing cars as "borrowing." They might acknowledge that what they did was illegal, but claim that they were "just having a little fun."

Denial of a Victim Some boys thought of themselves as avengers. Vandalizing a teacher's car was done to get revenge for an unfair grade, while shoplifting was a way to even the score with "crooked" store owners. In short, even if the boys did accept responsibility and admit that someone had gotten hurt, they protected their self-concept by claiming that the people "deserved what they got."

Condemnation of the Condemners Another technique the boys used was to deny that others had the right to judge them. They might accuse people who pointed their fingers at them of being "a bunch of hypocrites": The police were "on the take," teachers had "pets," and parents cheated on their taxes. In short, they said, "Who are *they* to accuse *me* of something?"

Appeal to Higher Loyalties A final technique the boys used to justify their activities was to consider loyalty to the gang more important than the norms of society. They might say, "I had to help my friends. That's why I got in the fight." Not incidentally, the boy may have shot two members of a rival group, as well as a bystander!

degradation ceremony a term coined by Harold Garfinkel to refer to a ritual whose goal is to reshape someone's self by stripping away that individual's self-identity and stamping a new identity in its place

labeling theory the view that the labels people are given affect their own and others' perceptions of them, thus channeling their behavior into either deviance or conformity

techniques of neutralization ways of thinking or rationalizing that help people deflect (or neutralize) society's norms

In Sum: These five techniques of neutralization have implications far beyond this group of boys, for it is not only delinquents who try to neutralize the norms of mainstream society. Look again at these five techniques—don't they sound familiar? (1) "I couldn't help myself"; (2) "Who really got hurt?"; (3) "Don't you think she deserved that, after what *she* did?"; (4) "Who are *you* to talk?"; and (5) "I had to help my friends—wouldn't you have done the same thing?" All of us attempt to neutralize the moral demands of society, for neutralization helps us to sleep at night.

Embracing Labels: The Example of Outlaw Bikers.   Although most of us resist attempts to label us as deviant, some people revel in a deviant identity. Some teenagers, for example, make certain by their clothing, choice of music, hairstyles, and "body art" that no one misses their rejection of adult norms. Their status among fellow members of a subculture—within which they are almost obsessive conformists—is vastly more important than any status outside it.

One of the best examples of a group that embraces deviance is motorcycle gangs. Sociologist Mark Watson (1980/2006) did participant observation with outlaw bikers. He rebuilt Harleys with them, hung around their bars and homes, and went on "runs" (trips) with them. He concluded that outlaw bikers see the world as "hostile, weak, and effeminate." Holding this conventional world in contempt, gang members pride themselves on breaking its norms and getting in trouble, laughing at death, and treating women as lesser beings whose primary value is to provide them with services—especially sex. They pride themselves in looking "dirty, mean, and generally undesirable," taking pleasure in shocking people by their appearance and behavior. Outlaw bikers also regard themselves as losers, a factor that becomes woven into their unusual embrace of deviance.

The Power of Labels: The Saints and the Roughnecks.   We can see how powerful labeling is by referring back to the "Saints" and the "Roughnecks," research that was cited in Chapter 4 (page 119). As you recall, both groups of high school boys were "constantly occupied with truancy, drinking, wild parties, petty theft, and vandalism." Yet their teachers looked on one group, the Saints, as "headed for success" and the other group, the Roughnecks, as "headed for trouble." By the time they finished high school, not one Saint had been arrested, while the Roughnecks had been in constant trouble with the police.

Why did the members of the community perceive these boys so differently? Chambliss (1973/2007) concluded that this split vision was due to *social class*. As symbolic interactionists emphasize, social class is like a lens that focuses our perceptions. The Saints came from respectable, middle-class families, while the Roughnecks were

How powerful are labels? Consider Michael Vick: Great football player or cruel dog fighter? Rich sports hero or convict? Shown here is Vick's attorney giving a press conference after Vick was sentenced to 23 months in prison. After serving 19 months in prison, he was given another NFL contract.

from less respectable, working-class families. These backgrounds led teachers and the authorities to expect good behavior from the Saints but trouble from the Roughnecks. And, like the rest of us, teachers and police saw what they expected to see.

The boys' social class also affected their visibility. The Saints had automobiles, and they did their drinking and vandalism outside of town. Without cars, the Roughnecks hung around their own street corners, where their drinking and boisterous behavior drew the attention of police, confirming the negative impressions that the community already had of them.

The boys' social class also equipped them with distinct *styles of interaction*. When police or teachers questioned them, the Saints were apologetic. This show of respect for authority elicited a positive reaction from teachers and police, allowing the Saints to escape school and legal problems. The Roughnecks, said Chambliss, were "almost the polar opposite." When questioned, they were hostile. Even when they tried to assume a respectful attitude, everyone could see through it. Consequently, while teachers and police let the Saints off with warnings, they came down hard on the Roughnecks.

Certainly, what happens in life is not determined by labels alone, but the Saints and the Roughnecks did live up to the labels that the community gave them. As you may recall, all but one of the Saints went on to college. One earned a Ph.D., one became a lawyer, one a doctor, and the others business managers. In contrast, only two of the Roughnecks went to college. They earned athletic scholarships and became coaches. The other Roughnecks did not fare so well. Two of them dropped out of high school, later became involved in separate killings, and were sent to prison. One became a local bookie, and no one knows the whereabouts of the other.

How do labels work? Although the matter is complex, because it involves the self-concept and reactions that vary from one individual to another, we can note that labels open and close doors of opportunity. Unlike its meaning in sociology, the term *deviant* in everyday usage is emotionally charged with a judgment of some sort. This label can lock people out of conforming groups and push them into almost exclusive contact with people who have been similarly labeled.

In Sum: Symbolic interactionists examine how people's definitions of the situation underlie their deviating from or conforming to social norms. They focus on group membership (differential association), how people balance pressures to conform and to deviate (control theory), and the significance of people's reputations (labeling theory).

The central point of symbolic interactionism, that *deviance* involves a clash of competing definitions, is explored in the Mass Media box on the next page.

The Functionalist Perspective

When we think of deviance, its dysfunctions are likely to come to mind. Functionalists, in contrast, are as likely to stress the functions of deviance as they are to emphasize its dysfunctions.

Can Deviance Really Be Functional for Society?

Most of us are upset by deviance, especially crime, and assume that society would be better off without it. The classic functionalist theorist Emile Durkheim (1893/1933, 1895/1964), however, came to a surprising conclusion. Deviance, he said—including crime—is functional for society, for it contributes to the social order. Its three main functions are:

1. *Deviance clarifies moral boundaries and affirms norms.* A group's ideas about how people should think and act mark its *moral boundaries*. Deviant acts challenge those boundaries. To call a member into account is to say, in effect, "You broke an important rule, and we cannot tolerate that." Punishing deviants affirms the group's norms and clarifies what it means to be a member of the group.

2. *Deviance promotes social unity.* To affirm the group's moral boundaries by punishing deviants fosters a "we" feeling among the group's members. In saying, "You can't get away with that," the group affirms the rightness of its own ways.

MASS MEDIA In SOCIAL LIFE

Pornography and the Mainstream: Freedom Versus Censorship

Pornography vividly illustrates one of the sociological principles discussed in this chapter: the relativity of deviance. It is not the act, but reactions to the act, that make something deviant. Consider pornography on the Internet.

Porn surfers have a wide variety of choices. Sites are indexed by race–ethnicity, sex, hair color, age, weight, heterosexuality, homosexuality, singles, groups, and sexual activity. Sites feature teenagers, cheerleaders, sneaky shots, and "grannies who still think they have it." Some sites offer only photographs, others video and sound. There also are live sites. After agreeing to the hefty per-minute charges, you can command your "model" to do almost anything your heart desires.

What is the problem? Why can't people exchange nude photos electronically if they want to? Or watch others having sex online, if someone offers that service? Although some people object to any kind of sex site, what disturbs many are the sites that feature bondage, torture, rape, bestiality (humans having sex with animals), and sex with children.

The Internet abounds with sites where people "meet" online to discuss some topic. No one is bothered by sites that feature Roman architecture or rap music or sports, of course, but those that focus on how to torture women are another matter. So are those that offer lessons on how to seduce grade school children—or that extol the delights of having sex with three-year-olds.

The state and federal governments have passed laws against child pornography, and the police seize computers of suspects and search them for illegal pictures. The penalties can be severe. When photos of children in sex acts were found on an Arizona man's computer, he was sentenced to 200 years in prison (Greenhouse 2007). When he appealed his sentence as unconstitutional (cruel, unusual), his sentence was upheld. To exchange pictures of tortured and sexually abused women remains legal.

The issue of censorship is front and center in the debate about pornography. While some people want to ban pornography, others, even those who find it immoral, say that we must tolerate it. No matter how much we may disagree with a point of view, or even find it repugnant, they say, we must allow communications about it. This includes photos and videos. If we let the government censor the Internet in any way, it will stretch that inch into a mile and censor the expression of other things it doesn't like—such as criticism of government officials (Foley 2008).

As this debate continues, pornography is moving into the mainstream. The online sex industry now has an annual trade show, Internext. Predictions at Internext are that hotels will soon offer not just sex videos on demand but also live images of people having sex (Johnston 2007). In its struggle for legitimacy, the sex industry is trying to get banks to invest in it—and to be listed on the stock exchanges (Richtel 2007). As social views change, this is likely to happen.

For Your Consideration

Can you disprove the central point of the symbolic interactionists—that an activity is deviant only because people decide that it is deviant? You may use any examples, but you cannot invoke God or moral absolutes in your argument, as they are outside the scope of sociology. Sociology cannot decide moral issues, even in extreme cases.

On pornography and censorship: Do you think it should be legal to exchange photos of women being sexually abused or tortured? Should it be legal to discuss ways to seduce children? If not, on what basis should these activities be banned? If we make them illegal, then what other communications should we prohibit? On what basis?

---

3. *Deviance promotes social change.* Groups do not always agree on what to do with people who push beyond their accepted ways of doing things. Some group members may even approve of the rule-breaking behavior. Boundary violations that gain enough support become new, acceptable behaviors. Deviance, then, may force a group to rethink and redefine its moral boundaries, helping groups—and whole societies—to adapt to changing circumstances.

Strain Theory: How Social Values Produce Deviance

Functionalists argue that crime is a *natural* part of society, not an aberration or some alien element in our midst. Mainstream values can even generate crime. Consider what sociologists Richard Cloward and Lloyd Ohlin (1960) identified as the crucial problem of the industrialized world: the need to locate and train its talented people—whether they were born into wealth or into poverty—so that they can take over the key technical jobs of society. When children are born, no one knows which ones will have the ability to become dentists, nuclear physicists, or engineers. To get the most talented people to compete with one another, society tries to motivate *everyone* to strive for success. It does this by arousing discontent—making people feel dissatisfied with what they have so they will try to "better" themselves.

We are quite successful in getting almost everyone to want **cultural goals,** success of some sort, such as wealth or prestige. But we aren't very successful in equalizing access to the **institutionalized means,** the legitimate ways to reach those goals. As sociologist Robert Merton (1956, 1968) analyzed socialization into success and the blocked access to it, he developed **strain theory.** *Strain* refers to the frustrations people feel when they want success but find their way to it blocked. It is easy to identify with mainstream norms (such as working hard or pursuing higher education) when they help you get ahead, but when they don't seem to be getting you anywhere, you feel frustrated. You might even feel wronged by the system. If mainstream rules seem illegitimate, you experience a gap that Merton called *anomie,* a sense of normlessness.

As part of living in society, all of us have to face these cultural goals and institutionalized means. Table 8.1 compares the various ways that people react to them. The first reaction, which Merton said is the most common, is *conformity,* using socially acceptable means to try to reach cultural goals. In industrialized societies most people try to get good jobs, a good education, and so on. If well-paid jobs are unavailable, they take less desirable jobs. If they are denied access to Harvard or Stanford, they go to a state university. Others take night classes and go to vocational schools. In short, most people take the socially acceptable path.

Four Deviant Paths.   The remaining four responses, which are deviant, represent reactions to the strain people feel between the goals they want and their access to the institutionalized means to reach them. Let's look at each. *Innovators* are people who accept the goals of society but use illegitimate means to try to reach them. Crack dealers, for instance, accept the goal of achieving wealth, but they reject the legitimate avenues for doing so. Other examples are embezzlers, robbers, and con artists.

The second deviant path is taken by people who become discouraged and give up on achieving cultural goals. Yet they still cling to conventional rules of conduct. Merton called this response *ritualism.* Although ritualists have given up on getting ahead at work, they survive by rigorously following the rules of their job. Teachers whose idealism is shattered (who are said to suffer from "burnout"), for example, remain in the classroom, where they teach without enthusiasm. Their response is considered deviant because they cling to the job even though they have abandoned the goal, which may have been to stimulate young minds or to make the world a better place.

People who choose the third deviant path, *retreatism,* reject both the cultural goals and the institutionalized means of achieving them. Some people stop pursuing success and retreat into alcohol or drugs. Although their path to withdrawal is considerably different, women who enter a convent or men a monastery are also retreatists.

The final type of deviant response is *rebellion.* Convinced that their society is corrupt, rebels, like retreatists, reject both society's goals and its institutionalized means. Unlike retreatists, however, rebels seek to give society new goals, as well as new means for reaching them. Revolutionaries are the most committed type of rebels.

---

cultural goals the objectives held out as legitimate or desirable for the members of a society to achieve

institutionalized means approved ways of reaching cultural goals

strain theory Robert Merton's term for the strain engendered when a society socializes large numbers of people to desire a cultural goal (such as success), but withholds from some the approved means of reaching that goal; one adaptation to the strain is crime, the choice of an innovative means (one outside the approved system) to attain the cultural goal

---

TABLE 8.1   How People Match Their Goals to Their Means

Do They Feel the Strain That Leads to Anomie?	Mode of Adaptation	Cultural Goals	Institutionalized Means
No	Conformity	Accept	Accept
	Deviant Paths:		
	1. Innovation	Accept	Reject
Yes	2. Ritualism	Reject	Accept
	3. Retreatism	Reject	Reject
	4. Rebellion	Reject/Replace	Reject/Replace

Source: Based on Merton 1968.

illegitimate opportunity structure opportunities for crimes that are woven into the texture of life

white-collar crime Edwin Sutherland's term for crimes committed by people of respectable and high social status in the course of their occupations; for example, bribery of public officials, securities violations, embezzlement, false advertising, and price fixing

corporate crime crimes committed by executives in order to benefit their corporation

In Sum: Strain theory underscores the sociological principle that deviants are the product of society. Mainstream social values (cultural goals and institutionalized means to reach those goals) can produce strain (frustration, dissatisfaction). People who feel this strain are more likely than others to take the deviant (nonconforming) paths summarized in Table 8.1.

Illegitimate Opportunity Structures: Social Class and Crime

Over and over in this text, you have seen the impact of social class on people's lives—and you will continue to do so in coming chapters. Let's look now at how social class produces distinct styles of crime.

Street Crime.   In applying strain theory, functionalists point out that industrialized societies have no trouble socializing the poor into wanting to own things. Like others, the poor are bombarded with messages urging them to buy everything from Xboxes and iPods to designer jeans and new cars. Television and movies are filled with images of middle-class people enjoying luxurious lives. The poor get the message—all full-fledged Americans can afford society's many goods and services.

Yet, the most common route to success, the school system, presents a bewildering world. Run by the middle class, schools are at odds with the background of the poor. What the poor take for granted is unacceptable, questioned, and mocked. Their speech, for example, is built around nonstandard grammar and is often laced with what the middle class considers obscenities. Their ideas of punctuality and their poor preparation in reading and paper-and-pencil skills also make it difficult to fit in. Facing such barriers, the poor are more likely than their more privileged counterparts to drop out of school. Educational failure, of course, slams the door on most legitimate avenues to financial success.

It is not that the poor are left without opportunities for financial success. Woven into life in urban slums is what Cloward and Ohlin (1960) called an **illegitimate opportunity structure.** An alternative door to success opens: "hustles" such as robbery, burglary, drug dealing, prostitution, pimping, gambling, and other crimes (Sánchez-Jankowski 2003; Anderson 1978, 1990/2006). Pimps and drug dealers, for example, present an image of a glamorous life—people who are in control and have plenty of "easy money." For many of the poor, the "hustler" becomes a role model.

It should be easy to see, then, why street crime attracts disproportionate numbers of the poor. In the Down-to-Earth Sociology box on the next page, let's look at how gangs are part of the illegitimate opportunity structure that beckons disadvantaged youth.

White-Collar Crime.   Like the poor, the *forms* of crime of the more privileged classes also match their life situation. And how different their illegitimate opportunities are! Physicians don't hold up cabbies, but they do cheat Medicare. Investment managers like Bernie Madoff run fraudulent schemes that cheat customers around the world. Mugging, pimping, and burgling are not part of this more privileged world, but evading income tax, bribing public officials, and embezzling are. Sociologist Edwin Sutherland (1949) coined the term **white-collar crime** to refer to crimes that people of respectable and high social status commit in the course of their occupations.

A special form of white-collar crime is **corporate crime,** crimes committed by executives in order to benefit their corporation. For example, to increase corporate profits, Sears executives

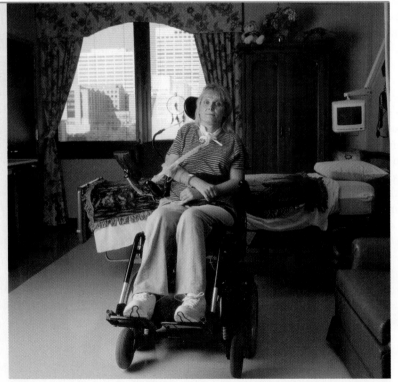

White collar crime usually involves only the loss of property, but not always. To save money, Ford executives kept faulty Firestone tires on their Explorers. The cost? The lives of over 200 people. Shown here in Houston is one of their victims. She survived a needless accident, but was left a quadraplegic. Not one Ford executive spent even a single day in jail.

Down-to-Earth Sociology
Islands in the Street: Urban Gangs in the United States

For more than ten years, sociologist Martín Sánchez-Jankowski (1991) did participant observation of thirty-seven African American, Chicano, Dominican, Irish, Jamaican, and Puerto Rican gangs in Boston, Los Angeles, and New York City. The gangs earned money through gambling, arson, mugging, armed robbery, and selling moonshine, drugs, guns, stolen car parts, and protection. Sánchez-Jankowski ate, slept, and fought with the gangs, but by mutual agreement he did not participate in drug dealing or other illegal activities. He was seriously injured twice during the study.

Contrary to stereotypes, Sánchez-Jankowski did not find that the motive for joining was to escape a broken home (there were as many members from intact families as from broken homes) or to seek a substitute family (the same number of boys said they were close to their families as those who said they were not). Rather, the boys joined to gain access to money, to have recreation (including girls and drugs), to maintain anonymity in committing crimes, to get protection, and to help the community. This last reason may seem surprising, but in some neighborhoods, gangs protect residents from outsiders and spearhead political change (Kontos et al. 2003). The boys also saw the gang as an alternative to the dead-end—and deadening—jobs held by their parents.

Neighborhood residents are ambivalent about gangs. On the one hand, they fear the violence. On the other hand, many of the adults once belonged to gangs, some gangs provide better protection than the police, and gang members are the children of people who live in the neighborhood.

Particular gangs will come and go, but gangs will likely always remain part of the city. As functionalists point out, gangs fulfill needs of poor youth who live on the margins of society.

For Your Consideration
What functions do gangs fulfill (what needs do they meet)? Suppose that you have been hired as an urban planner for the city of Los Angeles. How could you arrange to meet the needs that gangs fulfill in ways that minimize violence and encourage youth to follow mainstream norms?

---

defrauded $100 million from victims so poor that they had filed for bankruptcy. To avoid a criminal trial, Sears pleaded guilty. This frightened the parent companies of Macy's and Bloomingdales, which were doing similar things, and they settled out of court (McCormick 1999). Citigroup is notorious for stealing from the poor. In 2004, this firm had to pay $70 million for its crimes (O'Brien 2004). But, like a career criminal, it continued its law-breaking ways. The firm "swept" money from its customers' credit cards, even from the cards of people who had died. Caught red-handed once again—even stealing from the dead—in 2008 this company was forced to pay another $18 million (Read 2008). *Not one of the corporate thieves at Sears, Macy's, Bloomingdales, or Citigroup spent a day in jail.*

Seldom is corporate crime taken seriously, even when it results in death. One of the most notorious corporate crimes was committed by Firestone executives. They decided to recall faulty tires in Saudi Arabia and Venezuela and to allow them to remain on U.S. vehicles. This decision cost the lives of about 200 Americans (White et al. 2001). The photo on the previous page shows another human cost. Yet not a single Firestone executive went to jail.

Consider this: Under federal law, causing the death of a worker by *willfully* violating safety rules is a misdemeanor punishable by up to six months in prison. Yet to harass a wild burro on federal lands is punishable by a year in prison (Barstow and Bergman 2003).

At $400 billion a year (Reiman 2004), "crime in the suites" actually costs more than "crime in the streets." This refers only to dollar costs. No one has yet figured out a way to compare, for example, the suffering experienced by a rape victim with the pain felt by an elderly couple who have lost their life savings to white-collar fraud.

Fear, however, centers on street crime, especially the violent stranger who will change your life forever. As the Social Map on the next page shows, the chances of such an

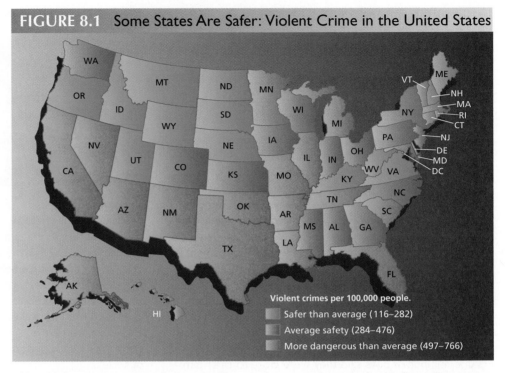

FIGURE 8.1   Some States Are Safer: Violent Crime in the United States

Violent crimes per 100,000 people.

Safer than average (116–282)

Average safety (284–476)

More dangerous than average (497–766)

Note: Violent crimes are murder, rape, robbery, and aggravated assault. As this figure illustrates, violent crime varies widely among the states. The chance of becoming a victim of these crimes is ten times higher in South Carolina, the most dangerous state, than in Maine, the safest state. Washington, D.C., not a state, is in a class by itself. Its rate of 1,508 is *thirteen* times higher than Maine's rate.

Source: By the author. Based on *Statistical Abstract of the United States* 2009:Table 297.

encounter depend on where you live. You can see that entire regions are safer—or more dangerous than—others. In general, the northern states are safer, and the southern states more dangerous.

Gender and Crime.   Gender is not just something we are or do. It is a feature of society that surrounds us from birth. As it pushes us, as male or female, into different corners in life, gender offers and nurtures some behaviors while it withdraws and dries up others. The opportunity to commit crime is one of the many consequences of how society sets up a gender order. The social changes that opened business and the professions to women also brought new opportunities for women to commit crime. Table 8.2 shows some of those changes, the increase in crime by women—from car theft to possessing illegal weapons.

In Sum: Functionalists stress that just as the social classes differ in opportunities for income and education, so they differ in opportunities for crime. As a result, street crime is higher among the lower social classes and white-collar crime higher among the higher social classes. The growing crime rates of women illustrate how changing gender roles have given women more access to what sociologists call "illegitimate opportunities."

TABLE 8.2   Women and Crime: What a Difference a Few Years Make

Of all those arrested, what percentage are women?

Crime	1992	2006	Change
Car theft	10.8%	17.8%	+65%
Burglary	9.2%	14.4%	+57%
Stolen property	12.5%	18.8%	+50%
Aggravated assault	14.8%	20.7%	+40%
Drunken driving	13.8%	20.0%	+45%
Robbery	8.5%	11.2%	+32%
Arson	13.4%	16.7%	+25%
Larceny/theft	32.1%	37.7%	+17%
Illegal drugs	16.4%	18.9%	+15%
Forgery and counterfeiting	34.7%	39.1%	+13%
Fraud	42.1%	44.5%	+6%
Illegal Weapons	7.5%	8.0%	+7%

Source: By the author. Based on *Statistical Abstract of the United States* 2009:Table 312.

The Conflict Perspective

criminal justice system the system of police, courts, and prisons set up to deal with people who are accused of having committed a crime

Class, Crime, and the Criminal Justice System

> Sioux Manufacturing in North Dakota made helmets for the U.S. ground troops in Iraq and Afghanistan. Two former managers reported that the company had set their looms to use less Kevlar—a fabric that deflects some shrapnel and bullets—than they were supposed to. The charge was serious, for doing this would endanger U.S. soldiers, perhaps causing some to die.
>
> But would anyone actually do such a thing? Government officials investigated, and found that the accusation was true. Employees had even doctored records to show that the company had used the correct amount of Kevlar. (Lambert 2008)

What was the punishment for a crime this serious? When the executives of Sioux Manufacturing were put on trial, for how long were they sentenced to prison? Actually, those who ordered this crime weren't even put on trial, and no one spent even a night in jail. The company just paid a fine—and then the government gave them another contract to make more helmets. Of course, they had to reset their looms.

Contrast this with poor people who are caught stealing cars and sent to prison for years. How can a legal system that proudly boasts "justice for all" be so inconsistent? According to conflict theory, this question is central to the analysis of crime and the **criminal justice system**—the police, courts, and prisons that deal with people who are accused of having committed crimes. Let's see what conflict theorists have to say about this.

The Law as an Instrument of Oppression

Conflict theorists regard power and social inequality as the main characteristics of society. They stress that the power elite uses the criminal justice system to protect its position of power and privilege. The idea that the law operates impartially to bring justice, they say, is a cultural myth promoted by the capitalist class. They point out that the law is really an instrument of oppression, a tool designed by the powerful to maintain their privileged position (Chambliss 2000, 1973/2007; Spitzer 1975; Reiman 2004).

With their large numbers, the working class and those below them pose a special threat to the power elite. Receiving the least of society's material rewards, they hold the

In early capitalism, children were employed alongside adults. At that time, just as today, most street criminals came from the *marginal working class*, as did the boys shown in this 1891 photo taken at a coal mine in Shenandoah, Pennsylvania.

"If you want justice, it's two hundred dollars an hour. Obstruction of justice runs a bit more."

The cartoonist's hyperbole makes an excellent commentary on the social class disparity of our criminal justice system. Not only are the crimes of the wealthy not as likely to come to the attention of authorities as are the crimes of the poor, but when they do, the wealthy can afford legal expertise that the poor cannot.

potential to rebel and overthrow the current social order (see Figure 10.5 on page 271). To prevent this, the law comes down hard on its members who get out of line. The working poor and the underclass are a special problem. They are the least rooted in society. They have few skills and only low-paying, part-time, or seasonal work—if they have jobs at all. Because their street crimes threaten the social order that keeps the elite in power, they are punished severely. From this class come *most* of the prison inmates in the United States.

The criminal justice system, then, does not focus on the executives of corporations and the harm they do through manufacturing unsafe products, creating pollution, and manipulating prices. Yet the violations of the capitalist class cannot be ignored totally, for if they become too outrageous or oppressive they might outrage the working class, encouraging them to rise up and revolt. To prevent this, a flagrant violation by a member of the capitalist class is occasionally prosecuted. The publicity given to the case helps to stabilize the social system by providing evidence of the "fairness" of the criminal justice system.

The powerful, however, are usually able to bypass the courts altogether, appearing instead before an agency that has no power to imprison (such as the Federal Trade Commission). These agencies are directed by people from wealthy backgrounds who sympathize with the intricacies of the corporate world. It is they who oversee most cases of manipulating the price of stocks, insider trading, violating fiduciary duty, and so on. Is it surprising, then, that the typical sanction for corporate crime is a token fine?

What do you think would happen if groups that have been denied access to power gain that access? You might surmise that one of the things they would change would be the legal system. This is precisely what is occurring now. Racial–ethnic minorities and homosexuals, for example, have more political power today than ever before in our history. In line with conflict theory, a new category called *hate crime* has been formulated. We analyze this change in a different context on pages 221–222.

In Sum: Conflict theorists stress that the power elite uses the legal system to control workers and to stabilize the social order, all with the goal of keeping itself in power. The poor pose a threat, for if they rebel as a group they can dislodge members of the power elite from their place of privilege. To prevent this, the power elite makes certain that heavy penalties come down on those whose crimes could upset the social order.

Reactions to Deviance

Whether it involves cheating on a sociology quiz or holding up a liquor store, any violation of norms invites reaction. Before we examine reactions in the United States, let's take a little side trip to Greenland, an island nation three times the size of Texas located between Canada and Denmark. I think you'll enjoy this little excursion in the Cultural Diversity box on page 217.

Street Crime and Prisons

Let's turn back to the United States. Figure 8.2 on page 216 shows the increase in the U.S. prison population. To get an idea of how huge this increase is, consider this: Not able to build prisons fast enough to hold all of their incoming prisoners, the states and federal government have hired private companies to operate additional prisons for them. About 120,000 prisoners are held in these "for-profit" prisons (Sabol and Couture 2008). Actually, the United States has even more prisoners than shown in Figure 8.2, since this total does not include jail inmates. If we add them, the total comes to 2.3 million people—about one out of every 140 citizens.

Not only does the United States have more prisoners than any other nation in the world, but it also has a larger percentage of its population in prison as well (Warren et al. 2008).

Who are these prisoners? Let's compare them with the U.S. population. As you look at Table 8.3, several things may strike you. Most prisoners (62 percent) are younger than 35, and almost all prisoners are men. Then there is this remarkable statistic: Although African Americans make up just 12.8 percent of the U.S. population, close to *half* of all prisoners are African Americans. On any given day, *one out of every nine* African American men ages 20 to 34 is in jail or prison. (For Latinos, the rate is one of twenty-six; for whites one of one hundred) (Warren et al. 2008.)

Finally, note how marriage and education—two of the major techniques society has of "anchoring" us—provide protection from prison. *Most* prisoners have never married. And look at the power of education, a major component of social class. As I mentioned earlier, social class funnels some people into the criminal justice system and diverts others away from it. You can see how people who drop out of high school have a high chance of ending up in prison—and how unlikely it is for a college graduate to have this unwelcome destination in life.

For about the past twenty years or so, the United States has followed a "get tough" policy. One of the most significant changes was the "three-strikes-and-you're-out" laws. When someone is convicted of a third felony, judges are required to give a mandatory sentence, sometimes life imprisonment. While few of us would feel sympathy if a man convicted of a third brutal rape or a third murder were sent to prison for life, these laws have had unanticipated consequences, as you will see in the following Thinking Critically section.

TABLE 8.3 Inmates in U.S. State Prisons		
Characteristics	Percentage of Prisoners with These Characteristics	Percentage of U.S. Population with These Characteristics
Age		
18–24	26.4%	9.9%
25–34	35.4%	13.5%
35–44	25.2%	14.8%
45–54	10.4%	14.3%
55 and older	1.0%	22.7%
Race–Ethnicity		
African American	47.3%	12.8%
White	36.9%	66.9%
Latino	14.2%	14.4%
Asian Americans	0.6%	4.3%
Native Americans	0.9%	1.0%
Sex		
Male	93.4%	49.3%
Female	6.3%	50.7%
Marital Status		
Never married	59.8%	28.2%
Divorced	15.5%	10.2%
Married	17.3%	58.6%
Widowed	1.1%	6.4%
Education		
Less than high school	39.7%	14.8%
High school graduate	49.0%	32.2%
Some college	9.0%	25.4%
College graduate	2.4%	27.6%

Source: By the author. Based on *Sourcebook of Criminal Justice Statistics* 2003:Tables 6.000b, 6.28; 2006:Tables 6.34, 6.45; *Statistical Abstract of the United States* 2009:Tables 8, 10, 18, 56, 223.

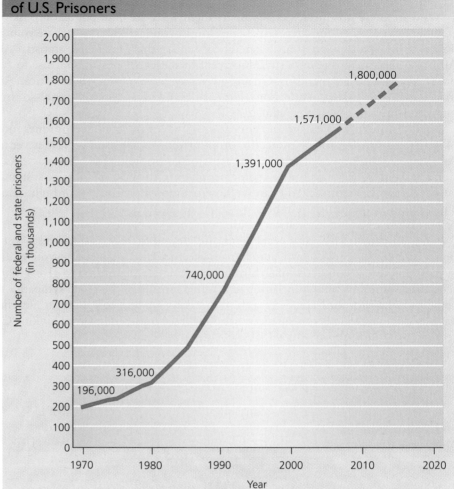

FIGURE 8.2   How Much Is Enough? The Explosion in the Number of U.S. Prisoners

Between 1970 and 2007, the U.S. population increased **48** percent, while the number of prisoners increased **816** percent, a rate that is *17 times greater* than population growth. If the number of prisoners had grown at the same rate as the U.S. population, we would have about 286,000 prisoners, only one-eighth of today's total. Or if the U.S. population had increased at the same rate as that of U.S. prisoners, the U.S. population would be 1,673,000,000—approximately the population of China and all of Europe combined.

Sources: By the author. Based on *Statistical Abstract of the United States* 1995: Table 349; 2009: Table 333. The broken line is the author's estimate.

ThinkingCRITICALLY

"Three Strikes and You're Out!" Unintended Consequences of Well-Intended Laws

As the violent crime rate soared in the 1980s, Americans grew fearful. They demanded that their lawmakers do something. Politicians heard the message, and they responded by passing the "three-strikes" law. Anyone who is convicted of a third felony receives an automatic mandatory sentence. Judges are not allowed to consider the circumstances. Some mandatory sentences carry life imprisonment.

In their haste to appease the public, the politicians did not limit the three-strike laws to *violent* crimes. And they did not consider that some minor crimes are considered felonies. As the functionalists would say, this has led to unanticipated consequences.

Cultural Diversity around the World

"What Kind of Prison Is This?"

The prison in Nuuk, the capital of Greenland, has no wall around it. It has no fence. It doesn't even have bars.

Meeraq Lendenhann, a convicted rapist, walked out of prison. He didn't run or hide. He just walked out. Meeraq wasn't escaping. He went to a store he likes to shop at, bought a CD of his favorite group, U2, and then walked back to the prison.

If Meeraq tires of listening to music, he can send e-mail and play games on a computer. Like the other prisoners, he also has a personal TV with satellite hookup.

One woman prisoner who said she was going to a beauty salon got sidetracked and went to a bar instead. When it got late and she was quite drunk, she called the prison and asked someone to come and get her.

The prison holds 60 prisoners—the country's killers, rapists, and a few thieves. The prisoners leave the prison to work at regular jobs, where they average $28,000 or so a year. But they have to return to the prison after work. And they are locked into their rooms at 9:30 P.M.

The prisoners have to work, because the prison charges them $150 a week for room and board. The extra money goes into their savings accounts or to help support their families.

If someone from another culture asks about the prisoners running away, the head of the prison says, "Where would they run? It's warm inside, and cold outside."

And if they ran away they would miss breakfast—a buffet of five kinds of imported cheese, various breads, marmalade, honey, coffee, and tea.

And they would miss out on their free guns. A major summer sport for Greenlanders is hunting reindeer and seals. Prisoners don't want to miss out on the fun, so if they ask, they are given shotguns.

But gun use isn't as easy as it sounds. Judges have set a severe requirement: The prisoners have to be accompanied

This photo was taken inside a "cell" at Nuuk—private room, personal TV with satellite connection, VCR, adjustable reading lamp, radio-CD player, and window to the outside. The inmate's coffee maker is on the other side of the room.

by armed guards. If that isn't bad enough, the judges have added another requirement—that the prisoners not get drunk while they hunt.

For Your Consideration

Greenland's unique approach to prisons arose out of its history of hunting and fishing for a living. If men are locked up, they won't be able to hunt or fish, and their families will suffer. The main goal of Greenland's prison is to integrate offenders into society, and their treatment in prison helps them ease back into village life after they have served their sentence. The incorrigibles, those who remain dangerous—about 20 men—are sent to a prison in Copenhagen, Denmark. Meeraq, the rapist, is given injections of Androcur, a testosterone-reducing drug that lowers his sex drive. Alcoholics are given Antabuse, a drug that triggers nasty reactions if someone drinks alcohol.

How do you think we could apply Greenland's approach to the United States?

—Based on Naik 2004.

Here are some actual cases:

- In Los Angeles, a 27-year-old man who stole a pizza was sentenced to 25 years in prison (Cloud 1998).
- In Sacramento, a man passed himself off as Tiger Woods and went on a $17,000 shopping spree. He was sentenced to 200 years in prison (Reuters 2001).
- In California, Michael James passed a bad check for $94. He was sentenced to 25 years to life (Jones 2008).
- In Utah, a 25-year-old sold small bags of marijuana to a police informant. The judge who sentenced the man to 55 years in prison said the sentence was unjust, but he had no choice (Madigan 2004).

• In New York City, a man who was about to be sentenced for selling crack said to the judge, "I'm only 19. This is terrible." He then hurled himself out of a courtroom window, plunging to his death sixteen stories below (Cloud 1998).

For Your Consideration

Apply the symbolic interactionist, functionalist, and conflict perspectives to the three-strikes laws. For *symbolic interactionism,* what do these laws represent to the public? How does your answer differ depending on what part of "the public" you are referring to? For *functionalism,* who benefits from these laws? What are some of their functions? Their dysfunctions? For the *conflict perspective,* what groups are in conflict? Who has the power to enforce their will on others?

The Decline in Violent Crime

As you have seen, judges have put more and more people in prison, and legislators have passed the three-strikes laws. As these changes occurred, the crime rate dropped sharply, which has led to a controversy in sociology. Some sociologists conclude that getting tough on criminals is the main reason that violent crime dropped (Conklin 2003). Others point to higher employment, a drop in drug use, and even abortion (Rosenfeld 2002; Reiman 2004; Blumstein and Wallman 2006). This matter is not yet settled, but both tough sentencing and the economy seem to be important factors.

recidivism rate the proportion of released convicts who are rearrested

capital punishment the death penalty

Recidivism

If a goal of prisons is to teach their clients to stay away from crime, they are colossal failures. We can measure their failure by the **recidivism rate**—the percentage of former prisoners who are rearrested. For people sent to prison for crimes of violence, within just three years of their release, two out of three (62 percent) are rearrested, and half (52 percent) are back in prison (*Sourcebook of Criminal Justice Statistics* 2003:Table 6.52). Looking at Figure 8.3, which gives a breakdown of three-year recidivism by type of crime, it is safe to conclude that prisons do not teach people that crime doesn't pay.

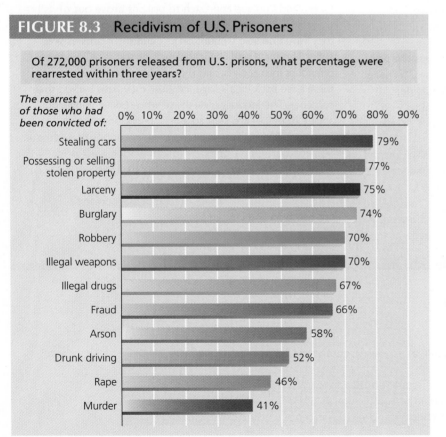

FIGURE 8.3   Recidivism of U.S. Prisoners

Of 272,000 prisoners released from U.S. prisons, what percentage were rearrested within three years?

The rearrest rates of those who had been convicted of:

Stealing cars	79%
Possessing or selling stolen property	77%
Larceny	75%
Burglary	74%
Robbery	70%
Illegal weapons	70%
Illegal drugs	67%
Fraud	66%
Arson	58%
Drunk driving	52%
Rape	46%
Murder	41%

Note: The individuals were not necessarily rearrested for the same crime for which they had originally been imprisoned.

Source: By the author. Based on *Sourcebook of Criminal Justice Statistics* 2003:Table 6.50.

The Death Penalty and Bias

As you know, **capital punishment,** the death penalty, is the most extreme measure the state takes. As you also know, the death penalty arouses impassioned opposition and support. Advances in DNA testing have given opponents of the death penalty a strong argument: Innocent people have been sent to death row, and some have been executed. Others are just as passionate about retaining the death penalty. They point to such crimes as those of the serial killers discussed in the Down-to-Earth Sociology box on page 220.

Apart from anyone's personal position on the death penalty, it certainly is clear that the death penalty is not administered evenly. Consider geography: The

Beneath the humor of this cartoon lies a serious point about the high *recidivism rate* of U.S. prisoners.

Social Map below shows that where people commit murder greatly affects their chances of being put to death.

The death penalty also shows social class bias. As you know from news reports, it is rare for a rich person to be sentenced to death. Although the government does not collect statistics on social class and the death penalty, this common observation is borne out by the education of the prisoners on death row. *Half* of the prisoners on death row (51 percent) have not finished high school (*Sourcebook of Criminal Justice Statistics* 2007:Table 6.81).

There is also a gender bias in the death penalty. It is so strong that it is almost unheard of for a woman to be sentenced to death, much less executed. Although women commit 9.6 percent of the murders, they make up only 1.7 percent of death row inmates (*Sourcebook of Criminal Justice Statistics* 2007:Tables 6.82, 6.83). Even on death row, the gender bias continues, for the state is more likely to execute a man than a woman. As Figure 8.5 shows, less than 1 percent of the 4,958 executions in the United States since 1930 have been of women. This gender bias could reflect the women's previous offenses and the relative brutality of their murders, but we need research to determine if this is so.

Bias was once so flagrant that it put a stop to the death penalty. Donald Partington (1965), a lawyer in Virginia, was shocked by the bias he saw in the courtroom, and he

FIGURE 8.4   Executions in the United States

Executions since 1977, when the death penalty was reinstated.

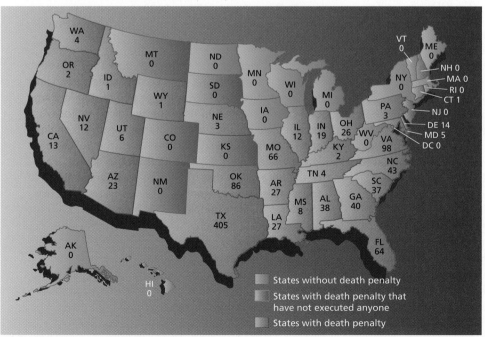

Source: By the author. Based on *Statistical Abstract of the United States* 2009:Table 340. I added the 2005 execution in Connecticut, missed by the source.

FIGURE 8.5   Who Gets Executed? Gender Bias in Capital Punishment

99.1%

0.9%

Men   Women

Source: By the author. Based on *Statistical Abstract of the United States* 2009:Table 339.

Down-to-Earth Sociology
The Killer Next Door: Serial Murderers in Our Midst

Here is my experience with serial killers. As I was watching television one night, I was stunned by the images. Television cameras showed the Houston police digging up dozens of bodies from under a boat storage shed. Fascinated, I waited impatiently for spring break. A few days later, I drove from Illinois to Houston, where 33-year-old Dean Corll had befriended Elmer Wayne Henley and David Brooks, two teenagers from broken homes. Together, they had killed twenty-seven boys. Elmer and David would pick up young hitchhikers and deliver them to Corll to rape and kill. Sometimes they even brought him their own high school classmates.

I talked to one of Elmer's neighbors, as he was painting his front porch. His 15-year-old son had gone to get a haircut one Saturday morning. That was the last time he saw his son alive. The police refused to investigate. They insisted that his son had run away. On a city map, I plotted the locations of the homes of the local murder victims. Many clustered around the homes of the teenage killers.

I decided to spend my coming sabbatical writing a novel on this case. To get into the minds of the killers, I knew that I would have to "become" them day after day for months. Corll kept a piece of plywood in his apartment. In each of its corners, he had cut a hole. He and the boys would spread-eagle their handcuffed victims on this board, torturing them for hours. Sometimes, they would even pause to order pizza. As such details emerged, I became uncertain that I could recover psychologically from such an immersion into torture and human degradation, and I decided not to write the book.

My interviews in Houston confirmed what has since become common knowledge about serial killers: They lead double lives so successfully that their friends and family are unaware of their criminal activities. Henley's mother swore to me that her son couldn't possibly be guilty—he was a good boy. Some of Elmer's high school friends told me that that his being involved in homosexual rape and murder was ridiculous—he was interested only in girls. I was interviewing them in Henley's bedroom, and for proof they pointed to a pair of girls' panties that were draped across a lamp shade.

Serial murder is the killing of victims in three or more separate events. The murders may occur over several days, weeks, or years. The elapsed time between murders distinguishes serial killers from *mass murderers*, those who do their killing all at once. Here are some infamous examples:

One of the striking traits of most serial killers is how they blend in with the rest of society. Ted Bundy, shown here, was remarkable in this respect. Almost everyone who knew this law student liked him. Even the Florida judge who found him guilty said that he would have liked to have him practice law in his court, but, as he added, "You went the wrong way, partner." (Note the term partner—used even after Bundy was convicted of heinous crimes.)

- During the 1960s and 1970s, Ted Bundy raped and killed dozens of women in four states.
- Between 1979 and 1981, Wayne Williams killed 28 boys and young men in Atlanta.
- Between 1974 and 1991, Dennis Rader killed 10 people in Wichita, Kansas. Rader had written to the newspapers, proudly calling himself the BTK (Bind, Torture, and Kill) strangler.
- In the late 1980s and early 1990s, Aileen Wuornos hitchhiked along Florida's freeways. She killed 7 men after having had sex with them.
- The serial killer with the most victims appears to be Harold Shipman, a physician in Manchester, England. From 1977 to 2000, during house calls Shipman gave lethal injections to 230 to 275 of his elderly female patients.

Is serial murder more common now than it used to be? Not likely. In the past, police departments had little communication with one another, and seldom did anyone connect killings in different jurisdictions. Today's more efficient communications, investigative techniques, and DNA matching make it easier for the police to know when a serial killer is operating in an area. Part of the perception that there are more serial killers today is also due to ignorance of our history: In our frontier past, for example, serial killers went from ranch to ranch.

For Your Consideration
Do you think that serial killers should be given the death penalty? Why or why not? How do your social locations influence your opinion?

decided to document it. He found that 2,798 men had been convicted for rape and attempted rape in Virginia between 1908 and 1963—56 percent whites and 44 percent blacks. For attempted rape, 13 had been executed. For rape, 41 men had been executed. *All those executed were black.* Not one of the whites was executed.

After listening to evidence like this, in 1972 the Supreme Court ruled in *Furman v. Georgia* that the death penalty, as applied, was unconstitutional. The execution of prisoners stopped—but not for long. The states wrote new laws, and in 1977 they again began to execute prisoners. Since then, 65 percent of those put to death have been white and 35 percent African American (*Statistical Abstract* 2009:Table 339). (Latinos are evidently counted as whites in this statistic.) While living on death row is risky for anyone, the risk is higher for African Americans and Latinos who killed whites. They are more likely to be executed (Jacobs et al. 2007). The most accurate predictor of who will be put to death, though, is somewhat surprising: Those who have the least education are the most likely to be executed (Karamouzis and Harper 2007). Table 8.4 shows the race–ethnicity of the prisoners who are on death row.

TABLE 8.4	The Race–Ethnicity of the 3,316 Prisoners on Death Row	
	Percentage	
	on Death Row	in U.S. Population
Whites	45%	67%
African Americans	42%	13%
Latinos	11%	14%
Asian Americans	1%	4%
Native Americans	1%	1%

Source: By the author. Based on *Sourcebook of Criminal Justice Statistics* 2008:Table 6.80 and Figure 12.5 of this text.

Legal Change

Did you know that it is a crime in Saudi Arabia for a woman to drive a car (Fattah 2007)? A crime in Florida to sell alcohol before 1 P.M. on Sundays? Or illegal in Wells, Maine, to advertise on tombstones? As has been stressed in this chapter, deviance, including the form called *crime,* is so relative that it varies from one society to another, and from one group to another within the same society. Crime also varies from one time period to another, as opinions change or as different groups gain access to power. We discuss one of these changes in the following Thinking Critically section.

ThinkingCRITICALLY
Changing Views: Making Hate a Crime

Because crime consists of whatever acts authorities decide to assign that label, new crimes emerge from time to time. A prime example is juvenile delinquency, which Illinois lawmakers designated a separate type of crime in 1899. Juveniles committed crimes before 1899, of course, but youths were not considered to be a separate type of lawbreaker. They were just young people who committed crimes, and they were treated the same as adults who committed the same crime. Sometimes new technology leads to new crimes. Motor vehicle theft, a separate crime in the United States, obviously did not exist before the automobile was invented.

Hate crimes *range from murder and injury to defacing property with symbols of hatred. This photo was taken in Detroit, Michigan.*

In the 1980s, another new crime was born when state governments developed the classification **hate crime,** crimes motivated by *bias* (dislike, hatred) against someone's race–ethnicity, religion, sexual orientation, disability, or national origin. Before this, people attacked others or destroyed their property out of these same motivations, but then the motivation was not the issue. If someone injured or killed another person because of that person's race–ethnicity, religion, sexual orientation, national origin, or disability, he or she was charged with assault or murder. Today, motivation has become a central issue, and hate crimes carry more severe sentences than do the same acts that do not have hatred as their motive. Table 8.5 on the next page summarizes the victims of hate crimes.

We can be certain that the "evolution" of crime is not yet complete. As society changes and as different groups gain access to power, we can expect the definitions of crime to change accordingly.

For Your Consideration

Why should we have a separate classification called hate crime? Why aren't the crimes of assault, robbery, and murder adequate? As one analyst (Sullivan 1999) said, "Was the brutal murder of gay college student Matthew Shepard in Laramie, Wyoming, in 1998 (a hate crime) worse than the abduction, rape, and murder of an eight-year-old Laramie girl by a pedophile (not a hate crime) that same year?"

How do you think your social location (race–ethnicity, gender, social class, sexual orientation, or physical ability) affects your opinion?

The Trouble with Official Statistics

Both the findings of symbolic interactionists (that stereotypes operate when authorities deal with groups such as the Saints and the Roughnecks) and the conclusion of conflict theorists (that the criminal justice system serves the ruling elite) demonstrate the need

serial murder the killing of several victims in three or more separate events

hate crime a crime that is punished more severely because it is motivated by hatred (dislike, hostility, animosity) of someone's race–ethnicity, religion, sexual orientation, disability, or national origin

police discretion the practice of the police, in the normal course of their duties, to either arrest or ticket someone for an offense or to overlook the matter

medicalization of deviance to make deviance a medical matter, a symptom of some underlying illness that needs to be treated by physicians

for caution in interpreting official statistics. Crime statistics do not have an objective, independent existence. They are not like oranges that you pick out in a grocery store. Rather, crime statistics are a human creation. One major element in producing them is the particular laws that exist. Another is how those laws are enforced. Still another is how officials report their statistics. Change these factors, and the statistics also change.

Consider this: According to official statistics, working-class boys are more delinquent than middle-class boys. Yet, as we have seen, who actually gets arrested for what is influenced by social class, a point that has far-reaching implications. As symbolic interactionists point out, the police follow a symbolic system as they enforce the law. Ideas of "typical criminals" and "typical good citizens," for example, permeate their work. The more a suspect matches their stereotypes of a lawbreaker (which they call "criminal profiles"), the more likely that person is to be arrested. **Police discretion,** the decision whether to arrest someone or even to ignore a matter, is a routine part of police work. Consequently, official crime statistics reflect these and many other biases.

In Sum: Reactions to deviants vary from such mild sanctions as frowns and stares to such severe responses as imprisonment and death. Some sanctions are formal—court hearings, for example—but most are informal, as when friends refuse to talk to each other. One sanction is to label someone a deviant, which can have powerful consequences for the person's life, especially if the label closes off conforming activities and opens deviant ones. The degradation ceremony, in which someone is publicly labeled "not one of us," is a powerful sanction. So is imprisonment. Official statistics must be viewed with caution, for they reflect biases.

TABLE 8.5	Hate Crimes
Directed Against	**Number of Victims**
Race–Ethnicity	
African Americans	3,332
Whites	1,054
Latinos	819
Multiracial	320
Asian Americans	239
Native Americans	75
Religion	
Jews	1,144
Muslims	208
Catholics	86
Protestants	65
Sexual Orientation	
Homosexual	1,422
Male Homosexual	913
Female Homosexual	202
General	387
Heterosexual	29
Bisexual	21
Disabilities	
Mental	74
Physical	21

Note: A victim can be an individual, a business, or an institution. Number is the cumulative victims from year 2000.

Source: By the author. Based on *Statistical Abstract of the United States* 2009:Table 310.

The Medicalization of Deviance: Mental Illness

Another way in which society deals with deviance is to "medicalize" it. Let's look at what this entails.

Neither Mental Nor Illness? To *medicalize* something is to make it a medical matter, to classify it as a form of illness that properly belongs in the care of physicians. For the past hundred years or so, especially since the time of Sigmund Freud (1856–1939), the Viennese physician who founded psychoanalysis, there has been a growing tendency toward the **medicalization of deviance.** In this view, deviance, including crime, is a sign of mental sickness. Rape, murder, stealing, cheating, and so on are external symptoms of internal disorders, consequences of a confused or tortured mind.

Thomas Szasz (1986, 1996, 1998), a renegade in his profession of psychiatry, argues that *mental illnesses are neither mental nor illnesses. They are simply problem behaviors.* Some behaviors that are called mental illnesses have organic causes; that is, they are *physical* illnesses that result in unusual perceptions or behavior. Some depression, for example, is caused by a chemical imbalance in the brain, which can be treated by drugs. The depression, however, may appear as crying, long-term sadness, and lack of interest in family, work, school, or one's appearance. When people are disturbed by someone's deviance *and* when they cannot find a satisfying explanation for

People whose behaviors violate norms often are called mentally ill. "Why else would they do such things?" is a common response to deviant behaviors that we don't understand. Mental illness is a label that contains the assumption that there is something wrong "within" people that "causes" their disapproved behavior. The surprise with this man, who changed his legal name to "Scary Guy," is that he speaks at schools across the country, where he promotes acceptance, awareness, love, and understanding.

why the person is "like that," they often say that a "sickness in the head" is causing the unacceptable behavior.

Attention-deficit disorder (ADD) is an excellent example. As Szasz says, "No one explains where this disease came from, why it didn't exist 50 years ago. No one is able to diagnose it with objective tests." It is diagnosed by a teacher or a parent complaining about a child misbehaving. Misbehaving children have been a problem throughout history, but now their problem behavior has become a sign of mental illness.

All of us have troubles. Some of us face a constant barrage of problems as we go through life. Most of us continue the struggle, perhaps encouraged by relatives and friends and motivated by job, family responsibilities, religious faith, and life goals. Even when the odds seem hopeless, we carry on, not perfectly, but as best we can.

Some people, however, fail to cope well with life's challenges. Overwhelmed, they become depressed, uncooperative, or hostile. Some strike out at others; and some, in Merton's terms, become retreatists and withdraw into their apartments or homes, refusing to come out. These are *behaviors, not mental illnesses,* stresses Szasz. They may be inappropriate ways of coping, but they are behaviors, not mental illnesses. Szasz concludes that "mental illness" is a myth foisted on a naive public. Our medical profession uses pseudoscientific jargon that people don't understand so it can expand its area of control and force nonconforming people to accept society's definitions of "normal."

Szasz's controversial claim forces us to look anew at the forms of deviance that we usually refer to as mental illness. To explain behavior that people find bizarre, he directs our attention not to causes hidden deep within the "subconscious," but, instead, to how people learn such behaviors. To ask, "What is the origin of someone's inappropriate or bizarre behavior?" then becomes similar to asking "Why do some women steal?" "Why do some men rape?" "Why do some teenagers cuss their parents and stalk out of the room, slamming the door?" *The answers depend on those people's particular experiences in life, not on an illness in their mind.* In short, some sociologists find Szasz's renegade analysis refreshing because it indicates that *social experiences,* not some illness of the mind, underlie bizarre behaviors—as well as deviance in general.

Mental illness is common among the homeless. This woman is sleeping in a doorway in New York City.

The Homeless Mentally Ill

Jamie was sitting on a low wall surrounding the landscaped courtyard of an exclusive restaurant. She appeared unaware of the stares elicited by her layers of mismatched clothing, her matted hair and dirty face, and the shopping cart that overflowed with her meager possessions.

After sitting next to Jamie for a few minutes, I saw her point to the street and concentrate, slowly moving her finger horizontally. I asked her what she was doing.

"I'm directing traffic," she replied. "I control where the cars go. Look, that one turned right there," she said, now withdrawing her finger.

"Really?" I said.

After a while she confided that her cart talked to her.

"Really?" I said again.

"Yes," she replied. "You can hear it, too." At that, she pushed the shopping cart a bit.

"Did you hear that?" she asked.

When I shook my head, she demonstrated again. Then it hit me. She was referring to the squeaking wheels!

I nodded.

When I left Jamie, she was pointing to the sky, for, as she told me, she also controlled the flight of airplanes.

To most of us, Jamie's behavior and thinking are bizarre. They simply do not match any reality we know. Could you or I become like Jamie?

Suppose for a bitter moment that you are homeless and have to live on the streets. You have no money, no place to sleep, no bathroom. You do not know *if* you are going to eat, much less where. You have no friends or anyone you can trust. You live in constant fear of rape and other violence. Do you think this might be enough to drive you over the edge?

Consider just the problems involved in not having a place to bathe. (Shelters are often so dangerous that many homeless people prefer to sleep in public settings.) At first, you try to wash in the restrooms of gas stations, bars, the bus station, or a shopping center. But you are dirty, and people stare when you enter and call the management when they see you wash your feet in the sink. You are thrown out and told in no uncertain terms never to come back. So you get dirtier and dirtier. Eventually, you come to think of being dirty as a fact of life. Soon, maybe, you don't even care. The stares no longer bother you—at least not as much.

No one will talk to you, and you withdraw more and more into yourself. You begin to build a fantasy life. You talk openly to yourself. People stare, but so what? They stare anyway. Besides, they are no longer important to you.

Jamie might be mentally ill. Some organic problem, such as a chemical imbalance in her brain, might underlie her behavior. But perhaps not. How long would it take you to exhibit bizarre behaviors if you were homeless—and hopeless? The point is that *living on the streets can cause mental illness*—or whatever we want to label socially inappropriate behaviors that we find difficult to classify. *Homelessness and mental illness are reciprocal:* Just as "mental illness" can cause homelessness, so the trials of being homeless, of living on cold, hostile streets, can lead to unusual thinking and behaviors.

The Need for a More Humane Approach

As Durkheim (1895/1964:68) pointed out, deviance is inevitable—even in a group of saints.

> Imagine a society of saints, a perfect cloister of exemplary individuals. Crimes, properly so called, will there be unknown; but faults which appear invisible to the layman will create there the same scandal that the ordinary offense does in ordinary society.

With deviance inevitable, one measure of a society is how it treats its deviants. Our prisons certainly don't say much good about U.S. society. Filled with the poor, uneducated, and unskilled, they are warehouses of the unwanted. White-collar criminals continue to get by with a slap on the wrist while street criminals are punished severely. Some deviants, who fail to meet current standards of admission to either prison or mental hospital, take refuge in shelters, as well as in cardboard boxes tucked away in urban recesses. Although no one has *the* answer, it does not take much reflection to see that there are more humane approaches than these.

Because deviance is inevitable, the larger issues are to find ways to protect people from deviant behaviors that are harmful to themselves or others, to tolerate those behaviors that are not harmful, and to develop systems of fairer treatment for deviants. In the absence of fundamental changes that would bring about an equitable social system, most efforts are, unfortunately, like putting a Band-Aid on a gunshot wound. What we need is a more humane social system, one that would prevent the social inequalities that are the focus of the next four chapters.

SUMMARY *and* REVIEW

What Is Deviance?

Deviance (the violation of norms) is relative. What people consider deviant varies from one culture to another and from group to group within the same society. As symbolic interactionists stress, it is not the act, but the reactions to the act, that make something deviant. All groups develop systems of **social control** to punish **deviants**—those who violate their norms. Pp. 198–200.

How do sociological and individualistic explanations of deviance differ?

To explain why people deviate, sociobiologists and psychologists look for reasons *within* the individual, such as **genetic predispositions** or **personality disorders.** Sociologists, in contrast, look for explanations *outside* the individual, in social experiences. Pp. 200–201.

The Symbolic Interactionist Perspective

How do symbolic interactionists explain deviance?

Symbolic interactionists have developed several theories to explain deviance such as **crime** (the violation of norms that are written into law). According to **differential association** theory, people learn to deviate by associating with others. According to **control theory,** each of us is propelled toward deviance, but most of us conform because of an effective system of inner and outer controls. People who have less effective controls deviate. Pp. 201–203.

   Labeling theory focuses on how labels (names, reputations) help to funnel people into or divert them away from deviance. People who commit deviant acts often use **techniques of neutralization** to deflect social norms. Pp. 203–207.

The Functionalist Perspective

How do functionalists explain deviance?

Functionalists point out that deviance, including criminal acts, is functional for society. Functions include affirming norms and promoting social unity and social change. According to **strain theory,** societies socialize their members into desiring **cultural goals.** Many people are unable to achieve these goals in socially acceptable ways—that is, by **institutionalized means.** *Deviants,* then, are people who either give up on the goals or use disapproved means to attain them. Merton identified five types of responses to cultural goals and institutionalized means: conformity,

innovation, ritualism, retreatism, and rebellion. **Illegitimate opportunity theory** stresses that some people have easier access to illegal means of achieving goals. Pp. 207–212.

The Conflict Perspective

How do conflict theorists explain deviance?

Conflict theorists take the position that the group in power imposes its definitions of deviance on other groups. From this perspective, the law is an instrument of oppression used by the powerful to maintain their position of privilege. The ruling class uses the **criminal justice system** to punish the crimes of the poor while diverting its own criminal activities away from this punitive system. Pp. 213–214.

Reactions to Deviance

What are common reactions to deviance in the United States?

In following a "get-tough" policy, the United States has imprisoned millions of people. African Americans and Latinos make up a disproportionate percentage of U.S. prisoners. The death penalty shows biases by geography, social class, gender, and race–ethnicity. In line with conflict theory, as groups gain political power, their views are reflected in the criminal code. **Hate crime** legislation was considered in this context. Pp. 214–222.

Are official statistics on crime reliable?

The conclusions of both symbolic interactionists (that the police operate with a large measure of discretion) and conflict theorists (that a power elite controls the legal system) indicate that we must be cautious when using crime statistics. Pp. 222–223.

What is the medicalization of deviance?

The medical profession has attempted to **medicalize** many forms of **deviance,** claiming that they represent mental illnesses. Thomas Szasz disagrees, asserting that they are problem behaviors, not mental illnesses. The situation of homeless people indicates that problems in living can lead to bizarre behavior and thinking. Pp. 223–225.

What is a more humane approach?

Deviance is inevitable, so the larger issues are to find ways to protect people from deviance that harms themselves and others, to tolerate deviance that is not harmful, and to develop systems of fairer treatment for deviants. P. 225.

THINKING CRITICALLY *ABOUT* Chapter 8

1. Select some deviance with which you are personally familiar. (It does not have to be your own—it can be something that someone you know did.) Choose one of the three theoretical perspectives to explain what happened.

2. As is explained in the text, deviance can be mild. Recall some instance in which you broke a social rule in dress, etiquette, or speech. What was the reaction? Why do you think people reacted like that? What was your response to their reactions?

3. What do you think should be done about the U.S. crime problem? What sociological theories support your view?

ADDITIONAL RESOURCES

What can you find in MySocLab? mysoclab www.mysoclab.com

- Complete Ebook
- Practice Tests and Video and Audio activities
- Mapping and Data Analysis exercises

- Sociology in the News
- Classic Readings in Sociology
- Research and Writing advice

Where Can I Read More on This Topic?

Suggested readings for this chapter are listed at the back of this book.

chapter

Global Stratification

Haiti

L et's contrast three "average" families from around the world:

For Getu Mulleta, 33, and his wife, Zenebu, 28, of rural Ethiopia, life is a constant struggle to avoid starvation. They and their seven children live in a 320-square-foot manure-plastered hut with no electricity, gas, or running water. They have a radio, but the battery is dead. The family farms teff, a grain, and survives on $130 a year.

> **They live in a 320-square-foot manure-plastered hut with no electricity, gas, or running water.**

The Mulletas' poverty is not due to a lack of hard work. Getu works about eighty hours a week, while Zenebu puts in even more hours. "Housework" for Zenebu includes fetching water, cleaning animal stables, and making fuel pellets out of cow dung for the open fire over which she cooks the family's food. Like other Ethiopian women, she eats after the men.

In Ethiopia, the average male can expect to live to age 48, the average female to 50.

The Mulletas' most valuable possession is their oxen. Their wishes for the future: more animals, better seed, and a second set of clothing.

＊ ＊ ＊ ＊ ＊

In Guadalajara, Mexico, Ambrosio and Carmen Castillo Balderas and their five children, ages 2 to 10, live in a four-room house. They also have a walled courtyard, where the family spends a good deal of time. They even have a washing machine, which is hooked up to a garden hose that runs to a public water main several hundred yards away. Like most Mexicans, they do not have a telephone, nor do they own a car.

Unlike many, however, they own a refrigerator, a stereo, and a recent purchase that makes them the envy of their neighbors: a television.

Ambrosio, 29, works full-time as a wholesale distributor of produce. He also does welding on the side. The family's total annual income is $3,600. They spend 57 percent of their income on food. Carmen works about 60 hours a week taking care of their children and keeping their home spotless. The neatness of their home stands in stark contrast to the squalor of their neighborhood, whose dirt roads are covered in litter. As in many other Mexican neighborhoods, public utilities and roadwork do not keep pace with people's needs.

The average life expectancy for males in Mexico is 70. For females, it is 76.

The Castillo Balderas' most valued possessions are their refrigerator and television. Their wish for the future: a truck.

＊ ＊ ＊ ＊ ＊

229

Springfield, Illinois, is home to the Kellys—Rick, 36, Patti, 34, Julie, 10, and Michael, 7. The Kellys live in a three-bedroom, 2½-bath, 2,524-square-foot, carpeted ranch-style house, with a fireplace, central heating and air conditioning, a basement, and a two-car garage. Their home is equipped with a refrigerator, washing machine, clothes dryer, dishwasher, garbage disposal, vacuum cleaner, food processor, microwave, and convection stovetop and oven. They also own six telephones (three cellular), four color televisions (two high-definition), two CD players, two digital cameras, digital camcorder, two DVD players, iPod, Wii, a computer, and a printer-scanner-fax machine, not to mention two blow dryers, an answering machine, a juicer, and an espresso coffee maker. This count doesn't include such items as electric can openers, battery-powered toothbrushes, or the stereo-radio-CD/DVD players in their pickup truck and SUV.

Rick works forty hours a week as a cable splicer for a telephone company. Patti teaches school part-time. Together they make $58,407, plus benefits. The Kellys can choose from among dozens of superstocked supermarkets. They spend $4,883 for food they eat at home, and another $3,710 eating out, a total of 15 percent of their annual income.

In the United States, the average life expectancy is 75 for males, 80 for females.

On the Kellys' wish list are a new hybrid car with satellite radio, a 200-gigabyte laptop with Bluetooth wi-fi, a 50-inch plasma TV with surround sound, a DVD camcorder, a boat, a motor home, an ATV, and, oh, yes, farther down the road, an in-ground heated swimming pool. They also have an eye on a cabin at a nearby lake.

Sources: Menzel 1994; *Statistical Abstract* 2009:Tables 98, 666, 673, 929.

Systems of Social Stratification

Some of the world's nations are wealthy, others poor, and some in between. This division of nations, as well as the layering of groups of people within a nation, is called *social stratification*. Social stratification is one of the most significant topics we shall discuss in this book, for, as you saw in the opening vignette, it profoundly affects our life chances—from our access to material possessions to the age at which we die.

The Mulleta family of Ethiopia, described in the opening vignette.

Social stratification also affects the way we think about life. Look at the photo on the previous page. If you had been born into this family, you would expect hunger to be a part of life and would not expect all of your children to survive. You would also be illiterate and would assume that your children would be as well. In contrast, to be born into either of the other two families featured in our opening vignette would give you quite a different picture of the world. If you were one of the U.S. parents, for example, you would expect your children not only to survive, but to go to college as well. You can see that social stratification brings with it our ideas of what we can expect out of life.

Social stratification is a system in which groups of people are divided into layers according to their relative property, power, and prestige. It is important to emphasize that social stratification does not refer to individuals. It is a way of ranking large groups of people into a hierarchy according to their relative privileges.

It is also important to note that *every society stratifies its members.* Some societies have greater inequality than others, but social stratification is universal. In addition, in every society of the world, *gender* is a basis for stratifying people. On the basis of their gender, people are either allowed or denied access to the good things offered by their society.

Let's consider four major systems of social stratification: slavery, caste, estate, and class.

> **social stratification** the division of large numbers of people into layers according to their relative property, power, and prestige; applies to both nations and to people within a nation, society, or other group
>
> **slavery** a form of social stratification in which some people own other people

Slavery

Slavery, whose essential characteristic is that *some individuals own other people,* has been common throughout world history. The Old Testament even lays out rules for how owners should treat their slaves. So does the Koran. The Romans also had slaves, as did the Africans and Greeks. In classical Greece and Rome, slaves did the work, freeing citizens to engage in politics and the arts. Slavery was most widespread in agricultural societies and least common among nomads, especially hunters and gatherers (Landtman 1938/1968). As we examine the major causes and conditions of slavery, you will see how remarkably slavery has varied around the world.

Causes of Slavery.   Contrary to popular assumption, slavery was usually based not on racism but on one of three other factors. The first was *debt.* In some societies, creditors would enslave people who could not pay their debts. The second was *crime.* Instead of being killed, a murderer or thief might be enslaved by the victim's family as compensation for their loss. The third was *war.* When one group of people conquered another, they often enslaved some of the vanquished. Historian Gerda Lerner (1986) notes that women were the first people enslaved through warfare. When tribal men raided another group, they killed the men, raped the women, and then brought the women back as slaves. The women were valued for sexual purposes, for reproduction, and for their labor.

Roughly twenty-five hundred years ago, when Greece was but a collection of city-states, slavery was common. A city that became powerful and conquered another city would enslave some of the vanquished. Both slaves and slaveholders were Greek. Similarly, when Rome became the supreme power of the Mediterranean area about two thousand years ago, following the custom of the time, the Romans enslaved some of the Greeks they had conquered. More educated than their conquerors, some of these slaves served as tutors in Roman homes. Slavery, then, was a sign of debt, of crime, or of defeat in battle. It was not a sign that the slave was viewed as inherently inferior.

Conditions of Slavery.   The conditions of slavery have varied widely around the world. *In some places, slavery was temporary.* Slaves of the Israelites were set free in the year of jubilee, which occurred every fifty years. Roman slaves ordinarily had the right to buy themselves out of slavery. They knew what their purchase price was, and some were able to meet this price by striking a bargain with their

$1200 TO 1250 DOLLARS ! FOR NEGROES ! !

THE undersigned wishes to purchase a large lot of NEGROES for the New Orleans market. I will pay $1200 to $1250 for No. 1 young men, and $850 to $1000 for No. 1 young women. In fact I will pay more for likely

NEGROES,

Than any other trader in Kentucky. My office is adjoining the Broadway Hotel, on Broadway, Lexington, Ky., where I or my Agent can always be found.

WM. F. TALBOTT.
LEXINGTON, JULY 2, 1853.

Under *slavery*, humans are sold like a commodity. Wm. F. Talbott bought slaves in Kentucky for the market in New Orleans.

bonded labor (indentured service) a contractual system in which someone sells his or her body (services) for a specified period of time in an arrangement very close to slavery, except that it is entered into voluntarily

ideology beliefs about the way things ought to be that justify social arrangements

owner and selling their services to others. In most instances, however, slavery was a lifelong condition. Some criminals, for example, became slaves when they were given life sentences as oarsmen on Roman war ships. There they served until death, which often came quickly to those in this exhausting service.

Slavery was not necessarily inheritable. In most places, the children of slaves were slaves themselves. But in some instances, the child of a slave who served a rich family might even be adopted by that family, becoming an heir who bore the family name along with the other sons or daughters of the household. In ancient Mexico, the children of slaves were always free (Landtman 1938/1968:271).

Slaves were not necessarily powerless and poor. In almost all instances, slaves owned no property and had no power. Among some groups, however, slaves could accumulate property and even rise to high positions in the community. Occasionally, a slave might even become wealthy, loan money to the master, and, while still a slave, own slaves himself or herself (Landtman 1938/1968). This, however, was rare.

Slavery in the New World. A gray area between contract labor and slavery is **bonded labor,** also called **indentured service.** Many people who wanted to start a new life in the American colonies were unable to pay their passage across the ocean. Ship captains would transport them on credit, and colonists would "buy their paper" when they arrived. This arrangement provided passage for the penniless, payment for the ship's captain, and, for wealthier colonists, servants for a set number of years. During that specified period, the servants were required by law to serve their master. If they ran away, they became outlaws who were hunted down and forcibly returned. At the end of their period of indenture, they became full citizens, able to live where they chose and free to sell their labor (Main 1965; Elkins 1968).

When there were not enough indentured servants to meet the growing need for labor, some colonists tried to enslave Native Americans. This attempt failed miserably, in part because when Indians escaped, they knew how to survive in the wilderness and were able to make their way back to their tribe. The colonists then turned to Africans, who were being brought to North and South America by the Dutch, English, Portuguese, and Spanish.

Because slavery has a broad range of causes, some analysts conclude that racism didn't lead to slavery, but, rather, that slavery led to racism. Finding it profitable to make people slaves for life, U.S. slave owners developed an **ideology,** beliefs that justify social arrangements. Ideology leads to a perception of the world that makes current social arrangements seem necessary and fair. The colonists developed the view that their slaves were inferior. Some even said that they were not fully human. In short, the colonists wove elaborate justifications for slavery, built on the presumed superiority of their own group.

To make slavery even more profitable, slave states passed laws that made slavery *inheritable;* that is, the babies born to slaves became the property of the slave owners (Stampp 1956). These children could be sold, bartered, or traded. To strengthen their control, slave states passed laws making it illegal for slaves to hold meetings or to be away from the master's premises without carrying a pass (Lerner 1972). As sociologist W. E. B. Du Bois (1935/1992:12) noted, "gradually the entire white South became an armed camp to keep Negroes in slavery and to kill the black rebel."

The Civil War did not end legal discrimination. For example, until 1954 many states operated separate school systems for blacks and whites. Until the 1950s, in order to keep the races from "mixing," it was illegal in Mississippi for a white and an African

During my research in India, I interviewed this 8-year-old girl. Mahashury is a *bonded laborer* who was exchanged by her parents for a 2,000 rupee loan (about $14). To repay the loan, Mahashury must do construction work for one year. She will receive one meal a day and one set of clothing for the year. Because this centuries-old practice is now illegal, the master bribes Indian officials, who inform him when they are going to inspect the construction site. He then hides his bonded laborers. I was able to interview and photograph Mahashury because her master was absent the day I visited the construction site.

American to sit together on the same seat of a car! There was no outright ban on blacks and whites being in the same car, however, so whites could employ African American chauffeurs.

Slavery Today.   Slavery has again reared its ugly head in several parts of the world. The Ivory Coast, Mauritania, Niger, and Sudan have a long history of slavery, and not until the 1980s was slavery made illegal in Mauritania and Sudan (Ayittey 1998). It took until 2003 for slavery to be banned in Niger (Polgreen 2008). Although officially abolished, slavery in this region continues, the topic of the Mass Media box on the next page.

The enslavement of children for work and sex is a problem in Africa, Asia, and South America (*Trafficking in Persons Report* 2008). A unique form of child slavery occurs in Kuwait, Qatar, and Saudi Arabia. There, little boys are held in captivity because they are prized as jockeys in camel races. Facing organized opposition to this unique form of human trafficking, the United Arab Emirates is replacing boy jockeys with robots (Khan 2007).

Caste

The second system of social stratification is caste. In a **caste system,** status is determined by birth and is lifelong. Someone who is born into a low-status group will always have low status, no matter how much that person may accomplish in life. In sociological terms, a caste system is built on ascribed status (discussed on pages 99–100). Achieved status cannot change an individual's place in this system.

Societies with this form of stratification try to make certain that the boundaries between castes remain firm. They practice **endogamy,** marriage within their own group, and prohibit intermarriage. Elaborate rules about *ritual pollution*—touching an inferior caste contaminates the superior caste—keeps contact between castes to a minimum.

India's Religious Castes.   India provides the best example of a caste system. Based not on race but on religion, India's caste system has existed for almost three thousand years (Chandra 1993a; Jaffrelot 2006). India's four main castes are depicted in Table 9.1. These four castes are subdivided into about three thousand subcastes, or *jati*. Each *jati* specializes in a particular occupation. For example, one subcaste washes clothes, another sharpens knives, and yet another repairs shoes.

The lowest group listed in Table 9.1, the Dalit, make up India's "untouchables." If a Dalit touches someone of a higher caste, that person becomes unclean. Even the shadow of an untouchable can contaminate. Early morning and late afternoons are especially risky, for the long shadows of these periods pose a danger to everyone higher up the caste system.

caste system a form of social stratification in which people's statuses are determined by birth and are lifelong

endogamy the practice of marrying within one's own group

TABLE 9.1 India's Caste System	
Caste	Occupation
Brahman	Priests and teachers
Kshatriya	Rulers and soldiers
Vaishya	Merchants and traders
Shudra	Peasants and laborers
Dalit (untouchables)	The outcastes; degrading or polluting labor

In a *caste system*, status is determined by birth and is lifelong. At birth, these women received not only membership in a lower caste but also, because of their gender, a predetermined position in that caste. When I photographed these women, they were carrying sand to the second floor of a house being constructed in Andhra Pradesh, India.

MASS MEDIA In SOCIAL LIFE

What Price Freedom? Slavery Today

Children of the Dinka tribe in rural Sudan don't go to school. They work. Their families depend on them to tend the cattle that are essential to their way of life.

On the morning of the raid, ten-year-old Adhieu had been watching the cattle. "We were very happy because we would soon leave the cattle camps and return home to our parents. But in the morning, there was shooting. There was yelling and crying everywhere. My uncle grabbed me by the hand, and we ran. We swam across the river. I saw some children drowning. We hid behind a rock."

By morning's end, 500 children were either dead or enslaved. Their attackers were their fellow countrymen—Arabs from northern Sudan. The children who were captured were forced to march hundreds of miles north. Some escaped on the way. Others tried to—and were shot (Akol 1998).

Journalists provided devastating accounts: In the United States, public television (PBS) ran film footage of captive children in chains. And escaped slaves recounted their ordeal in horrifying detail (Salopek 2003; Mende and Lewis 2005).

Although the United States bombed Kosovo (in Serbia) into submission for its crimes against humanity, in the face of this outrage it remained largely silent. A cynic might say that Kosovo was located at a politically strategic spot in Europe, but Sudan occupies an area of Africa in which the U.S. and European powers have had little interest. A cynic might add that these powers fear Arab retaliation, which might take the form of oil embargoes and terrorism. A cynic might also suggest that outrages against black Africans are not as significant to these powers as those against white Europeans. Finally, a cynic might add that this indifference will end as Sudan's oil reserves become more strategic to Western interests.

When the world's most powerful governments didn't act on behalf of the slaves, private groups stepped in.

A representative of Christian Solidarity International (on the left) is paying $13,200 in Sudanese money to free the 132 slaves shown in the background.

One was Switzerland's Christian Solidarity International (CSI). CSI sent Arab "retrievers" to northern Sudan, where they either bought or abducted slaves. CSI paid the retrievers $100 per slave. Critics claimed that buying slaves, even to free them, encourages slavery. The money provides motivation to enslave people in order to turn around and sell them. Certainly $100 is a lot of money in Sudan, where people are lucky to make $66 a month (*Statistical Abstract* 2009:Table 1305).

CSI said that this was a bogus argument. What is intolerable, they said, is to leave women and children in slavery where they are deprived of their freedom and families and are beaten and raped by brutal masters.

For Your Consideration

What do you think about buying the freedom of slaves? Can you suggest a workable alternative? Why do you think the U.S. government remained largely silent about this issue, when it invaded other countries such as Serbia and Haiti for human rights abuses? Do you think that, perhaps, political motivations outweigh human rights motivations? If not, why the silence in the face of slavery?

With the media coverage of this issue, some U.S. high schools—and even grade schools—raised money to participate in slave buyback programs. If you were a school principal, would you encourage this practice? Why or why not?

Consequently, Dalits are not allowed in some villages during these times. Anyone who becomes contaminated must follow *ablution*, or washing rituals, to restore purity.

Although the Indian government formally abolished the caste system in 1949, centuries-old practices cannot be eliminated so easily, and the caste system remains part of everyday life in India (Beckett 2007). The ceremonies people follow at births, marriages, and deaths, for example, are dictated by caste (Chandra 1993a). The upper castes dread the upward mobility of the untouchables, sometimes resisting it even with murder and ritual suicide (Crossette 1996; Trofimov 2007). From personal observations in India, I can add that in some villages Dalit children are not allowed in the government schools. If they try to enroll, they are beaten.

An untouchable summed up his situation in life this way:

> At the tea stalls, we have separate cups to drink from, chipped and caked with dirt. We have to walk for 15 minutes to carry water to our homes, because we're not allowed to use the taps in the village that the upper castes use. We're not allowed into temples. When I attended school, my friends and I were forced to sit outside the classroom. The upper caste children would not allow us even to touch the football they played with. We played with stones instead. (Guru and Sidhva 2001)

South Africa. In South Africa, Europeans of Dutch descent, a numerical minority called Afrikaners, used to control the government, the police, and the military. They used these sources of power to enforce a system called **apartheid** (ah-PAR-tate), the separation of the races. Everyone was classified by law into one of four groups: Europeans (whites), Africans (blacks), Coloureds (mixed races), and Asians. These classifications determined where people could live, work, and go to school. It also established where they could swim or see movies—for by law whites were not allowed to mix socially with the others.

After years of trade sanctions and sports boycotts, in 1990 Afrikaners began to dismantle their caste system, and in 1994 Nelson Mandela, a black, was elected president. Black Africans no longer have to carry special passes, public facilities are integrated, and all racial–ethnic groups have the right to vote and to hold office. Although apartheid has been dismantled, its legacy haunts South Africa. Whites still dominate the country's social institutions, and most blacks remain uneducated and poor. Many new rights—such as the right to higher education, to eat in restaurants, even to see a doctor—are of little use to people who can't afford them. Political violence has been replaced by old-fashioned crime. Even though the U.S. murder rate is so high it intimidates foreigners, South Africa's murder rate is *six* times higher (*Crime Situation . . .* 2008:Table 1; *Statistical Abstract* 2009:Table 295). Apartheid's legacy of prejudice, bitterness, and hatred appears destined to fuel racial tensions for generations to come.

A U.S. Racial Caste System. Before leaving the subject of caste, we should note that when slavery ended in the United States, it was replaced by a *racial caste system*. From the moment of birth, everyone was marked for life (Berger 1963/2007). In this system, *all* whites, even if they were poor and uneducated, considered themselves to have a higher status than *all* African Americans. As in India and South Africa, the upper caste, fearing pollution from the lower caste, prohibited intermarriage and insisted on separate schools, hotels, restaurants, and even toilets and drinking fountains in public facilities. In the South, when any white met any African American on a sidewalk, the African American had to move aside—which the untouchables of India still must do when they meet someone of a higher caste (Deliege 2001).

Estate

During the middle ages, Europe developed an **estate stratification system.** There were three groups, or estates. The *first estate* was made up of the nobility, the wealthy families who ruled the country. This group owned the land, which was the source of wealth at that time. The nobility did no farming themselves, or any "work" for that matter. Work was considered beneath their dignity, something to be done by servants. The nobility's responsibility was to administer their lands and to live "genteel" lives worthy of their high position.

The *second estate* consisted of the clergy. The Roman Catholic Church was a political power at this time. It also owned vast amounts of land and collected taxes from everyone who lived within the boundaries of a parish. The church's power was so great that in order to be crowned, kings had to obtain the pope's permission.

To prevent their vast land holdings from being carved into smaller chunks, members of the nobility practiced *primogeniture,* allowing only firstborn sons to inherit land. The other sons had to find some way to support themselves, and joining the clergy was a favored way. (Other ways included becoming an officer in the military or practicing law.)

apartheid the enforced separation of racial–ethnic groups as was practiced in South Africa

estate stratification system the stratification system of medieval Europe, consisting of three groups or estates: the nobility, clergy, and commoners

class system a form of social stratification based primarily on the possession of money or material possessions

social mobility movement up or down the social class ladder

The church was appealing because priests held lifetime positions and were guaranteed a comfortable living. At that time, the church sold offices, and, for example, a wealthy man could buy the position of bishop for his son, which guaranteed a high income.

The *third estate* consisted of the commoners. Known as *serfs,* they belonged to the land. If someone bought or inherited land, the serfs came with it. Serfs were born into the third estate, and they died within it, too. The rare person who made it out of the third estate was a man who was knighted for extraordinary bravery in battle or someone "called" into a religious vocation.

Women in the Estate System.   Women belonged to the estate of their husbands. Women in the first estate had no occupation, for, as in the case of their husbands, work was considered beneath their dignity. Their responsibility was to administer the household, overseeing the children and servants. The women in the second estate, nuns, were the exception to the rule that women belonged to the estate of their husbands, as the Roman Catholic clergy did not marry. Women of the third estate shared the hard life of their husbands, including physical labor and food shortages. In addition, they faced the peril of rape by men of the first estate. A few commoners who caught the eye of men of the first estate did marry and join them in the first estate. This, however, was rare.

Class

As we have seen, stratification systems based on slavery, caste, and estate are rigid. The lines drawn between people are firm, and there is little or no movement from one group to another. A **class system,** in contrast, is much more open, for it is based primarily on money or material possessions, which can be acquired. This system, too, is in place at birth, when children are ascribed the status of their parents, but, in this system, unlike the others, individuals can change their social class by what they achieve (or fail to achieve) in life. In addition, no laws specify people's occupations on the basis of birth or prohibit marriage between the classes.

A major characteristic of the class system, then, is its relatively fluid boundaries. A class system allows **social mobility,** movement up or down the class ladder. The potential for improving one's life—or for falling down the class ladder—is a major force that drives people to go far in school and to work hard. In the extreme, the family background that a child inherits at birth may present such obstacles that he or she has little chance of climbing very far—or it may provide such privileges that it makes it almost impossible to fall down the class ladder. Because social class is so significant for our own lives, we will focus on class in the next chapter.

In early industrialization, children worked alongside adults. Their 10 to 12 hour workdays were often spent in dangerous, filthy conditions. One of the early efforts to abolish child labor is shown in this 1890 photo from Philadelphia.

Global Stratification and the Status of Females

In *every* society of the world, gender is a basis for social stratification. In no society is gender the sole basis for stratifying people, but gender cuts across *all* systems of social stratification—whether slavery, caste, estate, or class (Huber 1990). In all these systems, on the basis of their gender, people are sorted into categories and given different access to the good things available in their society.

Apparently these distinctions always favor males. It is remarkable, for example, that in *every* society of the world men's earnings are higher than women's. Men's dominance is even more evident when we consider female circumcision (see the box on page 306). That most of the world's illiterate are females also drives home women's relative position in society. Of the several hundred million adults who cannot read, about two-thirds are women (UNESCO 2006). Because gender is such a significant factor in what happens to us in life, we shall focus on it more closely in Chapter 11.

The Global Superclass

The growing interconnections among the world's wealthiest people have produced a *global superclass*, one in which wealth and power are more concentrated than ever before. There are only about 6,000 members of this superclass—*the richest 1,000 of them have more wealth than the 2½ billion poorest people on this planet* (Rothkopf 2008:37). Almost all of them are white, and except as wives and daughters, few women are an active part of the superclass. We will have more to say about the superclass in Chapter 14, but for now, let's just stress their incredible wealth. There is nothing in history to compare with what you see in Figure 9.1.

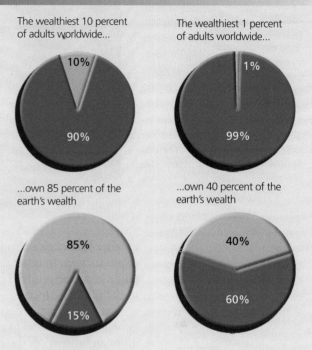

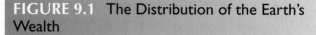

FIGURE 9.1 The Distribution of the Earth's Wealth

The wealthiest 10 percent of adults worldwide...

10%

90%

...own 85 percent of the earth's wealth

85%

15%

The wealthiest 1 percent of adults worldwide...

1%

99%

...own 40 percent of the earth's wealth

40%

60%

Source: Rothkopf 2008:37.

What Determines Social Class?

In the early days of sociology, a disagreement arose about the meaning of social class. Let's compare how Marx and Weber analyzed the issue.

Karl Marx: The Means of Production

As we discussed in Chapter 1, as agricultural society gave way to an industrial one, masses of peasants were displaced from their traditional lands and occupations. Fleeing to cities, they competed for the few available jobs. Paid only a pittance for their labor, they wore rags, went hungry, and slept under bridges and in shacks. In contrast, the factory owners built mansions, hired servants, and lived in the lap of luxury. Seeing this great disparity between owners and workers, Karl Marx (1818–1883) concluded that social class depends on a single factor: people's relationship to the **means of production**—the tools, factories, land, and investment capital used to produce wealth (Marx 1844/1964; Marx and Engels 1848/1967).

Marx argued that the distinctions people often make among themselves—such as clothing, speech, education, paycheck, the neighborhood they live in, even the car they drive—are superficial matters. These things camouflage the only dividing line that counts. There are just two classes of people, said Marx: the **bourgeoisie** (*capitalists*), those who own the means of production, and the **proletariat** (*workers*), those who work for the owners. In short, people's relationship to the means of production determines their social class.

Marx did recognize other groups: farmers and peasants; a *lumpenproletariat* (people living on the margin of society, such as beggars, vagrants, and criminals); and a middle group of self-employed professionals. Marx did not consider these groups social classes, however,

means of production the tools, factories, land, and investment capital used to produce wealth

bourgeoisie Marx's term for capitalists, those who own the means of production

proletariat Marx's term for the exploited class, the mass of workers who do not own the means of production

Taken at the end of the 1800s, these photos illustrate the contrasting worlds of *social classes* produced by capitalism. The sleeping boys shown in this classic 1890 photo by Jacob Riis sold newspapers in London. They did not go to school, and they had no home. The children on the right, Cornelius and Gladys Vanderbilt, are shown in front of their parents' estate. They went to school and did not work. You can see how the social locations illustrated in these photos would have produced different orientations to life and, therefore, politics, ideas about marriage, values, and so on—the stuff of which life is made.

for they lack **class consciousness**—a shared identity based on their position in the means of production. In other words, they did not perceive themselves as exploited workers whose plight could be resolved by collective action. Marx thought of these groups as insignificant in the future he foresaw—a workers' revolution that would overthrow capitalism.

The capitalists will grow even wealthier, Marx said, and the hostilities will increase. When workers come to realize that capitalists are the source of their oppression, they will unite and throw off the chains of their oppressors. In a bloody revolution, they will seize the means of production and usher in a classless society—and no longer will the few grow rich at the expense of the many. What holds back the workers' unity and their revolution is **false class consciousness,** workers mistakenly thinking of themselves as capitalists. For example, workers with a few dollars in the bank may forget that they are workers and instead see themselves as investors, or as capitalists who are about to launch a successful business.

Max Weber: Property, Power, and Prestige

Max Weber (1864–1920) was an outspoken critic of Marx. Weber argued that property is only part of the picture. *Social class,* he said, has three components: property, power, and prestige (Gerth and Mills 1958; Weber 1922/1978). Some call these the three P's of social class. (Although Weber used the terms *class, power,* and *status,* some sociologists find *property, power,* and *prestige* to be clearer terms. To make them even clearer, you may wish to substitute *wealth* for *property.*)

Property (or wealth), said Weber, is certainly significant in determining a person's standing in society. On that point he agreed with Marx. But, added Weber, ownership is not the only significant aspect of property. For example, some powerful people, such as managers of corporations, *control* the means of production even though they do not *own* them. If managers can control property for their own benefit—awarding themselves huge bonuses and magnificent perks—it makes no practical difference that they do not own the property that they use so generously for their own benefit.

Power, the second element of social class, is the ability to control others, even over their objections. Weber agreed with Marx that property is a major source of power, but he added that it is not the only source. For example, prestige can be turned into power. Two well-known examples are actors Arnold Schwarzenegger, who became governor of California, and Ronald Reagan, who was elected governor of California and president of the United States. Figure 9.2 shows how property, power, and prestige are interrelated.

Prestige, the third element in Weber's analysis, is often derived from property and power, for people tend to admire the wealthy and powerful. Prestige, however, can be based on other factors. Olympic gold medalists, for example, might not own property or be powerful, yet they have high prestige. Some are even able to exchange their

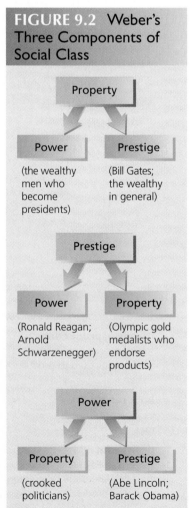

FIGURE 9.2　Weber's Three Components of Social Class

Property

Power　Prestige

(the wealthy men who become presidents)　(Bill Gates; the wealthy in general)

Prestige

Power　Property

(Ronald Reagan; Arnold Schwarzenegger)　(Olympic gold medalists who endorse products)

Power

Property　Prestige

(crooked politicians)　(Abe Lincoln; Barack Obama)

prestige for property—such as those who are paid a small fortune for endorsing a certain brand of sportswear or for claiming that they start their day with "the breakfast of champions." In other words, property and prestige are not one-way streets: Although property can bring prestige, prestige can also bring property.

In Sum: For Marx, the only distinction that counted was property, more specifically people's relationship to the means of production. Whether we are owners or workers decides everything else, for this determines our lifestyle and shapes our orientation to life. Weber, in contrast, argued that social class has three components—a combination of property, power, and prestige.

Why Is Social Stratification Universal?

What is it about social life that makes all societies stratified? We shall first consider the explanation proposed by functionalists, which has aroused much controversy in sociology, and then explanations proposed by conflict theorists.

The Functionalist View: Motivating Qualified People

Functionalists take the position that the patterns of behavior that characterize a society exist because they are functional for that society. Because social inequality is universal, inequality must help societies survive. But how?

Davis and Moore's Explanation.   Two functionalists, Kingsley Davis and Wilbert Moore (1945, 1953), wrestled with this question. They concluded that stratification of society is inevitable because

1. Society must make certain that its positions are filled.
2. Some positions are more important than others.
3. The more important positions must be filled by the more qualified people.
4. To motivate the more qualified people to fill these positions, society must offer them greater rewards.

To flesh out this functionalist argument, consider college presidents and military generals. The position of college president is more important than that of student because the president's decisions affect a large number of people, including many students. College presidents are also accountable for their performance to boards of trustees. It is the same with generals. Their decisions affect many people and sometimes even determine life and death. Generals are accountable to superior generals and to the country's leader.

Why do people accept such high-pressure positions? Why don't they just take less demanding jobs? The answer, said Davis and Moore, is that society offers greater rewards—prestige, pay, and benefits—for its more demanding and accountable positions. To get highly qualified people to compete with one another, some positions offer a salary of $2 million a year, country club membership, a private jet and pilot, and a chauffeured limousine. For less demanding positions, a $30,000 salary without fringe benefits is enough to get hundreds of people to compete. If a job requires rigorous training, it, too, must offer more salary and benefits. If you can get the same pay with a high school diploma, why suffer through the many tests and term papers that college requires?

Tumin's Critique of Davis and Moore.   Davis and Moore tried to explain *why* social stratification is universal; they were not attempting to justify social inequality. Nevertheless, their

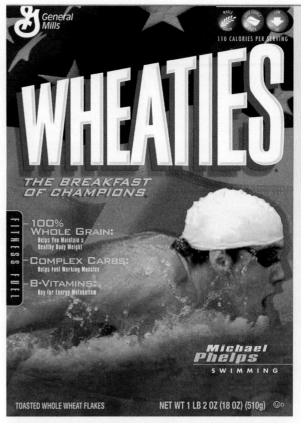

Prestige can sometimes be converted into property or power. Michael Phelps, the winner of 8 gold medals in the Beijing Olympics, gained endorsements worth millions. When a photo of Phelps smoking marijuana was posted on the Internet, sponsors like Wheaties quickly pulled their endorsements.

class consciousness Marx's term for awareness of a common identity based on one's position in the means of production

false class consciousness Marx's term to refer to workers identifying with the interests of capitalists

Sisters Venus and Serena Williams have dominated the women's tennis world for over a decade. To determine the social class of athletes as highly successful as the Williams sisters, shown here after having won gold medals at the Beijing Olympics, presents a sociological puzzle. With their fame and growing wealth, what do you think their social class is? Why?

view makes many sociologists uncomfortable, for they see it as coming close to justifying the inequalities in society. Its bottom line seems to be, The people who contribute more to society are paid more, while those who contribute less are paid less.

Melvin Tumin (1953) was the first sociologist to point out what he saw as major flaws in the functionalist position. Here are three of his arguments.

First, how do we know that the positions that offer the higher rewards are more important? A heart surgeon, for example, saves lives and earns much more than a garbage collector, but this doesn't mean that garbage collectors are less important to society. By helping to prevent contagious diseases, garbage collectors save more lives than heart surgeons do. We need independent methods of measuring importance, and we don't have them.

Second, if stratification worked as Davis and Moore described it, society would be a **meritocracy;** that is, positions would be awarded on the basis of merit. But is this what we have? The best predictor of who goes to college, for example, is not ability but income: The more a family earns, the more likely their children are to go to college (Carnevale and Rose 2003; Belley and Lochner 2007). Not merit, then, but money—another form of the inequality that is built into society. In short, people's positions in society are based on many factors other than merit.

Third, if social stratification is so functional, it ought to benefit almost everyone. Yet social stratification is *dysfunctional* for many. Think of the people who could have made valuable contributions to society had they not been born in slums, dropped out of school, and taken menial jobs to help support their families. Then there are the many who, born female, are assigned "women's work," thus ensuring that they do not maximize their mental abilities.

In Sum: Functionalists argue that some positions are more important to society than others. Offering higher rewards for these positions motivates more talented people to take them. For example, to get highly talented people to become surgeons—to undergo years of rigorous training and then cope with life-and-death situations, as well as malpractice suits—that position must provide a high payoff.

meritocracy a form of social stratification in which all positions are awarded on the basis of merit

The Conflict Perspective: Class Conflict and Scarce Resources

Conflict theorists don't just criticize details of the functionalist argument. Rather, they go for the throat and attack its basic premise. Conflict, not function, they stress, is the reason that we have social stratification. Let's look at the major arguments.

Mosca's Argument.   Italian sociologist Gaetano Mosca argued that every society will be stratified by power. This is inevitable, he said in an 1896 book titled *The Ruling Class,* because:

1. No society can exist unless it is organized. This requires leadership of some sort in order to coordinate people's actions.
2. Leadership (or political organization) requires inequalities of power. By definition, some people take leadership positions, while others follow.
3. Because human nature is self-centered, people in power will use their positions to seize greater rewards for themselves.

There is no way around these facts of life, added Mosca. Social stratification is inevitable, and every society will stratify itself along lines of power.

Marx's Argument.   If he were alive to hear the functionalist argument, Karl Marx would be enraged. From his point of view, the people in power are not there because of superior traits, as the functionalists would have us believe. This view is an ideology that members of the elite use to justify their being at the top—and to seduce the oppressed into believing that their welfare depends on keeping quiet and following authorities. What is human history, Marx asked, except the chronicle of class struggle? All of human history is an account of small groups of people in power using society's resources to benefit themselves and to oppress those beneath them—and of oppressed groups trying to overcome that oppression.

Marx predicted that the workers will revolt. Capitalist ideology now blinds them, but one day class consciousness will throw off that blindfold and expose the truth. When workers realize their common oppression, they will rebel. The struggle to control the means of production may be covert at first, taking such forms as work slowdowns and industrial sabotage. Ultimately, however, resistance will break out into the open. The revolution will not be easy, for the bourgeoisie control the police, the military, and even the educational system, where they implant false class consciousness in the minds of the workers' children.

Current Applications of Conflict Theory.   Just as Marx focused on overarching historic events—the accumulation of capital and power and the struggle between workers and capitalists—so do some of today's conflict sociologists. In analyzing global stratification and global capitalism, they look at power relations among nations, how national elites control workers, and how power shifts as capital is shuffled among nations (Sklair 2001).

Other conflict sociologists, in contrast, examine conflict wherever it is found, not just as it relates to capitalists and workers. They examine how groups *within the same class* compete with one another for a larger slice of the pie (Schellenberg 1996; Collins 1988, 1999). Even within the same industry, for example, union will fight against union for higher salaries, shorter hours, and more power. A special focus has been conflict between racial–ethnic groups as they compete for education, housing, and even prestige—whatever benefits society has to offer. Another focus has been relations between women and men, which conflict theorists say are best understood as a conflict over power—over who controls society's resources. Unlike functionalists, conflict theorists say that just beneath the surface of what may appear to be a tranquil society lies conflict that is barely held in check.

Lenski's Synthesis

As you can see, functionalist and conflict theorists disagree sharply. Is it possible to reconcile their views? Sociologist Gerhard Lenski (1966) thought so. He suggested that surplus is the key. He said that the functionalists are right when it comes to groups that don't accumulate a surplus, such as hunting and gathering societies. These societies give a greater share of their resources to those who take on important tasks, such as warriors who risk their lives in battle. It is a different story, said Lenski, with societies that accumulate surpluses. In them, groups fight over the surplus, and the group that wins becomes an elite. This dominant group rules from the top, controlling the groups below it. In the resulting system of social stratification, where you are born in that society, not personal merit, becomes important.

divine right of kings the idea that the king's authority comes from God; in an interesting gender bender, also applies to queens

In Sum: Conflict theorists stress that in every society groups struggle with one another to gain a larger share of their society's resources. Whenever a group gains power, it uses that power to extract what it can from the groups beneath it. This elite group also uses the social institutions to keep itself in power.

How Do Elites Maintain Stratification?

Suppose that you are part of the ruling elite of your society. What can you do to make sure you don't lose your privileged position? Besides the use of force, the key is to control people's ideas, information, and technology.

Soft Control Versus Force

Let's take our primary lesson from the estate system of medieval Europe that we just reviewed. Land was the primary source of wealth—and only the nobility and the church could own land. Almost everyone was a peasant (or serf) who worked for these powerful landowners. The peasants farmed the land, took care of the livestock, and built the roads and bridges. Each year, they had to turn over a designated portion of their crops to their feudal lord. Year after year, for centuries, they did so. Why?

Controlling People's Ideas.   Why didn't the peasants rebel and take over the land themselves? There were many reasons, not the least of which was that the nobility and church controlled the army. Coercion, however, goes only so far, for it breeds hostility and nourishes rebellion. How much more effective it is to get the masses to *want* to do what the ruling elite desires. This is where *ideology* (beliefs that justify the way things are) comes into play, and the nobility and clergy used it to great effect. They developed an ideology known as the **divine right of kings**—the idea that the king's authority comes directly from God. The king delegates authority to nobles, who, as God's representatives, must be obeyed. To disobey is a sin against God; to rebel is to merit physical punishment on earth and eternal suffering in hell.

Controlling people's ideas can be remarkably more effective than using brute force. Although this particular ideology governs few minds today, the elite in *every* society develops ideologies to justify its position at the top. For example, around the world, schools

The *divine right of kings* was an ideology that made the king God's direct representative on earth—to administer justice and punish evildoers. This theological-political concept was supported by the Roman Catholic Church. Shown here is Pope Pius VII directing the consecration of Napoleon as Emperor and Josephine as Empress on December 2, 1804.

teach that their country's form of government—*no matter what form of government that is*—is good. Religious leaders teach that we owe obedience to authority, that laws are to be obeyed. To the degree that their ideologies are accepted by the masses, the elite remains securely in power.

Ideology is so powerful that it also sets limits on the elite. Although leaders use ideas to control people, the people can also insist that their leaders conform to those same ideas. Pakistan is an outstanding example. If Pakistani leaders depart from fundamentalist Islamic ideology, their position is in jeopardy. For example, regardless of their personal views, Pakistani leaders cannot support Western ideas of morality. If they were to allow women to wear short skirts in public, for example, not only would they lose their positions of leadership but perhaps also their lives. To protect their position within a system of stratification, leaders, regardless of their personal opinions, must conform at least outwardly to the controlling ideas.

Controlling Information. To maintain their positions of power, elites try to control information and stifle criticism. For those who can get away with it, fear is a favorite tactic. In Thailand, you can be put in prison for criticizing the king or his family (Grant 2009). It was worse in Saddam Hussein's Iraq, where the penalty for telling a joke about Hussein was having your tongue cut out (Nordland 2003). Lacking such power, the ruling elites of democracies rely on covert means. A favorite tactic of U.S. presidents is to withhold information "in the interest of national security," a phrase that usually translates as "in the interest of protecting me."

Controlling Technology. The new technology has become a powerful tool for the power elites. Without leaving a trace, programs can read the entire contents of a computer in a second. Security cameras—"Tiny Brothers"—have sprouted almost everywhere. Face-recognition systems can scan a crowd of thousands, instantly matching the scans with digitized files of individuals. With these devices, the elite can monitor citizens without anyone knowing they are being watched. Dictators have few checks on how they use this technology, but in democracies, checks and balances, such as requiring court orders for search and seizure, help to curb their abuse. Such restraints on power always frustrate officials, so they are delighted with our new Homeland Security laws that allow them to spy on citizens without their knowledge.

The new technology, however, is a two-edged sword. Just as it gives the elite powerful tools for monitoring citizens, it also makes it more difficult for them to control information. With international borders meaning nothing to satellite communications, e-mail, and the Internet, information (both true and fabricated) flies around the globe in seconds. Internet users also have free access to some versions of PGP (Pretty Good Privacy), a code that no government has been able to break. Then, too, there is zFone, a voice encryption for telephone calls that prevents wiretappers from understanding what people are saying.

To stifle criticism, Chinese leaders have put tight controls on Internet cafes and search engines (Hutton 2007; James 2009). Unable to do this, U.S. officials have distributed fake news reports to be broadcast to the nation (Barstow and Stein 2005). We are still in the early stages of the new technology, so we will see how this cat and mouse game plays out.

In Sum: To maintain stratification, the elite tries to dominate its society's institutions. In a dictatorship, the elite makes the laws. In a democracy, the elite influences the laws. In both, the elite controls the police and military and can give orders to crush a rebellion—or to run the post office or air traffic control if workers strike. With force having its limits, especially the potential of provoking resistance, most power elites prefer to keep themselves in power by peaceful means, especially by influencing the thinking of their people.

Comparative Social Stratification

Now that we have examined systems of social stratification, considered why stratification is universal, and looked at how elites keep themselves in power, let's compare social stratification in Great Britain and in the former Soviet Union. In the next chapter, we'll look at social stratification in the United States.

Social Stratification in Great Britain

Great Britain is often called England by Americans, but England is only one of the countries that make up the island of Great Britain. The others are Scotland and Wales. In addition, Northern Ireland is part of the United Kingdom of Great Britain and Northern Ireland.

Like other industrialized countries, Great Britain has a class system that can be divided into a lower, a middle, and an upper class. Great Britain's population is about evenly divided between the middle class and the lower (or working) class. A tiny upper class, perhaps 1 percent of the population, is wealthy, powerful, and highly educated.

Compared with Americans, the British are very class conscious (Kerswill 2006). Like Americans, they recognize class distinctions on the basis of the type of car a person drives or the stores someone patronizes. But the most striking characteristics of the British class system are language and education. Because these often show up in distinctive speech, accent has a powerful impact on British life. Accent almost always betrays class. As soon as someone speaks, the listener is aware of that person's social class—and treats him or her accordingly (Sullivan 1998).

Education is the primary way by which the British perpetuate their class system from one generation to the next. Almost all children go to neighborhood schools. Great Britain's richest 5 percent, however—who own *half* the nation's wealth—send their children to exclusive private boarding schools (which, strange to the American ear, they call "public" schools). There the children of the elite are trained in subjects that are considered "proper" for members of the ruling class. An astounding 50 percent of the students at Oxford and Cambridge, the country's most prestigious universities, come from this 5 percent of the population. To illustrate how powerfully this system of stratified education affects the national life of Great Britain, sociologist Ian Robertson (1987) said,

> Eighteen former pupils of the most exclusive of [England's high schools], Eton, have become prime minister. Imagine the chances of a single American high school producing eighteen presidents!

Social Stratification in the Former Soviet Union

Heeding Karl Marx's call for a classless society, Vladimir Ilyich Lenin (1870–1924) and Leon Trotsky (1879–1940) led a revolution in Russia in 1917. They, and the nations that followed their banner, never claimed to have achieved the ideal of communism, in which all contribute their labor to the common good and receive according to their needs. Instead, they used the term *socialism* to describe the intermediate step between capitalism and communism, in which social classes are abolished but some inequality remains.

To tweak the nose of Uncle Sam, the socialist countries would trumpet their equality and point a finger at glaring inequalities in the United States. These countries, however, also were marked by huge disparities in privilege. Their major basis of stratification was membership in the Communist party. Party members decided who would gain admission to the better schools or obtain the more desirable jobs and housing. The equally qualified son or daughter of a nonmember would be turned down, for such privileges came with demonstrated loyalty to the party.

The Communist party, too, was highly stratified. Most members occupied a low level, where they fulfilled such tasks as spying on fellow workers. For this, they might get easier jobs in the factory or occasional access to special stores to purchase hard-to-find goods. The middle level consisted of bureaucrats who were given better than average access to resources and privileges. At the top level was a small elite: party members who enjoyed not only power but also limousines, imported delicacies, vacation homes, and even servants and hunting lodges. As with other stratification systems around the world, women held lower positions in the party. This was evident at each year's May Day, when the top members of the party reviewed the latest weapons paraded in Moscow's Red Square. Photos of these events showed only men.

The leaders of the USSR became frustrated as they saw the West thrive. They struggled with a bloated bureaucracy, the inefficiencies of central planning, workers who did the minimum because they could not be fired, and a military so costly that it spent one of every eight of the nation's rubles (*Statistical Abstract* 1993:1432, table dropped in later editions). Socialist ideology did not call for their citizens to be deprived, and in an attempt to turn things around, the Soviet leadership initiated reforms. They allowed elections to be held in which more than one candidate ran for an office. (Before this, voters had a choice of only one candidate per office.) They also sold huge chunks of state-owned businesses to the public. Overnight, making investments to try to turn a profit changed from a crime into a respectable goal.

Russia's transition to capitalism took a bizarre twist. As authority broke down, a powerful Mafia emerged (Varese 2005; Mesure 2008). These criminal groups are headed by gangsters, corrupt government officials (including members of the former KGB, now FSB), and crooked businessmen. In some towns, they buy the entire judicial system—the police force, prosecutors, and judges. They assassinate business leaders, reporters, and politicians who refuse to cooperate. They amass wealth, launder money through banks they control, and buy luxury properties in popular tourist areas in South America, Asia, and Europe. A favorite is Marbella, a watering and wintering spot on Spain's Costa del Sol.

As Moscow reestablishes its authority, Mafia ties have brought wealth to some of the members of this central government. This group of organized criminals is taking its place as part of Russia's new capitalist class.

Global Stratification: Three Worlds

As was noted at the beginning of this chapter, just as the people within a nation are stratified by property, power, and prestige, so are the world's nations. Until recently, a simple model consisting of First, Second, and Third Worlds was used to depict global stratification. *First World* referred to the industrialized capitalist nations, *Second World* to the communist (or socialist) countries, and *Third World* to any nation that did not fit into the first two categories. The breakup of the Soviet Union in 1989 made these terms outdated. In addition, although *first, second,* and *third* did not mean "best," "better," and "worst," they implied it. An alternative classification that some now use—developed, developing, and undeveloped nations—has the same drawback. By calling ourselves "developed," it sounds as though we are mature and the "undeveloped" nations are somehow retarded.

To resolve this problem, I use more neutral, descriptive terms: *Most Industrialized, Industrializing,* and *Least Industrialized* nations. We can measure industrialization with no judgment implied as to whether a nation's industrialization represents "development," ranks it "first," or is even desirable at all. The intention is to depict on a global level the three primary dimensions of social stratification: property, power, and prestige. The Most Industrialized Nations have much greater property (wealth), power (they usually get their way in international relations), and prestige (they are looked up to as world leaders). The three families sketched in the opening vignette illustrate the far-reaching effects of global stratification.

The Most Industrialized Nations

The Most Industrialized Nations are the United States and Canada in North America; Great Britain, France, Germany, Switzerland, and the other industrialized countries of western Europe; Japan in Asia; and Australia and New Zealand in the area of the world known as Oceania. Although there are variations in their economic systems, these nations are capitalistic. As Table 9.2 shows, although these nations have only 16 percent of the world's people, they possess 31 percent of the earth's land. Their wealth is so enormous that even their poor live better and longer lives than do the average citizens of the Least Industrialized Nations. The Social Map on pages 246–247 shows the tremendous disparities in income among the world's nations.

TABLE 9.2 Distribution of the World's Land and Population

	Land	Population
Most Industrialized Nations	31%	16%
Industrializing Nations	20%	16%
Least Industrialized Nations	49%	68%

Sources: Computed from Kurian 1990, 1991, 1992.

FIGURE 9.3   Global Stratification: Income[1] of the World's Nations

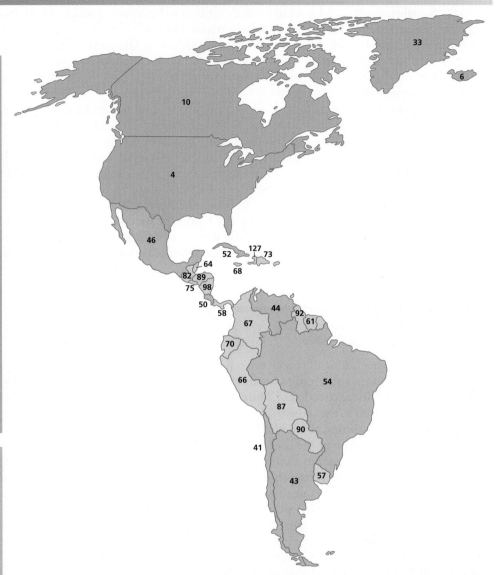

The Most Industrialized Nations

	Nation	Income per Person
1	Luxembourg	$79,400
2	Norway	$53,300
3	Singapore	$49,900
4	United States	$45,800
5	Hong Kong	$42,000
6	Iceland	$40,400
7	Switzerland	$40,100
8	Austria	$39,300
9	Netherlands	$39,000
10	Canada	$38,600
11	Sweden	$37,500
12	Australia	$37,300
13	Denmark	$37,200
14	Belgium	$36,200
15	Finland	$36,000
16	United Kingdom	$35,000
17	Germany	$34,100
18	Japan	$33,500
19	France	$32,600
20	Italy	$30,900
21	Taiwan	$30,100
22	Slovenia	$28,000
23	New Zealand	$27,200
24	Israel	$26,600
25	Korea, South	$25,000
26	Czech Republic	$24,500

The Industrializing Nations

	Nation	Income per Person
27	Ireland	$46,600
28	Spain	$33,600
29	Greece	$30,600
30	Estonia	$21,800
31	Portugal	$21,800
32	Slovakia	$20,200
33	Greenland	$20,000
34	Hungary	$19,300
35	Latvia	$17,700
36	Lithuania	$16,800
37	Poland	$16,200
38	Croatia	$15,500
39	Russia	$14,800
40	Malaysia	$14,500
41	Chile	$14,300
42	Gabon	$14,000
43	Argentina	$13,100
44	Venezuela	$12,800
45	Libya	$12,400
46	Mexico	$12,400
47	Turkey	$12,000
48	Bulgaria	$11,800
49	Mauritius	$11,300
50	Costa Rica	$11,100
51	Romania	$11,100
52	Cuba	$11,000
53	South Africa	$9,700
54	Brazil	$9,500

The Least Industrialized Nations

	Nation	Income per Person		Nation	Income per Person
55	Botswana[2]	$14,300	72	Algeria	$6,700
56	Kazakhstan	$11,000	73	Dominican	
57	Uruguay	$10,800		Republic	$6,600
58	Panama	$10,700	74	Bosnia	$6,100
59	Belarus	$10,600	75	El Salvador	$6,000
60	Lebanon	$10,300	76	Albania	$5,800
61	Suriname	$8,700	77	Armenia	$5,800
62	Macedonia	$8,400	78	China	$5,400
63	Azerbaijan	$8,000	79	Turkmenistan	$5,300
64	Belize	$7,900	80	Bhutan	$5,200
65	Angola	$7,800	81	Namibia	$5,200
66	Peru	$7,600	82	Guatemala	$5,100
67	Colombia	$7,400	83	Egypt	$5,000
68	Jamaica	$7,400	84	Jordan	$4,700
69	Tunisia	$7,400	85	Swaziland	$4,700
70	Ecuador	$7,200	86	Syria	$4,700
71	Ukraine	$7,000	87	Bolivia	$4,400

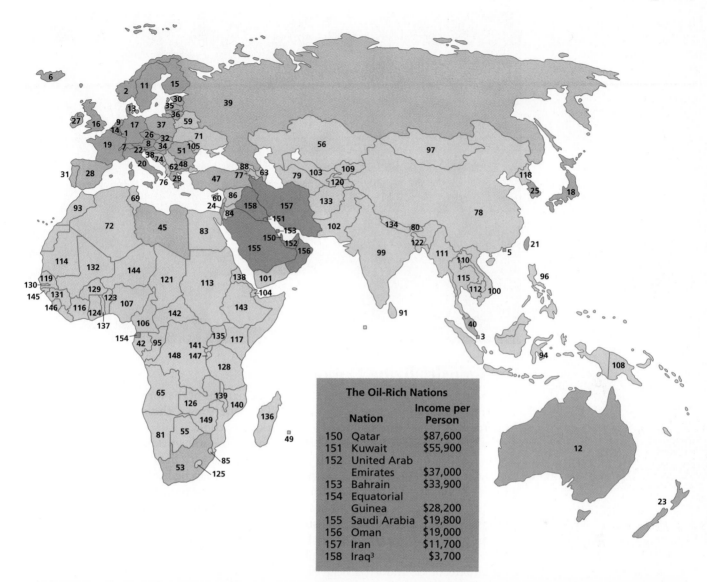

The Oil-Rich Nations

	Nation	Income per Person
150	Qatar	$87,600
151	Kuwait	$55,900
152	United Arab Emirates	$37,000
153	Bahrain	$33,900
154	Equatorial Guinea	$28,200
155	Saudi Arabia	$19,800
156	Oman	$19,000
157	Iran	$11,700
158	Iraq[3]	$3,700

The Least Industrialized Nations

	Nation	Income per Person		Nation	Income per Person		Nation	Income per Person		Nation	Income per Person
88	Georgia	$4,400	105	Moldova	$2,300	120	Tajikistan	$1,600	137	Togo	$900
89	Honduras	$4,300	106	Cameroon	$2,200	121	Chad	$1,500	138	Eritrea	$800
90	Paraguay	$4,000	107	Nigeria	$2,100	122	Bangladesh	$1,400	139	Malawi	$800
91	Sri Lanka	$4,000	108	Papua-New Guinea	$2,100	123	Benin	$1,400	140	Mozambique	$800
92	Guyana	$3,700	109	Krygyzstan	$2,000	124	Ghana	$1,400	141	Rwanda	$800
93	Morocco	$3,700	110	Laos	$2,000	125	Lesotho	$1,400	142	Central African Republic	$700
94	Indonesia	$3,600	111	Burma (Myanmar)	$1,900	126	Zambia	$1,400	143	Ethiopia	$700
95	Congo, Rep.	$3,400	112	Cambodia	$1,900	127	Haiti	$1,300	144	Niger	$700
96	Philippines	$3,200	113	Sudan	$1,900	128	Tanzania	$1,300	145	Guinea-Bissau	$600
97	Mongolia	$2,900	114	Mauritania	$1,800	129	Burkina Faso	$1,200	146	Sierra Leone	$600
98	Nicaragua	$2,800	115	Thailand	$1,800	130	Gambia	$1,200	147	Burundi	$300
99	India	$2,600	116	Cote d'Ivoire	$1,700	131	Guinea	$1,100	148	Congo, Dem. Rep.	$300
100	Vietnam	$2,600	117	Kenya	$1,700	132	Mali	$1,100	149	Zimbabwe	$200
101	Yemen	$2,500	118	Korea, North	$1,700	133	Afghanistan	$1,000			
102	Pakistan	$2,400	119	Senegal	$1,700	134	Nepal	$1,000			
103	Uzbekistan	$2,400				135	Uganda	$1,000			
104	Djibouti	$2,300				136	Madagascar	$900			

[1]Income is a country's purchasing power parity based on a country's Gross Domestic Product, where the value of a country's goods and services are valued at prices prevailing in the United States. Totals vary from year to year and should be considered as approximations.
[2]Botswana's income is based largely on its diamond mines.
[3]Iraq's oil wealth has been disrupted by war.

Source: By the author. Based on *CIA World Factbook* 2008.

The contrast between poverty and wealth is a characteristic of all contemporary societies. This photo of a woman begging with her sick daughter while shoppers retrieve cash from ATM machines was taken in Beijing, China.

The Industrializing Nations

The Industrializing Nations include most of the nations of the former Soviet Union and its former satellites in eastern Europe. As Table 9.2 shows, these nations account for 20 percent of the earth's land and 16 percent of its people.

The dividing points between the three "worlds" are soft, making it difficult to know how to classify some nations. This is especially the case with the Industrializing Nations. Exactly how much industrialization must a nation have to be in this category? Although soft, these categories do pinpoint essential differences among nations. Most people who live in the Industrializing Nations have much lower incomes and standards of living than do those who live in the Most Industrialized Nations. The majority, however, are better off than those who live in the Least Industrialized Nations. For example, on such measures as access to electricity, indoor plumbing, automobiles, telephones, and even food, most citizens of the Industrializing Nations rank lower than those in the Most Industrialized Nations, but higher than those in the Least Industrialized Nations. As you saw in the opening vignette, stratification affects even life expectancy.

The benefits of industrialization are uneven. Large numbers of people in the Industrializing Nations remain illiterate and desperately poor. Conditions can be gruesome, as we explore in the following Thinking Critically section.

Thinking CRITICALLY

Open Season: Children as Prey

What is childhood like in the Industrializing Nations? The answer depends on who your parents are. If you are the son or daughter of rich parents, childhood can be pleasant—a world filled with luxuries and even servants. If you are born into poverty, but live in a rural area where there is plenty to eat, life can still be good—although there may be no books, television, and little education. If you live in a slum, however, life can be horrible—worse even than in the slums of the Most Industrialized Nations. Let's take a glance at a notorious slum in Brazil.

Not enough food—this you can take for granted—along with wife abuse, broken homes, alcoholism, drug abuse, and a lot of crime. From your knowledge of slums in the

Most Industrialized Nations, you would expect these things. What you may not expect, however, are the brutal conditions in which Brazilian slum (*favela*) children live.

Sociologist Martha Huggins (Huggins et al. 2002) reports that poverty is so deep that children and adults swarm through garbage dumps to try to find enough decaying food to keep them alive. You might also be surprised to discover that the owners of some of these dumps hire armed guards to keep the poor out—so that they can sell the garbage for pig food. And you might be shocked to learn that some shop owners have hired hit men, auctioning designated victims to the *lowest* bidder!

Life is cheap in the poor nations—but death squads for children? To understand this, we must first note that Brazil has a long history of violence. Brazil also has a high rate of poverty, has only a tiny middle class, and is controlled by a small group of families who, under a veneer of democracy, make the country's major decisions. Hordes of homeless children, with no schools or jobs, roam the streets. To survive, they wash windshields, shine shoes, beg, and steal (Huggins and Rodrigues 2004).

The "respectable" classes see these children as nothing but trouble. They hurt business, for customers feel intimidated when they see begging children—especially teenaged males—clustered in front of stores. Some shoplift; others dare to sell items that place them in competition with the stores. With no effective social institutions to care for these children, one solution is to kill them. As Huggins notes, murder sends a clear message—especially if it is accompanied by ritual torture: gouging out the eyes, ripping open the chest, cutting off the genitals, raping the girls, and burning the victim's body.

Not all life is bad in the Industrializing Nations, but this is about as bad as it gets.

For Your Consideration

Death squads for children also operate in the slums of the Philippines ("Death Squads . . ." 2008). Do you think there is anything the Most Industrialized Nations can do about this situation? Or is it, though unfortunate, just an "internal" affair that is up to the particular nation to handle as it wishes?

The Least Industrialized Nations

In the Least Industrialized Nations, most people live on small farms or in villages, have large families, and barely survive. These nations account for 68 percent of the world's people but only 49 percent of the earth's land.

Poverty plagues these nations to such an extent that some families actually *live* in city dumps. This is hard to believe, but look at the photos on pages 250–251, which I took in Phnom Penh, the capital of Cambodia. Although wealthy nations have their pockets of poverty, *most* people in the Least Industrialized nations are poor. *Most* of them have no running water, indoor plumbing, or access to trained teachers or physicians. As we will review in Chapter 20, most of the world's population growth is occurring in these nations, placing even greater burdens on their limited resources and causing them to fall farther behind each year.

Modifying the Model

To classify countries into Most Industrialized, Industrializing, and Least Industrialized is helpful in that it pinpoints significant differences among them. But then there are the oil-rich nations of the Middle East, the ones that provide much of the gasoline that fuels the machinery of the Most Industrialized Nations. Although these nations are not industrialized, some have become immensely wealthy. To classify them simply as Least Industrialized would gloss

Homeless people sleeping on the streets is a common sight in India's cities. I took this photo in Chennai (formerly Madras).

The Dump People

Working and Living and Playing in the City Dump of Phnom Penh, Cambodia

I **went to Cambodia to inspect** orphanages, to see how well the children were being cared. for. While in Phnom Penh, Cambodia's capital, I was told about people who live in the city dump. *Live* there? I could hardly believe my ears. I knew that people made their living by picking scraps from the city dump, but I didn't know they actually lived among the garbage. This I had to see for myself.

I did. And there I found a highly developed social organization—an intricate support system. Because words are inadequate to depict the abject poverty of the Least Industrialized Nations, these photos can provide more insight into these people's lives than anything I could say.

This is a typical sight—family and friends working together. The trash, which is constantly burning, contains harmful chemicals. Why do people work under such conditions? Because they have few options. It is either this or starve.

The people live at the edge of the dump, in homemade huts (visible in the background). This woman, who was on her way home after a day's work, put down her sack of salvaged items to let me take her picture.

...er the garbage arrives by truck, people stream around it, struggling to ...he first to discover something of value. To sift through the trash, the ...kers use metal picks, like the one this child is holding. Note that ...dren work alongside the adults.

The children who live in the dump also play there. These children are riding bicycles on a "road," a packed, leveled area of garbage that leads to their huts. The huge stacks in the background are piled trash. Note the ubiquitous Nike.

...e of my many surprises was to find food stands in the dump. Although this one ...narily offers drinks and snacks, others serve more substantial food. One even has ...rs for its customers.

I was surprised to learn that ice is delivered to the dump. This woman is using a hand grinder to crush ice for drinks for her customers. The customers, of course, are other people who also live in the dump.

Not too many visitors to Phnom Penh tell a cab driver to take them to the city dump. The cabbie looked a bit perplexed, but he did as I asked. Two cabs are shown here because my friends insisted on accompanying me.

I know they were curious themselves, but my friends had also discovered that the destinations I want to visit are usually not in the tourist guides, and they wanted to protect me.

...he day's end, the workers wash at the community ...p. This hand pump serves all their water needs— ...ing, washing, and cooking. There is no indoor ...bing. The weeds in the background serve that ...ose. Can you imagine drinking water that comes ...below this garbage dump?
...es M. Henslin, all photos

TABLE 9.3 An Alternative Model of Global Stratification

Four Worlds of Development

1. Most Industrialized Nations
2. Industrializing Nations
3. Least Industrializing Nations
4. Oil-rich, nonindustrialized nations

over significant distinctions, such as their modern hospitals, extensive prenatal care, desalinization plants, abundant food and shelter, high literacy, and computerized banking. On the Social Map on pages 246–247, I classify them separately. Table 9.3 reflects this distinction.

Kuwait is an excellent example. Kuwait is so wealthy that almost none of its citizens work for a living. The government simply pays them an annual salary just for being citizens. Everyday life in Kuwait still has its share of onerous chores, of course, but migrant workers from the poor nations do most of them. To run the specialized systems that keep Kuwait's economy going, Kuwait imports trained workers from the Most Industrialized Nations.

How Did the World's Nations Become Stratified?

How did the globe become stratified into such distinct worlds? The commonsense answer is that the poorer nations have fewer resources than the richer nations. As with many commonsense answers, however, this one, too, falls short. Many of the Industrializing and Least Industrialized Nations are rich in natural resources, while one Most Industrialized Nation, Japan, has few. Three theories explain how global stratification came about.

Colonialism

The first theory, **colonialism,** stresses that the countries that industrialized first got the jump on the rest of the world. Beginning in Great Britain about 1750, industrialization spread throughout western Europe. Plowing some of their profits into powerful armaments and fast ships, these countries invaded weaker nations, making colonies out of them (Harrison 1993). After subduing these weaker nations, the more powerful countries left behind a controlling force in order to exploit the nations' labor and natural resources. At one point, there was even a free-for-all among the industrialized European countries as they rushed to divide up an entire continent. As they sliced Africa into pieces, even tiny Belgium got into the act and acquired the Congo, which was *seventy-five* times larger than itself.

The purpose of colonialism was to establish *economic colonies*—to exploit the nation's people and resources for the benefit of the "mother" country. The more powerful European countries would plant their national flags in a colony and send their representatives to run the government, but the United States usually chose to plant corporate flags in a colony and let these corporations dominate the territory's government. Central and South America are prime examples. There were exceptions, such as the conquest of the Philippines, which President McKinley said was motivated by the desire "to educate the Filipinos, and uplift and civilize and Christianize them" (Krugman 2002).

Colonialism, then, shaped many of the Least Industrialized Nations. In some instances, the Most Industrialized Nations were so powerful that when dividing their spoils, they drew lines across a map, creating new states without regard for tribal or cultural considerations (Kifner 1999). Britain and France did just this as they divided up North Africa and parts of the Middle East—which is why the national boundaries of Libya, Saudi Arabia, Kuwait, and other countries are so straight. This legacy of European conquests is a background factor in much of today's racial–ethnic and tribal violence: Groups with no history of national identity were incorporated arbitrarily into the same political boundaries.

World System Theory

The second explanation of how global stratification came about was proposed by Immanuel Wallerstein (1974, 1979, 1990). According to **world system theory,** industrialization led to four groups of nations. The first group consists of the *core nations,* the countries that industrialized first (Britain, France, Holland, and later Germany), which

colonialism the process by which one nation takes over another nation, usually for the purpose of exploiting its labor and natural resources

world system theory economic and political connections that tie the world's countries together

grew rich and powerful. The second group is the *semiperiphery*. The economies of these nations, located around the Mediterranean, stagnated because they grew dependent on trade with the core nations. The economies of the third group, the *periphery*, or fringe nations, developed even less. These are the eastern European countries, which sold cash crops to the core nations. The fourth group of nations includes most of Africa and Asia. Called the *external area*, these nations were left out of the development of capitalism altogether. The current expansion of capitalism has changed the relationships among these groups. Most notably, eastern Europe and Asia are no longer left out of capitalism.

The **globalization of capitalism**—the adoption of capitalism around the world—has created extensive ties among the world's nations. Production and trade are now so interconnected that events around the globe affect us all. Sometimes this is immediate, as happens when a civil war disrupts the flow of oil, or—perish the thought—as would be the case if terrorists managed to get their hands on nuclear or biological weapons. At other times, the effects are like a slow ripple, as when a government adopts some policy that gradually impedes its ability to compete in world markets. All of today's societies, then, no matter where they are located, are part of a *world system*.

The interconnections are most evident among nations that do extensive trading with one another. The following Thinking Critically section explores implications of Mexico's *maquiladoras*.

globalization of capitalism capitalism (investing to make profits within a rational system) becoming the globe's dominant economic system

ThinkingCRITICALLY

When Globalization Comes Home: *Maquiladoras* South of the Border

Two hundred thousand Mexicans rush to Juarez each year, fleeing the hopelessness of the rural areas in pursuit of a better life. They have no running water or plumbing, but they didn't have any in the country either, and here they have the possibility of a job, a weekly check to buy food for the kids.

The pay is $100 for a 48-hour work week, about $2 an hour (Harris 2008).

This may not sound like much, but it is more than twice the minimum daily wage in Mexico.

Assembly-for-export plants, known as *maquiladoras,* dot the Mexican border (Wise and Cypher 2007). The North American Free Trade Agreement (NAFTA) allows U.S. companies to import materials to Mexico without paying tax and to then export the finished products into the United States, again without tax. It's a sweet deal: few taxes and $17 a day for workers starved for jobs.

That these workers live in shacks, with no running water or sewage disposal is not the employers' concern.

Nor is the pollution. The stinking air doesn't stay on the Mexican side of the border. Neither does the garbage. Heavy rains wash torrents of untreated sewage and industrial

A photo taken inside a maquiladora *in Matamoros, Mexico. The steering wheels are for U.S. auto makers.*

The home of a maquiladora *worker.*

wastes into the Rio Grande (Lacey 2007).

There is also the loss of jobs for U.S. workers. Six of the fifteen poorest cities in the United States are located along the sewage-infested Rio Grande. NAFTA didn't bring poverty to these cities. They were poor before this treaty, but residents resent the jobs they've seen move across the border (Thompson 2001).

What if the *maquiladora* workers organize and demand better pay? Farther south, even cheaper labor beckons. Guatemala and Honduras will gladly take the *maquiladoras*. Mexico has already lost many of its *maquiladora* jobs to places where people even more desperate will work for even less (Brown 2008).

Many Mexican politicians would say that this presentation is one-sided. "Sure there are problems," they would say, "but that is always how it is when a country industrializes. Don't you realize that the *maquiladoras* bring jobs to people who have no work? They also bring roads, telephone lines, and electricity to undeveloped areas." "In fact," said Vicente Fox, when he was the president of Mexico, "workers at the *maquiladoras* make more than the average salary in Mexico—and that's what we call fair wages" (Fraser 2001).

For Your Consideration

Let's apply our three theoretical perspectives. Conflict theorists say that capitalists try to weaken the bargaining power of workers by exploiting divisions among them. In what is known as the *split labor market,* capitalists pit one group of workers against another to lower the cost of labor. How do you think that *maquiladoras* fit this conflict perspective?

When functionalists analyze a situation, they identify its functions and dysfunctions. What functions and dysfunctions of *maquiladoras* do you see?

Do *maquiladoras* represent exploitation or opportunity? As symbolic interactionists point out, reality is a perspective based on one's experience. What multiple realities do you see here?

Culture of Poverty

The third explanation of global stratification is quite unlike the other two. Economist John Kenneth Galbraith (1979) claimed that the cultures of the Least Industrialized Nations hold them back. Building on the ideas of anthropologist Oscar Lewis (1966a, 1966b), Galbraith argued that some nations are crippled by a **culture of poverty,** a way of life that perpetuates poverty from one generation to the next. He explained it this way: Most of the world's poor people are farmers who live on little plots of land. They barely produce enough food to survive. Living so close to the edge of starvation, they have little room for risk—so they stick closely to tried-and-true, traditional ways. To experiment with new farming techniques is to court disaster, for failure would lead to hunger and death.

Their religion also encourages them to accept their situation, for it teaches fatalism: the belief that an individual's position in life is God's will. For example, in India, the Dalits are taught that they must have done very bad things in a previous life to suffer so. They are supposed to submit to their situation—and in the next life maybe they'll come back in a more desirable state.

culture of poverty the assumption that the values and behaviors of the poor make them fundamentally different from other people, that these factors are largely responsible for their poverty, and that parents perpetuate poverty across generations by passing these characteristics to their children

Evaluating the Theories

Most sociologists prefer colonialism and world system theory. To them, an explanation based on a culture of poverty places blame on the victim—the poor nations themselves. It points to characteristics of the poor nations, rather than to international political arrangements that benefit the Most Industrialized Nations at the expense of the poor nations. But even taken together, these theories yield only part of the picture. None of these theories, for example, would have led anyone to expect that after World War II, Japan would become an economic powerhouse: Japan had a religion that stressed fatalism, two of its major cities had been destroyed by atomic bombs, and it had been stripped of its colonies.

Each theory, then, yields but a partial explanation, and the grand theorist who will put the many pieces of this puzzle together has yet to appear.

neocolonialism the economic and political dominance of the Least Industrialized Nations by the Most Industrialized Nations

Maintaining Global Stratification

Regardless of how the world's nations became stratified, why do the same countries remain rich year after year, while the rest stay poor? Let's look at two explanations of how global stratification is maintained.

Neocolonialism

Sociologist Michael Harrington (1977) argued that when colonialism fell out of style it was replaced by **neocolonialism.** When World War II changed public sentiment about sending soldiers and colonists to exploit weaker countries, the Most Industrialized Nations turned to the international markets as a way of controlling the Least Industrialized Nations. By selling them goods on credit—especially weapons that their elite desire so they can keep themselves in power—the Most Industrialized Nations entrap the poor nations with a circle of debt.

As many of us learn the hard way, owing a large debt and falling behind on payments puts us at the mercy of our creditors. So it is with neocolonialism. The *policy* of selling weapons and other manufactured goods to the Least Industrialized Nations on credit turns those countries into eternal debtors. The capital they need to develop their own industries goes instead as payments toward the debt, which becomes bloated with mounting interest.

The maintenance of global stratification has many faces, including these. This woman in Georgia cries at her destroyed apartment after Russia reasserted its control over South Ossetia in 2008.

Keeping these nations in debt forces them to submit to trading terms dictated by the neo-colonialists (Carrington 1993; S. Smith 2001).

Relevance Today.   Neocolonialism might seem remote from our own lives, but its heritage affects us directly. Consider the oil-rich Middle Eastern countries, our two wars in the Persian Gulf, and the terrorism that emanates from this region (*Strategic Energy Policy* 2001; Mouawad 2007). Although this is an area of ancient civilizations, the countries themselves are recent. Great Britain created Saudi Arabia, drawing its boundaries and even naming the country after the man (Ibn Saud) whom British officials picked to lead it. This created a debt for the Saudi family, which for decades it repaid by providing low-cost oil, which the Most Industrialized Nations need to maintain their way of life. When other nations pumped less oil—no matter the cause, whether revolution or an attempt to raise prices—the Saudis helped keep prices low by making up the shortfall. In return, the United States (and other nations) overlooked the human rights violations of the Saudi royal family, keeping them in power by selling them the latest weapons. This mutually sycophantic arrangement continues, but fluctuations in oil supplies have disrupted its effectiveness.

Multinational Corporations

Multinational corporations, companies that operate across many national boundaries, also help to maintain the global dominance of the Most Industrialized Nations. In some cases, multinational corporations exploit the Least Industrialized Nations directly. A prime example is the United Fruit Company, which used to control national and local politics in Central America. This U.S. corporation ran Central American nations as fiefdoms for the company's own profit while the U.S. Marines waited in the wings. An occasional invasion to put down dissidents reminded regional politicians of the military power that backed U.S. corporations.

Most commonly, however, it is simply by doing business that multinational corporations help to maintain international stratification. A single multinational corporation may manage mining operations in several countries, manufacture goods in others, and market its products around the globe. No matter where the profits are made, or where they are reinvested, the primary beneficiaries are the Most Industrialized Nations, especially the one in which the multinational corporation has its world headquarters.

Buying Political Stability.   In their pursuit of profits, the multinational corporations need cooperative power elites in the Least Industrialized Nations (Sklair 2001; Wise and Cypher 2007). In return for funneling money to the elites and selling them modern weapons, the corporations get a "favorable business climate"—that is, low taxes and cheap labor. The corporations politely call the money they pay to the elites "subsidies" and "offsets"—which are much prettier to the ear than "bribes." Able also to siphon money from their country's tax system and government spending, these elites live a sophisticated upper-class life in the major cities of their home country. Although most of the citizens of these countries live a hard-scrabble life, the elites are able to send their children to prestigious Western universities, such as Oxford, the Sorbonne, and Harvard.

You can see how this cozy arrangement helps to maintain global stratification. The significance of these payoffs is not so much the genteel lifestyles that they allow the elites to maintain, but the translation of the payoffs into power. They allow the elites to purchase high-tech weapons with which they oppress their people and preserve their positions of dominance. The result is a political stability that keeps alive the diabolical partnership between the multinational corporations and the national elites.

Unanticipating Consequences.   This, however, is not the full story. An unintentional by-product of the multinationals' global search for cheap resources and labor is to modify global stratification. When these corporations move manufacturing from the Most Industrialized Nations to the Least Industrialized Nations, they not only exploit cheap labor but they also bring jobs and money to these nations. Although workers in the Least Industrialized Nations are paid a pittance, it is more than they can earn elsewhere. With new factories come opportunities to develop skills and accumulate a capital base from which local elites can launch their own factories.

multinational corporations
companies that operate across
national boundaries; also called
transnational corporations

The Pacific Rim nations provide a remarkable example. In return for providing the "favorable business climate" just mentioned, multinational corporations invested billions of dollars in the "Asian tigers" (Hong Kong, Singapore, South Korea, and Taiwan). These nations have developed such a strong capital base that they have begun to rival the older capitalist countries. This has also made them subject to capitalism's "boom and bust" cycles, and workers and investors in these nations, including those in the *maquiladoras* that you just read about, are having their dreams smashed as capitalism suffers its current downturn.

Technology and Global Domination

The race between the Most and Least Industrialized Nations to develop and apply the new technologies might seem like a race between a marathon runner and someone with a broken leg. Can the outcome be in doubt? As the multinational corporations amass profits, they are able to invest huge sums in the latest technology while the Least Industrialized Nations are struggling to put scraps on the table. So it would appear, but the race is not this simple. Although the Most Industrialized Nations have a seemingly insurmountable head start, some of the other nations are shortening the distance between themselves and the front-runners. With cheap labor making their manufactured goods inexpensive, China and India are exporting goods on a massive scale. They are using the capital from these exports to adopt high technology to modernize their infrastructure (transportation, communication, electrical, and banking systems), with the goal of advancing their industry. Although global domination remains in the hands of the West, it could be on the verge of a major shift from West to East.

Unintended Public Relations.   Bono and others have used the media in a campaign to get G8 to forgive the debts of some of the poorest of the world's nations. (G8 is the Group of Eight, an association of wealthy and powerful nations—Canada, France, Germany, Italy, Japan, Russia, the United Kingdom, and the United States—that meet annually to discuss global issues.) Their efforts made a good story, which the mass media loved to promote. G8, however, knows how to milk the media, too. To cancel the debts of poor nations amidst television reporters and global drum rolls projects an image of good-hearted capitalists having mercy on the poor. Although G8 had written these debts off as uncollectible in the first place, the publicity that accompanied their pronouncements helps to soften opposition to the global dominance of capitalism.

Strains in the Global System

It is never easy to maintain global stratification. At the very least, a continuous stream of unanticipated events forces the elite to stay on their toes, and at times huge currents of history threaten to sweep them aside. As secure as a system of stratification can seem, it always contains unresolved issues. Contradictions can be covered up for a while, but inevitably they rear up. Some are just little dogs nipping at the heels of the world's elites, bringing issues that can be resolved with a few tanks or bombs—or, better, with a scowl and the threat to bomb some small nation into submission. Other issues are of a broader nature, part of huge historical shifts. Baring their teeth, they snarlingly demand change, even the rearrangement of global power.

Such events are rare, but when they come they bring cataclysmic disruptions. We are now living through such a time. The far-reaching economic-political changes in Russia and China have been accompanied by huge cracks in a creaking global banking system. Caught unaware, the global powers have desperately pumped trillions of dollars into their economic-political systems. As curious as we are about the outcome and as much as our lives are affected, we don't know the end point of this current strain in the global system and the power elites' desperate attempts to patch up the most glaring inconsistencies in their global domination. As this process of realignment continues, however, it is likely to sweep all of us into its unwelcome net.

SUMMARY *and* REVIEW

Systems of Social Stratification

What is social stratification?

Social stratification refers to a hierarchy of privilege based on property, power, and prestige. Every society stratifies its members, and in every society men as a group are placed above women as a group. Pp. 230–231.

What are four major systems of social stratification?

Four major stratification systems are slavery, caste, estate, and class. The essential characteristic of **slavery** is that some people own other people. Initially, slavery was based not on race but on debt, punishment for crime, or defeat in battle. Slavery could be temporary or permanent and was not necessarily passed on to one's children. North American slavery was gradually buttressed by a racist **ideology.** In a **caste system,** status is determined by birth and is lifelong. The **estate system** of feudal Europe consisted of the nobility, clergy, and peasants (serfs). A **class system** is much more open than these other systems, for it is based primarily on money or material possessions. Industrialization encourages the formation of class systems. Gender cuts across all forms of social stratification. Pp. 231–237.

What Determines Social Class?

Karl Marx argued that a single factor determines social class: If you own the means of production, you belong to the **bourgeoisie;** if you do not, you are one of the **proletariat.** Max Weber argued that three elements determine social class: *property, power,* and *prestige.* Pp. 237–239.

Why Is Social Stratification Universal?

To explain why stratification is universal, functionalists Kingsley Davis and Wilbert Moore argued that to attract the most capable people to fill its important positions, society must offer them greater rewards. Melvin Tumin said that if this view were correct, society would be a **meritocracy,** with positions awarded on the basis of merit. Gaetano Mosca argued that stratification is inevitable because every society must have leadership, which by definition means inequality. Conflict theorists argue that stratification is the outcome of an elite emerging as groups struggle for limited resources. Gerhard Lenski suggested a synthesis between the functionalist and conflict perspectives. Pp. 239–242.

How Do Elites Maintain Stratification?

To maintain social stratification within a nation, the ruling class adopts an ideology that justifies its current arrangements. It also controls information and uses technology. When all else fails, it turns to brute force. Pp. 242–243.

Comparative Social Stratification

What are key characteristics of stratification systems in other nations?

The most striking features of the British class system are speech and education. In Britain, accent reveals social class, and almost all of the elite attend "public" schools (the equivalent of U.S. private schools). In the former Soviet Union, communism was supposed to abolish class distinctions. Instead, it merely ushered in a different set of classes. Pp. 243–245.

Global Stratification: Three Worlds

How are the world's nations stratified?

The model presented here divides the world's nations into three groups: the Most Industrialized, the Industrializing, and the Least Industrialized. This layering represents relative property, power, and prestige. The oil-rich nations are an exception. Pp. 245–252.

How Did the World's Nations Become Stratified?

The main theories that seek to account for global stratification are **colonialism, world system theory,** and the **culture of poverty.** Pp. 252–255.

Maintaining Global Stratification

How do elites maintain global stratification?

There are two basic explanations for why the world's countries remain stratified. **Neocolonialism** is the ongoing dominance of the Least Industrialized Nations by the Most Industrialized Nations. The second explanation points to the influence of **multinational corporations.** The new technology gives further advantage to the Most Industrialized Nations. Pp. 255–257.

Strains in the Global System

What strains are showing up in global stratification?

All stratification systems have contradictions that threaten to erupt, forcing the system to change. Currently, capitalism is in crisis, and we seem to be experiencing a global shift in economic (and, ultimately political) power from the West to the East. P. 257.

THINKING CRITICALLY *ABOUT* Chapter 9

1. How do slavery, caste, estate, and class systems of social stratification differ?

2. Why is social stratification universal?

3. How do elites maintain stratification (keep themselves in power)?

4. What shifts in global stratification seem to be taking place? Why?

ADDITIONAL RESOURCES

What can you find in MySocLab?   mysoclab   www.mysoclab.com

- Complete Ebook
- Practice Tests and Video and Audio activities
- Mapping and Data Analysis exercises

- Sociology in the News
- Classic Readings in Sociology
- Research and Writing advice

Where Can I Read More on This Topic?

Suggested readings for this chapter are listed at the back of this book.

10

Social Class in the United States

Florida

Ah, New Orleans, that fabled city on the Mississippi Delta. Images from its rich past floated through my head—pirates, treasure, intrigue. Memories from a pleasant vacation stirred my thoughts—the exotic French Quarter with its enticing aroma of Creole food and sounds of earthy jazz drifting through the air.

I was startled by a sight so out of step with the misery and despair that I stopped and stared.

The shelter for the homeless, however, forced me back to an unwelcome reality. The shelter was like those I had visited in the North, West, and East—only dirtier. The dirt, in fact, was the worst that I had encountered during my research, and this shelter was the only one to insist on payment in exchange for sleeping in one of its filthy beds.

The men looked the same—disheveled and haggard, wearing that unmistakable expression of despair—just like the homeless anywhere in the country. Except for the accent, you wouldn't know what region you were in. Poverty wears the same tired face wherever you are, I realized. The accent may differ, but the look remains the same.

I had grown used to the sights and smells of abject poverty. Those no longer surprised me. But after my fitful sleep with the homeless, I saw something that did. Just a block or so from the shelter, I was startled by a sight so out of step with the misery and despair I had just experienced that I stopped and stared.

Indignation swelled within me. Confronting me were life-size, full-color photos mounted on the transparent Plexiglas shelter of a bus stop. Staring back at me were images of finely dressed men and women proudly strutting about as they modeled elegant suits, dresses, diamonds, and furs.

A wave of disgust swept over me. "Something is cockeyed in this society," I thought, as my mind refused to stop juxtaposing these images of extravagance with the suffering I had just witnessed.

social class according to Weber, a large group of people who rank close to one another in wealth, prestige, and power; according to Marx, one of two groups: capitalists who own the means of production or workers who sell their labor

property material possessions: animals, bank accounts, bonds, buildings, businesses, cars, furniture, land, and stocks

wealth the total value of everything someone owns, minus the debts

income money received, usually from a job, business, or assets

The disjunction that I felt in New Orleans was triggered by the ads, but it was not the first time that I had experienced this sensation. Whenever my research abruptly transported me from the world of the homeless to one of another social class, I experienced a sense of disjointed unreality. Each social class has its own way of being, and because these fundamental orientations to the world contrast so sharply, the classes do not mix well.

What Is Social Class?

If you ask most Americans about their country's social class system, you are likely to get a blank look. If you press the matter, you are likely to get an answer like this: "There are the poor and the rich—and then there are you and I, neither poor nor rich." This is just about as far as most Americans' consciousness of social class goes. Let's try to flesh out this idea.

Our task is made somewhat difficult because sociologists have no clear-cut, agreed-on definition of social class (Lareau and Conley 2008). As was noted in the last chapter, conflict sociologists (of the Marxist orientation) see only two social classes: those who own the means of production and those who do not. The problem with this view, say most sociologists, is that it lumps too many people together. Teenage "order takers" at McDonald's who work for $15,000 a year are lumped together with that company's executives who make $500,000 a year—because they both are workers at McDonald's, not owners.

Most sociologists agree with Weber that there is more to social class than just a person's relationship to the means of production. Consequently, most sociologists use the components Weber identified and define **social class** as a large group of people who rank closely to one another in property, power, and prestige. These three elements separate people into different lifestyles, give them different chances in life, and provide them with distinct ways of looking at the self and the world.

Let's look at how sociologists measure these three components of social class.

Property

Property comes in many forms, such as buildings, land, animals, machinery, cars, stocks, bonds, businesses, furniture, jewelry, and bank accounts. When you add up the value of someone's property and subtract that person's debts, you have what sociologists call **wealth.** This term can be misleading, as some of us have little wealth—especially most college students. Nevertheless, if your net total comes to $10, then that is your wealth. (Obviously, wealth as a sociological term does not mean wealthy.)

Distinguishing Between Wealth and Income. Wealth and income are sometimes confused, but they are not the same. Where *wealth* is a person's net worth, **income** is a flow of money. Income has many sources: The most common is a business or wages, but other sources are rent, interest, or royalties, even alimony, an allowance, or gambling. Some people have much wealth and little income. For example, a farmer may own much land (a form of wealth), but bad weather, combined with the high cost of fertilizers and machinery, can cause the income to dry up. Others have much income and little wealth. An executive with a $250,000 annual income may be debt-ridden. Below the surface prosperity—the exotic vacations, country club membership, private schools for the children, sports cars, and an elegant home—the credit cards may be maxed out, the sports cars in danger of being repossessed, and the mortgage payments "past due." Typically, however, wealth and income go together.

A mere one-half percent of Americans owns over a quarter of the entire nation's wealth. Very few minorities are numbered among this 0.5 percent. An exception is Oprah Winfrey, who has had an ultra-successful career in entertainment and investing. Worth $1.3 billion, she is the 215th richest person in the United States. Winfrey, who has given millions of dollars to help minority children, is shown here as she talks with Tom Cruise.

Distribution of Property. Who owns the property in the United States? One answer, of course, is "everyone." Although this statement has some merit, it overlooks how the nation's property is divided among "everyone."

Overall, Americans are worth a hefty sum, about $44 trillion (*Statistical Abstract* 2009:Table 701). This includes all real estate, stocks, bonds, and business assets in the entire country. Figure 10.1 shows how highly concentrated this wealth is. Most wealth, 70 percent, is owned by only *10 percent* of the nation's families. As you can also see from this figure, 1 percent of Americans own one-third of all the U.S. assets.

Distribution of Income. How is income distributed in the United States? Economist Paul Samuelson (Samuelson and Nordhaus 2005) put it this way: "If we made an income pyramid out of a child's blocks, with each layer portraying $500 of income, the peak would be far higher than Mount Everest, but most people would be within a few feet of the ground."

Actually, if each block were 1½-inches tall, the typical American would be just *10 feet off the ground,* for the average per capita income in the United States is about $39,000 per year. (This average income includes every American, even children.) The typical family climbs a little higher, for most families have more than one worker, and together they average about $58,000 a year. Compared with the few families who are on the mountain's peak, the average U.S. family would find itself only 15 feet off the ground (*Statistical Abstract* 2009:Tables 659, 674). Figure 10.2 portrays these differences.

The fact that some Americans enjoy the peaks of Mount Everest while most—despite their efforts—make it only 10 to 15 feet up the slope presents a striking image of income inequality in the United States. Another picture emerges if we divide the U.S. population into five equal groups and rank them from highest to lowest income. As Figure 10.3 on the next page shows, the top 20 percent of the population receive *half* (50.4 percent) of all income in the United States. In contrast, the bottom 20 percent of Americans receive only 3.4 percent of the nation's income.

Two features of Figure 10.3 are outstanding. First, notice how little change there has been in the distribution of income through the years. Second, look at how income inequality decreased from 1935 to 1970. *Since 1970, the richest 20 percent of U.S. families have grown richer, while the poorest 20 percent have grown poorer.* Despite numerous government

FIGURE 10.2
Distribution of the Income of Americans

Some U.S. families have incomes that exceed the height of Mt. Everest, 29,028 feet

Average U.S. family income $58,000 or 15 feet

Average U.S. individual income $39,000 or 10 feet

If a 1½-inch child's block equals $500 of income, the average individual's annual income of $39,000 would represent a height of 10 feet, and the average family's annual income of $58,000 would represent a height of 15 feet. The income of some families, in contrast, would represent a height greater than that of Mt. Everest.

Source: By the author.

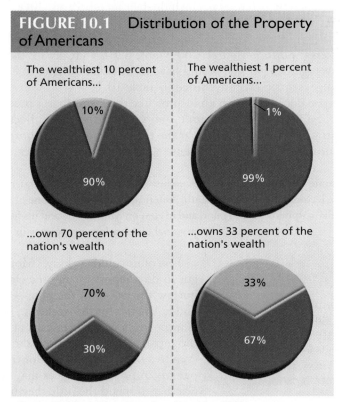

FIGURE 10.1 Distribution of the Property of Americans

The wealthiest 10 percent of Americans...

10%

90%

...own 70 percent of the nation's wealth

70%

30%

The wealthiest 1 percent of Americans...

1%

99%

...owns 33 percent of the nation's wealth

33%

67%

Source: By the author. Based on Beeghley 2008.

FIGURE 10.3 The More Things Change, the More They Stay the Same: Dividing the Nation's Income

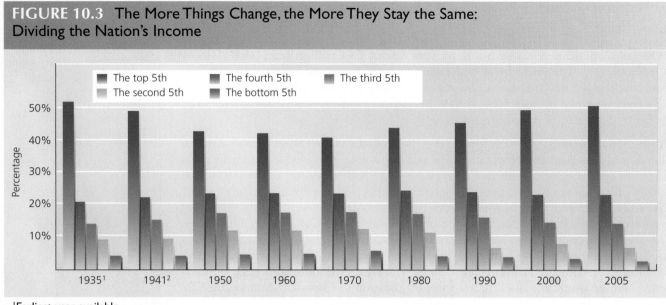

¹Earliest year available.
²No data for 1940.
Source: By the author. Based on *Statistical Abstract* 1960:Table 417; 1970:Table 489; 2009:Table 675.

antipoverty programs, the poorest 20 percent of Americans receive *less* of the nation's income today than they did decades ago. The richest 20 percent, in contrast, are receiving more, almost as much as they did in 1935.

The chief executive officers (CEOs) of the nation's largest corporations are especially affluent. The *Wall Street Journal* surveyed the 200 U.S. companies with the largest revenue to find out what they paid their CEOs ("*The Wall Street Journal* Survey. . ." 2009). Their median compensation (including salaries, bonuses, and stock options) came to $7,600,000 a year. (*Median* means that half received more than this amount, and half less.)

The CEOs' income—which does *not* include their income from interest, dividends, or rents, or the value of company-paid limousines and chauffeurs, airplanes and pilots, and private boxes at the symphony and sporting events—is *200 times* higher than the average pay of U.S. workers (*Statistical Abstract* 2009:Table 626). To really see the disparity, consider this: The average U.S. worker would have to work *2,800 years* to earn the amount received by the highest-paid executive listed in Table 10.1.

Imagine how you could live with an income like this. And that is precisely the point. Beyond these cold numbers lies a dynamic reality that profoundly affects people's lives. The difference in wealth between those at the top and those at the bottom of the U.S. class structure means that people experience vastly different lifestyles. For example,

a colleague of mine who was teaching at an exclusive Eastern university piqued his students' curiosity when he lectured on poverty in Latin America. That weekend, one of the students borrowed his parents' corporate jet and pilot, and in class on Monday, he and his friends related their personal observations on poverty in Latin America.

Few of us could ever say, "Mom and Dad, I've got to do a report for my soc class, so I need to borrow the jet—and the pilot—to run down to South America for the weekend." What a lifestyle! Contrast this with Americans at the low end of the income ladder who lack the funds to travel even to a neighboring town for the weekend. For parents in poverty, choices may revolve around whether to spend the little they have at the laundromat or on milk for the baby. The elderly might

TABLE 10.1 The 5 Highest-Paid CEOs

Executive	Company	Compensation
1. Sanjay Jha	Motorola	$104 million
2. Ray Irani	Occidental Petroleum	$50 million
3. Robert Iger	Disney	$50 million
4. Vikram Pandit	Citigroup	$38 million
5. Louis Camilleri	Philip Morris	$36 million

Note: Compensation includes salary, bonuses, and stock options.
Source: "*The Wall Street Journal* Survey. . ." 2009.

have to choose between purchasing the medicines they need or buying food. In short, divisions of wealth represent not "mere" numbers, but choices that make vital differences in people's lives. Let's explore this topic in the Down-to-Earth Sociology box below.

Down-to-Earth Sociology
How the Super-Rich Live

It's good to see how other people live. It gives us a different perspective on life. Let's take a glimpse at the life of John Castle (his real name). After earning a degree in physics at MIT and an MBA at Harvard, John went into banking and securities, where he made more than $100 million (Lublin 1999).

Wanting to be connected to someone famous, John bought President John F. Kennedy's "Winter White House," an oceanfront estate in Palm Beach, Florida. John spent $11 million to remodel the 13,000-square-foot house so that it would be more to his liking. Among those changes: adding bathrooms numbers 14 and 15. He likes to show off John F. Kennedy's bed and also the dresser that has the drawer labeled "black underwear," carefully hand-lettered by Rose Kennedy.

At his beachfront estate, John gives what he calls "refined feasts" to the glitterati ("On History . . ." 1999). If he gets tired of such activities—or weary of swimming in the Olympic-size pool where JFK swam the weekend before his assassination—John entertains himself by riding one of his thoroughbred horses at his nearby 10-acre ranch. If this fails to ease his boredom, he can relax aboard his custom-built 42-foot Hinckley yacht.

The yacht is a real source of diversion. John once boarded it for an around-the-world trip. He didn't stay on board, though—just joined the cruise from time to time. A captain and crew kept the vessel on course, and whenever John felt like it he would fly in and stay a few days. Then he would fly back to the States to direct his business. He did this about a dozen times, flying perhaps 150,000 miles. An interesting way to go around the world.

How much does a custom-built Hinckley yacht cost? John can't tell you. As he says, "I don't want to know what anything costs. When you've got enough money, price doesn't make a difference. That's part of the freedom of being rich."

Right. And for John, being rich also means paying $1,000,000 to charter a private jet to fly Spot, his Appaloosa horse, back and forth to the vet. John didn't want Spot to have to endure a long trailer ride. Oh, and of course, there was the cost of Spot's medical treatment, another $500,000.

Other wealthy people spend extravagantly, too. Lee Tachman threw a four-day party for three friends. They

How do the super-rich live? This photo helps give you an idea of how different their lifestyles are from most of ours. Shown here is Wayne Huizenga, who is featured in this box, with one of his vintage automobiles.

had massages, ate well, took rides in a helicopter, a fighter jet, Ferraris, and Lamborghinis, and did a little paintballing—all for the bargain price of $50,000. At the 1 Oak Lounge in New York City, some customers pay $35,000 for a bottle of champagne (Haughney and Konigsberg 2008). Of course, it is a large bottle.

Parties are fun, but what if you want privacy? You can buy that, too. Wayne Huizenga, the founder of Blockbuster, who sold a half ownership in the Miami Dolphins for $550 million ("Builder Stephen . . ." 2008), bought a 2,000-acre country club, complete with an 18-hole golf course, a 55,000-square-foot-clubhouse, and 68 slips for visiting vessels. The club is so exclusive that its only members are Wayne and his wife (Fabrikant 2005).

Charles Simonyi has even outdone having your own country club. He bought a $25 million ticket for a rocket ride to the International Space Station. Simonyi liked the experience so much that he bought a second ticket (Leo 2008). No frequent flyer miles included. But at the rate prices are increasing, $50 million isn't worth what it used to be anyway.

For Your Consideration
What effects has social class had on your life? (Go beyond possessions to values, orientations, and outlooks on life.) How do you think you would see the world differently if you were John Castle, Lee Tachman, Charles Simonyi, or Mrs. Wayne Huizenga?

Power

Like many people, you may have said to yourself, "Sure, I can vote, but the big decisions are always made despite what I might think. Certainly *I* don't make the decision to send soldiers to Afghanistan or Iraq. *I* don't launch missiles into Iraq or Pakistan. *I* don't decide to raise taxes, lower interest rates, or spend $700 billion to bail out Wall Street fools and felons."

And then another part of you may say, "But I do participate in these decisions through my representatives in Congress, and by voting for president." True enough—as far as it goes. The trouble is, it just doesn't go far enough. Such views of being a participant in the nation's "big" decisions are a playback of the ideology we learn at an early age—an ideology that Marx said is promoted by the elites to both legitimate and perpetuate their power. Sociologists Daniel Hellinger and Dennis Judd (1991) call this the "democratic facade" that conceals the real source of power in the United States.

Back in the 1950s, sociologist C. Wright Mills (1956) was criticized for insisting that **power**—the ability to get your way despite resistance—was concentrated in the hands of a few, for his analysis contradicted the dominant ideology of equality. As was discussed in earlier chapters, Mills coined the term **power elite** to refer to those who make the big decisions in U.S. society.

Mills and others have stressed how wealth and power coalesce in a group of like-minded individuals who share ideologies, values, and world views. These individuals belong to the same private clubs, vacation at the same exclusive resorts, and even hire the same bands for their daughters' debutante balls. Their shared backgrounds and vested interests reinforce their view of both the world and their special place in it (Domhoff 1999a, 2006). This elite wields extraordinary power in U.S. society, so much so that *most* U.S. presidents have come from this group—millionaire white men from families with "old money" (Baltzell and Schneiderman 1988).

Continuing in the tradition of Mills, sociologist William Domhoff (1990, 2006) argues that this group is so powerful that the U.S. government makes no major decision without its approval. He analyzed how this group works behind the scenes with elected officials to determine both foreign and domestic policy—from setting Social Security taxes to imposing trade tariffs. Although Domhoff's conclusions are controversial—and alarming—they certainly follow logically from the principle that wealth brings power, and extreme wealth brings extreme power.

Prestige

Occupations and Prestige.   What are you thinking about doing after college? Chances are, you don't have the option of lolling under palm trees at the beach. Almost all of us have to choose an occupation and go to work. Look at Table 10.2 to see how the career you are considering stacks up in terms of **prestige** (respect or regard). Because we are moving toward a global society, this table also shows how the rankings given by Americans compare with those of the residents of sixty other countries.

Why do people give more prestige to some jobs than to others? If you look at Table 10.2, you will notice that the jobs at the top share four features:

1. They pay more.
2. They require more education.
3. They entail more abstract thought.
4. They offer greater autonomy (independence, or self-direction).

If you look at the bottom of the list, you can see that people give less prestige to jobs with the opposite characteristics: These jobs are low-paying, require less preparation or education, involve more physical labor, and are closely supervised. In short, the professions and the white-collar jobs are at the top of the list, the blue-collar jobs at the bottom.

One of the more interesting aspects of these rankings is how consistent they are across countries and over time. For example, people in every country rank college professors higher than nurses, nurses higher than social workers, and social workers

power the ability to get your way, even over the resistance of others

power elite C. Wright Mills' term for the top people in U.S. corporations, military, and politics who make the nation's major decisions

prestige respect or regard

higher than janitors. Similarly, the occupations that were ranked high 25 years ago still rank high today—and likely will rank high in the years to come.

Displaying Prestige.   People want others to acknowledge their prestige. In times past, in some countries only the emperor and his family could wear purple—for it was the royal color. In France, only the nobility could wear lace. In England, no one could sit while the king was on his throne. Some kings and queens required that subjects walk backward as they left the room—so that they would not "turn their back" on the "royal presence."

Concern with displaying prestige has not let up. Military manuals specify who must salute whom. The U.S. president enters a room only after everyone else attending the function is present (to show that the president isn't waiting for others). Everyone must also be standing when the president enters. In the courtroom, bailiffs, sometimes armed, make certain that everyone stands when the judge enters.

Do you try to display prestige? Think about your clothing. How much more are you willing to pay for clothing that bears some hot "designer" label? Purses, shoes, jeans, and shirts—many of us pay more if they have some little symbol than if they don't. As we wear them proudly, aren't we actually proclaiming, "See, I had the money to buy this particular item!"? For many of us, prestige is a primary factor in deciding which college to attend. Everyone knows how the prestige of a generic sheepskin from Regional State College compares with a degree from Harvard, Princeton, Yale, or Stanford.

Status symbols vary with social class. Clearly, only the wealthy can afford certain items, such as yachts and huge estates—or the $35,000 bottle of champagne mentioned in the box on page 265. But beyond affordability lies a class-based preference in status symbols. For example, people who are striving to be upwardly mobile flaunt labels on their clothing or conspicuously carry shopping bags from prestigious stores to show that they have "arrived." The wealthy, who regard the symbols of the "common" classes as cheap and showy, flaunt their own status symbols, such as $50,000 Rolex watches and $40,000 diamond earrings. Like the other classes, they, too, try to outdo one another. They boast about who has the longest yacht or casually mention that they have a helicopter fly them to their golf game (Fabrikant 2005)—or that they stayed at the $30,000-a-night room at the Four Seasons in New York City (Feuer 2008).

TABLE 10.2   Occupational Prestige: How the United States Compares with 60 Countries

Occupation	United States	Average of 60 Countries
Physician	86	78
Supreme Court judge	85	82
College president	81	86
Astronaut	80	80
Lawyer	75	73
College professor	74	78
Airline pilot	73	66
Architect	73	72
Biologist	73	69
Dentist	72	70
Civil engineer	69	70
Clergy	69	60
Psychologist	69	66
Pharmacist	68	64
High school teacher	66	64
Registered nurse	66	54
Professional athlete	65	48
Electrical engineer	64	65
Author	63	62
Banker	63	67
Veterinarian	62	61
Police officer	61	40
Sociologist	61	67
Journalist	60	55
Classical musician	59	56
Actor or actress	58	52
Chiropractor	57	62
Athletic coach	53	50
Social worker	52	56
Electrician	51	44
Undertaker	49	34
Jazz musician	48	38
Real estate agent	48	49
Mail carrier	47	33
Secretary	46	53
Plumber	45	34
Carpenter	43	37
Farmer	40	47
Barber	36	30
Store sales clerk	36	34
Truck driver	30	33
Cab driver	28	28
Garbage collector	28	13
Waiter or waitress	28	23
Bartender	25	23
Lives on public aid	25	16
Bill collector	24	27
Factory worker	24	29
Janitor	22	21
Shoe shiner	17	12
Street sweeper	11	13

Note. For five occupations not located in the 1994 source, the 1991 ratings were used: Supreme Court judge, astronaut, athletic coach, lives on public aid, and street sweeper.

Sources: Treiman 1977, Appendices A and D; Nakao and Treas 1991; 1994: Appendix D.

How do you set yourself apart in a country so rich that of its 4.6 million people 79,000 are millionaires? Saeed Khouri (on the right), at an auction in Abu Dhabi paid $14 million for the license plate "1." His cousin was not as fortunate. His $9 million was enough to buy only "5."

Status Inconsistency

Ordinarily, we have a similar rank on all three dimensions of social class—property, power, and prestige. The homeless men in the opening vignette are an example of these three dimensions lined up. Such people are **status consistent.** Some people, however, have a mixture of high and low ranks. This condition, called **status inconsistency,** leads to some interesting situations.

Sociologist Gerhard Lenski (1954, 1966) analyzed how people try to maximize their **status,** their position in a social group. Individuals who rank high on one dimension of social class but lower on others want people to judge them on the basis of their highest status. Others, however, who are trying to maximize their own position, may respond to status-inconsistent individuals according to their lowest ranking.

A classic study of status inconsistency was done by sociologist Ray Gold (1952). After apartment-house janitors unionized in Chicago, they made more money than some of the tenants whose garbage they carried out. Tenants became upset when they saw their janitors driving more expensive cars than they did. Some attempted to "put the janitor in his place" by making "snotty" remarks to him. For their part, the janitors took delight in knowing "dirty" secrets about the tenants, gleaned from their garbage.

Individuals with status inconsistency, then, are likely to confront one frustrating situation after another (Heames et al. 2006). They claim the higher status, but are handed the lower one. The significance of this condition, said Lenski (1954), is that such people tend to be more politically radical. An example is college professors. Their prestige is very high, as we saw in Table 10.2, but their incomes are relatively low. Hardly anyone in U.S. society is more educated, and yet college professors don't even come close to the top of the income pyramid. In line with Lenski's prediction, the politics of most college professors are left of center. This hypothesis may also hold true among academic departments; that is, the higher a department's average pay, the less radical are the members' politics. Teachers in departments of business and medicine, for example, are among the most highly paid in the university—and they also are the most politically conservative.

Instant wealth, the topic of the Down-to-Earth Sociology box on the next page, provides an interesting case of status inconsistency.

status consistency ranking high or low on all three dimensions of social class

status inconsistency ranking high on some dimensions of social class and low on others; also called status discrepancy

status the position that someone occupies in a social group

Down-to-Earth Sociology
The Big Win: Life After the Lottery

Status inconsistency is common for lottery winners, whose new wealth is vastly greater than their education and occupational prestige. Shown here are John and Sandy Jarrell of Chicago, after they learned that they won $22 million. How do you think this will affect their lives?

" "If I just win the lottery, life will be good. These problems I've got, they'll be gone. I can just see myself now."

So goes the dream. And many Americans shell out megabucks every week, with the glimmering hope that "Maybe this week, I'll hit it big."

Most are lucky to get $20, or maybe just win another scratch-off ticket.

But there are the big hits. What happens to these winners? Are their lives all wine, roses, and chocolate afterward?

We don't have any systematic studies of the big winners, so I can't tell you what life is like for the average winner. But several themes are apparent from reporters' interviews.

The most common consequence of hitting it big is that life becomes topsy-turvy (Bernstein 2007). All of us are rooted somewhere. We have connections with others that provide the basis for our orientations to life and how we feel about the world. Sudden wealth can rip these moorings apart, and the resulting *status inconsistency* can lead to a condition sociologists call **anomie.**

First comes the shock. As Mary Sanderson, a telephone operator in Dover, New Hampshire, who won $66 million, said, "I was afraid to believe it was real, and afraid to believe it wasn't." Mary says that she never slept worse than her first night as a multimillionaire. "I spent the whole time crying—and throwing up" (Tresniowski 1999).

Reporters and TV camera operators appear on your doorstep. "What are you going to do with all that money?" they demand. You haven't the slightest idea, but in a daze you mumble something.

Then come the calls. Some are welcome. Your Mom and Dad call to congratulate you. But long-forgotten friends and distant relatives suddenly remember how close they really are to you—and strangely enough, they all have emergencies that your money can solve. You even get calls from strangers who have ailing mothers, terminally ill kids, sick dogs . . .

You have to unplug the phone and get an unlisted number.

You might be flooded with marriage proposals. You certainly didn't become more attractive or sexy overnight—or did you? Maybe money makes people sexy.

You can no longer trust people. You don't know what their real motives are. Before, no one could be after your money because you didn't have any. You may even fear kidnappers. Before, this wasn't a problem—unless some kidnapper wanted the ransom of a seven-year-old car.

The normal becomes abnormal. Even picking out a wedding gift is a problem. If you give the usual toaster, everyone will think you're stingy. But should you write a check for $25,000? If you do, you'll be invited to every wedding in town—and everyone will expect the same.

Here is what happened to some lottery winners:

When Alex Snelius of Chicago won $67 million, he lost his friends (Bernstein 2007). For some reason, they thought he should give them a large annual gift. As Alex's daughter says about Alex's (former) best friend, "He was like, 'Put me on your payroll.'"

As a tip, a customer gave a lottery ticket to Tonda Dickerson, a waitress at the Waffle House in Grand Bay, Alabama. She won $10 million. (Yes, just like the Nicholas Cage movie, *It Could Happen to You.*) Her co-workers sued her, saying that they had always agreed to split such winnings ("House Divided" 1999).

Then there is Michael Klinebiel of Rahway, New Jersey. When he won $2 million, his mother, Phyllis, said that half of it was hers, that she and her son had pooled $20 a month for years to play the lottery. He said they had done this—but he had bought the winning ticket on his own. Phyllis sued her son ("Sticky Ticket" 1998).

When Mack Metcalf, a forklift operator in Corbin, Kentucky, hit the jackpot for $34 million, he fulfilled a dream: He built and moved into a replica of George Washington's Mount Vernon home. Then his life fell apart—his former wife sued him, his current wife divorced him, and his new girlfriend got $500,000 while he was drunk. Within three years of his "good" fortune, Metcalf had drunk himself to death (Dao 2005).

Winners who avoid *anomie* seem to be people who don't make sudden changes in their lifestyle or their behavior. They hold onto their old friends and routines—the anchors in life that give them identity and a sense of belonging. Some even keep their old jobs—not for the money, of course, but because the job anchors them to an identity with which they are familiar and comfortable.

Sudden wealth, in other words, poses a threat that has to be guarded against.

And I can just hear you say, "I'll take the risk!"

For Your Consideration

How do you think your life would change if you won a lottery jackpot of $10 million?

Sociological Models of Social Class

The question of how many social classes there are is a matter of debate. Sociologists have proposed several models, but no single model has gained universal support. There are two main models: one that builds on Marx, the other on Weber.

Updating Marx

As Figure 10.4 illustrates, Marx argued that there are just two classes—capitalists and workers—with membership based solely on a person's relationship to the means of production. Sociologists have criticized this view, saying that these categories are too broad. For example, because executives, managers, and supervisors don't own the means of production, they would be classified as workers. But what do these people have in common with assembly-line workers? The category of "capitalist" is also too broad. Some people, for example, employ a thousand workers, and their decisions directly affect a thousand families.

Compare these people with a man I know in Godfrey, Illinois, who used to fix cars in his backyard. As Frank gained a following, he quit his regular job, and in a few years he put up a building with five bays and an office. Frank is now a capitalist, for he employs five or six mechanics and owns the tools and the building (the "means of production"). But what does he have in common with a factory owner who controls the lives of one thousand workers? Not only is Frank's work different but so are his lifestyle and the way he looks at the world.

To resolve this problem, sociologist Erik Wright (1985) suggests that some people are members of more than one class at the same time. They occupy what he calls **contradictory class locations.** By this, Wright means that a person's position in the class structure can generate contradictory interests. For example, the automobile mechanic-turned-business owner may want his mechanics to have higher wages because he, too, has experienced their working conditions. At the same time, his current interests—making profits and remaining competitive with other repair shops—lead him to resist pressures to raise their wages.

Because of such contradictory class locations, Wright modified Marx's model. As summarized in Table 10.3, Wright identifies four classes: (1) *capitalists,* business owners who employ many workers; (2) *petty bourgeoisie,* small business owners; (3) *managers,* who sell their own labor but also exercise authority over other employees; and (4) *workers,* who simply sell their labor to others. As you can see, this model allows finer divisions than the one Marx proposed, yet it maintains the primary distinction between employer and employee.

Problems persist, however. For example, in which category would we place college professors? And as you know, there are huge differences in the power of managers. An executive at Toyota, for example, may manage a thousand workers, while a shift manager at McDonald's may be responsible for only a handful. They, too, have little in common.

Updating Weber

Sociologists Joseph Kahl and Dennis Gilbert (Gilbert and Kahl 1998; Gilbert 2003) developed a six-tier model to portray the class structure of the United States and other capitalist countries. Think of this model, illustrated in Figure 10.5 on the next page, as a ladder. Our discussion starts with the highest rung and moves downward. In line with Weber, on each lower rung you find less property (wealth), less power, and less prestige. Note that in this model education is also a primary measure of class.

The Capitalist Class.   Sitting on the top rung of the class ladder is a powerful elite that consists of just 1 percent of the U.S. population. As you saw in Figure 10.1 on page 263, this capitalist class is so wealthy that it owns one–third of all the nation's assets. *This tiny 1 percent is worth more than the entire bottom 90 percent of the country* (Beeghley 2008).

Power and influence cling to this small elite. They have direct access to top politicians, and their decisions open or close job opportunities for millions of people. They even help

---

FIGURE 10.4   Marx's Model of the Social Classes

Capitalists
(*Bourgeoisie,* those who own the means of production)

Workers
(*Proletariat,* those who work for the capitalists)

Inconsequential Others
(beggars, etc.)

TABLE 10.3   Wright's Modification of Marx's Model of the Social Classes

1. Capitalists
2. Petty bourgeoisie
3. Managers
4. Workers

---

anomie Durkheim's term for a condition of society in which people become detached from the norms that usually guide their behavior

contradictory class locations Erik Wright's term for a position in the class structure that generates contradictory interests

FIGURE 10.5   The U.S. Social Class Ladder

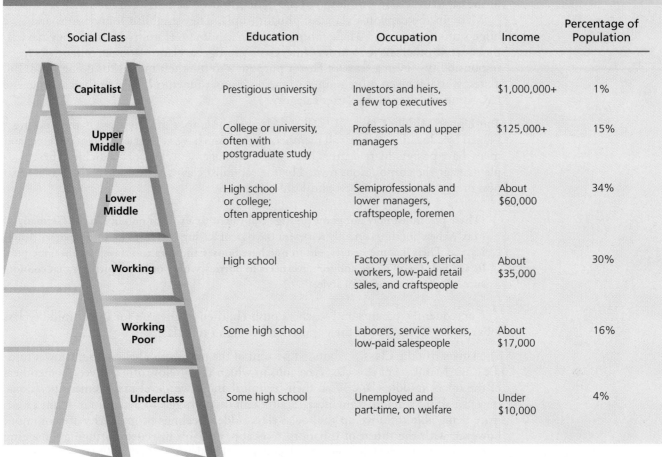

Social Class	Education	Occupation	Income	Percentage of Population
Capitalist	Prestigious university	Investors and heirs, a few top executives	$1,000,000+	1%
Upper Middle	College or university, often with postgraduate study	Professionals and upper managers	$125,000+	15%
Lower Middle	High school or college; often apprenticeship	Semiprofessionals and lower managers, craftspeople, foremen	About $60,000	34%
Working	High school	Factory workers, clerical workers, low-paid retail sales, and craftspeople	About $35,000	30%
Working Poor	Some high school	Laborers, service workers, low-paid salespeople	About $17,000	16%
Underclass	Some high school	Unemployed and part-time, on welfare	Under $10,000	4%

Source: Based on Gilbert and Kahl 1998 and Gilbert 2003; income estimates are modified from Duff 1995.

to shape the consciousness of the nation: They own our major media and entertainment outlets—newspapers, magazines, radio and television stations, and sports franchises. They also control the boards of directors of our most influential colleges and universities. The super-rich perpetuate themselves in privilege by passing on their assets and social networks to their children.

The capitalist class can be divided into "old" and "new" money. The longer that wealth has been in a family, the more it adds to the family's prestige. The children of "old" money seldom mingle with "common" folk. Instead, they attend exclusive private schools where they learn views of life that support their privileged position. They don't work for wages; instead, many study business or become lawyers so that they can manage the family fortune. These old-money capitalists (also called "blue-bloods") wield vast power as they use their extensive political connections to protect their economic empires (Sklair 2001; Domhoff 1990, 1999b, 2006).

At the lower end of the capitalist class are the *nouveau riche,* those who have "new money." Although they have made fortunes in business, the stock market, inventions, entertainment, or sports, they are outsiders to the upper class. They have not attended the "right" schools, and they don't share the social networks that come with old money. Not blue-bloods, they aren't trusted to have the right orientations to life. Even their "taste" in clothing and status symbols is suspect (Fabrikant 2005). Donald Trump, whose money is "new," is not listed in the *Social Register,* the "White Pages" of the blue-bloods that lists the most prestigious and wealthy one-tenth of 1 percent of the U.S. population. Trump says he "doesn't care," but he reveals his true feelings by adding that his heirs will be in it (Kaufman 1996).

With a fortune of $57 billion, Bill Gates, a cofounder of Microsoft Corporation, is the second wealthiest person in the world. His 40,000-square-foot home (sometimes called a "technopalace") in Seattle, Washington, was appraised at $110 million.

He is probably right, for the children of the new-moneyed can ascend into the top part of the capitalist class—if they go to the right schools *and* marry old money.

Many in the capitalist class are philanthropic. They establish foundations and give huge sums to "causes." Their motivations vary. Some feel guilty because they have so much while others have so little. Others seek prestige, acclaim, or fame. Still others feel a responsibility—even a sense of fate or purpose—to use their money for doing good. Bill Gates, who has given more money to the poor and to medical research than anyone else has, seems to fall into this latter category.

The Upper Middle Class.　Of all the classes, the upper middle class is the one most shaped by education. Almost all members of this class have at least a bachelor's degree, and many have postgraduate degrees in business, management, law, or medicine. These people manage the corporations owned by the capitalist class or else operate their own business or profession. As Gilbert and Kahl (1998) say,

> [These positions] may not grant prestige equivalent to a title of nobility in the Germany of Max Weber, but they certainly represent the sign of having "made it" in contemporary America. . . . Their income is sufficient to purchase houses and cars and travel that become public symbols for all to see and for advertisers to portray with words and pictures that connote success, glamour, and high style.

Consequently, parents and teachers push children to prepare for upper-middle-class jobs. About 15 percent of the population belong to this class.

The Lower Middle Class.　About 34 percent of the population belong to the lower middle class. Members of this class have jobs in which they follow orders given by members of the upper middle class. With their technical and lower-level management positions, they can afford a mainstream lifestyle, although they struggle to maintain it. Many anticipate being able to move up the social class ladder. Feelings of insecurity are common, however, with the threat of inflation, recession, and job insecurity bringing a nagging sense that they might fall down the class ladder (Kefalas 2007).

The distinctions between the lower middle class and the working class on the next rung below are more blurred than those between other classes. In general, however, members of the lower middle class work at jobs that have slightly more prestige, and their incomes are generally higher.

The Working Class.　About 30 percent of the U.S. population belong to this class of relatively unskilled blue-collar and white-collar workers. Compared with the lower middle class, they have less education and lower incomes. Their jobs are also less secure, more routine, and more closely supervised. One of their greatest fears is that of being laid off during a recession. With only a high school diploma, the average member of the working class has little hope of climbing up the class ladder. Job changes usually bring "more of the

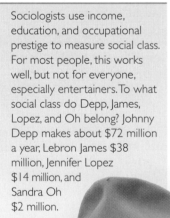

Sociologists use income, education, and occupational prestige to measure social class. For most people, this works well, but not for everyone, especially entertainers. To what social class do Depp, James, Lopez, and Oh belong? Johnny Depp makes about $72 million a year, Lebron James $38 million, Jennifer Lopez $14 million, and Sandra Oh $2 million.

same," so most concentrate on getting ahead by achieving seniority on the job rather than by changing their type of work. They tend to think of themselves as having "real jobs" and regard the "suits" above them as paper pushers who have no practical experience (Morris and Grimes 2005).

The Working Poor.   Members of this class, about 16 percent of the population, work at unskilled, low-paying, temporary and seasonal jobs, such as sharecropping, migrant farm work, housecleaning, and day labor. Most are high school dropouts. Many are functionally illiterate, finding it difficult to read even the want ads. They are not likely to vote (Beeghley 2008), for they believe that no matter what party is elected to office, their situation won't change.

Although they work full time, millions of the working poor depend on food stamps and donations from local food pantries to survive on their meager incomes (O'Hare 1996b). It is easy to see how you can work full time and still be poor. Suppose that you are married and have a baby 3 months old and another child 3 years old. Your spouse stays home to care for them, so earning the income is up to you. But as a high-school dropout, all you can get is a minimum wage job. At $7.25 an hour, you earn $290 for 40 hours. In a year, this comes to $15,080—before deductions. Your nagging fear—and recurring nightmare—is of ending up "on the streets."

The Underclass.   On the lowest rung, and with next to no chance of climbing anywhere, is the **underclass.** Concentrated in the inner city, this group has little or no connection with the job market. Those who are employed—and some are—do menial, low-paying, temporary work. Welfare, if it is available, along with food stamps and food pantries, is their main support. Most members of other classes consider these people the "ne'er-do-wells" of society. Life is the toughest in this class, and it is filled with despair. About 4 percent of the population fall into this class.

The homeless men described in the opening vignette of this chapter, and the women and children like them, are part of the underclass. These are the people whom most Americans wish would just go away. Their presence on our city streets bothers passersby from the more privileged social classes—which includes just about everyone. "What are those obnoxious, dirty, foul-smelling people doing here, cluttering up my city?" appears to be a common response. Some people react with sympathy and a desire to do something. But what? Almost all of us just shrug our shoulders and look the other way, despairing of a solution and somewhat intimidated by their presence.

The homeless are the "fallout" of our postindustrial economy. In another era, they would have had plenty of work. They would have tended horses, worked on farms, dug ditches, shoveled coal, and run the factory looms. Some would have explored and settled the West. The prospect of gold would have lured others to California, Alaska, and Australia. Today, however, with no frontiers to settle, factory jobs scarce, and farms that are becoming technological marvels, we have little need for unskilled labor.

"There are plenty of jobs around. People just don't want to work."

A primary sociological principle is that people's views are shaped by their social location. Many people from the middle and upper classes cannot understand how anyone can work and still be poor.

Consequences of Social Class

The man was a C student throughout school. As a businessman, he ran an oil company (Arbusto) into the ground. A self-confessed alcoholic until age forty, he was arrested for drunk driving. With this background, how did he become president of the United States?

Accompanying these personal factors was the power of social class. George W. Bush was born the grandson of a wealthy senator and the son of a businessman who himself became president of the United States after serving as a member of the House of Representatives, director of the CIA, and head of the Republican party. For high school, he went to an elite

underclass a group of people for whom poverty persists year after year and across generations

private prep school, Andover; for his bachelor's degree to Yale; and for his MBA to Harvard. He was given $1 million to start his own business. When that business (Arbusto) failed, Bush fell softly, landing on the boards of several corporations. Taken care of even further, he was made the managing director of the Texas Rangers baseball team and allowed to buy a share of the team for $600,000, which he sold for $15 million.

When it was time for him to get into politics, Bush's connections financed his run for governor of Texas and then for the presidency.

Does social class matter? And how! Think of each social class as a broad subculture with distinct approaches to life, so significant that it affects almost every aspect of our lives—our health, family life, education, religion, politics, and even our experiences with crime and the criminal justice system. Let's look at how social class affects our lives.

Physical Health

If you want to get a sense of how social class affects health, take a ride on Washington's Metro system. Start in the blighted Southeast section of downtown D.C. For every mile you travel to where the wealthy live in Montgomery County in Maryland, life expectancy rises about a year and a half. By the time you get off, you will find a twenty-year gap between the poor blacks where you started your trip and the rich whites where you ended it (Cohen 2004).

The principle is simple: As you go up the social-class ladder, health increases. As you go down the ladder, health decreases (Hout 2008). Age makes no difference. Infants born to the poor are more likely to die before their first birthday, and a larger percentage of poor people in their old age—whether 75 or 95—die each year than do the elderly who are wealthy.

How can social class have such dramatic effects? While there are many reasons, here are three basic ones. First, social class opens and closes doors to medical care. Consider this example:

Terry Takewell (his real name), a 21-year-old diabetic, lived in a trailer park in Somerville, Tennessee. When Zettie Mae Hill, Takewell's neighbor, found the unemployed carpenter drenched with sweat from a fever, she called an ambulance. Takewell was rushed to Methodist Hospital, where he had an outstanding bill of $9,400.

When the hospital administrator learned of the admission, he went to Takewell's room, got him out of bed, and escorted him to the parking lot. There, neighbors found him under a tree and took him home.

Takewell died about twelve hours later.

Zettie Mae Hill said, "I didn't think a hospital would just let a person die like that for lack of money." (Based on Ansberry 1988)

Why was Terry Takewell denied medical treatment and his life cut short? The fundamental reason is that health care in the United States is not a citizens' right but a commodity for sale. Unlike the middle and upper classes, few poor people have a personal physician, and they often spend hours waiting in crowded public health clinics. When the poor are hospitalized, they are likely to find themselves in understaffed and underfunded public hospitals, treated by rotating interns who do not know them and cannot follow up on their progress.

A second reason is lifestyles, which are shaped by social class. People in the lower classes are more likely to smoke, eat a lot of fats, be overweight, abuse drugs and alcohol, get little exercise, and practice unsafe sex (Chin et al. 2000; Navarro 2002; Liu 2007). This, to understate the matter, does not improve people's health.

There is a third reason, too. Life is hard on the poor. The persistent stresses they face cause their bodies to wear out faster (Spector 2007). The rich find life better. They have fewer problems and more resources to deal with the ones they have. This gives them a sense of control over their lives, a source of both physical and mental health.

Mental Health

Sociological studies from as far back as the 1930s have found that the mental health of the lower classes is worse than that of the higher classes (Faris and Dunham 1939; Srole et al. 1978; Pratt et al. 2007). Greater mental problems are part of the higher stress that accompanies poverty. Compared with middle- and upper-class Americans, the poor have less job security and lower wages. They are more likely to divorce, to be the victims of crime, and to have more physical illnesses. Couple these conditions with bill collectors and the threat of eviction, and you can see how they can deal severe blows to people's emotional well-being.

People higher up the social class ladder experience stress in daily life, of course, but their stress is generally less, and their coping resources are greater. Not only can they afford vacations, psychiatrists, and counselors, but *their class position also gives them greater control over their lives, a key to good mental health.*

Family Life

Social class also plays makes a significant difference in family life, in our choice of spouse, our chances of getting divorced, and how we rear our children.

Choice of Husband or Wife.   Members of the capitalist class place strong emphasis on family tradition. They stress the family's history, even a sense of purpose or destiny in life (Baltzell 1979; Aldrich 1989). Children of this class learn that their choice of husband or wife affects not just them, but the entire family, that it will have an impact on the "family line." These background expectations shrink the field of "eligible" marriage partners, making it narrower than it is for the children of any other social class. As a result, parents in this class play a strong role in their children's mate selection.

Divorce.   The more difficult life of the lower social classes, especially the many tensions that come from insecure jobs and inadequate incomes, leads to higher marital friction and a greater likelihood of divorce. Consequently, children of the poor are more likely to grow up in broken homes.

What a difference social class makes in our lives! Shown here are model Kimora Lee Simmons in her home in Saddle River, New Jersey, and Nakeva Narcisse and her daughter in their home in Port Sulphur, Lousiana. Can you see why these women see the world in highly distinctive ways? How do you think social class affects their politics and aspirations in life?

Child Rearing.   As discussed on page 81, lower-class parents focus more on getting their children to follow rules and obey authority, while middle-class parents focus more on developing their children's creative and leadership skills (Lareau and Weininger 2008). Sociologists have traced this difference to the parents' occupation (Kohn 1977). Lower-class parents are closely supervised at work, and they anticipate that their children will have similar jobs. Consequently, they try to teach their children to defer to authority. Middle-class parents, in contrast, enjoy greater independence at work. Anticipating similar jobs for their children, they encourage them to be more creative. Out of these contrasting orientations arise different ways of disciplining children; lower-class parents are more likely to use physical punishment, while the middle classes rely more on verbal persuasion.

Working-class and middle-class parents also have different ideas about how children develop (Lareau 2002; Bodovsky and Farkas 2008). Working-class parents think that children develop naturally—they sort of unfold from within. If parents provide comfort, food, shelter, and other basic support, the child's development will take care of itself. Middle-class parents, in contrast, think that children need a lot of guidance to develop correctly. Among the consequences of these contrasting orientations is that middle-class parents read to their children more, make more efforts to prepare them for school, and encourage play and extracurricular activities that they think will help develop their children's mental and social skills.

Education

As we saw in Figure 10.5 on page 271, education increases as one goes up the social class ladder. It is not just the amount of education that changes, but also the type of education. Children of the capitalist class bypass public schools. They attend exclusive private schools where they are trained to take a commanding role in society. Prep schools such as Andover, Groton, and Phillips Exeter Academy teach upper-class values and prepare their students for prestigious universities (Cookson and Persell 2005; Beeghley 2008).

Keenly aware that private schools can be a key to upward social mobility, some upper-middle-class parents do their best to get their children into the prestigious preschools that feed into these exclusive prep schools. Although some preschools cost $23,000 a year, they have a waiting list (Rohwedder 2007). Parents even solicit letters of recommendation for their 2- and 3-year-olds. Such parental involvement and resources are major reasons why children from the more privileged classes are more likely to go to college—and to graduate.

Religion

One area of social life that we might think would not be affected by social class is religion. ("People are just religious, or they are not. What does social class have to do with it?") As we shall see in Chapter 18, however, the classes tend to cluster in different denominations. Episcopalians, for example, are more likely to attract the middle and upper classes, while Baptists draw heavily from the lower classes. Patterns of worship also follow class lines: The lower classes are attracted to more expressive worship services and louder music, while the middle and upper classes prefer more "subdued" worship.

Politics

As I have stressed throughout this text, people perceive events from their own corner in life. Political views are no exception to this symbolic interactionist principle, and the rich and the poor walk different political paths. The higher that people are on the social class ladder, the more likely they are to vote for Republicans (Hout 2008). In contrast, most members of the working class believe that the government should intervene in the economy to provide jobs and to make citizens financially secure. They are more likely to vote for Democrats. Although the working class is more liberal on *economic* issues (policies that increase government spending), it is more conservative on *social* issues (such as opposing abortion and the Equal Rights Amendment) (Houtman 1995; Hout 2008). People toward the bottom of the class structure are also less likely to be politically active—to campaign for candidates or even to vote (Gilbert 2003; Beeghley 2008).

Crime and Criminal Justice

If justice is supposed to be blind, it certainly is not when it comes to one's chances of being arrested (Henslin 2008). In Chapter 8 (pages 210–212), we discussed how the social classes commit different types of crime. The white-collar crimes of the more privileged classes are more likely to be dealt with outside the criminal justice system, while the police and courts deal with the street crimes of the lower classes. One consequence of this class standard is that members of the lower classes are more likely to be in prison, on probation, or on parole. In addition, since those who commit street crimes tend to do so in or near their own neighborhoods, the lower classes are more likely to be robbed, burglarized, or murdered.

The Changing Economy

"They are so quiet," I thought, as I watched the homeless men at breakfast, most sitting in silence, slowly eating their food or staring into a cup of coffee. "What do they have to talk about, anyway"? I realized. Where they are going to panhandle? How many cans they expect to collect? The soup kitchen they are going to visit at noon?

Two major forces in today's world are the globalization of capitalism and rapidly changing technology. If the United States does not remain competitive by producing low-cost, high-quality, state-of-the-art goods and services, its economic position will decline. We will face dwindling opportunities—fewer jobs, shrinking paychecks, and vast downward social mobility. The men in the homeless shelter, high school dropouts, are technological know-nothings. Of what value are they to a rapidly changing technological society trying to compete on a global level? They have no productive place in it. Zero. This self-esteem and the feelings of belonging that come from work and paychecks have been pulled out from under them.

The upheaval in the economy does not affect all social classes in the same way. For the *capitalist class*, globalization is a dream come true: By minimizing the obstacles of national borders, capitalists are able to move production to countries that provide cheaper labor. They can produce components in one country, assemble them in another, and market the product throughout the world. Members of the *upper middle class* are well prepared for this change. Their higher education enables them to take a leading role in managing this global system for the capitalist class or for using the new technology to advance in their professions.

Below these two most privileged classes, changes in capitalism and technology add to the insecurities of life. As job markets shift, the skills of many in the *lower middle class* become outdated. Those who work at specialized crafts are especially at risk, for changing markets and technology can reduce or even eliminate the need for their skills. People in lower management are more secure, for they can transfer their skills from one job to another.

From this middle point on the ladder down, these changes in capitalism and technology hit people the hardest. The threat of plant closings haunts the *working class,* for they have few alternatives. The *working poor* are even more vulnerable, for they have even less to offer in the new job market. As unskilled jobs dry up, workers are tossed into the industrial garbage bin. Lacking technical skills, they fear the fate of the homeless.

Social Mobility

No aspect of life, then—from work and family life to politics—goes untouched by social class. Because life is so much more satisfying in the more privileged classes, people strive to climb the social class ladder. What affects their chances?

Three Types of Social Mobility

There are three basic types of social mobility: intergenerational, structural, and exchange. **Intergenerational mobility** refers to a change that occurs between generations—when grown-up children end up on a different rung of the social class ladder from the one

intergenerational mobility the change that family members make in social class from one generation to the next

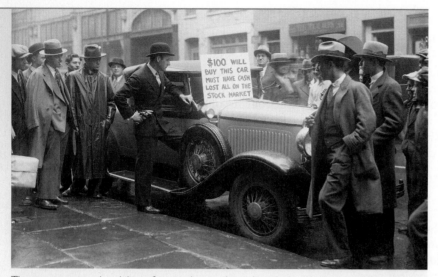

The term *structural mobility* refers to changes in society that push large numbers of people either up or down the social class ladder. A remarkable example was the stock market crash of 1929 when thousands of people suddenly lost immense amounts of wealth. People who once "had it made" found themselves standing on street corners selling apples or, as depicted here, selling their possessions at fire-sale prices. The crash of 2008 brought similar problems to untold numbers of people.

occupied by their parents. If the child of someone who sells used cars graduates from college and buys a Toyota dealership, that person experiences **upward social mobility.** Conversely, if a child of the dealership's owner parties too much, drops out of college, and ends up selling cars, he or she experiences **downward social mobility.**

We like to think that individual efforts are the reason people move up the class ladder—and their faults the reason they move down. In these examples, we can identify hard work, sacrifice, and ambition on the one hand, versus indolence and substance abuse on the other. Although individual factors such as these do underlie social mobility, sociologists consider **structural mobility** to be the crucial factor. This second basic type of mobility refers to changes in society that cause large numbers of people to move up or down the class ladder.

To understand *structural mobility,* think about how changes in society (its *structure*) drive some people down the social class ladder and lift others up. When computers were invented, for example, new types of jobs appeared overnight. Huge numbers of people attended workshops and took crash courses, switching from blue-collar to white-collar work. In contrast, others were thrown out of work as technology bypassed their jobs. Individual effort was certainly involved—for some seized the opportunity while others did not—but the underlying cause was a huge social change that transformed the *structure* of work. This happens during depressions, too, when opportunities disappear, forcing millions of people downward on the class ladder. In this instance, too, their changed status is due less to individual behavior than to *structural* changes in society.

The third type of social mobility, **exchange mobility,** occurs when large numbers of people move up and down the social class ladder, but, on balance, the proportions of the social classes remain about the same. Suppose that a million or so working-class people are trained in some new technology, and they move up the class ladder. Suppose also that because of a surge in imports, about a million skilled workers have to take lower-status jobs. Although millions of people change their social class, there is, in effect, an *exchange* among them. The net result more or less balances out, and the class system remains basically untouched.

Women in Studies of Social Mobility

In classic studies to determine how much social mobility there is, sociologists concluded that about half of sons passed their fathers on the social class ladder, about one-third stayed at the same level, and about one-sixth moved down (Blau and Duncan 1967; Featherman 1979). Feminists objected. They said that it wasn't good science to ignore daughters and that assigning women the class of their husband assumed that wives had no social class position of their own (Davis and Robinson 1988). The male sociologists of the time brushed off these objections, replying that too few women were in the labor force to make a difference.

These sociologists simply hadn't caught up with the times. The gradual but steady increase of women working for pay had caught them unprepared. Although sociologists now include women in their research on social mobility, determining how the social class of married women is related to that of their husbands is still in its infancy (McCall 2008). Sociologists Elizabeth Higginbotham and Lynn Weber (1992) studied 200 women from

upward social mobility
movement up the social class ladder

downward social mobility
movement down the social class ladder

structural mobility
movement up or down the social class ladder that is due to changes in the structure of society, not to individual efforts

exchange mobility about the same numbers of people moving up and down the social class ladder, such that, on balance, the social class system shows little change

working-class backgrounds who had become administrators, managers, and professionals in Memphis. Almost without exception, their parents had implanted ideas of success in them while they were still little girls, encouraging them to postpone marriage and get an education. This research confirms how important the family is in the socialization process. It also supports the observation that the primary entry to the upper middle class is a college education. At the same time, if there had not been a *structural* change in society, the millions of new positions that women occupy would not exist.

Bleeding people's savings, destroying jobs, and forcing people from their homes, the global economic crisis has forced many into *downward social mobility*.

Interpreting Statistics on Social Mobility

The United States is famous worldwide for its intergenerational mobility. That children can pass their parents on their way up the social class ladder is one of the attractions of this country. How much mobility is there? It turns out that most apples don't fall far from the tree. Of children who are born to the poorest 10 percent of Americans, about a third are still there when they are grown up. Similarly, of children who are born to the richest 10 percent of families, about a third stay there, too (Krueger 2002).

But is the glass half empty or half full? The answer depends on what part of these findings you emphasize. We can also put it this way: Two-thirds of the very poorest kids move up, and two-thirds of the very richest kids drop down. That is a lot of social mobility. What is the truth then? It depends on what you want to make of these findings. Remember that statistics don't lie, but liars use statistics. In this case, you can stress either part of these findings, depending on what you want to prove. Within all this, we don't want to lose sight of the broader principle: As with George W. Bush, the benefits that high-income parents enjoy tend to keep their children afloat. In contrast, the obstacles that low-income parents confront tend to weigh their children down.

The Pain of Social Mobility

If you were to be knocked down the social class ladder, you know it would be painful. But are you aware that it also hurts to climb this ladder? Sociologist Steph Lawler (1999) found that British women who had moved from the working class to the middle class were caught between two worlds—their working-class background and their current middle-class life. The women's mothers found their daughters' middle-class ways "uppity," and they criticized their daughters' tastes in furniture and food, their speech, even the way they reared their children. As you can expect, this put a lot of strain on the relationship between daughters and mothers. Studying working-class parents in Boston, sociologists Richard Sennett and Jonathan Cobb (1972/1988) found something similar. The parents had made deep sacrifices—working two jobs, postponing medical care—just so their children could go to college. They, of course, expected their children to appreciate their sacrifice. But again, the result was two worlds of experience. The children's educated world was so unlike that of their parents that children and parents had difficulty talking to one another. Not surprisingly, the parents felt betrayed and bitter.

Some of those who make the jump from the working to the middle class always feel a tearing away of their roots and never become comfortable with their new social class (Morris and Grimes 2005). The Cultural Diversity box on the next page discusses other costs that come with the climb up the social class ladder.

Cultural Diversity in the United States

Social Class and the Upward Social Mobility of African Americans

The overview of social class presented in this chapter doesn't apply equally to all the groups that make up U.S. society. Consider geography: What constitutes the upper class of a town of 5,000 people will differ from that of a city of a million. With fewer extremes of wealth and occupation, in small towns family background and local reputation are more significant.

So it is with racial–ethnic groups. All racial–ethnic groups are marked by social class, but what constitutes a particular social class can differ from one group to another—as well as from one historical period to another. Consider social class among African Americans (Cole and Omari 2003).

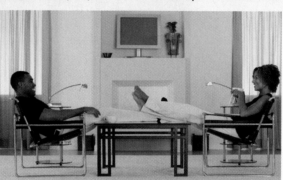

The earliest class divisions can be traced to slavery—to slaves who worked in the fields and those who worked in the "big house." Those who worked in the plantation home were exposed more to the customs, manners, and forms of speech of wealthy whites. Their more privileged position—which brought with it better food and clothing, as well as lighter work—was often based on skin color. Mulattos, lighter-skinned slaves, were often chosen for this more desirable work. One result was the development of a "mulatto elite," a segment of the slave population that, proud of its distinctiveness, distanced itself from the other slaves. At this time, there also were free blacks. Not only were they able to own property but some even owned black slaves.

After the War Between the States (as the Civil War is known in the South), these two groups, the mulatto elite and the free blacks, formed an upper class. Proud of their earlier status, they distanced themselves from

other blacks. From these groups came most of the black professionals.

After World War II, the black middle class expanded as African Americans entered a wider range of occupations. Today, more than half of all African American adults work at white-collar jobs, about 22 percent at the professional or managerial level (Beeghley 2008). An unwelcome cost greets many African Americans who move up the social class ladder: an uncomfortable distancing from their roots, a separation from significant others—parents, siblings, and childhood friends (hooks 2000). The upwardly mobile enter a world unknown to those left behind, one that demands not only different appearance and speech, but also different values, aspirations, and ways of viewing the world. These are severe challenges to the self and often rupture relationships with those left behind.

An additional cost is a subtle racism that lurks beneath the surface of some work settings, poisoning what could be easy, mutually respectful interaction. To be aware that white co-workers perceive you as different—as a stranger, an intruder, or "the other"—engenders frustration, dissatisfaction, and cynicism. To cope, many nourish their racial identity and stress the "high value of black culture and being black" (Lacy and Harris 2008). Some move to neighborhoods of upper-middle-class African Americans, where they can live among like-minded people who have similar experiences (Lacy 2007).

For Your Consideration

In the box on upward social mobility on page 84, we discussed how Latinos face a similar situation. Why do you think this is? What connections do you see among upward mobility, frustration, and racial–ethnic identity? How do you think that the upward mobility of whites is different? Why?

Poverty

Many Americans find that the "limitless possibilities" of the American dream are quite elusive. As illustrated in Figure 10.5 on page 271, the working poor and underclass together form about one-fifth of the U.S. population. This translates into a huge number, about 60 million people. Who are these people?

Drawing the Poverty Line

To determine who is poor, the U.S. government draws a **poverty line.** This measure was set in the 1960s, when poor people were thought to spend about one-third of their incomes on food. On the basis of this assumption, each year the government computes a low-cost food budget and multiplies it by 3. Families whose incomes are less than this amount are classified as poor; those whose incomes are higher—even by a dollar—are determined to be "not poor."

This official measure of poverty is grossly inadequate. Poor people actually spend only about 20 percent of their incomes on food, so to determine a poverty line, we ought to multiply their food budget by 5 instead of 3 (Uchitelle 2001). Another problem is that mothers who work outside the home and have to pay for child care are treated the same as mothers who don't have this expense. The poverty line is also the same for everyone across the nation, even though the cost of living is much higher in New York than in Alabama. In addition, much of the income of the poor goes uncounted: food stamps, rent assistance, subsidized child care, and the earned income tax credit (Kaufman 2007).

That a change in the poverty line would instantly make millions of people poor—or take away their poverty—would be laughable, if it weren't so serious. (The absurdity has not been lost on Parker and Hart, as you can see from their cartoon below). Although this line is arbitrary, because it is the official measure of poverty, we'll use it to see who in the United States is poor. Before we do this, though, compare your ideas of the poor with the stereotypes explored in the Down-to-Earth Sociology box on the next page.

Who Are the Poor?

Geography.   As you can see from the Social Map on page 283, the poor are not distributed evenly among the states. Notice the clustering of poverty in the South, a pattern that has prevailed for more than 150 years.

A second aspect of geography is also significant. The rate of rural poverty (16 percent) is higher than the national average of 12 percent. What is different about rural poverty? The rural poor are less likely to be single parents and more likely to be married and to have jobs. Compared with urban Americans, the rural poor are less educated, and the jobs available to them pay less than similar jobs in urban areas (Lichter and Crowley 2002; Arsneault 2006).

Geography, however, is not the main factor in poverty. The greatest predictors of poverty are race–ethnicity, education, and the sex of the person who heads the family. Let's look at these factors.

High rates of rural poverty have been a part of the United States from its origin to the present. This 1937 photo shows a 32-year old woman in California who had seven children and no food.

poverty line the official measure of poverty; calculated to include incomes that are less than three times a low-cost food budget

WIZARD OF ID

This cartoon pinpoints the arbitrary nature of the *poverty line.* This almost makes me think that the creators of the Wizard of Id have been studying sociology.

Down-to-Earth Sociology
Taking Another Fun Quiz: Exploring Stereotypes About the Poor

Do you hold any of these stereotypes? Can you tell which are true and which are not?

Most poor people are lazy. They are poor because they do not want to work. *False.* Half of the poor are either too old or too young to work: About 40 percent are under age 18, and another 10 percent are age 65 or older. About 30 percent of the working-age poor work at least half the year.

Most of the poor are trapped in a cycle of poverty that few escape. *False.* Long-term poverty is the exception. Most poverty lasts less than a year (Lichter and Crowley 2002). Only 12 percent remain in poverty for five or more consecutive years (O'Hare 1996a). Most children who are born in poverty are *not* poor as adults (Ruggles 1989; Corcoran 2001).

There is more poverty in rural than in urban areas. *True.* We'll review this in the following section.

Most African Americans are poor. *False.* This one was easy. We just reviewed some statistics in the box on upward mobility on page 280—plus you have the bar chart below.

Most of the poor are African Americans. *False.* Look at the second part of Figure 10.6. *There are more poor whites than any other group.* The combined total of poor African Americans, Latinos, and Native Americans, however, is larger than the total of poor whites.

Most of the poor are single mothers and their children. *False.* About 38 percent of the poor match this stereotype, but 34 percent of the poor live in married-couple families, 22 percent live alone or with nonrelatives, and 6 percent live in other settings.

Most of the poor live in the inner city. *False.* About 42 percent of the poor do live in the inner city, but 36 percent live in the suburbs, and 22 percent live in small towns and rural areas.

Most of the poor live on welfare. *False.* Only about 25 percent of the income of poor adults comes from welfare. About half comes from wages and pensions, and about 22 percent from Social Security.

On a percentage basis, more children than adults are poor. *True.* (Okay, no one holds this stereotype. I just want to make this important point. We'll come back to it shortly.)

For Your Consideration

What stereotypes of the poor do you (or people you know) hold? How would you test these stereotypes?

Sources: O'Hare 1996a, 1996b, with other sources as indicated.

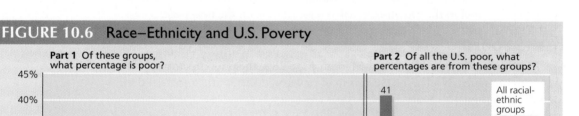

FIGURE 10.6   Race–Ethnicity and U.S. Poverty

Part 1 Of these groups, what percentage is poor?

Part 2 Of all the U.S. poor, what percentages are from these groups?

[Legend: All racial-ethnic groups; White Americans; Asian Americans; Latinos; African Americans; Native Americans; Others]

[Part 1 data — Overall: 12, 10, 10, 21, 24, 27¹; The elderly age 65 and over: 9, 8, 12, 19, 23, 17, 14, 12; Children under age 18: 27, 33]

[Part 2 data: 41, 3, 22, 21, 1, 12²]

¹The source does not break this total down by age. ²Others consists of people who identify themselves as being of ancestry other than the groups listed here plus those who claim membership in two or more racial–ethnic groups.

Note: Only these groups are listed in the source. The poverty line on which this figure is based is $20,614 for a family of four.
Source: By the author. Based on *Statistical Abstract of the United States 2009*: Tables 35, 688, and 691.

FIGURE 10.7 Patterns of Poverty

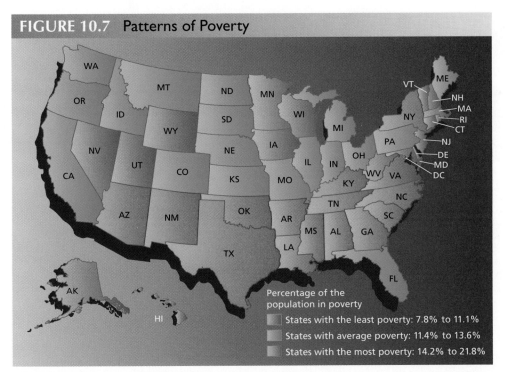

Percentage of the population in poverty

	States with the least poverty: 7.8% to 11.1%
	States with average poverty: 11.4% to 13.6%
	States with the most poverty: 14.2% to 21.8%

Note: Poverty varies tremendously from one state to another. In the extreme, poverty is about three times greater in Mississippi (21.8%) than in Maryland (7.8%).

Source: By the author. Based on *Statistical Abstract of the United States* 2009: Table 687.

Race–Ethnicity. One of the strongest factors in poverty is race–ethnicity. As Figure 10.6 shows, only 10 percent of Asian Americans and whites are poor. In contrast, 21 percent of Latinos live in poverty, while the total jumps even higher, to 24 percent for African Americans and 27 percent for Native Americans. Because whites are, by far, the largest group in the United States, their much lower rate of poverty still translates into larger numbers. As a result, there are more poor whites than poor people of any other racial–ethnic group.

Education. You are aware that education is a vital factor in poverty, but you may not know just how powerful it is. Figure 10.8 on the next page shows that 3 of 100 people who finish college end up in poverty, but 1 of every 4 people who drop out of high school is poor. As you can see, the chances that someone will be poor become less with each higher level of education. Although this principle applies regardless of race–ethnicity, this figure shows that at every level of education, race–ethnicity makes an impact.

The Feminization of Poverty. One of the best indicators of whether or not a family is poor is family structure. Families headed by both a mother and father are the least likely to be poor, and families headed by only a mother are the most likely to be poor (*Statistical Abstract* 2009: Table 676). The reason for this can be summed up in this one statistic: Women average only 70 percent of what men earn. (If you want to jump ahead, go to Figure 11.8 on page 318.)

Beyond the awareness of most Americans are the rural poor, such as this family in Maine. With low education and few good gobs available, life is hardscrabble. What do you think the future holds for these children?

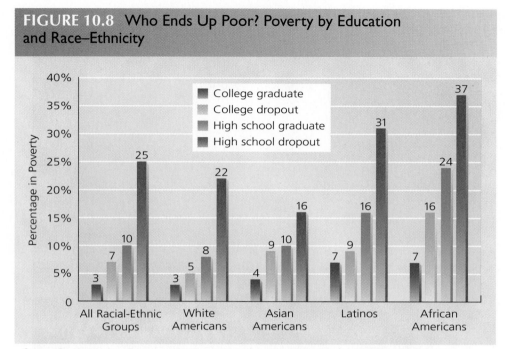

FIGURE 10.8 Who Ends Up Poor? Poverty by Education and Race–Ethnicity

Source: By the author. Based on *Statistical Abstract of the United States* 2007:Table 694.

With our high rate of divorce combined with our high number of births to single women, mother-headed families have become more common. Sociologists call this association of poverty with women the **feminization of poverty.**

Old Age.   As Figure 10.6 on page 282 shows, the elderly are *less* likely than the general population to be poor. This is quite a change. It used to be that growing old increased people's chances of being poor, but government policies to redistribute income—Social Security and subsidized housing, food stamps, and medical care—slashed the rate of poverty among the elderly. Figure 10.6 also shows how the prevailing racial–ethnic patterns carry over into old age. You can see how much more likely an elderly African American, Latino, or Native American is to be poor than an elderly white or Asian American.

Children of Poverty

Children are more likely to live in poverty than are adults or the elderly. This holds true regardless of race–ethnicity, but from Figure 10.6 on page 282, you can see how much greater poverty is among Latino, African American, and Native American children. That millions of U.S. children are reared in poverty is shocking when one considers the wealth of this country and the supposed concern for the well-being of children. This tragic aspect of poverty is the topic of the following Thinking Critically section.

ThinkingCRITICALLY

The Nation's Shame: Children in Poverty

One of the most startling statistics in sociology is shown in Figure 10.6 on page 282. Look at the rate of childhood poverty: For Asian Americans, 1 of 8 children is poor; for whites, 1 of 7; for Latinos, 1 of 4; and for African Americans, an astounding 1 of 3. These percentages translate into incredible numbers—approximately *13 million* children.

[the] feminization of poverty refers to the situation that most poor families in the U.S. are headed by women

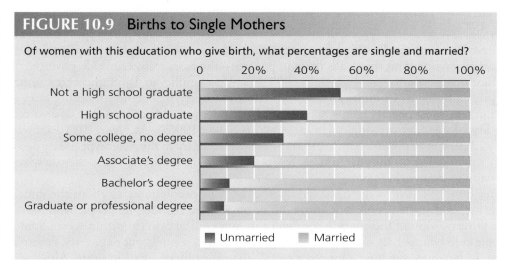

FIGURE 10.9   Births to Single Mothers

Of women with this education who give birth, what percentages are single and married?

Not a high school graduate
High school graduate
Some college, no degree
Associate's degree
Bachelor's degree
Graduate or professional degree

■ Unmarried   ■ Married

Note: Based on a national sample of all U.S. births in the preceding 12 months.
Source: Dye 2005.

Why do so many U.S. children live in poverty? A major reason is the large number of births to women who are not married, about 1.5 million a year. This number has increased sharply. In 1960, 1 of 20 U.S. children was born to a single woman. Today that total is about *eight times higher,* and single women now account for 2 of 5 (39 percent) of all U.S. births (*Statistical Abstract* 2009:Table 87).

By itself, though, births to single women don't cause poverty. Consider the obvious: Children born to wealthy single women aren't reared in poverty. Then consider this: Although the U.S. birth rate to single women is not the highest in the industrialized world, *our rate of child poverty is the highest in the industrialized world* (Rainwater and Smeeding 2003). In countries where the birth rate to single women is higher than ours but where child poverty is lower, the government provides extensive support for rearing these children—from day care to health checkups and medicine. As the cause of their poverty, then, why can't we point to government support for children—or the lack of it?

Apart from the matter of government policy, births to single women follow patterns that have a negative impact on their children's welfare. The less education a single woman has, the more likely she is to bear children. As you can see from Figure 10.9, births to single women drop with each gain in education. As you know, people with lower education earn less, so this means that the single women who can least afford children are those most likely to give birth. Their children are likely to face the obstacles to building a satisfying life that poverty entails. They are more likely to die in infancy, to go hungry, to be malnourished, to develop more slowly, and to have more health problems. They also are more likely to drop out of school, to become involved in criminal activities, and to have children while still in their teens—thus perpetuating a cycle of poverty.

For Your Consideration

With education so important to obtain jobs that pay well, in light of Figure 10.9, what programs would you suggest for helping women attain more education? What programs would you suggest for reducing child poverty? Be specific and practical.

The Dynamics of Poverty

Some have suggested that the poor get trapped in a **culture of poverty** (Lewis 1966a; Gorsky 2008). They assume that the values and behaviors of the poor "make them fundamentally different from other Americans, and that these factors are largely responsible for their continued long-term poverty" (Ruggles 1989:7).

culture of poverty the assumption that the values and behaviors of the poor make them fundamentally different from other people, that these factors are largely responsible for their poverty, and that parents perpetuate poverty across generations by passing these characteristics to their children

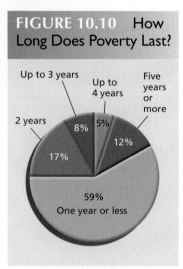

FIGURE 10.10 How Long Does Poverty Last?

Up to 3 years

Up to 4 years

Five years or more

2 years

8%   5%

12%

17%

59%
One year or less

Source: Gottschalk et al. 1994:89.

Lurking behind this concept is the idea that the poor are lazy people who bring poverty on themselves. Certainly, some individuals and families match this stereotype—many of us have known them. But is a self-perpetuating culture—one that poor people transmit across generations and that locks them in poverty—the basic reason for U.S. poverty?

Researchers who began following 5,000 poor U.S. families in 1968 uncovered some surprising findings. Contrary to stereotypes, most poverty is short-lived, lasting only a year or less. Most poverty comes about because of a dramatic life change such as divorce, the loss of a job, or even the birth of a child (O'Hare 1996a). As Figure 10.10 shows, only 12 percent of poverty lasts five years or longer. Contrary to the stereotype of lazy people content to live off the government, few poor people enjoy poverty—and they do what they can to avoid being poor.

Yet from one year to the next, the number of poor people remains about the same. This means that the people who move out of poverty are replaced by people who move *into* poverty. Most of these newly poor will also move out of poverty within a year. Some people even bounce back and forth, never quite making it securely out of poverty. Poverty, then, is dynamic, touching a lot more people than the official totals indicate. Although 13 percent of Americans may be poor at any one time, twice that number—about one-fourth of the U.S. population—is or has been poor for at least a year.

Why Are People Poor?

Two explanations for poverty compete for our attention. The first, which sociologists prefer, focuses on *social structure*. Sociologists stress that *features of society* deny some people access to education or the learning of job skills. They emphasize racial–ethnic, age, and gender discrimination, as well as changes in the job market—the closing of plants, the elimination of unskilled jobs, and the increase in marginal jobs that pay poverty wages. In short, some people find their escape route from poverty to a better life blocked.

A competing explanation focuses on the *characteristics of individuals* that are assumed to contribute to poverty. Sociologists reject individualistic explanations such as laziness and lack of intelligence, viewing these as worthless stereotypes. Individualistic explanations that sociologists reluctantly acknowledge include dropping out of school, bearing children in the teen years, and averaging more children than women in the other social classes. Most sociologists are reluctant to speak of such factors in this context, for they appear to blame the victim, something that sociologists bend over backward not to do.

The tension between these competing explanations is of more than just theoretical interest. Each explanation affects our perception and has practical consequences, as is illustrated in the following Thinking Critically section.

Thinking CRITICALLY
The Welfare Debate: The Deserving and the Undeserving Poor

Throughout U.S. history, Americans have divided the poor into two types: the deserving and the undeserving. The deserving poor are people who, in the public mind, are poor through no fault of their own. Most of the working poor, such as the Lewises, are considered deserving:

Nancy and Ted Lewis are in their early 30s and have two children. Ted works three part-time jobs, earning $13,000 a year; Nancy takes care of the children and house and is not employed. To make ends meet, the Lewises rely on food stamps, Medicaid, and housing subsidies.

The undeserving poor, in contrast, are viewed as people who brought on their own poverty. They are freeloaders who waste their lives in laziness, alcohol and drug abuse, and promiscuous sex. They don't deserve help, and, if given anything, will waste it on their dissolute lifestyles. Some would see Joan as an example:

> Joan, her mother, and her two brothers and two sisters lived on welfare. Joan started having sex at 13, bore her first child at 15, and, now, at 23, is expecting her fourth child. Her first two children have the same father, the third a different father, and Joan isn't sure who fathered her coming child. Joan parties most nights, using both alcohol and whatever drugs are available. Her house is filthy, the refrigerator usually empty, and social workers have threatened to take away her children.

This division of the poor into deserving and undeserving underlies the heated debate about welfare. "Why should we use *our* hard-earned money to help *them*? They are just going to waste it. Of course, there are others who want to get back on their feet, and helping them is okay."

For Your Consideration

Why do people make a distinction between deserving and undeserving poor? Should we let some people starve because they "brought poverty upon themselves"? Should we let children go hungry because their parents are drug abusers? Does "unworthy" mean that we should not offer assistance to people who "squander" the help they are given?

In contrast to thinking of poor people as deserving or undeserving, use the sociological perspective to explain poverty without blaming the victim. What *social* conditions (conditions of society) create poverty? Are there *social* conditions that produce the lifestyles that the middle class so despises?

Welfare Reform

After decades of criticism, the U.S. welfare system was restructured in 1996. A federal law—the Personal Responsibility and Work Opportunity Reconciliation Act—requires states to place a lifetime cap on welfare assistance and compels welfare recipients to look for work and to take available jobs. The maximum length of time that someone can collect welfare is five years. In some states, it is less. Unmarried teen parents must attend school and live at home or in some other adult-supervised setting.

This law set off a storm of criticism. Some called it an attack on the poor. Defenders replied that the new rules would rescue people from poverty. They would transform welfare recipients into self-supporting and hard-working citizens—and reduce welfare costs. National welfare rolls plummeted, dropping by about 60 percent (Urban Institute 2006). Two out of five who left welfare also moved out of poverty (Hofferth 2002).

This is only the rosy part of the picture, however. Three of five are still in poverty or are back on welfare. A third of those who were forced off welfare have no jobs (Hage 2004; Urban Institute 2006). Some can't work because they have health problems. Others lack transportation. Some are addicted to drugs and alcohol. Still others are trapped in economically depressed communities where there are no jobs. Then there are those who have jobs, but earn so little that they remain in poverty. Consider one of the "success stories":

> **JoAnne Sims, 37, lives in Erie, New York, with her 7-year-old daughter Jamine. JoAnne left welfare, and now earns $7.25 an hour as a cook for Head Start. Her 37-hour week brings $268 before deductions. With the help of medical benefits and a mother who provides child care, JoAnne "gets by." She says, "From what I hear, a lot of us who went off welfare are still poor . . . let me tell you, it's not easy." (Peterson 2000; earnings updated)**

Conflict theorists have an interesting interpretation of welfare. They say that the purpose of welfare is not to help people, but, rather, to maintain a *reserve labor force*. It is designed to keep the unemployed alive during economic downturns until their labor is needed during the next economic boom. The 1996 law that reduced the welfare rolls fits this

deferred gratification doing without something in the present in the hope of achieving greater gains in the future

Horatio Alger myth the belief that due to limitless possibilities anyone can get ahead if he or she tries hard enough

model, as it was passed during the longest economic boom in U.S. history. Recessions are inevitable, however, and just as inevitable is surging unemployment. In line with conflict theory, we can predict that during the coming recession, welfare rules will be softened—in order to keep the reserve labor force ready for the next time they are needed.

Deferred Gratification

One consequence of a life of deprivation punctuated by emergencies—*and of viewing the future as promising more of the same*—is a lack of **deferred gratification,** giving up things in the present for the sake of greater gains in the future. It is difficult to practice this middle-class virtue if one does not have a middle-class surplus—or middle-class hope.

In a classic 1967 study of black streetcorner men, sociologist Elliot Liebow noted that the men did not defer gratification. Their jobs were low-paying and insecure, their lives pitted with emergencies. With the future looking exactly like the present, and any savings they did manage gobbled up by emergencies, it seemed pointless to save for the future. The only thing that made sense from their perspective was to enjoy what they could at that moment. Immediate gratification, then, was not the cause of their poverty, but, rather, its consequence. Cause and consequence loop together, however, for their immediate gratification helped perpetuate their poverty. For another look at this "looping," see the Down-to-Earth Sociology box on the next page, in which I share my personal experiences with poverty.

If both causes are at work, why do sociologists emphasize the structural explanation? Reverse the situation for a moment. Suppose that members of the middle class drove old cars that broke down, faced threats from the utility company to shut off the electricity and heat, and had to make a choice between paying the rent or buying medicine and food and diapers. How long would they practice deferred gratification? Their orientations to life would likely make a sharp U-turn.

Sociologists, then, do not view the behaviors of the poor as the cause of their poverty, but, rather, as the result of their poverty. Poor people would welcome the middle-class opportunities that would allow them the chance to practice the middle-class virtue of deferred gratification. Without those opportunities, though, they just can't afford it.

Where Is Horatio Alger? The Social Functions of a Myth

In the late 1800s, Horatio Alger was one of the country's most popular authors. The rags-to-riches exploits of his fictional boy heroes and their amazing successes in overcoming severe odds motivated thousands of boys of that period. Although Alger's characters have disappeared from U.S. literature, they remain alive and well in the psyche of Americans. From real-life examples of people of humble origin who climbed the social class ladder, Americans know that anyone who really tries can get ahead. In fact, they believe that most Americans, including minorities and the working poor, have an average or better-than-average chance of getting ahead—obviously a statistical impossibility (Kluegel and Smith 1986).

The accuracy of the **Horatio Alger myth** is less important than the belief that limitless possibilities exist for everyone. Functionalists would stress that this belief is functional for society. On the one hand, it encourages people to compete for higher positions, or, as the song says, "to reach for the highest star." On the other hand, it places blame for failure squarely on the individual. If you don't make it—in the face of ample opportunities to get ahead—the fault must be your own. The Horatio Alger myth helps to stabilize society: Since the fault is viewed as the individual's, not society's, current social arrangements can be regarded as satisfactory. This reduces pressures to change the system.

As Marx and Weber pointed out, social class penetrates our consciousness, shaping our ideas of life and our "proper" place in society. When the rich look at the world around them, they sense superiority and anticipate control over their own destiny. When the poor look around them, they are more likely to sense defeat and to anticipate that unpredictable forces will batter their lives. Both rich and poor know the dominant ideology, that their particular niche in life is due to their own efforts, that the reasons for success—or failure—lie solely with the self. Like fish that don't notice the water, people tend not to perceive the effects of social class on their own lives.

A society's dominant ideologies are reinforced throughout the society, including its literature. Horatio Alger provided inspirational heroes for thousands of boys. The central theme of these many novels, immensely popular in their time, was rags to riches. Through rugged determination and self-sacrifice, a boy could overcome seemingly insurmountable obstacles to reach the pinnacle of success. (Girls did not strive for financial success, but were dependent on fathers and husbands.)

Down-to-Earth Sociology
Poverty: A Personal Journey

I was born in poverty. My parents, who could not afford to rent a house or apartment, rented the tiny office in their minister's house. That is where I was born.

My father began to slowly climb the social class ladder. His fitful odyssey took him from laborer to truck driver to the owner of a series of small businesses (tire repair shop, bar, hotel), then to vacuum cleaner salesman, and back to bar owner. He converted a garage into a house. Although it had no indoor plumbing or insulation (in northern Minnesota!), it was a start. Later, he bought a house, and then he built a new home. After that we moved into a trailer, and then back to a house. My father's seventh-grade education was always an obstacle. Although he never became wealthy, poverty eventually became a distant memory for him.

My social class took a leap—from working class to upper middle class—when, after attending college and graduate school, I became a university professor. I entered a world that was unknown to my parents, one that was much more pampered and privileged. I had opportunities to do research, to publish, and to travel to exotic places. My reading centered on sociological research, and I read books in Spanish as well as in English. My father, in contrast, never read a book in his life, and my mother read only detective stories and romance paperbacks. One set of experiences isn't "better" than the other, just significantly different in determining what windows of perception it opens onto the world.

My interest in poverty, which was rooted in my own childhood experiences, stayed with me. I traveled to a dozen or so skid rows across the United States and Canada, talking to homeless people and staying in their shelters. In my own town, I spent considerable time with people on welfare, observing how they lived. I constantly marveled at the connections between *structural* causes of poverty (low education and skills, undependable transportation, the lack of unskilled jobs) and *personal* causes (the *culture of poverty*—alcohol and drug abuse, multiple out-of-wedlock births, frivolous spending, all-night partying, and a seeming incapacity to keep appointments—except to pick up the welfare check).

Sociologists haven't unraveled this connection, and as much as we might *like* for only structural causes to apply, clearly *both* are at work (Duneier 1999:122). The situation can be illustrated by looking at the perennial health problems I observed among the poor—the constant colds, runny noses, backaches, and injuries. The health problems stem from the *social structure* (less access to medical care, less capable physicians, drafty houses, little knowledge about nutrition, and more dangerous jobs). At the same time, *personal* characteristics—hygiene, eating habits, and overdrinking—cause health problems. Which is the cause and which the effect? Both, of course, for one loops into the other. The medical problems (which are based on both personal and structural causes) feed into the poverty these people experience, making them less able to perform their jobs successfully—or even to show up at work regularly. What an intricate puzzle for sociologists!

By the Numbers: *Then and Now*

The richest 20% of Americans receive this percentage of the nation's income

1970	NOW
41%	51%

The poorest 20% of Americans receive this percentage of the nation's income

1970	NOW
6%	3%

Frequency of births outside of marriage

1960	NOW
1 in 20	8 in 20

SUMMARY *and* REVIEW

What Is Social Class?

What is meant by the term social class?

Most sociologists have adopted Weber's definition of **social class:** a large group of people who rank closely to one another in terms of property (wealth), power, and prestige. **Wealth**—consisting of the value of property and income—is concentrated in the upper classes. From the 1930s to the 1970s, the trend in the distribution of wealth in the United States was toward greater equality. Since that time, it has been toward greater inequality. Pp. 262–265.

Power is the ability to get one's way even though others resist. C. Wright Mills coined the term **power elite** to refer to the small group that holds the reins of power in business, government, and the military. **Prestige** is linked to occupational status. People's rankings of occupational prestige have changed little over the decades and are similar from country to country. Globally, the occupations that bring greater prestige are those that pay more, require more education and abstract thought, and offer greater independence. Pp. 266–267.

What is meant by the term status inconsistency?

Status is social position. Most people are **status consistent;** that is, they rank high or low on all three dimensions of social class. People who rank higher on some dimensions than on others are status inconsistent. The frustrations of **status inconsistency** tend to produce political radicalism. Pp. 268–269.

Sociological Models of Social Class

What models are used to portray the social classes?

Erik Wright developed a four-class model based on Marx: (1) capitalists (owners of large businesses), (2) petty bourgeoisie (small business owners), (3) managers, and (4) workers. Kahl and Gilbert developed a six-class model based on Weber. At the top is the capitalist class. In descending order are the upper middle class, the lower middle class, the working class, the working poor, and the **underclass.** Pp. 270–273.

Consequences of Social Class

How does social class affect people's lives?

Social class leaves no aspect of life untouched. It affects our chances of benefiting from the new technology, dying early, becoming ill, receiving good health care, and getting divorced. Social class membership also affects child rearing, educational attainment, religious affiliation, political participation, the crimes people commit, and contact with the criminal justice system. Pp. 273–277.

Social Mobility

What are three types of social mobility?

The term **intergenerational mobility** refers to changes in social class from one generation to the next. **Structural mobility** refers to changes in society that lead large numbers of people to change their social class. **Exchange mobility** is the movement of large numbers of people from one class to another, with the net result that the relative proportions of the population in the classes remain about the same. Pp. 277–280.

Poverty

Who are the poor?

Poverty is unequally distributed in the United States. Racial–ethnic minorities (except Asian Americans), children, households headed by women, and rural Americans are more likely than others to be poor. The poverty rate of the elderly is less than that of the general population. Pp. 281–286.

Why are people poor?

Some social analysts believe that characteristics of *individuals* cause poverty. Sociologists, in contrast, examine *structural* features of society, such as employment opportunities, to find the causes of poverty. Sociologists generally conclude that life orientations are a consequence, not the cause, of people's position in the social class structure. Pp. 286–289.

How is the Horatio Alger myth functional for society?

The **Horatio Alger myth**—the belief that anyone can get ahead if only he or she tries hard enough—encourages people to strive to get ahead. It also deflects blame for failure from society to the individual. P. 288.

THINKING CRITICALLY *ABOUT* Chapter 10

1. The belief that the United States is the land of opportunity draws millions of legal and illegal immigrants to the United States each year. How do the materials in this chapter support or undermine this belief?

2. How does social class impact your life?

3. What social mobility has your own family experienced? In what ways has this affected your life?

ADDITIONAL RESOURCES

What can you find in MySocLab? mysoclab www.mysoclab.com

- Complete Ebook
- Practice Tests and Video and Audio activities
- Mapping and Data Analysis exercises

- Sociology in the News
- Classic Readings in Sociology
- Research and Writing advice

Where Can I Read More on This Topic?

Suggested readings for this chapter are listed at the back of this book.

Chapter 11

Sex and Gender

Afghanistan

I n Tunis, the capital of Tunisia, on Africa's northern coast, I met some U.S. college students and spent a couple of days with them. They wanted to see the city's red light district, but I wondered whether it would be worth the trip. I already had seen other red light districts, including the unusual one in Amsterdam where a bronze statue of a female prostitute lets you know you've entered the area; the state licenses the women and men, requiring that they have medical checkups (certificates must be posted); and the prostitutes add a sales tax to the receipt they give customers. The prostitutes sit behind lighted picture windows while customers stroll along the narrow canal side streets and browse from the outside. Tucked among the brothels are day care centers, bakeries, and clothing stores. Amsterdam itself is an unusual place—you can smoke marijuana in cafes, but not tobacco.

> In front of each open door stood a young woman. I could see . . . a well-worn bed.

I decided to go with them. We ended up on a wharf that extended into the Mediterranean. Each side was lined with a row of one-room wooden shacks, crowded one against the next. In front of each open door stood a young woman. Peering from outside into the dark interiors, I could see that each door led to a tiny room with a well-worn bed.

The wharf was crowded with men who were eyeing the women. Many of the men wore sailor uniforms from countries that I couldn't identify.

As I looked more closely, I could see that some of the women had runny sores on their legs. Incredibly, with such visible evidence of their disease, customers still sought them out. Evidently, the $2 price was too low to resist.

With a sick feeling in my stomach and the desire to vomit, I kept a good distance between the beckoning women and myself. One tour of the two-block area was more than sufficient.

Somewhere nearby, out of sight, I knew that there were men whose wealth derived from exploiting these women who were condemned to live short lives punctuated by fear and misery.

In this chapter, we examine **gender stratification**—males' and females' unequal access to property, power, and prestige. Gender is especially significant because it is a *master status;* that is, it cuts across *all* aspects of social life. No matter what we attain in life, we carry the label *male* or *female.* These labels convey images and expectations about how we should act. They not only guide our behavior but also serve as a basis of power and privilege.

In this chapter's fascinating journey, we shall look at inequality between the sexes both around the world and in the United States. We shall explore whether it is biology or culture that makes us the way we are and review sexual harassment, unequal pay, and violence against women. This excursion will provide a good context for understanding the power differences between men and women that lead to situations such as the one described in our opening vignette. It should also give you insight into your own experiences with gender.

Issues of Sex and Gender

When we consider how females and males differ, the first thing that usually comes to mind is **sex,** the *biological characteristics* that distinguish males and females. *Primary sex characteristics* consist of a vagina or a penis and other organs related to reproduction. *Secondary sex characteristics* are the physical distinctions between males and females that are not directly connected with reproduction. These characteristics become clearly evident at puberty when males develop more muscles and a lower voice, and gain more body hair and height, while females develop breasts and form more fatty tissue and broader hips.

Gender, in contrast, is a *social,* not a biological characteristic. **Gender** consists of whatever behaviors and attitudes a group considers proper for its males and females. Consequently, gender varies from one society to another. Whereas *sex* refers to male or female, *gender* refers to masculinity or femininity. In short, you inherit your sex, but you learn your gender as you are socialized into the behaviors and attitudes your culture asserts are appropriate for your sex.

As the photo montage on the next page illustrates, the expectations associated with gender differ around the world. They vary so greatly that some sociologists suggest that we replace the terms *masculinity* and *femininity* with *masculinities* and *femininities.*

The sociological significance of gender is that it is a device by which society controls its members. Gender sorts us, on the basis of sex, into different life experiences. It opens and closes doors to property, power, and even prestige. Like social class, gender is a structural feature of society.

Before examining inequalities of gender, let's consider why the behaviors of men and women differ.

Gender Differences in Behavior: Biology or Culture?

Why are most males more aggressive than most females? Why do women enter "nurturing" occupations, such as teaching young children and nursing, in far greater numbers than men? To answer such questions, many people respond with some variation of "They're just born that way."

Is this the correct answer? Certainly biology plays a significant role in our lives. Each of us begins as a fertilized egg. The egg, or ovum, is contributed by our mother, the sperm that fertilizes the egg by our father. At the very instant the egg is fertilized, our sex is determined. Each of us receives twenty-three chromosomes from the ovum and twenty-three from the sperm. The egg has an X chromosome. If the sperm that fertilizes the egg also has an X chromosome, we become a girl (XX). If the sperm has a Y chromosome, we become a boy (XY).

That's the biology. Now, the sociological question is, Does this biological difference control our behavior? Does it, for example, make females more nurturing and submissive and males more aggressive and domineering? Almost all sociologists take the side of "nurture" in this "nature versus nurture" controversy, but a few do not, as you can see from the Thinking Critically section on pages 296–297.

gender stratification males' and females' unequal access to property, power, and prestige

sex biological characteristics that distinguish females and males, consisting of primary and secondary sex characteristics

gender the behaviors and attitudes that a society considers proper for its males and females; masculinity or femininity

Mexico

Jordan

Kenya

Ethiopia

Brazil

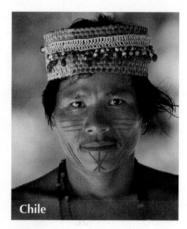

Chile

India

Tibet

Standards of Gender

Each human group determines its ideas of "maleness" and "femaleness." As you can see from these photos of four women and four men, standards of gender are arbitrary and vary from one culture to another. Yet, in its ethnocentrism, each group thinks that its preferences reflect what gender "really" is. As indicated here, around the world men and women try to make themselves appealing by aspiring to their group's standards of gender

ThinkingCRITICALLY
Biology Versus Culture—Culture Is the Answer

Sociologist Cynthia Fuchs Epstein (1988, 1999, 2007) stresses that differences between the behavior of males and females are solely the result of social factors—specifically, socialization and social control. Her argument is as follows:

1. The anthropological record shows greater equality between the sexes in the past than we had thought. In earlier societies, women, as well as men, hunted small game, made tools, and gathered food. In hunting and gathering societies, the roles of both women and men are less rigid than those indicated by stereotypes. For example, the Agta and Mbuti are egalitarian. This proves that hunting and gathering societies exist in which women are not subordinate to men. Anthropologists claim that in these societies women have a separate but equal status.

2. The types of work that men and women do in each society are determined not by biology but by social arrangements. Few people can escape these arrangements, and almost everyone works within his or her assigned narrow range. This division of work by gender serves the interests of men, and both informal customs and formal laws enforce it. When these socially constructed barriers are removed, women's work habits are similar to those of men.

Cynthia Fuchs Epstein, whose position in the ongoing "nature versus nurture" debate is summarized here.

3. Biology "causes" some human behaviors, but they are related to reproduction or differences in body structure. These differences are relevant for only a few activities, such as playing basketball or "crawling through a small space."

4. Female crime rates are rising in many parts of the world. This indicates that aggression, which is often considered a male behavior dictated by biology, is related instead to social factors. When social conditions permit, such as when women become lawyers, they, too, become "adversarial, assertive, and dominant." Not incidentally, another form of this "dominant behavior" is the challenges that women make to the biased views about human nature proposed by men.

In short, rather than "women's incompetence or inability to read a legal brief, perform brain surgery, [or] to predict a bull market," social factors—socialization, gender discrimination, and other forms of social control—create gender differences in behavior. Arguments that assign "an evolutionary and genetic basis" to explain differences in the behaviors of women and men are simplistic. They "rest on a dubious structure of inappropriate, highly selective, and poor data, oversimplification in logic and in inappropriate inferences by use of analogy."

ThinkingCRITICALLY
Biology Versus Culture—Biology Is the Answer

Sociologist Steven Goldberg (1974, 1986, 1993, 2003) finds it astonishing that anyone should doubt "the presence of core-deep differences in males and females, differences of temperament and emotion we call masculinity and femininity." Goldberg's argument—that it is not environment but inborn differences that "give masculine and feminine direction to the emotions and behaviors of men and women"—is as follows:

1. The anthropological record shows that all societies for which evidence exists are (or were) **patriarchies** (societies in which men-as-a-group dominate women-as-a-group). Stories about long-lost **matriarchies** (societies in which women-as-a-group dominate men-as-a-group) are myths.

2. In all societies, past and present, the highest statuses are associated with men. In every society, politics is ruled by "hierarchies overwhelmingly dominated by men."

3. Men dominate societies because they "have a lower threshold for the elicitation of dominance behavior . . . a greater tendency to exhibit whatever behavior is necessary in any environment to attain dominance in hierarchies and male–female encounters and relationships." Men are more willing "to sacrifice the rewards of other motivations—the desire for affection, health, family life, safety, relaxation, vacation and the like—in order to attain dominance and status."

4. Just as a 6-foot woman does not prove the social basis of height, so exceptional individuals, such as highly achieving and dominant women, do not refute "the physiological roots of behavior."

Steven Goldberg, whose position in the ongoing "nature versus nurture" debate is summarized here.

In short, there is only one valid interpretation of why every society from that of the Pygmy to that of the Swede associates dominance and attainment with men. Male dominance of society is "an inevitable resolution of the psychophysiological reality." Socialization and social institutions merely *reflect*—and sometimes exaggerate—inborn tendencies. Any interpretation other than inborn differences is "wrongheaded, ignorant, tendentious, internally illogical, discordant with the evidence, and implausible in the extreme." The argument that males are more aggressive because they have been socialized that way is equivalent to the claim that men can grow mustaches because boys have been socialized that way.

To acknowledge this reality is *not* to defend discrimination against women. Approval or disapproval of what societies have done with these basic biological differences is not the issue. The point is that biology leads males and females to different behaviors and attitudes—regardless of how we feel about this or whether we wish it were different.

patriarchy a society in which men as a group dominate women as a group; authority is vested in males

matriarchy a society in which women as a group dominate men as a group; authority is vested in females

The Dominant Position in Sociology

The dominant sociological position is that we behave the way we do because of social factors, not biology. Our visible differences of sex do not come with meanings built into them. Rather, each human group makes its own interpretation of these physical differences and assigns males and females to separate groups. In these groups, people learn what is expected of them and are given different access to property, power, prestige, and other privileges available in their society.

Most sociologists find compelling the argument that if biology were the principal factor in human behavior, all around the world we would find women behaving in one way and men in another. In fact, however, ideas of gender vary greatly from one culture to another—and, as a result, so do male–female behaviors.

Opening the Door to Biology

The matter of "nature" versus "nurture" is not so easily settled, however, and some sociologists acknowledge that biological factors are involved in some human behavior other than reproduction and childbearing (Udry 2000). Alice Rossi, a feminist sociologist and former president of the American Sociological Association, has suggested that women are better prepared biologically for "mothering" than are men. Rossi (1977, 1984) says that women are more sensitive to the infant's soft skin and to their nonverbal communications. She stresses that the issue is not either biology or society. Instead, nature provides biological predispositions, which are then overlaid with culture.

To see why the door to biology is opening just slightly in sociology, let's consider a medical accident and a study of Vietnam veterans.

A Medical Accident.   The drama began in 1963, when 7-month-old identical twin boys were taken to a doctor for a routine circumcision (Money and Ehrhardt 1972). The inept physician, who was using a heated needle, turned the electric current too high and accidentally burned off the penis of one of the boys. You can imagine the parents' disbelief—and then their horror—as the truth sank in.

What can be done in a situation like this? The damage was irreversible. The parents were told that their boy could never have sexual relations. After months of soul-searching and tearful consultations with experts, the parents decided that their son should have a sex-change operation. When he was 22 months old, surgeons castrated the boy, using the skin to construct a vagina. The parents then gave the child a new name, Brenda, dressed him in frilly clothing, let his hair grow long, and began to treat him as a girl. Later, physicians gave Brenda female steroids to promote female pubertal growth (Colapinto 2001).

At first, the results were promising. When the twins were 4 years old, the mother said (remember that the children are biologically identical):

> One thing that really amazes me is that she is so feminine. I've never seen a little girl so neat and tidy. . . . She likes for me to wipe her face. She doesn't like to be dirty, and yet my son is quite different. I can't wash his face for anything. . . . She is very proud of herself, when she puts on a new dress, or I set her hair. . . . She seems to be daintier. (Money and Ehrhardt 1972)

About a year later, the mother described how their daughter imitated her while their son copied his father:

> I found that my son, he chose very masculine things like a fireman or a policeman. . . . He wanted to do what daddy does, work where daddy does, and carry a lunch kit. . . . [My daughter] didn't want any of those things. She wants to be a doctor or a teacher. . . . But none of the things that she ever wanted to be were like a policeman or a fireman, and that sort of thing never appealed to her. (Money and Ehrhardt 1972)

David Reimer, whose story is recounted here.

If the matter were this clear-cut, we could use this case to conclude that gender is determined entirely by nurture. Seldom are things in life so simple, however, and a twist occurs in this story. Despite this promising start and her parents' coaching, Brenda did not adapt well to femininity. She preferred to mimic her father shaving, rather than her mother putting on makeup. She rejected dolls, favoring guns and her brother's toys. She liked rough-and-tumble games and insisted on urinating standing up. Classmates teased her and called her a "cavewoman" because she walked like a boy. At age 14, she was expelled from school for beating up a girl who teased her. Despite estrogen treatment, she was not attracted to boys, and at age 14, in despair over her inner turmoil, she was thinking of suicide. In a tearful confrontation, her father told her about the accident and her sex change.

"All of a sudden everything clicked. For the first time, things made sense, and I understood who and what I was," the twin said of this revelation. David (his new name) then had testosterone shots and, later, surgery to partially reconstruct a penis. At age 25, he married a woman and adopted her children (Diamond and Sigmundson 1997; Colapinto 2001). There is an unfortunate end to this story, however. In 2004, David committed suicide.

The Vietnam Veterans Study. Time after time, researchers have found that boys and men who have higher levels of testosterone tend to be more aggressive. In one study, researchers compared the testosterone levels of college men in a "rowdy" fraternity with those of men in a fraternity that had a reputation for academic achievement and social responsibility. Men in the "rowdy" fraternity had higher levels of testosterone (Dabbs et al. 1996). In another study, researchers found that prisoners who had committed sex crimes and acts of violence against people had higher levels of testosterone than those who had committed property crimes (Dabbs et al. 1995). The samples were small, however, leaving the nagging uncertainty that these findings might be due to chance.

Then in 1985, the U.S. government began a health study of Vietnam veterans. To be certain that the study was representative, the researchers chose a random sample of 4,462 men. Among the data they collected was a measurement of testosterone. This sample supports earlier studies showing that men who have higher levels of testosterone tend to be more aggressive and to have more problems as a consequence. When the veterans with higher testosterone levels were boys, they were more likely to get in trouble with parents and teachers and to become delinquents. As adults, they were more likely to use hard drugs, to get into fights, to end up in lower-status jobs, and to have more sexual partners. Those who married were more likely to have affairs, to hit their wives, and, it follows, to get divorced (Dabbs and Morris 1990; Booth and Dabbs 1993).

This makes it sound like biology is the basis for behavior. Fortunately for us sociologists, there is another side to this research, and here is where *social class,* the topic of our previous chapter, comes into play. High-testosterone men from lower social classes are more likely to get in trouble with the law, do poorly in school, or mistreat their wives than are high-testosterone men from higher social classes (Dabbs and Morris 1990). *Social* factors such as socialization, subcultures, life goals, and self-definitions are significant in these men's behavior. Discovering how social factors work in combination with testosterone level, then, is of great interest to sociologists.

Sociologists study the social factors that underlie human behavior, the experiences that mold us, funneling us into different directions in life. The research on Vietnam veterans discussed in the text indicates how the sociological door is opening slowly to also consider biological factors in human behavior. This 1966 photo shows orderlies rushing a wounded soldier to an evacuation helicopter.

In Sum: The findings are preliminary, but significant and provocative. They indicate that human behavior is not a matter of either nature or nurture, but of the two working together. Some behavior that we sociologists usually assume to be due entirely to socialization is apparently influenced by biology. In the years to come, this should prove to be an exciting—and controversial—area of sociological research. One level of research will be to determine whether any behaviors are due only to biology. The second level will be to discover the ways that social factors modify biology. The third level will be, in sociologist Janet Chafetz's (1990:30) phrase, to determine how "different" becomes translated into "unequal."

Gender Inequality in Global Perspective

Around the world, gender is *the* primary division between people. Every society sorts men and women into separate groups and gives them different access to property, power, and prestige. These divisions *always* favor men-as-a-group. After reviewing the historical record, historian and feminist Gerda Lerner (1986) concluded that "there is not a single society known where women-as-a-group have decision-making power over men (as a group)." Consequently, sociologists classify females as a *minority group*. Because females outnumber males, you may find this strange. The term *minority group* applies, however, because it refers to people who are discriminated against on the basis of physical or cultural characteristics, regardless of their numbers (Hacker 1951). For an overview of gender discrimination in Iran, see the Mass Media in Social Life box on the next page.

How Females Became a Minority Group

Have females always been a minority group? Some analysts speculate that in hunting and gathering societies, women and men were social equals (Leacock 1981; Hendrix 1994) and that horticultural societies also had less gender discrimination than is common today (Collins et al. 1993). In these societies, women may have contributed about 60 percent of the group's total food. Yet, around the world, gender is the basis for discrimination. How, then, did it happen that women became a minority group? Let's consider the primary theory that has been proposed.

The Origins of Patriarchy

The major theory of the origin of *patriarchy*—men dominating society—points to social consequences of human reproduction (Lerner 1986; Friedl 1990). In early human history, life was short. To balance the high death rate and maintain the population, women had to give birth to many children. This brought severe consequences for women. To survive, an infant needed a nursing mother. With a child at her breast or in her uterus, or one carried on her hip or on her back, women were physically encumbered. Consequently, around the world women assumed tasks that were associated with the home and child care, while men took over the hunting of large animals and other tasks that required both greater speed and longer absences from the base camp (Huber 1990).

As a result, men became dominant. It was the men who left camp to hunt animals, who made contact with other tribes, who traded with these groups, and who quarreled and waged war with them. It was also the men who made and controlled the instruments of death, the weapons that were used for hunting and warfare. It was they who accumulated possessions in trade and gained prestige by returning to the camp triumphantly, leading captured prisoners or bringing large animals they had killed to feed the tribe. In contrast, little prestige was given to the routine, taken-for-granted activities of women—who were not perceived as risking their lives for the group. Eventually, men took over society. Their sources of power were their weapons, items of trade, and knowledge gained from contact with other groups. Women became second-class citizens, subject to men's decisions.

Is this theory correct? Remember that the answer lies buried in human history, and there is no way of testing it. Male dominance may be the result of some entirely different cause. For example, anthropologist Marvin Harris (1977) proposed that because most men are stronger than most women and survival in tribal groups

Men's work? Women's work? Customs in other societies can blow away stereotypes. As is common throughout India, these women are working on road construction.

required hand-to-hand combat, men became the warriors, and women became the reward that enticed men to risk their lives in battle. Frederick Engels proposed that patriarchy came with the development of private property (Lerner 1986; Jacobs 2007). He could not explain why private property should have produced male dominance, however. Gerda Lerner (1986) suggests that patriarchy may even have had different origins in different places.

Whatever its origins, a circular system of thought evolved. Men came to think of themselves as inherently superior—based on the evidence that they dominated society. They shrouded many of their activities with secrecy and constructed elaborate rules and rituals

MASS MEDIA In SOCIAL LIFE

Women in Iran: The Times Are Changing, Ever So Slowly

A woman's testimony in court is worth half that of a man's testimony.

A woman may inherit from her parents only half what her brother inherits.

A woman who has sex with a man who is not her husband can be stoned to death.

A woman who refuses to cover her hair in public can receive 80 lashes with a whip.

Not exactly equality.

As you would expect, Iranian women don't like it. Until now, though, there was little that they could do. Women are controlled by their fathers until they marry, and after marriage they come under the control of their husbands.

For the most part, they didn't know that life could be different.

Now the mass media are spearheading change in gender relations. There is a new literacy: Iranian women are logging onto the Internet, and they are reading books. Satellite television is also beaming new information across geographic lines, bringing pictures of other ways of life, of an unfamiliar equality and mutual respect between women and men.

Thanks to the mass media, their eyes are being opened to the fact that not all the women in the world live under the thumbs of men. From this awareness is coming the realization that they don't have to live like this either, that there really is a potential for new relationships.

This awareness and the glimmer of hope that another way of life can be theirs are leading to an incipient women's movement.

As in Afghanistan, the movement is still small—and protest remains dangerous. Some women have been fined, and for others it is worse. Alieh Eghamdoust, for example, is serving a three-year jail sentence for participating in a women's demonstration. Other protestors

The incipient women's movement in Iran is a sign of changing times. These students at a university in Iran indicate changing lifestyles and ideas.

find brutality at home, from their husbands, fathers, or brothers.

Despite the danger, women are continuing to protest. They are even pressing for new rights in the Iranian courts. They are demanding divorce from abusive husbands—and some are getting it.

Not much has changed yet. A man can still divorce his wife whenever he wants, while a woman who wants to divorce a husband must go through a lengthy procedure and never can be sure she will be granted the divorce. A husband also gets automatic custody of any children over the age of seven.

But as women continue their struggle, change will come. One sign of hope: Fewer women are being stoned to death.

This, at least, is a beginning.

For Your Consideration

What do you think gender relations will be like in Iran ten years from now? Why?

If the women's movement in Iran becomes popular and effective, do you think that the relationship between men and women will be about the same as it is in the United States? Why or why not?

Based on Fathi 2009; Semple 2009.

Anthropologist George Murdock surveyed 324 traditional societies worldwide. In all of them, some work was considered "men's work," while other tasks were considered "women's work." He found that hunting is almost universally considered "men's work." These men, who live on the steppes of Mongolia, ride reindeer when they go hunting.

to avoid "contamination" by females, whom they openly deemed inferior by that time. Even today, patriarchy is always accompanied by cultural supports designed to justify male dominance—such as designating certain activities as "not appropriate" for women.

As tribal societies developed into larger groups, men, who enjoyed their power and privileges, maintained their dominance. Long after hunting and hand-to-hand combat ceased to be routine, and even after large numbers of children were no longer needed to maintain the population, men held on to their power. Male dominance in contemporary societies, then, is a continuation of a millennia-old pattern whose origin is lost in history.

Sex Typing of Work

Anthropologist George Murdock (1937) analyzed data that researchers had reported on 324 societies around the world. He found that in all of them, activities are *sex typed*. In other words, every society associates certain activities with one sex or the other. He also found that activities that are considered "female" in one society may be considered "male" in another. In some groups, for example, taking care of cattle is women's work, while other groups assign this task to men.

A theory of how *patriarchy* originated centers on childbirth. Because only women give birth, they assumed tasks associated with home and child care, while men hunted and performed other survival tasks that required greater strength, speed, and absence from home. Following in the steps of her female ancestors, this woman in Yangshou, China, while she works, takes care of her grandchild.

There was one exception, metalworking, which was considered men's work in all of the societies that Murdock examined. Making weapons, pursuing sea mammals, and hunting were almost universally the domain of men, but in a few societies women participated in these activities. Although Murdock found no specific work that was universally assigned only to women, he did find that making clothing, cooking, carrying water, and grinding grain were almost always female tasks. In a few societies, however, such activities were regarded as men's work.

From Murdock's cross-cultural survey, we can conclude that nothing about biology requires men and women to be assigned different work. Anatomy does not have to equal destiny when it comes to occupations, for as we have seen, pursuits that are considered feminine in one society may be deemed masculine in another, and vice versa. On pages 304–305 is a photo essay on women at work in India that underscores this point.

Gender and the Prestige of Work

You might ask whether this division of labor really illustrates social inequality. Does it perhaps simply represent each group's arbitrary ways of dividing up labor, not gender discrimination?

This could be the case, except for this finding: *Universally, greater prestige is given to male activities—regardless of what those activities are* (Linton 1936; Rosaldo 1974). If taking care of goats is men's work, then the care of goats is considered important and carries high prestige, but if it is women's work, it is considered less important and is given less prestige. Let's take an example closer to home. When delivering babies was "women's work" and was done by midwives, it was given low prestige. But when men took over this task, they became "baby doctors" with high prestige (Ehrenreich and English 1973). In short, it is not the work that provides the prestige, but the sex with which the work is associated.

Other Areas of Global Discrimination

Let's briefly consider four additional aspects of global gender discrimination. Later, when we focus on the United States, we shall examine these topics in greater detail.

The Global Gap in Education. Almost 1 billion adults around the world cannot read; two-thirds are women (UNESCO 2008). Illiteracy is especially common in Africa and the Middle East, but is not limited to those areas. In North America, only about half of the women in Haiti can read and write ("Women of . . . " 2002). The United Nations has made it a priority to increase literacy and monitors each country's progress. The statistics the United Nations uses, though, underestimate the problem. Some people are counted as literate if they can write their name (Falkenberg 2008).

The Global Gap in Politics. In 2008, Rwanda became the first country in the world to elect more women (56 percent) than men to its national legislature (Pflanz 2008). It is typical for women to be highly underrepresented in politics, for on average, women make up just 18 percent of the world's national legislative bodies (UNIFEM 2008). In some countries, such as Papua New Guinea, the total is only 1 percent.

The Global Gap in Pay. In every nation, women average less pay than men. In the United States, full-time working women average only 72 percent of what men make (see Figure 11.8 on page 318). In some countries, women make much less than this.

Global Violence Against Women. A global human rights issue is violence against women. Historical examples are foot binding in China, witch burning in Europe, and *suttee* (burning the living widow with the body of her dead husband) in India. Today we have rape, wife beating, female infanticide, and the kidnapping of women to be brides. There is also forced prostitution, which was probably the case in our opening vignette. Another notorious example is female circumcision, the topic of the Cultural Diversity box on page 306.

"Honor killings" are another form of violence against women. In some societies, such as Pakistan, Jordan, and Kurdistan, a woman who is thought to have brought disgrace on her family is killed by a male relative—usually a brother or her husband, but sometimes her father or uncles. What threat to the family's honor can be so severe that the men kill a daughter, wife, or sister? The usual reason is sex outside of marriage. Even a woman who has been raped is in danger of becoming the victim of an honor killing (Zoepf 2007; Falkenberg 2008). Killing the girl or woman removes the "stain" she has brought to the family and restores its honor in the community. Sharing this view, the police in these countries generally ignore honor killings, viewing them as private family matters.

In Sum: Inequality is not some accidental, hit-or-miss affair. Rather, each society's institutions work together to maintain the group's particular forms of inequality. Customs, often venerated throughout history, both justify and maintain these arrangements. In some cases, the prejudice and discrimination directed at females are so extreme they result in their enslavement and death.

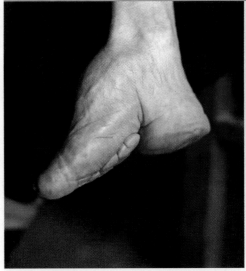

Foot binding was practiced in China until about 1900. Tiny feet were a status symbol. They made it difficult for a woman to walk, indicating that a woman's husband did not need his wife's labor. To make the feet even smaller, sometime's the baby's feet were broken and wrapped tightly. Some baby's toes were cut off. This photo was taken in Yunnan Province, China.

Work and Gender:
Women at Work in India

t raveling through India was both a pleasant and an eye-opening experience. The country is incredibly diverse, the people friendly, and the land culturally rich. For this photo essay, wherever I went—whether city, village, or countryside—I took photos of women at work.

From these photos, you can see that Indian women work in a wide variety of occupations. Some of their jobs match traditional Western expectations, and some diverge sharply from our gender stereotypes. Although women in India remain subservient to men—with the women's movement hardly able to break the cultural surface—women's occupations are hardly limited to the home. I was surprised at some of the hard, heavy labor that Indian women do.

Indian women are highly visible in public places. A storekeeper is as likely to be a woman as a man. This woman is selling glasses of water at a beach on the Bay of Bengal. The structure on which her glasses rest is built of sand.

The villages of India have no indoor plumbing. Instead, each village has a well with a hand pump, and it is the women's job to fetch the water. This is backbreaking work, for, after pumping the water, the women wrestle the heavy buckets onto their heads and carry them home. This was one of the few occupations I saw that was limited to women.

Women also take care of livestock. It looks as though this woman dressed up and posed for her photo, but this is what she was wearing and doing when I saw her in the field and stopped to talk to her. While the sheep are feeding, her job is primarily to "be" there, to make certain the sheep don't wander off or that no one steals them.

Sweeping the house is traditional work for Western women. So it is in India, but the sweeping has been extended to areas outside the home. These women are sweeping a major intersection in Chennai. When the traffic light changes here, the women will continue sweeping, with the drivers swerving around them. This was one of the few occupations that seems to be limited to women.

As in the West, food preparation in India is traditional women's work. Here, however, food preparation takes an unexpected twist. Having poured rice from the 60-pound sack onto the floor, these women in Chittoor search for pebbles or other foreign objects that might be in the rice.

When I saw this unusual sight, I had to stop and talk to the workers. From historical pictures, I knew that belt-driven machines were common on U.S. farms 100 years ago. This one in Tamil Nadu processes sugar cane. The woman feeds sugar cane into the machine, which disgorges the stalks on one side and sugar cane juice on the other.

I visited quarries in different parts of India, where I found men, women, and children hard at work in the tropical sun. This woman works 8 1/2 hours a day, six days a week. She earns 40 rupees a day (about ninety cents). Men make 60 rupees a day (about $1.35). Like many quarry workers, this woman is a bonded laborer. She must give half of her wages to her master.

This woman belongs to the Dhobi subcaste, whose occupation is washing clothes. She stands waist deep at this same spot doing the same thing day after day. The banks of this canal in Hyderabad are lined with men and women of her caste, who are washing linens for hotels and clothing for more well-to-do families.

A common sight in India is women working on construction crews. As they work on buildings and on highways, they mix cement, unload trucks, carry rubble, and, following Indian culture, carry loads of bricks atop their heads. This photo was taken in Raipur, Chhattisgarh.

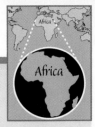

Cultural Diversity around the World

Female Circumcision

"Lie down there," the excisor suddenly said to me [when I was 12], pointing to a mat on the ground. No sooner had I laid down than I felt my frail, thin legs grasped by heavy hands and pulled wide apart. . . . Two women on each side of me pinned me to the ground . . . I underwent the ablation of the labia minor and then of the clitoris. The operation seemed to go on forever. I was in the throes of agony, torn apart both physically and psychologically. It was the rule that girls of my age did not weep in this situation. I broke the rule. I cried and screamed with pain . . . !

Afterwards they forced me, not only to walk back to join the other girls who had already been excised, but to dance with them. I was doing my best, but then I fainted. . . . It was a month before I was completely healed. When I was better, everyone mocked me, as I hadn't been brave, they said. (Walker and Parmar 1993:107–108)

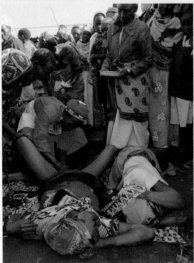

Circumcision in Kapchorwa, Uganda

Worldwide, between 100 million and 140 million females have been circumcised, mostly in Muslim Africa and in some parts of Malaysia and Indonesia (World Health Organization 2008). In Egypt, 97 percent of the women have been circumcised, the same as in Indonesia (Douglas 2005; Slackman 2007). In some cultures, the surgery occurs seven to ten days after birth, but in others it is not performed until girls reach adolescence. Among most groups, it takes place between the ages of 4 and 8. Because the surgery is usually done without anesthesia, the pain is so excruciating that adults hold the girl down. In urban areas, physicians sometimes perform the operation; in rural areas, a neighborhood woman usually does it.

In some cultures, only the girl's clitoris is cut off; in others, more is removed. In Sudan, the Nubia cut away most of the girl's genitalia, then sew together the remaining outer edges. They bind the girl's legs from her ankles to her waist for several weeks while scar tissue closes up the vagina. They leave a small opening the diameter of a pencil for the passage of urine and menstrual fluids. When a woman marries, the opening is cut wider to permit sexual intercourse. Before a woman gives birth, the opening is enlarged further. After birth, the vagina is again sutured shut; this cycle of surgically closing and opening begins anew with each birth.

What are the reasons for circumcising girls? Some groups believe that it reduces female sexual desire, making it more likely that a woman will be a virgin at marriage and, afterward, remain faithful to her husband. Others think that women can't bear children if they aren't circumcised.

The surgery has strong support among many women. Some mothers and grandmothers even insist that the custom continue. Their concern is that their daughters marry well, and in some of these societies uncircumcised women are considered impure and are not allowed to marry.

Feminists respond that female circumcision is a form of ritual torture to control female sexuality. They point out that men dominate the societies that practice it.

Change is on its way: A social movement to ban female circumcision has developed, and the World Health Organization has declared that female circumcision is a human rights issue. Fifteen African countries have now banned the circumcision of females. Without sanctions, though, these laws accomplish little. In Egypt, which prohibited female circumcision in 1996, almost all girls continue to be circumcised (Corbett 2008).

For Your Consideration

Do you think it is legitimate for the members of one culture to interfere with the customs of another culture? If so, under what circumstances? What makes us right and them wrong? What if some African nation said that some U.S. custom is wrong? How would you respond to this Somali woman who said, "The Somali woman doesn't need an alien woman telling her how to treat her private parts."

Sources: As cited, and Lightfoot-Klein 1989; Merwine 1993; Chalkley 1997; Collymore 2000; Tuhus-Dubrow 2007; UNIFEM 2008.

Gender Inequality in the United States

As we review gender inequality in the United States, let's begin by taking a brief look at how change in this vital area of social life came about. Before we do so, though, you might enjoy the historical snapshot presented in the Down-to-Earth Sociology box on the next page.

feminism the philosophy that men and women should be politically, economically, and socially equal; organized activities on behalf of this principle

Fighting Back: The Rise of Feminism

In the nation's early history, the second-class status of U.S. women was taken for granted. A husband and wife were legally one person—him (Chafetz and Dworkin 1986). Women could not vote, buy property in their own name, make legal contracts, or serve on juries. How could things have changed so much in the last hundred years that these examples sound like fiction?

A central lesson of conflict theory is that power yields privilege; like a magnet, power draws society's best resources to the elite. Because men tenaciously held onto their privileges and used social institutions to maintain their position, basic rights for women came only through prolonged and bitter struggle.

Feminism—the view that biology is not destiny and that stratification by gender is wrong and should be resisted—met with strong opposition, both by men who had privilege to lose and by women who accepted their status as morally correct. In 1894, for example, Jeannette Gilder said that women should not have the right to vote because "Politics is too public, too wearing, and too unfitted to the nature of women" (Crossen 2003).

Feminists, then known as suffragists, struggled against such views. In 1916, they founded the National Woman's Party, and in 1917 they began to picket the White House. After picketing for six months, the women were arrested. Hundreds were sent to prison, including Lucy Burns, a leader of the National Woman's Party. The extent to which these women had threatened male privilege is demonstrated by how they were treated in prison.

> Two men brought in Dorothy Day [the editor of a periodical that promoted women's rights], twisting her arms above her head. Suddenly they lifted her and brought her body down twice over the back of an iron bench. . . . They had been there a few minutes when Mrs. Lewis, all doubled over like a sack of flour, was thrown in. Her head struck the iron bed and she fell to the floor senseless. As for Lucy Burns, they handcuffed her wrists and fastened the handcuffs over [her] head to the cell door. (Cowley 1969)

ALICE PAUL
GOT SEVEN MONTHS
BECAUSE
SHE OPPOSED A POLITICAL PARTY
WE DEMAND
THAT SHE BE TREATED AS A
POLITICAL OFFENDER

THE SUFFRAGE PRISONERS
WERE ARRESTED FOR A
POLITICAL OFFENSE.
WE DEMAND
THAT THEY BE TREATED AS
POLITICAL OFFENDERS.

TO ASK FREEDOM
FOR WOMEN IS NOT
A CRIME
SUFFRAGE PRISONER
SHOULD NOT BE TREATED
AS CRIMINALS

The "first wave" of the U.S. women's movement met enormous opposition. The women in this 1920 photo had just been released after serving two months in jail for picketing the White House. Lucy Burns, mentioned on this page, is the second woman on the left. Alice Paul, who was placed in solitary confinement and is a subject of this 1920 protest, is featured in the photo circle of early female sociologists in Chapter 1, page 17.

Down-to-Earth Sociology
Women and Smoking: Let's Count the Reasons

(A humorous, but serious, look at historical changes in gender)

Why Women Shouldn't Smoke

1. Smoking ruins a woman's reputation and turns her into a tramp.
   "A man may take out a woman who smokes for a good time, but he won't marry her, and if he does, he won't stay married."

   Editorial in the Washington Post, *1914*

2. Women who smoke drive young men wild, break up families, and even make men kill.
   "Young fellows go into our restaurants to find women folks sucking cigarettes. What happens? The young fellows lose all respect for the women, and the next thing you know the young fellows, vampired by these smoking women, desert their homes, their wives and children, rob their employers and even commit murder so that they can get money to lavish on these smoking women."

   A New York City alderman

3. It just doesn't look good (but it can be elegant).
   "To smoke in public is always bad taste in a woman. In private she may be pardoned if she does it with sufficient elegance."

   Alexandre Duval, a Parisian restaurateur, 1921

4. Smoking is so un-motherlike.
   It "coarsens" women and "detracts from the ideal of fine motherhood."

   The executive board of the Cleveland Boy Scouts, 1928

5. Smoking is a horrible evil that ruins women's sleep; plus it is bad for their skin.
   "The cigarette habit indulged by women tends to cause nervousness and insomnia and ruins the complexion. This is one of the most evil influences in American life today."

   Hugh S. Cumming, surgeon general of the U.S., 1920

6. Women just aren't as good as men at smoking.
   "Women really don't know how to smoke. One woman smoking one cigarette at a dinner table will stir up more smoke than a whole tableful of men smoking cigars. They don't seem to know what to do with the smoke. Neither do they know how to hold their cigarettes properly. They make a mess of the whole performance."

   The manager of a Manhattan hotel

An ad from 1929

(And with cancer, you'll lose even more weight!)

Why Women Should Smoke

1. It helps avoid those bad body parts.
   "You can't hide fat, clumsy ankles. When tempted to overindulge, reach for a Lucky."

   The American Tobacco Company, 1930s

Opposition to women's smoking was so strong that the police in New York City warned women not to light up—even in their own cars. Women's colleges also got into the act. Smith College students who were seen smoking, even off campus, were given a demerit. This was serious—three demerits and a woman would be kicked out of college.

Despite the opposition, more and more women began to smoke, evidently feeling that having "fat, clumsy ankles" was worse than risking their reputations. (In case you are wondering about those ankles, with women's clothing of the time, that's about all that men could see.)

For Your Consideration

Why do you think there was such strong opposition to women smoking in the early 1900s? What is the relationship between women smoking at this time and women's evolving political rights? Here is an historical statement that connects them: "If it were a question between their smoking and their voting, and they would promise to stay at home and smoke, I would say let them smoke."

Sen. Joseph Bailey of Texas, 1918

Source: Based on Crossen 2008.

This *first wave* of the women's movement had a radical branch that wanted to reform all the institutions of society and a conservative branch whose concern was to win the vote for women (Freedman 2001). The conservative branch dominated, and after the right to vote was won in 1920, the movement basically dissolved.

The *second wave* began in the 1960s. Sociologist Janet Chafetz (1990) points out that up to this time most women thought of work as a temporary activity intended to fill the time between completing school and getting married. To see how children's books reinforced such thinking, see Figure 11.1. As more women took jobs and began to regard them as careers, however, they began to compare their working conditions with those of men. This shift in their reference group changed the way women viewed their conditions at work. The result was a second wave of protest against gender inequalities. The goals of this second wave (which continues today) are broad, ranging from raising women's pay to changing policies on violence against women.

A *third wave* of feminism has emerged. Three main aspects are apparent. The first is a greater focus on the problems of women in the Least Industrialized Nations (Spivak 2000; Hamid 2006). Some are fighting battles against conditions long since overcome by women in the Most Industrialized Nations. The second is a criticism of the values that dominate work and society. Some feminists argue that competition, toughness, calloused emotions, and independence represent "male" qualities and need to be replaced with cooperation, connection, openness, and interdependence (England 2000). A third aspect is the removal of impediments to women's love and sexual pleasure (Crawford 2007). As this third wave develops, we can assume that it, too, will have its liberal and conservative branches.

Although U.S. women enjoy fundamental rights today, gender inequality continues to play a central role in social life. Let's first consider everyday life, the most pervasive form of gender inequality.

Gender Inequality in Everyday Life

One of the more common and significant aspects of gender discrimination in everyday life is the devaluation of femininity.

Devaluation of Things Feminine.   In general, a higher value is placed on things considered masculine, for masculinity symbolizes strength and success while femininity is often perceived in terms of weakness and lack of accomplishment. People are often unaware that they make these relative evaluations, but if you listen carefully you can hear them pop up in their speech. Let's take a quick historical glance at one of these indicators. It might even be one that you have used:

FIGURE 11.1   Teaching Gender

Mother and Sally

Mother can sew.
Jane can sew.

The "Dick and Jane" readers were the top selling readers in the United States in the 1940s and 1950s. In addition to reading, they taught "gender messages." What gender message do you see here?

Housework is "women's work," a lesson girls should learn early in life.

Father

"I will help," said Dick.
"I will help you with the pigs."

What does this page teach children other than how to read the word "Father"? (Look above to see what Jane and Mother are doing.)

Besides learning words like "pigs" (relevant at that historical period), boys and girls also learned that rough outside work was for men.

Source: From *Dick and Jane: Fun with Our Family*, Illustrations © copyright 1951, 1979, and *Dick and Jane: We Play Outside*, copyright © 1965, Pearson Education, Inc., published by Scott, Foresman and Company. Used with permission.

Sociologist Samuel Stouffer headed a research team that produced *The American Soldier* (1949), a classic study of World War II combat soldiers. To motivate their men, officers used feminine terms as insults. If a man showed less-than-expected courage or endurance, an officer might say, "Whatsa matter, Bud—got lace on your drawers?" ["Drawers" was a term for shorts or underpants.] A generation later, as officers trained soldiers to fight in Vietnam, they still used accusations of femininity to motivate their men. Drill sergeants would mock their troops by saying, "Can't hack it, little girls?" (Eisenhart 1975). The practice continues. Male soldiers who show hesitation during maneuvers are mocked by others, who call them girls (Miller 1997/2007).

The same thing happens in sports. Anthropologist Douglas Foley (1990/2006), who studied high school football in Texas, reports that coaches insult boys who don't play well by shouting that they are "wearing skirts." In her research, sociologist Donna Eder (1995) heard junior high boys call one another "girl" when they didn't hit hard enough in football. When they play basketball, boys of this age also call one another a "woman" when they miss a basket (Stockard and Johnson 1980). In professional hockey, if players are not rough enough on the ice, their teammates call them "girls" (Gallmeier 1988:227).

These insults roll so easily off the tongues of men in sports and war that it is easy to lose sight of their significance, that they represent a devaluation of females. Sociologists Stockard and Johnson (1980:12) hit the nail on the head when they pointed out, "There is no comparable phenomenon among women, for young girls do not insult each other by calling each other 'man.'"

As discussed in Chapter 2, our background assumptions focus our perception, making some things invisible. Much of our male–female interaction in everyday life is like this. Perhaps the Down-to-Earth Sociology box below will pry open those windows just a bit. That, at least, is its intention. After this excursion, we'll look at how gender shows up in health care.

Gender Inequality in Health Care

Medical researchers were perplexed. Reports were coming in from all over the country: Women were twice as likely as men to die after coronary bypass surgery. Researchers at Cedars-Sinai Medical Center in Los Angeles checked their own records. They found that of 2,300 coronary bypass patients, 4.6 percent of the women died as a result of the surgery, compared with 2.6 percent of the men.

These findings presented a sociological puzzle. To solve it, researchers first turned to biology (Bishop 1990). In coronary bypass surgery, a blood vessel is taken from one part of the body and stitched to an artery on the surface of the heart. Perhaps the surgery was more difficult to do on women because of their smaller arteries. To find out,

Down-to-Earth Sociology
Where Are the Cheerleaders? (Male, That Is)

Whenever I attend a high school or college football or basketball game, I see a group of slender young women in short, brightly colored skirts who jump into the air and cheer wildly as the boys make a basket, a touchdown, or do something exciting. At girls' games, I see no group of boys in bright colors, shaking pom-poms, and jumping into the air as they lead cheers when the girls make a score or do something exciting.

"Well, of course not," some would reply, "because . . . "

For Your Consideration
Do you think that having female cheerleaders for boys' sports and not having male cheerleaders for girls' sports is a form of gender discrimination? Why or why not?

A cheerleader in Seattle

researchers measured the amount of time that surgeons kept patients on the heart-lung machine while they operated. They were surprised to learn that women spent *less* time on the machine than men. This indicated that the surgery was not more difficult to perform on women.

As the researchers probed, a surprising answer unfolded: unintended sexual discrimination. When women complained of chest pains, their doctors took them only *one tenth as seriously* as when men made the same complaints. How do we know this? Doctors were *ten* times more likely to give men exercise stress tests and radioactive heart scans. They also sent men to surgery on the basis of abnormal stress tests, but they waited until women showed clear-cut symptoms of heart disease before sending them to surgery. Patients who have surgery after heart disease is more advanced are more likely to die during and after heart surgery.

Although these findings have been publicized among physicians, the problem continues (Jneid et al. 2008). Perhaps as more women become physicians, the situation will change, since female doctors are more sensitive to women's health problems. For example, they are more likely to order Pap smears and mammograms (Lurie et al. 1993). In addition, as more women join the faculties of medical schools, we can expect that women's health problems will receive more attention in the training of physicians. Even this might not do it, however, as no one knows how stereotyping of the sexes produces this deadly discrimination, and women, too, hold our cultural stereotypes.

In contrast to unintentional sexism in heart surgery, there is a type of surgery that is a blatant form of discrimination against women. This is the focus of the Down-to-Earth Sociology box on the next page.

Gender Inequality in Education

To catch a glimpse of the past can give us a context for interpreting and appreciating the present. In many instances, as we saw in the box on women and smoking on page 308, change has been so extensive that the past can seem like it is from a different planet. So it is with education. Until 1832, women were not even allowed to attend college with men. When women were admitted to colleges attended by men—first at Oberlin College in Ohio—they had to wash the male students' clothing, clean their rooms, and serve them their meals (Flexner 1971/1999).

Female organs were a special focus of concern for the men who controlled education. They said that these organs dominated women's minds, making them less qualified than men for higher education. These men viewed menstruation as a special obstacle to women's success in education. It made women so feeble that they could hardly continue with their schooling, much less anything else in life. Here is how Dr. Edward Clarke, of Harvard University, put it:

> **A girl upon whom Nature, for a limited period and for a definite purpose, imposes so great a physiological task, will not have as much power left for the tasks of school, as the boy of whom Nature requires less at the corresponding epoch. (Andersen 1988)**

Because women are so much weaker than men, Clarke urged them to study only one-third as much as young men. And, of course, in their weakened state, they were advised to not study at all during menstruation.

From grade school through college, male sports have been emphasized, and women's sports underfunded. Due to federal laws (*Title IX*), the funding gap has closed considerably, and there is an increasing emphasis on women's accomplishments in sports. Shown here are U. S. A.'s Mia Hamm (L) and Brazil's Elaine Moura, outstanding soccer players.

Down-to-Earth Sociology
Cold-Hearted Surgeons and Their Women Victims

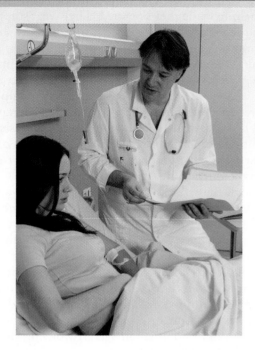

Sociologist Sue Fisher (1986), who did participant observation in a hospital, was surprised to hear surgeons recommend total hysterectomy (removal of both the uterus and the ovaries) *when no cancer was present.* When she asked why, the male doctors explained that the uterus and ovaries are "potentially disease producing." They also said that these organs are unnecessary after the childbearing years, so why not remove them? Doctors who reviewed hysterectomies confirm this bias: Three out of four of these surgeries are, in their term, inappropriate (Broder et al. 2000).

Greed is a powerful motivator in many areas of social life, and it rears its ugly head in surgical sexism. Surgeons make money when they do hysterectomies, and the more of them that they do, the more money they make. Since women, to understate the matter, are reluctant to part with these organs, surgeons find that they have to "sell" this operation. As you read how one resident explained the "hard sell" to sociologist Diana Scully (1994), you might think of a used car salesperson:

> You have to look for your surgical procedures; you have to go after patients. Because no one is crazy enough to come and say, "Hey, here I am. I want you to operate on me." You have to sometimes convince the patient that she is really sick—if she is, of course [laughs], and that she is better off with a surgical procedure.

Used-car salespeople would love to have the powerful sales weapon that these surgeons have at their disposal: To "convince" a woman to have this surgery, the doctor puts on a serious face and tells her that the examination has turned up *fibroids* in her uterus—and they *might* turn into *cancer.* This statement is often sufficient to get the woman to buy the surgery. She starts to picture herself lying at death's door, her sorrowful family gathered at her death bed. Then the used car salesperson—I mean,

the surgeon—moves in to clinch the sale. Keeping a serious face and emitting an "I-know-how-you-feel" look, the surgeon starts to make arrangements for the surgery. What the surgeon withholds is the rest of the truth—that a lot of women have fibroids, that fibroids usually do *not* turn into cancer, and that the patient has several alternatives to surgery.

In case it is difficult for someone to see how this is sexist, let's change the context just a little. Let's suppose that there are female surgeons whose income depends on their selling a specialized operation. To sell it, they systematically suggest to older men that they get castrated—since "that organ is no longer necessary, and it might cause disease."

For Your Consideration
Hysterectomies are now so common that one of three U.S. women eventually has her uterus surgically removed (Whiteman et al. 2008). Why do you think that surgeons are so quick to operate? How can women find alternatives to surgery?

Like out-of-fashion clothing, these ideas were discarded, and women entered college in growing numbers. As Figure 11.2 on the next page shows, by 1900 one-third of college students were women. The change has been so extensive that 56 percent of today's college students are women. This overall average differs with racial–ethnic groups, as you can see from Figure 11.3 on the next page. African Americans have the fewest men relative to women, and Asian Americans the most. As another indication of how extensive the change is, women now earn 58 percent of all bachelor's degrees and 60 percent of all master's degrees (*Statistical Abstract* 2009:Table 288). As discussed in the Down-to-Earth Sociology box on page 314, it might be time for affirmative action for men.

FIGURE 11.2 Changes in College Enrollment, by Sex

What percentages of U.S. college students are female and male?

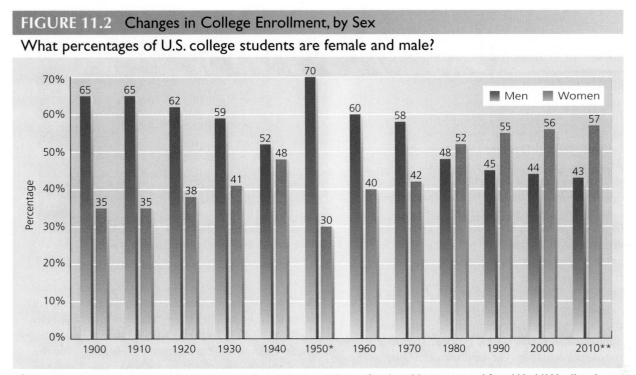

*This sharp drop in female enrollment occurred when large numbers of male soldiers returned from World War II and attended college under the new GI Bill of Rights.
** Projection by U. S. Department of Education 2008.

Source: By the author. Based on *Statistical Abstract of the United States* 1938:Table 114; 1959:Table 158; 1991:Table 261; 2009:Table 272.

FIGURE 11.3 College Students, by Sex and Race–Ethnicity

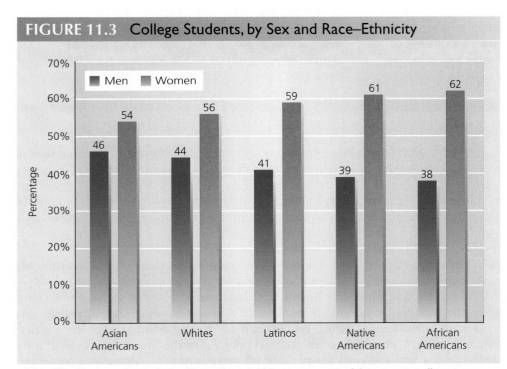

Note: This figure can be confusing. To read it, ask: What percentage of the group in college are men or women? (For example, what percentage of Asian American college students are men or women?)

Source: By the author. Based on *Statistical Abstract of the United States* 2008:Table 272; 2009:Table 272.

Down-to-Earth Sociology
Affirmative Action for Men?

The idea that we might need affirmative action *for men* was first proposed by psychologist Judith Kleinfeld (2002a). Many met this suggestion with laughter. After all, men dominate societies around the world, and they have done so for millennia. The discussion in this chapter has shown that as men exercised that dominance, they also suppressed and harmed women. To think that men would ever need affirmative action seems laughable at best.

In contrast to this reaction, let's pause, step back and try to see whether the idea has some merit. Look again at Figures 11.2 and 11.3 on page 313. Do you see that women have not only caught up with men, but that they also have passed them up? Do you see that this applies to all racial–ethnic groups? That this is not a temporary situation, like lead cars changing place at the Indy 500, is apparent from the statistics the government publishes each year. For decades, women have steadily added to their proportion of college student enrollment and the degrees they earn.

This accomplishment is laudable, but what about the men? Why have they fallen behind? With college enrollment open equally to both men and women, why don't enrollment and degrees now match the relative proportions of women and men in the population (51 percent and 49 percent)? Although no one yet knows the reasons for this—and there are a lot of suggestions being thrown about—some have begun to consider this a problem in need of a solution. In a first,

With fewer men than women in college, is it time to consider affirmative action for men?

Clark University in Massachusetts has begun a support program for men to help them adjust to their minority status (Gibbs 2008). I assume that other colleges will follow, as these totals have serious implications for the future of society—just as they did when fewer women were enrolled in college.

For Your Consideration

Do you think that women's and men's current college enrollments and degrees represent something other than an interesting historical change? Why do you think that men have fallen behind? Do you think anything should be done about this imbalance? If so, what? Behind the scenes, so as not to get anyone upset, some colleges have begun to reject more highly qualified women to get closer to a male–female balance (Kingsbury 2007). What do you think about this?

Figure 11.4 on the next page illustrates another major change. From this figure, you can see how women have increased their share of professional degrees. The greatest change is in dentistry: In 1970, across the entire United States, only 34 women earned degrees in dentistry. Today, about 2,000 women become dentists each year. As you can also see, almost as many women as men now graduate from U.S. medical and law schools. With the change so extensive and firm, I anticipate that women will soon outnumber men in earning these professional degrees.

With these extensive changes, it would seem that gender equality has been achieved, or at least almost so, and in some instances—as with the changed sex ratio in college—we have a new form of gender inequality. If we look closer, however, we find something beneath the surface. Underlying these degrees is *gender tracking;* that is, college degrees tend to follow gender, which reinforces male–female distinctions. Here are two extremes: Men earn 94 percent of the associate degrees in the "masculine" field of construction trades, while women are awarded 89 percent of the associate degrees in the "feminine" field of library science (*Statistical Abstract* 2009:Table 290). Because gender socialization gives men and women different orientations to life, they enter college with gender-linked aspirations. Socialization—not some presumed innate characteristic—channels men and women into different educational paths.

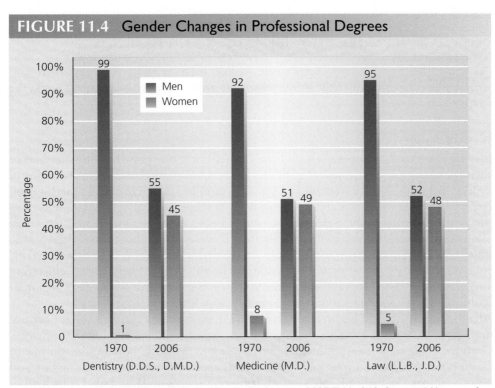

FIGURE 11.4   Gender Changes in Professional Degrees

Source: By the author. Based on *Digest of Education Statistics* 2007: Table 269; *Statistical Abstract of the United States* 2009: Table 293.

If we follow students into graduate school, we see that with each passing year the proportion of women drops. Table 11.1 below gives us a snapshot of doctoral programs in the sciences. Note how aspirations (enrollment) and accomplishments (doctorates earned) are sex linked. In five of these doctoral programs, men outnumber women, and in three, women outnumber men. In *all* of them, however, women are less likely to complete the doctorate.

If we follow those who earn doctoral degrees to their teaching careers at colleges and universities, we find gender stratification in rank and pay. Throughout the United States, women are less likely to become full professors, the highest-paying and most prestigious rank. In both private and public colleges, professors average more than twice the salary of instructors (*Statistical Abstract* 2009: Table 284). Even when women do become full professors, their average pay is less than that of men who are full professors (AAUP 2009: Table 5).

TABLE 11.1   Doctorates in Science, By Sex

Field	Students Enrolled		Doctorates Conferred		Completion Ratio* (Higher or Lower Than Expected)	
	Women	Men	Women	Men	Women	Men
Agriculture	48%	52%	40%	60%	−17	+15
Mathematics	36%	64%	30%	70%	−17	+ 9
Computer sciences	25%	75%	21%	79%	−16	+ 5
Social sciences	53%	47%	46%	54%	−13	+15
Biological sciences	56%	44%	49%	51%	−13	+16
Physical sciences	32%	68%	28%	72%	−13	+ 6
Engineering	23%	77%	20%	80%	−13	+ 4
Psychology	75%	25%	71%	29%	− 5	+16

*The formula for the completion ratio is X minus Y divided by Y, where X is the doctorates conferred and Y is the proportion enrolled in a program.

Source: By the author. Based on *Statistical Abstract of the United States* 2009: Tables 779, 782.

Gender Inequality in the Workplace

To examine the work setting is to make visible basic relations between men and women. Let's begin with one of the most remarkable areas of gender inequality at work, the pay gap.

The Pay Gap

One of the chief characteristics of the U.S. workforce is a steady growth in the numbers of women who work for wages outside the home. Figure 11.5 shows that in 1890 about one of every five paid workers was a woman. By 1940, this ratio had grown to one of four; by 1960 to one of three; and today it is almost one of two. As shown on this figure, the projections are that the ratio will remain 55 percent men and 45 percent women for the next few years.

Women who work for wages are not distributed evenly throughout the United States. From the Social Map on the next page, you can see that where a woman lives makes a difference in how likely she is to work outside the home. Why is there such a clustering among the states? The geographical patterns that you see on this map reflect regional-subcultural differences about which we currently have little understanding.

After college, you might like to take a few years off, travel around Europe, sail the oceans, or maybe sit on a beach in some South American paradise and drink piña coladas. But chances are, you are going to go to work instead. Since you have to work, how would you like to make an extra $650,000 on your job? If this sounds appealing, read on. I'm going to reveal how you can make an extra $1,356 a month between the ages of 25 and 65. Is this hard to do? Actually, it is simple for some and impossible for others. As Figure 11.7 on the next page shows, all you have to do is be born a male. If we compare full-time workers, based on current differences in earnings, this is how much more money the *average male* can expect to earn over the course of his career. Now if you want to boost that monthly difference to $2,482 for a whopping career total of $1,192,000, be both a male and a college graduate. Hardly any single factor pinpoints gender discrimination better than these totals. As you can see from Figure 11.7, the pay gap shows up at *all* levels of education.

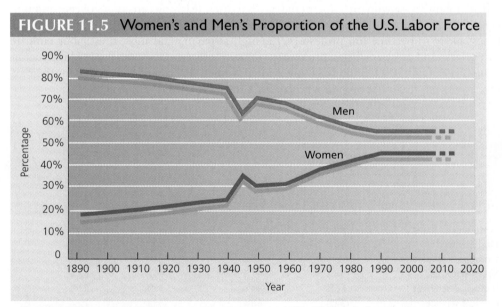

FIGURE 11.5 **Women's and Men's Proportion of the U.S. Labor Force**

Note: Pre-1940 totals include women 14 and over; totals for 1940 and after are for women 16 and over. Broken lines are the author's projections.

Sources: By the author. Based on 1969 *Handbook on Women Workers*, 1969:10; *Manpower Report to the President*, 1971:203, 205; Mills and Palumbo, 1980:6, 45; *Statistical Abstract of the United States* 2009:Table 568.

FIGURE 11.6 Women in the WorkForce

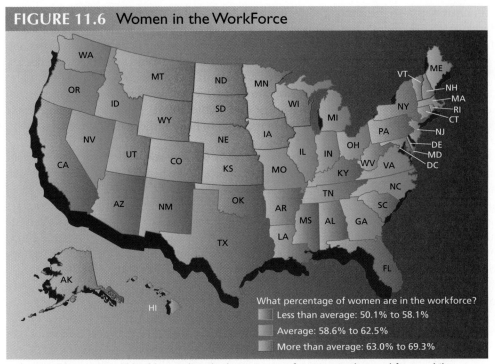

What percentage of women are in the workforce?
- Less than average: 50.1% to 58.1%
- Average: 58.6% to 62.5%
- More than average: 63.0% to 69.3%

Note: At 50.1 percent, West Virginia has the lowest rate of women in the workforce, while North Dakota, at 69.3 percent, has the highest.

Source: By the author. Based on *Statistical Abstract of the United States* 2009:Table 573.

FIGURE 11.7 The Gender Pay Gap, by Education[1]

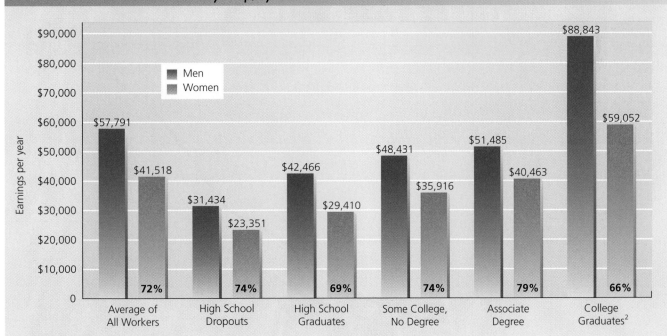

[1]Full-time workers in all fields. The percentage at the bottom of each red bar indicates the women's average percentage of the men's income.
[2]Bachelor's and all higher degrees, including professional degrees.

Source: By the author. Based on *Statistical Abstract of the United States* 2009: Table 681.

The pay gap is so great that U.S. women who work full-time average *only 72 percent* of what men are paid. As you can see from Figure 11.8 below, the pay gap used to be even worse. The gender gap in pay occurs not only in the United States but also in *all* industrialized nations.

If $1,192,000 in additional earnings isn't enough, how would you like to make another $166,000 extra at work? If so, just make sure that you are not only a man but also a *tall* man. Over their lifetimes, men who are over 6 feet tall average $166,000 more than men who are 5 feet 5 inches or less (Judge and Cable 2004). Taller women also make more than shorter women. But even when it comes to height, the gender pay gap persists, and tall men make more than tall women.

What logic can underlie the gender pay gap? As we just saw, college degrees are gender linked, so perhaps this gap is due to career choices. Maybe women are more likely to choose lower-paying jobs, such as teaching grade school, while men are more likely to go into better-paying fields, such as business and engineering. Actually, this is true, and researchers have found that about *half* of the gender pay gap is due to such factors. And the balance? It consists of a combination of gender discrimination (Jacobs 2003; Roth 2003) and what is called the "child penalty"—women missing out on work experience and opportunities while they care for children (Hundley 2001; Chaker and Stout 2004).

For college students, the gender gap in pay begins with the first job after graduation. You might know of a particular woman who was offered a higher salary than most men in her class, but she would be an exception. On average, men enjoy a "testosterone bonus," and employers start them out at higher salaries than women (Fuller and Schoenberger

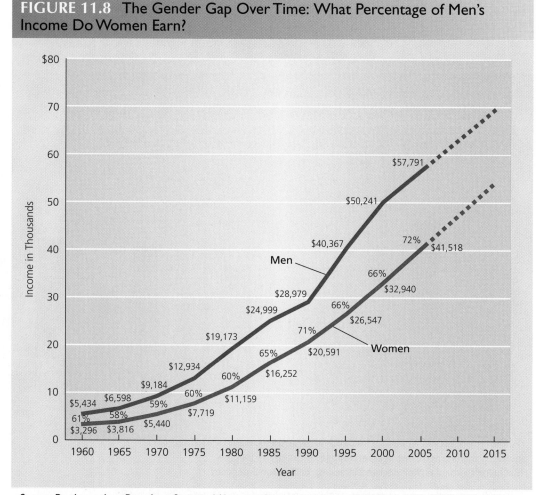

FIGURE 11.8   The Gender Gap Over Time: What Percentage of Men's Income Do Women Earn?

Source: By the author. Based on *Statistical Abstract of the United States* 1995:Table 739; 2002:Table 666; 2009:Table 681, and earlier years. Broken lines indicate the author's estimate.

1991; Harris et al. 2005). Depending on your sex, then, you will either benefit from the pay gap or be victimized by it.

As a final indication of the extent of the U.S. gender pay gap, consider this. Of the nation's top 500 corporations (the so-called Fortune 500), only 12 are headed by women (Kaufman and Hymowitz 2008). The highest number of these positions ever held by women is 13. I examined the names of the CEOs of the 350 largest U.S. corporations, and I found that your best chance to reach the top is to be named (in this order) John, Robert, James, William, or Charles. Edward, Lawrence, and Richard are also advantageous names. Amber, Katherine, Leticia, and Maria apparently draw a severe penalty. Naming your baby girl John or Robert might seem a little severe, but it could help her reach the top. (I say this only slightly tongue-in-cheek. One of the few women to head a Fortune 500 company—before she was fired and given $21 million severance pay—had a man's first name: Carleton Fiorina of Hewlett-Packard. Carleton's first name is actually Cara, but knowing what she was facing in the highly competitive business world, she dropped this feminine name to go by her masculine middle name.)

The Cracking Glass Ceiling

What keeps women from breaking through the **glass ceiling,** the mostly invisible barrier that prevents women from reaching the executive suite? The "pipelines" that lead to the top of a company are its marketing, sales, and production positions, those that directly affect the corporate bottom line (Hymowitz 2004; DeCrow 2005). Men, who dominate the executive suite, stereotype women as being good at "support" but less capable than men of leadership (Belkin 2007). They steer women into human resources or public relations. Successful projects in these positions are not appreciated in the same way as those that bring corporate profits—and bonuses for their managers.

Another reason the glass ceiling is so powerful is that women lack mentors—successful executives who take an interest in them and teach them the ropes. Lack of a mentor is no trivial matter, for mentors can provide opportunities to develop leadership skills that open the door to the executive suite (Hymowitz 2007; Mattioli 2008).

The glass ceiling is cracking, however (Hymowitz 2004; Belkin 2007). A look at women who have broken through reveals highly motivated individuals with a fierce competitive spirit who are willing to give up sleep and recreation for the sake of career advancement.

As the *glass ceiling* slowly cracks, women are gradually gaining entry into the top positions in society. In 2009, Ellen Kullman, shown here, became the first female CEO of DuPont, a company founded in 1802.

glass ceiling the mostly invisible barrier that keeps women from advancing to the top levels at work

Dilbert

One of the frustrations felt by many women in the labor force is that no matter what they do, they hit a glass ceiling. Another is that to succeed they feel forced to abandon characteristics they feel are essential to their self.

sexual harassment the abuse of one's position of authority to force unwanted sexual demands on someone

They also learn to play by "men's rules," developing a style that makes men comfortable. In addition, women who began their careers twenty to thirty years ago are now running major divisions within the largest companies (Hymowitz 2004). With this background, some of these women have begun to emerge as the new CEOs.

When women break through the cracking glass ceiling, they still confront stereotypes of gender that portray them in less favorable light than men. The women have negotiated these stereotypes on their way to the top, so they know how to handle them. Occasionally, however, the stereotypes of male dominance lead to humorously awkward situations. When Nancy Andrews (2007), who became the first female dean of the Duke University School of Medicine, visited a school in North Carolina, she took her family with her. "As we entered," she says, "the school principal vigorously shook my husband's hand and welcomed him, saying, 'You must be the man of the moment.' Unfortunately," she adds, "it didn't cross his mind that I might be the 'woman of the moment.'"

Sexual Harassment—and Worse

Sexual harassment—unwelcome sexual attention at work or at school, which may affect a person's job or school performance or create a hostile environment—was not recognized as a problem until the 1970s. Before this, women considered unwanted sexual comments, touches, looks, and pressure to have sex to be a personal matter.

With the prodding of feminists, women began to perceive unwanted sexual advances at work and school as part of a *structural* problem. That is, they began to realize that the issue was more than a man here or there doing obnoxious things because he was attracted to a woman; rather, men were using their positions of authority to pressure women to have sex. Now that women have moved into positions of authority, they, too, have become sexual harassers (Wayne et al. 2001). With most authority still vested in men, however, most of the sexual harassers are men.

As symbolic interactionists stress, labels affect our perception. Because we have the term *sexual harassment,* we perceive actions in a different light than did our predecessors. The meaning of sexual harassment is vague and shifting, however, and court cases constantly change what this term does and does not include (Anderson 2006). Originally, sexual desire was an element of sexual harassment, but no longer. This changed when the U.S. Supreme Court considered the lawsuit of a homosexual who had been tormented by his supervisors and fellow workers. The Court ruled that sexual desire is not necessary—that sexual harassment laws also apply to homosexuals who are harassed by heterosexuals while on the job (Felsenthal 1998). By extension, the law applies to heterosexuals who are sexually harassed by homosexuals.

Central to sexual harassment is the abuse of power, a topic that is explored in the following Thinking Critically section.

ThinkingCRITICALLY

Sexual Harassment and Rape of Women in the Military

WOMEN RAPED AT WEST POINT! MORE WOMEN RAPED AT THE U.S. AIR FORCE ACADEMY!

So shrieked the headlines and the TV news teasers. For once, the facts turned out to be just as startling. Women cadets, who were studying to become officers in the U.S. military, had been sexually assaulted by their fellow cadets.

And when the women reported the attacks, *they* were the ones who were punished. The women found themselves charged with drinking alcohol and socializing with upperclassmen.

Women in the military being sexually harassed by male soldiers knows no geographical limits. Shown here is Anjali Gupta, a Flying Officer in India's Air Force, who was court martialed for insubordination after she lodged complaints against a superior officer.

For the most part, the women's charges against the men were ignored. The one man who faced a court martial was acquitted (Schemo 2003a).

This got the attention of Congress. Hearings were held, and the commander of the Air Force Academy was replaced.

A few years earlier, several male Army sergeants at Aberdeen Proving Ground in Maryland had been accused of forcing sex on unwilling female recruits (McIntyre 1997). The drill sergeants, who claimed that the sex was consensual, were found guilty of rape. One married sergeant, who pled guilty to having consensual sex with eleven trainees (adultery is a crime in the Army), was convicted of raping another six trainees a total of eighteen times and was sentenced to twenty-five years in prison.

The Army appointed a blue-ribbon panel to investigate sexual harassment in its ranks. When Sgt. Major Gene McKinney, the highest-ranking of the Army's 410,000 noncommissioned officers, was appointed to this committee, former subordinates accused *him* of sexual harassment (Shenon 1997). McKinney was relieved of his duties and court-martialed. Found not guilty of sexual harassment, but guilty of obstruction of justice, McKinney was reprimanded and demoted. His embittered accusers claimed the Army had sacrificed them for McKinney.

Rape in the military is not an isolated event. Researchers who interviewed a random sample of women veterans found that four of five had experienced sexual harassment during their military service, and 30 percent had been victims of attempted or completed rape. Three-fourths of the women who had been raped did not report their assault (Sadler et al. 2003). A study of women graduates of the Air Force Academy showed that 12 percent had been victims of rape or attempted rape (Schemo 2003b). In light of such findings, the military appointed a coordinator of sexual assault at every military base (Stout 2005). Sexual assaults continue, however (Dreazen 2008).

After the U.S. military was sent to Iraq and Afghanistan, the headlines again screamed rape, this time in the Persian Gulf. Again, the headlines were right. And once again, Congress held hearings (Schmitt 2004). With assaults continuing and Congress still putting pressure on the military, the Army held an emergency summit attended by eighty generals (Dreazen 2008). We'll have to see how long this cycle of rape followed by hearings followed by rape repeats itself before adequate reforms are put in place.

For Your Consideration

How can we set up a structure to minimize sexual harassment and rape in the military? Can we do this and still train men and women together? Can we do this and still have men and women sleep in the same barracks and on the same ships? Be specific about the structure you would establish.

Gender and Violence

One of the consistent characteristics of violence in the United States—and the world—is its gender inequality. That is, females are more likely to be the victims of males, not the other way around. Let's briefly review this almost one-way street in gender violence as it applies to the United States.

Violence Against Women

In the Thinking Critically section above, we considered rape in the military; on page 303, we examined violence against women in other cultures; on page 312, we reviewed a form of surgical violence; and in Chapter 16 we shall review violence in the home. Here, due to space limitations, we can review only briefly some primary features of violence.

Forcible Rape.   Being raped is a common fear of U.S. women, a fear that is far from groundless. As high as the official rate of rape is, the real rate is even higher. As pointed out in Chapter 5, page 133, the National Crime Victimization Survey shows that the real rate is about 40 percent higher than the number reported to the police. Since the official rate is 6.1 per 10,000 females, the actual rate would be 8.4 (*Statistical Abstract* 2009: Table 303). This would be 1 of every 1,200 U.S. females *each year.* Despite this high number, women are safer now than they were ten and twenty years ago, as the rape rate has declined.

Although any woman can be a victim of sexual assault—and victims include babies and elderly women—the typical victim is 16 to 19 years old. As you can see from Table 11.2, sexual assault peaks at those ages and then declines.

Women's most common fear seems to be that of strangers—who, appearing as though from nowhere, abduct and beat and rape them. Contrary to the stereotypes that underlie these fears, most victims know their attacker. As you can see from Table 11.3, about one of three rapes is committed by strangers.

Date (Acquaintance) Rape.   What has shocked so many about date rape (also known as *acquaintance rape*) are studies showing that it is common (Littleton et al. 2008). Researchers who used a representative sample of courses to survey the students at Marietta College, a private school in Ohio, found that 2.5 percent of the women had been physically forced to have sex (Felton et al. 2001). This was just one college, but a study using a nationally representative sample of women enrolled in U.S. colleges and

TABLE 11.2	Rape Victims
Age	Rate per 1,000 Females
12–15	2.3
16–19	3.9
20–24	2.5
25–34	1.4
35–49	0.7
50–64	0.3
65 and Older	0.08

Source: By the author. A ten-year average, based on *Statistical Abstract of the United States* 2000:Table 354; 2001:Table 341; 2002:Table 303; 2003:Table 295; 2004:Table 322; 2005:Table 306; 2006:Table 308; 2007:Table 311; 2008:Table 313; 2009:Table 305.

TABLE 11.3	Relationship of Victims and Rapists
Relationship	Percentage
Relative	7%
Known Well	34%
Casual Acquaintance	24%
Stranger	34%
Not Reported	1%

Sources: By the author. A ten-year average, based on *Statistical Abstract of the United States* 1999:Table 355; 2000:Table 342; 2001:Table 304; 2002:Table 296; 2003:Table 323; 2004-2005:Table 307; 2006:Table 311; 2007:Table 315; 2008:Table 316; 2009:Table 306.

universities with 1,000 students or more came up with similar findings. Of these women, 1.7 percent had been raped during the preceding six months, and another 1.1 percent had been victims of attempted rape (Fisher et al. 2000).

Think about the huge numbers involved. With about 11 million women enrolled in college, 2.8 percent (1.7 plus 1.1) means that over a quarter of a million college women were victims of rape or of attempted rape *in just the past six months.* (This conclusion assumes that the rate is the same in colleges with fewer than 1,000 students, which has not been verified.) Most of the women told a friend what happened, but only *5 percent* reported the crime to the police (Fisher et al. 2003). The most common reason for not reporting was thinking that the event "was not serious enough." The next most common reason was being unsure whether a crime had been committed. Many women were embarrassed and didn't want others, especially their family, to know what happened. Others felt there was no proof ("It would be my word against his"), feared reprisal from the man, or feared the police (Fisher et al. 2000). Sometimes a rape victim feels partially responsible because she knows the person, was drinking with him, went to his place voluntarily, or invited him to her place. As a physician who treats victims of date rape said, "Would you feel responsible if someone hit you over the head with a shovel—just because you knew the person?" (Carpenito 1999).

Murder.   All over the world, men are more likely than women to be killers. Figure 11.9 illustrates this gender pattern in U.S. murders. Note that although females make up about 51 percent of the U.S. population, they don't even come close to making up 51 percent of the nation's killers. As you can see from this figure, when women are murdered, about 9 times out of 10 the killer is a man.

Violence in the Home.   In the family, too, women are the typical victims. Spouse battering, marital rape, and incest are discussed in Chapter 16, pages 490–492. Two forms of violence against women—honor killings and genital circumcision—are discussed on pages 303 and 306.

Feminism and Gendered Violence.   Feminist sociologists have been especially effective in bringing violence against women to the public's attention. Some use symbolic interactionism, pointing out that to associate strength and virility with violence—as is done in many cultures—is to promote violence. Others use conflict theory. They argue that men are losing power, and that some men turn violently against women as a way to reassert their declining power and status (Reiser 1999; Meltzer 2002).

Solutions.   There is no magic bullet for this problem of gendered violence, but to be effective, any solution must break the connection between violence and masculinity. This would require an educational program that encompasses schools, churches, homes, and the media. Given the gun-slinging heroes of the Wild West and other American icons, as well as the violent messages that are so prevalent in the mass media, including video games, it is difficult to be optimistic that a change will come any time soon.

Our next topic, women in politics, however, gives us much more reason for optimism.

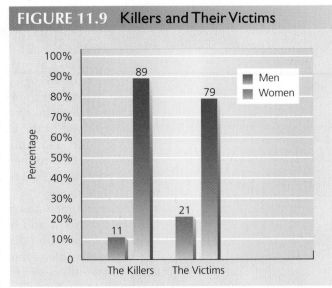

FIGURE 11.9   Killers and Their Victims

Source: By the author. Based on *Statistical Abstract of the United States* 2008:Table 318; 2009:Table 300.

Although women are severely underrepresented in U.S. politics, the situation is changing, at least gradually. Shown here is Nancy Pelosi, the Speaker of the U.S. House of Representatives, as she signs the financial bailout plan passed by the House.

The Changing Face of Politics

Women could take over the United States! Think about it. Eight million more women than men are of voting age, and more women than men vote in U.S. national elections. As Table 11.4 shows, however, men greatly outnumber women in political office. Despite the gains women have made in recent elections, since 1789 almost 2,000 men have served in the U.S. Senate, but only 38 women have served, including 17 current senators. Not until 1992 was the first African American woman (Carol Moseley-Braun) elected to the U.S. Senate. No Latina or Asian American woman has yet been elected to the Senate (National Women's Political Caucus 1998; *Statistical Abstract* 2009:Table 390).

Why are women underrepresented in U.S. politics? First, women are still underrepresented in law and business, the careers from which most politicians emerge. Most women also find that the irregular hours needed to run for office are incompatible with their role as mother. Fathers, in contrast, whose traditional roles are more likely to take them away from home, are less likely to feel this conflict. Women are also less likely to have a supportive spouse who is willing to play an unassuming background role while providing solace, encouragement, child care, and voter appeal. Finally, preferring to hold on to their positions of power, men have been reluctant to incorporate women into centers of decision making or to present them as viable candidates.

These conditions are changing. In 2002, Nancy Pelosi was the first woman to be elected by her colleagues as minority leader of the House of Representatives. Five years later, in 2007, they chose her as the first female Speaker of the House. These posts made her the most powerful woman ever in Congress. Another occurred in 2008 when Hillary Clinton came within a hair's breadth of becoming the presidential nominee of the Democratic party. That same year, Sarah Palin was chosen as the Republican vice-presidential candidate. We can also note that more women are becoming corporate executives, and, as indicated in Figure 11.4 (on page 314), more women are also becoming lawyers. In these positions, women are traveling more and making statewide and national contacts. Another change is that child care is increasingly seen as a responsibility of both mother and father. With this generation's fundamental change in women's political participation, it is only a matter of time until a woman occupies the Oval Office.

TABLE 11.4 U.S. Women in Political Office		
	Percentage of Offices Held by Women	Number of Offices Held By Women
National Office		
U.S. Senate	17%	17
U.S. House of Representatives	17%	74
State Office		
Governors	16%	8
Lt. Governors	18%	9
Attorneys General	8%	4
Secretaries of State	24%	12
Treasurers	22%	11
State Auditors	12%	6
State Legislators	24%	1,734

Source: Center for American Women and Politics 2007, 2008a, b.

Glimpsing the Future—With Hope

Women's fuller participation in the decision-making processes of our social institutions has shattered stereotypes that tended to limit females to "feminine" activities and push males into "masculine" ones. As structural barriers continue to fall and more activities are de-gendered, both males and females will have greater freedom to pursue activities that are more compatible with their abilities and desires as individuals.

As females and males develop a new consciousness both of their capacities and of their potential, relationships will change. Distinctions between the sexes will not disappear, but there is no reason for biological differences to be translated into social inequalities. If current trends continue, we may see a growing appreciation of sexual differences coupled with greater equality of opportunity—which has the potential of transforming society (Gilman 1911/1971; Offen 1990). If this happens, as sociologist Alison Jaggar (1990) observed, gender equality can become less a goal than a background condition for living in society.

By the Numbers: *Then and Now*

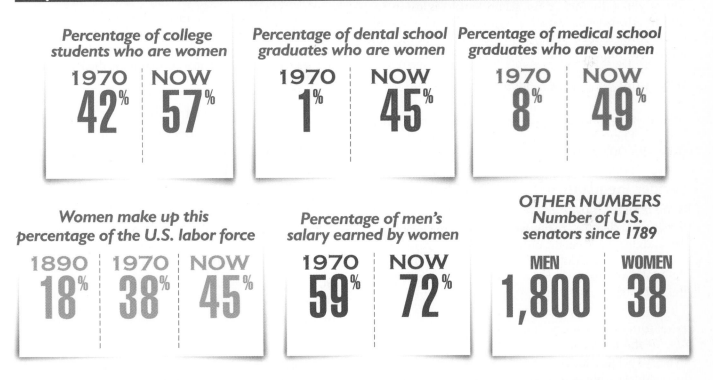

Percentage of college students who are women
1970 **42**% | NOW **57**%

Percentage of dental school graduates who are women
1970 **1**% | NOW **45**%

Percentage of medical school graduates who are women
1970 **8**% | NOW **49**%

Women make up this percentage of the U.S. labor force
1890 **18**% | 1970 **38**% | NOW **45**%

Percentage of men's salary earned by women
1970 **59**% | NOW **72**%

OTHER NUMBERS Number of U.S. senators since 1789
MEN **1,800** | WOMEN **38**

SUMMARY *and* REVIEW

Issues of Sex and Gender

What is gender stratification?

The term **gender stratification** refers to unequal access to property, power, and prestige on the basis of sex. Each society establishes a structure that, on the basis of sex and gender, opens and closes doors to its privileges. P. 294.

How do sex and gender differ?

Sex refers to biological distinctions between males and females. It consists of both primary and secondary sex characteristics. **Gender,** in contrast, is what a society considers proper behaviors and attitudes for its male and female members. Sex physically distinguishes males from females; gender refers to what people call "masculine" and "feminine." P. 294.

Why do the behaviors of males and females differ?

The "nature versus nurture" debate refers to whether differences in the behaviors of males and females are caused by inherited (biological) or learned (cultural) characteristics. Almost all sociologists take the side of nurture. In recent years, however, sociologists have begun to cautiously open the door to biology. Pp. 294–299.

Gender Inequality in Global Perspective

Is gender stratification universal?

George Murdock surveyed information on tribal societies and found that all of them have sex-linked activities and give greater prestige to male activities. **Patriarchy,** or male dominance, appears to be universal. Besides work, other areas of discrimination include education, politics, and violence. Pp. 299–300.

How did females become a minority group?

The origin of discrimination against females is lost in history, but the primary theory of how females became a minority group in their own societies focuses on the physical limitations imposed by childbirth. Pp. 301–302.

What forms does gender inequality take around the world?

Its many forms include inequalities in education, politics, and pay. There is also violence, including female circumcision. Pp. 302–306.

Gender Inequality in the United States

Is the feminist movement new?

In what is called the "first wave," feminists made political demands for change in the early 1900s—and were met with hostility, and even violence. The "second wave" began in the 1960s and continues today. A "third wave" is emerging. Pp. 307–308.

What forms does gender inequality take in everyday life, health care, and education?

In everyday life, a lower value is placed on things feminine. In health care, physicians don't take women's health complaints as seriously as those of men, and they exploit women's fears, performing unnecessary hysterectomies. In education, more women than men attend college, but many choose fields that are categorized as "feminine." More women than men also earn college degrees. Women are less likely to complete the doctoral programs in science. Fundamental change is indicated by the growing numbers of women in law and medicine. Pp. 308–315.

Gender Inequality in the Workplace

How does gender inequality show up in the workplace?

All occupations show a gender gap in pay. For college graduates, the lifetime pay gap runs over a million dollars in favor of men. **Sexual harassment** also continues to be a reality of the workplace. Pp. 316–321.

Gender and Violence

What is the relationship between gender and violence?

Overwhelmingly, the victims of rape and murder are females. Female circumcision and honor killing are special cases of violence against females. Conflict theorists point out that men use violence to maintain their power and privilege. Pp. 322–323.

The Changing Face of Politics

What is the trend in gender inequality in politics?

A traditional division of gender roles—women as child care providers and homemakers, men as workers outside the home—used to keep women out of politics. Women continue to be underrepresented in politics, but the trend toward greater political equality is firmly in place. P. 324.

Glimpsing the Future—with Hope

How might changes in gender roles and stereotypes affect our lives?

In the United States, women are more involved in the decision-making processes of our social institutions. Men, too, are reexamining their traditional roles. New gender expectations may be developing, ones that allow both males and females to pursue more individual, less stereotypical interests. P. 325.

THINKING CRITICALLY *ABOUT* Chapter 11

1. What is your position on the "nature versus nurture" (biology or culture) debate? What materials in this chapter support your position?

2. Why do you think that the gender gap in pay exists all over the world?

3. What do you think can be done to reduce gender inequality?

ADDITIONAL RESOURCES

What can you find in MySocLab? mysoclab www.mysoclab.com

- Complete Ebook
- Practice Tests and Video and Audio activities
- Mapping and Data Analysis exercises

- Sociology in the News
- Classic Readings in Sociology
- Research and Writing advice

Where Can I Read More on This Topic?

Suggested readings for this chapter are listed at the back of this book.

Chapter 12

Race and Ethnicity

Idaho

I magine that you are an African American man living in Macon County, Alabama, during the Great Depression of the 1930s. Your home is a little country shack with a dirt floor. You have no electricity or running water. You never finished grade school, and you make a living, such as it is, by doing odd jobs. You haven't been feeling too good lately, but you can't afford a doctor.

You have just become part of one of the most callous experiments of all time.

Then you hear incredible news. You rub your eyes in disbelief. It is just like winning the lottery! If you join *Miss Rivers' Lodge* (and it is free to join), you will get free physical examinations at Tuskegee University *for life*. You will even get free rides to and from the clinic, hot meals on examination days, and a lifetime of free treatment for minor ailments.

You eagerly join *Miss Rivers' Lodge*.

After your first physical examination, the doctor gives you the bad news. "You've got bad blood," he says. "That's why you've been feeling bad. Miss Rivers will give you some medicine and schedule you for your next exam. I've got to warn you, though. If you go to another doctor, there's no more free exams or medicine."

You can't afford another doctor anyway. You are thankful for your treatment, take your medicine, and look forward to the next trip to the university.

What has really happened? You have just become part of what is surely slated to go down in history as one of the most callous experiments of all time, outside of the infamous World War II Nazi and Japanese experiments. With heartless disregard for human life, the U.S. Public Health Service told 399 African American men that they had joined a social club and burial society called *Miss Rivers' Lodge*. What the men were *not* told was that they had syphilis, that there was no real Miss Rivers' Lodge, that the doctors were just using this term so they could study what happened when syphilis went untreated. For forty years, the "Public Health Service" allowed these men to go without treatment for their syphilis—and kept testing them each year—to study the progress of the disease. The "public health" officials even had a control group of 201 men who were free of the disease (Jones 1993).

By the way, the men did receive a benefit from "Miss Rivers Lodge," a free autopsy to determine the ravages of syphilis on their bodies.

329

race a group whose inherited physical characteristics distinguish it from other groups

genocide the systematic annihilation or attempted annihilation of a people because of their presumed race or ethnicity

Laying the Sociological Foundation

As unlikely as it seems, this is a true story. It really did happen. Seldom do race and ethnic relations degenerate to this point, but reports of troubled race relations surprise none of us. Today's newspapers and TV news shows regularly report on racial problems. Sociology can contribute greatly to our understanding of this aspect of social life—and this chapter may be an eye-opener for you. To begin, let's consider to what extent race itself is a myth.

Race: Myth and Reality

With its more than 6.5 billion people, the world offers a fascinating variety of human shapes and colors. People see one another as black, white, red, yellow, and brown. Eyes come in shades of blue, brown, and green. Lips are thick and thin. Hair is straight, curly, kinky, black, blonde, and red—and, of course, all shades of brown.

As humans spread throughout the world, their adaptations to diverse climates and other living conditions resulted in this profusion of complexions, hair textures and colors, eye hues, and other physical variations. Genetic mutations added distinct characteristics to the peoples of the globe. In this sense, the concept of **race**—a group of people with inherited physical characteristics that distinguish it from another group—is a reality. Humans do, indeed, come in a variety of colors and shapes.

In two senses, however, race is a myth, a fabrication of the human mind. The *first* myth is the idea that any race is superior to others. All races have their geniuses—and their idiots. As with language, no race is superior to another.

Ideas of racial superiority abound, however. They are not only false but also dangerous. Adolf Hitler, for example, believed that the Aryans were a superior race, responsible for the cultural achievements of Europe. The Aryans, he said, were destined to establish a superior culture and usher in a new world order. This destiny required them to avoid the "racial contamination" that would come from breeding with inferior races; therefore, it became a "cultural duty" to isolate or destroy races that threatened Aryan purity and culture.

Put into practice, Hitler's views left an appalling legacy—the Nazi slaughter of those they deemed inferior: Jews, Slavs, gypsies, homosexuals, and people with mental and physical disabilities. Horrific images of gas ovens and emaciated bodies stacked like cordwood haunted the world's nations. At Nuremberg, the Allies, flush with victory, put the top Nazis on trial, exposing their heinous deeds to a shocked world. Their public executions, everyone assumed, marked the end of such grisly acts.

Obviously, they didn't. In the summer of 1994 in Rwanda, Hutus slaughtered about 800,000 Tutsis—mostly with machetes (Cowell 2006). A few years later, the Serbs in Bosnia massacred Muslims, giving us the new term "ethnic cleansing." As these events sadly attest, **genocide,** the attempt to destroy a group of people because of their presumed race or ethnicity, remains alive and well. Although more recent killings are not accompanied by swastikas and gas ovens, the perpetrators' goal is the same.

The *second* myth is that "pure" races exist. Humans show such a mixture of physical characteristics—in skin color, hair texture, nose shape, head shape, eye color, and so on—that there are no "pure" races. Instead of falling into distinct types that are clearly separate from one another, human characteristics flow endlessly together. The mapping of the human genome system shows that humans are strikingly homogenous, that so-called racial groups differ from one another only once in a thousand subunits of the genome (Angler 2000; Frank 2007). As you can see from the example of Tiger Woods, discussed in the Cultural Diversity box on the next page, these minute gradations make any attempt to draw lines of race purely arbitrary.

Humans show remarkable diversity. Shown here is just one example—He Pingping, from China, who at 2 feet 4 inches, is the world's shortest man, and Svetlana Pankratova, from Russia, who, according to the *Guiness Book of World Records,* is the woman with the longest legs. Race-ethnicity shows similar diversity.

Cultural Diversity in the United States

Tiger Woods: Mapping the Changing Ethnic Terrain

Tiger Woods, perhaps the top golfer of all time, calls himself *Cablinasian*. Woods invented this term as a boy to try to explain to himself just who he was—a combination of Caucasian, Black, Indian, and Asian (Leland and Beals 1997; Hall 2001). Woods wants to embrace all sides of his family.

Like many of us, Tiger Woods' heritage is difficult to specify. Analysts who like to quantify ethnic heritage put Woods at one-quarter Thai, one-quarter Chinese, one-quarter white, an eighth Native American, and an eighth African American. From this chapter, you know how ridiculous such computations are, but the sociological question is why many people consider Tiger Woods an African American. The U.S. racial scene is indeed complex, but a good part of the reason is simply that this is the label the media placed on him. "Everyone has to fit somewhere" seems to be our attitude. If they don't, we grow uncomfortable. And for Tiger Woods, the media chose African American.

Tiger Woods as he answers questions at a news conference.

The United States once had a firm "color line"—barriers between racial–ethnic groups that you didn't dare cross, especially in dating or marriage. This invisible barrier has broken down, and today such marriages are common (*Statistical Abstract* 2009:Table 59). Several campuses have interracial student organizations. Harvard has two, one just for students who have one African American parent (Leland and Beals 1997).

As we enter unfamiliar ethnic terrain, our classifications are bursting at the seams. Consider how Kwame Anthony Appiah, of Harvard's Philosophy and Afro-American Studies Departments, described his situation:

> "My mother is English; my father is Ghanaian. My sisters are married to a Nigerian and a Norwegian. I have nephews who range from blond-haired kids to very black kids. They are all first cousins. Now according to the American scheme of things, they're all black—even the guy with blond hair who skis in Oslo." (Wright 1994)

I marvel at what racial experts the U.S. census takers once were. When they took the census, which is done every ten years, they looked at people and assigned them a race. At various points, the census contained these categories: mulatto, quadroon, octoroon, Negro, black, Mexican, white, Indian, Filipino, Japanese, Chinese, and Hindu. Quadroon (one-fourth black and three-fourths white) and octoroon (one-eighth black and seven-eighths white) proved too difficult to "measure," and these categories were used only in 1890. Mulatto appeared in the 1850 census, but disappeared in 1930. The Mexican government complained about Mexicans being treated as a race, and this category was used only in 1930. I don't know whose idea it was to make Hindu a race, but it lasted for three censuses, from 1920 to 1940 (Bean et al. 2004; Tafoya et al. 2005).

Continuing to reflect changing ideas about race–ethnicity, censuses have become flexible, and we now have many choices. In the 2000 census, we were first asked to declare whether we were or were not "Spanish/Hispanic/Latino." After this, we were asked to check "one or more races" that we "consider ourselves to be." We could choose from White; Black, African American, or Negro; American Indian or Alaska Native; Asian Indian, Chinese, Filipino, Japanese, Korean, Vietnamese, Native Hawaiian, Guamanian or Chamorro, Samoan, and other Pacific Islander. If these didn't do it, we could check a box called "Some Other Race" and then write whatever we wanted.

Perhaps the census should list Cablinasian, after all. We could also have ANGEL for African-Norwegian-German-English-Latino Americans, DEVIL for those of Danish-English-Vietnamese-Italian-Lebanese descent, and STUDENT for Swedish-Turkish-Uruguayan-Danish-English-Norwegian-Tibetan Americans. As you read farther in this chapter, you will see why these terms make as much sense as the categories we currently use.

For Your Consideration

Just why do we count people by "race" anyway? Why not eliminate race from the U.S. census? (Race became a factor in 1790 during the first census. To determine the number of representatives from each state, slaves were counted as three-fifths of whites!) Why is race so important to some people? Perhaps you can use the materials in this chapter to answer these questions.

The reason I selected these photos is to illustrate how seriously we must take all preaching of hatred and of racial supremacy, even though it seems to come from harmless or even humorous sources. The strange-looking person with his hands on his hips, who is wearing *lederhosen*, traditional clothing of Bavaria, Germany, is Adolf Hitler. He caused this horrific scene at the Landsberg concentration camp, which, as shown here, the U.S. military forced German civilians to view.

Although large groupings of people can be classified by blood type and gene frequencies, even these classifications do not uncover "race." Rather, race is so arbitrary that biologists and anthropologists cannot even agree on how many "races" there are (Smedley and Smedley 2005). Ashley Montagu (1964, 1999), a physical anthropologist, pointed out that some scientists have classified humans into only two "races," while others have found as many as two thousand. Montagu (1960) himself classified humans into forty "racial" groups. As the Down-to-Earth Sociology box on page 333 illustrates, even a plane ride can change someone's race!

The *idea* of race, of course, is far from a myth. Firmly embedded in our culture, it is a powerful force in our everyday lives. That no race is superior and that even biologists cannot decide how people should be classified into races is not what counts. "I know what I see, and you can't tell me any different" seems to be the common attitude. As was noted in Chapter 4, sociologists W. I. and D. S. Thomas (1928) observed that "If people define situations as real, they are real in their consequences." In other words, people act on perceptions and beliefs, not facts. As a result, we will always have people like Hitler and, as illustrated in our opening vignette, officials like those in the U.S. Public Health Service who thought that it was fine to experiment with people whom they deemed inferior. While few people hold such extreme views, most people appear to be ethnocentric enough to believe that their own race is—at least just a little—superior to others.

Ethnic Groups

In contrast to *race,* which people use to refer to supposed biological characteristics that distinguish one group of people from another, **ethnicity** and **ethnic** refer to cultural characteristics. Derived from the word *ethnos* (a Greek word meaning "people" or "nation"), *ethnicity* and *ethnic* refer to people who identify with one another on the basis of common ancestry and cultural heritage. Their sense of belonging may center on their nation or region of origin, distinctive foods, clothing, language, music, religion, or family names and relationships.

People often confuse the terms *race* and *ethnic group.* For example, many people, including many Jews, consider Jews a race. Jews, however, are more properly considered an ethnic group, for it is their cultural characteristics, especially their religion, that bind them together. Wherever Jews have lived in the world, they have intermarried. Consequently,

ethnicity (and **ethnic)** having distinctive cultural characteristics

Down-to-Earth Sociology

Can a Plane Ride Change Your Race?

At the beginning of this text (page 8), I mentioned that common sense and sociology often differ. This is especially so when it comes to race. According to common sense, our racial classifications represent biological differences between people. Sociologists, in contrast, stress that what we call races are *social* classifications, not biological categories.

Sociologists point out that *our "race" depends more on the society in which we live than on our biological characteristics.* For example, the racial categories common in the United States are merely one of *numerous* ways by which people around the world classify physical appearances. Although various groups use different categories, each group assumes that its categories are natural, merely a response to visible biology.

To better understand this essential sociological point—that race is more social than it is biological—consider this: In the United States, children born to the same parents are all of the same race. "What could be more natural?" Americans assume. But in Brazil, children born to the same parents may be of different races—if their appearances differ. "What could be more natural?" assume Brazilians.

Consider how Americans usually classify a child born to a "black" mother and a "white" father. Why do they usually say that the child is "black"? Wouldn't it be equally as logical to classify the child as "white"? Similarly, if a child has one grandmother who is "black," but all her other ancestors are "white," the child is often considered "black." Yet she has much more "white blood" than "black blood." Why, then, is she considered "black"? Certainly not because of biology. Such thinking is a legacy of slavery. In an attempt to preserve the "purity" of their "race" in the face of the many children whose fathers were white slave masters and whose mothers were black slaves, whites classified anyone with even a "drop of black blood" as black. They actually called this the "one-drop" rule.

Even a plane trip can change a person's race. In the city of Salvador in Brazil, people classify one another by color of skin and eyes, breadth of nose and lips, and color and curliness of hair. They use at least

What "race" are these two Brazilians? Is the child's "race" different from her mother's "race"? The text explains why "race" is such an unreliable concept that it changes even with geography.

seven terms for what we call white and black. Consider again a U.S. child who has "white" and "black" parents. If she flies to Brazil, she is no longer "black"; she now belongs to one of their several "whiter" categories (Fish 1995).

If the girl makes such a flight, would her "race" actually change? Our common sense revolts at this, I know, but it actually would. We want to argue that because her biological characteristics remain unchanged, her race remains unchanged. This is because we think of race as biological, when *race is actually a label we use to describe perceived biological characteristics.* Simply put, the race we "are" depends on our social location—on who is doing the classifying.

"Racial" classifications are also fluid, not fixed. Even now, you can see change occurring in U.S. classifications. The category "multiracial," for example, indicates changing thought and perception.

For Your Consideration

How would you explain to "Joe and Suzie Six-Pack" that race is more a social classification than a biological one? Can you come up with any arguments to refute this statement? How do you think our racial-ethnic categories will change in the future?

minority group people who are singled out for unequal treatment and who regard themselves as objects of collective discrimination

dominant group the group with the most power, greatest privileges, and highest social status

Jews in China may have Chinese features, while some Swedish Jews are blue-eyed blonds. The confusion of race and ethnicity is illustrated in the photo below.

Minority Groups and Dominant Groups

Sociologist Louis Wirth (1945) defined a **minority group** as people who are singled out for unequal treatment and who regard themselves as objects of collective discrimination. Worldwide, minorities share several conditions: Their physical or cultural traits are held in low esteem by the dominant group, which treats them unfairly, and they tend to marry within their own group (Wagley and Harris 1958). These conditions tend to create a sense of identity among minorities (a feeling of "we-ness"). In some instances, even a sense of common destiny emerges (Chandra 1993b).

Surprisingly, a minority group is not necessarily a *numerical* minority. For example, before India's independence in 1947, a handful of British colonial rulers dominated tens of millions of Indians. Similarly, when South Africa practiced apartheid, a smaller group of Afrikaners, primarily Dutch, discriminated against a much larger number of blacks. And all over the world, as we discussed in the previous chapter, females are a minority group. Accordingly, sociologists refer to those who do the discriminating not as the *majority,* but, rather, as the **dominant group,** for regardless of their numbers, this is the group that has the greater power and privilege.

Possessing political power and unified by shared physical and cultural traits, the dominant group uses its position to discriminate against those with different—and supposedly inferior—traits. The dominant group considers its privileged position to be the result of its own innate superiority.

Emergence of Minority Groups.   A group becomes a minority in one of two ways. The *first* is through the expansion of political boundaries. With the exception of females, tribal societies contain no minority groups. Everyone shares the same culture, including the same language, and belongs to the same group. When a group expands its political boundaries, however, it produces minority groups if it incorporates people with different customs, languages, values, or physical characteristics into the same political entity and discriminates against them. For example, in 1848, after defeating Mexico in war, the United States took over the Southwest. The Mexicans living there, who had been the dominant group prior to the war, were transformed

Because ideas of *race* and *ethnicity* are such a significant part of society, all of us are classified according to those concepts. This photo illustrates the difficulty such assumptions posed for Israel. The Ethiopians, shown here as they arrived in Israel, although claiming to be Jews, looked so different from other Jews that it took several years for Israeli authorities to acknowledge this group's "true Jewishness."

into a minority group, a master status that has influenced their lives ever since. Referring to his ancestors, one Latino said, "We didn't move across the border—the border moved across us."

A *second* way in which a group becomes a minority is by migration. This can be voluntary, as with the millions of people who have chosen to move from Mexico to the United States, or involuntary, as with the millions of Africans who were brought in chains to the United States. (The way females became a minority group represents a third way, but, as discussed in the previous chapter, no one knows just how this occurred.)

How People Construct Their Racial–Ethnic Identity

Some of us have a greater sense of ethnicity than others. Some of us feel firm boundaries between "us" and "them." Others have assimilated so extensively into the mainstream culture that they are only vaguely aware of their ethnic origins. With interethnic marriage common, some do not even know the countries from which their families originated— nor do they care. If asked to identify themselves ethnically, they respond with something like "I'm Heinz 57—German and Irish, with a little Italian and French thrown in—and I think someone said something about being one-sixteenth Indian, too."

Why do some people feel an intense sense of ethnic identity, while others feel hardly any? Figure 12.1 portrays four factors, identified by sociologist Ashley Doane, that heighten or reduce our sense of ethnic identity. From this figure, you can see that the keys are relative size, power, appearance, and discrimination. If your group is relatively small, has little power, looks different from most people in society, and is an object of discrimination, you will have a heightened sense of ethnic identity. In contrast, if you belong to the dominant group that holds most of the power, look like most people in the society, and feel no discrimination, you are likely to experience a sense of "belonging"—and to wonder why ethnic identity is such a big deal.

We can use the term **ethnic work** to refer to the way people construct their ethnicity. For people who have a strong ethnic identity, this term refers to how they enhance and maintain their group's distinctions—from clothing, food, and language to religious practices and holidays. For people whose ethnic identity is not as firm, it refers to attempts to recover their ethnic heritage, such as trying to trace family lines or visiting the country or region of their family's origin. As illustrated by the photo essay on the next page many Americans are engaged in ethnic work. This has confounded the experts, who thought that the United States would be a *melting pot,* with most of its groups blending into a sort of ethnic stew. Because so many Americans have become fascinated with their "roots," some analysts have suggested that "tossed salad" is a more appropriate term than "melting pot."

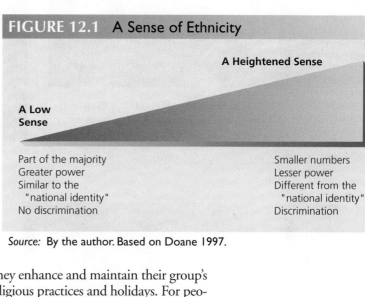

FIGURE 12.1   A Sense of Ethnicity

A Heightened Sense

A Low Sense

Part of the majority	Smaller numbers
Greater power	Lesser power
Similar to the "national identity"	Different from the "national identity"
No discrimination	Discrimination

Source: By the author. Based on Doane 1997.

Prejudice and Discrimination

With prejudice and discrimination so significant in social life, let's consider the origin of prejudice and the extent of discrimination.

Learning Prejudice

Distinguishing Between Prejudice and Discrimination.   Prejudice and discrimination are common throughout the world. In Mexico, Mexicans of Hispanic descent discriminate against Mexicans of Native American descent; in Israel, Ashkenazi Jews, primarily of European descent, discriminate against Sephardi Jews from the Muslim world. In some places, the elderly discriminate against the young; in others, the young discriminate against the elderly. And all around the world, men discriminate against women.

ethnic work activities designed to discover, enhance, or maintain ethnic and racial identity

Ethnic Work
Explorations in Cultural Identity

Ethnic work refers to the ways that people establish, maintain, protect, and transmit their ethnic identity. As shown here, among the techniques people use to forge ties with their roots are dress, dance, and music.

Many African Americans are trying to get in closer contact with their roots. To do this, some use musical performances, as with this group in Philadelphia, Pennsylvania. Note the five-year old who is participating.

Having children participate in ethnic celebrations is a common way of passing on cultural heritage. Shown here is a Thai girl in Los Angeles getting final touches before she performs a temple dance.

Folk dancing (doing a traditional dance of one's cultural heritage) is often used to maintain ethnic identity Shown here is a man in Arlington, Virginia, doing a Bolivian folk dance.

Many European Americans are also involved in ethnic work, attempting to maintain an identity more precise than "from Europe." These women of Czech ancestry are performing for a Czech community in a small town in Nebraska.

Many Native Americans have maintained continuous identity wit their tribal roots. This Nisqually mother is placing a traditional headdress on her daughter for a reenactment of a wedding ceremor

Discrimination is an *action*—unfair treatment directed against someone. Discrimination can be based on many characteristics: age, sex, height, weight, skin color, clothing, speech, income, education, marital status, sexual orientation, disease, disability, religion, and politics. When the basis of discrimination is someone's perception of race, it is known as **racism.** Discrimination is often the result of an *attitude* called **prejudice**—a prejudging of some sort, usually in a negative way. There is also *positive prejudice*, which exaggerates the virtues of a group, as when people think that some group (usually their own) is more capable than others. Most prejudice, however, is negative and involves prejudging a group as inferior.

Learning from Association.   As with our other attitudes, we are not born with prejudice. Rather, we learn prejudice from the people around us. In a fascinating study, sociologist Kathleen Blee (2005) interviewed women who were members of the KKK and Aryan Nations. Her first finding is of the "ho hum" variety: Most women were recruited by someone who already belonged to the group. Blee's second finding, however, holds a surprise: Some women learned to be racists *after* they joined the group. They were attracted to the group not because it matched their racist beliefs but because someone they liked belonged to it. Blee found that their racism was not the *cause* of their joining but, rather, the *result* of their membership.

This classic photo from 1956 illustrates the learning of prejudice.

The Far-Reaching Nature of Prejudice.   It is amazing how much prejudice people can learn. In a classic article, psychologist Eugene Hartley (1946) asked people how they felt about several racial and ethnic groups. Besides Negroes, Jews, and so on, he included the Wallonians, Pireneans, and Danireans—names he had made up. Most people who expressed dislike for Jews and Negros also expressed dislike for these three fictitious groups.

Hartley's study shows that prejudice does not depend on negative experiences with others. It also reveals that people who are prejudiced against one racial or ethnic group also tend to be prejudiced against other groups. People can be, and are, prejudiced against people they have never met—and even against groups that do not exist!

The neo-Nazis and the Ku Klux Klan base their existence on prejudice. These groups believe that race is real, that white is best, and that society's surface conceals underlying conspiracies (Ezekiel 2002). What would happen if a Jew attended their meetings? Would he or she survive? In the Down-to-Earth Sociology box on the next page, sociologist Raphael Ezekiel reveals some of the insights he gained during his remarkable study of these groups.

Internalizing Dominant Norms.   People can even learn to be prejudiced against their *own* group. A national survey of black Americans conducted by black interviewers found that African Americans think that lighter-skinned African American women are more attractive than those with darker skin (Hill 2002). Sociologists call this *the internalization of the norms of the dominant group.*

To study the internalization of dominant norms, psychologists Mahzarin Banaji and Anthony Greenwald created the *Implicit Association Test.* In one version of this test, good and bad words are flashed on a screen along with photos of African Americans and whites. Most subjects are quicker to associate positive words (such as "love," "peace," and "baby") with whites and negative words (such as "cancer," "bomb," and "devil") with blacks. Here's the clincher: This is true for *both* white and black subjects (Dasgupta et al. 2000; Greenwald and Krieger 2006). Apparently, we all learn the *ethnic maps* of our culture and, along with them, their route to biased perception.

Individual and Institutional Discrimination

Sociologists stress that we should move beyond thinking in terms of **individual discrimination,** the negative treatment of one person by another. Although such behavior creates problems, it is primarily an issue between individuals. With their focus on the broader

discrimination an act of unfair treatment directed against an individual or a group

prejudice an attitude or prejudging, usually in a negative way

racism prejudice and discrimination on the basis of race

individual discrimination the negative treatment of one person by another on the basis of that person's perceived characteristics

Down-to-Earth Sociology
The Racist Mind

Sociologist Raphael Ezekiel wanted to get a close look at the racist mind. The best way to study racism from the inside is to do participant observation (see pages 133–134). But Ezekiel is a Jew. Could he study these groups by participant observation? To find out, Ezekiel told Ku Klux Klan and neo-Nazi leaders that he wanted to interview them and attend their meetings. He also told them that he was a Jew. Surprisingly, they agreed. Ezekiel published his path-breaking research in a book, *The Racist Mind* (1995). Here are some of the insights he gained during his fascinating sociological adventure:

> [The leader] builds on mass anxiety about economic insecurity and on popular tendencies to see an Establishment as the cause of economic threat; he hopes to teach people to identify that Establishment as the puppets of a conspiracy of Jews. [He has a] belief in exclusive categories. For the white racist leader, it is profoundly true . . . that the socially defined collections we call races represent fundamental categories. A man is black or a man is white; there are no in-betweens. Every human belongs to a racial category, and all the members of one category are radically different from all the members of other categories. Moreover, race represents the essence of the person. A truck is a truck, a car is a car, a cat is a cat, a dog is a dog, a black is a black, a white is a white. . . . These axioms have a rock-hard quality in the leaders' minds; the world is made up of racial groups. That is what exists for them.
>
> Two further beliefs play a major role in the minds of leaders. First, life is war. The world is made of distinct racial groups; life is about the war between these groups. Second, events have secret causes, are never what they seem superficially. . . . Any myth is plausible, as long as it involves intricate plotting. . . . It does not matter to him what others say. . . . He lives in his ideas and in the little

world he has created where they are taken seriously. . . . Gold can be made from the tongues of frogs; Yahweh's call can be heard in the flapping swastika banner. (pp. 66–67)

Who is attracted to the neo-Nazis and Ku Klux Klan? Here is what Ezekiel discovered:

> [There is a] ready pool of whites who will respond to the racist signal. . . . This population [is] always hungry for activity—or for the talk of activity—that promises dignity and meaning to lives that are working poorly in a highly competitive world. . . . Much as I don't want to believe it, [this] movement brings a sense of meaning—at least for a while—to some of the discontented. To struggle in a cause that transcends the individual lends meaning to life, no matter how ill-founded or narrowing the cause. For the young men in the neo-Nazi group . . . membership was an alternative to atomization and drift; within the group they worked for a cause and took direct risks in the company of comrades. . . .
>
> When interviewing the young neo-Nazis in Detroit, I often found myself driving with them past the closed factories, the idled plants of our shrinking manufacturing base. The fewer and fewer plants that remain can demand better educated and more highly skilled workers. These fatherless Nazi youths, these high-school dropouts, will find little place in the emerging economy . . . a permanently underemployed white underclass is taking its place alongside the permanent black underclass. The struggle over race merely diverts youth from confronting the real issues of their lives. Not many seats are left on the train, and the train is leaving the station. (pp. 32–33)

For Your Consideration
Use functionalism, conflict theory, and symbolic interaction to explain how the leaders and followers of these hate groups view the world. Use these same perspectives to explain why some people are attracted to the message of hate.

---

picture, sociologists encourage us to examine **institutional discrimination,** that is, to see how discrimination is woven into the fabric of society. Let's look at two examples.

Home Mortgages.   Bank lending provides an excellent illustration of institutional discrimination. When a 1991 national study showed that minorities had a harder time getting mortgages, bankers said that favoring whites might *look* like discrimination, but it wasn't: Loans go to those with better credit histories, and that's what whites have. Researchers then compared the credit histories of the applicants. They found that even when applicants had identical credit, African Americans and Latinos were *60 percent* more likely to be rejected (Thomas 1991, 1992).

A new revelation surfaced with the subprime debacle that threw the stock market into a tailspin and led the U.S. Congress to put the next generation deeply in debt for the foibles of this one. Look at Figure 12.2 (on the next page). The first thing you will notice is that minorities are still more likely to be turned down for a loan. You can see that this happens whether their incomes are below or above the median income of their community. Beyond this hard finding lies another just as devastating. In the credit crisis that caused so many to lose their homes, African

institutional discrimination
negative treatment of a minority group that is built into a society's institutions; also called *systemic discrimination*

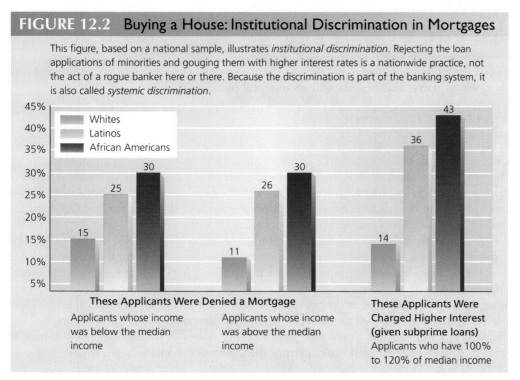

FIGURE 12.2   Buying a House: Institutional Discrimination in Mortgages

This figure, based on a national sample, illustrates *institutional discrimination*. Rejecting the loan applications of minorities and gouging them with higher interest rates is a nationwide practice, not the act of a rogue banker here or there. Because the discrimination is part of the banking system, it is also called *systemic discrimination*.

Source: By the author. Based on Kochbar and Gonzalez-Barrera 2009.

Americans and Latinos were hit harder than whites. There are many reasons for this, but the last set of bars on this figure reveals one of them: Banks purposely targeted minorities to charge higher interest rates. Over the lifetime of a loan, these higher monthly payments mean paying an extra $100,000 to $200,000 (Powell and Roberts 2009). Another consequence of the higher payments was that African Americans and Latinos were more likely to lose their homes.

Health Care.   Discrimination does not have to be deliberate. It can occur even though no one is aware of it: neither those being discriminated against *nor* those doing the discriminating. White patients, for example, are more likely than either Latino or African American patients to receive knee replacements and coronary bypass surgery (Skinner et al. 2003; Popescu 2007). Treatment after a heart attack follows a similar pattern: Whites are more likely than blacks to be given cardiac catheterization, a test to detect blockage of blood vessels. This study of 40,000 patients holds a surprise: Both black *and* white doctors are more likely to give this preventive care to whites (Stolberg 2001).

Researchers do not know why race–ethnicity is a factor in medical decisions. With both white and black doctors involved, we can be certain that physicians *do not intend* to discriminate. In ways we do not yet understand—but which could be related to the implicit bias that apparently comes with the internalization of dominant norms—discrimination is built into the medical delivery system (Green et al. 2007). Race seems to work like gender: Just as women's higher death rates in coronary bypass surgery can be traced to implicit attitudes about gender (see pages 310–311), so also race–ethnicity becomes a subconscious motivation for giving or denying access to advanced medical procedures.

The stark contrasts shown in Table 12.1 indicate that institutional discrimination can be a life-and-death matter. In childbirth, African American mothers are *three* times as likely to die as white mothers, while their babies are more than *twice* as likely to die during their first year of life. This is not a matter of biology, as though African American mothers and children are more fragile. It is a matter of *social* conditions, primarily those of nutrition and medical care.

TABLE 12.1   Race–Ethnicity and Mother/Child Deaths[1]

	Infant Deaths	Maternal Deaths
White Americans	5.7	11.1
African Americans	13.7	36.5

[1]The national database used for this table does not list these totals for other racial–ethnic groups. *White* refers to non-Hispanic whites. *Infant deaths* refers to the number of deaths per year of infants under 1 year old per 1,000 live births. *Maternal deaths* refers to the number of deaths per 100,000 women who give birth in a year.

Source: Statistical Abstract of the United States 2009:Table 110.

Theories of Prejudice

Social scientists have developed several theories to explain prejudice. Let's first look at psychological explanations, then at sociological ones.

Psychological Perspectives

Frustration and Scapegoats.   In 1939, psychologist John Dollard suggested that prejudice is the result of frustration. People who are unable to strike out at the real source of their frustration (such as debt and unemployment) look for someone to blame. They unfairly blame their troubles on a **scapegoat**—often a racial–ethnic or religious minority—and this person or group becomes a target on which they vent their frustrations. Gender and age are also common targets of scapegoating.

Even mild frustration can increase prejudice. A team of psychologists led by Emory Cowen (1959) measured the prejudice of a group of students. They then gave the students two puzzles to solve, making sure the students did not have enough time to solve them. After the students had worked furiously on the puzzles, the experimenters shook their heads in disgust and said that they couldn't believe the students hadn't finished such a simple task. They then retested the students and found that their scores on prejudice had increased. The students had directed their frustrations outward, transferring them to people who had nothing to do with the contempt the experimenters had shown them.

The Authoritarian Personality.   Have you ever wondered whether personality is a cause of prejudice? Maybe some people are more inclined to be prejudiced, and others more fairminded. For psychologist Theodor Adorno, who had fled from the Nazis, this was no idle speculation. With the horrors he had observed still fresh in his mind, Adorno wondered whether there might be a certain type of person who is more likely to fall for the racist spewings of people like Hitler, Mussolini, and those in the Ku Klux Klan.

To find out, Adorno (Adorno et al. 1950) tested about two thousand people, ranging from college professors to prison inmates. To measure their ethnocentrism, anti-Semitism (bias against Jews), and support for strong, authoritarian leaders, he gave them three tests. Adorno found that people who scored high on one test also scored high on the other two. For example, people who agreed with anti-Semitic statements also said that governments should be authoritarian and that foreign ways of life pose a threat to the "American" way.

Adorno concluded that highly prejudiced people are insecure conformists. They have deep respect for authority and are submissive to authority figures. He termed this the **authoritarian personality.** These people believe that things are either right or wrong. Ambiguity disturbs them, especially in matters of religion or sex. They become anxious when they confront norms and values that are different from their own. To view people who differ from themselves as inferior assures them that their own positions are right.

Adorno's research stirred the scientific community, stimulating more than a thousand research studies. In general, the researchers found that people who are older, less educated, less intelligent, and from a lower social class are more likely to be authoritarian. Critics say that this doesn't indicate a particular personality, just that the less educated are more prejudiced—which we already knew (Yinger 1965; Ray 1991). Nevertheless, researchers continue to study this concept (Nicol 2007).

Sociological Perspectives

Sociologists find psychological explanations inadequate. They stress that the key to understanding prejudice cannot be found by looking *inside* people, but, rather, by examining conditions *outside* them. For this reason, sociologists focus on how social environments influence prejudice. With this background, let's compare functionalist, conflict, and symbolic interactionist perspectives on prejudice.

Functionalism.   In a telling scene from a television documentary, journalist Bill Moyers interviewed Fritz Hippler, a Nazi intellectual who at age 29 was put in charge of the entire German film industry. Hippler said that when Hitler came to power the Germans were

scapegoat an individual or group unfairly blamed for someone else's troubles

authoritarian personality Theodor Adorno's term for people who are prejudiced and rank high on scales of conformity, intolerance, insecurity, respect for authority, and submissiveness to superiors

no more anti-Semitic than the French, and probably less so. He was told to increase anti-Semitism in Germany. Obediently, Hippler produced movies that contained vivid scenes comparing Jews to rats—with their breeding threatening to infest the population.

Why was Hippler told to create hatred? Prejudice and discrimination were functional for the Nazis. Germany was on its knees at this time. It had been defeated in World War I and was being devastated by fines levied by the victors. The middle class was being destroyed by runaway inflation. The Jews provided a scapegoat, a common enemy against which the Nazis could unite Germany. In addition, the Jews owned businesses, bank accounts, fine art, and other property that the Nazis could confiscate. Jews also held key positions (as university professors, reporters, judges, and so on), which the Nazis could fill with their own flunkies. In the end, hatred also showed its dysfunctional side, as the Nazi officials hanged at Nuremberg discovered.

Prejudice becomes practically irresistible when state machinery is used to advance the cause of hatred. To produce prejudice, the Nazis harnessed government agencies, the schools, police, courts, and mass media. The results were devastating. Recall the identical twins featured in the Down-to-Earth Sociology box on page 65. Jack and Oskar had been separated as babies. Jack was brought up as a Jew in Trinidad, while Oskar was reared as a Catholic in Czechoslovakia. Under the Nazi regime, Oskar learned to hate Jews, unaware that he himself was a Jew.

That prejudice is functional and is shaped by the social environment was demonstrated by psychologists Muzafer and Carolyn Sherif (1953). In a boys' summer camp, they assigned friends to different cabins and then had the cabin groups compete in sports. In just a few days, strong in-groups had formed. Even lifelong friends began to taunt one another, calling each other "crybaby" and "sissy." The Sherif study teaches us several important lessons about social life. Note how it is possible to arrange the social environment to generate either positive or negative feelings about people, and how prejudice arises if we pit groups against one another in an "I win, you lose" situation. You can also see that prejudice is functional, how it creates in-group solidarity. And, of course, it is obvious how dysfunctional prejudice is, when you observe the way it destroys human relationships.

Conflict Theory.   Conflict theorists also analyze how groups are pitted against one another. Their focus, however, is on how this arrangement benefits those with power. They begin by noting that workers want better food, health care, housing, education, and leisure. To attain these goals, workers need jobs that pay well. If workers are united, they can demand higher wages and better working conditions. Divisions, in contrast, weaken them and prevent united action. To divide them and keep wages down, business owners use two main tactics.

The first tactic is to keep workers insecure. Fear of unemployment works especially well. The unemployed serve as a **reserve labor force.** Business owners draw on the unemployed to expand production during economic booms, and when the economy contracts, they release these workers to rejoin the ranks of the unemployed. The lesson is not lost on workers who have jobs. They fear eviction and worry about having their cars and furniture repossessed. Many know they are just one paycheck away from ending up "on the streets." This helps to keep workers docile.

The second tactic to weaken labor is to exploit racial–ethnic divisions (Patterson 2007). In the 1800s, when white workers in California went on strike, owners of factories replaced them with Chinese workers. When Japanese workers in Hawaii struck, owners of plantations hired Koreans (Jeong and You 2008). This division of workers along racial–ethnic and gender lines is known as a **split labor market** (Du Bois 1935/1992; Roediger 2002). Although today's exploitation is more subtle, fear and suspicion continue to split workers. Whites are aware that other racial–ethnic groups are ready to take their jobs, African Americans often perceive Latinos as competitors (Cose 2006), and men know that women are eager to get promoted. All of this helps to keep workers in line.

The consequences are devastating, say conflict theorists. Just like the boys in the Sherif experiment, African Americans, Latinos, whites, and others see themselves as able to make gains only at the expense of members of the other groups. Sometimes this rivalry shows up along very fine racial–ethnic lines, such as that in Miami between Haitians and African

reserve labor force the unemployed; unemployed workers are thought of as being "in reserve"—capitalists take them "out of reserve" (put them back to work) during times of high production and then put them back "in reserve" (lay them off) when they are no longer needed

split labor market workers split along racial, ethnic, gender, age, or any other lines; this split is exploited by owners to weaken the bargaining power of workers

selective perception seeing certain features of an object or situation, but remaining blind to others

Americans, who distrust each other as competitors. Divisions among workers deflect anger and hostility away from the power elite and direct these powerful emotions toward other racial and ethnic groups. Instead of recognizing their common class interests and working for their mutual welfare, workers learn to fear and distrust one another.

Symbolic Interactionism. While conflict theorists focus on the role of the owner (or capitalist) class in exploiting racial and ethnic divisions, symbolic interactionists examine how labels affect perception and create prejudice.

How Labels Create Prejudice: Symbolic interactionists stress that *the labels we learn affect the way we perceive people.* Labels cause **selective perception;** that is, they lead us to see certain things while they blind us to others. If we apply a label to a group, we tend to perceive its members as all alike. We shake off evidence that doesn't fit (Simpson and Yinger 1972). Racial and ethnic labels are especially powerful. They are shorthand for emotionally charged stereotypes. As you know, the term *nigger* is not neutral. Nor are *honky, cracker, spic, mick, kike, limey, kraut, dago, guinea,* or any of the other scornful words people use to belittle ethnic groups. Such words overpower us with emotions, blocking out rational thought about the people to whom they refer (Allport 1954).

Labels and the Self-Fulfilling Stereotype: Some stereotypes not only justify prejudice and discrimination but also produce the behavior depicted in the stereotype. We examined this principle in Chapter 4 in the box on beauty (page 110). Let's consider Group X. According to stereotypes, the members of Group X are lazy, so they don't deserve good jobs. ("They are lazy and undependable and wouldn't do the job well.") Denied the better jobs, most members of Group X are limited to doing "dirty work," the jobs few people want but that are thought appropriate for "that kind" of people. Since much "dirty work" is sporadic, members of Group X are often seen "on the streets." The sight of their idleness reinforces the original stereotype of laziness. The discrimination that created the "laziness" in the first place passes unnoticed.

To apply these three theoretical perspectives and catch a glimpse of how amazingly different things were in the past, read the Down-to-Earth Sociology box on the next page.

Global Patterns of Intergroup Relations

In their studies of racial–ethnic relations around the world, sociologists have found six basic ways that dominant groups treat minority groups. These patterns are shown in Figure 12.3. Let's look at each.

FIGURE 12.3   Global Patterns of Intergroup Relations: A Continuum

Inhumanity ←→ Humanity

Rejection ←→ Acceptance

Genocide	Population Transfer	Internal Colonialism	Segregation	Assimilation	Multiculturalism (Pluralism)
The dominant group tries to destroy the minority group (e.g., Germany and Rwanda)	The dominant group expels the minority group (e.g., Native Americans forced onto reservations)	The dominant group exploits the minority group (e.g., low-paid, menial work)	The dominant group structures the social institutions to maintain minimal contact with the minority group (e.g., the U.S. South before the 1960s)	The dominant group absorbs the minority group (e.g., American Czechoslovakians)	The dominant group encourages racial and ethnic variation; when successful, there is no longer a dominant group (e.g., Switzerland)

Down-to-Earth Sociology
The Man in the Zoo

The Bronx Zoo in New York City used to keep a 22-year-old pygmy in the Monkey House. The man—and the orangutan he lived with—became the most popular exhibit at the zoo. Thousands of visitors would arrive daily and head straight for the Monkey House. Eyewitnesses to what they thought was a lower form of human in the long chain of evolution, the visitors were fascinated by the pygmy, especially by his sharpened teeth.

To make the exhibit even more alluring, the zoo director had animal bones scattered in front of the man.

I know it sounds as though I must have made this up, but this is a true story. The World's Fair was going to be held in St. Louis in 1904, and the Department of Anthropology wanted to show villages from different cultures. They asked Samuel Verner, an explorer, if he could bring some pygmies to St. Louis to serve as live exhibits. Verner agreed, and on his next trip to Africa, in the Belgian Congo he came across Ota Benga (or Otabenga), a pygmy who had been enslaved by another tribe. Benga, then about age 20, said he was willing to go to St. Louis. After Verner bought Benga's freedom for some cloth and salt, Benga recruited another half dozen pygmies to go with them.

After the World's Fair, Verner took the pygmies back to Africa. When Benga found out that a hostile tribe had wiped out his village and killed his family, he asked Verner if he could return with him to the United States. Verner agreed.

When they returned to New York, Verner ran into financial trouble and wrote some bad checks. No longer able to care for Benga, Verner left him with friends at the American Museum of Natural History. After a few weeks, they grew tired of Benga's antics and turned him over to the Bronx Zoo. The zoo officials put Benga on display in the Monkey House, with this sign:

The African Pygmy, 'Ota Benga.' Age 23 years. Height 4 feet 11 inches. Weight 103 pounds. Brought from the Kasai River, Congo Free State, South Central Africa by Dr. Samuel P. Verner. Exhibited each afternoon during September

Ota Benga, 1906, on exhibit in the Bronx Zoo.

Exhibited with an orangutan, Benga became a sensation. An article in the *New York Times* said it was fortunate that Benga couldn't think very deeply, or else living with monkeys might bother him.

When the Colored Baptist Ministers' Conference protested that exhibiting Benga was degrading, zoo officials replied that they were "taking excellent care of the little fellow." They added that "he has one of the best rooms at the primate house." (I wonder what animal had the best room.)

Not surprisingly, this reply didn't satisfy the ministers. When they continued to protest, zoo officials decided to let Benga out of his cage. They put a white shirt on him and let him walk around the zoo. At night, Benga slept in the monkey house.

Benga's life became even more miserable. Zoo visitors would follow him, howling, jeering, laughing, and poking at him. One day, Benga found a knife in the feeding room of the Monkey House and flourished it at the visitors. Zoo officials took the knife away.

Benga then made a little bow and some arrows and began shooting at the obnoxious visitors. This ended the fun for the zoo officials. They decided that Benga had to leave.

After living in several orphanages for African American children, Benga ended up working as a laborer in a tobacco factory in Lynchburg, Virginia.

Always treated as a freak, Benga was desperately lonely. In 1916, at about the age of 32, in despair that he had no home or family to return to in Africa, Benga ended his misery by shooting himself in the heart.

—Based on Bradford and Blume 1992; Crossen 2006; Richman 2006.

For Your Consideration

1. See what different views emerge as you apply the three theoretical perspectives (functionalism, symbolic interactionism, and conflict theory) to exhibiting Benga at the Bronx Zoo.
2. How does the concept of ethnocentrism apply to this event?
3. Explain how the concepts of prejudice and discrimination apply to what happened to Benga.

compartmentalize to separate acts from feelings or attitudes

population transfer the forced movement of a minority group

Genocide

Last century's two most notorious examples of genocide occurred in Europe and Africa. In Germany during the 1930s and 1940s, Hitler and the Nazis attempted to destroy all Jews. In the 1990s, in Rwanda, the Hutus tried to destroy all Tutsis. One of the horrifying aspects of these slaughters was that the killers did not crawl out from under a rock someplace. Rather, they were ordinary people. In some cases, they were even the victims' neighbors and friends. Their killing was facilitated by labels that singled out the victims as enemies who deserved to die (Huttenbach 1991; Browning 1993; Gross 2001).

To better understand how ordinary people can participate in genocide, let's look at an example from the United States. To call the Native Americans "savages," as U.S. officials and white settlers did, was to label them as inferior, as somehow less than human. This identification made it easier to justify killing the Native Americans in order to take their resources.

> When gold was discovered in northern California in 1849, the fabled "Forty-Niners" rushed in. In this region lived 150,000 Native Americans. To get rid of them, the white government put a bounty on their heads. It even reimbursed the whites for their bullets. The result was the slaughter of 120,000 Native American men, women, and children. (Schaefer 2004)

Most Native Americans died not from bullets, however, but from the diseases the whites brought with them. Measles, smallpox, and the flu came from another continent, and the Native Americans had no immunity against them (Dobyns 1983; Schaefer 2004). The settlers also ruthlessly destroyed the Native Americans' food supply (buffalos, crops). As a result, about *95 percent* of Native Americans died (Thornton 1987; Churchill 1997).

The same thing was happening in other places. In South Africa, the Dutch settlers viewed the native Hottentots as jungle animals and totally wiped them out. In Tasmania, the British settlers stalked the local aboriginal population, hunting them for sport and sometimes even for dog food.

Labels are powerful. Those that dehumanize help people to **compartmentalize**—to separate their acts of cruelty from their sense of being good and moral people. To regard members of some group as inferior or even less than human means that it is okay to treat them inhumanely. This allows people to kill—and still retain a good self-concept (Bernard et al. 1971). In short, *labeling the targeted group as inferior or even less than fully human facilitates genocide.*

Population Transfer

There are two types of **population transfer:** indirect and direct. *Indirect transfer* is achieved by making life so miserable for members of a minority that they leave "voluntarily." Under the bitter conditions of czarist Russia, for example, millions of Jews made this "choice." *Direct transfer* occurs when a dominant group expels a minority. Examples include the U.S. government relocating Native Americans to reservations and transferring Americans of Japanese descent to internment camps during World War II.

In the 1990s, a combination of genocide and population transfer occurred in Bosnia and Kosovo, parts of the former Yugoslavia. A hatred nurtured for centuries had been kept under wraps by Tito's iron-fisted rule from 1944 to 1980. After Tito's death, these suppressed, smoldering hostilities soared to the sur-

Amid fears that Japanese Americans were "enemies within" who would sabotage industrial and military installations on the West Coast, in the early days of World War II Japanese Americans were transferred to "relocation camps." Note the identification ("baggage") tags on this woman and her child as they await relocation. The photo was taken in May 1942.

face, and Yugoslavia split into warring factions. When the Serbs gained power, Muslims rebelled and began guerilla warfare. The Serbs vented their hatred by what they termed **ethnic cleansing:** They terrorized villages with killing and rape, forcing survivors to flee in fear.

Internal Colonialism

In Chapter 9, the term *colonialism* was used to refer to one way that the Most Industrialized Nations exploit the Least Industrialized Nations (p. 252). Conflict theorists use the term **internal colonialism** to describe the way in which a country's dominant group exploits minority groups for its economic advantage. The dominant group manipulates the social institutions to suppress minorities and deny them full access to their society's benefits. Slavery, reviewed in Chapter 9, is an extreme example of internal colonialism, as was the South African system of *apartheid*. Although the dominant Afrikaners despised the minority, they found its presence necessary. As Simpson and Yinger (1972) put it, who else would do the hard work?

Segregation

Internal colonialism is often accompanied by **segregation**—the separation of racial or ethnic groups. Segregation allows the dominant group to maintain social distance from the minority and yet to exploit their labor as cooks, cleaners, chauffeurs, nannies, factory workers, and so on. In the U.S. South until the 1960s, by law African Americans and whites had to use separate public facilities such as hotels, schools, swimming pools, bathrooms, and even drinking fountains. In thirty-eight states, laws prohibited marriage between blacks and whites. Violators could be sent to prison (Mahoney and Kooistra 1995; Crossen 2004b). The last law of this type was repealed in 1967 (Spickard 1989). In the villages of India, an ethnic group, the Dalits (untouchables), is forbidden to use the village pump. Dalit women must walk long distances to streams or pumps outside of the village to fetch their water (author's notes).

Assimilation

Assimilation is the process by which a minority group is absorbed into the mainstream culture. There are two types. In *forced assimilation,* the dominant group refuses to allow the minority to practice its religion, to speak its language, or to follow its customs. Before the fall of the Soviet Union, for example, the dominant group, the Russians, required that Armenian children attend schools where they were taught in Russian. Armenians could celebrate only Russian holidays, not Armenian ones. *Permissible assimilation,* in contrast, allows the minority to adopt the dominant group's patterns in its own way and at its own speed.

Multiculturalism (Pluralism)

A policy of **multiculturalism,** also called **pluralism,** permits or even encourages racial–ethnic variation. The minority groups are able to maintain their separate identities, yet participate freely in the country's social institutions, from education to politics. Switzerland provides an outstanding example of multiculturalism. The Swiss population includes four ethnic groups: French, Italians, Germans, and Romansh. These groups have kept their own languages, and they live peacefully in political and economic unity. Multiculturalism has been so successful that none of these groups can properly be called a minority.

As immigrants assimilate into a new culture, they learn and adapt new customs. These Muslim girls at an elementary school in Dearborn, Michigan, are in the process of assimilating into U.S. culture.

ethnic cleansing a policy of eliminating a population; includes forcible expulsion and genocide

internal colonialism the policy of exploiting minority groups for economic gain

segregation the policy of keeping racial-ethnic groups apart

assimilation the process of being absorbed into the mainstream culture

multiculturalism (also called *pluralism*) a philosophy or political policy that permits or encourages ethnic differences

pluralism the diffusion of power among many interest groups that prevents any single group from gaining control of the government

FIGURE 12.4 Race–Ethnicity of the U.S. Population

African Americans 12%
Latinos 15%
Asian Americans 4%
Native Americans 1%
Whites 66%
Claim two or more races 1.4%

Source: By the author. See Figure 12.5.

Racial–Ethnic Relations in the United States

Writing about race–ethnicity is like stepping onto a minefield: One never knows where to expect the next explosion. Even basic terms are controversial. The term *African American,* for example, is rejected by those who ask why this term doesn't include white immigrants from South Africa. Some people classified as African Americans also reject this term because they identify themselves as blacks. Similarly, some Latinos prefer the term *Hispanic American,* but others reject it, saying that it ignores the Indian side of their heritage. Some would limit the term *Chicanos*—commonly used to refer to Americans from Mexico—to those who have a sense of ethnic oppression and unity; they say that it does not apply to those who have assimilated.

No term that I use here, then, will satisfy everyone. Racial–ethnic identity is fluid, constantly changing, and all terms carry a risk as they take on politically charged meanings. Nevertheless, as part of everyday life, we classify ourselves and one another as belonging to distinct racial-ethnic groups. As Figures 12.4 and 12.5 show, on the basis of these

Notes: This figure, which follows convention and lists Latinos as a separate category, brings into focus the problem of counting "racial–ethnic" groups. Because Latinos can be of any racial–ethnic group, I have reduced the total of the groups with which they self-identify by the number of Latinos who identify with those groups.
[a]Interestingly, this total is *six* times higher than all the Irish who live in Ireland.
[b]Includes French Canadian.
[c]Includes "Scottish-Irish."
[d]Most Latinos trace at least part of their ancestry to Europe.
[e]In descending order, the largest groups of Asian Americans are from China, the Philippines, India, Korea, Vietnam, and Japan. See Figure 12.10. Also includes those who identify themselves as Native Hawaiian or Pacific Islander.
[f]Includes Native Alaskans
[g]Includes Native Hawaiians

FIGURE 12.5 U.S. Racial–Ethnic Groups

Americans of European Descent 198,744,000 66.4%		
German	49,523,000	16.5%
Irish[a]	34,679,000	11.6%
English/British	29,046,000	9.7%
Italian	17,235,000	5.8%
French[b]	11,796,000	3.9%
Scottish[c]	11,148,000	3.7%
Polish	9,771,000	3.3%
Dutch	5,079,000	1.7%
Norwegian	4,601,000	1.5%
Swedish	4,260,000	1.4%
Russian	3,010,000	1.0%
Welsh	1,928,000	0.6%
Czech	1,883,000	0.6%
Hungarian	1,522,000	0.5%
Danish	1,434,000	0.5%
Portuguese	1,379,000	0.5%
Greek	1,291,000	0.4%
Swiss	1,017,000	0.3%
Others	8,142,000	2.7%

Americans of African, Asian, North, Central, and South American, and Pacific Island Descent 96,563,000 32.2%		
Latino[d]	44,321,000	14.8%
African American	36,690,000	12.3%
Asian American[e]	12,881,000	4.3%
Native American[f]	2,259,000	0.75%
Pacific Islander[g]	412,000	0.1%

Americans Who Claim Two or More Race–Ethnicities		
	4,091,000	1.4%

Percentage of Americans: 0   4%   8%   12%   16%   20%

USA–the land of diversity

Source: By the author. Based on *Statistical Abstract of the United States* 2008: Tables 9, 51.

self-identities, whites make up 66 percent of the U.S. population, minorities (African Americans, Asian Americans, Latinos, and Native Americans) 32 percent. Between 1 and 2 percent claim membership in two or more racial–ethnic groups.

As you can see from the Social Map below, the distribution of dominant and minority groups among the states seldom comes close to the national average. This is because minority groups tend to be clustered in regions. The extreme distributions are represented by Maine and Vermont, each of which has only 5 percent minority, and by Hawaii, where minorities outnumber whites 75 percent to 25 percent. With this as background, let's review the major groups in the United States, going from the largest to the smallest.

European Americans

Perhaps the event that best illustrates the racial view of the nation's founders occurred at the first Continental Congress of the United States. There they passed the Naturalization Act of 1790, declaring that only white immigrants could apply for citizenship. The sense of superiority and privilege of **WASPs** (white Anglo-Saxon Protestants) was not limited to their ideas of race. They also viewed white Europeans from countries other than England as inferior. They held disdainful stereotypes of **white ethnics**—immigrants from Europe whose language and other customs differed from theirs. They despised the Irish, viewing them as dirty, lazy drunkards, but they also painted Germans, Poles, Jews, Italians, and others with similar disparaging brushstrokes.

To get an idea of how intense the feelings of the WASPs were, consider this statement by Benjamin Franklin regarding immigrants from Germany:

> Why should the Palatine boors (Germans) be suffered to swarm into our settlements and by herding together establish their language and manners to the exclusion of ours? Why should Pennsylvania, founded by the English, become a colony of aliens, who will shortly be so numerous as to germanize us instead of our anglifying them? (In Alba and Nee 2003:17)

The political and cultural dominance of the WASPs placed intense pressure on immigrants to assimilate into the mainstream culture. The children of most immigrants embraced the new way of life and quickly came to think of themselves as Americans

white ethnics white immigrants to the United States whose cultures differ from WASP culture

WASP White Anglo-Saxon Protestant; narrowly, an American

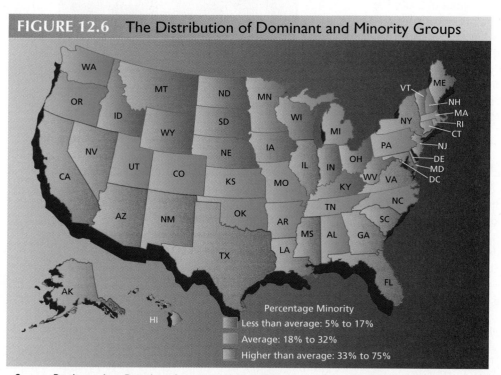

FIGURE 12.6   The Distribution of Dominant and Minority Groups

Percentage Minority
Less than average: 5% to 17%
Average: 18% to 32%
Higher than average: 33% to 75%

Source: By the author. Based on *Statistical Abstract of the United States* 2009:Table 18.

rather than as Germans, French, Hungarians, and so on. They dropped their distinctive customs, especially their language, often viewing them as symbols of shame. This second generation of immigrants was sandwiched between two worlds: "the old country" of their parents and their new home. Their children, the third generation, had an easier adjustment, for they had fewer customs to discard. As immigrants from other parts of Europe assimilated into this Anglo-American culture, the meaning of WASP expanded to include them.

In Sum: Because Protestant English immigrants settled the colonies, they established the culture—from the dominant language to the dominant religion. Highly ethnocentric, they regarded as inferior the customs of other groups. Because white Europeans took power, they determined the national agenda to which other ethnic groups had to react and conform. Their institutional and cultural dominance still sets the stage for current ethnic relations, a topic that is explored in the Down-to-Earth Sociology box below.

Down-to-Earth Sociology
Unpacking the Invisible Knapsack: Exploring Cultural Privilege

O vert racism in the United States has dropped sharply, but doors still open and close on the basis of the color of our skin. Whites have a difficult time grasping the idea that good things come their way because they are white. They usually fail to perceive how "whiteness" operates in their own lives.

Peggy McIntosh, of Irish descent, began to wonder why she was so seldom aware of her race–ethnicity, while her African American friends were so conscious of theirs. She realized that people are not highly aware of things that they take for granted—and that "whiteness" is a "taken-for-granted" background assumption of U.S. society. (You might want to review Figure 12.1 on page 335.) To explore this, she drew up a list of taken-for-granted privileges that come with her "whiteness," what she calls her "invisible knapsack." Because she is white, McIntosh (1988) says:

One of the cultural privileges of being white in the United States is less suspicion of wrongdoing.

1. When I go shopping, store detectives don't follow me.
2. If I don't do well as a leader, I can be sure people won't say that it is because of my race.
3. When I watch television or look at the front page of the paper, I see people of my race presented positively.
4. When I study our national heritage, I see people of my color and am taught that they made our country great.
5. To protect my children, I do not have to teach them to be aware of racism.
6. I can talk with my mouth full and not have people put this down to my color.

7. I can speak at a public meeting without putting my race on trial.
8. I can achieve something and not be "a credit to my race."
9. If a traffic cop pulls me over, I can be sure that it isn't because I'm white.
10. I can be late to a meeting without people thinking I was late because "That's how *they* are."

For Your Consideration

Can you think of other "background privileges" that come to whites because of their skin color? (McIntosh's list contains forty-six items.) Why are whites seldom aware that they carry an "invisible knapsack"?

Latinos (Hispanics)

A Note on Terms.   Before reviewing major characteristics of Latinos, it is important to stress that *Latino* and *Hispanic* refer not to a race but to ethnic groups. Latinos may identify themselves racially as black, white, or Native American. Some Latinos who have an African heritage refer to themselves as Afro-Latinos (Navarro 2003).

Numbers, Origins, and Location.   When birds still nested in the trees that would be used to build the *Mayflower,* Latinos had already established settlements in Florida and New Mexico (Bretos 1994). Today, Latinos are the largest minority group in the United States. As shown in Figure 12.7, about 29 million people trace their origin to Mexico, 4 million to Puerto Rico, 1 to 2 million to Cuba, and about 8 million to Central or South America.

Although Latinos are officially tallied at 44 million, another 9 million Latinos are living here illegally. About 7 million are from Mexico, and the rest from Central and South America (*Statistical Abstract* 2009:Table 46; Passel and Cohn 2009). Most Latinos are legal residents, but each year more than *1 million* Mexicans are arrested and returned to Mexico, most as they are trying to cross the border (Office of Immigration Statistics 2008). Each year, about 300,000 elude detection and make it to the United States. With this vast migration, about 20 million more Latinos live in the United States than Canadians (33 million) live in Canada. As Figure 12.8 shows, two-thirds live in just four states: California, Texas, Florida, and New York. (Also see Figure 20.8 on page 603.)

The massive unauthorized entry into the United States has aroused intense public concern. Despite protests from environmental groups and the Mexican government, U.S. officials have begun to build a 670-mile-long wall on the U.S. side of the border. A group of civilians called the Minutemen also patrols the border, but unofficially. To avoid conflict with the U.S. Border Patrol, the Minutemen do not carry guns. A second unofficial group, the Techno Patriots, also patrols the border, using computers and thermal imaging cameras. When they confirm illegal crossings, they call the Border Patrol, whose agents make the arrests (Archibold and Preston 2008; Marino 2008). Despite walls and patrols, as long as there is a need for unskilled labor and millions of Mexicans live in poverty, this flow of undocumented workers will continue. To gain insight into why, see the Cultural Diversity box on the next page.

Spanish Language.   The Spanish language distinguishes most Latinos from other U.S. ethnic groups. With 34 million people speaking Spanish at home, the United States has become one of the largest Spanish-speaking nations in the world (*Statistical Abstract* 2009: Table 52). Because about half of Latinos are unable to speak English, or can do so only with difficulty, many millions face a major obstacle to getting good jobs.

The growing use of Spanish has stoked controversy (Fund 2007). Perceiving the prevalence of Spanish as a threat, Senator S. I. Hayakawa of California initiated an "English-only" movement in 1981. The constitutional amendment that he sponsored never got off the ground, but thirty states have passed laws that declare English their official language.

Diversity.   For Latinos, country of origin is highly significant. Those from Puerto Rico, for example, feel that they have little in common with people from Mexico, Venezuela, or El Salvador—just as earlier immigrants from Germany, Sweden, and England felt they had little in common with one another. A sign of these divisions is that many refer to themselves in terms of their country of origin, such as *puertorriqueños* or *cubanos,* rather than as Latino or Hispanic.

As with other ethnic groups, Latinos are separated by social class. The half-million Cubans who fled Castro's rise to power in 1959, for example, were mostly well-educated, well-to-do professionals or businesspeople. In contrast, the "boat people"

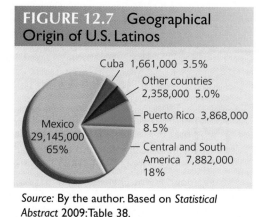

FIGURE 12.7 Geographical Origin of U.S. Latinos

Cuba 1,661,000 3.5%
Other countries 2,358,000 5.0%
Puerto Rico 3,868,000 8.5%
Central and South America 7,882,000 18%
Mexico 29,145,000 65%

Source: By the author. Based on *Statistical Abstract* 2009:Table 38.

FIGURE 12.8 Where U.S. Latinos Live

New Mexico 2%
Colorado 2%
New Jersey 3%
Arizona 4%
Illinois 4%
New York 7%
Florida 8%
Texas 19%
California 29%
Other States 22%

Source: By the author. Based on *Statistical Abstract of the United States* 2009:Table 18.

Cultural Diversity in the United States

The Illegal Travel Guide

Manuel was a drinking buddy of Jose, a man I had met in Colima, Mexico. At 45, Manuel was friendly, outgoing, and enterprising.

Manuel, who had lived in the United States for seven years, spoke fluent English. Preferring to live in his hometown in Colima, where he palled around with his childhood friends, Manuel always seemed to have money and free time.

When Manuel invited me to go on a business trip with him, I accepted. I never could figure out what he did for a living or how he could afford a car, a luxury that none of his friends had. As we traveled from one remote village to another, Manuel would sell used clothing that he had heaped in the back of his older-model Ford station wagon.

At one stop, Manuel took me into a dirt-floored, thatched-roof hut. While chickens ran in and out, Manuel whispered to a slender man who was about 23 years old. The poverty was overwhelming.

A man and woman from Mexico crossing the Rio Grande on their way to Texas.

Juan, as his name turned out to be, had a partial grade school education. He also had a wife, four hungry children under the age of 5, and two pigs—his main food supply. Although eager to work, Juan had no job, for there was simply no work available in this remote village.

As we were drinking a Coke, which seems to be the national beverage of Mexico's poor, Manuel explained to me that he was not only selling clothing—he was also lining up migrants to the United States. For a fee, he would take a man to the border and introduce him to a "wolf," who would help him cross into the promised land.

When I saw the hope in Juan's face, I knew nothing would stop him. He was borrowing every cent he could from every friend and relative to scrape the money together. Although he risked losing everything if apprehended and he would be facing unknown risks, Juan would make the trip, for wealth beckoned on the other side. He knew people who had been to the United States and spoke glowingly of its opportunities. Manuel, of course, the salesman he was, stoked the fires of hope.

Looking up from the children playing on the dirt floor with chickens pecking about them, I saw a man who loved his family. In order to make the desperate bid for a better life, he would suffer an enforced absence, as well as the uncertainties of a foreign culture whose language he did not know.

Juan opened his billfold, took something out, and slowly handed it to me. I looked at it curiously. I felt tears as I saw the tenderness with which he handled this piece of paper. It was his passport to the land of opportunity: a Social Security card made out in his name, sent by a friend who had already made the trip and who was waiting for Juan on the other side of the border.

It was then that I realized that the thousands of Manuels scurrying about Mexico and the millions of Juans they are transporting can never be stopped, for only the United States can fulfill their dreams of a better life.

For Your Consideration

The vast stream of immigrants crossing illegally across the Mexican–U.S. border has become a national issue. What do you think is the best way to deal with this issue? Why?

who fled later were mostly lower-class refugees, people with whom the earlier arrivals would not have associated in Cuba. The earlier arrivals, who are firmly established in Florida and who control many businesses and financial institutions, distance themselves from the more recent immigrants.

These divisions of national origin and social class are a major obstacle to political unity. One consequence is a severe underrepresentation in politics. Because Latinos make up 14.8 percent of the U.S. population, we might expect thirteen or fourteen U.S. Senators to be Latino. How many are there? *Three.* In addition, Latinos hold only 5 percent of the

For millions of people, the United States represents a land of opportunity and freedom from oppression. Shown here are Cubans who reached the United States by transforming their 1950s truck into a boat.

seats in the U.S. House of Representatives (*Statistical Abstract* 2009:Table 388; 2009 election updates).

The potential political power of Latinos is remarkable, and in coming years we will see more of this potential realized. As Latinos have become more visible in U.S. society and more vocal in their demands for equality, they have come face to face with African Americans who fear that Latino gains in employment and at the ballot box will come at their expense (Hutchinson 2008). Together, Latinos and African Americans make up more than one-fourth of the U.S. population. If these two groups were to join together, their unity would produce an unstoppable political force.

Comparative Conditions.   To see how Latinos are doing on some major indicators of well-being, look at Table 12.2 on the next page. As you can see, compared with white Americans and Asian Americans, Latinos have less income, higher unemployment, and more poverty. They are also less likely to own their homes. Now look at how closely Latinos rank with African Americans and Native Americans. From this table, you can also see how significant country of origin is. People from Cuba score higher on all these indicators of well-being, while those from Puerto Rico score lower.

The significance of country or region of origin is also underscored by Table 12.3. You can see that people who trace their roots to Cuba attain more education than do those who come from other areas. You can also see that that Latinos are the most likely to drop out of high school and the least likely to graduate from college. In a postindustrial society that increasingly requires advanced skills, these totals indicate that huge numbers of Latinos will be left behind.

African Americans

After slavery was abolished, the Southern states passed legislation (*Jim Crow* laws) to segregate blacks and whites. In 1896, the U.S. Supreme Court ruled in *Plessy v. Ferguson* that it was a reasonable use of state power to require "separate but equal" accommodations for blacks. Whites used this ruling to strip blacks of the political power they had gained after the Civil War. Declaring political primaries to be "white," they prohibited blacks from voting in them. Not until 1944 did the Supreme Court rule that political primaries weren't "white" and were open to all voters. White politicians then passed laws that only people who could read could vote—and they determined that most African Americans were illiterate. Not until 1954 did African Americans gain the legal right to attend the same public schools as whites, and well into the 1960s the South was still openly—and legally—practicing segregation.

TABLE 12.2   Race–Ethnicity and Comparative Well-Being[1]

	Income		Unemployment		Poverty		Home Ownership	
Racial–Ethnic Group	Median Family Income	Compared to Whites	Percentage Unemployed	Compared to Whites	Percentage Below Poverty Line	Compared to Whites	Percentage Who Own Their Homes	Compared to Whites
Whites	$62,300	—	3.2%	—	9.0%	—	73.7%	—
Latinos	$37,387	39% lower	3.6%	13% higher	21.8%	142% higher	48.8%	34% lower
Country or Area of Origin								
Cuba	NA[2]	NA	2.2%	31% lower	10.7%	19% higher	62.7%	20% lower
Central and South America	NA	NA	NA	NA	16.3%	81% higher	37.3%	49% lower
Mexico	NA	NA	3.6%	13% higher	23.8%	164% higher	50.8%	31% lower
Puerto Rico	NA	NA	4.4%	38% higher	25.3%	181% higher	39.6%	46% lower
African Americans	$36,075	42% lower	6.8%	113% higher	25.6%	184% higher	45.8%	38% lower
Asian Americans[3]	$69,159	9% higher	2.5%	22% lower	11.5%	28% higher	59.1%	20% lower
Native Americans	$38,558	40% lower	NA	NA	25.4%	182% higher	56.0%	24% lower

[1]Data are from 2005 and 2006.
[2]Not Available
[3]Includes Pacific Islanders

Source: By the author. Based on *Statistical Abstract of the United States* 2008: Tables 36, 39, 609.

TABLE 12.3   Race–Ethnicity and Education

	Education Completed				Doctorates		
Racial–Ethnic Group	Less than High School	High School	Some College	College (BA or Higher)	Number Awarded	Percentage of all U.S. Doctorates[1]	Percentage of U.S. Population
Whites	11.0%	30.3%	28.7%	30.0%	30,261	79.0%	66.4%
Latinos	40.6%	27.0%	20.2%	12.2%	1,824	4.8%	14.8%
Country or Area of Origin							
Cuba	26.5%	30.4%	18.4%	24.7%	NA	NA	
Puerto Rico	27.8%	33.7%	24.7%	13.8%	NA	NA	
Central and South America	37.6%	25.6%	18.3%	18.5%	NA	NA	
Mexico	47.7%	26.6%	17.4%	8.3%	NA	NA	
African Americans	20.1%	32.9%	29.7%	17.3%	3,056	8.0%	12.3%
Asian Americans	14.4%	16.8%	19.7%	49.1%	2,911	7.6%	4.3%
Native Americans	23.6%	31.2%	31.5%	13.6%	237	0.6%	0.8%

[1]Percentage after the doctorates awarded to nonresidents are deducted from the total.

Source: By the author. Based on *Statistical Abstract of the United States* 2008: Tables 36, 44, 293 and Figure 12.5 of this text.

Until the 1960s, the South's public facilities were segregated. Some were reserved for whites, others for blacks. This *apartheid* was broken by blacks and whites who worked together and risked their lives to bring about a fairer society. Shown here is a 1963 sit-in at a Woolworth's lunch counter in Jackson, Mississippi. Sugar, ketchup, and mustard are being poured over the heads of the demonstrators.

The Struggle for Civil Rights

It was 1955, in Montgomery, Alabama. As specified by law, whites took the front seats of the bus, and blacks went to the back. As the bus filled up, blacks had to give up their seats to whites.

When Rosa Parks, a 42-year-old African American woman and secretary of the Montgomery NAACP, was told that she would have to stand so that white folks could sit, she refused (Bray 1995). She stubbornly sat there while the bus driver raged and whites felt insulted. Her arrest touched off mass demonstrations, led 50,000 blacks to boycott the city's buses for a year, and thrust an otherwise unknown preacher into a historic role.

Reverend Martin Luther King, Jr., who had majored in sociology at Morehouse College in Atlanta, Georgia, took control. He organized car pools and preached nonviolence. Incensed at this radical organizer and at the stirrings in the normally compliant black community, segregationists also put their beliefs into practice—by bombing the homes of blacks and dynamiting their churches.

Rising Expectations and Civil Strife.   The barriers came down, but they came down slowly. In 1964, Congress passed the Civil Rights Act, making it illegal to discriminate on the basis of race. African Americans were finally allowed in "white" restaurants, hotels, theaters, and other public places. Then in 1965, Congress passed the Voting Rights Act, banning the fraudulent literacy tests that the Southern states had used to keep African Americans from voting.

African Americans then experienced what sociologists call **rising expectations.** They expected that these sweeping legal changes would usher in better conditions in life. In contrast, the lives of the poor among them changed little, if at all. Frustrations built up, exploding in Watts in 1965, when people living in that ghetto of central Los Angeles took to the streets in the first of what were termed the *urban revolts*. When a white supremacist assassinated King on April 4, 1968, inner cities across the nation erupted in fiery violence. Under threat of the destruction of U.S. cities, Congress passed the sweeping Civil Rights Act of 1968.

rising expectations the sense that better conditions are soon to follow, which, if unfulfilled, increases frustration

Continued Gains.   Since then, African Americans have made remarkable gains in politics, education, and jobs. At 10 percent, the number of African Americans in the U.S. House of

In 2009, Barack Obama was sworn in as the 44th president of the United States. He is the first minority to achieve this political office.

Representatives is almost *three times* what it was a generation ago (*Statistical Abstract* 1989: Table 423; 2009:Table 390). As college enrollments increased, the middle class expanded, and today half of all African American families make more than $40,000 a year. One in five earns more than $75,000, and one in nine over $100,000 (*Statistical Abstract* 2009:Table 672). Contrary to stereotypes, the average African American family is *not* poor.

African Americans have become prominent in politics. Jesse Jackson (another sociology major) competed for the Democratic presidential nomination in 1984 and 1988. In 1989, L. Douglas Wilder was elected governor of Virginia, and in 2006 Deval Patrick became governor of Massachusetts. These accomplishments, of course, pale in comparison to the election of Barack Obama as president of the United States in 2008.

Current Losses.   Despite these remarkable gains, African Americans continue to lag behind in politics, economics, and education. Only *one* U.S. Senator is African American, but on the basis of the percentage of African Americans in the U.S. population we would expect about twelve. As Tables 12.2 and 12.3 on page 352 show, African Americans average only 58 percent of white income, have much more unemployment and poverty, and are less likely to own their home or to have a college education. That half of African American families have incomes over $40,000 is only part of the story. Table 12.4 shows the other part—that almost one of every five African American families makes less than $15,000 a year.

The upward mobility of millions of African Americans into the middle class has created two worlds of African American experience—one educated and affluent, the other uneducated and poor. Concentrated among the poor are those with the least hope, the most despair, and the violence that so often dominates the evening news. Although homicide rates have dropped to their lowest point in thirty-five years, African Americans are *six* times as likely to be murdered as are whites (*Statistical Abstract* 2009:Table 301). Compared with whites, African Americans are about *eight* times more likely to die from AIDS (*Statistical Abstract* 2009:Table 121).

TABLE 12.4	Race–Ethnicity and Income Extremes	
	Less than $15,000	Over $100,000
Asian Americans	6.7%	36.2%
Whites	6.7%	25.4%
African Americans	18.7%	11.9%
Latinos	13.5%	11.4%

Note: These are family incomes. Only these groups are listed in the source.

Source: By the author: Based on *Statistical Abstract of the United States* 2009:Table 672.

Race or Social Class? A Sociological Debate.   This division of African Americans into "haves" and "have-nots" has fueled a sociological controversy. Sociologist William Julius Wilson (1978, 2000, 2007) argues that social class has become more important than race in determining the life chances of African Americans. Before civil rights legislation, he says, the African American experience was dominated by race. Throughout the United States, African Americans were excluded from avenues of economic advancement: good schools and good jobs. When civil rights laws opened new opportunities, African Americans seized them. Just as legislation began to open doors to African Americans, however, manufacturing jobs dried up, and many blue-collar jobs were moved to the suburbs. As better-educated African Americans obtained middle-class, white-collar jobs and moved out of the inner city, left behind were those with poor education and few skills.

Wilson stresses how significant these two worlds of African American experience are. The group that is stuck in the inner city lives in poverty, attends poor schools, and faces dead-end jobs or welfare. This group is filled with hopelessness and despair, combined with apathy or hostility. In contrast, those who have moved up the social class ladder live in comfortable homes in secure neighborhoods. Their jobs provide decent incomes, and they send their children to good schools. With their middle-class experiences shaping their views on life, their aspirations and values have little in common with those of African Americans who remain poor. According to Wilson, then, social class—not race—is the most significant factor in the lives of African Americans.

Some sociologists reply that this analysis overlooks the discrimination that continues to underlie the African American experience. They note that African Americans who do the same work as whites average less pay (Willie 1991; Herring 2002) and even receive fewer tips (Lynn et al. 2008). This, they argue, points to racial discrimination, not to social class.

What is the answer to this debate? Wilson would reply that it is not an either-or question. My book is titled The **Declining** Significance of Race, he would say, not The **Absence** of Race. Certainly racism is still alive, he would add, but today social class is more central to the African American experience than is racial discrimination. He stresses that we need to provide jobs for the poor in the inner city—for work provides an anchor to a responsible life (Wilson 1996, 2007).

Racism as an Everyday Burden.   Racism, though more subtle than it used to be, still walks among us (Perry 2006; Crowder and South 2008). Since racism has become more subtle, it takes more subtle methods to uncover it. In one study, researchers sent out 5,000 résumés in response to help wanted ads in the Boston and Chicago Sunday papers (Bertrand and Mullainathan 2002). The résumés were identical, except for the names of the job applicants. Some applicants had white-sounding names, such as Emily and Brandon, while others had black-sounding names, such as Lakisha and Jamal. Although the qualifications of the supposed job applicants were identical, the white-sounding names elicited *50 percent* more callbacks than the black-sounding names. The Down-to-Earth Sociology box on the next page presents another study of subtle racism.

African Americans who occupy higher statuses enjoy greater opportunities and face less discrimination. The discrimination that they encounter, however, is no less painful. Unlike whites of the same social class, they sense discrimination hovering over them. Here is how an African American professor described it:

> [One problem with] being black in America is that you have to spend so much time thinking about stuff that most white people just don't even have to think about. I worry when I get pulled over by a cop. . . . I worry what some white cop is going to think when he walks over to our car, because he's holding on to a gun. And I'm very aware of how many black folks accidentally get shot by cops. I worry when I walk into a store, that someone's going to think I'm in there shoplifting. . . . And I get resentful that I have to think about things that a lot of people, even my very close white friends whose politics are similar to mine, simply don't have to worry about. (Feagin 1999:398)

Sociologists disagree about the relative significance of race and social class in determining social and economic conditions of African Americans. William Julius Wilson, shown here, is an avid proponent of the social class side of this debate.

Down-to-Earth Sociology
Stealth Racism in the Rental Market: What You Reveal by Your Voice

The past often sounds unreal. Discrimination in public accommodations was once standard—and legal. With today's changed laws and the vigilance of groups such as the NAACP and the Jewish Anti-Defamation League, no hotel, restaurant, or gas station would refuse service on the basis of race–ethnicity. There was even a time when white racists could lynch African Americans and Asian Americans without fear of the law. When they could no longer do that, they could still burn crosses on their lawns. Today, such events will make the national news, and the perpetrators will be prosecuted. If local officials won't do their job, the FBI will step in.

Yesterday's overt racism has been replaced with today's stealth racism (Pager 2007; Lynn et al. 2008). There are many forms, but here's one: Sociologist Douglas Massey was talking with his undergraduate students at the University of Pennsylvania about how Americans identify one another racially by their speech. In his class were whites who spoke middle-class English, African Americans who spoke middle-class English with a black accent, and African Amer-

Unlike today, racial discrimination used to be overt. These Ku Klux Klan members are protesting the 1964 integration of a restaurant in Atlanta, Georgia.

icans who spoke a dialect known as Black English Vernacular. Massey and his students decided to investigate how voice is used to discriminate in the housing market. They designed standard identities for the class members, assigning them similar incomes, jobs, and education. They also developed a standard script and translated it into Black English Vernacular. The students called on 79 apartments that were advertised for rent in newspapers. The study was done blindly, with these various English speakers not knowing how the others were being treated.

What did they find? Compared with whites, African Americans were less likely to get to talk to rental agents, who often used answering machines to screen calls. When they did get through, they were less likely to be told that an apartment was available, more likely to have to pay an application fee, and more likely to be asked about their credit history. Students who posed as lower-class blacks (speakers of Black English Vernacular) had the least access to apartments. Figure 12.9 summarizes the percentages of callers who were told an apartment was available.

As you can see from this figure, in all three language groups women experienced more discrimination than men, another indication of the gender inequality we discussed in the previous chapter. For African American women, sociologists use the term *double bind,* meaning that they are discriminated against both because they are African Americans and because they are women.

For Your Consideration
Missing from this study are "White English Vernacular" speakers—whites whose voice identifies them as members of the lower class. If they had been included, where do you think they would place on Figure 12.9?

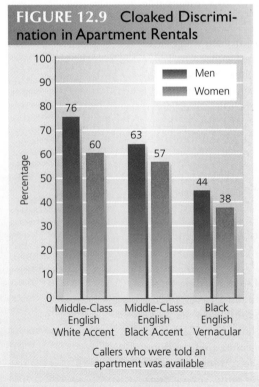

FIGURE 12.9   Cloaked Discrimination in Apartment Rentals

Men
Women

- Middle-Class English White Accent: 76 (Men), 60 (Women)
- Middle-Class English Black Accent: 63 (Men), 57 (Women)
- Black English Vernacular: 44 (Men), 38 (Women)

Percentage

Callers who were told an apartment was available

Source: Massey and Lundy 2001.

Asian Americans

I have stressed in this chapter that our racial–ethnic categories are based more on social considerations than on biological ones. This point is again obvious when we examine the category Asian American. As Figure 12.10 shows, those who are called Asian Americans came to the United States from many nations. *With no unifying culture or "race," why should these people of so many backgrounds be clustered together and assigned a single label?* The reason is that others perceive them as a unit. Think about it. What culture or race–ethnicity do Samoans and Vietnamese have in common? Or Laotians and Pakistanis? Or people from Guam and those from China? Those from Japan and those from India? Yet all these groups—and more—are lumped together and called Asian Americans. Apparently, the U.S. government is not satisfied until it is able to pigeonhole everyone into some racial–ethnic category.

Since *Asian American* is a standard term, however, let's look at the characteristics of the 13 million people who are lumped together and assigned this label.

FIGURE 12.10 The Country of Origin of Asian Americans

Source: By the author. Based on *Statistical Abstract of the United States* 2006:Table 24.

A Background of Discrimination. From their first arrival in the United States, Asian Americans confronted discrimination. Lured by gold strikes in the West and an urgent need for unskilled workers to build the railroads, 200,000 Chinese immigrated between 1850 and 1880. When the famous golden spike was driven at Promontory, Utah, in 1869 to mark the completion of the railroad to the West Coast, white workers prevented Chinese workers from being in the photo—even though Chinese made up 90 percent of Central Pacific Railroad's labor force (Hsu 1971).

After the railroad was complete, the Chinese took other jobs. Feeling threatened by their cheap labor, Anglos formed vigilante groups to intimidate them. They also used the law. California's 1850 Foreign Miner's Act required Chinese (and Latinos) to pay a fee of $20 a month in order to work—when wages were a dollar a day. The California Supreme Court ruled that Chinese could not testify against whites (Carlson and Colburn 1972). In 1882, Congress passed the Chinese Exclusion Act, suspending all Chinese immigration for ten years. Four years later, the Statue of Liberty was dedicated. The tired, the poor, and the huddled masses it was intended to welcome were obviously not Chinese.

When immigrants from Japan arrived, they encountered *spillover bigotry,* a stereotype that lumped Asians together, depicting them as sneaky, lazy, and untrustworthy. After Japan attacked Pearl Harbor in 1941, conditions grew worse for the 110,000 Japanese Americans who called the United States their home. U.S. authorities feared that Japan would invade the United States and that the Japanese Americans would fight on Japan's side. They also feared that Japanese Americans would sabotage military installations on the West Coast. Although no Japanese American had been involved in even a single act of sabotage, on February 19, 1942, President Franklin D. Roosevelt ordered that everyone who was *one-eighth Japanese or more* be confined in detention centers (called "internment camps"). These people were charged with no crime, and they had no trials. Japanese ancestry was sufficient cause for being imprisoned.

Diversity. As you can see from Tables 12.2 and 12.4 on pages 352 and 354, the income of Asian Americans has outstripped that of all groups, including whites. This has led to the stereotype that all Asian Americans are successful. Are they? Their poverty rate is actually higher than that of whites, as you can also see from Table 12.2. As with Latinos, country of origin is significant: Poverty is unusual among Chinese and Japanese Americans, but it clusters among Americans from Southeast Asia. Altogether, between 1 and 2 million Asian Americans live in poverty.

Reasons for Success. The high average income of Asian Americans can be traced to three major factors: family life, educational achievement, and assimilation into mainstream culture. Of all ethnic groups, including whites, Asian American children are the most likely to grow up with two parents and the least likely to be born to a single mother (*Statistical Abstract* 2009:Tables 68, 85). (If you want to jump ahead, look at Figure 16.6 on

Of the racial–ethnic groups in the United States, Asian Americans have the highest rate of intermarriage.

page 475.) Common in these families is a stress on self-discipline, thrift, and hard work (Suzuki 1985; Bell 1991). This early socialization provides strong impetus for the other two factors.

The second factor is their unprecedented rate of college graduation. As Table 12.3 on page 352 shows, 49 percent of Asian Americans complete college. To realize how stunning this is, compare this rate with that of the other groups shown on this table. This educational achievement, in turn, opens doors to economic success.

The most striking indication of the third factor, assimilation, is a high rate of intermarriage. Of Asian Americans who graduate from college, about 40 percent of the men and 60 percent of the women marry a non-Asian American (Qian and Lichter 2007). The intermarriage of Japanese Americans is so extensive that two of every three of their children have one parent who is not of Japanese descent (Schaefer 2004). The Chinese are close behind (Alba and Nee 2003).

Asian Americans are becoming more prominent in politics. With more than half of its citizens being Asian American, Hawaii has elected Asian American governors and sent several Asian American senators to Washington, including the two now serving there (Lee 1998, *Statistical Abstract* 2009:Table 300). The first Asian American governor outside of Hawaii was Gary Locke, who served from 1997 to 2005 as governor of Washington, a state in which Asian Americans make up less than 6 percent of the population. In 2008 in Louisiana, Piyush Jindal became the first Indian American governor.

Native Americans

"I don't go so far as to think that the only good Indians are dead Indians, but I believe nine out of ten are—and I shouldn't inquire too closely in the case of the tenth. The most vicious cowboy has more moral principle than the average Indian."

—Said in 1886 by Teddy Roosevelt
(President of the United States 1901–1909)

Diversity of Groups.   This quote from Teddy Roosevelt provides insight into the rampant racism of earlier generations. Yet, even today, thanks to countless grade B Westerns, some Americans view the original inhabitants of what became the United States as wild, uncivilized savages, a single group of people subdivided into separate tribes. The European immigrants to the colonies, however, encountered diverse groups of people with a variety of cultures—from nomadic hunters and gatherers to people who lived in wooden houses in settled agricultural communities. Altogether, they spoke over 700 languages (Schaefer 2004). Each group had its own norms and values—and the usual ethnocentric pride in its own culture. Consider what happened in 1744 when the colonists of Virginia offered college scholarships for "savage lads." The Iroquois replied:

"Several of our young people were formerly brought up at the colleges of Northern Provinces. They were instructed in all your sciences. But when they came back to us, they were bad runners, ignorant of every means of living in the woods, unable to bear either cold or hunger, knew neither how to build a cabin, take a deer, or kill an enemy. . . . They were totally good for nothing."

They added, "If the English gentlemen would send a dozen or two of their children to Onondaga, the great Council would take care of their education, bring them up in really what was the best manner and make men of them." (Nash 1974; in McLemore 1994)

Native Americans, who numbered about 10 million, had no immunity to the diseases the Europeans brought with them. With deaths due to disease—and warfare, a much lesser cause—their population plummeted. The low point came in 1890, when the census reported only 250,000 Native Americans. If the census and the estimate of the original population are accurate, Native Americans had been reduced to about *one-fortieth* their original size. The population has never recovered, but Native Americans now number over 2 million (see Figure 12.5 on page 346). Native Americans, who today speak 150 different languages, do not think of themselves as a single people who fit neatly within a single label (McLemore 1994).

From Treaties to Genocide and Population Transfer.   At first, the Native Americans tried to accommodate the strangers, since there was plenty of land for both the few new-comers and themselves. Soon, however, the settlers began to raid Indian villages and pillage their food supplies (Horn 2006). As wave after wave of settlers arrived, Pontiac, an Ottawa chief, saw the future—and didn't like it. He con-vinced several tribes to unite in an effort to push the Euro-peans into the sea. He almost succeeded, but failed when the English were reinforced by fresh troops (McLemore 1994).

A pattern of deception evolved. The U.S. government would make treaties to buy some of a tribe's land, with the promise to honor forever the tribe's right to what it had not sold. European immigrants, who continued to pour into the United States, would then disregard these boundaries. The tribes would resist, with death tolls on both sides. The U.S. government would then intervene—not to enforce the treaty, but to force the tribe off its lands. In its relentless drive west-ward, the U.S. government embarked on a policy of geno-cide. It assigned the U.S. cavalry the task of "pacification," which translated into slaughtering Native Americans who "stood in the way" of this territorial expansion.

The acts of cruelty perpetrated by the Europeans against Native Americans appear endless, but two are especially no-table. The first is the Trail of Tears. The U.S. government adopted a policy of population transfer (see Figure 12.3 on page 342), which it called *Indian Removal.* The goal was to

The Native Americans stood in the way of the U.S. government's westward expansion. To seize their lands, the government followed a policy of *genocide,* later replaced by *population transfer.* This depiction of Apache shepherds being attacked by the U.S. Cavalry is by Rufus Zogbaum, a popular U.S. illustrator of the 1880s.

confine Native Americans to specified areas called *reservations.* In the winter of 1838–1839, the U.S. Army rounded up 15,000 Cherokees and forced them to walk a thousand miles from the Carolinas and Georgia to Oklahoma. Coming from the South, many of the Cherokees wore only light clothing. Conditions were so brutal that about 4,000 of those who were forced to make this midwinter march died along the way. The second, the symbolic end to Native American resistance to the European expansion, took place in 1890 at Wounded Knee, South Dakota. There the U.S. cavalry gunned down 300 men, women, and children of the Dakota Sioux tribe. After the massacre, the soldiers threw the bodies into a mass grave (Thornton 1987; Lind 1995; DiSilvestro 2006).

The Invisible Minority and Self-Determination.   Native Americans can truly be called the invisible minority. Because about half live in rural areas and one-third in just three states—Oklahoma, California, and Arizona—most other Americans are hardly aware of a Native American presence in the United States. The isolation of about half of Native Americans on reservations further reduces their visibility (Schaefer 2004).

The systematic attempts of European Americans to destroy the Native Americans' way of life and their forced resettlement onto reservations continue to have deleterious effects. The rate of suicide of Native Americans is the highest of any racial–ethnic group, and their life expectancy is lower than that of the nation as a whole (Murray et al. 2006; Centers for Disease Control 2007b). Table 12.3 on page 352 shows that their education also lags behind most groups: Only 14 percent graduate from college.

Native Americans are experiencing major changes. In the 1800s, U.S. courts ruled that Native Americans did not own the land on which they had been settled and had no right to develop its resources. They made Native Americans wards of the state, and the Bureau of Indian Affairs treated them like children (Mohawk 1991; Schaefer 2004). Then, in the 1960s, Native Americans won a series of legal victories that gave them control over reservation lands. With this legal change, many Native American tribes have opened businesses—ranging from fish canneries to industrial parks that serve metropolitan areas. The Skywalk, opened by the Hualapai, which offers breathtaking views of the Grand Canyon, gives an idea of the varieties of businesses to come.

It is the casinos, though, that have attracted the most attention. In 1988, the federal government passed a law that allowed Native Americans to operate gambling establishments on reservations. Now over 200 tribes operate casinos. *They bring in $26 billion a year, twice as much as all the casinos in Las Vegas* (Werner 2007; *Statistical Abstract* 2009: Table 1218). The Oneida tribe of New York, which has only 1,000 members, runs a casino that nets $232,000 a year for each man, woman, and child (Peterson 2003). This huge amount, however, pales in comparison with that of the Mashantucket Pequot tribe of Connecticut. With only 700 members, the tribe brings in more than $2 million a day just from slot machines (Rivlin 2007). Incredibly, one tribe has only *one* member: She has her own casino (Bartlett and Steele 2002).

A highly controversial issue is *separatism*. Because Native Americans were independent peoples when the Europeans arrived and they never willingly joined the United States, many tribes maintain the right to remain separate from the U.S. government. The chief of the Onondaga tribe in New York, a member of the Iroquois Federation, summarized the issue this way:

> For the whole history of the Iroquois, we have maintained that we are a separate nation. We have never lost a war. Our government still operates. We have refused the U.S. government's reorganization plans for us. We have kept our language and our traditions, and when we fly to Geneva to UN meetings, we carry Hau de no sau nee passports. We made some treaties that lost some land, but that also confirmed our separate-nation status. That the U.S. denies all this doesn't make it any less the case. (Mander 1992)

One of the most significant changes for Native Americans is **pan-Indianism.** This emphasis on common elements that run through their cultures is an attempt to develop an identity that goes beyond the tribe. Pan-Indianism ("We are all Indians") is a remarkable example of the plasticity of ethnicity. It embraces and substitutes for individual tribal identities the label "Indian"—originally imposed by Spanish and Italian sailors, who thought they had reached the shores of India. As sociologist Irwin Deutscher (2002:61) put it, "The peoples who have accepted the larger definition of who they are, have, in fact, little else in common with each other than the stereotypes of the dominant group which labels them."

Native Americans say that it is they who must determine whether they want to establish a common identity and work together as in pan-Indianism or to stress separatism and identify solely with their own tribe; to assimilate into the dominant culture or to remain apart from it; to move to cities or to remain on reservations; or to operate casinos or to engage only in traditional activities. "Such decisions must be ours," say the Native Americans. "We are sovereign, and we will not take orders from the victors of past wars."

Looking Toward the Future

Back in 1903, sociologist W. E. B. Du Bois said, "The problem of the twentieth century is the problem of the color line—the relation of the darker to the lighter races." Incredibly, over a hundred years later, the color line remains one of the most volatile topics facing the nation. From time to time, the color line takes on a different complexion, as with the war on terrorism and the corresponding discrimination directed against people of Middle Eastern descent.

In another hundred years, will yet another sociologist lament that the color of people's skin still affects human relationships? Given our past, it seems that although racial–ethnic walls will diminish, even crumble at some points, the color line is not likely to disappear. Let's close this chapter by looking at two issues we are currently grappling with, immigration and affirmative action.

pan-Indianism a movement that focuses on common elements in the cultures of Native Americans in order to develop a cross-tribal self-identity and to work toward the welfare of all Native Americans

The Immigration Debate

Throughout its history, the United States has both welcomed immigration and feared its consequences. The gates opened wide (numerically, if not in attitude) for waves of immigrants in the 1800s and early 1900s. During the past twenty years, a new wave of immigration has brought close to a million new residents to the United States each year. Today, more immigrants (38 million) live in the United States than at any other time in the country's history (*Statistical Abstract* 2007: Table 5; 2009:Table 39).

In contrast to earlier waves, in which immigrants came almost exclusively from western Europe, the current wave of immigrants is so diverse that it is changing the U.S. racial–ethnic mix. If current trends in immigration (and birth) persist, in about fifty years the "average" American will trace his or her ancestry to Africa, Asia, South America, the Pacific Islands, the Middle East—almost anywhere but white Europe. This change is discussed in the Cultural Diversity box on the next page.

In some states, the future is arriving much sooner than this. In California, racial–ethnic minorities have become the majority. California has 21 million minorities and 16 million whites (*Statistical Abstract* 2009:Table 18). Californians who request new telephone service from Pacific Bell can speak to customer service representatives in Spanish, Korean, Vietnamese, Mandarin, Cantonese—or English.

As in the past, there is concern that "too many" immigrants will change the character of the United States. "Throughout the history of U.S. immigration," write sociologists Alejandro Portes and Rubén Rumbaut (1990), "a consistent thread has been the fear that the 'alien element' would somehow undermine the institutions of the country and would lead it down the path of disintegration and decay." A hundred years ago, the widespread fear was that the immigrants from southern Europe would bring communism with them. Today, some fear that Spanish-speaking immigrants threaten the primacy of the English language. In addition, the age-old fear that immigrants will take jobs away from native-born Americans remains strong. Finally, minority groups that struggled for political representation fear that newer groups will gain political power at their expense.

Affirmative Action

Affirmative action in our multicultural society lies at the center of a national debate about racial–ethnic relations. In this policy, initiated by President Kennedy in 1961, goals based on race (and sex) are used in hiring, promotion, and college admission. Sociologist Barbara Reskin (1998) examined the results of affirmative action. She concluded that although it is difficult to separate the results of affirmative action from economic booms and busts and the greater numbers of women in the workforce, affirmative action has had a modest impact.

The results may have been modest, but the reactions to this program have been anything but modest. Affirmative action has been at the center of controversy for almost two generations. Liberals, both white and minority, say that this program is the most direct way to level the playing field of economic opportunity. If whites are passed over, this is an unfortunate cost that we must pay if we are to make up for past discrimination. In contrast, conservatives, both white and minority, agree that opportunity should be open to all, but claim that putting race (or sex) ahead of an individual's training and ability to perform a job is reverse discrimination. Because of their race (or sex), qualified people who had nothing to do with past inequality are discriminated against. They add that affirmative action stigmatizes the people who benefit from it, because it suggests that they hold their jobs because of race (or sex), rather than merit.

Cultural Diversity in the United States

Glimpsing the Future: The Shifting U.S. Racial–Ethnic Mix

During the next twenty-five years, the population of the United States is expected to grow by about 22 percent. To see what the U.S. population will look like at that time, can we simply add 22 percent to our current racial–ethnic mix? The answer is a resounding no. As you can see from Figure 12.11, some groups will grow much more than others, giving us a different-looking United States. Some of the changes in the U.S. racial–ethnic mix will be dramatic. In twenty-five years, one of every nineteen Americans is expected to have an Asian background, and in the most dramatic change, almost one of four is expected to be of Latino ancestry.

The basic causes of this fundamental shift are the racial–ethnic groups' different rates of immigration and birth. Both will change the groups' proportions of the U.S. population, but immigration is by far the more important. From Figure 12.11, you can see that the proportion of non-Hispanic whites is expected to shrink, that of Native Americans to remain the same, that of African Americans to increase slightly, and that of Latinos to increase sharply.

For Your Consideration

This shifting racial–ethnic mix is one of the most significant events occurring in the United States. To better understand its implications, apply the three theoretical perspectives.

Use the *conflict perspective* to identify the groups that are likely to be threatened by this change. Over what resources are struggles likely to develop? What impact do you think this changing mix might have on European Americans? On Latinos? On African Americans? On Asian Americans? On Native Americans? What changes in immigration laws (or their enforcement) can you anticipate?

To apply the *symbolic interactionist perspective*, consider how groups might perceive one another differently as their proportion of the population changes. How do you think that this changed perception will affect people's behavior?

To apply the *functionalist perspective*, try to determine how each racial-ethnic group will benefit from this changing mix. How will other parts of society (such as businesses) benefit? What functions and dysfunctions can you anticipate for politics, economics, education, or religion?

FIGURE 12.11   Projections of the Racial–Ethnic Makeup of the U.S. Population

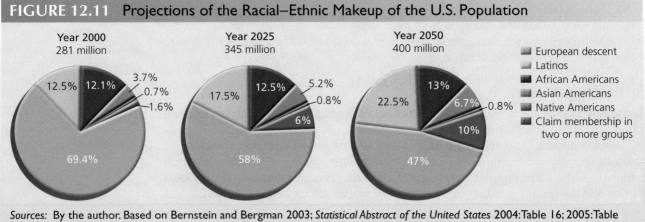

Year 2000 — 281 million: 69.4%, 12.5%, 12.1%, 3.7%, 0.7%, 1.6%

Year 2025 — 345 million: 58%, 17.5%, 12.5%, 5.2%, 0.8%, 6%

Year 2050 — 400 million: 47%, 22.5%, 13%, 6.7%, 0.8%, 10%

Legend:
- European descent
- Latinos
- African Americans
- Asian Americans
- Native Americans
- Claim membership in two or more groups

Sources: By the author. Based on Bernstein and Bergman 2003; *Statistical Abstract of the United States* 2004: Table 16; 2005: Table 16. I modified the projections based on the new census category of membership in two or more groups and trends in interethnic marriage.

This national debate crystallized with a series of controversial rulings. One of the most significant was *Proposition 209,* a 1996 amendment to the California state constitution. This amendment made it illegal to give preference to minorities and women in hiring, promotion, and college admissions. Despite appeals by a coalition of civil rights groups, the U.S. Supreme Court upheld this California law.

A second significant ruling was made by the Supreme Court of Michigan in 2003. White students who had been denied admission to the University of Michigan claimed that they had been discriminated against because less qualified applicants had been admitted on the basis of their race. The Court ruled that universities can give minorities an edge in admissions, but there must be a meaningful review of individual applicants. Mechanical systems, such as giving extra points because of race, are unconstitutional. This murky message satisfied no one, as no one knew what it really meant.

To remove ambiguity, opponents of affirmative action put amendments to several state constitutions on the ballot. The amendments, which make it illegal for public institutions to even consider race or sex in hiring, in awarding contracts, or in college admissions, failed in some states, such as Colorado, but became law in Michigan and Nebraska (Lewin 2007; Kaufman and Fields 2008).

With constitutional battles continuing, the issue of affirmative action in a multicultural society is likely to remain center stage for quite some time.

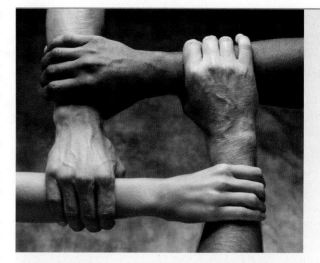

The United States is the most racially–ethnically diverse society in the world. This can be our central strength, with our many groups working together to build a harmonious society, a stellar example for the world. Or it can be our Achilles heel, with us breaking into feuding groups, a Balkanized society that marks an ill-fitting end to a grand social experiment. Our reality will probably fall somewhere between these extremes.

By the Numbers: *Then and Now*

Percentage of Americans who claim membership in these groups:

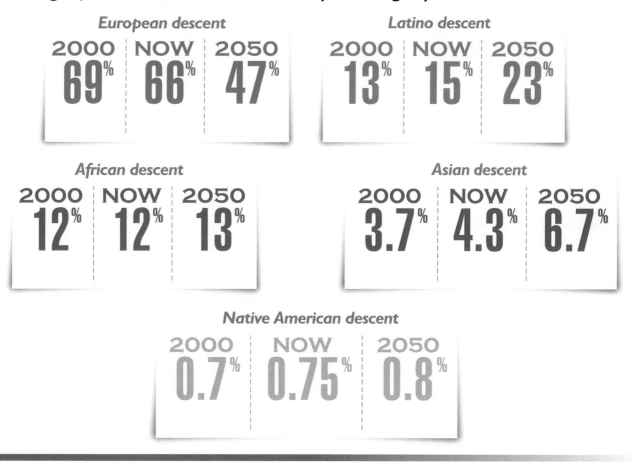

European descent

2000	NOW	2050
69%	66%	47%

Latino descent

2000	NOW	2050
13%	15%	23%

African descent

2000	NOW	2050
12%	12%	13%

Asian descent

2000	NOW	2050
3.7%	4.3%	6.7%

Native American descent

2000	NOW	2050
0.7%	0.75%	0.8%

Toward a True Multicultural Society

The United States has the potential to become a society in which racial–ethnic groups not only coexist, but also respect one another—and thrive—as they work together for mutually beneficial goals. In a true multicultural society, the minority groups that make up the United States would participate fully in the nation's social institutions while maintaining their cultural integrity. Reaching this goal will require that we understand that "the biological differences that divide one race from another add up to a drop in the genetic ocean." For a long time, we have given racial categories an importance they never merited. Now we need to figure out how to reduce them to the irrelevance they deserve. In short, we need to make real the abstraction called equality that we profess to believe (Cose 2000).

SUMMARY *and* REVIEW

Laying the Sociological Foundation

How is race both a reality and a myth?

In the sense that different groups inherit distinctive physical traits, race is a reality. There is no agreement regarding what constitutes a particular race, however, or even how many races there are. In the sense of one race being superior to another and of there being pure races, race is a myth. The *idea* of race is powerful, shaping basic relationships among people. Pp. 330–331.

How do race and ethnicity differ?

Race refers to inherited biological characteristics; **ethnicity,** to cultural ones. Members of ethnic groups identify with one another on the basis of common ancestry and cultural heritage. Pp. 331–334.

What are minority and dominant groups?

Minority groups are people who are singled out for unequal treatment by members of the **dominant group,** the group with more power and privilege. Minorities originate with migration or the expansion of political boundaries. Pp. 334–335.

What heightens ethnic identity, and what is "ethnic work"?

A group's relative size, power, physical characteristics, and amount of discrimination heighten or reduce ethnic identity. **Ethnic work** is the process of constructing and maintaining an ethnic identity. For people without a firm ethnic identity, ethnic work is an attempt to recover one's ethnic heritage. For those with strong ties to their culture of origin, ethnic work involves enhancing group distinctions. P. 335.

Prejudice and Discrimination

Why are people prejudiced?

Prejudice is an attitude, and **discrimination** is an action. Like other attitudes, prejudice is learned in association with others. Prejudice is so extensive that people can show prejudice against groups that don't even exist. Minorities also internalize the dominant norms, and some show prejudice against their own group. Pp. 335–337.

How do individual and institutional discrimination differ?

Individual discrimination is the negative treatment of one person by another, while **institutional discrimination** is negative treatment that is built into social institutions. Institutional discrimination can occur without the awareness of either the perpetrator or the object of discrimination. Discrimination in health care is one example. Pp. 337–339.

Theories of Prejudice

How do psychologists explain prejudice?

Psychological theories of prejudice stress the **authoritarian personality** and frustration displaced toward **scapegoats.** P. 340.

How do sociologists explain prejudice?

Sociological theories focus on how different social environments increase or decrease prejudice. *Functionalists* stress the benefits and costs that come from discrimination. *Conflict theorists* look at how the groups in power exploit racial–ethnic divisions in order to control workers and maintain power. *Symbolic interactionists* stress how labels create **selective perception** and self-fulfilling prophecies. Pp. 340–342.

Global Patterns of Intergroup Relations

What are the major patterns of minority and dominant group relations?

Beginning with the least humane, they are **genocide, population transfer, internal colonialism, segregation, assimilation,** and **multiculturalism (pluralism).** Pp. 342–345.

Racial–Ethnic Relations in the United States

What are the major racial–ethnic groups in the United States?

From largest to smallest, the major groups are European Americans, Latinos, African Americans, Asian Americans, and Native Americans. P. 346.

What are some issues in racial–ethnic relations and characteristics of minority groups?

Latinos are divided by social class and country of origin. African Americans are increasingly divided into middle and lower classes, with two sharply contrasting worlds of experience. On many measures, Asian Americans are bet-ter off than white Americans, but their well-being varies with their country of origin. For Native Americans, the primary issues are poverty, nationhood, and settling treaty obligations. The overarching issue for minorities is over-coming discrimination. Pp. 347–360.

Looking Toward the Future

What main issues dominate U.S. racial–ethnic relations?

The main issues are immigration, affirmative action, and how to develop a true multicultural society. The answers affect our future. Pp. 360–363.

THINKING CRITICALLY *ABOUT* Chapter 12

1. How many races do your friends or family think there are? Do they think that one race is superior to the others? What do you think their reaction would be to the sociological position that racial categories are primarily social?

2. A hundred years ago, sociologist W. E. B. Du Bois said, "The problem of the twentieth century is the problem of the color line—the relation of the darker to the lighter races." Why do you think that the color line remains one of the most volatile topics facing the nation?

3. If you were appointed head of the U.S. Civil Service Commission, what policies would you propose to reduce racial–ethnic strife in the United States? Be ready to explain the sociological principles that might give your proposals a higher chance of success.

ADDITIONAL RESOURCES

What can you find in MySocLab? mysoclab www.mysoclab.com

- Complete Ebook
- Practice Tests and Video and Audio activities
- Mapping and Data Analysis exercises

- Sociology in the News
- Classic Readings in Sociology
- Research and Writing advice

Where Can I Read More on This Topic?

Suggested readings for this chapter are listed at the back of this book.

chapter

13

The Elderly

Argentina

In 1928, Charles Hart, who was working on his Ph.D. in anthropology, did fieldwork with the Tiwi people, who live on an island off the northern coast of Australia. Because every Tiwi belongs to a clan, they assigned Hart to the bird (Jabijabui) clan and told him that a particular woman was his mother. Hart described the woman as "toothless, almost blind, withered." He added that she was "physically quite revolting and mentally rather senile." He then recounted this remarkable event:

> [They would] put the old woman in the hole and fill it in with earth until only her head was showing.

Toward the end of my time on the islands an incident occurred that surprised me because it suggested that some of them had been taking my presence in the kinship system much more seriously than I had thought. I was approached by a group of about eight or nine senior men. . . . They were the senior members of the Jabijabui clan and they had decided among themselves that the time had come to get rid of the decrepit old woman who had first called me son and whom I now called mother. . . . As I knew, they said, it was Tiwi custom, when an old woman became too feeble to look after herself, to "cover her up." This could only be done by her sons and brothers and all of them had to agree beforehand, since once it was done, they did not want any dissension among the brothers or clansmen, as that might lead to a feud. My "mother" was now completely blind, she was constantly falling over logs or into fires, and they, her senior clansmen, were in agreement that she would be better out of the way. Did I agree?

I already knew about "covering up." The Tiwi, like many other hunting and gathering peoples, sometimes got rid of their ancient and decrepit females. The method was to dig a hole in the ground in some lonely place, put the old woman in the hole and fill it in with earth until only her head was showing. Everybody went away for a day or two and then went back to the hole to discover to their great surprise, that the old woman was dead, having been too feeble to raise her arms from the earth. Nobody had "killed" her; her death in Tiwi eyes was a natural one. She had been alive when her relatives last saw her. I had never seen it done, though I knew it was the custom, so I asked my brothers if it was necessary for me to attend the "covering up."

They said no and that they would do it, but only after they had my agreement. Of course I agreed, and a week or two later we heard in our camp that my "mother" was dead, and we all wailed and put on the trimmings of mourning. (C. W. M. Hart in Hart and Pilling 1979:125–126.)

367

Aging in Global Perspective

We won't deal with the question of whether it was moral or ethical for Hart to agree that the old woman should be "covered up." What is of interest for our purposes is how the Tiwi treated their frail elderly—or, more specifically, their frail *female* elderly. You probably noticed that the Tiwi "covered up" only old women. As was noted in Chapter 11, females are discriminated against throughout the world. As this incident makes evident, in some places that discrimination extends even to death.

Every society must deal with the problem of people growing old, and of some becoming frail. Although few societies choose to bury old people alive, all societies must decide how to allocate limited resources among their citizens. With the percentage of the population that is old increasing in many nations, these decisions are generating tensions between the generations.

The Social Construction of Aging

The way the Tiwi treated frail elderly women reflects one extreme of how societies cope with aging. Another extreme, one that reflects an entirely different attitude, is illustrated by the Abkhasians, an agricultural people who live in a mountainous region of Georgia, a republic of the former Soviet Union. The Abkhasians pay their elderly high respect and look to them for guidance. They would no more dispense with their elderly by "covering them up" than we would "cover up" a sick child in our culture.

The Abkhasians may be the longest-lived people on earth. Many claim to live past 100—some beyond 120 and even 130 (Benet 1971; Robbins 2006). Although it is difficult to document the accuracy of these claims, government records indicate that an extraordinary number of Abkhasians do live to a very old age.

The man riding the horse is Temir Tarba, who was 100 years old when the photo was taken. As discussed in the text, the Abkhasians have an extraordinarily large number of elderly, but due to a lack of records, there are questions about their exact age.

Three main factors appear to account for their long lives. The first is their diet, which consists of little meat, much fresh fruit, vegetables, garlic, goat cheese, cornmeal, buttermilk, and wine. The second is their lifelong physical activity. They do slow down after age 80, but even after the age of 100 they still work about four hours a day. The third factor—a highly developed sense of community—lies at the very heart of the Abkhasian culture. From childhood, each individual is integrated into a primary group and remains so throughout life. There is no such thing as a nursing home, nor do the elderly live alone. Because they continue to work and contribute to the group's welfare, the elderly aren't a burden to anyone. They don't vegetate, nor do they feel the need to "fill time" with bingo and shuffleboard. In short, the elderly feel no sudden rupture between what they "were" and what they "are."

The examples of the Tiwi and the Abkhasians reveal an important sociological principle: Like gender, aging is *socially constructed.* That is, nothing in the nature of aging summons forth any particular viewpoint. Rather, attitudes toward the aged are rooted in society and, therefore, differ from one social group to another. As we shall see, even the age at which people are considered old depends not on biology, but on culture.

Industrialization and the Graying of the Globe

As was noted in previous chapters, industrialization is occurring worldwide. With industrialization comes a higher standard of living, including more food, a purer water supply, and more effective ways of fighting the diseases that kill children. As a result, when a country industrializes, more of its people reach older ages. The Social Map on the next page illustrates this principle.

From this global map, you can see that the industrialized countries have the highest percentage of elderly. The range among nations is broad, from just 1 of 45 citizens in nonindustrialized Uganda to *nine* times greater than this—1 of 5—in postindustrial Japan (*Statistical Abstract* 2009:Table 1290). In just two decades, *half* the population of Italy and Japan will be older than 50 (Kinsella and

Phillips 2005). The graying of the globe is so new that *two-thirds of all people who have ever passed age 50 in the history of the world are alive today* (Zaslow 2003).

As a nation's elderly population increases, so, too, does the bill its younger citizens pay to provide for their needs. This expense has become a major social issue. Although Americans complain that Social Security taxes are too high, the U.S. rate of 15.3 percent is comparatively low. Polish workers are hit the hardest; they pay 37 percent of their wages into social security. Workers in Austria, France, Greece, Holland, and Hungary pay only slightly less (*Statistical Abstract* 2008:Tables 527, 1326). Workers in the Least Industrialized Nations pay no social security taxes. There, families are expected to take care of their own elderly, with no help from the government.

As the numbers of elderly continue to grow, analysts have become alarmed about future liabilities for their care (Sanderson and Scherbov 2008). This issue is especially troubling in western Europe and Japan, which have the largest percentage of citizens over the age of 60. The basic issue is, How can nations provide high-quality care for their growing numbers of elderly without burdening future generations with impossible taxes? Although more and more nations around the world are confronting this issue, no one has found a solution yet.

Except for interaction within families, age groups in Western cultures are usually kept fairly separate. This combination of an old folks home and day care center in Japan is an interesting contrast to the Western approach.

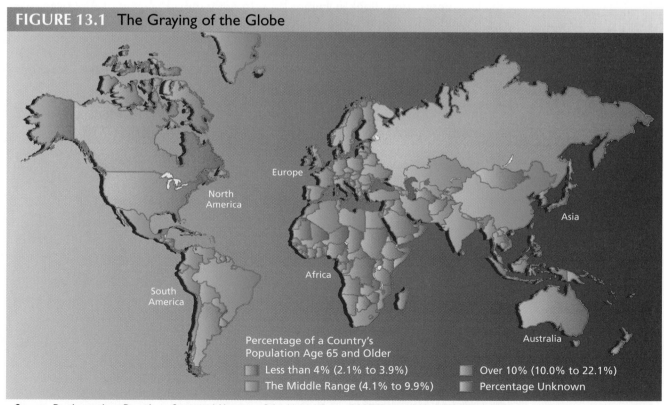

FIGURE 13.1   The Graying of the Globe

Europe

North America

Asia

Africa

South America

Australia

Percentage of a Country's Population Age 65 and Older

◼ Less than 4% (2.1% to 3.9%)   ◼ Over 10% (10.0% to 22.1%)
◼ The Middle Range (4.1% to 9.9%)   ◼ Percentage Unknown

Source: By the author. Based on *Statistical Abstract of the United States* 2007:Table 1309; 2009:Table 1290.

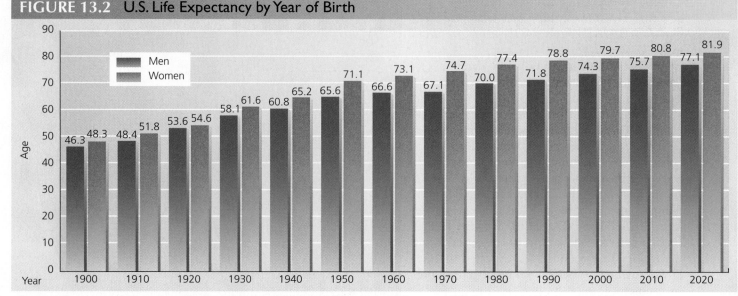

FIGURE 13.2   U.S. Life Expectancy by Year of Birth

Sources: By the author. Based on *Historical Statistics of the United States, Colonial Times to 1970,* Bicentennial Edition, Part I, Series B, 107–115; *Statistical Abstract of the United States* 2009: Table 100.

life expectancy the number of years that an average person at any age, including newborns, can expect to live

graying of America the growing percentage of older people in the U.S. population

The Graying of America

As Figure 13.2 illustrates, the United States is part of this global trend. This figure shows how U.S. **life expectancy,** the number of years people can expect to live, has increased since 1900. To me, and perhaps to you, it is startling to realize that a hundred years ago the average American could not even expect to see age 50. Since then, we've added about *30* years to our life expectancy, and Americans born today can expect to live into their 70s or 80s.

The term **graying of America** refers to this growing percentage of older people in the U.S. population. Look at Figure 13.3. In 1900 only 4 percent of Americans were age 65 and older. Today about 13 percent are. The average 65-year-old can expect to live another 19 years (*Statistical Abstract* 2009: Table 103). U.S. society has become so "gray" that, as Figure 13.4 shows, the median age has almost *doubled* since 1850. Today, there are 8 million *more* elderly Americans than there are teenagers (*Statistical*

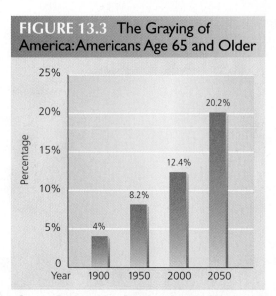

FIGURE 13.3 The Graying of America: Americans Age 65 and Older

Source: By the author. Based on *Statistical Abstract of the United States* 2009: Table 10, and earlier years.

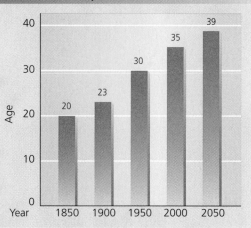

FIGURE 13.4 The Median Age of the U.S. Population

Source: By the author. Based on *Statistical Abstract of the United States* 2000: Table 14; 2009: Table 10, and earlier years.

FIGURE 13.5   Life Expectancy in Global Perspective

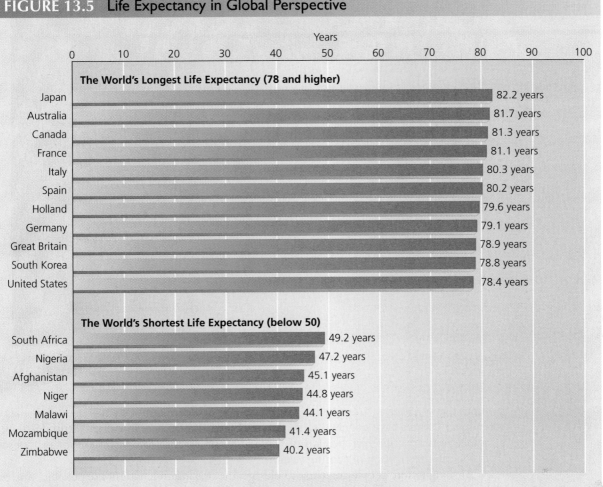

Note: The countries listed in the source with a life expectancy higher than the United States and those with a life expectancy less than 50 years. The totals are for year 2010. All the countries in the top group are industrialized, and none of those in the bottom group is.

Source: By the author. Based on *Statistical Abstract of the United States* 2009:Table 1295.

Abstract 2009:Table 7). Despite this vast change, as Figure 13.5 shows, life expectancy in the United States is far from the world's highest. With its overall average of 82, Japan holds this record.

As anyone who has ever visited Florida has noticed, the elderly population is not distributed evenly around the country. (As Jerry Seinfeld sardonically noted, "There's a law that when you get old, you've got to move to Florida.") The Social Map on the next page shows how uneven this distribution is.

Race–Ethnicity and Aging. Just as the states have different percentages of elderly, so do the racial–ethnic groups that make up the United States. As you can see from Table 13.1, whites have the highest percentage of elderly and Latinos the lowest. The difference is so great that the proportion of elderly whites (15.3 percent) is almost three

TABLE 13.1   Race–Ethnicity and Aging

	AGE				Total 65 and Over
	Median	65–74	75–84	85+	
Whites	40.8	7.6%	5.4%	2.3%	15.3%
Asian Americans	35.4	5.3%	2.9%	1.0%	9.2%
African Americans	31.1	4.7%	2.6%	1.0%	8.3%
Native Americans	30.3	4.3%	2.1%	0.8%	7.2%
Latinos	27.6	3.1%	1.8%	0.6%	5.5%
U.S. Average	36.6	6.4%	4.3%	1.8%	12.5%

Source: By the author. Based on *Statistical Abstract of the United States* 2009:Table 9.

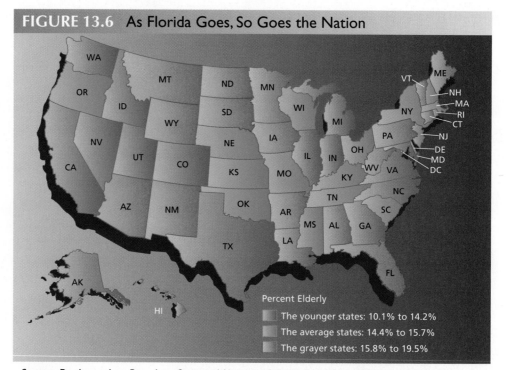

FIGURE 13.6   As Florida Goes, So Goes the Nation

Percent Elderly

The younger states: 10.1% to 14.2%
The average states: 14.4% to 15.7%
The grayer states: 15.8% to 19.5%

Source: By the author. Based on *Statistical Abstract of the United States* 2009: Table 17. Projections to 2015.

times that of Latinos (5.5 percent). The percentage of older Latinos is small because so many younger Latinos have migrated to the United States. Differences in cultural attitudes about aging, family relationships, work histories, and health practices will be important areas of sociological investigation in coming years.

Although more people are living to old age, the maximum length of life possible, the **life span,** has not increased. No one knows, however, just what that maximum is. We do know that it is at least 122, for this was the well-documented age of Jeanne Louise Calment of France at her death in 1997. If the birth certificate of Tuti Yusupova in Uzbekistan proves to be genuine, her age of 128 would indicate that the human life span may exceed even this number by a comfortable margin. It is also likely that advances in genetics will extend the human life span—perhaps to hundreds of years—a topic we will return to later. For now, let's see the different pictures of aging that emerge when we apply the three theoretical perspectives.

The Symbolic Interactionist Perspective

We saw how industrialization changed the way earlier Americans viewed the elderly. To see how social factors affect our own views, let's begin by asking how culture "signals" to people that they are "old." Then let's consider how ideas about the elderly are changing and how stereotypes and the mass media influence our perceptions of aging.

When Are You "Old"?

Changing Perceptions as You Age.   You probably can remember when you thought that a 12-year-old was "old"—and anyone older than that, beyond reckoning. You probably were 5 or 6 at the time. Similarly, to a 12-year-old, someone who is 21 seems "old." To someone who is 21, 30 may mark the point at which one is no longer "young," and 40 may seem very old. As people add years, "old" gradually recedes further from the self. To people who turn 40, 50 seems old; at 50, the late 60s look old—not the early 60s, for the passing of years seems to accelerate as we age, and at 50 age 60 doesn't seem so far away.

In Western culture, most people have difficulty applying the label "old" to themselves. In the typical case, they have become used to what they see in the mirror. The changes

life span the maximum length of life of a species; for humans, the longest that a human has lived

have taken place gradually, and each change, if it has not exactly been taken in stride, has been accommodated. Consequently, it comes as a shock to meet a long-lost friend and see how much that person has changed. At class reunions, *each* person can hardly believe how much older *the others* appear!

Four Factors in Our Decision.   If there is no fixed age line that people cross, then what makes someone "old"? Sociologists have identified several factors that spur people to apply the label of old to themselves.

The first factor is *biology*. One person may experience "signs" of aging earlier than others: wrinkles, balding, aches, difficulty in doing something that he or she used to take for granted. Consequently, one person will *feel* "old" at an earlier or later age than others.

A second factor is *personal history* or biography. An accident that limits someone's mobility, for example, can make that person feel old sooner than others. Or consider a woman who gave birth at 16 and has a daughter who, in turn, has a child

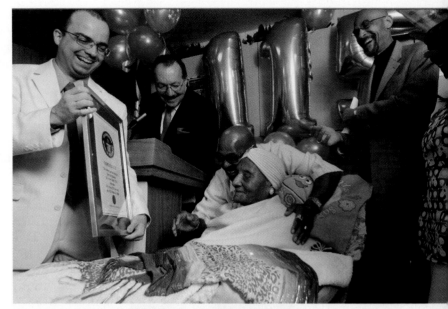

At age 115, Gertrude Baines is the world's oldest living person. Baines, whose parents were former slaves, was born in Georgia in 1894. The world's record for age that has been documented by a birth certificate is held by Jeanne Calment of France who died in 1997 at the age of 122.

at 18. She has become a biological grandmother at age 34. It is most unlikely, however, that she will play any stereotypical role—spending the day in a rocking chair, for example—but *knowing* that she is a grandmother has an impact on her self-concept. At a minimum, she must *deny* that she is old.

Then there is **gender age,** the relative value that a culture places on men's and women's ages. For example, graying hair on a man, and even a few wrinkles, may be perceived as signs of "maturity," while on a woman, those same features may indicate that she is getting "old." "Mature" and "old," of course, carry different meanings; most of us like to be called mature, but few of us like to be called old. Similarly, around the world, most men are able to marry younger spouses than women can. Maria might be an exception and marry Bill, who is fourteen years younger than she. But in most marriages in which there is a fourteen-year age gap, the odds greatly favor the wife being the younger of the pair. This is not biology in action; rather, it is the social construction of appearance and gender age.

The fourth factor in deciding when people label themselves as "old" is timetables, the signals societies use to inform their members that old age has begun. Since there is no automatic age at which people become "old," these timetables vary around the world. One group may choose a particular birthday, such as the 60th or 65th, to signal the onset of old age. Other groups do not even have birthdays, making such numbers meaningless. In the West, retirement is sometimes a cultural signal of the beginning of old age—which is one reason that some people resist retirement.

Changing Perceptions of the Elderly

At first, the audience sat quietly as the developers explained their plans to build a high-rise apartment building. After a while, people began to shift uncomfortably in their seats. Then they began to show open hostility.

"That's too much money to spend on those people," said one.

"You even want them to have a swimming pool?" asked another incredulously.

Finally, one young woman put their attitudes in a nutshell when she asked, "Who wants all those old people around?"

When physician Robert Butler (1975, 1980) heard these complaints about plans to build apartments for senior citizens, he began to realize how deeply antagonistic feelings toward the elderly can run. He coined the term **ageism** to refer to prejudice, discrimination, and hostility directed against people because of their age. Let's see how ageism developed in U.S. society.

gender age the relative value placed on men's and women's ages

ageism prejudice, discrimination, and hostility directed against people because of their age; can be directed against any age group, including youth

When does old age begin? And what activities are appropriate for the elderly? From this photo that I took of Munimah, a 65-year-old bonded laborer in Chennai, India, you can see how culturally relative these questions are. No one in Chennai thinks it is extraordinary that this woman makes her living by carrying heavy rocks all day in the burning, tropical sun. Working next to her in the quarry is her 18-year-old son, who breaks the rocks into the size that his mother carries.

Shifting Meanings.   As we have seen, there is nothing inherent in old age to produce any particular attitude, negative or not. Some historians point out that in early U.S. society old age was regarded positively (Cottin 1979; Fleming et al. 2003). In colonial times, growing old was seen as an accomplishment because so few people made it to old age. With no pensions, the elderly continued to work at jobs that changed little over time. They were viewed as storehouses of knowledge about work skills and sources of wisdom about how to live a long life.

The coming of industrialization eroded these bases of respect. The better sanitation and medical care allowed more people to reach old age, and no longer was being elderly an honorable distinction. Industrialization's new forms of mass production also made young workers as productive as the elderly. Coupled with mass education, this stripped away the elderly's superior knowledge (Cowgill 1974; Hunt 2005). In the Cultural Diversity box on the next page, you can see how a similar process is now occurring in China as it, too, industrializes.

A basic principle of symbolic interactionism is that we perceive both ourselves and others according to the symbols of our culture. What old age means to people has followed this principle. When the meaning of old age changed from an asset to a liability, not only did younger people come to view the elderly differently but the elderly also began to perceive themselves in a new light. This shift in meaning is demonstrated in the way people lie about their age: They used to claim that they were older than they were, but now they say that they are younger than they are (Clair et al. 1993).

Once again, the meaning of old age is shifting—and this time in a positive direction. This is largely because most of today's U.S. elderly can take care of themselves financially, and many are well-off. As the vast numbers of the baby boom generation enter their elderly years, their better health and financial strength will contribute to still more positive images of the elderly. If this symbolic shift continues, the next step—now in process—is to celebrate old age as a time of renewal. Old age will be viewed not as a period that precedes death, but, rather, as a new stage of growth.

Even in scholarly theories, perceptions of the elderly have become more positive. A theory that goes by the mouthful *gerotranscendence* was developed by Swedish sociologist Lars Tornstam. The thrust of this theory is that as people grow old they transcend their more limited views of life. They become less self-centered and begin to feel more at one with the universe. Coming to see things as less black and white, they develop more subtle ways of viewing right and wrong and tolerate more ambiguity (Manheimer 2005; Wadensten 2007). This theory is not likely to be universal. I have seen some elderly people grow softer and more spiritual, but I have also seen others grow bitter, close up, and become even more judgmental of others. The theory's limitations should become apparent shortly.

Stereotypes, which play such a profound role in social life, are a basic area of sociological investigation. In contemporary society, the mass media are a major source of stereotypes.

Cultural Diversity around the World

China: Changing Sentiment About the Elderly

As she contemplates her future, Zhao Chunlan, a 71-year-old widow, smiles shyly, with evident satisfaction. She has heard about sons abandoning their aged parents. She has even heard whispering about abuse.

But Zhao has no such fears.

It is not that her son is so devoted that he would never swerve from his traditional duty to his mother. Rather, it is a piece of paper that has eased Zhao's mind. Her 51-year-old son has signed a support agreement: He will cook her special meals, take her to medical checkups, even give her the largest room in his house and put the family's color television in it (Sun 1990).

The high status of the elderly in China is famed around the world: The elderly are considered a source of wisdom, given honored seating at both family and public gatherings—even venerated after death in ancestor worship.

Although this outline may represent more ideal than real culture, it appears to generally hold true—for the past, that is. Today, the authority of elders has eroded, leading to less respect from the adult children (Yan 2003; Fan 2008). For some, the cause is the children's success in the new market economy, which places them in a world unknown to their parents (Chen 2005). But other structural reasons are also tearing at the bonds between generations, especially the longer life expectancy that has come with industrialization. The change is startling: In 1950, China's life expectancy was 41 years. It has now jumped to 70 years (Li 2004). China's elderly

This grandfather in Beijing is teaching calligraphy to his granddaughter. As China industrializes and urbanizes, its society is changing, including the structure of relationships that nurture the elderly.

population is growing so rapidly that the country has 112 million elderly—8.3 percent of its population (*Statistical Abstract* 2009:Table 1290).

China's policy that allows each married couple only one child has created a problem for the support of the elderly. With such small families, the responsibility for supporting aged parents falls on fewer shoulders. The problem is that many younger couples must now support four elderly parents (Zhang and Goza 2007). Try putting yourself in that situation, and see how it would interfere with your plans for life. Can you see how it might affect your attitudes toward your aging parents—and toward your in-laws?

Alarmed by signs that parent–child bonds are weakening, some local officials require adult children to sign support agreements for their aged parents. One province has come up with an ingenious device: To get a marriage license, a couple must sign a contract pledging to support their parents after they reach age 60 (Sun 1990). "I'm sure he would do right by me, anyway," says Zhao, "but this way I know he will."

For Your Consideration

Do you think we could solve our Social Security crisis by requiring adult children to sign a parental support agreement in order to get a marriage license? Why or why not? What do you think Chinese officials can do to solve the problem of supporting these huge and growing numbers?

The Influence of the Mass Media

In Chapter 3 (pages 78–80), we noted that the mass media help to shape our ideas about both gender and relationships between men and women. As a powerful source of symbols, the media also influence our ideas of the elderly, the topic of the Mass Media box on the next page.

In Sum: Symbolic interactionists stress that old age has no inherent meaning. There is nothing about old age to automatically summon forth responses of honor and respect, as with the Abkhasians, or any other response. Culture shapes how we perceive the elderly, including the way we view our own aging. In short, the social modifies the biological.

MASS MEDIA In SOCIAL LIFE

The Cultural Lens: Shaping Our Perceptions of the Elderly

The mass media profoundly influence our perception of others. What we hear and see on television and in the movies, the songs we listen to, the books and magazines we read—all become part of the cultural lens through which we view the world. Without our knowing it, the media subtly shape our images of people. They influence how we view minorities and dominant groups; men, women, and children; people with disabilities; people from other cultures—and the elderly.

The shaping of our images and perception of the elderly is subtle, so much so that it usually occurs without our awareness. The elderly, for example, are underrepresented on television and in most popular magazines. This leaves a covert message—that the elderly are of little consequence and can be safely ignored.

The media also reflect and reinforce stereotypes of *gender age.* Older male news anchors are likely to be retained, while female anchors who turn the same age are more likely to be transferred to less visible positions. Similarly, in movies older men are more likely to play romantic leads—and to play them opposite much younger rising stars.

Although usually subtle, the message is not lost. The more television that people watch, the more they perceive the elderly in negative terms. The elderly, too, internalize these negative images, which, in turn, influences the ways they view themselves. These images are so powerful that they affect the elderly's health, even the way they walk (Donlon et al. 2005).

We become fearful of growing old, and we go to great lengths to deny that this is happening to us. Fear and denial play into the hands of advertisers, of course, who exploit our concerns about losing our youth.

In some cultures, Demi Moore, 44, would be considered elderly. Moore is shown here with her husband, Ashton Kutcher, 29. Almost inevitably, when there is a large age gap between a husband and wife, it is the husband who is the older one. The marriage of Kutcher and Moore is a reversal of the typical pattern of gender age.

They help us deny this biological reality by selling us hair dyes, skin creams, and other products that are designed to conceal even the appearance of old age. For these same reasons, plastic surgeons do a thriving business as they remove telltale signs of aging.

The elderly's growing numbers and affluence translate into economic clout and political power. It is inevitable, then, that the media's images of the elderly will change. An indication of that change is shown in the photo above.

For Your Consideration

What other examples of fear and denial of growing old are you familiar with? What examples of older men playing romantic leads with younger women can you give? Of older women and younger men? Why do you think we have gender age?

The Functionalist Perspective

Functionalists analyze how the parts of society work together. Among the components of society are **age cohorts**—people who were born at roughly the same time and who pass through the life course together. Although you don't see them, age cohorts have a huge impact on your life. When you finish college, for example, if the age cohort nearing retirement is large (a "baby boom" generation), more jobs will be available. In contrast, if it is a small group (a "baby bust" generation), fewer jobs open up. Let's look at theories that focus on how people adjust to retirement.

age cohort people born at roughly the same time who pass through the life course together

Disengagement Theory

Think about how disruptive it would be if the elderly left their jobs only when they died or became incompetent. How does society get the elderly to leave their positions so younger people can take them? According to **disengagement theory,** developed by Elaine Cumming and William Henry (1961), this is the function of pensions. Pensions get the elderly to *disengage* from their positions and hand them over to younger people. Retirement, then, is a mutually beneficial arrangement between two parts of society.

Cumming (1976) also examined disengagement from the individual's perspective. She pointed out that people start to disengage long before retirement. During middle age, they sense that the end of life is closer than its start. As they realize that their time is limited, they begin to assign priority to goals and tasks. Disengagement begins in earnest when their children leave home and increases with retirement and eventually widowhood.

Changing Forms of "Disengagement." And how do the elderly "disengage" today? Few quit their jobs and sit in rocking chairs watching the world go by. With computers, the Internet, and new types of work, the dividing line between work and retirement has blurred. Less and less does retirement mean an end to work. Millions of workers just slow down. Some stay at their jobs, but put in fewer hours. Others work as consultants part-time. Some switch careers, even though they are in their 60s, some even in their 70s. Many never "retire"—at least not in the sense of sinking into a recliner or being forever on the golf course.

Evaluation of the Theory. Disengagement theory came under attack almost as soon as the ink dried on the theorists' paper. One of the main criticisms is that this theory contains an implicit bias against older people—assumptions that the elderly disengage from productive social roles and then sort of slink into oblivion (Manheimer 2005). Instead of disengaging, say the critics, the elderly *exchange* one set of roles for another (Jerrome 1992). The elderly's new roles, which often center on friendship, are no less satisfying to them than their earlier roles. These new roles are less visible to researchers, however, who tend to have a youthful orientation—and who show their bias by assuming that productivity is the measure of self-worth. If disengagement theory is ever resurrected, it must also come to grips with our new patterns of "disengagement."

Activity Theory

Are retired people more satisfied with life? (All that extra free time and not having to kow-tow to a boss must be nice.) Are intimate activities more satisfying than formal ones? Such questions are the focus of **activity theory.** Although we could consider this theory from other perspectives, we are examining it from the functionalist perspective because its focus is how disengagement is functional or dysfunctional.

Evaluation of the Theory. A study of retired people in France found that some people are happier when they are more active, but others are happier when they are less involved (Keith 1982). Similarly, most people find informal, intimate activities, such as spending time with friends, to be more satisfying than formal activities. But not everyone does. In one study, 2,000 retired U.S. men reported formal activities to be as important as informal ones. Even solitary activities, such as doing home repairs, had about the same impact as

> **disengagement theory** the view that society is stabilized by having the elderly retire (disengage from) their positions of responsibility so the younger generation can step into their shoes
>
> **activity theory** the view that satisfaction during old age is related to a person's amount and quality of activity

Researchers are exploring factors that can make old age an enjoyable period of life, those conditions that increase people's mental, social, emotional, and physical well-being. As research progresses, do you think we will reach the point where the average old person will be in this woman's physical condition?

intimate activities on these men's life satisfaction (Beck and Page 1988). It is the same for spending time with adult children. "Often enough" for some parents is "not enough" or even "too much" for others. In short, researchers have discovered the obvious: What makes life satisfying for one person doesn't work for another. (This, of course, can be a source of intense frustration for retired couples.)

Continuity Theory

Another theory of how people adjust to growing old is **continuity theory.** As its name implies, the focus of this theory is on how the elderly maintain ties with their past (Kinsella and Phillips 2005). When they retire, many people take on new roles that are similar to the ones they gave up. For example, a former CEO might serve as a consultant, a retired electrician might do small electrical repairs, or a pensioned banker might take over the finances of her church. Researchers have found that people who are active in multiple roles (wife, author, mother, intimate friend, church member, etc.) are better equipped to handle the changes that growing old entails. They have also found that with their greater resources, people from higher social classes adjust better to the challenges of aging.

Evaluation of the Theory.   The basic criticism of continuity theory is that it is too broad (Hatch 2000). We all have anchor points based on our particular experiences in life, and we all rely on them to make adjustments to the changes we encounter. This applies to people of all ages beyond infancy. This theory is really a collection of loosely connected ideas, with no specific application to the elderly.

In Sum: The *broader* perspective of the functionalists is how society's parts work together to keep society running smoothly. Although it is inevitable that younger workers replace the elderly, this transition could be disruptive. To entice the elderly out of their positions so that younger people can take over, the elderly are offered pensions. Functionalists also use a *narrower* perspective, focusing on how individuals adjust to their retirement. The findings of this narrower perspective are too mixed to be of much value—except that people who have better resources and are active in multiple roles adjust better to old age (Crosnoe and Elder 2002).

Because U.S. workers do not have to retire by any certain age, it is also important to study how people decide to keep working or to retire in the first place. After they retire, how do they reconstruct their identities and come to terms with their changed life? As the United States grows even grayer, these should prove productive areas of sociological theory and research.

The Conflict Perspective

As you know, the conflict perspective's guiding principle of social life is how social groups struggle to control power and resources. How does this apply to society's age groups? Regardless of whether the young and old recognize it, say conflict theorists, they are opponents in a struggle that threatens to throw society into turmoil. Let's look at how the passage of Social Security legislation fits the conflict view.

Fighting for Resources: Social Security Legislation

In the 1920s, before Social Security provided an income for the aged, two-thirds of all citizens over 65 had no savings and could not support themselves (Holtzman 1963; Crossen 2004a). The fate of workers sank even deeper during the Great Depression, and in 1930 Francis Townsend, a physician, started a movement to rally older citizens. He soon had one-third of all Americans over age 65 enrolled in his Townsend Clubs. They demanded that the federal government impose a national sales tax of 2 percent to provide $200 a month for every person over 65 ($2,100 a month in today's money). In 1934, the Townsend Plan went before Congress. Because it called for such high payments and many were afraid that it would destroy people's incentive to save for the future, members of

continuity theory the focus of this theory is how people adjust to retirement by continuing aspects of their earlier lives

Congress looked for a way to reject the plan without appearing to oppose the elderly. When President Roosevelt announced his own, more modest Social Security plan in 1934, Congress embraced it (Schottland 1963; Amenta 2006).

To provide jobs for younger people, the new Social Security law required that workers retire at age 65. It did not matter how well people did their work, or how much they needed the pay. For decades, the elderly protested. Finally, in 1986, Congress eliminated mandatory retirement. Today, almost 90 percent of Americans retire by age 65, but most do so voluntarily. No longer can they be forced out of their jobs simply because of their age. Let's look at what has happened to this groundbreaking legislation since it was passed.

dependency ratio the number of workers who are required to support each dependent person—those 65 and older and those 15 and under

ThinkingCRITICALLY

The Social Security Trust Fund: There Is No Fund, and You Can't Trust It

Each month, the Social Security Administration mails checks to 49 million people. Across the country, 200 million U.S. workers pay into the Social Security system, looking to it to provide for their basic necessities—and even a little more than that—in their old age (*Statistical Abstract* 2009: Tables 525, 526).

How dependable is Social Security? The short answer is "Don't bet your old age on it."

The first problem is well known. Social Security is not a bank account. The money taken from our checks is not deposited into our individual accounts. No money in the Social Security system is attached to anyone's name. At retirement, we don't withdraw the money we paid into Social Security. Instead, the government writes checks on money that it collects from current workers. When these workers retire, they, too, will be paid, not from their own savings, but from money collected from others who are still working.

The Social Security system is like a giant chain letter—it works as long as enough new people join the chain. If you join early enough, you'll collect more than you paid in—but if you join toward the end, you're simply out of luck. And, say some conflict theorists, we are nearing the end of the chain. The shift in the **dependency ratio**—the number of people who collect Social Security compared with the number of workers who contribute to it—is especially troubling. As Figure 13.7 shows, sixteen workers used to support each person who was collecting Social Security. Now the dependency ratio has dropped to four to one. In another generation, it could hit two to one. If this happens, Social Security taxes could become so high that they stifle the country's economy. To prevent this, Congress raised Social Security taxes and established a Social Security trust fund. Supposedly, this fund has trillions of dollars. But does it?

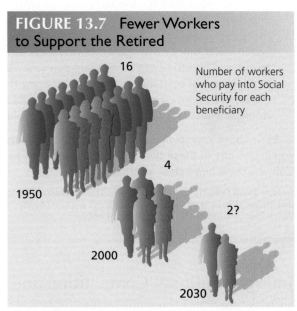

FIGURE 13.7 Fewer Workers to Support the Retired

16

Number of workers who pay into Social Security for each beneficiary

1950

4

2000

2?

2030

Source: By the author. Based on Social Security Administration; *Statistical Abstract of the United States* 2009: Tables 525, 526.

This question takes us to the root of the crisis, or, some would say, the fraud. In 1965, President Lyndon Johnson was bogged down in a war in Vietnam. To conceal the war's costs from the public, he arrived at the diabolical solution of forcing the Social Security Administration to invest only in U.S. Treasury bonds, a form of government IOUs. This put the money collected for Social Security into the general fund, where Johnson could siphon it off to finance the war. Politicians love this easy source of money, and they continue the fraud. They use the term "off budget" to refer to the Social Security money they spend. And *each year, they spend it all.*

Suppose that you buy a $10,000 U.S. Treasury bond. The government takes your $10,000 and hands you a document that says it owes you $10,000 plus interest. This is how Social Security works. The Social Security Administration (SSA) collects the money from workers, pays the retired, disabled, and survivors of deceased workers, and then hands the excess over to the U.S. government. The government, in turn, gives IOUs to the SSA in the form of U.S. Treasury bonds. The government spends the money on whatever it wants—whether that means building roads and schools, subsidizing tobacco crops, or buying bombs and fighting a war in some far off place.

Suppose you are spending more money than you make. You talk Aunt Mary into loaning you some money, and you give her an IOU. If you don't count what you owe Aunt Mary, you have a surplus. The government simply does not count those huge IOUs that it owes the elderly. Instead, it reports a fake surplus to the public.

This arrangement is a politician's dream. Politicians grab the money from the workers and hand the workers giant IOUs. And then they pretend that they haven't even spent that money.

The Gramm-Rudman law, which was designed to limit the amount of federal debt, does *not* count the money that the government "borrows" from Social Security. It is as though the debt owed to Social Security does not exist—and to politicians it doesn't. To politicians, Social Security is a magical money machine. A wave of their magical wand produces billions from thin air. Are those just numbers on paper? Or are they money that has been confiscated from workers? Ask workers whose paychecks are hit by that magical wand.

One analyst (Sloan 2001) put the matter pithily: "The Social Security trust fund isn't a fund, and you shouldn't trust it."

For Your Consideration

Here are two proposals to solve this problem.

1. Raise the age at which Social Security payments begin to 70.
2. Keep the retirement age the same, but put what workers pay as Social Security taxes into their own individual retirement accounts. Most proposals to do this lack controls to make the system work. Here are controls: A board, independent of the government, would select money managers to invest these accounts in natural resources, real estate, stocks, and bonds—both foreign and domestic. Annually, the board would review the performance of each money manager, retaining those who do the best job and replacing the others. All investment results would be published, and individuals could select the management team that they prefer. No one could withdraw funds before retirement.

How about your own Social Security? Do you prefer to retain the current system? Do you prefer one of these two proposals? Neither is perfect. What problems might each have? Can you think of a better alternative?

Sources: Smith 1986; Hardy 1991; Genetski 1993; Stevenson 1998; *Statistical Abstract* 2009. Government publications that list Social Security receipts as deficits can be found in *Monthly Treasury Statement of Receipts and Outlays,* the *Winter Treasury Bulletin,* and the *Statement of Liabilities and Other Financial Commitments of the United States Government.*

Intergenerational Competition and Conflict

Social Security came about not because the members of Congress had generous hearts, but out of a struggle between competing interest groups. As conflict theorists stress, equilibrium between competing groups is only a temporary balancing of oppositional forces, one that can be upset at any time. Following this principle, could conflict between the elderly and the young be in our future? Let's consider this possibility.

If you listen closely, you can hear ripples of grumbling—complaints that the elderly are getting more than their fair share of society's resources. The huge costs of Social Security and Medicare are a special concern. *One of every three* tax dollars (35 percent) is spent on these two programs (*Statistical Abstract* 2009:Table 455). As Figure 13.8 shows, Social Security payments were $781 million in 1950; now they run *750 times* higher. Now look at Figure 13.9 on the next page, which shows the nation's medical bill to care for the elderly. Like gasoline poured on a bonfire, these soaring costs may well fuel a coming intergenerational showdown.

Figure 13.10 on the next page shows another area of concern that can fuel an intergenerational conflict. You can see how greatly the condition of the elderly improved as the government transferred resources to them. But look also at the matching path of children's poverty. Even with its recent decline, children's poverty is just as high now as it was in 1967. Certainly the decline in the elderly's rate of poverty did not come at the expense of the nation's children. Congress could have decided to finance the welfare of children just as it has that of the elderly. It has chosen not to. One fundamental reason, following conflict theorists, is that the children have not launched as broad an assault on Congress. Simply put, the lobbyists for the elderly have put more grease in the political reelection machine.

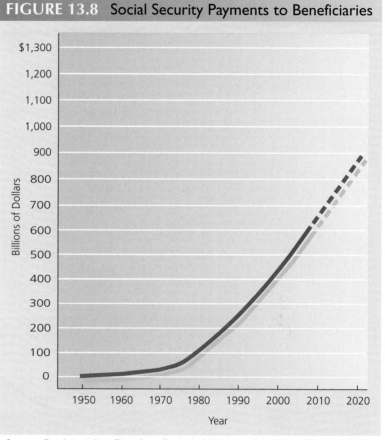

FIGURE 13.8 Social Security Payments to Beneficiaries

Source: By the author. Based on *Statistical Abstract of the United States* 1997: Table 518; 2009:Table 455. Broken line indicates the author's projections.

Figure 13.10 could be another indicator of a coming intergenerational storm. If we take a 10 percent poverty rate as a goal for the nation's children—just to match what the government has accomplished for the elderly—where would the money come from? If the issue gets pitched as a case of money going to one group at the expense of another group, it can divide the generations. To get people to think that they must choose between pathetic children and suffering old folks can splinter them into opposing groups, breaking their power to work together to improve society. The Down-to-Earth Sociology box on page 383 examines stirrings of resentment that could become widespread.

Fighting Back

Some organizations work to protect the gains of the elderly. Let's consider two.

The Gray Panthers. The Gray Panthers, who claim 20,000 members, are aware how easily the public can be split along age lines (Gray Panthers n.d.). This organization encourages people of all ages to work for the welfare of *both* the old and the young. On the micro level, their goal is to help people develop positive self-concepts (Kuhn 1990), and on the macro level, to build a base so broad that it can challenge institutions that oppress the poor, whatever their age, and fight attempts to pit people against one another along age lines. One indication of their effectiveness is that Gray Panthers frequently testify before congressional committees concerning pending legislation.

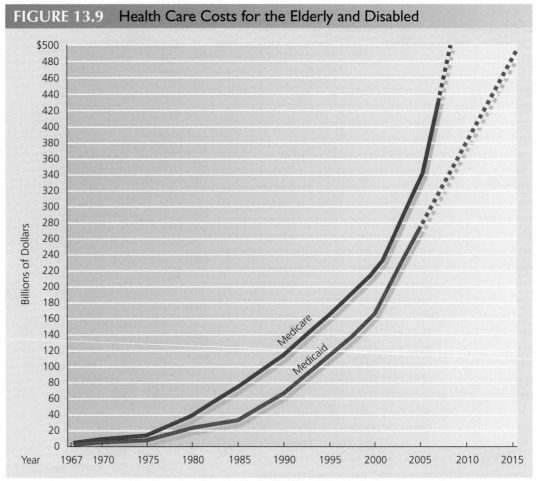

FIGURE 13.9 Health Care Costs for the Elderly and Disabled

Note: Medicare is intended for the elderly and disabled, Medicaid for the poor. About 23 percent of Medicaid payments ($63 billion) go to the elderly (*Statistical Abstract* 2009: Table 140).

Source: By the author. Based on *Statistical Abstract, of the United States* various years, and 2009: Tables 137, 140. Broken lines indicate the author's projections.

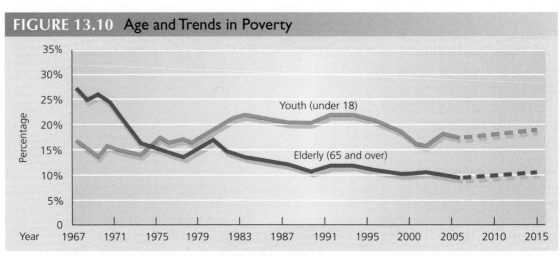

FIGURE 13.10 Age and Trends in Poverty

Source: By the author. *Statistical Abstract of the United States*, various years, and 2009: Table 691. Broken lines indicate the author's projections.

Down-to-Earth Sociology
Stirrings of Resentment About the U.S. Elderly

In the past, most U.S. elderly were poor. Social Security has been so successful that, as we saw in Figure 10.6 on page 282, the poverty rate of today's elderly is *less* than the national average. Many of the elderly who draw Social Security don't need it. Despite our economic crisis, many elderly still travel about the country in motor homes and spend huge amounts on recreation. The golf courses, although thinned, continue to be popular with retired Americans. The cruise ships still wend their way to exotic destinations. Is the relative prosperity of the elderly in the midst of economic hardships for many creating resentments?

There are indications that it is. Many younger people have begun to question "senior citizen discounts." "Why should old folks pay less for a meal or for a hotel room than I do?" they wonder. Some of the younger know their parents' situation: They have paid off their home, own investment property, collect a private pension from their former employer, *and* collect social security. Why should they—or anyone else—be automatically entitled to a "senior citizen discount," they wonder. . . .

In one of the more bizarre reactions to the growing political power of the elderly, one of our senators, who just happened to head the Senate Committee on Social Security, called the retired "greedy geezers" who demand government handouts while they "tee off near their second homes in Florida" (Duff 1995). Of course, senators say most anything if they feel it is popular. This particular senator later retired, quickly grabbed his generous Senate pension, and became a "greedy geezer" himself, teeing off from his own second home.

Attitudes toward the elderly have undergone major shifts during the short history of the United States. As the economic circumstances of the elderly improve, attitudes are changing once again.

Another indication of changing sentiment is that some have begun to argue that we should ration medical care for the elderly (Thau 2001). Open-heart surgery is a favorite example. For people in their 80s, this costly operation prolongs life by only two or three years. Since our resources are limited, they say it makes more sense to pay for a kidney transplant for a child, whose life might be prolonged by fifty years.

For Your Consideration

These questions, brought up only tentatively in the United States, are being asked more openly in countries that have larger proportions of elderly. In Austria, for example, even resentments about old age pensions have become front page news (Aichinger 2007). How do you see future relationships between the elderly and the younger?

Finally, if seniors have it so good, why do you see so many of them working at Wal-Mart?

The American Association of Retired Persons.   The AARP also champions legislation to benefit the elderly. With 39 million members, this organization has political clout. It monitors federal and state legislation and mobilizes its members to act on issues affecting their welfare. A statement of displeasure about some proposed law from the AARP can trigger tens of thousands of telephone calls, telegrams, letters, and e-mails from irate elderly citizens. To protect their chances of reelection, politicians try not to cross swords with the AARP. As you can expect, critics claim that this organization is too powerful, that it muscles its way to claim more than its share of the nation's resources.

In Sum: All of these points—from Social Security and Medicare to organizations that lobby for the elderly—support our position, say conflict theorists. Age groups are one of society's many groups that are competing for scarce resources. At some point, conflict is the inevitable result.

FIGURE 13.11
The Elderly Who Are Widowed

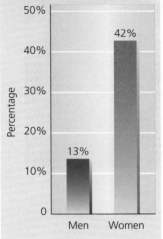

Source: By the author. Based on *Statistical Abstract of the United States* 2009:Table 33.

FIGURE 13.12
The Elderly Who Live with a Spouse

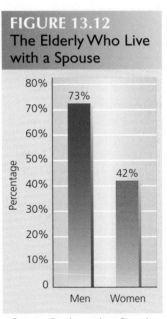

Source: By the author. Based on *Statistical Abstract of the United States* 2009:Table 33.

Recurring Problems

"When I get old, will I be able to take care of myself? Will I become frail and unable to get around? Will I end up in some nursing home, in the hands of strangers who don't care about me?" These are common concerns of people as they age. Let's first examine gender and the elderly and then the problems of nursing homes, abuse, and poverty.

Gender and the Elderly

In Chapter 11, we examined how gender influences our lives. The impact of gender doesn't stop when we get old. Because most women live longer than most men, women are more likely to experience the loneliness and isolation that widowhood often brings. This is one implication of Figure 13.11, which shows how much more likely women are to be widowed. This difference in mortality also leads to different living arrangements in old age. Figure 13.12 shows how much more likely elderly men are to be living with their wives than elderly women are to be living with their husbands. Another consequence is that most patients in nursing homes are women.

Before we review nursing homes, I think you will enjoy reading the Down-to-Earth Sociology box on the next page. It will give you a glimpse of some of the variety that exists among the elderly, as well as how people carry gender roles into old age.

Nursing Homes

In one nursing home, the nurses wrote in the patient's chart that she had a foot lesion. She actually had gangrene and maggots in her wounds (Rhone 2001). In another nursing home— supposedly a premier retirement home in Southern California—a woman suffered a stroke in her room. Her "caretakers" didn't discover her condition for 15 hours. She didn't survive. (Morin 2001)

Most elderly are cared for by their families, but at any one time a million and a half Americans age 65 and over are in nursing homes. This comes to about 4 percent of the nation's elderly (*Statistical Abstract* 2009:Tables 8, 187). Some patients return home after only a few weeks or a few months. Others die after a short stay. Overall, about one half of elderly women and one-third of elderly men spend at least some time in nursing homes.

Nursing home residents are *not typical* of the elderly. Three of four are age 75 or older. Almost all (80 percent) are widowed or divorced, or have never married, leaving them without family to care for them. Most of these elderly are in such poor health that they need help to bathe, dress, and eat (Centers for Disease Control and Prevention 2008d).

Understaffing, Dehumanization, and Death. It is difficult to say good things about nursing homes. The literature on nursing homes, both popular and scientific, is filled with horror stories of neglected and abused patients. *Ninety percent* of nursing homes fail federal inspections for health and safety (Pear 2008). With events like those in the quotation that opens this section, Congress ordered a national study of nursing homes. The researchers found that in nursing homes that are understaffed, patients are more likely to have bedsores and to be malnourished, underweight, and dehydrated. *Ninety percent* of nursing homes are understaffed (Pear 2002).

It is easy to see why nursing homes are understaffed. Who—if he or she has a choice— works for poverty-level wages in a place that smells of urine, where you have to clean up feces, and where you are surrounded by dying people? Forty to one hundred percent of nursing home staff quit each year (DeFrancis 2002).

But all the criticisms of nursing homes pale in comparison with this finding: Compared with the elderly who have similar health conditions but remain home, those who go to nursing homes tend to get sicker and to die sooner (Wolinsky et al. 1997). This is a remarkable finding. Could it be, then, that a function of nursing homes is to dispose of

Down-to-Earth Sociology
Feisty to the End: Gender Roles Among the Elderly

This image of my father makes me smile—not because he was arrested as an old man, but, rather, because of the events that led to his arrest. My dad had always been a colorful character, ready with endless, ribald jokes and a hearty laugh. He carried these characteristics into his old age.

In his late 70s, my dad was living in a small apartment in a complex for the elderly in Minnesota. The adjacent building was a nursing home, the next destination for the residents of these apartments. None of them liked to think about this "home," because no one survived it—yet they all knew that this would be their destination. Under the watchful eye of these elderly neighbors, care in the nursing home was fairly good. Until they were transferred to this unwelcome last stopping-place, life for them went on "as usual" in the complex for the elderly.

According to the police report and my dad's account, here is what happened:

> Dad was sitting in the downstairs lounge with other residents, waiting for the mail to arrive, a daily ritual that the residents looked forward to. For some reason known only to him, my dad hooked his cane under the dress of an elderly woman, lifted up her skirt, and laughed. Understandably, this upset her, as well as her husband, who was standing next to her. Angry, the man moved toward my father, threatening him.
>
> I say "moved," rather than "lunged," because this man was using a walker. My dad started to run away from this threat. Actually, "run" isn't quite the right word. "Hobbled" would be a better term.
>
> My dad fled as fast as he could using his cane, while the other man pursued him as fast as he could using his walker. Wheezing and puffing, the two went from the lounge into the long adjoining hall, pausing now and then to catch their breath. Tiring the most, the other man gave up the pursuit. He then called the police.
>
> When the police officer arrived, he said, "Uncle Marv, I'm sorry, but I'm going to have to arrest you." (This event occurred in a small town, and the officer assigned this case turned out to be Dad's nephew.)

During their elderly years, men and women continue to exhibit aspects of the gender roles that they learned and played in their younger years.

> Dad went before a judge, who could hardly keep a straight face. He gave Dad a small fine and warned him to behave himself. The apartment manager also gave Dad a warning: One more incident, and he would have to move out of the complex.
>
> Dad's wife wasn't too happy about the situation, either.

This event was brought to mind by a newspaper account of a fight that broke out at the food bar of a retirement home ("Melee Breaks" . . . 2004). It seems that one elderly man criticized the way another man was picking through the salad. When a fight broke out between the two, several elderly people were hurt as they tried either to intervene or to flee.

For Your Consideration
People carry their personalities, values, and other traits into old age. Among these characteristics are gender roles. What examples of gender roles do you see in the events related here? Are you familiar with how old people continue to show their femininity or masculinity?

the frail and unwanted elderly? If so, could we consider nursing homes the Western equivalent of the Tiwi's practice of "covering up," which we reviewed in this chapter's opening vignette?

Perhaps this judgment is too harsh. But there are alternatives, and yet we continue with the depressing nursing homes that all of us want to avoid. We explore more pleasant alternatives in the Down-to-Earth Sociology box on the next page.

Down-to-Earth Sociology
Do You Want to Live in a Nursing Home?

You have just turned 75—or 85—or 95, and the dreaded moment has come. You know you've been a "little" forgetful lately, but it couldn't be this bad. That's a county sheriff's vehicle that just pulled up to your house. You know they're going to take you to a nursing home.

"Over my dead body!" you shout to no one, as you begin to frantically barricade the door. "They're not coming in here. I'd rather die!"

While one deputy diverts your attention at the front door, another crawls in a back window. He grabs you from behind, pins your frail arms behind you while he opens the door with the other hand. The two deputies drag you screaming and kicking to their car.

These members of a Wii bowling team illustrate the developing concept of homes for the elderly: active old people enjoying themselves in home-like settings.

* * *

But wait a minute. It didn't happen like that at all. Instead, you were packed up and waiting—with a big grin on your face. "Finally, I get to go to the home for the elderly," you say to yourself, as you open the door to welcome the two officials who are going to take you to live with your new friends.

"That first version is a little extreme—barricade and all—but so is the second one," you might say, adding, "Never in my life would I want to live in a nursing home!" That reaction is understandable. The isolation, the coldness, the harried staff, the neglect, people calling you "dearie" and talking to you like you're a child, the antipsychotic drugs given to people who have no psychosis, to "calm" anyone who gets out of line—make nursing homes depressing, feared places.

Do nursing homes have to be like this? Can't we do better—a lot better? Could we even turn them into places so warm and inviting that the second version of our little story could be true—that you would look forward to living there when you are old?

Some visionaries say that we can transform nursing homes into warm, inviting places. They started with a clean piece of paper and asked how we could redesign nursing homes so they enhance or maintain people's quality of life. The model they came up with doesn't look or even feel like a nursing home. (And it certainly doesn't smell like one.) In Green Houses, as they are called, elderly people live in a homelike setting (Lagnado 2008). Instead of a sterile hallway lined with rooms, 10 to 12 residents live in a carpeted ranch-style house. They re-

ceive medical care suited to their personal needs, share meals at a communal dining table, and, if they want to, they can cook together in an open kitchen. As shown in the photo above, they can even play virtual sports on plasma televisions. This home-like setting fosters a sense of community among residents and staff.

Taking a different approach, the elderly themselves are developing a second model, neighborhood support groups. The goal is to avoid nursing homes altogether, no matter how good they might be. In some areas, such as Beacon Hill in Boston, the neighborhood support group replaces the caring, nearby adult children that many lack (Gross 2007). In return for annual dues, just a phone call away are screened carpenters, house cleaners—even someone to drop by and visit. In one version of these neighborhood support groups, members exchange services. Those who are still able to fix faucets, for example, do so. They bank that time, exchanging it for something they need, such as transportation to the doctor. This concept, simple and promising, lets the elderly live in their own homes, remaining in the neighborhood they know so well and in which they feel comfortable.

For Your Consideration
Of the two models presented here, Green Houses and neighborhood support groups, which would you prefer if you were elderly? Why? What are the limitations of each model?

In old age, as in all other stages of the life course, people find life more pleasant if they have friends and enough money to meet their needs. How do you think that an elderly man who lives by himself in a rundown camper finds life? How about elderly married people who get together for lunch with friends of many years? While neither welcomes old age, you can see what a difference social factors make in how people experience this time of life.

Elder Abuse

You've probably heard stories of elder abuse, about residents of nursing homes being pushed, grabbed, shoved, or shouted at. Some of the elderly in nursing homes are also abused sexually (Ramsey-Klawsnik et al. 2008). Others are abused at home, by family members who exploit them financially or abuse them physically.

While abuse of the elderly certainly occurs, it is not typical. Less than 4 percent of the U.S. elderly experience financial abuse, and less than 1 percent are abused physically (Laumann et al. 2008). Few of the abusers are "mean" people. One of the most common reasons for abuse is that a family member has run out of patience. The husband of a woman who was suffering from Alzheimer's disease said this to the social scientists who interviewed him

> **Frustration reaches a point where patience gives out. I've never struck her, but sometimes I wonder if I can control myself. . . . This is . . . the part of her care that causes me the frustration and the loss of patience. What I tell her, she doesn't register. Like when I tell her, "You're my wife." "You're crazy," she says. (Pillemer and Suitor 1992)**

This quote is not intended to excuse any abuse, but, rather, to gain insight into why anyone would abuse a family member. From what this husband said, we can glean some insight into the stress that comes with caring for a person who is dependent, demanding, and uncomprehending. Since most people who care for the elderly undergo stress but are not violent toward those they care for, however, we do not have the answer to why some caregivers become violent. For this, we must await future research.

More important than understanding the causes of abuse, however, is preventing the elderly from being abused in the first place. There is little that can be done about abuse at home by relatives—except to enforce current laws when abuse comes to the attention of authorities. For home-care and nursing home workers, in contrast, we can require background checks to screen out people who have been convicted of robbery, rape, and other violence. This is similar to requiring background checks of preschool workers in order to screen out people who have been convicted of molesting children. Such laws are only a first step to solving this problem. They will not prevent abuse, only avoid the obvious.

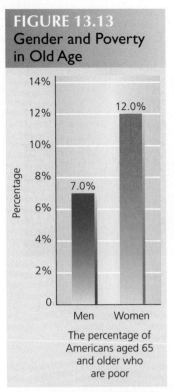

FIGURE 13.13
Gender and Poverty
in Old Age

The percentage of
Americans aged 65
and older who
are poor

Source: By the author. Based on
Statistical Abstract of the United
States 2009:Table 33.

The Elderly Poor

Many elderly live in nagging fear of poverty. Not knowing how long they will live nor how much inflation they will face, they fear that they will outlive their savings. How realistic is this fear? Statistics don't apply to any individual case, but they help us to understand how earlier social patterns carry over to the elderly as a group.

Gender and Poverty.   As reviewed in Chapter 11, during their working years most women earn less than men. Figure 13.13 shows how this pattern follows women and men into their old age. As you can see, elderly women are about 70 percent more likely than elderly men to be poor.

Race–Ethnicity and Poverty.   As we reviewed earlier, Social Security has lifted most elderly Americans out of poverty, and today's elderly are less likely than the average American to be poor. There is poverty among the elderly, of course, and it follows the racial–ethnic patterns of the general society. From Figure 13.14, you can see how much less likely elderly whites and Asian Americans are to be poor than are African Americans and Latinos.

The Sociology of Death and Dying

Have you ever noticed how people use language to try to distance themselves from death? We have constructed *linguistic masks*, ways to refer to death without using the word itself. Instead of dead, we might say "gone," "passed on," "no longer with us," or "at peace now." We don't have space to explore this fascinating characteristic of social life, but we can take a brief look at why sociologists emphasize that dying is more than a biological event.

Industrialization and the New Technology

Before industrialization, death was no stranger. The family took care of the sick at home, and the sick died at home. Because life was short, *most* children saw a sibling or parent die (Blauner 1966). As noted in Chapter 1 (page 26), the family even prepared corpses for burial. Industrialization changed this. As secondary groups came to dominate society, the process of dying was placed in the hands of professionals in hospitals. Dying now takes place behind closed doors—isolated, remote, and managed by strangers. As a result, for most of us death has become something strange and alien.

Not only did new technologies remove the dying from our presence, but they also created *technological life*—a form of existence that lies between life and death, but is neither (Cerulo and Ruane 1996). The "brain dead" in our hospitals have no self. Their "person" is gone—dead—yet our technology keeps the body alive. This muddles the boundary between life and death, which used to seem so certain.

For most of us, however, that boundary will remain firm, and we will face a definite death. Some of us will even learn in advance that we will die shortly. If so, how are we likely to cope with this knowledge? Let's look at what researchers have found.

Death as a Process

Let me share an intimate event from my own life.

When my mother was informed that she had inoperable lung cancer, she went into a vivid stage of denial. If she later went through anger or negotiation, she kept it to herself. After a short depression, she experi-

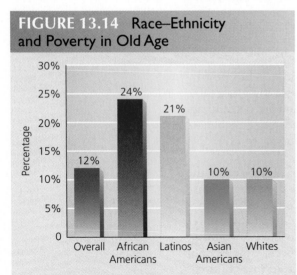

FIGURE 13.14   Race–Ethnicity
and Poverty in Old Age

Source: By the author. Based on *Statistical Abstract of the
United States* 2009:Table 689.

enced a longer period of questioning why this was happening to her. After coming to grips with the fact that she was going to die soon, she began to make her "final arrangements." The extent of those preparations soon became apparent.

After her funeral, my two brothers and I went to her apartment, as she had instructed us. There, to our surprise, attached to each item in every room—from the bed and the television to the boxes of dishes and knickknacks—was a piece of masking tape with one of our names on it. At first we found this strange. We knew she was an orderly person, but to this extent? As we sorted through her things, reflecting on why she had given certain items to whom, we began to appreciate the "closure" she had given to this aspect of her material life.

Psychologist Elisabeth Kübler-Ross (1969/2008) studied how people cope during the *living–dying interval,* that period between discovering they are going to die soon and death itself. After interviewing people who had been informed that they had an incurable disease, she concluded that people who come face to face with their own death go through five stages:

1. *Denial.* At first, people cannot believe that they are going to die. ("The doctor must have made a mistake. Those test results can't be right.") They avoid the topic of death and situations that remind them of it.
2. *Anger.* After a while, they acknowledge that they are going to die, but they view their death as unjust. ("I didn't do anything to deserve this. So-and-so is much worse than I am, and she's in good health. It isn't right that I should die.")
3. *Negotiation.* Next, the individual tries to get around death by making a bargain with God, with fate, or even with the disease itself. ("I need one more Thanksgiving with my family. I never appreciated them as much as I should have. Let me just hold out until then.")
4. *Depression.* During this stage, people become resigned to their death, but they grieve because their life is about to end, and they have no power to change the course of events.
5. *Acceptance.* In this final stage, people come to terms with their impending death. They put their affairs in order—make wills, pay bills, instruct their children to take care of the surviving parent. They also express regret at not having done certain things when they had the chance. Devout Christians are likely to talk about the hope of salvation and their desire to be in heaven with Jesus.

Dying is more individualized than this model indicates. Not everyone, for example, tries to make bargains. What is important sociologically is that *death is a process,* not just an event. People who expect to die soon face a reality quite different from the one experienced by those of us who expect to be alive years from now. Their impending death powerfully affects their thinking and behavior.

Hospices

What a change. In earlier generations, life was short, and people took death at an early age for granted. Today, we take it for granted that most people will see old age. Due to advances in medical technology and better public health practices, *most* deaths in the United States (about 75 percent) occur after age 65. People want to die with dignity, in the comforting presence of friends and relatives, but hospitals, to put the matter bluntly, are awkward places in which to die. There people experience what sociologists call *institutional death*—they die surrounded by strangers in formal garb, in sterile rooms filled with machines, in an organization that puts its routines ahead of patients' needs.

Hospices emerged as a way to reduce the emotional and physical burden of dying—and to lower the costs of death. Hospice care is built around the idea that the people who are dying and their families should control the process of dying. The term **hospice** originally referred to a place, but now it generally refers to home care. Services are brought into

hospice a place (or services brought to someone's home) for the purpose of giving comfort and dignity to a dying person

a dying person's home—from counseling and managing pain to such basic help as providing babysitters or driving the person to a doctor or lawyer. During the course of a year, more than a million people are in hospice care in the United States. These services have become so popular that two of five Americans receive hospice care prior to their deaths (National Hospice 2008).

Whereas hospitals are dedicated to prolonging life, hospice care is dedicated to providing dignity in death and making people comfortable during the *living–dying interval*. In the hospital, the focus is on the patient; in hospice care, the focus switches to both the dying person and his or her friends and family. In the hospital, the goal is to make the patient well; in hospice care, it is to relieve pain and suffering and make death easier to bear. In the hospital, the primary concern is the individual's physical welfare; in hospice care, although medical needs are met, the primary concern is the individual's social—and, in some instances, spiritual—well-being.

Suicide and Age

We noted in Chapter 1 how Durkheim stressed that suicide has a *social* base. Suicide, he said, is much more than an individual act. Each country, for example, has its own suicide rate, which remains quite stable year after year. In the United States, we can predict that 31,000 people will commit suicide this year. If we are off by more than 1,000, it would be a surprise. As we saw in Figure 1.1 (page 13), we can also predict that Americans will choose firearms as the most common way to kill themselves and that hanging will come in second. We can also be certain that this year more men than women will kill themselves, and more people in their 60s than in their 20s. It is this way year after year.

Statistics often fly in the face of the impressions we get from the mass media, and here we have such an example. Although the suicides of young people are given much publicity, such deaths are relatively rare. The suicide rate of adolescents is *lower* than that of adults of any age. It is the elderly who have the highest suicide rate, especially those age 75 and over. Because adolescents have such a low overall death rate, however, suicide does rank as their third leading cause of death—after accidents and homicide (*Statistical Abstract* 2009:Table 115).

These findings on suicide are an example of the primary sociological point stressed throughout this text: Recurring patterns of human behavior—whether education, marriage, work, crime, use of the Internet, or even suicide—represent underlying social forces. Consequently, if no basic change takes place in the social conditions under which the groups that make up U.S. society live, you can expect these same patterns of suicide to prevail five to ten years from now.

Adjusting to Death

The feelings that people experience after the death of a loved one often surprise them. Along with grief and loneliness, they may feel guilt, anger, or even relief. During the period of mourning that follows, usually one or two years, the family members come to terms with the death. In addition to sorting out their feelings, they also reorganize their family system to deal with the absence of the person who was so important to it.

In general, when death is expected, family members find it less stressful. They have begun to cope with the coming death by managing a series of smaller losses, including the person's inability to fulfill his or her usual roles or to do specific tasks. They also have been able to say a series of goodbyes to their loved one. In contrast, unexpected deaths—accidents, suicides, and murders—bring greater emotional shock. The family members have had no time to get used to the idea that the individual is going to die. One moment, the person is here; the next, he or she is gone. The sudden death gave them no chance to say goodbye or to bring any form of "closure" to their relationship.

Looking Toward the Future

Let's not lose sight of one of the major changes stressed in this chapter—that for the first time in human history huge numbers of people are becoming elderly. It is inevitable that such a fundamental change will have a powerful impact on societies around the world, so much so that it might even transform them. We don't have space to explore such potential transformations, which are only speculative at the moment, so let's try to catch a glimpse of what is happening with the elderly themselves.

A New Model of Aging

As huge numbers of Americans move into old age, the elderly have begun not only to challenge the demeaning stereotypes of the aged but also to develop new models of aging. These new approaches build on the idea that old age should not be viewed as "a-time-close-to-death," but, rather, as a new period of life, one with its specific challenges, to be sure, but also one to be enjoyed, even celebrated. This new time of life provides unique opportunities to pursue interests, to develop creativity, and to enhance the appreciation of life's beauty and one's place in it. Let's look at how this new model is being applied.

Creative Aging. In the 1970s, as larger numbers of people became elderly, many said that having endless amounts of leisure time was not their idea of how to enjoy being old. Pioneering the view that old age is a time to embark on new learning, they promoted free, space-available, noncredit attendance at colleges and universities, group travel to historical sites around the world, and the writing of memoirs about the past.

In the second phase, which we are just entering, emphasis is being placed on mental growth and enhancing people's creative abilities. An example is "The Colony," a retirement home in Hollywood, where the emphasis is on the arts. Residents write and perform plays, make sculptures, write and record songs, paint, and write novels (Brown 2006). Some residents, who did none of these things during their preretirement years, have become so good that they perform on radio and television.

More and more, the goal of the elderly is to enjoy themselves—and with more resources at their disposal, more and more are able to do so. The goal of the Red Hat Society, with chapters around the nation, is simply for women to have fun.

This approach to aging is new, so we don't know the directions it will take. But if this emphasis continues, it will change how the younger generations view the elderly—as well as how the elderly view themselves. The stereotype of despondent, disengaged old people might even be replaced with a stereotype of robust, engaged, thriving older adults (Manheimer 2005). No stereotype will encompass the reality of the elderly, of course, as the aged differ among themselves as much as younger people differ. Cultural differences will remain, as will those of social class. "The Colony," for example, with its emphasis on developing creativity, is directed toward the middle class. It seems certain that the poor, with their fewer resources, will not be affected as directly by creative aging.

The Impact of Technology

Throughout this text, we have examined some of the deep impacts that technology is having on our lives. To close this chapter, I would like you to reflect on how technological breakthroughs might affect your own life as you grow older.

ThinkingCRITICALLY

How Long Do You Want to Live? Approaching Methuselah

Would you like to live to 200? To 500? To 1,000?

Such a question may strike you as absurd. But with our new and still developing technology, science may stretch the life span to limits unheard of since biblical days.

We are just at the beginning stages of genetic engineering, and ahead of us may lie a brave new world. Technicians may be able to snip out our bad DNA and replace it with more compliant bits. The caps at the ends of our chromosomes, the telomeres, shrink as we age, causing the cells to die. An enzyme called telomerase may be able to modify this process, allowing cells to reproduce many more times than they currently are able to (Demidov 2005).

By manipulating genes, scientists have been able to extend the life span of worms by six times. Humans have these same genes. A human life span six times longer than what we now have would take the longest living people to over 600 (Chase 2003). We are only peering over the edge of the future, glimpsing what might be possible. Some optimistic geneticists predict that some people will live 1,000 years or longer (Gorman 2003; Vincent 2006).

Some geneticists compare the human body to a house (Gorman 2003). A house keeps standing not because it is built to last forever, but because people keep repairing it. In this envisioned future of scientific advances, we will use stem cells to grow spare body parts—livers, hearts, kidneys, fingers, and so on. As parts of our body wear out, we will replace them.

In grade school, many of us heard stories about Ponce de Leon, an explorer from Spain who searched for the fountain of youth. He eventually "discovered" Florida, but the fountain of youth eluded him. In our perpetual search for immortality, could we be discovering what eluded Ponce de Leon?

For Your Consideration

Let's assume that biomedical science does stretch the human life span, that living to be 150 or 200 becomes common. If people retire at age 65, how could society afford to support them for 100 years or so? People can't work much past 70, for—and this may be the basic flaw in this scenario of a brave new world—even with new body parts, the world would not be filled with 200-year-olds who functioned as though they were 25. They would be very old people, subject to the diseases and debilities that come with advanced age. If Medicare costs are bulging at the seams now, what would they be like in such a world?

Finally, how would you answer this question: Is the real issue how we can live longer, or how we can live better? Because of medical advances, public health, and better nutrition, millions of today's elderly enjoy good health. This is leading to a new view of old age—from a time of decay and death to a time of opportunity to pursue interests and develop talents, to obtain a fresh perspectives and a growing sense of satisfaction with life.

By the Numbers: *Then and Now*

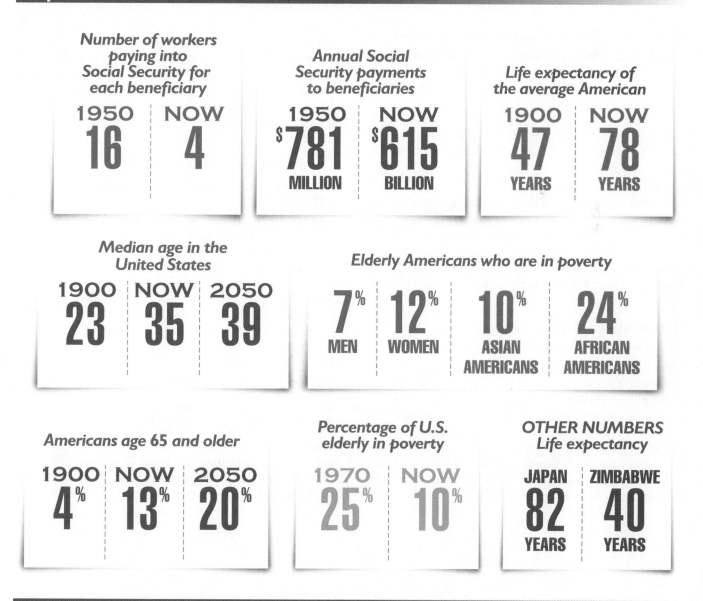

Number of workers paying into Social Security for each beneficiary

1950	NOW
16	4

Annual Social Security payments to beneficiaries

1950	NOW
$781 MILLION	$615 BILLION

Life expectancy of the average American

1900	NOW
47 YEARS	78 YEARS

Median age in the United States

1900	NOW	2050
23	35	39

Elderly Americans who are in poverty

7% MEN	12% WOMEN	10% ASIAN AMERICANS	24% AFRICAN AMERICANS

Americans age 65 and older

1900	NOW	2050
4%	13%	20%

Percentage of U.S. elderly in poverty

1970	NOW
25%	10%

OTHER NUMBERS Life expectancy

JAPAN	ZIMBABWE
82 YEARS	40 YEARS

SUMMARY *and* REVIEW

Aging in Global Perspective

How are the elderly treated around the world?

No single set of attitudes, beliefs, or policies regarding the aged characterizes the world's nations. Rather, they vary from exclusion and killing to integration and honor. The global trend is for more people to live longer. P. 368.

What does the social construction of aging mean?

Nothing in the nature of aging produces any particular set of attitudes. Rather, attitudes toward the elderly are rooted in culture and differ from one social group to another. Pp. 368–369.

What does the phrase "graying of America" mean?

The phrase **graying of America** refers to the growing percentage of Americans who reach old age. The costs of Social Security and health care for the elderly have become major social issues. Pp. 370–372.

The Symbolic Interactionist Perspective

What factors influence perceptions of aging?

Symbolic interactionists stress that aging is socially constructed. That is, no age has any particular built-in meaning; rather, we use cultural cues to define age. Four factors influence when people label themselves as "old": biological changes, biographical events, **gender age,** and cultural timetables. Cross-cultural comparisons demonstrate how culture shapes the ways that people experience aging. **Ageism,** negative reactions to the elderly, is based on stereotypes. Pp. 372–376.

The Functionalist Perspective

How is retirement functional for society?

Functionalists focus on how the withdrawal of the elderly from positions of responsibility benefits society. **Disengagement theory** examines retirement as a device for ensuring that a society's positions of responsibility are passed smoothly from one generation to the next. **Activity theory** examines how people adjust when they disengage from productive roles. **Continuity theory** focuses on how people adjust to growing old by maintaining their roles and coping techniques. Pp. 376–378.

The Conflict Perspective

How do the younger and the elderly compete for scarce resources?

Social Security legislation is an example of one generation making demands on another generation for limited resources. As the number of retired people grows, there are relatively fewer workers to support them. The Social Security Trust Fund may be a gigantic fraud perpetrated by the power elite on the nation's workers. Organizations such as the Gray Panthers and the AARP watch out for the interests of the elderly. Pp. 378–383.

Recurring Problems

What are some of the problems that today's elderly face?

Women are more likely to live alone and to be poor. At any one time, about 4 percent of the elderly live in nursing homes. Nursing homes are understaffed, and neglecting patients is common. Those most likely to abuse the elderly are members of their own family. Poverty in old age, greatly reduced through government programs, reflects the gender and racial–ethnic patterns of poverty in the general society. Pp. 384–388.

The Sociology of Death and Dying

How does culture affect the way we experience death and dying?

Like old age, death is much more than a biological event. Industrialization brought with it modern medicine, hospitals—and dying in a formal setting surrounded by strangers. Kübler-Ross identified five stages in the dying process, which, though insightful, do not characterize all people. **Hospices** are a cultural device designed to overcome the negative aspects of dying in hospitals. Suicide is most common after age 75. Pp. 388–390.

Looking Toward the Future

What technological developments can be a wild card in social planning for the aged?

The huge numbers of elderly who are in good health are fostering a new view of old age—as a time of creativity and personal development. Technological breakthroughs may stretch the human **life span.** If so, it is difficult to see how younger workers would be able to support retired people for 100 years or longer. Pp. 391–393.

THINKING CRITICALLY *ABOUT* Chapter 13

1. How does culture influence people's ideas about the elderly and when old age begins? Can you identify cultural changes that are likely to affect your own perceptions of the onset of old age and of the elderly?

2. How do the symbolic interactionist, functionalist, and conflict perspectives on the elderly differ?

3. If you were appointed to head the U.S. Department of Health and Human Services, how would you improve the nation's nursing homes?

ADDITIONAL RESOURCES

What can you find in MySocLab? mysoclab www.mysoclab.com

- Complete Ebook
- Practice Tests and Video and Audio activities
- Mapping and Data Analysis exercises

- Sociology in the News
- Classic Readings in Sociology
- Research and Writing advice

Where Can I Read More on This Topic?

Suggested readings for this chapter are listed at the back of this book.

1-MOS 0.005 0.01%   3-MOS 0.030 0.02%

Crude Oil (Jan) (@CL.1)
44.05 ▼3.93 [-8.1
One Week ▲5.53%

50.0
47.5
45.0
42.5
40.0

Mon   Tue   Wed

REAKING   TECHNICAL TRADE:
NEWS   OIL PRICES THIS WEE

9   XL Capital   3 00 ▼0.4

K@7.80 ▼0   Resource

The Economy

New York City

If you are like most students, you are wondering how changes in the economy are going to affect your chances of getting a good job. Let's see if we can shed some light on this question. We'll begin with this story:

"Not Monday already," Kim groaned as the alarm went off. "There must be a better way of starting the week." With her eyes still closed, she pressed the snooze button on the clock (from Germany) to sneak another ten minutes' sleep. In what seemed like just thirty seconds, the alarm once again shrilly insisted that she get up and face the week.

She said to herself, "If people were more like me, this country would be in better shape."

Still bleary-eyed after her shower, Kim peered into her closet and picked out a silk blouse (from China), a plaid wool skirt (from Scotland), and leather shoes (from Italy). She nodded, satisfied, as she added a pair of simulated pearls (from Taiwan). Running late, she hurriedly ran a brush (from Mexico) through her hair. As Kim wolfed down a bowl of cereal (from the United States) topped with milk (from the United States), bananas (from Costa Rica), and sugar (from the Dominican Republic), she turned on her kitchen television (from Korea) to listen to the weather forecast.

Gulping the last of her coffee (from Brazil), Kim grabbed her briefcase (from India), purse (from Spain), and jacket (from Malaysia), left her house, and quickly climbed into her car (from Japan). As she glanced at her watch (from Switzerland), she hoped that the traffic would be in her favor. She muttered to herself as she pulled up at a stoplight (from Great Britain) and eyed her gas gauge. She muttered again when she pulled into a station and paid for gas (from Saudi Arabia), for the price had risen over the weekend. "My paycheck never keeps up with prices," she moaned.

When Kim arrived at work, she found the office abuzz. Six months ago, New York headquarters had put the company up for sale, but there had been no takers. The big news was that both a Chinese company and a Canadian company had put in bids over the weekend. No one got much work done that day, as the whole office speculated about how things might change.

As Kim walked to the parking lot after work, she saw a tattered "Buy American" bumper sticker on the car next to hers. "That's right," she said to herself. "If people were more like me, this country would be in better shape."

The Transformation of Economic Systems

Although this vignette may be slightly exaggerated, many of us are like Kim: We use a multitude of products from around the world, and yet we're concerned about our country's ability to compete in global markets. Today's **economy**—our system of producing and distributing goods and services—differs radically from past economies. The products that Kim uses make it apparent that today's economy knows no national boundaries. To better understand how global forces affect the U.S. economy—and your life—let's begin by summarizing the sweeping historical changes we reviewed in Chapter 6.

Preindustrial Societies: The Birth of Inequality

The earliest human groups, *hunting and gathering societies,* had a **subsistence economy.** In small groups of about twenty-five to forty, people lived off the land. They gathered plants and hunted animals in one location and then moved to another place as these sources of food ran low. Because these people had few possessions, they did little trading with one another. With no excess to accumulate, as was mentioned in Chapter 6, everybody owned as much (or, really, as little) as everyone else.

Then people discovered how to breed animals and cultivate plants. The more dependable food supply in what became *pastoral and horticultural societies* allowed humans to settle down in a single place. Human groups grew larger, and for the first time in history, it was no longer necessary for everyone to work at producing food. Some people became leather workers, others weapon makers, and so on. This new division of labor produced a surplus, and groups traded items with one another. The primary sociological significance of surplus and trade is this: They fostered *social inequality,* for some people accumulated more possessions than others. The effects of that change remain with us today.

The plow brought the next major change, ushering in *agricultural societies.* Plowing the land made it more productive, allowing even more people to specialize in activities other than producing food. More specialized divisions of labor followed, and trade expanded. Trading centers then developed, which turned into cities. As power passed from the heads of families and clans to a ruling elite, social, political, and economic inequalities grew.

The commonsense meaning of market is a place where people exchange or buy and sell goods. Such old-fashioned markets remain common in the Least Industrialized Nations, such as this floating one in Bangkok, Thailand. Here people find the social interaction every bit as rewarding as the goods and money that they exchange.

Industrial Societies: The Birth of the Machine

The steam engine, invented in 1765, ushered in *industrial societies*. Based on machines powered by fuels, these societies created a surplus unlike anything the world had seen. This, too, stimulated trade among nations and brought even greater social inequality. A handful of individuals opened factories and exploited the labor of many.

Then came more efficient machines. As the surpluses grew even greater, the emphasis gradually changed—from producing goods to consuming them. In 1912, sociologist Thorstein Veblen coined the term **conspicuous consumption** to describe this fundamental change in people's orientations. By this term, Veblen meant that the Protestant ethic identified by Weber—an emphasis on hard work, savings, and a concern for salvation (discussed on page 176)—was being replaced by an eagerness to show off wealth by the "elaborate consumption of goods."

Postindustrial Societies: The Birth of the Information Age

In 1973, sociologist Daniel Bell noted that *a new type of society was emerging*. This new society, which he called the *postindustrial society*, has six characteristics: (1) a service sector so large that *most* people work in it, (2) a vast surplus of goods, (3) even more extensive trade among nations, (4) a wider variety and quantity of goods available to the average person, (5) an information explosion, and (6) a *global village*—that is, the world's nations are linked by fast communications, transportation, and trade.

Biotech Societies: The Merger of Biology and Economics

As we discussed in Chapter 6, we may be on the verge of yet another new type of society. This one is being ushered in by advances in biology, especially the deciphering of the human genome system. While the specifics of this new society have yet to unfold, the marriage of biology and economics should yield even greater surpluses and more extensive trade. The global village will continue to expand. The technological advances that will emerge in this new society may also allow us to lead longer and healthier lives. As history is our guide, it also may create even greater inequality between the rich and poor nations.

Implications for Your Life

The broad changes in societies that I have just sketched may seem to be abstract matters, but they are far from irrelevant to your life. Whenever society changes, so do our lives. Consider the information explosion. When you graduate from college, you will most likely do some form of "knowledge work." Instead of working in a factory, you will manage information or design, sell, or service products. The type of work you do has profound implications for your life. It produces social networks, nurtures attitudes, and even affects how you view yourself and the world. To better understand this, consider how vastly different your outlook on life would be if you were one of the children discussed in the Cultural Diversity box on the next page.

It is the same with the global village. Think of the globe as being divided into three neighborhoods—the three worlds of industrialization and postindustrialization that we reviewed in Chapter 9. Some nations are located in the poor part of the village. Their citizens do menial work and barely eke out a living. Life is so precarious that some even starve to death, while their fellow villagers in the rich neighborhood feast on the best that the globe has to offer. It's the same village, but what a difference the neighborhood makes.

Now visualize any one of the three neighborhoods. Again you will see gross inequalities. Not everyone who lives in the poor neighborhood is poor, and some areas of the rich neighborhood are packed with poor people. The United States is the global economic leader, occupying the most luxurious mansion in the best neighborhood and is spearheading the new biotech society.

conspicuous consumption
Thorstein Veblen's term for a change from the Protestant ethic to an eagerness to show off wealth by the consumption of goods

Cultural Diversity around the World

The Child Workers

Nine-year-old Alone Banda works in an abandoned quarry in Zambia. Using a bolt, he breaks rocks into powder. In a week, he makes enough powder to fill half a cement bag. Alone gets $3 for the half bag.

The amount is pitiful, but without it he and his grandmother would starve to death.

It is still a slow death for Alone. Robbed of his childhood and breathing rock dust continuously, Alone is likely to come down with what the quarry workers call a "heavy chest," an early sign of silicosis.

Some of the children who work at the quarry are only 7 years old. As one mother said, "If I feel pity for them, what are they going to eat?" (Wines 2006a).

In Ghana, 6-year-old Mark Kwadwo, who weighs about 30 pounds, works for a fisherman. For up to fourteen hours a day, seven days a week, he paddles a boat and takes fish out of nets. If Mark doesn't paddle hard enough, or pull in the fish from the nets fast enough, Takyi hits him on the head with a paddle. Exhausted, Mark falls asleep at night in a mud hut that he shares with five other boys.

Mark is too little to dive, but he knows what is coming when he is older. His fear is that he will dive to free a tangled net—and never resurface.

"I prefer to have my boy home with me," says the mother of Kwabena, whom she leased to the fisherman four years ago when Kwabena was 7, "but I need the money to survive."

The answer to "What is the proper role of children in an economy?" varies by social class, culture, economic development, and historical period. On the top is a boy working in a Pennsylvania coal mine about 1880. On the bottom is a girl working in a rice field in Madagascar today.

Kwabena's mother has received $66 for the four years' work (LaFraniere 2006).

Some children work in construction (see the photo on page 232), others in factories (Barboza 2008). Children work as miners, pesticide sprayers, street vendors, and household servants. They weave carpet in India, race camels in the Middle East, and, all over the world, work as prostitutes. The poverty in some areas is so severe that the few dollars the children earn makes the difference between life and death. In Ghana, where Mark works on the fishing boat, two out of three people live on less than $1 a day (LaFraniere 2006).

Besides poverty, there is also a cultural factor. In many parts of the world, people view children differently than we do in the West. The idea that children have the right to be educated and to be spared from adult burdens is fairly new in history. A major factor shaping our views of life is economics, and when prosperity comes to these other countries, so will this new perspective.

For Your Consideration

How do you think the wealthier nations can help alleviate the suffering of child workers? Before industrialization, and for a period afterwards, having children work was also common in the West. Just because our economic system has changed, bringing with it different ideas of childhood and of the rights of children, what right do we have to impose our changed ideas on other nations?

The Transformation of the Medium of Exchange

As each type of economy evolved, so, too, did the **medium of exchange,** the means by which people value and exchange goods and services. As we review the changes summarized in the time-event line at the bottom of this page, you'll see how the medium of exchange reflects a country's economy.

Earliest Mediums of Exchange

Hunting and gathering and pastoral and horticultural societies produced little surplus, and people **bartered,** directly exchanging one item for another. In later societies, surpluses grew and trade expanded, making barter too cumbersome. People then developed new ways of placing values on goods and services so they could trade them. Let's look at how the medium of exchange was transformed.

Medium of Exchange in Agricultural Societies

Although bartering continued in agricultural societies, people increasingly came to use **money,** a medium of exchange that places a value on items. In most places, money consisted of gold and silver coins. A coin's weight and purity determined the amount of goods or services it could purchase. In some places, people made purchases with **deposit receipts.** These receipts transferred ownership to a specified number of ounces of gold or silver, or bushels of grain, or to a specified amount of other goods that were on deposit in a warehouse or bank. Toward the end of the agricultural period, deposit receipts became formalized into **currency** (paper money). Each piece of paper represented a specific amount of gold or silver stored in a warehouse. Currency and deposit receipts represented **stored value.** No more currency or deposit receipts could be issued than the total amount of gold or silver in the warehouse. Gold and silver coins continued to circulate alongside the deposit receipts and currency.

Medium of Exchange in Industrial Societies

With few exceptions, bartering became a thing of the past in industrial societies. Gold was replaced by paper currency, which, in the United States, could be exchanged for gold stored at Fort Knox. This policy was called the **gold standard.** As long as each dollar represented a specified amount of gold, the number of dollars that could be issued was limited. Toward the end of this period, U.S. paper money could no longer be exchanged for gold or silver. Instead, there was **fiat money,** currency issued by a government that is not backed by stored value.

When fiat money replaced stored value, coins made of precious metals disappeared from circulation. People considered these coins more valuable, and they were unwilling to part with them. In the United States, gold coins disappeared first, followed by the largest silver coin, the dollar. Then, as inferior metals (copper, zinc, and nickel) replaced the smaller silver coins, people began to hoard these silver coins, and they, too, disappeared from circulation.

Even without a gold standard that restricts the amount of currency issued to the amount of stored value, governments have a practical limit on the amount of paper money they can distribute. In general, prices increase if a government issues currency at a rate higher than the growth of its **gross domestic product (GDP),** the total goods and services that a country produces. This condition, **inflation,** means that each unit of currency will purchase fewer goods and services. Governments try to control inflation, for high inflation is a destabilizing influence.

medium of exchange the means by which people place a value on goods and services in order to make an exchange—for example, currency, gold, and silver

barter the direct exchange of one item for another

money any item (from sea shells to gold) that serves as a medium of exchange; today, currency is the most common form

deposit receipt a receipt stating that a certain amount of goods is on deposit in a warehouse or bank; the receipt is used as a form of money

currency paper money

stored value the goods that are stored and held in reserve that back up (or provide the value for) a currency

gold standard paper money backed by gold

fiat money currency issued by a government that is not backed by stored value

gross domestic product (GDP) the amount of goods and services produced by a nation

inflation an increase in prices

FIGURE 14.1   Changes in the Medium of Exchange

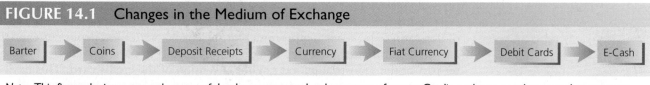

Barter → Coins → Deposit Receipts → Currency → Fiat Currency → Debit Cards → E-Cash

Note: This figure depicts a general course of development, not a hard sequence of events. Credit cards are not shown, as they are not a medium of exchange but an IOU, a version of merchants' charge accounts.
Source: By the author.

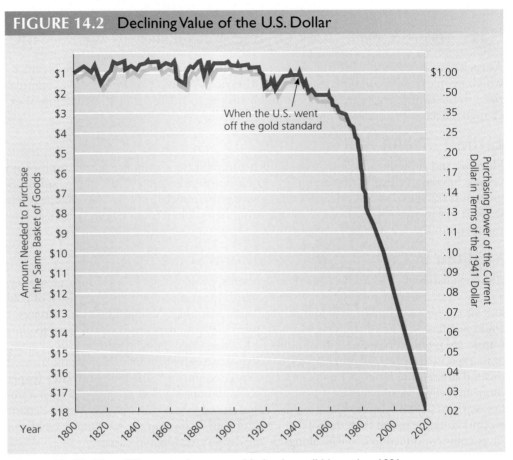

FIGURE 14.2   Declining Value of the U.S. Dollar

Source: Modified from "Alternative Investment Market Letter," November 1991.

As you can see from Figure 14.2 as long as the gold standard limited the amount of currency, the purchasing power of the dollar remained relatively stable. When the United States left the gold standard in 1937, the dollar no longer represented stored value, and it plunged in value. Today, the dollar is but a skinny shadow of its former self, retaining only about 5 percent of its earlier purchasing power—and shrinking rapidly.

Inflation in the United States is usually mild, less than 5 percent a year. People get used to gradual increases in prices. High inflation, in contrast, makes life difficult, and when inflation goes wild, it upsets everything. How would you like to pay $800,000 for a little bread roll? Or $1,000,000 for a chicken? How about $417 for a single piece of scratchy toilet paper? These are actual prices in Zimbabwe, where inflation has run wild (Wines 2006b; Bearak 2008). A Coke was really high, $15,000,000,000 (Walker and Higgins 2008). That was at noon. By dinner, of course, it cost a few million more (all prices in Zimbabwean money, not U.S. dollars).

After World War I, Germany was ravaged by high inflation, which helped to usher Hitler into power. Look at the photos to the left. The large, beautiful bill—which I bought in an antique shop—looks and feels as though it had been engraved. Although it is only 100 marks, with this 1908 bill you could buy a car. The smaller bills of 200,000 and 1 million marks, churned out by the German mint in 1923 at the height of inflation after World War I, look and feel like Monopoly money. With them, you could buy a loaf of bread—if you rushed to the store before the price rose.

In industrialized societies, checking accounts became common. A *check* is a type of deposit receipt, for it is a promise that the check's writer has deposited enough currency in the warehouse (the bank or credit union) to cover the check. The latter part of the industrial period saw the invention of the **credit card.** This device allows someone who has been approved for a specified amount of credit to purchase goods without an immediate exchange of money—either metal, currency, or check. The owner of the credit card is then billed for the purchase.

Medium of Exchange in Postindustrial Societies

During the first part of the postindustrial (or information) society, paper money circulated freely. Paper money then became less common, gradually being replaced by checks and credit cards. The next development was the **debit card,** a device that electronically withdraws the cost of an item from the cardholder's bank account. Like the check, the debit card is a type of deposit receipt, for it transfers ownership of currency on deposit.

The latest evolution of money is **e-cash,** money stored on a company's computer that can be transferred over the Internet to anyone who has an account with that company. E-cash can be used for making purchases and for paying bills. We can use the term *e-currency* to refer to the most common form of e-cash. E-currency represents an amount recorded in a government's paper money, such as so many dollars or euros.

The second form of e-cash is *electronic gold,* which represents a balance in units of gold. A transaction in e-gold is actually the transfer of ownership to a specified amount of gold, which the owner has stored in a bank's vault. E-gold takes us back to the time when people made transactions in gold and silver—this time, in contrast, using an electronic form for the exchange. The value of an electronic gold account goes up or down depending on the price of gold. Because electronic gold is not issued by any national government, it does not represent the transfer of euros or dollars or any other currency. This makes electronic gold a non-national money that can be used by citizens of any government. Governments dislike the development of e-cash, in general, as the transactions bypass banks, making it difficult for governments to monitor the financial activities of their citizens. E-gold poses a special threat, for it even bypasses government-issued currencies. Consequently, we can expect extensive legislation to help governments regain control over money.

credit card a device that allows its owner to purchase goods and to be billed later

debit card a device that allows its owner to charge purchases against his or her bank account

e–cash digital money that is stored on computers; it is of two types, e-currency and e-gold

capitalism an economic system characterized by the private ownership of the means of production, the pursuit of profit, and market competition

laissez-faire capitalism unrestrained manufacture and trade (literally "hands off" capitalism)

World Economic Systems

Now that we have sketched the main historical changes in the means of exchange, let's compare capitalism and socialism, the two main economic systems in force today. This will help us to understand where the United States stands in the world economic order.

Capitalism

People who live in a capitalist society may not understand its basic tenets, even though they see them reflected in their local shopping malls and fast-food chains. Table 14.1 distills the many businesses of the United States down to their basic components. As you can see, **capitalism** has three essential features: (1) *private ownership of the means of production* (individuals own the land, machines, and factories); (2) *market competition* (competing with one another, the owners decide what to produce and set the prices for their products); and (3) *the pursuit of profit* (the owners try to sell their products for more than what they cost).

No country has pure capitalism. Pure capitalism, known as **laissez-faire capitalism** (literally "hands off" capitalism), means that the government doesn't interfere in the market.

TABLE 14.1　Comparing Capitalism and Socialism	
Capitalism	**Socialism**
1. Individuals own the means of production.	1. The public owns the means of production.
2. Based on competition, the owners determine production and set prices.	2. Central committees plan production and set prices; no competition.
3. The pursuit of profit is the reason for distributing goods and services.	3. No profit motive in the distribution of goods and services.

welfare (or state) capitalism an economic system in which individuals own the means of production but the state regulates many economic activities for the welfare of the population

monopoly the control of an entire industry by a single company

The current form of U.S. capitalism is **welfare** or **state capitalism.** Private citizens own the means of production and pursue profits, but they do so within a vast system of laws designed to protect the welfare of the population.

Consider this example:

Suppose that you discover what you think is a miracle tonic: It will grow hair, erase wrinkles, and dissolve excess fat. If your product works, you will become an overnight sensation—not only a multimillionaire, but also the toast of television talk shows and the darling of Hollywood.

But don't count on your money or fame yet. You still have to reckon with market restraints, the laws and regulations of welfare capitalism that limit your capacity to produce and sell. First, you must comply with local and state laws. You must obtain a business license and a state tax number that allows you to buy your ingredients without paying sales taxes. Then come the federal regulations. You cannot simply take your product to local stores and ask them to sell it; you first must seek approval from federal agencies that monitor compliance with the Pure Food and Drug Act. This means that you must prove that your product will not cause harm to the public. Your manufacturing process is also subject to federal, state, and local laws concerning fraud, hygiene, and the disposal of hazardous wastes.

Suppose that you overcome these obstacles, and your business prospers. Other federal agencies will monitor your compliance with laws concerning racial, sexual, and disability discrimination; minimum wages; and Social Security taxes. State agencies will examine your records to see whether you have paid unemployment taxes and sales taxes. Finally, as your shadowy business partner, the Internal Revenue Service will look over your shoulder and demand about 35 percent of your profits.

To see how welfare or state capitalism developed in the United States, let's go back to an earlier era. Back in the 1800s, when capitalism was in its infancy, you could have made your "magic" potion at home and sold it at any store willing to handle it. You could have advertised that it cured baldness, erased wrinkles, and dissolved fat, for no agency existed to monitor your product or your claims. As you can see from the 1885 poster below, this is precisely what thousands of individuals did at that time. They made "elixirs" in their basements and gave them whimsical names such as "Granny's Miracle Medicine" and "Elixir of Health and Happiness." They might claim that their product could restore sexual potency, purge the intestines, and make people more intelligent. These tonics often made people feel better, for many elixirs were braced with alcohol—and even cocaine (Ashley 1975). (The *Coca* in Coca-Cola refers to cocaine, which this "pick-me-up" drink contained until 1903.) To protect the public's health, in 1906 the federal government passed the Pure Food and Drug Act and began to regulate products.

John D. Rockefeller's remarkable success in unregulated markets helps to explain why the government began to regulate capitalism. After a ruthless drive to eliminate competition, Rockefeller managed to corner the U.S. oil and gasoline market (Chernow 1998). He slashed prices and then doubled them after driving out the competition. He even sabotaged competitors' pipelines and refineries (Josephson 1949). With his competitors crippled or eliminated, his company, Standard Oil, was able to dictate prices to the entire nation. Rockefeller had achieved the capitalist's dream, a **monopoly,** the control of an entire industry by a single company.

Rockefeller had played the capitalist game too well, however, for he had wiped out one of its

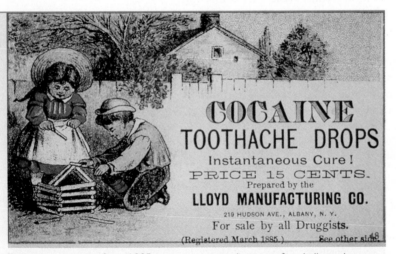

This advertisement from 1885 represents an early stage of capitalism when individuals were free to manufacture and market products with little or no interference from the government. Today, the production and marketing of goods take place under detailed, complicated government laws and regulations.

essential components: competition. Consequently, to protect this cornerstone of capitalism, the federal government passed antimonopoly legislation and broke up Standard Oil. Today, the top firms in each industry—such as General Electric in household appliances—must obtain federal approval before acquiring another company in the same industry. If the government determines that one firm dominates a market, it can force that company to *divest* (sell off) some of the businesses it owns.

Another characteristic of welfare capitalism is that although the government encourages competition, it establishes its own monopoly over what it calls "common good" items. These are items and services presumed essential for the common good of the citizens, such as armed forces, highways, and sewers.

Socialism

As shown in Table 14.1 on page 403, **socialism** also has three essential components: (1) public ownership of the means of production, (2) central planning, and (3) the distribution of goods without a profit motive.

In socialist economies, the government owns the means of production—not only the factories but also the land, railroads, oil wells, and gold mines. Unlike capitalism, in which **market forces**—supply and demand—determine both what will be produced and the prices that will be charged, a central committee decides that the country needs X number of toothbrushes, Y toilets, and Z shoes. The committee decides how many of each will be produced, which factories will produce them, what price will be charged for the items, and where they will be distributed.

Socialism is designed to eliminate competition, for goods are sold at predetermined prices regardless of the demand for an item or the cost of producing it. The goal is not to make a profit, nor is it to encourage the consumption of goods that are in low demand (by lowering the price) or to limit the consumption of hard-to-get goods (by raising the price). Rather, the goal is to produce goods for the general welfare and to distribute them according to people's needs, not their ability to pay.

In a socialist economy *everyone* in the economic chain works for the government. The members of the central committee who set production goals are government employees, as are the supervisors who implement their plans, the factory workers who produce the merchandise, the truck drivers who move it, and the clerks who sell it. Those who buy the items may work at different jobs—in offices, on farms, or in day care centers—but they, too, are government employees.

Just as capitalism does not exist in a pure form, neither does socialism. Although the ideology of socialism calls for resources to be distributed according to need and not the ability to pay, socialist countries found it necessary to pay higher salaries for some jobs in order to entice people to take on greater responsibilities. Factory managers, for example, always earned more than factory workers. These differences in pay follow the functionalist argument of social stratification presented in Chapter 9 (pages 239–240). By narrowing the huge pay gaps that characterize capitalist nations, however, socialist nations established considerably greater equality of income.

Dissatisfied with the greed and exploitation of capitalism and the lack of freedom and individuality of socialism, Sweden and Denmark developed **democratic socialism** (also called *welfare socialism*). In this form of socialism, both the state and individuals produce and distribute goods and services. The government owns and runs the steel, mining, forestry, and energy concerns, as well as the country's telephones, television stations, and airlines. Remaining in private hands are the retail stores, farms, factories, and most service industries.

Ideologies of Capitalism and Socialism

Not only do capitalism and socialism have different approaches to producing and distributing goods but they also represent opposing belief systems. *Capitalists* believe that market forces should determine

---

socialism an economic system characterized by the public ownership of the means of production, central planning, and the distribution of goods without a profit motive

market forces the law of supply and demand

democratic socialism a hybrid economic system in which the individual ownership of businesses is mixed with the state ownership of industries thought essential to the public welfare, such as the postal service and the delivery of medicine and utilities

Successful capitalists can buy most things in life, including trophy wives. Some trade their entrepreneurial success (money, property, sometimes fame) for younger, beautiful women. Fred Thompson, age 66, a successful, wealthy actor and trial lawyer who also served as U.S. Senator from Tennessee, is married to Jeri Kehn, age 42.

both products and prices. They also believe that profits are good for humanity. The potential to make money stimulates people to produce and distribute goods, as well as to develop new products. Society benefits, as the result is a more abundant supply of goods at cheaper prices.

Socialists take an opposite view of profits. They consider them to be immoral. An item's value is based on the work that goes into it, said Karl Marx. The only way there can be profit, he stressed, is by paying workers less than the value of their labor. Profit, then, is an *excess value* that has been withheld from workers. Socialists believe that the government should protect workers from this exploitation. To do so, the government should own the means of production, using them not to generate profit but to produce items that match people's needs, not their ability to pay.

Capitalists and socialists paint each other in such stark colors that *each perceives the other system as one of exploitation.* Capitalists believe that socialists violate people's basic right to make their own decisions and to pursue opportunity. Socialists believe that capitalists violate people's basic right to be free from poverty. With each side claiming moral superiority while viewing the other as a threat to its very existence, the last century witnessed the world split into two main blocs. In what was known as the *Cold War,* the West armed itself to defend and promote capitalism, the East to defend and promote socialism.

Тов. Ленин ОЧИЩАЕТ землю от нечисти.

Throughout most of the twentieth century, capitalism and communism were pitted against one another in a deadly struggle. Each thought of itself as the correct economic form, and each viewed the other as an evil to be eradicated. In support of this view of essential goodness and evil, proponents of each system launched global propaganda campaigns. This poster from about 1920 says: "Comrade Lenin cleanses the filth from the earth." Those being swept away are rich royalty at the top, the clergy (lower left), and capitalists (lower right).

Criticisms of Capitalism and Socialism

The primary criticism leveled against capitalism is that it leads to social inequality. Capitalism, say its critics, produces a tiny top layer of wealthy people who exploit an immense bottom layer of poorly paid workers. Another criticism is that the tiny top layer wields vast political power. Those few who own the means of production reap huge profits, accrue power, and get legislation passed that goes against the public good.

The primary criticism leveled against socialism is that it does not respect individual rights. Others (in the form of some government body) control people's lives. They decide where people will live, work, and go to school. In China, they even decide how many children women may bear (Mosher 1983, 2006). Critics also argue that central planning is grossly inefficient and that socialism is not capable of producing much wealth. They say that its greater equality really amounts to giving almost everyone an equal chance to be poor.

The Convergence of Capitalism and Socialism

Regardless of the validity of these mutual criticisms, as nations industrialize they come to resemble one another. They urbanize, encourage higher education, and produce similar divisions of labor (such as professionals and skilled technicians; factory workers and factory managers). Similar values also emerge (Kerr 1983). By itself, this tendency would make capitalist and socialist nations grow more alike, but another factor also brings them closer to one another (Form 1979): Despite their incompatible ideologies, both capitalist and socialist systems have adopted features from the other.

That capitalism and socialism are growing similar is known as **convergence theory.** Fundamental changes in socialist countries give evidence for this coming hybrid, or mixed, economy. Russians suffered from the production of shoddy goods, they were plagued by shortages, and their standard of living lagged severely behind that of the West. To try to catch up, in the 1980s and

1990s the rulers of Russia made the private ownership of property legal and abandoned communism. Making a profit—which had been a crime—was encouraged. China joined the change, but kept a communist government. In its converged form of "capunism," capitalists joined the Communist party. The convergence is so great that when the Western governments began stimulus plans to counter the economic crisis, China joined in with a huge stimulus plan of its own (Batson 2009). Even Western banks have been welcomed in China, so they can provide specialized services to China's 300,000 new millionaires (Reuters 2008). Perhaps the point that best summarizes this remarkable change is this: Some textbooks in China now give more space to Bill Gates than to Mao (Guthrie 2008). The Cultural Diversity box below provides a glimpse of the new capitalism in China.

Cultural Diversity around the World

The New Capitalism in China

Socialism has the virtue of making people more equal. Socialism's equality, however, translates into distributing poverty throughout a society. Under socialism, almost everyone becomes equally poor.

Capitalism, in contrast, has the virtue of producing wealth. A lot of people remain poor, however, leaving a sharp contrast in wealth and poverty, one that produces envy and sometimes creates social unrest.

Chinese leaders realized the wealth-producing capacity of capitalism and wanted that for their people. In the Chinese version they produced—capitalism directed by communists—wealth is being produced. In all the world's history, this new capitalism has lifted the largest number of people out of poverty in the shortest time. The poor who are left behind, however, aren't happy when their land is taken from them to help make others wealthy. The anger and resentment have kept the Party busy, for its army has had to squelch a lot of riots.

In Beijing, the capital of China, stands a mansion built by Zhang Yuchen. This is no ordinary mansion, like those built by China's other newly rich. This imposing building is a twin of the Chateau de Maisons-Laffitte, an architectural landmark on the Seine River outside Paris. At a cost of $50 million, the Beijing replica matches the original edifice detail for detail. The architects even used the original blueprints of the French chateau, and the building features the same Chantilly stone (Kahn 2004, 2007b).

The cost of this Chinese version of the chateau was actually greater than $50 million. The acreage set aside

Like a debutante being introduced to society, the Chinese comcapitalists presented themselves on the world stage at the Beijing Olympics. This photo is from the games' closing ceremonies.

for the mansion and a housing development of luxury homes made eight hundred farmers landless.

But not to worry. The spiked fence, the moat, and the armed guards—looking sharp in their French-style uniforms complete with capes and kepis—keep the peasants out of the chateau.

In most places, you need connections to become wealthy. In China, this means connections with the Communist Party, for this group still holds the power. Yuchen has those connections. As a member of the Party, it was his job to direct Beijing's construction projects. With his deep connections, Yuchen was able to get the wheat fields farmed by the peasants rezoned from farmland to a "conservation area." He was even able to divert a river so he could build the moat around the chateau, one of the finishing touches on his architectural wonder.

It isn't as though the peasants have been left with nothing. As part of Yuchen's deal to get the land, he gives $45 a month to each of the elderly. And the younger peasants can work in the vineyards that Yuchen is planting. French wine will top off the project.

For Your Consideration

When China has completed its transition to capitalism, what do you think the final version will look like (that is, what characteristics do you think it will have)? Where will the top Party leaders fit in the class system that is emerging? Why? (To answer this, consider the connections and resources of the elite.)

Changes in capitalism also support this theory. The United States has adopted many socialist practices. One of the most obvious is the government taking money from some individuals to pay for the benefits it gives to others. Examples include unemployment compensation (taxes paid by workers are distributed to those who no longer produce a profit); subsidized housing (shelter, paid for by the many, is given to the poor and elderly, with no motive of profit); welfare (taxes from the many are distributed to the needy); a minimum wage (the government, not the employer, determines the minimum that workers receive); and Social Security (the retired do not receive what they paid into the system, but, rather, money that the government collects from current workers). Finally, in 2008 when Wall Street and auto firms started to buckle, the government stepped in to shore up these businesses, even buying ownership in some of these firms, firing CEOs, and setting salary limits. Such an embrace of socialist principles indicates that the United States has produced its own version of a mixed economy.

Convergence seems to be unfolding before our very eyes. On the one hand, capitalists have assumed, reluctantly, that their system should provide workers with at least minimal support during unemployment, extended illness, and old age—and in some instances that the government should buy company stock. On the other hand, socialist leaders have admitted, also reluctantly, that profit and private ownership do motivate people to work harder.

Social life is sometimes stranger than fiction, and here is a fascinating possibility. Like two cars heading toward each other, these two economic systems do not converge. Rather, each passes the other, continuing in the direction it is headed. The capitalist nations end up adopting so many features of socialism while the former socialistic nations adopt so many features of capitalism that each is transformed into something close to what the other was. Could this theory, which we can call *transmergence,* indicate something that is even possible? Consider this. An article in *Pravda,* Russia's main newspaper and the former propaganda organ of the Soviet Communist Party, warned the United States not to travel farther on the road to socialism (Mishin 2009). These new capitalists said that by bailing out private companies—such as becoming owners of banks and automobile manufacturers—the United States is choosing a path that is "dangerously Marxist."

The Functionalist Perspective on the Globalization of Capitalism

Capitalism has integrated the world's countries, making them all part of the same broader economic unit. When the economic crisis hit the United States, it spread quickly around the world. The leaders of the top 20 producers of consumer goods met in Washington to see what steps they could take to head off the crisis. Chinese leaders said that no one should worry about them not being a team player, that they realized that any action they took would affect other nations. (Yardley and Brasher 2008)

The globalization of capitalism may be the most significant economic change in the past 100 years. Its impact on our lives may rival that of the Industrial Revolution. As Louis Gallambos, a historian of business, says, "This new global business system will change the way everyone lives and works" (Zachary 1995).

The New Global Division of Labor

To apply functionalism to the globalization of capitalism, let's step back a moment and look at the nature of work. You know that work is functional for society. Only because people work can we have electricity, hospitals, schools, automobiles, and homes. Beyond this obvious point, however, lies a basic sociological principle: *Work binds us together.* As you may recall from Chapter 4, Emile Durkheim noted that because farmers do the same type of work, they share a similar view of the world. Durkheim used the term **mechanical solidarity** to refer to the sense of unity that comes from doing similar activities.

mechanical solidarity
Durkheim's term for the unity (a shared consciousness) that people feel as a result of performing the same or similar tasks

In their march toward globalization, multinational companies locate their corporate headquarters in one country, manufacture their components in another country, assemble them in still another, and sell the finished product throughout the world. These are some of the 14,000 workers in Nike shoe factories in Indonesia.

When an agricultural society industrializes, people work at many different types of jobs. As the division of labor grows, people come to feel less solidarity with one another. Grape pickers in California, for example, may feel that they have little in common with workers who make aircraft in Missouri. Yet, what each worker does contributes to the economic system and, therefore, to the welfare of the others. Because they are *like the separate organs that make up the same body,* Durkheim called this type of unity **organic solidarity.**

Durkheim had observed the beginning of a global process. With our new *global division of labor,* each of us now depends on workers around the globe. If we live in California or New York—or even Michigan—we depend on workers in Tokyo to produce cars. Tokyo workers, in turn, depend on Saudi Arabian workers to pump oil and South American workers to operate ships that deliver that oil. We may not feel a sense of unity with one another, but the same global economic web links all of us.

This process, now engulfing the world, is still in its early stage. As corporations expand into new areas, they have hit some unexpected cultural hurdles, the topic of the Cultural Diversity box on the next page.

Capitalism in a Global Economy

Corporate Capitalism.   That capitalism could become the world's dominant economic force can be traced to a social invention called the corporation. A **corporation** is a business that is treated legally as a person. A corporation can make contracts, incur debts, sue and be sued. Its liabilities and obligations, however, are separate from those of its owners. For example, each shareholder of Ford Motor Company—whether he or she has 1 or 100,000 shares—owns a portion of the company. However, Ford, not its individual owners, is responsible for fulfilling its contracts and paying its debts. The term **corporate capitalism** is used to indicate that corporations dominate the economy.

Separation of Ownership and Management.   One of the most surprising aspects of corporations is their separation of ownership and management. Unlike most businesses, it is not the owners—those who own the company's stock—who run the day-to-day affairs of the company (Sklair 2001). Instead, managers run the corporation, and they are able to treat it *as though it were their own.* The result is the "ownership of wealth without

organic solidarity
Durkheim's term for the interdependence that results from the division of labor; people depending on others to fulfill their jobs

corporation a business enterprise, often jointly owned, whose assets, liabilities, and obligations are separate from those of its owners; as a legal entity, it can enter into contracts, assume debt, and sue and be sued

corporate capitalism the domination of an economic system by giant corporations

Cultural Diversity around the World

Doing Business in the Global Village

The globalization of capitalism means that businesspeople face cultural hurdles as they market products in other countries. Some of the cultural mistakes they make as they try to clear these hurdles are downright humorous.

In trying to reach Spanish-speaking Americans and Mexico's growing middle class, some companies have stumbled over their Spanish. Parker Pen was using a slogan "It won't leak in your pocket and embarrass you." The translation, however, came out as "It won't leak in your pocket and make you pregnant." Frank Perdue's cute chicken slogan "It takes a strong man to make a tender chicken" didn't fare any better in Spanish. It came out as "It takes an aroused man to make a chicken affectionate." And when American Airlines launched a "Fly in Leather" campaign to promote its leather seats in first class, the Mexican campaign stumbled just a bit. "Fly in Leather" (*vuela en cuero*), while literally correct, came out as "Fly Naked." I suppose that slogan did appeal to some (Archbold and Harmon 2001).

United States

The Spanish market is so huge that it keeps enticing companies to run marketing campaigns. The American Dairy Association made a hit in the United States with its humorous campaign, "Got Milk?" In Mexico, though, the Spanish translation read "Are you lactating?" All those mouths with white milk on them suddenly took on new meaning. Coors didn't fare any better. Their slogan, "Turn It Loose," was a hit in the United States, but in Spanish it came out as "Get Diarrhea."

Then there is Hershey's new candy bar, *Cajeta Elegancita,* marketed to Spanish-speaking customers. While *cajeta* can mean nougat, its most common meaning is "little box." The literal translation of *cajeta elegancita* is elegant or fancy little box. Some customers are snickering about this one, too, for *cajeta* is also slang for an intimate part of the female anatomy ("Winner . . ." 2006).

It isn't only Spanish that has given U.S. companies problems. Vicks decided to sell its cough drops in

Japan

Germany. In German, the "v" is pronounced "f." Unfortunately, this made Vicks sound like the "f" word in English, which is just what ficks means in German.

Cultural mistakes are a two-way street, of course. A Swedish company makes Electrolux, a vacuum cleaner. Their cute slogan reads just fine in Swedish, but the translation for their U.S. ads came out as "Nothing sucks like an Electrolux."

Some businesspeople have managed to avoid such problems. They have seized profit opportunities in cultural differences. For example, Japanese women are embarrassed by the sounds they make in public toilets. To drown out the offensive sounds, they flush the toilet an average of 2.7 times a visit (Iori 1988). This wastes a lot of water, of course. Seeing this cultural trait as an opportunity, a U.S. entrepreneur developed a battery-powered device that is mounted in the toilet stall. When a woman activates the device, it emits a 25-second flushing sound. A toilet-sound duplicator may be useless in our culture, but the Japanese have bought thousands of them.

To be accepted in another culture, sometimes even the product has to be changed. In a process called *transcreation*, cartoons designed originally for one audience are modified to match the tastes of an audience in another culture. The illustration in this box shows this process. At the top is the U.S. version of the Powerpuff Girls; at the bottom is how the Powerpuff Girls appear on Japanese television. Portraying Blossom, Buttercup, and Bubbles as leggy and dressed in skimpy outfits has broadened their appeal considerably: Not only do little girls look forward to this cartoon on Saturday mornings, but so do many adult Japanese men (Fowler and Chozick 2007).

For Your Consideration

1. Why is it often difficult to do business across cultures?
2. How can businesspeople avoid cross-cultural mistakes?
3. If a company makes a cultural blunder, what should it do?

appreciable control, and control of wealth without appreciable ownership" (Berle and Means 1932). Sociologist Michael Useem (1984) put it this way:

> When few owners held all or most of a corporation's stock, they readily dominated its board of directors, which in turn selected top management and ran the corporation. Now that a firm's stock [is] dispersed among many unrelated owners, each holding a tiny fraction of the total equity, the resulting power vacuum allow[s] management to select the board of directors; thus management [becomes] self-perpetuating and thereby acquire[s] de facto control over the corporation.
>
> Management determines its own salaries, sets goals and awards itself bonuses for meeting them, authorizes market surveys, hires advertising agencies, determines marketing strategies, and negotiates with unions. The management's primary responsibility to the owners is to produce profits.

Because of this power vacuum, at their annual meetings the stockholders ordinarily rubber-stamp management's recommendations. It is so unusual for this *not* to happen that these rare cases are called a **stockholders' revolt.** The irony of this term is generally lost, but remember that in such cases it is not the workers who are rebelling at the control of the owners but the owners who are rebelling at the control of the workers!

Functions and Dysfunctions on a Global Scale

The globalization of capitalism has forged a new world structure. Three primary trading blocs have emerged: North and South America, dominated by the United States; Europe, dominated by Germany; and Asia, dominated by Japan and China. Functionalists stress that this new global division benefits not only the multinational giants but also the citizens of the world.

Consider free trade. Free trade increases competition, which, in turn, drives the search for greater productivity. This lowers prices and brings a higher standard of living. Free trade also has dysfunctions. As production moves to countries where labor costs are lower, millions of U.S., U.K., French, and German workers have lost their jobs. Functionalists point out that this is merely a temporary dislocation. As the Most Industrialized Nations lose production jobs, their workers shift into service and high-tech jobs. Meanwhile, some of the poor of the Least Industrialized Nations have new jobs and the chance for a better life.

The adjustment is not easy. As the U.S. steel industry lost out to global competition, for example, the closings of plants created "rust belts" in the northern states. The globalization of capitalism has also brought special challenges to small towns, which were already suffering long-term losses because of urbanization. Their struggle to survive is the topic of the photo essay on the next two pages. The most visible dysfunction, however, is the global economic crisis, discussed in the Cultural Diversity box on page 414.

The Conflict Perspective on the Globalization of Capitalism

Conflict theorists say that to place the focus on global interdependence is to miss the point. What we should look at is the interconnected power of the wealthy and how they use it to exploit workers.

The Changing Inner Circle of Corporate Capitalism

Table 14.2 on page 415 lists the world's twenty-five largest **multinational corporations**— companies that operate across national borders. You can see that the largest multinationals are spread around eleven countries. You can also see the dominance of the United States. What is not apparent from this list is the decline of the United States and the rise of China. In the preceding year, twelve U.S. companies were on this list of the world's twenty-five largest companies—and none from China. Now it is nine from the United States and three from China.

stockholders' revolt the refusal of a corporation's stockholders to rubber-stamp decisions made by its managers

multinational corporations companies that operate across national boundaries; also called *transnational corporations*

Small Town USA

Struggling to Survive

all across the nation, small towns are struggling to survive. Parents and town officials are concerned because so few young adults remain in their home town. There is little to keep them there, and when they graduate from high school, most move to the city. With young people leaving and old ones dying, the small towns are shriveling.

How can small towns contend with cutthroat global competition when workers in some countries are paid a couple of dollars a day? Even if you open a store, down the road Wal-Mart sells the same products for about what you pay for them—and offers much greater variety.

There are exceptions: Some small towns are located close to a city, and they receive the city's spillover. A few possess a rare treasure—some unique historical event or a natural attraction—that draws visitors with money to spend. Most of the others, though, are drying up, left in a time warp as history shifts around them. This photo essay tells the story.

People do whatever they can to survive. This enterprising proprietor uses the building for an unusual combination of purposes: a "plant world," along with the sale of milk, eggs, bread, and, in a quaint southern touch, cracking pecans.

The small towns are filled with places like this—small businesses, locally owned, that have enough clientele for the owner and family to eke out a living. They have to offer low prices because there is a fast-food chain down the road. Fixing the sign? That's one of those "I'll get-to-its."

I was struck by the grandiosity of people's dreams, at least as reflected in the names that some small-towners give their businesses. Donut Palace has a nice ring to it—inspiring thoughts of wealth and royalty (note the crowns). Unfortunately, like so many others, this business didn't make it.

In striking contrast to the grandiosity of some small town business names is the utter simplicity of others. Cafe tells everyone that some type of food and drinks are served here. Everyone in this small town knows the details.

One of the few buildings consistently in good repair in the small towns is the U.S. Post Office. Although its importance has declined in the face of telecommunications, for "small towners" the post office still provides a vital link with the outside world.

With little work available, it is difficult to afford adequate housing. This house, although cobbled together and in disrepair, is a family's residence.

There is no global competition for this home-grown business. Shirley has located her sign on a main highway just outside Niceville, Florida. By the looks of the building, business could be better.

This is a successful business. The store goes back to the early 1900s, and the proprietors have capitalized on the "old timey" atmosphere.

This general store used to be the main business in the area; it even has a walk-in safe. It has been owned by the same family since the 1920s, but is no longer successful. To get into the building, I had to find out where the owner (shown here) lived, knock on her door, and then wait while she called around to find out who had the keys.

Cultural Diversity (Unity) around the World

When Capitalism Fails: Consequences for All of Us

If there were any doubt that we live in an integrated world united by capitalism, that doubt was erased with the economic crisis that stunned the world in 2008. What started as a financial problem with a few Wall Street firms spread to a full-blown credit crisis in the United States, then morphed into a banking–financial crisis that spread across the globe. Stock markets in New York plunged. So did those in Tokyo, Moscow, London, Berlin, and Beijing. The prices of houses and commercial property dropped not just in Los Angeles and Miami but also in Lisbon and Hong Kong. I was in Spain at the time, and you could actually see the crisis: Cranes on construction sites suddenly idled, when just a week or so before they had been carrying building materials to scores of workers.

The economic crisis moved quickly from an American to a global problem. This billboard in Seoul represents the drop in value of the South Korean won.

Panic hit. Banks refused to loan money, even to customers who were quite profitable. The thinking was, Who knows what might really be lurking in the company's accounting records? Millions of U.S. homeowners fell behind on their mortgage and credit card payments. Foreclosures became so common that it was not unusual to drive down a neighborhood street and see multiple "bank repossessed properties" for sale.

The heads of General Motors, Ford, and Chrysler—who just a short time before had been reporting rosy futures to their stockholders—stood hats-in-hand before Congress, begging for a handout, pleading that without help they would have to close up their factories in a few months, the not-so-hidden threat that if they didn't get their share of the newly-printed billions then millions of workers related to the auto industry would be walking the streets. Congress almost gave in, but not quite. They said to come back with a plan—adding that it didn't look good for these executives to fly to Washington in private jets when they were begging for money.

These three did come back—this time letting the media know they were driving to Washington, and in gas-saving hybrid vehicles. Congress relented and gave out cash—billions of dollars to those outstretched hands. Ford turned it down, but Chrysler took it. GM grabbed it, asked for more, and promptly went belly up.

Although the Europeans thought at first that they could stay above the "American" financial crisis, banks in England, Spain, and France suddenly discovered that they, too, were holding billions in bad loans. Frightened, panicked depositors demanded their money, a crisis that hit so suddenly and severely that to prevent strikes and riots, the European governments stepped in and guaranteed their banks' deposits. "If they can't return your money, we'll print more and give it to you" was their overnight response. That was sufficient to quiet the depositors.

Russians, too, started to grumble. The good times that they had just started to enjoy under capitalism—after so many decades of communist shoddiness and shortages—started to evaporate before their eyes. Seeing the writing on the wall, Vladimir Putin appeared on prime-time television to soothe his constituents. "We won't let the problems of those bad foreigners become ours," he told his stone-eyed skeptics. But as the price of oil, on which Putin's new empire depended, plunged, so did the confidence of the Russians—and, with it, Putin's political security. The former Soviet slave states—from the Baltic to Poland—felt themselves crushed by the economic crisis. Their rush to capitalism and the EU money that flowed to them had made them feel financially secure. But as the reality of the crisis began to sink in, their newfound pride in economic development and its cornucopia of consumer goods began to come crashing down around them. As the Ukrainians watched in horror, their currency, the *hryvnia*, lost half its value in just three months. Now how can you live with that? At first, China, too, felt smugly immune from the West's problems, but as the West cut its consumption, factory orders declined. Panicked, some newly wealthy owners grabbed whatever money there was left and fled to parts unknown. Suddenly dumped, millions of urban immigrants returned dejected to their villages.

An economically integrated world? And how! United by capitalism—with good times rolling around the globe, and bad times shaking the globe.

For Your Consideration

What effects has the economic crisis had on your life? How do you think it will affect your future? Why is the phrase, the globalization of capitalism, an accurate one?

TABLE 14.2 The World's Largest Corporations

Rank	Company	Country	Industry	Sales ($bil)	Profits ($bil)	Assets ($bil)
1	General Electric	United States	Conglomerates	183	17	798
2	Royal Dutch Shell	Netherlands	Oil & Gas Operations	458	26	278
3	Toyota Motor	Japan	Consumer Durables	263	17	325
4	ExxonMobil	United States	Oil & Gas Operations	426	45	228
5	BP	United Kingdom	Oil & Gas Operations	361	21	228
6	HSBC Holdings	United Kingdom	Banking	142	6	2,520
7	AT&T	United States	Telecommunications Services	124	13	265
8	Wal-Mart Stores	United States	Retailing	406	13	163
9	Banco Santander	Spain	Banking	96	13	1,319
10	Chevron	United States	Oil & Gas Operations	255	24	161
11	Total	France	Oil & Gas Operations	223	15	165
12	ICBC	China	Banking	54	11	1,188
13	Gazprom	Russia	Oil & Gas Operations	97	27	277
14	PetroChina	China	Oil & Gas Operations	114	20	145
15	Volkswagen Group	Germany	Consumer Durables	158	7	244
16	JPMorgan Chase	United States	Banking	101	4	2,175
17	GDF Suez	France	Utilities	116	9	233
18	ENI	Italy	Oil & Gas Operations	158	13	140
19	Berkshire Hathaway	United States	Diversified Financials	108	5	267
20	Vodafone	United Kingdom	Telecommunications Services	70	13	252
21	Mitsubishi UFJ Financial	Japan	Banking	61	6	1,931
22	Procter & Gamble	United States	Household & Personal Products	84	14	138
23	CCB-China Construction Bank	China	Banking	43	9	903
24	Verizon Communications	United States	Telecommunications Services	97	6	202
25	Petrobras-Petroleo Brasil	Brazil	Oil & Gas Operations	92	14	121

Note: Size is measured by sales, market value, assets, and profits.

Source: "Global 2000," 2009.

The heads of these top twenty-five corporations wield power beyond their own companies. Not only do they move capital around the globe, but they also serve on the boards of directors of their nation's most influential foundations and universities. Although in competition with one another, they are united by a common interest—making capitalism flourish (Carroll and Carson 2003; Rothkopf 2008).

The *inner circles* that head a country's top corporations have access to high-level politicians, which they use to promote legislation favorable to big business. Some also use those contacts for more sinister purposes. In the 1950s, the newly elected president of Guatemala, Jacobo Árbenz, wanted workers to get higher wages. The largest employer in Guatemala, The United Fruit Company, a U.S. corporation, opposed this plan. The CIA then funded and trained an army, which overthrew Árbenz (Shefner 2008). In 1973, another U.S. company, the International Telephone & Telegraph Company (ITT), joined the CIA in a plot that led to the assassination of Salvador Allende, the president of Chile (Coleman 1995; Rohter 2002). In 2009, a Dutch company, Royal Dutch Shell, paid $16 million to settle a claim that it was complicit in hanging a man who led a protest against the company's destruction of the environment (Mouawad 2009).

How would you like to be a fly on the wall as such a conspiracies develop? Here's your chance. Listen as the CEO of a leading aircraft manufacturer talks to a ranking member of the Senate's Armed Services Committee:

Here's the deal. I want to sell a plane to Muammar Qaddafi and he wants to buy one. But we have sanctions in place that won't let me sell to him. The U.S. wants the guy dead. So, what I'm thinking is, if you help me get the okay to sell him the plane, I'll build it with explosive bolts connecting the wings to the fuselage. Then, one day he's up flying over the Med and we push a button. He's gone. I make my sale. Everyone's happy. (Rothkopf 2008:xix)

The CEO was wrong, of course, not just morally, but in his facts. Not everyone would be happy about such an arrangement—at least not Qaddafi and his family. By the way, the senator didn't take the CEO up on his offer.

Most economic-political connections are not sinister. Most consist of politicians passing legislation to protect corporate profits. But the interests between business and politics do overlap to such a degree that business leaders have even been able to get a sitting U.S. president to help them sell airplanes. Here is the report from the Associated Press (October 29, 1995):

The White House celebrated Saudi Arabia's $6 billion purchase of U.S.-made airplanes Thursday, calling it a victory for both American manufacturers and the Clinton administration. . . . President Clinton helped broker the sale. . . . Prince Bandar bin Sultan, [Saudi Arabia's] minister of defense and aviation, credited Clinton for closing the purchase. *Clinton personally pitched the quality of the U.S. planes to Saudi King Fahd.* [Italics added]
. . . The Clinton Administration worked this sale awfully damn hard because of the president's commitment to promoting U.S. business abroad. . . . He has done that routinely, instructed his ambassadors and his diplomats to put the economic interests of Americans forward as they conduct their diplomacy.

Although the president wasn't selling underarm deodorant, it was the same principle.

Concentration of Power

Conflict theorists stress how power is concentrated in the capitalist class described on pages 270–271. A tool that unites and magnifies their power is **interlocking directorates.** Individuals serve on the board of directors of several major companies, and so do their fellow board members. Like a spider's web that starts at the center and fans out in all directions, these overlapping memberships join the top companies into a single network. As one chief executive said:

If you serve on, say, six outside boards, each of which has, say . . . five experts in one or another subject, you have a built-in panel of thirty friends who are experts who you meet regularly, automatically each month, and you really have great access to ideas and information. You're joining a club, a very good club. (Useem 1984)

This is not just a characteristic of capitalism in the United States, but of capitalism throughout the world.

The Global Superclass

The overlapping memberships of the globe's top multinational companies enfold their leaders into a small circle that we can call the **global superclass** (Rothkopf 2008). The superclass is not only extremely wealthy, as we reviewed in Chapter 9 (see Figure 9.1 on page 237), but it is also extremely powerful. These people have access to the top circles of political power around the globe. Here is how a member of this superclass describes these tight connections:

Every country has its large financial institutions that are central to the development of that country, and everyone else in finance knows somebody who will know the head of one of those companies. That person knows a senior person in their government that could be useful in a situation. . . . the key is the network. . . . it is twenty, thirty, fifty people worldwide who ultimately drive the decisions. (Rothkopf 2008:129–130)

interlocking directorates the same people serving on the board of directors of several companies

global superclass a small group of highly interconnected individuals in which wealth and power are so concentrated that they make the world's major decisions

Twenty to fifty individuals who make the world's major decisions! Could this possibly be true? The individual who said this, Stephen Schwarzman, is an insider who was describing the way things work at the top. Pay attention to this real-life example of how this interconnected global power works out in practice:

> When Schwarzman, the head of a major U.S. investment company, had a problem with some policy of the German government, he called a German friend. The friend arranged for Schwarzman to meet with the Chancellor of Germany. After listening to Schwarzman, the Chancellor agreed to support a change in Germany's policy.

This high concentration of power is new on the world scene. Although hidden from view, it is highly significant for our lives—and for everyone around the world. The decisions of this global superclass affect our present and future.

Global Investing

"This Bud's for you!" —Thanks to InBev, a Belgian brewer
"Fill up at Shell!" —Thanks to a Dutch refinery
"Tums for your tummy!"—Thanks to Beecham Group, a British corporation

Corporations have expanded well beyond their national borders, as illustrated by the Social map below and the one on the next page. Cross-border investments have become so extensive that about 1 of every 22 U.S. employees—over 5 million people—works for a business owned by people in other countries (*Statistical Abstract* 2009:Table 1253).

Although we take multinational corporations for granted—as well as their cornucopia of products—their power and presence are new to the world scene. As multinational corporations do business across national borders, they tend to become detached from the interests and values of their country of origin. The head of Intel made this revealing statement, "Intel can thrive today and never hire another American. It is not our intention, but we can do that." (Rothkopf 2008:120). These global giants move investments and production from one part of the globe to another—with no concern for consequences other than profits.

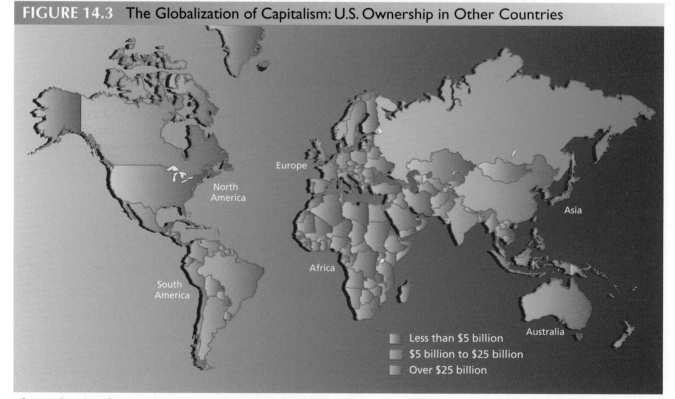

FIGURE 14.3   The Globalization of Capitalism: U.S. Ownership in Other Countries

Less than $5 billion
$5 billion to $25 billion
Over $25 billion

Source: Based on *Statistical Abstract of the United States* 2009:Table 1256.

FIGURE 14.4   The Globalization of Capitalism: Foreign Ownership of U.S. Business

Businesses in which at least 10 percent of the voting interest is controlled by a non-U.S. owner.

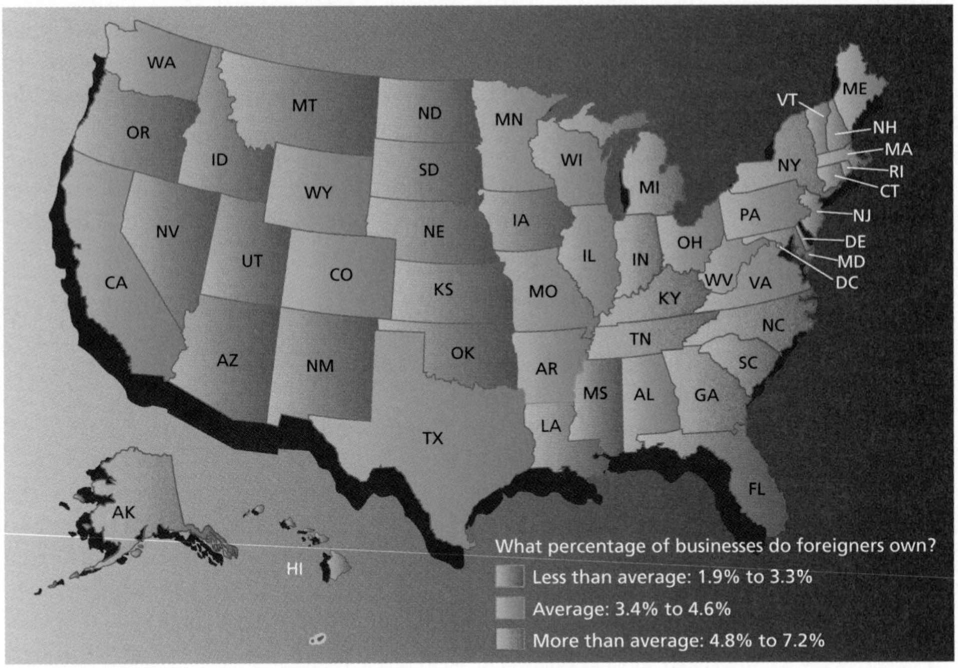

What percentage of businesses do foreigners own?

- Less than average: 1.9% to 3.3%
- Average: 3.4% to 4.6%
- More than average: 4.8% to 7.2%

Source: Based on *Statistical Abstract of the United States* 2009:Table 1253.

How opening or closing factories affects workers is of no concern to them. With profit their moral guide, the conscience of multinational corporations is written in dollar signs.

This primary allegiance to profits and market share, rather than to their workers or to any country, accompanied by a web of interconnections that span the globe, is of high sociological significance. The shift in orientation and organization is so new, however, that we don't yet know its implications. But we can consider two stark contrasts. The first: Removed from tribal loyalties and needing easy access across national boundaries, the global interconnections of the multinational corporations could unite the world's nations and produce global peace. The second: They could create a New World Order dominated by a handful of corporate leaders. If so, we all may find ourselves at the mercy of a global elite in a system of interconnected societies, directed by the heads of the world's corporate giants. We will discuss this possibility in the next chapter.

Work in U.S. Society

With this broad, even global, background, let's turn our focus on work in U.S. society.

The Transition to Postindustrial Society

Analysts often use the term *postindustrial society* to describe the United States. Figure 14.5 illustrates why this term is appropriate. The change shown in this figure is without parallel in human history. In the 1800s, most U.S. workers were farmers. Today, farmers make up about 1 percent of the workforce. With the technology of the 1800s, a typical farmer produced

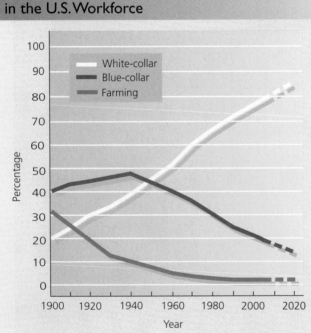

FIGURE 14.5   The Revolutionary Change in the U.S. Workforce

- White-collar
- Blue-collar
- Farming

Source: By the author. Based on *Statistical Abstract of the United States,* various years, and 2009:Tables 596, 1324.

enough food to feed five people. With today's powerful machinery and hybrid seeds, a farmer now feeds about eighty. In 1940, about half of U.S. workers wore a blue collar; then changing technology shrank the market for blue-collar jobs. White-collar work continued its ascent, reaching the dominant position it holds today.

When you look at Figure 14.5, the change in type of work is readily apparent, but what you see here is merely the surface. The significance of this change in work is that it indicates the arrival of a new type of society. To live in a postindustrial society is to live in a different world. Not only is your work different but so are your lifestyle, your relationships, the age at which you marry, the amount of education you attain, the number of children you have, your attitudes and values, and even the way you view the world.

Women and Work

Let's look at another major change that has transformed our world, the unprecedented increase in the numbers of women who work for wages. In Chapter 11 (Figure 11.5, page 316), you saw how this number has increased so greatly that today almost half of all U.S. workers are women. Look at Figure 14.6 to see how the United States ranks among other Western nations.

Researchers have found two primary distinctions between women and men in the world of work. First, women seem to be more concerned than men with maintaining

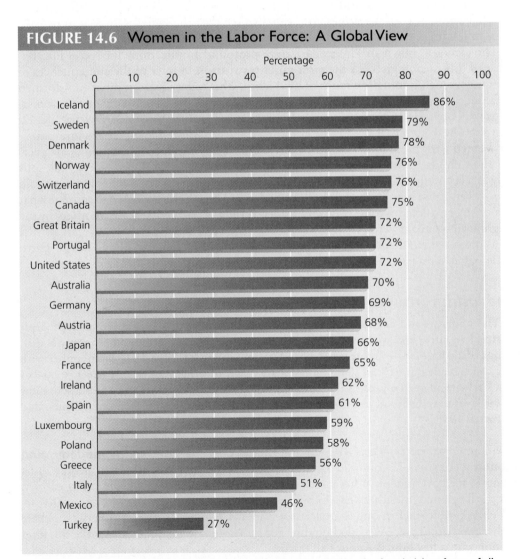

FIGURE 14.6   Women in the Labor Force: A Global View

Percentage

Country	Percentage
Iceland	86%
Sweden	79%
Denmark	78%
Norway	76%
Switzerland	76%
Canada	75%
Great Britain	72%
Portugal	72%
United States	72%
Australia	70%
Germany	69%
Austria	68%
Japan	66%
France	65%
Ireland	62%
Spain	61%
Luxembourg	59%
Poland	58%
Greece	56%
Italy	51%
Mexico	46%
Turkey	27%

Note: Female labor force participation rates are derived by dividing the female labor force of all ages by the female population ages 15–64. These totals include women who work part-time.

Source: By the author. Based on *Statistical Abstract of the United States* 2009: Table 1322.

a balance between their work and family lives (Statham et al. 1988; Caproni 2004). Second, men and women tend to follow different models for success: Men seem to place more emphasis on individualism, power, and competition, while women seem more likely to stress collaboration, encouragement, and helping (Miller-Loessi 1992; Mayer et al. 2008).

Note the caution with which I have presented these findings—the use of *seem to* and *tend to*. I am not convinced that there are any substantial or essential differences between women's and men's orientations to work. The few studies that we have on this topic could be tapping core differences—or they could be measuring temporary tendencies owing to women having more recently entered the paid workforce. If so, as women's work experiences accumulate, these differences will disappear. It will be interesting to see what happens as more women reach the top levels of their professions and attain the more powerful positions in the business world.

How likely is it that a woman will be in the labor force? Figure 14.7a on the next page shows how working for wages increases with each level of education. This is probably because women who have more education find more satisfying work—and get higher pay. Figure 14.7b shows the influence of marital status. You can see that single women are the most likely to work for wages; married women follow closely behind; and divorced, widowed, and separated women are the least likely to be in the workforce. From Figure 14.7c, you can see that African American women are the most likely to be in the workforce, but that race–ethnicity makes little difference in whether women work for wages. You can also see that the racial–ethnic groups have been following a parallel course.

The changes shown in Figure 14.7 have profound implications for social life. Because of this, sociologists use the term **quiet revolution** to refer to the consequences of so many women joining the ranks of paid labor. This quiet revolution has transformed self-concepts, spending patterns, and relations at work. It has also changed relationships with boyfriends, husbands, and children. It has even transformed views of life. I'll give just one example. It used to be considered most undesirable—perhaps immoral—for women with preschoolers to work for wages. Believing that they would be neglecting their children and that neighbors would talk, mothers of preschoolers took jobs only as a last resort. Now, as Figure 14.7d shows, *most* mothers of preschoolers have paid jobs—even those who have children under age 3. The neighbors don't gossip, for what was once considered wrong is now considered right—and most of the mothers in the neighborhood are at work.

As discussed in Chapter 11, women face discrimination at work. The Down-to-Earth Sociology box on page 422 explores how some women cope with this discrimination.

The Underground Economy

> The underground economy. The term has a sinister ring—suggestive of dope deals struck in alleys and wads of bills hastily exchanged. The underground economy is this, but it is a lot more—and it is usually a lot more innocent. If you pay the plumber with a check made out to "cash," if you purchase a pair of sunglasses from a street vendor or a kitchen gadget at a yard sale, if you so much as hand a neighbor's kid a $20 bill to mow the lawn or to baby sit, you are participating in the underground economy. (Pennar and Farrell 1993)

quiet revolution the fundamental changes in society that follow when vast numbers of women enter the workforce

underground economy exchanges of goods and services that are not reported to the government and thereby escape taxation

Also known as the *informal economy* and the *off-the-books economy*, the **underground economy** consists of economic activities—whether legal or illegal—that people don't report to the government. What interests most of us is not unreported babysitting money, but the illegal activities that people could not report even if they wanted to. As a 20-year-old child care worker in one of my classes who also worked as a prostitute two or three nights a week told me, "Why do I do this? For the money! Where else can I make this kind of money in a few hours? And it's all tax free."

FIGURE 14.7 Women in the Labor Force: The U.S. Experience

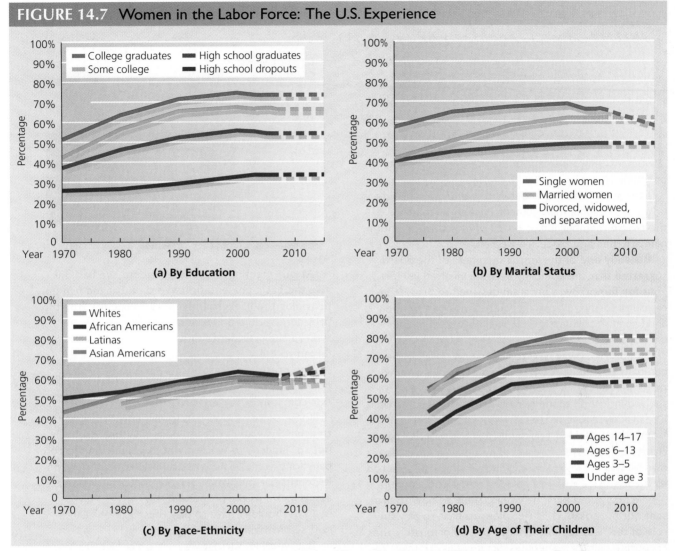

(a) By Education

Legend: College graduates, High school graduates, Some college, High school dropouts

(b) By Marital Status

Legend: Single women, Married women, Divorced, widowed, and separated women

(c) By Race-Ethnicity

Legend: Whites, African Americans, Latinas, Asian Americans

(d) By Age of Their Children

Legend: Ages 14–17, Ages 6–13, Ages 3–5, Under age 3

Note: To understand this figure, ask "What percentage of Group X is working for wages?" The broken lines in Part C are government projections; the other broken lines indicate projections by the author.

Sources: By the author. Based on *Statistical Abstract of the United States* 1989: Tables 638, 639, 640; 1990: Tables 625, 627, 637; 2001: Table 578; 2009: Tables 568, 572, 577, 579.

The largest source of illegal income is probably drug dealing. Twenty million Americans currently use illegal drugs (*Statistical Abstract* 2009: Tables 7, 199). To serve them, billions of dollars flow from users to sellers and to their networks of growers, importers, processors, transporters, dealers, and enforcers. These particular networks are so huge that each year the police arrest more than a million Americans for illegal drug activities (*Statistical Abstract* 2009: Table 312).

The million or so illegal immigrants who enter the United States each year are also part of the underground economy. Often called *undocumented workers* (referred to as *los sin documentos* in Mexico), they work for employers who either ignore their fake Social Security cards or pay them in cash. I asked a housekeeper from Mexico who had entered the United States illegally if she had a "green card" (the card given to immigrants who enter the country legally). She said that she did, adding, "They're sold on the street like candy."

Down-to-Earth Sociology
Women in Business: Maneuvering the Male Culture

I work for a large insurance company. Of its twenty-five hundred employees, about 75 percent are women. Only 5 percent of the upper management positions, however, are held by women.

I am one of the more fortunate women, for I hold a position in middle management. I am also a member of the twelve-member junior board of directors, of whom nine are men and three are women.

Recently one of the female members of the board suggested that the company become involved in Horizons for Tomorrow, a program designed to provide internships for disadvantaged youth. Two other women and I spent many days developing a proposal for our participation.

The problem was how to sell the proposal to the company president. From past experiences, we knew that if he saw it as a "woman's project" it would be shelved into the second tier of "maybes." He hates what he calls "aggressive bitches."

We three decided, reluctantly, that the proposal had a chance only if it were presented by a man. We decided that Bill was the logical choice. We also knew that we had to "stroke" Bill if we were going to get his cooperation.

We first asked Bill if he would "show us how to present our proposal." (It is ridiculous to have to play the role of the "less capable female," but, unfortunately, the corporate culture sometimes dictates this strategy.) To clinch matters, we puffed up Bill even more by saying, "You're the logical choice for the next chairmanship of the board."

Bill, of course, came to our next planning session, where we "prepped" *him* on what to say.

At our meeting with the president, we had Bill give the basic presentation. We then backed *him* up, providing the background and rationale for why the president should endorse the project. As we answered the president's questions, we carefully deferred to Bill.

The president's response? "An excellent proposal," he concluded, "an appropriate project for our company."

To be successful, we had to maneuver through the treacherous waters of the "hidden culture" (actually not so "hidden" to women who have been in the company for a while). The proposal was not sufficient on its merits, for the "who" behind a proposal is at least as significant as the proposal itself.

"We shouldn't have to play these games," Laura said, summarizing our feelings.

But we all know that we have no choice. To become labeled "pushy" is to commit "corporate suicide"—and we're no fools.

Source: Written by an insurance executive in the author's introductory sociology class who, out of fear of retaliation at work, has chosen to remain anonymous.

When terrorists struck the World Trade Center, 43 restaurant workers were killed. Of them, 12 were working with fake Social Security cards (Cleeland 2001). Undocumented workers from China work primarily in Chinese restaurants and in New York's garment industry. Many from India and Pakistan work in fast-food restaurants (Rosenbaum 1998). Those from Mexico and Central and South America are concentrated in California and Texas, but they disperse throughout the country. They do housework, pick lettuce on farms, sew garments in clandestine sweatshops, clean rooms in hotels, and serve food at restaurants. For the most part, they do the low-paying and dirty jobs that U.S. citizens try to avoid. The rest of us benefit from their labor, for they bring us cheaper goods and services.

Because of its subterranean nature, no one knows the exact size of the underground economy, but it probably runs around 10 percent of the regular economy (Barta 2009). Since the official gross domestic product of the United States is about $14 trillion (*Statistical Abstract* 2009:Table 645), the underground economy probably totals well over $1 trillion a year. It is so huge that it distorts the official statistics of the country's gross domestic product. It also costs the IRS billions of dollars a year in lost taxes.

Stagnant Paychecks

With our extensive automation, the productivity of U.S. workers has increased year after year, making them some of the most productive in the world (*Statistical Abstract* 2009:Table 1342). One might think, therefore, that their pay would be increasing. This brings us to a disturbing trend.

Look at Figure 14.8. The gold bars show current dollars. These are the dollars the average worker finds in his or her paycheck. You can see that since 1970 the average pay of U.S. workers has soared from just over $3 an hour to over $17 an hour. Workers today are bringing home more than *five* times as many dollars as workers used to.

But let's strip away the illusion. Look at the green bars, which show the dollars adjusted for inflation, the *buying power* of those paychecks. You can see how inflation has suppressed the value of the dollars that workers earn. Today's workers, with their $17 an hour, can buy little more than workers in 1970 could with their "measly" $3 an hour. The question is not "How could workers live on just $3 an hour back then?" but, rather, *"How can workers get by on a 29-cent-an-hour raise that it took 37 years to get?"* Incredibly, despite their having more years of college and more technical training, despite the use of computers, and much higher productivity, the average worker's purchasing power increased just 29 cents an hour between 1970 and 2007.

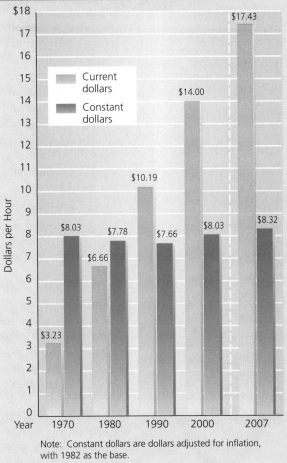

FIGURE 14.8 Average Hourly Earnings of U.S. Workers in Current and Constant Dollars

Note: Constant dollars are dollars adjusted for inflation, with 1982 as the base.

Source: By the author. Based on *Statistical Abstract of the United States* 1992:Table 650; 1999:Table 698; 2009:Table 622.

Patterns of Work and Leisure

Suppose that it is 1860 and you work for a textile company in Lowell, Massachusetts. When you arrive at work one day, you find that the boss has posted a new work rule: "All workers will have to come in at the same time and remain until quitting time." Like the other workers, you feel outrage. You join them as they shout, "This is slavery!" and march out of the plant, indignant at such a preposterous rule. (Zuboff 1991)

This is a true story. The workers were angry because up until then, they had been able to come and go when they wanted. Let's consider how patterns of work and leisure are related to the transformation of economies.

Effects of Industrialization. Hunting and gathering societies provide enormous amounts of **leisure,** time not taken up by work or necessary activities such as eating and sleeping. Assuming they didn't live in a barren place or have to deal with some calamitous event, such as drought or pestilence, it did not take long for people to hunt and gather what they needed for the day. In fact, *most of their time was leisure,* and the rhythms of nature were an essential part of their lives. Agricultural economies

leisure time not taken up by work or necessary activities

also allowed much leisure, for, at least in the western hemisphere, work peaked with the spring planting, let up in the summer, and then peaked again with the fall harvest. During the winter work again receded, for by this time the harvest was in, animals had been slaughtered, food had been preserved and stored, and wood had been laid up.

Industrialization, however, broke this harnessing of work to seasonal rhythms. Going against all of human history, bosses and machines began to dictate when work was to be done. Workers resisted, clinging to their traditional patterns. After working for several weeks—or even just a few days—a worker would disappear, only to reappear when money ran out. For most workers, enjoying leisure was considerably more important than amassing money (Weber 1958/1904–1905). Since regular, efficient production brought more profits, bosses began to insist that all workers start work at the same time. To workers of that period, this seemed like slavery. Today, in contrast, work patterns that corporations and bosses impose on us have become part of the taken-for-granted cultural rhythms that coordinate our lives.

FIGURE 14.9
Leisure and the Life Course: The "U" Curve of Leisure

Most Leisure Time

Early childhood ... Old age

Years after parenthood

Teen years

Years of parenthood

Least Leisure Time

Source: By the author.

Trends in Leisure. It is not the activity itself that makes something leisure, but the purpose for which it is done. Consider driving a car. If you do it for pleasure, it is leisure, but if you are a cabbie or if you must commute to the office, it is work. If done for enjoyment, horseback riding and reading a book are leisure—but these activities are work for jockeys and students.

Patterns of leisure change with the life course, following the U-curve shown on Figure 14.9. Young children enjoy the most leisure, but teenagers still have considerably more leisure than their parents. Parents with small children have the least leisure, but after the children leave home, leisure picks up again. After the age of 60 or so, the amount of leisure for adults peaks.

Compared with workers during early industrialization, today's workers have far more leisure. A hundred years ago the work week was half again as long as today's, for then workers had to be at their machines 60 hours a week. When workers unionized, they demanded a shorter work week. Over the years, the work week has gradually shrunk. In Germany the work week is 35 hours, with Friday afternoons usually taken off. Volkswagen was the world's first multinational corporation to adopt a 30-hour work week. In addition, German workers get six weeks of paid vacation a year. A strange thing has happened in the United States, though. This trend toward more leisure has reversed course. U.S. workers now average over 1,800 hours of work a year, as much as workers in Japan (Gornick and Heron 2006).

Teleworking. Just as the Industrial Revolution took workers from home to factory and office, so our technological revolution has allowed two million workers to leave the office and work at home (Shellenbarger 2008). Corporations save office space, and workers avoid traffic jams. Managers often fret about a loss of control over workers, and teleworking does produce mixed results. For some workers, out of sight means that it's time to goof off. Without the structure that forces them to quit at the end of the day, others go on 24/7 work binges (Johnson 2004).

Work is more than just the job a person performs. Although the paycheck is the typical motivation for taking a job, friendships at work become so significant that they affect even the self-concept. It isn't surprising that teleworkers miss the camaraderie of their office mates. Lacking face-to-face communications with co-workers and bosses, they are also deprived of nonverbal cues—the facial expressions and body language—that are so essential for our understanding one another. E-mail helps, but it isn't the same as seeing the look on Bob's and Mary's faces when they tell a joke or repeat the latest office gossip. Some teleworkers power up at coffee houses, just so they can see the faces of others (Cava 2006).

Many teleworkers find work at home to be a soulless experience. Here is what a student who read this text reported:

My husband is still working as a software engineer. His company "wired" most of their employees for home offices. So he now works from home and has a boss in another state whom he rarely sees in person. He misses his "community" at the office and often, out of the blue, will just go in for a few hours for no good reason. He's usually disappointed, though, because most everyone else works at home, and he finds few people to chat with. His company recognizes this as a big problem. It's hard to keep the team spirit, so they have tried to gently "mandate" once a week togetherness lunches. But it's not the same as everyday contact.

Teleworkers, of course, enjoy not having a boss breathing down their necks, and they revel in the ability to plan their days or even to take an afternoon off to visit the zoo when the kids don't have school. And they don't miss the traffic jams, either.

Global Capitalism and Our Future

Global capitalism has had vital effects on all of our lives, and it will continue to do so. Let's look at just one more aspect of our changing economic times.

The New Economic System and the Old Divisions of Wealth

Suppose that you own a business that manufactures widgets. You are paying your workers an average of *$20 an hour* (including their fringe benefits, vacation pay, sick pay, unemployment benefits, Social Security, and so on). Widgets similar to yours are being manufactured in Thailand, where workers are paid *$8 a day*. Those imported widgets are being sold in the same stores that feature your widgets.

How long do you think you could stay in business? Even if your workers were willing to drop their pay in half—which they aren't willing to do—you would still be undersold.

What do you do? Your choices are simple. You can continue as you are and go broke, try to find some other product to manufacture (which, if successful, will soon be made in Thailand or India or China)—or you can close up your plants here and manufacture your widgets in Thailand.

As capitalism globalizes, it is not just the products but also the cultures of the dominant capitalist nations that are exported around the world. The music of Canadian Avril Lavigne, shown here in Shanghai, China, brings not only melodies and words but also ideas and orientations to life.

What happens when oil tankers wear out? They go to Bangladesh, where they are turned into scrap. These workers, an expendable part of the global economic system that we are all a part of, are exposed to PCBs, asbestos, and other toxins. For this, they earn $1 a day.

The many changes that the globalization of capitalism is bringing include stark choices for U.S. manufacturers. These are not easy times for them. One wrong decision can destroy a generation of wealth and privilege. Despite the treachery of changing markets, however, for the most part they open for investors the opportunity for greater profits.

And for workers? One disruption after another. High insecurity with layoffs, plant closings, and the prospect of more of the same. The insecurity is especially hard-hitting on the most desperate of workers, the less-skilled and all those who live from paycheck to paycheck. No matter how hard they work, how can they compete with people overseas who work for peanuts? They suffer the wrenching adjustments that come from having their jobs pulled out from under them, looking for work and finding only jobs that pay lower wages—if that—watching their savings go down the drain, postponing their retirement, and seeing their children disillusioned about the future.

What about the wealthy? Aren't they hurt by shifting economics, too? Is it really true that with the huge global competition in manufacturing, distribution, and service, the wealthy are doing well? Aren't they, perhaps, being hurt like the workers are? As I mentioned, some rich individuals do make wrong decisions. They can get on the wrong side of investments and lose their collective shirts. In general, though, it is the workers who suffer. The wealthy continue to do just fine in our challenging economic times. How can I be so sure, you might be wondering. Take a look at Figure 14.10.

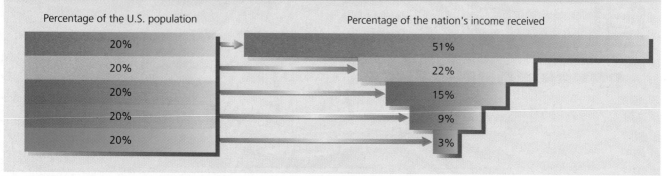

FIGURE 14.10   The Inverted Income Pyramid: The Proportion of Income Received by Each Fifth of the U.S. Population

Percentage of the U.S. population	Percentage of the nation's income received
20%	51%
20%	22%
20%	15%
20%	9%
20%	3%

Source: By the author. Based on *Statistical Abstract of the United States* 2009: Table 675.

By the Numbers: *Then and Now*

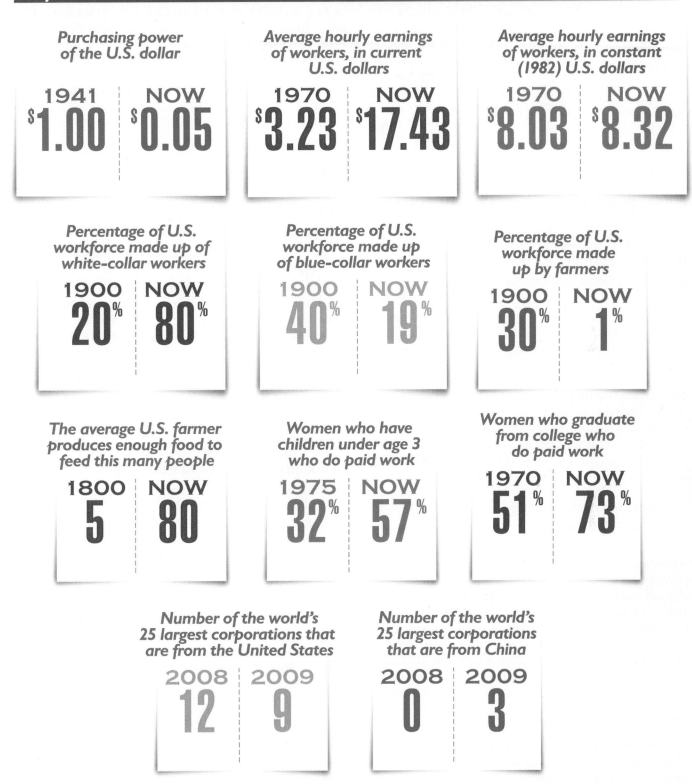

Purchasing power of the U.S. dollar

1941 | NOW
$1.00 | $0.05

Average hourly earnings of workers, in current U.S. dollars

1970 | NOW
$3.23 | $17.43

Average hourly earnings of workers, in constant (1982) U.S. dollars

1970 | NOW
$8.03 | $8.32

Percentage of U.S. workforce made up of white-collar workers

1900 | NOW
20% | 80%

Percentage of U.S. workforce made up of blue-collar workers

1900 | NOW
40% | 19%

Percentage of U.S. workforce made up by farmers

1900 | NOW
30% | 1%

The average U.S. farmer produces enough food to feed this many people

1800 | NOW
5 | 80

Women who have children under age 3 who do paid work

1975 | NOW
32% | 57%

Women who graduate from college who do paid work

1970 | NOW
51% | 73%

Number of the world's 25 largest corporations that are from the United States

2008 | 2009
12 | 9

Number of the world's 25 largest corporations that are from China

2008 | 2009
0 | 3

Each rectangle on the left of this figure represents a fifth of the U.S. population, about 60 million people. The rectangles of the inverted pyramid on the right show the percentage of the nation's income that goes to each fifth of the population. You can see that half—51 percent—of the entire country's income goes to the richest fifth of Americans. Only 3 percent goes to the poorest fifth. This gap has been growing over the years, and it now is greater than it has been in generations. Despite the vast changes forced on us by the transition to a postindustrial economy, our income inequalities have been perpetuated, even enlarged. The common folk saying that the rich are getting richer and the poor are getting poorer is certainly an apt observation, well supported by social research. What implications of this division of the nation's wealth do you see for our future?

SUMMARY *and* REVIEW

The Transformation of Economic Systems

How are economic systems linked to types of societies?

In early societies (hunting and gathering), small groups lived off the land and produced little or no surplus. Economic systems grew more complex as people discovered how to domesticate animals and grow plants (pastoral and horticultural societies), farm (agricultural societies), and manufacture (industrial societies). As people produced a *surplus,* trade developed. Trade, in turn, brought social inequality as some people accumulated more than others. Service industries dominate the postindustrial societies. If a biotech society is emerging, it is too early to know its consequences. Pp. 398–400.

The Transformation of the Medium of Exchange

How has the medium of exchange evolved?

A **medium of exchange** is any means by which people exchange goods and services. In hunting and gathering and pastoral and horticultural societies, people **bartered** goods and services. In agricultural societies, **money** came into use, and evolved into **currency,** or paper money, representing a specific amount of gold or silver on deposit. Postindustrial societies rely increasingly on electronic transfer of funds in the form of **credit cards, debit cards,** and **e-cash.** Pp. 401–403.

World Economic Systems

How do the major economic systems differ?

The world's two major economic systems are capitalism and socialism. In **capitalism,** private citizens own the means of production and pursue profits. In **socialism,** the state owns the means of production and has no goal of profit. Adherents of each have developed ideologies that defend their own systems and paint the other as harmful or even evil. As expected from **convergence theory,** each system has adopted features of the other. Pp. 403–408.

The Functionalist Perspective on the Globalization of Capitalism

How does functionalism apply to the globalization of capitalism?

From the functionalist perspective, work is a basis of social solidarity. Traditional societies have **mechanical solidarity;** people perform similar tasks and identify with one another. Industrialization brings **organic solidarity,** interdependence based on the division of labor. This process has continued to the point that we now are developing a global division of labor. **Corporations,** with their separation of ownership and management, underlie the success of capitalism. Pp. 408–411.

The Conflict Perspective on the Globalization of Capitalism

How does a conflict perspective apply to the globalization of capitalism?

Conflict theorists, who focus on power, note that global capitalism is a means by which capitalists exploit workers. From the major owners of the **multinational corporations** come an *inner circle.* While workers lose jobs to automation, the inner circle maintains its political power and profits from the new technology. The term **corporate capitalism** indicates that giant corporations dominate capitalism today. Power and wealth have become so concentrated that a **global superclass** has arisen. Pp. 411–418.

Work in U.S. Society

How has the workforce changed?

In the transition to a postindustrial society, the number of farm workers has plummeted, blue-collar work has shrunk, and most people work at service jobs. Pp. 418–420.

What is the underground economy?

The **underground economy** consists of any money-making enterprise not reported to the government, from babysitting to prostitution. The size of the underground economy runs about 10 percent of the regular economy. Pp. 420–423.

*How have patterns of work and
leisure changed?*

In hunting and gathering societies, most time was
leisure. In agricultural societies, work was dictated by
the seasons. Industrialization reduced workers' leisure,
but workers have now gained some leisure back. Americans and Japanese work more hours per week than
do the workers of any other industrialized nation.
Pp. 423–425.

Global Capitalism and Our Future

*How do the old divisions of wealth fare
in global capitalism?*

The wealthy can make mistakes that jeopardize their economic
welfare, but it is primarily the workers who face the most precarious survival during our current economic dislocations.
Global capitalism has brought more of the old inequalities,
with the wealthy getting a larger share of the economic pie
and the poorest even less than previously. Pp. 425–427.

THINKING CRITICALLY *ABOUT* Chapter 14

1. What global forces are affecting the U.S. economy? What consequences are they having? How do they affect your own life?
2. What are the major characteristics and ideologies of capitalism and socialism? What changes are taking place in these economic systems?
3. How can anyone say that the average U.S. worker hasn't gotten ahead in recent years, when the average hourly wage has jumped from $3 to $17 an hour? What implications does this have for your own future?

ADDITIONAL RESOURCES

What can you find in MySocLab? mysoclab www.mysoclab.com

- Complete Ebook
- Practice Tests and Video and Audio activities
- Mapping and Data Analysis exercises
- Sociology in the News
- Classic Readings in Sociology
- Research and Writing advice

Where Can I Read More on This Topic?

Suggested readings for this chapter are listed at the back of this book.

chapter 15

Politics

Washington, D.C.

I n 1949, George Orwell wrote *1984,* a book about a time in the future in which the government, known as "Big Brother," dominates society, dictating almost every aspect of each individual's life. Even loving someone is considered sinister—a betrayal of the supreme love and total allegiance that all citizens owe Big Brother.

Despite the danger, Winston and Julia fall in love. They delight in each other, but they must meet furtively, always with the threat of discovery hanging over their heads. When informers turn them in, interrogators separate Julia and Winston and try to destroy their affection and restore their loyalty to Big Brother.

> **Even loving someone is considered sinister—a betrayal of the supreme love and total allegiance that all citizens owe Big Brother.**

Winston's tormentor is O'Brien, who straps Winston into a chair so tightly that he can't even move his head. O'Brien explains that inflicting pain is not always enough to break a person's will, but everyone has a breaking point. There is some worst fear that will push anyone over the edge.

O'Brien tells Winston that he has discovered his worst fear. Then he sets a cage with two starving giant sewer rats on the table next to Winston. O'Brien picks up a hood connected to the door of the cage and places it over Winston's head. He then explains that when he presses the lever, the door of the cage will slide up, and the rats will shoot out like bullets and bore straight into Winston's face. Winston's eyes, the only part of his body that he can move, dart back and forth, revealing his terror. Speaking so quietly that Winston has to strain to hear him, O'Brien adds that the rats sometimes attack the eyes first, but sometimes they burrow through the cheeks and devour the tongue. When O'Brien places his hand on the lever, Winston realizes that the only way out is for someone else to take his place. But who? Then he hears his own voice screaming, "Do it to Julia! . . . Tear her face off. Strip her to the bones. Not me! Julia! Not me!"

Orwell does not describe Julia's interrogation, but when Julia and Winston see each other later, they realize that each has betrayed the other. Their love is gone. Big Brother has won.

Winston's and Julia's misplaced loyalty had made them political heretics, a danger to the state, for every citizen had the duty to place the state above all else in life. To preserve the state's dominance over the individual, their allegiance to one another had to be stripped from them. As you see, it was.

Although seldom this dramatic, politics is always about power and authority. Let's explore this topic that is so significant for our lives.

431

politics the exercise of power and attempts to maintain or to change power relations

power the ability to carry out your will, even over the resistance of others

micropolitics the exercise of power in everyday life, such as deciding who is going to do the housework or use the remote control

macropolitics the exercise of large-scale power, the government being the most common example

authority power that people consider legitimate, as rightly exercised over them; also called *legitimate power*

coercion power that people do not accept as rightly exercised over them; also called *illegitimate power*

Micropolitics and Macropolitics

The images that come to mind when we think of *politics* are associated with government: kings, queens, coups, dictatorships, people running for office, voting. These are examples of politics, but the term actually has a much broader meaning. **Politics** refers to *power relations wherever they exist,* including those in everyday life. As Weber (1922/1978) said, **power** is the ability to get your way even over the resistance of others. You can see the struggle for power all around you. When workers try to gain the favor of their bosses, they are attempting to maneuver into a stronger position. Students do the same with their teachers. Power struggles are also part of family life, such as when parents try to enforce a curfew over the protests of a reluctant daughter or son. Ever have a struggle over the remote control to the TV? All these examples illustrate attempts to gain power—and, thus, are political actions. *Every group, then, is political, for in every group there is a power struggle of some sort.* Symbolic interactionists use the term **micropolitics** to refer to the exercise of power in everyday life (Schwartz 1990).

In contrast, **macropolitics**—the focus of this chapter—refers to the exercise of power over a large group. Governments—whether dictatorships or democracies—are examples of macropolitics. Because authority is essential to macropolitics, let's begin with this topic.

Power, Authority, and Violence

To exist, every society must have a system of leadership. Some people must have power over others. As Max Weber (1913/1947) pointed out, we perceive power as either legitimate or illegitimate. *Legitimate* power is called **authority.** This is power that people accept as right. In contrast, *illegitimate* power—called **coercion**—is power that people do not accept as just.

The ultimate foundation of any political order is violence. At no time is this more starkly demonstrated than when a government takes a human life. Shown in this 1940 photo from Mississippi is a man who is about to be executed. He was convicted of killing his wife.

Imagine that you are on your way to buy the hot new cell phone that is on sale for $250. As you approach the store, a man jumps out of an alley and shoves a gun in your face. He demands your money. Frightened for your life, you hand over your $250. After filing a police report, you head back to college to take a sociology exam. You are running late, so you step on the gas. As you hit 85, you see flashing blue and red lights in your rearview mirror. Your explanation about the robbery doesn't faze the officer—or the judge who hears your case a few weeks later. She first lectures you on safety and then orders you to pay $50 in court costs plus $10 for every mile over 65. You pay the $250.

The mugger, the police officer, and the judge—all have power, and in each case you part with $250. What, then, is the difference? The difference is that the mugger has no authority. His power is *illegitimate*—he has no *right* to do what he did. In contrast, you acknowledge that the officer has the right to stop you and that the judge has the right to fine you. They have authority, or *legitimate* power.

Authority and Legitimate Violence

As sociologist Peter Berger observed, it makes little difference whether you willingly pay the fine that the judge levies against you or refuse to pay it. The court will get its money one way or another.

> There may be innumerable steps before its application [of violence], in the way of warnings and reprimands. But if all the warnings are disregarded, even in so slight a matter as paying a traffic ticket, the last thing that will happen is that a couple of cops show up at the door

with handcuffs and a Black Maria [billy club]. Even the moderately courteous cop who hands out the initial traffic ticket is likely to wear a gun—just in case. (Berger 1963)

The *government*, then, also called the **state**, claims a monopoly on legitimate force or violence. This point, made by Max Weber (1946, 1922/1978)—that the state claims both the exclusive right to use violence and the right to punish everyone else who uses violence—is crucial to our understanding of politics. If someone owes you a debt, you cannot take the money by force, much less imprison that person. The state, in contrast, can. The ultimate proof of the state's authority is that you cannot kill someone because he or she has done something that you consider absolutely horrible—but the state can. As Berger (1963) summarized this matter, *"Violence is the ultimate foundation of any political order."*

Before we explore the origins of the modern state, let's first look at a situation in which the state loses legitimacy.

The Collapse of Authority.   Sometimes the state oppresses its people, and they resist their government just as they do a mugger. The people cooperate reluctantly—with a smile if that is what is required—while they eye the gun in the hand of the government's representatives. But, as they do with a mugger, when they get the chance, they take up arms to free themselves. **Revolution,** armed resistance with the intent to overthrow and replace a government, is not only a people's rejection of a government's claim to rule over them but also their rejection of its monopoly on violence. In a revolution, people assert that right for themselves. If successful, they establish a new state in which they claim the right to monopolize violence.

What some see as coercion, however, others see as authority. Consequently, while some people are ready to take up arms against a government, others remain loyal to it, willingly defend it, and perhaps even die for it. *The more that its power is seen as legitimate, then, the more stable a government is.*

But just why do people accept power as legitimate? Max Weber (1922/1978) identified three sources of authority: traditional, rational–legal, and charismatic. Let's examine each.

Traditional Authority

Throughout history, the most common basis for authority has been tradition. **Traditional authority,** which is based on custom, is the hallmark of tribal groups. In these societies, custom dictates basic relationships. For example, birth into a particular family makes an individual the chief, king, or queen. As far as members of that society are concerned, this is the right way to determine who shall rule because "We've always done it this way."

Gender relations often open a window on traditional authority. For example, as shown in the photo to the right, in the villages around the Mediterranean, widows were expected to wear only black until they remarried. This generally meant that they wore black for the rest of their lives. By law, a widow was free to wear any color she wanted to, but custom dictated otherwise. Tradition was so strong that if a widow violated this dress code by wearing a color other than black, she was perceived as having profaned the memory of her deceased husband and was ostracized by the community.

When a traditional society industrializes, its transformation undermines traditional authority. Social change brings with it new experiences. This opens up new perspectives on life, and no longer does traditional authority go unchallenged. In some villages of Italy, for example, you can still see old women dressed in black from head to toe—and you immediately know their marital status. Younger widows, however, are likely to be indistinguishable from other women.

For centuries, widows in Mediterranean countries, such as this widow in Italy, were expected to dress in black and to mourn for their husbands the rest of their lives. Widows conformed to this expression of lifetime sorrow not because of law, but because of custom. As industrialization erodes traditional authority, fewer widows follow this practice.

state a political entity that claims monopoly on the use of violence in some particular territory; commonly known as a country

revolution armed resistance designed to overthrow and replace a government

traditional authority authority based on custom

rational–legal authority
authority based on law or written rules and regulations; also called *bureaucratic authority*

charismatic authority
authority based on an individual's outstanding traits, which attract followers

Although traditional authority declines with industrialization, it never dies out. Even though we live in a postindustrial society, parents continue to exercise authority over their children *because* parents always have had such authority. From generations past, we inherit the idea that parents should discipline their children, choose their children's doctors and schools, and teach their children religion and morality.

Rational–Legal Authority

The second type of authority, **rational–legal authority,** is based not on custom but on written rules. *Rational* means reasonable, and *legal* means part of law. Thus *rational–legal* refers to matters that have been agreed to by reasonable people and written into law (or regulations of some sort). The matters that are agreed to may be as broad as a constitution that specifies the rights of all members of a society or as narrow as a contract between two individuals. Because bureaucracies are based on written rules, rational–legal authority is sometimes called *bureaucratic authority.*

Rational–legal authority comes from the *position* that someone holds, not from the person who holds that position. In the United States, for example, the president's authority comes from the legal power assigned to that office, as specified in a written constitution, not from custom or the individual's personal characteristics. In rational–legal authority, everyone—no matter how high the office held—is subject to the organization's written rules. In governments based on traditional authority, the ruler's word may be law; but in those based on rational–legal authority, the ruler's word is subject to the law.

Charismatic Authority

A few centuries back, in 1429, the English controlled large parts of France. When they prevented the coronation of a new French king, a farmer's daughter heard a voice telling her that God had a special assignment for her—that she should put on men's clothing, recruit an army, and go to war against the English. Inspired, Joan of Arc raised an army, conquered cities, and defeated the English. Later that year, her visions were fulfilled as she stood next to Charles VII while he was crowned king of France. (Bridgwater 1953)

Joan of Arc is an example of **charismatic authority,** the third type of authority Weber identified. (*Charisma* is a Greek word that means a gift freely and graciously given [Arndt and Gingrich 1957].) People are drawn to a charismatic individual because they believe that individual has been touched by God or has been endowed by nature with exceptional qualities (Lipset 1993). The armies did not follow Joan of Arc because it was the custom to do so, as in traditional authority. Nor did they risk their lives alongside her because she held a position defined by written rules, as in rational–legal authority. Instead, people followed her because they were attracted by her outstanding traits. They saw her as a messenger of God, fighting on the side of justice, and they accepted her leadership because of these appealing qualities.

The Threat Posed by Charismatic Leaders.   Kings and queens owe allegiance to tradition, and presidents to written laws. To what, however, do charismatic leaders owe allegiance? Their authority resides in their ability to attract followers, which is often based on their sense of a special mission or calling. Not tied to tradition or the regulation of law, charismatic leaders pose a threat to the established political order. Following their personal inclination, charismatic leaders can inspire followers to disregard—or even to overthrow—traditional and rational–legal authorities.

This threat does not go unnoticed, and traditional and rational–legal authorities often oppose charismatic leaders. If they are not careful, however, their opposition may arouse even more positive sentiment in favor of the charismatic leader, who might be viewed

One of the best examples of *charismatic authority* is Joan of Arc. Uncomfortable at portraying Joan of Arc wearing only a man's coat of armor, the artist had made certain she is wearing plenty of makeup, and also has added a ludicrous skirt.

as an underdog persecuted by the powerful. Occasionally the Roman Catholic Church faces such a threat, as when a priest claims miraculous powers that appear to be accompanied by amazing healings. As people flock to this individual, they bypass parish priests and the formal ecclesiastical structure. This transfer of allegiance from the organization to an individual threatens the church hierarchy. Consequently, church officials may encourage the priest to withdraw from the public eye, perhaps to a monastery, to rethink matters. This defuses the threat, reasserts rational–legal authority, and maintains the stability of the organization.

Authority as Ideal Type

Weber's classifications—traditional, rational–legal, and charismatic—represent ideal types of authority. As noted on pages 179–180, *ideal type* does not refer to what is ideal or desirable, but to a composite of characteristics found in many real-life examples. A particular leader, then, may show a combination of characteristics.

An example is John F. Kennedy, who combined rational–legal and charismatic authority. As the elected head of the U.S. government, Kennedy represented rational–legal authority. Yet his mass appeal was so great that his public speeches aroused large numbers of people to action. When in his inaugural address Kennedy said, "Ask not what your country can do for you; ask what you can do for your country," millions of Americans were touched. When Kennedy proposed a Peace Corps to help poorer countries, thousands of idealistic young people volunteered for challenging foreign service.

Charismatic and traditional authority can also overlap. The Ayatollah Khomeini of Iran, for example, was a religious leader, holding the traditional position of ayatollah. His embodiment of the Iranian people's dreams, however, as well as his austere life and devotion to principles of the Koran, gave him such mass appeal that he was also a charismatic leader. Khomeini's followers were convinced that God had chosen him, and his speeches could arouse tens of thousands of followers to action.

In rare instances, then, traditional and rational–legal leaders possess charismatic traits. This is unusual, however, and most authority is clearly one type or another.

Charismatic authorities can be of any morality, from the saintly to the most bitterly evil. Like Joan of Arc, Adolf Hitler attracted throngs of people, providing the stuff of dreams and arousing them from disillusionment to hope. This poster from the 1930s, titled *Es Lebe Deutschland* ("Long Live Germany"), illustrates the qualities of leadership that Germans of that period saw in Hitler.

The Transfer of Authority

The orderly transfer of authority from one leader to another is crucial for social stability. Under traditional authority, people know who is next in line. Under rational–legal authority, people might not know who the next leader will be, but they do know how that person will be selected. South Africa provides a remarkable example of the orderly transfer of authority under a rational–legal organization. This country had been ripped apart by decades of racial–ethnic strife, including horrible killings committed by each side. Yet, by maintaining its rational–legal authority, the country was able to transfer power peacefully from the dominant group led by President de Klerk to the minority group led by Nelson Mandela.

Charismatic authority has no rules of succession, making it less stable than either traditional or rational–legal authority. Because charismatic authority is built around a single individual, the death or incapacitation of a charismatic leader can mean a bitter struggle for succession. To avoid this, some charismatic leaders make arrangements for an orderly transition of power by appointing a successor. This step does not guarantee orderly succession, of course, for the followers may not have the same confidence in the designated heir as did the charismatic leader. A second strategy is for the charismatic leader to build an organization. As the organization develops rules or regulations, it transforms itself into a rational–legal organization. Weber used the term the **routinization of charisma** to refer to the transition of authority from a charismatic leader to either traditional or rational–legal authority.

routinization of charisma the transfer of authority from a charismatic figure to either a traditional or a rational–legal form of authority

city-state an independent city whose power radiates outward, bringing the adjacent area under its rule

monarchy a form of government headed by a king or queen

democracy a government whose authority comes from the people; the term, based on two Greek words, translates literally as "power to the people"

direct democracy a form of democracy in which the eligible voters meet together to discuss issues and make their decisions

representative democracy a form of democracy in which voters elect representatives to meet together to discuss issues and make decisions on their behalf

Types of Government

How do the various types of government—monarchies, democracies, dictatorships, and oligarchies—differ? As we compare them, let's also look at how the state arose and why the concept of citizenship was revolutionary.

Monarchies: The Rise of the State

Early societies were small and needed no extensive political system. They operated more like an extended family. As surpluses developed and societies grew larger, cities evolved—perhaps around 3500 B.C. (Fischer 1976). **City-states** then came into being, with power radiating outward from the city like a spider's web. Although the ruler of each city controlled the immediate surrounding area, the land between cities remained in dispute. Each city-state had its own **monarchy,** a king or queen whose right to rule was passed on to the monarch's children. If you drive through Spain, France, or Germany, you can still see evidence of former city-states. In the countryside, you will see only scattered villages. Farther on, your eye will be drawn to the outline of a castle on a faraway hill. As you get closer, you will see that the castle is surrounded by a city. Several miles farther, you will see another city, also dominated by a castle. Each city, with its castle, was once a center of power.

City-states often quarreled, and wars were common. The victors extended their rule, and eventually a single city-state was able to wield power over an entire region. As the size of these regions grew, the people slowly began to identify with the larger region. That is, they began to see distant inhabitants as "we" instead of "they." What we call the *state*—the political entity that claims a monopoly on the use of violence within a territory—came into being.

This classic painting by Archibald Willard, "Spirit of '76," depicts a generic scene from the War of Independence, which allowed the U.S. experiment with *democracy* to proceed. In this war, drummers and fifers actually led some charges. And young boys were some of the drummers.

Democracies: Citizenship as a Revolutionary Idea

The United States had no city-states. Each colony, however, was small and independent like a city-state. After the American Revolution, the colonies united. With the greater strength and resources that came from political unity, they conquered almost all of North America, bringing it under the power of a central government.

The government formed in this new country was called a **democracy.** (Derived from two Greek words—*demos* [common people] and *kratos* [power]—*democracy* literally means "power to the people.") Because of the bitter antagonisms associated with the revolution against the British king, the founders of the new country were distrustful of monarchies. They wanted to put political decisions into the hands of the people.

This was not the first democracy the world had seen, but such a system had been tried before only with smaller groups. Athens, a city-state of Greece, practiced democracy 2,500 years ago, with each free male above a certain age having the right to be heard and to vote. Members of some Native American tribes, such as the Iroquois, also elected their chiefs, and in some, women were able to vote and to hold the office of chief. (The Incas and Aztecs of Mexico and Central America had monarchies.)

Because of their small size, tribes and cities were able to practice **direct democracy.** That is, they were small enough for the eligible voters to meet together, express their opinions, and then vote publicly—much like a town hall meeting today. As populous and spread out as the United States was, however, direct democracy was impossible, and the founders invented **representative democracy.**

Certain citizens (at first only white male landowners) voted for men to represent them in Washington. Later, the vote was extended to men who didn't own property, to African American men, and, finally, to women. The Internet could further increase voter participation and even allow direct democracy to develop, issues explored in the Mass Media box on the next page.

Today we take the concept of citizenship for granted. What is not evident to us is that this idea had to be envisioned in the first place. There is nothing natural about citizenship; it is simply one way in which people choose to define themselves. Throughout most of human history, people were thought to *belong* to a clan, to a tribe, or even to a ruler. The idea of **citizenship**—that by virtue of birth and residence people have basic rights—is quite new to the human scene.

The concept of representative democracy based on citizenship—perhaps the greatest gift the United States has given to the world—was revolutionary. Power was to be vested in the people

Democracy (or "democratization") is a global social movement. People all over the world yearn for the freedoms that are taken for granted in the Western democracies. Shown here is a man in a remote village in Indonesia, where democracy has gained a foothold.

themselves, and government was to flow from the people. That this concept was revolutionary is generally forgotten, but its implementation meant *the reversal of traditional ideas. It made the government responsive to the people's will, not the people responsive to the government's will.* To keep the government responsive to the needs of its citizens, people were expected to express dissent. In a widely quoted statement, Thomas Jefferson observed that

> **A little rebellion now and then is a good thing. . . . It is a medicine necessary for the sound health of government. . . . God forbid that we should ever be twenty years without such a rebellion. . . . The tree of liberty must be refreshed from time to time with the blood of patriots and tyrants. (In Hellinger and Judd 1991)**

The idea of **universal citizenship**—of *everyone* having the same basic rights by virtue of being born in a country (or by immigrating and becoming a naturalized citizen)—flowered slowly, and came into practice only through fierce struggle. When the United States was founded, for example, this idea was still in its infancy. Today, it seems inconceivable to Americans that sex or race–ethnicity should be the basis for denying anyone the right to vote, hold office, make a contract, testify in court, or own property. For earlier generations of property-owning white American men, however, it seemed just as inconceivable that women, racial–ethnic minorities, and the poor should be *allowed* such rights.

Over the years, then, rights have been extended, and in the United States citizenship and its privileges now apply to all. No longer do sex, race–ethnicity, or owning property determine the right to vote, testify in court, and so on. These characteristics, however, do influence whether one votes, as we shall see in a later section on voting patterns.

Dictatorships and Oligarchies: The Seizure of Power

If an individual seizes power and then dictates his will to the people, the government is known as a **dictatorship.** If a small group seizes power, the government is called an **oligarchy.** The occasional coups in Central and South America and Africa, in which military leaders seize control of a country, are often oligarchies. Although one individual may be named president, often it is military officers, working behind the scenes, who make the decisions. If their designated president becomes uncooperative, they remove him from office and appoint another.

Monarchies, dictatorships, and oligarchies vary in the amount of control they wield over their citizens. **Totalitarianism** is almost *total* control of a people by the government. In Nazi

citizenship the concept that birth (and residence or naturalization) in a country imparts basic rights

universal citizenship the idea that everyone has the same basic rights by virtue of being born in a country (or by immigrating and becoming a naturalized citizen)

dictatorship a form of government in which an individual has seized power

oligarchy a form of government in which a small group of individuals holds power; the rule of the many by the few

totalitarianism a form of government that exerts almost total control over people

MASS MEDIA In SOCIAL LIFE

Politics and Democracy: The Promise and Threat of the Internet

"Politics is just like show business."
—Ronald Reagan

The Internet holds tremendous promise for democracy, but does it also pose a threat to democracy? Let's first consider its advantages for politics.

Politicians find the Internet to be a powerful tool. Candidates set up Web sites, state their position on issues, and send newsletters to hundreds of thousands of supporters. Through their home pages, blogs, and lists of online contacts, they also organize their supporters and raise funds for their cause.

The Internet is also a powerful tool for citizens. Blogs, online petitions, and other expressions of political sentiment don't go unnoticed. Even Chinese leaders listen to the opinions that their people express on Web sites. When officials in China were deciding whether to award a Japanese company a contract to build a bullet train between Beijing and Shanghai, there was an online outpouring of resentment against the Japanese for not atoning for their war crimes in China. Communist officials dropped Japan from consideration.

The Internet's potential for politics is so powerful that it could even transform the way we vote and pass laws. "Televoting" could even replace our representational democracy with a form of direct democracy. No longer would we have to travel to polling places in rain and snow. More people would probably vote, for they could cast their ballots from the comfort of their own living rooms and offices. For many matters, the Internet might even allow us to bypass politicians entirely. Online, we could decide issues that politicians now resolve for us.

With these potential benefits, how could the new technology pose a threat to democracy?

Under its constitutional system, the United States is remarkably stable: Power is transferred peacefully—even when someone of an unusual background wins an election. Arnold Schwarzenegger, shown here is his role in Batman and Robin, *was elected and reelected governor of California.*

Some fear that the Internet isn't safe for voting. With no poll watchers, how would threats, promises, or gifts in return for votes be detected? There is also the threat of hackers, so proficient that they even find ways to break into "secure" financial and government sites. Proponents counter with a litany of the shortcomings of other voting methods—that ballot boxes can be stuffed and that electronic voting machines can be rigged with chips to redistribute votes already cast (Duffy 2006).

Others raise a more fundamental issue: Direct democracy could become a detour around the U.S. Constitution's system of checks and balances, which was designed to safeguard us from the "tyranny of the majority." To determine from a poll that 51 percent of adults hold a certain opinion on an issue is one thing—that information can guide our leaders. But to have 51 percent of televoters determine a law is not the same as having elected representatives argue the merits of a proposal in public and then try to balance the interests of the many groups that make up their constituency.

Others counter this argument, saying that before people televote, the merits of a proposal would be debated vigorously in newspapers, on radio and television, and on the Internet itself. Voters would certainly be no less informed than they now are. As far as balancing interest groups is concerned, that would take care of itself, for people from all interest groups would participate in televoting.

For Your Consideration

Do you think that direct democracy would be superior to representative democracy? How about the issue of the "tyranny of the majority"? (This means that the interests of smaller groups—whether defined by race–ethnicity, region, or any other factor—are overwhelmed by the voting power of the majority.) How can we use the mass media and the Internet to improve government?

Sources: Diamond and Silverman 1995; Hutzler 2004; Duffy 2006; Seib and Harwood 2008.

Germany, Hitler organized a ruthless secret police force, the Gestapo, which searched for any sign of dissent. Spies even watched how moviegoers reacted to newsreels, reporting those who did not respond "appropriately" (Hippler 1987). Saddam Hussein acted just as ruthlessly toward Iraqis. The lucky ones who opposed Hussein were shot; the unlucky ones had their eyes gouged out, were bled to death, or were buried alive (Amnesty International 2005). The punishment for telling a joke about Hussein was to have your tongue cut out.

People around the world find great appeal in the freedom that is inherent in citizenship and representative democracy. Those who have no say in their government's decisions, or who face prison or even death for expressing dissent, find in these ideas the hope for a brighter future. With today's electronic communications, people no longer remain ignorant of whether they are more or less politically privileged than others. This knowledge produces pressure for greater citizen participation in government—and for governments to respond to their citizens' concerns. As electronic communications develop further, this pressure will increase.

The U.S. Political System

With this global background, let's examine the U.S. political system. We shall consider the two major political parties, compare the U.S. political system with other democratic systems, and examine voting patterns and the role of lobbyists and PACs.

Political Parties and Elections

After the founding of the United States, numerous political parties emerged. By the time of the Civil War, however, two parties dominated U.S. politics: the Democrats, who in the public mind are associated with the working class, and the Republicans, who are associated with wealthier people (Burnham 1983). In pre-elections, called *primaries,* the voters decide who will represent their party. The candidates chosen by each party then campaign, trying to appeal to the most voters. The Social Map on the next page shows how Americans align themselves with political parties.

Although the Democrats and Republicans represent somewhat different philosophical principles, each party represents slightly different slices from the center, making it difficult to distinguish a conservative Democrat from a liberal Republican. The extremes are easy to discern, however. Deeply committed Democrats support legislation that transfers income from those who are richer to those who are poorer or that controls wages, working conditions, and competition. Deeply committed Republicans, in contrast, oppose such legislation.

Those who are elected to Congress may cross party lines. That is, some Democrats vote for legislation proposed by Republicans, and vice versa. This happens because officeholders support their party's philosophy, but not necessarily its specific proposals. When it comes to a particular bill, such as raising the minimum wage, some conservative Democrats may view the measure as unfair to small employers and vote with the Republicans against the bill. At the same time, liberal Republicans—feeling that the proposal is just, or sensing a dominant sentiment in voters back home—may side with its Democratic backers.

Regardless of their differences and their public quarrels, the Democrats and Republicans represent *different slices of the center.* Although each party may ridicule the opposing party and promote different legislation—and they do fight hard battles—they both firmly support such fundamentals of U.S. political philosophy as free

The Democrats and the Republicans represent slightly different slices of the political center. Yet some candidates arouse extremes of ire and admiration, as did vice-presidential candidate Sarah Palin. Palin is shown here in her governor's office in Anchorage, Alaska. The decoration on her couch indicates one of the reasons for the emotions she aroused.

FIGURE 15.1 Which Political Party Dominates?

■ Democrat States
■ Republican States

Note: Domination by a political party does not refer to votes for president or Congress. This social map is based on the composition of the states' upper and lower houses. When different parties dominate a state's houses, the total number of legislators was used. In Nebraska, where no parties are designated, the percentage vote for president was used.

Source: By the author. Based on *Statistical Abstract of the United States* 2009:Table 395.

public education; a strong military; freedom of religion, speech, and assembly; and, of course, capitalism—especially the private ownership of property.

Third parties sometimes play a role in U.S. politics, but to gain power, they must also support these centrist themes. Any party that advocates radical change is doomed to a short life. Because most Americans consider a vote for a third party a waste, third parties do notoriously poorly at the polls. Two exceptions are the Bull Moose party, whose candidate, Theodore Roosevelt, won more votes in 1912 than Robert Taft, the Republican presidential candidate, and the United We Stand (Reform) party, founded by billionaire Ross Perot, which won 19 percent of the vote in 1992. Amidst internal bickering, the Reform Party declined rapidly, dropping to 8 percent of the presidential vote in 1996, and then off the political map (Bridgwater 1953; *Statistical Abstract* 1995:Table 437; 2009: Table 381).

Contrast with Democratic Systems in Europe

We tend to take our political system for granted and to assume that any other democracy looks like ours—even down to having two major parties. Such is not the case. To gain a comparative understanding, let's look at the European system.

Although both their system and ours are democracies, there are fundamental distinctions between the two (Lind 1995). First, elections in most of Europe are not winner-take-all. In the United States, a simple majority determines an election. For example, if a Democrat wins 51 percent of the votes cast in an electoral district, he or she takes office. The Republican candidate, who may have won 49 percent, loses everything. Most European countries, in contrast, base their elections on a system of **proportional representation;** that is, the seats in the legislature are divided according to the proportion of votes that each party receives. If one party wins 51 percent of the vote, for example, that party is awarded 51 percent of the seats; while a party with 49 percent of the votes receives 49 percent of the seats.

proportional representation an electoral system in which seats in a legislature are divided according to the proportion of votes that each political party receives

Second, proportional representation encourages minority parties, while the winner-take-all system discourages them. In a proportional representation system, if a party can get 10 percent of the voters to support its candidate, it will get 10 percent of the seats. This system encourages the formation of **noncentrist parties,** those that propose less popular ideas, such as the shutting down of nuclear power reactors. In the United States, in contrast, 10 percent of the votes means 0 seats. So does 49 percent of the votes. This pushes parties to the center: If a party is to have any chance of "taking it all," it must strive to obtain broad support. For this reason, the United States has **centrist parties.**

The proportional representation system bestows publicity and power on noncentrist parties. Winning a few seats in the national legislature allows even a tiny party to gain access to the media throughout the year, which helps keep its issues alive. Small parties also gain power beyond their numbers. Because votes are fragmented among the many parties that compete in elections, seldom does a single party gain a majority of the seats in the legislature. To muster the required votes, the party with the most seats must form a **coalition government** by aligning itself with one or more of the smaller parties. A party with only 10 or 15 percent of the seats, then, may be able to trade its vote on some issues for the larger party's support on others. Because coalitions often fall apart, these governments tend to be less stable than that of the United States. Italy, for example, has had 62 different governments since World War II (some lasting as little as two weeks, none longer than four years) (Fisher and Provoledo 2008). During this same period, the United States has had twelve presidents. Seeing the greater stability of the U.S. government, the Italians have voted that three-fourths of their Senate seats will be decided on the winner-take-all system (Katz 2006).

noncentrist party a political party that represents less popular ideas

centrist party a political party that represents the center of political opinion

coalition government a government formed by two or more political parties working together to obtain a ruling majority

Voting Patterns

Year after year, Americans show consistent voting patterns. From Table 15.1 on the next page, you can see that the percentage of people who vote increases with age. This table also shows how significant race–ethnicity is. Non-Hispanic whites are more likely to vote than are African Americans, although when Barack Obama ran for president in 2008, their totals were almost identical. Latinos and Asian Americans are less likely to vote than are Whites and African Americans. A crucial aspect of the socialization of newcomers to the United States is to learn the U.S. political system, the topic of the Cultural Diversity box on page 443.

From Table 15.1, you can see how voting increases with education—that college graduates are almost twice as likely to vote as are high school graduates. You can also see how much more likely the employed are to vote. And look at how powerful income is in determining voting. At each higher income level, people are more likely to vote. Finally, note that women are more likely than men to vote.

Social Integration. How can we explain the voting patterns shown in Table 15.1? It is useful to look at the extremes. You can see that those who are most likely to vote are the older, more educated, affluent, and employed. Those who are least likely to vote are the younger, less educated, poor, and unemployed. From these extremes, we can draw this principle: The more that people feel they have a stake in the political system, the more likely they are to vote. They have more to protect, and they feel that voting can make a difference. In effect, people who have been rewarded more by the political and economic system feel more socially integrated. They vote because they perceive that elections make a difference in their lives, including the type of society in which they and their children live.

Alienation and Apathy. In contrast, those who gain less from the system—in terms of education, income, and jobs—are more likely to feel alienated from politics. Perceiving themselves as outsiders, many feel hostile toward the government.

From *The Wall Street Journal*, permission Cartoon Features Syndicate.

TABLE 15.1   Who Votes for President?

	1988	1992	1996	2000	2004	2008
Overall						
Americans Who Voted	57%	61%	54%	55%	58%	64%
Age						
18–20	33%	39%	31%	28%	41%	44%
21–24	46%	46%	33%	35%	43%	52%
25–34	48%	53%	43%	44%	47%	57%
35–44	61%	64%	55%	55%	57%	63%
45–64	68%	70%	64%	64%	67%	69%
65 and older	69%	70%	67%	68%	69%	70%
Sex						
Male	56%	60%	53%	53%	62%	61%
Female	58%	62%	56%	56%	65%	66%
Race–Ethnicity						
Whites	64%	70%	61%	62%	67%	66%
African Americans	55%	59%	53%	57%	60%	65%
Asian Americans	NA	54%	46%	44%	45%	48%
Latinos	48%	52%	44%	55%	47%	50%
Education						
High school dropouts	41%	41%	34%	34%	40%	39%
High school graduates	55%	58%	49%	49%	56%	55%
College dropouts	65%	69%	61%	60%	69%	68%
College graduates	78%	81%	73%	72%	74%	79%
Marital Status						
Married	NA	NA	66%	67%	71%	70%
Divorced	NA	NA	50%	53%	58%	59%
Labor Force						
Employed	58%	64%	55%	56%	60%	66%
Unemployed	39%	46%	37%	35%	46%	55%
Income[1]						
Under $20,000	NA	NA	NA	NA	48%	53%
$20,000 to $30,000	NA	NA	NA	NA	58%	59%
$30,000 to $40,000	NA	NA	NA	NA	62%	63%
$40,000 to $50,000	NA	NA	NA	NA	69%	66%
$50,000 to $75,000	NA	NA	NA	NA	72%	71%
$75,000 to $100,000	NA	NA	NA	NA	78%	76%
Over $100,000	NA	NA	NA	NA	81%	80%

[1]The primary source used different income categories for 2004, making the data from earlier presidential election years incompatible.

Sources: By the author. Data on marital status are from Casper and Bass 1998, Jamieson et al. 2002, and Holder 2006. Data on income are from Holder 2006. The other data are from U.S. Census Bureau, Current Population Survey; *Statistical Abstract of the United States* 1991:Table 450; 1997:Table 462; 2009:Table 400; Lopez and Taylor 2009; McDonald 2009; Advance Release 2009. Thanks to John Paul DeWitt for reworking the advance data.

Some feel betrayed, believing that politicians have sold out to special-interest groups. They are convinced that all politicians are liars.

From Table 15.1, we see that many highly educated people with good incomes also stay away from the polls. Many people do not vote because of **voter apathy,** or indifference. Their view is that "next year will just bring more of the same, regardless of who is in office." A common attitude of those who are apathetic is "What difference will my one vote make when there are millions of voters?" Many also see little difference between the two major political parties. Alienation and apathy are so widespread that only about *half* of the nation's eligible voters cast ballots in presidential and congressional elections (*Statistical Abstract* 2009:Table 402).

voter apathy indifference and inaction on the part of individuals or groups with respect to the political process

Cultural Diversity in the United States

The Politics of Immigrants: Power, Ethnicity, and Social Class

That the United States is the land of immigrants is a truism. Every schoolchild knows that since the English Pilgrims landed on Plymouth Rock, group after group has sought relief from hardship by reaching U.S. shores. Some, such as the Irish immigrants in the late 1800s and early 1900s, left to escape brutal poverty and famine. Others, such as the Jews of czarist Russia, fled religious persecution. Some sought refuge from lands ravaged by war. Others, called entrepreneurial immigrants, came primarily for better economic opportunities. Still others were sojourners who planned to return home after a temporary stay. Some, not usually called immigrants, came in chains, held in bondage by earlier immigrants.

Today, the United States is in the midst of its second largest wave of immigration. In the largest wave, immigrants accounted for 15 percent of the U.S. population. Almost all of those immigrants in the late 1800s and early 1900s came from Europe. In our current wave, immigrants make up about 13 percent of the U.S. population, with a mix that is far more diverse: Immigration from Europe has slowed to a trickle, with twice as many of our recent immigrants coming from Asia as from Europe (*Statistical Abstract* 2009: Table 39, 43). In the past 20 years, about 20 million immigrants have settled legally in the United States, and another 12 million are here illegally (*Statistical Abstract* 2009: Tables 44, 46).

In the last century, U.S.-born Americans feared that immigrants would bring socialism or communism with them. Today's fear is that the millions of immigrants from Spanish-speaking countries threaten the primacy of the English language. Last century brought a fear that immigrants would take jobs away from U.S.-born citizens. This fear has returned. In addition, African Americans fear a

Theses immigrants, coming through Ellis Island in New York about 1900, don't look like "Americans." But just as their clothing and hair styles will soon change to blend in with "Americans," so their orientations to life will also change.

loss of political power as immigrants from Mexico and Central and South America swell the Latino population.

What path do immigrants take to political activity? In general, immigrants first organize as a group on the basis of *ethnicity* rather than *class*. They respond to common problems, such as discrimination and issues associated with adapting to a new way of life. This first step in political activity reaffirms their cultural identity. As sociologists Alejandro Portés and Ruben Rumbaut (1990) note, "By mobilizing the collective vote and by electing their own to office, immigrant minorities have learned the rules of the democratic game and absorbed its values in the process."

Immigrants, then, don't become "American" overnight. Instead, they begin by fighting for their own interests as an ethnic group—as Irish, Italians, and so on. As Portés and Rumbaut note, as a group gains representation somewhat proportionate to its numbers, a major change occurs: At that point, social class becomes more significant than race–ethnicity. Note that the significance of race–ethnicity in politics does not disappear, but that it recedes in importance.

Irish immigrants to Boston illustrate this pattern. Banding together on the basis of ethnicity, they built a power base that put the Irish in political control of Boston. As the significance of ethnicity faded, social class became prominent. Ultimately, they saw John F. Kennedy, one of their own, from the upper class, sworn in as president of the United States. Yet, being "Irish" continues to be a significant factor in Boston politics.

For Your Consideration

Try to project the path to political participation of the many millions of new U.S. immigrants. What obstacles will they have to overcome? Why do you think their path will or will not be similar to that of the earlier U.S. immigrants?

The Gender and Racial–Ethnic Gap in Voting.   Historically, men and women voted the same way, but now we have a *political gender gap*. That is, men and women are somewhat more likely to vote for different presidential candidates. As you can see from Table 15.2 below, men are more likely to favor the Republican candidate, while women are more likely to vote for the Democratic candidate. This table also illustrates the much larger racial–ethnic gap in politics. Note how few African Americans vote for a Republican presidential candidate.

As we saw in Table 15.1, voting patterns reflect life experiences, especially people's economic conditions. On average, women earn less than men, and African Americans earn less than whites. As a result, at this point in history, women and African Americans tend to look more favorably on government programs that redistribute income, and they are more likely to vote for Democrats. As you can see in Table 15.2, Asian American voters, with their higher average incomes, are an exception to this pattern. The reason could be a lesser emphasis on individualism in the Asian American subculture.

Lobbyists and Special-Interest Groups

Suppose that you are president of the United States, and you want to make milk more affordable for the poor. As you check into the matter, you find that part of the reason that prices are high is because the government is paying farmers billions of dollars a year in price supports. You propose to eliminate these subsidies.

Immediately, large numbers of people leap into action. They contact their senators and representatives and hold news conferences. Your office is flooded with calls, faxes, and e-mail.

Reuters and the Associated Press distribute pictures of farm families—their Holsteins grazing contentedly in the background—and inform readers that your harsh proposal will destroy these hard-working, healthy, happy, good Americans who are struggling to make a living. President or not, you have little chance of getting your legislation passed.

TABLE 15.2	How the Two-Party Presidential Vote Is Split					
	1988	1992	1996	2000	2004	2008[1]
Women						
Democrat	50%	61%	65%	56%	53%	57%
Republican	50%	39%	35%	44%	47%	41%
Men						
Democrat	44%	55%	51%	47%	46%	45%
Republican	56%	45%	49%	53%	54%	52%
African Americans						
Democrat	92%	94%	99%	92%	90%	96%
Republican	8%	6%	1%	8%	10%	2%
Whites						
Democrat	41%	53%	54%	46%	42%	46%
Republican	59%	47%	46%	54%	58%	52%
Latinos						
Democrat	NA	NA	NA	61%	58%	66%
Republican	NA	NA	NA	39%	42%	31%
Asian Americans						
Democrat	NA	NA	NA	62%	77%	62%
Republican	NA	NA	NA	38%	23%	38%

[1]The totals are less than 100 percent because of votes for other candidates.

Sources: *Statistical Abstract of the United States* 1999:Table 464; 2002:Table 372; 2009:Table 382; Gallup Poll 2008a; Advance Release 2009; McDonald 2009; Current Population Survey 2009.

What happened? The dairy industry went to work to protect its special interests. A **special-interest group** consists of people who think alike on a particular issue and who can be mobilized for political action. The dairy industry is just one of thousands of such groups that employ **lobbyists,** people who are paid to influence legislation on behalf of their clients. Special-interest groups and lobbyists have become a major force in U.S. politics. Members of Congress who want to be reelected must pay attention to them, for they represent blocs of voters who share a vital interest in the outcome of specific bills. Well financed and able to contribute huge sums, lobbyists can deliver votes to you—or to your opponent.

Some members of Congress who lose an election have a pot of gold waiting for them. So do people who have served in the White House as assistants to the president. With their influence and contacts swinging open the doors of the powerful, they are sought after as lobbyists (Revkin and Wald 2007). Some can demand $2 million a year (Shane 2004). *Half* of the top one hundred White House officials go to work for or advise the same companies they regulated while they worked for the president (Ismail 2003).

With the news media publicizing how special-interest groups influence legislation, Congress felt pressured to pass a law to limit the amount of money that any individual or organization can donate to a candidate. This law also requires that all contributions over $500 be made public. The politicians didn't want their bankroll cut, of course, so they immediately looked for ways to get around the law they had just passed. It didn't take long to find the loophole—which they might have built in purposely. "Handlers" solicit donations from hundreds or even thousands of donors—each contribution within the legal limit–and turn the large amount over to the candidate. Special-interest groups use the same technique. They form **political action committees (PACs)** to solicit contributions from many, and then use that large amount to influence legislation.

PACs are powerful, for they bankroll lobbyists and legislators. To influence politics, about 4,000 PACs shell out about $150 million a year to their candidates (*Statistical Abstract* 2009:Tables 404, 405). PACs give money to candidates to help get them elected, and after their election give "honoraria" (gifts of money) to senators who agree to say a few words at a breakfast. A few PACs represent broad social interests such as environmental protection. Most, however, represent the financial interests of specific groups, such as the banking, dairy, defense, and oil industries.

Congress also made it illegal for former senators to lobby for two years after they leave office. How do they manage to get around this law? Even simpler. It's all in the name. They flout the law by hiring themselves out to lobbying firm as *strategic advisors.* They then lobby—excuse me—"strategically advise" their former colleagues ("It's So Much Nicer . . ." 2008).

PACs in U.S. Elections

Suppose that you want to run for the U.S. Senate. To have a chance of winning, not only do you have to shake hands around the state, be photographed hugging babies, and eat a lot of chicken dinners at local civic organizations, but you also must send out hundreds of thousands of pieces of mail to solicit votes and raise financial support. During the home stretch, your TV ads can cost hundreds of thousands of dollars a week. If you are an *average* candidate for the Senate, you will spend several million dollars on your campaign (*Statistical Abstract* 2009:Table 408).

special-interest group a group of people who support a particular issue and who can be mobilized for political action

lobbyists people who influence legislation on behalf of their clients

political action committee (PAC) an organization formed by one or more special-interest groups to solicit and spend funds for the purpose of influencing legislation

THE INTRICATE MECHANICS OF GOVERNMENT

PUBLIC ENTRANCE

LOBBYIST ENTRANCE

© '06 WILEY INK, INC.
DIST. BY UNIVERSAL PRESS SYNDICATE 9-22 WILEYINK@EARTHLINK.NET
GOCOMICS.COM

anarchy a condition of law-lessness or political disorder caused by the absence or collapse of governmental authority

pluralism the diffusion of power among many interest groups that prevents any single group from gaining control of the government

checks and balances the separation of powers among the three branches of U.S. government—legislative, executive, and judicial—so that each is able to nullify the actions of the other two, thus preventing any single branch from dominating the government

Now suppose that it is only a few weeks from the election. You are exhausted from a seemingly endless campaign, and the polls show you and your opponent neck and neck. Your war chest is empty. The representatives of a couple of PACs pay you a visit. One says that his organization will pay for a mailing, while the other offers to buy TV and radio ads. You feel somewhat favorable toward their positions anyway, and you accept. Once elected, you owe them. When legislation that affects their interests comes up for vote, their representatives call you—on your private cell phone—and tell you how they want you to vote. It would be political folly to double-cross them.

It is said that the first duty of a politician is to get elected—and the second duty is to get reelected. If you are an average senator, to finance your reelection campaign you must raise over $2,500 *every single day* of your six-year term (Maldin 2008). It is no wonder that money has been dubbed the "mother's milk of politics."

Criticism of Lobbyists and PACs.   The major criticism leveled against lobbyists and PACs is that their money, in effect, buys votes. Rather than representing the people who elected them, legislators support the special interests of groups that have the ability to help them stay in power. The PACs that have the most clout in terms of money and votes gain the ear of Congress. To politicians, the sound of money talking apparently sounds like the voice of the people.

Even if the United States were to outlaw PACs, special-interest groups would not disappear from U.S. politics. Lobbyists walked the corridors of the Senate long before PACs, and since the time of Alexander Graham Bell they have carried the unlisted numbers of members of Congress. For good or for ill, lobbyists play an essential role in the U.S. political system.

Who Rules the United States?

With lobbyists and PACs wielding such influence, just whom do U.S. senators and representatives really represent? This question has led to a lively debate among sociologists.

The Functionalist Perspective: Pluralism

Functionalists view the state as having arisen out of the basic needs of the social group. To protect themselves from oppressors, people formed a government and gave it the monopoly on violence. The risk is that the state can turn that force against its own citizens. To return to the example used earlier, states have a tendency to become muggers. Thus, people must find a balance between having no government—which would lead to **anarchy,** a condition of disorder and violence—and having a government that protects them from violence, but that also may turn against them. When functioning well, then, the state is a balanced system that protects its citizens both from one another *and* from government.

What keeps the U.S. government from turning against its citizens? Functionalists say that **pluralism,** a diffusion of power among many special-interest groups, prevents any one group from gaining control of the government and using it to oppress the people (Polsby 1959; Dahl 1961, 1982; Newman 2006). To keep the government from coming under the control of any one group, the founders of the United States set up three branches of government: the executive branch (the president), the judiciary branch (the courts), and the legislative branch (the Senate and House of Representatives). Each is sworn to uphold the Constitution, which guarantees rights to citizens, and each can nullify the actions of the other two. This system, known as **checks and balances,** was designed to ensure that no one branch of government dominates the others.

In Sum: Our pluralist society has many parts—women, men, racial–ethnic groups, farmers, factory and office workers, religious organizations, bankers, bosses, the unemployed, the retired—as well as such broad categories as the rich, middle class, and poor. No group dominates. Rather, as each group pursues its own interests, it is balanced by other groups that are pursuing theirs. To attain their goals, groups must negotiate with one another and make compromises. This minimizes conflict. Because these groups have political muscle to flex at the polls, politicians try to design policies that please as many groups as they can. This, say functionalists, makes the political system responsive to the people, and no one group rules.

power elite C. Wright Mills' term for the top people in U.S. corporations, military, and politics who make the nation's major decisions

ruling class another term for the power elite

The Conflict Perspective: The Power Elite

If you focus on the lobbyists scurrying around Washington, stress conflict theorists, you get a blurred image of superficial activities. What really counts is the big picture, not its fragments. The important question is, Who holds the power that determines the country's overarching policies? For example, who determines interest rates—and their impact on the price of our homes? Who sets policies that encourage the transfer of jobs from the United States to countries where labor costs less? And the ultimate question of power: Who is behind the decision to go to war?

Sociologist C. Wright Mills (1956) took the position that the country's most important matters are not decided by lobbyists or even by Congress. Rather, the decisions that have the greatest impact on the lives of Americans—and people across the globe—are made by a **power elite**. As depicted in Figure 15.2, the power elite consists of the top leaders of the largest corporations, the most powerful generals and admirals of the armed forces, and certain elite politicians—the president, the president's cabinet, and senior members of Congress who chair the major committees. It is they who wield power, who make the decisions that direct the country and shake the world.

Are the three groups that make up the power elite—the top business, political, and military leaders—equal in power? Mills said that they were not, but he didn't point to the president and his staff or even to the generals and admirals as the most powerful. The most powerful, he said, are the corporate leaders. Because all three segments of the power elite view capitalism as essential to the welfare of the country, Mills said that business interests take center stage in setting national policy. (Remember the incident mentioned in the previous chapter (page 416) of a U.S. president selling airplanes.)

Sociologist William Domhoff (1990, 2006) uses the term **ruling class** to refer to the power elite. He focuses on the 1 percent of Americans who belong to the super-rich, the powerful capitalist class analyzed in Chapter 10 (pages 270–272). Members of this class control our top corporations and foundations, even the boards that oversee our major universities. It is no accident, says Domhoff, that from this group come most members of the president's cabinet and the ambassadors to the most powerful countries of the world.

In Sum: Conflict theorists take the position that a *power elite,* whose connections extend to the highest centers of power, determines the economic and political conditions under which the rest of the country operates (Domhoff 1990, 1998, 2007). They say that we should not think of the power elite (or ruling class) as some secret group that meets to agree on specific matters. Rather, the group's unity springs from the members having similar backgrounds and orientations to life. All have attended prestigious private schools, belong to exclusive clubs, and are millionaires many times over. Their behavior stems not from some grand conspiracy to control the country but from a mutual interest in solving the problems that face big business.

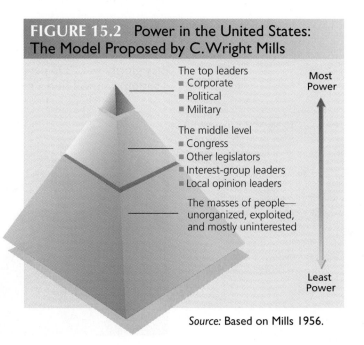

FIGURE 15.2 Power in the United States: The Model Proposed by C. Wright Mills

The top leaders
- Corporate
- Political
- Military

The middle level
- Congress
- Other legislators
- Interest-group leaders
- Local opinion leaders

The masses of people—unorganized, exploited, and mostly uninterested

Most Power

Least Power

Source: Based on Mills 1956.

Which View Is Right?

The functionalist and conflict views of power in U.S. society cannot be reconciled. Either competing interests block any single group from being dominant, as functionalists assert, or a power elite oversees the major decisions of the United States, as conflict theorists maintain. The answer may have to do with the level you look at. Perhaps at the middle level of power depicted in Figure 15.2, the competing groups do keep each other at bay, and none is able to dominate. If so, the functionalist view would apply to this level. But which level holds the key to U.S. power? Perhaps the functionalists have not looked high enough, and activities at the peak remain invisible to them. On that level, does an elite dominate? To protect its mutual interests, does a small group make the major decisions of the United States?

Sociologists passionately argue this issue, but with mixed data, we don't yet know the answer. We await further research.

War and Terrorism: Implementing Political Objectives

Some students wonder why I include war and terrorism as topics of politics. The reason is that war and terrorism are tools used to try to accomplish political goals. The Prussian military analyst Carl von Clausewitz, who entered the military at the age of twelve and rose to the rank of major-general, put it best when he said "War is merely a continuation of politics by other means."

Let's look at this aspect of politics.

Is War Universal?

war armed conflict between nations or politically distinct groups

Although human aggression and individual killing characterize all human groups, war does not. **War,** armed conflict between nations (or politically distinct groups) is simply *one option* that groups choose for dealing with disagreements, but not all societies choose this option. The Mission Indians of North America, the Arunta of Australia, the Andaman Islanders of the South Pacific, and the Inuit (Eskimos) of the Arctic, for example, had procedures to handle aggression and quarrels, but they did not have organized battles that pitted one tribe or group against another. These groups do not even have a word for war (Lesser 1968).

How Common Is War?

One of the contradictions of humanity is that people long for peace while at the same time they glorify war. "Do people really glorify war?" you might ask. If you read the history or a nation, you will find a recounting of a group's major battles—and the exploits of the he-

Few want to say that we honor war, but we do. Its centrality in the teaching of history and the honoring of the patriots who founded a country are two indications. A third is the display of past weapons in parks and museums. Shown here is an open-air museum in Kiev, Ukraine, where the instruments of war have become children's toys.

roes of those battles. And if you look around a country, you are likely to see monuments to generals, patriots, and battles scattered throughout the land. From May Day parades in Moscow's Red Square to the Fourth of July celebrations in the United States and the Cinco de Mayo victory marches in Mexico, war and revolution are interwoven into the fabric of national life.

War is so common that a cynic might say it is the normal state of society. Sociologist Pitirim Sorokin (1937–1941) counted the wars in Europe from 500 B.C. to A.D. 1925. He documented 967 wars, an average of one war every two to three years. Counting years or parts of a year in which a country was at war, at 28 percent Germany had the lowest record of warfare. Spain's 67 percent gave it the dubious distinction of being the most war-prone. Sorokin found that Russia, the land of his birth, had experienced only one peaceful quarter-century during the entire previous thousand years. Since the time of William the Conqueror, who took power in 1066, England had been at war an average of 56 out of each 100 years. It is worth noting the history of the United States in this regard: Since 1850, it has intervened militarily around the world about 160 times, an average of *once a year* (Kohn 1988; current events).

Why Nations Go to War

Why do nations choose war as a means to handle disputes? Sociologists answer this question not by focusing on factors *within* humans, such as aggressive impulses, but by looking for *social* causes—conditions in society that encourage or discourage combat between nations.

Sociologist Nicholas Timasheff (1965) identified three essential conditions of war. The first is an antagonistic situation in which two or more states confront incompatible objectives. For example, each may want the same land or resources. The second is a cultural tradition of war. Because their nation has fought wars in the past, the leaders of a group see war as an option for dealing with serious disputes with other nations. The third is a "fuel" that heats the antagonistic situation to a boiling point, so that politicians cross the line from thinking about war to actually waging it.

Timasheff identified seven such "fuels." He found that war is likely if a country's leaders see the antagonistic situation as an opportunity to achieve one or more of these objectives:

1. *Revenge:* settling "old scores" from earlier conflicts
2. *Power:* dominating a weaker nation
3. *Prestige:* defending the nation's "honor"
4. *Unity:* uniting rival groups within their country
5. *Position:* protecting or exalting the leaders' positions
6. *Ethnicity:* bringing under their rule "our people" who are living in another country
7. *Beliefs:* forcibly converting others to religious or political beliefs

Timasheff's analysis is excellent, and you can use these three essential conditions and seven fuels to analyze any war. They will help you understand why politicians at that time chose this political action.

Costs of War

One side effect of the new technologies stressed in this text is a higher capacity to inflict death. During World War I, bombs claimed fewer than 3 of every 100,000 people in England and Germany. With World War II's more powerful airplanes and bombs, these deaths increased a hundredfold, to 300 of every 100,000 civilians (Hart 1957). Our killing capacity has increased so greatly that if a nuclear war were fought, the death rate could be 100 percent. War is also costly in terms of money. As shown in Table 15.3, the United States has spent $8 trillion on twelve of its wars.

TABLE 15.3	What U.S. Wars Cost
American Revolution	$3,434,000,000
War of 1812	$1,080,000,000
Mexican War	$1,908,000,000
Civil War	$77,591,000,000
Spanish-American War	$6,996,000,000
World War I	$636,000,000,000
World War II	$5,191,666,000,000
Korean War	$440,748,000,000
Vietnam War	$946,367,000,000
Gulf War	$95,016,000,000
Iraq War	$657,000,000,000
Afghanistan	$173,000,000,000
Total	$8,230,806,000,000

Note: These totals are in 2008 dollars. Where a range was listed, I used the mean. The 1967 dollar totals listed in *Statistical Abstract* were multiplied by 6.36, the inflation rate between 1967 and 2008. The cost of the Gulf War from the *New York Times*, given in 2002 dollars, was multiplied by its inflation figure, 1.18.

Not included are veterans' benefits, which run about $90 billion a year; interest payments on war loans; and the ongoing expenditures of the military, currently about $650 billion a year. Nor are these costs reduced by the financial benefits to the United States, such as the acquisition of California, Texas, Arizona, and New Mexico during the Mexican War.

The military costs for the numerous U.S. involvements in "small" clashes such as the Barbary Coast War of 1801–1805 and others more recently in Grenada, Panama, Somalia, Haiti, and Kosovo are not listed in the sources.

Sources: "In Perspective" 2003; Belasco 2008; Stiglitz 2008; *Statistical Abstract of the United States* 1993:Table 553; 2009:Table 485.

Despite its massive costs in lives and property, warfare remains a common way to pursue political objectives. For about seven years, the United States fought in Vietnam—at a cost of 59,000 American and about 2 million Vietnamese lives (Hellinger and Judd 1991). For nine years, the Soviet Union waged war in Afghanistan—with a death toll of about 1 million Afghans and perhaps 50,000 Soviet soldiers (Armitage 1989; Binyon 2001). An eight-year war between Iran and Iraq cost about 400,000 lives. Cuban mercenaries in Africa and South America brought an unknown number of deaths. Civil wars in Africa, Asia, and South America claimed hundreds of thousands of lives, mostly of civilians. Also unknown is the number of lives lost in fighting the Taliban in Afghanistan and in the wars with Iraq, but they, too, run into the hundreds of thousands.

The hatred and vengeance of adults becomes the children's heritage. The headband of this 4-year-old Palestinian boy reads: "Friends of Martyrs."

A Special Cost of War: Dehumanization

Proud of his techniques, the U.S. trainer was demonstrating to the South American soldiers how to torture a prisoner. As the victim screamed in anguish, the trainer was interrupted by a phone call from his wife. His students could hear him say, "A dinner and a movie sound nice. I'll see you right after work." Hanging up the phone, he then continued the lesson. (Stockwell 1989)

War exacts many costs in addition to killing people and destroying property. One of the most remarkable is its effect on morality. Exposure to brutality and killing often causes **dehumanization,** the process of reducing people to objects that do not deserve to be treated as humans. From the quote above, you can see how numb people's conscience can become, allowing them to participate in acts they would ordinarily condemn. To help understand how this occurs, read the Down-to-Earth Sociology box on the next page.

Success and Failure of Dehumanization.   Dehumanization can be remarkably effective in protecting people's mental adjustment. During World War II, surgeons, who were highly sensitive to patients' needs in ordinary medical situations, became capable of mentally denying the humanity of Jewish prisoners. By thinking of Jews as "lower people" (*untermenschen*), they were able to mutilate them just to study the results.

Dehumanization does not always insulate the self from guilt, however, and its failure to do so can bring severe consequences. During the war, while soldiers are surrounded by buddies who agree that the enemy is less than human and deserve to be brutalized, it is easier for such definitions to remain intact. After returning home, the dehumanizing definitions can break down, and many soldiers find themselves disturbed by what they did during the war. Although most eventually adjust, some cannot, such as the soldier from California who wrote this note before putting a bullet through his brain (Smith 1980):

dehumanization the act or process of reducing people to objects that do not deserve the treatment accorded humans

I can't sleep anymore. When I was in Vietnam, we came across a North Vietnamese soldier with a man, a woman, and a three- or four-year-old girl. We had to shoot them all. I can't get the little girl's face out of my mind. I hope that God will forgive me . . . I can't.

Down-to-Earth Sociology
How Can "Good" People Torture Others?

When the Nuremberg Trials revealed the crimes of the Nazis to the world, people wondered what kind of abnormal, bizarre humans could have carried out those horrific acts. The trials, however, revealed that the officials who authorized the torture and murder of Jews and the soldiers who followed those orders were ordinary, "good" people (Hughes 1962/2005). This revelation came as a shock to the world.

Prisoner at Abu Ghraib Prison, Iraq

Later, we learned that in Rwanda Hutus hacked their Tutsi neighbors to death. Some Hutu teachers even killed their Tutsi students. Similar revelations of "good" people torturing prisoners have come from all over the world—Cambodia, Iraq, Afghanistan, Mexico. We have also learned that when the torturers finish their "work," they go home to their families, where they are ordinary fathers and husbands.

Let's try to understand how "good, ordinary people" can torture prisoners and still feel good about themselves. Consider the four main characteristics of dehumanization (Bernard et al. 1971):

1. *Increased emotional distance from others.* People stop identifying with others, no longer seeing them as having qualities similar to themselves. They perceive them as "the enemy," or as objects of some sort. Sometimes they think of their opponents as less than human, or even not as people at all.
2. *Emphasis on following orders.* The individual clothes acts of brutality in patriotic language: To follow orders is "a soldier's duty." Torture is viewed as a tool that helps soldiers do their duty. People are likely to say "I don't like doing this, but I have to follow orders—and someone has to do the 'dirty work.'"
3. *Inability to resist pressures.* Ideas of morality take a back seat to fears of losing your job, losing the respect of peers, or having your integrity and loyalty questioned.
4. *A diminished sense of personal responsibility.* People come to see themselves as only small cogs in a large machine. The higher-ups who give the orders are thought to have more complete or even secret information that justifies the torture. The thinking becomes, "Those who make the decisions are responsible, for they are in a position to judge what is right and wrong. In my low place in the system, who am I to question these acts?"

Sociologist Martha Huggins (2004) interviewed Brazilian police who used torture to extract confessions. She identified a *fifth* method that torturers sometimes use: They *blame the victim.* "He was just stupid. If he had confessed in the first place, he wouldn't have been tortured." This technique removes the blame from the torturer—who is just doing a job—and places it on the victim.

A *sixth* technique of neutralization was used by U.S. government officials who authorized the torture of terrorists. Their technique of neutralization was to say that what they authorized was *not* torture. Rather, in their words, they authorized "enhanced techniques" of interrogation (Shane 2008). A fair summary of their many statements on this topic would be "What we authorized is a harsh, but necessary, method of questioning prisoners, selectively used on designated individuals, to extract information to protect Americans." In one of these approved interrogation techniques, called waterboarding, the interrogators would force a prisoner's head backward and pour water over his or her face. The gag reflex would force the prisoner to inhale water, producing an intense sensation of drowning. When the interrogators stopped pouring the water, they would ask their questions again. If they didn't get a satisfactory answer, they continued the procedure. With an outcry from humanitarian groups and some members of Congress, waterboarding was banned (Shenon 2008).

In several contexts in this book, I have emphasized how important labels are in social life. Notice how powerful they are in this situation. Calling waterboarding "not torture" means that it becomes "not torture"—for those who authorize and practice it. This protects the conscience, allowing the individuals who authorize or practice torture to retain the sense of a "good" self.

One of my students, a Vietnam veteran, who read this section, told me, "You missed the major one we used. We killed kids. Our dehumanizing technique was this saying, 'The little ones are the soldiers of tomorrow.'"

Such sentiments may be more common than we suppose—and the killers' and torturers' uniforms don't have to display swastikas.

For Your Consideration

Do you think you could torture people? Instead of just saying, "Of course not!" think about this: If "good, ordinary" people can become torturers, why not you? Aren't you a "good, ordinary" person? To answer this question properly, then, let's rephrase it: Based on what you read here, what conditions could get you to cooperate in the torture of prisoners?

terrorism the use of violence or the threat of violence to produce fear in order to attain political objectives

Terrorism

Mustafa Jabbar, in Najaf, Iraq, is proud of his first born, a baby boy, but he said, "I will put mines in the baby and blow him up." (Sengupta 2004)

How can feelings run so deep that a father would sacrifice his only son? Some groups nourish hatred, endlessly chronicling the injustices and atrocities of their archenemy. Stirred in a cauldron of bitterness, antagonism can span generations, its embers sometimes burning for centuries. The combination of perceived injustice and righteous hatred produces a desire to strike out and hurt an enemy. If a group is weaker than its enemy, however, what options does it have? Unable to meet its more powerful opponent on the battlefield, one option is **terrorism,** violence intended to create fear in order to bring about political objectives. And, yes, that can mean blowing up your only child. Stronger groups sometimes use terrorism, too, but this is "just because they can." They revel in their power and delight in seeing their opponents suffer.

Suicide terrorism, a weapon sometimes chosen by the weaker group, captures headlines around the world. Among the groups that have used suicide terrorism are the Palestinians against the Israelis and the Iraqis against U.S. troops. The suicide terrorism that has had the most profound effects on our lives is the attack on the World Trade Center and the Pentagon under the direction of Osama bin Laden. What kind of sick people become suicide terrorists? This is the topic of the Down-to-Earth Sociology box on the next page.

The suicide attacks on New York and Washington are tiny in comparison with the threat of weapons of mass destruction. If terrorists unleash biological, nuclear, or chemical weapons, the death toll could run in the millions. We've had a couple of scares. Criminal opportunists, who don't care who their customers are, have tried to smuggle enriched uranium out of Europe. Their shipment was intercepted just before it landed in terrorist hands (Sheets and Broad 2007a, b). This chilling possibility was brought home to Americans in 2001 when anthrax powder was mailed to a few select victims.

It is sometimes difficult to tell the difference between war and terrorism. This is especially so in civil wars when the opposing sides don't wear uniforms and attack civilians. Africa is embroiled in such wars. In the Down-to-Earth Sociology box on page 454, we look at one aspect of these wars, that of child soldiers.

Sowing the Seeds of Future Wars and Terrorism

Selling War Technology. Selling advanced weapons to the Least Industrialized Nations sows the seeds of future wars and terrorism. When a Least Industrialized Nation buys high-tech weapons, its neighbors get nervous, which sparks an arms race among them (Broad and Sanger 2007). Table 15.4 shows that the United States is, by far, the chief merchant of death. Russia and Great Britain place a distant second and third.

This table also shows the major customers in the business of death. Two matters are of interest. First, India, where the average annual income is only $600 and Egypt, where it is only $1,500, are some of the world's biggest spenders. Second, the huge purchase of arms by Saudi Arabia indicates that U.S. dollars spent on oil tend to return to the United States. There is, in reality, an exchange of arms for oil, with dollars the medium of exchange. As mentioned in Chapter 9 (page 256), Saudi Arabia cooperates with the United States by trying to keep oil prices down and, in return, the United States props up its dictators.

The seeds of future wars and terrorism are also sown by nuclear proliferation. Some Least Industrialized Nations, such as India, China, and North Korea, possess nuclear weapons. So does Pakistan, whose head of nuclear development

TABLE 15.4 The Business of Death	
The Top Arms Sellers	**The Top Arms Buyers**
1. $28 billion, United States	1. $19 billion, Saudi Arabia
2. $16 billion, Russia	2. $9 billion, China
3. $12 billion, Great Britain	3. $7 billion, United Arab Emirates
4. $9 billion, France	4. $6 billion, Egypt
5. $3 billion, China	5. $6 billion, India
6. $2 billion, Israel	6. $4 billion, Israel
7. $1 billion, Germany	7. $4 billion, Taiwan
8. $1 billion, Ukraine	8. $3 billion, South Korea

Note: For years 2001–2004.

Source: By the author. Based on Grimmett 2005:Tables 2F, 2I.

Down-to-Earth Sociology
Who Are the Suicide Terrorists? Testing Your Stereotypes

What does a suicide bomber look like? Iraqi police arrested this girl, who was wearing an explosives vest.

We carry a lot of untested ideas around in our heads, and we use those ideas to make sense out of our experiences. When something happens, we place the event into a mental file of "similar events," which gives us a way of interpreting it. This is a normal process, and all of us do it all the time. Without stereotypes—ideas of what people, things, and events are like—we could not get through everyday life.

As we traverse society, our files of "similar people" and "similar events" usually provide adequate interpretations. That is, the explanations we get from our interpreting process usually satisfy our "need to understand." Sometimes, however, our files for classifying people and events leave us perplexed, not knowing what to make of things. For most of us, terrorism is like this. We don't know any terrorists or suicide bombers, so it is hard to imagine someone becoming one.

Let's see if we can flesh out those mental files a bit. Sociologist Marc Sageman (2008a, 2008b) wondered about terrorists, too. Finding that his mental files were inadequate to understand them, he decided that research might provide the answer. Sageman had an unusual advantage for gaining access to data—he had been in the CIA. Through his contacts, he studied 400 al-Qaeda terrorists who had targeted the United States. He was able to examine thousands of pages of their trial records.

So let's use Sageman's research to test some common ideas. I think you'll find that the data blow away stereotypes of terrorists.

- Here's a common stereotype. Terrorists come from backgrounds of poverty. Cunning leaders take advantage of their frustration and direct it toward striking out at an enemy. Not true. Three-quarters of the terrorists came from the middle and upper classes.
- How about this image, then—the deranged loner? We carry around images like this concerning serial and mass murderers. It is a sort of catch-all stereotype that we have. These people can't get along with anyone; they stew in their loneliness and misery; and all this bubbles up in misapplied violence. You know, the workplace killer sort of image, loners "going postal." Not this one, either. Sageman found that 90 percent of the terrorists came from caring, intact families. On top of this, 73 percent were married, and most of them had children.
- Let's try another one. Terrorists are ignorant people, so those cunning leaders can manipulate them easily. We have to drop this one, too. Sageman found that 63

percent of the terrorists had gone to college. Three-quarters worked in professional and semi-professional occupations. Many were scientists, engineers, and architects.

What? Most terrorists are intelligent, educated, family-oriented, professional people? How can this be? Sageman found that these people had gone through a process of radicalization. Here was the trajectory:

1. *Moral outrage.* They became incensed about something that they felt was terribly wrong.
2. *Ideology.* They interpreted their moral outrage within a radical, militant interpretation of Islamic teachings.
3. *Shared outrage and ideology.* They found like-minded people, often on the Internet, especially in chat rooms.
4. *Group decision:* They decided that an act of terrorism was called for.

To understand terrorists, then, it is not the individual that we need to look at. We need to focus on *group dynamics*, how the group influences the individual and how the individual influences the group (as we studied in Chapter 6). In one sense, however, the image of the loner does come close. Seventy percent of these terrorists committed themselves to extreme acts while they were living away from the country where they grew up. They became homesick, sought out people like themselves, and ended up at radical mosques where they learned a militant script.

Constantly, then, sociologists seek to understand the relationship between the individual and the group. This fascinating endeavor sometimes blows away stereotypes.

For Your Consideration

1. How do you think we can reduce the process of radicalization that turns people into terrorists?
2. Sageman concludes that this process of radicalization has produced networks of homegrown, leaderless terrorists, ones that don't need al-Qaeda to direct them. He also concludes that this process will eventually wear itself out. Do you agree? Why or why not?

Down-to-Earth Sociology
Child Soldiers

A boy soldier in Liberia.

When rebels entered 12-year-old Ishmael Beah's village in Sierra Leone, they lined up the boys (Beah 2007). One of the rebels said, "We are going to initiate you by killing these people. We will show you blood and make you strong."

Before the rebels could do the killing, shots rang out and the rebels took cover. In the confusion, Ishmael escaped into the jungle. When he returned, he found his family dead and his village burned.

With no place to go and rebels attacking the villages, killing, looting, and raping, Ishmael continued to hide in the jungle. As he peered out at a village one day, he saw a rebel carrying the head of a man, which he held by the hair. With blood dripping from where the neck had been, Ishmael said that the head looked as though it were still feeling its hair being pulled.

Months later, government soldiers found Ishmael. The "rescue" meant that he had to become a soldier—on their side, of course.

Ishmael's indoctrination was short but to the point. Hatred is a strong motivator.

> "You can revenge the death of your family, and make sure that more children do not lose their parents," the lieutenant said. "The rebels cut people's heads off. They cut open pregnant women's stomachs and take the babies out and kill them. They force sons to have sex with their mothers. Such people do not deserve to live. This is why we must kill every single one of them. Think of it as destroying a great evil. It is the highest service you can perform for your country."

Along with thirty other boys, most of whom were ages 13 to 16, with two just 7 and 11, Ishmael was trained to shoot and clean an AK-47.

Banana trees served for bayonet practice. With thoughts of disemboweling evil rebels, the boys would slash at the leaves.

The things that Ishmael had seen, he did.

Killing was difficult at first, but after a while, as Ishmael says, "killing became as easy as drinking water."

The corporal thought that the boys were sloppy with their bayonets. To improve their performance, he held a contest. He chose five boys and placed them opposite five prisoners with their hands tied. He told the boys to slice the men's throats on his command. The boy whose prisoner died the quickest would win the contest.

"I stared at my prisoner," said Ishmael. "He was just another rebel who was responsible for the death of my family. The corporal gave the signal with a pistol shot, and I grabbed the man's head and sliced his throat in one fluid motion. His eyes rolled up, and he looked me straight in the eyes before they suddenly stopped in a frightful glance. I dropped him on the ground and wiped my bayonet on him. I reported to the corporal who was holding a timer. I was proclaimed the winner. The other boys clapped at my achievement."

"No longer was I running away from the war," adds Ishmael. "I was in it. I would scout for villages that had food, drugs, ammunition, and the gasoline we needed. I would report my findings to the corporal, and the entire squad would attack the village. We would kill everyone."

Ishmael was one of the lucky ones. Of the approximately 300,000 child soldiers worldwide, Ishmael is one of the few who has been rescued and given counseling at a UNICEF rehabilitation center. Ishmael has also had the remarkable turn of fate of graduating from college in the United States and becoming a permanent U.S. resident.

For Your Consideration
1. Why are there child soldiers?
2. What can be done to prevent the recruitment of child soldiers? Why don't we just pass a law that requires a minimum age to serve in the military?
3. How can child soldiers be helped? What agencies can take what action?

Based on Beah 2007; quotations are summaries.

sold blueprints for atomic bombs to North Korea, Libya, and Iran (Perry et al. 2007). As I write this, Iran and North Korea are furiously following those blueprints, trying to develop their own nuclear weapons. In the hands of terrorists or a dictator who wants to settle grudges—whether nationalistic or personal—these weapons can mean nuclear blackmail or nuclear destruction, or both.

Making Alignments and Protecting Interests.   The current alignments of the powerful nations also sow the seeds of future conflicts. The seven richest, most powerful, and most technologically advanced nations (Canada, France, Germany, Great Britain, Italy, Japan, and the United States) formed a loose alliance which they called G7 (the Group of 7). The goal was to coordinate their activities so they could perpetuate their global dominance, divide up the world's markets, and regulate global economic activity. Although Russia did not qualify for membership on the basis of wealth, power, or technology, the other nations feared Russia's nuclear arsenal and invited Russia as an observer at its annual summits. Russia became a full member in 2002, and the organization is now called G8. Because China has increased both its economic clout and its nuclear arsenal, it has been invited to be an observer—a form of trial membership.

G8, soon to be G9, may be a force for peace—if these nations can agree on how to divide up the world's markets and force weaker nations to cooperate. Dissension became apparent in 2003, however, when the United States attacked Iraq, with the support of only Great Britain and Italy from this group. On several occasions, U.S. officials have vowed that the United States will not allow Iran to become a nuclear power. If the United Nations does not act and if a course similar to that which preceded the Iraq War is followed, the United States, with the support of Great Britain, will bomb Iran's nuclear facilities. An alternative course of action is for the United States to quietly give the go-ahead to Israel to do the bombing. One way or the other, the United States will protect its interests in this oil-rich region of the world.

It does not take much imagination to foresee the implications of these current alignments: the propping up of cooperative puppet governments that support the interests of G8, the threat of violence to those that do not cooperate, and the inevitable resistance—including the use of terrorism—of various ethnic groups to the domination of these more powerful countries. With these conditions in place, the perpetuation of war and terrorism is guaranteed.

A New World Order?

War and terrorism, accompanied as they so often are by torture and dehumanization, are tools that some nations use to dominate other nations. So far, their use to dominate the globe has failed. A New World Order, however, might be ushered in, not by war, but by nations cooperating for economic reasons. Perhaps the key political event in our era is the globalization of capitalism. Why the term *political*? Because politics and economics are twins, with each setting the stage for the other.

Trends Toward Unity

As discussed in the previous chapter, the world's nations are almost frantically embracing capitalism. In this pursuit, they are forming cooperative, economic–political units. The United States, Canada, and Mexico have formed a North American Free-Trade Association (NAFTA). Eventually, all of North and South America may belong to such an organization. Ten Asian countries with a combined population of a half billion people have formed a regional trading partnership called ASEAN (Association of South East Asian Nations). Struggling for dominance is an even more encompassing group called the *World Trade Organization*. These coalitions of trading partners, along with the Internet, are making national borders increasingly insignificant.

The European Union (EU) may indicate a unified future. Transcending their national boundaries, twenty-seven European countries (with a combined population of 450 million) formed this economic and political unit. These nations have adopted a single, cross-national

All governments—all the time—use propaganda to influence public opinion. During times of war, the propaganda becomes more obvious. Note how ugly Hitler and Tojo are depicted on the World War II poster from the United States—and this is just an ad to prevent forest fires! In the other poster, the Italian government exposes what Americans are "really" like—in case any Italians are going soft.

currency, the Euro, which has replaced their marks, francs, liras, lats, and pesetas. The EU has also established a military staff in Brussels, Belgium (Mardell 2007).

Could this process continue until there is just one state or empire that envelops the earth? It is possible. The United Nations is striving to become the legislative body of the world, wanting its decisions to supersede those of any individual nation. The UN operates a World Court (formally titled the International Court of Justice). It also has a rudimentary army and has sent "peacekeeping" troops to several nations.

Strains in the Global System

Although the globalization of capitalism and its encompassing trade organizations could lead to a single world government, the strains in the developing global system are so great that they threaten to rip the system apart. As noted in Chapter 9, it certainly isn't easy to maintain global stratification. Unresolved items constantly rear up, demanding realignments of the current arrangements of power. Although these pressures are resolved on a short-term basis, over time their accumulative weight leads to a gradual shift in global stratification.

If we take a broad historical view, we see that groups and cultures can dominate only so long. They always come to an end, to be replaced by another group or culture. The process of decline is usually slow and can last hundreds of years (Toynbee 1946), but in our speeded-up existence, the future looms into the present at a furious rate. If the events of the past century indicate the future, the decline of U.S. dominance—like that of Great Britain—will come fairly quickly, although certainly not without resistance and bloodshed. What the new political arrangements of world power will look like is anyone's guess, although there are indications that point to the ascendancy of China. Certainly the political arrangements of the present will give way, creating a new world for future generations.

Building upon what we know about political power, we can be certain that whatever the particular shape of future stratification, a political elite will be directing it, using its resources to bolster its position, making alliances across international boundaries designed to continue its dominance. Perhaps this process as it is currently unfolding will lead to a one-world government. Only time will tell. In the meantime, a major blockage to global unity is national patriotism and ethnic loyalties, a topic explored in the following Thinking Critically section, which closes this chapter.

ThinkingCRITICALLY

Nationalism and Ethnic Loyalties: Roadblocks to the New World Order

Nation or state? What's the difference? The world has about 5,000 *nations,* people who share a language, culture, territory, and political organization. A *state* is another name for "country." Claiming a monopoly on violence over a territory, a state may contain many nations. The Cataluns are one of the nations within the state called Spain. The Chippewa and Sioux are two nations within the state called the United States. The world's 5,000 nations have existed for hundreds, some even for thousands, of years. In contrast, most of the world's states have been around only since World War II.

The nations that exist within states usually ended up there through conquest, leaving a bitter harvest of resentment. Nation identity, much more personal and intense, usually trumps state identity. The Palestinians who live within Israel's borders, for example, do not identify themselves as Israelis. The Oromos in Ethiopia, who have more members than do three-quarters of the states in the United Nations, do not think of themselves as Ethiopians. The 22 million Kurds don't consider themselves first and foremost to be Iranians, Iraqis, Syrians, or Turks.

That nations are squeezed into states with which they don't identify is the nub of the problem. Nigeria has about 450 nations, India 350, Brazil 180, the former USSR 130, and Ethiopia 90. Most states are controlled by a power elite that operates by a simple principle: Winner takes all. To keep itself in power, this elite controls foreign investment and aid, levies taxes—and buys weapons. A state obtains great wealth by confiscating the resources of the nations under its control. The specifics are endless—Native American land in North and South America, oil from the Kurds in Iraq, gold from the aborigines of Australia. When nations resist, the result is armed conflict—and sometimes genocide.

G8's attempt to establish a New World Order can be viewed as a drive to divide the world's resources on a global scale. The unexpected roadblock is the resurgence of **nationalism**—identity with and loyalty to a nation. Nationalism strikes chords of emotions so deep that people will kill—or give up their own lives. When nationalism erupts in a shooting war, the issues and animosities are understood only faintly by those who are not a party to them; but nurtured in a nation's folklore and collective memory, they remain vividly alive to the participants.

nationalism a strong identification with a nation, accompanied by the desire for that nation to be dominant

The outcome of our present arrangements is seemingly contradictory: local shooting wars alongside global coalitions. The local conflicts come as nations struggle to assert their identity and control, the coalitions as G8 tries to divide the globe into regional trading blocs. With G8's power, David is not likely to defeat Goliath this time. Yet there is a spoiler. Where David had five small stones and needed only one, some nations have discovered that terrorism is a powerful weapon. This, too, has become part of the balance of global political power.

For Your Consideration

Do you think we will have a one-world government? Why or why not? If so, when? If a nation possesses self-identity and a common history and culture, should it have the right to secede from a state?

Sources: Clay 1990; Ohmae 1995; Marcus 1996; Hechter 2000; Kaplan 2003; Zakaria 2008.

The depths of the roadblock to the New World Order were made apparent in the 2008 conflict between Georgia and South Ossetia, especially when Russia intervened militarily. Shown here is a Georgian woman crying over soldiers buried in the rubble.

By the Numbers: *Then and Now*

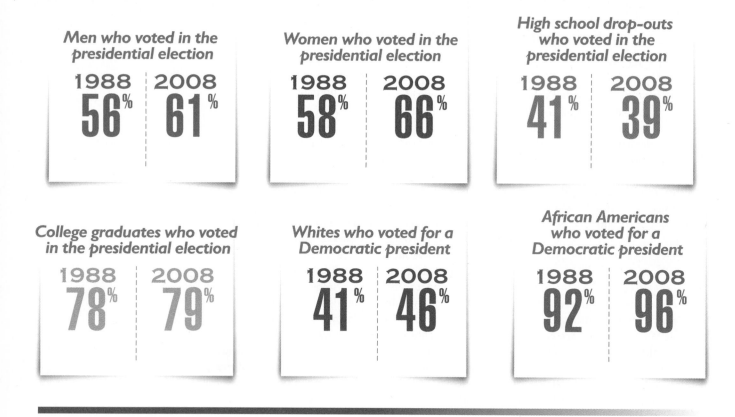

Men who voted in the presidential election		Women who voted in the presidential election		High school drop-outs who voted in the presidential election	
1988	2008	1988	2008	1988	2008
56%	61%	58%	66%	41%	39%

College graduates who voted in the presidential election		Whites who voted for a Democratic president		African Americans who voted for a Democratic president	
1988	2008	1988	2008	1988	2008
78%	79%	41%	46%	92%	96%

SUMMARY *and* REVIEW

Micropolitics and Macropolitics

What is the difference between micropolitics and macropolitics?

The essential nature of **politics** is **power,** and every group is political. The term **micropolitics** refers to the exercise of power in everyday life. **Macropolitics** refers to large-scale power, such as governing a country. P. 432.

Power, Authority, and Violence

How are authority and coercion related to power?

Authority is power that people view as legitimately exercised over them, while **coercion** is power they consider unjust. The **state** is a political entity that claims a monopoly on violence over some territory. If enough people consider a state's power illegitimate, **revolution** is possible. Pp. 432–433.

What kinds of authority are there?

Max Weber identified three types of authority. In **traditional authority,** power is derived from custom—patterns set down in the past serve as rules for the present. In **rational–legal authority** (also called *bureaucratic authority*), power is based on law and written procedures. In **charismatic authority,** power is derived from loyalty to an individual to whom people are attracted. Charismatic authority, which undermines traditional and rational–legal authority, has built-in problems in transferring authority to a new leader. Pp. 433–435.

Types of Government

How are the types of government related to power?

In a **monarchy,** power is based on hereditary rule; in a **democracy,** power is given to the ruler by citizens; in a **dictatorship,** power is seized by an individual; and in an **oligarchy,** power is seized by a small group. Pp. 436–439.

The U.S. Political System

What are the main characteristics of the U.S. political system?

The United States has a "winner take all" system, in which a simple majority determines the outcome of elections. Most European democracies, in contrast, have **proportional representation;** legislative seats are allotted according to the percentage of votes each political party receives. Pp. 439–441.

Voter turnout is higher among people who are more socially integrated—those who sense a greater stake in the outcome of elections, such as the more educated and well-to-do. **Lobbyists** and **special-interest groups,** such as **political action committees** (PACs), play a significant role in U.S. politics. Pp. 441–446.

Who Rules the United States?

Is the United States controlled by a ruling class?

In a view known as **pluralism,** functionalists say that no one group holds power, that the country's many competing interest groups balance one another. Conflict theorists, who focus on the top level of power, say that the United States is governed by a **power elite,** a **ruling class** made up of the top corporate, political, and military leaders. At this point, the matter is not settled. Pp. 446–448.

War and Terrorism: Implementing Political Objectives

How are war and terrorism related to politics—and what are their costs?

War and **terrorism** are both means of attempting to accomplish political objectives. Timasheff identified three essential conditions of war and seven fuels that ignite antagonistic situations into war. His analysis can be applied to terrorism. Because of technological advances in killing, the costs of war in terms of money spent and human lives lost have escalated. Another cost is **dehumanization,** whereby people no longer see others as worthy of human treatment. This paves the way for torture and killing. Pp. 448–455.

A New World Order?

Is humanity headed toward a world political system?

The globalization of capitalism and the trend toward regional economic and political unions may indicate that a world political system is developing. Oppositional forces are global economic crises, ethnic loyalties, and **nationalism**. Pp. 455–458.

THINKING CRITICALLY *ABOUT* Chapter 15

1. What are the three sources of authority, and how do they differ from one another?

2. What does biological terrorism have to do with politics? What does the globalization of capitalism have to do with politics?

3. Apply the findings on "Why Nations Go to War" (page 449) to a recent war that the United States has been a part of.

ADDITIONAL RESOURCES

What can you find in MySocLab? mysoclab www.mysoclab.com

- Complete Ebook
- Practice Tests and Video and Audio activities
- Mapping and Data Analysis exercises

- Sociology in the News
- Classic Readings in Sociology
- Research and Writing advice

Where Can I Read More on This Topic?

Suggested readings for this chapter are listed at the back of this book.

Chapter

Marriage and Family

London

" Hold still. We're going to be late," said Sharon as she tried to put shoes on 2-year-old Michael, who kept squirming away.

Finally succeeding with the shoes, Sharon turned to 4-year-old Brittany, who was trying to pull a brush through her hair. "It's stuck, Mom," Brittany said.

"Well, no wonder. Just how did you get gum in your hair? I don't have time for this, Brittany. We've got to leave."

> "Yes, he did," Brittany said, crossing her arms defiantly as she kicked her brother's seat.

Getting to the van fifteen minutes behind schedule, Sharon strapped the kids in, and then herself. Just as she was about to pull away, she remembered that she had not checked the fridge for messages.

"Just a minute, kids. I'll be right back."

Running into the house, she frantically searched for a note from Tom. She vaguely remembered him mumbling something about being held over at work. She grabbed the Post-It and ran back to the van.

"He's picking on me," complained Brittany when her mother climbed back in.

"Oh, shut up, Brittany. He's only 2. He can't pick on you."

"Yes, he did," Brittany said, crossing her arms defiantly as she stretched out her foot to kick her brother's seat.

"Oh, no! How did Mikey get that smudge on his face? Did you do that, Brit?"

Brittany crossed her arms again, pushing out her lips in her classic pouting pose.

As Sharon drove to the day care center, she tried to calm herself. "Only two more days of work this week, and then the weekend. Then I can catch up on housework and have a little relaxed time with the kids. And Tom can finally cut the grass and buy the groceries," she thought. "And maybe we'll even have time to make love. Boy, that's been a long time."

At a traffic light, Sharon found time to read Tom's note. "Oh, no. That's what he meant. He has to work Saturday. Well, there go those plans."

What Sharon didn't know was that her boss had also made plans for Sharon's Saturday. And that their emergency Saturday babysitter wouldn't be available. And that Michael was coming down with the flu. And that Brittany would follow next. And that . . .

polygyny a form of marriage in which men have more than one wife

polyandry a form of marriage in which women have more than one husband

family two or more people who consider themselves related by blood, marriage, or adoption

household people who occupy the same housing unit

nuclear family a family consisting of a husband, wife, and child(ren)

family of orientation the family in which a person grows up

family of procreation the family formed when a couple's first child is born

"There just isn't enough time to get everything done!" Most of us have this complaint, but it is especially true for working parents of young children. Unlike parents in the past, today's young parents find themselves without the support that used to be taken for granted: stay-at-home moms who provided stability to the neighborhood, husbands whose sole income was enough to support a wife and several children, a safe neighborhood where even small children could play outside, and grandmas who could pitch in during emergencies.

Those days are gone, most likely forever. Today, more and more families are like Sharon and Tom's. They are harried, working more but haunted by debt, and seeming to have less time for one another. In this chapter, we shall try to understand what is happening to the U.S. family and to families worldwide.

Marriage and Family in Global Perspective

To better understand U.S. patterns of marriage and family, let's first look at how customs differ around the world. This will give us a context for interpreting our own experience with this vital social institution.

What Is a Family?

"What is a family, anyway?" asked William Sayres in an article on this topic. In posing this question, he (1992) meant that although the family is so significant to humanity that it is universal—every human group in the world organizes its members in families—the world's cultures display so much variety that the term *family* is difficult to define. For example, although the Western world regards a family as a husband, wife, and children, other groups have family forms in which men have more than one wife (**polygyny**) or women more than one husband (**polyandry**). How about the obvious? Can we define the family as the approved group into which children are born? Then we would be overlooking the Banaro of New Guinea. In this group, a young woman must give birth *before* she can marry—and she *cannot* marry the father of her child (Murdock 1949).

What if we were to define the family as the unit in which parents are responsible for disciplining children and providing for their material needs? This, too, is not universal. Among the Trobriand Islanders, it is not the parents but the wife's eldest brother who is responsible for providing the children's discipline and their food (Malinowski 1927).

Such remarkable variety means that we have to settle for a broad definition. A **family** consists of people who consider themselves related by blood, marriage, or adoption. A **household,** in contrast, consists of people who occupy the same housing unit—a house, apartment, or other living quarters.

We can classify families as **nuclear** (husband, wife, and children) and **extended** (including people such as grandparents, aunts, uncles, and cousins in addition to the nuclear unit). Sociologists also refer to the **family of orientation** (the family in which an individual grows up) and the **family of procreation** (the family that is formed when a couple has its first child).

Often one of the strongest family bonds is that of mother–daughter. The young artist, an eleventh grader, wrote: "This painting expresses the way I feel about my future with my child. I want my child to be happy and I want her to love me the same way I love her. In that way we will have a good relationship so that nobody will be able to take us apart. I wanted this picture to be alive; that is why I used a lot of bright colors."

What Is Marriage?

We have the same problem here. For just about every element you might regard as essential to marriage, some group has a different custom.

Consider the sex of the bride and groom. Until recently, this was taken-for-granted. Then in the 1980s and 1990s, several European countries legalized same-sex marriages. In 2003, so did Canada, followed by several U.S. states. In 2008, California approved same-sex marriages, and a few months later banned them.

Same-sex marriages sound so new, but when Columbus landed in the Americas, some Native American tribes were already practicing same-sex marriages. Through a ceremony called the *berdache,* a man or woman who wanted to be a member of the opposite sex was officially *declared* to have his or her sex changed. The "new" man or woman put on the clothing of the opposite sex, performed the tasks associated with his or her new sex, and was allowed to marry.

Even sexual relationships don't universally characterize marriage. The Nayar of Malabar never allow a bride and groom to have sex. After a three-day celebration of the marriage, they send the groom packing—and never allow him to see his bride again (La Barre 1954). This can be a little puzzling to figure out, but it works like this: The groom is "borrowed" from another tribe for the ceremony. Although the Nayar bride can't have sex with her husband, after the marriage she can have approved lovers from her tribe. This system keeps family property intact—along matrilineal lines.

At least one thing has to be universal in marriage—that the bride and groom are alive. So you would think. But even in such a basic matter we find an exception. On the Loess Plateau in China, if a man dies without a wife, his parents look for a dead woman to be his bride. After finding one—from parents willing to sell their dead unmarried daughter— the dead man and woman are married and then buried together. Happy that their son will have intimacy in the afterlife, the parents throw a party to celebrate the marriage (Fremson 2006). This is an ancient Chinese practice, and it used to be that the couple was buried in a double coffin (Yao 2002).

With such encompassing cultural variety, we can define **marriage** this way—a group's approved mating arrangements, usually marked by a ritual of some sort (the wedding) to indicate the couple's new public status.

marriage a group's approved mating arrangements, usually marked by a ritual of some sort

Common Cultural Themes

Despite this diversity, several common themes run through marriage and family. As Table 16.1 illustrates, all societies use marriage and family to establish patterns of mate selection, descent, inheritance, and authority. Let's look at these patterns.

TABLE 16.1   Common Cultural Themes: Marriage in Traditional and Industrialized Societies

Characteristic	Traditional Societies	Industrial (and Postindustrial) Societies
What is the structure of marriage?	*Extended* (marriage embeds spouses in a large kinship network of explicit obligations)	*Nuclear* (marriage brings fewer obligations toward the spouse's relatives)
What are the functions of marriage?	Encompassing (see the six functions listed on p. 465)	More limited (many functions are fulfilled by other social institutions)
Who holds authority?	*Patriarchal* (authority is held by males)	Although some patriarchal features remain, authority is divided more equally
How many spouses at one time?	Most have one spouse (*monogamy*), while some have several (*polygamy*)	One spouse
Who selects the spouse?	Parents, usually the father, select the spouse	Individuals choose their own spouse
Where does the couple live?	Couples usually reside with the groom's family (*patrilocal residence*), less commonly with the bride's family (*matrilocal residence*)	Couples establish a new home (*neolocal residence*)
How is descent figured?	Usually figured from male ancestors (*patrilineal kinship*), less commonly from female ancestors (*matrilineal kinship*)	Figured from male and female ancestors equally (*bilineal kinship*)
How is inheritance figured?	Rigid system of rules; usually patrilineal, but can be matrilineal	Highly individualistic; usually bilineal

Source: By the author.

Mate Selection.   Each human group establishes norms to govern who marries whom. If a group has norms of **endogamy,** it specifies that its members must marry *within* their group. For example, some groups prohibit interracial marriage. In some societies, these norms are written into law, but in most cases they are informal. In the United States, most whites marry whites, and most African Americans marry African Americans—not because of any laws but because of informal norms. In contrast, norms of **exogamy** specify that people must marry *outside* their group. The best example of exogamy is the **incest taboo,** which prohibits sex and marriage among designated relatives.

As you can see from Table 16.1 on the previous page, how people find mates varies around the world, from fathers selecting them, with no input from those who are to marry, to the highly individualistic, personal choices common in Western cultures. Changes in mate selection are the focus of the Sociology and the New Technology box on the next page.

Descent.   How are you related to your father's father or to your mother's mother? The answer to this question is not the same all over the world. Each society has a **system of descent,** the way people trace kinship over generations. We use a **bilineal system,** for we think of ourselves as related to *both* our mother's and our father's sides of the family. "Doesn't everyone?" you might ask. Ours, however, is only one logical way to reckon descent. Some groups use a **patrilineal system,** tracing descent only on the father's side; they don't think of children as being related to their mother's relatives. Others follow a **matrilineal system,** tracing descent only on the mother's side, and not considering children to be related to their father's relatives. The Naxi of China, for example, don't even have a word for father (Hong 1999).

Inheritance.   Marriage and family—in whatever form is customary in a society—are also used to determine rights of inheritance. In a bilineal system, property is passed to both males and females, in a patrilineal system only to males, and in a matrilineal system (the rarest form), only to females. No system is natural. Rather, each matches a group's ideas of justice and logic.

Authority.   Historically, some form of **patriarchy,** a social system in which men dominate women, has formed a thread that runs through all societies. Contrary to what some think, there are no historical records of a true **matriarchy,** a social system in which women as a group dominate men as a group. Our marriage and family customs, then, developed within a framework of patriarchy. Although U.S. family patterns are becoming more **egalitarian,** or equal, some of today's customs still reflect their patriarchal origin. One of the most obvious examples is U.S. naming patterns. Despite some changes, the typical bride still takes the groom's last name, and children usually receive the father's last name.

Marriage and Family in Theoretical Perspective

As we have seen, human groups around the world have many forms of mate selection, ways to trace descent, and ways to view the parent's responsibility. Although these patterns are arbitrary, each group perceives its own forms of marriage and family as natural. Now let's see what pictures emerge when we view marriage and family theoretically.

The Functionalist Perspective: Functions and Dysfunctions

Functionalists stress that to survive, a society must fulfill basic functions (that is, meet its basic needs). When functionalists look at marriage and family, they examine how they are related to other parts of society, especially the ways that marriage and family contribute to the well-being of society.

endogamy the practice of marrying within one's own group

exogamy the practice of marrying outside one's own group

incest taboo the rule that prohibits sex and marriage among designated relatives

system of descent how kinship is traced over the generations

bilineal (system of descent) a system of reckoning descent that counts both the mother's and the father's side

patrilineal (system of descent) a system of reckoning descent that counts only the father's side

matrilineal (system of descent) a system of reckoning descent that counts only the mother's side

patriarchy a group in which men as a group dominate women as a group; authority is vested in males

matriarchy a society in which women as a group dominate men as a group

egalitarian authority more or less equally divided between people or groups (in marriage, for example, between husband and wife)

SOCIOLOGY and the NEW TECHNOLOGY

Finding a Mate: Not the Same as It Used to Be

Things haven't changed entirely. Boys and girls still get interested in each other at their neighborhood schools, and men and women still meet at college. Friends still serve as matchmakers and introduce friends, hoping they might click. People still meet at churches and bars, at the mall and at work.

But the Internet is bringing fundamental changes. Dating sites advertise that they offer thousands of potential companions, lovers, or spouses. For a low monthly fee, you can meet the person of your dreams.

The photos on these sites are fascinating. Some seem to be lovely people, warm, attractive, and vivacious, and one wonders why they are posting their photos and personal information online. Do they have some secret flaw that they need to do this? Others seem okay, although perhaps a bit needy. Then there are the pitiful, and one wonders whether they will ever find a mate, or even a hookup, for that matter. Some are desperate, begging for someone—anyone—to contact them: women who try for sexy poses, exposing too much flesh, suggesting the promise of at least a good time, and men who try their best to look like hulks, their muscular presence promising the same.

The Internet dating sites are not filled with losers, although there are plenty of them. Many regular, ordinary people post their profiles, too. And some do find the person of their dreams—or at least adequate

Snapshots

© Jason Love/www.CartoonStock.com

Tall, Dark, and Handsome chats with Buxom Blonde.

matches. With Internet postings losing their stigma, electronic matchmaking is becoming an acceptable way to find a mate.

Matchmaking sites tout "thousands of eligible prospects." Unfortunately, the prospects are spread over the nation, and few people want to invest in a plane ticket only to find that the "prospect" doesn't even resemble the posted photo. You can do a search for your area, but there are likely to be few candidates from it.

Not to worry. More technology to the rescue. The ease and comfort of "dating on demand." You sit at home, turn on your TV, and use your remote to search for your partner. Your local cable company has done all the hard work—hosting singles events at bars and malls, where they tape singles talking about themselves and what they are looking for in a mate (Grant 2005).

You can view the videos free. And if you get interested in someone, for just a small fee you can contact the individual.

Now all you need to do is to hire a private detective—also available online for another fee—to see if this engaging person is already married, has a dozen kids, has been sued for paternity or child support, or is a child molester or a rapist.

For Your Consideration

What is your opinion of electronic dating sites? Have you used one? Would you consider using an electronic dating site (if you were single and unattached)? Why or why not?

Why the Family Is Universal.   Although the form of marriage and family varies from one group to another, the family is universal. The reason for this, say functionalists, is that the family fulfills six needs that are basic to the survival of every society. These needs, or functions, are (1) economic production, (2) socialization of children, (3) care of the sick and aged, (4) recreation, (5) sexual control, and (6) reproduction. To make certain that these functions are performed, every human group has adopted some form of the family.

Functions of the Incest Taboo.   Functionalists note that the incest taboo helps families to avoid *role confusion*. This, in turn, facilitates the socialization of children. For example, if father–daughter incest were allowed, how should a wife treat her daughter—as a daughter, as a subservient second wife, or even as a rival? Should the daughter consider her mother as a mother, as the first wife, or as a rival? Would her father be a father or a lover? And would the wife be the husband's main wife, a secondary wife—or even the "mother of the other wife" (whatever role that might be)? And if the daughter had a child by her father, what relationships would everyone have? Maternal incest would also lead to complications every bit as confusing as these.

The incest taboo also forces people to look outside the family for marriage partners. Anthropologists theorize that *exogamy* was especially functional in tribal societies, for it forged alliances between tribes that otherwise might have killed each other off. Today, exogamy still extends both the bride's and the groom's social networks by adding and building relationships with their spouse's family and friends.

Isolation and Emotional Overload.   As you know, functionalists also analyze dysfunctions. One of those dysfunctions comes from the relative isolation of today's nuclear family. Because extended families are enmeshed in large kinship networks, their members can count on many people for material and emotional support. In nuclear families, in contrast, the stresses that come with crises such as the loss of a job—or even the routine pressures of a harried life, as depicted in our opening vignette—are spread among fewer people. This places greater strain on each family member, creating *emotional overload.* In addition, the relative isolation of the nuclear family makes it vulnerable to a "dark side"—incest and various other forms of abuse, matters that we examine later in this chapter.

The Conflict Perspective: Struggles Between Husbands and Wives

Anyone who has been married or who has seen a marriage from the inside knows that—despite a couple's best intentions—conflict is a part of marriage. Conflict inevitably arises between two people who live intimately and who share most everything in life—from their goals and checkbooks to their bedroom and children. At some point, their desires and approaches to life clash, sometimes mildly and sometimes quite harshly. Conflict among married people is so common that it is the grist of soap operas, movies, songs, and novels.

Throughout the generations, power has been a major source of conflict between wives and husbands: Husbands have had much more power, and wives have resented it. In the United States, as you know, the change has been far-reaching. Do your think that one day wives will have more power than their husbands? Maybe they already do. Look at Figure 16.1. Based on a national sample, this figure shows who makes decisions concerning the family's finances and purchases, what to do on the weekends, and even what to watch on television. As you can see, wives now have more control over the family purse and make more of these decisions than do their husbands. These findings are a surprise, and we await confirmation by future studies.

For those marriages marked by the heat of conflict or the coldness of indifference, divorce is a common solution. Divorce can mark the end of the relationship and its problems, or it can merely indicate a changed legal relationship within which the couple's problems persist as they continue to quarrel about finances and children. We will return to the topic of divorce later in this chapter.

The Symbolic Interactionist Perspective: Gender, Housework, and Child Care

Changes in Traditional Orientations.   Throughout the generations, housework and child care have been regarded as "women's work," and men have resisted getting involved. As more women began to work for wages, however, men came to feel pressure to do housework and to be more involved in the care of their children. But no man wanted to be thought of as a sissy or under the control of a woman, a sharp conflict with his culturally rooted feelings of

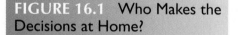

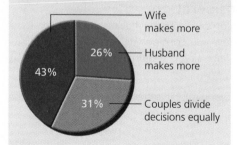

FIGURE 16.1   Who Makes the Decisions at Home?

- 43% — Wife makes more
- 26% — Husband makes more
- 31% — Couples divide decisions equally

Note: Based on a nationally representative sample, with questions on who chooses weekend activities, buys things for the home, decides what to watch on television, and manages household finances.
Source: Morin and Cohn 2008.

manhood and the reputation he wanted to maintain among his friends and family.

As women put in more hours at paid work, men gradually began to do more housework and to take on more responsibility for the care of their children. When men first began to change diapers—at least openly—it was big news. Comedians even told jokes about Mr. Mom, giving expression to common concerns about a future of feminized men. (Could Mr. Mom go to war and defend the country?)

Ever so slowly, cultural ideas changed, and housework, care of children, and paid labor came to be regarded as the responsibilities of both men and women. (And ever so gradually, women have become soldiers.) Let's examine these changing responsibilities in the family.

Who Does What?   Figure 16.2 illustrates several significant changes that have taken place in U.S. families. The first is likely to surprise you. If you look closely at this figure, you will see that not only are husbands spending more time taking care of the children but so are wives. This is fascinating: *Both* husbands and wives are spending more time in child care.

How can children be getting *more* attention from their parents than they used to? This flies in the face of our mythical past, the *Leave-It-to-Beaver* images that color our perception of the present. It also contradicts images like that in our opening vignette, of both mothers and fathers working as they struggle to support themselves and their children. We know that

In Hindu marriages, the roles of husband and wife are firmly established. Neither this woman, whom I photographed in Chittoor, India, nor her husband question whether she should carry the family wash to the village pump. Women here have done this task for millennia. As India industrializes, as happened in the West, who does the wash will be questioned—and may eventually become a source of strain in marriage.

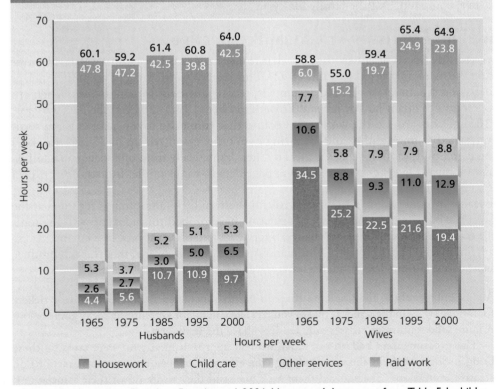

FIGURE 16.2   In Two-Paycheck Marriages, How Do Husbands and Wives Divide up Their Responsibilities?

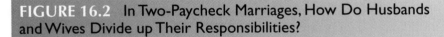

Source: By the author. Based on Bianchi et al. 2006. Housework hours are from Table 5.1, child care from Table 4.1, and work hours and total hours from Table 3.4. Other services is derived by subtracting the hours for housework, child care, and paid work from the total hours.

families are not leisurely lolling through their days as huge paychecks flow in, so if parents are spending more time with their children, just where is the time coming from?

Today's parents are squeezing out more hours for their children by spending less time on social activities and by participating less in organizations. But this accounts for only some of the time. Look again at Figure 16.2, but this time focus on the hours that husbands and wives spend doing housework. Although men are doing more housework than they used to, women are spending so much less time on housework that the total hours that husbands and wives spend on housework have dropped from 38.9 to 29.1 hours a week. This leaves a lot more time to spend with the children.

Does this mean that today's parents aren't as fussy about housework as their parents were, and today's houses are dirtier and messier? That is one possibility. Or technology could be the explanation. Perhaps microwaves, dishwashers, more efficient washing machines and clothes dryers, and wrinkle-free clothing have saved hours of drudgery, leaving home hygiene about the same as before (Bianchi et al. 2006). The time savings from the "McDonaldization" we discussed in Chapter 7, with people eating more "fast foods," are also substantial. It is likely that both explanations are true.

Finally, from Figure 16.2, you can see that husbands and wives spend their time differently. In what sociologists call a *gendered division of labor,* husbands still take the primary responsibility for earning the income and wives the primary responsibility for taking care of the house and children. You can also see that a shift is taking place in this traditional gender orientation: Wives are spending more time earning the family income, while husbands are spending more time on housework and child care. In light of these trends and with changing ideas of gender—of what is considered appropriate for husbands and wives—we can anticipate greater marital equality in the future.

The Family Life Cycle

We have seen how the forms of marriage and family vary widely, looked at marriage and family theoretically, and examined major changes in family relationships. Now let's discuss love, courtship, and the family life cycle.

Love and Courtship in Global Perspective

Until recently, social scientists thought that romantic love originated in western Europe during the medieval period (Mount 1992). This is strange, for ancient accounts, such as Genesis and 1 Samuel in the Old Testament, record stories of romantic love. When anthropologists William Jankowiak and Edward Fischer (1992) surveyed the data available on 166 societies around the world, they found that **romantic love**—people being sexually attracted to one another and idealizing each other—showed up in 88 percent (147) of these groups. Ideas of love, however, can differ dramatically from one society to another. As the Cultural Diversity box on the next page details, for example, Indians don't expect love to occur until *after* marriage.

Because love plays such a significant role in Western life—and often is regarded as the *only* proper basis for marriage—social scientists have probed this concept with the tools of the trade: experiments, questionnaires, interviews, and observations. In a fascinating experiment, psychologists Donald Dutton and Arthur Aron discovered that fear can produce romantic love (Rubin 1985). Here's what they did.

About 230 feet above the Capilano River in North Vancouver, British Columbia, a rickety footbridge sways in the wind. It makes you feel like you might fall into the rocky gorge below. A more solid footbridge crosses only ten feet above the shallow stream.

The experimenters had an attractive woman approach men who were crossing these bridges. She told them she was studying "the effects of exposure to scenic attractions on creative expression." She showed them a picture, and they wrote down their associations. The sexual imagery in their stories showed that the men on the unsteady, frightening bridge were more sexually aroused than were the men on the solid bridge. More of these men also called the young woman afterward—supposedly to get information about the study.

romantic love feelings of sexual attraction accompanied by an idealization of the other

Cultural Diversity around the World

India

East Is East and West Is West: Love and Arranged Marriage in India

After Arun Bharat Ram returned to India with a degree from the University of Michigan, his mother announced that she wanted to find him a wife. Arun would be a good catch anywhere: 27 years old, educated, well-mannered, intelligent, handsome—and, not incidentally, heir to a huge fortune.

Arun's mother already had someone in mind. Manju came from a middle-class family and was a college graduate. Arun and Manju met in a coffee shop at a luxury hotel—along with both sets of parents. He found her pretty and quiet. He liked that. She was impressed that he didn't boast about his background.

After four more meetings, including one at which the two young people met by themselves, the parents asked their children whether they were willing to marry. Neither had any major objections.

This billboard in Chennai, India, caught my attention. As the text indicates, even though India is industrializing, most of its people still follow traditional customs. This billboard is a sign of changing times.

The Prime Minister of India and fifteen hundred other guests came to the wedding.

"I didn't love him," Manju says. "But when we talked, we had a lot in common." She then adds, "But now I couldn't live without him. I've never thought of another man since I met him."

Despite India's many changes, parents still arrange about 90 percent of marriages. Unlike the past, however, today's couples have veto power over their parents' selection. Another innovation is that the prospective bride and groom are allowed to talk to each other before the wedding—unheard of a generation or two ago.

Why do Indians have arranged marriages? And why does this practice persist, even among the educated and upper classes? We can also ask why the United States has such an individualistic approach to marriage.

The answers to these questions take us to two sociological principles. First, *a group's marriage practices match its values.* Individual mate selection matches U.S. values of individuality and independence, while arranged marriages match the Indian value of children deferring to parental authority. To Indians, allowing unrestricted dating would mean entrusting important matters to inexperienced young people.

Second, *a group's marriage practices match its patterns of social stratification.* Arranged marriages in India affirm caste lines by channeling marriage within the same caste. Unchaperoned dating would encourage premarital sex, which, in turn, would break down family lines. Virginity at marriage, in contrast, assures the upper castes that they know who fathered the children. Consequently, Indians socialize their children to think that parents have superior wisdom in these matters. In the United States, where family lines are less important and caste is an alien concept, the practice of young people choosing their own dating partners mirrors the relative openness of our social class system.

These different backgrounds have produced contrasting ideas of love. Americans idealize love as something mysterious, a passion that suddenly seizes an individual. Indians view love as a peaceful feeling that develops when a man and a woman are united in intimacy and share life's interests and goals. For Americans, love just "happens," while for Indians the right conditions create love. Marriage is one of those right conditions.

The end result is this startling difference: *For Americans, love produces marriage—while for Indians, marriage produces love.*

For Your Consideration

What advantages do you see to the Indian approach to love and marriage? Could the Indian system work in the United States? Why or why not? Do you think that love can be created? Or does love suddenly "seize" people? What do you think love is anyway?

Sources: Based on Gupta 1979; Bumiller 1992; Sprecher and Chandak 1992; Dugger 1998; Gautham 2002; Easley 2003, Berger 2007; Swati and Ey 2008.

homogamy the tendency of people with similar characteristics to marry one another

You may have noticed that this research was really about sexual attraction, not love. The point, however, is that romantic love usually begins with sexual attraction. Finding ourselves sexually attracted to someone, we spend time with that person. If we discover mutual interests, we may label our feelings "love." Apparently, then, *romantic love has two components.* The first is emotional, a feeling of sexual attraction. The second is cognitive, a label that we attach to our feelings. If we attach this label, we describe ourselves as being "in love."

Marriage

In the typical case, marriage in the United States is preceded by "love," but, contrary to folklore, whatever love is, it certainly is not blind. That is, love does not hit us willy-nilly, as if Cupid had shot darts blindly into a crowd. If it did, marital patterns would be unpredictable. An examination of who marries whom, however, reveals that love is socially channeled.

The Social Channels of Love and Marriage.   The most highly predictable social channels are age, education, social class, and race–ethnicity. For example, a Latina with a college degree whose parents are both physicians is likely to fall in love with and marry a Latino slightly older than herself who has graduated from college. Similarly, a girl who drops out of high school and whose parents are on welfare is likely to fall in love with and marry a man who comes from a background similar to hers.

Sociologists use the term **homogamy** to refer to the tendency of people who have similar characteristics to marry one another. Homogamy occurs largely as a result of *propinquity,* or spatial nearness. That is, we tend to "fall in love" with and marry people who live near us or whom we meet at school, church, or work. The people with whom we associate are far from a random sample of the population, for social filters produce neighborhoods, schools, and places of worship that follow racial–ethnic and social class lines.

As with all social patterns, there are exceptions. Although 93 percent of Americans who marry choose someone of their same racial–ethnic background, 7 percent do not. Because there are 60 million married couples in the United States, those 7 percent add up, totaling over 4 million couples (*Statistical Abstract* 2009: Table 59).

One of the more dramatic changes in U.S. marriage patterns is the increase in marriages between African Americans and whites. Today it is difficult to realize how norm-shattering such marriages used to be, but they used to be illegal in 40 states (Staples 2008). Mississippi had the most extreme penalty for interracial marriage: *life in prison* (Crossen 2004b). Despite the risks, a few couples crossed the "color line," but it took the social upheaval of the 1960s to break this barrier permanently. In 1967, the U.S. Supreme Court struck down the state laws that prohibited such marriages.

Figure 16.3 illustrates this change. Look at the race–ethnicity of the husbands and wives in these marriages, and you will see that here, too, Cupid's arrows don't hit random targets. Why do you think this particular pattern exists?

Childbirth

Ideal Family Size.   The number of children that Americans consider ideal has changed over the years, with preferences moving to smaller families. Figure 16.4 shows this change, based on questions the Gallup organization has been asking since the 1930s. Religion shows an interesting divide, not between Protestants and Roman Catholics, who give the same

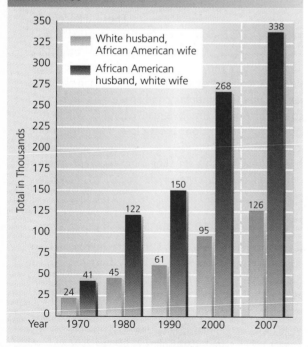

FIGURE 16.3   Marriages Between Whites and African Americans: The Race–Ethnicity of the Husbands and Wives

Legend:
- White husband, African American wife
- African American husband, white wife

Year / values:
- 1970: 24, 41
- 1980: 45, 122
- 1990: 61, 150
- 2000: 95, 268
- 2007: 126, 338

Source: By the author. *Based on Statistical Abstract of the United States* 1990: Table 53; 2009: Table 59.

FIGURE 16.4 The Number of Children Americans Think Are Ideal

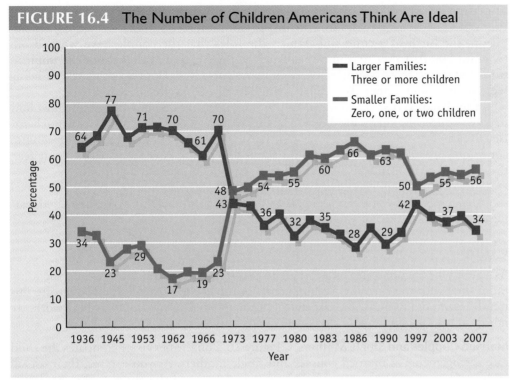

Legend:
- Larger Families: Three or more children
- Smaller Families: Zero, one, or two children

Source: Gallup Poll, June 26, 2007.

answers, but by church attendance. Those who attend services more often prefer larger families than those who attend less often. The last couple of polls have revealed a rather unexpected divide: Younger Americans (ages 18 to 34) prefer larger families than do those who are older than 34 (Gallup Poll, June 26, 2007).

Marital Satisfaction. Sociologists have found that after the birth of a child marital satisfaction usually decreases (Claxton and Perry-Jenkins 2008; Simon 2008). To

The average woman in the United States gives birth to two children. "Average" is made up of the extremes of zero children to the 18 of Michelle Duggar and her husband Jim Bob of Rogers, Arkansas. The couple is shown here after the birth of their 18th child. One child was not present when the photo was taken.

understand why, recall from Chapter 6 that a dyad (two persons) provides greater intimacy than a triad (after adding a third person, interaction must be shared). In addition, the birth of a child unbalances the roles that the couple have worked out (Knauth 2000). To move from the abstract to the concrete, think about the implications for marriage of coping with a fragile newborn's 24-hour-a-day needs of being fed, soothed, and diapered—while having less sleep and greater expenses.

Yet husbands and wives continue to have children, not because they don't know how to avoid conceiving them, but because having their own child brings them so much satisfaction. New parents bubble over with joy, saying things like, "There's no feeling to compare with holding your own child in your arms. Those little hands, those tiny feet, those big eyes, that little nose, that sweet face . . ." and they gush on and on.

This is why there really is no equivalent to parents. It is *their* child, and no one else takes such delight in a baby's first steps, its first word, and so on. Let's turn, then, to child rearing.

Child Rearing

As you saw in Figure 16.2, today's parents—both mothers and fathers—are spending more time with their children than parents did in the 1970s and 1980s. Despite this trend, with mothers and fathers spending so many hours away from home at work, we must ask: Who's minding the kids while the parents are at work?

Married Couples and Single Mothers.   Figure 16.5 on the next page compares the child care arrangements of married couples and single mothers. As you can see, their overall arrangements are similar. A main difference is the role of the child's father while the mother is at work. For married couples, about one of five children is cared for by the father, while for single mothers, care by the father drops in half to one of ten. As you can see, grandparents and other relatives help fill the gap left by the absent father. Single mothers also rely more on organized day care.

Day Care.   Figure 16.5 also shows that about one of four children is in day care. The broad conclusions of research on day care were reported in Chapter 3 (page 82). Apparently only a minority of U.S. day care centers offer high-quality care as measured by whether they provide safety, stimulating learning activities, and emotional warmth (Bergmann 1995; Blau 2000). A primary reason for this dismal situation is the low salaries paid to day care workers, who average only about $16,000 a year ("Child Day Care Services" 2009).

It is difficult for parents to judge the quality of day care, since they don't know what takes place when they are not there. If you ever look for day care, two factors best predict that children will receive quality care: staff who have taken courses in early childhood development and a low ratio of children per staff member (Blau 2000; Belsky et al. 2007). If you have nagging fears that your children might be neglected or even abused, choose a center that streams live Web cam images on the Internet. While at work, you can "visit" each room of the day care center via cyberspace and monitor your toddler's activities and care.

Nannies.   For upper-middle-class parents, nannies have become a popular alternative to day care centers. Parents love the one-on-one care. They also like the convenience of in-home care, which eliminates the need to transport the child to an unfamiliar environment, reduces the chances that the child will catch illnesses, and eliminates the hardship of parents having to take time off from work when their child becomes ill. A recurring problem, how-

"Your attitude is sucking all the fulfillment out of motherhood."

One of the most demanding, exasperating—and also fulfilling—roles in life is that of parent. To really appreciate this cartoon, perhaps one has to have experienced this part of the life course.

ever, is tensions between the parents and the nanny: jealousy that the nanny might see the first step, hear the first word, or—worse yet—be called "mommy." There are also tensions over different discipline styles; disdain on the part of the nanny that the mother isn't staying home with her child; and feelings of guilt or envy as the child cries when the nanny leaves but not when the mother goes to work.

Social Class.   Do you think that social class makes a difference in how people rear their children? If you answered "yes," you are right. But what difference? And why? Sociologists have found that working-class parents tend to think of children as wildflowers that develop naturally. Middle-class parents, in contrast, are more likely to think of children as garden flowers that need a lot of nurturing if they are to bloom (Lareau 2002). These contrasting views make a world of difference Working-class parents are more likely to set limits on their children and then let them choose their own activities, while middle-class parents are more likely to try to push their children into activities that they think will develop the children's thinking and social skills.

Sociologist Melvin Kohn (1963, 1977; Kohn and Schooler 1969) also found that the type of work that parents do has an impact on how they rear their children. Because members of the working class are closely supervised on their jobs, where they are expected to follow explicit rules, their concern is less with their children's motivation and more with their outward conformity. These parents are more apt to use physical punishment—which brings about outward conformity without regard for internal attitude. Middle-class workers, in contrast, are expected to take more initiative on the job. Consequently, middle-class parents have more concern that their children develop curiosity and self-expression. They are also more likely to withdraw privileges or affection than to use physical punishment.

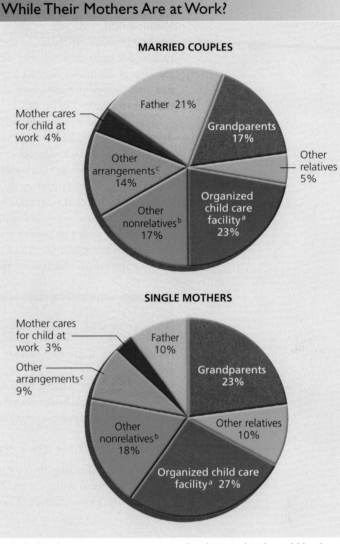

FIGURE 16.5 Who Takes Care of Preschoolers While Their Mothers Are at Work?

MARRIED COUPLES

- Father 21%
- Grandparents 17%
- Other relatives 5%
- Organized child care facility[a] 23%
- Other nonrelatives[b] 17%
- Other arrangements[c] 14%
- Mother cares for child at work 4%

SINGLE MOTHERS

- Father 10%
- Grandparents 23%
- Other relatives 10%
- Organized child care facility[a] 27%
- Other nonrelatives[b] 18%
- Other arrangements[c] 9%
- Mother cares for child at work 3%

[a] Includes day care centers, nursery schools, preschools, and Head Start programs.
[b] Includes in-home babysitters and other nonrelatives providing care in either the child's or the provider's home.
[c] Includes self-care and no regular arrangements.

*Source: America's Children 2005:*Table POP8.B.

Family Transitions

The later stages of family life bring their own pleasures to be savored and problems to be solved. Let's look at two transitions—staying home longer and adjusting to widowhood.

"Adultolescents" and the Not-So-Empty Nest.   When the last child leaves home, the husband and wife are left, as at the beginning of their marriage, "alone together." This situation, sometimes called the *empty nest*—is not as empty as it used to be. With prolonged education and the high cost of establishing a household, U.S. children are leaving home later. Many stay home during college, and others move back after college. Some (called "boomerang children") strike out on their own, but then find the cost or responsibility too great and return home. Much to their own disappointment, some even leave and return to the parents' home several times. As a result, 42 percent of all U.S. 25- to 29-year-olds are living with their parents (U.S. Census Bureau 2007a:Table A2).

Although these "adultolescents" enjoy the protection of home, they have to work out issues of remaining dependent on their parents at the same time that they are grappling with concerns and fears about establishing independent lives. For the parents, "boomerang children" mean not only a disruption of routines but also disagreements about turf, authority, and responsibilities—items they thought were long ago resolved.

Widowhood.   As you know, women are more likely than men to become widowed. There are two reasons for this: On average, women live longer than men, and they usually marry men older than they are. For either women or men, the death of a spouse tears at the self, clawing at identities that had merged through the years. With the one who had become an essential part of the self gone, the survivor, as in adolescence, once again confronts the perplexing question "Who am I?"

The death of a spouse produces what is called the *widowhood effect*. The impact of the death is so strong that it increases the chances that the surviving spouse will die earlier than expected. The "widowhood effect" is not even across the board, however, and those who have gone through anticipatory grief suffer fewer health consequences (Elwert and Christakis 2008). This is apparently because they knew their spouse was going to die, and they were able to make preparations that smoothed the transition—from arranging finances to preparing themselves psychologically for being alone (Hiltz 1989). You can see how saying goodbye and cultivating treasured last memories would help people adjust to the impending death of an intimate companion. Sudden death, in contrast, rips the loved one away, offering no chance for this predeath healing.

Diversity in U.S. Families

As we review some of the vast diversity of U.S. families, it is important to note that we are not comparing any of them to *the* American family. There is no such thing. Rather, family life varies widely throughout the United States. We have already seen in several contexts how significant social class is in our lives. Its significance will continue to be evident as we examine diversity in U.S. families.

African American Families

Note that the heading reads African American *families,* not *the* African American family. There is no such thing as *the* African American family any more than there is *the* white family or *the* Latino family. The primary distinction is not between African Americans and

There is no such thing as *the* African American family, any more than there is *the* Native American, Asian American, Latino, or Irish American family. Rather, each racial–ethnic group has different types of families, with the primary determinant being social class.

other groups, but between social classes (Willie and Reddick 2003). Because African Americans who are members of the upper class follow the class interests reviewed in Chapter 10—preservation of privilege and family fortune—they are especially concerned about the family background of those whom their children marry (Gatewood 1990). To them, marriage is viewed as a merger of family lines. Children of this class marry later than children of other classes.

Middle-class African American families focus on achievement and respectability. Both husband and wife are likely to work outside the home. A central concern is that their children go to college, get good jobs, and marry well—that is, marry people like themselves, respectable and hardworking, who want to get ahead in school and pursue a successful career.

African American families in poverty face all the problems that cluster around poverty (Wilson 1987, 1996; Anderson 1990/2006; Venkatesh 2006). Because the men are likely to have few skills and to be unemployed, it is difficult for them to fulfill the cultural roles of husband and father. Consequently, these families are likely to be headed by a woman and to have a high rate of births to single women. Divorce and desertion are also more common than among other classes. Sharing scarce resources and "stretching kinship" are primary survival mechanisms. People who have helped out in hard times are considered brothers, sisters, or cousins to whom one owes obligations as though they were blood relatives; and men who are not the biological fathers of their children are given fatherhood status (Stack 1974; Hall 2008). Sociologists use the term *fictive kin* to refer to this stretching of kinship.

From Figure 16.6 you can see that, compared with other groups, African American families are the least likely to be headed by married couples and the most likely to be headed by women. Because African American women tend to go farther in school than African American men, they are more likely than women in other racial–ethnic groups to marry men who are less educated than themselves (Eshleman 2000; Harford 2008).

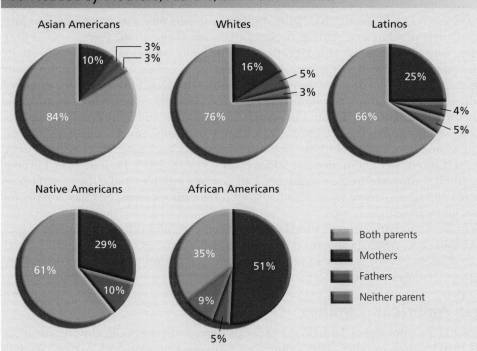

FIGURE 16.6   Family Structure: U.S. Families with Children Under Age 18 Headed by Mothers, Fathers, and Both Parents

Sources: By the author. For Native Americans, "American Community . . ." 2004. For other groups, *Statistical Abstract of the United States* 2009: Table 68.

As with other groups, there is no such thing as *the* Latino family. Some Latino families speak little or no English, while others have assimilated into U.S. culture to such an extent that they no longer speak Spanish.

Latino Families

As Figure 16.6 shows, the proportion of Latino families headed by married couples and women falls in between that of whites and Native Americans. The effects of social class on families, which I just sketched, also apply to Latinos. In addition, families differ by country of origin. Families from Mexico, for example, are more likely to be headed by a married couple than are families from Puerto Rico (*Statistical Abstract* 2009:Table 38). The longer that Latinos have lived in the United States, the more their families resemble those of middle-class Americans (Saenz 2004).

With such wide variety, experts disagree on what is distinctive about Latino families. Some researchers have found that Latino husbands-fathers play a stronger role than husbands-fathers in white and African American families (Vega 1990; Torres et al. 2002). Others point to the Spanish language, the Roman Catholic religion, and a strong family orientation coupled with a disapproval of divorce, but there are Latino families who are Protestants, don't speak Spanish, and so on. Still others emphasize loyalty to the extended family, with an obligation to support the extended family in times of need (Cauce and Domenech-Rodriguez 2002), but this, too, is hardly unique to Latino families. Descriptions of Latino families used to include **machismo**—an emphasis on male strength, sexual vigor, and dominance—but *machismo* decreases with each generation in the United States and is certainly not limited to Latinos (Hurtado et al. 1992; D. Wood 2001; Torres et al. 2002). Compared to their husbands, Latina wives-mothers tend to be more family-centered and display more warmth and affection for their children, but this is probably true of all racial–ethnic groups.

With such diversity among Latino families, you can see how difficult it is to draw generalizations. The sociological point that runs through all studies of Latino families, however, is this: Social class is more important in determining family life than is either being Latino or a family's country of origin.

Asian American Families

As you can see from Figure 16.6 on the previous page, Asian American children are more likely than children in other racial–ethnic groups to grow up with both parents. As with the other groups, family life also reflects social class. In addition, because Asian Americans

machismo an emphasis on male strength, high sexuality, and dominance

emigrated from many different countries, their family life reflects those many cultures (Jeong and You 2008). As with Latino families, the more recent their immigration, the more closely their family life reflects the patterns in their country of origin (Glenn 1994; Jeong and You 2008).

Despite such differences, sociologist Bob Suzuki (1985), who studied Chinese American and Japanese American families, identified several distinctive characteristics of Asian American families. Although Asian Americans have adopted the nuclear family structure, they tend to retain Confucian values that provide a framework for family life: humanism, collectivity, self-discipline, hierarchy, respect for the elderly, moderation, and obligation. Obligation means that each member of a family owes respect to other family members and has a responsibility never to bring shame on the family. Conversely, a child's success brings honor to the family (Zamiska 2004). To control their children, Asian American parents are more likely to use shame and guilt than physical punishment.

Seldom does the ideal translate into the real, and so it is here. The children born to Asian immigrants confront a bewildering world of incompatible expectations—those of the new culture and those of their parents. As a result, they experience more family conflict and mental problems than do children of Asian Americans who are not immigrants (Meyers 2006; Ying and Han 2008).

Native American Families

Perhaps the single most significant issue that Native American families face is whether to follow traditional values or to assimilate into the dominant culture (Frosch 2008). This primary distinction creates vast differences among families. The traditionals speak native languages and emphasize distinctive Native American values and beliefs. Those who have assimilated into the broader culture do not.

Figure 16.6 on page 475 depicts the structure of Native American families. You can see how close it is to that of Latinos. In general, Native American parents are permissive with their children and avoid physical punishment. Elders play a much more active role in their children's families than they do in most U.S. families: Elders, especially grandparents, not only provide child care but also teach and discipline children. Like others, Native American families differ by social class.

To search for *the* Native American family would be fruitless. There are rural, urban, single-parent, extended, nuclear, rich, poor, traditional, and assimilated Native American families, to name just a few. Shown here is an Onondaga Nation family. The wife is a teacher; the husband a Webmaster.

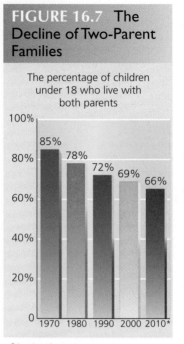

FIGURE 16.7 The Decline of Two-Parent Families

The percentage of children under 18 who live with both parents

*Author's estimate.
Source: By the author. Based on *Statistical Abstract of the United States* 1995:Table 79; 2009:Table 65.

In Sum: From this brief review, you can see that race–ethnicity signifies little for understanding family life. Rather, social class and culture hold the keys. The more resources a family has, the more it assumes the characteristics of a middle-class nuclear family. Compared with the poor, middle-class families have fewer children and fewer unmarried mothers. They also place greater emphasis on educational achievement and deferred gratification.

One-Parent Families

Another indication of how extensively U.S. families are changing is the increase in one-parent families. From Figure 16.7, you can see that the percentage of U.S. children who live with two parents (not necessarily their biological parents) has dropped sharply. The concerns—even alarm—that are often expressed about one-parent families may have more to do with their poverty than with children being reared by one parent. Because women head most one-parent families, these families tend to be poor. Although most divorced women earn less than their former husbands, about 85 percent of children of divorce live with their mothers (Aulette 2002).

To understand the typical one-parent family, then, we need to view it through the lens of poverty, for that is its primary source of strain. The results are serious, not just for these parents and their children but also for society. Children from one-parent families are more likely to have behavioral problems in school, to drop out of school, to get arrested, to have physical health problems, to have emotional problems, and to get divorced (McLanahan and Sandefur 1994; Menaghan et al. 1997; McLanahan and Schwartz 2002; Amato and Cheadle 2005; Wen 2008). If female, they are more likely to have sex at a younger age and to bear children while still unmarried teenagers.

Families Without Children

While most married women give birth, about one of five do not (Dye 2008). This is *double* what it was twenty years ago. As you can see from Figure 16.8, childlessness varies by racial–ethnic group, with whites and Latinas representing the extremes. Some couples are infertile, but most childless couples have made a *choice* to not have children—and they prefer the term *childfree* rather than *childless.* Some decide before marriage that they will never have children, often to attain a sense of freedom—to pursue a career, to be able to change jobs, to travel, and to have less stress (Letherby 2002; Koropeckyj-Cox 2007). In many cases, the couple has simply postponed the date they were going to have their first child until either it was too late to have children or it seemed too uncomfortable to add a child to their lifestyle.

With trends firmly in place—more education and careers for women, advances in contraception, legal abortion, the high cost of rearing children, and an emphasis on possessing more material things—the proportion of women who never bear children is likely to increase. Consider this statement in a newsletter:

> We are DINKS (Dual Incomes, No Kids). We are happily married. I am 43; my wife is 42. We have been married for almost twenty years. . . . Our investment strategy has a lot to do with our personal philosophy: "You can have kids—or you can have everything else!"

Many couples who are not childless by choice desperately want to have children, and they keep trying to do so. Coming to the soul-wrenching conclusion that they can never bear children, many decide to adopt. Some, in contrast, turn to solutions not available to previous generations, the topic of our Sociology and the New Technology box on the next page.

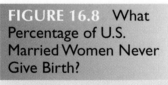

FIGURE 16.8 What Percentage of U.S. Married Women Never Give Birth?

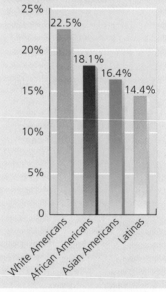

Source: By the author. Based on women ages 40–44 in Dye 2008.

SOCIOLOGY and the NEW TECHNOLOGY

Rent-a-Womb: "How Much for Your Uterus?"

Let's suppose that you are a married woman—easier, of course, for some to suppose than others. Let's also suppose that you've been trying to get pregnant for several years and that nothing has worked. You and your husband have tried the usual techniques: sex at a certain time of the month, lying on your back, legs up after sex, and so on. Nothing.

You've both been examined by doctors, probed and tested. Everything is fine. You've taken some fertility drugs. Nothing. You've even taken some "just in case" pills that your doctor prescribed. Still nothing.

OK, hard to admit, but you even did some of the superstitious things that your aunt told you to try. Still nothing.

Your gynecologist has told you about surrogacy, that for a fee a woman will rent her womb to you. A fertility expert will mix your egg and your husband's sperm in a little dish and insert the fertilized egg inside a woman who will bear the child for you.

The cost? About $50,000 or so. It might as well be ten times as high. You can't afford it anyway.

Then you hear about a clinic in India. For $15,000, including your plane ticket and hotel, you can get the whole procedure: your egg fertilized and transferred to a young Indian woman, the woman's care including a balanced diet, the hospitalization, the doctor, the delivery, and the necessary papers filed. You even get to look over the young women who are offering their uteruses for rent and pick out one you like. She'll become like part of your family. Or something like that.

Outsourcing pregnancy. What a creative use of capitalism.

No matter how you try, though, you can't get the $15,000 together? Or maybe you have a fear of flying?

Or maybe you think that surrogacy in India is taking advantage of women in poverty?

So have you exhausted all alternatives? Not by a long shot. There are always friends and relatives. OK, none of them is willing. But if no one else, maybe your own old mother can revitalize her womb once more?

Sound too far-fetched to be even a possibility?

Not at all. This is just what Kim Coseno asked her 56-year old mother to do. And her mother agreed. That's their picture on this page. And, yes, Kim's mother did a great job. She delivered triplets for Kim and her husband Joe.

And she didn't charge anything either.

For Your Consideration

If you really wanted children and were not able to get pregnant (or it is your wife in this situation), would you consider surrogacy? Why or why not? Do you think that hiring a poor woman in India to be a surrogate mother for your child is exploitation? (The surrogate mothers are paid several thousand dollars, when the annual Indian wage is about $600.) What do you think about the birth of the triplets shown in the photo below?

Based on Spring 2006; Mukherjee 2007; Associated Press 2008.

An egg from the younger woman shown here in Mayfield Heights, Ohio, was fertilized by her husband and implanted in her mother, the older woman who is holding the triplets. This older woman gave birth to the triplets, making her both the triplets' surrogate mother and grandmother.

blended family a family whose members were once part of other families

Blended Families

The **blended family,** one whose members were once part of other families, is an increasingly significant type of family in the United States. Two divorced people who marry and each bring their children into a new family unit form a blended family. With divorce common, millions of children spend some of their childhood in blended families. I've never seen a better description of how blended families complicate family relationships than what one of my freshman students wrote:

> I live with my dad. I should say that I live with my dad, my brother (whose mother and father are also my mother and father), my half sister (whose father is my dad, but whose mother is my father's last wife), and two stepbrothers and stepsisters (children of my father's current wife). My father's wife (my current stepmother, not to be confused with his second wife who, I guess, is no longer my stepmother) is pregnant, and soon we all will have a new brother or sister. Or will it be a half brother or half sister?
>
> If you can't figure this out, I don't blame you. I have trouble myself. It gets very complicated around Christmas. Should we all stay together? Split up and go to several other homes? Who do we buy gifts for, anyway?

Gay and Lesbian Families

Although a handful of U.S. states allow people of the same sex to marry, 40 states have laws that do not allow same-sex marriages (McKinley and Goostein 2008). Walking a fine conceptual tightrope, some states recognize "registered domestic partnerships," giving legal status to same-sex unions but avoiding the term *marriage.* The result is that most gay and lesbian couples lack both legal marriage and the legal protection of registered "partnerships."

Gay and lesbian couples live throughout the United States, but about half live in just twenty cities, with the greatest concentrations in San Francisco, Los Angeles, Atlanta, New York City, and Washington, D.C. About one-fifth of gay and lesbian couples were previously married to heterosexuals. Twenty-two percent of female couples and 5 percent of male couples have children from their earlier heterosexual marriages (Bianchi and Casper 2000).

What are same-sex relationships like? Like everything else in life, these couples cannot be painted with a single brush stroke. Social class, as it does for opposite-sex couples, significantly shapes orientations to life. Sociologists Philip Blumstein and Pepper Schwartz (1985), who interviewed same-sex couples, found their main struggles to be housework, money, careers, problems with relatives, and sexual adjustment. If these sound familiar, they should be, as they are precisely the same problems that heterosexual couples face. Some find that their sexual orientation brings discrimination, which can add stress to their relationship (Todosijevic et al. 2005). The children they rear have about the same adjustment as children reared by heterosexual parents and are no more likely to have a gay or lesbian sexual orientation (Perrin 2002; "Lesbian and Gay Parenting" 2005). Same-sex couples are more likely to break up, and one argument for legalizing gay marriages is that this will make these relationships more stable. Where same-sex marriages are legal, like opposite-sex marriages, to break them requires negotiating around legal obstacles.

Being fought in U.S. courts is whether or not marriage should be limited to heterosexual couples. This lesbian couple was married in San Francisco, California, in 2008 but later that year California voters passed *Proposition 8,* which limits marriage to men and women.

Trends in U.S. Families

As is apparent from this discussion, marriage and family life in the United States is undergoing a fundamental shift. Let's examine other indicators of this change.

Postponing Marriage and Childbirth

Figure 16.9 below illustrates one of the most significant changes in U.S. marriages. As you can see, the average age of first-time brides and grooms declined from 1890 to about 1950. In 1890, the typical first-time bride was 22, but by 1950, she had just left her teens. For about twenty years, there was little change. Then in 1970, the average age started to increase sharply. *Today's average first-time bride and groom are older than at any other time in U.S. history.*

Since postponing marriage is today's norm, it may come as a surprise to many readers to learn that *most* U.S. women used to be married by the time they reached age 24. To see this remarkable change, look at Figure 16.10 on the next page. Postponing marriage has become so common that the percentage of women of this age who are unmarried is now more than *double* what it was in 1970. Another consequence of postponing marriage is that the average age at which U.S. women have their first child is 25.2, also the highest in U.S. history (Mathews and Hamilton 2002; Martin et al. 2007).

Why have these changes occurred? The primary reason is cohabitation. Although Americans have postponed the age at which they first marry, they have *not* postponed the age at which they first set up housekeeping with someone of the opposite sex. Let's look at this trend.

Cohabitation

Figure 16.11 on the next page shows the increase in **cohabitation,** adults living together in a sexual relationship without being married. This figure is one of the most remarkable in sociology. Hardly ever do we have totals that rise this steeply and consistently. Cohabitation is *ten times* more common today than it was in the 1970s. From a furtive activity, cohabitation has moved into the mainstream, and today most couples who marry have cohabited (Popenoe 2008). Cohabitation has become so common that about 40 percent of U.S. children will spend some time in a cohabiting family (Scommegna 2002).

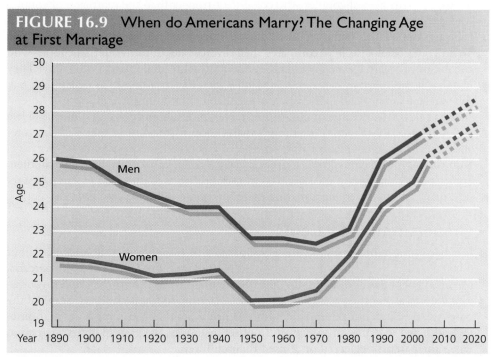

FIGURE 16.9   When do Americans Marry? The Changing Age at First Marriage

Note: This is the median age at first marriage. The broken lines indicate the author's estimate.

Source: By the author. Based on U.S. Census Bureau 2008.

cohabitation unmarried couples living together in a sexual relationship

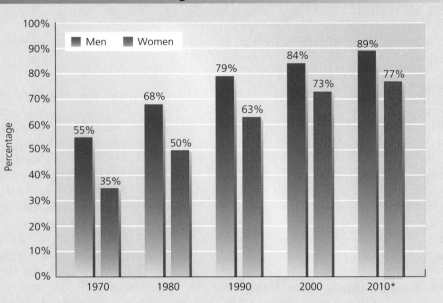

FIGURE 16.10   Americans Ages 20–24 Who Have Never Married

*Author's projection.

Source: By the author. Based on *Statistical Abstract of the United States* 1993: Table 60; 2002: Table 48; 2009: Table 56.

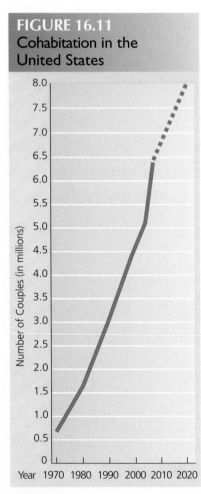

FIGURE 16.11
Cohabitation in the United States

Note: Broken line indicates author's estimate

Source: By the author. Based on U.S. Bureau of the Census 2007b and *Statistical Abstract of the United States* 1995: Table 60; 2009: Table 62.

Commitment is the essential difference between cohabitation and marriage. In marriage, the assumption is permanence; in cohabitation, couples agree to remain together for "as long as it works out." For marriage, individuals make public vows that legally bind them as a couple; for cohabitation, they simply move in together. Marriage requires a judge to authorize its termination; if a cohabiting relationship sours, the couple separates, telling friends and family that "it didn't work out." As you know, many cohabiting couples marry, but do you know how this is related to what cohabitation means to them? Let's explore this in our Down-to-Earth Sociology box on the next page.

Are the marriages of couples who cohabited stronger than the marriages of couples who did not live together before they married? It would seem they would be, that cohabiting couples have had the chance to work out real-life problems prior to marriage. To find out, sociologists have compared their divorce rates. It turns out that couples who cohabit before marriage are *more* likely to divorce (Lichter and Qian 2008). Why? They had that living-together experience, and only then did they decide to marry. The reason, suggest some sociologists, is because cohabiting relationships are so easy to end (Dush et al. 2003). Because of this, people are less picky about choosing someone to live with ("It's probably a temporary thing") than choosing someone to marry ("This is really serious"). After couples cohabit, however, many experience a push toward marriage. Some of this "push" comes from simply having common possessions, pets, and children. Some comes from family and friends—from subtle hints to direct statements. As a result, many end up marrying a partner that they would not otherwise have chosen.

Grandparents as Parents

It is becoming more common for grandparents to rear their grandchildren. About 6 percent of U.S. children are being reared by their grandparents, twice the percentage of a generation ago (Lagnado 2009). The main reason for these *skipped-generation families* is that the parents are incapable of caring for their children. Some of the parents have died, but the most common reasons are that the parents are ill, homeless, addicted to drugs, or in prison. In other instances, the grandparents stepped in when the parents neglected or abused their children.

Caring for grandchildren can bring great satisfaction. The grandparents know that their grandchildren are in loving hands, they build strong emotional bonds with

Down-to-Earth Sociology
"You Want Us to Live Together? What Do You Mean By That?"

What has led to the surge of cohabitation in the United States? Let's consider two fundamental changes in U.S. culture.

The first is changed ideas of sexual morality. It is difficult for today's college students to grasp the sexual morality that prevailed before the 1960s sexual revolution. Almost everyone used to consider sex before marriage to be immoral. Premarital sex existed, to be sure, but it took place furtively and often with guilt. To live together before marriage was called "shacking up," and the couple was said to be "living in sin." A double standard prevailed. It was the woman's responsibility to say no to sex before marriage. Consequently, she was considered to be the especially sinful one in cohabitation.

The second cultural change is the high U.S. divorce rate. Although the rate has declined since 1980, today's young adults have seen more divorce than any prior generation. This makes marriage seem fragile, as if it isn't going to last regardless of how much you try to make it work. This is scary. Cohabitation reduces the threat by offering a relationship of intimacy in which divorce is impossible. You can break up, but you can't get divorced.

From the outside, all cohabitation may look the same, but not to the people who are living together. As you can see from Table 16.2, for about 10 percent of couples, cohabitation is a substitute for marriage. These couples consider themselves married but for some reason don't want a marriage certificate. Some object to marriage on philosophical grounds ("What difference does a piece of paper make?"); others do not yet have a legal divorce from a spouse. Almost half of cohabitants (46 percent) view cohabitation as a step on the path to marriage. For them, cohabitation is more than "going steady" but less than engagement. Another 15 percent of couples are simply "giving it a try." They want to see what marriage to one another might be like. For the least committed, about 29 percent, cohabitation is a form of dating. It provides a dependable source of sex and emotional support.

If you look at these couples a half dozen years after they began to live together, you can see how important these different levels of commitment are. As you can see from Table 16.2, couples who view cohabitation as a substitute for marriage are the least likely to marry and the most likely to continue to cohabit. For couples who see cohabitation as a step toward marriage, the outcome is just the opposite: They are the most likely to marry and the least likely to still be cohabiting. Couples who are the most likely to break up are those who "tried" cohabitation and those for whom cohabitation was a form of dating.

For Your Consideration
Can you explain why the meaning of cohabitation makes a difference in whether couples marry? Can you classify cohabiting couples you know into these four types? Do you think there are other types? If so, what?

TABLE 16.2	What Cohabitation Means: Does It Make a Difference?				
			After 5 to 7 years		
				Of Those Still Together	
What Cohabitation Means	Percent of Couples	Split Up	Still Together	Married	Cohabitating
Substitute for Marriage	10%	35%	65%	37%	63%
Step toward Marriage	46%	31%	69%	73%	27%
Trial Marriage	15%	51%	49%	66%	34%
Coresidential Dating	29%	46%	54%	61%	39%

Source: Recomputed from Bianchi and Casper 2000.

them, and they are able to transmit their family values. But taking over as parents also brings stress: the unexpected responsibilities of parenthood, the squeezed finances, the need to continue working when they were anticipating retirement, conflict with the parents of the children, and feeling trapped (Waldrop and Weber 2001; Lumpkin 2008). This added wear and tear takes its toll, and these grandparents are more likely than others to be depressed (Letiecq et al. 2008).

The "Sandwich Generation" and Elder Care

The "sandwich generation" refers to people who find themselves sandwiched between and responsible for two other generations, their children and their own aging parents. Typically between the ages of 40 and 55, these people find themselves pulled in two different directions. Many feel overwhelmed as these competing responsibilities collide. Some are plagued with guilt and anger because they can be in only one place at a time and have little time to pursue personal interests.

Concerns about elder care have gained the attention of the corporate world, and half of the 1,000 largest U.S. companies offer elder care assistance to their employees (Hewitt Associates 2004). This assistance includes seminars, referral services, and flexible work schedules to help employees meet their responsibilities without missing so much work. Why are companies responding more positively to the issue of elder care than to child care? Most CEOs are older men whose wives stayed home to take care of their children, so they don't understand the stresses of balancing work and child care. In contrast, nearly all have aging parents, and many have faced the turmoil of trying to cope with both their parents' needs and those of work and their own family.

With people living longer, this issue is likely to become increasingly urgent.

Divorce and Remarriage

The topic of family life would not be complete without considering divorce. Let's first try to determine how much divorce there really is.

Ways of Measuring Divorce

You probably have heard that the U.S. divorce rate is 50 percent, a figure that is popular with reporters. The statistic is true in the sense that each year almost half as many divorces are granted as there are marriages performed. The totals are 2.16 million marriages and about 1.04 million divorces (*Statistical Abstract* 2009:Table 123).

What is wrong, then, with saying that the divorce rate is about 50 percent? Think about it for a moment. Why should we compare the number of divorces and marriages that take place during the same year? The couples who divorced do not—with rare exceptions—come from the group that married that year. The one number has *nothing* to do with the other, so these statistics in no way establish the divorce rate.

What figures should we compare, then? Couples who divorce come from the entire group of married people in the country. Since the United States has 60,000,000 married couples, and a little over 1 million of them get divorced in a year, the divorce rate for any given year is less than 2 percent. A couple's chances of still being married at the end of a year are over 98 percent—not bad odds—and certainly much better odds than the mass media would have us believe. As the Social Map on the next page shows, the "odds"—if we want to call them that—depend on where you live.

Over time, of course, each year's small percentage adds up. A third way of measuring divorce, then, is to ask, "Of all U.S. adults, what percentage are divorced?" Figure 16.13 on the next page answers this question. You can see how divorce has increased over the years and how race–ethnicity makes a difference for the likelihood that couples will divorce. If you look closely, you can also see that the rate of divorce has slowed down.

Figure 16.13 shows us the percentage of Americans who are currently divorced, but we get yet another answer if we ask the question, "What percentage of Americans have *ever* been divorced?" This percentage increases with each age group, peaking when people reach their 50s. Forty percent of women in their 50s have been divorced at some point in their

" I NOW PRONOUNCE YOU SECOND HUSBAND AND FOURTH WIFE."

This fanciful depiction of marital trends may not be too far off the mark.

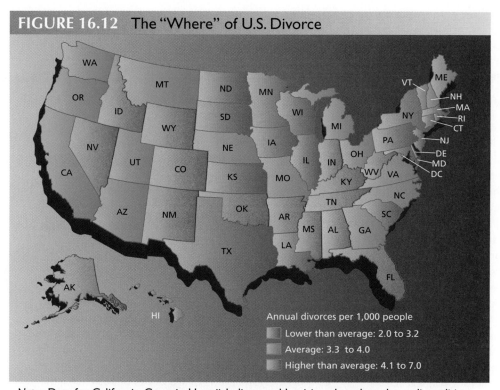

FIGURE 16.12   The "Where" of U.S. Divorce

Annual divorces per 1,000 people
- Lower than average: 2.0 to 3.2
- Average: 3.3 to 4.0
- Higher than average: 4.1 to 7.0

Note: Data for California, Georgia, Hawaii, Indiana, and Louisiana, based on the earlier editions in the source, have been decreased by the average decrease in U.S. divorce.

Source: By the author. Based on *Statistical Abstract of the United States* 1995: Table 149; 2002: Table 111; 2009: Table 123.

lives; for men, the total is 43 percent ("Marital History . . ." 2004). Looked at in this way, a divorce rate of 50 percent, then, is fairly accurate.

What most of us want to know is what *our* chances of divorce are. It is one thing to know that a certain percentage of Americans are divorced, but have sociologists found out anything that will tell me about *my* chances of divorce? This is the topic of the Down-to-Earth Sociology box on the next page.

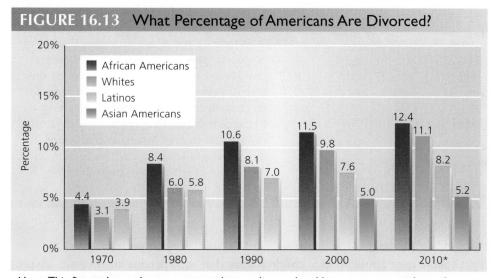

FIGURE 16.13   What Percentage of Americans Are Divorced?

Legend:
- African Americans
- Whites
- Latinos
- Asian Americans

Year	African Americans	Whites	Latinos	Asian Americans
1970	4.4	3.1	3.9	
1980	8.4	6.0	5.8	
1990	10.6	8.1	7.0	
2000	11.5	9.8	7.6	5.0
2010*	12.4	11.1	8.2	5.2

Note: This figure shows the percentage who are divorced and have not remarried, not the percentage who have *ever* divorced. Only these racial–ethnic groups are listed in the source. The source only recently added data on Asian Americans. *Author's estimate

Source: By the author. Based on *Statistical Abstract of the United States* 1995: Table 58; 2009: Table 56.

Down-to-Earth Sociology
"What Are Your Chances of Getting Divorced?"

Divorces are often messy. To settle the question of who gets the house, a couple in Cambodia sawed their house in half.

It is probably true that over a lifetime about half of all marriages fail (Whitehead and Popenoe 2004). If you have that 50 percent figure dancing in your head while you are getting married, you might as well make sure that you have an escape door open even while you're saying "I do."

Not every group carries the same risk of divorce. For some, the risk is much higher; for others, much lower. Let's look at some factors that reduce people's risk. As Table 16.3 shows, sociologists have worked out percentages that you might find useful. As you can see, people who go to college, participate in a religion, wait to get married before having children, and earn higher incomes have a much better chance that their marriage will last. You can also see that having parents who did not divorce is significant. If you reverse these factors, you will see how the likelihood of divorce increases for people who have a baby before they marry, who marry in their teens, and so on. It is important to note, however, that these factors reduce the risk of divorce for groups of people, not for any particular individual.

Three other factors increase the risk for divorce, but for these, sociologists have not computed percentages:

The first will probably strike you as strange—if a couple's firstborn child is a girl (Ananat and Michaels 2007; Dahl and Moretti 2008). Apparently, men prefer sons, and if the firstborn is a boy, the father is more likely to stick around. The second factor is more obvious: The more co-workers you have who are of the opposite sex, the more likely you are to get divorced (McKinnish 2007). (I'm sure you can figure out why.) No one knows the reason for the third factor: working with people who are recently divorced (Aberg 2003). It could be that divorced people are more likely to "hit" on their fellow workers—and human nature being what it is . . .

For Your Consideration

Why do you think that people who go to college have a lower risk of divorce? How would you explain the other factors shown in Table 16.3? What other factors discussed in this chapter indicate a greater or lesser risk of divorce?

Why can't you figure your own chances of divorce by starting with some percentage (say 30 percent likelihood of divorce for the first 10 years of marriage) and then reducing it according to this table (subtracting 13 percent of the 30 percent for going to college, and so on)? To better understand this, you might want to read the section on the misuse of statistics on page 493.

TABLE 16.3	What Reduces the Risk of Divorce?
Factors that Reduce People's People's Chances of Divorce	**How Much Does This Decrease the Risk of Divorce?**
Some college (vs. high-school dropout)	−13%
Affiliated with a religion (vs. none)	−14%
Parents not divorced	−14%
Age 25 or over at marriage (vs. under 18)	−24%
Having a baby 7 months or longer after marriage (vs. before marriage)	−24%
Annual income over $25,000 (vs. under $25,000)	−30%

Note: These percentages apply to the first ten years of marriage.
Source: Whitehead and Popenoe 2004.

Children of Divorce

Each year, more than 1 million U.S. children learn that their parents are divorcing. Numbers like this are cold. They don't tell us what divorce feels like, what the children experience. In the Down-to-Earth Sociology box on the next page, we try to catch a glimpse of this.

Children whose parents divorce are more likely than children reared by both parents to experience emotional problems, both during childhood and after they grow up (Amato and

Down-to-Earth Sociology
Caught Between Two Worlds: The Children of Divorce

The statistics can tell you how many couples divorce, how many children these couples have, and other interesting information. But the numbers can't tell what divorce is like—how children feel their world falling apart when they learn their parents are going to get a divorce. Or how torn apart they feel when they are shuffled from one house to another.

Elizabeth Marquardt, a child of divorce herself, did a national study of children of divorce. In her book, *Between Two Worlds* (2005), she weaves her own experiences with those of the people she interviewed, taking us into the thought world of children who are being pulled apart by their parents.

It's the many little things that the statistics don't touch. The children feel like they are growing up in two families, not one. This creates painful complications that make the children feel like insiders *and* outsiders in their parents' worlds. They are outsiders when they look or act like one of the parents. This used to be a mark of an insider, a part of the family to which the child and the two parents belonged. But now it reminds one parent of the former spouse, someone they want to forget. And those children who end up with different last names than one of their parents—what a dramatic symbol of *outsider* that is. And when children learn something about one parent that they can't tell the other parent—which happens often—how uncomfortable they feel at being unable to share this information. Outsider–insider again.

What information do you share, anyway—or what do you *not* dare to share—as you travel from one world to the other? What do you say when dad asks if mom has a boyfriend? Is this supposed to be a secret? Will dad get mad if you tell him? Will he feel hurt? You don't want him to get angry or to feel hurt. Yet you don't want to keep secrets. And will mom get mad if you tell dad? It's all so complicated for a kid.

Marquardt says that as a child of divorce she tried to keep her two worlds apart, but they sometimes collided. At her mom's house, she could say that things were "screwed up." But if she used "screwed up" at her dad's

The custody and support of children are often a major source of contention in divorces. Shown here is Britney Spears, whose battle for the custody of her children and her court-ordered support of her former husband, Kevin Federline, made news around the world.

house, he would correct her, saying, "*Messed* up." He meant the best for her, teaching her better language, but this left her feeling silly and ashamed. Things like this, little to most people, are significant to kids who feel pinched between their parents' differing values, beliefs, and life styles.

To shuttle between two homes is to enter and leave different worlds—feeling things in common with each, but also sensing distances from each. And then come the strange relationships—their parents' girlfriends or boyfriends. Eventually come new blended families, which may not blend so easily, those that bring the new stepmom or stepdad, and perhaps their children. And then there are the new break-ups, with a recurring cycle of supposedly permanent relationships. What a complicated world for a child to traverse.

Marquardt pinpoints the dilemma for the child of divorce when she says, Being with one parent always means *not* being with the other.

For Your Consideration

If you are a child of divorce, did you have two worlds of experience? Were your experiences like those mentioned here? If you lived with both parents, how do you think your life has been different because your parents didn't divorce?

Sobolewski 2001; Weitoft et al. 2003). They are also more likely to become juvenile delinquents (Wallerstein et al. 2001) and less likely to complete high school, to attend college, and to graduate from college (McLanahan and Schwartz 2002). Finally, the children of divorce are themselves more likely to divorce (Wolfinger 2003), perpetuating a marriage–divorce cycle.

Is the greater maladjustment of the children of divorce a serious problem? This question initiated a lively debate between two researchers, both psychologists. Judith Wallerstein

serial fatherhood a pattern of parenting in which a father, after a divorce, reduces contact with his own children, serves as a father to the children of the woman he marries or lives with, then ignores these children, too, after moving in with or marrying another woman

claims that divorce scars children, making them depressed and leaving them with insecurities that follow them into adulthood (Wallerstein et al. 2001). Mavis Hetherington replies that 75 to 80 percent of children of divorce function as well as children who are reared by both of their parents (Hetherington and Kelly 2003).

Without meaning to weigh in on either side of this debate, it doesn't seem to be a simple case of the glass being half empty or half full. If 75 to 80 percent of children of divorce don't suffer long-term harm, this leaves one-fourth to one-fifth who do. Any way you look at it, one-fourth or one-fifth of a million children each year is a lot of kids who are having a lot of problems.

What helps children adjust to divorce? Children of divorce who feel close to both parents make the best adjustment, and those who don't feel close to either parent make the worst adjustment (Richardson and McCabe 2001). Other studies show that children adjust well if they experience little conflict, feel loved, live with a parent who is making a good adjustment, and have consistent routines. It also helps if their family has adequate money to meet its needs. Children also adjust better if a second adult can be counted on for support (Hayashi and Strickland 1998). Urie Bronfenbrenner (1992) says this person is like the third leg of a stool, giving stability to the smaller family unit. Any adult can be the third leg, he says—a relative, friend, or even a former mother-in-law—but the most powerful stabilizing third leg is the father, the ex-husband.

As mentioned, when the children of divorce grow up and marry, they are more likely to divorce than are adults who grew up in intact families. Have researchers found any factors that increase the chances that the children of divorce will have successful marriages? Actually, they have. They are more likely to have a lasting marriage if they marry someone whose parents did not divorce. These marriages have more trust and less conflict. If both husband and wife come from broken families, however, it is not good news. Those marriages tend to have less trust and more conflict, leading to a higher chance of divorce (Wolfinger 2003).

Grandchildren of Divorce

Paul Amato and Jacob Cheadle (2005), the first sociologists to study the grandchildren of people who had divorced, found that the effects of divorce continue across generations. Using a national sample, they compared grandchildren—those whose grandparents had divorced with those whose grandparents had not divorced. Their findings are astounding. The grandchildren of divorce have weaker ties to their parents, don't go as far in school,

It is difficult to capture the anguish of the children of divorce, but when I read these lines by the fourth-grader who drew these two pictures, my heart was touched:

Me alone in the park . . .

All alone in the park.

My Dad and Mom are divorced

that's why I'm all alone.

This is me in the picture with my son.

We are taking a walk in the park.

I will never be like my father.

I will never divorce my wife and kid.

and don't get along as well with their spouses. As these researchers put it, when parents divorce, the consequences ripple through the lives of children who are not yet born.

The Absent Father and Serial Fatherhood

With divorce common and mothers usually granted custody of the children, a new fathering pattern has emerged. In this pattern, known as **serial fatherhood,** a divorced father maintains high contact with his children during the first year or two after the divorce. As the man develops a relationship with another woman, he begins to play a fathering role with the woman's children and reduces contact with his own children. With another breakup, this pattern may repeat. Relationships are so broken that 31 percent of children who live apart from their fathers have contact with their father less than once a month—and this includes phone calls. Another 30 percent have no contact with their father (Stewart 2003). For many men, fatherhood has apparently become a short-term commitment.

The Ex-Spouses

Anger, depression, and anxiety are common feelings at divorce. But so is relief. Women are more likely than men to feel that divorce is giving them a "new chance" in life. A few couples manage to remain friends through it all—but they are the exception. The spouse who initiates the divorce usually gets over it sooner (Kelly 1992; Wang and Amato 2000) and remarries sooner (Sweeney 2002).

Divorce does not necessarily mean the end of a couple's relationship. Many divorced couples maintain contact because of their children (Fischer et al. 2005). For others, the "continuities," as sociologists call them, represent lingering attachments (Vaughan 1985; Masheter 1991; author's file 2005). The former husband may help his former wife paint a room or move furniture; she may invite him over for a meal or to watch television. They might even go to dinner or to see a movie together. Some couples even continue to make love after their divorce.

We don't yet know the financial impact of divorce. Studies used to show that divorce lowered women's income by a third (Seltzer 1994), but current research indicates that the finances of the average woman with minor children are either unchanged or actually improve after divorce (Bedard and Deschenes 2005; Ananat and Michaels 2007). There seem to be three reasons: divorced women work more hours, some move in with their parents, and others marry or cohabit with men who do better financially than their husbands did. We need more research to resolve this question.

Remarriage

Despite the number of people who emerge from divorce court swearing "Never again!" many do remarry. The rate at which they remarry, however, has slowed, and today only half of women who divorce remarry (Bramlett and Mosher 2002). Figure 16.14 shows how significant race–ethnicity is in determining whether women remarry. Comparable data are not available for men.

As Figure 16.15 shows, most divorced people marry other divorced people. You may be surprised that the women who are most likely to remarry are young mothers and those with less education (Glick and Lin 1986; Schmiege et al. 2001). Apparently women who are more educated and more independent (no children) can afford to be more selective. Men are more likely than women to remarry, perhaps because they have a larger pool of potential mates.

How do remarriages work out? The divorce rate of remarried people *without* children is the same as that of first marriages. Those who bring children into a new marriage, however, are more likely to divorce again (MacDonald and DeMaris 1995). Certainly these relationships are more complicated and stressful. A lack of clear norms to follow may also play a role (Coleman et al. 2000). As sociologist Andrew Cherlin (1989) noted, we lack satisfactory names for stepmothers, stepfathers, stepbrothers, stepsisters, stepaunts, stepuncles, stepcousins, and stepgrandparents. At the very least, these are awkward terms to use, but they also represent ill-defined relationships.

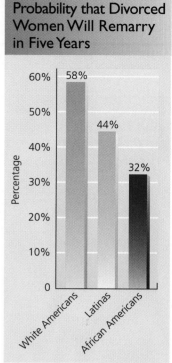

FIGURE 16.14 The Probability that Divorced Women Will Remarry in Five Years

Note: Only women and these groups are listed in the source.
Source: By the author. Based on Bramlett and Mosher 2002.

FIGURE 16.15 The Marital History of U.S. Brides and Grooms

■ First marriage of bride and groom
■ Remarriage of bride and groom
■ First marriage of bride, remarriage of groom
■ First marriage of groom, remarriage of bride

Source: By the author. Based on *Statistical Abstract of the United States* 2000:Table 145. Table dropped in later editions.

Two Sides of Family Life

Let's first look at situations in which marriage and family have gone seriously wrong and then try to answer the question of what makes marriage work.

The Dark Side of Family Life: Battering, Child Abuse, Marital Rape, and Incest

The dark side of family life involves events that people would rather keep in the dark. We shall look at spouse battering, child abuse, rape, and incest.

Spouse Battering.   To study spouse abuse, some sociologists have studied just a few victims in depth (Goetting 2001), while others have interviewed nationally representative samples of U.S. couples (Straus and Gelles 1988; Straus 1992). Although not all sociologists agree (Dobash et al. 1992, 1993; Pagelow 1992), Murray Straus concludes that husbands and wives are about equally likely to attack one another. If gender equality exists here, however, it certainly vanishes when it comes to the effects of violence—85 percent of the injured are women (Rennison 2003). A good part of the reason, of course, is that most husbands are bigger and stronger than their wives, putting women at a physical disadvantage in this literal battle of the sexes. The Down-to-Earth Sociology box on the next page discusses why some women remain with their abusive husbands.

Violence against women is related to the sexist structure of society, which we reviewed in Chapter 11, and to the socialization that we analyzed in Chapter 3. Because they grew up with norms that encourage aggression and the use of violence, some men feel that it is their right to control women. When frustrated in a relationship—or even by events outside it—some men become violent. The basic sociological question is how to socialize males to handle frustration and disagreements without resorting to violence (Rieker et al. 1997). We do not yet have this answer.

Child Abuse.

> I answered an ad about a lakeside house in a middle-class neighborhood that was for sale by owner. As the woman showed me through her immaculate house, I was surprised to see a plywood box in the youngest child's bedroom. About 3 feet high, 3 feet wide, and 6 feet long, the box was perforated with holes and had a little door with a padlock. Curious, I asked what it was. The woman replied matter-of-factly that her son had a behavior problem, and this was where they locked him for "time out." She added that other times they would tie him to a float, attach a line to the dock, and put him in the lake.
>
> I left as soon as I could. With thoughts of a terrorized child filling my head, I called the state child abuse hotline.

As you can tell, what I saw upset me. Most of us are bothered by child abuse—helpless children being victimized by their parents and other adults who are supposed to love, protect, and nurture them. The most gruesome of these cases make the evening news: The 4-year-old girl who was beaten and raped by her mother's boyfriend, passed into a coma, and three days later passed out of this life; the 6- to 10-year-old children whose stepfather videotaped them engaging in sex acts. Unlike these cases, which made headlines in my area, most child abuse is never brought to our attention: the children who live in filth, who are neglected—left alone for hours or even days at a time—or who are beaten with extension cords—cases like the little boy I learned about when I went house hunting.

Child abuse is extensive. Each year, U.S. authorities receive about 2 million reports of children being abused or neglected. About 900,000 of these cases are substantiated (*Statistical Abstract* 2009:Table 330). The excuses that parents make are incredible. Of those I have read, the most fantastic is what a mother said to a Manhattan judge, "I slipped

Down-to-Earth Sociology
"Why Doesn't She Just Leave?" The Dilemma of Abused Women

"Why would she ever put up with violence?" is a question on everyone's mind. From the outside, it looks so easy. Just pack up and leave. "I know I wouldn't put up with anything like that."

Yet this is not what typically happens. Women tend to stay with their men after they are abused. Some stay only a short while, to be sure, but others remain in abusive situations for years. Why?

Sociologist Ann Goetting (2001) asked this question, too. To learn the answer, she interviewed women who had made the break. She wanted to find out what it was that set them apart. How were they able to leave, when so many women couldn't seem to? She found that

1. They had a positive self-image.
   Simply put, they believed that they deserved better.
2. They broke with old ideas.
   They did not believe that a wife had to stay with her husband no matter what.
3. They found adequate finances.
   For some, this was easy. But others had to save for years, putting away just a dollar or two a week.
4. They had supportive family and friends.
   A support network served as a source of encouragement to help them rescue themselves.

If you take the opposite of these four characteristics, you can understand why some women put up with abuse: They don't think they deserve anything better, they believe it is their duty to stay, they don't think they can make it financially, and they lack a supportive network. These four factors are not of equal importance to all women, of course. For some, the lack of finances is the most important, while for others, it is their low self-concept. The lack of a supportive network is also significant.

There are two additional factors: The woman must define her husband's acts as abuse that warrants her leaving, and she must decide that he is not going to change. If she defines her husband's acts as normal, or

Spouse abuse is one of the most common forms of violence. Shown here are police pulling a woman from her bathroom window, where she had fled from her husband, who was threatening to shoot her.

perhaps as deserved in some way, she does not have a motive to leave. If she defines his acts as temporary, thinking that her husband will change, she is likely to stick around to try to change her husband.

Sociologist Kathleen Ferraro (2006) reports that when she was a graduate student, her husband "monitored my movements, eating, clothing, friends, money, make-up, and language. If I challenged his commands, he slapped or kicked me or pushed me down." Ferraro was able to leave only after she defined her husband's acts as intolerable abuse—not simply that she was caught up in an unappealing situation that she had to put up with—and after she decided that her husband was not going to change. Fellow students formed the supportive network that Ferraro needed to act on her new definition. Her graduate mentor even hid her from her husband after she left him.

For Your Consideration
On the basis of these findings, what would you say to a woman whose husband is abusing her? How do you think battered women's shelters fit into this explanation? What other parts of this puzzle can you think of— such as the role of love?

in a moment of anger, and my hands accidentally wrapped around my daughter's windpipe" (LeDuff 2003).

Marital or Intimacy Rape.   Sociologists have found that marital rape is more common than is usually supposed. For example, between one-third and one-half of women who seek help at shelters for battered women are victims of marital rape (Bergen 1996). Women at shelters, however, are not representative of U.S. women. To get a better answer of how common marital rape is, sociologist Diana Russell (1990) used a sampling technique that allows generalization, but only to San Francisco. She found that 14 percent of married women report that their husbands have raped them. Similarly, 10 percent of a representative sample of Boston women interviewed by sociologists David Finkelhor and Kersti Yllo (1985, 1989) reported that their husbands had used physical force to compel them to have sex. Compared with victims of rape by strangers or acquaintances, victims of marital rape are less likely to report the rape (Mahoney 1999).

With the huge numbers of couples who are cohabiting, we need a term that includes sexual assault in these relationships. Perhaps, then, we should use the term *intimacy rape.* And intimacy rape is not limited to men who sexually assault women. Sociologist Lori Girshick (2002) interviewed lesbians who had been sexually assaulted by their partners. In these cases, both the victim and the offender were women. Girshick points out that if the pronoun "he" were substituted for "she" in her interviews, a reader would believe that the events were being told by women who had been battered and raped by their husbands. Like wives who have been raped by their husbands, these victims, too, suffered from shock, depression, and self-blame.

Incest.   Sexual relations between certain relatives (for example, between brothers and sisters or between parents and children) constitute **incest.** Incest is most likely to occur in families that are socially isolated (Smith 1992). Sociologist Diana Russell (n.d.) found that incest victims who experience the greatest trauma are those who were victimized the most often, whose assaults occurred over longer periods of time, and whose incest was "more intrusive"—for example, sexual intercourse as opposed to sexual touching.

Who are the offenders? The most common incest is apparently between brothers and sisters, with the sex initiated by the brother (Canavan et al. 1992; Carlson et al. 2006). With no random samples, however, we don't know for sure. Russell found that uncles are the most common offenders, followed by first cousins, stepfathers, brothers, and, finally, other relatives ranging from brothers-in-law to stepgrandfathers. All studies indicate that incest between mothers and their children is rare, more so than between fathers and their children.

The Bright Side of Family Life: Successful Marriages

Successful Marriages.   After examining divorce and family abuse, one could easily conclude that marriages seldom work out. This would be far from the truth, however, for about three of every five married Americans report that they are "very happy" with their marriages (Whitehead and Popenoe 2004). (Keep in mind that each year divorce eliminates about a million unhappy marriages.) To find out what makes marriage successful, sociologists Jeanette and Robert Lauer (1992) interviewed 351 couples who had been married fifteen years or longer. Fifty-one of these marriages were unhappy, but the couples stayed together for religious reasons, because of family tradition, or "for the sake of the children."

Of the others, the 300 happy couples, all

1. Think of their spouse as their best friend
2. Like their spouse as a person
3. Think of marriage as a long-term commitment
4. Believe that marriage is sacred
5. Agree with their spouse on aims and goals
6. Believe that their spouse has grown more interesting over the years
7. Strongly want the relationship to succeed
8. Laugh together

Sociologist Nicholas Stinnett (1992) used interviews and questionnaires to study 660 families from all regions of the United States and parts of South America. He found that happy families

incest sexual relations between specified relatives, such as brothers and sisters or parents and children

1. Spend a lot of time together
2. Are quick to express appreciation
3. Are committed to promoting one another's welfare
4. Do a lot of talking and listening to one another
5. Are religious
6. Deal with crises in a positive manner

There are three more important factors: Marriages are happier when the partners get along with their in-laws (Bryant et al. 2001), find leisure activities that they both enjoy (Crawford et al. 2002), and agree on how to spend money (Bernard 2008).

Symbolic Interactionism and the Misuse of Statistics

Many students express concerns about their own marital future, a wariness born out of the divorce of their parents, friends, neighbors, relatives—even their pastors and rabbis. They wonder about their chances of having a successful marriage. Because sociology is not just about abstract ideas, but is really about our lives, it is important to stress that you are an individual, not a statistic. That is, if the divorce rate were 33 percent or 50 percent, this would *not* mean that if you marry, your chances of getting divorced are 33 percent or 50 percent. That is a misuse of statistics—and a common one at that. Divorce statistics represent all marriages and have absolutely *nothing* to do with any individual marriage. Our own chances depend on our own situations—especially the way we approach marriage.

To make this point clearer, let's apply symbolic interactionism. From a symbolic interactionist perspective, we create our own worlds. That is, because our experiences don't come with built-in meanings, we interpret our experiences and act accordingly. As we do so, we can create a self-fulfilling prophecy. For example, if we think that our marriage might fail, we are more likely to run when things become difficult. If we think that our marriage is going to work out, we are more likely to stick around and to do things to make the marriage successful. The folk saying "There are no guarantees in life" is certainly true, but it does help to have a vision that a good marriage is possible and that it is worth the effort to achieve.

The Future of Marriage and Family

What can we expect of marriage and family in the future? Despite its many problems, marriage is in no danger of becoming a relic of the past. Marriage is so functional that it exists in every society. Consequently, the vast majority of Americans will continue to find marriage vital to their welfare.

Certain trends are firmly in place. Cohabitation, births to single women, age at first marriage, and parenting by grandparents will increase. As more married women join the workforce, wives will continue to gain marital power. The number of elderly will increase, and more couples will find themselves sandwiched between caring for their parents and rearing their own children.

Our culture will continue to be haunted by distorted images of marriage and family: the bleak ones portrayed in the mass media and the rosy ones perpetuated by cultural myths. Sociological research can help to correct these distortions and allow us to see how our own family experiences fit into the patterns of our culture. Sociological research can also help to answer the big question: How do we formulate social policies that will support and enhance family life?

By the Numbers: *Then and Now*

Americans who want 3 or more children

1936	NOW
64%	34%

Americans who want 0, 1, or 2 children

1936	NOW
34%	56%

Number of marriages with a white wife and an African American husband

1970	NOW
41,000	338,000

Number of hours per week husbands do housework

1970	NOW
4.4	9.7

Percentage of children under age 18 who live with both parents

1970	NOW
85%	66%

Number of cohabitating couples

1970	NOW
500,000	6,400,000

Percentage of white Americans divorced

1970	NOW
3.1%	11.1%

Percentage of African Americans divorced

1970	NOW
4.4%	12.4%

Average age of first-time bride

1970	NOW
21	26

Women ages 20–24 who have never married

1970	NOW
35%	77%

SUMMARY *and* REVIEW

Marriage and Family in Global Perspective

What is a family—and what themes are universal?

Family is difficult to define. There are exceptions to every element that one might consider essential. Consequently, **family** is defined broadly—as people who consider themselves related by blood, marriage, or adoption. Universally, **marriage** and family are mechanisms for governing mate selection, reckoning descent, and establishing inheritance and authority. Pp. 462–464.

Marriage and Family in Theoretical Perspective

What is a functionalist perspective on marriage and family?

Functionalists examine the functions and dysfunctions of family life. Examples include the **incest taboo** and how weakened family functions increase divorce. Pp. 464–466.

What is a conflict perspective on marriage and family?

Conflict theorists focus on inequality in marriage, especially unequal power between husbands and wives. P. 466.

What is a symbolic interactionist perspective on marriage and family?

Symbolic interactionists examine the contrasting experiences and perspectives of men and women in marriage. They stress that only by grasping the perspectives of wives and husbands can we understand their behavior. Pp. 466–468.

The Family Life Cycle

What are the major elements of the family life cycle?

The major elements are love and courtship, marriage, childbirth, child rearing, and the family in later life. Most mate selection follows predictable patterns of age, social class, race–ethnicity, and religion. Child-rearing patterns vary by social class. Pp. 468–474.

Diversity in U.S. Families

How significant is race–ethnicity in family life?

The primary distinction is social class, not race–ethnicity. Families of the same social class are likely to be similar, regardless of their race–ethnicity. Pp. 474–478.

What other diversity do we see in U.S. families?

Also discussed are one-parent, childless, **blended,** and gay and lesbian families. Each has its unique characteristics, but social class is significant in determining their primary characteristics. Poverty is especially significant for single-parent families, most of which are headed by women. Pp. 478–480.

Trends in U.S. Families

What major changes characterize U.S. families?

Three changes are postponement of first marriage, an increase in **cohabitation,** and more grandparents serving as parents to their grandchildren. With more people living longer, many middle-aged couples find themselves sandwiched between rearing their children and taking care of their aging parents. Pp. 480–484.

Divorce and Remarriage

What is the current divorce rate?

Depending on what numbers you choose to compare, you can produce almost any rate you wish, from 50 percent to less than 2 percent. P. 484.

How do children and their parents adjust to divorce?

Divorce is difficult for children, whose adjustment problems often continue into adulthood. Most divorced fathers do not maintain ongoing relationships with their children. Financial problems are usually greater for the former wives. The rate of remarriage has slowed. Pp. 485–489.

Two Sides of Family Life

What are the two sides of family life?

The dark side is abuse—spouse battering, child abuse, marital rape, and **incest.** All these are acts that revolve around the misuse of family power. The bright side is that most people find marriage and family to be rewarding. Pp. 490–493.

The Future of Marriage and Family

What is the likely future of marriage and family?

We can expect cohabitation, births to unmarried women, age at first marriage, and parenting by grandparents to increase. The growing numbers of women in the workforce are likely to continue to shift the balance of marital power. P. 493.

THINKING CRITICALLY *ABOUT* Chapter 16

1. Functionalists stress that the family is universal because it provides basic functions for individuals and society. What functions does your family provide? Hint: In addition to the section "The Functionalist Perspective," also consider the section "Common Cultural Themes."

2. Explain why social class is more important than race–ethnicity in determining a family's characteristics.

3. Apply this chapter's contents to your own experience with marriage and family. What social factors affect your family life? In what ways is your family life different from that of your grandparents when they were your age?

ADDITIONAL RESOURCES

What can you find in MySocLab? mysoclab   www.mysoclab.com

- Complete Ebook
- Practice Tests and Video and Audio activities
- Mapping and Data Analysis exercises

- Sociology in the News
- Classic Readings in Sociology
- Research and Writing advice

Where Can I Read More on This Topic?

Suggested readings for this chapter are listed at the back of this book.

Chapter

17

Education

Mississippi

Kathy Spiegel was upset. Horace Mann, the school principal in her hometown in Oregon, had asked her to come to his office. He explained that Kathy's 11-year-old twins had been acting up in class. They were disturbing other children and the teacher—and what was Kathy going to do about this?

Kathy didn't want to tell Mr. Mann what he could do with the situation. *That* would have gotten her kicked out of the office. Instead, she bit her tongue and said she would talk to her daughters.

> **Kathy's 11-year-old twins were disturbing other children and the teacher— and what was Kathy going to do about this?**

* * * * *

On the other side of the country, Jim and Julia Attaway were pondering their own problem. When they visited their son's school in the Bronx, they didn't like what they saw. The boys looked like they were junior gang members, and the girls dressed and acted as though they were sexually active. Their own 13-year-old son had started using street language at home, and it was becoming increasingly difficult to communicate with him.

* * * * *

In Minneapolis, Denzil and Tamika Jefferson were facing a much quieter crisis. They found life frantic as they hurried from one school activity to another. Their 13-year-old son attended a private school, and the demands were so intense that it felt like the junior year in high school. They no longer seemed to have any relaxed family time together.

* * * * *

In Atlanta, Jaime and Maria Morelos were upset at the ideas that their 8-year-old daughter had begun to express at home. As devout first-generation Protestants, Jaime and Maria felt moral issues were a top priority, and they didn't like what they were hearing.

* * * * *

Kathy talked the matter over with her husband, Bob. Jim and Julia discussed their problem, as did Denzil and Tamika and Jaime and Maria. They all came to the same conclusion: The problem was not their children. The problem was the school their children attended. All four sets of parents also came to the same solution: home schooling for their children.

497

education a formal system of teaching knowledge, values, and skills

Home schooling might seem to be a radical solution to today's education problems, but it is one that the parents of over a million U.S. children have chosen. We'll come back to this topic, but, first, let's take a broad look at education.

The Development of Modern Education

To provide a background for understanding our own educational system, let's look first at education in earlier societies, then trace the development of universal education.

Education in Earlier Societies

Earlier societies had no separate social institution called education. They had no special buildings called schools and no people who earned their living as teachers. Rather, as an ordinary part of growing up, children learned what was necessary to get along in life. If hunting or cooking were the essential skills, then parents and other relatives taught them to the children. *Education was synonymous with acculturation,* learning a culture. It still is in today's tribal groups.

In some societies—such as China, Greece, and North Africa—when a sufficient surplus developed, a separate institution for education appeared. Some people then devoted themselves to teaching, while those who had the leisure—the children of the wealthy—became their students. In ancient China, for example, Confucius taught a few select pupils, while in Greece, Aristotle, Plato, and Socrates taught science and philosophy to upper-class boys. Education, then, came to be something distinct from informal acculturation. **Education** is a group's *formal* system of teaching knowledge, values, and skills. Such instruction stood in marked contrast to the learning of traditional skills such as farming or hunting, for it was intended to develop the mind. Education flourished during the period roughly marked by the birth of Christ, then slowly died out. During the Dark Ages of Europe, monks kept the candle of enlightenment burning. Except for a handful of the wealthy and some members of the nobility, only the monks could read and write. Although the monks delved into philosophy, they focused on learning Greek, Latin, and Hebrew so that they could study the Bible and writings of early church leaders. The Jews also kept formal learning alive as they studied the Torah. In the Arab world, the center of learning was Baghdad, where the focus was on the Koran, poetry, philosophy, linguistics, and astronomy.

Formal education remained limited to those who had the leisure to pursue it. (The word *school* comes from the Greek word *scholé* meaning "leisure.") Industrialization transformed education, for some of the machinery and new types of jobs required workers to read, write, and work accurately with numbers—the classic three R's of the nineteenth century (Reading, 'Riting, and 'Rithmetic).

Industrialization and Universal Education

After the American Revolution, the founders of the new republic were concerned that the many contrasting religious and ethnic groups (nationalities) would make the nation unstable. To help create a uniform national culture, Thomas Jefferson and Noah Webster proposed universal schooling. Standardized texts would instill patriotism and

In hunting and gathering societies, there is no separate social institution called *education.* Instead, children learn from their parents and elders. These boys in South Africa are learning survival skills as their grandfather shows them lizard tracks in the sand.

teach the principles of representative government (Hellinger and Judd 1991). If this new political experiment were to succeed, they reasoned, it would need educated citizens who were capable of making sound decisions and voting wisely. A national culture remained elusive, however, and the country remained politically fragmented into the 1800s. Many states even considered themselves to be near-sovereign nations.

Education reflected this disunity. There was no comprehensive school system, just a hodgepodge of independent schools. Public schools even charged tuition. Lutherans, Presbyterians, and Roman Catholics operated their own schools (Hellinger and Judd 1991). Children of the rich attended private schools. Children of the poor received no formal education—nor did slaves. High school was considered higher education (hence the name *high* school), and only the wealthy could afford it. College, too, was beyond the reach of almost everyone.

This 1902 photo from Tuskegee, Alabama, provides a glimpse into the past, when free public education, pioneered in the United States, was still in its infancy. In these one-room rural schools, a single teacher had charge of grades 1 to 8. Children were assigned a grade not by age but by mastery of subject matter.

Horace Mann, an educator from Massachusetts, found it deplorable that parents with an average income could not afford to send their children to grade school. In 1837 he proposed that "common schools," supported through taxes, be established throughout his state. Mann's idea spread, and state after state began to provide free public education. It is no coincidence that universal education and industrialization occurred at the same time. As they observed the transformation of the economy, political and civic leaders recognized the need for an educated workforce. They also feared the influx of "foreign" values and, like the founders of the country, looked on public education as a way to "Americanize" immigrants (Hellinger and Judd 1991).

mandatory education laws
laws that require all children to attend school until a specified age or until they complete a minimum grade in school

By 1918, all U.S. states had **mandatory education laws** requiring children to attend school, usually until they completed the eighth grade or turned 16, whichever came first. By this time, schooling had become widespread, and graduation from the eighth grade marked the end of education for most people. "Dropouts" at that time were students who did not complete grade school.

As industrialization progressed and fewer people made their living from farming, even more years of formal education came to be regarded as essential to the well-being of society. As graduation from high school became more common, more students wanted a college education. Free education stopped with high school, however, and with the distance to the nearest college too far and the cost of tuition and lodging too great, most high school graduates were unable to attend college. As is discussed in the Down-to-Earth Sociology box on the next page, this predicament gave birth to community colleges. Figure 17.1 shows the incredible change in

FIGURE 17.1   Educational Achievement in the United States

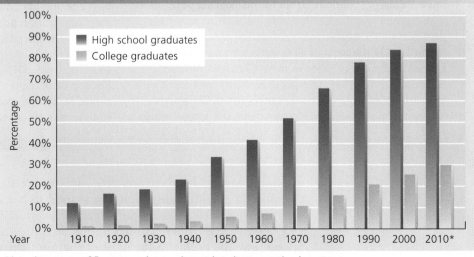

Note: Americans 25 years and over. Asterisk indicates author's estimate.

Sources: By the author. Based on National Center for Education Statistics 1991:Table 8; *Statistical Abstract of the United States* 2009:Table 221.

Down-to-Earth Sociology
Community Colleges: Facing Old and New Challenges

I attended a junior college in Oakland, California. From there, with fresh diploma in hand, I transferred to a senior college—a college in Fort Wayne, Indiana, that had no freshmen or sophomores.

I didn't realize that my experimental college matched the vision of some of the founders of the community college movement. In the early 1900s, they foresaw a system of local colleges that would be accessible to the average high school graduate—a system so extensive that it would be unnecessary for universities to offer courses at the freshman and sophomore levels (Manzo 2001).

A group with an equally strong opinion questioned whether preparing high school graduates for entry to four-year colleges and universities should be the goal of junior colleges. They insisted that the purpose of junior colleges should be vocational preparation, to equip people for the job market as electricians and other technicians. In some regions, where the proponents of transfer dominated, the admissions requirements for junior colleges were higher than those of Yale (Pedersen 2001). This debate was never won by either side, and you can still hear its echoes today (Van Noy et al. 2008).

The name *junior* college also became a problem. Some felt that the word *junior* made their institution sound as though it weren't quite a real college. A struggle to change the name ensued, and several decades ago *community* college won out.

The name change didn't settle the debate about whether the purpose was preparing students to transfer to universities or training them for jobs, however. Community colleges continue to serve this dual purpose.

Community colleges have become such an essential part of the U.S. educational system that almost two of every five (37 percent) of all undergraduates in the United States are enrolled in them (*Statistical Abstract* 2009:Table 270). They have become the major source of the nation's emergency medical technicians, firefighters, nurses, and police officers. Most students are *nontraditional*

Community colleges have opened higher education to millions of students who would not otherwise have access to college because of cost or distance.

students: Many are age 25 or older, are from the working class, have jobs and children, and attend college part-time (Bryant 2001; Panzarella 2008).

To help students who are not seeking occupational certificates transfer to four-year colleges and universities, many community colleges work closely with top-tier public and private universities (Chaker 2003b). Some provide admissions guidance on how to enter flagship state schools. Others coordinate courses, making sure that they match the university's title and numbering system, as well as its rigor of instruction and grading. More than a third offer honors programs that prepare talented students to transfer with ease into these schools (Padgett 2005).

Community colleges face the challenges of securing adequate budgets in the face of declining resources, adjusting to changing job markets, and maintaining quality instruction. Other challenges include offering effective remedial courses, meeting the shifting needs of students, such as teaching students for whom English is a second language, and providing on-campus day care for parents. In their quest to help students complete college, community colleges are also working to improve their orientation programs and to find better ways to monitor their students' progress (Panzarella 2008).

For Your Consideration
Do you think the primary goal of community colleges should be to prepare students for jobs or to prepare them to transfer to four-year colleges and universities? Why?

educational achievement. As you can see, receiving a bachelor's degree is now *twice* as common as completing high school used to be. Two of every three (66 percent) high school graduates enter college (*Statistical Abstract* 2009:Table 267).

One of seven Americans has not made it through high school, however, which leads to economic problems for most of them for the rest of their lives (*Statistical Abstract* 2009:Table 221). The Social Map on the next page shows how unevenly distributed high school graduation is among the states. You may want to compare this Social Map with the one on page 283 that shows how poverty is distributed among the states.

FIGURE 17.2 Not Making It: Dropping Out of High School

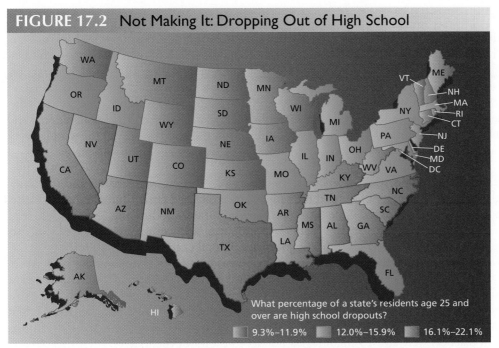

What percentage of a state's residents age 25 and over are high school dropouts?

☐ 9.3%–11.9%   ☐ 12.0%–15.9%   ☐ 16.1%–22.1%

Note: The states vary widely. The extremes range from 9.3 percent in Minnesota to 22.1 percent in Mississippi.

Source: By the author. Based on *Statistical Abstract of the United States* 2009:Table 225.

Education in Global Perspective

To further place our own educational system in perspective, let's look at education in three countries at different levels of industrialization. This will help us see how education is related to a nation's culture and its economy.

Education in the Most Industrialized Nations: Japan

A central sociological principle of education is that a nation's education reflects its culture. Because a core Japanese value is solidarity with the group, the Japanese discourage competition among individuals. In the workforce, people who are hired together work as a team. They are not expected to compete with one another for promotions; instead, they are promoted as a group (Ouchi 1993). Japanese education reflects this group-centered approach to life. Children in grade school work as a group, all mastering the same skills and materials. On any one day, children all over Japan study the same page from the same textbook ("Less Rote . . ." 2000).

In a fascinating cultural contradiction, college admissions in Japan are highly competitive. The Scholastic Assessment Test (SAT), taken by college-bound high school juniors and seniors in the United States, is voluntary, but Japanese seniors who want to attend college must take a national test. U.S. students who perform poorly on their tests can usually find some college to attend—as long as their parents can pay the tuition. Until recently, in Japan only the top scorers—rich and poor alike—were admitted to college. This is changing. Because of Japan's low birth rate, the pool of students has shrunk and Japan's colleges have begun to compete for students (McNeill 2008). As in the United States, children from the richer families score higher on college admission tests and are more likely to go to college. In each country, to be born into a richer family means to inherit privileges—among them having more highly educated parents, from grade school through high school being expected to bring home top grades, and enjoying cultural experiences that translate into higher test scores.

Education in the Industrializing Nations: Russia

After the Russian Revolution of 1917, the Soviet Communist party changed the nation's educational system. At that time, as in most countries, education was limited to children of the elite. The communists expanded the educational system until eventually it encompassed all children. Following the sociological principle that education reflects culture, the new government made certain that socialist values dominated its schools, for it saw education as a means to undergird the new political system. As a result, schoolchildren were taught that capitalism was evil and that communism was the salvation of the world. Every classroom was required to prominently display photographs of Lenin and Stalin.

Education, including college, was free. Just as the economy was directed from central headquarters in Moscow, so was education. Schools stressed mathematics and the natural sciences. Each school followed the same state-prescribed curriculum, and all students in the same grade used the same textbooks. To prevent critical thinking, which might lead to criticisms of communism, few courses in the social sciences were taught, and students memorized course materials, repeating lectures on oral exams (Deaver 2001).

Russia's switch from communism to capitalism brought a change in culture—especially new ideas about profit, private property, and personal freedom. This, in turn, meant that the educational system had to adjust to the country's changing values and views of the world. Not only did the photos of Lenin and Stalin come down, but also, for the first time, private, religious, and even foreign-run schools were allowed. For the first time as well, teachers were able to encourage students to think for themselves.

The problems that Russia confronted in "reinventing" its educational system are mind-boggling. Tens of thousands of teachers who had been teaching students to memorize Party-dictated political answers had to learn new methods of instruction. As the economy faltered during Russia's early transition to capitalism, school budgets dwindled. Some teachers went unpaid for months; instead of money, at one school teachers were given toilet paper and vodka (Deaver 2001). Teachers are now paid regularly (and in money), but the salaries are low. University professors average only $300 to $500 a month (Nemtsova 2008). Abysmal salaries have encouraged corruption, and some students pay for good grades and for admission to the better schools ("Russia Sets Out to . . ." 2007).

Because it is true of education everywhere, we can confidently predict that Russia's educational system will continue to reflect its culture. Its educational system will glorify Russia's historical exploits and reinforce its values and world views—no matter how they might change.

Education in the Least Industrialized Nations: Egypt

Education in the Least Industrialized Nations stands in sharp contrast to that in the industrialized world. Because most of the citizens of these nations work the land or take care of families, there is little emphasis on formal schooling. Mandatory attendance laws are not enforced. As we saw in Figure 9.3 (pages 248–249), many people in the Least Industrialized Nations live on less than $1,000 a year. Consequently, in some of these nations few children go to school beyond the first couple of grades. Figure 17.3 on the next page contrasts education in China with that of the United States. As was once common around

The poverty of the Least Industrialized Nations carries over to their educational systems. This school in Bangladesh is better off than some, which have no books, paper, or even buildings, just a blackboard on the street.

the globe, it is primarily the wealthy in the Least Industrialized Nations who have the means and the leisure for formal education—especially anything beyond the basics. As an example, let's look at education in Egypt.

Several centuries before the birth of Christ, Egypt's world-renowned centers of learning produced such acclaimed scientists as Archimedes and Euclid. The primary areas of study during this classic period were astronomy, geography, geometry, mathematics, medicine, philosophy, and physics. The largest library in the world was at Alexandria. Fragments from the papyrus manuscripts of this library, which burned to the ground, have been invaluable in deciphering ancient manuscripts. After Rome defeated Egypt, however, education declined and has never regained its former prominence.

Although the Egyptian constitution guarantees five years of free grade school for all children, many poor children receive no education at all. For those who do attend school, qualified teachers are few, and classrooms are crowded (Cook 2001). As a result, one-third of Egyptian men and over half of Egyptian women are illiterate (UNESCO 2005). Those who go beyond the five years of grade school attend a preparatory school for three years. High school also lasts for three years. During the first two years, all students take the same courses, but during the third year they specialize in arts, science, or mathematics. The emphasis has been on memorizing facts to pass national tests. As concerns have grown that this approach leaves minds less capable of evaluating life and opens the door to religious extremism, some Egyptian educators are pressing for critical thinking to be added to the curriculum (Gauch 2006). So far the government has been slow to respond, and little has changed (Dhillon et al. 2008).

The Functionalist Perspective: Providing Social Benefits

A central position of functionalism is that when the parts of society are working properly, each contributes to the well-being or stability of that society. The positive things that people intend their actions to accomplish are known as **manifest functions.** The positive consequences they did not intend are called **latent functions.** Let's look at the functions of education.

Teaching Knowledge and Skills

Education's most obvious manifest function is to teach knowledge and skills—whether the traditional three R's or their more contemporary counterparts, such as computer literacy. Each generation must train the next to fill the group's significant positions. Because our postindustrial society needs highly educated people, the schools supply them.

But testing in algebra or paragraph construction to sell gizmos at Radio Shack? Sociologist Randall Collins (1979) observed that industrialized nations have become **credential societies.** By this, he means that employers use diplomas and degrees as *sorting devices* to determine who is eligible for a job. Because employers don't know potential workers, they depend on schools to weed out the incapable. For example, when you graduate from college, potential employers will presume that you are a responsible person—that you have shown up for numerous classes, have turned in scores of assignments, and have demonstrated basic writing and thinking skills. They will then graft their particular job skills onto this foundation, which has been certified by your college.

In some cases, job skills must be mastered before you are allowed to do the work. On-the-job training was once adequate to become an engineer or an airline pilot, but with changes in information and technology it is no longer sufficient. This is precisely why doctors display their credentials so prominently. Their framed degrees declare that an institution of higher learning has certified them to work on your body.

Cultural Transmission of Values

Another manifest function of education is the **cultural transmission of values,** a process by which schools pass on a society's core values from one generation to the next. Consequently,

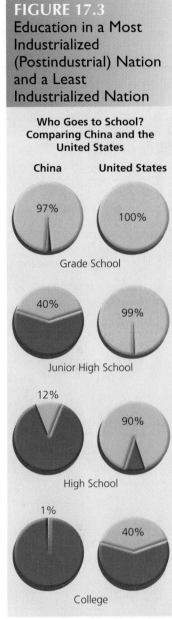

FIGURE 17.3

Education in a Most Industrialized (Postindustrial) Nation and a Least Industrialized Nation

Who Goes to School? Comparing China and the United States

China   United States

97%   100%

Grade School

40%   99%

Junior High School

12%   90%

High School

1%   40%

College

Note: These are initial attendance rates, not completion rates. The U.S. junior high school total is the author's estimate.

Sources: Brauchli 1994; Kahn 2004; Zeng and Wang 2007; *Statistical Abstract of the United States* 2009: Tables 215, 217, 264.

"Hey, how come no diplomas?" "Oh, I'm self-taught."

The cartoonist captures a primary reason that we have become a credential society.

schools in a socialist society stress values of socialism, while schools in a capitalist society teach values that support capitalism. U.S. schools, for example, stress the significance of private property, individualism, and competition.

Regardless of a country's economic system, loyalty to the state is a cultural value, and schools around the world teach patriotism. U.S. schools—as well as those of Russia, France, China, and other countries around the world—extol the society's founders, their struggle for freedom from oppression, and the goodness of the country's social institutions. Seldom is this function as explicit as it is in Japan, where the law requires that schools "cultivate a respect for tradition and culture, and love for the nation and homeland" (Nakamura 2006).

To visualize what the functionalists mean, consider how differently a course in U.S. history would be if taught in Cuba, Iran, and Muncie, Indiana.

Social Integration

Schools also bring about *social integration.* They promote a sense of national identity by having students salute the flag and sing the national anthem. One of the best examples of how U.S. schools promote political integration is how they have taught mainstream ideas and values to tens of millions of immigrants. Coming to regard themselves as Americans, the immigrants gave up their earlier national and cultural identities (Carper 2000; Thompson 2009).

This integrative function of education goes far beyond making people similar in their appearance, speech or even ways of thinking. *To forge a national identity is to stabilize the political system.* If people identify with a society's institutions and *perceive them as the basis of their own welfare,* they have no reason to rebel. This function is especially significant when it comes to the lower social classes, from which most social revolutionaries emerge. The wealthy already have a vested interest in maintaining the status quo, but getting the lower classes to identify with a social system *as it is* goes a long way toward preserving the system in its current state.

People with disabilities often have found themselves left out of the mainstream of society. To overcome this, U.S. schools have added a manifest function, **mainstreaming,** or inclusion. This means that educators try to incorporate students with disabilities into regular school activities. As a matter of routine policy, students with disabilities used to be placed in special classes or schools. There, however, they learned to adjust to a specialized situation, leaving them ill prepared to cope with the dominant world. To overcome this, U.S. schools have added a manifest function, mainstreaming, or inclusion. As in the photo on the next page, this means that educators try to incorporate students with disabilities into regular school activities. Wheelchair ramps are provided for people who cannot walk; interpreters who use sign language may attend classes with those who cannot hear. Most students who are blind attend special schools, as do people with severe learning disabilities. Most mainstreaming seems to go fairly smoothly, but mainstreaming students with serious emotional and behavioral problems disrupts classrooms, frustrates teachers, and increases teacher turnover (Tomsho and Golden 2007). Overall, one half of students with disabilities now attend school in regular classrooms (U.S. Department of Education 2007).

Gatekeeping

Gatekeeping, or determining which people will enter what occupations, is another function of education. One type of gatekeeping is *credentialing*—using diplomas and degrees to determine who is eligible for a job—which opens the door of opportunity for some and closes it to others. Gatekeeping is often accomplished by **tracking,** sorting students into different educational programs on the basis of their perceived abilities. Some U.S. high

mainstreaming helping people to become part of the mainstream of society

gatekeeping the process by which education opens and closes doors of opportunity; another term for the *social placement* function of education

tracking in education, the sorting of students into different programs on the basis of perceived abilities

schools funnel students into one of three tracks: general, college prep, or honors. Students on the lowest track are likely to go to work after high school, or to take vocational courses. Those on the highest track usually attend prestigious colleges. Those in between usually attend a local college or regional state university. The impact is lifelong, affecting opportunities for jobs, income, and lifestyle. Schools have retreated from formal tracking, but placing students in "ability groups" and "advanced" classes serves the same purpose (Lucas 1999; Tach and Farkas 2003).

Gatekeeping sorts people on the basis of merit, said functionalists Talcott Parsons (1940), Kingsley Davis, and Wilbert Moore (Davis and Moore 1945). They pioneered a view known as **social placement,** arguing that some jobs require few skills and can be performed by people of lesser intelligence. Other jobs, however, such as that of physician, require high intelligence and advanced education. To motivate capable people to postpone gratification and to put up with years of rigorous education, rewards of high income and prestige are offered. Thus, functionalists look at education as a system that, to benefit society, sorts people according to their abilities and ambitions.

Replacing Family Functions

Over the years, the functions of U.S. schools have expanded, and they now rival some family functions. Child care is an example. Grade schools do double duty as babysitters for families in which both parents work, or for single working mothers. Child care has always been a latent function of formal education, for it was an unintended consequence. Now, however, with two wage earners in most families, child care has become a manifest function, and some schools offer child care both before and after the school day. Some high schools even provide nurseries for the children of their teenaged students (Bosman 2007). Another function is providing sex education, and, as in 500 school-based health centers, birth control (Elliott 2007). This has stirred controversy, for some families resent schools taking this function away from them. Disagreement over values has fueled the social movement for home schooling, featured in our opening vignette and in the Down-to-Earth Sociology box on the next page.

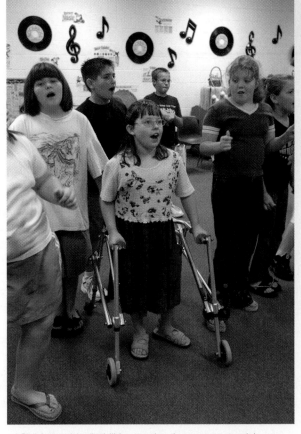

Children with disabilities used to be sent to special schools. In a process called *mainstreaming* or inclusion, they now attend regular schools. Shown here is a girl with cerebral palsy participating in music class in Gun Barrel City, Texas.

Other Functions

Education also fulfills other functions. One is *matchmaking.* Because most students are unmarried, it is at high school and college that many people meet their future spouses. The sociological significance is that schools funnel people into marriage with mates of similar background, interests, and education. Schools are also a source of *social networks;* some students make lifetime friendships, while others make contacts that benefit their careers. Schools also help to *reduce the unemployment rate.* To keep millions of young people in the classroom is to keep them out of the job market. Schools also *stabilize society* by keeping these millions off the streets, where they might be holding demonstrations and demanding change in the political system.

Another function of schools is to provide employment. With 49 million students in grade and high schools, and another 18 million enrolled in college, U.S. education is big business. Elementary and secondary schools provide jobs for over 4 million teachers and staff, while another 3 million teachers and staff work at colleges and universities (*Statistical Abstract* 2009:Tables 233, 248, 268, 285). Others earn their living in industries that service schools—from publishing textbooks to building schools and manufacturing pencils, paper, desks, and computers.

social placement a function of education—funneling people into a society's various positions

Down-to-Earth Sociology
Home Schooling: The Search for Quality and Values

Over a million U.S. students are homeschooled, including these two brothers in Maple Grove, Minnesota, who are taught by their mother.

"You're doing WHAT? You're going to teach your kids at home?" is the typical, incredulous response to parents who decide to home school their children. The unspoken questions are, "How can you teach? You're not trained. And taking your kids out of the public schools—Do you want your kids to be dumb and social misfits?"

The home-schooling movement was small at first, just a trickle of parents who were dissatisfied with the rigidity of the school bureaucracy, lax discipline, incompetent teachers, low standards, lack of focus on individual needs, and, in some instances, hostility to their religion. That trickle grew into a social movement, and now 1,100,000 U.S. children are being taught at home (*Statistical Abstract* 2008:Table 228).

Home schooling is far from new. In the colonial era, home schooling was the *typical* form of education (Carper 2000). Today's home-schooling movement is restoring this earlier pattern, but it also reflects a fascinating shift in U.S. politics. Political and religious *liberals* began the contemporary home-schooling movement in the 1950s and 1960s. Their objection was that the schools were too conservative. Then the schools changed, and in the 1970s and 1980s, political and religious *conservatives* embraced home schooling (Lines 2000; Stevens 2001). Their objection was that the schools were too liberal. Other parents have no political motivation. They are homeschooling their children because of concerns about safety at school and the lack of individual attention (Cooper and Sureau 2007; MacFarquhar 2008).

Does home schooling work? Can parents who are not trained as teachers actually teach? To find out, researchers tested 21,000 home schoolers across the nation (Rudner 1999). The results were astounding. The median scores for every test at every grade were in the 70th to 80th percentiles. The home schoolers outscored students in both public and Catholic schools.

The basic reason for the stunning success of home schooling appears to be the parents' involvement in their children's education. Home schoolers receive an intense, one-on-one education. Their curriculum—although it includes the subjects that are required by the state—is designed around the student's interests and needs. Ninety percent of students are taught by their mothers, ten percent by their fathers (Lines 2000). The parents' income is also above average.

We do not know what these home schoolers' test scores would have been if they had been taught in public schools. With their parents' involvement in their education, they likely would have done very well there, too. In addition, although the Rudner study was large, it was not a random sample, and we cannot say how the *average* home schooler is doing. But, then, we have no random sample of all public school students, either.

What about the children's social skills? Since they don't attend school with dozens and even hundreds of other students, do they become social misfits? The studies show that they do just fine on this level, too, that they even have fewer behavior problems than children who attend conventional schools (Lines 2000). Contrary to stereotypes, home-schooled children are not isolated. As part of their educational experience, their parents take them to libraries, museums, factories, and nursing homes (Medlin 2000). Some home schoolers also participate in the physical education and sports programs of the public schools. For social activities, many of the children meet with other homeschooled children and go on field trips together. Parents have also formed regional and national home-schooling associations and hold national sports championships (Cooper and Sureau 2007; Drape 2008). The same companies that sell class rings to public high schools also sell class rings to home schoolers (McGinn and McLure 2003).

How about getting into college? How can home-schooled children be admitted without official transcripts? This has been a problem, but as homeschooling has become widespread, colleges have adjusted. Now three of four colleges have procedures for admitting home schoolers (Cooper and Sureau 2007).

For Your Consideration
Why do you think that home schooling has become so popular? Do you think this social movement could eventually become a threat to U.S. public schools? Would you consider home schooling your children? Why or why not?

A Surprising Latent Function.   Researchers have found a surprising effect of education: On average, the farther that people go in school, the longer they live. Americans who drop out of high school live to an average age of 75, but those who go beyond high school live to an average age of 82 (Meara et al. 2008). The most likely reasons are that the more educated live healthier (better diets and less smoking) and have better jobs, higher pay, and superior medical services.

The Conflict Perspective: Perpetuating Social Inequality

Unlike functionalists, who look at the benefits of education, conflict theorists examine how *the educational system reproduces the social class structure.* By this, they mean that schools perpetuate the social divisions of society and help members of the elite to maintain their dominance.

Let's look, then, at how education is related to social classes, how it helps people inherit the life opportunities that were laid down before they were born.

The Hidden Curriculum

The term **hidden curriculum** refers to the attitudes and the unwritten rules of behavior that schools teach in addition to the formal curriculum. Examples are obedience to authority and conformity to mainstream norms. Conflict theorists stress that the hidden curriculum helps to perpetuate social inequalities.

To understand this central point, consider the way English is taught. Schools for the middle class—whose teachers know where their students are headed—stress "proper" English and "good" manners. In contrast, the teachers in inner-city schools—who also know where *their* students are headed—allow ethnic and street language in the classroom. Each type of school is helping to reproduce the social class structure. That is, each is preparing students to work in positions similar to those of their parents. The social class of some children destines them for higher positions. For these jobs, they need "refined" speech and manners. The social destiny of others is low-status jobs. For this type of work, they need only to obey rules (Bowles and Gintis 1976; 2002). Teaching these students "refined" speech and manners would be a wasted effort. In other words, even the teaching of English and manners helps keep the social classes intact across generations.

From the conflict perspective, even kindergarten has a hidden curriculum, as the Down-to-Earth Sociology box on the next page illustrates.

Tilting the Tests: Discrimination by IQ

Even intelligence tests help to keep the social class system intact. Let's look at an example. How would you answer this question?

> **A symphony is to a composer as a book is to a(n) ___**
> **___ paper ___ sculptor ___ musician ___ author ___ man**

You probably had no difficulty coming up with "author" as your choice. Wouldn't any intelligent person have done so?

In point of fact, this question raises a central issue in intelligence testing. Not all intelligent people would know the answer. This question contains *cultural biases.* Children from some backgrounds

Stressing that education reproduces a country's social class system, conflict theorists point out that the social classes attend separate schools. There they learn perspectives of the world that match their place in it. Shown here are students at a private school in Argentina. What do you think this school's *hidden curriculum* is?

Down-to-Earth Sociology
Kindergarten as Boot Camp

After he did participant observation in a kindergarten, sociologist Harry Gracey (1991/2007) concluded that kindergarten is a sort of boot camp for education. Here, tender students from diverse backgrounds are molded into a compliant group that will, on command, follow classroom routines. "Show and tell," for example, does more than allow children to be expressive. It also teaches them to talk only when they are asked to speak. ("It's your turn, Jarmay.") The format instructs children to request permission to talk ("Who knows what Adela has?") by raising a hand and being acknowledged. This ritual also teaches children to acknowledge the teacher's ideas as superior. She alone has the capacity to evaluate what students say and do.

Gracey also found a *hidden curriculum* in other activities he observed. Whether students were drawing pictures, listening to music, eating snacks, or resting, the teachers would scold talkative students and give approval to those who conformed. In short, the children received the message that the teacher—and, by inference, the entire school system—is the authority.

This, Gracey concluded, is not a side issue—it is *the* purpose of kindergarten. The kindergarten teacher's job is to teach children to "follow orders with unquestioning obedience." It is to "create and enforce a rigid social structure in the classroom through which they effectively control the behavior of most of the children for most of the school day."

This produces three kinds of students: (1) *"good"* students, those who submit to school-imposed discipline and come to identify with it; (2) *"adequate"* students, those who submit to the school's discipline but do not identify with it; and (3) *"bad"* students, those who refuse to submit to school routines. Children in the third category are called "problem children." To bring them into line, tougher drill sergeants—the principal and the school psychologist—are called in. If that doesn't work, the problem children are drugged into docility with Ritalin.

These early lessons extend beyond the classroom. As Gracey notes, school serves as a boot camp to prepare students for the routines of the work world, both on the assembly line and at the office. School helps turn children into docile workers who follow the routines imposed by "the company."

For Your Consideration

Gracey has a negative reaction to teaching so much discipline in kindergarten. What is your reaction? How else can schools exist if students don't listen quietly to their teachers? What would happen if students didn't learn obedience to authority early and later questioned what they were being taught?

---

are more familiar with the concepts of symphonies, composers, and sculptors than are other children. Consequently, the test is tilted in their favor.

To make the bias clearer, try to answer this question:

If you throw two dice and "7" is showing on the top, what is facing down?
____ *seven* ____ *snake eyes* ____ *box cars* ____ *little Joes* ____ *eleven*

Adrian Dove (n.d.), a social worker in Watts, a poor area of Los Angeles, suggested this question. Its cultural bias should be obvious—that it allows children from certain social backgrounds to perform better than others. Unlike the first question, this one is not tilted to the middle-class experience. In other words, IQ (intelligence quotient) tests measure not only intelligence but also acquired knowledge.

You should now be able to perceive the bias of IQ tests that use such words as *composer* and *symphony*. A lower-class child may have heard about rap, rock, gangsta, or jazz, but not about symphonies. One consequence of this bias to the middle-class experience is that the children of the poor score lower on IQ tests. Then, to match their supposedly inferior intelligence, these children are assigned to less demanding courses. Their inferior education helps them reach their social destiny, their lower-paying jobs in adult life. As conflict theorists view them, then, IQ tests are another weapon in an arsenal designed to maintain the social class structure across the generations.

Stacking the Deck: Unequal Funding

As you can see from the Social Map at right, the amount spent on educating children varies widely among the states. Although there is no one-for-one match, in general, the states that spend more on education have higher quality schools. A main reason is that they attract more highly qualified teachers. Conflict theorists go beyond this, however, and stress the sig-

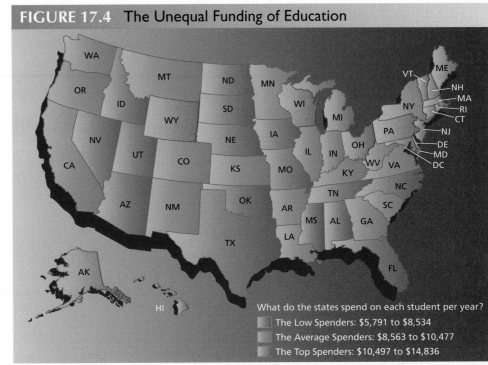

FIGURE 17.4   The Unequal Funding of Education

What do the states spend on each student per year?
- The Low Spenders: $5,791 to $8,534
- The Average Spenders: $8,563 to $10,477
- The Top Spenders: $10,497 to $14,836

Note: Some states spend more than twice as much to educate their students. The range is from $5,791 in Arizona to $14,836 in Vermont. At $17,152, the District of Columbia is in a class by itself.

Source: By the author. Based on *Statistical Abstract of the United States* 2009: Table 251.

nificance of *how* U.S. schools are funded. Because public schools are supported largely by local property taxes, the richer communities (where property values and incomes are higher) have more to spend on their children, and the poorer communities have less to spend on theirs. Consequently, the richer communities can offer higher salaries and take their pick of the most highly qualified and motivated teachers. They can also afford to buy the latest textbooks, computers, and software, as well as offer courses in foreign languages, music, and the arts. This, stress conflict theorists, means that in *all* states the deck is stacked against the poor.

The Correspondence Principle

In a classic analysis, conflict sociologists Samuel Bowles and Herbert Gintis (1976, 2002) used the term **correspondence principle** to refer to how schools reflect society. This term means that what is taught in a nation's schools *corresponds* to the characteristics of that society. Here are some examples.

Characteristics of Society	**Characteristics of Schools**
1. Capitalism	1. Encourage competition
2. Social inequality	2. Unequal funding of schools
3. Social class bias	3. Funnel children of the poor into job training programs that demand little thinking
4. Bureaucratic structure of corporations	4. Provide a model of authority in the classroom
5. Need for submissive workers	5. Make students submissive, as in the kindergarten boot camp
6. Need for dependable workers	6. Enforce punctuality in attendance and homework
7. Need to maintain armed forces	7. Promote patriotism

correspondence principle the sociological principle that schools correspond to (or reflect) the social structure of their society

FIGURE 17.5   Who Goes to College? Comparing Social Class and Ability in Determining College Attendance

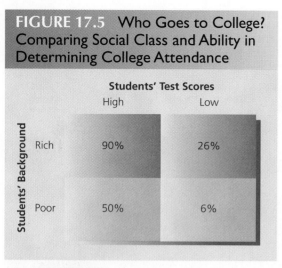

Source: Bowles 1977.

FIGURE 17.6   The Funneling Effects of Education: Race-Ethnicity

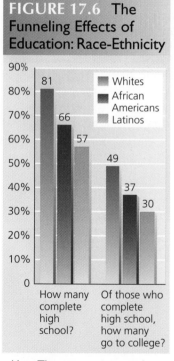

Note: The source gives totals only for these three groups.

Source: By the author. Based on *Statistical Abstract of the United States* 2009:Table 270.

Conflict theorists conclude that the correspondence principle demonstrates that the U.S. educational system is designed to turn students into dependable workers who will not question their bosses. It also is intended to produce some who are innovators in thought and action, but who can still be counted on to be loyal to the social system as it exists (Olneck and Bills 1980).

The Bottom Line: Family Background

The end result of unequal funding, IQ tests, and the other factors we have discussed is this: Family background is more important than test scores in predicting who attends college. In a classic study, sociologist Samuel Bowles (1977) compared the college attendance of the brightest 25 percent of high school students with that of the intellectually weakest 25 percent. Figure 17.5 shows the results. Of the *brightest* 25 percent of high school students, 90 percent of those from affluent homes went to college, while only half of those from low-income homes did. Of the *intellectually weakest* students, 26 percent from affluent homes went to college, while only 6 percent from poorer homes did so.

Other sociologists have confirmed this classic research. Anthony Carnevale and Stephen Rose (2003) compared students' college attendance with their intellectual abilities and their parents' social class. Regardless of personal abilities, children from more well-to-do families are more likely not only to go to college but also to attend the nation's most elite schools. This, in turn, piles advantage upon advantage, because they get higher-paying and more prestigious jobs when they graduate. The elite colleges are the icing on the cake of these students' more privileged birth.

Conflict theorists point out that the educational system reproduces not only the U.S. social class structure but also its racial–ethnic divisions. From Figure 17.6, you can see that, compared with whites, African Americans and Latinos are much less likely to complete high school and, of those who do, much less likely to go to college. Because adults without college degrees usually end up with low-paying, dead-end jobs, you can see how this supports the conflict view—that education is helping to reproduce the racial–ethnic structure for the next generation.

Table 17.1 below gives us another snapshot of the significance of race–ethnicity and college attendance. From this table, you can see that whites are the most likely to attend four-year colleges, which supports the conflict perspective. But you can also see that African Americans are the most likely to attend private colleges, which does not support this perspective. You can also see, however, that Latinos and Native Americans are less likely to attend private colleges. This, coupled with their being less likely to attend college in the first place, helps to perpetuate some of society's racial–ethnic divisions.

In Sum: U.S. schools closely reflect the U.S. social class system. They equip the children of the elite with the tools they need to maintain their dominance, while they prepare the children of the poor for lower-status positions. Because education's doors of opportunity swing wide open for some but have to be pried open by others, conflict theorists say that the educational system perpetuates social inequality across generations (or, as they often phrase it, helps to reproduce the social class structure). In fact, they add, this is one of its primary purposes.

TABLE 17.1   Types of College and Race–Ethnicity

	Public	Private	2-Year	4-Year
Whites	74%	26%	35%	65%
African Americans	71%	29%	41%	59%
Asian Americans	78%	22%	38%	62%
Latinos	81%	19%	52%	48%
Native Americans	81%	19%	46%	54%

Source: By the author. Based on *Statistical Abstract of the United States* 2009:Table 270.

The Symbolic Interactionist Perspective: Teacher Expectations

Functionalists look at how education benefits society, and conflict theorists examine how education perpetuates social inequality. Symbolic interactionists, in contrast, study face-to-face interaction in the classroom. They have found that the expectations of teachers have profound consequences for their students.

The Rist Research

Why do some people get tracked into college prep courses and others into vocational ones? There is no single answer, but in what has become a classic study, sociologist Ray Rist came up with some intriguing findings. Rist (1970, 2000) did participant observation in an African American grade school with an African American faculty. He found that after only eight days in the classroom, the kindergarten teacher felt that she knew the children's abilities well enough to assign them to three separate worktables. To Table 1, Mrs. Caplow assigned those she considered to be "fast learners." They sat at the front of the room, closest to her. Those whom she saw as "slow learners," she assigned to Table 3, located at the back of the classroom. She placed "average" students at Table 2, in between the other tables.

This seemed strange to Rist. He knew that the children had not been tested for ability, yet their teacher was certain that she could identify the bright and slow children. Investigating further, Rist found that social class was the underlying basis for assigning the children to the different tables. Middle-class students were separated out for Table 1, and children from poorer homes were assigned to Tables 2 and 3. The teacher paid the most attention to the children at Table 1, who were closest to her, less to Table 2, and the least to Table 3. As the year went on, children from Table 1 perceived that they were treated better and came to see themselves as smarter. They became the leaders in class activities and even ridiculed children at the other tables, calling them "dumb." Eventually, the children at Table 3 disengaged themselves from many classroom activities. At the end of the year, only the children at Table 1 had completed the lessons that prepared them for reading.

This early tracking stuck. Their first-grade teacher looked at the work these students had done, and she placed students from Table 1 at her Table 1. She treated her tables much as the kindergarten teacher had, and the children at Table 1 again led the class.

The children's reputations continued to follow them. The second-grade teacher reviewed their scores and also divided her class into three groups. The first she named the "Tigers" and, befitting their name, gave them challenging readers. Not surprisingly, the Tigers came from the original Table 1 in kindergarten. The second group she called the "Cardinals." They came from the original Tables 2 and 3. Her third group consisted of children she had failed the previous year, whom she called the "Clowns." The Cardinals and Clowns were given less advanced readers.

Rist concluded that *each child's journey through school was determined by the eighth day of kindergarten!* As we saw with the Saints and Roughnecks, in Chapter 4, labels can be so powerful that they can set people on courses of action that affect the rest of their lives.

Education can be a dangerous thing. Socrates, who taught in Greece about 400 years before the birth of Christ, was forced to take poison because his views challenged those of the establishment. Usually, however, educators reinforce the perspectives of the elite, teaching students to take their place within the social structure. This 1787 painting, "The Death of Socrates," is by J. L. David (1748–1825).

What occurred was a **self-fulfilling prophecy.** This term, coined by sociologist Robert Merton (1949/1968), refers to a false assumption of something that is going to happen but which then comes true simply because it was predicted. For example, if people believe an unfounded rumor that a credit union is going to fail because its officers have embezzled their money, they all rush to the credit union to demand their money. The prediction—although originally false—is now likely to come true.

The Rosenthal-Jacobson Experiment

Let's look at another classic example of the self-fulfilling prophecy in education. This one, too, holds some surprises. All of us know about teacher expectations—that some teachers have higher standards and expect work of a higher quality. Teacher expectations, however, also work at a very subtle level. In a famous experiment, social psychologists Robert Rosenthal and Lenore Jacobson (1968) told the teachers in a San Francisco grade school that they had developed a predictive test of children's abilities. After testing their students, they told them which students would probably "spurt" ahead during the year. They told the teachers to watch these students' progress, but not to let the students or their parents know about the test results. At the end of the year, they tested the students again. As they predicted, the "spurters" had spurted: Their IQs had jumped ten to fifteen points!

Did Rosenthal and Jacobson become world-famous for developing a powerful scholastic aptitude test? Actually, they hadn't developed any test at all, much less something this astounding. They had just done another of those covert experiments. They had given routine IQ tests to the children and then had *randomly* chosen 20 percent of the students as "spurters." These students were *no* different from their classmates. The "spurting," though, was real. What had happened was a self-fulfilling prophecy: The teachers expected more from those particular students, and responding to subtle cues, these students learned more and performed better on the tests.

A good deal of research confirms that, *regardless of their abilities,* students who are expected to do better generally do better, and those who are expected to do poorly do poorly (Rosenthal 1998; McKown and Weinstein 2002, 2008). In short, expect dumb and you get dumb. Expect smart, and you get smart.

How Do Teacher Expectations Work?

Sociologist George Farkas (1990a, 1990b, 1996) became interested in how teacher expectations affect grades. Using a stratified sample of students in a large school district in Texas, he found that teacher expectations produced gender and racial–ethnic biases. *On the gender level:* Even though boys and girls had the same test scores, girls on average were given higher course grades. *On the racial–ethnic level:* Asian Americans who had the same test scores as the other groups averaged higher grades than did African Americans, Latinos, and whites.

At first, this may sound like more of the same old news—another case of discrimination. But this explanation doesn't fit, which is what makes the finding fascinating. Look at who the victims are. It is most unlikely that the teachers would be prejudiced against boys and whites. To interpret these unexpected results, Farkas used symbolic interactionism. He observed that some students "signal" to their teachers that they are "good students." They show an eagerness to cooperate, and they quickly agree with what the teacher says. They also show that they are "trying hard." The teachers pick up these signals and reward these "good students" with better grades. Girls and Asian Americans, the researcher concluded, are better at giving these signals so coveted by teachers.

We do not have enough information on how teachers communicate their expectations to students. Nor do we know much about how students "signal" messages to teachers. Perhaps you will become the educational sociologist who will shed more light on this significant area of human behavior.

self-fulfilling prophecy Robert Merton's term for an originally false assertion that becomes true simply because it was predicted

Problems in U.S. Education— and Their Solutions

Now that we've looked at some of the dynamics within the classroom, let's turn to three problems facing U.S. education—mediocrity, cheating, and violence—and consider their potential solutions.

Mediocrity

The Rising Tide of Mediocrity.   Since I know you love taking tests, let's see how you do on these three questions:

1. How many goals are on a basketball court? a. 1 b. 2 c. 3 d. 4
2. How many halves are in a college basketball game? a. 1 b. 2 c. 3 d. 4
3. How many points does a three-point field goal account for in a basketball game? a. 1 b. 2 c. 3 d. 4

I know that this sounds like a joke, but it isn't. Sociologist Robert Benford (2007) got his hands on a copy of a 20-question final examination given to basketball players who took a credit course on coaching principles at the University of Georgia. It is usually difficult to refer to athletes, sports, and academics in the same breath, but this is about as mediocre as mediocrity can get.

Let's move to a broader view of mediocrity, which plagues our educational system like pollution plagues gasoline engines:

- All Arizona high school sophomores took a math test. As you would expect, the test covered the math that sophomores should know. *One of ten passed.*
- In Tennessee, state officials were so pleased at *their* test results that they called a news conference. They boasted that 87 percent of their students were proficient at math—and they had the test results to prove it. When the federal government retested the students, the results dropped just a bit—to 21 percent (Dillon 2005b).
- These are appalling conditions, but the situation gets worse. Schools have reduced their standards so greatly that only *34 percent* of U.S. high school graduates are ready for college (Greene and Winters 2005).

How about our SAT tests? How are we doing on them? The news is mixed. First the good news. Look at Figure 17.7. You can see how the scores dropped from the 1960s to 1980. At that point, educators sounded an alarm—and even Congress expressed concern. School officials decided that they had better do something if they didn't want to lose their jobs. They raised their standards, and the SAT scores started to climb. The recovery in math is encouraging. Today's high school seniors now score the same in math as seniors did in the 1960s. Administrators are requiring more of teachers, and teachers are requiring more of students. Each is performing according to these higher expectations.

But then there is the bad news. Look at the verbal scores on Figure 17.7. Their drop from the 1960s was even larger than the drop in math, and they have not recovered. No one knows why these scores remain so low, but the usual suspects are rounded up: "dummied down" textbooks, less rigorous teaching, and less reading because of watching television and playing video and computer games. Today's

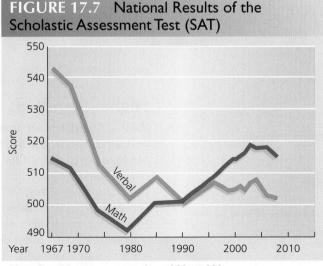

FIGURE 17.7   National Results of the Scholastic Assessment Test (SAT)

Note: Possible scores range from 200 to 800.

Source: By the author. Based on Jashik 2008; *Statistical Abstract of the United States* 2009:Table 258.

students perform so poorly that they couldn't handle analogies, which demand penetrating thinking. Rather than facing the bad news—which might force schools to do a better job of teaching, as they did with math—the makers of the SAT took the easy way out: They avoided embarrassment by eliminating the analogy part of the test.

How to Cheat on the SATs.   If you receive poor grades this semester, wouldn't you like to use a magic marker—to—presto!—change them into higher grades? I suppose every student would. Now imagine that you had that power. Would you use it?

Some people in authority apparently have found such a magic marker, and they have used it to raise our low national SAT scores. Table 274 of the 1996 edition of the *Statistical Abstract of the United States* reports that in 1995 only 8.3 percent of students earned 600 or more on the verbal portion of the SAT test. The very next edition, in 1997, however, holds a pleasant surprise. Table 276 tells us that it was really 21.9 percent of students who scored 600 or higher in 1995. Later editions of this source retain the higher figure. What a magic marker!

In the twinkle of an eye, we get another bonus. Somehow, between 1996 and 1997 the scores of *everyone* who took the test in previous years improved. Now that's the kind of power we all would like to have. Students, grab your report cards. Workers, change those numbers on your paycheck.

It certainly is easier to give easier tests than to teach more effectively. And this is what has happened to the SAT. The results were so embarrassing to U.S. educators that the SAT was made easier. Not only was testing on antonyms and analogies dropped, but the test was also shortened and students were given more time to answer the fewer questions. The test makers then "rescored" the totals of previous years to match the easier test. This "dummying down" of the SAT is a form of grade inflation, the topic to which we shall now turn.

Grade Inflation, Social Promotion, and Functional Illiteracy.   The letter grade C used to indicate average, and since more students are average than superior, high school teachers used to give about twice as many *C*'s as *A*'s. Now they give more *A*'s than *C*'s. Students aren't smarter—grading is just easier. Grades have become so inflated that some of today's *A*'s are the *C*'s of years past. **Grade inflation** is so pervasive that *46 percent* of all college freshmen have an overall high school grade point average of *A*. This is more than *twice* what it was in 1970 (*Statistical Abstract* 2009:Table 276). Grade inflation has also hit the Ivy League. At Harvard University, *half* of the course grades are *A*'s and *A*–'s. *Ninety* percent of Harvard students graduate with honors. To rein in "honor inflation," the Harvard faculty voted to limit the number of students who graduate with honors to 60 percent of a class (Hartocollis 2002; Douthat 2005).

Easy grades and declining standards have been accompanied by **social promotion,** passing students from one grade to the next even though they have not learned the basic materials. One result is **functional illiteracy,** high school graduates who never mastered even things they should have learned in grade school. They even have difficulty with reading and writing. Some high school graduates can't fill out job applications; others can't even figure out whether they get the right change at the grocery store.

Higher Standards

Raising Standards for Teachers.   It is one thing to identify problems, quite another to find solutions for them. How can we solve mediocrity? To offer a quality education, we need quality teachers. Don't we already have them? Most teachers are qualified and, if motivated, can do an excellent job. But a large number of teachers are not qualified. Consider just a couple of items. California requires that its teachers pass an educational skills test. California's teachers did so poorly that to get enough teachers to fill their classrooms, officials had to drop the passing grade to the 10th-grade level. These are college graduates who are teachers—and they are expected to perform at the 10th-grade level (Schemo 2002). I don't know about you, but I think this situation is a national disgrace. If we want to improve teaching, we need to insist that teachers meet high standards.

Our schools compete with private industry for the same pool of college graduates. If the starting salary in other fields is higher than it is in education, those fields will attract brighter, more energetic graduates. Figure 17.8 on the next page highlights the abysmal job we are doing in this competition for talent. Despite this, however, there is a shimmer of good news.

grade inflation higher grades given for the same work; a general rise in student grades without a corresponding increase in learning

social promotion passing students on to the next level even though they have not mastered basic materials

functional illiterate a high school graduate who has difficulty with basic reading and math

The SAT scores of those who are joining the ranks of teachers are climbing, and the average new teacher is now more qualified than those who began teaching several years ago (Gitomer 2007).

Raising Standards for Students. What else can we do to improve the quality of education? An older study by sociologists James Coleman and Thomas Hoffer (1987) provides helpful guidelines. They wanted to see why the test scores of students in Roman Catholic schools average 15 to 20 percent higher than those of students in public schools. Is it because Catholic schools attract better students, while public schools have to put up with everyone?

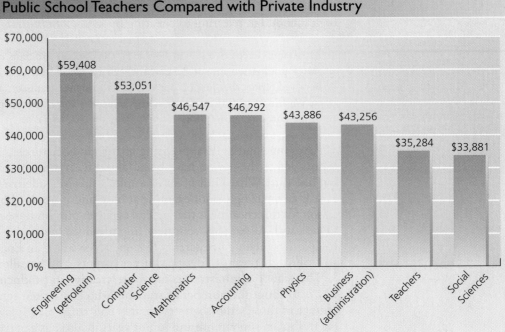

FIGURE 17.8 Starting Salaries of U.S. College Graduates, BA or BS Degree: Public School Teachers Compared with Private Industry

- Engineering (petroleum): $59,408
- Computer Science: $53,051
- Mathematics: $46,547
- Accounting: $46,292
- Physics: $43,886
- Business (administration): $43,256
- Teachers: $35,284
- Social Sciences: $33,881

Note: Starting salaries for BA or BS degree.

Sources: By the author. Based on American Federation of Teachers 2008; *Statistical Abstract of the United States* 2009: Table 287.

To find out, they tested 15,000 students in public and Catholic high schools.

Their findings? From the sophomore through the senior years, students at Catholic schools pull ahead of public school students by a full grade in verbal and math skills. The superior test performance of students in Catholic schools, they concluded, is due not to better students, but to higher standards. Catholic schools have not watered down their curricula as have public schools. The researchers also underscored the importance of parental involvement. Parents and teachers in Catholic schools reinforce each other's commitment to learning.

These findings support the basic principle reviewed earlier about teacher expectations: Students perform better when they are expected to meet higher standards. To this, you might want to reply, "Of course. I knew that. Who wouldn't?" Somehow, however, this basic principle is lost on many teachers, who end up teaching at a low level because they expect little of their students and have supervisors who accept low student performance. The reason, actually, is probably not their lack of awareness of such basics, but, rather, the organization that entraps them, a bureaucracy in which ritual replaces performance. To understand this point better, you may want to review Chapter 7.

A Warning About Higher Standards. If we raise standards, we can expect protest. It is less upsetting to use low standards and to tell students that they are doing well than it is to do rigorous teaching and use high standards to measure student performance. When Florida decided that its high school seniors needed to pass an assessment test in order to receive a diploma, 13,000 students failed the test. Parents of failed students banded together—not to demand better teaching but to pressure the state to drop the new test. They asked people to boycott Disney World and to not buy Florida orange juice (Candy 2003). What positive steps to improve their children's learning!

Let's look at a second problem in education.

On average, students in Roman Catholic schools score higher on national tests than students in public schools. Is it because Roman Catholic schools have better students, or because they do better teaching? The text reports the sociological findings.

Cheating

I'm not referring to the cheating you saw in your social studies or mathematics class in high school. I'm referring to cheating by *school administrators*. Listen to this:

> **Mississippi keeps two sets of books: In the one, statisticians crunch numbers and record the state's graduation rate at 87 percent. For its second set of books, statisticians crunch numbers and report that just 63 percent of its students graduate. They report the 87 percent rate to Washington. California does the same. Its totals are 83 percent and 67 percent. So do other states. (Dillon 2008)**

As strange and as disappointing as it sounds, it turns out that high school administrators across the nation have been faking their graduation rates. Why are they cheating like this? What kind of an example is this to students?

It is an amazingly poor example at best, and it needs to be exposed for what it is. The reason for this cheating is that federal agencies publish these reports, and states don't want to look bad. Also, the government might reduce the money states get from Washington. It's like a girl telling her parents that she received a B in English when she really received a D. She didn't want to disappoint her parents, and her allowance might be cut.

The school administrators are quite creative in producing their fake numbers. One way is to count the number of students who begin their senior year, and report the percentage of those seniors who graduate. This conveniently overlooks all their dropouts in the freshman, sophomore and junior years. It also has a perverse effect. Some administrators encourage high school students who are doing poorly to drop out before they reach their senior year. This way, they won't be counted as dropouts (Dillon 2008).

The solution to this problem is fairly simple. Develop a straightforward measurement of high school graduation and require all states to follow it. A simple measure is to compare the number of those who graduate from high school with those who entered high school in the ninth grade four years earlier, minus those who died and those who transferred out plus those who transferred in. Federal officials could spot-check records across the nation, publicize the names of any administrators who cheated on computing the rate, and make certain they were fired and could not receive another job in education for a minimum of five years. It is likely that honesty in reporting would jump immediately. Real graduation rates would help pinpoint where the problems are, helping us to know where to focus solutions. If you don't know where its broken, you don't know where to fix it.

Let's turn to the third problem.

Violence

Some U.S. schools have deteriorated to the point that safety is an issue. In these schools, uniformed guards and metal detectors have become permanent fixtures. Everywhere, school officials fear that "it could happen here." In an era of bomb threats and armed, roaming sociopaths, some states now require lockdown, or "Code Blue," drills: The classrooms—each equipped with a phone—are locked, the windows are locked, and the shades are drawn. The students are told to remain absolutely silent, while a school official wanders the halls, like an armed intruder, listening for the slightest sound that would indicate that someone was in a classroom (Kelley 2008).

School shootings are a national concern. For a surprising analysis of deaths at school, read the Mass Media box on the next page.

A Secure Learning Environment.   The first step in offering a good education is to keep students safe and free from fear. With the high rate of violence in the United States, we can expect some violence to spill over into the schools. To minimize this spillover, school administrators can expel all students who threaten the welfare of others. They also can refuse to tolerate threats, violence, and weapons. The zero tolerance policy for guns and other weapons on school property that school boards and administrators have adopted helps to make schools safer.

MASS MEDIA In SOCIAL LIFE

School Shootings: Exploring a Myth

The media sprinkle their reports of school shootings with such dramatic phrases as "alarming proportions," "outbreak of violence," and "out of control." They give us the impression that wackos walk our hallways, ready to spray our schools with gunfire. Parents used to consider schools safe havens, but no longer. Those naïve thoughts have been shattered by the bullets that have ripped through schools—or at least by the media's portrayal of growing danger and violence in our schools.

Have our schools really become war zones, as the mass media would have us believe? Certainly events such as those at Columbine High School and Virginia Tech are disturbing, but we need to probe deeper than newspaper headlines and televised images.

When we do, we find that the media's sensationalist reporting has created a myth. Contrary to "what everyone knows," *there is no trend toward greater school violence.* In fact, the situation is just the opposite—*the trend is toward greater safety.* Despite the dramatic school shootings that make headlines, as Table 17.2 shows, shooting deaths at schools are *decreasing.* The average number of annual shooting deaths for 1992 to 1999 is 30, which is *twice* as high as the annual average of 15 for 2000 to 2007.

This is not to say that school shootings are not a serious problem. Even one student being wounded or killed is too many. But, contrary to the impression fostered by the media, school shooting deaths have dropped sharply.

This is one reason that we need sociology: to quietly, dispassionately search for facts so we can better understand the events that shape our lives. The first requirement for solving any problem is accurate data, for how can we create rational solutions that are based on hysteria? The information presented in this box may not make for sensational headlines, but it does serve to explode one of the myths that the media have created.

This frame from a home video shows Eric Harris (on the left) and Dylan Klebold (on the right) as they pretend that they are searching for victims. They put their desires into practice in the infamous Columbine High School shootings.

For Your Consideration

How do you think we can reduce school shootings? How about school violence of any sort?

TABLE 17.2	Exploding a Myth: Deaths at U.S. Schools[1]				
			VICTIMS		
School Year	Shooting Deaths	Other Deaths[2]	Boys	Girls	Total
1992–1993	45	11	49	7	56
1993–1994	41	12	41	12	53
1994–1995	16	5	18	3	21
1995–1996	29	7	26	10	36
1996–1997	15	11	18	8	26
1997–1998	36	8	27	17	44
1998–1999	25	6	24	7	31
1999–2000	16	16	26	6	32
2000–2001	19	5	20	4	24
2001–2002	4	2	6	0	6
2002–2003	14	8	16	6	22
2003–2004	29	13	37	5	42
2004–2005	20	8	20	8	28
2005–2006	5	0	4	1	5
2006–2007	16	4	13	7	20
Total 1992–2007	330	114	343	101	446
Mean 1992–2007	22.0	7.6	22.9	6.7	29.6

[1]Includes all school-related homicides, even those that occurred on the way to or from school. Includes suicides, school personnel killed at school by other adults, and even adults who had nothing to do with the school but who were found dead on school property. Source does not report on deaths at colleges, only K–12 (kindergarten through high school).
[2]Beating, hanging, jumping, stabbing, slashing, strangling, or heart attack.

Source: By the author. Based on National School Safety Center 2009.

The Future of Education

Most of the changes that administrators make consist of minor adjustments to the current system of education: giving this test or that test, measuring progress this way or that way, requiring more memorization or less memorization, providing a core curriculum or more diversity, emphasizing more or less the contributions of minorities to mainstream culture, motivating teachers and students by this carrot or that carrot. All might be important in their own way, but each is a minute adjustment to the details of an existing—and flawed—system. In the meantime, technology is transforming education, changing what we learn and the way we learn it. To conclude the chapter, let's consider this major change.

SOCIOLOGY and the NEW TECHNOLOGY

Internet University: No Walls, No Ivy, No All Night Parties

Distance learning, courses taught to students who are not physically present with their instructor, is not new. For decades, we have had correspondence courses. Today, however, telecommunications have transformed distance learning. Satellites, computers, and video cameras are making cyber colleges part of mainstream education. Using video links, students are able to watch the professor on their screen. Clicking an icon, they can "raise their hands" to ask questions. Networking programs let the instructor know who is e-mailing others—and who is holding back. Tucked deeper in the software is a program that allows deans (supervisors) to scrutinize the instructors. The deans get reports, for example, that let them know how long it takes instructors to answer e-mail from students.

Broadening the experience of both students and instructors through cultural diversity is one of the

We may be seeing the beginning of technology's transformation of education. This avatar is of a teacher who is using Second Life *to teach a required writing course at Ball State University. Students select their own avatars. They roam this virtual world, asking other inhabitants of* Second Life *about their feelings of identity and then write a weekly blog on their observations.*

interesting potentials of distance learning. Students can enjoy stimulating international experiences without leaving the country. For example, sociology professors at the State University of New York and the State University of Belarus (Minsk, Russia) jointly taught an online course on Social Control. Coming from such different political experiences, the American and Russian students found that the course opened their eyes to different perspectives (Beaman 2003).

Why should formal education be limited to walled classrooms? Think of the possibilities the Net opens to us. We could study human culture and compare notes on eating, dating, or burial customs with fellow students in Thailand, Iceland, South Africa, Germany, Egypt, China, and Australia. We could write a joint paper in which we compare our experiences with one another, within the context of theories taught in the text, and then submit our paper to our mutual instructor.

Then there are students who don't fit in. They might not look like the "cool" students, and they certainly don't think like them. Some find school boring. Others find it a threatening place. For still others, an inability to focus, a tendency to drift off, puts them out of sync with both teachers and classmates. For students like these, virtual classes have become a viable alternative. The students can even enter an online classroom without their classmates noticing by clicking a "make yourself invisible" icon (White 2003).

Some teachers are using a format that combines classroom and distance learning. Instructors upload to a university Web site the lectures they give to a classroom of students, and students who missed class or who don't want to attend class sessions download them to their iPods. Some professors have their students listen to their recorded lectures and then use the classroom to involve their students in interactive discussion groups (Tyre 2005).

Of course, there are limitations. You couldn't give gym classes over the Net. Or could you? This, too is being done. In some schools, students can do any vig-orous exercise they want for 30 minutes, four times a week. They report their activity and heart rate to gym instructors, with their parents certifying their accuracy (Dillon 2005a).

As distance learning expands, will we eventually go from kindergarten to grad school with classmates from around the world? While this may sound intriguing, having no walls also means no joking in the hallway or dorm, no flirting after class, no getting together over a cup of coffee....

For Your Consideration
Do you think that at some point online teaching might totally replace traditional classrooms? Why or why not? What do you see as the advantages of on-line learning? Its disadvantages? If you were able to take all your college classes online and receive the same degree from the same college, would you? Why or why not?

By the Numbers: *Then and Now*

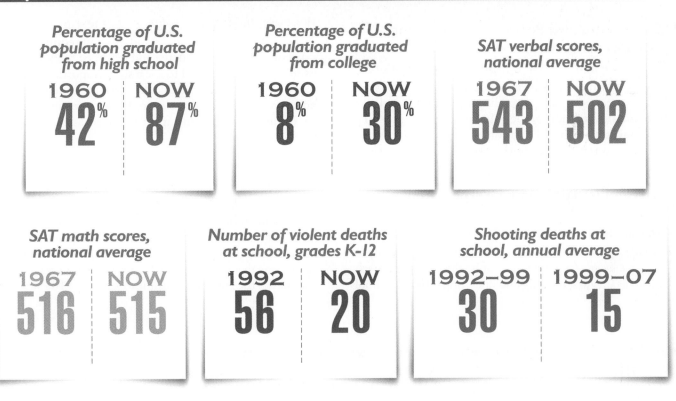

Percentage of U.S. population graduated from high school — 1960: 42% | NOW: 87%

Percentage of U.S. population graduated from college — 1960: 8% | NOW: 30%

SAT verbal scores, national average — 1967: 543 | NOW: 502

SAT math scores, national average — 1967: 516 | NOW: 515

Number of violent deaths at school, grades K-12 — 1992: 56 | NOW: 20

Shooting deaths at school, annual average — 1992-99: 30 | 1999-07: 15

SUMMARY *and* REVIEW

The Development of Modern Education

How did modern education develop?

In most of human history, **education** consisted of informal learning, equivalent to *acculturation.* In some earlier societies, centers of formal education did develop, such as among the Arabs, Chinese, Greeks, and Egyptians. Because modern education came about in response to industrialization, formal education is much less common in the Least Industrialized Nations. Pp. 498–500.

Education in Global Perspective

How does education compare among the Most Industrialized, Industrializing, and Least Industrialized Nations?

In general, formal education reflects a nation's economy. Consequently, education is extensive in the Most Industrialized Nations, undergoing vast change in the Industrializing Nations, and spotty in the Least Industrialized Nations. Japan, Russia, and Egypt provide examples of education in countries at three levels of industrialization. Pp. 501–503.

The Functionalist Perspective: Providing Social Benefits

What is the functionalist perspective on education?

Among the functions of education are the teaching of knowledge and skills, providing credentials, **cultural transmission of values,** social integration, **gatekeeping,** and **mainstreaming.** Functionalists also note that education has replaced some traditional family functions. Pp. 503–507.

The Conflict Perspective: Perpetuating Social Inequality

What is the conflict perspective on education?

The basic view of conflict theorists is that *education reproduces the social class structure;* that is, through such mechanisms as unequal funding and operating different schools for the elite and for the masses, education perpetuates a society's basic social inequalities from one generation to the next. Pp. 507–510.

The Symbolic Interactionist Perspective: Teacher Expectations

What is the symbolic interactionist perspective on education?

Symbolic interactionists focus on face-to-face interaction. In examining what occurs in the classroom, they have found that student performance tends to conform to teacher expectations, whether they are high or low. Pp. 511–512.

Problems in U.S. Education—and Their Solutions

What are the chief problems that face U.S. education?

The major problems are mediocrity (low achievement as shown by SAT scores and international comparisons), **grade inflation, social promotion, functional illiteracy,** faked data reported by school administrators, and violence. Pp. 513–514.

What are the potential solutions to these problems?

To restore high educational standards will require that we expect more of *both* students and teachers; school administrators can be required to use a single reporting measure based on objective, verifiable data; and, although we cannot prevent all school violence, for an effective learning environment we can and must provide basic security for students. Pp. 514–517.

The Future of U.S. Education

What development indicates the future of U.S. education?

Most changes in education represent rather minor and, in many cases, trivial tinkering with an existing system. Distance learning, in contrast, indicates a major change in education, one that will transform the way students are educated and, likely, the content of their learning. Pp. 518–519.

THINKING CRITICALLY *ABOUT* Chapter 17

1. How does education in the United States compare with education in Japan, Russia, and Egypt?

2. How have your experiences in education (including teachers and assignments) influenced your goals, attitudes, and values? How have your classmates influenced you? Be specific.

3. How do you think that U.S. schools can be improved?

ADDITIONAL RESOURCES

What can you find in MySocLab?   mysoclab   www.mysoclab.com

- Complete Ebook
- Practice Tests and Video and Audio activities
- Mapping and Data Analysis exercises

- Sociology in the News
- Classic Readings in Sociology
- Research and Writing advice

Where Can I Read More on This Topic?

Suggested readings for this chapter are listed at the back of this book.

Religion

India

Yearning for Zion What kind of a strange name for a ranch is this?

And what strange things are those people doing behind those locked gates? A 1,700-acre ranch with its own temple. Women who come into town to shop wearing homemade prairie dresses—like women wear in Western movies.

Strange people.

The rumors swirled. "Those are Mormons, and the men have a lot of wives." "Those aren't Mormons," someone said. "They are a breakaway group of some sort. And, yeah, I think the men do have a lot of wives."

> A female, claiming to be a 16-year-old, said she had been forced to marry a 50-year-old man.

"They're peaceful enough, though, so let them be. This is Texas, where a man can be what he wants to be—and so can a woman. Mind your own business."

"But they're so strange. Not just those dresses and that funny hairdo, but they got their own religion. And who knows what goes on behind those gates. They've got armed guards, and they won't let anyone in."

But they did let someone in. In fact, they let a lot of outsiders in.

The telephone call was anonymous. A female, claiming to be a 16-year-old, said she had been forced to marry a 50-year-old man, and he was abusing her. Ordinarily, an anonymous call doesn't merit much action, but the authorities jumped at this one. This was their chance to get behind those gates.

A judge had no problem signing search and arrest warrants, even though it was just an anonymous call. State troopers, officials from Child Protective Services, and even the famed Texas Rangers rushed to those locked gates. They were concerned that they might have another Waco on their hands (another place in Texas where federal officials who raided the compound of a religious group met armed resistance, and eighty-two of the sect's members were burned alive).

The police put up roadblocks to the ranch, and they brought in an armored vehicle. Unlike Waco, though, there was no resistance. The leaders of the *Yearning for Zion Ranch* were well aware of Waco. And they didn't relish having their wives and children burned to death.

The officials rushed in and quickly carried off 52 girls. Later, they came back, seizing a total of 468 children, both girls and boys.

It took a couple of months, but the mothers finally got their children back. Authorities were stunned when an appeals court ruled that the seizure of the children was illegal. They then issued arrest warrants for the group's leader and four other men, charging them with the sexual assault of a minor.

523

sacred Durkheim's term for things set apart or forbidden that inspire fear, awe, reverence, or deep respect

profane Durkheim's term for common elements of everyday life

religion according to Durkheim, beliefs and practices that separate the profane from the sacred and unite its adherents into a moral community

The anonymous caller was never identified. It could have been a prank call.

The group, which broke off from the Latter Day Saints in 1890, still believes that for a man to reach heaven's highest realms he must have three wives in this life.

—Based on Blumenthal 2008a, 2008b; Hylton 2008.

Seldom does the government swoop down on a religious group, but it does happen. One of the topics we shall consider in this chapter is the relationship of the dominant culture to cults, or new religions. Let's begin by asking what religion is.

What Is Religion?

All human societies are organized by some form of the family, as well as by some kind of economic system and political order. As we have seen, these key social institutions touch on aspects of life that are essential to human welfare. This chapter examines religion, another universal social institution.

Sociologists who do research on religion analyze the relationship between society and religion, and study the role that religion plays in people's lives. They do not try to prove that one religion is better than another. Nor is it their goal to verify or disprove anyone's faith. As was mentioned in Chapter 1, sociologists have no tools for deciding that one course of action is more moral than another, much less for determining that one religion is "the" correct one. Religion is a matter of faith—and sociologists deal with empirical matters, things they can observe or measure. When it comes to religion, then, sociologists study the effects of religious beliefs and practices on people's lives. They also analyze how religion is related to stratification systems. Unlike theologians, however, sociologists do not try to evaluate the truth of a religion's teachings.

Emile Durkheim was highly interested in religion, probably because he was reared in a mixed-religion family, by a Protestant mother and a Jewish father. Durkheim decided to find out what all religions have in common. After surveying religions around the world, in 1912 he published his findings in *The Elementary Forms of the Religious Life*. The book is complicated, but let's summarize Durkheim's three main findings. The first is that the world's religions are so varied that they have no specific belief or practice in common. The second is that all religions develop a community centering on their beliefs and practices. The third is that all religions separate the sacred from the profane. By **sacred,** Durkheim referred to aspects of life having to do with the supernatural that inspire awe, reverence, deep respect, even fear. By **profane,** he meant aspects of life that are not concerned with religion but, instead, are part of ordinary, everyday life.

Durkheim (1912/1965) summarized his conclusions by saying:

> A religion is a unified system of beliefs and practices relative to sacred things, that is to say, things set apart and forbidden—beliefs and practices which unite into one single moral community called a Church, all those who adhere to them.

Religion, then, has three elements:

1. *Beliefs* that some things are sacred (forbidden, set apart from the profane)
2. *Practices* (rituals) centering on the things considered sacred
3. *A moral community* (a church), which results from a group's beliefs and practices

When I visited a Hindu temple in Chattisgargh, India, I was impressed by the colorful and expressive statues on its roof. Here is a close-up of some of those figures, which represent some of the millions of gods that Hindus worship.

Durkheim used the word **church** in an unusual sense, to refer to any "moral community" centered on beliefs and practices regarding the sacred. In Durkheim's sense, *church* refers to Buddhists bowing before a shrine, Hindus dipping in the Ganges River, and Confucians offering food to their ancestors. Similarly, the term *moral community* does not imply morality in the sense familiar to most of us—of ethical conduct. Rather, a moral community is simply a group of people who are united by their religious practices—and that would include sixteenth-century Aztec priests who each day gathered around an altar to pluck out the beating heart of a virgin.

To better understand the sociological approach to religion, let's see what pictures emerge when we apply the three theoretical perspectives.

> **church** according to Durkheim, one of the three essential elements of religion—a moral community of believers; also refers to a large, highly organized religious group that has formal, sedate worship services with little emphasis on evangelism, intense religious experience, or personal conversion

The Functionalist Perspective

Functionalists stress that religion is universal because it meets universal human needs. Let's look at some of the functions—and dysfunctions—of religion.

Functions of Religion

Questions About Ultimate Meaning.   Around the world, religions provide answers to perplexing questions about ultimate meaning—such as the purpose of life, why people suffer, and the existence of an afterlife. Those answers give followers a sense of purpose, a framework in which to live. Instead of seeing themselves buffeted by random events in an aimless existence, believers see their lives as fitting into a divine plan.

Emotional Comfort.   The answers that religion provides about ultimate meaning also comfort people by assuring them that there is a purpose to life, even to suffering. Similarly, religious rituals that enshroud crucial events such as illness and death provide emotional comfort at times of crisis. The individual knows that others care and can find consolation in following familiar rituals.

Social Solidarity.   Religious teachings and practices unite believers into a community that shares values and perspectives ("we Jews," "we Christians," "we Muslims"). The religious rituals that surround marriage, for example, link the bride and groom with a broader community that wishes them well. So do other religious rituals, such as those that celebrate birth and mourn death.

Guidelines for Everyday Life.   The teachings of religion are not all abstractions. They also provide practical guidelines for everyday life. For example, four of the ten commandments delivered by Moses to the Israelites concern God, but the other six contain instructions for getting along with others, from how to avoid problems with parents and neighbors to warnings about lying, stealing, and having affairs.

The consequences for people who follow these guidelines can be measured. For example, people who attend church are less likely to abuse alcohol, nicotine, and illegal drugs than are people who don't go to church (Gillum 2005; Wallace et al 2007). In general, churchgoers follow a healthier lifestyle, and they live longer than people who don't go to church. How religion affects health is discussed in the Down-to-Earth Sociology box on the next page.

One of the many functions of religion is providing emotional comfort. This nun is ministering to a terminally ill cancer patient in Atlanta, Georgia.

Down-to-Earth Sociology
Religion and Health: What We Know and Don't Know

"After seeing the data, I think I should go to church," said Lynda Powell, an epidemiologist at Rush University Medical Center in Chicago (Helliker 2005).

Religious activity brings surprising health benefits.

This was the response of a non-church-going scientist when she saw the data on health and religion. Although scientists cannot determine the truth of any religion, they can study the effects of religion on people's lives. Health is one of those areas that can be measured, and the results are holding some surprises.

Powell, along with two colleagues, evaluated the published research on the effects of religion on health. They evaluated only research that met solid scientific criteria. For example, they threw out studies that didn't control for age, gender, or race–ethnicity, significant variables in health (Powell et al. 2003). The most outstanding finding? *People who attend religious services at least once a week have 25 percent fewer deaths than people who don't go to church.* Think about it: For every hundred deaths of non-churchgoers, there are only 75 deaths of people who attend church weekly.

How could this possibly be? Perhaps the churchgoers were already healthier. This wasn't the reason, though, for the researchers compared people who were at the same levels of health or illness.

How about healthier lifestyles? Churchgoers are less likely to smoke, to get drunk, and so on. Not this either. The researchers also controlled for lifestyle. Actually, the weekly churchgoers had 30 percent less mortality. When the researchers adjusted for lifestyle and social class, the difference in mortality dropped to 25 percent (Powell et al. 2003).

What explanation could there be, then? Remember that the researchers are scientists, so they aren't going to say "God." But they do suggest three mechanisms that might account for the lower mortality of churchgoers: finding a sense of self-worth and purpose in life; experiencing positive emotions; and learning calming ways of coping with crises.

The explanations suggested by the researchers could be correct, but we need further research to find out.

Is there anything about religion itself that could account for this remarkable reduction in mortality? Some researchers think they've put their finger on it: prayer. Prayer (or meditation) seems to change people's brain activity in a way that improves their immune response. Scientists are investigating this hypothesis (Kalb 2003).

One researcher points to something else about religion—the practice of forgiveness. It turns out that people who forgive easily are more likely to be in good psychological health. They are especially less likely to be depressed (Krause and Ellison 2003). To forgive someone who has done you wrong apparently brings release from feelings of resentment, bitterness, and hatred—but holding on to grudges rips you apart inside.

What have researchers found about praying for people who are sick? Does this help them get better? So far, most researchers haven't found any difference between people who are prayed for and those who are not (Benson et al. 2006). But researchers have encountered a problem. How do they find a control group of people who are not being prayed for? There is so much prayer—from parents, siblings, aunts and uncles, friends and neighbors—that some people don't even know they are being prayed for. I'm sure that researchers will solve this.

We are just at the initial stages of research on religion and health. At this point, we have hardly any answers, but we do have this remarkable finding about attending religious services and lower mortality rates. In fact, people who go to religious services more than once a week live 7½ years longer than those who don't attend religious services (Hummer et al. 1999; Hummer et al. 2004).

So, if you want to live longer . . .

For Your Consideration

If you attend a church, synagogue, or mosque, what difference do you think that your attendance makes in your life? How does your religion affect your lifestyle? What decisions would you have made differently if you did not practice your religion?

Social Control.   Religion not only provides guidelines for everyday life but also sets limits on people's behaviors. Most norms of a religious group apply only to its members, but nonmembers also feel a spillover. Religious teachings, for example, are incorporated into criminal law. In the United States, blasphemy and adultery were once crimes for which people could be arrested, tried, and sentenced. Some states still have laws that prohibit the sale of alcohol before noon on Sunday, laws whose purpose was to get people out of the saloons and into the churches.

Adaptation.   Religion can help people adapt to new environments. For example, it isn't easy for immigrants to adjust to the customs of a new land. By keeping their native language alive within a community of people who are going through similar experiences, religion serves as a bridge between the old and new: It provides both continuity with the immigrants' cultural past and encouragement to adapt to the new culture. This was the case for earlier U.S. immigrants from Europe, and it remains true today for immigrants from all over the globe. The thousands of Spanish-speaking churches around the United States are an outstanding example.

Support for the Government.   Most religions provide support for the government. An obvious example is the way some churches prominently display the U.S. flag. Some fly it in front of the church building, and many display both the U.S. flag and a church flag on stands at the front of their worship center. Religions that become hostile to the government—or even seem strange—can run into trouble, as in the example of our opening vignette.

For their part, governments reciprocate by supporting God. In the extreme, some governments sponsor a particular religion, ban or place a heavy hand on others, provide financial support for building churches, synagogues, mosques, and seminaries, and even pay salaries to the clergy. These religions are known as **state religions.** During the sixteenth and seventeenth centuries in Sweden, the government sponsored Lutheranism; in Switzerland, Calvinism; and in Italy, Roman Catholicism. In some Arab countries today, this is the practice regarding Islam.

In some instances, even though the government sponsors no particular religion, religious beliefs are embedded in a nation's life. This is called **civil religion** (Bellah 1970). For example, U.S. presidents—regardless of whether they are believers—invariably ask God to bless the nation in their inaugural speeches. U.S. officials take office by swearing that they will, in the name of God, fulfill their duty. Similarly, Congress opens each session with a prayer led by its own chaplain. The pledge of allegiance includes the phrase "one nation under God," and coins bear the inscription "In God We Trust."

Social Change.   Although religion is often so bound up with the prevailing social order that it resists social change, religion occasionally spearheads change. In the 1960s, for example, the civil rights movement, whose goal was to desegregate public facilities and abolish racial discrimination at southern polls, was led by religious leaders, especially leaders of African American churches such as Martin Luther King, Jr. Churches also served as centers at which demonstrators were trained and rallies were organized. Other churches were centers for resisting this change.

Functional Equivalents of Religion

If some component of society other than religion answers questions about ultimate meaning and provides emotional comfort and guidelines for daily life, sociologists call it a **functional equivalent** of religion. For some people, Alcoholics Anonymous is a functional equivalent of religion (Chalfant 1992). For others, it is psychotherapy, humanism, transcendental meditation, or even a political party.

> **state religions** a government-sponsored religion; also called ecclesia
>
> **civil religion** Robert Bellah's term for religion that is such an established feature of a country's life that its history and social institutions become sanctified by being associated with God
>
> **functional equivalent** a substitute that serves the same functions (or meets the same needs) as religion; for example, psychotherapy

Religion can promote social change, as was evident in the U.S. civil rights movement. Dr. Martin Luther King, Jr., a Baptist minister, shown here in his famous "I have a dream" speech, was the foremost leader of this movement.

Some functional equivalents are difficult to distinguish from a religion (Brinton 1965; Luke 1985). For example, communism had its prophets (Marx and Lenin), sacred writings (everything written by Marx, Engels, and Lenin, but especially the *Communist Manifesto*), high priests (the heads of the Communist party), sacred buildings (the Kremlin), shrines (Lenin's body on display in Red Square), rituals (the annual May Day parade in Red Square), and even martyrs (Cuba's Ché Guevara). Soviet communism was avowedly atheistic and tried to wipe out all traces of Christianity, Judaism, and Islam from its midst. It even replaced baptisms and circumcisions with state-sponsored rituals that dedicated the child to the state. The Communist party also devised its own rituals for weddings and funerals.

As sociologist Ian Robertson (1987) pointed out, however, there is a fundamental distinction between a religion and its functional equivalent. Although the substitute may perform similar functions, its activities are not directed toward God, gods, or the supernatural.

Dysfunctions of Religion

Functionalists also examine ways in which religion is *dysfunctional,* that is, how it can bring harmful results. Two dysfunctions are religious persecution and war and terrorism.

Religion as Justification for Persecution.   Beginning in the 1200s and continuing into the 1800s, in what has become known as the Inquisition, special commissions of the Roman Catholic Church tortured women to make them confess that they were witches and then burned them at the stake. In 1692, Protestant leaders in Salem, Massachusetts, executed twenty-one women and men who were accused of being witches. In 2001, in the Democratic Republic of the Congo, about 1,000 alleged witches were hacked to death (Jenkins 2002). In Angola, children who are accused of being witches are beaten and then killed or expelled (LaFraniere 2007). Similarly, it seems fair to say that the Aztec religion had its dysfunctions—at least for the virgins who were offered to appease angry gods. In short, religion has been used to justify oppression and any number of brutal acts.

War and Terrorism.   History is filled with wars based on religion—commingled with politics. Between the eleventh and fourteenth centuries, for example, Christian monarchs conducted nine bloody Crusades in an attempt to wrest control of the region they called the Holy Land from the Muslims. Terrorist acts, too, are sometimes committed in the name of religion, as discussed in the Down-to-Earth Sociology box on the next page.

The Symbolic Interactionist Perspective

Symbolic interactionists focus on the meanings that people give their experiences, especially how they use symbols. Let's apply this perspective to religious symbols, rituals, and beliefs to see how they help to forge a community of like-minded people.

Religious Symbols

Symbolic interactionists stress that a basic characteristic of humans is that they attach meaning to objects and events and then use representations of those objects or events to communicate with one another. Michaelangelo's *Pietà*, depicting Mary tenderly holding her son, Jesus, after his crucifixion, is one of the most acclaimed symbols in the Western world. It is admired for its beauty by believers and nonbelievers alike.

Suppose that it is about two thousand years ago and you have just joined a new religion. You have come to believe that a recently crucified Jew named Jesus is the Messiah, the Lamb of God offered for your sins. The Roman leaders are persecuting the followers of Jesus. They hate your religion because you and your fellow believers will not acknowledge Caesar as God. Christians are few in number, and you are eager to have fellowship with other believers. But how can you tell who is a believer? Spies are everywhere. The government has sworn to destroy this new religion, and you do not relish the thought of being fed to lions in the Colosseum.

You use a simple technique. While talking with a stranger, as though doodling absentmindedly in the sand or dust, you casually trace the outline of a fish. Only fellow believers know the meaning—that, taken together, the first letter of each word in the Greek sentence "Jesus (is) Christ the Son of God" spell the Greek word for fish. If the other person gives no response, you rub out the outline and continue the interaction as usual. If there is a response, you eagerly talk about your new faith.

Down-to-Earth Sociology
Terrorism and the Mind of God

> **WARNING: The "equal time" contents of this box are likely to offend just about everyone.**

After September 11, 2001, the question on many people's minds was some form of "How can people do such evil in the name of God?"

To answer this question, we need to broaden the context. The question is fine, but it cannot be directed solely at Islamic terrorists. If it is, it misses the point.

We need to consider other religions, too. For Christians, we don't have to go back centuries to the Inquisition or to the Children's Crusades. We only have to look at Ireland and the bombings in Belfast. There, Protestants and Catholics slaughtered each other in the name of God.

In the United States, we can consider the killing of abortion doctors. Paul Hill, a minister who was executed for killing a doctor in Florida, was convinced that his act was good, that he had saved the lives of unborn babies. Before his execution, he said that he was looking forward to heaven.

Since I want to give equal time to the major religions, we can't forget the Jews. Dr. Baruch Goldstein was convinced that Yahweh wanted him to take an assault rifle, go to the Tomb of the Patriarchs, and shoot into a crowd of praying Palestinian men and boys. His admirers built a monument on his grave (Juergensmeyer 2000).

Finally, for the sake of equality, let's not let the Hindus, Buddhists, and Sikhs off the hook. In India, these groups continue to slaughter one another. In the name of their gods, they attack the houses of worship of the others and blow one another up. (The Hindus are actually equal opportunists—they kill Christians, too. I visited Orissa, a state in India where Hindus had doused a jeep with gasoline and burned alive an Australian missionary and his two sons. This dysfunctional aspect of religion came alive for me in 2008 when Hindu leaders orchestrated riots throughout Orissa. Violently sweeping through the state, the rioters burned down churches and orphanages. People I know had to flee into the nearby jungles. When they returned, they found their homes looted and burned.)

None of these terrorists—Islamic, Christian, Jew, Sikh, Buddhist, or Hindu—represent the mainstream of their religion, but they do commit violence for religious reasons. How can they do so? Here are five elements that religious terrorists seem to have in common.

First, the individuals believe that they are under attack. Evil forces are bent on destroying the good of their world—whether that be their religion, their way of life, or unborn babies.

Religious violence, which goes back thousands of years, continues. Shown here is a Christian whose house was burned by Hindus in Orissa, India, in 2008.

Second, they become convinced that God wants the evil destroyed.

Third, they conclude that only violence will resolve the situation.

Fourth, they become convinced that God has chosen them for this task.

Fifth, these perspectives are nurtured by a community, a group in which the individuals find identity. This group may realize that most members of their faith do not support their views, but those others are mistaken. The smaller community holds the truth.

Under these conditions, morality is turned upside down. Killing becomes a moral act, a good done for a greater cause.

There is just enough truth in these points of view to keep the delusion alive. After all, wouldn't it have been better for the millions of victims of Hitler, Stalin, or Pol Pot if someone had had the nerve and foresight to kill them? Wouldn't their deaths and one's own self-sacrifice have been a greater good? Today, there are those bad Protestants, those bad Catholics, those bad Jews, those bad Palestinians, those bad abortionists, those bad Americans—an endless list. And the violence is for the Greater Good: what God wants.

Once people buy into this closed system of thought, they become convinced that they have access to the mind of God.

For Your Consideration

How do you think the type of thinking that leads to religiously-motivated violence can be broken?

All religions use symbols to provide identity and create social solidarity for their members. For Muslims, the primary symbol is the crescent moon and star; for Jews, the Star of David; for Christians, the cross. For members, these are not ordinary symbols, but sacred emblems that evoke feelings of awe and reverence. In Durkheim's terms, religions use symbols to represent what the group considers sacred and to separate the sacred from the profane.

A symbol is a condensed way of communicating. Worn by a fundamentalist Christian, for example, the cross says, "I am a follower of Jesus Christ. I believe that He is the Messiah, the promised Son of God, that He loves me, that He died to take away my sins, that He rose from the dead and is going to return to earth, and that through Him I will receive eternal life."

That is a lot to pack into one symbol—and it is only part of what the symbol means to a fundamentalist believer. To people in other traditions of Christianity, the cross conveys somewhat different meanings—but to all Christians, the cross is a shorthand way of expressing many meanings. So it is with the Star of David, the crescent moon and star, the cow (expressing to Hindus the unity of all living things), and the various symbols of the world's many other religions.

Rituals

Rituals, ceremonies or repetitive practices, are also symbols that help to unite people into a moral community. Some rituals, such as the bar mitzvah of Jewish boys and the holy communion of Christians, are designed to create in devout believers a feeling of closeness with God and unity with one another. Rituals include kneeling and praying at set times; bowing; crossing oneself; singing; lighting candles and incense; reading scripture; and following prescribed traditions at processions, baptisms, weddings, and funerals. The photo essay on pages 532–533 features annual rituals held in Spain during Holy Week.

Beliefs

Symbols, including rituals, develop from beliefs. The belief may be vague ("God is") or highly specific ("God wants us to prostrate ourselves and face Mecca five times each day"). Religious beliefs include not only *values* (what is considered good and desirable in life—how we ought to live) but also a **cosmology,** a unified picture of the world. For example, the Jewish, Christian, and Muslim belief that there is only one God, the creator of the universe, who is concerned about the actions of humans and who will hold us accountable for what we do, is a cosmology. It presents a unifying picture of the universe.

Religious Experience

The term **religious experience** refers to a sudden awareness of the supernatural or a feeling of coming into contact with God. Some people undergo a mild version, such as feeling closer to God when they look at a mountain, watch a sunset, or listen to a certain piece of music. Others report a life-transforming experience. St. Francis of Assisi, for example, said that he became aware of God's presence in every living thing.

Some Protestants use the term **born again** to describe people who have undergone such a life-transforming religious experience. These people say that they came to the realization that they had sinned, that Jesus had died for their sins, and that God wants them to live a new life. Their worlds become transformed. They look forward to the Resurrection and to a new life in heaven, and they see relationships with spouses, parents, children, and even bosses in a new light. They also report a need to make changes in how they interact with others so that their lives reflect their new, personal commitment to Jesus as their "Savior and Lord." They describe a feeling of beginning life anew; hence the term *born again.*

Community

Finally, the shared meanings that come through symbols, rituals, and beliefs (and for some, a religious experience) unite people into a moral community. People in a moral community feel a bond with one another, for their beliefs and rituals bind them

rituals ceremonies or repetitive practices; in religion, observances or rites often intended to evoke a sense of awe of the sacred

cosmology teachings or ideas that provide a unified picture of the world

religious experience a sudden awareness of the supernatural or a feeling of coming in contact with God

born again a term describing Christians who have undergone a religious experience so life-transforming that they feel they have become new persons together—and at the same time separate them from those who do not share their unique symbolic world. Mormons, for example, feel a "kindred spirit" (as it is often known) with other Mormons. Baptists, Jews, Jehovah's Witnesses, and Muslims feel similar bonds with members of their respective faiths.

As a symbol of their unity, members of some religious groups address one another as "brother" or "sister." "Sister Luby, we are going to meet at Brother and Sister Maher's on Wednesday" is a common way of expressing a message. The terms *brother* and *sister* are intended to symbolize a relationship so close that the individuals consider themselves members of the same family.

Community is powerful. Not only does it provide the basis for mutual identity but also it establishes norms that govern the behavior of its members. Members either conform or they lose their membership. In Christian churches, for example, an individual

One of the functions of religion is to create community—a sense of being connected with one another and, in this case, also a sense of being connected with God. To help accomplish this, religions often use rituals. Shown here are Javanese Muslim women in Surinam as they celebrate Id al Fatr at the end of Rammadan.

whose adultery becomes known, and who refuses to admit wrongdoing and ask forgiveness, may be banned from the church. He or she may be formally excommunicated, as in the Catholic tradition, or more informally "stricken from the rolls," as is the usual Protestant practice.

Removal from the community is a serious matter for people whose identity is bound up in that community. Sociologists John Hostetler (1980), William Kephart, and William Zellner (Kephart and Zellner 2001) describe the Amish practice of *shunning*—ignoring an offender in all situations. Persons who are shunned are treated as though they do not exist (for if they do not repent by expressing sorrow for their act, they have ceased to exist as members of the community). The shunning is so thorough that even family members, who themselves remain in good standing in the congregation, are not allowed to talk to the person being shunned. This obviously makes for some interesting times at the dinner table.

The Conflict Perspective

In general, conflict theorists are highly critical of religion. They stress that religion supports the status quo and helps to maintain social inequalities. Let's look at some of their analyses.

Opium of the People

Karl Marx, an avowed atheist who believed that the existence of God was impossible, set the tone for conflict theorists with his most famous statement on this subject: "Religion is the sigh of the oppressed creature, the sentiment of a heartless world. . . . It is the opium of the people" (Marx 1844/1964). By this statement, Marx meant that oppressed workers find escape in religion. For them, religion is like a drug that helps them to forget their misery. By diverting their thoughts toward future happiness in an afterlife, religion takes their eyes off their suffering in this world, reducing the possibility that they will rebel against their oppressors.

Holy Week in Spain

religious groups develop rituals designed to evoke memories, create awe, inspire reverence, and stimulate social solidarity. One of the primary means by which groups, religious and secular, accomplish these goals is through the display of symbols.

I took these photos during Holy Week in Spain—in Malaga and Almuñecar. Throughout Spain, elaborate processions feature *tronos* that depict the biblical account of Jesus' suffering, death, and resurrection. During the processions in Malaga, the participants walk slowly for about two minutes; then because of the weight of the *tronos*, they rest for about two minutes. This process repeats for about six hours each day.

A group of participants exiting the Church of the Incarnation for Malaga's Easter procession.

Bands, sometimes several of them, are part of the processions.

The procession in the village was more informal. This Roman soldier has an interesting way of participating—and keeping tabs—on his little daughter. The girl is distributing candy.

Parents gave a lot of attention to their children both during the preparations and during the processions. This photo was taken during one of the repetitive two-minute breaks.

During the short breaks at the night processions, children from the audience would rush to collect dripping wax to make wax balls. This was one way that the audience made themselves participants in the drama.

Beneath the costumes are townspeople and church members who know one another well. They enjoy themselves prior to the procession. This man is preparing to put on his hood.

Some *tronos* were so heavy that they required many men to carry them. (Some required over 100 men.) This photo was taken in Malaga, on Monday of Holy Week.

For the Good Friday procession, I was fortunate to be able to photograph the behind-the-scenes preparations, which are seldom seen by visitors. Shown here are finishing touches being given to the Mary figure.

The town square was packed with people awaiting the procession. From one corner of the square, the *trono* of Jesus was brought in. Then from another, that of Mary ("reuniting" them, as I was told). During this climactic scene, the priest on the balcony on the left read a message.

Philadelphia: Quäkerkirche.

This engraving is of a Quaker meeting in the 1700s when women sat on one side of the church, and men on the other. Some Jewish and Muslim groups continue this practice today. Do you think that sex-segregated seating supports the conflict perspective that religion reflects and legitimates social inequalities? Why or why not?

A Legitimation of Social Inequalities

Conflict theorists say that religion legitimates the social inequalities of the larger society. By this, they mean that religion teaches that the existing social arrangements of a society represent what God desires. For example, during the Middle Ages, Christian theologians decreed the *divine right of kings*. This doctrine meant that God determined who would become king and set him on the throne. The king ruled in God's place, and it was the duty of a king's subjects to be loyal to him (and to pay their taxes). To disobey the king was to disobey God.

In what was perhaps the supreme technique of legitimating the social order (and one that went even a step farther than the divine right of kings), the religion of ancient Egypt held that the pharaoh himself was a god. The emperor of Japan was similarly declared divine. If this were so, who could ever question his decisions? Today's politicians would give their right arm for such a religious teaching.

Conflict theorists point to many other examples of how religion legitimates the social order. In India, Hinduism supports the caste system by teaching that an individual who tries to change caste will come back in the next life as a member of a lower caste—or even as an animal. In the decades before the American Civil War, Southern ministers used scripture to defend slavery, saying that it was God's will—while Northern ministers legitimated *their* region's social structure by using scripture to denounce slavery as evil (Ernst 1988; Nauta 1993; White 1995).

Religion and the Spirit of Capitalism

Max Weber disagreed strongly with the conflict perspective that religion merely reflects and legitimates the social order and that it impedes social change by encouraging people to focus on the afterlife. In contrast, Weber said that religion's focus on the afterlife is a source of profound social change.

Like Marx, Weber observed the early industrialization of European countries. Weber wondered why some societies embraced capitalism while others held onto their traditional ways. Tradition was strong in all these countries, yet capitalism had transformed some while others remained untouched. As he explored this puzzle, Weber concluded that religion held the key to **modernization**—the transformation of traditional societies to industrial societies.

To explain his conclusions, Weber wrote *The Protestant Ethic and the Spirit of Capitalism* (1904–1905/1958). Because Weber's argument was presented in Chapter 7 (page 176), it is only summarized here.

modernization the transformation of traditional societies into industrial societies

1. Capitalism is not just a superficial change. Rather, capitalism represents a fundamentally different way of thinking about work and money. *Traditionally, people worked*

just enough to meet their basic needs, not so that they could have a surplus to invest. To accumulate money (capital) as an end in itself, not just to spend it, was a radical departure from traditional thinking. People even came to consider it a duty to invest money so they could make profits. They reinvested these profits to make even more profits. Weber called this new approach to work and money the **spirit of capitalism.**

2. Why did the spirit of capitalism develop in Europe and not, for example, in China or India, where the people had similar material resources and education? According to Weber, *religion was the key.* The religions of China and India, and indeed Roman Catholicism in Europe, encouraged a traditional approach to life, not thrift and investment. Capitalism appeared when Protestantism came on the scene.

3. What was different about Protestantism, especially Calvinism? John Calvin taught that God had predestined some people to go to heaven, and others to hell. Neither church membership nor feelings about your relationship with God could assure you that you were saved. You wouldn't know your fate until after you died.

4. This doctrine created intense anxiety: "Am I predestined to hell or to heaven?" Calvin's followers wondered. As they wrestled with this question, they concluded that church members have a duty to prove that they are one of God's elect and to live as though they are predestined to heaven—for good works are a demonstration of salvation.

5. This conclusion motivated Calvinists to lead moral lives *and* to work hard, to use their time productively, and to be frugal—for idleness and needless spending were signs of worldliness. Weber called this self-denying approach to life the **Protestant ethic.**

6. As people worked hard and spent money only on necessities (a pair of earrings or a second pair of dress shoes would have been defined as sinful luxuries), they had money left over. Because it couldn't be spent, this capital was invested, which led to a surge in production.

7. Weber's analysis can be summed up this way: The change in religion (from Catholicism to Protestantism, especially Calvinism) led to a fundamental change in thought and behavior (the *Protestant ethic*). The result was the *spirit of capitalism.* For this reason, capitalism originated in Europe and not in places where religion did not encourage capitalism's essential elements: the accumulation of capital and its investment and reinvestment.

"We're thinking maybe it's time you started getting some religious instruction. There's Catholic, Protestant, and Jewish—any of those sound good to you?"

For some Americans, religion is an "easy-going, makes-little-difference" matter, as expressed in this cartoon. For others, religious matters are firmly held, and followers find even slight differences of faith to be significant.

Although Weber's analysis has been influential, it has not lacked critics (Kalberg 2002). Hundreds of scholars have attacked it, some for overlooking the lack of capitalism in Scotland (a Calvinist country), others for failing to explain why the Industrial Revolution was born in England (not a Calvinist country). Hundreds of other scholars have defended Weber's argument, and sociologists continue to test Weber's theory (Basten and Betz 2008). There is currently no evidence that can definitively prove or disprove Weber's thesis.

At this point in history, the Protestant ethic and the spirit of capitalism are not confined to any specific religion or even to any one part of the world. Rather, they have become cultural traits that have spread to societies around the globe (Greeley 1964; Yinger 1970). U.S. Catholics have about the same approach to life as do U.S. Protestants. In addition, Hong Kong, Japan, Malaysia, Singapore, South Korea, and Taiwan—not exactly Protestant countries—have embraced capitalism. China, Russia, and Vietnam are in the midst of doing so.

spirit of capitalism Weber's term for the desire to accumulate capital—not to spend it, but as an end in itself—and to constantly reinvest it

Protestant ethic Weber's term to describe a self-denying, highly moral life accompanied by hard work and frugality

monotheism the belief that there is only one God

polytheism the belief that there are many gods

animism the belief that all objects in the world have spirits, some of which are dangerous and must be outwitted

The World's Major Religions

The largest of the thousands of religions in the world are listed in Figure 18.1 on the next page. Let's briefly review six of them.

Judaism

The origin of Judaism is traced to Abraham, who lived about four thousand years ago in Mesopotamia. Jews believe that God (Jahweh) made a covenant with Abraham, selecting his descendants as a chosen people—promising to make them "as numerous as the sands of the seashore" and to give them a special land that would be theirs forever. The sign of this covenant was the circumcision of males, which was to be performed when a boy was eight days old. Descent is traced through Abraham and his wife, Sarah, their son Isaac, and their grandson Jacob (also called Israel).

Joseph, a son of Jacob, was sold by his brothers into slavery and taken to Egypt. Following a series of hair-raising adventures, Joseph became Pharaoh's right-hand man. When a severe famine hit Canaan, where Jacob's family was living, Jacob and his eleven other sons fled to Egypt. Under Joseph's leadership, they were welcome. A subsequent Pharaoh, however, enslaved the Israelites. After about four hundred years, Moses, an Israelite who had been adopted by Pharaoh's daughter, confronted Pharaoh. He persuaded Pharaoh to release the slaves, who at that time numbered about 2 million. Moses led the Israelites out of Egypt, but before they reached their Promised Land, they spent forty years wandering in the desert. Sometime during those years, Moses delivered the Ten Commandments from Mount Sinai. Abraham, Isaac, Jacob, and Moses hold revered positions in Judaism. The events of their lives and the recounting of the early history of the Israelites are contained in the first five books of the Bible, called the Torah.

The founding of Judaism marked a fundamental change in religion, for it was the first religion based on **monotheism,** the belief that there is only one God. Prior to Judaism, religions were based on **polytheism,** the belief that there are many gods. In ancient Greek religion, for example, Zeus was the god of heaven and earth, Poseidon the god of the sea, and Athena the goddess of wisdom. Other groups followed **animism,** believing that all objects in the world have spirits, some of which are dangerous and must be outwitted.

Contemporary Judaism in the United States comprises three main branches: Orthodox, Reform, and Conservative. Orthodox Jews adhere to the laws espoused by Moses. They eat only foods prepared in a designated manner (kosher), observe the Sabbath in a traditional way, and segregate males and females in their religious services. During the 1800s, a group that wanted to make their practices more compatible with U.S. culture broke from this tradition. This liberal group, known as Reform Judaism, mostly uses English in its religious ceremonies and has much less ritual. The third branch, Conservative Judaism, falls somewhere between the other two. No branch has continued to practice polygyny (allowing a man to have more than one wife), the orig-

Religion, which provides community and identity, is often passed from the older to the younger. Shown here is a family of Hasidic Jews at the Sabbath table.

inal marriage custom of the Jews, which was outlawed by rabbinic decree about a thousand years ago.

The history of Judaism is marked by conflict and persecution. The Israelites were conquered by the Babylonians, and were again made slaves. After returning to Israel and rebuilding the temple, they were later conquered by the Romans, and, after their rebellion at Masada in A.D. 70 failed, they were exiled for almost two thousand years into other nations. During those centuries, they faced prejudice, discrimination, and persecution (called **anti-Semitism**) by many peoples and rulers. The most horrendous example was the Nazi Holocaust of World War II, when Hitler attempted to eliminate the Jews as a people. Under the Nazi occupation of Europe and North Africa, about 6 million Jews were slaughtered. Many died in gas ovens that were constructed for just this purpose.

Central to Jewish teaching is the requirement to love God and do good deeds. Good deeds begin in the family, where each member has an obligation toward the others. Sin is a conscious choice to do evil and must be atoned for by prayers and good works. Jews consider Jerusalem a holy city and believe that one day the Messiah will appear there, bringing redemption for them all.

Christianity

Christianity, which developed out of Judaism, is also monotheistic. Christians believe that Jesus is the Christ, the Messiah whom God promised the Jews.

Jesus was born in poverty, and traditional Christians believe his mother was a virgin. Within two years of his birth, Herod—named king of Palestine by Caesar, who had conquered Israel—was informed that people were saying a new king had been born. When they realized Herod had sent soldiers to kill the baby, Jesus' parents fled with him to Egypt. After Herod died, they returned, settling in the small town of Nazareth.

At about the age of thirty, Jesus began a preaching and healing ministry. His teachings challenged the contemporary religious establishment, and as his popularity grew, the religious leaders plotted to have him killed by the Romans. Christians interpret the death of Jesus as a blood sacrifice made to atone for their sins. They believe that through his death they have peace with God and will inherit eternal life.

The twelve main followers of Jesus, called *apostles,* believed that Jesus rose from the dead. They preached the need to be "born again," that is, to accept Jesus as Savior, give up selfish ways, and live a devout life. The new religion spread rapidly, and after an initial period of hostility on the part of imperial Rome—during which time believers were fed to the lions in the Coliseum—in A.D. 317 Christianity became the empire's official religion.

During the first thousand years of Christianity, there was only one church organization, directed from Rome. During the eleventh century, after disagreement over doctrine and politics, Greek Orthodoxy was declared independent of Rome. It was headquartered in Constantinople (now Istanbul, Turkey). During the Middle Ages, the Roman Catholic Church, which was aligned with the political establishment, became corrupt. Some Church offices, such as that of bishop, were sold for a set price. The Reformation, which was led by Martin Luther in the sixteenth century, was sparked by Luther's outrage that the forgiveness of sins (including those not yet committed) could be purchased by buying an "indulgence."

Although Martin Luther's original goal was to reform the Church, not divide it, the Reformation began a splintering of Christianity. The Reformation coincided with the breakup of feudalism, and as the ancient political structure came apart, people clamored for independence in both political and religious thought. Today, Christianity is the most popular religion in the world, with about 2 billion adherents. Christians are divided into hundreds of groups, some with doctrinal differences so slight that only members of the group can appreciate the extremely fine distinctions that they feel significantly separate them from others. The Social Map on the next page shows how some of these groups are distributed in the United States.

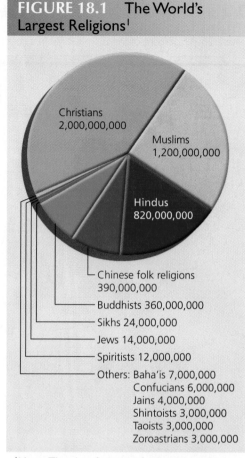

FIGURE 18.1   The World's Largest Religions[1]

Christians 2,000,000,000

Muslims 1,200,000,000

Hindus 820,000,000

Chinese folk religions 390,000,000

Buddhists 360,000,000

Sikhs 24,000,000

Jews 14,000,000

Spiritists 12,000,000

Others: Baha'is 7,000,000
Confucians 6,000,000
Jains 4,000,000
Shintoists 3,000,000
Taoists 3,000,000
Zoroastrians 3,000,000

[1]*Note:* The classification of religions is often confusing. Animists, for example, although numerous, are not listed as a separate group in the source. It is sometimes difficult to tell what groups are included in what categories.

Sources: "Adherents of . . . " 2003.

anti-Semitism prejudice, discrimination, and persecution directed against Jews

FIGURE 18.2   Church Membership: Dominant Religion, by County

When no religious group has 25 percent of the total membership in a county, that county is left blank. When two or more religious groups have 25–49 percent of the membership in a county, the largest is shown.

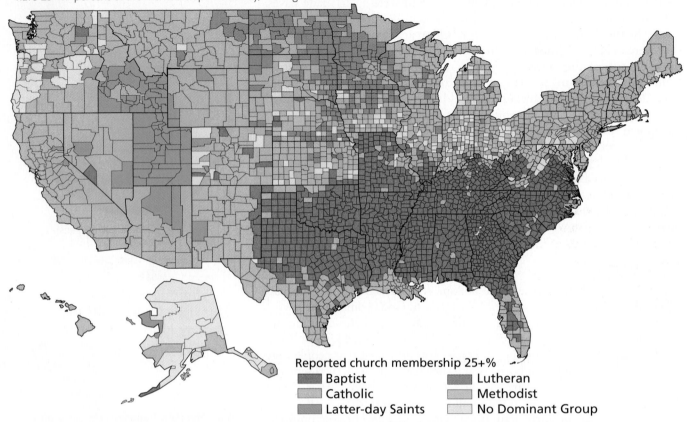

Reported church membership 25+%

Baptist   Lutheran
Catholic   Methodist
Latter-day Saints No Dominant Group

Source: Reprinted with permission from *Religious Congregations and Membership in the United States: 2000.* (Nashville: Glenmary Research Center, 2002). © Association of Statisticians of American Religious Bodies. All rights reserved.

Islam

Islam, whose followers are known as Muslims, began in the same part of the world as Judaism and Christianity. Islam, the world's third monotheistic religion, has over a billion followers. It was founded by Muhammad, who was born in Mecca (now in Saudi Arabia) in about A.D. 570. Muhammad married Khadija, a wealthy widow. About the age of 40, he reported that he had had visions from God. These, and his teachings, were later written down in a book called the Qur'an (Koran). Few paid attention to Muhammad, although Ali, his son-in-law, believed him. When he found out that there was a plot to murder him, Muhammad fled to Medina, where he found a more receptive audience. There he established a *theocracy* (a government based on the principle that God is king, God's laws are the statutes of the land, and priests are the earthly administrators of God). In A.D. 630 he returned to Mecca, this time as a conqueror (Bridgwater 1953).

After Muhammad's death, a struggle for control over the empire he had founded split Islam into two branches that remain today, the Sunni and the Shi'ite. The Shi'ites believe that the *imam* (the religious leader) is inspired as he interprets the Qur'an. They are generally more conservative and are inclined to **fundamentalism,** the belief that modern ways of life threaten religion and that the faith as it was originally practiced should be restored. The Sunnis, who do not share this belief, are generally more liberal, more accepting of social change.

Like the Jews, Muslims trace their ancestry to Abraham. Abraham fathered a son, Ishmael, by Hagar, his wife Sarah's Egyptian maid (Genesis 25:12). Ishmael had twelve

fundamentalism the belief that social change, especially in values, is threatening true religion and that the religion needs to go back to its fundamentals (roots, basic beliefs, and practices)

sons, from whom a good portion of today's Arab world is descended. For them also, Jerusalem is a holy city. The Muslims consider the Bibles of the Jews and the Christians to be sacred, but they take the Qur'an as the final word. They believe that the followers of Abraham and Moses (Jews) and Jesus (Christians) changed the original teachings and that Muhammad restored these teachings to their initial purity. It is the duty of each Muslim to make a pilgrimage to Mecca during his or her lifetime. Unlike the Jews, the Muslims continue to practice polygyny. They limit a man to four wives, however.

Hinduism

Unlike the other religions just described, Hinduism has no specific founder. Going back about four thousand years, Hinduism was the chief religion of India. The term *Hinduism,* however, is Western, and in India the closest term is *dharma* (law). Unlike Judaism, Christianity, and Islam, Hinduism has no canonical scripture, that is, no texts thought to be inspired by God. Instead, several books, including the Brahmanas, Bhagavad-Gita, and Upanishads, expound on the moral qualities that people should strive to develop. They also delineate the sacrifices people should make to the gods.

Hindus are *polytheists;* that is, they believe that there are many gods. They believe that one of these gods, Brahma, created the universe. Brahma, along with Shiva (the Destroyer) and Vishnu (the Preserver), form a triad that is at the center of modern Hinduism. A central belief is *karma,* spiritual progress. There is no final judgment, but, instead, **reincarnation,** a cycle of life, death, and rebirth. Death involves only the body. The soul continues its existence, coming back in a form that matches the individual's moral progress in the previous life (which centers on proper conduct in following the rules of one's caste). If an individual reaches spiritual perfection, he or she has attained *nirvana.* This marks the end of the cycle of death and rebirth, when the soul is reunited with the universal soul. When this occurs, *maya,* the illusion of time and space, has been conquered.

Some Hindu practices have been modified as a consequence of social protest—especially child marriage and *suttee,* the practice of cremating a surviving widow along with her deceased husband (Bridgwater 1953). Other ancient rituals remain unchanged, however, and include *kumbh mela,* a purifying washing in the Ganges River, which takes place every twelve years, and in which many millions participate.

reincarnation in Hinduism and Buddhism, the return of the soul (or self) after death in a different form

Worshippers of Ganesh, the elephant-headed god, during a festival in Mumbai, India

Buddhism

In about 600 B.C., Siddhartha Gautama founded Buddhism. (Buddha means the "enlightened one," a term Gautama was given by his disciples.) Gautama was the son of an upper-caste Hindu ruler in an area north of Benares, India. At the age of 29, he renounced his life of luxury and became an ascetic. Through meditation, he discovered the "four noble truths," which emphasize self-denial and compassion:

1. Existence is suffering.
2. The origin of suffering is desire.
3. Suffering ceases when desire ceases.
4. The way to end desire is to follow the "noble eightfold path."

The noble eightfold path consists of

1. Right belief
2. Right resolve (to renounce carnal pleasure and to harm no living creature)
3. Right speech
4. Right conduct
5. Right occupation or living
6. Right effort
7. Right-mindedness (or contemplation)
8. Right ecstasy

The central symbol of Buddhism is the eight-spoked wheel. Each spoke represents one aspect of the path. As with Hinduism, the ultimate goal of Buddhism is the cessation of rebirth and thereby of suffering. Buddhists teach that all things are temporary, even the self. Because all things are destined to pass away, there is no soul (Reat 1994).

Buddhism spread rapidly. In the third century B.C., the ruler of India adopted Buddhism and sent missionaries throughout Asia to spread the new teaching (Bridgwater 1953). By the fifth century A.D., Buddhism reached the height of its popularity in India, after which it died out. Buddhism, however, had spread to Ceylon, Burma, Tibet, Laos, Cambodia, Thailand, China, Korea, and Japan, where it flourishes today. With increased immigration from Asian nations, vigorous communities of Buddhists have developed in the United States (Cadge and Bender 2004).

Confucianism

About the time that Gautama lived, K'ung Fu-tsu (551–479 B.C.) was born in China. Confucius (his name strung together in English), a public official, was distressed by the corruption that he saw in government. Unlike Gautama, who urged withdrawal from social activities, Confucius urged social reform and developed a system of moral principles based on peace, justice, and universal order. His teachings were incorporated into writings called the *Analects*.

The basic moral principle of Confucianism is to maintain *jen,* sympathy or concern for other humans. The key to *jen* is to sustain right relationships—being loyal and placing morality above self-interest. In what is called the "Confucian Golden Rule," Confucius stated a basic principle for *jen:* to treat those who are subordinate to you as you would like to be treated by people superior to yourself. Confucius taught that right relationships within the family (loyalty, respect) should be the model for society. He also taught the "middle way," an avoidance of extremes.

Confucianism was originally atheistic, simply a set of moral teachings without reference to the supernatural. As the centuries passed, however, local gods were added to the teachings, and Confucius himself was declared a god. Confucius' teachings became the basis for the government of China. About A.D. 1000, the emphasis on meditation gave way to a stress on improvement through acquiring knowledge. This emphasis remained dominant until the twentieth century. By this time, the government had become rigid, and respect for the existing order had replaced respect for relationships (Bridgwater 1953). Following the Communist revolution of 1949, political leaders attempted to weaken the people's ties with Confucianism. They succeeded in part, but Confucianism remains embedded in Chinese culture.

Types of Religious Groups

Sociologists have identified four types of religious groups: cult, sect, church, and ecclesia. Why do some of these groups meet with hostility, while others tend to be accepted? For an explanation, look at Figure 18.3.

Let's explore what sociologists have found about these four types of religious groups. The summary that follows is a modification of analyses by sociologists Ernst Troeltsch (1931), Liston Pope (1942), and Benton Johnson (1963).

Cult

The word *cult* conjures up bizarre images—shaven heads, weird music, brainwashing—and even ritual suicide may come to mind. Cults, however, are not necessarily weird, and few practice "brainwashing" or bizarre rituals. In fact, *all religions began as cults* (Stark 1989). A **cult** is simply a new or different religion whose teachings and practices put it at odds with the dominant culture and religion. Because the term *cult* arouses such negative meanings in the public mind, however, some scholars prefer to use the term *new religion* instead. As is evident from the Cultural Diversity box on the next page, "new" can mean that an older religion from one culture has made its appearance in a culture that is not familiar with it.

Cults often originate with a **charismatic leader,** an individual who inspires people because he or she seems to have extraordinary qualities. **Charisma** refers to an outstanding gift or to some exceptional quality. People feel drawn to both the person and the message because they find something highly appealing about the individual—in some instances, almost a magnetic charm.

The most popular religion in the world began as a cult. Its handful of followers believed that an unschooled carpenter who preached in remote villages in a backwater country was the Son of God, that he was killed and came back to life. Those beliefs made the early Christians a cult, setting them apart from the rest of their society. Persecuted by both religious and political authorities, these early believers clung to one another for support.

cult a new religion with few followers, whose teachings and practices put it at odds with the dominant culture and religion

charismatic leader literally, someone to whom God has given a gift; in its extended sense, someone who exerts extraordinary appeal to a group of followers

Charisma literally, an extraordinary gift from God; more commonly, an outstanding, "magnetic" personality

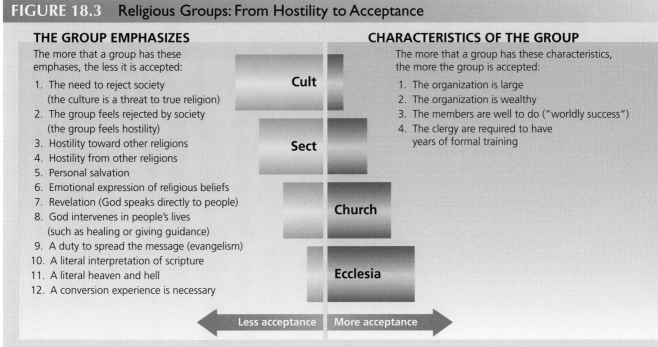

FIGURE 18.3 Religious Groups: From Hostility to Acceptance

THE GROUP EMPHASIZES

The more that a group has these emphases, the less it is accepted:

1. The need to reject society (the culture is a threat to true religion)
2. The group feels rejected by society (the group feels hostility)
3. Hostility toward other religions
4. Hostility from other religions
5. Personal salvation
6. Emotional expression of religious beliefs
7. Revelation (God speaks directly to people)
8. God intervenes in people's lives (such as healing or giving guidance)
9. A duty to spread the message (evangelism)
10. A literal interpretation of scripture
11. A literal heaven and hell
12. A conversion experience is necessary

CHARACTERISTICS OF THE GROUP

The more that a group has these characteristics, the more the group is accepted:

1. The organization is large
2. The organization is wealthy
3. The members are well to do ("worldly success")
4. The clergy are required to have years of formal training

Cult

Sect

Church

Ecclesia

Less acceptance ← → More acceptance

Note: Any religious organization can be placed somewhere on this continuum, based on its having "more" or "less" of these characteristics and emphases. The varying proportions of the rectangles are intended to represent the group's relative characteristics and emphases.

Sources: By the author. Based on Troeltsch 1931; Pope 1942; and Johnson 1963.

Cultural Diversity in the United States

Human Heads and Animal Blood: The Toleration of Religion

As the customs officials looked over the line of people who had just gotten off the plane from Haiti, there was nothing to make this particular woman stand out. She would have passed through without a problem, except for one thing: As the customs agents gave her luggage a routine search, they found something that struck them as somewhat unusual—a human head.

The head had teeth, hair, pieces of skin, and some dirt. It had evidently been dug up from some grave, probably in Haiti.

The 30-year-old woman, who lives in Florida, practiced Voodoo. The head was for her religious rituals.

The woman was arrested. She faces up to 15 years in prison for the crime of not filing a report that she was carrying "organic material" ("Mujer con Cabeza ..." 2006).

A follower of voodoo holding a chicken before it is sacrificed to the deity of fertility.

＊ ＊ ＊ ＊ ＊

The Santeros from Cuba who live in Florida sacrifice animals. They meet in apartments, where, following a Yoruba religion, they kill goats and chickens. Calling on their gods, they first ask permission to sacrifice the animals. After sacrificing them, they pour out the animals' blood, which opens and closes the doors of their destiny. They also cut off the animals' heads and place them at locations in the city that represent the four directions of a compass. This is done to terrorize their enemies and give them safety. The sacrificed heads also protect the city from hurricanes and other destructive forces.

When city officials in Hialeah, Florida, learned that the Santeros were planning to build a church in their city, they passed a law against the sacrifice of animals within the city limits. The Santeros appealed to the U.S. Supreme Court, claiming discrimination, because the law was directed against them. The Court ruled in their favor.

For Your Consideration

What do you think the limitations on religious freedom should be? Should people be allowed to sacrifice animals as part of their religious practices?

If the Santeros can sacrifice animals, why shouldn't people who practice Voodoo be able to use human heads if they want to? (Assume that the relatives of the dead person have given their permission.)

Many cut off associations with friends who didn't accept the new message. To others, the early Christians must have seemed deluded and brainwashed.

So it was with Islam. When Muhammad revealed his visions and said that God's name was really Allah, only a few people believed him. To others, he must have seemed crazy, deranged.

Each cult (or new religion) is met with rejection on the part of society. Its message is considered bizarre, its approach to life strange. Its members antagonize the majority, who are convinced that they have a monopoly on the truth. The new religion may claim messages from God, visions, visits from angels—some form of enlightenment or seeing the true way to God. The cult demands intense commitment, and its followers, who are confronting a hostile world, pull together in a tight circle, separating themselves from nonbelievers.

Most cults fail. Not many people believe the new message, and the cult fades into obscurity. Some, however, succeed and make history. Over time, large numbers of people may come to accept the message and become followers of the religion. If this happens, the new religion changes from a cult to a sect.

sect a religious group larger than a cult that still feels substantial hostility from and toward society

Sect

A **sect** is larger than a cult, but its members still feel tension between their views and the prevailing beliefs and values of the broader society. A sect may even be hostile to the society in which it is located. At the very least, its members remain uncomfortable with many of the emphases of the dominant culture; in turn, nonmembers tend to be uncomfortable with members of the sect.

Ordinarily, sects are loosely organized and fairly small. They emphasize personal salvation and an emotional expression of one's relationship with God. Clapping, shouting, dancing, and extemporaneous prayers are hallmarks of sects. Like cults, sects also stress **evangelism,** the active recruitment of new members.

If a sect grows, its members tend to gradually make peace with the rest of society. To appeal to a broader base, the sect shifts some of its doctrines, redefining matters to remove some of the rough edges that create tension between it and the rest of society. As the members become more respectable in the eyes of the society, they feel less hostility and little, if any, isolation. If a sect follows this course, as it grows and becomes more integrated into society, it changes into a church.

Church

At this point, the religious group is highly bureaucratized—probably with national and international headquarters that give direction to the local congregations, enforce rules about who can be ordained, and control finances. The relationship with God has grown less intense. The group is likely to have less emphasis on personal salvation and emotional expression. Worship services are likely to be more sedate, with sermons more formal, and written prayers read before the congregation. Rather than being recruited from the outside by fervent, personal evangelism, most new members now come from within, from children born to existing members. Rather than joining through conversion—seeing the new truth—children may be baptized, circumcised, or dedicated in some other way. At some designated age, children may be asked to affirm the group's beliefs in a confirmation or bar mitzvah ceremony.

Ecclesia

Finally, some groups become so well integrated into a culture, and so strongly allied with their government, that it is difficult to tell where one leaves off and the other takes over. In these *state religions,* also called **ecclesia,** the government and religion work together to try to shape society. There is no recruitment of members, for citizenship makes everyone a member. For most people in the society, the religion is part of a cultural identity, not an eye-opening experience. Sweden provides a good example of how extensively religion and government intertwine in an ecclesia. In the 1860s, all citizens had to memorize Luther's *Small Catechism* and be tested on it yearly (Anderson 1995). Today, Lutheranism is still associated with the state, but most Swedes come to church only for baptisms, marriages, and funerals.

Unlike cults and sects, which perceive God as personally involved with and concerned about an individual's life, ecclesias envision God as more impersonal and remote. Church services reflect this view of the supernatural, for they tend to be highly formal, directed by ministers or priests who, after undergoing rigorous training in approved schools or seminaries, follow prescribed rituals.

Examples of ecclesia include the Church of England (whose very name expresses alignment between church and state), the Lutheran church in Norway and Denmark, Islam in Iran and Iraq, and, during the time of the Holy Roman Empire, the Roman Catholic Church, which was the official religion for the region that is now Europe.

> **evangelism** an attempt to win converts
>
> **ecclesia** a religious group so integrated into the dominant culture that it is difficult to tell where the one begins and the other leaves off; also called a state religion

Like other aspects of culture, religion is filled with background assumptions that usually go unquestioned. In this photo, which I took in Amsterdam, what background assumption of religion is this woman violating?

Variations in Patterns

Obviously, not all religious groups go through all these stages—from cult to sect to church to ecclesia. Some die out because they fail to attract enough members. Others, such as the Amish, remain sects. And, as is evident from the few countries that have state religions, very few religions ever become ecclesias.

In addition, these classifications are not perfectly matched in the real world. For example, although the Amish are a sect, they place little or no emphasis on recruiting others. The early Quakers, another sect, shied away from emotional expressions of their beliefs. They would quietly meditate in church, with no one speaking, until God gave someone a message to share with others. Finally, some groups that become churches may retain a few characteristics of sects, such as an emphasis on evangelism or a personal relationship with God.

Although all religions began as cults, not all varieties of a particular religion begin that way. For example, some **denominations**—"brand names" within a major religion, such as Methodism or Reform Judaism—begin as splinter groups. Some members of a church disagree with *particular* aspects of the church's teachings (not its major message), and they break away to form their own organization.

When Religion and Culture Conflict

As we have seen, cults and sects represent a break with the past. This division presents a challenge to the social order, and often generates hostility. When religion and the culture in which it is embedded find themselves in conflict, how do they adapt?

First, the members of a religion may reject the dominant culture and have as little as possible to do with nonmembers of their religion. Like the Amish, they may withdraw into closed communities. As noted in the Cultural Diversity box on page 107, the Amish broke away from Swiss-German Mennonites in 1693. They try to preserve the culture of their ancestors, who lived in a simpler time when there were no televisions, movies, automobiles, computers—or even electricity. To do so, they emphasize family life and traditional male and female roles. They continue to wear the style of clothing that their ancestors wore three hundred years ago, to light their homes with oil lamps, and to speak German at home and in church. They also continue to reject radio, television, motorized vehicles, and education beyond the eighth grade. They do mingle with non-Amish when they shop in town—where their transportation (horse-drawn carriages), clothing, and speech set them apart.

In the *second* pattern, a cult or sect rejects only specific elements of the prevailing culture. For example, religious teachings may dictate that immodest clothing—short skirts, skimpy swimsuits, low-cut dresses, and so on—is immoral or that wearing makeup or going to the movies is wrong. Most elements of the main culture, however, are accepted. Although specific activities are forbidden, members of the religion are able to participate in most aspects of the broader society. They resolve this mild tension either by adhering to the religion or by "sneaking," doing the forbidden acts on the sly.

In the *third* pattern, the society rejects the religious group. Our opening vignette focused on an example, the seizure by Texan authorities of children from a Mormon splinter group. In the extreme, as with the early Christians, political leaders may even try to destroy the group. The Roman emperor declared the followers of Jesus to be enemies of Rome and ordered them to be hunted down and destroyed. In the United States, after mobs hounded the new Mormons out of several communities and then killed Joseph Smith, the founder of their religion, the Mormons decided to escape the dominant culture altogether. In 1847, they settled in a wilderness, in what is today Utah's Great Salt Lake Valley (Bridgwater 1953). The most remarkable example in the United States within the past couple of decades occurred in 1993 when U.S. authorities attacked and destroyed a cult called the Branch Davidians. Including the twenty-five children who died huddled next to their mothers, more than eighty people died.

denomination a "brand name" within a major religion; for example, Methodist or Baptist

Religion in the United States

To better understand religion in U.S. society, let's first find out who belongs to religious groups and then look at the groups they belong to.

Characteristics of Members

About 65 percent of Americans belong to a church, synagogue, or mosque. What are the characteristics of people who hold formal membership in a religion?

Social Class.   Religion in the United States is stratified by social class. As you can see from Figure 18.4 below, some religious groups are "top-heavy," and others are "bottom-heavy." The most top-heavy are Jews and Episcopalians; the most bottom-heavy are Assembly of God, Southern Baptists, and Jehovah's Witnesses. This figure provides further confirmation that churchlike groups tend to appeal to people who have more "worldly" success, while the more sectlike groups attract people who have less "worldly" success.

From this figure, you can see how *status consistency* (a concept we reviewed in Chapter 10, page 268) applies to religious groups. If a group ranks high (or low) on education, it is also likely to rank high (or low) on income and occupational prestige. Jews, for example, rank the highest on education, income, and occupational prestige, while Jehovah's Witnesses rank the lowest on these three measures of social class. As you can see, the Mormons are status inconsistent. They rank second in income, fourth in education, and tie for sixth in occupational prestige. Even more status inconsistent is the Assembly of God. Their members tie for third in occupational prestige but rank only eighth in income and ninth in education. This inconsistency is so jarring that there could be a problem with the sample.

Americans who change their social class also tend to change their religion. Their new social class experiences create changes in their ideas about the world, molding new preferences for music and styles of speech. Upwardly mobile people are likely to seek

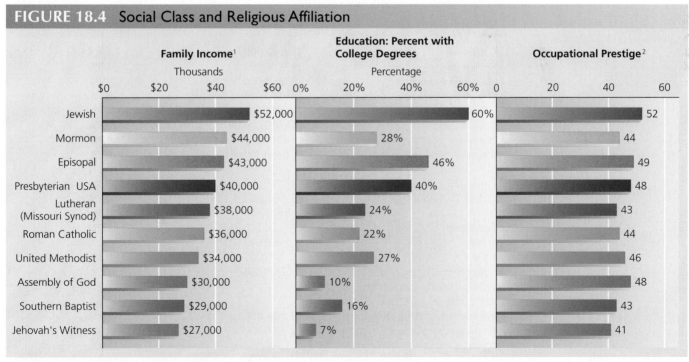

FIGURE 18.4   Social Class and Religious Affiliation

[1]Since the income data were reported, inflation has run approximately 27 percent.

[2]Higher numbers mean that more of the group's members work at occupations that have higher prestige, generally those that require more education and pay more. For more information on occupational prestige, see Table 10.2 on page 267.
Source: By the author. Based on Smith and Faris 2005.

a religion that draws more affluent people. An upwardly mobile Baptist, for example, may become a Methodist or a Presbyterian. For Roman Catholics, the situation is somewhat different. Because each parish is a geographical unit, Catholics who move into more affluent neighborhoods are also likely to be moving to a congregation that has a larger proportion of affluent members.

Race–Ethnicity.   It is common for religions around the world to be associated with race–ethnicity: Islam with Arabs, Judaism with Jews, Hinduism with Indians, and Confucianism with Chinese. Sometimes, as with Hinduism and Confucianism, a religion and a particular country are almost synonymous. Christianity is not associated with any one country, although it is associated primarily with Western culture.

In the United States, all major religious groups draw from the nation's many racial–ethnic groups. Like social class, however, race–ethnicity tends to cluster. People of Irish descent are likely to be Roman Catholics; those with Greek ancestors are likely to belong to the Greek Orthodox Church. African Americans are likely to be Protestants—more specifically, Baptists—or to belong to fundamentalist sects.

Although many churches are integrated, it is with good reason that Sunday morning between 10 and 11 A.M. has been called "the most segregated hour in the United States." African Americans tend to belong to African American churches, while most whites see only whites in theirs. The segregation of churches is based on custom, not on law.

Characteristics of Religious Groups

Let's examine features of the religious groups in the United States.

Diversity.   With its 300,000 congregations and hundreds of denominations, no religious group even comes close to being a dominant religion in the United States (*Statistical Abstract* 2009:Tables 74, 75). Table 18.1 illustrates some of this remarkable diversity.

TABLE 18.1   How U.S. Adults Identify with Religion

Religious Group	Number of Members	Percentage of U.S. Adults
Christian	**176,000,000**	**78.4%**
Protestant	115,000,000	51.3%
Evangelical churches	59,000,000	26.3%
Mainline churches	41,000,000	18.1%
Historical black churches	16,000,000	6.9%
Roman Catholic	54,000,000	23.9%
Mormon	3,800,000	1.7%
Jehovah's Witness	1,600,000	0.7%
Orthodox, Greek, Russian	1,400,000	0.6%
Other Christian	700,000	0.3%
Other Religions	**11,000,000**	**4.7%**
Jewish	3,800,000	1.7%
Buddhist	1,600,000	0.7%
Muslim	1,400,000	0.6%
Hindu	900,000	0.4%
Other faiths	2,700,000	1.2%
(Unitarians, New Age, Native American religions, Liberal)		
No Identity with a Religion	**36,000,000**	**16.1%**
Nothing in particular	27,000,000	12.1%
Agnostic	5,400,000	2.4%
Atheist	3,600,000	1.6%
Don't Know or Refused	**1,800,000**	**0.8%**

Note: Due to rounding, totals may not add to 100. Based on a sample of 35,000 of the 225 million Americans age 18 and over.

Source: U.S. Religious Landscape Survey 2008:5.

Pluralism and Freedom.   It is the U.S. government's policy not to interfere with religions. The government's position is that its obligation is to ensure an environment in which people can worship as they see fit. Religious freedom is so extensive that anyone can start a church and proclaim himself or herself a minister, revelator, or any other desired term. The exceptions to this hands-off policy are startling. As mentioned, the most notorious exception in recent times occurred in Waco, Texas. When armed agents of the Bureau of Alcohol, Tobacco, and Firearms attacked the compound of the Branch Davidians, an obscure religious group, eighty-two men, women, and children were burned to death. A second example is the focus of this chapter's opening vignette. A third is the government's infiltration of mosques to monitor the activities of Arab immigrants (Elinson 2004). Other limitations to this policy are discussed in the Cultural Diversity box on page 542.

Competition and Recruitment.   The many religious groups of the United States compete for clients. They even advertise in the Yellow Pages of the telephone directory and insert appealing advertising—under the guise of news—in the religion section of the Saturday or Sunday edition of the local newspapers

Commitment.   Americans are a religious people, and 42 percent report that they attend religious services each week (Gallup Poll 2008b). Sociologists have questioned this statistic, suggesting that the high total is due to an *interviewer effect*. Because people want to please interviewers, they stretch the truth a bit. To find out, sociologists Stanley Presser and Linda Stinson (1998) examined people's written reports (no interviewer present) on how they spent their Sundays. They concluded that about 30 percent or so do attend church each week.

Whether the percentage of weekly church attendance is 30 or 42, Americans are a religious people, and they back up their commitment with generous support for religion and its charities. Each year Americans donate about $97 billion to religious causes (*Statistical Abstract* 2009:Table 561). To appreciate the significance of this huge figure, keep in mind that, unlike a country in which there is an ecclesia, those billions of dollars are not forced taxes, but money that people give away.

Toleration.   The general religious toleration of Americans can be illustrated by three prevailing attitudes: (1) "All religions have a right to exist—as long as they don't try to brainwash or hurt anyone." (2) "With all the religions to choose from, how can anyone tell which one—if any—is true?" (3) "Each of us may be convinced about the truth of our religion—and that is good—but don't be obnoxious by trying to convince others that you have the exclusive truth."

Fundamentalist Revival.   As discussed in the Cultural Diversity box on the next page, the fundamentalist Christian churches are undergoing a revival. They teach that the Bible is literally true and that salvation comes only through a personal relationship with Jesus Christ. They also denounce what they see as the degeneration of U.S. culture: flagrant sex on television, in movies, and in videos; abortion; corruption in public office; premarital sex and cohabitation; and drug abuse. Their answer to these problems is firm, simple, and direct: People whose hearts are changed through religious conversion will change their lives. The mainstream churches, which offer a more remote God and less emotional involvement, fail to meet the basic religious needs of large numbers of Americans.

One result is that mainstream churches are losing members while the fundamentalists are gaining them. Figure 18.5 on page 549 depicts this change. The exception is the Roman Catholic Church, whose growth in North America is due primarily to immigration from Mexico and other Roman Catholic countries.

The Electronic Church.   What began as a ministry to shut-ins and those who do not belong to a church blossomed into its own type of church. Its preachers, called "televangelists," reach millions of viewers and raise millions of dollars. Some of its most famous ministries are those of Joyce Meyers, Pat Robertson (the 700 Club), Benny Hinn, Creflo Dollar, Kenneth Copeland, and Joel Osteen.

Many local ministers view the electronic church as a competitor. They complain that it competes for the attention and dollars of their members. Leaders of the electronic church reply that the money goes to good causes and that through its conversions, the electronic church feeds members into the local churches, strengthening, not weakening them.

Cultural Diversity in the United States

The New Face of Religion: Pentecostals and the Spanish-Speaking Immigrants

That millions of immigrants from Spanish-speaking countries have become part of the U.S. social scene is not news. That most of them are poor isn't news, either. Almost all the immigrants who came before them were poor, too.

What is news is that many of these Latinos are abandoning the Roman Catholic religion and are embracing a form of Protestantism called Pentecostalism. Pentecostals, often referred to by the derisive term, holy rollers, take the Bible literally. They believe there is a real heaven and hell. They lay hands on each other and pray for healings. They expect God to act in their lives in a personal way. They speak in tongues.

And they are noisily joyful about their faith.

Go into one of their storefront churches, such as those on Amsterdam Avenue in New York City—or in any of the thousands of little churches that have sprung up around the country. You'll hear music and clapping. The preachers talk about a God who is concerned about the troubles people are going through. They warn the congregation, too, about the dangers of sin—the adultery that seductively beckons; the downfall of drugs and alcohol; the dead end of laziness and extravagance. They also extol the values of thrift and hard work. As the preacher preaches, the congregation breaks out into "Amens." "Amen, brother! Bring it on!" will shout one person, while another says, "Amen, sister. Tell it like it is!"

The preachers know what they are talking about. They work at factory jobs during the day. They know what it is to sweat for a living and that J-O-B is really spelled B-R-O-K-E. Cantankerous bosses, unpaid bills, and paychecks that run out before the month does are part of their own lives.

Religion often helps immigrants adapt to their new culture. What indications of this do you see in this photo?

As people clap and sway to the sounds of the drums and guitars—like salsa music with religious lyrics—some pray silently in tongues. Others shout out the strange sounds. Some tongues, they believe, are messages straight from God. But no one can understand them unless someone else is given the interpretation. When this happens, people listen intently for what God has to say to them personally.

The worshippers don't come just for an hour on Sunday mornings. They come night after night, finding comfort in community and encouragement in the message and music. The services also allow them to express their emotions among like-minded people.

Pentecostalism is the fastest-growing religion in the United States, and there are perhaps 400 million Pentecostals worldwide. Although there are middle-class and college-educated Pentecostals, the middle-class arms don't open as wide. The appeal is mainly to the poor. When the poor make the transition to the middle class—as their religion, with its emphasis on work and thrift will help them do—they are likely to seek new forms of religious expression.

When this happens, we can expect that Pentecostalism will also adapt, that the form will remain recognizable, but the fervor will be lost. For now, though, it is the fervor—the intensity that connects the individuals to God and to one another—that is the driving force of this religion. The Pentecostals would phrase this a little differently. They would say that the fervor is merely the expression of the driving force of their religion, which is the Holy Spirit.

Either way you put it, these people are on fire. And that fire is burning a new imprint on the face of religion.

For Your Consideration
Why do you think the Pentecostals are growing so fast? What effect do you think they might have on mainstream Christianity?

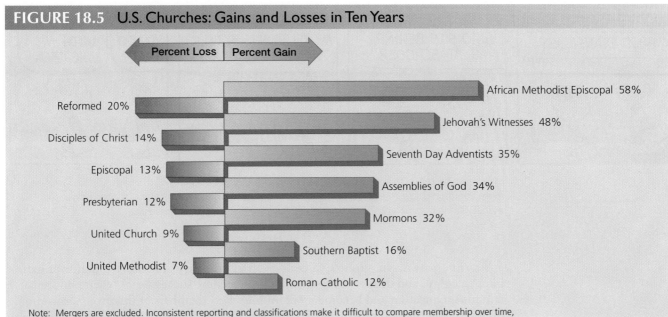

FIGURE 18.5   U.S. Churches: Gains and Losses in Ten Years

Percent Loss | Percent Gain

African Methodist Episcopal 58%
Jehovah's Witnesses 48%
Seventh Day Adventists 35%
Assemblies of God 34%
Mormons 32%
Southern Baptist 16%
Roman Catholic 12%

Reformed 20%
Disciples of Christ 14%
Episcopal 13%
Presbyterian 12%
United Church 9%
United Methodist 7%

Note: Mergers are excluded. Inconsistent reporting and classifications make it difficult to compare membership over time, making these totals only approximate.

Source: By the author. Recomputed from Jones et al. 2002.

Secularization of Religion and Culture

The term *secularization* refers to the process by which worldly affairs replace spiritual interests. (The term **secular** means "belonging to the world and its affairs.") As we shall see, both religions and cultures can become secularized.

The Secularization of Religion

> As the model, fashionably slender, paused before the head table of African American community leaders, her gold necklace glimmering above the low-cut bodice of her emerald-green dress, the hostess, a member of the Church of God in Christ, said, "It's now OK to wear more revealing clothes—as long as it's done in good taste." Then she added, "You couldn't do this when I was a girl, but now it's OK—and you can still worship God." (Author's files)

When I heard these words, I grabbed a napkin and quickly jotted them down, my sociological imagination stirred by their deep implication. As strange as it may seem, this simple event pinpoints the essence of why the Christian churches in the United States have splintered. Let's see how this could possibly be.

The simplest explanation for why Christians don't have just one church, or at most several, instead of the hundreds of sects and denominations that dot the U.S. landscape, is disagreements about doctrine (church teaching). As theologian and sociologist Richard Niebuhr pointed out, however, there are many ways of settling doctrinal disputes besides splintering off and forming other religious organizations. Niebuhr (1929) suggested that the answer lies more in *social* change than it does in *religious* conflict.

The explanation goes like this. As was noted earlier, when a sect becomes more churchlike, its members feel less tension with the mainstream culture. Quite likely, when a sect is first established, its founders and first members are poor, or at least not very successful in worldly pursuits. Feeling like strangers in the dominant culture, they derive a good part of their identity from their religion. In their church services and lifestyle, they stress how different their values are from those of the dominant culture. They are also likely to emphasize the joys of the coming afterlife, when they will be able to escape from their present pain.

secular belonging to the world and its affairs

In its technical sense, to evangelize means to "announce the Good News" (that Jesus is the Savior). In its more common usage, to evangelize means to make converts. As *Peanuts* so humorously picks up, evangelization is sometimes accomplished through means other than preaching.

As time passes, the group's values—such as frugality and the avoidance of gambling, alcohol, and drugs—help the members become successful. As their children attain more education and become more middle class, members of this group grow more respectable in the eyes of society. They no longer experience the alienation that was felt by the founders of their group. Life's burdens don't seem as heavy, and the need for relief through an afterlife becomes less pressing. Similarly, the pleasures of the world no longer appear as threatening to the "truth." As with the woman at the fashion show, people then attempt to harmonize their religious beliefs with their changing ideas about the culture.

This process is called the **secularization of religion**—shifting the focus from spiritual matters to the affairs of this world. Anyone familiar with today's mainstream Methodists would be surprised to know that they once were a sect. Methodists used to ban playing cards, dancing, and going to movies. They even considered circuses to be sinful. As Methodists grew more middle class, however, they began to change their views on sin. They started to dismantle the barriers that they had constructed between themselves and the outside world (Finke and Stark 1992).

Secularization leads to a splintering of the group, for adjusting to the secular culture displeases some of the group's members, especially those who have had less worldly success. These people still feel a gulf between themselves and the broader culture. For them, tension and hostility continue to be real. They see secularization as a desertion of the group's fundamental truths, a "selling out" to the secular world.

After futile attempts by die-hards to bring the group back to its senses, the group splinters. Those who protested the secularization of Methodism, for example, were kicked out—even though *they* represented the values around which the group had organized in the first place. The dissatisfied—who have come to be viewed as complainers—then form a sect that once again stresses its differences from the world; the need for more personal, emotional religious experiences; and salvation from the pain of living in this world. As time passes, the cycle repeats: adjustment to the dominant culture by some, continued dissatisfaction by others, and further splintering.

This process is not limited to sects, but also occurs in churches. When U.S. Episcopalians elected an openly gay bishop in 2003, some pastors and congregations splintered from the U.S. church and affiliated with the more conservative African archbishops. In an ironic twist, this made them mission congregations from Africa. Sociologists have not yet compared the income or wealth of those who stayed with the group that elected the gay bishop and those who joined the splinter groups. If such a study is done and it turns out that there is no difference, we will have to modify the secularization thesis.

The Secularization of Culture.   Just as religion can secularize, so can culture. Sociologists use the term **secularization of culture** to refer to a culture that was once

secularization of religion
the replacement of a religion's spiritual or "other worldly" concerns with concerns about "this world"

secularization of culture
the process by which a culture becomes less influenced by religion

heavily influenced by religion, but no longer retains much of that influence. The United States provides an example.

Despite attempts to reinterpret history, the Pilgrims and most of the founders of the United States were highly religious people. The Pilgrims were even convinced that God had guided them to found a new religious community whose members would follow the Bible. Similarly, many of the framers of the U.S. Constitution felt that God had guided them to develop a new form of government.

The clause in the Constitution that mandates the separation of church and state was *not* an attempt to keep religion out of government, but a (successful) device to avoid the establishment of a state religion like that in England. Here, people were to have the freedom to worship as they wished. The assumption of the founders was even more specific—that Protestantism represented the true religion.

The phrase in the Declaration of Independence, "All men are *created* equal," refers to a central belief in God as the creator of humanity. A member of the clergy opened Congress with prayer. Many colonial laws were based on principles derived explicitly from the Old and New Testaments. In some colonies, blasphemy was a crime, as was failing to observe the Sabbath. Similarly, sexual affairs were a crime; in some places adultery carried the death penalty. Even public kissing between husband and wife was considered an offense, punishable by placement in the public stocks (Frumkin 1967). In other words, religion permeated U.S. culture. It was part and parcel of how the colonists saw life. Their lives, laws, and other aspects of the culture reflected their religious beliefs.

As U.S. culture secularized, the influence of religion on public affairs diminished. No longer are laws based on religious principles. It has even become illegal to post the Ten Commandments in civic buildings. Overall, ideas of what is "generally good" have replaced religion as an organizing principle for the culture.

Underlying the secularization of culture is *modernization,* a term that refers to a society industrializing, urbanizing, developing mass education, and adopting science and advanced technology. Science and advanced technology bring with them a secular view of the world that begins to permeate society. They provide explanations for many aspects of life that people traditionally attributed to God. As a consequence, people come to depend much less on religion to explain life's events. Birth and death—and everything in between, from life's problems to its joys—are attributed to natural causes. When a society has secularized thoroughly, even religious leaders may turn to answers provided by biology, philosophy, psychology, sociology, and so on.

Although the secularization of U.S. culture means that religion has become less important in public life, *personal* religious involvement among Americans has not diminished. Rather, it has increased (Finke and Stark 1992). About 86 percent believe there is a God, and 81 percent believe there is a heaven. Not only do 63 percent claim membership in a church or synagogue, but, as we saw, on any given weekend somewhere between 30 and 42 percent of all Americans attend a worship service (Gallup 1990, 2008b).

Table 18.2 underscores the paradox. While the culture has secularized, church membership has increased. The proportion of Americans who belong to a church or synagogue is now about *three and a half* times higher than it was when the country was founded. As you can see, membership peaked in 1975. Church membership, of course, is only a rough indicator of how significant religion is in people's lives. Some church members are not particularly religious, while many intensely religious people—Lincoln, for one—never joined a church.

TABLE 18.2 Growth in Religious Membership	
Americans Who Belong to a Church or Synagogue	
Year	Percentage Who Claim Membership
1776	17%
1860	37%
1890	45%
1926	58%
1975	71%
2000	68%
2007	62%

Note: The sources do not contain data on mosque membership.

Sources: Finke and Stark 1992; *Statistical Abstract of the United States* 2002:Table 64; Gallup Poll 2007b.

The Future of Religion

Religion thrives in the most advanced scientific nations—and, as officials of Soviet Russia were disheartened to learn—in even the most ideologically hostile climate. Although the Soviet authorities threw believers into prison, people continued to practice their religions. Humans are inquiring creatures. As they reflect on life, they ask, What is the purpose of it all? Why are we born? Is there an afterlife? If so, where are we going? Out of these concerns arises this question: If there is a God, what does God want of us in this life? Does God have a preference about how we should live?

Science, including sociology, cannot answer such questions. By its very nature, science cannot tell us about four main concerns that many people have:

1. *The existence of God.* About this, science has nothing to say. No test tube has either isolated God or refuted God's existence.
2. *The purpose of life.* Although science can provide a definition of life and describe the characteristics of living organisms, it has nothing to say about ultimate purpose.
3. *An afterlife.* Science can offer no information on this at all, for it has no tests to prove or disprove a "hereafter."
4. *Morality.* Science can demonstrate the consequences of behavior, but not the moral superiority of one action compared with another. This means that science cannot even prove that loving your family and neighbor is superior to hurting and killing them. Science can describe death and measure consequences, but it cannot determine the moral superiority of any action, even in such an extreme example.

There is no doubt that religion will last as long as humanity lasts, for what could replace it? And if something did, and answered such questions, would it not be religion under a different name?

To close this chapter, let's try to glimpse the cutting edge of religious change.

A basic principle of symbolic interactionism is that meaning is not inherent in an object or event, but is determined by people as they interpret the object or event. Does this dinosaur skeleton "prove" evolution? Does it "disprove" creation? Such "proof" and "disproof" lie in the eye of the beholder, based on the background assumptions by which it is interpreted.

God on the Net: The Online Marketing of Religion

You want to pray right there at the Holy Land, but you can't leave home? No problem. Buy our special telephone card—now available at your local 7-11. Just record your prayer, and we'll broadcast it via the Internet at the site you choose. Press 1 for the holy site of Jerusalem, press 2 for the holy site of the Sea of Galilee, press 3 for the birthplace of Jesus, press 4 for . . . (Rhoads 2007)

This service is offered by a company in Israel. No discrimination. Open to Jews and Christians alike. Maybe with expansion plans for Muslims. Maybe to anyone, as long as they can pay $10 for a two-minute card.

You left India and now live in Kansas but you want to pray in Chennai? No problem. Order your *pujas* (prayers), and we'll have a priest say them in the temple of your choice. Just click how many you want. Food offerings for Vishnu included in the price. All major credit cards accepted (K. Sullivan 2007).

Erin Polzin, a 20-year-old college student, listens to a Lutheran worship service on the radio, confesses online, and uses PayPal to tithe. "I don't like getting up early," she says. "This is like going to church without really having to" (Bernstein 2003).

You can go to church in your pajamas, and you don't even have to comb your hair.

Muslims in France download sermons and join an invisible community of worshippers at virtual mosques. Jews in Sweden type messages that fellow believers in Jerusalem download and insert in the Western Wall. Christians in the United States make digital donations to the Crystal Cathedral. Buddhists in Japan seek enlightenment online. The Internet helps to level the pulpit: On the Net, the leader of a pagan group can compete directly with the Pope.

There are also virtual church services. Just choose an avatar, and you can walk around the virtual church. You can sing, kneel, pray, and listen to virtual sermons. You can talk to other avatars if you get bored (Feder 2004).

Some people have begun to "attend" church as avatars.

And, of course, you can use your credit card—a real one, not the virtual kind.

The Internet is also making it harder for religious groups to punish their rebels. Jacques Gaillot is a French Roman Catholic bishop who marches in public demonstrations for the poor. He also takes theological positions that upset the church hierarchy: The clergy should marry, women should be ordained, and homosexual partnerships should be blessed. Pope John Paul II took Gaillot's diocese away from him and gave him a nonexistent diocese in the Saharan desert of North Africa. This strategy used to work well to silence dissidents, but it didn't stop Gaillot. He uses the Internet to publicize his views (Huffstutter 1998; Williams 2003).

So does the Vatican at its Web site, which also offers virtual tours of its art galleries. But the real sign of changing times occurred in 2009 when the pope launched his own YouTube channel (Winfield 2009).

Some say that the Net has put us on the verge of a religious reformation as big as the one set off by Gutenberg's invention of the printing press. This sounds like an exaggeration, but perhaps it is true. We'll see.

For Your Consideration

We are gazing into the future. How do you think that the Internet might change religion? How can it replace the warm embrace of fellow believers? Do you think it can it bring comfort to someone who is grieving for a loved one?

By the Numbers: *Then and Now*

Percentage of Americans claiming membership in a church or synagogue

1776
17%

NOW
62%

SUMMARY *and* REVIEW

What Is Religion?
Durkheim identified three essential characteristics of **religion:** beliefs that set the **sacred** apart from the **profane, rituals,** and a moral community (a **church**). Pp. 524–525.

The Functionalist Perspective
What are the functions and dysfunctions of religion?

Among the functions of religion are answering questions about ultimate meaning; providing emotional comfort, social solidarity, guidelines for everyday life, social control, help in adapting to new situations, support for the government; and fostering social change. Nonreligious groups or activities that provide these functions are called **functional equivalents** of religion. Among the dysfunctions of religion are religious persecution and war and terrorism. Pp. 525–528.

The Symbolic Interactionist Perspective
What aspects of religion do symbolic interactionists study?

Symbolic interactionists focus on the meanings of religion for its followers. They examine religious symbols, **rituals,** beliefs, **religious experiences,** and the sense of community that religion provides. Pp. 528–531.

The Conflict Perspective
What aspects of religion do conflict theorists study?

Conflict theorists examine the relationship of religion to social inequalities, especially how religion reinforces a society's stratification system. Pp. 531–534.

Religion and the Spirit of Capitalism
What does the spirit of capitalism have to do with religion?

Max Weber saw religion as a primary source of social change. He analyzed how Calvinism gave rise to the **Protestant ethic,** which stimulated what he called the **spirit of capitalism.** The result was capitalism, which transformed society. Pp. 534–535.

The World's Major Religions
What are the world's major religions?

Judaism, Christianity, and Islam, all **monotheistic** religions, can be traced to the same Old Testament roots. Hinduism, the chief religion of India, has no specific founder, but Judaism (Abraham), Christianity (Jesus), Islam (Muhammad), Buddhism (Gautama), and Confucianism (K'ung Fu-tsu) do. Specific teachings and history of these religions are reviewed in the text. Pp. 536–540.

Types of Religious Groups
What types of religious groups are there?

Sociologists divide religious groups into cults, sects, churches, and ecclesias. All religions began as **cults.** Those that survive tend to develop into **sects** and eventually into **churches.** Sects, often led by **charismatic leaders,** are unstable. Some are perceived as threats and are persecuted by the state. **Ecclesias,** or state religions, are rare. Pp. 541–544.

Religion in the United States
What are the main characteristics of religion in the United States?

Membership varies by social class and race–ethnicity. The major characteristics are diversity, pluralism and freedom, competition, commitment, toleration, a fundamentalist revival, and the electronic church. Pp. 545–548.

What is the connection between secularization of religion and the splintering of churches?

Secularization of religion, a change in a religion's focus from spiritual matters to concerns of "this world," is the key to understanding why churches divide. Basically, as a cult or sect changes to accommodate its members' upward social class mobility, it changes into a church. Left dissatisfied are members who are not upwardly mobile. They tend to splinter off and form a new cult or sect, and the cycle repeats itself. Cultures permeated by religion also secularize. This, too, leaves many people dissatisfied and promotes social change. Pp. 549–551.

The Future of Religion

Although industrialization led to the **secularization of culture,** this did not spell the end of religion, as many social analysts assumed it would. Because science cannot answer questions about ultimate meaning, the existence of God or an afterlife, or provide guidelines for morality, the need for religion will remain. In any foreseeable future, religion will prosper. The Internet is likely to have far-reaching consequences on religion. Pp. 552–553.

THINKING CRITICALLY *ABOUT* Chapter 18

1. Since 9/11, many people have wondered how anyone can use religion to defend or promote terrorism. How does the Down-to-Earth Sociology box on terrorism and the mind of God on page 529 help to answer this question? How do the analyses of groupthink in Chapter 6 (pages 169–170) and dehumanization in Chapter 15 (pages 450–452) fit into your analysis?

2. How has secularization affected religion and culture in the United States (or of your country of birth)?

3. Why is religion likely to remain a strong feature of U.S. life—and remain strong in people's lives around the globe?

ADDITIONAL RESOURCES

What can you find in MySocLab? mysoclab www.mysoclab.com

- Complete Ebook
- Practice Tests and Video and Audio activities
- Mapping and Data Analysis exercises

- Sociology in the News
- Classic Readings in Sociology
- Research and Writing advice

Where Can I Read More on This Topic?

Suggested readings for this chapter are listed at the back of this book.

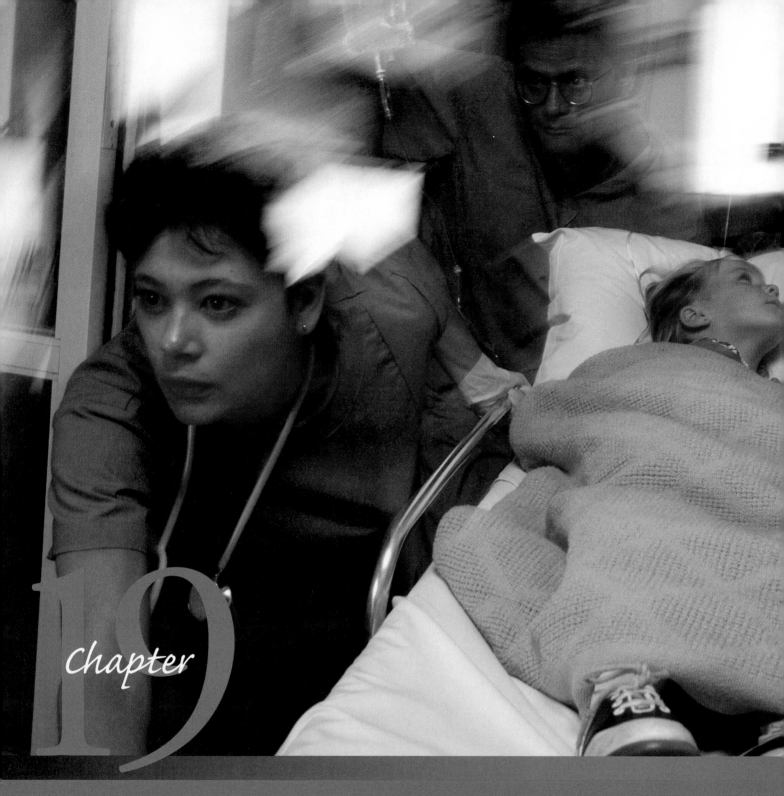

Chapter 19

Medicine and Health

Utah

I decided that it was not enough to just study the homeless—I had to help them. I learned that a homeless shelter in St. Louis, just across the river from where I was teaching, was going to help poor people save on utilities by installing free wood stoves in their homes. When their utilities are cut off, the next step is eviction and being forced onto the streets. It wasn't exactly applied sociology, but I volunteered.

He was crawling under cars at a traffic light—and they let him out in two days.

I was a little anxious about the coming training session on how to install stoves, as I had never done anything like this. Sociology hadn't trained me to be "handy with my hands," but with the encouragement of a friend, I decided to participate. As I entered the homeless shelter on that Saturday morning, I found the building in semidarkness. "They must be saving on electricity," I thought. Then I was greeted with an unnerving scene. Two police officers were chasing a naked man, who was running through the halls. They caught him. I watched as the elderly man, looking confused, struggled to put on his clothing. From the police, I learned that this man had ripped the wires out of the shelter's main electrical box; that was why there were no lights on.

I asked the officers where they were going to take the man, and they replied, "To Malcolm Bliss" (the state hospital). When I said, "I guess he'll be in there for quite a while," they replied, "Probably just a day or two. We picked him up last week—he was crawling under cars at a traffic light—and they let him out in two days."

The police then explained that the man must be a danger to himself or to others to be admitted as a long-term patient. Visualizing this old man crawling under stopped cars at an intersection, and considering how he had risked electrocution by ripping out the electrical wires with his bare hands, I marveled at the definition of "danger" that the psychiatrists must be using.

557

medicine one of the social institutions that sociologists study; a society's organized ways of dealing with sickness and injury

shaman the healing specialist of a tribe who attempts to control the spirits thought to cause a disease or injury; commonly called a witch doctor

health a human condition measured by four components: physical, mental, social, and spiritual

Sociology and the Study of Medicine and Health

This incident points to a severe problem in the delivery of medical care in the United States. In this chapter, we will examine why the poor often receive second-rate medical care and, in some instances, abysmal treatment. We'll also look at how skyrocketing costs have created ethical dilemmas such as the discharge of patients from hospitals before they are well and the potential rationing of medical care.

As we consider these issues, the role of sociology in studying **medicine**—a society's standard ways of dealing with illness and injury—will become apparent. For example, because medicine in the United States is a profession, a bureaucracy, and a big business, sociologists study how it is influenced by self-regulation, the bureaucratic structure, and the profit motive. Sociologists also study how illness and health are much more than biological matters—how, for example, they are related to cultural beliefs, lifestyle, and social class. Because of these emphases, the sociology of medicine is one of the applied fields of sociology. Many medical schools and even hospitals have sociologists on their staffs.

The Symbolic Interactionist Perspective

Let's begin, then, by examining how culture influences health and illness. This takes us to the heart of the symbolic interactionist perspective.

The Role of Culture in Defining Health and Illness

Suppose that one morning you look in the mirror and you see strange blotches covering your face and chest. Hoping against hope that it is not serious, you rush to a doctor. If the doctor said that you had "dyschromic spirochetosis," your fears would be confirmed.

Now, wouldn't everyone around the world draw the conclusion that your spots are symptoms of a disease? No, not everybody. In one South American tribe, this skin condition is so common that the few individuals who *aren't* spotted are seen as the unhealthy ones. They are even excluded from marriage because they are "sick" (Ackernecht 1947; Zola 1983).

Consider mental "illness" and mental "health." People aren't automatically "crazy" because they do certain things. Rather, they are defined as "crazy" or "normal" according to cultural guidelines. If an American talks aloud to spirits that no one else can see or hear, he or she is likely to be defined as insane—and, for everyone's good, locked up in a mental hospital. In some tribal societies, in contrast, someone who talks to invisible spirits might be honored for being in close contact with the spiritual world—and, for everyone's good, be declared a **shaman,** or spiritual intermediary. The shaman would then diagnose and treat medical problems.

"Sickness" and "health," then, are not absolutes, as we might suppose. Rather, they are matters of cultural definition. Around the world, each culture provides guidelines that its people use to determine whether they are "healthy" or "sick."

We define health and illness according to our culture. If almost everyone in a village had this skin disease, the villagers might consider it normal—and those without it the unhealthy ones. I photographed this infant in a jungle village in Orissa, India, so remote that it could be reached only by following a foot path.

The Components of Health

Back in 1941, international "health experts" identified three components of **health:** physical, mental, and social (World Health Organization 1946). They missed the focus of our previous chapter, however, and I have added a spiritual component to Figure 19.1. Even the dimensions of health, then, are subject to debate.

Even if we were to agree on the components of health, we would still be left with the question of what makes someone physically, mentally, socially, or spiritually healthy. Again, as symbolic interactionists stress, these are not objective matters. Rather, what is considered "health" or "illness" varies from culture to culture and, in a pluralistic society, even from group to group.

As with religion in the previous chapter, then, the concern of sociologists is not to define "true" health or "true" illness. Instead, it is to analyze how people's experiences affect their health, how people's ideas about health and illness affect their lives, and even how people determine that they are sick.

The Functionalist Perspective

Functionalists begin with an obvious point: If society is to function well, its people need to be healthy enough to perform their normal roles. This means that societies must set up ways to control sickness. One way they do this is to develop a system of medical care. Another way is to make rules that help keep too many people from "being sick." Let's look at how this works.

The Sick Role

Do you remember when your throat began to hurt, and when your mom or dad took your temperature the thermometer registered 102°F? Your parents took you to the doctor, and despite your protests that tomorrow was the first day of summer vacation (or some other important event), you had to spend the next three days in bed taking medicine.

Your parents forced you to play what sociologists call the "sick role." What do they mean by this term?

Elements of the Sick Role.   Talcott Parsons, the functionalist who first analyzed the **sick role,** pointed out that it has four elements—you are not held responsible for being sick, you are exempt from normal responsibilities, you don't like the role, and you will get competent help so you can return to your routines. People who seek approved help are given sympathy and encouragement; those who do not are given the cold shoulder. People who don't get competent help are considered responsible for being sick, are refused the right to claim sympathy from others, and are denied permission to be excused from their normal routines. They are considered to be wrongfully claiming the sick role.

Ambiguity in the Sick Role.   Instead of a fever of 102°F, suppose that the thermometer registers 99.5°F. Do you then "become" sick—or not? That is, do you decide to claim the sick role? Because most instances of illness are not as clear-cut as, say, a limb fracture, decisions to claim the sick role often are based more on social considerations than on physical conditions. Let's also suppose that you are facing a midterm, you are unprepared for it, and you are allowed to make up the test if you are ill. The more you think about the test, the worse you are likely to feel—which makes the need to claim the sick role seem more legitimate. Now assume that the thermometer still shows 99.5, but you have no test and your friends are coming over to take you out to celebrate your twenty-first birthday. You are not likely to play the sick role. Note that in both cases your physical condition is the same.

Gatekeepers to the Sick Role.   For children, parents are the primary *gatekeepers* to the sick role. That is, parents decide whether children's symptoms are sufficient to legitimize their claim that they are sick. Before parents call the school to excuse a child from class, they decide whether the child is faking or has genuine symptoms. If they determine that the symptoms are real, then they decide whether the symptoms are serious enough to keep the child home from school or even severe enough to take the child to a doctor. For adults, the gatekeepers to the sick role are physicians. Adults can bypass the gatekeeper for short periods, but employers will eventually insist on a "doctor's excuse." This can come in such forms as a "doctor's appointment" or insurance forms signed by the doctor. In sociological terms, these are ways of getting permission to play the sick role.

FIGURE 19.1   A Continuum of Health and Illness

Health
Excellent Functioning

P H Y S I C A L   M E N T A L   S O C I A L   S P I R I T U A L

Poor Functioning
Illness

sick role a social role that excuses people from normal obligations because they are sick or injured, while at the same time expecting them to seek competent help and cooperate in getting well

Gender Differences in the Sick Role.   Women are more willing than men to claim the sick role when they don't feel well. They go to doctors more frequently than men, and they are hospitalized more often than men (*Statistical Abstract* 2009:Tables 158, 160, 167). Apparently, the sick role does not match the *macho* image that most boys and men try to project. Most men try to follow the cultural ideal that they should be strong, keep pain to themselves, and "tough it out." The woman's model, in contrast, is more likely to involve sharing feelings and seeking help from others, characteristics that are compatible with the sick role.

The Conflict Perspective

As we stressed in earlier chapters, the primary focus of the conflict perspective is people's struggle over scarce resources. Health care is one of those resources. Let's first take a global perspective on medical care and then, turning our attention to the United States, we will analyze how one group secured a monopoly on U.S. health care.

Effects of Global Stratification on Health Care

In Chapter 9 (pages 252–253), we saw how the first nations to industrialize obtained the economic and military power that brought them riches and allowed them to dominate other nations. This eventually led to a global stratification of medical care, starkly evident in the photo below. For example, open heart surgery has become routine in the Most Industrialized Nations. The Least Industrialized Nations, in contrast, cannot afford the technology that open heart surgery requires. So it is with AIDS. In the United States and other rich nations, costly medicines have extended the lives of those who suffer from AIDS. Most people with AIDS in the Least Industrialized Nations can't afford these medicines. For them, AIDS is a death sentence.

Life expectancy and infant mortality rates also tell the story. Most people in the industrialized world can expect to live to about age 75, but *most* people in Afghanistan, Nigeria, and South Africa don't even make it to 50. Look at Figure 19.2 on the next page, which shows countries in which fewer than 7 of every 1,000 babies die before they are a

Global stratification in health care is starkly evident in this photo of patients in the Marastoon mental hospital in West Kabul, Afghanistan.

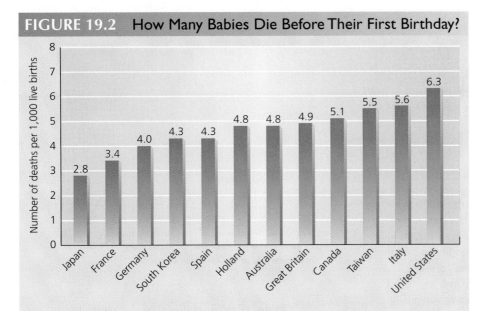

FIGURE 19.2   How Many Babies Die Before Their First Birthday?

Number of deaths per 1,000 live births

Japan	2.8
France	3.4
Germany	4.0
South Korea	4.3
Spain	4.3
Holland	4.8
Australia	4.8
Great Britain	4.9
Canada	5.1
Taiwan	5.5
Italy	5.6
United States	6.3

Note: Belgium, Czech Republic, and Greece are also likely to have lower infant mortality rates than that of the United States, but they were dropped from recent editions of the source.
Infant mortality is the number of babies that die before their first birthday, per 1,000 live births.

Source: By the author. Based on *Statistical Abstract of the United States* 2009:Table 1295.

year old. Then consider this: Afghanistan's infant mortality rate of 155 is *fifty-five* times higher than Japan's infant mortality rate (*Statistical Abstract* 2009:Table 1295).

Global stratification even helps to determine what diseases we get. Suppose that you had been born in a Least Industrialized Nation located in the tropics. During your much shorter life, you would face four major causes of illness and death: malaria (from mosquitoes), internal parasites (from contaminated water), diarrhea (from food and soil contaminated with human feces), and malnutrition. You would not face heart disease and cancer, for they are "luxury" diseases; that is, they are part of the industrialized world, where people live long enough to get them. As nations industrialize, health care and nutrition improve, and their citizens live longer. The diseases that used to be their primary killers decline, and residents begin to worry about cancer and heart attacks instead.

There is also the matter of social stratification *within* the Least Industrialized Nations. Many diseases that ravage the poor people in these countries could be brought under control if more money were spent on public health. Cheap drugs can prevent malaria, while safer water supplies and higher food production would go a long way toward eliminating the other major killers. The meager funds that these countries have at their disposal are not spent this way, however. Instead, having garnered the lion's share of the country's resources, the elite lavish it on themselves. For their own medical treatment, they even send a few students to top medical schools in the West. This gives them access to advanced technology—from X rays to life support systems. The poor of these nations, in contrast, go without even basic medical services and continue to die at an early age.

As the functionalists stress, human actions often have unanticipated consequences. So it is with the global stratification of health care. When the Most Industrialized Nations introduced hybrid seeds that increased the yields of grain, along with vaccinations and antibiotics to combat infectious diseases, the populations of the Least Industrialized Nations exploded. This stimulated mass migration to cities unprepared to receive vast numbers of poor people. In the next chapter, we will review these problems.

Before turning to medical care in the United States, let's consider the international black market in human organs. This stunning example of the inequality that arises from global stratification is the topic of the Down-to-Earth Sociology box on the next page.

Down-to-Earth Sociology

"Where Did You Get That New Liver?" The International Black Market in Human Body Parts

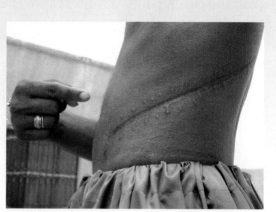

Organ exports from the poor to the wealthy: A Pakistani man who sold one of his kidneys.

The ability to transplant livers, lungs, kidneys, and even hearts and faces is one of the marvels of modern medicine. Advanced medical technology and the skills of surgeons have given life to people who just a short time ago were doomed to die.

But where do those organs come from?

You know about organ donors. You might even have checked a box on your driver's license that says it is okay for medical personnel to take your organs if you die in a car accident. Hospitals routinely ask dying patients—or their relatives—for permission to harvest body parts from the deceased.

But do you know about the international black market in human organs?

In Chapter 9, we discussed some of the horrible conditions faced by people living in the Least Industrialized Nations. It is important to keep these conditions in mind to understand why people in these countries "donate" their body parts.

> Jose da Silva has a lot of memories from childhood. One of the most vivid is the morning when seven children shared a single egg for breakfast.
>
> Today, da Silva will lift his shirt to show the scar where a kidney and rib were removed.
>
> Da Silva is one of twenty-three children of a woman in Brazil who sold her flesh to survive. As an adult, da Silva works for the Brazilian minimum wage, making $80 a month. When he heard that he could sell a kidney for $6,000, it was like a dream come true. It would take six years of hard work to make $6,000.

How da Silva's kidney became part of an international black market in human organs stretches back to Brooklyn, to a woman who had been on dialysis for fifteen years. This woman was on waiting lists for organ transplants—but so were another 60,000 Americans. "If you want to live," her doctor told her, "get a kidney any way you can."

Selling human organs is illegal in the United States, but the woman's husband heard about a group in Israel that traffics in human organs. His relatives in Tel Aviv made contact with this group, who had middlemen in Brazil. After da Silva agreed to sell one of his kidneys, he was flown to South Africa, where he was lodged in a safe house. The U.S. woman also flew to South Africa, where she was put up at a beach house.

Da Silva had to sign a statement that the woman was his cousin.

The transplant took place in a hospital. The South African doctors kept in contact with the woman's U.S. doctors, informing them of the woman's progress.

The woman paid $60,000 for da Silva's kidney. After da Silva was paid $6,000, the rest of the money went to the people who made the arrangements.

When word got out, there was a rush of Brazil's poor wanting to sell their kidneys—and to get a free trip to South Africa, where they expected to see lions, giraffes, and elephants. As the supply rose, the price for a kidney dropped to $3,000.

For Your Consideration

What is wrong with people selling their body parts, if they want to? Aren't poor people better off with one kidney and six years of extra earnings to buy a home, start a business, get out of debt, or take care of their families than with two kidneys and no such opportunities?

Source: Based on Rohter 2004.

Establishing a Monopoly on U.S. Health Care

Did you know that health care is the largest business in the United States? And did you know that it is the country's only legal monopoly? To understand how these remarkable facts developed, we first need to see how medicine became professionalized.

The Professionalization of Medicine.

Imagine that you are living in the American colonies in the 1700s and you want to become a physician. Will the entrance exams and required courses be difficult? Not really. You won't have any. You won't even need any formal education, for there is neither licensing nor medical school. You can simply ask a physician to train you. In return for the opportunity to learn, you'll be his assistant and help him with menial tasks. When you think that you have learned enough, you can hang out a sign and proclaim yourself a doctor. If you want to, you can even skip the apprenticeship. If you can convince people you are a good doctor, you'll make a living. If not, you'll have to turn to something else. The process was similar to how people can become automobile mechanics today.

In the 1800s, things began to change. A few medical schools opened, and there was some licensing of physicians. The medical schools of this period were like religions are today: They competed for clients and made different claims to the truth. One medical school would teach a particular idea about what caused illness and how to treat it, while another medical school would teach something else. Training was short, and often not even a high school diploma was required. There was no clinical training, and lectures went unchanged from year to year. The medical school at Harvard University took only two school years to complete—and the school year lasted only four months (Starr 1982; Rosenberg 1987; Riessman 1994).

Then came the 1900s. By 1906, the United States had 160 medical schools. The Carnegie Foundation asked Abraham Flexner, an educator, to evaluate them. Even the most inadequate schools opened their doors to Flexner, for they thought that gifts from the Carnegie Foundation would follow (Rodash 1982). In some schools, the laboratories consisted only of "a few vagrant test tubes squirreled away in a cigar box." Other schools had libraries with no books. Flexner advised that to raise standards, philanthropies should fund the most promising schools. They did, and the schools that were funded upgraded their facilities and were able to attract more capable faculty and students. In the face of higher standards and greater competition, most of the other schools had to close their doors.

The Flexner report (1910) led to the **professionalization of medicine.** When sociologists use the term *profession,* they mean something quite specific. What happened was that physicians began to (1) undergo a rigorous education; (2) claim a theoretical understanding of illness; (3) regulate themselves; (4) assert that they were performing a service for society (rather than just following self-interest); and (5) take authority over clients (Goode 1960; Freidson 2001).

The Monopoly of Medicine.

When medicine became a profession, it also became a monopoly, and this is the key to understanding our current situation. The group that gained control over U.S. medicine, the American Medical Association (AMA), managed to get laws passed that limited medical licenses to graduates of schools they controlled. By controlling the education and licensing of physicians, this group silenced most competing philosophies of medicine. The men in charge of this organization either refused to admit women to medical schools or severely limited their enrollment. In 1915, the AMA began to admit women members (Campbell and McCammon 2005).

The monopoly was so thorough that by law only this approved group—a sort of priesthood of medicine—was allowed to diagnose and treat medical problems. Only they knew what was right for people's health. Only they could scribble the secret language (Latin) on pieces of parchment (prescription forms) for translators (pharmacists) to decipher (Miner 1956/2007). This group of men became so powerful that it was even able to take childbirth away from midwives—the focus of the Down-to-Earth Sociology box on the next page.

professionalization of medicine the development of medicine into a specialty in which education becomes rigorous, and in which physicians claim a theoretical understanding of illness, regulate themselves, claim to be doing a service to society (rather than just following self-interest), and take authority over clients

Down-to-Earth Sociology

Giving Birth: From Women's Work to Men's Work

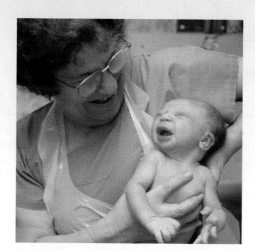

A midwife with the baby she just delivered

The history of midwifery helps us understand the professionalization of medicine and gives us insight into how the U.S. medical establishment came about. In the United States, as in Europe and elsewhere, pregnancy and childbirth were considered natural events. It was also considered natural that women would help women with them. Some midwives were trained to deliver babies; others were neighborhood women who had experience in childbirth. In many European countries, midwives were licensed by the state—as they still are.

Physicians wanted to expand their business, and taking over the management of childbirth was one way to do it. They encountered two major obstacles, however. The first you can expect: The midwives didn't want physicians to cut into their business. The second was ignorance. Almost all physicians were men, and they knew nothing about delivering babies. It was even considered indecent for a man to know much about pregnancy, and unheard of for a man to help a woman give birth.

Some physicians bribed midwives to sneak them into the bedrooms where women were giving birth. To say "sneaked" is no exaggeration, for they crawled on their hands and knees so that the mother-to-be wouldn't know that a man was present. Most physicians, however, weren't fortunate enough to find such cooperative midwives, and they trained with mannequins. Eventually, physicians were allowed to be present at births, but this was still considered indecent, because it meant that a man who was not a woman's husband might see the woman's private parts. To prevent this, the men had to fumble blindly under a sheet in a darkened room, their head decorously turned aside.

As physicians gained political power, they launched a ruthless campaign against their competitors. They attacked the midwives as "dirty, ignorant, and incompetent," even calling them a "menace to the health of the community." After physicians formed their union, the American Medical Association, they persuaded many states to pass laws that made it illegal for anyone but physicians to deliver babies. Some states, however, continue to allow nurse-midwives to practice. Even today, this struggle is not over; nurse-midwives and physicians sometimes still clash over who has the right to deliver babies.

Conflict theorists emphasize that this was not just a business matter but gender conflict—men sought to take control over what had been women's work. They stress that the men used their political connections to expand their business. Symbolic interactionists, without denying the political aspect, stress how the physicians manipulated symbols to win this struggle. They point to the information campaign that physicians launched to eliminate midwives, how they convinced the public that pregnancy and childbirth were not natural processes, but medical conditions that required the assistance of an able man. This new definition flew in the face of human history, for it had always been women who had helped women have babies. It created a new reality, transforming childbirth into "men's work." When this happened, the prestige of the work went up—and so did the price.

For Your Consideration

In Chapter 11, we learned an interesting principle of gender: Activities that are associated with women are given lower prestige than the activities that are associated with men. Managing childbirth is an example. As women come to dominate medicine, which seems likely, do you think the prestige of practicing medicine will decline? How about the income of physicians?

Sources: Wertz and Wertz 1981; Rodash 1982; Rothman 1994; Liptak 2006; Phillips 2007.

From its humble origins (no training or licensing required), medicine has grown into the largest business in the United States, one so powerful that it lobbies all state legislatures and the U.S. Congress. The AMA, which practices **fee-for-service**—payment to a physician in exchange for diagnosis and treatment—has become the only legal monopoly in the United States. The medical business consists not only of physicians but also of nurses, physician assistants, hospital personnel, pharmacists, insurance companies, corporations that own hospitals and nursing homes, and the huge research, manufacturing, and sales force that lies behind the drug industry.

fee-for-service payment to a physician to diagnose and treat a patient's medical problems

epidemiology the study of disease and disability patterns in a population

Historical Patterns of Health

Let's look at how the patterns of health and illness in the United States have changed. This will take us into the field of **epidemiology,** the study of how medical problems are distributed throughout a population.

Physical Health

Leading Causes of Death.   One way to see how the physical health of Americans has changed is to compare the leading causes of death in two time periods. To get an idea of how dramatic this change is, look at Figure 19.3. Note that four of the leading causes of death in 1900 don't even appear on today's list. Heart disease and cancer, which placed fourth and eighth in 1900, have now jumped to the top of the list, while tuberculosis and diarrhea, which were two of the top three killers in 1900, don't even show up in today's top ten. Similarly, diabetes and Alzheimer's disease didn't make the top ten in 1900, but they do now. These shifts indicate that extensive changes have occurred in society. Disease and death, then, are not only biological events. They are also *social* indicators, following the contours of social change.

Were Americans Healthier in the Past?   A second way to see how the physical health of Americans has changed is to ask if they are healthier—or sicker—than they used to be. This question brings us face to face with the definitional problem discussed earlier. "Healthy" by whose standards? An additional problem is that many of today's diseases, such as Alzheimer's, went unrecognized in the past. One way around these problems is to look at mortality rates. If Americans used to live longer, we can assume they were healthier. Because most people today live longer than their ancestors, however, we can conclude that contemporary Americans are healthier.

Some may think that this conclusion flies in the face of our polluted air and water—and of our high rates of heart disease and cancer shown in Figure 19.3. And it does. Sometimes older people say, "When I was a kid, hardly anyone died from cancer, and now it seems almost everyone does." What they say is true, but what they overlook is that most cancers strike older people, so when life expectancy is shorter, fewer people die from cancer. Also, in the past, most cancer went unrecognized. People were simply said to have died of "old age" or "heart failure."

Mental Health

When it comes to mental health, we have no way to make good comparisons with earlier times. Some people picture an idyllic past: There was little mental illness because almost everyone grew up with two loving parents, married for life, and lived in harmony in close-knit families with everyone helping one another. But do we have any facts? We need solid measures of mental illness or mental health, not stories of how things used to be that make the past look better than it was (Coontz 2000). Idyllic pasts like this never existed—except in people's imaginations. All groups have their share of mental problems—and beliefs that mental illness is worse today represent a perception, not measured reality. Perhaps there was less mental illness in the past, but

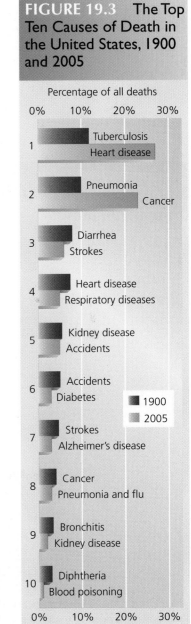

FIGURE 19.3   The Top Ten Causes of Death in the United States, 1900 and 2005

Percentage of all deaths

1. Tuberculosis / Heart disease
2. Pneumonia / Cancer
3. Diarrhea / Strokes
4. Heart disease / Respiratory diseases
5. Kidney disease / Accidents
6. Accidents / Diabetes
7. Strokes / Alzheimer's disease
8. Cancer / Pneumonia and flu
9. Bronchitis / Kidney disease
10. Diphtheria / Blood poisoning

■ 1900
■ 2005

Sources: By the author. Based on National Center for Health Statistics; *Statistical Abstract of the United States* 2009:Table 115.

the *opposite* could also be true. Since we don't even know how much mental illness there is today (Scheff 1999), how can we judge how much there was in the past?

Issues in Health Care

Let's turn to issues in health care in the United States.

Medical Care: A Right or a Commodity?

> Nataline Sarkisyan, a 17-year-old cancer patient, waited for a liver transplant that never came. Livers were available, but her health insurer refused to pay for the operation. Nataline's hospital, UCLA Medical Center, said it would do the transplant, but only if the family paid $75,000 upfront.
>
> The family managed to get that money together, but then the hospital demanded $300,000 to care for Nataline after surgery. That was impossible for the family to raise, and Nataline died. (Martinez 2008)

A primary controversy in the United States is whether medical care is a right or a commodity—something offered for sale. If medical care is a right, then all citizens should have access to similar medical care. If medical care is a commodity, then, as with automobiles and clothing, the rich will have access to one type of care, and the poor to another.

But why should there even be a question of which it is? The event quoted above makes it starkly clear that medical care in the United States is *not* the right of citizens. Medical care is a commodity for sale. Those who have more money can afford quality health care; those who have little money have to settle for less, or even for none. The many attempts to replace this commodity system with some form of national medical care have been futile.

The skyrocketing cost of medical care doesn't make things easier. Look at Figure 19.4. In 1960, health care cost the average American $150 a year. Today, the total has jumped to $6,500. Consider this: In 1960, a 17-inch black-and-white television cost $150, the same as the average amount people spent on medical care. If the cost of televisions had risen the same as the cost of health care, a *17-inch black-and-white* television would now cost $6,500. The jump in medical costs includes more advanced and expensive medical technology and medicines (as well as many more elderly people and costly malpractice insurance), so to try to keep this comparison accurate, assume that the television is also more advanced, say 32 inches, color, and digital. But it still costs $6,500. On top of this, the average American would have to buy a new television every year!

It is difficult to grasp how reasonable medical costs used to be. Look at the hospital

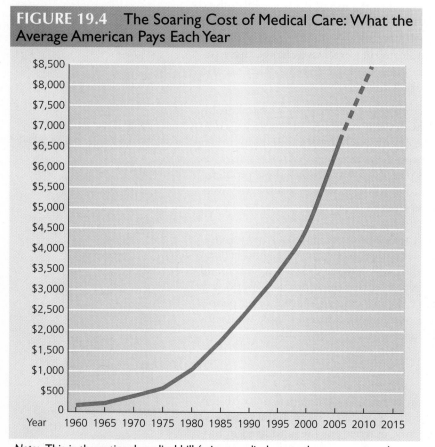

FIGURE 19.4   The Soaring Cost of Medical Care: What the Average American Pays Each Year

Note: This is the national medical bill (minus medical research, structures, and equipment) divided by the total population. The average American pays half this amount out of pocket and by insurance.

Source: By the author. Based on *Statistical Abstract of the United States* 2009: Table 127, and earlier years.

```
                    — STATEMENT —
        Grande Ronde Hospital Association
                  LA GRANDE, OREGON
                      7-21-62
                       DATE


            Mr.
            1902 Washington
            La Grande, Ore.


            RE:  Martha E

  DATE
  ADMITTED   7-18-62          TO    7-21-62        ROOM   220

  Balance Due
  General Care   3  days @ $  18.00              54.00
  Operating Room   circumcision                  10.00
  Anesthetic                                      2.50
  Medicines                                       3.10
  Surgical Dressings                              2.25
  Delivery Room                                  20.00
  Laboratory                                      3.00
  X-Ray
  Oxygen
  Treatments
  Special Drugs
  Nursery                                        18.00
  Bracelet                                        1.00

                           total               113.85
  Accounts not paid when due are subject to interest charge.
```

bill reproduced above. This is the entire amount billed by the private hospital for the delivery of a child. The $113.85 included 3 days stay for the mother and child, the delivery room, the anesthetic, even the circumcision.

Social Inequality

Recall the opening vignette—about the naked man in the homeless shelter who was being taken to the state mental hospital. This event lays bare our **two-tier system of medical care.** A middle-class or rich person who had mental problems would visit a private psychiatrist, not be sent to a state mental hospital—or to jail, where poor people with mental illnesses often end up. Of course, he or she would not have been in that shelter in the first place. Because health care is a commodity—and, today, a costly one—those who can afford it buy superior health care, while, for the most part, the poor get leftovers. In short, medical care is like automobiles—new sports cars for the wealthy and worn-out used cars for the poor.

Since 1939, sociologists have found what they call "an inverse correlation between mental problems and social class"; that is, the lower the social class, the more mental problems there are. This finding has been confirmed in numerous studies (Faris and Dunham 1939; Srole et al. 1978; National Center for Health Statistics 2004; Schoenborn 2004). It is not difficult to understand why people in the lower social classes have greater mental problems, for they bear the many stresses that poverty thrusts on them. Compared with middle- and upper-class Americans, the poor have less job security and lower wages, and are hounded by bill collectors. They are also more likely to divorce, to be victims of violent crime, and to abuse alcohol. Such conditions deal severe blows to emotional well-being.

two-tier system of medical care a system of medical care in which the wealthy receive superior medical care and the poor inferior medical care

These same stresses are also bad for physical health. Unlike the middle and upper classes, few poor people have a personal physician, and some of them spend hours waiting in emergency rooms and public health clinics. After waiting most of a day, some don't even get to see a doctor; they are simply told to come back the next day (Fialka 1993; Goldstein 2008). When hospitalized, the poor are likely to find themselves in understaffed and underfunded public hospitals, where they are treated by rotating interns who do not know them and do not follow up on their progress.

Figure 19.5 portrays the relationship between income and illness. "Illness" refers to both physical and mental health problems. This is a significant figure, for it illustrates how higher income protects people from illness.

Malpractice Lawsuits and Defensive Medicine

> **"I'm looking for something else to do, because medicine is no longer fun. Every time I treat a patient, I wonder if this is the one who is going to turn around and sue me."**
>
> —Said by an anxious physician to your author.

Some analysts have concluded—seriously—that physicians used to kill more patients than they cured. This might be true. Physicians did leave a trail of death. They didn't know about germs, they didn't wash their hands before surgery or childbirth, and their beliefs about the cause of sickness were not exactly helpful. In the 1800s, doctors thought that "bad fluids" caused sickness. To get rid of these bad fluids, they used four techniques: (1) bleeding (cutting a vein or using leeches to drain out "bad" blood); (2) blistering (applying packs so hot they burned the skin, causing "bad pus" to drain); (3) vomiting (giving patients liquids that made them vomit up the bad fluids); and (4) purging (giving patients substances that caused diarrhea).

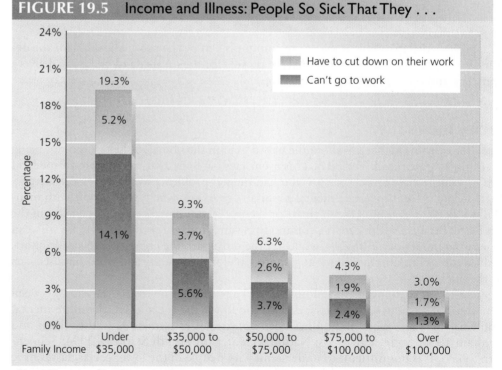

FIGURE 19.5   Income and Illness: People So Sick That They . . .

Legend:
- Have to cut down on their work
- Can't go to work

Family Income	Under $35,000	$35,000 to $50,000	$50,000 to $75,000	$75,000 to $100,000	Over $100,000
Total	19.3%	9.3%	6.3%	4.3%	3.0%
Have to cut down on their work	5.2%	3.7%	2.6%	1.9%	1.7%
Can't go to work	14.1%	5.6%	3.7%	2.4%	1.3%

Note: These totals refer to families, not to individuals. The first bar means that 14.1 percent of families whose annual incomes are below $35,000 have a family member age 18 or over who is so sick that he or she cannot go to work—not that 14.1 percent of all people whose incomes are below $35,000 are so sick that they cannot go to work. The percentages of illness refer to any given day.

Source: By the author. Based on Adams et al. 2008: Table 6.

Not surprisingly, these treatments killed some patients. Back then there were no medical malpractice suits; but today, with our vastly superior medical care, malpractice suits are common. Why? Previously, the law didn't allow patients to recover damages. The thinking was, "People make mistakes," and that includes doctors. Today, physicians are held to much higher standards—and they are not excused for making mistakes. As indicated by the quote that opened this section, malpractice suits are like a sword dangling over the heads of physicians. Suspended only by a rotting thread, the sword will fall, but they don't know when. To protect themselves, physicians practice **defensive medicine.** They consult with colleagues and order lab tests not because the patient needs them but because the doctors want to leave a paper trail in case they are sued. These consultations and tests—done for the doctor's benefit, not the patient's—run medical bills up even higher.

defensive medicine medical practices done not for the patient's benefit but in order to protect a physician from malpractice suits

Medical Incompetence

A woman went into the hospital with a problem with her lungs. Her surgeon did a hysterectomy.

A man had surgery to remove a cancerous kidney. The surgeon removed the healthy one instead.

A man was supposed to have a circumcision, but the surgeon mistakenly removed both testicles.

No, I'm not making these up. These are actual cases (Steinhauer and Fessenden 2001; Seiden and Barach 2006). There is also the woman who had the wrong foot amputated, the man who . . . In fact, some physicians operate on the wrong patient altogether. There are about 4,000 wrong-patient, wrong-side, or wrong-procedure surgeries a year in the United States (Senders and Kenzki 2008). To prevent surgeons from removing the wrong body part, some hospitals require the doctor to mark in indelible ink on the patient's body where the incision is to be made, and to have both patient and doctor sign their names at that spot.

Mistakes in U.S. hospitals kill 44,000 to 98,000 patients each year. Most medical care takes place in clinics and doctors' offices, not hospitals—so the total is likely to be at least *double* this already huge number (Reisman 2003). *If death from medical errors were an official classification, it would rank as the sixth leading cause of death in the United States (Statistical Abstract 2009:Table 115).* Doctors have developed an interesting term to refer to these needless deaths—and no it isn't "death by incompetence" or "killed by doctors." Instead, they have chosen this innocuous term: "adverse events." (These deaths and injuries are certainly "adverse" from the perspective of the patient and family.) One of these adverse events is shown in the photo to the right.

The situation is so bad that the Institute of Medicine has proposed that we establish a Federal Center for Patient Safety. All medical deaths and injuries would be reported to the Center. Just as the Federal Aviation Agency investigates each plane crash, the Center would investigate each medical injury and death. Based on the cause it pinpointed, the Center would set up guidelines to reduce similar events. If this proposal were implemented, prospective patients could even check out the hospital they are thinking of using, to see how many people their doctors have injured or killed through incompetence or negligence.

We all forget things, including doctors. Just as our forgetfulness causes problems in our everyday lives, so it causes problems in medicine. In an interesting experiment to help doctors remember, surgeons in eight countries were required to use a simple checklist ("Did you check the patient's identification bracelet? Did you check for allergies. Did you ..."). The results were dramatic. *Patient deaths dropped by 40 percent* (Goldstein 2009). Physicians are gradually discovering what airline pilots learned long ago: With lives at stake, don't rely on your memory to make sure you've done everything before taking off.

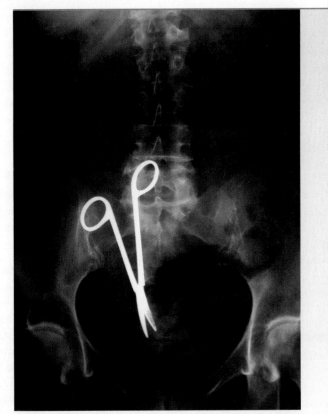

In our era of scientific medicine, the errors made by doctors and nurses are astounding. Surgeons in Sydney, Australia, left this pair of scissors inside a patient.

Depersonalization: The Medical Cash Machine

Mary Duffy, who runs a food service business in San Jose, California, was recovering from surgery. As she was lying in her hospital bed, a group of white-coated strangers came in. Without a word, a man leaned over, pulled back her blanket, and stripped her nightgown from her shoulders. He then began to lecture about carcinomas to the group standing around the bed. As the half dozen medical students stared at Mrs. Duffy's naked body, the doctor spoke his first words to Mrs. Duffy, asking, "Have you passed gas yet?" (Carey 2005)

One of the main complaints that patients have about doctors and nurses is **depersonalization.** As was the case with Mrs. Duffy, patients feel as though they are being treated like cases and diseases, not as individuals. Some also get the impression that they are viewed as cash machines, as walking ATMs. While talking to patients, some physicians seem to be counting minutes and tabulating dollars so that they can move on to the next ATM and extract more money. After all, any extra time spent with a patient is money down the drain.

Although some students start medical school with lofty motives, desiring to "treat the whole person," it doesn't take long for them to learn to depersonalize patients. Sociologists Jack Haas and William Shaffir (1993), who did participant observation at McMaster University in Canada, discovered how this happens. As vast amounts of information are thrown at medical students, their feelings for patients are overpowered by the need to be efficient. Consider what this student told the researchers:

> Somebody will say, "Listen to Mrs. Jones's heart. It's just a little thing flubbing on the table." *And you forget about the rest of her . . .* and it helps in learning in the sense that you can go in to a patient, put your stethoscope on the heart, listen to it, and walk out . . . . The advantage is that *you can go in a short time and see a patient, get the important things out of the patient, and leave.*

Unconscious patients, the dying, and the dead are transformed into special objects for practicing their skills (Berger et al. 2002). Listen to what this student said to Haas and Shaffir.

> You don't know the people that are under anesthesia—just practice putting the tube in, and the person wakes up with a sore throat, and well, it's just sort of a part of the procedure. . . . Someone comes in who has croaked [and you say], "Well, come on. Here is a chance to practice your intubation" [inserting a tube in the throat].

Conflict of Interest

Sandy was surprised when her doctor brought another person with him to her examination. She would have been even more surprised to learn that this other person was a pharmaceutical sales representative who had paid the doctor to be present at the examination. (Petersen 2002)

The representative had paid Sandy's doctor so he could attend the examination and recommend his company's drugs to treat her. Although this representative carried things a little farther than most, drug companies often pay doctors to prescribe their brands of drugs. One doctor received $300,000 for recommending to other doctors that they prescribe a particular drug to their patients (Petersen 2003). Other physicians publish research in medical journals on products in which they are investors (Abelson 2008). Some surgeons invest in medical supply companies that sell the products they use in surgery. Patients are charged $1,000 for each screw used in spinal-fusion surgery, for example, with a profit of $900 on each screw (Abelson 2006).

You can see the conflict of interest. Did the physician use an extra screw in surgery because the patient needed it or to get a share of the additional $900 profit? Is the doctors' research on a medical product in which they have invested money unbiased, or is it slanted

depersonalization dealing with people as though they were objects; in the case of medical care, as though patients were merely cases and diseases, not people

to increase the sales of the product? Some drug companies even ghostwrite articles for medical journals that present research about how good their drugs are—and then look for doctors to list as authors (Ross et al. 2008). With conflict of interest so powerful, new laws are being passed to curb these practices (Meier 2009).

At Harvard University, the conflict of interest with drug companies has taken an interesting turn. Medical students have protested that when their professors are receiving money from a pharmaceutical company, what they teach is no longer objective. In response to their protest, teachers in the medical school must now inform their students of all ties they have with drug companies (Wilson 2009).

Medical Fraud

One doctor billed Medicare for treatment of a patient's eye—the only problem was that the patient was missing that eye (Levy 2003). A dentist charged Medicare for 991 procedures in a single day. In a typical workday, that would come to one every 36 seconds (Levy and Luo 2005). A psychiatrist in California had sex with his patient—and charged Medicaid for the time. (Geis et al. 1995)

Today's medical fraud is more sophisticated than this Specto-Chrome of years past, a machine that could cure anything with colored lights, but the goal is always the same, money.

These are not isolated incidents—they are just some of the most outrageous. With 3 million Medicare claims filed every day, physicians are not likely to be audited (Johnson 2008). Many doctors have not been able to resist the temptation to cheat.

Do you recall the section on white collar crime in Chapter 8, where I pointed out that some white-collar crime goes far beyond money, that it harms and kills people? So it is with this white-collar crime. A pharmacist in Kansas City was so driven by greed that he diluted the drugs he sold for patients in chemotherapy (Belluck 2001). And what do you think Guidant Corporation did when it discovered that its heart defibrillators, which are surgically implanted in patients, could short-circuit and kill patients? Tell the patients and doctors? You would think so. Instead, the company kept selling the defective model while it developed a new one. Several patients died when their defibrillators short-circuited (Meier 2005, 2006).

Then there is Bayer, that household name you trust when you reach for aspirin. Bayer also makes Trasylol, a drug given after heart surgery. Bayer found that its drug had a few slight side effects—it could increase the risk of strokes, damage kidneys, and cause heart failure and death. Did Bayer warn doctors that they might be killing their patients? Not at all. In Bayer's own words, it "mistakenly did not inform" the Federal Drug Administration of the study (Harris 2006). In the same vein that Bayer made its statement, I will assume that the $200 million annual sales of this drug had nothing to do with Bayer making this mistake.

Greed can be so enticing that it ensnares even outstanding individuals, distorting their ethics and sense of reality. A top medical researcher at Harvard who was also the head of pediatric research at Massachusetts General Hospital told the drug company, Johnson & Johnson, that if they funded his research, his findings would benefit the company (Harris 2009). No honest researcher knows in advance what research findings will be.

Sexism and Racism in Medicine

In Chapter 11 (pages 310–311), we saw that physicians don't take women's health complaints as seriously as they do those of men. As a result, surgeons operate on women after the women's heart disease has progressed farther, which makes it more likely that the women will die from the disease. This sexism is so subtle that the physicians are not even

medicalization the transformation of a human condition into a matter to be treated by physicians

euthanasia mercy killing

aware that they are discriminating against women. Some sexism in medicine, in contrast, is blatant. One of the best examples is the bias against women's reproductive organs that we reviewed in Chapter 11 (page 312).

Racism is also an unfortunate part of medical practice. In Chapter 12, we reviewed racism in surgery and in health care after heart attacks. You might want to review these materials on page 339.

The Medicalization of Society

As we have seen, childbirth and women's reproductive organs have come to be defined as medical matters. Sociologists use the term **medicalization** to refer to the process of turning something that was not previously considered a medical issue into a medical matter. "Bad" behavior is an example. If a psychiatric model is followed, crime becomes not willful behavior that should be punished, but a symptom of unresolved mental problems that were created during childhood. These problems need to be treated by doctors. The human body is a favorite target of medicalization. Characteristics that once were taken for granted—such as wrinkles, acne, balding, sagging buttocks and chins, bulging stomachs, and small breasts—have become medical problems, all in need of treatment by physicians.

As usual, the three theoretical perspectives give us contrasting views of the medicalization of such human conditions. Symbolic interactionists would stress that there is nothing inherently medical about wrinkles, acne, balding, sagging chins, and so on. It is a matter of definition: People used to consider such matters as normal problems of life; now they are starting to redefine them as medical problems. Functionalists would stress that the medicalization of such conditions is functional for the medical establishment. It strengthens the medical establishment by broadening its customer base. Conflict sociologists would argue that such medicalization indicates the growing power of the medical establishment: The more conditions of life that physicians can medicalize, the greater their profits and power.

Medically Assisted Suicide

To consider medically assisted suicide takes us face to face with controversial issues that are both disturbing and difficult to resolve. Should doctors be able to write lethal prescriptions for terminally ill patients? Some take the position that this will relieve suffering and help people to die with dignity. Others say that such laws would simply legalize murder. Let's explore these issues in the following Thinking Critically section.

Thinking CRITICALLY
Should Doctors Be Allowed to Kill Patients?

Except for the name, this is a true story:

> Bill Simpson, in his 70s, had battled leukemia for years. After his spleen was removed, he developed an abdominal abscess. It took another operation to drain it. A week later, the abscess filled and required more surgery. Again the abscess returned. Simpson began to go in and out of consciousness. His brother-in-law suggested euthanasia. The surgeon injected a lethal dose of morphine into Simpson's intravenous feeding tubes.

At a medical conference in which **euthanasia,** mercy killing, was discussed, a cancer specialist who had treated thousands of patients announced that he had kept count of the patients who had asked him to help them die. "There were 127 men and women," he said. He paused, and then added, "And I saw to it that 25 of them got their wish." Thousands of other physicians have done the same (Nuland 1995).

When a doctor ends a patient's life, such as by injecting a lethal drug, it is called *active euthanasia.* To withhold life support (nutrients or liquids) is called *passive euthanasia.* To remove life support, such as disconnecting a patient from oxygen falls somewhere in between. The result, of course, is the same.

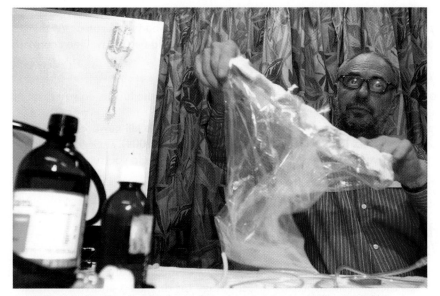

Dr. Phillip Nitschke ("Dr. Death") showing his euthanasia items at a "Killing Me Softly" conference in Sidney, Australia. The bag he is holding is connected by a hose to a generator and placed over someone's head. The individual dies by carbon dioxide poisoning.

Two images seem to dominate the public's ideas of euthanasia: One is of an individual devastated by chronic pain. The doctor mercifully helps to end that pain by performing euthanasia. The second is of a brain-dead individual—a human vegetable—who lies in a hospital bed, kept alive only by machines. How accurate are these images?

We have the example of Holland. There, along with Belgium, euthanasia is legal. Incredibly, in about 1,000 cases a year, physicians kill their patients without the patients' express consent. In one instance a doctor ended the life of a nun because he thought she would have wanted him to do so but was afraid to ask because it was against her religion. In another case, a physician killed a patient with breast cancer who said that she did *not* want euthanasia. In the doctor's words, "It could have taken another week before she died. I needed this bed" (Hendin 1997, 2000).

Some Dutch, concerned that they could be euthanized if they have a medical emergency, carry "passports" that instruct medical personnel that they wish to live. Most Dutch, however, support euthanasia. Many carry another "passport," one that instructs medical personnel to carry out euthanasia (Shapiro 1997).

In Michigan, Dr. Jack Kevorkian, a pathologist (he didn't treat patients—he studied diseased tissues) decided that regardless of laws, he had the right to help people commit suicide. He did, 120 times. Here is how he described one of those times:

> I started the intravenous dripper, which released a salt solution through a needle into her vein, and I kept her arm tied down so she wouldn't jerk it. This was difficult as her veins were fragile. And then once she decided she was ready to go, she just hit the switch and the device cut off the saline drip and through the needle released a solution of thiopental that put her to sleep in ten to fifteen seconds. A minute later, through the needle flowed a lethal solution of potassium chloride. (Denzin 1992)

Kevorkian taunted authorities. He sometimes left bodies in vans and dropped them off at hospitals. Although he provided the poison, as well as a "death machine" that he developed to administer the poison, and he watched patients pull the lever that released the drugs, Kevorkian never touched that lever. Frustrated Michigan prosecutors tried Kevorkian for murder four times, but four times juries refused to convict him. Then Kevorkian made a fatal mistake. On national television, he played a videotape showing him giving a lethal injection to a man who was dying from Lou Gehrig's disease. Prosecutors put Kevorkian on trial again. This time, he was convicted of second-degree murder and was sentenced to 10 to 25 years in prison. Kevorkian was released after 8 years. To get out, he had to promise not to kill anyone else (Wanzer 2007).

Only in Oregon (since 1997) and Washington (since 2008) is it legal for doctors to assist in suicide, and only under strict rules. If Kevorkian had lived in Oregon or Washington, and he hadn't begun killing patients until those years, he would never have been convicted.

For Your Consideration

Do you think Oregon and Washington are right? Why? In the future, do you think other states will approve medically assisted suicide?

In addition to what is reported here, Dutch doctors also kill newborn babies who have serious birth defects (Smith 1999; "Piden en Holanda . . ." 2004). Their justification is that if these children live they would not have "quality of life." Would you support this?

Curbing Costs: From Health Insurance to Rationing Medical Care

We have seen some of the reasons why the cost of medical care in the United States has soared: advanced—and expensive—technology for diagnosis and treatment, a growing elderly population, tests performed as defensive measures rather than for medical reasons, malpractice insurance, and health care as a commodity to be sold to the highest bidder. As long as these conditions exist, the price of medical care will continue to outpace inflation. Let's look at some attempts to reduce costs.

Health Maintenance Organizations. Some medical companies—health maintenance organizations (HMOs)—charge an annual fee in exchange for providing medical care to a company's employees. Prices are lower because HMOs bid against one another. Whatever money is left over at the end of the year is the HMO's profit. While this arrangement eliminates unnecessary medical treatment, it can also reduce *necessary* treatment. The results are anything but pretty.

> Over her doctor's strenuous objections, a friend of mine was discharged from the hospital even though she was still bleeding and running a fever. Her HMO representative said he would not authorize another day in the hospital. After suffering a heart attack, a man in Kansas City, Missouri, needed surgery that could be performed only at Barnes Hospital in St. Louis, Missouri. The HMO said, "Too bad. That hospital is out of our service area." The man died while appealing the HMO decision (Spragins 1996). Some doctors also have HMOs. One doctor, who works for a hospital, noticed a lump in her breast. She went to the x-ray department to get a mammogram, but her own hospital said she couldn't have one. Her HMO allowed one mammogram every two years, and she had had one 18 months before. After a formal appeal, she was granted an exception. She had breast cancer. ("What Scares Doctors?" 2006)

The basic question, of course, is: At what human cost do we reduce spending on medical treatment?

Diagnosis-Related Groups. To curb spiraling costs, the federal government has classified all illnesses into diagnosis-related-groups (DRGs) and has set an amount that it will pay for the

The cartoonist has captured an unfortunate reality of U.S. medicine.

treatment of each illness. Hospitals make a profit if they move patients through the system quickly—if they discharge patients before the allotted amount is spent. As a consequence, some patients are discharged before they have recovered. Others are refused admittance because they appear to have a "worse than average" case of a particular illness: If they take longer to treat, they will cost the hospital money instead of bringing them a profit.

dumping the practice of sending unprofitable patients to public hospitals

National Health Insurance

The van from Hollywood Presbyterian Hospital pulled up to the curbside in the center of skid row in Los Angeles, California. The driver got out and walked to the passenger side. As several people watched, she opened the door and helped a paraplegic man out. As she drove away, leaving the befuddled man, people shouted at her, "Where's his wheelchair? Where's his walker?"

Someone called 911. The police found the man crawling in the gutter, wearing a flimsy, soiled hospital gown and trailing a broken colostomy bag.

"I can't think of anything colder than that," said an L.A. detective. "It's the worst area of skid row." (Blankstein and Winton 2007)

This is a blatant example of **dumping,** hospitals discharging unprofitable patients. Seldom is dumping as dramatic as in this instance, but dumping is not unusual. Dumping is one consequence of a system that puts profit ahead of patient care. With 47 million Americans uninsured (*Statistical Abstract* 2009:Table 147), pressure has grown for the government to provide national health insurance. What patterns do you see in the Social Map below, which shows how the uninsured are distributed among the states?

Advocates of national health insurance point out that centralized, large-scale purchases of medical and hospital supplies will reduce costs. They also stress that national health insurance will solve the problem of the poor receiving inferior medical care. Opponents stress that national health insurance will bring expensive red tape. They also ask why anyone would think that federal agencies—such as those that run the post office—should be entrusted with administering something as vital as the nation's health care. Proponents reply that right now no one is in charge of it. This debate is not new, and even if some form of national health insurance is adopted, the arguments will continue.

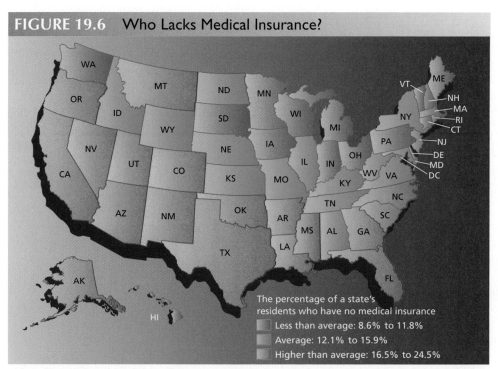

FIGURE 19.6   Who Lacks Medical Insurance?

The percentage of a state's residents who have no medical insurance
- Less than average: 8.6% to 11.8%
- Average: 12.1% to 15.9%
- Higher than average: 16.5% to 24.5%

Note: The range is broad, from 8.6 percent who lack medical insurance in Rhode Island to 24.5 percent in Texas.

Source: By the author. Based on *Statistical Abstract of the United States* 2009:Table 147.

Maverick Solutions

> Single ear infections $40
> Simple cuts with suture removal $95
> Ingrown toenail corrections $150

The Tennessee doctor who put this billboard up outside his clinic had grown tired of having to hire people to fill out and submit insurance claims, and then waiting to get paid, or having the forms rejected and having to resubmit them (Brown 2007). To avoid these frustrations and the cost of dealing with insurance companies, this doctor, like a few others, opened a *pay-as-you-go* clinic. No insurance allowed. Payments only by cash or credit card. With no billing costs, the doctors can charge less.

Other doctors are lowering costs by replacing individual consultations with *group care.* They meet with a group of patients who have similar medical conditions. Eight or ten pregnant women, for example, go in for their obstetrics checkup together. This allows the doctor more time to discuss medical symptoms and treatments, and, at the same time, to charge each patient less. The patients also benefit from the support and encouragement of people who are in their same situation (Bower 2003).

Rationing Medical Care.   The most controversial suggestion for how to reduce medical costs is to ration medical care. The argument is simple: We cannot afford to provide all the available technology to everyone, so we have to ration it. No easy answer has been found for this dilemma, the focus of the Sociology and the New Technology box on the next page.

Threats to Health

Let's look at major threats to health, both in the United States and worldwide.

HIV/AIDS

In 1981, the first case of AIDS (acquired immune deficiency syndrome) was documented. Since then, about 600,000 Americans have died from AIDS. As you can see from Figure 19.7,

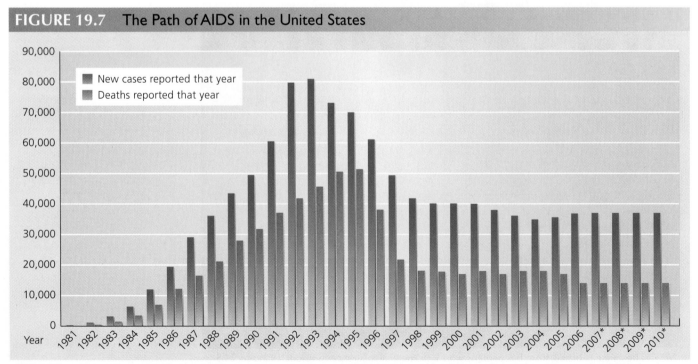

FIGURE 19.7   The Path of AIDS in the United States

Legend:
- New cases reported that year
- Deaths reported that year

Note: Alternative estimates indicate a higher incidence of new cases of HIV (Centers for Disease Control and Prevention 2008c).
*Indicates the author's projections.

Sources: By the author. Based on Centers for Disease Control and Prevention 2003:Table 21; 2008a:Tables 1, 7.

SOCIOLOGY and the NEW TECHNOLOGY

Who Should Live, and Who Should Die? The Dilemma of Rationing Medical Care

A 75-year old woman enters the emergency room, screaming and in tears from severe pain. She is suffering from metastatic cancer (cancer that has spread through her body). She has only weeks to live, and she needs immediate admittance to the intensive care unit.

At this same time, a 20-year old woman, severely injured in a car wreck, is wheeled into the emergency room. To survive, she must be admitted to the intensive care unit.

As you probably guessed, there is only one unoccupied bed left in intensive care. What do the doctors do?

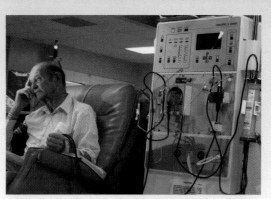

The high cost of some medical treatments, such as dialysis, shown here, has led to the issue of rationing medical care.

This story, not as far-fetched as you might think, distills a pressing situation that faces U.S. medical health care. Even though a particular treatment is essential to care for a medical problem, there isn't enough of it to go around to everyone who needs it. Other treatments are so costly that they could bankrupt society if they were made available to everyone who had a particular medical problem. Who, then, should receive the benefits of our new medical technology?

In the situation above, medical care would be rationed. The young woman would be admitted to intensive care, and the elderly person would be directed into some ward in the hospital. But what if the elderly woman had already been admitted to intensive care? Would physicians pull her out? That is not as easily done, but probably.

Consider the much less dramatic, more routine case of dialysis, the use of machines to cleanse the blood of people who are suffering from kidney disease. Dialysis is currently available to anyone who needs it, and the cost runs several billion dollars a year. Many wonder how the nation can afford to continue to pay this medical bill. Physicians in Great Britain act much like doctors would in our opening example. They ration dialysis informally, making bedside assessments of patients' chances of survival and excluding most older patients from this treatment (Aaron et al. 2005).

Modern medical technology is marvelous. People walk around with the hearts, kidneys, livers, lungs, and faces of deceased people. Eventually, perhaps, surgeons will be able to transplant brains. The costs are similarly astounding. Look again at Figure 19.4 on page 566. Our national medical bill runs more than $2 trillion a year (*Statistical*

Abstract 2009: Table 124). Frankly, I can't understand what a trillion of anything is. I've tried, but the number is just too high for me to grasp. Now there are two of these trillions to pay each year. Where can we get such fantastic amounts? How long can we continue to pay them? These questions haunt our medical system, making the question of medical rationing urgent.

The nation's medical bill will not flatten out. Rather, it is destined to increase. Medical technology, including new drugs, continues to advance—and to be costly. And we all want the latest, most advanced treatment. Then there is the matter we covered in Chapter 13, that people are living longer and the number of elderly is growing rapidly. It is the elderly who need the most medical care, especially during their last months of life.

The dilemma is harsh: If we ration medical treatment, many sick people will die. If we don't, we will indebt future generations even further.

For Your Consideration

At the heart of this issue lie questions not only of cost but also of fairness. If all of us can't have the latest, best, and most expensive medical care, then how can we distribute medical care fairly? Use ideas, concepts, and principles from this and other chapters to develop a proposal for solving this issue. How does this dilemma change if you view it from the contrasting perspectives of conflict theory, functionalism, and symbolic interactionism?

If we ration medical care, what factors would be fair to consider? If age is a factor, for example, should the younger or the older get preferred treatment? Why? If you are about 20 years old, your answer is likely to be a quick, "the younger." But is the matter really that simple? What about a 40-year old who has a 5-year old child, for example? Or a 55-year old nuclear physicist? Or the U.S. president? (OK, why bring that up? He or she will never get the same medical treatment as we get. But, wait, isn't that the point?)

With AIDS devastating Malawi and other areas of Africa, "coffin shops" have become a common sight. This one is in Blantyre, Malawi.

in the United States this disease has been brought under control. New cases peaked in 1993, and deaths peaked in 1995. This disease is far from conquered, however. Each year about 35,000 Americans are infected with the HIV virus, and about 14,000 die from it. For the 500,000 Americans who receive treatment, HIV/AIDS has become a chronic disease that they live with (Centers for Disease Control 2008a:Table 8).

Globally, in contrast, the epidemic is exploding, with 2.7 million new HIV infections a year (UNAIDS 2008). *Every minute* of every hour of every day, about 5 people become infected with HIV. Over 40 million people have died from AIDS, but the worst is yet to come. The most devastated area is sub-Saharan Africa. Although this region has just 10 percent of the world's population, it accounts for 67 percent of all people living with HIV and 72 percent of the world's deaths from AIDS. The death toll in this region is so high that the average person dies at age 50. The lowest life expectancy in the world is in Swaziland. There, the average person is dead by age 33 (Haub and Kent 2008). As Figure 19.8 illustrates, Africa is the hardest-hit region of the world.

Let's look at some of the major characteristics of this disease.

Origin. The question of how HIV/AIDS originated baffled scientists for two decades, but they finally traced its genetic sequences back to the Congo (Kolata 2001). Apparently, the virus was present in chimpanzees and was somehow transmitted to humans. How this crossover occurred is not known, but the best guess is that hunters were exposed to the animals' blood as they slaughtered them for meat.

The Transmission of HIV/AIDS. The only way a person can become infected with the HIV virus is if bodily fluids pass from one person to another. HIV is most commonly transmitted through blood, semen, and vaginal secretions, but nursing babies can also get HIV through the milk of their infected mothers. Since the HIV virus is present in all bodily fluids (including sweat, tears, spittle, and urine), some people think that HIV can also be transmitted in these forms. The U.S. Centers for Disease Control, however, stresses that HIV cannot be transmitted by casual contact in which traces of these fluids would be exchanged. Figure 19.9 on the next page compares how U.S. men and women get infected.

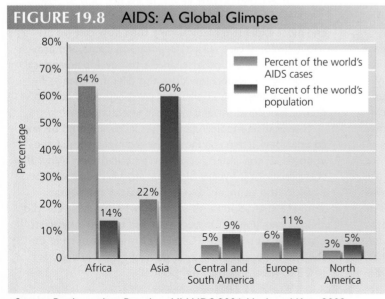

FIGURE 19.8   AIDS: A Global Glimpse

Legend:
- Percent of the world's AIDS cases
- Percent of the world's population

Region	Percent of the world's AIDS cases	Percent of the world's population
Africa	64%	14%
Asia	22%	60%
Central and South America	5%	9%
Europe	6%	11%
North America	3%	5%

Source: By the author. Based on UNAIDS 2006; Haub and Kent 2008.

Gender, Circumcision, and Race–Ethnicity. In the United States, AIDS hits men the hardest, but the proportion of women has been growing. In 1982, only 6 percent of AIDS cases were women, but today it is 26 percent (Centers for Disease Control 1997; 2008b). In sub-Saharan Africa, AIDS is more common among women (UNAIDS 2008). Researchers have found that circumcision reduces a man's chance of getting infected with HIV by about half (McNeil 2006). Because circumcision is not widely practiced in sub-Saharan Africa, to help stem the epidemic Israel is sending in circumcision teams (Kraft 2008).

HIV/AIDS is also related to race–ethnicity. One of the most startling examples is this: African American women are *19 times* more likely to come down with AIDS than are white women (Centers for Disease Control 2008b). Figure 19.10 on the next page summarizes racial–ethnic differences in this disease. The reason for the differences shown on this figure is *not* genetic. No racial–ethnic group is more susceptible to AIDS because of biological factors. Rather, risks differ because of *social* factors, such as the use of condoms and the number of drug users who share needles.

The Stigma of AIDS.   Recall how I stressed at the beginning of this chapter how social factors are essential to understanding health and illness. The stigma associated with AIDS is a remarkable example. Some people refuse even to be tested because they fear the stigma they would bear if they test HIV-positive. One unfortunate consequence is the continuing spread of AIDS by people who "don't want to know." Even some governments have put their heads in the sand. Chinese officials, for example, at first refused to admit that they had an AIDS problem, but now they are more open about it. If this disease is to be brought under control, its stigma must be overcome: AIDS must be viewed like any other lethal disease—as the work of a destructive biological organism.

Is There a Cure for AIDS?   As you saw on Figure 19.7 (page 576), the number of AIDS cases in the United States increased dramatically, reached a peak, and then declined. With such a remarkable decline, have we found a cure for AIDS?

With thousands of scientists doing research, the media have heralded each new breakthrough as a possible cure. The most promising treatment, the one that lies behind the drop in deaths shown in Figure 19.7, was spearheaded by David Ho, a virologist (virus researcher). If patients in the early stages of the disease take a "cocktail" of drugs (a combination of protease, fusion, and integrase inhibitors), their immune systems rebound. Antiretroviral therapy, as it is called, is not a cure, however. The virus remains, ready to flourish if the drugs are withdrawn.

While most praise this new treatment, some researchers warn that the cocktail could become this decade's penicillin. When penicillin was introduced, everyone was ecstatic about its effectiveness. However, over the years, the microbes that penicillin targets mutated, producing "super germs" against which we have

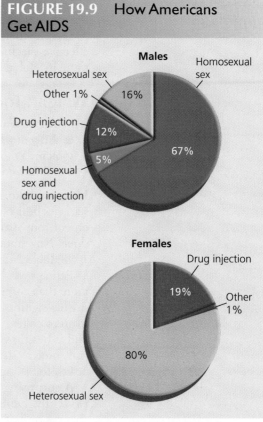

FIGURE 19.9   How Americans Get AIDS

Note: "Other" includes unknown and blood transfusion.

Source: Centers for Disease Control and Prevention 2008b.

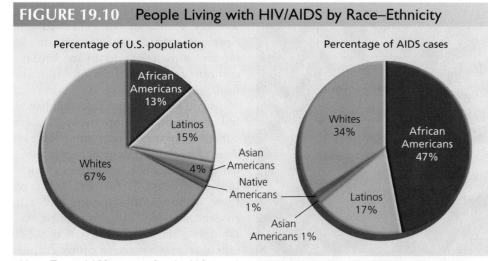

FIGURE 19.10   People Living with HIV/AIDS by Race–Ethnicity

Note: To total 100 percent for the U.S. population and distribute the "claim two or more race–ethnicities," I rounded the totals for whites and African Americans up.

Source: By the author. Based on Figure 12.5 of this text and Centers for Disease Control and Prevention 2008b.

little protection. If this happens with AIDS, a tsunami of a "super-AIDS" virus could hit the world with more fury than the first devastating wave.

Despite their frustrations, medical researchers remain hopeful that they will develop an effective vaccine. If so, many millions of lives will be saved. If not, this disease will continue its global death march.

Weight: Too Much and Too Little

When a friend from Spain visited, I asked him to comment on the things that struck him as different. He mentioned how surprised he was to see people living in metal houses. It took me a moment to figure out what he meant, but then I understood: He had never seen a mobile home. Then he added, "And there are so many fat Americans."

Is this a valid perception, or just some twisted ethnocentric observation by a foreigner? The statistics bear out his observation. Americans have added weight—and a lot of it. In 1980, one of four Americans was overweight. By 1990, this percentage had jumped to one of three. Now about *two-thirds* (65 percent) of Americans are overweight (*Statistical Abstract* 1998:Table 242; 2009:Table 203). We have become the fattest nation on earth.

Perhaps we should just shrug our shoulders and say, "So what?" Is obesity really anything more than someone's arbitrary idea of how much we should weigh? It turns out that obesity has significant costs. The first is quite unexpected: Obese high school girls are less likely to go to college (but there is no difference for overweight boys) (Crosnoe 2007). The second is health: Obese people are more likely to come down with diabetes, kidney disease, and some types of cancer (Centers for Disease Control and Prevention 2009a). Obesity's health toll is high, accounting for about 112,000 deaths a year (Flegal et al. 2007).

A surprising side-effect of being overweight is that it helps some people live longer. Evidently, being either seriously overweight (obese) or underweight increases people's chances of dying, but being a little overweight is good. No one yet knows the reason for this, but some suggest that having a few extra pounds reduces bad cholesterol (Centers for Disease Control 2005).

Alcohol and Nicotine

Many drugs, both legal and illegal, harm their users. Let's examine some of the health consequences of alcohol and nicotine, the two most frequently used legal drugs in the United States.

Alcohol.   Alcohol is *the* standard recreational drug of Americans. The *average* adult American drinks 25 gallons of alcoholic beverages per year—about 21 gallons of beer, 2 gallons of wine, and almost 2 gallons of whiskey, vodka, or other distilled spirits. Beer is so popular that Americans drink more of it than they do tea and fruit juices combined (*Statistical Abstract* 2009:Table 207).

As you know, despite laws that ban alcohol consumption before the age of 21, underage drinking is common. Table 19.1 shows that two-thirds of all high school students drink alcohol during their senior year. If getting drunk is the abuse of alcohol, then, without doubt, among high school students abusing alcohol is popular. As this table also shows, almost half of all high school seniors have been drunk during the past year, with 28 percent getting drunk during just the past month. From this table, you can also see what other drugs high school seniors use.

Everyone knows that drinking and driving don't mix. Here's what's left of a Ferrari in Newport Beach, California. The driver of the other car was arrested for drunk driving and vehicular manslaughter.

TABLE 19.1   What Drugs Have High School Seniors Used?

	In the past month?	In the past year?
Alcohol	43.1%	66.5%
How many have been drunk?	27.6%	45.6%
Nicotine (cigarettes)	20.4%	NA
Marijuana	19.4%	32.4%
Amphetamines	2.9%	6.8%
Barbiturates	2.8%	5.8%
Tranquilizers	2.6%	6.2%
Hallucinogens*	2.2%	5.0%
Cocaine	1.9%	4.4%
MDMA (Ecstasy)	1.8%	4.3%
LSD	1.1%	2.7%
Steroids	1.0%	1.5%
PCP	0.6%	1.1%
Heroin	0.5%	0.7%

* Other than LSD.

Source: By the author. Based on Johnston et al 2008a: Tables 2, 3.

In Table 19.2, we turn to college students. Among them, too, alcohol is the most popular drug, and four out of five of all college students have drunk alcohol during the past year, about two-thirds in the past month. About two of three have been drunk during the past year, almost half in just the past month. As you can see, women are slightly more likely to drink alcohol and to get drunk. In general, however, male college students are slightly more likely to use drugs.

Is alcohol bad for health? This beverage cuts both ways. One to two drinks a day for men and one drink a day for women reduces the risk of heart attacks, strokes, gallstones, and diabetes ("Alcohol" 2009). (Women weigh less on average and produce fewer enzymes that metabolize alcohol.) Beyond these amounts, however, alcohol scars the liver, damages the heart, and increases the risk of breast cancer. It also increases the likelihood of birth defects. One-third of the 43,000 Americans who die each year in vehicle accidents are drunk (*Statistical Abstract* 2009: Table 1070). Each year, 700,000 Americans seek treatment for alcohol problems (*Statistical Abstract* 2009: Table 198).

TABLE 19.2   What Drugs Have Full-Time College Students Used?

	In the past month?		In the past year?	
	Men	Women	Men	Women
Alcohol	67.2%	66.2%	80.1%	81.4%
How many have been drunk?	46.3%	47.1%	61.9%	66.7%
Nicotine (cigarettes)	21.8%	18.8%	32.2%	29.7%
Marijuana	20.2%	14.8%	35.8%	29.4%
Amphetamines	2.8%	3.2%	8.1%	6.2%
Hallucinogens*	2.2%	0.8%	7.3%	3.1%
Cocaine	1.8%	1.7%	6.3%	4.9%
Tranquilizers	1.6%	1.9%	1.3%	0.2%
Barbiturates	1.0%	1.6%	4.2%	3.2%
MDMA (Ecstasy)	0.5%	0.3%	1.4%	2.7%
LSD	0.7%	0.1%	2.2%	0.8%
Heroin	0.3%	0.1%	0.3%	0.1%

* Other than LSD.

Source: By the author. Based on Johnston et al. 2008b: Tables 8-2, 8-3.

Nicotine.

> Let's suppose that you are on your way to the airport to leave for a long-awaited vacation. You are listening to the radio and thinking about the palm trees and ocean waves of sunny Hawaii. Suddenly, an announcer breaks into your reverie with a flash bulletin: Terrorists have hidden bombs aboard five jumbo jets scheduled for takeoff today. The announcer pauses, then adds: "The authorities have not been able to find the bombs. Because they don't know which flights will crash, all flights will depart on schedule."
>
>   Five jets are going to crash. On each jet will be 200 passengers and crew. They will plummet from the skies, leaving a trail of agonizing screams as they meet their fiery destiny.

What would you do? My guess is that you would turn your car around and go home. Adios to Hawaii's beaches, and hello to your own backyard.

Nicotine use—with its creeping side-effects of emphysema and several types of cancer—kills about 400,000 Americans each year (Centers for Disease Control and Prevention 2009b). This is the equivalent of five fully loaded, 200-passenger jets with full crews crashing each and every day—leaving no survivors. Who in their right mind would take the risk that *their* plane will not be among those that crash? Yet this is the risk that smokers take.

Nicotine is, by far, the most lethal of all recreational drugs. Smoking causes cancer of the bladder, cervix, esophagus, kidneys, larynx, lungs, and other body organs. Smokers are more likely to have heart attacks and strokes, and even to come down with cataracts and pneumonia (Surgeon General 2005). The list of health problems related to smoking goes on and on.

Then there is secondhand smoke, which is estimated to kill 50,000 nonsmokers a year (Surgeon General 2006). This is the equivalent of another fully loaded jet going down every two days.

An antismoking campaign that stresses tobacco's health hazards has been so successful that smoking is banned on public transportation and in most offices, restaurants, and, in some states, even bars. Figure 19.11 shows how this antismoking message has hit home. In four decades, cigarette smoking has been cut by more than *half* among U.S. men, and almost that among U.S. women. As you look at this figure, you might be surprised to see that *most* men used to smoke.

Millions of Americans wouldn't think of flying if they knew that even one jet were going to crash—yet they continue to smoke. Why? The two major reasons are addiction and advertising. Nicotine may be as addictive as heroin (Tolchin 1988). While this may sound far-fetched, consider Buerger's disease:

> In this disease, the blood vessels, especially those supplying the legs, become so constricted that circulation is impaired whenever nicotine enters the bloodstream.
>
>   If a patient continues to smoke, gangrene may eventually set in. First a toe may have to be amputated, then the foot at the ankle, then the leg at the knee, and ultimately at the hip. . . . Patients are informed that if they will only stop smoking, it is virtually certain that the otherwise inexorable march of gangrene up the legs will be curbed. Yet surgeons report that some patients with Buerger's disease vigorously puff away in their hospital beds following a second or third amputation. (Brecher et al. 1972)

The second reason is advertising. Cigarette ads were banned from television in the 1980s, but cigarettes continue to be advertised in newspapers and magazines and on billboards. Cigarette companies spend huge amounts to encourage Americans to smoke—about $13 billion a year. This comes to $43 for every man, woman, and child in the entire country (Centers for Disease Control 2007b). Although the tobacco industry denies it, they target youth, often by associating cigarette smoking with success, high fashion, and independence. Despite these denials, Joe Camel, the industry's most blatant attempt to lure children to smoke, has been banned. (See the photo on the next page.) With fewer smokers in the United States, the tobacco companies have turned to recruiting victims in the least industrialized nations. Their efforts to increase nicotine addiction there have been quite successful, making nicotine deaths a serious problem in countries such as China (Gu et al. 2009).

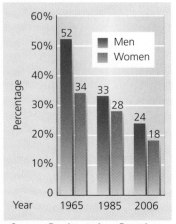

FIGURE 19.11   Who Is Still Smoking?

The Percentage of Americans Age 18 and Over Who Smoke Cigarettes

Source: By the author. Based on *Statistical Abstract of the United States* 2009: Table 196, and earlier years.

Disabling Environments

A **disabling environment** is one that is harmful to people's health. The health risk of some occupations is evident: Lumberjacking, riding rodeo bulls, and training lions are obvious examples. In many occupations, however, people become aware of the risk only years after they worked at jobs that they thought were safe. For example, during and after World War II, several million people worked with asbestos. The federal government estimates that one-quarter of them will die of cancer from having breathed asbestos particles. It is likely that many other substances also cause slowly developing cancers—including, ironically, some asbestos substitutes (Meier 1987; Hawkes 2001).

Industrialization increased the world's standard of living and brought better health to hundreds of millions of people. Ironically, industrialization also threatens to disable the basic environment of the human race, posing what may be the greatest health hazard of all time. The burning of carbon fuels has led to the *greenhouse effect,* a warming of the earth that may change the globe's climate, melt the polar ice caps, and flood the earth's coastal shores. The pollution of land, air, and water, especially through nuclear waste, pesticides, herbicides, and other chemicals, poses additional risks to life on our planet. We discuss these problems in Chapter 22.

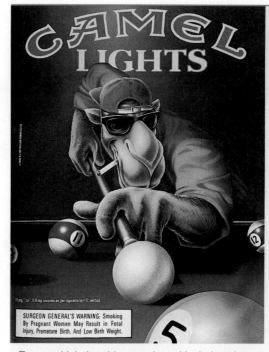

Do you think that this magazine ad is designed to make cigarettes appealing to male youth? Although tobacco industry officials denied that they were trying to entice youth to smoke, evidence such as this ad is overwhelmingly against them. It took pressure from the U.S. Congress to get R.J. Reynolds Tobacco Company to stop its Joe Camel ads.

Medical Experiments: Callous and Harmful

At times, physicians and government officials behave so arrogantly that they callously disregard people's health. Harmful medical experiments, though well-intentioned, are an excellent example. We can trace these experiments to 1895, with an attempt to find a way to immunize people against syphilis. In that year, Albert Neisser, a physician in Germany, injected young prostitutes—one was just 10 years old—with syphilis. Many came down with the disease (Proctor 1999). Let's look at two notorious instances in the United States.

The Tuskegee Syphilis Experiment.   To review this horrible experiment conducted by the U.S. Public Health Service, read the opening vignette for Chapter 12 (page 329). To summarize here, the U.S. Public Health Service did not tell 399 African American men in Mississippi that they had syphilis. Doctors examined them once a year, recording their symptoms, and letting the disease kill them.

The Cold War Experiments.

> Assume that you are a soldier stationed in Nevada, and the U.S. Army orders your platoon to march through an area in which an atomic bomb has just been detonated. Because you are a soldier, you obey. Nobody knows much about radiation, and you don't know that the army is using you as a guinea pig: It wants to see if you'll be able to withstand the fallout—without any radiation equipment. Or suppose you are a patient at the University of Rochester in 1946, and your doctor, whom you trust implicitly, says, "I am going to give you something to help you." You are pleased. But the injection, it turns out, is uranium (Noah 1994). He and a team of other doctors are conducting an experiment to find out how much uranium it will take to damage your kidneys. (U.S. Department of Energy 1995)

Like the Tuskegee experiment, radiation experiments like these were conducted on unsuspecting subjects simply because government officials wanted information. There were others, too. Some soldiers were given LSD. And in Palmetto, Florida, officials released whooping cough viruses into the air, killing a dozen children (Conahan 1994). In other tests, deadly chemical and biological agents, such as sarin, were sprayed onto naval ships to see if they were vulnerable. The sailors in these tests wore protective clothing, but were unaware that they had become white mice (Shanker 2002). In 2003, Congress approved a bill to provide health care for 5,842 soldiers harmed by these secret tests.

disabling environment an environment that is harmful to health

This two-headed dog is the result of an experiment by surgeons in Moscow. Do you think that grafting the puppy onto the adult dog, intended to advance techniques for transplanting human organs, is justified?

The Department of Veterans Affairs never learned the lesson, and they are still using veterans for testing drugs. But this time they get permission—by offering $30 a month to down-and-out veterans of Iraq and Afghanistan. When a drug turns out to have serious side effects, they delay telling their guinea pig veterans ("VA Testing . . ." 2008).

Playing God. To most of us, it is incredible that government officials and medical personnel would callously disregard human life, but it happens. Those in official positions sometimes reach a point where they think they can play God and determine who shall live and who shall die. And, obviously, the most expendable citizens are the poor and powerless. *It is inconceivable that the doctors who did the syphilis studies would have used wealthy and powerful subjects.* The elite are protected from such callous disregard of human rights and life. The only way the poor can be protected against such abuse of professional power is if we publicize each known instance of abuse and insist on vigorous prosecution of those who plan, direct, and carry out such experiments.

Do such things still happen? You can decide for yourself. Consider how medical researchers developed fetal surgery. Surgeons were intrigued with the idea of operating on unborn children. Not only did such surgery hold the possibility of extending medical knowledge but the pioneers would also get their names in prestigious medical journals and be applauded by their peers. Yet such experimental surgery could cost lives. To reduce the risk, the researchers first experimented on animals. Their next step in refining their skills was to operate on pregnant Puerto Rican women. Now that the procedures are proven, the main patients are the unborn of the white and affluent (Casper 1998). The steps taken in this process expose an underlying assumption about the value of life—from animals to Puerto Rican women to white women. It is almost as though the researchers viewed themselves as climbing an evolutionary ladder.

The Globalization of Disease

The year was 1918. Men and women, seemingly healthy the day before, collapsed and were soon dead. In the morning, men wheeled carts down the streets to pick up corpses that were left on porches like last night's trash. In a matter of months, a half million Americans died. Worldwide, the death toll reached between 20 million and 40 million. (Phillips 1998)

What silent killer had so abruptly hit the United States and most of the world? Incredibly, it was the flu. For some reason, still unknown, a particularly lethal variety of the common flu bug had suddenly appeared.

Medical researchers fear that something like this will happen again. If it does, today's global jet travel, unknown in 1918, may make the outbreak even more deadly. Global travel has destroyed the natural frontiers that used to contain diseases. In a matter of hours, today's airline passengers can spread a disease around the world. The resulting number of deaths could make the 1918 death toll seem puny by comparison.

Such are the fears. New diseases keep appearing on the world scene, and antibiotics are ineffective against many of them. When the Ebola virus made its surprise appearance in 1976, with its particularly hideous form of death, the only way it could be contained was to isolate an entire region of Zaire (Olshansky et al. 1997). When SARS (Severe Acute Respiratory Syndrome) appeared in 2003, the World Health Organization of the United Nations called emergency meetings, as did the Centers for Disease Control in the United States. The fear was that SARS would encircle the globe, killing millions of people in a short time. Each person with SARS was isolated, and cities and regions were declared off limits to visitors. The same thing has happened with outbreaks of Asian bird flu (avian influenza) and the Marburg virus in Angola that causes death from fever, diarrhea, vomiting, and bleeding (LaFraniere 2005). Officials are also fearful of a powerful new form of tuberculosis that appeared in South Africa (Wines 2007; Dugger 2008).

When such deadly diseases—for which there is no cure—break out, world health officials send out emergency medical teams to seal off the area. They have been successful in containing these diseases so far, but they fear that they won't always be so fortunate.

Treatment or Prevention?

Let's turn our attention again to the U.S. medical system. One promising alternative to the way U.S. medicine is usually practiced is to change the focus from the treatment of disease to its prevention. Let's consider this in the following Thinking Critically section.

Thinking CRITICALLY
How Will Your Lifestyle Affect Your Health?

Let's contrast Utah (home of the Mormons, who disapprove of alcohol, tobacco, extramarital sex, and even caffeine) with its adjacent state Nevada (home of a gambling industry that fosters rather different values and lifestyles). Although these two states have similar levels of income, education, urbanization, and medical care, Nevadans are more likely to die from cancer, car wrecks, heart attacks, kidney disease, lung diseases, and strokes. (*Statistical Abstract* 2009:Table 116)

As you can tell from this example, your lifestyle is fundamentally important for your health. Lifestyles can lead you down a road to disease and illness—or to health and wellness. Of course, you know this. Our schools and the mass media publicize the message that healthy living—exercising regularly, eating nutritious food, maintaining an optimal weight, not smoking, avoiding alcohol abuse, and not having a lot of sexual partners—leads to better health and a longer life. It doesn't take much reading to know that fatty, low-fiber foods bring disease and that a diet rich in fruits and leafy, green vegetables stimulates health. Yet the message of how greatly lifestyle affects health falls on many deaf ears.

Although millions of Americans exercise regularly and watch their diet and weight, millions more gorge on potato chips, cookies, and soft drinks during their mesmerized hours of watching television and wielding joy sticks. A shorter life and the misery of sickness are simply not on people's minds while snacks, reruns, and video games beckon. Prevention requires work, while illness requires only a doctor's prescription.

Most doctors, too, are attuned to writing prescriptions for health problems instead of focusing on preventive medicine and "wellness." When patients see their doctor, they don't want to hear "Lose weight, exercise, and don't forget to eat your vegetables." Who wants to pay for that? You can get that message from your mother free. Patients want to leave their doctor's office with the message, "You've got such-and such"—and a comforting prescription in hand to cure such-and such. Frankly, doctors make money writing prescriptions for sick people, and to get physicians to turn their focus to "wellness," we will have to make "wellness" profitable. Under our current fee-for-service system, if doctors and hospitals prevent illness, they lose money. Perhaps, then as some have suggested, we can pay doctors and hospitals a fee for keeping people well. "Wellness" programs can be profitable. Many companies have found that their medical bills are lower if they help their employees stay healthy so they don't become patients (Conlin 2007).

For Your Consideration

First, place the focus on yourself. How can you apply this information to live a healthier life?

Second, consider the broader picture, comprehensive "wellness" and prevention. How can we improve disabling environments, decrease the use of harmful drugs, and stop businesses from spewing industrial wastes into the air and using our rivers and oceans as industrial sewers? How can we eliminate ads designed to seduce youth to use deadly drugs? How about ads designed to get adults to tell their doctors what drugs they want? Finally, since we live in a global village, how can we establish international controls and cooperation so we can create a global health-producing environment?

The Future of Medicine

What will the practice of medicine be like in the future? You can expect current issues to remain, such as the financing of health care, the extent it should be an individual or governmental responsibility. Other issues mentioned in this chapter will also remain, such as social inequality, malpractice lawsuits, and depersonalization. Some, such as conflicts of interest and incompetence, will scandalize the medical profession. New diseases will also appear, for which we will have to find new treatments. Beyond such carryover issues, two trends seem to be shaping the future of medicine, alternative medicine and technology.

Alternative Medicine

It is likely that despite attempts of the American Medical Association to enforce a conforming view of illness and health, competing views and practices will demand equal time. An example is **alternative medicine**, also called *nontraditional medicine*. This term often refers to medical practices imported from Asian cultures. From the perspective of traditional Western medical theory and practice, most alternative medicine makes no sense. Regarding it as the superstitious practices of ignorant people, Western doctors usually turn a scornful and hostile eye at alternative medicine. They first ridiculed acupuncture, for example, because it violated their understanding of how the body works. But with patients reporting results such as pain relief, acupuncture has slowly been accepted in U.S. medical practice.

Many U.S. patients have begun to demand alternatives, and the U.S. medical establishment has started to listen. Although the change is slow, in some places the Western and Eastern approaches to medical care are being combined. In two hospitals in Savannah, Georgia, standard and alternative doctors work alongside one another. Patients are given traditional treatment accompanied by yoga, meditation, and shirodhara, in which warm herbalized sesame oil is slowly dripped onto the patient's forehead. Patients may also choose polarity therapy (to unblock energy), biofeedback, Chinese face-lifting, and aromatherapy (Abelson and Brown 2002). Hospitals affiliated with Stanford University, the University of Maryland School of Medicine, and Harvard Medical School have also begun to offer a touch of alternative medicine (Keates 2003; Waldholz 2003).

The change is just a trickle at this point, but what is sociologically significant is that alternative medicine has begun to make inroads into the exclusive club run by the U.S. medical establishment.

alternative medicine (also called *nontraditional medicine*) medical treatment other than that of standard Western medicine; often refers to practices that originate in Asia, but may also refer to taking vitamins not prescribed by a doctor

Using leeches, an old medical treatment, is making a come-back. Researchers have found that the chemicals the leeches inject when they bite relieve symptoms of arthritis and other conditions.

Technology

Technology is certainly destined to have profound effects on medicine. Let's close this chapter with a look at just one aspect of these coming changes, one that, with a strange twist, will bring medicine closer to its roots, that of doctors making house calls.

SOCIOLOGY and the NEW TECHNOLOGY

Making Virtual House Calls: Visiting Your Doctor Online

No more taking time off of work, filling out lengthy paperwork or spending hours to visit your local Doctors office. Just visit one of our online doctors today were available 24/7. Sign up and a Doctor or Nurse will be with you in minutes.

—Quoted from an online medical site (whose quality of English may or may not be indicative of its doctors' practice of medicine)

U.S. medicine is finally moving into the digital age. In some places, you can log online and have a face-to-face consultation (via Webcam) with your doctor. Not only can you describe your symptoms, but you can also use your computer camera to show you doctor what hurts.

After looking, listening, and asking questions—the usual thing—the physician gives advice and writes a prescription. The physician files the prescription with your local pharmacy, which will deliver it to your door.

Great for rural areas, where there is a shortage of physicians. And also great for people who want to avoid traffic jams, germ-infested doctors' offices, and, of course, those outdated magazines.

Meg Young was running a 102-degree fever when she arrived in Boston. She considered going to a hospital emergency room, but instead she went to her hotel room. There she went online and hooked up with her primary doctor in California. After she described her symptoms, he said she had a bacterial infection. He prescribed an antibiotic, which she picked up from a drugstore near her hotel.

"I couldn't have been happier to not sit up in some hospital half the night," she said.

It is easy to see why some patients find virtual house calls appealing. They also hold high appeal for some doctors.

If you are an online physician, just like your patient you don't have to fight traffic. You don't even have the expense of running an office, paying nurses and utilities. On top of this, you don't even have to see patients in person. To avoid contact with all of those germs is a nice side benefit. You get to sit at your computer, talk to your patient, view some part of their body, and write a prescription. This process also cuts down on the boring chit-chat. And getting paid is no

Well, not quite, but coming soon in some form. Already, doctors can perform surgery on patients who are in distant locations, even thousands of miles away. Telesurgery is performed through a combination of robotics and live imaging.

problem. Patients don't get to "see" you until after their credit card has been approved.

Seeing the profit opportunity in this developing new medical "specialty" of "online medical expert," entrepreneurs have already started to move in. Some companies will arrange the online visits, maintain records, and handle credit cards and insurance reimbursements.

Having a physician just a click away, around the clock, seven days a week is just the beginning. Eventually, the virtual house calls will be made from mobile phone to mobile phone. Talk about a time saver. Snap an image of what hurts, and you will be able to visit your doctor while you are driving your car.

Of course, if you get too involved in the house call, after a crunching noise, you might be using your camera phone to show more injuries than you intended.

Based on Costello 2008; Miller 2009; Song 2009.

For Your Consideration

Which would you prefer—visiting your doctor online or in his or her office? Why? Do you think that virtual house calls are the wave of the future or an experiment that will disappoint and be discarded?

By the Numbers: *Then and Now*

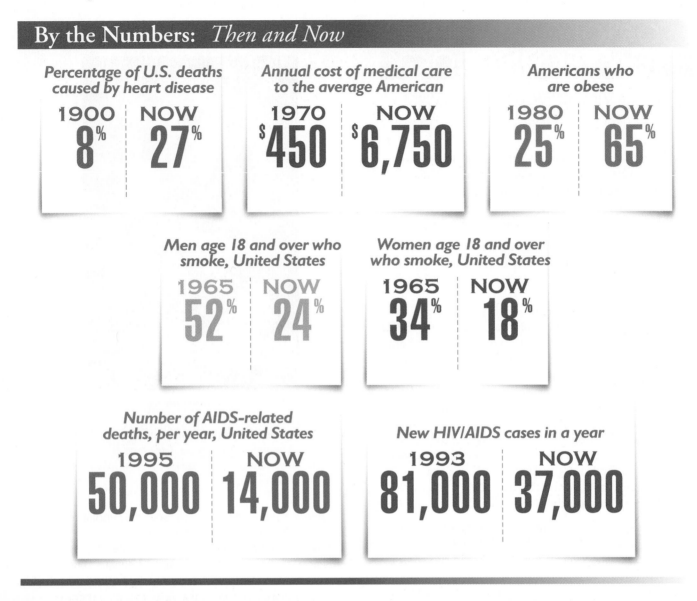

Percentage of U.S. deaths caused by heart disease

1900	NOW
8%	27%

Annual cost of medical care to the average American

1970	NOW
$450	$6,750

Americans who are obese

1980	NOW
25%	65%

Men age 18 and over who smoke, United States

1965	NOW
52%	24%

Women age 18 and over who smoke, United States

1965	NOW
34%	18%

Number of AIDS-related deaths, per year, United States

1995	NOW
50,000	14,000

New HIV/AIDS cases in a year

1993	NOW
81,000	37,000

SUMMARY *and* REVIEW

Sociology and the Study of Medicine and Health

What is the role of sociology in the study of medicine?
Sociologists study **medicine** as a social institution. As practiced in the United States, three of its primary characteristics are professionalization, bureaucracy, and the profit motive. P. 558.

The Symbolic Interactionist Perspective

What is the symbolic interactionist perspective on health and illness?
Health is not only a biological matter but is also intimately related to society. Illness is also far from an objective condition, for illness is always viewed from the framework of culture. The definitions applied to physical and mental conditions vary from one group to another. Pp. 558–559.

The Functionalist Perspective

What is the functionalist perspective on health and illness?
Functionalists stress that in return for being excused from their usual activities, people have to accept the **sick role.** They must assume responsibility for seeking competent medical help and cooperate in getting well so they can quickly resume normal activities. Pp. 559–560.

The Conflict Perspective

What is the conflict perspective on health and illness?
Health care is one of the scarce resources for which groups compete. In 1910, the education of physicians came under the control of a group of men who eliminated most of their competition and turned medicine into a monopoly that has become the largest business in the United States. On a global level, health care follows the stratification that we studied in Chapter 9. The best health care is

available in the Most Industrialized Nations, the worst in the Least Industrialized Nations. Pp. 560–565.

Historical Patterns of Health

How have health patterns changed over time?

Patterns of disease in the United States have changed so extensively that of today's top ten killers, four did not even show up on the 1900 top ten list. Because most Americans live longer than their ancestors did, we can conclude that contemporary Americans are healthier. For mental illness, we have no idea how the current rate of mental illness compares with that of the past, for we have no baselines from which to make comparisons. Pp. 565–566.

Issues in Health Care

How does treating health care as a commodity lead to social inequalities?

Because health care is a commodity to be sold to the highest bidder, the United States has a two-tier system of medical care in which the poor receive inferior health care for both their mental and physical illnesses. Pp. 566–568.

What are some other problems in U.S. health care?

One problem is defensive medicine, which refers to medical procedures that are done for the physician's benefit, not for the benefit of the patient. Intended to protect physicians from lawsuits, these tests and consultations add huge amounts to the nation's medical bill. Other problems are incompetence, depersonalization, conflict of interest, medical fraud, and racism and sexism. Pp. 568–572.

What is the controversy over physicians helping people end their lives?

People's bodies can be kept alive by technology even when they have no brain waves. This leads to questions about the meaning of life and when to "pull the plug." Doctors giving prescriptions to end life is also an issue, fueled by research findings on **euthanasia** in Holland. Pp. 572–574.

What attempts have been made to cut medical costs?

Health maintenance organizations (HMOs) and diagnosis-related groups (DRGs) are among the measures that have been taken to reduce medical costs. Proposals for national health insurance have ended in controversy, but the most controversial proposal is to ration medical care. Pp. 574–576.

Threats to Health

What are some threats to the health of Americans?

Threats to the health of Americans include AIDS, which has stabilized in the United States but is devastating sub-Saharan Africa; obesity and thinness; alcohol and nicotine; **disabling environments;** unethical experiments, of which the Tuskegee syphilis experiments and the Cold War radiation experiments are two examples; and the globalization of disease. Pp. 576–586.

The Future of Medicine

What is the future of medicine?

Many present aspects of medicine will continue into the future, but **alternative medicine** and technology are likely to shape the future of medicine. Pp. 586–587.

THINKING CRITICALLY *ABOUT* Chapter 19

1. A major issue in this chapter is the tension between medicine as a right and medicine as a commodity. What arguments support each side of this issue?

2. How does lifestyle affect health? What does this have to do with sociology?

3. Have you had an experience with alternative medicine? Or do you know someone who has? If so, how did the treatment (and the theory underlying the cause of the medical problem) differ from standard medical practice?

ADDITIONAL RESOURCES

What can you find in MySocLab? mysoclab www.mysoclab.com

- Complete Ebook
- Practice Tests and Video and Audio activities
- Mapping and Data Analysis exercises

- Sociology in the News
- Classic Readings in Sociology
- Research and Writing advice

Where Can I Read More on This Topic?

Suggested readings for this chapter are listed at the back of this book.

chapter

20

Population and Urbanization

Nigeria

The image still haunts me. There stood Celia, age 30, her distended stomach visible proof that her thirteenth child was on its way. Her oldest was only 14 years old! A mere boy by our standards, he had already gone as far in school as he ever would. Each morning, he joined the men to work in the fields. Each evening around twilight, I saw him return home, exhausted from hard labor in the subtropical sun.

I was living in Colima, Mexico, and Celia and Angel had invited me for dinner.

> There stood Celia, age 30, her distended stomach visible proof that her thirteenth child was on its way.

Their home clearly reflected the family's poverty. A thatched hut consisting of only a single room served as home for all fourteen members of the family. At night, the parents and younger children crowded into a double bed, while the eldest boy slept in a hammock. As in many homes in the village, the other children slept on mats spread on the dirt floor—despite the crawling scorpions.

The home was meagerly furnished. It had only a gas stove, a table, and a cabinet where Celia stored her few cooking utensils and clay dishes. There were no closets; clothes hung on pegs in the walls. There also were no chairs, not even one. I was used to the poverty in the village, but this really startled me. The family was too poor to afford even a single chair.

Celia beamed as she told me how much she looked forward to the birth of her next child. Could she really mean it? It was hard to imagine that any woman would want to be in her situation.

Yet Celia meant every word. She was as full of delighted anticipation as she had been with her first child—and with all the others in between.

How could Celia have wanted so many children—especially when she lived in such poverty? That question bothered me. I couldn't let it go until I understood why.

This chapter helps to provide an answer.

591

demography the study of the size, composition, growth, and distribution of human populations

Malthus theorem an observation by Thomas Malthus that although the food supply increases arithmetically (from 1 to 2 to 3 to 4 and so on), population grows geometrically (from 2 to 4 to 8 to 16 and so forth)

Population in Global Perspective

Celia's story takes us into the heart of **demography,** the study of the size, composition, growth, and distribution of human populations. It brings us face to face with the question of whether we are doomed to live in a world so filled with people that there will be very little space for anybody. Will our planet be able to support its growing population? Or are chronic famine and mass starvation the sorry fate of most earthlings?

Let's look at how concern about population growth began.

A Planet with No Space for Enjoying Life?

The story begins with the lowly potato. When the Spanish *conquistadores* found that people in the Andes Mountains ate this vegetable, which was unknown in Europe, they brought some home to cultivate. At first, Europeans viewed the potato with suspicion, but gradually it became the main food of the lower classes. With a greater abundance of food, fertility increased, and the death rate dropped. Europe's population soared, almost doubling during the 1700s (McKeown 1977; McNeill 1999).

Thomas Malthus (1766–1834), an English economist, saw this surging growth as a sign of doom. In 1798, he wrote a book that became world famous, *An Essay on the Principle of Population* (1798). In it, Malthus proposed what became known as the **Malthus theorem.** He argued that although population grows geometrically (from 2 to 4 to 8 to 16 and so forth), the food supply increases only arithmetically (from 1 to 2 to 3 to 4 and so on). This meant, he claimed, that if births go unchecked, the population of a country, or even of the world, will outstrip its food supply.

The New Malthusians

Was Malthus right? This question has become a matter of heated debate among demographers. One group, which can be called the *New Malthusians,* is convinced that today's situation is at least as grim as—if not grimmer than—Malthus ever imagined. For example, *the world's population is growing so fast that in just the time it takes you to read this chap-*

In earlier generations, large farm families were common. Having many children was functional—more hands to help with planting, harvesting, and food preparation. As the country industrialized and urbanized and children became expensive and nonproducing, the size of families shrank. This photo was taken in 1938 in Crowley, Louisiana.

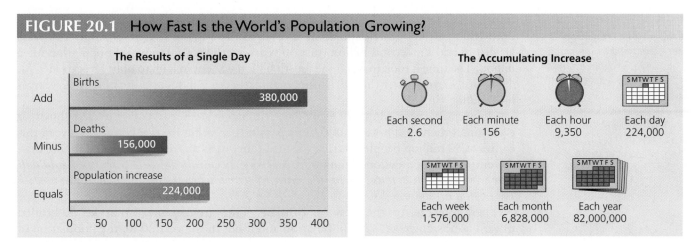

FIGURE 20.1 How Fast Is the World's Population Growing?

The Results of a Single Day

Add — Births — 380,000

Minus — Deaths — 156,000

Equals — Population increase — 224,000

(scale: 0 50 100 150 200 250 300 350 400)

The Accumulating Increase

Each second 2.6
Each minute 156
Each hour 9,350
Each day 224,000

Each week 1,576,000
Each month 6,828,000
Each year 82,000,000

Source: By the author. Based on Haub and Kent 2008.

ter, another 20,000 to 40,000 babies will be born! By this time tomorrow, the earth will have about 224,000 more people to feed. This increase goes on hour after hour, day after day, without letup. For an illustration of this growth, see Figure 20.1.

The New Malthusians point out that the world's population is following an **exponential growth curve.** This means that if growth doubles during approximately equal intervals of time, it suddenly accelerates. To illustrate the far-reaching implications of exponential growth, sociologist William Faunce (1981) retold an old parable about a poor man who saved a rich man's life. The rich man was grateful and said that he wanted to reward the man for his heroic deed.

> The man replied that he would like his reward to be spread out over a four-week period, with each day's amount being twice what he received on the preceding day. He also said he would be happy to receive only one penny on the first day. The rich man immediately handed over the penny and congratulated himself on how cheaply he had gotten by.
>
> At the end of the first week, the rich man checked to see how much he owed and was pleased to find that the total was only $1.27. By the end of the second week he owed only $163.83. On the twenty-first day, however, the rich man was surprised to find that the total had grown to $20,971.51. When the twenty-eighth day arrived the rich man was shocked to discover that he owed $1,342,177.28 for that day alone and that the total reward had jumped to $2,684,354.56!

This is precisely what alarms the New Malthusians. They claim that humanity has just entered the "fourth week" of an exponential growth curve. Figure 20.2 shows why they

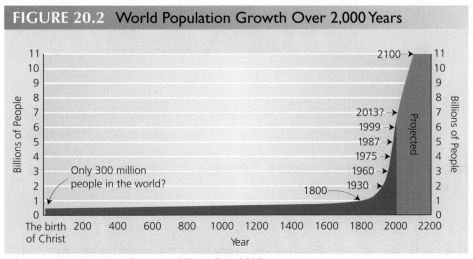

FIGURE 20.2 World Population Growth Over 2,000 Years

(y-axis: Billions of People, 0–11)

Only 300 million people in the world?

The birth of Christ — 200 400 600 800 1000 1200 1400 1600 1800 2000 2200 (Year)

1800
1930
1960 →
1975 →
1987 →
1999 →
2013? →
2100 →

Projected

Sources: Modified from Piotrow 1973; McFalls 2007.

exponential growth curve
a pattern of growth in which numbers double during approximately equal intervals, showing a steep acceleration in the later stages

demographic transition a three-stage historical process of population growth: first, high birth rates and high death rates; second, high birth rates and low death rates; and third, low birth rates and low death rates; a fourth stage in which deaths outnumber births has made its appearance in the Most Industrialized Nations

think the day of reckoning is just around the corner. It took from the beginning of time until 1800 for the world's population to reach its first billion. It then took only 130 years (1930) to add the second billion. Just 30 years later (1960), the world population hit 3 billion. The time it took to reach the fourth billion was cut in half, to only 15 years (1975). Then just 12 years later (in 1987), the total reached 5 billion, and in another 12 years it hit 6 billion (in 1999).

On average, every minute of every day, 156 babies are born. As Figure 20.1 shows, at each sunset the world has 224,000 more people than it did the day before. In a year, this comes to 82 million people. During the next four years, this increase will total more than the entire U.S. population. Think of it this way: *In just the next 12 years, the world will add as many people as it did during the entire time from when the first humans began to walk the earth until the year 1800.*

These totals terrify the New Malthusians. They are convinced that we are headed toward a showdown between population and food. In the year 2050, the population of just India and China is expected to be more than the entire world's population was in 1950 (Haub and Kent 2008). It is obvious that we will run out of food if we don't curtail population growth. Soon we are going to see more televised images of pitiful, starving children.

The Anti-Malthusians

All of this seems obvious, and no one wants to live shoulder-to-shoulder and fight for scraps. How, then, can anyone argue with the New Malthusians?

An optimistic group of demographers, whom we can call the *Anti-Malthusians,* paint a far different picture. They believe that Europe's **demographic transition** provides a more accurate glimpse into the future. This transition is diagrammed in Figure 20.3. During most of its history, Europe was in Stage 1. Its population remained about the same from year to year, for high death rates offset the high birth rates. Then came Stage 2, the "population explosion" that so upset Malthus. Europe's population surged because birth rates remained high while death rates went down. Finally, Europe made the transition to Stage 3: The population stabilized as people brought their birth rates into line with their lower death rates.

This, say the Anti-Malthusians, will also happen in the Least Industrialized Nations. Their current surge in population growth simply indicates that they have reached Stage 2

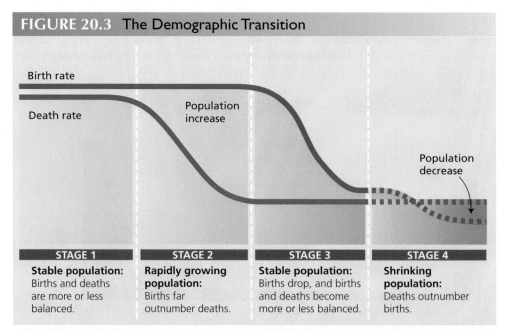

FIGURE 20.3   The Demographic Transition

Birth rate

Death rate

Population increase

Population decrease

STAGE 1	STAGE 2	STAGE 3	STAGE 4
Stable population: Births and deaths are more or less balanced.	**Rapidly growing population:** Births far outnumber deaths.	**Stable population:** Births drop, and births and deaths become more or less balanced.	**Shrinking population:** Deaths outnumber births.

Note: The standard demographic transition is depicted by Stages 1–3. Stage 4 has been suggested by some Anti-Malthusians.

of the demographic transition. Hybrid seeds, medicine from the Most Industrialized Nations, and purer public drinking water have cut their death rates, while their birth rates have remained high. When they move into Stage 3, as surely they will, we will wonder what all the fuss was about. In fact, their growth is already slowing.

Who Is Correct?

As you can see, both the New Malthusians and the Anti-Malthusians have looked at historical trends and projected them onto the future. The New Malthusians project continued world growth and are alarmed. The Anti-Malthusians project Stage 3 of the demographic transition onto the Least Industrialized Nations and are reassured.

There is no question that the Least Industrialized Nations are in Stage 2 of the demographic transition. The question is, Will these nations enter Stage 3? After World War II, the West exported its hybrid seeds, herbicides, and techniques of public hygiene around the globe. Death rates plummeted in the Least Industrialized Nations as their food supply increased and health improved. Because their birth rates stayed high, their populations mushroomed. This alarmed demographers, just it had Malthus 200 years earlier. Some predicted worldwide catastrophe if something were not done immediately to halt the population explosion (Ehrlich and Ehrlich 1972, 1978).

We can use the conflict perspective to understand what happened when this message reached the leaders of the industrialized world. They saw the mushrooming populations of the Least Industrialized Nations as a threat to the global balance of power they had so carefully worked out. With swollen populations, the poorer countries might demand a larger share of the earth's resources. The leaders found the United Nations to be a willing tool, and they used it to spearhead efforts to reduce world population growth. The results have been remarkable. The annual growth of the Least Industrialized Nations has dropped 29 percent, from an average of 2.1 percent a year in the 1960s to 1.5 percent today (Haub and Yinger 1994; Haub and Kent 2008).

The New Malthusians and Anti-Malthusians have greeted this news with significantly different interpretations. For the Anti-Malthusians, this slowing of growth is the signal they had been waiting for: Stage 3 of the demographic transition has begun. First, the death rate in the Least Industrialized Nations fell—now, just as they predicted, birth rates are also falling. Did you notice, they would say, if they looked at Figure 20.2, that it took twelve years to add the fifth billion to the world's population—and also twelve years to add the sixth billion? Population momentum is slowing. The New Malthusians reply that a slower growth rate still spells catastrophe—it just takes longer for it to hit.

The Anti-Malthusians also argue that our future will be the opposite of what the New Malthusians worry about: There are going to be too few children in the world, not too many. The world's problem will not be a population explosion, but **population shrinkage**—populations getting smaller. They point out that births in sixty-five countries have already dropped so low that those countries no longer produce enough children to maintain their populations. About half of the countries of Europe fill more coffins than cradles (Haub and Kent 2008). Apparently, they all would if it were not for immigration from Africa.

Some Anti-Malthusians even predict a "demographic free fall" (Mosher 1997). As more nations enter Stage 4 of the demographic transition, the world's population will peak at about 8 or 9 billion, then begin to grow smaller. Two hundred years from now, they say, we will have a lot fewer people on earth.

Who is right? It simply is too early to tell. Like the proverbial pessimists who see the glass of water half empty, the New Malthusians interpret changes in world population growth negatively. And like the eternal optimists who see the same glass half full, the Anti-Malthusians view the figures positively. Sometime during our lifetime we should know the answer.

Why Are People Starving?

Pictures of starving children gnaw at our conscience. We live in such abundance, while these children and their parents starve before our very eyes. Why don't they have enough food? Is it because there are too many of them, or simply because the abundant food the world produces does not reach them?

population shrinkage the process by which a country's population becomes smaller because its birth rate and immigration are too low to replace those who die and emigrate

Photos of starving people, such as this mother and her child, haunt Americans and other members of the Most Industrialized Nations. Many of us wonder why, when some are starving, we should live in the midst of such abundance, often overeating and even casually scraping excess food into the garbage. We even have eating contests to see who can eat the most food in the least time. The text discusses reasons for such disparities.

The Anti-Malthusians make a point that seems irrefutable. As Figure 20.4 on the next page shows, *there is more food for each person in the world now than there was in 1950.* Although the world's population has more than doubled since 1950, improved seeds and fertilizers have made more food available for *each* person on earth. Even more food may be on the way, for bioengineers are making breakthroughs in agriculture. Despite droughts and civil wars, the global production of meat, fish, and cereals (grains and rice) continues to increase ("Food Outlook" 2008; "Crop Prospects" 2009).

Then why do people die of hunger? From Figure 20.4, we can conclude that people don't starve because the earth produces too little food, but because particular places lack food. Droughts and wars are the main reasons. Just as droughts slow or stop food production, so does war. In nations ravaged by civil war, opposing sides either confiscate or burn crops, and farmers flee to the cities (Thurow 2005; Gettleman 2009). While some countries suffer like this, others are producing more food than their people can consume. At the same time that countries of Africa are hit by drought and civil wars—leaving a swath of starving people—the U.S. government pays farmers to *reduce* their crops. The United States' problem is too much food; West Africa's is too little.

The New Malthusians counter with the argument that the world's population is still growing and that we don't know how long the earth will continue to produce enough food. They add that the recent policy of turning food (such as corn and sugar cane) into biofuels (such as gasoline and diesel fuel) is short-sighted, posing a serious threat to the world's food supply. They also remind us of the penny doubling each day. It is only a matter of time, they insist, until the earth no longer produces enough food—not "if," but "when."

Both the New Malthusians and the Anti-Malthusians have contributed significant ideas, but theories will not eliminate famines. Starving children are going to continue to peer out at us from our televisions and magazines, their tiny, shriveled bodies and bloated stomachs nagging at our conscience and imploring us to do something. Regardless of the underlying causes of this human misery, it has a simple solution: Food can be transferred from nations that have a surplus.

These pictures of starving Africans leave the impression that Africa is overpopulated. Why else would all those people be starving? The truth, however, is far different. Africa has 23 percent of the earth's land, but only 14 percent of the earth's population (Haub and Kent 2008). Africa even has vast areas of fertile land that have not yet been farmed. The reason for famines in Africa, then, *cannot* be too many people living on too little land.

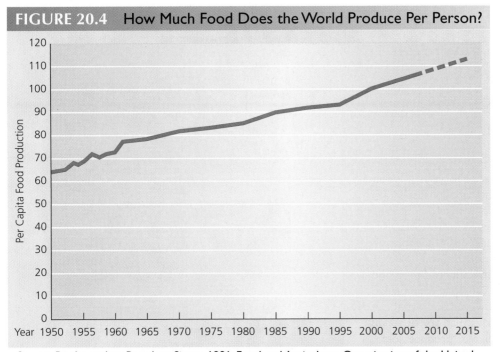

FIGURE 20.4   How Much Food Does the World Produce Per Person?

Source: By the author. Based on Simon 1981; Food and Agriculture Organization of the United Nations 2006; *Statistical Abstract of the United States* 2009: Table 1326.

Population Growth

Even if starvation is the result of a maldistribution of food rather than overpopulation, the fact remains that the Least Industrialized Nations are growing *thirteen times faster* than the Most Industrialized Nations (Haub and Kent 2008). At these rates, it will take 500 years for the average Most Industrialized Nation to double its population, but just 40 years for the average Least Industrialized Nation to do so. Figure 20.5 puts the matter in stark perspective. So does the Down-to-Earth Sociology box on the next page.

Why the Least Industrialized Nations Have So Many Children

Why do people in the countries that can least afford it have so many children? Let's go back to the chapter's opening vignette and try to figure out why Celia was so happy about having her thirteenth child. It will help if we apply the symbolic interactionist perspective. We must take the role of the other so that we can understand the world of Celia and Angel as *they* see it. As our culture does for us, their culture provides a perspective on life that guides their choices. Celia and Angel's culture tells them that twelve children are *not* enough, that they ought to have a thirteenth—as well as a fourteenth and fifteenth. How can this be? Let's consider three reasons why bearing many children plays a central role in their lives—and in the lives of millions upon millions of poor people around the world.

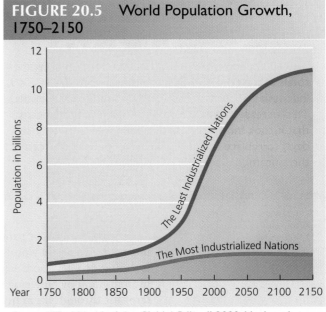

FIGURE 20.5   World Population Growth, 1750–2150

Source: "The World of the Child 6 Billion" 2000; Haub and Kent 2008.

Down-to-Earth Sociology
How the 2004 Tsunami Can Help Us to Understand Population Growth

This photo was snapped at Koh Raya in Thailand, just as the tsunami wave of December 26, 2004, landed.

On December 26, 2004, the world witnessed the worst tsunami in modern history. As the giant waves rolled over the shores of unsuspecting countries, they swept away people from all walks of life—from lowly sellers of fish to wealthy tourists visiting the fleshpots of Sri Lanka. In all, 286,000 people died.

In terms of lives lost, this was not the worst single disaster the world had seen. Several hundred thousand people had been killed in China's Tangshan earthquake in 1976. In terms of geography, however, this was the broadest. It involved more countries than any other disaster in modern history. And, unlike its predecessors, this tsunami occurred during a period of instantaneous, global reporting of events.

As news of the tsunami was transmitted around the globe, the response was almost immediate. Aid poured in—in unprecedented amounts. Governments gave over $3 billion. Citizens pitched in, too, from Little Leaguers and religious groups to the "regulars" at the local bars.

I want to use the tsunami disaster to illustrate the incredible population growth that is taking place in the Least Industrialized Nations. My intention is not to dismiss the tragedy of these deaths, for they were horrible—as were the maiming of so many, the sufferings of families, and the lost livelihoods.

Let's consider Indonesia first. With 233,000 deaths, this country was hit the hardest. At the time, Indonesia had an annual growth rate of 1.6 percent (its "rate of natural increase," as demographers call it). With a population of 220 million, Indonesia was growing by 3,300,000 people each year (Haub 2004). (I'm using the totals at the time of the tsunami. As I write this in 2009, Indonesia's population has already soared to 240 million.) This increase, coming to 9,041 people each day, means that it took Indonesia less than four weeks (twenty-six days) to replace the huge number of people it lost to the tsunami.

The next greatest loss of lives took place in Sri Lanka. With its lower rate of natural increase of 1.3 and its smaller population of 19 million, it took Sri Lanka a little longer to replace the 31,000 people it lost: forty-six days.

India was the third hardest hit. With India's 1 billion people and its 1.7 rate of natural increase, India was adding 17 million people to its population each year—46,575 people each day. At an increase of 1,940 people per hour, India took just 8 or 9 hours to replace the 16,000 people it lost to the tsunami.

The next hardest hit was Thailand. It took Thailand four or five days to replace the 5,000 people that it lost.

For the other countries, the losses were smaller: 298 for Somalia, 82 for the Maldives; 68 for Malaysia; 61 for Myanmar, 10 for Tanzania, 2 for Bangladesh, and 1 for Kenya ("Tsunami deaths . . ." 2005).

Again, I don't want to detract from the horrifying tragedy of the 2004 tsunami. But by using this event as a comparative backdrop, we can gain a better grasp of the unprecedented population growth that is taking place in the Least Industrialized Nations.

First is the status of parenthood. In the Least Industrialized Nations, motherhood is the most prized status a woman can achieve. The more children a woman bears, the more she is thought to have achieved the purpose for which she was born. Similarly, a man proves his manhood by fathering children. The more children he fathers, especially sons, the better—for through them his name lives on.

Second, the community supports this view. Celia and those like her live in *Gemeinschaft* communities, where people share similar views of life. To them, children are a sign of

God's blessing. By producing children, people reflect the values of their community, achieve status, and are assured that they are blessed by God. It is the barren woman, not the woman with a dozen children, who is to be pitied.

You can see how these factors provide strong motivations for bearing many children. There is also another powerful incentive: For poor people in the Least Industrialized Nations, children are *economic assets*. Like Celia and Angel's eldest son, children begin contributing to the family income at a young age. (See Figure 20.6.) But even more important: Children are the equivalent of our Social Security. In the Least Industrialized Nations, the government does not provide social security or medical and unemployment insurance. This motivates people to bear *more* children, for when parents become too old to work, or when no work is to be found, their children take care of them. The more children they have, the broader their base of support.

To those of us who live in the Most Industrialized Nations, it seems irrational to have many children. And *for us it would be*. Understanding life from the framework of people who are living it, however—the essence of the symbolic interactionist perspective—reveals how it makes perfect sense to have many children. Consider this report by a government worker in India:

> **Thaman Singh (a very poor man, a water carrier) . . .** welcomed me inside his home, gave me a cup of tea (with milk and "market" sugar, as he proudly pointed out later), and said: "You were trying to convince me that I shouldn't have any more sons. Now, you see, I have six sons and two daughters and I sit at home in leisure. They are grown up and they bring me money. One even works outside the village as a laborer. You told me I was a poor man and couldn't support a large family. Now, you see, because of my large family I am a rich man." (Mamdani 1973)

FIGURE 20.6   Why the Poor Need Children

Children are an economic asset in the Least Industrialized Nations. Based on a survey in Indonesia, this figure shows that boys and girls can be net income earners for their families by the age of 9 or 10.

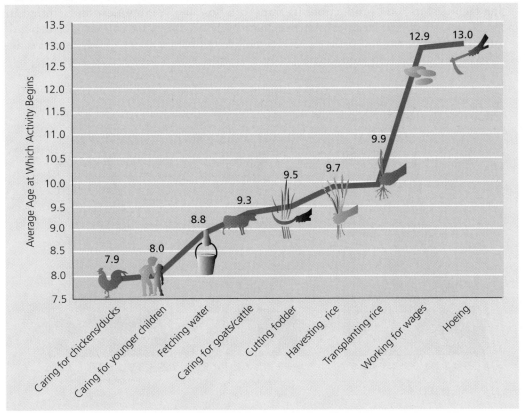

Source: U.N. Fund for Population Activities.

population pyramid a graph that represents the age and sex of a population (see Figure 20.7)

Conflict theorists offer a different view of why women in the Least Industrialized Nations bear so many children. Feminists argue that women like Celia have internalized values that support male dominance. In Latin America, *machismo*—an emphasis on male virility and dominance—is common. To father many children, especially sons, shows that a man is sexually potent, giving him higher status in the community. From a conflict perspective, then, the reason poor people have so many children is that men control women's reproductive choices.

Implications of Different Rates of Growth

The result of Celia and Angel's desire for many children—and of the millions of Celias and Angels like them—is that Mexico's population will double in forty years. In contrast, women in the United States are having so few children that if it weren't for immigration, the U.S. population would begin to shrink. To illustrate population dynamics, demographers use **population pyramids.** These depict a country's population by age and sex. Look at Figure 20.7, which shows the population pyramids of the United States, Mexico, and the world.

To see why population pyramids are important, I would like you to imagine a miracle. Imagine that, overnight, Mexico is transformed into a nation as industrialized as the United States. Imagine also that overnight the average number of children per woman drops to 2.1, the same as in the United States. If this happened, it would seem that Mexico's population would grow at the same rate as that of the United States, right?

But this isn't what would happen. Instead, the population of Mexico would grow much faster than that of the United States. To see why, look again at the population pyramids. You can see that a much higher percentage of Mexican women are in their childbearing years. Even if Mexico and the United States had the same birth rate (2.1 children per woman), a larger percentage of women in Mexico would be giving birth, and Mexico's population would grow faster. As demographers like to phrase this, Mexico's *age structure* gives it greater *population momentum.*

With its population momentum and higher birth rate, Mexico's population will double in forty years. The implications of a doubling population are mind-boggling. *Just to stay even,* within forty years Mexico must double the number of available jobs and housing facilities; its food production; its transportation and communication facilities; its water, gas, sewer, and electrical systems; and its schools, hospitals, churches, civic buildings, theaters, stores, and parks. If Mexico fails to double them, its already meager standard of living will drop even further.

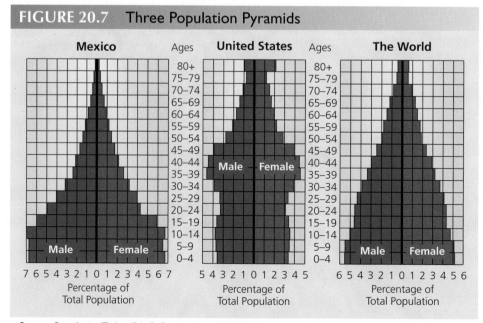

FIGURE 20.7   Three Population Pyramids

Source: Population Today, 26, 9, September 1998:4, 5.

Conflict theorists point out that a declining standard of living poses the threat of political instability—protests, riots, even revolution—and, in response, repression by the government. Political instability in one country can spill into others, threatening an entire region's balance of power. Fearing such disruptions, leaders of the Most Industrialized Nations are using the United Nations to direct a campaign of worldwide birth control. With one hand they give agricultural aid, IUDs, and condoms to the masses in the Least Industrialized Nations—while, with the other, they sell weapons to the elites in these countries. Both actions, say conflict theorists, serve the same purpose: promoting political stability in order to maintain the dominance of the Most Industrialized Nations in global stratification.

The Three Demographic Variables

How many people will live in the United States fifty years from now? What will the world's population be then? These are important questions. Educators want to know how many schools to build. Manufacturers want to anticipate changes in the market for their products. The government needs to know how many doctors, engineers, and executives to train. Politicians want to know how many people will be paying taxes—and how many young people will be available to fight a war.

To project the future of populations, demographers use three **demographic variables:** fertility, mortality, and migration. Let's look at each.

Fertility.   The number of children that the average woman bears is called the **fertility rate.** The world's overall fertility rate is 2.6, which means that during her lifetime the average woman in the world bears 2.6 children. At 2.1, the fertility rate of U.S. women is considerably less (Haub and Kent 2008). A term that is sometimes confused with fertility is **fecundity,** the number of children that women are *capable* of bearing. This number is rather high, as some women have given birth to 30 children (McFalls 2007).

The region of the world that has the highest fertility rate is Middle Africa, where the average woman gives birth to 6.1 children; the lowest is Eastern and Southern Europe, where the average woman bears 1.4 children (Haub and Kent 2008). As you can see from Table 20.1, Macao has the world's lowest fertility rate. There, the average woman gives birth to only 1.0 children. Five of the lowest-birth countries are in Asia. The rest are located in Europe. The countries with the highest birth rate are also clustered. With the exception of Afghanistan and Timor-Leste in Asia, all of them are in Africa. Niger and Guinea-Bissau in West Africa tie for the record for the world's highest birth rate. There, the average woman gives birth to 7.1 children, *seven* times as many children as the average woman in Macao.

To compute the fertility rate of a country, demographers analyze the government's records of births. From these, they figure the country's **crude birth rate,** the annual number of live births per 1,000 population. There can be considerable slippage here, of course. The birth records in many of the Least Industrialized Nations are haphazard, at best.

Mortality.   The second demographic variable is measured by the **crude death rate,** the annual number of deaths per 1,000 people. It, too, varies widely around the world. The highest death rate is 31, a record held by Swaziland in Africa. At 2, the world's record for the lowest death rate is tied by three oil-rich countries: Kuwait, Qatar, and United Arab Emirates (Haub and Kent 2008).

demographic variables the three factors that influence population growth: fertility, mortality, and net migration

fertility rate the number of children that the average woman bears

fecundity the number of children that women are capable of bearing

crude birth rate the annual number of live births per 1,000 population

crude death rate the annual number of deaths per 1,000 population

TABLE 20.1   Extremes in Childbirth

Where Do Women Give Birth to the Fewest Children?		Where Do Women Give Birth to the Most Children?	
Country	Number of Children	Country	Number of Children
Macao	1.0	Guinea-Bissau	7.1
Hong Kong	1.0	Niger	7.1
Taiwan	1.1	Afghanistan	6.8
Slovakia	1.2	Angola	6.8
Andorra	1.2	Burundi	6.8
Bosnia-Herzegovina	1.2	Liberia	6.8
Germany	1.3	Somalia	6.7
Hungary	1.3	Timor-Leste	6.7
Japan	1.3	Uganda	6.7
South Korea	1.3	Mali	6.6

Note: Several other countries also average 1.3 children per woman.

Source: Haub and Kent 2008.

Current U.S. immigration shows great diversity of origin. These individuals were part of 3,000 who took their oath of citizenship at Fenway Park in Boston.

Migration. The third demographic variable is *migration,* the movement of people from one area to another. There are two types of migration. The first type occurs when people move from one region to another within the same country. During and after World War II, in what is known as "The Great Migration," millions of African Americans moved from the South to the North. In a historical shift, many are now returning to the South to participate in its growing economy, to enjoy its warmer climate, and to renew ties with family roots (Frey 2004, 2006).

The second type of migration occurs when people move from one country to another. Demographers use the term **net migration rate** to refer to the difference between the number of *immigrants* (people moving into a country) and *emigrants* (people moving out of a country) per 1,000 people. Unlike fertility and mortality, migration does not affect the global population, for people are simply shifting their residence from one country or region to another.

What motivates people to give up the security of their family and friends to move to a country with a strange language and unfamiliar customs? To understand migration, we need to look at both push and pull factors. The *push* factors are what people want to escape: poverty or persecution for their religious and political ideas. The *pull* factors are the magnets that draw people to a new land, such as opportunities for education, better jobs, the freedom to worship or to discuss political ideas, and a more promising future for their children. After "migrant paths" are established, immigration often accelerates—networks of kin and friends attract more people from the same nation, even from the same villages.

Around the world, the flow of migration is from the Least Industrialized Nations to the industrialized countries. By far, the United States is the world's number one choice. The United States admits more immigrants each year than all the other nations of the world combined. Thirty-eight million residents—one of every eight Americans—were born in other countries (*Statistical Abstract* 2009:Table 43). Table 20.2 below shows where recent U.S. immigrants were born. With the economic crisis, this flow has slowed. Not only are fewer migrants arriving, but many who have lost their jobs are returning to their home countries (Barta and Millman 2009).

net migration rate the difference between the number of immigrants and emigrants per 1,000 population

TABLE 20.2   Country of Birth of Authorized U.S. Immigrants

North America	**2,500,000**	Iran	79,000	Brazil	85,000
Mexico	1,199,000	Bangladesh	64,000	Ecuador	77,000
Cuba	196,000	Taiwan	64,000	Guyana	56,000
Dominican Republic	194,000			Venezuela	53,000
Canada	124,000	**Europe**	**1,043,000**	Argentina	35,000
El Salvador	194,000	Ukraine	119,000		
Guatemala	122,000	Russia	113,000	**Africa**	**526,000**
Jamaica	121,000	United Kingdom	111,000	Nigeria	70,000
		Poland	92,000	Ethiopia	67,000
Asia	**2,473,000**	Bosnia and Herzegovina	85,000	Egypt	47,000
India	473,000	Germany	56,000	Ghana	42,000
China	447,000	Romania	40,000	Somalia	36,000
Philippines	415,000	Albania	35,000	South Africa	24,000
Vietnam	215,000				
Korea	147,000	**South America**	**617,000**		
Pakistan	97,000	Colombia	171,000		
		Peru	99,000		

Note: Totals are for the top countries of origin for 2001–2007, the latest years available.

Source: By the author. Based on *Statistical Abstract of the United States* 2009:Table 49.

To escape grinding poverty, such as that which surrounds Celia and Angel, millions of people also enter the United States illegally. Although it may seem surprising, as Figure 20.8 shows, U.S. officials have sufficient information on these approximately 12 million people to estimate their country of origin.

Experts cannot agree about whether immigrants are a net contributor to the U.S. economy or a drain on it. Some economists claim that immigrants benefit the economy. After subtracting what immigrants collect in welfare, what they cost the medical and school systems, and then adding what they produce in jobs and taxes, they conclude that immigrants produce more than they cost (Council of Economic Advisers 2007). Looking at the same data, other economists conclude that immigrants drain taxpayers of billions of dollars a year (Davis and Weinstein 2002). Evidence seems strong that immigrants lower the income of the native-born Americans with whom they compete (Borjas 2004, 2005, 2006). The fairest conclusion seems to be that the more educated immigrants produce more than they cost, while the less educated cost more than they produce.

Problems in Forecasting Population Growth

The total of the three demographic variables—fertility, mortality, and net migration—gives us a country's **growth rate,** the net change after people have been added to and subtracted from a population. What demographers call the **basic demographic equation** is quite simple:

Growth rate = births – deaths + net migration

If population increase depended only on biology, the demographer's job would be easy. But social factors—wars, economic booms and busts, plagues, and famines—push rates of birth and death and migration up or down. As is shown in the Cultural Diversity box on the next page, even infanticide can affect population growth. Politicians also complicate projections. Sometimes governments try to persuade women to bear fewer—or more—children. When Hitler decided that Germany needed more "Aryans," the German government outlawed abortion and offered cash bonuses to women who gave birth. The population increased. Today, European leaders are alarmed that their birth rates have dropped so low that their populations will shrink. With its population dropping, Russia's leaders are offering cash payments to women who have children (Chivers 2006).

In China, we find the opposite situation. Many people know that China tries to limit population growth with its "One couple, one child" policy, but few know how ruthlessly officials enforce this policy. Steven Mosher (2006), an anthropologist who did fieldwork in China, revealed that—whether she wants it or not—after the birth of her first child, each woman is fitted with an IUD (intrauterine device). If a woman has a second child, she is sterilized. If a woman gets pregnant without government permission (yes, you read that right), the fetus is aborted. If she does not consent to an abortion, one is performed on her anyway—even if she is nine months pregnant. No unmarried woman is allowed to give birth; any unmarried woman who gets pregnant is arrested and forced to have an abortion. In some areas, authorities allow women to have a second child—if their first one was a girl (Jacobs 2008).

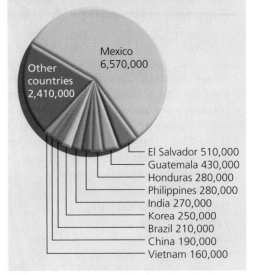

FIGURE 20.8   Country of Origin of Unauthorized Immigrants to the United States

Mexico 6,570,000
Other countries 2,410,000
El Salvador 510,000
Guatemala 430,000
Honduras 280,000
Philippines 280,000
India 270,000
Korea 250,000
Brazil 210,000
China 190,000
Vietnam 160,000

Source: By the author. Based on *Statistical Abstract of the United States* 2009:Table 46.

growth rate the net change in a population after adding births, subtracting deaths, and either adding or subtracting net migration

basic demographic equation the growth rate equals births minus deaths plus net migration

The Chinese government uses billboards to remind people of its "one couple, one child" policy. The fat on the child's face on this billboard in Chengdu carries an additional message—that curtailing childbirth brings prosperity, abundant food for all. The portrayal of a girl baby is part of the government's attempt to reduce female infanticide.

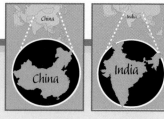

Cultural Diversity around the World

Killing Little Girls: An Ancient and Thriving Practice

"The Mysterious Case of the Missing Girls" could have been the title of this box. Around the globe, for every 100 girls born, about 105 boys are born. In China, however, for every 100 baby girls, there are 120 baby boys. Given China's huge population, this means that China has several million fewer baby girls than it should have. Why?

The answer is *female infanticide,* the killing of baby girls. When a Chinese woman goes into labor, the village midwife sometimes grabs a bucket of water. If the newborn is a girl, she is plunged into the water before she can draw her first breath.

At the root of China's sexist infanticide is economics. The people are poor, and they have no pensions. When parents can no longer work, sons support them. In contrast, a daughter must be married off, at great expense, and at that point, her obligations transfer to her husband and his family.

In the past few years, the percentage of boy babies has grown. The reason, again, is economics, but this time it has a new twist. As China opened the door to capitalism, travel and trade opened up—but primarily to men, for it is not thought appropriate for women to travel alone. With men finding themselves in a better position to bring profits home to the family, parents have one more reason to want male children.

This woman in New Delhi, India, is participating in a protest against sex-selective abortion.

The gender ratio is so lopsided that for people in their 20s there are six bachelors for every five potential brides. Concerned about this gender imbalance, officials have begun a campaign to stop the drowning of girl babies. They are also trying to crack down on the abortions of female fetuses.

It is likely that the preference for boys, and the resulting female infanticide, will not disappear until the social structures that perpetuate sexism are dismantled. This is unlikely to take place until women hold as much power as men, a development that, should it ever occur, apparently lies far in the future.

In the meantime, politicians have become concerned about a primary sociological implication of female infanticide—that large numbers of young men who cannot marry pose a political threat. These "bare branches," as they are referred to in China, disgruntled and lacking the stabilizing influences of marriage and children, could become a breeding ground for political dissent. This threat could motivate the national elites to take steps against female infanticide.

For Your Consideration

What do you think can be done to reduce female infanticide? Why do you think this issue receives so little publicity and is not a priority with world leaders?

Sources: Jordan 2000; Dugger 2001; Eckholm 2002; French 2004; Riley 2004; Sang-Hun 2007; Yardley 2007.

Although government policies can change a country's growth rate, the main factor is not the government, but industrialization. *In every country that industrializes, the birth rate declines.* Not only does industrialization open up economic opportunities but it also makes rearing children more expensive. Children require more education and remain dependent longer. Significantly, the basis for conferring status also changes—from having many children to attaining education and displaying material wealth. People like Celia and Angel in our opening vignette begin to see life differently, and their motivation to have many children drops sharply. Not knowing how rapidly industrialization will progress or how quickly changes in values and reproductive behavior will follow adds to the difficulty of making accurate projections.

Consider what the U.S. population might be in the year 2050. Between now and then, will we have **zero population growth**? (Every 1,000 women would give birth to 2,100 children,

zero population growth
women bearing only enough children to reproduce the population

the extra 100 children making up for those who do not survive or reproduce.) What percentage of women will go to college? (Educated women bear fewer children.) How many immigrants will we have? Will some devastating disease appear? Because of these many unknowns, demographers play it safe by making several projections of population growth, each depending on an "if" scenario. Figure 20.9 shows their three projections of the U.S. population.

Let's turn to a different aspect of population, where people live. Because more and more people around the world are living in cities, we shall concentrate on urban trends and urban life.

Urbanization

As I was climbing a steep hill in Medellin, Colombia, in a district called El Tiro, my informant, Jaro, said, "This used to be a garbage heap." I stopped to peer through the vegetation alongside the path we were on, and sure enough, I could see bits of refuse still sticking out of the dirt. The "town" had been built on top of garbage.

This was just the first of my many revelations that day. The second was that El Tiro was so dangerous that the Medellin police refused to enter it. I shuddered for a moment, but I had good reason to trust Jaro. He had been a pastor in El Tiro for several years, and he knew the people well. I knew that if I stayed close to him I would be safe.

Actually, El Tiro was safer now than it had been. A group of young men had banded together to make it so, Jaro told me. A sort of frontier justice prevailed. The vigilantes told the prostitutes and drug dealers that there would be no prostitution or drug dealing in El Tiro and to "take it elsewhere." They killed anyone who robbed or killed someone. And they even made families safer—they would beat up any man who got drunk and beat "his" woman. With the threat of instant justice, the area had become much safer.

Jaro then added that each household had to pay the group a monthly fee, which turned out to be less than a dollar in U.S. money. Each business had to pay a little more. For this, they received security.

As we wandered the streets of El Tiro, it did look safe—but I still stayed close to Jaro. And I wondered about this group of men who had made the area safe. What kept them from turning on the residents? Jaro had no answer. When Jaro pointed to two young men, whom he said were part of the ruling group, I asked if I could take their picture. They refused. I did not try to snap one on the sly.

My final revelation was El Tiro itself. On the next two pages you can see some of the things I saw that day.

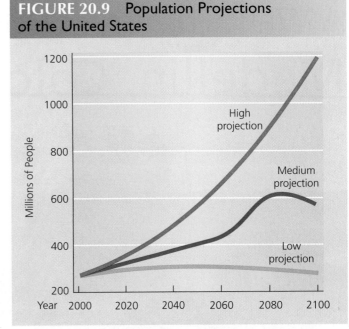

FIGURE 20.9 Population Projections of the United States

Note: The projections are based on different assumptions of fertility, mortality, and, especially, immigration.

Source: By the author. Based on *Statistical Abstract of the United States* 2002: Table 3.

Early cities were small economic centers surrounded by walls to keep out enemies. These cities had to be fortresses, for they were constantly under threat. Pictured in this 1884 illustration is an attack on Paris in 885.

A Walk Through El Tiro
Medellin, Colombia

This is the "richer" area below El Tiro. As you can see, some of the residents own cars.

Kids are kids the world over. These children don't know they are poor. They are having a great time playing on a pile of dirt in the street.

Almost at the top of the garbage heap, I saw this boy in front of his house. His mother hung out the family's wash to dry.

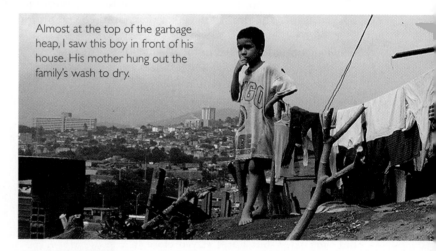

This is one of my favorite photos. The woman is happy that she has a home—and proud of what she has done with it. What I find remarkable is the flower garden she so carefully tends, and has taken great effort to protect from children and dogs. I can see the care she would take of a little suburban home.

© James M. Henslin, all photos

The road to El Tiro. On the left, going up the hill, is a board walk. To the right is a meat market (carnicería). Note the structure above the meat market, where the family that runs the store lives.

It doesn't take much skill to build your own house in El Tiro. A hammer and saw, some nails, and used lumber will provide most of what you need. This man is building his house on top of another house.

El Tiro has home delivery.

An infrastructure has developed to serve El Tiro. This woman is waiting in line to use the only public telephone.

"What does an El Tiro home look like inside?," I kept wondering. Then Jaro, my guide (on the left), took me inside the home of one of his parishioners. Amelia keeps a neat house, with everything highly organized.

What do people do to make a living in El Tiro? Anything they can. This man is sharpening a saw in front of his home.

city a place in which a large number of people are permanently based and do not produce their own food

urbanization the process by which an increasing proportion of a population lives in cities and has a growing influence on the culture

metropolis a central city surrounded by smaller cities and their suburbs

In this second part of the chapter, I will try to lay the context for understanding urban life—and El Tiro. Let's begin by first finding out how the city itself came about.

The Development of Cities

Cities are not new to the world scene. Perhaps as early as 7,000 years ago, people built small cities with massive defensive walls, such as biblically famous Jericho (Homblin 1973). Cities on a larger scale appeared about 3500 B.C., around the time that writing was invented (Chandler and Fox 1974; Hawley 1981). At that time, cities emerged in several parts of the world—first in Mesopotamia (Iran and Iraq) and later in the Nile, Indus, and Yellow River valleys, in West Africa, along the shores of the Mediterranean, in Central America, and in the Andes (Fischer 1976; Flanagan 1990). In the Americas, the first city was Caral, in what is now Peru (Fountain 2001).

The key to the origin of cities is the development of more efficient agriculture (Lenski and Lenski 1987). Only when farming produces a surplus can some people stop producing food and gather in cities to spend time in other economic pursuits. A **city**, in fact, can be defined as a place in which a large number of people are permanently based and do not produce their own food. The invention of the plow about 5,000 years ago created widespread agricultural surpluses, stimulating the development of towns and cities.

Most early cities were tiny, merely a collection of a few thousand people in agricultural centers or on major trade routes. The most notable exceptions are two cities that reached 1 million residents for a brief period of time before they declined—Changan (Xi'an) in China about A.D. 800 and Baghdad in Persia (Iraq) about A.D. 900 (Chandler and Fox 1974). Even Athens at the peak of its power in the fifth century B.C. had only about 250,000 inhabitants. Rome, at its peak, may have had a million people or more, but as the Roman empire declined, the city of Rome became only a collection of villages (Palen 2008).

Two hundred years ago, the only city in the world that had a population of more than a million was Peking (Beijing), China (Chandler and Fox 1974). As Figure 20.10 shows, today the world has over 400 cities with more than a million residents. Behind this surge lies the Industrial Revolution, which not only drew people to cities by providing work but which also stimulated rapid transportation and communication. These, in turn, allowed the efficient movement of people, resources, products, and especially today, information—essential factors (called *infrastructure*) that allow large cities to exist.

The Process of Urbanization

Although cities are not new to the world scene, **urbanization**—the movement of masses of people to cities, which then have a growing influence on society—is quite recent in world history. In 1800 only 3 percent of the world's population lived in cities (Hauser and Schnore 1965), but by 2008, for the first time in history, more people lived in cities than in rural areas. Although urbanization is taking place around the globe, as you can see from Table 20.3 it is quite uneven.

To understand the city's attraction, we need to consider the "pulls" of urban life. Because of its exquisite division of labor, the city offers incredible variety—music ranging from rap and salsa to death metal and classical, shops that feature imported delicacies from around the world and those that sell special foods for vegetarians and diabetics. Cities also offer anonymity, which so many find refreshing in light of the tighter controls of village and small-town life. And, of course, the city offers work.

Some cities have grown so large and have so much influence over a region that the term *city* is no longer adequate to describe them. The term **metropolis** is used instead. This term refers to a central city sur-

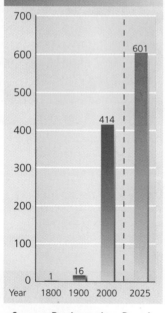

FIGURE 20.10

A Global Boom: Cities with Over One Million Residents

Sources: By the author. Based on Chandler and Fox 1974; Brockerhoff 2000; United Nations 2008.

TABLE 20.3   Urbanization and Industrial Development

	Percent Urban
Least Industrialized Nations	28%
Industrializing Nations	44%
Most Industrialized Nations	75%

Source: By the author. Based on United Nations 2008; Haub and Kent 2008.

rounded by smaller cities and their suburbs. They are linked by transportation and communication and connected economically, and sometimes politically, through county boards and regional governing bodies. St. Louis is an example.

> Although this name, St. Louis, properly refers to a city of 350,000 people in Missouri, it also refers to another 3 million people who live in more than a hundred separate towns in both Missouri and Illinois. Altogether, the region is known as the "St. Louis or Bi-State Area." Although these towns are independent politically, they form an economic unit. They are linked by work (many people in the smaller towns work in St. Louis or are served by industries from St. Louis), by communications (they share the same area newspaper and radio and television stations), and by transportation (they use the same interstate highways, the Bi-State Bus system, and international airport). As symbolic interactionists would note, shared symbols (the Arch, the Mississippi River, Busch Brewery, the Cardinals, the Rams, the Blues—both the hockey team and the music) provide the residents a common identity.
>
> Most of the towns run into one another, and if you were to drive through this metropolis, you would not know that you were leaving one town and entering another—unless you had lived there for some time and were aware of the fierce small-town identifications and rivalries that coexist within this overarching identity.

Some metropolises have grown so large and influential that the term **megalopolis** is used to describe them. This term refers to an overlapping area consisting of at least two metropolises and their many suburbs. Of the twenty or so megalopolises in the United States, the three largest are the Eastern seaboard running from Maine to Virginia, the area in Florida between Miami, Orlando, and Tampa, and California's coastal area between San Francisco and San Diego. The California megalopolis extends into Mexico and includes Tijuana and its suburbs.

This process of urban areas turning into a metropolis, and a metropolis developing into a megalopolis, occurs worldwide. When a city's population hits 10 million, it is called a **megacity.** In 1950, New York City was the only megacity in the world, but today there are nineteen (United Nations 2008). Megacities are growing so rapidly that by the year 2025 there are expected to be twenty-seven. The largest of these are shown in Figure 20.11. As you can see, most megacities are located in the Least Industrialized Nations.

megalopolis an urban area consisting of at least two metropolises and their many suburbs

megacity a city of 10 million or more residents

FIGURE 20.11   The 20 Largest Cities in the World.*

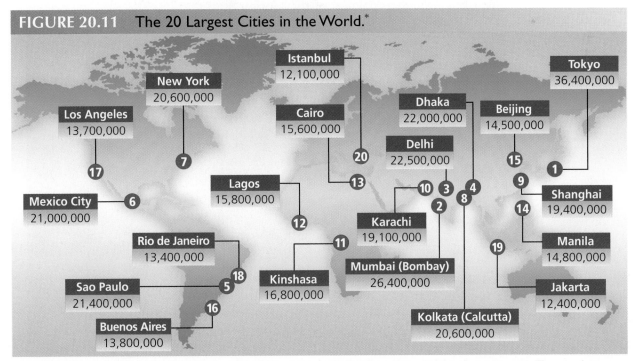

City	Population
Tokyo	36,400,000
Istanbul	12,100,000
New York	20,600,000
Dhaka	22,000,000
Beijing	14,500,000
Los Angeles	13,700,000
Cairo	15,600,000
Delhi	22,500,000
Mexico City	21,000,000
Lagos	15,800,000
Shanghai	19,400,000
Rio de Janeiro	13,400,000
Karachi	19,100,000
Manila	14,800,000
Sao Paulo	21,400,000
Kinshasa	16,800,000
Mumbai (Bombay)	26,400,000
Jakarta	12,400,000
Buenos Aires	13,800,000
Kolkata (Calcutta)	20,600,000

*Includes contiguous cities. Los Angeles, for example, includes Long Beach, and New York includes Newark. The populations are projections for year 2025.

Source: By the author. Based on United Nations 2008: Table 3.

U.S. Urban Patterns

From Country to City. In its early years, the United States was almost exclusively rural. In 1790, only about 5 percent of Americans lived in cities. By 1920, this figure had jumped to 50 percent. Urbanization has continued without letup, and today 79 percent of Americans live in cities.

The U.S. Census Bureau divides the country into 274 **metropolitan statistical areas (MSAs).** Each MSA consists of a central city of at least 50,000 people and the urbanized areas linked to it. About three of five Americans live in just fifty or so MSAs. As you can see from the Social Map below, like our other social patterns, urbanization is uneven across the United States.

From City to City. As Americans migrate in search of work and better lifestyles, some cities increase in population while others shrink. Table 20.4 on the next page compares the fastest-growing U.S. cities with those that are losing people. This table reflects a major shift of people, resources, and power between regions of the United States. As you can see, five of the ten fastest-growing cities are in the West, and five are in the South. Of the ten declining cities, six are in the Northeast, three in the South, and one in the West. New Orleans, a special case, has not yet recovered from Hurricane Katrina.

Between Cities. As Americans migrate, **edge cities** have developed to meet their needs. This term refers to clusters of buildings and services near the intersection of major highways. These areas of shopping malls, hotels, office parks, and apartment complexes are not cities in the traditional sense. Rather than being political units with their own mayor or city manager, they overlap political boundaries and include parts of several cities or towns. Yet, edge cities—such as Tysons Corner near Washington, DC, and those clustering along the LBJ Freeway near Dallas, Texas—provide a sense of place to those who live or work there.

Within the City. Another U.S. urban pattern is **gentrification,** the movement of middle-class people into rundown areas of a city. What draws the middle class are the low

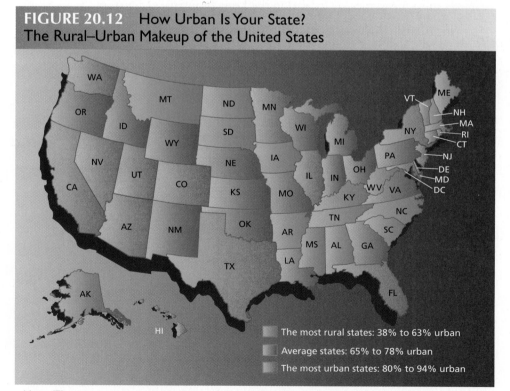

**FIGURE 20.12 How Urban Is Your State?
The Rural–Urban Makeup of the United States**

The most rural states: 38% to 63% urban
Average states: 65% to 78% urban
The most urban states: 80% to 94% urban

Note: The most rural state is Vermont (38% urban). The most urban states are California and New Jersey (94% urban).

Source: By the author. Based on *Statistical Abstract of the United States* 2009: Table 28.

TABLE 20.4	The Shrinking and the Fastest-Growing Cities		
The Shrinking Cities		**The Fastest-Growing Cities**	
1. −21.7%	New Orleans, LA	1. +33.9%	Cape Coral–Ft. Myers, FL
2. −5.4%	Youngstown, OH	2. +33.5%	Las Vegas, NV
3. −3.6%	Buffalo–Niagara Falls, NY	3. +31.4%	Raleigh, NC
4. −3.1%	Pittsburgh, PA	4. +30.9%	Provo, UT
5. −2.5%	Cleveland, OH	5. +28.5%	Phoenix, AZ
6. −2.3%	Beaumont, TX	6. +27.9%	Austin, TX
7. −2.0%	Scranton, PA	7. +26.4%	Boise City, ID
8. −1.8%	Charleston, WV	8. +25.6%	Naples, FL
9. −1.7%	Utica-Rome, NY	9. +25.5%	Fayetteville, AR
10. −1.6%	Huntington, WV	10. +25.5%	Ocala, FL

Note: Population change from 2000 to 2007.

Source: By the author. Based on *Statistical Abstract of the United States* 2009: Table 19.

prices for large houses that, although deteriorated, can be restored. With gentrification comes an improvement in the appearance of the neighborhood—freshly painted buildings, well-groomed lawns, and the absence of boarded-up windows.

Gentrification received a black eye because it was thought that the more well-to-do newcomers displaced the poorer residents, that they took over their turf, so to speak. While there certainly are tensions with the newcomers (Anderson 1990, 2006), a recent study indicates that gentrification also draws middle-class minorities to the neighborhood and improves their incomes (McKinnish et al. 2008). We will have to see if further research confirms this finding.

The usual pattern is for the gentrifiers to be whites and the earlier residents to be minorities, but in the Harlem neighborhood of New York City, both groups are African Americans. As is discussed in the Down-to-Earth Sociology box on the next page, as middle-class and professional African Americans reclaim this area, an infrastructure—which includes everything from Starbucks coffee shops to dentists—is following. So are soaring real estate prices.

From City to Suburb. The term **suburbanization** refers to people moving from cities to **suburbs**, the communities located just outside a city. Suburbanization is not new. The Mayan city of Caracol (in what is now Belize) had suburbs, perhaps even with specialized subcenters, the equivalent of today's strip malls (Wilford 2000). The extent to which people have left U.S. cities in search of their dreams is remarkable. In 1920, about 15 percent of Americans lived in the suburbs, and today over half of all Americans live in them (Palen 2008).

After the racial integration of U.S. schools in the 1950s and 1960s, whites fled the city. Starting around 1970, minorities also began to move to the suburbs, where in some they have become the majority. "White flight" appears to have ended (Dougherty 2008a). Although only a trickle at this point, the return of whites to the city is significant enough that in Washington, D.C., and San Francisco, California, some black churches and businesses are making the switch to a white clientele. In a reversal of patterns, some black churches are now fleeing the city, following their parishioners to the suburbs.

Smaller Centers. The most recent urban trend is the development of *micropolitan areas.* A *micropolis* is a city of 10,000 to 50,000 residents that is not a suburb (McCarthy 2004), such as Gallup, New Mexico, or Carbondale, Illinois. Most micropolises are located "next to nowhere." They are fairly self-contained in terms of providing work, housing, and entertainment, and few of their residents commute to urban centers for work. Micropolises are growing, as residents of both rural and urban areas find their cultural attractions and conveniences appealing, especially in the absence of the city's crime and pollution.

The Rural Rebound

The desire to retreat to a safe haven has led to a migration to rural areas that is without precedent in the history of the United States. Some small farming towns are making a comeback, their boarded-up stores and schools once again open for business and learning.

suburbanization the migration of people from the city to the suburbs

suburb a community adjacent to a city

Down-to-Earth Sociology
Reclaiming Harlem: A Twist in the Invasion–Succession Cycle

The story is well known. The inner city is filled with crack, crime, and corruption. It stinks from foul, festering filth strewn on the streets and piled up around burned-out buildings. Only those who have no choice live in these desolate, despairing areas where danger lurks around every corner.

What is not so well known is that affluent African Americans are reclaiming some of these areas.

Howard Sanders was living the American Dream. After earning a degree from Harvard Business School, he took a position with a Manhattan investment firm. He lived in an exclusive apartment on Central Park West, but he missed Harlem, where he had grown up. He moved back, along with his wife and daughter.

African American lawyers, doctors, professors, and bankers are doing the same.

What's the attraction? The first is nostalgia, a cultural identification with the Harlem of legend and folklore. It was here that black writers and artists lived in the 1920s, here that the blues and jazz attracted young and accomplished musicians.

The second reason is that Harlem offers housing values, such as five-bedroom homes with 6,000 square feet, some with Honduran mahogany. Some brownstones are only shells and have to be rebuilt from the inside out. Others are in perfect condition.

What is happening is the rebuilding of a community. Some people who "made" it want to be role models. They want children in the community to see them going to and returning from work.

When the middle class moved out of Harlem, so did its amenities. Now that young professionals are moving back in, the amenities are returning. There were no coffee shops, restaurants, jazz clubs, florists, copy centers, dentist and optometrist offices, or art galleries—the types of things urbanites take for granted. Now there are.

The police are also helping to change the character of Harlem. No longer do they just rush in, sirens wailing, to confront emergencies and shootouts. Instead, the police have become a normal part of this urban scene. Not only have they shut down the open-air drug markets, but they

Social class preferences in music styles and volume are a source of tension between the old and new residents of Harlem. New residents have complained about these musicians at Marcus Garvey Park.

are even enforcing laws against public urination and vagrancy. The greater safety of the area is attracting even more of the middle class.

Two of the strongest signs of the change are that former president Clinton chose to locate his office here, and Magic Johnson opened a Starbucks and a multiplex.

There is another side of the story, of course, the tension between the old timers, the people who were already living in Harlem, and the newcomers, the investment bankers and professionals who are moving back and trying to rediscover their roots. Sometimes cultural differences become a problem. The old timers like loud music, for example, while the newcomers prefer a more sedate lifestyle. On a more serious level are the tenants' associations that protest the increase in rents and the homeowners' associations that fight to keep renters out of their rehabilitated areas. All are African Americans. The issue is not race, but social class antagonisms.

The "invasion-succession cycle," as sociologists call it, is continuing, but this time with a twist—a flight back in.

For Your Consideration
Would you be willing to move into an area of high crime in order to get a good housing bargain? How do you think the economic crisis—with the loss of jobs and falling real estate prices—will affect Harlem?

Sources: Based on Cose 1999; McCormick 1999b; Leland 2003; Hampson 2005; Hyra 2006; Beveridge 2008; Williams 2008; Haughney 2009.

In some cases, towns have even become too expensive for families that had lived there for decades (Dougherty 2008b).

The "push" factors for this fundamental shift are fears of urban crime and violence. The "pull" factors are safety, lower cost of living, and more living space. Interstate highways have made airports—and the city itself—accessible from longer distances. With satellite communications, cell phones, fax machines, and the Internet, people can be "plugged in"—connected with others around the world—even though they live in what just a short time ago were remote areas.

Listen to the wife of one of my former students as she explains why she and her husband moved to a rural area, three hours from the international airport that they fly out of each week:

> I work for a Canadian company. Paul works for a French company, with headquarters in Paris. He flies around the country doing computer consulting. I give motivational seminars to businesses. When we can, we drive to the airport together, but we often leave on different days. I try to go with my husband to Paris once a year.
>
> We almost always are home together on the weekends. We often arrange three- and four-day weekends, because I can plan seminars at home, and Paul does some of his consulting from here.
>
> Sometimes shopping is inconvenient, but we don't have to lock our car doors when we drive, and the new Wal-Mart superstore has most of what we need. E-commerce is a big part of it. I just type in www—whatever, and they ship it right to my door. I get make-up and books online. I even bought a part for my stove.
>
> Why do we live here? Look at the lake. It's beautiful. We enjoy boating and swimming. We love to walk in this parklike setting. We see deer and wild turkeys. We love the sunsets over the lake. (author's files)

She added, "I think we're ahead of the learning curve," referring to the idea that their lifestyle is a wave of the future.

Models of Urban Growth

In the 1920s, Chicago was a vivid mosaic of immigrants, gangsters, prostitutes, the homeless, the rich, and the poor—much as it is today. Sociologists at the University of Chicago studied these contrasting ways of life. One of these sociologists, Robert Park, coined the term **human ecology** to describe how people adapt to their environment (Park and Burgess 1921; Park 1936). (This concept is also known as *urban ecology.*) The process of urban growth is of special interest to sociologists. Let's look at four main models they developed.

The Concentric Zone Model

To explain how cities expand, sociologist Ernest Burgess (1925) proposed a *concentric-zone model.* As shown in part A of Figure 20.13 on the next page, Burgess noted that a city expands outward from its center. Zone 1 is the central business district. Zone 2, which encircles the downtown area, is in transition. It contains rooming houses and deteriorating housing, which Burgess said breed poverty, disease, and vice. Zone 3 is the area to which thrifty workers have moved in order to escape the zone in transition and yet maintain easy access to their work. Zone 4 contains more expensive apartments, residential hotels, single-family homes, and exclusive areas where the wealthy live. Commuters live in Zone 5, which consists of suburbs or satellite cities that have grown up around transportation routes.

Burgess intended this model to represent "the tendencies of any town or city to expand radially from its central business district." He noted, however, that no "city fits perfectly this ideal scheme." Some cities have physical obstacles such as a lake, river, or railroad that cause their expansion to depart from the model. Burgess also noted that businesses had begun to deviate from the model by locating in outlying zones (see Zone 10). That was in 1925. Burgess didn't know it, but he was seeing the beginning of a major shift that led businesses away from downtown areas to suburban shopping malls. Today, these malls account for most of the country's retail sales.

human ecology Robert Park's term for the relationship between people and their environment (such as land and structures); also known as *urban ecology*

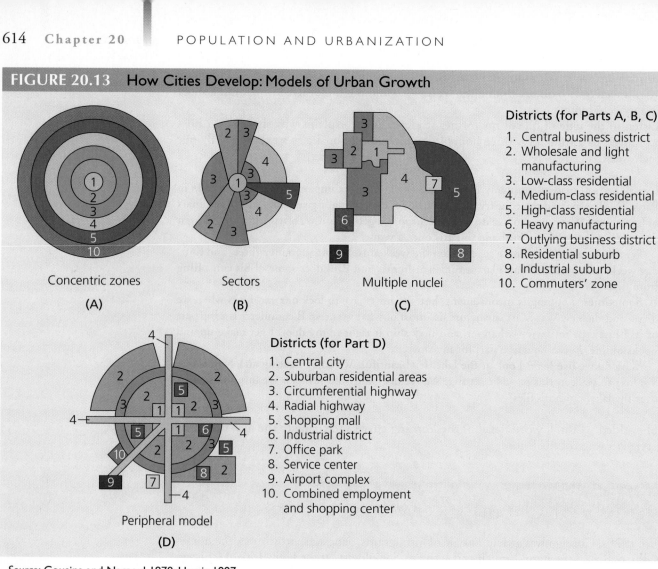

FIGURE 20.13   How Cities Develop: Models of Urban Growth

Concentric zones
(A)

Sectors
(B)

Multiple nuclei
(C)

Districts (for Parts A, B, C)

1. Central business district
2. Wholesale and light manufacturing
3. Low-class residential
4. Medium-class residential
5. High-class residential
6. Heavy manufacturing
7. Outlying business district
8. Residential suburb
9. Industrial suburb
10. Commuters' zone

Peripheral model
(D)

Districts (for Part D)

1. Central city
2. Suburban residential areas
3. Circumferential highway
4. Radial highway
5. Shopping mall
6. Industrial district
7. Office park
8. Service center
9. Airport complex
10. Combined employment and shopping center

Source: Cousins and Nagpaul 1970; Harris 1997.

The Sector Model

Sociologist Homer Hoyt (1939, 1971) noted that a city's concentric zones do not form a complete circle, and he modified Burgess' model of urban growth. As shown in part B of Figure 20.13, a concentric zone can contain several sectors—one of working-class housing, another of expensive homes, a third of businesses, and so on—all competing for the same land.

An example of this dynamic competition is what sociologists call an **invasion–succession cycle.** Poor immigrants and rural migrants settle in low-rent areas. As their numbers swell, they spill over into adjacent areas. Upset by their presence, the middle class moves out, which expands the sector of low-cost housing. The invasion-succession cycle is never complete, for later another group will replace this earlier one. The cycle, in fact, can go full circle. As discussed in the Down-to Earth Sociology box on page 612, in Harlem there has been a switch in the sequence: The "invaders" are the middle class

The Multiple-Nuclei Model

Geographers Chauncey Harris and Edward Ullman noted that some cities have several centers or nuclei (Harris and Ullman 1945; Ullman and Harris 1970). As shown in part C of Figure 20.13, each nucleus contains some specialized activity. A familiar example is the clustering of fast-food restaurants in one area and automobile dealers in another. Sometimes similar activities are grouped together because they profit from cohesion; retail districts, for example, draw more customers if there are more stores. Other clustering occurs because some types of land use, such as factories and expensive homes, are incompatible with one another. One result is that services are not spread evenly throughout the city.

invasion–succession cycle
the process of one group of people displacing a group whose racial–ethnic or social class characteristics differ from their own

The Peripheral Model

Chauncey Harris (1997) also developed the peripheral model shown in part D of Figure 20.13. This model portrays the impact of radial highways on the movement of people and services away from the central city to the city's periphery, or outskirts. It also shows the development of industrial and office parks.

Critique of the Models

These models tell only part of the story. They are time bound, for medieval cities didn't follow these patterns (see the photo on page 605). In addition, they do not account for urban planning policies. England, for example, has planning laws that preserve green belts (trees and farmlands) around the city. This prevents urban sprawl: Wal-Mart cannot buy land outside the city and put up a store; instead, it must locate in the downtown area with the other stores. Norwich has 250,000 people—yet the city ends abruptly in a green belt where pheasants skitter across plowed fields while sheep graze in verdant meadows (Milbank 1995).

If you were to depend on these models, you would be surprised when you visit the cities of the Least Industrialized Nations. There, the wealthy often claim the inner city, where fine restaurants and other services are readily accessible. Tucked behind walls and protected from public scrutiny, they enjoy luxurious homes and gardens. The poor, in contrast, especially rural migrants, settle in areas outside the city—or, as in the case of El Tiro, featured in the photo essay on pages 606–607, on top of piles of garbage in what used to be the outskirts of a city. This topic is discussed in the Cultural Diversity box on the next page.

City Life

Life in cities is filled with contrasts. Let's look at two of those contrasts, alienation and community.

Alienation in the City

In a classic essay, sociologist Louis Wirth (1938) noted that urban dwellers live anonymous lives marked by segmented and superficial encounters. This type of relationship, he said, undermines kinship and neighborhood, the traditional bases of social control and feelings of solidarity. Urbanites then grow aloof and indifferent to other people's problems. In short, the price of the personal freedom that the city offers is alienation. Seldom, however, does alienation get to this point:

> In crowded traffic on a bridge going into Detroit, Deletha Word bumped the car ahead of her. The damage was minor, but the driver, Martell Welch, jumped out. Cursing, he pulled Deletha from her car, pushed her onto the hood, and began beating her. Martell's friends got out to watch. One of them held Deletha down while Martell took a car jack and smashed Deletha's car. Scared for her life, Deletha broke away, fleeing to the bridge's railing. Martell and his friends taunted her, shouting, "Jump, bitch, jump!" Deletha plunged to her death. (*Newsweek*, September 4, 1995). Welch was convicted of second degree murder and sentenced to 16 to 40 years in prison.

This certainly is not an ordinary situation, but anyone who lives in a large city knows that it is prudent to be alert to danger. Even a minor traffic accident can explode into road rage. And you never know who that stranger in the mall—or even next door–really is. Few city dwellers cower in fear, of course, but a common response to the potential of urban danger is to be wary and to "mind your own business." At a minimum, to deal with the crowds of strangers with whom they temporarily share the same urban space, urbanites avoid needless interaction with others and are absorbed in their own affairs. The most common reason for impersonality and self-interest is not fear of danger, however, but the impossibility of dealing with crowds as individuals and the need to find focus within the many stimuli that come buzzing in from the bustle of the city (Berman et al. 2008).

Cultural Diversity around the World

Why City Slums Are Better Than the Country: Urbanization in the Least Industrialized Nations

At the bottom of a ravine near Mexico City is a bunch of shacks. Some of the parents have 14 children. "We used to live up there," Señora Gonzalez gestured toward the mountain, "in those caves. Our only hope was one day to have a place to live. And now we do." She smiled with pride at the jerry-built shacks...each one had a collection of flowers planted in tin cans. "One day, we hope to extend the water pipes and drainage—perhaps even pave . . . ."

And what was the name of her community? Señora Gonzalez beamed. "Esperanza!" (McDowell 1984:172)

Esperanza is the Spanish word for hope.

What started as a trickle has become a torrent. In 1930, only one Latin American city had over a million people—now fifty do! The world's cities are growing by one million people each week (Brockerhoff 2000). The rural poor are flocking to the cities at such a rate that, as we saw in Figure 20.11 on page 609, these nations now contain *most* of the world's largest cities.

When migrants move to U.S. cities, they usually settle in rundown housing near the city's center. The wealthy live in suburbs and luxurious city enclaves. Migrants to cities of the Least Industrialized Nations, in contrast, establish illegal squatter settlements outside the city. There they build shacks from scrap boards, cardboard, and bits of corrugated metal. Even flattened tin cans are scavenged for building material. The squatters enjoy no city facilities—

It is difficult for Americans to grasp the depth of poverty that is the everyday life of hundreds of millions of people across the world. This photo was taken in Bombay, India. In the background, is one of India's main financial centers.

roads, public transportation, water, sewers, or garbage pickup. After thousands of squatters have settled an area, the city reluctantly acknowledges their right to live there and adds bus service and minimal water lines. Hundreds of people use a single spigot. About *5 million* of Mexico City's residents live in such squalid conditions, with hundreds of thousands more pouring in each year.

Why this rush to live in the city under such miserable conditions? On the one hand are the "push" factors that come from the breakdown of traditional rural life. More children are surviving because of a safer water supply and modern medicine. As rural populations multiply, the parents no longer have enough land to divide among their children. With neither land nor jobs, there is hunger and despair. On the other hand are the "pull" factors that draw people to the cities—jobs, schools, housing, and even a more stimulating life.

How will the Least Industrialized Nations adjust to this vast migration? Authorities in Brazil, Guatemala, Venezuela, and other countries have sent in the police and even the army to evict the settlers. Force doesn't work. After a violent dispersal, the settlers return—and others stream in. The roads, water and sewer lines, electricity, schools, and public facilities must be built. But these poor countries don't have the resources to build them. As wrenching as the adjustment will be, to survive these countries must—and somehow will—make the transition. They have no choice.

For Your Consideration

What solutions do you see to the vast migration to the cities of the Least Industrialized Nations?

Community in the City

I don't want to give the impression that the city is inevitably alienating. Far from it. Many people find that living in the city is a pleasant experience. There are good reasons that millions around the world are rushing to live there. And there is another aspect of the attack on Deletha Word. After Deletha went over the railing, two men jumped in after her, risking injury and their own lives in a futile attempt to save her. Some urbanites, then, are far from alienated.

To the contrary, many people find community in the city. Sociologist Herbert Gans, a symbolic interactionist who did participant observation in the West End of Boston, was so impressed with the area's sense of community that he titled his book *The Urban Villagers* (1962). In this book, which has become a classic in sociology, Gans said:

> After a few weeks of living in the West End, my observations—and my perceptions of the area—changed drastically. The search for an apartment quickly indicated that the individual units were usually in much better condition than the outside or the hallways of the buildings. Subsequently, in wandering through the West End, and in using it as a resident, I developed a kind of selective perception, in which my eye focused only on those parts of the area that were actually being used by people. Vacant buildings and boarded-up stores were no longer so visible, and the totally deserted alleys or streets were outside the set of paths normally traversed, either by myself or by the West Enders. The dirt and spilled-over garbage remained, but, since they were concentrated in street gutters and empty lots, they were not really harmful to anyone and thus were not as noticeable as during my initial observations.
>
> Since much of the area's life took place on the street, faces became familiar very quickly. I met my neighbors on the stairs and in front of my building. And, once a shopping pattern developed, I saw the same storekeepers frequently, as well as the area's "characters" who wandered through the streets everyday on a fairly regular route and schedule. In short, the exotic quality of the stores and the residents also wore off as I became used to seeing them.

The city doesn't have to be an anomic, unfriendly place. This elderly man who fell onto the sidewalk in Vienna is helped by concerned strangers. (After I snapped this photo, a police officer approached me and asked why I took it.)

In short, Gans found a *community*, people who identified with the area and with one another. Its residents enjoyed networks of friends and acquaintances. Despite the area's substandard buildings, most West Enders had chosen to live here. *To them, this was a low-rent district, not a slum.*

Most West Enders had low-paying, insecure jobs. Other residents were elderly, living on small pensions. Unlike the middle class, these people didn't care about their "address." The area's inconveniences were something they put up with in exchange for cheap housing. In general, they were content with their neighborhood.

Who Lives in the City?

Whether people find alienation or community in the city depends on whom you are talking about. As with almost everything in life, social class is especially significant. The greater security enjoyed by the city's wealthier residents reduces alienation and increases satisfaction with city life (Santos 2009). There also are different types of urban dwellers, each with distinctive experiences. As we review the five types that Gans (1962, 1968, 1991) identified, try to see where you fit.

The Cosmopolites.   These are the intellectuals, professionals, artists, and entertainers who have been attracted to the city. They value its conveniences and cultural benefits.

The Singles.   Usually in their early 20s to early 30s, the singles have settled in the city temporarily. For them, urban life is a stage in their life course. Businesses and services, such as singles bars and apartment complexes, cater to their needs and desires. After they marry, many move to the suburbs.

The Ethnic Villagers.   Feeling a sense of identity, working-class members of the same ethnic group band together. They form tightly knit neighborhoods that resemble villages and small towns. Family- and peer-oriented, they try to isolate themselves from the dangers and problems of urban life.

The Deprived.   Destitute, emotionally disturbed, and having little income, education, or work skills, the deprived live in neighborhoods that are more like urban jungles than urban villages. Some of them stalk those jungles in search of prey. Neither predator nor prey has much hope for anything better in life—for themselves or for their children.

The Trapped.   These people don't live in the area by choice, either. Some were trapped when an ethnic group "invaded" their neighborhood and they could not afford to move. Others found themselves trapped in a downward spiral. They started life in a higher social class, but because of personal problems—mental or physical illness or addiction to alcohol or other drugs—they drifted downward. There also are the elderly who are trapped by poverty and not wanted elsewhere. Like the deprived, the trapped suffer from high rates of assault, mugging, and rape.

Critique.   You probably noticed this inadequacy in Gans' categories, that you can be both a cosmopolite and a single. You might have noticed also that you can be these two things and an ethnic villager as well. Gans also seems to have missed an important type of city dweller—the people who live in the city who don't stand out in any way. They work and marry there and quietly raise their families. They aren't cosmopolites, singles, or ethnic villagers. Neither are they deprived nor trapped. Perhaps we can call these the "Just Plain Folks."

In Sum: Within the city's rich mosaic of social diversity, not all urban dwellers experience the city in the same way. Each group has its own lifestyle, and each has distinct experiences. Some people welcome the city's cultural diversity and mix with several groups. Others find community by retreating into the security of ethnic enclaves. Still others feel trapped and deprived. To them, the city is an urban jungle. It poses threats to their health and safety, and their lives are filled with despair.

Where do you think these people fit in Gans' classification of urban dwellers?

The Norm of Noninvolvement and the Diffusion of Responsibility

Urban dwellers try to avoid intrusions from strangers. As they go about their everyday lives in the city, they follow a *norm of noninvolvement.*

> To do this, we sometimes use props such as newspapers to shield ourselves from others and to indicate our inaccessibility for interaction. In effect, we learn to "tune others out." In this regard, we might see the [iPod] as the quintessential urban prop in that it allows us to be tuned in and tuned out at the same time. It is a device that allows us to enter our own private world and thereby effectively to close off encounters with others. The use of such devices protects our "personal space," along with our body demeanor and facial expression (the passive "mask" or even scowl that persons adopt on subways). (Karp et al. 1991)

Social psychologists John Darley and Bibb Latané (1968) ran the series of experiments featured in Chapter 6, pages 162–163. In their experiments, they uncovered the *diffusion of responsibility*—the more bystanders there are, the less likely people are to help. As a group grows, people's sense of responsibility becomes diffused, with each person assuming that *another* will do the responsible thing. "With these other people here, it is not *my* responsibility," they reason.

The diffusion of responsibility helps to explain why people can ignore the plight of others. Those who did nothing to intervene in the attack on Deletha Word were *not* uncaring people. Each felt that others might do something. Then, too, there was the norm of noninvolvement—helpful for getting people through everyday city life but, unfortunately, dysfunctional in some crucial situations.

To this dispassionate analysis of diffusion of responsibility and norm of noninvolvement, we can add this: These people were scared. They didn't want to get hurt. The fears nurtured by events like the sudden attack on a motorist, as well as the city's many rapes and muggings, make many people want to retreat to a safe haven. This topic is discussed in the Down-to-Earth Sociology box below.

Down-to-Earth Sociology
Urban Fear and the Gated Fortress

To protect themselves, primarily from the poor, the upper middle class increasingly seeks sanctuary behind gated communities. This photo was taken in Florida.

Gated neighborhoods—where gates open and close to allow or prevent access to a neighborhood—are not new. They always have been available to the rich. What is new is the rush of the upper middle class to towns where they pay high taxes to keep all of the town's facilities private. Even the city's streets are private.

Towns cannot discriminate on the basis of religion or race–ethnicity, but they can—and do—discriminate on the basis of social class. Klahanie, Washington, is an excellent example. Begun in 1985, it was supposed to take twenty years to develop. With its winding streets, pavilions, gardens, swimming pools, parks, private libraries, infant-toddler playcourt, and 25 miles of hiking-bicycling-running trails on 900 acres of open space, Easter egg hunts, and Fourth of July parties, demand for the $300,000 to $500,000 homes nestled by a lake in this private community exceeded supply (Egan 1995; Klahanie Association Web site 2009).

As the upper middle class flees urban areas and tries to build a bucolic dream, we will see many more private towns. A strong sign of the future is Celebration, a town of 20,000 people planned and built by the Walt Disney Company just five minutes from Disney World. Celebration boasts the usual school, hospital, and restaurants. In addition, Celebration offers a Robert Trent Jones golf course, walking and bicycling paths, a hotel with a lighthouse tower and bird sanctuary, a health and fitness center with a rock-climbing wall, and its own cable TV channel. With fiber-optic technology, the residents of private communities can remain locked within their sanctuaries and still be connected to the outside world.

For Your Consideration

Community involves a sense of togetherness, an identifying with one another. Can you explain how this concept also contains the idea of separateness from others (not just in the example of gated communities)? What will our future be if we become a nation of gated communities, where middle-class homeowners withdraw into private domains, separating themselves from the rest of the nation?

As cities evolve, so does architecture. Designed to look like an Arabian sail ship, this building, the world's second largest hotel, is located on an artificial island in Dubai, United Arab Emirates. As a sign of changing times, the building was designed by a British architect and built by a South African construction company.

Urban Problems and Social Policy

To close this chapter, let's look at the primary reasons that U.S. cities have declined, and then consider the potential of urban revitalization.

Suburbanization

The U.S. city has been the loser in the transition to the suburbs. As people moved out of the city, businesses and jobs followed. White-collar corporations, such as insurance companies, were the first to move their offices to the suburbs. They were soon followed by manufacturers. This process has continued so relentlessly that today twice as many manufacturing jobs are located in the suburbs as in the city (Palen 2008). As the city's tax base shrank, it left a budget squeeze that affected not only parks, zoos, libraries, and museums, but also the city's basic services—its schools, streets, sewer and water systems, and police and fire departments.

This shift in population and resources left behind people who had no choice but to stay in the city. As we reviewed in Chapter 12, sociologist William Julius Wilson says that this exodus transformed the inner city into a ghetto. Left behind were families and individuals who, lacking training and skills, were trapped by poverty, unemployment, and welfare dependency. Also left behind were those who prey on others through street crime. The term *ghetto*, says Wilson, "suggests that a fundamental social transformation has taken place...that groups represented by this term are collectively different from and much more socially isolated from those that lived in these communities in earlier years" (quoted in Karp et al. 1991).

City Versus Suburb.   Having made the move out of the city—or having been born in a suburb and preferring to stay there—suburbanites want the city to keep its problems to itself. They reject proposals to share suburbia's revenues with the city and oppose measures that would allow urban and suburban governments joint control over what has become a contiguous mass of people and businesses. Suburban leaders generally believe that it is in their best interests to remain politically, economically, and socially separate from their nearby city. They do not mind going to the city to work, or venturing there on weekends for the diversions it offers, but they do not want to help pay the city's expenses.

It is likely that the mounting bill ultimately will come due, however, and that suburbanites will have to pay for their uncaring attitude toward the urban disadvantaged. Karp et al. (1991) put it this way:

> It may be that suburbs can insulate themselves from the problems of central cities, at least for the time being. In the long run, though, there will be a steep price to pay for the failure of those better off to care compassionately for those at the bottom of society.

Our occasional urban riots may be part of that bill—perhaps just the down payment.

Suburban Flight.   In some places, the bill is coming due quickly. As they age, some suburbs are becoming mirror images of the city that their residents so despise. Suburban crime, the flight of the middle class, a shrinking tax base, and eroding services create a spiraling sense of insecurity, stimulating more middle-class flight (Palen 2008; Katz and Bradley 2009). Figure 20.14 on the next page illustrates this process, which is new to the urban-suburban scene.

Disinvestment and Deindustrialization

As the cities' tax base shrank and their services declined, neighborhoods deteriorated, and banks began **redlining**: Afraid of loans going bad, bankers would draw a line around a

redlining a decision by the officers of a financial institution not to make loans in a particular area

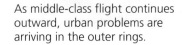

FIGURE 20.14   Urban Growth and Urban Flight

50 years ago	25 years ago	Now

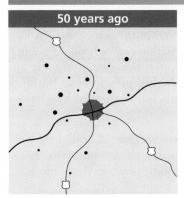 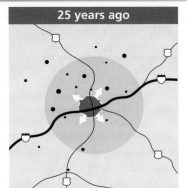

At first, the city and surrounding villages grew independently.

As city dwellers fled urban decay, they created a ring of suburbs.

As middle-class flight continues outward, urban problems are arriving in the outer rings.

problem area on a map and refuse to make loans for housing or businesses there. This **disinvestment** (withdrawal of investment) pushed these areas into further decline. Youth gangs, muggings, and murders are common in these areas, but good jobs are not. All are woven into this process of disinvestment.

The globalization of capitalism has also left a heavy mark on U.S. cities. As we reviewed in Chapter 14, to compete in the global market, many U.S. industries abandoned local communities and moved their factories to countries where labor costs are lower. This process, called **deindustrialization,** made U.S. industries more competitive, but it eliminated millions of U.S. manufacturing jobs. Lacking training in the new information technologies, many poor people are locked out of the benefits of the postindustrial economy that is engulfing the United States. Left behind in the inner cities, many live in despair.

The Potential of Urban Revitalization

Social policy usually takes one of two forms. The first is to tear down and rebuild—something that is fancifully termed **urban renewal.** The result is the renewal of an area—but *not* for the benefit of its inhabitants. Stadiums, high-rise condos, luxury hotels, and boutiques replace run-down, cheap housing. Outpriced, the area's inhabitants are displaced into adjacent areas.

The second is some sort of **enterprise zone,** a designated area of the city that offers economic incentives, such as reduced taxes, to businesses that move into it. Although the intention is good, the usual result is failure. Most businesses refuse to locate in high-crime areas. Those that do relocate pay a high price for security and losses from crime, which can eat up the tax savings. If workers are hired from within the problem area and the jobs pay a decent wage, which most do not, the workers move to better neighborhoods—which doesn't help the area (Lemann 1994). After all, who chooses to live with the fear of violence?

A form of the enterprise zone, called *Federal Empowerment Zones,* has brought some success. In addition to tax breaks, this program offers low-interest loans targeted for redeveloping an area. It is, in effect, the opposite of disinvestment, which devastates areas. The Down-to-Earth Sociology box on page 612 featured the renaissance of Harlem. Stimulating this change was the designation of Harlem as a Federal Empowerment Zone. The economic incentives lured grocery stores, dry cleaners, and video stores, attracting urbanites who expect such services. As middle-class people moved back in, the demand for more specialty shops followed. A self-feeding cycle of investment and hope began, replacing the self-feeding cycle of despair, crime, and drug use that accompanies disinvestment.

U.S. cities can be revitalized and made into safe and decent places to live. There is nothing in the nature of cities that turns them into dangerous slums. If U.S. cities are to change,

disinvestment the withdrawal of investments by financial institutions, which seals the fate of an urban area

deindustrialization the process of industries moving out of a country or region

urban renewal the rehabilitation of a rundown area, which usually results in the displacement of the poor who are living in that area

enterprise zone the use of economic incentives in a designated area to encourage investment

U.S. suburbs were once unplanned, rambling affairs that took irregular shapes as people moved away from the city. Today's suburbs tend to be planned to precise details even before the first resident moves in. This photo is of a suburb outside of Venice, CA.

they need to become top agenda items of the U.S. government. Adequate resources in terms of money and human talents must be focused on overcoming urban woes. That we are beginning to see success in Harlem, Chicago's North Town, and even in formerly riot-torn East Los Angeles indicates that the transformation can be brought about.

Replacing old buildings with new ones, however, is not the answer. Instead, we need to apply sociological principles of building community. Here are three guiding principles suggested by sociologist William Flanagan (1990):

Scale. Regional and national planning is necessary. Local jurisdictions, with their many rivalries, competing goals, and limited resources, end up with a hodgepodge of mostly unworkable solutions.

Livability. Cities must be appealing and meet human needs, especially the need of community. This will attract the middle classes into the city, which will increase its tax base. In turn, this will help finance the services that make the city more livable.

Social justice. In the final analysis, social policy must be evaluated by how it affects people. "Urban renewal" programs that displace the poor for the benefit of the middle class and wealthy do not pass this standard. The same would apply to solutions that create "livability" for select groups but neglect the poor and the homeless.

Most actions taken to solve urban problems are window dressings for politicians who want to *appear* as though they are doing something constructive. The solution is to avoid Band-Aids that cover up the problems that hurt our quality of life and to address their *root* causes—poverty, poor schools, crimes of violence, lack of jobs, and an inadequate tax base to provide the amenities that enhance our quality of life and attract people to the city.

By the Numbers: *Then and Now*

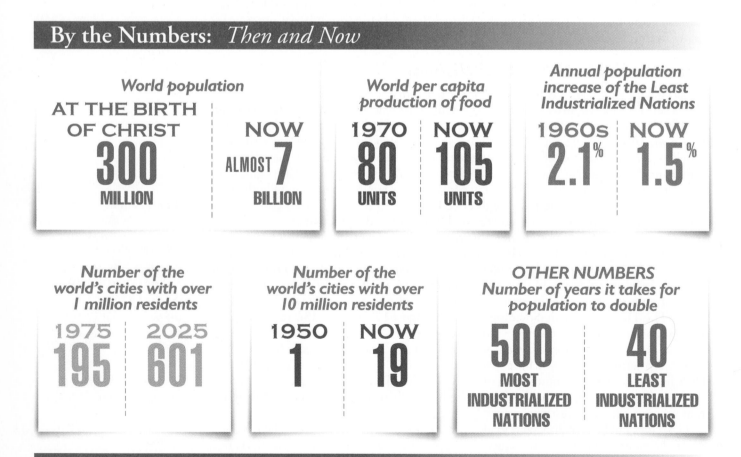

World population

AT THE BIRTH OF CHRIST
300 MILLION

NOW
ALMOST **7** BILLION

World per capita production of food

1970
80 UNITS

NOW
105 UNITS

Annual population increase of the Least Industrialized Nations

1960s
2.1%

NOW
1.5%

Number of the world's cities with over 1 million residents

1975
195

2025
601

Number of the world's cities with over 10 million residents

1950
1

NOW
19

OTHER NUMBERS Number of years it takes for population to double

500 MOST INDUSTRIALIZED NATIONS

40 LEAST INDUSTRIALIZED NATIONS

SUMMARY *and* REVIEW

A Planet with No Space for Enjoying Life?

What debate did Thomas Malthus initiate?

In 1798, Thomas Malthus analyzed the surge in Europe's population. He concluded that the world's population will outstrip its food supply. The debate between today's New Malthusians and those who disagree, the Anti-Malthusians, continues. Pp. 592–595.

Why are people starving?

Starvation is not due to a lack of food in the world, for there is now *more* food for each person in the entire world than there was fifty years ago. Rather, starvation is the result of a maldistribution of food, which is primarily due to drought and civil war. Pp. 595–597.

Population Growth

Why do people in the poor nations have so many children?

In the Least Industrialized Nations, children are often viewed as gifts from God. In addition, they cost little to rear, contribute to the family income at an early age, and provide the parents' social security. These are powerful motivations to have large families. Pp. 597–601.

What are the three demographic variables?

To compute population growth, demographers use *fertility, mortality,* and *migration.* They follow the **basic demographic equation,** births minus deaths plus net migration equals the growth rate. Pp. 601–603.

Why is forecasting population difficult?

A nation's growth rate is affected by unanticipated variables—from economic cycles, wars, and famines to industrialization and government policies. Pp. 603–605.

The Development of Cities

How are cities related to farming and the Industrial Revolution?

Cities can develop only if there is an agricultural surplus large enough to free people from food production. The primary impetus to the development of cities was the invention of the plow. After the Industrial Revolution stimulated rapid transportation and communication, cities grew quickly. Today **urbanization** is so extensive that some cities have become **metropolises,** dominating the areas adjacent to them. Some metropolises spill over into each other, forming a **megalopolis.** Pp. 605–611.

What is the rural rebound?

As people flee cities and suburbs, the population of most U.S. rural counties is growing. This is a fundamental departure from a trend that had been in place for a couple of hundred years. Pp. 611–613.

Models of Urban Growth

What models of urban growth have been proposed?

The primary models are concentric zone, sector, multiple-nuclei, and peripheral. These models fail to account for ancient and medieval cities, many European cities, cities in the Least Industrialized Nations, and urban planning. Pp. 613–615.

City Life

Who lives in the city?

Some people experience **alienation** in the city; others find **community** in it. What people find depends largely on their background and urban networks. Five types of people who live in cities are cosmopolites, singles, ethnic villagers, the deprived, and the trapped. Pp. 615–619.

Urban Problems and Social Policy

Why have U.S. cities declined?

Three primary reasons for the decline of U.S. cities are **suburbanization** (as people moved to the suburbs, the tax base of cities eroded and services deteriorated), **disinvestment** (banks withdrawing their financing), and **deindustrialization** (which caused a loss of jobs). Pp. 620–621.

What social policy can salvage U.S. cities?

Three guiding principles for developing urban social policy are scale, livability, and social justice. Pp. 621–622.

THINKING CRITICALLY *ABOUT* Chapter 20

1. Do you think that the world is threatened by a population explosion? Use data from this chapter to support your position.

2. Why do people find alienation or community in the city?

3. What are the causes of urban problems, and what can we do to solve those problems?

Collective Behavior and Social Movements

Texas

The news spread like wildfire. A police officer had been killed. In just twenty minutes, the white population was armed and heading for the cabin. Men and mere boys, some not more than 12 years old, carried rifles, shotguns, and pistols.

The mob, now swollen to about four hundred, surrounded the log cabin. Tying a rope around the man's neck, they dragged him to the center of town. While the men argued about the best way to kill him, the women and children shouted their advice—some to hang him, others to burn him alive.

One of the men poured oil over him. Another lit a match.

Someone pulled a large wooden box out of a store and placed it in the center of the street. Others filled it with straw. Then they lifted the man, the rope still around his neck, and shoved him head first into the box. One of the men poured oil over him. Another lit a match.

As the flames shot upward, the man managed to lift himself out of the box, his body a mass of flames. Trying to shield his face and eyes from the fire, he ran the length of the rope, about twenty feet, when someone yelled, "Shoot!" In an instant, dozens of shots rang out. Men and boys walked to the lifeless body and emptied their guns into it.

They dragged the man's body back to the burning box, then piled on more boxes from the stores, and poured oil over them. Each time someone threw on more oil and the flames shot upward, the crowd roared shouts of approval.

Standing about seventy-five feet away, I could smell the poor man's burning flesh. No one tried to hide their identity. I could clearly see town officials help in the burning. The inquest, dutifully held by the coroner, concluded that the man met death "at the hands of an enraged mob unknown to the jury." What else could he conclude? Any jury from this town would include men who had participated in the man's death.

They dug a little hole at the edge of the street, and dumped in it the man's ashes and what was left of his body.

The man's name was Sam Pettie, known by everybody to be quiet and inoffensive. I can't mention my name. If I did, I would be committing suicide.

—Based on a May 1914 letter to *The Crisis*

625

collective behavior extraordinary activities carried out by groups of people; includes lynchings, rumors, panics, urban legends, and fads and fashions

collective mind Gustave LeBon's term for the tendency of people in a crowd to feel, think, and act in extraordinary ways

circular reaction Robert Park's term for a back-and-forth communication among the members of a crowd whereby a "collective impulse" is transmitted

Collective Behavior

Why did people in this little town "go mad"? These men—and the women who shouted suggestions about how to kill the captured man—were ordinary, law-abiding citizens. Even some of the "pillars of the community" joined in the vicious killing of Sam Pettie, who may well have been innocent.

Lynching is a form of **collective behavior,** actions by a group of people who bypass the usual norms governing their behavior and do something unusual (Turner and Killian 1987; Harper and Leicht 2002). Collective behavior is a broad term. It includes not only such violent acts as lynchings and riots but also rumors, panics, fads, and fashions. Before examining its specific forms, let's look at theories that seek to explain collective behavior.

Early Explanations: The Transformation of the Individual

When people can't figure something out, they often resort to using "madness" as an explanation. People may say, "She went 'off her rocker'—that's why she drove her car into the river." "He must have 'gone nuts,' or he wouldn't have shot into the crowd." Early explanations of collective behavior were linked to such assumptions. Let's look at how these ideas developed.

How the Crowd Transforms the Individual

The study of collective behavior began when Charles Mackay (1814–1889), a British journalist, noticed that "country folks," who ordinarily are reasonable sorts of people, sometimes "went mad" and did "disgraceful and violent things" when they formed a crowd. The best explanation Mackay (1852) could come up with was that people had a "herd mentality"—they were like a herd of cows that suddenly stampede.

About fifty years later, Gustave LeBon (1841–1931), a French psychologist, built on this initial idea. In an 1895 book, LeBon stressed how people feel anonymous in crowds, less accountable for what they do. Some even develop feelings of invincibility and come to think that they can do almost anything. A **collective mind** develops, he said, and people are swept up by almost any suggestion. Then contagion, something like mass hypnosis, takes over, releasing the destructive instincts that society so carefully represses.

Robert Park (1864–1944), a U.S. sociologist who studied in Germany and wrote a 1904 dissertation on the nature of the crowd, was influenced by LeBon (McPhail 1991). After Park joined the faculty at the University of Chicago, he added the ideas of social unrest and circular reaction. He said,

Social unrest . . . is transmitted from one individual to another . . . so that the manifestations of discontent in A [are] communicated to B, and from B reflected back to A. (Park and Burgess 1921)

Park used the term **circular reaction** to refer to this back-and-forth communication. Circular reaction, he

Race relations in the United States have gone through many stages, some of them very tense. This photo was taken in Birmingham, Alabama, in 1963, at the height of the Civil Rights Movement. The fire department is dispersing demonstrators who are protesting segregation.

said, creates a "collective impulse" that comes to "dominate all members of the crowd." If "collective impulse" sounds just like LeBon's "collective mind," that's because it really is. As noted, Park was influenced by LeBon, and his slightly different term did not change the basic idea at all.

The Acting Crowd

Herbert Blumer (1900–1987), who studied under Park, synthesized LeBon's and Park's ideas. As you can see from Figure 21.1, Blumer (1939) identified five stages that precede what he called an **acting crowd,** an excited group that moves toward a goal. This model still dominates today's police manuals on crowd behavior (McPhail 1989). Let's apply it to the killing of Sam Pettie.

1. *A background of tension or unrest.* At the root of collective behavior is a background condition of tension or unrest. Disturbed about some condition of society, people become apprehensive. This makes them vulnerable to rumors and suggestions. Sam Pettie was killed during the early 1900s. At this time, southern life was in upheaval. With the country industrializing, millions of Americans were moving from farm to city in search of jobs, and from South to North. Left behind were many poor, rural southerners, white and black, who faced a bleak future. In addition, African Americans were questioning the legitimacy of their low status and deprivation.

2. *Exciting event.* An exciting event occurs, one so startling that people become preoccupied with it. In this instance, that event was the killing of a police officer.

3. *Milling.* Next comes **milling,** people standing or walking around, talking about the exciting event. A circular reaction then sets in. Picking up cues about the "right" way to think and feel, people reinforce them in one another. Members of the mob that killed Sam Pettie milled only a short time, but while they did so they became increasingly agitated as they discussed the officer's death.

4. *A common object of attention.* In this stage, people's attention becomes riveted on some aspect of the event. They get caught up in the collective excitement. In this case, people's attention turned to Sam Pettie. Someone may have said that he had been talking to the officer or that they had been arguing.

acting crowd an excited group of people who move toward a goal

milling a crowd standing or walking around as they talk excitedly about some event

---

FIGURE 21.1   Blumer's Model of How an Acting Crowd Develops

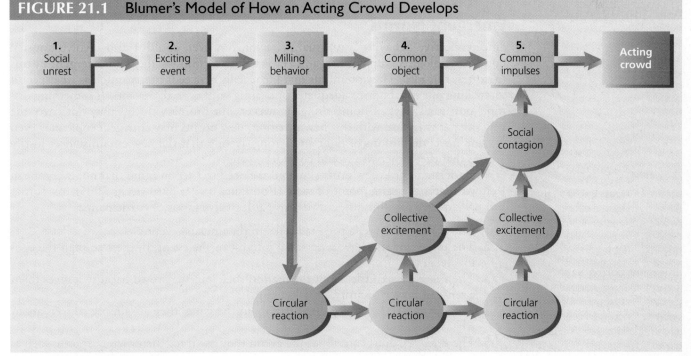

Source: Based on McPhail 1991:11.

5. *Common impulses.* People get the feeling that they are in agreement about what should be done. These common impulses are stimulated by *social contagion,* a sense of excitement that is passed from one person to another. In this instance, people concluded that only the killer's immediate death would be adequate vengeance.

Acting crowds aren't always negative or destructive, as this one was. Some involve spontaneous demonstrations directed against oppression. Nor are they all serious, for students having a food fight in a cafeteria are also acting crowds.

The Contemporary View: The Rationality of the Crowd

If we were to see a lynching—or a screaming mob or a prison riot—most of us might agree with LeBon that some sort of "madness" had swept over the crowd. Sociologists today, however, point out that beneath the chaotic surface, crowds are actually quite rational (Yamaguchi 2000; Horowitz 2001). They point out that crowd participants take deliberate steps to reach some goal. As sociologist Clark McPhail (1991) says, even a lynch mob is cooperative—someone gets the rope while others hold the victim, some tie the knot, and others hoist the body. This is exactly what you saw in Pettie's execution—the men working together: the rope, the boxes, the straw, and the oil.

The Minimax Strategy

A general principle of human behavior is that we try to minimize our costs and maximize our rewards. Sociologist Richard Berk (1974) called this a **minimax strategy.** The fewer costs and the more rewards we anticipate from something, the more likely we are to do it. For example, if we think that others will approve an act, the chances increase that we will do it. Whether someone is yelling for the referee's blood after a bad call in a football game, or shouting for real blood as a member of a lynch mob, this principle applies. In short, whether people are playing a video game with a few friends or are part of a mob, the principles of human behavior remain the same.

Emergent Norms

Since collective behavior is unusual behavior, however, could it also involve unusual norms? Sociologists Ralph Turner and Lewis Killian (1987) use the term **emergent norms** to express this idea. They point out that life usually proceeds pretty much as we expect it to, making our usual norms adequate for dealing with everyday events. If something disrupts our usual ways of doing things, however, our ordinary norms may not cover the new situation. To deal with this new situation, new norms may emerge. People may even develop novel definitions of right and wrong, feeling that the new circumstances justify actions that they otherwise would consider wrong.

To understand how new norms emerge, we need to keep in mind that not everyone in a crowd shares the same point of view (Rodríguez 1994; Surowiecki 2005). As Turner and Killian (1987) point out, crowds have at least five kinds of participants:

1. The *ego-involved* feel a personal stake in the unusual event.
2. The *concerned* also have a personal interest in the event, but less so than the ego-involved.
3. The *insecure* care little about the matter; they join the crowd because it gives them a sense of power, security, or belonging.
4. The *curious spectators* also care little about the issue; they are simply curious about what is going on.
5. The *exploiters* don't care about the event; they use it for their own purposes, such as hawking food or T-shirts. For them, a rock concert would serve just as well.

minimax strategy Richard Berk's term for the efforts people make to minimize their costs and maximize their rewards

emergent norms Ralph Turner and Lewis Killian's term for the idea that people develop new norms to cope with a new situation; used to explain crowd behavior

The "ego-involved" are the most important for setting the crowd on a particular course of action. Some of them make suggestions about what should be done; others simply start doing something. As the "concerned" join in, they, too, influence the crowd. If things get heated up, the "insecure" and the "curious spectators" may also join in. Although the "exploiters" are unlikely to participate, they do lend passive support to the crowd. A common mood completes the stage for new norms to emerge: Activities that are "not OK" in everyday life now may seem "OK"—whether they involve throwing bottles at the cops or shouting obscenities at the college president.

This analysis of emergent norms helps us to see that collective behavior is *rational*. The crowd, for example, does not consider all suggestions made by the ego-involved to be equal: To be acceptable, suggestions must match predispositions that the crowd already has. This current view, then, is a far cry from earlier interpretations that people are so transformed by a crowd that they go out of their minds.

riot violent crowd behavior directed at people and property

Forms of Collective Behavior

Sociologists analyze collective behavior the same way they do other forms of behavior. They ask their usual questions about interaction, such as How do people influence one another? What is the significance of the participants' age, gender, race–ethnicity, and social class? How did they perceive the situation? How did their perceptions get translated into action? In other words, sociologists view collective behavior as the actions of ordinary people who are responding to extraordinary situations.

In addition to lynchings, collective behavior includes riots, rumors, panics, mass hysteria, moral panics, fads, fashions, and urban legends. Let's look at each.

Riots

The nation watched in horror. White Los Angeles police officers had been caught on videotape beating an African American traffic violator with their nightsticks. The videotape showed the officers savagely bringing their nightsticks down on a man prostrate at their feet. Television stations around the United States—and the world—broadcast the pictures to stunned audiences.

When the officers went on trial for beating the man identified as Rodney King, how could the verdict be anything but guilty? Yet a jury consisting of eleven whites and one Asian American found the officers innocent of using excessive force. The result was a riot—violent crowd behavior directed at people and property. Within minutes of the verdict, angry crowds began to gather in Los Angeles. That night, mobs set fire to businesses, and looting and arson began in earnest. The rioting spread to other cities, including Atlanta, Tampa, Las Vegas, and even Madison, Wisconsin. Whites and Koreans were favorite targets of violence.

Americans sat transfixed before their television sets as they saw parts of Los Angeles go up in flames and looters carrying television sets and lugging sofas in full view of the Los Angeles Police Department, which took no steps to stop them. Seared into the public's collective consciousness was the sight of Reginald Denny, a 36-year-old white

In this photo from the Los Angeles riot of 1992, can you identify emergent norms?

truck driver who had been yanked from his truck. As Denny sat dazed in the street, Damian Williams, laughing, broke the truck driver's skull with a piece of concrete.

On the third night, after 4,000 fires had been set and more than thirty people killed, President George Bush announced on national television that the U.S. Justice Department had appointed prosecutors to pursue federal charges against the police officers. The president stated that he had ordered the Seventh Infantry, SWAT teams, and the FBI into Los Angeles. He also federalized the California National Guard and placed it under the command of Gen. Colin Powell, the chairman of the Joint Chiefs of Staff. Rodney King went on television and tearfully pleaded for peace.

The Los Angeles riot was the bloodiest since the Civil War. Before it was over, fifty-four people lost their lives, more than 2,000 people were treated in hospital emergency rooms, thousands of businesses were burned, and about $1 billion of property was destroyed. Two of the police officers were later sentenced to two years in prison on federal charges, and King was awarded $3.8 million in damages. (Rose 1992; Stevens and Lubman 1992; Cannon 1998; "Rodney King" 2007)

The *background conditions* of urban riots are frustration and anger brought on by feelings of deprivation. Frustration and anger simmer in people who feel that they have been denied jobs and justice and are being singled out by the police. If a *precipitating event* brings these pent-up feelings to a boiling point, they can erupt in collective violence. All these conditions existed in the Los Angeles riot, with the jury's verdict being the precipitating event.

Sociologists have found that it is not only the deprived who participate in riots. The first outbursts over the Rodney King verdict didn't come from the poorest neighborhoods, but, rather, from stable neighborhoods. Similarly, after the assassination of Dr. Martin Luther King, Jr., in 1968, when many U.S. cities erupted in riots, even people with good jobs participated (McPhail 1991). Why would middle-class people participate in riots? The answer, says sociologist Victor Rodríguez (1994), is the same: frustration and anger. Even minorities with good jobs and middle-class lives are sometimes treated as second-class citizens, creating simmering resentments that a precipitating event brings to the surface.

Also participating in riots are opportunists—people who feel neither rage at their situation in life nor outrage at the precipitating event. For them, a riot is a handy event. Not only do they get to participate in something exciting, but they also get an opportunity to loot stores.

In Sum: *The event that precipitates a riot is important, but so is the riot's general context.* Both must be present. The precipitating event is the match that lights the fuel, but the fuel is the background of resentment, tension, and unrest. Beneath what may appear to be a placid surface can lie seething rage. To be set ablaze, it takes but a match, such as the Rodney King verdict.

Rumors

Obscene, subliminal messages from the Magic Kingdom?

In *The Lion King*, Simba, the cuddly lion star, stirs up a cloud of dust that, floating off the screen, spells S-E-X. In *The Little Mermaid,* the bishop who is presiding over a wedding, becomes noticeably aroused. And in *Aladdin,* the handsome young title character murmurs, "All good children, take off your clothes."

Ann Runge, a mother of eight who owned stacks of Disney animated videos, said, "I felt as though I had entrusted my kids to pedophiles." (Bannon 1995)

A **rumor** is unverified information about some topic of interest that is passed from one person to another. Thriving on conditions of ambiguity, rumors fill in missing information (Turner 1964; DiFonzo 2008). In response to this particular rumor, Disney reported that Aladdin really says "Scat, good tiger, take off and go." The line is hard to understand, however, leaving enough ambiguity for others to hear what they want to hear, and even to insist that the line is an invitation to a teenage orgy. Similar ambiguity remains with Simba's dust and the aroused bishop.

rumor unfounded information spread among people

Most rumors are short-lived. They arise in a situation of ambiguity, only to dissipate when they are replaced by factual information—or by another rumor. Occasionally, however, a rumor has a long life.

> In the eighteenth and nineteenth centuries, for no known reason, healthy people would grow weak and slowly waste away. No one understood the cause, and people said they had consumption (now called tuberculosis). People were terrified as they saw their loved ones wither into shells of their former selves. With no one knowing when the disease would strike, or who its next victim would be, the rumor began that some of the dead had turned into vampire-like beings. At night, they were coming back from the grave and draining the life out of the living. The evidence: loved ones who wasted away before people's very eyes.
>
> To kill these ghoulish "undead," people began to sneak into graveyards. They would dig up a grave, remove the leg bones and place them crossed on the skeleton's chest, then lay the skull at the feet, forming a skull and crossbones. Having thus killed the "undead," they would rebury the remains. These rumors and the resulting mutilations of the dead continued off and on in New England until the 1890s. (Sledzik and Bellantoni 1994)

Rumors have swirled around the Magic Kingdom's supposed plots to undermine the morality of youth. Could Mickey Mouse be a dark force, and these children his victims? As humorous as this may be, some have taken these rumors seriously.

Why do rumors thrive? The three main factors are importance, ambiguity, and source. Rumors deal with a subject that is important to an individual, they replace ambiguity with some form of certainty, and they are attributed to a credible source. An office rumor may be preceded by "Jane overheard the boss say that . . ."

Rumors thrive on ambiguity and fears, for where people know the facts about a situation a rumor has no life. Surrounded by unexplained illnesses and deaths, however, the New Englanders speculated about why people wasted away. Their conclusion seems bizarre to us, but it provided answers to bewildering events. The Disney rumor may have arisen from fears that the moral fabric of modern society is decaying.

Not only are most rumors short-lived, but most are also of little consequence. As discussed in the Down-to-Earth Sociology box on the next page, however, some rumors not only disrupt people's lives but also lead to the destruction of entire communities.

Rumors usually pass directly from one person to another, although, as with the Tulsa riot, they can originate from the mass media. As the Down-to-Earth Sociology box on page 633 illustrates, the Internet, too, has become a source of rumors.

Panics

The Classic Panic

> In 1938, on the night before Halloween, a radio program of dance music was interrupted by a report that explosions had been observed on the surface of Mars. The announcer added that a cylinder of unknown origin had been discovered embedded in the ground on a farm in New Jersey. The radio station then switched to the farm, where a breathless reporter gave details of horrible-looking Martians coming out of the cylinder. Their death-ray weapons had destructive powers unknown to humans. An astronomer then confirmed that Martians had invaded the Earth.

Perhaps six million Americans heard this radio program. Many missed the announcement at the beginning and somewhere in the middle that this was a dramatization of H. G. Wells' *The War of the Worlds*. Thinking that Martians had really invaded the earth, thousands grabbed their weapons and hid in their basements or ran into the streets. Hundreds bundled up their families and jumped into their cars, jamming the roads as they headed to who knows where.

Panic occurs when people become so fearful that they cannot function normally and may even flee a situation they perceive as threatening. Looking down from our superior place of wisdom, the reaction to this radio program certainly seems humorous. But we need to ask why these people panicked. Psychologist Hadley Cantril (1941) attributed the reaction to widespread

panic the condition of being so fearful that one cannot function normally and may even flee

Down-to-Earth Sociology
Rumors and Riots: An Eyewitness Account of the Tulsa Riot

A family moving after the riot in Tulsa. Note that the man on the passenger side is holding a rifle.

In 1921, a race riot ripped Tulsa, Oklahoma, apart. And it all began with a rumor (Gates 2004). Up to this time, Tulsa's black community had been vibrant and prosperous. Many blacks owned their own businesses and competed successfully with whites. Then on May 31, everything changed after a black man was accused of assaulting a white girl.

Buck Colbert Franklin (Franklin and Franklin 1997), a black attorney in Tulsa at the time, was there. Here is what he says:

> Hundreds of men with drawn guns were approaching from every direction, as far I could see as I stood at the steps of my office, and I was immediately arrested and taken to one of the many detention camps. Even then, airplanes were circling overhead dropping explosives upon the buildings that had been looted, and big trucks were hauling all sorts of furniture and household goods away.

Unlike more recent U.S. riots, these were white looters who were breaking in and burning the homes and businesses of blacks.

Franklin continues:

> Soon I was back upon the streets, but the building where I had my office was a smoldering ruin, and all my lawbooks and office fixtures had been consumed by flames. I went to where my roominghouse had stood a few short hours before, but it was in ashes, with all my clothes and the money to be used in moving my family. As far as one could see, not a Negro dwellinghouse or place of business stood.... Negroes who yesterday were wealthy, living in beautiful homes in ease and comfort, were now beggars, public charges, living off alms.

The rioters burned all black churches, including the imposing Zion Baptist church, which had just been completed. When they finished destroying homes and businesses, block after block lay in ruins, as though a tornado had swept through the area.

And what about the young man who had been accused of assault, the event that precipitated the riot? Franklin says that the police investigated and found that there had been no assault. All the man had done was accidentally step on a lady's foot in a crowded elevator, and, as Franklin says, "She became angry and slapped him, and a fresh, cub newspaper reporter, without any experience and no doubt anxious for a byline, gave out an erroneous report through his paper that a Negro had assaulted a white girl."

For Your Consideration

It is difficult to place ourselves in such a historical mind-set to imagine that stepping on someone's foot could lead to such destruction, but it did. Can you apply the sociological findings on both rumors and riots to explain the riot at Tulsa? Why do you think that so many whites believed this rumor, and why were some of them so intent on destroying this thriving black community? If "seething rage" underlies riots, it should apply to this one, too. What "seething rage" (or resentments or feelings of injustice) do you think were involved?

---

anxiety about world conditions. The Nazis were marching in Europe, and millions of Americans (correctly, as it turned out) were afraid that the United States would get involved in this conflict. War jitters, he said, created fertile ground for the broadcast to touch off a panic.

Contemporary analysts, however, question whether there even was a panic. Sociologist William Bainbridge (1989) acknowledges that some people did become frightened and that a few actually did get in their cars and drive like maniacs. But he says that most of this famous panic was an invention of the news media. Reporters found a good story, and, as some journalists do, they milked it, exaggerating as they went along.

Bainbridge points to a 1973 event in Sweden. To dramatize the dangers of atomic power, Swedish Radio broadcast a play about an accident at a nuclear power plant. Knowing about the 1938 broadcast in the United States, Swedish sociologists were waiting to see what would happen. Might some people fail to realize that it was a dramatization and panic at the threat of ruptured reactors spewing out radioactive gases? The sociologists found no

Down-to-Earth Sociology
You Could Be Next: Danger on the Internet

Life is uncertain, even perilous. That new neighbor who just moved in across the street could be a child molester, the guy next door a rapist. Evil lurks everywhere, and, who knows, you or some little kid could be the next victim.

Or so it can seem. And within this sea of uncertainty comes the Net to feed our gnawing suspicions. Here is an e-mail that I received (reproduced exactly as the original):

> Please, read this very carefully. . . . then send it out to all the people online that you know. Something like this is nothing to take casually; this is something that you do want to pay attention to.
>
> If a guy with a screen-name of SlaveMaster contacts you, do not answer. DO NOT TALK TO THIS PERSON. DO NOT ANSWER ANY OF HIS/HER INSTANT MESSAGES/E-MAIL.
>
> He has killed 56 women (so far) that he has talked to on the Internet.
>
> PLEASE SEND OUT TO ALL THE WOMEN ON YOUR BUDDY LIST. ALSO ASK THEM TO PASS THIS ON.
>
> He has been on Yahoo and AOL and Excite so far. This is no joke!!!

PLEASE SEND THIS TO MEN TOO . . . JUST IN CASE!!!

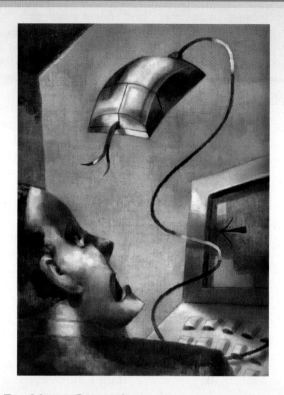

For Your Consideration

How do the three main factors associated with rumors—importance, ambiguity, and source—apply to this note? In what ways do they not apply?

---

panic. A few people did become frightened. Some telephoned family members and the police; others shut windows to keep out the radioactivity—reasonable responses, considering what they thought had occurred.

Yet the Swedish media reported a panic! Apparently, a reporter had telephoned two police departments and learned that each had received calls from concerned citizens. With a deadline hanging over his head, the reporter decided to gamble. He reported that police and fire stations were jammed with citizens, people were flocking to the shelters, and others were fleeing south (Bainbridge 1989).

When panics do occur, they can have devastating consequences.

On September 1, 2005, hundreds of thousands of Iraqis were walking to the tomb of a Shiite martyr. When someone spotted what he thought was a suicide bomber, the rumor spread quickly through the crowd. Thousands of pilgrims who were crossing a bridge scrambled for safety, crushing and trampling to death about 1,000 people.

It is not difficult to understand why these people panicked. At the time, suicide bombers were appearing out of nowhere, raining destruction and death on crowds. To run was a logical response. The consequences, however, were devastating.

Some panics occur because of the fear of getting trapped by fire. Like the Iraqis in the example above, in a frantic effort to escape, hundreds of people lunge for the same exit. Such a panic occurred on Memorial Day weekend in 1977 at the Beverly Hills Supper Club in Southgate, Kentucky.

About half of the Club's 2,500 patrons were crowded into the Cabaret Room. A fire, which began in a small banquet room near the front of the building, burned undetected until it was

role extension the incorporation of additional activities into a role

mass hysteria an imagined threat that causes physical symptoms among a large number of people

beyond control. When employees discovered the fire, they warned patrons. People began to exit in orderly fashion, but when flames rushed in, they trampled one another in a furious attempt to reach the exits. The exits were blocked by masses of screaming people trying to push their way through all at once. The writhing bodies at the exits created further panic among the remainder, who pushed even harder to force their way through the bottlenecks. One hundred sixty-five people died. All but two were within thirty feet of two exits in the Cabaret Room.

Sociologists who studied this panic found the same thing that researchers have discovered in analyzing other disasters. *Not everyone panics.* In disturbances, many people continue to act responsibly (Clarke 2002). Especially important are primary bonds. Parents help their children, for example (Morrow 1995). Gender roles also persist, and more men help women than women help men (Johnson 1993). Even work roles continue to guide some behavior. Sociologists Drue Johnston and Norris Johnson (1989) found that only 29 percent of the employees of the Beverly Hills Supper Club left when they learned of the fire. As noted in Table 21.1, most of the workers helped customers, fought the fire, or searched for friends and relatives.

Sociologists use the term **role extension** to describe the actions of most of these employees. By this term, they mean that the workers extended their occupational role so that it included other activities. Servers, for example, extended their role to include helping people to safety. How do we know that giving help was an extension of their occupational role and not simply a general act of helping? Johnston and Johnson found that servers who were away from their assigned stations returned to them in order to help *their* customers.

In some life-threatening situations in which we might expect panic, we find that a sense of order prevails instead. This seems to have been the case during the attack on the World Trade Center when, at peril to their own lives, people helped injured friends and even strangers escape down many flights of stairs. These people, it would seem, were highly socialized into the collective good, and had a highly developed sense of empathy. But even that is a weak answer. We simply don't know why these people didn't panic when so many others do under threatening situations.

Mass Hysteria

Let's look **mass hysteria,** where an imagined threat causes physical symptoms among large numbers of people. I think you'll enjoy the Down-to-Earth Sociology box on the next page.

Moral Panics

"They touched me down there. Then they killed a horse. They said if I told they would kill my sister."

"They took off my clothes. Then they got in a space ship and flew away."

"It was awful when they killed the baby. There was blood all over."

What would you think if you heard little children saying things like this? You probably would shake your head and wonder what kind of TV shows they had been watching.

But not if you were an investigator in the 1980s in the United States. At that time, rumors swept the country that day care centers were run by monsters who were sexually molesting the little kids.

Prosecutors believed the children who told these stories. They knew their statements about space ships and aliens weren't true, but maybe little pets had been killed and families threatened. There was no evidence, but interrogators kept hammering away at the children. Kids who kept saying that nothing had happened were said to be "in denial."

Prosecutors took their cases to court, and juries believed the kids. That there was no evidence bothered some people, but images of helpless little children—naked, tied up, and

TABLE 21.1 Employees' First Action After Learning of the Fire	
Action	**Percentage**
Left the building	29%
Helped others to leave	41%
Fought or reported the fire	17%
Continued routine activities	7%
Other (e.g., looked for a friend or relative)	5%

Note: Based on interviews with 95 of the 160 employees present at the time of the fire: 48 men and 47 women.
Source: Based on Johnston and Johnson 1989.

Down-to-Earth Sociology
Mass Hysteria

Let's look at five events.

Several hundred years ago, a strange thing happened near Naples, Italy. When people were bitten by tarantulas, not only did they feel breathless and have fast-beating hearts but they also felt unusual sexual urges. As though that weren't enough, they also felt an irresistible urge to dance—and to keep dancing to the point of exhaustion.

The disease was contagious. Even people who hadn't been bitten came down with the same symptoms. The situation got so bad that instead of gathering the summer harvest, whole villages would dance in a frenzy.

A lot of remedies were tried, but nothing seemed to work except music. Bands of musicians traveled from village to village, providing relief to the victims of *tarantism* by playing special "tarantula" music (Bynum 2001).

* * * * *

In the year 2001, in New Delhi, the capital of India, a "monkey-man" stalked people who were sleeping on rooftops during the blistering summer heat. He clawed and bit a hundred victims. People would wake up screaming that the monkey-man was after them. One man was killed when he jumped off the roof of his house during one of the monkey-man's many attacks ("'Monkey' . . . " 2001).

There was no apelike killer.

* * * * *

At the United Arab Emirates University in Al-Ain, twenty-three female students rushed to the hospital emergency room after escaping from a fire in their dormitory. As you might expect from people who barely escaped burning to death, they were screaming, weeping, shaking, and fainting (Amin et al. 1997).

But there was no fire. A student had been burning incense in her room. The fumes of the burning incense had been mistaken for the smell of a fire.

* * * * *

People across France and Belgium became sick after drinking Coca-Cola. After a quick investigation, "experts" diagnosed the problem as "bad carbon dioxide and a fungicide." Coke recalled 15 *million* cases of its soft drink ("Coke . . . " 1999).

Later investigations revealed that there was nothing wrong with the drink.

* * * * *

In McMinville, Tennessee, a teacher smelled a "funny odor." Students and teachers began complaining of

This 1938 photo was taken in Grover's Mill, New Jersey, after the broadcast of H. G. Wells' The War of the Worlds. *The man is guarding against an attack of Martians.*

headaches, nausea, and a shortness of breath. The school was evacuated, and doctors treated more than 100 people at the local hospital. Authorities found nothing.

A few days later, a second wave of illness struck. This time, the Tennessee Department of Health shut the high school down for two weeks. They dug holes in the foundation and walls and ran snake cameras through the ventilation and heating ducts. They even tested the victims' blood (Adams 2000).

Nothing unusual was found.

* * * * *

"It's all in their heads," we might say. In one sense, we would be right. There was no external, objective cause of the illnesses from tarantism or Coca-Cola. There was no "monkey-man," no fire, nor any chemical contaminant at the school.

In another sense, however, we would be wrong to say that it is "all in their heads." The symptoms that these people experienced were real. They had real headaches and stomach aches. They did vomit and faint. And they did experience unusual sexual urges and the desire to dance until they could no longer stand.

There is no explanation for mass hysteria except suggestibility. Experts might use fancy words to try to explain it, but once you cut through their terms, you find that they are really saying, "It happens." Mass hysteria occurs in many cultures, which indicates that it follows basic principles of human behavior. Someday, we will understand these principles.

For Your Consideration
What do you think causes mass hysteria? Have you ever been part of mass hysteria?

In the 1980s, a *moral panic* regarding child molesters working at day care centers swept the United States. Shown here is Peggy McMartin Buckey, age 74, who was tried and acquitted of such charges in California. At the time, "everyone" (except the jury) knew she was guilty.

sexually assaulted—it was all too much. The ghoulish child care workers were sent to prison. To say anything in their defense was to defend child molesters from hell.

Moral panics occur when large numbers of people become concerned, even fearful, about some behavior that they believe threatens morality, and when the fear is out of proportion to any actual danger (Bandes 2007; Denham 2008). The threat is perceived as enormous, and hostility builds toward those deemed responsible.

The media fed this moral panic. Each new revelation about day care centers sold papers and brought viewers to their TVs. The situation grew so bad that day care workers across the country became suspects. Only fearfully did parents leave their children in day care centers. Despite intensive investigations, the stories of children supposedly subjected to bizarre sexual rituals were never substantiated.

Like other panics, moral panics center on a sense of danger. In the 1980s and 1990s, strangers were supposedly snatching thousands of U.S. children from playgrounds, city streets, and their own backyards. Parents became fearful, perplexed at how society could have gone to hell in a handbasket. The actual number of stranger kidnappings in the United States per year was between 64 and 300 (Bromley 1991; Simons and Willie 2000), about the same as it is now ("Nonfamily Abducted Children" 2002).

Rumors often feed moral panics. In the 1990s, a rumor swept the country that Satanists were buying some of these missing children. The Satanists would sexually abuse the children, then ritually murder them. People appeared who said they were eyewitnesses to these sacrifices. They were convincing as they told their pitiful stories to horrified audiences. Even though this rumor and the eyewitness reports were outlandish, many believed them because the stories filled in missing information: who was abducting and doing what to those supposedly thousands of missing children. The police investigated, but, like the sexploitation of the nursery school children, no evidence substantiated the reports.

Like rumors, moral panics thrive on uncertainty, fear, and anxiety. With so many mothers working outside the home, concerns can grow that children are receiving inadequate care. Linked with fears about declining morality and stoked by the publicity given high-profile cases of child abuse, these concerns can give birth to the idea that pedophiles and child killers are lurking almost everywhere. After all, they could be, couldn't they? Is it, then, such a stretch from could to are?

Fads and Fashions

A **fad** is a novel form of behavior that briefly catches people's attention. The new behavior appears suddenly and spreads by imitation and identification with people who are already involved in the fad. Reports by the mass media help to spread the fad. After a short life, the fad fades away, although it may reappear from time to time (Aguirre et al. 1993; Best 2006).

Fads come in many forms. Very short, intense fads are called *crazes*. They appear suddenly and are gone almost as quickly. "Tickle Me Elmo" dolls and Beanie Babies were object crazes. There also are behavior crazes, such as streaking, which lasted only a couple of months in 1974; as a joke, an individual or a group would run nude in some public place. "Flash mobs" was a behavior craze of 2003; alerted by e-mail messages, individuals would gather at a specified time, do something, such as point toward the ceiling of a mall, and then, without a word, disperse. As fads do, this one has reappeared, and likely will drop into oblivion. (See the box on pranking on page 183.)

Even administrators of businesses, colleges, and universities can get caught up in fads. For about ten years, quality circles were a fad; these were supposedly an effective way of

moral panic a fear that grips a large number of people over the possibility that some evil threatens the well-being of society; followed by hostility, sometimes violence, toward those thought responsible

fad a temporary pattern of behavior that catches people's attention

getting workers and management to cooperate and develop innovative techniques to increase production. This administrative fad peaked in 1983, then quickly dropped from sight (Strang and Macy 2001). There are also fads in child rearing—permissive versus directive, spanking versus non-spanking. Our food is subject to fads as well; recent fads include tofu, power drinks, and herbal supplements. Fads in dieting also come and go, with many seeking the perfect diet, and practically all leaving the fad diet disillusioned.

Some fads involve millions of people but still die out quickly. In the 1950s, the hula hoop was so popular that stores couldn't keep them in stock. Children cried and pleaded for these brightly colored plastic hoops. Across the nation, children—and even adults—held contests to see who could keep the hoops up the longest or who could rotate the most hoops at one time. Then, in a matter of months it was over, and parents wondered what to do with these items, which seemed useless for any other purpose. Hula hoops can again be found in toy stores, but now they are just another toy.

When a fad lasts, it is called a **fashion.** Some fashions, as with clothing and furniture, are the result of a coordinated international marketing system that includes designers, manufacturers, advertisers, and retailers. By manipulating the tastes of the public, they sell billions of dollars of products. Fashion, however, also refers to hairstyles, to the design and colors of buildings, and even to the names that parents give their children (Lieberson 2000). Sociologist John Lofland (1985) pointed out that fashion also applies to common expressions, as demonstrated by these roughly comparable terms: "Neat!" in the 1950s, "Right on!" in the 1960s, "Really!" in the 1970s, "Awesome!" in the 1980s, "Bad!" in the 1990s, "Sweet" and "Tight" in the early 2000s, "Hot" in the middle 2000s, and, recurringly, "Cool."

The medical/media complex is so effective at molding self images in order to sell its products that even people without wrinkles think they need botox.

Urban Legends

Did you hear about Kristi and Paul? They were parked at Bluewater Bay, listening to the radio, when the music was interrupted by an announcement that a rapist-killer had escaped from prison. Instead of a right hand, he had a hook. Kristi said they should leave, but Paul laughed and said there wasn't any reason to go. When they heard a strange noise and Kristi screamed, Paul agreed to take her home. When Kristi opened the door, she heard something clink. It was a hook hanging on the door handle!

For decades, some version of "The Hook" has circulated among Americans. It has appeared as a "genuine" letter in "Dear Abby," and some of my students heard it in grade school. **Urban legends** are stories with an ironic twist that sound realistic but are false. Although untrue, they usually are told by people who believe that they happened.

Here is another one:

A horrible thing happened. This girl in St. Louis kept smelling something bad. The smell wouldn't leave even when she took showers. She finally went to the doctor, and it turned out that her insides were rotting. She had gone to the tanning salon too many times, and her insides were cooked.

Folklorist Jan Brunvand (1981, 1984, 2004) reports that urban legends are passed on by people who often think that the event happened just one or two people down the line of transmission, sometimes to a "friend of a friend." These stories have strong appeal and gain their credibility by naming specific people or citing particular events. Note the details of where Kristi and Paul were. Brunvand views urban legends as "modern morality stories"; each one teaches a moral lesson about life.

If we apply Brunvand's analysis to these two urban legends, three principles emerge. First, these stories serve as warnings. "The Hook" warns young people that they should be careful about where they go, with whom they go, and what they do when they get there. The

fashion a pattern of behavior that catches people's attention and lasts longer than a fad

urban legend a story with an ironic twist that sounds realistic but is false

social movement a large group of people who are organized to promote or resist some social change

proactive social movement a social movement that promotes some social change

reactive social movement a social movement that resists some social change

social movement organization an organization whose purpose is to promote the goals of a social movement

tanning salon story warns people about the dangers of new technology. Second, these stories are related to social change: "The Hook" to changing sexual morality, the tanning salon to changing technology. Third, each is calculated to instill fear: We should all be afraid, for dangers abound. They lurk in the dark countryside, or even at our neighborhood tanning salon.

These principles can be applied to an urban legend that made the rounds in the late 1980s. I heard several versions of this one; each narrator swore that it had just happened to a friend of a friend.

> Jerry (or whoever) went to a nightclub last weekend. He met a good-looking woman, and they hit it off. They spent the night in a motel. When he got up the next morning, the woman was gone. When he went into the bathroom, he saw a message scrawled on the mirror in lipstick: "Welcome to the wonderful world of AIDS."

Social Movements

When the Nazis, a small group of malcontents in Bavaria, first appeared on the scene in the 1920s, the world found their ideas laughable. This small group believed that the Germans were a race of supermen (*Ubermenschen*) and that they would launch a Third Reich (reign or nation) that would control the world for a thousand years. Their race destined them for greatness; lesser races would serve them.

The Nazis started as a little band of comic characters who looked as though they had stepped out of a grade B movie (see the photo on page 332). From this inauspicious start, the Nazis gained such power that they threatened to overthrow Western civilization. How could a little man with a grotesque moustache, surrounded by a few sycophants in brown shirts, ever come to threaten the world? Such things don't happen in real life—only in novels or movies—the deranged nightmare of some author with an overactive imagination. Only this was real life. The Nazis' appearance on the human scene caused the deaths of millions of people and changed the course of world history.

Social movements, the second major topic of this chapter, hold the answer to Hitler's rise to power. **Social movements** consist of large numbers of people who organize either to promote or to resist social change. Members of social movements hold strong ideas about what is wrong with the world—or some part of it—and how to make things right. Other examples include the civil rights movement, the white supremacist movement, the women's movement, the animal rights movement, and the environmental movement.

At the heart of social movements lies a sense of injustice (Klandermans 1997). Some find a particular condition of society intolerable, and their goal is to promote social change. Theirs is called a **proactive social movement.** Others, in contrast, feel threatened because some condition of society is changing, and they *react* to resist that change. Theirs is a **reactive social movement.**

Social movements involve large numbers of people who, upset about some condition in society, organize to do something about it. Shown here is Al Gore, who has spearheaded a movement centered on promoting clean and renewable energy to solve global warming.

To further their goals, people establish **social movement organizations.** Those who want to promote social change develop organizations such as the National Association for the Advancement of Colored People (NAACP). In contrast, those who are trying to resist these particular changes form organizations such as the Ku Klux Klan or Aryan Nations. To recruit followers and publicize their grievances, leaders of social movements use attention-getting devices, from marches and protest rallies to sit-ins and boycotts. These "media events" can be quite effective.

Social movements are like a rolling sea, observed sociologist Mayer Zald (1992). During one period, few social movements may appear, but shortly afterward, a wave of them rolls in, each competing for the public's attention. Zald suggests that a *cultural crisis* can give birth to a wave of social movements. By this, he means that there are times when a society's institutions fail to keep up with social change. During these times many people's needs go unfulfilled, unrest follows, and attempting to bridge this gap, people form and become active in social movements.

Types and Tactics of Social Movements

Let's see what types of social movements there are and then examine their tactics.

Types of Social Movements

Since social change is their goal, we can classify social movements according to their *target* and the *amount of change* they seek. Look at Figure 21.2. If you read across, you will see that the first two types of social movements target *individuals*. **Alterative social movements** seek to *alter* some specific behavior. An example is the Woman's Christian Temperance Union, a powerful social movement of the early 1900s. Its goal was to get people to stop drinking alcohol. Its members were convinced that if they could shut down the saloons, such problems as poverty and wife abuse would go away. **Redemptive social movements** also target individuals, but their goal is *total* change. An example is a religious social movement that stresses conversion. In fundamentalist Christianity, for example, when someone converts to Christ, the entire person is supposed to change, not just some specific behavior. Self-centered acts are to be replaced by loving behaviors toward others as the convert becomes, in their terms, a "new creation."

The next two types of social movements target *society*. (See cells 3 and 4 of Figure 21.2) **Reformative social movements** seek to *reform* some specific aspect of society. The animal rights movement, for example, seeks to reform the ways in which society views and treats animals. **Transformative social movements,** in contrast, seek to *transform* the social order itself. Its members want to replace the social order with their vision of the good society. Revolutions, such as those in the American colonies, France, Russia, and Cuba, are examples.

One of the more interesting examples of transformative social movements is millenarian social movements, which are based on prophecies of impending calamity. Of particular interest is a type of millenarian movement called a *cargo cult* (Worsley 1957). About one hundred years ago, Europeans colonized the Melanesian Islands of the South Pacific. Ships from the home countries of the colonizers arrived one after another, each loaded with items the Melanesians had never seen. As the Melanesians watched the cargo being unloaded, they expected that some of it would go to them. Instead, it all went to the Europeans. Melanesian prophets then revealed the secret of this exotic merchandise. Their own ancestors were manufacturing and sending the cargo to them, but the colonists were intercepting the merchandise. Since the colonists were too strong to fight and too selfish to share the cargo, there was little the Melanesians could do.

Then came a remarkable self-fulfilling prophecy. Melanesian prophets revealed that if the people would destroy their crops and food and build harbors, their ancestors would see their sincerity and send the cargo directly to them. The Melanesians did so. When the colonial administrators of the island saw that the natives had destroyed their crops and were just sitting in the hills waiting for the cargo ships to arrive, they informed the home government. The prospect of thousands of islanders patiently starving to death was too horrifying to allow. The British government fulfilled the prophecy by sending ships to the islands loaded with cargo earmarked for the Melanesians.

As Figure 21.2 indicates, some social movements have a global orientation. As with many aspects of life in our new global economy, numerous issues that concern people transcend national boundaries. Participants of **transnational social movements** (also called *new social movements*) want to change some specific condition that cuts across societies. (See Cell 5 of Figure 21.2.) These social movements often center on improving the quality of life (Melucci 1989). Examples are the women's movement, labor movement, and the environmental movement (Smith et al. 1997; Walter 2001; Tilly 2004).

alterative social movement a social movement that seeks to alter only some specific aspects of people and institutions

redemptive social movement a social movement that seeks to change people and institutions totally, to redeem them

reformative social movement a social movement that seeks to reform some specific aspects of society

transformative social movement a social movement that seeks to change society totally, to transform it

millenarian social movement a social movement based on the prophecy of coming social upheaval

transnational social movement a social movement whose emphasis is on some condition around the world, instead of on a condition in a specific country; also known as *new social movements*

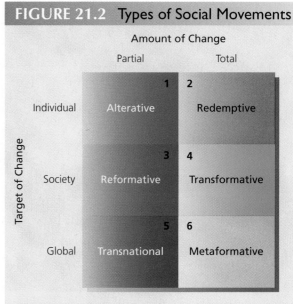

FIGURE 21.2 Types of Social Movements

	Amount of Change	
	Partial	Total
Individual	1 Alterative	2 Redemptive
Society	3 Reformative	4 Transformative
Global	5 Transnational	6 Metaformative

Target of Change

Sources: The first four types are from Aberle 1966; the last two are by the author.

metaformative social movement a social movement that has the goal to change the social order not just of a country or two, but of a civilization, or even of the entire world

public in this context, a dispersed group of people relevant to a social movement; the sympathetic and hostile publics have an interest in the issues on which a social movement focuses; there is also an unaware or indifferent public

Cell 6 in Figure 21.2 represents a rare type of social movement. The goal of **metaformative social movements** is to change the social order itself—not just of a specific country, but of an entire civilization, or even the whole world. Their objective is to change concepts and practices of race–ethnicity, class, gender, family, religion, government, and the global stratification of nations. These were the aims of the communist social movement of the early to middle twentieth century and the fascist social movement of the 1920s to 1940s. (The fascists consisted of the Nazis in Germany, the Black Shirts of Italy, and other groups throughout Europe and the United States.)

Today, we are witnessing another metaformative social movement, that of Islamic fundamentalism. Like other social movements before it, this movement is not united, but consists of many separate groups with differing goals and tactics. Al-Qaeda, for example, would not only cleanse Islamic societies of Western influences—which they contend are demonic and degrading to men, women, and morality—but also replace Western civilization with an extremist form of Islam. This frightens both Muslims and non-Muslims, who hold sharply differing views of what constitutes quality of life. If the Islamic fundamentalists—like the communists or fascists before them—have their way, they will usher in a New World Order fashioned after their particular views of the good life.

Tactics of Social Movements

The leaders of a social movement can choose from a variety of tactics. Should they boycott, stage a march, or hold an all-night candlelight vigil? Or should they bomb a building, burn down a research lab, or assassinate a politician? To understand why the leaders of social movements choose their tactics, let's examine a group's levels of membership, the publics it addresses, and its relationship to authorities.

Levels of Membership.   Figure 21.3 on the next page shows the composition of social movements. Beginning at the center and moving outward are three levels of membership. At the center is the inner core, those most committed to the movement. The inner core sets the group's goals, timetables, and strategies. People at the second level are also committed to the movement, but somewhat less so than the inner core. They can be counted on to show up for demonstrations and to do the grunt work—help with mailings, pass out petitions and leaflets, make telephone calls. The third level consists of a wider circle of people who are less committed and less dependable. Their participation depends on convenience—if an activity doesn't interfere with something else they want to do, they participate.

The tactics that a group uses depend largely on the backgrounds and predispositions of the inner core. Because of their differing backgrounds, some members of the inner core may be predisposed to engaging in peaceful, quiet demonstrations, or even placing informational ads in newspapers. Others may prefer heated, verbal confrontations. Still others may tend toward violence. Tactics also depend on the number of committed members. Different tactics are called for if the inner core can count on seven hundred—or only seven—committed members to show up.

The Publics.   Outside the group's membership is the **public,** a dispersed group of people who may have an interest in the issue. As you can see from Figure 21.3, there are three types of publics. Just outside the third circle of members, and blending into it, is the *sympathetic* public. Although their sympathies lie with the movement, these people have no commitment to it. Their sympathies with the movement's goals, however, make them prime candidates for recruitment. The second public is *hostile.* The movement's values go against its own, and it wants to stop the so-

As the text explains, people have many reasons for joining social movements. One reason that some people participate in the animal rights movement is illustrated by this photo, which evokes in many an identity with animals.

cial movement. The third public consists of *disinterested* people. They are either unaware of the social movement or, if they are aware, are indifferent to it.

In selecting tactics, the leaders pays attention to these publics. The sympathetic public is especially significant, because it is the source of new members and support at the ballot box. Leaders avoid tactics that they think might alienate the sympathetic public and seek strategies that will elicit sympathy from this group. To make themselves appear to be victims—people whose rights are being trampled on—leaders may even force a confrontation with the hostile public. Tactics directed toward the indifferent or unaware public are designed to neutralize their indifference and increase their awareness.

Relationship to Authorities.   In determining tactics, the movement's relationship to authorities is also significant. This is especially true when it comes to choosing between peaceful and violent actions. If a social movement is *institutionalized*—accepted by authorities—violence will not be directed toward the authorities, for they are on the movement's side. This, however, does not rule out using violence against the opposition. In contrast, if authorities are hostile to a social movement, they may become the object of aggression or violence. For example, because the goal of a transformative (revolutionary) social movement is to replace the government, the movement and the government are clearly on a collision course.

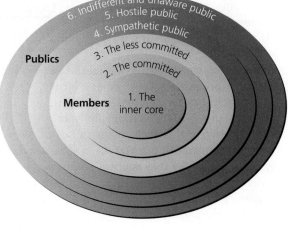

FIGURE 21.3   The Membership and Publics of Social Movements

Source: By the author.

Propaganda and the Mass Media

The leaders of social movements try to manipulate the mass media to influence **public opinion,** how people think about some issue. The right kind of publicity enables the leaders to arouse sympathy and to lay the groundwork for recruiting more members. Pictures of bloodied, dead baby seals, for example, go a long way toward getting a group's message across.

A key to understanding social movements, then, is **propaganda.** Although this word often evokes negative images, it actually is a neutral term. Propaganda is simply the presentation of information in an attempt to influence people. Its original meaning was positive. *Propaganda* referred to a committee of cardinals of the Roman Catholic Church whose assignment was the care of foreign missions. (They were to *propagate*—multiply or spread—the faith.) The term has traveled a long way since then, however, and today it usually refers to one-sided information designed to distort reality.

Propaganda, in the sense of organized attempts to influence public opinion, is a part of everyday life. Our news is filled with propaganda, as various interest groups—from retailers to the government—try to manipulate our perceptions of the world. Our movies, too, although seemingly intended as simply entertainment devices, are actually propaganda vehicles. The basic techniques that underlie propaganda are discussed in the Down-to-Earth Sociology box on the next page.

The mass media play such a crucial role that we can say they are the gatekeepers to social movements. If those who control and work in the mass media—from owners to reporters—are sympathetic to some particular "cause," you can be sure that it will receive sympathetic treatment. If the social movement goes against their views, however, it likely will be ignored or receive unfavorable treatment. If you ever get the impression that the media are trying to manipulate your opinions and attitudes—even your feelings—on some particular issue or social movement, you probably are right. Far from providing unbiased reporting, the media are under the control and influence of people who have an agenda. To the materials in the Down-to-Earth Sociology box on propaganda, then, we need to add the biases of the media establishment—the topics it chooses to publicize, those it chooses to ignore, and its favorable and unfavorable treatment of issues and movements.

Sociology can be a liberating discipline (Berger 1963/2007). Sociology sensitizes us to *multiple realities;* that is, for any single point of view on some topic, there are competing points of view. Each represents reality as people see it, their distinct experiences having led

public opinion how people think about some issue

propaganda in its broad sense, the presentation of information in the attempt to influence people; in its narrow sense, one-sided information used to try to influence people

Down-to-Earth Sociology

"Tricks of the Trade"—Deception and Persuasion in Propaganda

Sociologists Alfred and Elizabeth Lee (1939) found that propaganda relies on seven basic techniques, which they termed "tricks of the trade." To be effective, the techniques should be subtle, with the audience unaware that their minds and emotions are being manipulated. If propaganda is effective, people will not know why they support something, but they'll fervently defend it. Becoming familiar with these techniques can help you keep your mind and emotions from being manipulated.

You probably know immediately why the photo on the left is propaganda, but do you know why the photo on the right is propaganda?

Name calling. This technique aims to arouse opposition to the competing product, candidate, or policy by associating it with negative images. By comparison, one's own product, candidate, or policy is attractive. Republicans who call Democrats "soft on crime" and Democrats who call Republicans "insensitive to the poor" are using this technique.

Glittering generality. Essentially the opposite of the first technique, this one surrounds the product, candidate, or policy with images that arouse positive feelings. "She's a real Democrat" has little meaning, but it makes the audience feel that something substantive has been said. "This Republican stands for individual rights" is so general that it is meaningless; yet the audience thinks that it has heard a specific message about the candidate.

Transfer. In its positive form, this technique associates the product, candidate, or policy with something the public approves of or respects. You might not be able to get by with saying "Coors is patriotic," but surround a beer with images of the country's flag, and beer drinkers will get the idea that it is more patriotic to drink this brand of beer than some other kind. In its negative form, this technique associates the product, candidate, or policy with something generally disapproved of by the public.

Testimonials. Famous individuals endorse a product, candidate, or policy. David Beckham lends his name to Gillette, and Beyoncé tells you that L'Oréal is a great line of cosmetics. In the negative form of this technique, a despised person is associated with the competing product. If propagandists (called "spin doctors" in politics) could get away with it, they would show Osama bin Laden announcing support for a candidate they oppose.

Plain folks. Sometimes it pays to associate the product, candidate, or policy with "just plain folks." "If Mary or John Q. Public likes it, you will, too." A political candidate who kisses babies, puts on a hard hat, and has lunch at McDonald's while photographers "catch him (or her) in the act" is using the "plain folks" strategy. "I'm just a regular person" is the message of the presidential candidate who poses for photographers in jeans and work shirt—while making certain that the chauffeur-driven Mercedes does not show up in the background.

Card stacking. The aim of this technique is to present only positive information about what you support, and only negative information about what you oppose. The intent is to make it sound as though there is only one conclusion a rational person can draw. Falsehoods, distortions, and illogical statements are often used.

Bandwagon. "Everyone is doing it" is the idea behind this technique. Emphasizing how many other people buy the product or support the candidate or policy conveys the message that anyone who doesn't join in is on the wrong track.

The Lees (1939) added, "Once we know that a speaker or writer is using one of these propaganda devices in an attempt to convince us of an idea, we can separate the device from the idea and see what the idea amounts to on its own merits."

For Your Consideration

What propaganda techniques have you seen or heard recently? Recall not just product ads but also TV programs, political ads, movies, and newspaper articles. Explain why they were propaganda, not simply a source of information or entertainment.

them to different perceptions. Consequently, different people find opposing points of view equally compelling. Although the committed members of a social movement are sincere—and perhaps even make sacrifices for "the cause"—theirs is but one view of the world. If other sides were presented, the issue would look quite different.

Why People Join Social Movements

As we have seen, social movements are fed by a sense of injustice—a conviction that we can no longer tolerate some condition of society. However, not everyone who feels this way joins a social movement. Why do some join, but not others? Sociologists have found that recruitment generally follows channels of social networks. That is, people most commonly join a social movement because they have friends and acquaintances already in it (McCarthy and Wolfson 1992; Snow et al. 1993a).

Let's look at three explanations for why people join social movements.

Mass Society Theory

To explain why people are attracted to social movements, sociologist William Kornhauser (1959) proposed **mass society theory.** Kornhauser argued that many people feel isolated because they live in a **mass society**—an impersonal, industrialized, highly bureaucratized society. Social movements fill this void by offering a sense of belonging.

This theory has been criticized severely (Thomson 2005). When sociologist Doug McAdam and his colleagues (McAdam et al. 1988) interviewed people who had risked their lives in the civil rights movement, they found that these participants had strong roots in families and communities. They were motivated by a desire to right wrongs and to overcome injustices—not to escape isolation. Even the Nazis attracted many people who were firmly rooted in their communities (Oberschall 1973). Finally, the most isolated of all, the homeless, generally do not join anything—except food lines.

Deprivation Theory

A second explanation for why people join social movements is *deprivation theory.* According to this theory, people who feel deprived—whether it be of money, justice, status, or privilege—join social movements with the hope of redressing their grievances. This theory may seem so obvious that it needs no evidence. Don't the thousands of African Americans who participated in the civil rights movement of the 1950s and 1960s and the World War I soldiers who marched on Washington after Congress refused to pay their promised bonuses provide ample evidence that the theory is true?

Deprivation theory does provide a starting point. But there is more to the matter than this. About 150 years ago, Alexis de Tocqueville (1856/1955) made a telling observation. Both the peasants of Germany and the peasants of France were living under deprived conditions. According to deprivation theory, if revolution were to occur we would expect it to take place in both countries. Only the French peasants rebelled and overthrew their king, however. The reason, said de Tocqueville, is *relative* deprivation. The living conditions of the French peasants had been improving, and they could foresee even better circumstances ahead. German peasants, in contrast, had never experienced anything but depressed conditions, and they had no comparative basis for feeling deprived.

According to **relative deprivation theory,** then, it is not people's actual deprivation that matters. The key to participation in social movements is *relative* deprivation—what people *think* they should have relative to what others have, or relative to their own efforts, abilities, status, or even their perceived future. Relative deprivation theory, which has provided insight into revolutions, holds a surprise. Because improving conditions fuel human desire for even better conditions, *improving* conditions can spark revolutions—which is why revolution occurred in France, not Germany. As Figure 21.4 shows, revolutions tend to occur when people's expectations outstrip the change they experience. It is likely that we can also apply this principle to riots.

mass society theory an explanation for why people participate in a social movement based on the assumption that the movement offers them a sense of belonging

mass society industrialized, highly bureaucratized, impersonal society

relative deprivation theory in this context, the idea that people join social movements based on what they think they should have compared with what others have

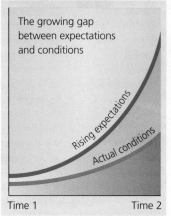

FIGURE 21.4
Relative Deprivation and Revolution

The growing gap between expectations and conditions

Rising expectations

Actual conditions

Time 1   Time 2

agent provocateur someone who joins a group in order to spy on it or to sabotage it by provoking its members to commit extreme acts

Relative deprivation also explains an interesting aspect of the civil rights movement. Relatively well-off African Americans—college students and church leaders—were at the center of the sit-ins, marches, and boycotts in the South during the 1950s and 1960s. They went to restaurants and lunch counters that were reserved for whites. When refused service, they sat peacefully while curses and food were heaped on them (Morris 1993). You might want to review the photo on page 353. Why did they subject themselves to such treatment? Remember that according to relative deprivation theory, what is significant is not what we have or don't have, but with whom we compare ourselves. The African American demonstrators compared themselves with whites of similar status, and they perceived themselves as deprived.

How about the white, middle-class college students and the white church leaders from the North? They, too, risked their lives when they joined the Southern protesters. They weren't comparing themselves with people whose situation was better than their own. Nor was their own personal welfare at stake. Relative deprivation theory doesn't help us here. We need to look at the *moral* reasons for their involvement (McAdam et al. 1988; Jasper 2007). Let's consider that motivation in social movements.

Moral Issues and Ideological Commitment

As sociologist James Jasper (2007) points out, we will miss the *basic* reason for many people's involvement in social movements if we overlook the moral issue—people getting upset about the injustice that others experience and wanting to do something about it. Some people join because of *moral shock*—a sense of outrage at finding out what is "really" going on. For people who view a social movement in moral terms, great issues hang in the balance. They feel they must choose sides and do what they can to help right wrongs. As sociologists put it, they join because of *ideological commitment* to the movement.

Many members on *both* sides of the abortion issue, for example, perceive their involvement in such terms. Similarly, activists in the animal rights movement are convinced that there can be no justification for making animals suffer in order to make safer products for humans. Activists in the peace and environmental movements and those who protest against global capitalism view nuclear weapons, pollution, and global power in similar moral terms. It is for moral reasons that they risk arrest and ridicule for their demonstrations. For them, to *not* act would be an inexcusable betrayal of future generations. The *moral* component of a social movement, then, is a primary reason for many people's involvement.

The Michigan militia is not run by the federal or state governments or any government agency. It is a private organization, made up of individuals who fear increasing government control over individual freedoms. It is likely that their membership includes state and federal agents who have infiltrated the group.

A Special Case: The Agent Provocateur

Agent provocateurs are a unique type of participant in social movements. These are agents of the government or even of the opposing sides of a social movement whose job is to spy on the leaders and perhaps to sabotage their activities. Some are recruited from the membership itself—people who are willing to betray their friends in the organization for a few Judas dollars. Others are police or members of a rival group who infiltrate the movement.

The radical social change advocated by some social movements poses a threat to the power elite. In such cases, the use of agent provocateurs is not surprising. What may be surprising, however, is that some agents convert to the social movement they have infiltrated. Sociologist Gary Marx (1993) explains that to be credible, agents must share at least some of the class, age, gender, racial–ethnic, or religious characteristics of the group. This background makes the agents more likely to be sympathetic to the movement's goals and to become disenchanted with trying to harm the group. To be effective, agents must also work their way into the center of the group. This requires that they spend time with the group's committed members. As these agents spend time building trust, they often are cut off from their own group. The point of view they represent can start to recede in their minds, to be replaced with concerns about betraying and deceiving people who now trust them as friends.

What also may be surprising is how far some agents are willing to go. During the 1960s, when a wave of militant social movements streamed across the United States, the FBI recruited agent provocateurs to sabotage some of these groups. These agents provoked illegal activities that otherwise would not have occurred: They set the leadership up for arrest and, in some instances, set them up for death. Two examples will let us see how agent provocateurs operate (Marx 1993). In a plot by a group called the Black Liberation Front to blow up the Statue of Liberty, one of the four men involved was an undercover agent. It was he who drew up the plans and even provided funds to pay for the dynamite and rent the car. In another instance, the FBI paid $36,500 to two members of the White Knights of the Ku Klux Klan to bomb a Jewish businessman's home. The two walked into the FBI trap, one was killed and the other was arrested.

In Sum: There is no single reason that people join social movements. Most people join because they have friends and acquaintances already in the movement. Some join because of moral convictions, others to further their own careers. Still others join because they find a valued identity, or even because it is fun. Some even participate although they *don't want to.* The Cuban government, for example, compels people to turn out for mass demonstrations to show support of the Communist regime (Aguirre 1993). As we just saw, police agents may join social movements in order to spy on them and sabotage their activities. As in all other activities in life, people remain a complex bundle of motivations—a challenge for sociologists to unravel.

On the Success and Failure of Social Movements

Some social movements have brought about extensive social change, but most are not successful. Let's look at the reasons for their success or failure.

The Rocky Road to Success

Social movements come, and social movements go—and most go quietly without leaving much of an impact on society. Why? To exist, a social movement must focus on a problem that concerns a large number of people. Broad problems, however, are embedded deeply in society. This means that minor tinkering with something superficial won't solve the problem. Just as the problem touches many interrelated components of society, so the solutions must be broad. No quick fix is available for such social conditions, so the social movement must last for years—and longevity brings its own risks. As social movements lose momentum, their leaders often turn inward, focusing their energies more on keeping the organization going than on working toward the solution of the problem that is the reason for the movement's existence.

Some social movements, in contrast, leave a heritage that changes a society and even world history. The civil rights movement and the women's movement, for example, became powerful forces for social change. Their agitation for change was so successful that they turned society onto different paths. In another direction was the fascist social movement mentioned earlier. Led by Hitler in Germany and Mussolini in Italy, this social movement turned the world upside down. Like anything else in life, the consequences of social movements can be good or bad. What they all have in common is social change, either to promote it or to resist it. With a changing society such as ours, we can anticipate that new social movements will be a regular feature of our social landscape.

Seeing the stages that social movements go through can help us to better understand why social movements succeed or fail. Let's look at these stages.

The Stages of Social Movements

Sociologists have identified five stages in the growth and maturity of social movements (Lang and Lang 1961; Mauss 1975; Spector and Kitsuse 1977; Jasper 1991; Tilly 2004):

1. *Initial unrest and agitation.* During this first stage, people are upset about some condition in society and want to change it. Leaders emerge who verbalize people's feelings and crystallize issues. Most social movements fail at this stage. Unable to gain enough support, after a brief flurry of activity, they fade away.

2. *Resource mobilization.* A crucial factor that enables social movements to make it past the first stage is **resource mobilization.** By this term, sociologists mean organizing and using resources such as time, money, information, mailing lists, and people's skills. It also includes using communications technology such as cell phones, Internet sites, blogs, and tweets—and getting the attention of the mass media. For the Civil Rights Movement, these resources included access to churches to organize protests (Mirola 2003).

   In some groups, the members mobilize these resources. Other groups, lacking capable leadership, turn to "guns for hire," outside specialists who sell their services. As sociologists John McCarthy and Mayer Zald (1977; Zald and McCarthy 1987) point out, even though large numbers of people may be upset over some condition of society, without resource mobilization they are only upset people, perhaps even agitators, but they do not constitute a social movement.

3. *Organization.* A division of labor is set up. The leaders make policy decisions, and the rank and file do the daily tasks necessary to keep the movement going. There is still much collective excitement about the issue, the movement's focal point of concern.

4. *Institutionalization.* At this stage, the movement has developed a bureaucracy, the type of formal hierarchy that was described in Chapter 7. Control lies in the hands of career officers, who may care more about their own position in the organization than the movement for which the organization's initial leaders made sacrifices. The collective excitement diminishes.

5. *Decline and death.* During this phase, managing the day-to-day affairs of the organization dominates the leadership. A change in public sentiment may even have occurred, and there may no longer be a group of committed people who share a common cause. The movement eventually withers away, although a small staff can remain for years until the last of the funds are drained.

Resurgence

The final stage of decline and death can be postponed for decades, perhaps even for generations, as events breath new life into a social movement and as committed, fresh blood replaces faltering leaders. The outstanding example is the abortion movement, whose prochoice and prolife sides continue to energize one another. To close this chapter, let's look at this social movement.

ThinkingCRITICALLY

Which Side of the Barricades? Prochoice and Prolife as a Social Movement

No issue so divides Americans as abortion. Although most Americans take more moderate views, on one side are some who believe that abortion should be permitted under any circumstance, even during the last month of pregnancy. They are matched by individuals on the other side who are convinced that abortion should never be allowed under any circumstances, not even in the case of rape or incest or during the first month of pregnancy. This polarization constantly breathes new life into the movement.

When the U.S. Supreme Court made its 1973 decision, *Roe v. Wade,* that states could not prohibit abortion, the prochoice side relaxed. Victory was theirs, and they thought their

With sincere people on both sides of the issue—equally committed and equally convinced that their side is right—abortion is destined to remain a controversial force in U.S. life.

opponents would quietly fade away. Instead, large numbers of Americans were disturbed by what they saw as the legal right to murder unborn children.

The views of the two sides could not be more incompatible. Those who favor choice view the 1.2 million abortions that are performed annually in the United States as examples of women exercising their basic reproductive rights. Those who gather under the prolife banner see these abortions as legalized murder. To the prochoice side, those who oppose abortion are blocking women's rights—they would force women to continue pregnancies they want to terminate. To the prolife side, those who advocate choice are perceived as condoning murder—they would sacrifice their unborn children for the sake of school, career, or convenience.

There is no way to reconcile these contrary views. Each sees the other as unreasonable and extremist. And each uses propaganda by focusing on worst-case scenarios: prochoice images of young women raped at gunpoint, forced to bear the children of rapists; prolife images of women who are eight months pregnant killing their babies instead of nurturing them.

With no middle ground, these views remain in perpetual conflict. As each side fights for what it considers to be basic rights, it reinvigorates the other. When in 1989 the U.S. Supreme Court decided in *Webster v. Reproductive Services* that states could restrict abortion, one side mourned it as a defeat and the other hailed it as a victory. Seeing the political battle going against them, the prochoice side regrouped for a determined struggle. The prolife side, sensing judicial victory within its grasp, gathered forces for a push to complete the overthrow of *Roe v. Wade*.

In 1992, this goal of the prolife side almost became reality in *Casey v. Planned Parenthood*. In a 6–3 decision, the Supreme Court upheld the right of states to make women wait 24 hours between confirming their pregnancy and getting an abortion; to require girls under 18 to obtain the consent of one parent; and to require that women be given materials which describe the fetus and that they be informed about alternatives to abortion. In the same case, however, by a 5–4 decision, the Court ruled that a wife does not have to inform her husband if she intends to have an abortion. In 2007, in another 5–4 decision, the Court ruled a certain type of abortion procedure illegal. The names given this late-term procedure represent the ongoing struggle: One side calls it an "intact dilation and evacuation," while the other side terms it a "partial-birth abortion."

The struggle of the opposing sides is usually a quiet affair, but it makes headlines each time the Senate is asked to confirm a president's nominee to the U.S. Supreme Court. To watch these hearings is to view, in miniature, irreconcilable views of reality. This social movement also makes headlines when opposing sides confront one another in street drama, each wielding signs in the attempt to capture the attention of the mass media. There is also the rare, but more powerfully headline-grabbing assassination of doctors who perform abortions. National attention was focused briefly on Wichita, Kansas, for example, when George Tiller, who specialized in late-term abortions, was shot to death at his church, a murder disavowed by prolife organizations.

With emotions raw and convictions firm, this social movement cannot end unless an overwhelming majority of Americans commit to one side or the other. Short of this, every legislative and judicial outcome—including the extremes of a constitutional amendment that declares abortion to be either murder or a woman's right—is a victory to one and a defeat to the other. To committed activists, no battle is ever complete. Rather, each action is only one small part of a long, hard-fought, moral struggle.

For Your Consideration

The last stage of a social movement is decline and death. Why hasn't this social movement declined? Under what conditions will it decline and die?

The longer the duration of the pregnancy, the fewer the number of Americans who approve of abortion. How do you feel about abortion during the third month versus the seventh month? The first month versus the ninth month? What do you think about abortion in cases of rape and incest? Can you identify some of the social reasons that underlie your opinions?

Sources: Williams 1995; Douthat 2008; Crary 2009; *Statistical Abstract of the United States* 2009: Table 97.

SUMMARY *and* REVIEW

Early Explanations: The Transformation of the Individual

How did early theorists explain the ways that crowds affect people?

Early theorists of **collective behavior** argued that crowds transform people. Charles Mackay used the term *herd mentality* to explain why people did wild things when they were in crowds. Gustave LeBon said that a **collective mind** develops, and people are swept away by suggestions. Robert Park said that collective unrest develops, which, fed by a **circular reaction,** leads to collective impulses. Pp. 626–627.

What are the five stages of crowd behavior?

Herbert Blumer identified five stages that crowds go through before they become an **acting crowd:** social unrest, an exciting event, **milling,** a common object of attention, and common impulses. Pp. 627–628.

The Contemporary View: The Rationality of the Crowd

What is the current view of crowd behavior?

Current theorists view crowds as rational. Richard Berk suggested a **minimax strategy;** that is, people try to minimize their costs and maximize their rewards, regardless of whether they are alone, with friends, or in crowds. In **emergent norm theory,** Ralph Turner and Lewis Killian suggest that new norms emerge that allow people to do things in crowds that they otherwise would not do. Pp. 628–629.

Forms of Collective Behavior

What forms of collective behavior are there?

Forms of **collective behavior** include lynchings, **riots, rumors, panics, mass hysteria, moral panics, fads, fashions,** and **urban legends.** Conditions of uncertainty and discontent provide fertile ground for collective behavior. Each form of collective behavior provides a way of dealing with these conditions. Pp. 629–638.

Types and Tactics of Social Movements

What types of social movements are there?

Social movements consist of large numbers of people who organize to promote or resist social change. Depending on their target (individuals or society) and the amount of social change that is desired (partial or complete), social movements can be classified as **alterative, redemptive, reformative, transformative, transnational,** and **metaformative.** Pp. 638–640.

How do social movement leaders select their tactics?

Leaders choose tactics on the basis of a group's levels of membership, its **publics,** and its relationship to authorities. The three levels of membership are *the inner core, the committed,* and *the less committed.* The predispositions of the inner core are crucial in choosing tactics, but so is the public they want to address. If relationships with authorities are bad, the chances of aggressive or violent tactics increase. Pp. 640–641.

How are the mass media related to social movements?

The mass media are gatekeepers for social movements. Because the media's favorable or unfavorable coverage affects

public opinion, leaders choose tactics with the media in mind. Leaders also use **propaganda** to further their causes. Pp. 641–643.

Why People Join Social Movements

Why do people join social movements?

People often join social movements simply because they know others in the movement. In addition, according to **mass society theory,** social movements relieve feelings of isolation created by an impersonal, bureaucratized society. According to **relative deprivation theory,** people join movements to redress their grievances. A sense of justice, morality, values, and ideological commitment also motivate people to join social movements. **Agent provocateurs** illustrate that even people who oppose a cause may participate in it. Pp. 643–645.

On the Success and Failure of Social Movements

Why do social movements succeed or fail?

Groups that appeal to few people cannot succeed. To appeal broadly in order to attain **resource mobilization,** the movement must focus on broad concerns. These concerns are embedded deeply in society, which makes success difficult. Sociologists have identified five stages of social movements: initial unrest and agitation, mobilization, organization, institutionalization, and decline and death. Resurgence of a declining social movement is possible. In the social movement around abortion, opposing sides revitalize one another. Pp. 645–648.

THINKING CRITICALLY *ABOUT* Chapter 21

1. Describe the different forms of collective behavior, and explain why people participate in collective behavior.

2. Use sociological findings to analyze a rumor or an urban legend you have heard or a fad you've participated in.

3. Analyze a social movement of your choice according to the sociological principles and findings reviewed in this chapter.

ADDITIONAL RESOURCES

What can you find in MySocLab? mysoclab www.mysoclab.com

- Complete Ebook
- Practice Tests and Video and Audio activities
- Mapping and Data Analysis exercises

- Sociology in the News
- Classic Readings in Sociology
- Research and Writing advice

Where Can I Read More on This Topic?

Suggested readings for this chapter are listed at the back of this book.

22

Social Change
and the Environment

India

Among technology's amazing feats is the capacity to transplant livers, hearts, and other organs from one person to another. Because body parts deteriorate quickly, a surgical team that harvests them is called *before* a patient dies. This team is not allowed in the patient's room before the death—just to be sure it doesn't get impatient and do something rash. The team has to wait for another doctor—who is not a member of the team—to declare the patient dead.

They have the nagging feeling that maybe they won't really be dead when the surgeons start to harvest their organs.

Ruben Navarro, a disabled, brain-damaged 25-year-old, was admitted to Sierra Vista Regional Medical Center in San Luis Obispo, California. Dr. Hootan Roozrokh, a highly trained surgical specialist was called in, but he and his team didn't wait for Navarro to die. After Navarro's breathing tubes were removed, they entered his room, knives impatient and ready for Navarro to take his last gasp. Most people die within a few minutes after their breathing tubes are removed, but Navarro kept on breathing, while the transplant team grew increasingly impatient, knives dangling uselessly at their side.

Dr. Roozrokh ordered that Navarro be given morphine and Ativan—ten to twenty times the normal dosages. Later he ordered that Navarro be given Betadine, "a substance that may cause death if ingested." When Navarro still hung in there, Roozrokh suggested that Navarro really was dead, that the electronic monitors were not showing a heartbeat but, instead, just "pulseless electronic activity."

Dr. Laura Lubarsky, assigned by the hospital to determine when Navarro was dead—so that those waiting surgical knives weren't put to use prematurely—disagreed. Using a stethoscope, she said she could hear Navarro's heart beating.

A slow, agonizing eight hours later, Navarro's heart finally gave up.

Finally! But it was too late. You can imagine the disappointment Dr. Roozrokh felt. Navarro's death had been so slow that his organs had deteriorated and were worthless as transplants.

What a wasted day for Roozrokh (for Navarro, too, of course). But the worst was yet to come for Roozrokh.

After thinking about what happened for a couple of days, a nurse broke the medical norm against squealing on doctors. The sheriff investigated, and the district attorney ordered Dr. Roozrokh arrested. Roozrokh was charged with the felonies of abusing a dependent adult, administering a harmful substance (Betadine), and

social change the alteration of culture and societies over time

prescribing a controlled substance (morphine) without a legitimate medical purpose. A jury found Dr. Roozrokh not guilty.

Many people don't want to sign consent forms to have their organs removed after their death. Some feel repugnance at the thought of having someone cut up their bodies after they die. Others have the nagging feeling that maybe they won't really be dead when the surgeons start to harvest their organs.

That's ridiculous. Of course, they'll be dead. The surgeons will make sure of that.

Or will they? To be sure a heart doesn't start beating on its own, surgeons have to wait at least five minutes to remove a heart. "Too long," said doctors at Denver's Children's Hospital, who decided that they can declare a baby dead without the baby being brain dead. And using a new technique, they remove the baby's heart within seventy-five seconds of declaring it dead. Some physicians are saying, "Not so fast. That baby isn't really dead!" And they add, "If the heart can be restarted in another baby, it could have been restarted in the donor baby."

—Based on Committee on Non-Heart-Beating Transplantation II 2000; Armstrong 2008; Associated Press 2008; Chawkins 2008; Elsworth 2008; McKinley 2008; Parilla 2008.

If you want a better understanding of society—and your own life—you need to understand social change, probably the main characteristic of social life today. As we shall see in this chapter, technology, such as that which allows us to transplant human organs from one person to another, is a driving force behind this change.

How Social Change Transforms Social Life

Social change, a shift in the characteristics of culture and society, is such a vital part of social life that it has been a recurring theme throughout this book. To make this theme more explicit, let's review the main points about social change that we looked at in the preceding chapters.

Social change comes in many forms. Shown here are students in a Fort Myer, Virginia, elementary school on the first day of desegregation in 1954. The school, operated by the military for the children of military personnel, was desegregated by order of the Defense Department.

The Four Social Revolutions

You know that we are in the midst of rapid social change and that this change is occurring around the world. Why is this happening? The first thing to understand is that today's social change is the result of forces that were set in motion thousands of years ago, beginning with the domestication of plants and animals. This first social revolution allowed hunting and gathering societies to develop into horticultural and pastoral societies (see pages 148–150). The plow brought about the second social revolution, from which agricultural societies emerged. The third social revolution, prompted by the invention of the steam engine, ushered in the Industrial Revolution. Now we are in the midst of the fourth social revolution, stimulated by the invention of the microchip. The process of change has accelerated so greatly that the mapping of the human genome system could be pushing us into yet another new type of society, one based on biotechnology.

From *Gemeinschaft* to *Gesellschaft*

Although our society has changed extensively—think of how life was for your grandparents—we have seen only the tip of the iceberg. By the time this fourth—and perhaps fifth—social revolution is full-blown, little of our current way of life will remain. This assumption is based on what happened in our earlier social revolutions.

Consider the change from agricultural to industrial society. It isn't just the surface that changed, such as people living in cities instead of on farms. (See Table 7.1 on page 174.) People's lives had been built around the reciprocal obligations (such as exchanging favors) that are essential to kinship, social status, and friendship. When people moved to the city, many intimate relationships were replaced by impersonal associations built around paid work, contracts, and money. As reviewed on page 106, sociologists use the terms *Gemeinschaft* and *Gesellschaft* to indicate this fundamental shift in society.

Traditional, or *Gemeinschaft*, societies are small, rural, and slow-changing. Men dominate social life, and, as has been established for centuries, the divisions of labor between men and women are rigid. People live in extended families, have little formal education, treat most illnesses at home, tend to see morals in absolute terms, and consider the past the key for dealing with the present. In contrast, modern, or *Gesellschaft*, societies are large, urbanized, fast-changing, with more fluid divisions of labor between the sexes. In the third stage of the demographic transition, people have smaller families and low rates of infant mortality. They prize formal education, are future-oriented, have higher incomes, and enjoy vastly more material possessions.

The Industrial Revolution and Capitalism

As you can see, these are not just surface changes. The switch from *Gemeinschaft* to *Gesellschaft* society transformed people's social relationships and their orientations to life. In his analysis of this transition, Karl Marx stressed that when feudal society broke up, it threw people off the land, creating a surplus of labor. When these desperate masses moved to cities, they were exploited by capitalists, the owners of the means of production (factories, machinery, tools). This set in motion antagonistic relationships between capitalists and workers that remain today.

Max Weber traced capitalism to the Protestant Reformation (see page 176). He noted that the Reformation stripped Protestants of the assurance that church membership saved them. As they agonized over heaven and hell, they concluded that God did not want the elect to live in uncertainty. Surely God would give a sign to assure them that they were predestined to heaven. That sign, they decided, was prosperity. An unexpected consequence of the Reformation, then, was to make Protestants work hard and be thrifty. This created an economic surplus, which stimulated capitalism. In this way, Protestantism laid the groundwork for the Industrial Revolution that transformed the world.

The Protestant Reformation ushered in not only religious change but also, as Max Weber analyzed, fundamental social-economic change. Before capitalism, only the nobility and higher clergy could afford such possessions as those shown in this 1533 painting of French ambassadors by Hans Holbein, the Younger.

TABLE 22.1   Comparing Traditional and Industrialized (and Information) Societies

Characteristics	Traditional Societies	Industrialized (and Information) Societies
General Characteristics		
Social change	Slow	Rapid
Size of group	Small	Large
Religious orientation	More	Less
Education	Informal	Formal
Place of residence	Rural	Urban
Family size	Larger	Smaller
Infant mortality	High	Low
Life expectancy	Short	Long
Health care	Home	Hospital
Temporal orientation	Past	Future
Demographic transition	First stage	Third stage (or Fourth)
Material Relations		
Industrialized	No	Yes
Technology	Simple	Complex
Division of labor	Simple	Complex
Income	Low	High
Material possessions	Few	Many
Social Relationships		
Basic organization	*Gemeinschaft*	*Gesellschaft*
Families	Extended	Nuclear
Respect for elders	More	Less
Social stratification	Rigid	More open
Statuses	More ascribed	More achieved
Gender equality	Less	More
Norms		
View of morals	Absolute	Relativistic
Social control	Informal	Formal
Tolerance of differences	Less	More

Source: By the author.

The sweeping changes ushered in by the Industrial Revolution, called **modernization,** are summarized on Table 22.1. The traits listed on this table are *ideal types* in Weber's sense of the term, for no society exemplifies all of them to the maximum degree. Actually, our new technology has created a remarkable unevenness in the characteristics of nations, making them a mixture of the traits shown on this table. For example, Uganda is a traditional society, but the elite have computers, have smaller families, emphasize formal education, and so on. Thus the characteristics shown in Table 22.1 should be interpreted as "more" or "less" rather than "either-or."

When technology changes, societies change. Consider how technology from the industrialized world transforms traditional societies. When the West exported medicine to the Least Industrialized Nations, for example, death rates dropped while birth rates remained high. As a result, the population exploded. It brought hunger, uprooting masses of people who migrate to cities that have little industrialization to support them. The photo essay on pages 606–607 and the Cultural Diversity box on page 616 focus on some of these problems.

Social Movements

Social movements often reveal the cutting edge of social change. Upset by some aspect of society, people band together to express their feelings, even their outrage. They organize to demand change, or to resist some change they don't like. Because social movements form around issues that bother large numbers of people, they indicate areas of society in which there is great pressure for change. With globalization, these issues increasingly cut across international boundaries, indicating areas of discontent and sweeping change that affect many millions of people in different cultures (see pages 638–648).

Conflict, Power, and Global Politics

In our fast-paced world, we pay most attention to changes that directly affect our own lives. Mostly out of sight is one of the most significant changes of all, the shifting arrangements of power among nations. By the sixteenth century, global divisions had begun to emerge. Nations with the most advanced technology (at that time, the swiftest ships and the most powerful cannons) became wealthy through *colonialism,* conquering other nations and taking control of their resources. As capitalism emerged, those nations that industrialized first exploited the resources of countries that had not yet industrialized. According to *world system theory,* this made the nonindustrialized nations dependent and unable to develop their own resources (see pages 252–253).

G7 Plus.   Since World War II, a realignment of the world's powers (called *geopolitics*) has resulted in a triadic division of the globe: a Japan-centered East (soon to be dominated by China), a Germany-centered Europe, and a United States–centered western hemisphere. These three powers, along with four lesser ones—Canada, France, Great

modernization the transformation of traditional societies into industrial societies

Britain, and Italy—formed G7, meaning the "Group of 7." Fear of Russia's nuclear arsenal and an attempt to gain Russia's cooperation in global affairs prompted G7 to let Russia join their elite club, forming G8. The fragility of Russia's membership, which depends on its continued cooperation, became apparent with the armed conflict in Georgia in 2008, as well as with the snarling and insults member nations have thrown at one another since then.

No longer can this group ignore the growing wealth and power of China. Wanting to recapture its glories of centuries past, China is expanding its domain of influence. Bowing to the inevitable and attempting to reduce the likelihood of conflict as China steps on turf claimed by others, G8 has allowed China to become an observer at its annual summits. As mentioned in Chapter 11, if China cooperates adequately, the next step will be to incorporate China into this exclusive club.

Each year, the leaders of the world's eight most powerful nations meet in a secluded place to make world-controlling decisions. And each year, protesters demonstrate near the site. This photo was taken at G8's 2009 meeting at L'Aquila, Italy.

Dividing Up the World.   At their annual meetings, these world powers set policies to guide global economic affairs. Their goal is to perpetuate their global dominance. Essential to this goal is trying to maintain access to abundant, cheap oil—which requires that they dominate the Middle East, not letting it become an independent power. To the degree that these nations fail to implement policies and international relations that further their own interests, they undermine the New World Order they are trying to orchestrate.

Two Threats to This Coalition of Powers.   There are two major threats to the global divisions that this group is trying to work out. The first is dissension within. Currently, Russia is at the center of the intrafamilial feuding that threatens this coalition of powers. Because Russia is still stinging after losing its empire and wants a more powerful presence on the world stage, it is quick to perceive insult and threat—and to retaliate. In the dead of winter of 2006 and again in 2008, amidst a dispute with Ukraine over the price of gas, Russia turned off the oil supply that runs from it through Ukraine to western Europe, endangering lives in several countries (Crossland 2006; Kramer 2009). Russia also threatened to aim its missiles at cities in Europe if the United States didn't back down from its plan to put missiles in Poland as part of a missile-defense shield (Blomfield 2007). Russia even went as far as threatening a nuclear attack on Poland (McElroy 2008). Despite snarling back and forth, it is likely that these nations will resolve their tensions—including the coming ones with China—realign their structure of power successfully, and work out their New World Order.

I was in Riga, Latvia, as Russia's feud with the other powers began to unfold. While there, I took the photos on the next page, a foreshadowing of the armed conflict in Georgia.

The second threat is the resurgence of ethnic rivalries and conflicts. In Europe, ethnic violence in the former Yugoslavia split the country into seven nations. Ossetians and Georgians recently killed one another, the Flemish say they are not Belgian, and Turks in Germany live in fear of the young Germans who threaten their lives. In Africa, violence erupts between Kenya's Kalenjin and Kikuyu, and in Nigeria the Igbo won't let the government count them because, as they say, "We are not Nigerian." Ethnic conflicts threaten the peace in many parts of the world—from the United States and Mexico in North America to China and Vietnam in Asia. We do not know how long the lid can be kept on these seemingly bottomless ethnic antagonisms or whether they will ever play themselves out.

For global control, the Most Industrialized Nations require political and economic stability, both in their own backyards and in those countries that provide the raw materials essential for their industrial machine. This explains why they care little when African

Armored vehicles blocked streets when NATO held a summit in Riga, Latvia, in 2006. Disregarding broadcast warnings to stay off the streets, I wandered around the city, taking photos. I expected to be stopped, perhaps arrested, but I wasn't.

Angry that NATO was meeting in Latvia, a country Russia still claims as its own, Vladimir Putin, then the president of Russia, boycotted the meetings. I took this photo from an apartment window overlooking the ship on which NATO held secret meetings on November 29.

nations self-destruct in ethnic slaughter but refuse to tolerate interethnic warfare in their own neighborhoods. To let interethnic warfare in Bosnia, Kosovo, or Georgia go unchecked would be to tolerate conflict that could spread and engulf Europe. In contrast, the deaths of hundreds of thousands of Tutsis in Rwanda carried little or no political significance for these powerful countries.

The Africa Connections. The Most Industrialized Nations have begun to perceive connections between Africa and their own interests, however, and their attitudes and actions have begun to change. They are realizing that African poverty and political corruption breed political unrest. In addition, with political stability, Africa, as the world's last largely untapped market, could provide a huge outlet for their underutilized economic machine. Then, too, there are Africa's vast mineral resources—and oil reserves that could counterbalance those of the unstable Middle East. As a result, the United States has raised funds for African AIDS victims and, as in Liberia, Somalia, and Darfur, has begun to intervene in African politics.

Information Technology. Just as the development of armaments in the fourteenth and fifteenth centuries had an impact on global stratification, so, too, today's information revolution is destined to have similar far-reaching consequences. Those nations that make the most significant advances in information technology gain tremendous advantage in the world's race for dominance. Which nations will do so? The forecast points to an inevitable conclusion—the continued global dominance by the Most Industrialized Nations, including China as it joins this group. The fly in the ointment is the development of nuclear weapons by a state such as Iran or North Korea, which can upset all balances of power.

Theories and Processes of Social Change

Social change has always fascinated theorists. Earlier in the text, we reviewed the theories of Karl Marx and Max Weber, which we just summarized. Of the many other attempts to explain why societies change, we shall consider just four: the evolution of societies, natural cycles, conflict and power, and the pioneering views of sociologist William Ogburn.

Evolution from Lower to Higher

Evolutionary theories of how societies change are of two types, unilinear and multilinear. *Unilinear* theories assume that all societies follow the same path: Each evolves from simpler to more complex forms. This journey takes each society through uniform sequences (Barnes 1935). Of the many versions of this theory, the one proposed by Lewis Morgan (1877) once dominated Western thought. Morgan said that all societies go through three stages: savagery, barbarism, and civilization. In Morgan's eyes, England, his own society, was the epitome of civilization. All other societies were destined to follow the same path.

Multilinear views of evolution replaced unilinear theories. Instead of assuming that all societies follow the same sequence, multilinear theorists proposed that different routes lead to the same stage of development. Although the paths all lead to industrialization, societies need not pass through the same sequence of stages on their journey (Sahlins and Service 1960; Lenski and Lenski 1987).

Central to all evolutionary theories, whether unilinear or multilinear, is the assumption of *cultural progress.* Tribal societies are assumed to have a primitive form of human culture. As these societies evolve, they will reach a higher state—the supposedly advanced and superior form that characterizes the Western world. Growing appreciation of the rich diversity—and complexity—of tribal cultures discredited this idea. In addition, Western culture is now in crisis (poverty, racism, war, terrorism, sexual assaults, unsafe streets) and is no longer regarded as the apex of human civilization. Consequently, the idea of cultural progress has been cast aside, and evolutionary theories have been rejected (Eder 1990; Smart 1990).

Despite the globe's vast social change, people all over the world continue to make race a fundamental distinction. Shown here is a Ukrainian being measured to see if he is really "full lipped" enough to be called a Tartar.

Natural Cycles

Cyclical theories attempt to account for the rise of entire civilizations. Why, for example, did Egypt, Greece, and Rome wield such power and influence, only to crest and then decline? Cyclical theories assume that civilizations are like organisms: They are born, enjoy an exuberant youth, come to maturity, and then decline as they reach old age. They finally die (Hughes 1962).

The cycle does exist, but why? Historian Arnold Toynbee (1946) said that each civilization faces challenges to its existence. Groups work out solutions to these challenges, as they must be to continue. But those solutions are not satisfactory to all. The ruling elite manages to keep the remaining oppositional forces under control, even though they "make trouble" now and then. At a civilization's peak, however, when it has become an empire, the ruling elite loses its capacity to keep the masses in line "by charm rather than by force." Over time, the fabric of society rips apart. Force may hold the empire together for hundreds of years, but the civilization is doomed.

In a book that provoked widespread controversy, *The Decline of the West* (1926–1928), Oswald Spengler, a high school teacher in Germany, proposed that Western civilization had passed its peak and was in decline. Although the West succeeded in overcoming the crises provoked by Hitler and Mussolini, as Toynbee noted, civilizations don't end in sudden collapse. Because the decline can last hundreds of years, perhaps the crisis in Western civilization mentioned earlier (poverty, rape, murder, and so on) indicates that Spengler was right, and we are now in decline. If so, it appears that China is waiting on the horizon to be the next global power and to forge a new civilization.

Conflict over Power

Long before Toynbee, Karl Marx identified a recurring process of social change. He said that each *thesis* (a current arrangement of power) contains its own *antithesis* (contradiction or opposition). A struggle develops between the thesis and its antithesis, leading to a *synthesis* (a new arrangement of power). This new social order, in turn, becomes a thesis that will be challenged by its own antithesis, and so on. Figure 22.1 gives a visual summary of this process.

FIGURE 22.1
Marx's Model of Historical Change

Thesis
(some current arrangement of power)

+

Antithesis
(contradictions in the arrangement of power)

Synthesis
(a new arrangement of power)

Process continues throughout history

Classless state

Source: By the author.

dialectical process (of history) each arrangement of power (a thesis) contains contradictions (antitheses) which make the arrangement unstable and which must be resolved; the new arrangement of power (a synthesis) contains its own contradictions; this process of balancing and unbalancing continues throughout history as groups struggle for power and other resources

invention the combination of existing elements and materials to form new ones; identified by William Ogburn as one of three processes of social change

discovery a new way of seeing reality; identified by William Ogburn as one of three processes of social change

According to Marx's view (called a **dialectical process** of history), each ruling group sows the seeds of its own destruction. Consider capitalism. Marx said that capitalism (the thesis) is built on the exploitation of workers (an antithesis, or built-in opposition). With workers and owners on a collision course, the dialectical process will not stop until workers establish a classless state (the synthesis).

The analysis of G7 in the previous section follows conflict theory. G7's current division of the globe's resources and markets is a thesis. Resentment on the part of have-not nations is an antithesis. If one of the Least Industrialized Nations gains in military power, that nation will press for a redistribution of resources. With their nuclear weapons, China, India, Pakistan, Russia, and, soon, Iran and North Korea fit this scenario. So do the efforts of al-Qaeda to change the balance of power between the Middle East and the industrialized West. Any rearrangement of power (the new synthesis) will contain its own antitheses. These may be ethnic hostilities, or leaders feeling that their country has been denied its fair share of resources. These antitheses will haunt the rearrangement of power and must at some point be resolved into another synthesis. The process repeats.

Ogburn's Theory

Sociologist William Ogburn (1922/1938, 1961, 1964) proposed a theory of social change that is based largely on technology. As you can see from Table 22.2, he said that technology changes society by three processes: invention, discovery, and diffusion. Let's consider each.

Invention.   Ogburn defined **invention** as a combining of existing elements and materials to form new ones. We usually think of inventions as being only material items, such as computers, but there also are *social inventions*. We have considered many social inventions in this text including democracy and citizenship (pages 436–437), capitalism (pages 174–176, 403–405), socialism (pages 405–406), bureaucracy (pages 176–185), the corporation (pages 187–191, 409–411), and in Chapter 11, gender equality. We saw how these social inventions had far-reaching consequences on people's relationships. Material inventions can also affect social life deeply, and in this chapter we will examine how the automobile and the computer have transformed society.

Discovery.   Ogburn identified **discovery,** a new way of seeing reality, as a second process of change. The reality is already present, but people see it for the first time. An example is Columbus' "discovery" of North America, which had consequences so huge that they

TABLE 22.2 Ogburn's Processes of Social Change			
Process of Change	What It is	Examples	Social Changes
Invention	Combination of existing elements to form new ones	1. Cars 2. Computers 3. Graphite composites	1. Urban sprawl and long commutes to work 2. Telework and Global Positioning System 3. New types of building construction
Discovery	New way of seeing some aspect of the world	1. Columbus—N. America 2. Gold in California 3. DNA	1. Realignment of global power 2. Westward expansion of United States 3. Positive identification of criminals
Diffusion	Spread of an invention or discovery	1. Airplanes 2. Money 3. Condom	1. Global tourism 2. Global trade 3. Smaller families

Note: For each example, there are many changes. For some of the changes ushered in by the automobile and computer, see pages 663–670. You can also see that any particular change, such as global trade, depends not just on one item, but on several preceding changes.
Source: By the author.

altered the course of human history. This example also illustrates another principle: A discovery brings extensive change only when it comes at the right time. Other groups, such as the Vikings, had already "discovered" North America in the sense of learning that a new land existed—obviously no discovery to the Native Americans already living in it. Viking settlements disappeared into history, however, and Norse culture was untouched by the discovery.

Diffusion.   Ogburn stressed how **diffusion,** the spread of an invention or discovery from one area to another, can have extensive effects on people's lives. Consider an object as simple as the axe. When missionaries introduced steel axes to the Aborigines of Australia, it upset their whole society. Before this, the men controlled axe-making. They used a special stone that was available only in a remote region, and fathers passed axe-making skills on to their sons. Women had to request permission to use the axe. When steel axes became common, women also possessed them, and the men lost both status and power (Sharp 1995).

Diffusion also includes the spread of social inventions and ideas. As we saw in Chapter 15, the idea of citizenship changed political structures around the world. It swept away monarchs as an unquestioned source of authority. The idea of gender equality is now circling the globe. To those who are used to this concept, it is surprising to think that the idea that it is wrong to withhold rights on the basis of someone's sex is revolutionary. Like citizenship, gender equality is destined to transform basic human relationships and entire societies.

Cultural Lag.   Ogburn coined the term **cultural lag** to refer to how some elements of a culture lag behind the changes that come from invention, discovery, and diffusion. Technology, he suggested, usually changes first, with culture lagging behind. In other words, we play catch-up with changing technology, adapting our customs and ways of life to meet its needs.

Culture contact is the source of *diffusion,* the spread of an *invention* or *discovery* from one area to another. Shown here with a camera phone is a farmer in China. A few years ago, he was cut off from almost everyone except fellow villagers. How do you think modern communications will affect his orientation to life?

Evaluation of Ogburn's Theory.   Some find Ogburn's analysis too one-directional, saying that it makes technology the cause of almost all social change. They point out that how people adapt to technology is only one part of the story. The other part is that people take control over technology. People develop or adapt the technology they need, and they selectively use it. You read about the Amish on page 107, a good example, as they reject technologies they perceive as threatening to their culture.

Think of technology and social change as a two-way street: Just as technology stimulates social change, so social change stimulates technology. Last century, the Nazi armies marching across Europe stimulated the United States to develop the atomic bomb. Today, the growing number of elderly is spurring the development of new medical technologies, such as those used to treat Alzheimer's disease. Similarly, our changing perspectives about people with disabilities—that they should not be shunted aside but should participate in society's mainstream—has triggered the development of new types of wheelchairs and prosthetic devices that allow people who cannot move their legs to play basketball, participate in the Special Olympics, and even compete in rigorous downhill wheelchair races. The street is so two-way that their greater visibility and participation, in turn, are changing attitudes toward people with disabilities.

In fairness to Ogburn, we must note that he never said that technology is the only force for social change. Nor did he assert that people are passive pawns in the face of overwhelming technological forces. He did stress, though, that the material culture (technology) usually changes first, and the symbolic culture (people's ideas and ways of life) follows. This direction still holds. As with the organ transplants featured in the chapter's

diffusion the spread of an invention or a discovery from one area to another; identified by William Ogburn as one of three processes of social change

cultural lag Ogburn's term for human behavior lagging behind technological innovations

opening vignette, technology underlies the rapid change that is engulfing us today. And we are still playing catch-up with technology, with the computer especially, which is transforming society and, with it, our way of life.

How Technology Changes Society

As you may recall from Chapter 2, *technology* has a double meaning. It refers to both the *tools,* the items used to accomplish tasks, and the skills or procedures needed to make and use those tools. Technology refers to tools as simple as a comb and as complicated as a computer. Technology's second meaning—the skills or procedures needed to make and use tools—refers in this case not only to the procedures used to manufacture combs and computers but also to those that are required to "produce" an acceptable hairdo or to go online. Apart from its particulars, technology always refers to *artificial means of extending human abilities.*

All human groups make and use technology, but the chief characteristic of technology in postindustrial societies (also called **postmodern societies**) is that it greatly extends our abilities to communicate, to travel, and to retrieve and analyze information. These *new technologies,* as they are called, allow us to do what had never been done before: to transplant organs; to communicate almost instantaneously anywhere on the globe; to probe space; to travel greater distances faster; and to store, retrieve, and analyze vast amounts of information.

Change is rapid. Desktop computers are giving way to laptops—and some laptops are being replaced by handheld devices that contain keyboards and cameras. And this is just the beginning. In our coming biotech society, we may even "wear" computers, storing data on holograms located in our own proteins (bacteriorhodopsin) (Guessous et al. 2004). Our journey to the future is going to have so many twists and turns that no one knows what our life will be like. It is intriguing, however, to try to peer over the edge of the present to catch a glimpse of that future.

The Sociological Significance of Technology

The sociological significance of technology is how it changes our way of life. When a technology is introduced into a society, it forces other parts of society to give way. In fact, *new technologies can reshape society.* Let's look at four ways that technology changes social life.

Changes in Social Organization. Technology changes how people organize themselves. In Chapter 6, we discussed how, before machine technology was developed, most people worked at home; the new power-driven machinery required them to leave their families and go to a place called a factory. In the first factories, each worker still made an entire item. Then it was discovered that production increased if each worker performed only a specific task. One worker would hammer on a single part, or turn a certain number of bolts, and then someone else would take the item and do some other repetitive task before a third person took over, and so on. Henry Ford built on this innovation by developing

THE FAR SIDE® BY GARY LARSON

In the days before television

the assembly line: Instead of workers moving to the parts, machines moved the parts to the workers. In addition, the parts were made interchangeable and easy to attach (Womack et al. 1991).

Changes in Ideology. Technology also spurs ideology. Karl Marx noted that when workers did repetitive tasks on just a small part of a product, they did not feel connected to the finished product. No longer did they think of the product as "theirs." As Marx put it, workers had become *alienated* from the product of their labor, an **alienation** that breeds dissatisfaction and unrest.

Marx stressed that before factories came on the scene, workers owned their tools. This made them independent. If workers didn't like something, they would pack up their hammers and saws and leave. They would build a wagon or make a table for someone else. The factory was a great contrast, for there the capitalists owned the tools and machinery. This ownership transferred power to the capitalists, who used it to extract every ounce of sweat and blood they could. The workers had to submit, for desperate unemployed workers were lined up, eager to take the place of anyone who left. This exploitation, Marx believed, would lead to a workers' revolution: One day, workers would decide that they had had enough. They would unite, violently take over the means of production, and establish a workers' state.

The new technology that led to this unbalanced power also led to a change in ideology. As capitalists made huge profits from their factories, they developed the ideology that maximizing profits was a moral, even spiritual, endeavor. Profits benefited society—and pleased God as well. Followers of Marx, in turn, built ideologies of socialism to attack capitalism. In their view, profit comes only by exploiting workers, for workers are the true owners of society's resources.

Changes in Conspicuous Consumption. Just as ideology follows technology, so does ostentatious consumption. If technology is limited to clubbing animals, then animal skins are valued. No doubt primitive men and women who wore the skins of some especially unusual or dangerous animal walked with their heads held high—while their neighbors, wearing the same old sheepskins, looked on in envy. With technological change, Americans make certain that their clothing and accessories (sunglasses, handbags, and watches) have trendy labels prominently displayed. They also proudly display their cars, boats, and second homes. In short, while envy and pride may be basic to human nature, the particular material display depends on the state of technology.

Changes in Social Relationships. Technology also changes how people relate to one another. When men left home to work in factories, they became isolated from much of the everyday lives of their families. One consequence of becoming relative strangers to their wives and children was more divorce. As more women were drawn from the home to offices and factories, there were similar consequences—greater isolation from husbands and children and even more fragile marriages. A counter-trend is now in force, as the newer technology allows millions of workers to work at home. One consequence may be a strengthening of families and a reduction of divorce.

To get a better idea of how technology shapes our way of life, let's consider the changes ushered in by the automobile and the computer.

When Old Technology Was New: The Impact of the Automobile

About 100 years ago, the automobile was a new technology. It certainly had a profound impact on social life—and continues to influence our lives today. Let's look at some of the ways in which this invention has shaped U.S. society.

Displacement of Existing Technology. In a process that began in earnest when Henry Ford began to mass-produce the Model T in 1908, the automobile gradually pushed aside the old technology. People found automobiles to be cleaner, more reliable, and more economical than horses. People even thought that cars would lower their taxes, for no longer

alienation Marx's term for workers' lack of connection to the product of their labor; caused by their being assigned repetitive tasks on a small part of a product—this leads to a sense of powerlessness and normlessness; others use the term in the general sense of not feeling a part of something

would the public have to pay to clean up the tons of horse manure that accumulated on city streets (Flink 1990). Humorous as it sounds now, they also thought that automobiles would eliminate the cities' parking problems, for an automobile took up only half as much space as a horse and buggy.

Effects on Cities.   The automobile stimulated suburbanization. By the 1920s, Americans had begun to leave the city. They found that they could commute to jobs in the city from outlying areas where they enjoyed more space and lower taxes (Preston 1979). Eventually, this exodus to the suburbs produced urban sprawl and reduced the cities' tax base, contributing, as discussed in Chapter 20, to many of the problems that U.S. cities experience today.

Changes in Architecture.   The automobile's effects on commercial architecture are easy to see—from the huge parking lots that loop around shopping malls to the drive-up windows at banks and fast-food restaurants. Not so apparent is how the automobile altered the architecture of U.S. homes (Flink 1990). Before cars came on the scene, each home had a stable in the back where the family kept its horse and buggy. As first, people parked their cars there, as it required no change in architecture. Then, in three steps, home architecture changed. First, new homes were built with a detached garage. It was located, like the stable, at the back of the home. As the automobile became more essential to the U.S. family, the garage was incorporated into the home. It was moved from the back yard to the side of the house, and was connected by a breezeway. In the final step, the breezeway was removed, and the garage was integrated into the home. This allowed people to enter their automobiles without going outside.

Changed Courtship Customs and Sexual Norms.   By the 1920s, the automobile was used extensively for dating. This removed children from the watchful eye of parents and undermined parental authority. The police began to receive complaints about "night riders" who parked their cars along country lanes, "doused their lights, and indulged in orgies" (Brilliant 1964). Automobiles became so popular for courtship that by the 1960s about 40 percent of marriage proposals took place in them (Flink 1990).

In 1925 Jewett introduced cars with a foldout bed, as did Nash in 1937. The Nash version became known as "the young man's model" (Flink 1990). Mobile lovemaking has declined since the 1970s, primarily because changed sexual norms have made bedrooms easily accessible to the unmarried.

In the photo on the left, Henry Ford proudly displays his 1905 car, the latest in automobile technology. As is apparent, especially from the spokes on the car's wheels, new technology builds on existing technology. At the time this photo was taken, who could have imagined that this vehicle would transform society? The photo on the right of Mazda's Taiki, a concept car.

Effects on Women's Roles.   The automobile may also lie at the heart of the way women's roles have changed in U.S. society. To see how, we first need to see what a woman's life was like before the automobile. Historian James Flink (1990) described it this way:

> Until the automobile revolution, in upper-middle-class households groceries were either ordered by phone and delivered to the door or picked up by domestic servants or the husband on his way home from work. Iceboxes provided only very limited space for the storage of perishable foods, so shopping at markets within walking distance of the home was a daily chore. The garden provided vegetables and fruits in season, which were home-canned for winter consumption. Bread, cakes, cookies, and pies were home-baked. Wardrobes contained many home-sewn garments.
>
> Mother supervised the household help and worked alongside them preparing meals, washing and ironing, and housecleaning. In her spare time she mended clothes, did decorative needlework, puttered in her flower garden, and pampered a brood of children. Generally, she made few family decisions and few forays alone outside the yard. She had little knowledge of family finances and the family budget. The role of the lower-middle-class housewife differed primarily in that far less of the household work was done by hired help, so that she was less a manager of other people's work, more herself a maid-of-all-work around the house.

Because automobiles required skill to operate rather than strength, women were able to drive as well as men. This new mobility freed women physically from the narrow confines of the home. As Flink (1990) observed, the automobile changed women "from producers of food and clothing into consumers of national-brand canned goods, prepared foods, and ready-made clothes. The automobile permitted shopping at self-serve supermarkets outside the neighborhood and in combination with the electric refrigerator made buying food a weekly rather than a daily activity." When women began to do the shopping, they gained greater control over the family budget, and as their horizons extended beyond the confines of the home, they also gained different views of life.

In Sum: The automobile helped transform society, including views of courtship and sexuality. It had a special impact on women's roles at home, including their relationship with their husbands. It altered women's attitudes as it transformed their opportunities and stimulated them to participate in areas of social life not connected with the home.

No one attributes such fundamental changes in relationships and values solely to the automobile, of course, for many historical events, as well as many other technological changes, occurred during this same period, each making its own contribution to social change. Even this brief overview of the social effects of the automobile, however, illustrates that technology is much more than just a tool—that it exerts profound influence on social life.

We are now living through another invention that is having profound effects on our lives. Let's consider the impact of that technological marvel, the computer.

The Cutting Edge of Change

Changes in Social Relationships.   Although the computer is part of our daily lives, most of us never think about it. We are pleased with the computer's capacity to make life easier. The ease and speed of digital communications, such as being able to type just one message and send it instantaneously to everyone in our address book, bring special pleasure. Many of us also welcome the new ways that we are able to relate socially, the topic of the Sociology and the New Technology box on the next page.

Concerns About the Computer.   Some people have deep reservations about our computerized society. They worry that errors will creep into computerized records, that their privacy will be invaded, or that their identity will be stolen. Then there is the matter of political control. Increasingly, governments monitor citizens, and the computer certainly makes it easier for them to do so. Chinese authorities are issuing identity cards with a chip that includes not just the individual's name and address but also education, work history, religion, ethnicity, medical insurance, police record, landlord's phone number, and—to enforce the country's "one child" policy—the individual's reproductive history (Bradsher 2007).

SOCIOLOGY and the NEW TECHNOLOGY

From Electronic Toy to Political Weapon: Twittering in the Digital Age

Evan Williams, co-founder of Twitter

Why would anyone want to Twitter? Do you really want to know the up-to-the-minute and by-the-minute blow-by-blow detailed activities and thoughts of your friends? All those instantaneous, brief messages (up to 140 characters, like a mobile phone text) recounting feelings ("I'm so down today"), work problems ("boss is mad at me again"), and activities ("making a sandwich—ham, cheese, egg, and ketchup—yummy").

So, who cares?

This doesn't make sense—until you try it.

Ben Haley thought that such streaming trivia ("tweets") was absurd, but for the fun of it, he and his friends signed on to Twitter. Each day, he was greeted with a page of one- or two-line notes. At first the stream of trivia made no sense. But then he found himself caught up in his friends' lives as never before. Starting to sense the rhythm of their lives, he found himself checking and rechecking his account several times a day, sometimes several times an hour.

When a friend came down with a virus, Haley could tell from the updates that she was getting worse, and he became aware when she was turning the corner. He followed his friends' emotions as they went through their days—from scoring successes to finding themselves in hell. Even the daily sandwich-making started to make sense, part of the rhythm of that person's life.

When Haley and his friends get together (physically), they don't have to ask, "What have you been up to?" They already know—and in more detail than practically any friends have had in history. Instead, their topics begin from threads of the updates, as though they are picking up a conversation in the middle.

Ambient awareness is the name social scientists have given to this not-being-there-and yet-being-there. The term *digital co-presence* or even *twittering* might be bet-

ter, but whatever you call it, the computer, with all its related gizmos, is changing social life. As this more recent one unfolds, other changes will be in hot pursuit—each nudging adjustments in our lives.

Technology often has uses and implications for social life that go far beyond the expectations and even imaginations of its developers. So it is with Twitter. Without warning, this electronic toy that helped people keep up with one another was turned into a political weapon. As Iranians protested election fraud in 2009, they used Twitter to bypass censors so they could organize mass protests. Then they used Twitter to transmit up-to-the-minute information on their demonstrations to friends—and to the world.

For Your Consideration

How are you keeping up with your friends' lives and letting them keep up with yours? Do you use Twitter? Facebook? Or FriendFeed, Jaiku, Plurk, or Pownce? How many messages, including mobile phone texts and IMs, do you send friends and family a day? A week? How are the various forms of instant messaging affecting your relationships?

How do you think Twitter might become a political weapon in the United States?

Based on Thompson 2008; Liedtke 2009; Stanley 2009.

The U.S. government might outdo even this. The Federal Drug Administration has approved an identity chip the size of a grain of rice that can be injected under the skin (Stein 2004). Designed to store a patient's medical records, the chip will include the individual's name, address, age, weight, height, hair and skin color, and race–ethnicity. It could, of course, also include the names and addresses of our friends and associates—even any suspected acts of disloyalty. The chip can be activated by a scanner, so none of us would even know that we were under surveillance. It isn't difficult to jump from the capacities of this chip to Orwell's Big Brother society.

The computer has changed our lives, and here is an illustration of how computers have changed. This 1946 photo is of the ENIAC, the world's first computer, which weighed 30 tons, was eight feet high, three feet deep, and 100 feet long. The iPhone G3 held by the college student superimposed on this photo has more power than the ENIAC.

At this point, let's consider how the computer is changing education, the workplace, business, and the waging of war. We'll then consider its likely effects on social inequality.

Computers in Education. Because of computers, students can take courses in Russian, German, and Spanish—even when their schools have no teachers who speak these languages. Even though they have no sociology instructors, they can take courses in the sociology of gender, race, social class, or even sex, and sports. (The comma is important. It isn't sex and sports. That course isn't offered—yet.)

We've barely begun to harness the power of computers, but I imagine that the day will come when you will be able to key in the terms *social interaction* and *gender,* select your preference of historical period, geographical site, age, and ethnic group—and the computer will spew out text, maps, moving images, and sounds. You will be able to compare sexual discrimination in the military in 1985 and today, or the price of marijuana in Los Angeles and New Orleans. If you wish, the computer will give you a test—geared to the level of difficulty you choose—so that you can check your mastery of the material.

Distance learning, courses taught to students who are not physically present with their instructor, will become such a part of mainstream education that most students will take at least some of their high school, college, and graduate courses through this arrangement. Cameras in laptops allow everyone in the class to see everyone else, even though the students live in different countries. Imagine this—and likely it soon will be a reality: Your fellow students in a course on diversity in human culture will be living in Thailand, South Africa, Latvia, Egypt, China, and Australia. With zero-cost conference calls and e-mail and file exchanges, you will be able to compare your countries' customs on eating, dating, marriage, family, or burial—whatever is of interest to you. You can then write a team paper in which you compare your experiences with one another, applying the theories taught in the text, and then e-mail your paper to your mutual instructor.

Computers in the Workplace. The computer is also transforming the workplace. At the simplest level, it affects how we do our work. For example, I wrote the first two editions of this book on a computer, and a printer produced a copy of the manuscript. A series of archaic, precomputer processes followed: I sent the printed copy via the postal service to an editor, who physically handled the manuscript and sent it to others who did the same. The manuscript, marked up in red pencil, was then returned to me, and I mailed back a revised copy. The process was primitive, much the same as would have occurred during Benjamin Franklin's day—only without the quill and pony.

Practice soon caught up with potential. My editors and I zap text back and forth electronically. I may be in the United States or Europe or South America, while they are in Connecticut, Massachusetts, and Oregon. It makes no difference. I print nothing, and until the final step in the process, send no papers. Even then, I have the option of skipping the paper copy, but I like to handle the actual pages. Although the distances are greater, the time lapse has shrunk. For me, the process is marvelous testimony of our changing world—and, perhaps, unsettling confirmation of our steady steps into a brave new world.

On a deeper level, the computer also changed social relationships. I used to take my manuscript to a university secretary, wait several days for her to type it, and then retrieve it. With electronic manuscripts, no secretary is involved. This enhanced social relationships, for I made fewer demands on the department secretary. It also reduced tensions, for it eliminated the necessity of the secretary making excuses when she didn't have the manuscript ready on time (when I had seen her doing crossword puzzles).

For some, including myself, the computer has also reversed the change in work location that industrialization ushered in. As discussed earlier, industrialization shifted much work from home to factory and office. Now several million workers remain home while satellite communications connect them with their supervisors, customers, and fellow workers at locations around the country—or even on the other side of the globe. This could be the beginning of another historical shift, one that brings families closer together.

Computers in Business and Finance.   The advanced technology of businesses used to consist of cash registers and adding machines. Connections to the outside world were managed by telephone. Today, those same businesses are electronically "wired" to suppliers, salespeople, and clients around the country—and around the world. Computers track sales of items, tabulate inventory, and set in motion the process of reordering and restocking. Their detailed reports of sales alert managers to changes in their customers' tastes or preferences. For retail giants like Wal-Mart, the computer reports changing shopping patterns and preferences in products by region.

National borders have become meaningless as computers instantaneously transfer billions of dollars from one country to another. No "cash" changes hands in these transactions. The money consists of digits in computer memory banks. In the same day, this digitized money can be transferred from the United States to Switzerland, from there to the Grand Cayman Islands, and then to the Isle of Mann. Its zigzag, instantaneous path around the globe leaves few traces for sleuths to follow. "Where's my share?" governments around the world are grumbling, as they consider how to control—and tax—this new technology.

Computers are also having a major impact on the way war is fought, the topic of the Sociology and the New Technology box on the next page.

Technology, which drives much social change, is at the forefront of our information revolution. This revolution, based on the computer chip, allows reality to cross with fantasy, a merging that sometimes makes it difficult to tell where one ends and the other begins. A computer projects an image onto the front of the coat, making its wearer "invisible."

SOCIOLOGY and the NEW TECHNOLOGY

The Coming Star Wars

Star Wars is on its way.

The Predator is an unmanned plane that flies thousands of feet above enemy lines and beams streaming video back to the base. Sensors from the Global Positioning System report the Predator's precise location. When operators at the base identify a target, they press a button; the Predator beams a laser onto the target, and the operators launch guided bombs (Barry and Thomas 2001). The enemy doesn't know what hit them. They see neither the Predator nor the laser. Perhaps, however, just before they are blown to bits, they do hear the sound of an incoming bomb (Barry 2001).

Warfighter I is a camera that uses hyperspectral imaging, a way of identifying objects by detecting their "light signatures." This camera is so precise that it can report from space whether a field of grain contains natural or genetically altered grain—and whether the grain has adequate nitrogen. The military use of this camera? It can also locate tanks that are camouflaged or even hiding under trees (Hitt 2001).

Robot soldiers are on their way. In a project called Future Combat Systems, the Pentagon is developing robots that will see and react like humans. They might not look like humans. In fact, they might look like hummingbirds—or tractors, or cockroaches. They will gather intelligence, search buildings, and fire weapons (Weiner 2005a). The first robots were put to use in Iraq, but they were primitive versions, remote-controlled devices that dispose of bombs. The next ones are likely to have the capacity to drive vehicles.

The Pentagon is building its own Internet, the Global Information Grid (GIG). The goal of GIG, encircling the globe, is grandiose: to give the Pentagon a "God's eye view" of every enemy everywhere (Weiner 2004).

All this is but a prelude. The U.S. Defense Department is planning to "weaponize" space. Concerned that other nations will also launch intelligence-gathering devices and space weapons, the United States is set to launch microsatellites the size of a suitcase. These satellites will be able to pull alongside an enemy satellite and, using a microwave gun, fry its electronic system.

Coming also is a laser whose beam will bounce off a mirror in space, making the night battlefield visible to ground soldiers who are wearing special goggles. Also on its way is a series of Star Wars weapons: space-based

The pilotless Predator

lasers, pyrotechnic electromagnetic pulsers, holographic decoys, suppression clouds, oxygen suckers, robo-bugs—and whatever else the feverish imaginations of military planners can devise.

The Air Force has nicknamed one of it space programs "Rods from God." Tungsten cylinders would be hurled from space at targets on the ground. Striking at speeds of 7,000 miles an hour, the rods would have the force of a small nuclear weapon. In another program, radio waves would be directed to targets on the earth. As the Air Force explains it, the power of the radio waves could be "just a tap on the shoulder—or they could turn you into toast" (Weiner 2005b).

We are on the edge of a surrealistic world. Politicians and the military assume that it is normal both to dominate the world and to weaponize space. The chilling reality is reflected in a report by a congressional commission: "Every medium—air, land and sea—has seen conflict. Reality indicates that space will be no different" (Hitt 2001). A Republican or a Democratic president—this makes no difference either. As Barack Obama said to the military: "We need greater investment in advanced technology, . . . like unmanned aerial vehicles and electronic warfare capabilities" (Findlater 2009).

For Your Consideration

Do you think we should militarize space? What if other countries do the same? In 2006, China launched a missile to shoot down one of its own orbiting satellites, which could indicate that it is ready to play this deadly space game. What do you think of this comment, made to Congress by the head of the U.S. Air Force Space Command? "We must establish and maintain space superiority. It's the American way of fighting" (Weiner 2005b).

Cyberspace and Social Inequality

We've already stepped into our future. The Net gives us access to libraries of electronic information. We utilize software that sifts, sorts, and transmits text, images, sound, and video. We zap messages and images to people on the other side of the globe—or even in our own homes, dorm, or office. Our world has become linked by almost instantaneous communications, with information readily accessible around the globe. Few places can still be called "remote."

This new technology carries severe implications for national and global stratification. On the national level, computer technology could perpetuate present inequalities: We could end up with information have-nots, primarily inner-city residents cut off from the flow of information on which prosperity depends. Or this technology could provide an opportunity to break out of the inner city and the rural centers of poverty. On the global level, the question is similar, but on a grander scale, taking us to one of the more profound issues of this century: Will unequal access to advanced technology destine the Least Industrialized Nations to a perpetual pauper status? Or will access to this new technology be their passport to affluence?

In Sum: As technology wraps itself around us, changing our society, our culture, and our everyday lives, we confront four primary issues: What type of future will technology lead us into? Will technology liberate us or make us slaves of Big Brother? Will the new technology perpetuate or alleviate social inequalities on both national and global levels? And finally, and perhaps most ominously, will the technology that is transforming the face of war and being used "over there" come back to haunt us in our own land?

The Growth Machine Versus the Earth

Of all the changes swirling around us, those that affect the natural environment seem to hold the most serious implications for human life.

Underlying today's environmental decay is the globalization of capitalism, which I have stressed throughout this text. To maintain their dominance and increase their wealth, the Most Industrialized Nations, spurred by multinational corporations, continue to push for economic growth. At the same time, the Industrializing Nations, playing catch-up, are striving to develop their economies. Meanwhile, the Least Industrialized Nations are anxious to enter the race: Because they start from even farther behind, they have to strive for even faster growth.

Many people are convinced that the earth cannot withstand such an onslaught. Global economic production creates extensive pollution, and faster-paced production means faster-paced destruction of our environment. The photos to the left illustrate just the tip of the iceberg. In this relentless pursuit of economic development, many animal species have been driven to the verge of extinction—or are already gone forever. If the goal is a **sustainable environment,** a world system in which we use our physical environment to meet our needs without destroying humanity's future, we cannot continue to trash the earth. In short, the ecological message is incompatible with an economic message that implies it is OK to rape the earth if it makes someone money.

Before looking at the social movement that has emerged about this issue, let's examine major environmental problems. We'll begin with pollution in the Most Industrialized Nations.

Sumatran Tiger
Fewer than 400, Indonesia

Texas Ocelot
Fewer than 250, southern United States, northern Mexico

Mountain Bongo
About 50, Kenya

Gaur
About 36,000, Southeast Asia

Environmental Problems in the Most Industrialized Nations

Although even tribal groups produced pollution, the frontal assault on the natural environment did not begin in earnest until nations industrialized. Industrialization was equated with progress and prosperity. For the Most Industrialized Nations, the slogan has been "Growth at any cost."

Industrial growth did come, but at a high cost. Despite their destruction of the environment and the dangers they pose to people's health, much toxic waste has simply been dumped onto the land, into our streams and lakes, and into the ocean. Formerly pristine streams have been turned into polluted sewers, and the water supply of some cities is unfit to drink. On the Social Map below, you can see the locations of the worst hazardous waste sites in the United States. These sites represent corporate garbage, some of it subsidized by *corporate welfare*, the topic of the Down-to-Earth Sociology box on the next page. A special problem is our nuclear power plants, supposedly a solution to the problem of the "dirty" generation of electricity. Nuclear plants produce wastes that remain lethal for thousands of years. We simply don't know what to do with these piles of deadly garbage (Vergakis 2009).

The major polluters are the Most Industrialized Nations. Our follies include harming the ozone layer in order to have the convenience of aerosol spray bottles, refrigerators, and air conditioners. With limited space to address this issue, I would like to focus on an overarching aspect of the pollution of our environment, the burning of fossil fuels.

Fossil Fuels and Global Warming.   Burning fossil fuels to run factories, motorized vehicles, and power plants has been especially harmful. Figure 22.3 on page 671 illustrates how burning fossil fuels produces **acid rain,** which kills animal and plant life. The situation is so bad that fish can no longer survive in some lakes in Canada and the northeastern United States.

An invisible but infinitely more serious consequence is the **greenhouse effect.** Burning fossil fuels releases gases that, like the glass of a greenhouse, allow sunlight to enter the earth's atmosphere freely but inhibit the release of heat. It is as though the gases

acid rain rain containing sulfuric and nitric acids (burning fossil fuels release sulfur dioxide and nitrogen oxide that become sulfuric and nitric acids when they react with moisture in the air)

greenhouse effect the buildup of carbon dioxide in the earth's atmosphere that allows light to enter freely but inhibits the release of heat; believed to cause global warming

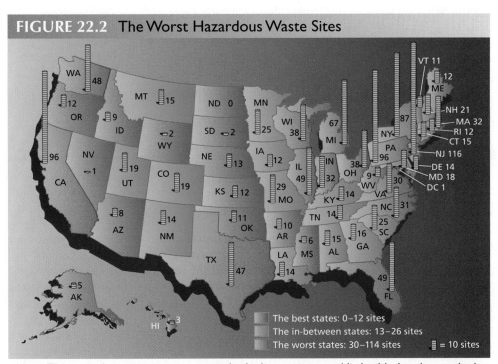

FIGURE 22.2   The Worst Hazardous Waste Sites

Note: These are the waste sites so outstandingly threatening to public health that they made the national priority list. New Jersey is in a class by itself. This small state has 20 more hazardous waste sites than its nearest competitor, Pennsylvania, with 96.

Source: By the author. Based on *Statistical Abstract of the United States* 2009: Table 367.

Down-to-Earth Sociology
Corporate Welfare: How to Get Paid to Pollute

Welfare is one of the most controversial topics in the United States. It arouses the ire of many wealthy and middle-class Americans, who view the poor who collect welfare as parasites. But have you heard about **corporate welfare.** This term refers to handouts that are given to corporations. Some states will reduce a company's taxes if it locates within the state or if it remains after threatening to leave. Some states provide land and buildings at bargain prices. The reason: jobs.

Corporate welfare even goes to companies that foul our land, water, and air. Borden Chemicals and Plastics in Louisiana has released clouds of hazardous chemicals so thick that to protect drivers, the police have sometimes had to shut down the highway that runs near the plant. Borden has even buried hazardous wastes without a permit. The groundwater beneath its plant is contaminated, threatening the aquifer that provides drinking water for residents of Louisiana and Texas.

Borden's pollution has cost the company dearly: $3.6 million in fines, $3 million to clean up the groundwater, and $400,000 for local emergency response units. That's a hefty $7 million. But if we add corporate welfare, the company didn't make out so badly. With $15 million in reduced and canceled property taxes, Borden has enjoyed a net gain of $8 million (Bartlett and Steele 2001). And that's not counting the savings the company racked up by not having to properly dispose of its toxic wastes in the first place.

Louisiana has added a novel twist to corporate welfare. It offers an incentive to help start-up companies.

Exxon Mobil refinery, Baton Rouge, Louisiana
High rates of cancer in this area? Couldn't be the pollution. Must be something they ate.

This itself isn't novel; the owners of that little "mom and pop" grocery store on your corner may have received some benefits when they first opened. Louisiana's twist is what it counts as a start-up company. One of these little start-ups is called Exxon Mobil Corp., one of the world's richest companies. Although the original enterprise that evolved into Exxon Mobil opened for business in 1870, its property taxes were slashed by $213 million under this program for start-ups. Another little company that the state figured could use a nudge to help it get started was Shell Oil Co., which had $140 million slashed from its taxes (Bartlett and Steele 2001). Then there were International Paper, Dow Chemical, Union Carbide, Boise Cascade, Georgia Pacific, and another tiny one called Procter & Gamble.

For Your Consideration
Apply the functionalist, symbolic interactionist, and conflict perspectives to corporate welfare. Which do you think provides the best explanation of corporate welfare? Why?

---

corporate welfare the financial incentives (tax breaks, subsidies, and even land and stadiums) given to corporations in order to attract them to an area or induce them to remain

global warming an increase in the earth's temperature due to the greenhouse effect

have smudged the windows of our earth's greenhouse, and our planet can no longer breathe the way it should. The buildup of heat is causing **global warming:** Glaciers are melting and the seas are rising, threatening to flood the world's shorelines. Some island nations will disappear, washed away into the ocean (Kanter and Revkin 2007). As the climate boundaries move north several hundred miles, many animal and plant species will become extinct.

For decades, scientists argued about global warming. Many said that it was part of a natural cycle that the earth goes through. Some even said that it did not exist. As evidence accumulated, more and more scientists concluded that global warming did exist and that human activity—primarily the burning of coal and oil—was its cause. Today, the world's leading climate scientists, forming the United Nations' Intergovernmental Panel on

FIGURE 22.3 Acid Rain

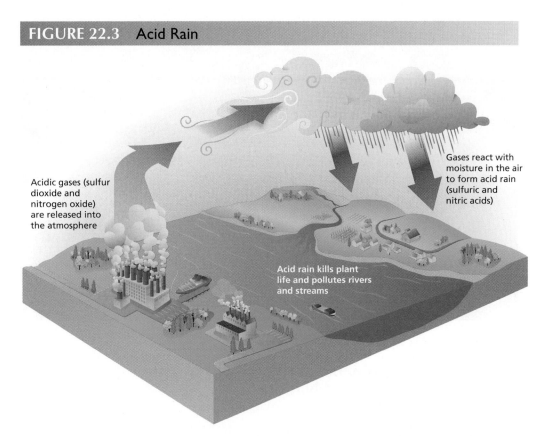

Acidic gases (sulfur dioxide and nitrogen oxide) are released into the atmosphere

Gases react with moisture in the air to form acid rain (sulfuric and nitric acids)

Acid rain kills plant life and pollutes rivers and streams

Climate Change, have concluded that global warming is "unequivocal" and that human activity is its main driver (Rosenthal and Revkin 2007). The Most Industrialized Nations have agreed to cut in half the emissions that cause the greenhouse effect (Stolberg 2008). If they don't, the consequences are likely to be catastrophic.

The Energy Shortage and Multinational Corporations. If you ever read about an energy shortage, you can be sure that what you read is false. There is no energy shortage, nor can there ever be. We can produce unlimited low-cost power, which can help to raise the living standards of humans across the globe. The sun, for example, produces more energy than humanity could ever use. Boundless energy is also available from the tides and the winds. In some cases, we need better technology to harness these sources of energy; in others, we need only to apply the technology we already have.

Burning fossil fuels in internal combustion engines is the main source of pollution in the Most Industrialized Nations. Of the technologies being developed to use alternative sources of energy in vehicles, the most prominent is the gas-electric hybrid. Some of these cars are expected to eventually get several hundred miles per gallon of gasoline. The hybrid, however, is simply a bridge until vehicles powered by fuel cells become practical. Fuel cells convert hydrogen into electricity; water, instead of carbon monoxide, will come out of a car's exhaust pipe.

Environmental Injustice. Unequal power has led to **environmental injustice**—minorities and the poor being the ones who suffer the most from the effects of pollution (Laszewski 2008). Industries locate where land is cheaper, which is *not* where the wealthy live. Nor will the rich allow factories to spew pollution near their homes. As a result, low-income communities, which are often inhabited by minorities, are more likely to be exposed to pollution. Sociologists have studied, formed, and joined *environmental justice* groups that fight to close polluting plants and block construction of polluting industries.

environmental injustice
refers to how minorities and the poor are harmed the most by environmental pollution

Rising sea levels? No problem for the Lilypad, floating self-contained cities of 50,000 inhabitants envisioned for the future.

Environmental Problems in the Industrializing and Least Industrialized Nations

The Industrializing Nations are also major polluters. Of the world's 40 most polluted cities, 36 are in China (World Bank 2007:Figure 5). The nine thousand chemical plants along its banks have turned China's Yangtze River into an industrial sewer (Zakaria 2008). China's pollution is so great that it now emits more carbon dioxide than does the United States (Rosenthal 2008). Like the Russians before them, Chinese who dare to speak out about pollution are arrested and sent to prison (Feshbach 1992; J. Kahn 2007c). As China secures its place in the industrialized world, its leaders will place more emphasis on controlling pollution.

Some of the Least Industrialized Nations lack environmental protection laws, which has not gone unnoticed by opportunists in the Most Industrialized Nations. Some companies produce chemicals in these nations that are outlawed in their own countries (Smith 1995; Mol 2001). Others dump industrial wastes in these countries (Polgreen and Simons 2006). Alarmed at the growing environmental destruction, the World Bank, the monetary arm of the Most Industrialized Nations, has pressured the Least Industrialized Nations to reduce pollution. When New Delhi officials tried to comply, workers blocked traffic and set fires, closing down the city for several days (Freund 2001). Understandably, the basic concern of workers is to provide food for their families first, and to worry about the environment later. With this in mind, the global financial crisis does not bode well for reducing our planet's pollution.

A special concern is the rain forests. Although they cover just 6 percent of the earth's land area, the rain forests are home to *one-half* of all the earth's plant and animal species (Frommer 2007). Despite our knowledge that the rain forests are essential for humanity's welfare, we seem bent on destroying them for the sake of timber and farms. In the process, we extinguish plant and animal species, perhaps thousands a year. As biologists remind us, once a species is lost, it is gone forever.

As the rain forests disappear, so do the Indian tribes who live in them. With their extinction goes their knowledge of the environment, the topic of the Cultural Diversity box on the next page. Like Esau who traded his birthright for a bowl of porridge, we are exchanging our future for some lumber, farms, and pastures.

The Environmental Movement

Concern about environmental problems has produced a worldwide social movement. One result is *green parties,* political parties whose central issue is the environment. In some European countries, these parties have made a political impact. In Germany, for example,

Cultural Diversity around the World

The Rain Forests: Lost Tribes, Lost Knowledge

In the past 100 years, 90 of Brazil's 270 Indian tribes have disappeared. Other tribes have moved to villages as ranchers and gold miners have taken over their lands. Tribal knowledge is lost as group members adapt to village life.

Tribal groups are not ignorant people who barely survive. On the contrary, these groups have developed intricate forms of social organization and possess knowledge that has accumulated over thousands of years. The Kayapo Indians, for example, who belong to one of the Amazon's endangered tribes, use 250 types of wild fruit and hundreds of nut and tuber species. They cultivate thirteen types of bananas, eleven kinds of manioc (cassava), sixteen strains of sweet potato, and seventeen kinds of yams. Many of these varieties are unknown to non-Indians. The Kayapo also use thousands of medicinal plants, one of which contains a drug that is effective against intestinal parasites.

A Pishta girl of the Yine tribe in the Peruvian Amazon. The way of life of the world's few remaining rain forest tribes is threatened.

Until recently, Western scientists dismissed tribal knowledge as superstitious and worthless. Now, however, some have come to realize that to lose tribes is to lose valuable knowledge. In the Central African Republic, a man whose chest was being eaten away by an amoeboid infection lay dying because the microbes did not respond to drugs. Out of desperation, the Roman Catholic nuns who were treating him sought the advice of a native doctor. He applied crushed termites to the open wounds. To the amazement of the nuns, the man made a remarkable recovery.

With this example, I don't mean to imply that these tribes have medicine superior to ours, just that we can learn from their experience with nature. The disappearance of the rain forests means the destruction of plant species that may have healing properties. Some of the discoveries from the rain forests have been astounding. The needles from a Himalayan tree in India contain taxol, a drug that is effective against ovarian and breast cancer. A flower from Madagascar is used in the treatment of leukemia; a frog in Peru produces a painkiller that is more powerful, but less addictive, than morphine (Wolfensohn and Fuller 1998).

On average, one tribe of Amazonian Indians has been lost each year for the past century—because of violence, greed for their lands, and exposure to infectious diseases against which these people have little resistance. Ethnocentrism underlies much of this assault. Perhaps the extreme is represented by the cattle ranchers in Colombia who killed eighteen Cueva Indians. The cattle ranchers were perplexed when they were put on trial for murder. They asked why they should be charged with a crime, since everyone knew that the Cuevas were animals, not people. They pointed out that there was even a verb in Colombian Spanish, *cuevar,* which means "to hunt Cueva Indians." So what was their crime, they asked? The jury found them not guilty because of "cultural ignorance."

For Your Consideration
What do you think we can do to stop the destruction of the rain forests?

Sources: Durning 1990; Gorman 1991; Linden 1991; Stipp 1992; Nabhan 1998; Simons 2006.

the Green Party has won seats in the national legislature. Green parties have had little success in the United States, but in the 2000 election, a green party headed by Ralph Nader arguably tipped the balance and gave the presidential election to George W. Bush.

Activists in the environmental movement generally seek solutions in politics, education, and legislation. Despairing that pollution continues, that the rain forests are still being cleared, and that species are becoming extinct, some activists are convinced that the planet is doomed unless urgent steps are taken. Choosing a more radical course, they use extreme tactics to try to arouse indignation among the public and to force the government to act. Convinced that they stand for true morality, many are willing to break the law and go to jail for their actions. Such activists are featured in the following Thinking Critically section.

ThinkingCRITICALLY

Ecosabotage

Chaining oneself to a giant Douglas fir that is slated for cutting, tearing down power lines and ripping up survey stakes, driving spikes into redwood trees, sinking whaling vessels, and torching SUVs and Hummers—are these the acts of dangerous punks who have little understanding of the needs of modern society? Or are they the acts of brave men and women who are willing to put their freedom, and even their lives, on the line on behalf of the earth itself?

To understand why **ecosabotage**—actions taken to sabotage the efforts of people who are thought to be legally harming the environment—is taking place, consider the Medicine Tree, a 3,000-year-old redwood in the Sally Bell Grove near the northern California coast. Georgia Pacific, a lumber company, was determined to cut down the Medicine Tree, the oldest and largest of the region's redwoods, which rests on a sacred site of the Sinkyone Indians. Members of Earth First! chained themselves to the tree. After they were arrested, the sawing began. Other protesters jumped over the police-lined barricade and stood defiantly in the path of men wielding axes and chain saws. A logger swung an axe and barely missed a demonstrator. At that moment, the sheriff radioed a restraining order, and the cutting stopped.

Julia "Butterfly" Hill lived for two years in this 1,000-year-old redwood tree, which she named Luna. The Pacific Lumber Company finally agreed to save the tree and a 200-foot buffer zone.

How many 3,000-year-old trees remain on our planet? Does our desire for fences and picnic tables for backyard barbecues justify cutting them down? Issues like these—as well as the slaughter of seals and whales, the destruction of the rain forests, and the drowning of dolphins in mile-long drift nets—spawned Earth First! and other organizations devoted to preserving the environment, such as Greenpeace, Rain Forest Action Network, the Ruckus Society, and the Sea Shepherds.

"We feel like there are insane people who are consciously destroying our environment, and we are compelled to fight back," explains a member of one of the militant groups. "No compromise in defense of Mother Earth!" says another. "With famine and death approaching, we're in the early stages of World War III," adds another.

Radical environmentalists represent a broad range of activities and purposes. They are united neither on tactics nor on goals. Most envision a simpler lifestyle that will consume less energy and reduce pressure on the earth's resources. Some want to stop a specific action, such as the killing of whales. Others want to destroy all nuclear weapons and dismantle nuclear power plants. Some want everyone to become a vegetarian. Still others want the earth's population to drop to one billion, roughly what it was in 1800. Some even want humans to return to hunting and gathering societies. These groups are so splintered that Dave Foreman—the founder of Earth First!—quit his own organization when it became too confrontational for his taste.

Radical groups have had some successes. They have brought a halt to the killing of dolphins off Japan's Iki Island, achieved a ban on whaling, established trash recycling programs, and saved hundreds of thousands of acres of trees, including, of course, the Medicine Tree.

For Your Consideration

Should we applaud ecosaboteurs or jail them? As symbolic interactionists stress, it all depends on how you view their actions. And as conflict theorists emphasize, your view likely depends on your social location. That is, if you own a lumber company, you will see ecosaboteurs

ecosabotage actions taken to sabotage the efforts of people who are thought to be legally harming the environment

differently than a camping enthusiast will. How does your own view of ecosaboteurs depend on your life situation? What effective alternatives to ecosabotage are there for people who are convinced that we are destroying the very life support system of our planet?

Sources: Carpenter 1990; Eder 1990; Foote 1990; Parfit 1990; Reed and Benet 1990; Knickerbocker 2003; Gunther 2004; Fattig 2007.

Environmental Sociology

A specialization within sociology is **environmental sociology,** whose focus is the relationship between human societies and the environment (Dunlap and Catton 1979, 1983; Bell 2009). Environmental sociology is built around these key ideas:

1. The physical environment should be a significant variable in sociological investigation.
2. Human beings are but one species among many that depend on the natural environment.
3. Because of feedback to nature, human actions have many unintended consequences.
4. The world is finite, so there are physical limits to economic growth.
5. Economic expansion requires increased extraction of resources from the environment.
6. Increased extraction of resources leads to ecological problems.
7. These ecological problems place limits on economic expansion.
8. Governments create environmental problems by encouraging the accumulation of capital.
9. For the welfare of humanity, environmental problems must be solved.

The goal of environmental sociology is not to stop pollution or nuclear power but, rather, to study how humans (their cultures, values, and behavior) affect the physical environment and how the physical environment affects human activities. Not surprisingly, environmental sociology attracts environmental activists, and the Section on Environment and Technology of the American Sociological Association tries to influence governmental policies (American Sociological Association n.d.).

environmental sociology
a specialty within sociology whose focus is how humans affect the environment and how the environment affects humans

Technology and the Environment: The Goal of Harmony. It is inevitable that humans will continue to develop new technologies. But the abuse of our environment by those

Pollution in the Industrializing Nations has become a major problem. Shown here is a child swimming in the waters of Cilincing Beach in Jakarta, Indonesia.

The social movement that centers on the environment has become global. In all nations, people are concerned about the destruction of the earth's resources. This photo is a sign of changing times. Instead of jumping on this beached whale and carving it into pieces, these Brazilians are doing their best to save its life.

technologies is not inevitable. To understate the matter, the destruction of our planet is an unwise choice.

If we are to live in a world that is worth passing on to coming generations, we must seek harmony between technology and the natural environment. This will not be easy. At one extreme are people who claim that to protect the environment we must eliminate industrialization and go back to a tribal way of life. At the other extreme are people who are blind to the harm being done to the natural environment, who want the entire world to industrialize at full speed. Somewhere, there must be a middle ground, one that recognizes not only that industrialization is here to stay but also that we *can* control it, for it is our creation. Controlled, industrialization can enhance our quality of life; uncontrolled, it will destroy us.

It is essential, then, that we develop ways to reduce or eliminate the harm that technology does to the environment. This includes mechanisms to monitor the production and use of technology and the disposal of its wastes. The question, of course, is whether we have the resolve to take the steps necessary to preserve the environment for future generations. What is at stake is nothing less than the welfare of planet Earth. Surely that is enough to motivate us to make wise choices.

SUMMARY *and* REVIEW

How Social Change Transforms Social Life

What major trends have transformed the course of human history?

The primary changes in human history are the four social revolutions (domestication, agriculture, industrialization, and information); the change from *Gemeinschaft* to *Gesellschaft* societies; capitalism and industrialization; and global stratification. Social movements indicate cutting edges of social change. Ethnic conflicts and power rivalries threaten the global divisions that the Most Industrialized Nations have worked out. We may also be on the cutting edge of a new biotech society. Pp. 652–656.

Theories and Processes of Social Change

What are the main theories of social change?

Evolutionary theories assume that societies move from the same starting point to some similar ending point. *Unilinear* theories assume the same evolutionary path for every society, while *multilinear* theories assume that different paths lead

to the same stage of development. *Cyclical* theories view civilizations as going through a process of birth, youth, maturity, decline, and death. Conflict theorists view social change as inevitable, for each *thesis* (basically an arrangement of power) contains *antitheses* (contradictions). A new *synthesis* develops to resolve these contradictions, but it, too, contains contradictions that must be resolved, and so on. This is called a **dialectical** process. Pp. 656–658.

What is Ogburn's theory of social change?

William Ogburn identified technology as the basic cause of social change, which comes through three processes: **invention, discovery,** and **diffusion.** The term **cultural lag** refers to symbolic culture lagging behind changes in technology. Pp. 658–660.

How Technology Changes Society

How does new technology affect society?

Because technology is an organizing force of social life, changes in technology can have profound effects. The automobile and the computer were used as extended examples. The computer is changing the way we learn, work, do business, and fight wars. We don't yet know whether information technologies will help to perpetuate or to reduce social inequalities on both a national and a global level. Pp. 660–668.

The Growth Machine Versus the Earth

What are the environmental problems of the Most Industrialized Nations?

The environmental problems of the Most Industrialized Nations range from smog and acid rain to the **greenhouse effect. Global warming** is likely to have severe consequences for the world. Burning fossil fuels in internal combustion engines lies at the root of many environmental problems. The location of factories and hazardous waste sites creates **environmental injustice,** environmental problems having a greater impact on minorities and the poor. Pp. 668–672.

Do the Industrializing and Least Industrialized Nations have environmental problems?

The rush of the Least Industrialized Nations to industrialize is adding to the planet's environmental decay. The pollution in China is so severe that China now emits more carbon dioxide than the United States does. Environmental activists in China are arrested and imprisoned. The world is facing a basic conflict between the lust for profits through the exploitation of the earth's resources and the need to establish a **sustainable environment.** P. 672.

What is the environmental movement?

The environmental movement is an attempt to restore a healthy environment for the world's people. This global social movement takes many forms, from peaceful attempts to influence the political process to **ecosabotage.** Pp. 673–674.

What is environmental sociology?

Environmental sociology is not an attempt to change the environment, but, rather, is a study of the relationship between humans and the environment. Environmental sociologists are generally also environmental activists. Pp. 674–676.

THINKING CRITICALLY *ABOUT* Chapter 22

1. How has social change affected your life? Be specific—what changes, how? Does Ogburn's theory help to explain your experiences? Why or why not?

2. In what ways does technology change society?

3. Do you think that a sustainable environment should be a goal of the world's societies? Why or why not? If so, what practical steps do you think we can take to produce a sustainable environment?

ADDITIONAL RESOURCES

What can you find in MySocLab? mysoclab www.mysoclab.com

- Complete Ebook
- Practice Tests and Video and Audio activities
- Mapping and Data Analysis exercises

- Sociology in the News
- Classic Readings in Sociology
- Research and Writing advice

Where Can I Read More on This Topic?

Suggested readings for this chapter are listed at the back of this book.

As you explored social life in this textbook, I hope that you found yourself thinking along with me. If so, you should have gained a greater understanding of why people think, feel, and act as they do—as well as insights into why *you* view life the way you do. Developing your sociological imagination was my intention in writing this book. I have sincerely wanted to make sociology come alive for you.

Majoring in Sociology

If you feel a passion for peering beneath the surface—for seeking out the social influences in people's lives, and for seeing these influences in your own life—this is the best reason to major in sociology. As you take more courses in sociology, you will continue this enlightening process of social discovery. Your sociological perspective will grow, and you will become increasingly aware of how social factors underlie human behavior.

In addition to people who have a strong desire to continue this fascinating process of social discovery, there is a second type of person whom I also urge to major in sociology. Let's suppose that you have a strong, almost unbridled sense of wanting to explore many aspects of life. Let's also assume that because you have so many interests, you can't make up your mind about what you want to do with your life. You can think of so many things you'd like to try, but for each one there are other possibilities that you find equally as compelling. Let me share what one student who read this text wrote me:

I'd love to say what my current major is—if only I truly knew. I know that the major you choose to study in college isn't necessarily the field of work you'll be going into. I've heard enough stories of grads who get jobs in fields that are not even related to their majors to believe it to a certain extent. My only problem is that I'm not even sure what it is I want to study, or what I truly want to be in the future for that matter.

The variety of choices I have left open for myself are very wide, which creates a big problem, because I know I have to narrow it down to just one, which isn't something easy at all for me. It's like I want to be the best and do the best (medical doctor), yet I also wanna do other things (such as being a paramedic, or a cop, or firefighter, or a pilot), but I also realize I've only got one life to live. So the big question is: What's it gonna be?

This note reminded me of myself. In my reply, I said:

You sound so much like myself when I was in college. In my senior year, I was plagued with uncertainty about what would be the right course for my life. I went to a counselor and took a vocational aptitude test. I still remember the day when I went in for the test results. I expected my future to be laid out for me, and I hung on every word. But then I heard the counselor say, "Your tests show that mortician should be one of your vocational choices."

Mortician! I almost fell off my chair. That choice was so far removed from anything that I wanted that I immediately gave up on such tests.

I like your list of possibilities: physician, cop, firefighter, and paramedic. In addition to these, mine included cowboy, hobo, and beach bum. One day, I was at the dry cleaners (end of my sophomore year in college), and the guy standing next to me was a cop. We talked about his job, and when I left the dry cleaners, I immediately went to the police station to get an application. I found out that I had to be 21, and I was just 20. I went back to college.

I'm very happy with my choice. As a sociologist, I am able to follow my interests. I was able to become a hobo (or at least a traveler and able to experience different cultural settings). As far as being a cop, I developed and taught a course in the sociology of law.

One of the many things I always wanted to be was an author. I almost skipped graduate school to move to Greenwich Village and become a novelist. The problem was that I was too timid, too scared of the unknown—and I had no support at all—to give it a try. My ultimate choice of sociologist has allowed me to fulfill this early dream.

It is sociology's breadth that is so satisfying to those of us who can't seem to find the limit to our interests, who can't pin ourselves down to just one thing in life. Sociology covers *all* of social life. Anything and everything that people do is part of sociology. For those of us who feel such broad, and perhaps changing interests, sociology is a perfect major.

But what if you already have a major picked out, yet you really like thinking sociologically? You can *minor* in sociology. Take sociology courses that continue to pique your sociological imagination. Then after college, continue to stimulate your sociological interests through your reading, including novels. This ongoing development of your sociological imagination will serve you well as you go through life.

But What Can You Do With a Sociology Major?

I can just hear someone say: "That's fine for you, since you became a sociologist. I don't want to go to graduate school, though. I just want to get my bachelor's degree and get out of college and get on with life. So, how can a bachelor's in sociology help me?"

This is a fair question. Just what can you do with a bachelor's degree in sociology?

A few years ago, in my sociology department we began to develop a concentration in applied sociology. At that time, since this would be a bachelor's degree, I explored this very question. I was surprised at the answer: *Almost anything!*

It turns out that most employers don't care what you major in. (Exceptions are some highly specialized fields such as nursing, computers, and engineering.) *Most* employers just want to make certain that you have completed college, and for most of them one degree is the same as another. *College provides the base on which the employer builds.*

Because you have your bachelor's degree—no matter what it is in—employers assume that you are a responsible person. This credential implies that you have proven yourself: You were able to stick with a four-year course, you showed up for classes, listened to lectures, took notes, passed tests, and carried out whatever assignments you were given. On top of this base of presumed responsibility, employers add the specifics necessary for you to perform their particular work, whether that be in sales or service, in insurance, banking, retailing, marketing, product development, or whatever.

If you major in sociology, you don't have to look for a job as a sociologist. If you ever decide to go on for an advanced degree, that's fine. But such plans are not necessary. The bachelor's in sociology can be your passport to most types of work in society.

Final Note

I want to conclude by stressing the reason to major in sociology that goes far beyond how you are going to make a living. It is the sociological perspective itself, the way of thinking and understanding that sociology provides. Wherever your path in life may lead, the sociological perspective will accompany you.

You are going to live in a fast-paced, rapidly changing society that, with all its conflicting crosscurrents, is going to be in turmoil. The sociological perspective will cast a different light on life's events, allowing you to perceive them in more insightful ways. As you watch television, attend a concert, converse with a friend, listen to a boss or co-worker—you will be more aware of the social contexts that underlie such behavior. The sociological perspective that you develop as you major in sociology will equip you to view what happens in life differently from someone who does not have your sociological background. Even events in the news will look different to you.

The final question that I want to leave you with, then, is, "If you enjoy sociology, why not major in it?"

With my best wishes for your success in life,

Jim Henslin

GLOSSARY

achieved statuses positions that are earned, accomplished, or involve at least some effort or activity on the individual's part

acid rain rain containing sulfuric and nitric acids (burning fossil fuels release sulfur dioxide and nitrogen oxide that become sulfuric and nitric acids when they react with moisture in the air)

acting crowd an excited group of people who move toward a goal

activity theory the view that satisfaction during old age is related to a person's amount and quality of activity

age cohort people born at roughly the same time who pass through the life course together

ageism prejudice, discrimination, and hostility directed against people because of their age; can be directed against any age group, including youth

agent provocateur someone who joins a group in order to spy on it and to sabotage it by provoking its members to commit extreme acts

agents of socialization people or groups that affect our self-concept, attitudes, behaviors, or other orientations toward life

aggregate individuals who temporarily share the same physical space but who do not see themselves as belonging together

agricultural revolution the second social revolution, based on the invention of the plow, which led to agricultural societies

agricultural society a society based on large-scale agriculture

alienation Marx's term for workers' lack of connection to the product of their labor; caused by workers being assigned repetitive tasks on a small part of a product—this leads to a sense of powerlessness and normlessness; others use the term in the general sense of not feeling a part of something

alterative social movement a social movement that seeks to alter only some specific aspects of people and institutions

alternative medicine medical treatment other than that of standard Western medicine; often refers to practices that originate in Asia, but may also refer to taking vitamins not prescribed by a doctor

anarchy a condition of lawlessness or political disorder caused by the absence or collapse of governmental authority

animism the belief that all objects in the world have spirits, some of which are dangerous and must be outwitted

anomie Durkheim's term for a condition of society in which people become detached from the usual norms that guide their behavior

anticipatory socialization the process of learning in advance an anticipated future role or status

anti-Semitism prejudice, discrimination, and persecution directed against Jews

apartheid the separation of racial–ethnic groups as was practiced in South Africa

applied sociology the use of sociology to solve problems—from the micro level of classroom interaction and family relationships to the macro level of crime and pollution

ascribed status a position an individual either inherits at birth or receives involuntarily later in life

assimilation the process of being absorbed into the mainstream culture

authoritarian leader an individual who leads by giving orders

authoritarian personality Theodor Adorno's term for people who are prejudiced and rank high on scales of conformity, intolerance, insecurity, respect for authority, and submissiveness to superiors

authority power that people consider legitimate, as rightly exercised over them; also called *legitimate power*

back stage places where people rest from their performances, discuss their presentations, and plan future performances

background assumption a deeply embedded, common understanding of how the world operates and of how people ought to act

barter the direct exchange of one item for another

basic demographic equation the growth rate equals births minus deaths plus net migration

basic or **pure sociology** sociological research for the purpose of making discoveries about life in human groups, not for making changes in those groups

bilineal (system of descent) a system of reckoning descent that counts both the mother's and the father's side

biotech society a society whose economy increasingly centers on the application of genetics—human genetics for medicine, and plant and animal genetics for the production of food and materials

blended family a family whose members were once part of other families

body language the ways in which people use their bodies to give messages to others

bonded labor (indentured service) a contractual system in which someone sells his or her body (services) for a specified period of time in an arrangement very close to slavery, except that it is entered into voluntarily

born again a term describing Christians who have undergone a religious experience so life-transforming that they feel they have become new persons

bourgeoisie Marx's term for capitalists, those who own the means of production

bureaucracy a formal organization with a hierarchy of authority and a clear division of labor; emphasis on impersonality of positions and written rules, communications, and records

capital punishment the death penalty

capitalism an economic system characterized by the private ownership of the means of production, the pursuit of profit, and market competition

cargo cult a social movement in which South Pacific islanders destroyed their possessions in the anticipation that their ancestors would ship them new goods

case study an intensive analysis of a single event, situation, or individual

caste system a form of social stratification in which people's statuses are determined by birth and are lifelong

category people, objects, and events that have similar characteristics and are classified together

centrist party a political party that represents the center of political opinion

charisma literally, an extraordinary gift from God; more commonly, an outstanding, "magnetic" personality

charismatic authority authority based on an individual's outstanding traits, which attract followers

charismatic leader literally, someone to whom God has given a gift; in its extended sense, someone who exerts extraordinary appeal to a group of followers

checks and balances the separation of powers among the three branches of U.S. government—legislative, executive, and judicial—so that each is able to nullify the actions of the other two, thus preventing any single branch from dominating the government

church according to Durkheim, one of the three essential elements of religion—a moral community of believers; also refers to a large, highly organized religious group that has formal, sedate worship services with little emphasis on evangelism, intense religious experience, or personal conversion

circular reaction Robert Park's term for a back-and-forth communication among the members of a crowd whereby a "collective impulse" is transmitted

citizenship the concept that birth (and residence or naturalization) in a country imparts basic rights

city a place in which a large number of people are permanently based and do not produce their own food

G

city-state an independent city whose power radiates outward, bringing the adjacent area under its rule

civil religion Robert Bellah's term for religion that is such an established feature of a country's life that its history and social institutions become sanctified by being associated with God

class conflict Marx's term for the struggle between capitalists and workers

class consciousness Marx's term for awareness of a common identity based on one's position in the means of production

class system a form of social stratification based primarily on the possession of money or material possessions

clique a cluster of people within a larger group who choose to interact with one another

closed-ended questions questions that are followed by a list of possible answers to be selected by the respondent

coalition the alignment of some members of a group against others

coalition government a government in which a country's largest party aligns itself with one or more smaller parties

coercion power that people do not accept as rightly exercised over them; also called *illegitimate power*

cohabitation unmarried couples living together in a sexual relationship

collective behavior extraordinary activities carried out by groups of people; includes lynchings, rumors, panics, urban legends, fads, and fashions

collective mind Gustave LeBon's term for the tendency of people in a crowd to feel, think, and act in extraordinary ways

colonialism the process by which one nation takes over another nation, usually for the purpose of exploiting its labor and natural resources

common sense those things that "everyone knows" are true

compartmentalize to separate acts from feelings or attitudes

conflict theory a theoretical framework in which society is viewed as composed of groups that are competing for scarce resources

conspicuous consumption Thorstein Veblen's term for a change from the thrift, savings, and investments of the Protestant ethic to showing off wealth through spending and the display of possessions

continuity theory the focus of this theory is how people adjust to retirement by continuing aspects of their earlier lives

contradictory class locations Erik Wright's term for a position in the class structure that generates contradictory interests

control group the subjects in an experiment who are not exposed to the independent variable

control theory the idea that two control systems—inner controls and outer controls—work against our tendencies to deviate

convergence theory the view that as capitalist and socialist economic systems each adopt features of the other, a hybrid (or mixed) economic system will emerge

corporate capitalism the domination of an economic system by giant corporations

corporate crime crimes committed by executives in order to benefit their corporation

corporate welfare the financial incentives (tax breaks, subsidies, and even land and stadiums) given to corporations in order to attract them to an area or induce them to remain

corporation a business enterprise whose assets, liabilities, and obligations are separate from those of its owners; as a legal entity, it can enter into contracts, assume debt, and sue and be sued

correspondence principle the sociological principle that schools correspond to (or reflect) the social structure of their society

cosmology teachings or ideas that provide a unified picture of the world

counterculture a group whose values, beliefs, norms, and related behaviors place its members in opposition to the broader culture

credential society the use of diplomas and degrees to determine who is eligible for jobs, even though the diploma or degree may be irrelevant to the actual work

credit card a device that allows its owner to purchase goods and to be billed later

crime the violation of norms written into law

criminal justice system the system of police, courts, and prisons set up to deal with people who are accused of having committed a crime

crude birth rate the annual number of live births per 1,000 population

crude death rate the annual number of deaths per 1,000 population

cult a new religion with few followers, whose teachings and practices put it at odds with the dominant culture and religion

cultural diffusion the spread of cultural traits from one group to another; includes both material and nonmaterial cultural traits

cultural goals the objectives held out as legitimate or desirable for the members of a society to achieve

cultural lag Ogburn's term for human behavior lagging behind technological innovations

cultural leveling the process by which cultures become similar to one another; refers especially to the process by which Western culture is being exported and diffused into other nations.

cultural relativism not judging a culture but trying to understand it on its own terms.

cultural transmission of values the process of transmitting values from one group to another; often refers to how cultural traits are transmitted across generations; in education, the ways in which schools transmit a society's culture, especially its core values

cultural universal a value, norm, or other cultural trait that is found in every group

culture of poverty the assumption that the values and behaviors of the poor make them fundamentally different from other people, that these factors are largely responsible for their poverty, and that parents perpetuate poverty across generations by passing these characteristics to their children

culture the language, beliefs, values, norms, behaviors, and even material objects that characterize a group and are passed from one generation to the next

culture shock the disorientation that people experience when they come in contact with a fundamentally different culture and can no longer depend on their taken-for-granted assumptions about life

currency paper money

defensive medicine medical practices done not for the patient's benefit but in order to protect physicians from malpractice suits

deferred gratification forgoing something in the present in the hope of achieving greater gains in the future

degradation ceremony a term coined by Harold Garfinkel to refer to a ritual whose goal is to remake someone's self by stripping away that individual's self-identity and stamping a new identity in its place

dehumanization the act or process of reducing people to objects that do not deserve the treatment accorded humans

deindustrialization the process of industries moving out of a country or region

democracy a government whose authority comes from the people; the term, based on two Greek words, translates literally as "power to the people"

democratic leader an incdividual who leads by trying to reach a consensus

democratic socialism a hybrid economic system in which the individual ownership of businesses is mixed with the state ownership of industries thought essential to the public welfare, such as the postal service, natural resources, the medical delivery system, and mass transportation

demographic transition a three-stage historical process of change in the size of populations: first, high birth rates and high death rates; second, high birth rates and low death rates; and third, low birth rates and low death rates; a fourth stage of population shrinkage in which deaths outnumber births has made its appearance in the Most Industrialized Nations

demographic variables the three factors that change the size of a population: fertility, mortality, and net migration

demography the study of the size, composition, growth or shrinkage, and distribution of human populations

denomination a "brand name" within a major religion; for example, Methodist or Baptist

dependency ratio the number of workers who are required to support each dependent person—those 65 and older and those 15 and under

dependent variable a factor in an experiment that is changed by an independent variable

depersonalization dealing with people as though they were objects; in the case of medical care, as though patients were merely cases and diseases, not people

deposit receipt a receipt stating that a certain amount of goods is on deposit in a warehouse or bank; the receipt is used as a form of money

deviance the violation of norms (or rules or expectations)

dialectical process (of history) each arrangement of power (a thesis) contains contradictions (antitheses) which make the arrangement unstable and which must be resolved; the new arrangement of power (a synthesis) contains its own contradictions; this process of balancing and unbalancing continues throughout history as groups struggle for power and other resources

dictatorship a form of government in which an individual has seized power

differential association Edwin Sutherland's term to indicate that people who associate with some groups learn an "excess of definitions" of deviance, increasing the likelihood that they will become deviant

diffusion the spread of an invention or a discovery from one area to another; identified by William Ogburn as one of three processes of social change

direct democracy a form of democracy in which the eligible voters meet together to discuss issues and make their decisions

disabling environment an environment that is harmful to health

discovery a new way of seeing reality; identified by William Ogburn as one of three processes of social change

discrimination an act of unfair treatment directed against an individual or a group

disengagement theory the view that society is stabilized by having the elderly retire (disengage from) their positions of responsibility so the younger generation can step into their shoes

disinvestment the withdrawal of investments by financial institutions, which seals the fate of an urban area

divine right of kings the idea that the king's authority comes from God; in an interesting gender bender, also applies to queens

division of labor the splitting of a group's or a society's tasks into specialties

documents in its narrow sense, written sources that provide data; in its extended sense, archival material of any sort, including photographs, movies, CDs, DVDs, and so on

domestication revolution the first social revolution, based on the domestication of plants and animals, which led to pastoral and horticultural societies

dominant group the group with the most power, greatest privileges, and highest social status

downward social mobility movement down the social class ladder

dramaturgy an approach, pioneered by Erving Goffman, in which social life is analyzed in terms of drama or the stage; also called *dramaturgical analysis*

dumping the practice of sending unprofitable patients to public hospitals

dyad the smallest possible group, consisting of two persons

e–cash digital money that is stored on computers

ecclesia a religious group so integrated into the dominant culture that it is difficult to tell where the one begins and the other leaves off; also called a *state religion*

economy a system of producing and distributing goods and services

ecosabotage actions taken to sabotage the efforts of people who are thought to be legally harming the environment

edge city a large clustering of service facilities and residential areas near highway intersections that provides a sense of place to people who live, shop, and work there

education a formal system of teaching knowledge, values, and skills

egalitarian authority more or less equally divided between people or groups (in heterosexual marriage, for example, between husband and wife)

ego Freud's term for a balancing force between the id and the demands of society

electronic community individuals who regularly interact with one another on the Internet and who think of themselves as belonging together

emergent norms Ralph Turner and Lewis Killian's term for the idea that people develop new norms to cope with a new situation; used to explain crowd behavior

endogamy the practice of marrying within one's own group

enterprise zone the use of economic incentives in a designated area to encourage investment

environmental injustice refers to how minorities and the poor are harmed the most by environmental pollution

environmental sociology a specialty within sociology whose focus is how humans affect the environment and how the environment affects humans

epidemiology the study of patterns of disease and disability in a population

estate stratification system the stratification system of medieval Europe, consisting of three groups or estates: the nobility, clergy, and commoners

ethnic cleansing a policy of eliminating a population; includes forcible expulsion and genocide

ethnic work activities designed to discover, enhance, or maintain ethnic and racial identity

ethnicity (and **ethnic**) having distinctive cultural characteristics

ethnocentrism the use of one's own culture as a yardstick for judging the ways of other individuals or societies, generally leading to a negative evaluation of their values, norms, and behaviors

ethnomethodology the study of how people use background assumptions to make sense out of life

euthanasia mercy killing

evangelism an attempt to win converts

exchange mobility about the same numbers of people moving up and down the social class ladder, such that, on balance, the social class system shows little change

experiment the use of control and experimental groups and dependent and independent variables to test causation

experimental group the group of subjects in an experiment who are exposed to the independent variable

exponential growth curve a pattern of growth in which numbers double during approximately equal intervals, showing a steep acceleration in the later stages

expressive leader an individual who increases harmony and minimizes conflict in a group; also known as a *socioemotional leader*

face-saving behavior techniques used to salvage a performance (interaction) that is going sour

fad a temporary pattern of behavior that catches people's attention

false class consciousness Marx's term to refer to workers identifying with the interests of capitalists

family two or more people who consider themselves related by blood, marriage, or adoption

family of orientation the family in which a person grows up

family of procreation the family formed when a couple's first child is born

fashion a pattern of behavior that catches people's attention and lasts longer than a fad

fecundity the number of children that women are capable of bearing

fee-for-service payment to a physician to diagnose and treat a patient's medical problems

feminism the philosophy that men and women should be politically, economically, and socially equal; organized activities on behalf of this principle

[the] **feminization of poverty** a condition of U.S. poverty in which most poor families are headed by women

feral children children assumed to have been raised by animals, in the wilderness, isolated from humans

fertility rate the number of children that the average woman bears

fiat money currency issued by a government that is not backed by stored value

folkways norms that are not strictly enforced

formal organization a secondary group designed to achieve explicit objectives

front stage places where people give performances

functional analysis a theoretical framework in which society is viewed as composed of various parts, each with a function that, when fulfilled, contributes to society's equilibrium; also known as *functionalism* and *structural functionalism*

functional equivalent a substitute that serves the same functions (or meets the same needs) as religion; for example, psychotherapy

functional illiterate a high school graduate who has difficulty with basic reading and math

fundamentalism the belief that social change, especially in values, is threatening true religion and that the religion needs to go back to its fundamentals (roots, basic beliefs and practices)

gatekeeping the process by which education opens and closes doors of opportunity; another term for the *social placement* function of education

Gemeinschaft a type of society in which life is intimate; a community in which everyone knows everyone else and people share a sense of togetherness

gender the behaviors and attitudes that a society considers proper for its males and females; masculinity or femininity

gender age the relative value placed on men's and women's ages

gender role the behaviors and attitudes expected of people because they are female or male

gender socialization the ways in which society sets children on different paths in life *because* they are male or female

gender stratification males' and females' unequal access to property, power, and prestige

generalizability the extent to which the findings from one group (or sample) can be generalized or applied to other groups (or populations)

generalization a statement that goes beyond the individual case and is applied to a broader group or situation

generalized other the norms, values, attitudes, and expectations of people "in general"; the child's ability to take the role of the generalized other is a significant step in the development of a self

genetic predisposition inborn tendencies (for example, a tendency to commit deviant acts)

genocide the systematic annihilation or attempted annihilation of a people because of their presumed race or ethnicity

gentrification middle-class people moving into a rundown area of a city, displacing the poor as they buy and restore homes

Gesellschaft a type of society that is dominated by impersonal relationships, individual accomplishments, and self-interest

gestures the ways in which people use their bodies to communicate with one another

glass ceiling the mostly invisible barrier that keeps women from advancing to the top levels at work

global warming an increase in the earth's temperature due to the greenhouse effect

globalization the extensive interconnections among nations due to the expansion of capitalism

globalization of capitalism capitalism (investing to make profits within a rational system) becoming the globe's dominant economic system

goal displacement an organization replacing old goals with new ones; also known as *goal replacement*

gold standard paper money backed by gold

grade inflation higher grades given for the same work; a general rise in student grades without a corresponding increase in learning

graying of America the growing percentage of older people in the U.S. population

greenhouse effect the buildup of carbon dioxide in the earth's atmosphere that allows light to enter freely but inhibits the release of heat; believed to cause global warming

gross domestic product (GDP) the amount of goods and services produced by a nation

group people who have something in common and who believe that what they have in common is significant; also called a *social group*

group dynamics the ways in which individuals affect groups and the ways in which groups influence individuals

groupthink a narrowing of thought by a group of people, leading to the perception that there is only one correct answer, in which to even suggest alternatives becomes a sign of disloyalty

growth rate the net change in a population after adding births, subtracting deaths, and either adding or subtracting net migration; can result in a negative number

hate crime a crime that is punished more severely because it is motivated by hatred (dislike, hostility, animosity) of someone's race–ethnicity, religion, sexual orientation, disability, or national origin

health a human condition measured by four components: physical, mental, social, and spiritual

hidden curriculum the unwritten goals of schools, such as teaching obedience to authority and conformity to cultural norms

homogamy the tendency of people with similar characteristics to marry one another

Horatio Alger myth the belief that due to limitless possibilities anyone can get ahead if he or she tries hard enough

horticultural society a society based on cultivating plants by the use of hand tools

hospice a place (or services brought to someone's home) for the purpose of giving comfort and dignity to a dying person

household people who occupy the same housing unit

human ecology Robert Park's term for the relationship between people and their environment

(such as land and structures); also known as *urban ecology*

humanizing a work setting organizing a workplace in such a way that it develops rather than impedes human potential

hunting and gathering society a human group that depends on hunting and gathering for its survival

hypothesis a statement of how variables are expected to be related to one another, often according to predictions from a theory

id Freud's term for our inborn basic drives

ideal culture a people's ideal values and norms; the goals held out for them

ideology beliefs about the way things ought to be that justify social arrangements

illegitimate opportunity structure opportunities for crimes that are woven into the texture of life

impression management people's efforts to control the impressions that others receive of them

incest sexual relations between specified relatives, such as brothers and sisters or parents and children

incest taboo the rule that prohibits sex and marriage among designated relatives

income money received, usually from a job, business, or assets

independent variable a factor that causes a change in another variable, called the dependent variable

Industrial Revolution the third social revolution, occurring when machines powered by fuels replaced most animal and human power

industrial society a society based on the harnessing of machines powered by fuels

inflation an increase in prices

in-groups groups toward which one feels loyalty

institutional discrimination negative treatment of a minority group that is built into a society's institutions; also called *systemic discrimination*

institutionalized means approved ways of reaching cultural goals

instrumental leader an individual who tries to keep the group moving toward its goals; also known as a *task-oriented leader*

intergenerational mobility the change that family members make in social class from one generation to the next

interlocking directorates the same people serving on the boards of directors of several companies

internal colonialism the policy of exploiting minority groups for economic gain

interview direct questioning of respondents

interviewer bias effects that interviewers have on respondents that lead to biased answers

invasion–succession cycle the process of one group of people displacing a group whose racial–ethnic or social class characteristics differ from their own

invention the combination of existing elements and materials to form new ones; identified by William Ogburn as one of three processes of social change

[the] iron law of oligarchy Robert Michels' term for the tendency of formal organizations to be dominated by a small, self-perpetuating elite

labeling theory the view that the labels people are given affect their own and others' perceptions of them, thus channeling their behavior into either deviance or conformity

laissez-faire leader an individual who leads by being highly permissive

language a system of symbols that can be combined in an infinite number of ways and can represent not only objects but also abstract thought

latent functions unintended beneficial consequences of people's actions

leader someone who influences other people

leadership styles ways in which people express their leadership

leisure time not taken up by work or necessary activities

life course the stages of our life as we go from birth to death

life expectancy the number of years that an average person at any age, including newborns, can expect to live

life span the maximum length of life of a species; for humans, the longest that a human has lived

lobbyists people who influence legislation on behalf of their clients

looking-glass self a term coined by Charles Horton Cooley to refer to the process by which our self develops through internalizing others' reactions to us

machismo an emphasis on male strength and dominance

macro-level analysis an examination of large-scale patterns of society

macropolitics the exercise of large-scale power, the government being the most common example

macrosociology analysis of social life that focuses on broad features of society, such as social class and the relationships of groups to one another; usually used by functionalists and conflict theorists

mainstreaming helping people to become part of the mainstream of society

Malthus theorem an observation by Thomas Malthus that although the food supply increases arithmetically (from 1 to 2 to 3 to 4 and so on), population grows geometrically (from 2 to 4 to 8 to 16 and so forth)

mandatory education laws laws that require all children to attend school until a specified age or until they complete a minimum grade in school

manifest functions the intended beneficial consequences of people's actions

market forces the law of supply and demand

marriage a group's approved mating arrangements, usually marked by a ritual of some sort

mass hysteria an imagined threat that causes physical symptoms among a large number of people

mass media forms of communication, such as radio, newspapers, and television that are directed to mass audiences

mass society industrialized, highly bureaucratized, impersonal society

mass society theory an explanation for why people participate in a social movement based on the assumption that the movement offers them a sense of belonging

master status a status that cuts across the other statuses that an individual occupies

material culture the material objects that distinguish a group of people, such as their art, buildings, weapons, utensils, machines, hairstyles, clothing, and jewelry

matriarchy a society in which women as a group dominate men as a group; authority is vested in females

matrilineal (system of descent) a system of reckoning descent that counts only the mother's side

[the] McDonaldization of society the process by which ordinary aspects of life are rationalized and efficiency comes to rule them, including such things as food preparation

means of production the tools, factories, land, and investment capital used to produce wealth

mechanical solidarity Durkheim's term for the unity (a shared consciousness) that people feel as a result of performing the same or similar tasks

medicalization the transformation of a human condition into a matter to be treated by physicians

medicalization of deviance to make deviance a medical matter, a symptom of some underlying illness that needs to be treated by physicians

medicine one of the social institutions that sociologists study; a society's organized ways of dealing with sickness and injury

medium of exchange the means by which people place a value on goods and services in order to make an exchange—for example, currency, gold, and silver

megacity a city of 10 million or more residents

megalopolis an urban area consisting of at least two metropolises and their many suburbs

meritocracy a form of social stratification in which all positions are awarded on the basis of merit

metaformative social movement a social movement that has the goal to change the social order not just of a country or two, but of a civilization, or even of the entire world

metropolis a central city surrounded by smaller cities and their suburbs

metropolitan statistical area (MSA) a central city and the urbanized counties adjacent to it

micro-level analysis an examination of small-scale patterns of society; such as how the members of a group interact

micropolitics the exercise of power in everyday life, such as deciding who is going to do the housework or use the remote control

microsociology analysis of social life that focuses on social interaction; typically used by symbolic interactionists

millenarian social movement a social movement based on the prophecy of coming social upheaval

milling a crowd standing or walking around as they talk excitedly about some event

minimax strategy Richard Berk's term for the efforts people make to minimize their costs and maximize their rewards

minority group people who are singled out for unequal treatment and who regard themselves as objects of collective discrimination

modernization the transformation of traditional societies into industrial societies

monarchy a form of government headed by a king or queen

money any item (from sea shells to gold) that serves as a medium of exchange; today, currency and credit cards are the most common forms

monopoly the control of an entire industry by a single company

monotheism the belief that there is only one God

moral panic a fear that some evil threatens the well-being of society grips a large number of people; followed by hostility, sometimes violence, toward those thought responsible

mores norms that are strictly enforced because they are thought essential to core values or the well-being of the group

multiculturalism (also called *pluralism*) a philosophy or political policy that permits or encourages ethnic differences

multinational corporations companies that operate across national boundaries; also called *transnational corporations*

nationalism a strong identification with a nation, accompanied by the desire for that nation to be dominant

natural sciences the intellectual and academic disciplines designed to comprehend, explain, and predict events in our natural environments

negative sanction an expression of disapproval for breaking a norm, ranging from a mild, informal reaction such as a frown to a formal reaction such as a prize or a prison sentence

neocolonialism the economic and political dominance of the Most Industrialized Nations over the Least Industrialized Nations

net migration rate the difference between the number of immigrants and emigrants per 1,000 population

new technology the emerging technologies of an era that have a significant impact on social life

noncentrist party a political party that represents less popular ideas

nonmaterial culture a group's ways of thinking (including its beliefs, values, and other assumptions about the world) and doing (its common patterns of behavior, including language and other forms of interaction); also called *symbolic culture*

nonverbal interaction communication without words through gestures, use of space, silence, and so on

norms expectations, or rules of behavior

nuclear family a family consisting of a husband, wife, and child(ren)

objectivity value neutrality in research

oligarchy a form of government in which a small group of individuals holds power; the rule of the many by the few

open-ended questions questions that respondents answer in their own words

operational definition the way in which a researcher measures a variable

organic solidarity Durkheim's term for the interdependence that results from the division of labor; as part of the same unit, we all depend on others to fulfill their jobs

out-groups groups toward which one feels antagonism

panic the condition of being so fearful that one cannot function normally and may even flee

participant observation or **fieldwork** research in which the researcher participates in a research setting while observing what is happening in that setting

pastoral society a society based on the pasturing of animals

patriarchy a group in which men as a group dominate women as a group; authority is vested in males

patrilineal (system of descent) a system of reckoning descent that counts only the father's side

patterns recurring characteristics or events

peer group a group of individuals, often of roughly the same age, who are linked by common interests and orientations

personality disorders the view that a personality disturbance of some sort causes an individual to violate social norms

Peter principle a tongue-in-cheek observation that the members of an organization are promoted for their accomplishments until they reach their level of incompetence; there they cease to be promoted, remaining at the level at which they can no longer do good work

pluralism the diffusion of power among many interest groups that prevents any single group from gaining control of the government

pluralistic society a society made up of many different groups

police discretion the practice of the police, in the normal course of their duties, to either arrest or ticket someone for an offense or to overlook the matter

political action committee (PAC) an organization formed by one or more special-interest groups to solicit and spend funds for the purpose of influencing legislation

politics the exercise of power and attempts to maintain or to change power relations

polyandry a form of marriage in which women have more than one husband

polygyny a form of marriage in which men have more than one wife

polytheism the belief that there are many gods

population pyramid a graph that represents the age and sex of a population (see Figure 20.7)

population shrinkage the process by which a country's population becomes smaller because its birth rate and immigration are too low to replace those who die and emigrate

population a target group to be studied

population transfer the forced movement of a minority group

positive sanction a reward or positive reaction for following norms, ranging from a smile to a material reward

positivism the application of the scientific approach to the social world

postindustrial (information) society a society based on information, services, and high technology, rather than on raw materials and manufacturing

postmodern society another term for postindustrial society; a chief characteristic is the use of tools that extend human abilities to gather and analyze information, to communicate, and to travel

poverty line the official measure of poverty; calculated to include incomes that are less than three times a low-cost food budget

power the ability to carry out one's will, even over the resistance of others

power elite C. Wright Mills' term for the top people in U.S. corporations, military, and politics who make the nation's major decisions

prejudice an attitude or prejudging, usually in a negative way

prestige respect or regard

primary group a small group characterized by intimate, long-term, face-to-face association and cooperation

proactive social movement a social movement that promotes some social change

profane Durkheim's term for common elements of everyday life

professionalization of medicine the development of medicine into a specialty in which education becomes rigorous, and in which physicians claim a theoretical understanding of

illness, regulate themselves, claim to be doing a service to society (rather than just following self-interest), and take authority over clients

proletariat Marx's term for the exploited class, the mass of workers who do not own the means of production

propaganda in its broad sense, the presentation of information in the attempt to influence people; in its narrow sense, one-sided information used to try to influence people

property material possessions: animals, bank accounts, bonds, buildings, businesses, cars, copyrights, furniture, land, and stocks

proportional representation an electoral system in which seats in a legislature are divided according to the proportion of votes that each political party receives

Protestant ethic Weber's term to describe the ideal of a self-denying, highly moral life accompanied by thrift and hard work and frugality

public opinion how people think about some issue

public sociology sociology being used for the public good; especially the sociological perspective (of how things are related to one another) guiding politicians and policy makers

public in this context, a dispersed group of people relevant to a social movement; the sympathetic and hostile publics have an interest in the issues on which a social movement focuses; there is also an unaware or indifferent public

questionnaires a list of questions to be asked of respondents

quiet revolution the fundamental changes in society that follow when vast numbers of women enter the workforce

race a group whose inherited physical characteristics distinguish it from other groups

racism prejudice and discrimination on the basis of race

random sample a sample in which everyone in the target population has the same chance of being included in the study

rapport (ruh-POUR) a feeling of trust between researchers and the people they are studying

rationality using rules, efficiency, and practical results to determine human affairs

[the] **rationalization of society** a widespread acceptance of rationality and social organizations that are built largely around this idea

rational–legal authority authority based on law or written rules and regulations; also called *bureaucratic authority*

reactive social movement a social movement that resists some social change

real culture the norms and values that people actually follow; as opposed to *ideal culture*

recidivism rate the percentage of released convicts who are rearrested

redemptive social movement a social movement that seeks to change people and institutions totally, to redeem them

redlining a decision by the officers of a financial institution not to make loans in a particular area

reference group a group whose standards we refer to as we evaluate ourselves

reformative social movement a social movement that seeks to reform some specific aspects of society

reincarnation in Hinduism and Buddhism, the return of the soul (or self) after death in a different form

relative deprivation theory in this context, the belief that people join social movements based on their evaluations of what they think they should have compared with what others have

reliability the extent to which research produces consistent or dependable results

religion according to Durkheim, beliefs and practices that separate the profane from the sacred and unite its adherents into a moral community

religious experience a sudden awareness of the supernatural or a feeling of coming in contact with God

replication the repetition of a study in order to test its findings

representative democracy a form of democracy in which voters elect representatives to meet together to discuss issues and make decisions on their behalf

research method (or **research design**) one of seven procedures that sociologists use to collect data: surveys, participant observation, case studies, secondary analysis, documents, experiments, and unobtrusive measures

reserve labor force the unemployed; unemployed workers are thought of as being "in reserve"—capitalists take them "out of reserve" (put them back to work) during times of high production and then put them "back in reserve" (lay them off) when they are no longer needed

resocialization the process of learning new norms, values, attitudes, and behaviors

resource mobilization a theory that social movements succeed or fail based on their ability to mobilize resources such as time, money, and people's skills

respondents people who respond to a survey, either in interviews or by self-administered questionnaires

revolution armed resistance designed to overthrow and replace a government

riot violent crowd behavior directed at people and property

rising expectations the sense that better conditions are soon to follow, which, if unfulfilled, increases frustration

rituals ceremonies or repetitive practices; in religion, observances or rites often intended to evoke a sense of awe of the sacred

role the behaviors, obligations, and privileges attached to a status

role conflict conflicts that someone feels *between* roles because the expectations attached to one role are incompatible with the expectations of another role

role extension a role being stretched to include activities that were not originally part of that role

role performance the ways in which someone performs a role; showing a particular "style" or "personality"

role strain conflicts that someone feels within a role

romantic love feelings of erotic attraction accompanied by an idealization of the other

routinization of charisma the transfer of authority from a charismatic figure to either a traditional or a rational–legal form of authority

ruling class another term for the power elite

rumor unfounded information spread among people

sacred Durkheim's term for things set apart or forbidden that inspire fear, awe, reverence, or deep respect

sample the individuals intended to represent the population to be studied

sanctions either expressions of approval given to people for upholding norms or expressions of disapproval for violating them

Sapir-Whorf hypothesis Edward Sapir and Benjamin Whorf's hypothesis that language creates ways of thinking and perceiving

scapegoat an individual or group unfairly blamed for someone else's troubles

science the application of systematic methods to obtain knowledge and the knowledge obtained by those methods

[the] **scientific method** the use of objective, systematic observations to test theories

secondary analysis the analysis of data that have been collected by other researchers

secondary group compared with a primary group, a larger, relatively temporary, more anonymous, formal, and impersonal group based on some interest or activity

sect a religious group larger than a cult that still feels substantial hostility from and toward society

secular belonging to the world and its affairs

secularization of culture the process by which a culture becomes less influenced by religion

secularization of religion the replacement of a religion's spiritual or "other worldly" concerns with concerns about "this world"

segregation the policy of keeping racial–ethnic groups apart

selective perception seeing certain features of an object or situation, but remaining blind to others

self the unique human capacity of being able to see ourselves "from the outside"; the views we internalize of how others see us

self-administered questionnaires questionnaires that respondents fill out

self-fulfilling prophecy Robert Merton's term for an originally false assertion that becomes true simply because it was predicted

self-fulfilling stereotype preconceived ideas of what someone is like that lead to the person's behaving in ways that match the stereotype

serial fatherhood a pattern of parenting in which a father, after a divorce, reduces contact with his own children, serves as a father to the children of the woman he marries or lives with, then ignores these children, too, after moving in with or marrying another woman

serial murder the killing of several victims in three or more separate events

sex biological characteristics that distinguish females and males, consisting of primary and secondary sex characteristics

sexual harassment the abuse of one's position of authority to force unwanted sexual demands on someone

shaman the healing specialist of a tribe who attempts to control the spirits thought to cause a disease or injury; commonly called a witch doctor

sick role a social role that excuses people from normal obligations because they are sick or injured, while at the same time expecting them to seek competent help and cooperate in getting well

significant other an individual who significantly influences someone's life

sign-vehicle the term used by Goffman to refer to how people use social setting, appearance, and manner to communicate information about the self

slavery a form of social stratification in which some people own other people

small group a group small enough for everyone to interact directly with all the other members

social change the alteration of culture and societies over time

social class according to Weber, a large group of people who rank close to one another in property, power and prestige; according to Marx, one of two groups: capitalists who own the means of production or workers who sell their labor

social construction of reality the use of background assumptions and life experiences to define what is real

social control a group's formal and informal means of enforcing its norms

social environment the entire human environment, including interaction with others

social facts Durkheim's term for a group's patterns of behavior

social inequality a social condition in which privileges and obligations are given to some but denied to others

social institution   the organized, usual, or standard ways by which society meets its basic needs

social integration   the degree to which members of a group or a society feel united by shared values and other social bonds; also known as *social cohesion*

social interaction   what people do when they are in one another's presence; includes communications at a distance

social location   the group memberships that people have because of their location in history and society

social mobility   movement up or down the social class ladder

social movement   a large group of people who are organized to promote or resist some social change

social movement organization   an organization to promote the goals of a social movement

social network   the social ties radiating outward from the self that link people together

social order   a group's usual and customary social arrangements, on which its members depend and on which they base their lives

social placement   a function of education—funneling people into a society's various positions

social promotion   passing students on to the next level even though they have not mastered basic materials

social sciences   the intellectual and academic disciplines designed to understand the social world objectively by means of controlled and repeated observations

social stratification   the division of large numbers of people into layers according to their relative property, power, and prestige; applies to both nations and to people within a nation, society, or other group

social structure   the framework that surrounds us, consisting of the relationships of people and groups to one another, which gives direction to and sets limits on behavior

socialism   an economic system characterized by the public ownership of the means of production, central planning, and the distribution of goods without a profit motive

socialization   the process by which people learn the characteristics of their group—the behaviors, knowledge, skills, attitudes, values, norms, and other orientations thought appropriate for them

society   people who share a culture and a territory

sociobiology   a framework of thought that views human behavior as the result of natural selection and considers biological factors to be a fundamental cause of human behavior

sociological perspective   understanding human behavior by placing it within its broader social context

sociology   the scientific study of society and human behavior

special-interest group   a group of people who support a particular issue and who can be mobilized for political action

spirit of capitalism   Weber's term for the desire to accumulate capital—not to spend it, but as an end in itself—and to constantly reinvest it

split labor market   workers split along racial–ethnic, gender, age, or any other lines; this split is exploited by owners to weaken the bargaining power of workers

state   a political entity that claims monopoly on the use of violence in some particular territory; commonly known as a country

state religion   a government-sponsored religion; also called *ecclesia*

status   the position that someone occupies in a social group

status consistency   ranking high or low on all three dimensions of social class

status inconsistency   ranking high on some dimensions of social class and low on others, also called *status discrepancy*

status set   all the statuses or positions that an individual occupies

status symbols   items used to identify a status

stereotype   assumptions of what people are like, whether true or false

stigma   "blemishes" that discredit a person's claim to a "normal" identity

stored value   the goods that are stored and held in reserve that back up (or provide the value for) a currency

strain theory   Robert Merton's term for the strain engendered when a society socializes large numbers of people to desire a cultural goal (such as success), but withholds from some the approved means of reaching that goal; one adaptation to the strain is crime, the choice of an innovative means (one outside the approved system) to attain the cultural goal

stratified random sample   a sample from selected subgroups of the target population in which everyone in those subgroups has an equal chance of being included in the research

street crime   crimes such as mugging, rape, and burglary

structural mobility   movement up or down the social class ladder that is due more to changes in the structure of society than to the actions of individuals

structured interviews   interviews that use closed-ended questions

subculture   the values and related behaviors of a group that distinguish its members from the larger culture; a world within a world

subjective meanings   the meanings that people give their own behavior

subsistence economy   a type of economy in which human groups live off the land and have little or no surplus

suburb   a community adjacent to a city

suburbanization   the migration of people from the city to the suburbs

superego   Freud's term for the conscience; the internalized norms and values of our social groups

survey   the collection of data by having people answer a series of questions

sustainable environment   a world system that takes into account the limits of the environment, produces enough material goods for everyone's needs, and leaves a heritage of a sound environment for the next generation

symbol   something to which people attach meanings and then use to communicate with others

symbolic culture   another term for nonmaterial culture

symbolic interactionism   a theoretical perspective in which society is viewed as composed of symbols that people use to establish meaning, develop their views of the world, and communicate with one another

system of descent   how kinship is traced over the generations

taboo   a norm so strong that it often brings revulsion if violated

taking the role of the other   putting oneself in someone else's shoes; understanding how someone else feels and thinks and thus anticipating how that person will act

teamwork   the collaboration of two or more people to manage impressions jointly

techniques of neutralization   ways of thinking or rationalizing that help people deflect (or neutralize) society's norms

technology   in its narrow sense, tools; its broader sense includes the skills or procedures necessary to make and use those tools

terrorism   the use of violence or the threat of violence to produce fear in order to attain political objectives

theory   a general statement about how some parts of the world fit together and how they work; an explanation of how two or more facts are related to one another

Thomas theorem   William I. and Dorothy S. Thomas' classic formulation of the definition of the situation: "If people define situations as real, they are real in their consequences."

total institution   a place that is almost totally controlled by those who run it, in which people are cut off from the rest of society and the society is mostly cut off from them

totalitarianism   a form of government that exerts almost total control over people

tracking   in education, the sorting of students into different programs on the basis of real or perceived abilities

traditional authority   authority based on custom

traditional society   a society in which the past is thought to be the best guide for the present; tribal, peasant, and feudal societies

transformative social movement   a social movement that seeks to change society totally, to transform it

transitional adulthood a term that refers to a period following high school when young adults have not yet taken on the responsibilities ordinarily associated with adulthood; also called *adultolescence*

transnational social movements social movements whose emphasis is on some condition around the world, instead of on a condition in a specific country; also known as *new social movements*

triad a group of three people

two-tier system of medical care a system of medical care in which the wealthy receive superior medical care and the poor inferior medical care

underclass a group of people for whom poverty persists year after year and across generations

underground economy exchanges of goods and services that are not reported to the government and thereby escape taxation

universal citizenship the idea that everyone has the same basic rights by virtue of being born in a country (or by immigrating and becoming a naturalized citizen)

unobtrusive measures ways of observing people so they do not know they are being studied

unstructured interviews interviews that use open-ended questions

upward social mobility movement up the social class ladder

urban legend a story with an ironic twist that sounds realistic but is false

urban renewal the rehabilitation of a rundown area, which usually results in the displacement of the poor who are living in that area

urbanization the process by which an increasing proportion of a population lives in cities and has a growing influence on the culture

validity the extent to which an operational definition measures what it is intended to measure

value cluster values that together form a larger whole

value contradiction values that contradict one another; to follow the one means to come into conflict with the other

value free the view that a sociologist's personal values or biases should not influence social research

values the standards by which people define what is desirable or undesirable, good or bad, beautiful or ugly

variable a factor thought to be significant for human behavior, which can vary (or change) from one case to another

Verstehen a German word used by Weber that is perhaps best understood as "to have insight into someone's situation"

voluntary associations groups made up of people who voluntarily organize on the basis of some mutual interest; also known as *voluntary memberships* and *voluntary organizations*

voter apathy indifference and inaction on the part of individuals or groups with respect to the political process

war armed conflict between nations or politically distinct groups

wealth the total value of everything someone owns, minus the debts

welfare (or **state**) **capitalism** an economic system in which individuals own the means of production but the state regulates many economic activities for the welfare of the population

white ethnics white immigrants to the United States whose cultures differ from WASP culture

white-collar crime Edwin Sutherland's term for crimes committed by people of respectable and high social status in the course of their occupations; for example, bribery of public officials, securities violations, embezzlement, false advertising, and price fixing

world system theory economic and political connections that tie the world's countries together

zero population growth women bearing only enough children to reproduce the population

Chapter 1: The Sociological Perspective

Allan, Kenneth D. *Explorations in Classical Sociological Theory: Seeing the Social World.* Thousand Oaks, Calif.: Pine Forge Press, 2006. The author's emphasis is on sociological theory as a guide for selecting research projects and interpreting the results.

Berger, Peter L. *Invitation to Sociology: A Humanistic Perspective.* New York: Doubleday, 1972. This analysis of how sociology applies to everyday life has become a classic in the field.

Brooks, Arthur C. *Gross National Happiness: Why Happiness Matters for America and How We Can Get More of It.* New York: Basic Books, 2008. To see how happiness, ordinarily considered to be an intensely personal matter, can be explained by the sociological perspective, read this book.

Charon, Joel M. *Symbolic Interactionism: An Introduction, an Interpretation, an Integration,* 9th ed. Upper Saddle River, N.J.: Prentice Hall, 2008. The author lays out the main points of symbolic interactionism, providing an understanding of why this perspective is important in sociology.

Geary, Daniel. *Radical Ambition: C. Wright Mills, the Left, and American Social Thought.* Berkeley: University of California Press, 2009. This overview of the life and times of C. Wright Mills places Mills' sociological analysis within broader trends in U.S. politics, thought, and culture.

Hedstrom, Peter. *Dissecting the Social: On the Principles of Analytical Sociology.* New York: Cambridge University Press, 2006. By examining the personal perspective of each theorist, the author shows how theoretical and historical perspectives apply to our understanding of the world.

Henslin, James M., ed. *Down to Earth Sociology: Introductory Readings,* 15th ed. New York: Free Press, 2010. This collection of readings about everyday life and social structure is designed to broaden the reader's understanding of society, and of the individual's place within it.

Jeffries, Vincent, ed. *Handbook of Public Sociology.* Lanham, MD: Rowman & Littlefield, 2009. The authors examine how sociology can be taken out of its academic isolation to engage wider audiences. Somewhat advanced reading.

Lengermann, Patricia Madoo, and Gillian Niebrugge. *The Women Founders: Sociology and Social Theory, 1830-1930.* Long Grove, Ill.: Waveland Press, 1998. Through their analyses and the writings they reprint, the authors/editors illuminate the struggles of female sociologists during the early period of sociology.

Mills, C. Wright. *The Sociological Imagination.* New York: Oxford University Press, 2000. First published in 1960, this classic analysis provides an overview of sociology from the framework of the conflict perspective.

Ritzer, George. *Classic Sociological Theory,* 5th ed. New York: McGraw-Hill, 2008. To help understand the personal and historical context of how theory develops, the author includes biographical sketches of the theorists.

Journals

Applied Behavioral Science Review, Clinical Sociology Review, International Clinical Sociology, Journal of Applied Sociology, The Practicing Sociologist, Sociological Practice: A Journal of Clinical and Applied Sociology, and *Sociological Practice Review* report the experiences of sociologists who work in applied settings, from peer group counseling and suicide prevention to recommending changes to school boards.

Contexts: Understanding People in Their Social Worlds, published by the American Sociological Association, uses a magazine format to present sociological research in a down-to-earth fashion.

Humanity & Society, the official journal of the Association for Humanist Sociology, publishes articles intended "to advance the quality of life of the world's people."

Qualitative Sociology, Symbolic Interaction, and Urban Life features articles on symbolic interactionism and analyses of everyday life.

Electronic Journals

Electronic Journal of Sociology (http://www.sociology.org) and *Sociological Research Online* (http://www.socresonline.org.uk) publish articles on various sociological topics. Access is free.

About Majoring in Sociology

You like sociology and perhaps are thinking about majoring in it, but what can you do with a sociology major? Be sure to check the epilogue of this book (pages 680–681). Also check out the resources that are available from the American Sociological Association. Go to www.asanet.org. This will bring you to the ASA's home page. Here, you can click around and get familiar with what this professional association offers students.

On the menu at the top of ASA's home page, click Students. This will bring you to a page that has links to resources for students. You may be interested in *The Student Sociologist,* a newsletter for students. The link, *Careers,* will take you to several free online publications, including those that feature information on careers in both basic and applied sociology. You will also see such links as the student forum, student involvement, and funding.

If you want to contact the ASA by snail mail or by telephone or fax, here is that information: American Sociological Association, 1430 K Street NW, Suite 600, Washington, D.C. 20005. Tel. (202) 383-9005. Fax (202) 638-0882. E-mail: Executive.Office@asanet.org

You might also be interested in how you can make a living with sociology.

Careers in Sociology Module. New York: Wadsworth, 2009, and Lambert, Stephen. *Great Jobs for Sociology Majors,* New York: McGraw-Hill, 2009. These two publications explore careers in sociology, from business and government to health care and the law.

Chapter 2: Culture

Borofsky, Robert, and Bruce Albert. *Yanomani: The Fierce Controversy and What We Can Learn from It.* Berkeley: University of California Press, 2006. The authors criticize the research on the Yanomani, including that by Chagnon in the next book, with an emphasis on anthropologists' lack of consideration for human rights.

Chagnon, Napoleon A. *Yanomamö: The Fierce People,* 5th ed. New York: Harcourt, Brace, Jovanovich, 1997. This account of a tribal people whose customs are extraordinarily different from ours will help you to see how arbitrary the choices are that underlie human culture. This research has aroused enormous controversy over human rights.

Davis, Wade, K. David Harrison, and Catherine Herbert Howell, eds. *Book of Peoples of the World: A Guide to Cultures.* New York: Random House, 2009. A panoramic view of over 200 ethnic groups across the world, from the Kallawaya of the Peruvian Andes, numbering fewer than 1,000, to the Bengalis of India, a group of 172 million.

Fulbeck, Kip. *Permanence: Tattoo Portraits.* New York: Chronicle Books, 2008. Through photographs of tattoos and the accounts of those who have those tattoos, you can gain insight and understanding of the tattoo subcultures, which are being adopted and modified by mainstreamers.

Griswold, Wendy. *Cultures and Societies in a Changing World,* 3rd ed. Thousand Oaks, Calif.: Pine Forge Press, 2008. Analyzes how culture shapes people's individual identity, including their norms, values, beliefs, and behavior; also indicates how globalization is changing cultures.

Inglis, David. *Culture and Everyday Life.* Oxford, UK: Routledge, 2006. An overview of how culture shapes, influences, and structures our everyday lives.

Jacobs, Mark D., and Nancy Weiss Hanrahan, eds. *The Blackwell Companion to the Sociology of Culture.* Malden, Mass.: Blackwell, 2005. The authors of these articles explore cultural systems, everyday life, identity, collective memory, and citizenship in a global economy.

Lenski, Gerhard, and Patrick Nolan. *Human Societies*, 10th ed. Boulder, Colo.: Paradigm, 2006. This wide-ranging examination of the fundamentals of human societies also analyzes social change, including globalization, outsourcing, the end of cheap oil, Islamic fundamentalism, and the rise of China.

Zellner, William W. *Countercultures: A Sociological Analysis*. New York: St. Martin's Press, 1995. The author's analysis of skinheads, the Ku Klux Klan, survivalists, satanists, the Church of Scientology, and the Unification Church (Moonies) helps us understand why people join countercultures.

Journals

Cultural Sociology and *Space for Difference* focus on sociological analyses of culture, with crossovers into art history, gender studies, human geography, racism, literary studies, and social activism.

Chapter 3: Socialization

Ariès, Philippe. *Centuries of Childhood: A Social History of Family Life*. New York: Vintage Books, 1972. The author analyzes how childhood in Europe during the Middle Ages differs from childhood today.

Blumer, Herbert. *George Herbert Mead and Human Conduct*. Lanham, Md.: AltaMira Press, 2004. An overview of symbolic interactionism by a sociologist who studied under Mead.

Greco, Monica, and Paul Stenner, eds. *Emotions: A Social Science Reader*. New York: Routledge, 2008. The authors examine the increasing significance of the study of emotions in the social sciences.

Grusec, Joan E., and Paul D. Hastings, eds. *Handbook of Socialization: Theory and Research*. New York: Guilford Press, 2007. Extensive overview of socialization from earliest childhood into adulthood.

Handel, Gerald, Spencer Cahill, and Frederick Elkin. *Children and Society: The Sociology of Children and Childhood Socialization*. New York: Oxford University Press, 2007. A symbolic interactionist perspective on childhood from birth to adolescence with an emphasis on the development of the self.

Hunt, Stephen J. *The Life Course: A Sociological Introduction*. New York: Palgrave McMillan, 2006. Gives an overview of the life course while considering what is distinct about a sociological approach to this topic.

Lareau, Annette. *Unequal Childhoods: Class, Race, and Family Life*. Berkeley: University of California Press, 2003. The author documents differences in child rearing in poor, working-class, and middle-class U.S. families.

Pugh, Allison J. *Longing and Belonging: Parents, Children, and Consumer Culture*. Berkeley: University of California Press, 2009. Through participant observation and interviewing, the author analyzes why parents, even though they are financially strapped, give in to their children's material wants.

Settersten, Richard A., Jr., and Timothy J. Owens, eds. *New Frontiers in Socialization*. Greenwich, Conn.: JAI Press, 2003. The authors of these articles focus on the adult years in the life course, examining the influence of families, neighborhoods, communities, friendship, education, work, volunteer associations, medical institutions, and the media.

Sociological Studies of Child Development: A Research Annual. Greenwich, Conn.: JAI Press, published annually. Along with theoretical articles, this publication reports on sociological research on the socialization of children.

Turmel, André. *A Historical Sociology of Childhood: Developmental Thinking, Categorization and Graphic Visualization*. New York: Cambridge University Press, 2008. The author examines how the idea of what a "normal" child is has changed over time.

Chapter 4: Social Structure and Social Interaction

Berry, Bonnie. *Beauty Bias: Discrimination and Social Power*. Westport, Conn.: Praeger, 2007. The subject is *lookism*: the many areas of discrimination, negative and positive, that are based on appearance.

Bogle, Kathleen A. *Hooking Up: Sex, Dating, and Relationships on Campus*. New York: New York University Press, 2008. An analysis of the sexual-social interaction of college students.

Cregan, Kate. *The Sociology of the Body: Mapping the Abstraction of Embodiment*. Beverly Hills, Calif.: Sage, 2006. Examines social influences on the body, the smallest unit of sociological analysis.

Day, Graham. *Community and Everyday Life*. New York: Routledge, 2006. The author reviews changing ideas and patterns of community, from urban to rural to communes and virtual communities.

Goffman, Erving. *The Presentation of Self in Everyday Life*. New York: Peter Smith, 1999. First published in 1959. This classic statement of dramaturgical analysis provides a different way of looking at everyday life. When I was a student, this was one of the most intellectually provocative books I read.

Seidman, Steven. *The Social Construction of Sexuality*. New York: W.W. Norton, 2004. The author explores how society influences our sexual choices, our beliefs about sexuality, and our sexual standards.

Tönnies, Ferdinand. *Community and Society (Gemeinschaft und Gesellschaft)*. New York: Dover, 2003. Originally published in 1887, this classic work, focusing on social change, provides insight into how society influences personality. Rather challenging reading.

Waskul, Dennis, and Phillip Vannini, eds. *Body/embodiment: Symbolic Interaction and the Sociology of the Body*. London: Ashgate, 2006. Using a symbolic interactionist perspective, the authors analyze the interrelationship of the body, the self, and social interaction.

Whyte, William Foote. *Street Corner Society: The Social Structure of an Italian Slum*, 4th ed. Chicago: University of Chicago Press, 1993. Originally published in 1943. The author's analysis of interaction in a U.S Italian slum demonstrates how social structure affects personal relationships.

Journals

Qualitative Sociology, Symbolic Interaction, and *Urban Life* feature articles on symbolic interactionism and analyses of everyday life.

Chapter 5: How Sociologists Do Research

Bryman, Alan. *Social Research Methods*, 3rd ed. Oxford: Oxford University Press, 2008. An overview of the research methods used by sociologists, with an emphasis on the logic that underlies these methods.

Creswell, John W. *Research Design: Qualitative, Quantitative, and Mixed Methods Approaches*, 3rd ed. Beverly Hills, Calif.: Sage, 2008. This introduction to research methods walks you through the research experience and helps you to understand when to use a particular method.

Drew, Paul, Geoffrey Raymond, and Darin Weinberg. *Talk and Interaction in Social Research Methods*. Thousand Oaks, Calif.: Sage, 2006. The authors stress the importance of talk in a variety of social research methods.

Lee, Raymond M. *Unobtrusive Methods in Social Research*. Philadelphia: Open University Press, 2000. This overview of unobtrusive ways of doing social research summarizes many interesting studies.

Lomand, Turner C. *Social Science Research: A Cross Section of Journal Articles for Discussion and Evaluation*, 5th ed. Los Angeles: Pyrczak, 2007. This overview of the methods of research used by sociologists includes articles on current topics.

Neuman, W. Lawrence. *Social Research Methods: Qualitative and Quantitative Approaches*, 6th ed. Boston: Allyn and Bacon, 2006. This "how-to" book of sociological research describes how sociologists gather data and the logic that underlies each method.

Schuman, Howard. *Method and Meaning in Polls and Surveys*. Cambridge, Mass.: Harvard University Press, 2008. Examines how the wording of questions can change findings and how to understand the results of surveys.

Whyte, William Foote. *Creative Problem Solving in the Field: Reflections on a Career*. Lanham, Md.: AltaMira Press, 1997. Focusing on his extensive field experiences, the author provides insight into the researcher's role in participant observation.

Wysocki, Diane Kholos, ed. *Readings in Social Research Methods*, 3rd ed. Belmont, Calif.: Wadsworth, 2008. The authors of these articles provide an overview of research methods.

Writing Papers for Sociology

Booth, Wayne C., Gregory G. Colomb, and Joseph M. Williams. *The Craft of Research*, 3rd ed. Chicago: University of Chicago Press, 2008. How to plan a paper, build an argument, anticipate and respond to the reservations of readers, and create introductions and conclusions that answer the demanding question, "So what?"

Richlin-Klonsky, Judith, William G. Roy, Ellen Strenski, and Roseann Giarusso, eds. The Sociology Writing Group. *A Guide to Writing Sociology Papers*, 6th ed. New York: Worth, 2007. The guide walks students through the steps in writing a sociology paper, from choosing the initial assignment to doing the research and turning in a finished paper. Also explains how to manage time and correctly cite sources.

Chapter 6: Societies to Social Networks

Cross, Robert, and Andrew Parker. *The Hidden Power of Social Networks: Understanding How Work* Really *Gets Done in Organizations*. Cambridge, Mass: Harvard Business School Press, 2004. Based on their research and experience in organizations, the authors explain how understanding networks can improve communication and productivity.

Homans, George C. *The Human Group*. New Brunswick, N.J.: Transaction, 2001. First published in 1950. In this classic work, the author develops the idea that all human groups share common activities, interactions, and sentiments.

Hughes, Richard L., Robert C. Ginnett, and Gordon J. Curphy. *Leadership: Enhancing the Lessons of Experience*, 5th ed. New York: McGraw-Hill, 2006. Supplementing empirical studies with illustrative anecdotes, the authors focus on what makes effective leaders.

Janis, Irving L. *Groupthink: Psychological Studies of Policy Decisions and Fiascoes*, 2nd ed. New York: Houghton Mifflin, 1982. Janis analyzes how groups can become cut off from alternatives, interpret evidence in light of their preconceptions, and embark on courses of action that they should have seen as obviously incorrect.

Newman, Mark, Albert-Laszlo Barabasi, and Duncan J. Watts, eds. *The Structure and Dynamics of Networks*, 6th ed. Princeton, N.J.: Princeton University Press, 2007. The authors of these papers analyze the significance of social networks for individuals and the functioning of society.

Purcell, Patrick, ed. *Networked Neighborhoods: The Connected Community in Context*. New York: Springer, 2007. The authors of these papers analyze the impact of the Internet on our social relationships, community, work patterns, and lifestyles.

Small, Mario Luis. *Unexpected Gains: Origins of Network Inequality in Everyday Life*. New York: Oxford University Press, 2009. The author's thesis is that some people have larger, more supportive, or useful networks because of the organization in which they participate: colleges, firms, gyms, day care centers, beauty salons, and churches.

Venkatesh, Sudhir. *Gang Leader for a Day: A Rogue Sociologist Takes to the Streets*. New York: Penguin Press, 2008. The adventures of a naïve graduate student in sociology as he explores a drug-dealing gang in a Chicago public housing project.

Wilson, Gerald L. *Groups in Context: Leadership and Participation in Small Groups*, 7th ed. New York: McGraw-Hill, 2005. An overview of principles and processes of interaction in small groups, with an emphasis on how to exercise leadership.

Chapter 7: Bureaucracy and Formal Organizations

Ackoff, Russell L., and Sheldon Rovin. *Beating the System: Using Creativity to Outsmart Bureaucracies*. San Francisco: Berrett-Koehler, 2005. This analysis can be applied to everyday situations, such as avoiding getting lost in a maze as you try to solve a problem with the phone company or some other bureaucracy.

Crouter, Ann C., and Alan Booth, eds. *Work-Life Policies*. Washington D.C.: Urban Institute Press, 2008. The authors examine work policies that make life better for both the employees and the company.

Fineman, Stephen, Gabriel Yiannis, and David P. Sims. *Organizing and Organizations*, 3rd ed. Thousand Oaks, Calif.: Sage, 2006. The authors draw on many firsthand accounts to help enliven the study of formal organizations.

Freidson, Eliot. *Professionalism: The Third Logic: On the Practice of Knowledge*. Chicago: University of Chicago Press, 2001. The author distinguishes professions, technical occupations, and crafts, analyzing how they differ by knowledge base, educational requirements, career paths, organization, and ideology.

Low, Albert. *Conflict and Creativity at Work: Human Roots of Corporate Life*. East Sussex, UK: Sussex University Press, 2008. The author's thesis is that employers have the obligation to structure work in such a way that it benefits the workers, which will result in greater creativity and better mental health.

Parkinson, C. Northcote. *Parkinson's Law*. Boston: Buccaneer Books, 1997. Although this exposé of the inner workings of bureaucracies is delightfully satirical, if what Parkinson analyzes were generally true, bureaucracies would always fail.

Ritzer, George. *The McDonaldization of Society: An Investigation into the Changing Character of Contemporary Life*, 5th ed. Thousand Oaks, Calif.: Pine Forge Press, 2007. The author examines how Durkheim's predictions about the rationalization of society are coming true in everyday life.

Tolbert, Pamela S., and Richard H. Hall. *Organizations: Structures, Processes, and Outcomes*, 10th ed. Upper Saddle River, N. J.: Prentice Hall, 2009. The focus of this review of the literature on social organizations is on the impacts that organizations have upon individuals and society.

Want, Jerome. *Corporate Culture: Illuminating the Black Hole*. New York: St. Martin's Press, 2007. The author uses real-life examples to show how culture determines the success of an organization.

Chapter 8: Deviance and Social Control

Clear, Todd R. *Imprisoning Communities: How Mass Incarceration Makes Disadvantaged Neighborhoods Worse*. New York: Oxford University Press, 2009. The author's thesis is that mass incarceration breaks up family and social networks; deprives siblings, spouses, and parents of emotional and financial support; and threatens the economic and political infrastructure of struggling neighborhoods.

Cusac, Anne-Marie. *Cruel and Unusual: The Culture of Punishment in America*. New Haven, Conn.: Yale University Press, 2009. The author analyzes why the United States has become more punitive toward lawbreakers.

Deflin, Mathieu. *Surveillance and Governance: Crime Control and Beyond*. Greenwich, Conn.: JAI Press, 2008. The use of increasingly powerful surveillance techniques to monitor terrorists and other violent criminals is usually taken for granted—but what is to keep those same methods from being turned against ordinary citizens?

Domanick, Joe. *Cruel Justice: Three Strikes and the Politics of Crime in America's Golden State*. Berkeley: University of California Press, 2004. A history of California's three-strikes law and the reaction to its unintended injustice.

Goffman, Erving. *Stigma: Notes on the Management of Spoiled Identity*. New York: Simon & Schuster, 1986. First published in 1968. The author outlines the social and personal reactions to "spoiled identity," appearances that—due to disability, weight, ethnicity, birth marks, and so on—do not match dominant expectations.

Goode, Erich, and D. Angus Vail, eds. *Extreme Deviance*. Thousand Oaks, Calif.: Pine Forge Press, 2007. As the authors of these articles examine behaviors that bring extreme negative reactions, they analyze vocabularies of motive, deviance neutralization, the acquisition of a deviant identity, and the formation of deviant subcultures.

Heiner, Robert, ed. *Deviance Across Cultures*. Oxford: Oxford University Press, 2007. Cross-cultural norms and behavior are the focus of this collection of classic and contemporary articles on deviance.

Parmentier, Stephen, and Elmar Weitekamp. *Crime and Human Rights*. Greenwich, Conn.: JAI Press, 2008. The authors analyze how the emphasis on human rights is changing the ways crime and criminal justice are viewed and how this is impacting the U.S. and European justice systems.

Rathbone, Cristina. *A World Apart: Women, Prison, and Life Behind Bars.* New York: Random House, 2006. A journalist's account of the four years she spent investigating MCI Framingham, the oldest women's prison in the United States.

Reiman, Jeffrey. *The Rich Get Richer and the Poor Get Prison: Ideology, Class, and Criminal Justice,* 8th ed. Boston: Allyn and Bacon, 2007. An analysis of how social class works to produce different types of criminals and different types of justice.

Simon, David R. *Elite Deviance,* 9th ed. Boston: Allyn & Bacon, 2008. A broad overview of deviance, from scandals to organized crime syndicates.

Journals

Contemporary Justice Review, Criminology and Public Policy, Deviant Behavior, and *Journal of Law and Society* examine the social forces that shape deviance and reaction to it.

Chapter 9: Global Stratification

Bales, Kevin, and Ron Soodalter. *The Slave Next Door: Human Trafficking and Slavery in America Today.* Berkeley: University of California Press, 2009. The authors' thesis is that there is slavery in the United States—from prostitutes to dishwashers, people work under threat of violence and cannot walk away—and that we can put an end to it.

Grusky, David B., ed. *Social Stratification: Class, Race, and Gender in Sociological Perspective.* Boulder, Colo.: Westview Press, 2008. This reader of over 100 articles and 1,000 pages examines almost every aspect of social stratification, from causes and consequences to likely futures.

Gu, George Zhibin, and Andre Gunder Frank. *China's Global Reach: Markets, Multinationals, and Globalization,* rev. ed. Palo Alto, Calif.: Fultus Corp., 2006. The author tries to identify the causes and consequences of global development, with a comparison of corporations in China and other nations.

Holzner, Burkart, and Leslie Holzner. *Transparency in Global Change: The Vanguard of the Open Society.* Pittsburgh: University of Pittsburgh Press, 2006. The tension between transparency and secrecy as information flows within and across international boundaries.

Lechner, Krank J., and John Boli, eds. *The Globalization Reader,* 3rd ed. Malden, Mass.: Wiley-Blackwell, 2008. A thorough introduction to globalization, including a link with environmentalism.

Ritzer, George. *The Globalization of Nothing.* 2nd ed. Thousand Oaks, Calif.: Pine Forge Press, 2007. The author expresses concerns about the short- and long-term effects of globalization.

Rothkopf, David. *Superclass: The Global Power Elite and the World They Are Making.* New York: Farrar, Straus and Giroux, 2008. The author of this overview of the world's wealthiest families has many connections with these elite, powerful people.

Sernau, Scott. *Worlds Apart: Social Inequalities in a Global Economy,* 2nd ed. Thousand Oaks, Calif.: Pine Forge Press, 2005. The author's thesis is that the market-driven global economy contributes to rather than reduces social inequality.

Wan, Ming. *The Political Economy of East Asia: Striving for Wealth and Power.* Washington, D.C.: CQ Press, 2008. The author analyzes the politics and policies that are increasing the power and wealth of east Asia.

Zakaria, Fareed. *The Post-American World.* New York: W.W. Norton, 2008. The author analyzes political and economic megatrends that are making fundamental changes in the distribution of world power.

Chapter 10: Social Class in the United States

Beeghley, Leonard. *The Structure of Social Stratification in the United States,* 5th ed. Boston: Pearson, 2008. The author presents a concise overview of the U.S. social classes.

Eitzen, D. Stanley, and Janis E. Johnston, eds. *Inequality: Social Class and Its Consequences.* Boulder, Colo.: Paradigm, 2007. Written from the conflict perspective (class struggle), these selections examine class formation, cultures, and politics.

Engels, Friedrich. *Condition of the Working Class in England.* Sydney, Australia: Read How You Want, 2007. First published as *Die Lage der arbeitenden Klasse in England,* in 1844. One of the significant books in world history, this analysis of people who lived in poverty (the working class of the time) is based on the author's research and parliamentary reports.

Gilbert, Dennis. *The American Class Structure in an Age of Growing Inequality,* 7th ed. Thousand Oaks, Calif.: Pine Forge Press, 2008. This basic text on the U.S. social class structure, filled with facts about class, grapples with the question of why social mobility in the United States is decreasing.

McNamee, Stephen J., and Robert K. Miller, *The Meritocracy Myth,* 2nd ed. Lanham, MD: Rowman & Littlefield, 2009. The authors evaluate talent, attitude, work ethic, and character as elements of merit and social status; race, heritage, and wealth as elements of nonmerit.

Newman, Katherine S., and Victor Tan Chen. *The Missing Class: Portraits of the Near Poor in America.* Boston: Beacon Press, 2007. The story of nine families who live on the edge of poverty: their experiences in education, leisure, child rearing, romance, work, the police, courts, welfare, shopping, and debt.

Perucci, Robert, and Earl Wyson. *The New Class Society,* 3rd ed. Lanham, Md.: Rowman and Littlefield, 2007. An overview of the U.S. social class structure, with the suggestion that no longer is there a middle class.

Sherman, Rachel. *Class Acts: Service and Inequality in Luxury Hotels.* Berkeley, Calif.: University of California Press, 2007. Based on participant observation, the author explores the relationship between workers and guests at a luxury hotel.

Sumner, William Graham. *What the Social Classes Owe to Each Other.* Charleston, South Carolina: BiblioBazaar, 2008. First published in 1883. Written when sociology had a largely conservative orientation, the author explains why the government should not redistribute wealth.

Van Galen, Jane A., and George W. Noblit, eds. *Late to Class: Social Class and Schooling in the New Economy.* Albany: State University of New York Press, 2007. The authors of these articles compare the educational experiences of poor, working-class, and middle-class students, illustrating how education reproduces social class and suggesting ways to open educational opportunity.

Journals

Journal of Children and Poverty and *Journal of Poverty* analyze issues that affect the quality of life of people who live in poverty.

Race, Gender, and Class publishes interdisciplinary articles on the topics listed in its title.

Chapter 11: Sex and Gender

Andersen, Margaret L. *Thinking About Women: Sociological Perspectives on Sex and Gender,* 8th ed. New York: Allyn and Bacon, 2008. An overview of the main issues of sex and gender in contemporary society, ranging from sexism and socialization to work and health.

Brettell, Caroline B., and Carolyn F. Sargent, eds. *Gender in Cross-Cultural Perspective,* 5th ed. Upper Saddle River, N.J.: Prentice Hall, 2008. The net is spread wide as the authors examine gender and biology, in prehistory, at home, and the division of labor, and the body, property, kinship, religion, politics, and the global economy.

Casey, Emma, and Lydia Martens, eds. *Gender and Consumption: Domestic Cultures and the Commercialization of Everyday Life.* Burlington, Vt.: Ashgate, 2007. The articles in this short book focus on how gender is constructed and communicated through the purchase and use of objects.

Colapinto, John. *As Nature Made Him: The Boy Who Was Raised as a Girl, P.S.* New York: Harper Perennial, 2006. A detailed account of the event summarized in this chapter of the boy whose penis was accidentally burned off.

DeFrancisco, Victoria Priun, and Catherine Helen Palczewski. *Communicating Gender Diversity: A Critical Approach.* Los Angeles: Sage 2007. Probably the polar opposite of the Colapinto book; gender is viewed not as something that people are but as something that people do; an emphasis on how gender is constructed through communication.

Fuller, Linda K., ed. *Sport, Rhetoric, and Gender: Historical Perspectives and Media Representations.* New York: Palgrave Macmillan, 2006. The articles in this short book focus on how gender is communicated in sports; includes both historical materials and contemporary case studies.

Gilbert, Paula Ruth, and Kimberly K. Eby, eds. *Violence and Gender: An Interdisciplinary Reader*. Upper Saddle River, N.J.: Prentice Hall, 2004. The authors of these articles examine violence and youth, the human body, war, intimacy, sports, the media, and how to prevent violence.

Gilman, Charlotte Perkins. *The Man-Made World or, Our Androcentric Culture*. New York: Charlton, 1911. Reprinted in 1971 by Johnson Reprint. This early book on women's liberation provides an excellent view of gender relations at the beginning of the last century.

Gonas, Lena, and Jan Ch Karlsson, eds. *Gender Segregation: Divisions of Work in Post-Industrial Welfare States*. Burlington, Vermont: Ashgate, 2006. This short book of ten articles focuses on the gendered division of labor.

Hanson, Sandra L. *Swimming Against the Tide: African American Girls in Science Education*. Philadelphia, PA.: Temple University Press, 2009. Examines how gender and race–ethnicity coalesce to discourage African American females from becoming scientists.

Johnson, Allan G. *Privilege, Power, and Difference*, 2nd ed. New York: McGraw-Hill, 2006. The author helps us see the nature and consequences of privilege and our connection to it.

McDonagh, Eileen, and Laura Pappano. *Playing with the Boys: Why Separate Is Not Equal in Sports*. New York: Oxford University Press, 2008. A detailed history of how women have challenged men's sports; filled with anecdotes and contains fascinating historical photos.

Nelson, Robert L., and William P. Bridges. *Legalizing Gender Inequality: Courts, Markets and Unequal Pay for Women in America*. New York: Cambridge University Press, 2008. The authors analyze how organizations produce pay disparities between the sexes and how the courts legitimate them.

Siltanen, Janet, and Andrea Doucet. *Gender Relations: Intersectionality and Beyond*. New York: Oxford University Press, 2008. The authors look at how gender differences and inequalities play out in the lives of men and women throughout the life course.

Journals

These journals focus on the role of gender in social life: *Feminist Studies; Gender and Behavior; Gender and Society; Forum in Women's and Gender Studies; Gender and History; Gender, Place and Culture: A Journal of Feminist Geography; Journal of Gender, Culture, and Health; Journal of Interdisciplinary Gender Studies; Journal of Men's Health and Gender; Sex Roles;* and *Signs: Journal of Women in Culture and Society*.

Chapter 12: Race and Ethnicity

Blackmon, Douglas A. *A Different Kind of Slavery, The Re-Enslavement of Black Americans from the Civil War to World War II*. New York, Doubleday, 2008. The author documents the horrible conditions African Americans suffered in Georgia during "post-slavery," especially in its criminal "justice" system.

Bullard, Robert D., and Beverly Wright, eds. *Race, Place, and Environmental Justice After Hurricane Katrina: Struggles to Reclaim, Rebuild, and Revitalize New Orleans and the Gulf Coast*. Boulder, Colo.: Westview Press, 2009. Among the other issues of race and place (geography) that the authors examine are the health and environment and what they call "the color of opportunity."

Glover, Karen S. *Racial Profiling: Research, Racism, and Resistance*. Lanham, MD: Rowman & Littlefield, 2009. The author analyzes racial profiling in traffic stops—associating criminality with race–ethnicity—in terms of the rights of citizenship.

Higginbotham, Elizabeth, and Margaret L. Andersen, eds. *Race and Ethnicity in Society: The Changing Landscape*, 2nd ed. Belmont, Calif.: Wadsworth, 2008. From race–ethnicity as a social issue to its relationship to beliefs, ideology, and personal identity, the authors provide a thorough overview of this topic.

Idler, Jose Enrique. *Officially Hispanic: Classification Policy and Identity*. Lanham, Md.: Lexington Books, 2007. How official categories are inadequate for representing the racial–ethnic experience.

Parrillo, Vincent N. *Strangers to These Shores: Race and Ethnic Relations in the United States,* 9th ed. Boston: Allyn and Bacon, 2009. This text reviews the experiences of more than 50 racial–ethnic groups.

Ross, Jeffrey Ian, and Larry Gould, eds. *Native Americans and the Criminal Justice System*. Boulder, Colo.: Paradigm, 2006. The authors of these articles address crime by Native Americans within historical, cultural, and legal contexts and the issue of criminal justices and tribal sovereignty.

Russell, James W. *Class and Race Formation in North America*. Toronto: University of Toronto Press, 2009. As the author explores how race–ethnicity and social class formed in Canada, Mexico, and the United States, he examines the effects and possible future consequences of NAFTA.

Schaefer, Richard T. *Race and Ethnicity in the United States,* 5th ed. Upper Saddle River, New Jersey: Prentice Hall, 2009. The data and analyses of this basic text can help cut through some of the emotional blinders that often accompany this topic.

Sutton, Mark Q. *An Introduction to Native North America,* 3rd ed. Boston: Allyn and Bacon, 2007. An overview of the cultures of Native Americans, with an emphasis on the effects of the European invasion.

White, Michael J., and Jennifer E. Glick. *Achieving Anew: How New Immigrants Do in American Schools, Jobs, and Neighborhoods*. New York: Russell Sage Foundation, 2009. This examination of immigrant life at school, at work, and in communities and shows that recent immigrants and their children are not forming an underclass but are making substantial progress in entering the mainstream.

Williams, Philip J., Timothy Steigenga, and Manual A. Vasquez, eds. *A Place to Be: Brazilian, Guatemalan, and Mexican Immigrants in Florida's New Destinations*. The authors analyze the challenges, resources, and strategies of immigrants as they form community and establish identity. Piscataway, New Jersey: Rutgers University Press, 2009.

Wilson, William Julius. *More Than Just Race: Being Black and Poor in the Inner City*. New York: W.W. Norton, 2009. The author analyzes both cultural and structural factors that maintain poverty in the inner city. Includes policy recommendations.

Zeitz, Joshua M. *White Ethnic New York: Jews, Catholics, and the Shaping of Postwar Politics*. Chapel Hill: University of North Carolina Press, 2007. Examines the sometimes contentious, fractious, and fragile coalition that became politically and culturally significant in this area of the United States.

Chapter 13: The Elderly

Booth, Alan, Ann C. Crouter, Suzanne Bianchi, , and Judith A. Seltzer. *Intergenerational Caregiving*. Washington, D.C.: Urban Institute Press, 2008. Considers effects on social policies of our changing family relationships: divorce, extramarital childbearing, cohabitation, remarriage, and longer life expectancy.

Buettner, Dan. *Blue Zones: Lessons for Living Longer from the People Who've Lived the Longest*. Washington, D.C.: National Geographic Society, 2008. The author interviewed elderly people around world to find out how lifestyles affect longevity.

Gass, Thomas Edward, and Bruce C. Vladeck. *Nobody's Home: Candid Reflections of a Nursing Home Aide*. Ithaca, N.Y.: ILR Press, 2004. A firsthand account of the reality of life in a nursing home.

Harris, Diana K., and Michael L. Benson. *Maltreatment of Patients in Nursing Homes: There Is No Safe Place*. New York: Routledge, 2006. An examination of the physical, financial, and psychological abuse of patients—restraints, verbal abuse, sexual abuse, the theft of belongings, childlike treatment, and learned helplessness.

Hooyman, Nancy, and H. Asuman Kiyak. *Social Gerontology: A Multidisciplinary Perspective*, 8th ed. Boston: Allyn and Bacon, 2008. As the authors consider factors that influence how people experience old age, they review differences by age and cohort, gender, race–ethnicity, sexual orientation, and socioeconomic status.

Nilan, Pam, and Carles Feixa, eds. *Global Youth? Hybrid Identities, Plural Worlds*. New York, Routledge, 2006. The authors of these articles report research on Eastern youth cultures.

Quadagno, Jill S. *Aging and the Life Course: An Introduction to Social Gerontology,* 4th ed. New York: McGraw-Hill, 2008. In this review of major issues in gerontology, the author examines how the quality of life that people experience in old age is the result of earlier choices, opportunities, and constraints.

Schaie, K. Warner, and Laura Carsgtensen. *Social Structures, Aging, and Self-Regulation in the Elderly.* New York: Springer, 2006. The focus is how social location, especially social class, influences the lives, even the brains, of the elderly; recommended for advanced students.

Schultz, James H., and Robert H. Binstock. *Aging Nation: The Economics and Politics of Growing Older in America.* Baltimore, MD: Johns Hopkins University Press, 2008. The authors look at the future in the light of faltering employer pensions, health care, workplace conditions, and entitlement programs.

Xi, Jieying, Yunxiao Sun, and Jin Jian Xiao, eds. *Chinese Youth in Transition.* Burlington, Vermont: Ashgate, 2006. The authors of these articles analyze the changing youth culture of China.

Journals

Elderly Latinos; The Gerontologist, Journal of Aging and Identity, Journal of Aging and Social Policy, Journal of Aging Studies, Journal of Cross-Cultural Gerontology, Journal of Elder Abuse and Neglect, Journal of Gerontology, Journal of Long Term Home Health Care, and *Journal of Women and Aging* focus on issues of aging, while *Youth and Society* and *Journal of Youth Studies* examine adolescent culture.

Chapter 14: The Economy

Bales, Kevin. *Documenting Disposable People: Contemporary Global Slavery.* Berkeley: Hayward Press, 2008. Documents human oppression to extract money from child labor in Bangladesh to sex slavery in the Ukraine.

Davis, Gerald F. *Managed by the Markets: How Finance Has Re-Shaped America.* New York: Oxford University Press, 2009. Analyzes how we got into the financial crisis and examines how the well-being of society is linked to financial markets.

Eitzen, D. Stanley, and Maxine Baca Zinn, eds. *Globalization: The Transformation of Social Worlds.* Belmont, Calif.: Wadsworth, 2008. The authors of these articles examine the process of globalization and analyze how globalization is reshaping society and groups within it.

Friedman, Thomas L. *The World Is Flat: A Brief History of the Twenty-First Century.* New York: Picador, 2007. Examines implications of it now being "possible for more people than ever to collaborate and compete in real time with more people on more different kinds of work from more different corners of the planet and on a more equal footing than at any previous time in the history of the world."

Kenway, Jane, Elizabeth Bullen, Johannah Fahey, and Simon Robb. *Haunting the Knowledge Economy.* New York: Routledge, 2007. The authors' thesis is that alongside the dominant knowledge economy lie alternative marginalized risk, libidinal, gift, and survival economies.

Lenin, Vladimir Ilyrich. *The Development of Capitalism in Russia.* Honolulu: University Press of the Pacific, 2004. An English translation of Lenin's 1899 book.

Noland, Marcus, and Howard Pack. *The Arab Economies in a Changing World.* Washington, D.C.: Institute for International Economies, 2007. Places the economies of the Middle East in global context, comparing them with other transition economies.

Stiglitz, Joseph E. *Making Globalization Work.* New York: W. W. Norton, 2008. The author suggests ways that globalization can benefit the poor and rich alike and solve the problems of the indebtedness of developing countries, international fiscal instability, and worldwide pollution.

Sweet, Stephen A., and Peter F. Meiksins. *Changing Contours of Work: Jobs and Opportunities in the New Economy.* Thousand Oaks, Calif.: Pine Forge Press, 2008. The authors examine historical changes in work, explain how U.S. workers have become part of an integrated global workforce, and make recommendations for how the new economy can help overcome inequality and serve human dignity.

Volti, Rudi. *An Introduction to the Sociology of Work and Occupations.* Thousand Oaks, Calif.: Pine Forge Press, 2008. Reviewing work from hunting and gathering societies to the information age, this basic introduction to the sociology of work stresses the impact of globalization on work today.

Chapter 15: Politics

Amnesty International. *Amnesty International Report.* London: Amnesty International Publications, published annually. Summarizes human rights violations around the world, country by country, listing specific instances and names.

Beah, Ishmael. *A Long Way Gone: Memoirs of a Boy Soldier.* New York: Farrar, Straus, and Giroux, 2007. This first-person account of a boy who was forced into being a soldier in Sierra Leone provides an understanding of the social dynamics that transform young teenagers into rapists, torturers, and killers.

Domhoff, G. William. *Who Rules America? Power and Politics,* 5th ed. New York: McGraw-Hill, 2006. An analysis of how the multinational corporations dominate the U.S. government.

DuBois, William, and R. Dean Wright. *Politics in the Human Interest.* Lanham, Md.: Lexington Books, 2007. The authors explain how we can use sociology to change politics so it serves the interests of the people.

Harrison, Lawrence E. *The Central Liberal Truth: How Politics Can Change a Culture and Save It From Itself.* New York: Oxford University Press, 2008. Based on research on cultural values in dozens of nations, the author examines which values, beliefs, and attitudes best promote democracy, social justice, and prosperity.

Lazreg, Marnia. *Torture and the Twilight of Empire: From Algiers to Baghdad.* Princeton, New Jersey: Princeton University Press, 2007. Examines the connection between colonial domination and torture, looking at the French experience in Algeria and that of the United States in Iraq and Afghanistan.

Mills, C. Wright. *The Power Elite,* 2nd ed. New York: Textbook, 2003. First published in 1956. This classic analysis elaborates the conflict thesis summarized in this chapter—that U.S. society is ruled by the nation's top corporate leaders, together with elites from the military and political institutions.

Nash, Kate. *Contemporary Political Sociology: Globalization, Politics, and Power.* Malden, Mass.: Blackwell, 2008. This overview of the sociology of politics makes the point that globalization is ushering in a major transition, from the nation-state to the internationalized state.

Paxton, Pamela, and Melanie M. Hughes. *Women, Politics, and Power: A Global Perspective.* Thousand Oaks, Calif.: Pine Forge Press, 2007. The authors survey women's political participation in many countries and regions of the world.

Research in Political Sociology: A Research Annual. Greenwich, Conn.: JAI Press, published annually. Analyzes political topics of vital concern to our well-being; recommended for advance students, as the findings and theories can be difficult and abstract.

Toussaint, Laura L. *The Contemporary U.S. Peace Movement.* New York: Routledge, 2009. The author examines the impact on the peace movement of the governent's attempt to control dissent since 9/11.

Journals

Many sociology journals publish articles on politics, but these focus on this area of social life: *American Political Science Review, Behavioral Sciences of Terrorism and Political Aggression, Journal of Political and Military Sociology, Social Policy,* and *Social Politics.*

Chapter 16: Marriage and Family

Agger, Ben, and Beth Anne Shelton. *Fast Families, Virtual Children: A Critical Sociology of Families and Schooling.* Boulder, Colo.: Paradigm, 2007. The authors analyze how technology has changed the way families conduct their lives, rear their children, and try to maintain a boundary between work and home.

Amato, Paul R., Alan Booth, David R. Johnson, and Stacy J. Rogers. *Alone Together: How Marriage in American Is Changing.* Cambridge, Mass.: Harvard University Press, 2007. The authors' controversial thesis is that the significance of marriage is declining, that marriage is becoming just one lifestyle choice among many.

Bianchi, Suzanne M., John P. Robinson, and Melissa A. Milkie. *Changing Rhythms of American Family Life.* New York: Russell Sage, 2007. Based on time-diaries, the authors conclude that despite their greater participation in the paid labor force U.S. mothers spend just as much time with their children as the previous generation of women did.

Conley, Dalton. *The Pecking Order: A Bold New Look at How Family and Society Determine Who We Become.* New York: Random House, 2009. Analyzes how the inequality in families—children ending up in different social classes—is related to the larger social forces that envelop the family: gender expectations, the cost of education, divorce, early loss of a parent, geographic mobility, religious and sexual orientation, trauma, and even luck and accidents.

Coontz, Stephanie. *Marriage, a History: How Love Conquered Marriage.* New York: Penguin 2006. This analysis of how the fundamental orientations to marriage have changed contains enlightening excerpts from the past.

Epstein, Cynthia Fuchs, and Arne L. Kalleberg, eds. *Fighting for Time: Shifting Boundaries of Work and Social Life.* New York: Russell Sage, 2006. Explores changes in the time people spend at work and the consequences of those changes for individuals and families.

McAdoo, Harriet Pipes, ed. *Black Families,* 4th ed. Beverly Hills, Calif.: Sage, 2007. The authors of these 23 articles analyze gender relations, family patterns, religion, social policy, and even funerary practices of African Americans.

Stone, Pamela. *Opting Out? Why Women Really Quit Careers and Head Home.* Berkeley: University of California Press, 2007. A study of high-achieving, highly educated, privileged women who quit their fast-paced professional work in order to become stay-at-home mothers—their decision, the transition, and the consequences.

Sullivan, Andrew, ed. *Same-Sex Marriage: Pro and Con.* New York: Random House, 2009. In this even-handed anthology, the editor brings together arguments and opinions concerning same-sex marriage.

Wallace, Harvey. *Family Violence: Legal, Medical, and Social Perspectives,* 5th ed. Boston: Allyn and Bacon, 2008. This overview of violence, from stalking to sexual harassment to sexual violence in the workplace, includes case studies.

Journals

Family Relations, The History of the Family, International Journal of Sociology of the Family, Journal of Comparative Family Studies, Journal of Divorce, Journal of Divorce and Remarriage, Journal of Family and Economic Issues, Journal of Family Issues, Journal of Family Violence, Journal of Marriage and Family, and *Marriage and Family Review* publish articles on almost every aspect of marriage and family life.

Chapter 17: Education

Ansalone, George. *Exploring Unequal Achievement in the Schools: The Social Construction of Failure.* Lanham, MD: Rowman & Littlefield, 2009. The author's thesis is that unequal achievement in school is facilitated both by student attributes including gender, race, and class and by educational structures and policies.

Attewell, Paul, David Lavin, Thurston Domina, and Tana Levey. *Passing the Torch: Does Higher Education for the Disadvantaged Pay Off Across the Generations?* New York: Russell Sage, 2007. This study of women from poor families who attended college under open admission programs shows that their children are more likely to succeed in school and to earn college degrees themselves.

Ballantine, Jeanne H., and Floyd Hammock. *The Sociology of Education: A Systemic Analysis,* 6th ed. Upper Saddle River, N.J.: Prentice Hall, 2008. A basic reader that covers current issues in education, and the social processes that underlie education.

Cotterill, Pamela, Sue Jackson, and Gayle Letherby, ed. *Challenges and Negotiations for Women in Higher Education.* Dordrecht, Netherlands: Springer, 2007. A short book of just twelve articles; addresses issues women face in higher education, from feeling unwelcome to juggling families and schooling.

Graham, Patricia Albjerg. *Schooling America: How the Public Schools Meet the Nation's Changing Needs.* New York: Oxford University Press, 2007. Examines the relationship between changes in society since 1900 and the educational response to these changing needs.

Grant, Gerald. *Hope and Despair in the American City: Why There Are No Bad Schools in Raleigh.* Cambridge, Mass.: Harvard University Press, 2009. The author compares the social class and racial–ethnic integration in the schools of Raleigh, North Carolina, with the segregation of the schools in Syracuse, New York.

Grubb, W. Norton. *The Money Myth: School Resources, Outcomes, and Equity.* New York: Russell Sage, 2009. The author's thesis is that educational success does not come from the money spent on schools but from leadership, instruction, and tracking policies.

Hess, Frederick M. *Common Sense School Reform.* New York: Palgrave Macmillan, 2005. Critical of current efforts to reform U.S. education, the author makes the case that reform needs to be based around accountability, competition, and leadership.

Kozol, Jonathan. *Ordinary Resurrections: Children in the Years of Hope.* New York: Crown, 2001. To listen as these children from a dismal neighborhood in South Bronx talk about life makes us more aware of the potential that schools have to transform the lives of children in poverty.

Stevens, Michael L. *Kingdom of Children: Culture and Controversy in the Homeschooling Movement.* Princeton: Princeton University Press, 2003. This analysis of the homeschooling movement, based on interviews and participant observation, contains numerous quotations that provide insight into why parents homeschool their children.

Journals

The following journals contain articles that examine almost every aspect of education: *Education and Urban Society, Harvard Educational Review, Sociology and Education,* and *Sociology of Education.*

Chapter 18: Religion

Cateura, Linda Brandi, and Omid Safi. *Voices of American Muslims.* New York: Hippocrene Books, 2006. U.S. Muslims describe their religion, experiences with suspicion and misunderstandings, and, in this heated period of terrorist attacks by Muslims, their devotion to the United States.

Christiano, Kevin, William H. Swatos, Jr., and Peter Kivisto. *Sociology of Religion: Contemporary Developments,* 2nd ed. Lanham, Md.: Rowman and Littlefield, 2008. Examines the foundations of the sociology of religion and charts changes in this field.

Covington, Dennis. *Salvation on Sand Mountain: Snake Handling and Redemption in Southern Appalachia.* New York: Penguin Books, 1995. A fascinating account by someone who became curious about snake handlers and in his research handled snakes himself.

Crawford, Suzanne. *Native American Religious Traditions.* Upper Saddle River, N.J.: Prentice Hall, 2006. An introduction to the religions traditions of the Lakota, Diné (Navajo), and Coast Salish tribes, placing them within their historical, social, and political contexts.

Edwards, Korie L. *The Elusive Dream: The Power of Race in Interracial Churches.* New York: Oxford University Press, 2008. In this study of a racially integrated church, the author found that African Americans conform to the expectations of white members.

Gilman, Sander. *Jewish Frontiers: Essays on Bodies, Histories, and Identities.* New York: Macmillan, 2003. Analyzes Jewish identity from the framework of living on a frontier, and the representation of this identity in the mass media.

Hicks, Douglas A. *With God on All Sides: Leadership in a Devout and Diverse America.* New York: Oxford University Press, 2009. The author analyzes how civic leaders need to and can turn the cacophony of beliefs and practices in their communities into a kind of citizenship worthy of the American tradition of religious freedom.

Juergensmeyer, Mark. *Terror in the Mind of God: The Global Rise of Religious Violence,* 3rd ed. Berkeley: University of California Press, 2003. The author's summaries of religious violence provide a rich background for understanding this behavior.

Smith, Christian, and Melinda Denton. *Soul Searching: The Religious and Spiritual Life of American Teenagers.* Oxford: Oxford University Press, 2006. U.S. teenagers describe the meaning of their spiritual life.

Thumma, Scott, and Dave Travis. *Beyond Megachurch Myths: What We Can Learn from America's Largest Churches.* New Jersey: Jossey-Bass, 2007. The authors analyze the similarities and diversities of the nation's megachurches, indicating how participants find community in the midst of the crowd.

Journals

These journals publish articles that focus on the sociology of religion: *Journal for the Scientific Study of Religion, Review of Religious Research,* and *Sociological Analysis: A Journal in the Sociology of Religion.*

Chapter 19: Medicine and Health

Aday, Lu Ann, ed. *Reinventing Public Health: Policies and Practices for a Healthy Nation.* Hoboken, New Jersey: Jossey-Bass, 2005. The authors analyze how public policy must respond to changing societal characteristics that influence a population's health.

Barber, Charles. *Comfortably Numb.* New York: Random House, 2009. The author examines the ways in which pharmaceutical companies first create the need for a drug and then rush to fill it.

Gabe, Jonathan, and Michael Calnan. *The New Sociology of the Health Service.* New York: Routledge, 2009. The authors analyze contemporary health services issues, including consumerism, technology, evidence-based practice, public health, managerialism, and social care.

Grob, Gerald N. *The Deadly Truth: A History of Disease in America.* Cambridge, Mass.: Harvard University Press, 2003. In this history of disease in the United States, the author stresses relationships among society, environment, and human health.

Henderson, Gail E., and Sue E. Estroff, et al., eds. *The Social Medicine Reader, Volume Two: Social and Cultural Contributions to Health, Difference, and Inequality,* 2nd ed. Durham, N.C.: Duke University Press, 2005. The authors combine first-person accounts with empirical studies, drawing on findings in sociology, anthropology, and the history of medicine.

Hilts, Philip J. *Rx for Survival: Why We Must Rise to the Global Health Challenge.* New York: Penguin, 2007. The author makes the case that we must take bold steps now in order to avoid a world crisis in disease that will make terrorism pale by comparison.

Reverby, Susan M., ed. *Tuskegee's Truths: Rethinking the Tuskegee Syphilis Study.* Chapel Hill: University of North Carolina Press, 2000. Analyses of the syphilis experiments conducted by the U.S. Public Health Service at Tuskegee Institute, which victimized African American men.

Sharp, Lesley A. A. *Strange Harvest: Organ Transplants, Denatured Bodies, and the Transformed Self.* Berkeley, Calif.: University of California Press, 2007. Analyzes how recipients of body organs, donor families, and medical specialists make sense of the transfer of body parts from the dead to the living.

Smedley, Brian D., Adrienne Y. Stith, and Alan R. Nelson, eds. *Unequal Treatment: Confronting Racial and Ethnic Disparities in Health Care.* Washington, D.C.: National Academies Press, 2003. The authors of these articles examine how stereotyping and biases on the part of health care providers, accompanied by barriers of language, geography, and culture, contribute to inequality in health care.

Weitz, Rose. *The Sociology of Health, Illness, and Health Care: A Critical Approach,* 5th ed. Belmont, Calif.: Wadsworth, 2009. With an emphasis on how gender, race–ethnicity, and social class affect people's experiences of health and illness, the author examines the health care system, alternative health care, and the experiences of those who live with illness or disability.

Journals

Health: An Interdisciplinary Journal for the Social Study of Health, Illness and Medicine, Journal of Health and Social Behavior, Research in the Sociology of Health Care, Social Science and Medicine, and *Sociological Practice: A Journal of Clinical and Applied Sociology* publish research articles and essays in the field of medical sociology.

Chapter 20: Population and Urbanization

Bull, Michael. *Sounds Moves: Ipod Culture and Urban Experience.* New York: Routledge, 2008. Using the example of the Apple iPod, the author analyzes how urbanites use sound to construct key areas of their daily lives.

Connelly, Matthew. *Fatal Misconception: The Struggle to Control World Population.* New Haven, Conn.: Yale University Press, 2008. Analyzes how the well-intentioned "breeding better people" (eugenics) movement of the twentieth century went wrong and caused extensive suffering.

Department of Agriculture. *Yearbook of Agriculture.* Washington, D.C.: Department of Agriculture, published annually. This yearbook focuses on specific aspects of U.S. agribusiness, especially international economies and trade.

Lang, Robert E., and Jennifer LeFurgy. *Boomburgs: The Rise of America's Accidental Cities.* Washington, D.C.: Brookings Institution Press, 2007. Contending that many fast-growing "cities" are really overgrown suburbs ("boomburgs"), the authors look at what attracts people to them and how they are governed.

Lin, Jan, and Christopher Mele, eds. *The Urban Sociology Reader.* New York: Routledge, 2006. The authors of these articles review major issues in urban change and development.

Palen, J. John. *The Urban World,* 8th ed. Boulder, Colo.: Paradigm Publishers, 2008. A short, basic text that summarizes major issues in urban sociology.

Rodriguez, Gregory. *Mongrels, Bastards, Orphans, and Vagabonds: Mexican Immigration and the Future of Race in America.* New York: Random House, 2007. A thorough overview, not just of the immigration of Mexicans to the United States, but also of the tense and changing relationships between Anglos and Mexican immigrants.

Wacquant, Loic. *Urban Outcasts: A Comparative Sociology of Advanced Marginality.* Malden, Mass.: Polity, 2008. This analysis of U.S. ghettos and French *banlieue* explores polarization, lived realities, and "reserved urban spaces."

Yaukey, David, and Douglas L. Anderton. *Demography: The Study of Human Population,* 3rd ed. Bellevue, Wash.: Waveland Press, 2007. Focusing on both the United States and the world, the authors analyze major issues in population.

Zhao, Zhongwei, and Fie Guo. *Transition and Challenge: China's Population at the Beginning of the 21st Century.* New York: Oxford University Press, 2007. The authors analyze implications of China's family planning policy, changes in marital patterns, high rural-urban migration, and falling birthrates coupled with a rising life expectancy.

Journals

City and Community, Journal of Rural Studies, Journal of Urban Affairs, Review of Regional and Urban Development Studies, Rural Sociology, and *Urban Studies* publish articles whose focus is the city, community, immigration, migration, rural life, and suburbs.

Chapter 21: Collective Behavior and Social Movements

Best, Joel. *Flavor of the Month: Why Smart People Fall for Fads.* Berkeley, Calif.: University of California Press, 2006. If you want to smile, perhaps even laugh, as you read a sociological account, this little book is for you.

Brunvand, Jan Harold. *Too Good to Be True: The Colossal Book of Urban Legends.* New York: W. W. Norton, 2002. In this collection of over 200 urban legends, you'll probably find some that you heard and thought were true.

Cohen, Stanley. *Folk Devils and Moral Panics,* 3rd ed. New York: Rutledge, 2003. The author's thesis is that the mass media create moral panics and stifle rational discussion about social problems.

DiFonzo, Nicholas. *The Watercooler Effect: A Psychologist Explores the Extraordinary Power of Rumors.* New York: Avery, 2008. Examines how rumors work and why; contains interesting examples.

Goodwin, Jeff, and James M. Jasper, eds. *The Social Movements Reader: Cases and Concepts, 2nd ed.* New York: Wiley-Blackwell, 2009. The authors answer such questions as why social movements occur, who joins them, who drops out, and what social movements accomplish.

Gupta, Dipak K. *Path to Collective Madness: A Study in Social Order and Political Pathology.* New York: Praeger, 2002. The author analyzes the process by which people participate in "collective madness"—such events as parents poisoning their children in Jonestown and the genocide of Rwanda.

Meyer, David S. *The Politics of Protest: Social Movements in America.* New York: Oxford University Press, 2006. Within the thesis that social movements create vital social change, the author examines mobilization, organization, strategies, identities, and the culture of social movements.

Schnapp, Jeffrey T., and Matthew Tiews, eds. *Crowds.* Stanford, Calif.: Stanford University Press, 2006. The role of crowds in modern life, based on Stanford University's "Big Humanities" project.

Solove, Daniel J. *The Future of Reputation: Gossip, Rumor, and Privacy on the Internet.* New Haven, Conn.: Yale University Press, 2007. In this analysis of how the free flow of information in a digital world liberates and constrains, the author examines issues of shaming, free speech, anonymity, privacy, and accountability.

Surowiecki, James. *The Wisdom of Crowds.* New York: Anchor, 2005. The author proposes that the collective knowledge of the people who make up crowds is greater than that of the individuals within them.

Tilly, Charles. *The Politics of Collective Violence.* New York: Cambridge University Press, 2003. The author analyzes causes, combinations, and settings that underlie collective violence and tries to identify ways to reduce violence.

Journal

Social Movement Studies examines the origins, development, organization, context, and impact of social movements.

Chapter 22: Social Change and the Environment

Bavistar, Amita, ed. *Contested Grounds: Essays on Nature, Culture, and Power.* New York: Oxford University Press, 2008. Examines such aspects of the environment as waste, scarcity, security, territory, sovereignty, conflict, expertise, and community from the perspective of power and culture.

Brown, Lester R., ed. *State of the World.* New York: Norton, published annually. Experts on environmental issues analyze environmental problems throughout the world; a New Malthusian perspective.

Conley, Dalton. *Elsewhere U.S.A.* New York, Random House, Inc., 2009. Examines how technological change (Internet, e-mail, Blackberrys) are changing our work and social relationships.

Council on Environmental Quality. *Environmental Quality.* Washington, D.C.: U.S. Government Printing Office, published annually. Each report evaluates the condition of some aspect of the environment.

Hannigan, John. *Environmental Sociology: A Social Constructionist Perspective,* 2nd ed. New York: Routledge, 2006. This basic text on environmental sociology links major disasters to environmental change and reviews the escalating global conflict over freshwater resources.

McKibben, Bill. *Deep Economy: The Wealth of Communities and the Durable Future.* New York: Holt, 2008. The author's thesis is that we are on the brink of environmental disaster and that we need to take corrective steps now.

Leichenko, Robin, and Karen O'Brien, *Environmental Change and Globalization: Double Exposures.* New York: Oxford University Press, 2008. Explores the connections between climate change and globalization and how these two processes are related to growing inequalities, growing vulnerabilities, and unsustainable rates of development.

Stahler-Sholk, Richard. *Latin American Social Movements in the Twenty-first Century: Resistance, Power, and Democracy.* Lanham, Md.: Rowman and Littlefield, 2008. Focuses on the involvement of socially marginalized Latin Americans in social movements, examining the origins, strategies, and outcomes of their opening.

Stewart, Charles J., Craig Allen Smith, and Robert E. Denton, Jr. *Persuasion and Social Movements,* 5th ed. Long Grove, Ill.: Waveland Press, 2007. The authors analyze social movements and countermovements in the light of identity, values, and culture, showing how people have shaped society collectively.

Zittrain, Jonathan L. *The Future of the Internet—And How to Stop It.* New Haven, Conn.: Yale University Press, 2009. The author expresses fears that new communications systems will mark the end of privacy.

Journals

Earth First! Journal and *Sierra,* magazines published by Earth First! and the Sierra Club respectively, are excellent sources for keeping informed of major developments in the environmental movement.

REFERENCES

All new references are printed in blue.

Aaron, Henry J., William B. Schwartz, and Melissa Cox. *Can We Say No? The Challenge of Rationing Health Care.* Washington, D.C.: Brookings Institution Press, 2005.

AAUP (American Association of University Professors). "2006–07 Report on the Economic Status of the Profession," April 2007.

AAUP. "2007–08 Report on the Economic Status of the Profession." Washington, D.C.: Author, February 2009.

Abelson, Reed. "Financial Ties Cited as Issue in Spine Study." *New York Times,* January 30, 2008.

Abelson, Reed. "The Spine as Profit Center." *New York Times,* December 30, 2006.

Abelson, Reed, and Patricia Leigh Brown. "Alternative Medicine Is Finding Its Niche in Nation's Hospitals." *New York Times,* April 14, 2002.

Aberg, Yvonne. *Social Interactions: Studies of Contextual Effects and Endogenous Processes.* Doctoral Dissertation, Department of Sociology, Stockholm University, 2003.

Aberle, David F., A. K. Cohen, A. K. David, M. J. Leng, Jr., and F. N. Sutton. "The Functional Prerequisites of a Society." *Ethics, 60,* January 1950:100–111.

Ackernecht, Erwin H. "The Role of Medical History in Medical Education." *Bulletin of the History of Medicine, 21,* 1947:135–145.

Adams, Noah. "All Things Considered." *New England Journal of Medicine* report. January 12, 2000.

Adams, P. F., P. M. Barnes, and J. L. Vickerie. "Summary Health Statistics for the U.S. Population: National Health Interview Survey, 2007." National Center for Health Statistics. *Vital Health Statistics, 10,* 238: November 2008.

Addams, Jane. *Twenty Years at Hull-House.* New York: Signet, 1981. First published in 1910.

"Adherents of All Religions, By Six Continental Areas." *World Almanac and Book of Facts, 2003.*

Adler, Patricia A., and Peter Adler. *Peer Power: Preadolescent Culture and Identity.* New Brunswick, N.J.: Rutgers University Press, 1998.

Adorno, Theodor W., Else Frenkel-Brunswick, D. J. Levinson, and R. N. Sanford. *The Authoritarian Personality.* New York: Harper & Row, 1950.

"Advance Release of the 2008-2009 ANES Panel Study." Ann Arbor, Michigan: American National Election Studies, 2009.

Aeppel, Timothy. "More Amish Women Are Tending to Business." *Wall Street Journal,* February 8, 1996:B1, B2.

Aguirre, Benigno E. "The Conventionalization of Collective Behavior in Cuba." In *Collective Behavior and Social Movements,* Russell I. Curtis, Jr., and Benigno E. Aquirre, eds. Boston: Allyn and Bacon, 1993:413–428.

Aguirre, Benigno E., E. L. Quarantelli, and Jorge L. Mendoza. "The Collective Behavior of Fads: The Characteristics, Effects, and Career of Streaking." In *Collective Behavior and Social Movements,* Russell L. Curtis, Jr., and Benigno E. Aguirre, eds. Boston: Allyn and Bacon, 1993:168–182.

Aichinger, Philipp von. "Junger Protest gegen Erhohung der Pensionen." *Die Presse* (Vienna), November 15, 2007:2.

Akol, Jacob. "Slavery in Sudan." *New African,* September 1998.

Alba, Richard, and Victor Nee. *Remaking the American Mainstream: Assimilation and Contemporary Immigration.* Cambridge, Mass.: Harvard University Press, 2003.

Albanese, Jennifer. Personal research for the author. March 2007.

Albert, Ethel M. "Women of Burundi: A Study of Social Values." In *Women of Tropical Africa,* Denise Paulme, ed. Berkeley: University of California Press, 1963:179–215.

"Alcohol: Balancing Risks and Benefits." Harvard School of Public Health, January 9, 2009.

Aldrich, Nelson W., Jr. *Old Money: The Mythology of America's Upper Class.* New York: Vintage Books, 1989.

Allport, Floyd. *Social Psychology.* Boston: Houghton Mifflin, 1954.

Alter, Alexandra. "Is This Man Cheating on His Wife?" *Wall Street Journal,* August 10, 2007.

Amato, Paul R., and Jacob Cheadle. "The Long Reach of Divorce: Divorce and Child Well-Being Across Three Generations." *Journal of Marriage and Family, 67,* February 2005:191–206.

Amato, Paul R., and Juliana M. Sobolewski. "The Effects of Divorce and Marital Discord on Adult Children's Psychological Well-Being." *American Sociological Review, 66,* 6, December 2001:900–921.

Amenta, Edwin. "The Social Security Debate, Now, and Then." *Contexts, 5,* 3, Summer 2006.

America's Children: Key National Indicators of Well-Being 2005. Washington, D.C.: Federal Interagency Forum on Child and Family Statistics, 2005.

"American Community Survey 2003." Washington, D.C.: U.S. Census Bureau, 2004.

American Federation of Teachers. "Survey and Analysis of Teacher Salary Trends 2007." Washington, D.C.: AFT Research and Information Services Department, 2008.

American Sociological Association. "An Invitation to Public Sociology." 2004.

American Sociological Association. "Code of Ethics and Policies and Procedures of the ASA Committee on Professional Ethics." Washington, D.C.: American Sociological Association, 1999.

American Sociological Association. "Section on Environment and Technology." Pamphlet, no date.

Amin, Yousreya, Emad Hamdi, et. al. "Mass Hysteria in an Arab Culture." *International Journal of Social Psychiatry, 43,* 4, Winter 1997:303–306.

Amnesty International. "Decades of Human Rights Abuse in Iraq." Online, 2005.

Ananat, Elizabeth O., and Guy Michaels. "The Effect of Marital Breakup on the Income Distribution of Women with Children." Centre for Economic Performance, CEP Discussion Paper dp0787, April 2007.

Andersen, Margaret L. *Thinking About Women: Sociological Perspectives on Sex and Gender.* New York: Macmillan, 1988.

Anderson, Chris. "NORC Study Describes Homeless." *Chronicle,* 1986:5, 9.

Anderson, Elijah. *A Place on the Corner.* Chicago: University of Chicago Press, 1978.

Anderson, Elijah. "Streetwise." In *Exploring Social Life: Readings to Accompany Essentials of Sociology, Sixth Edition,* 2nd ed., James M. Henslin, ed. Boston: Allyn and Bacon, 2006:147–156. Originally published 1990.

Anderson, Elijah. *Streetwise: Race, Class, and Change in an Urban Community.* Chicago: University of Chicago Press, 1990.

Anderson, Elizabeth. "Recent Thinking about Sexual Harassment: A Review Essay." *Philosophy & Public Affairs, 34,* 3, 2006:284–312.

Anderson, Nels. *Desert Saints: The Mormon Frontier in Utah.* Chicago: University of Chicago Press, 1966. First published in 1942.

Anderson, Philip. "God and the Swedish Immigrants." *Sweden and America,* Autumn 1995:17–20.

Anderson, Teresa A. "The Best Years of Their Lives." *Newsweek,* January 7, 1985:6.

Andrews, Nancy C. "Climbing through Medicine's Glass Ceiling." *New England Journal of Medicine, 357,* 19, November 8, 2007:1887–1889.

Ang, Audra. "In China, High-Tech Mixes With Tradition to Make Matches." *Houston Chronicle,* February 13, 2006.

Angier, Natalie. "Do Races Differ? Not Really, DNA Shows." *New York Times,* August 22, 2000.

Angwin, Julia. "How to Twitter." *Wall Street Journal,* March 7, 2009.

Ansberry, Clare. "Despite Federal Law, Hospitals Still Reject Sick Who Can't Pay." *Wall Street Journal,* November 29, 1988:A1, A4.

Aptheker, Herbert. "W. E. B. Du Bois: Struggle Not Despair." *Clinical Sociology Review, 8,* 1990:58–68.

R

Archbold, Ronna, and Mary Harmon. "International Success: Acceptance." Online: The Five O'clock Club, 2001.

Archibold, Randal C., and Julia Preston. "Homeland Security Stands by Its Fence." *New York Times*, May 21, 2008.

Arenson, Karen W. "(Big) Red Faces at Cornell Over E-Mail Error." *New York Times*, February 28, 2003.

Arías, Jesús. "La Junta rehabilita en Grenada casas que deberá tirar por ruina." *El Pais*, January 2, 1993:1.

Ariès, Philippe. *Centuries of Childhood*. R. Baldick, trans. New York: Vintage Books, 1965.

Arlacchi, P. *Peasants and Great Estates: Society in Traditional Calabria*. Cambridge, England: Cambridge University Press, 1980.

Armitage, Richard L. "Red Army Retreat Doesn't Signal End of U.S. Obligation." *Wall Street Journal*, February 7, 1989:A20.

Armstrong, David. "Hard Case: When Academics Double as Expert Witnesses." *Wall Street Journal*, June 22, 2007.

Armstrong, David. "New Technique to Transplant Hearts in Babies." *Wall Street Journal*, August 14, 2008.

Arndt, William F., and F. Wilbur Gingrich. *A Greek-English Lexicon of the New Testament and Other Early Christian Literature*. Chicago: University of Chicago Press, 1957.

Arsneault, Shelly. "Implementing Welfare Reform in Rural and Urban Communities: Why Place Matters." *American Review of Public Administration, 36, 2*, June 2006:173–188.

Asch, Solomon. "Effects of Group Pressure Upon the Modification and Distortion of Judgments." In *Readings in Social Psychology*, Guy Swanson, Theodore M. Newcomb, and Eugene L. Hartley, eds. New York: Holt, Rinehart and Winston, 1952.

Ashley, Richard. *Cocaine: Its History, Uses, and Effects*. New York: St. Martin's, 1975.

Associated Press. "Ohio Grandma Gives Birth to Daughter's Triplets." November 25, 2008.

Aulette, Judy Root. *Changing American Families*. Boston: Allyn and Bacon, 2002.

Ayittey, George B. N. "Black Africans Are Enraged at Arabs." *Wall Street Journal*, interactive edition, September 4, 1998.

Bainbridge, William Sims. "Collective Behavior and Social Movements." In *Sociology*, Rodney Stark. Belmont, Calif.: Wadsworth, 1989:608–640.

Baker, Harrison. "SOU Students Visit Nicaragua." *Ashland Daily Tidings*, September 8, 2008.

Bales, Robert F. "The Equilibrium Problem in Small Groups." In *Working Papers in the Theory of Action*, Talcott Parsons et al., eds. New York: Free Press, 1953:111–115.

Bales, Robert F. *Interaction Process Analysis*. Reading, Mass.: Addison-Wesley, 1950.

Baltzell, E. Digby. *Puritan Boston and Quaker Philadelphia*. New York: Free Press, 1979.

Baltzell, E. Digby, and Howard G. Schneiderman. "Social Class in the Oval Office." *Society, 25*, Sept/Oct, 1988:42–49.

Bandes, Susan. "The Lessons of Capturing the Friedmans: Moral Panic, Institutional Denial and Due Process." *Law, Culture and the Humanities, 3*, 2007:293–319.

Bannon, Lisa. "How a Rumor Spread About Subliminal Sex in Disney's 'Aladdin'." *Wall Street Journal*, October 24, 1995:A1, A6.

Barboza, David. "Child Labor Rings Reach China's Distant Villages." *New York Times*, May 10, 2008.

Barnes, Fred. "How to Rig a Poll." *Wall Street Journal*, June 14, 1995:A14.

Barnes, Harry Elmer. *The History of Western Civilization*, Vol. 1. New York: Harcourt, Brace, 1935.

Barnes, Helen. "A Comment on Stroud and Pritchard: Child Homicide, Psychiatric Disorder and Dangerousness." *British Journal of Social Work, 31, 3*, June 2001.

Barry, John. "A New Breed of Soldier." *Newsweek*, December 10, 2001:24–31.

Barry, John, and Evan Thomas. "Dropping the Bomb." *Newsweek*, June 25, 2001.

Barstow, David, and Lowell Bergman. "Death on the Job, Slaps on the Wrist." *Wall Street Journal*, January 10, 2003.

Barstow, David, and Robin Stein. "Between News and P. R., More Blurred Lines Found." *New York Times*, March 13, 2005.

Barta, Patrick. "The Rise of the Underground." *New York Times*, March 14, 2009.

Barta, Patrick, and Joel Millman. "The Great U-Turn." *Wall Street Journal*, June 6, 2009.

Bartlett, Donald L., and James B. Steele. "Paying a Price for Polluters." *Time*, June 24, 2001:72–80.

Bartlett, Donald L., and James B. Steele. "Wheel of Misfortune." *Time*, December 16, 2002:44–58.

Basten, Christoph, and Frank Betz. "Max Weber's Protestant Ethic in Contemporary Switzerland." Florence, Italy: European University Institute, November 2008.

Bates, Marston. *Gluttons and Libertines: Human Problems of Being Natural*. New York: Vintage Books, 1967. Quoted in Crapo, Richley H. *Cultural Anthropology: Understanding Ourselves and Others*, 5th ed. Boston: McGraw Hill, 2002.

Batson, Andrew. "China Stimulus Tweaks don't Redress Imbalances." *Wall Street Journal*, March 9, 2009.

Beah, Ishmael. *A Long Way Gone: Memoirs of a Boy Soldier*. New York: Farrar, Straus and Giroux, 2007.

Beals, Ralph L., and Harry Hoijer. *An Introduction to Anthropology*, 3rd ed. New York: Macmillan, 1965.

Beaman, Jean. "New York to Belarus: Sociology in International Distance-learning." *Footnotes*, February 2003:7.

Bean, Frank D., Jennifer Lee, Jeanne Batalova, and Mark Leach. "Immigration and Fading Color Lines in America." Washington, D.C.: Population Reference Bureau, 2004.

Bearak, Barry. "In Crisis, Zimbabwe Asks: Could Mugabe Lose?" *New York Times*, March 7, 2008.

Bearman, Peter S., and Hannah Bruckner. "Opposite-Sex Twins and Adolescent Same-Sex Attraction." *American Journal of Sociology, 107*, March 2002:1179–1205.

Beck, Scott H., and Joe W. Page. "Involvement in Activities and the Psychological Well-Being of Retired Men." *Activities, Adaptation, & Aging, 11, 1*, 1988:31–47.

Becker, Howard S. *Outsiders: Studies in the Sociology of Deviance*. New York: Free Press, 1966.

Beckett, Paul. "Caste Away." *Wall Street Journal*, June 23, 2007.

Beckman, Nils, Magda Waern, Deborah Gustafson, and Ingmar Skoog. "Secular Trends in Self Reported Sexual Activity and Satisfaction in Swedish 70 Year Olds: Cross Sectional Survey of Four Populations, 1971–2001." *BMJ*, 2008:1–7.

Bedard, Kelly, and Olivier Deschenes. "Sex Preference, Marital Dissolution, and the Economic Status of Women." *Journal of Human Resources, 40, 2*, 2005:411–434.

Beeghley, Leonard. *The Structure of Social Stratification in the United States*, 5th ed. Boston: Allyn & Bacon, 2008.

Begley, Sharon. "Twins: Nazi and Jew." *Newsweek, 94*, December 3, 1979:139.

Belasco, Amy. "CRS Report for Congress: The Cost of Iraq, Afghanistan, and Other Global War on Terror Operations Since 9/11." Washington, D.C.: Congressional Research Service, October 15, 2008.

Belkin, Lisa. "The Feminine Critique." *New York Times*, November 1, 2007.

Bell, Daniel. *The Coming of Post-Industrial Society: A Venture in Social Forecasting*. New York: Basic Books, 1973.

Bell, David A. "An American Success Story: The Triumph of Asian-Americans." In *Sociological Footprints: Introductory Readings in Sociology*, 5th ed., Leonard Cargan and Jeanne H. Ballantine, eds. Belmont, Calif.: Wadsworth, 1991: 308–316.

Bell, Michael Mayerfeld. *An Invitation to Environmental Sociology*. Los Angeles: Pine Forge Press, 2009.

Bellah, Robert N. *Beyond Belief*. New York: Harper & Row, 1970.

Belley, Philippe, and Lance Lochner. "The Changing Role of Family Income and Ability in Determining Educational Achievement." National Bureau of Economic Research, Working Paper 13527, October 2007.

Belluck, Pam. "Prosecutors Say Greed Drove Pharmacist to Dilute Drugs." *New York Times,* August 18, 2001.

Belsky, Jay. "Early Child Care and Early Child Development: Major Findings of the NICHD Study of Early Child Care." *European Journal of Developmental Psychology, 3,* 1, 2006:95–110.

Belsky, Jay, Deborah Lowe Vandell, Margaret Burchinall, K. Alison Clarke-Stewart, Kathleen McCartney, and Margaret Tresch Owen. "Are There Long-Term Effects of Early Child Care?" *Child Development, 78,* 2, March/April 2007:681–701.

Benet, Sula. "Why They Live to Be 100, or Even Older, in Abkhasia." *New York Times Magazine, 26,* December 1971.

Benford, Robert D. "The College Sports Reform Movement: Reframing the 'Educational' Industry." *The Sociological Quarterly, 48,* 2007:1–28.

Bennet, James. "Palestinian Mob Attacks Pollster Over Study on 'Right to Return.'" *New York Times,* July 14, 2003.

Benson, Herbert, Jeffrey A. Dusek, Jane B. Sherwood, et al. "Study of the Therapeutic Effects of Intercessory Prayer (STP) in Cardiac Bypass Patients: A Multicenter Randomized Trial of Uncertainty and Certainty of Receiving Intercessory Prayer." *American Heart Journal, 151,* 2006:934–942.

Bergen, Raquel Kennedy. *Wife Rape: Understanding the Response of Survivors and Service Providers.* Newbury Park, Calif.: Sage, 1996.

Berger, Arthur Asa. *Video Games: A Popular Culture Phenomenon.* New Brunswick, N.J.: Transaction Publishers, 2002.

Berger, Jeffrey T., Fred Rasner, and Eric J. Cassell. "Ethics of Practicing Medical Procedures on Newly Dead and Nearly Dead Patients." *Journal of General Internal Medicine, 17,* 2002:774–778.

Berger, Joseph. "Family Ties and the Entanglements of Caste." *New York Times,* October 24, 2004.

Berger, Peter L. *Invitation to Sociology: A Humanistic Perspective.* New York: Doubleday, 1963.

Berger, Peter. "Invitation to Sociology." In *Down to Earth Sociology: Introductory Readings,* 14th ed., James M. Henslin, ed. New York: The Free Press, 2007. First published in 1963.

Bergmann, Barbara R. "The Future of Child Care." Paper presented at the 1995 meetings of the American Sociological Association.

Berk, Laura E. *Child Development,* 8th ed. Boston: Allyn and Bacon, 2008.

Berk, Richard A. *Collective Behavior.* Dubuque, Iowa: Brown, 1974.

Berle, Adolf, Jr., and Gardiner C. Means. *The Modern Corporation and Private Property.* New York: Harcourt, Brace and World, 1932. As cited in Useem 1980:44.

Berman, Marc G., John Jonides, and Stephen Kaplan. "The Cognitive Benefits of Interacting with Nature." *Psychological Science, 19,* 12, 2008:1207–1212.

Bernard, Jessie. "The Good-Provider Role." In *Marriage and Family in a Changing Society,* 4th ed., James M. Henslin, ed. New York: Free Press, 1992:275–285.

Bernard, Tara Siegel. "The Key to Wedded Bliss? Money Matters." *New York Times,* September 10, 2008.

Bernard, Viola W., Perry Ottenberg, and Fritz Redl. "Dehumanization: A Composite Psychological Defense in Relation to Modern War." In *The Triple Revolution Emerging: Social Problems in Depth,* Robert Perucci and Marc Pilisuk, eds. Boston: Little, Brown, 1971:17–34.

Bernstein, David. "The $18-million Dollar Headache." *Chicago Magazine,* April 2007.

Bernstein, Elizabeth. "More Prayer, Less Hassle." *Wall Street Journal,* June 27, 2003:W3, W4.

Bernstein, Robert, and Mike Bergman. "Hispanic Population Reaches All-Time High of 38.8 Million, New Census Bureau Estimates Show." *U.S. Department of Commerce News,* June 18, 2003.

Berry, Bonnie. *Beauty Bias: Discrimination and Social Power.* Westport, CT: Praeger, 2007.

Bertrand, Marianne, and Sendhil Mullainathan. "Are Emily and Brendan More Employable than Lakish and Jamal? A Field Experiment on Labor Market Discrimination." Unpublished paper, November 18, 2002.

Best, Joel. *Flavor of the Month: Why Smart People Fall for Fads.* Berkeley: University of California Press, 2006.

Beveridge, Andrew A. "A Century of Harlem in New York City: Some Notes on Migration, Consolidation, Segregation, and Recent Developments." *City and Community, 7,* 4, December 2008:358–365.

Bialik, Carl. "'The Numbers Guy.' Ambitious Homeless Count Fills a Void, But Has Limitations." *Wall Street Journal,* March 3, 2006.

Bianchi, Suzanne M., and Lynne M. Casper. "American Families." *Population Bulletin, 55,* 4, December 2000:1–42.

Bianchi, Suzanne M., John P. Robinson, and Melissa A. Milkie. *Changing Rhythms of American Family Life.* New York: Russell Sage Foundation, 2006.

Bilefsky, Dan. "Albanian Custom Fades: Woman as Family Man." *New York Times,* June 25, 2008.

Billeaud, Jacques. "Arizona Sheriff Defends Illegal-Immigrant Sweeps." *Seattle Times,* April 26, 2008.

Binyon, Michael. "The Graveyard of Invading Armies." *The Times,* September 14, 2001.

Bird, Chloe E., and Patricia P. Rieker. "Gender Matters: An Integrated Model for Understanding Men's and Women's Health." *Social Science and Medicine, 48,* 6, March 1999:745–755.

Bishop, Jerry E. "Study Finds Doctors Tend to Postpone Heart Surgery for Women, Raising Risk." *Wall Street Journal,* April 16, 1990:B4.

Bjerklie, David, Andrea Dorfman, Wendy Cole, Jeanne DeQuine, Helen Gibson, David S. Jackson, Leora Moldofsky, Timothy Roche, Chris Taylor, Cathy Booth Thomas, and Dick Thompson. "Baby, It's You: And You, and You . . . " *Time,* February 19, 2001:47–57.

Blankstein, Andrew, and Richard Winton. "Paraplegic Allegedly 'Dumped' on Skid Row." *Los Angeles Times,* February 9, 2007.

Blassi, Joseph, and Michael Conte. "Employee Stock Ownership and Corporate Performance Among Public Companies." *Industrial and Labor Relations Review, 50,* 1, October 1996:60–79.

Blau, David M. "The Production of Quality in Child-Care Centers: Another Look." *Applied Developmental Science, 4,* 3, 2000:136–148.

Blau, Peter M., and Otis Dudley Duncan. *The American Occupational Structure.* New York: John Wiley, 1967.

Blauner, Robert. "Death and Social Structure." *Psychiatry, 29,* 1966:378–394.

Blee, Kathleen M. "Inside Organized Racism." In *Life in Society: Readings to Accompany Sociology A Down-to-Earth Approach, Seventh Edition,* James M. Henslin, ed. Boston: Allyn and Bacon, 2005:46–57.

Blomfield, Adrian. "Putin Vows to Aim Nukes at Europe." *London Daily Telegraph,* June 4, 2007.

Blumenthal, Ralph. "52 Girls Are Taken From Polygamist Sect's Ranch in Texas." *New York Times,* April 5, 2008a.

Blumenthal, Ralph. "Court Says Texas Illegally Seized Sect's Children." *New York Times,* May 23, 2008b.

Blumer, Herbert George. "Collective Behavior." In *Principles of Sociology,* Robert E. Park, ed. New York: Barnes and Noble, 1939:219–288.

Blumer, Herbert George. *Industrialization as an Agent of Social Change: A Critical Analysis,* David R. Maines and Thomas J. Morrione, eds. Hawthorne, N. Y.: Aldine de Gruyter, 1990.

Blumstein, Alfred, and Joel Wallman. "The Crime Drop and Beyond." *Annual Review of Law and Social Science, 2,* December 2006:125–146.

Blumstein, Philip, and Pepper Schwartz. *American Couples: Money, Work, Sex.* New York: Pocket Books, 1985.

Boaler, Jo. "Promoting 'Relational Equity' and High Mathematics Achievement Through an Innovative Mixed Ability Approach." *British Educational Research Journal,* 2008.

Bodovski, Katerina, and George Farkas. "'Concerted Cultivation' and Unequal Achievement in Elementary School." *Social Science Research, 37,* 2008:903–919.

Bond, Rod. "Group Size and Conformity." *Group Processes and Intergroup Relations, 8,* 4, 2005:331–354.

Booth, Alan, and James M. Dabbs, Jr. "Testosterone and Men's Marriages." *Social Forces, 72,* 2, December 1993:463–477.

Borjas, George J. "Increasing the Supply of Labor Through Immigration: Measuring the Impact on Native-born Workers." *Backgrounder,* May 2004:1–11.

Borjas, George J. "The Labor Market Impact of High-Skill Immigration." *National Bureau of Economic Research Working Paper* 11217, March 2005.

Borjas, George J. "Making It in America: Social Mobility in the Immigrant Population." *National Bureau of Economic Research Working Paper* 12088, March 2006.

Borsch-Supan, Axel, Ismail Duzgun, and Matthias Weiss. "Productivity and the Age Composition of Work Teams. Evidence from the Assembly Line." Harvard School of Public Health, working paper, April 17, 2007.

Bosman, Ciska M., et al. "Business Success and Businesses' Beauty Capital." National Bureau of Economic Research Working Paper: 6083, July 1997.

Bosman, Julie. "New York Schools for Pregnant Girls Will Close." *New York Times,* May 24, 2007.

Boulding, Elise. *The Underside of History.* Boulder, Colo.: Westview Press, 1976.

Boushey, Heather. "Strengthening the Middle Class: Ensuring Equal Pay for Women." Testimony Before the House Committee on Education and Labor. Washington, D.C.: Center for Economic and Policy Research, April 24, 2007.

Bower, Amanda. "The Semiprivate Checkup." *Time,* November 10, 2003.

Bowles, Samuel, and Herbert Gintis. "*Schooling in Capitalist America* Revisited." *Sociology of Education, 75,* 2002:1–18.

Bowles, Samuel, and Herbert Gintis. *Schooling in Capitalist America.* New York: Basic Books, 1976.

Bowles, Samuel. "Unequal Education and the Reproduction of the Social Division of Labor." In *Power and Ideology in Education,* J. Karabel and A. H. Halsely, eds. NY: Oxford University Press, 1977.

Bradford, Phillips Verner, and Harvey Blume. *Ota Benga: The Pygmy in the Zoo.* New York: Delta, 1992.

Brajuha, Mario, and Lyle Hallowell. "Legal Intrusion and the Politics of Fieldwork: The Impact of the Brajuha Case." *Urban Life, 14,* 4, January 1986:454–478.

Bramlett, M. D., and W. D. Mosher. "Cohabitation, Marriage, Divorce, and Remarriage in the United States." Hyattsville, Md.: National Center for Health Statistics, Vital Health Statistics, Series 23, Number 22, July 2002.

Brannon, Linda. *Gender: Psychological Perspectives,* 2nd ed. Boston: Allyn and Bacon, 1999.

Brauchli, Marcus W. "Wary of Education But Needing Brains, China Faces a Dilemma." *Wall Street Journal,* November 15, 1994:A1, A10.

Bray, Rosemary L. "Rosa Parks: A Legendary Moment, a Lifetime of Activism. *Ms., 6,* 3, November-December 1995:45–47.

"Brazil Arrests U.S. Pilot Over Obscene Gesture." Associated Press, January 15, 2004.

Brecher, Edward M., and the Editors of Consumer Reports. *Licit and Illicit Drugs.* Boston: Little, Brown, 1972.

Bretos, Miguel A. "Hispanics Face Institutional Exclusion." *Miami Herald,* May 22, 1994.

Bridgwater, William, ed. *The Columbia Viking Desk Encyclopedia.* New York: Viking Press, 1953.

Brilliant, Ashleigh E. *Social Effects of the Automobile in Southern Califronia during the 1920s.* Unpublished doctoral disertation University of California at Berkeley, 1964.

Brinkley, Christina. "Women in Power: Finding Balance in the Wardrobe." *Wall Street Journal,* January 24, 2008.

Brinton, Crane. *The Anatomy of Revolution.* New York: Vintage Books, 1965.

Broad, William J., and David E. Sanger. "With Eye on Iran, Rivals Also Want Nuclear Power." *New York Times,* April 15, 2007.

Brockerhoff, Martin P. "An Urbanizing World." *Population Bulletin, 55,* 3, September 2000:1–44.

Broder, Michael S., David E. Kanouse, Brian S. Mittman, and Steven J. Bernstein. "The Appropriateness of Recommendations for Hysterectomy." *Obstetrics and Gynecology, 95,* 2, February 2000:199–205.

Bromley, David G. "The Satanic Cult Scare." *Culture and Society,* May–June 1991:55–56.

Bronfenbrenner, Urie. "Principles for the Healthy Growth and Development of Children." In *Marriage and Family in a Changing Society,* 4th ed., James M. Henslin, ed. New York: Free Press, 1992:243–249.

Brooks-Gunn, Jeanne, Greg. J. Duncan, and Lawrence Aber, eds. *Neighborhood Poverty, Volume 1: Context and Consequences for Children.* New York: Russell Sage Foundation, 1997.

Brown, Alan S. "Mexico Redux." *Mechanical Engineering,* 2008.

Brown, Fred. "Maverick Doctor's Revolution: Services-for-Fee Clinic." *Knoxville News Sentinel,* August 20, 2007.

Brown, Patricia Leigh. "At New Rentals, the Aim Is to Age with Creativity." *Wall Street Journal,* September 10, 2006.

Browne, Beverly A. "Gender Stereotypes in Advertising on Children's Television in the 1990s: A Cross-National Analysis." *Journal of Advertising, 27,* 1, Spring 1998:83–96.

Browning, Christopher R. *Ordinary Men: Reserve Police Battalion 101 and the Final Solution in Poland.* New York: HarperPerennial, 1993.

Brunello, Giorgio, and Beatrice D'Hombres. "Does Body Weight Affect Wages? Evidence From Europe." *Economics and Human Biology, 5,* 2007:1–19.

Brunvand, Jan Harold. *Be Afraid, Be Very Afraid: The Book of Scary Urban Legends.* New York: W.W. Norton, 2004.

Brunvand, Jan Harold. *The Choking Doberman and Other "New" Urban Legends.* New York: Norton, 1984.

Brunvand, Jan Harold. *The Vanishing Hitchhiker: American Urban Legends and Their Meanings.* New York: Norton, 1981.

Bryant, Alyssa N. "Community College Students: Recent Findings and Trends." *Community College Review, 29,* 3, 2001:77–93.

Bryant, Chalandra M., Rand D. Conger, and Jennifer M. Meehan. "The Influence of In-Laws on Changes in Marital Success." *Journal of Marriage and the Family, 63, 3,* August 2001:614–626.

"Builder Stephen Ross Buys Half of Dolphins from Huizenga." *International Herald Tribune,* February 22, 2008.

Bumiller, Elisabeth. "First Comes Marriage—Then, Maybe, Love." In *Marriage and Family in a Changing Society,* 4th ed., James M. Henslin, ed. New York: Free Press, 1992:120–125.

Burawoy, Michael. "The Field of Sociology: Its Power and Its Promise." In *Public Sociology: Fifteen Eminent Sociologists Debate Politics and the Profession in the Twenty-first Century.* Berkeley: University of California Press, 2007:241–258.

Burger, Jerry M. "Replicating Milgram: Would People Still Obey Today?" *American Psychologist, 64,* 1, January 2009:1–11.

Burgess, Ernest W. "The Growth of the City: An Introduction to a Research Project." In *The City,* Robert E. Park et al., eds. Chicago: University of Chicago Press, 1925:47–62.

Burgess, Ernest W., and Harvey J. Locke. *The Family: From Institution to Companionship.* New York: American Book, 1945.

Burnham, Walter Dean. *Democracy in the Making: American Government and Politics.* Englewood Cliffs, N.J.: Prentice Hall, 1983.

Bush, Diane Mitsch, and Robert G. Simmons. "Socialization Processes Over the Life Course." In *Social Psychology: Sociological Perspectives,* eds. Morris Rosenberger and Ralph H. Turner. New Brunswick, N.J.:Transaction, 1990:133–164.

Butler, Robert N. "Ageism: Another Form of Bigotry." *Gerontologist, 9,* Winter 1980:243–246.

Butler, Robert N. *Why Survive? Being Old in America.* New York: Harper & Row, 1975.

Bynum, Bill. "Discarded Diagnoses." *Lancet, 358,* 9294, November 17, 2001:1736.

Cadge, Wendy, and Courtney Bender. "Yoga and Rebirth in America: Asian Religions Are Here to Stay." *Contexts,* Winter 2004:45–51.

Caforio, Giuseppe, ed. *Handbook of the Sociology of the Military.* New York: Springer, 2006.

Campbell, Karen E., and Holly J. McCammon. "Elizabeth Blackwell's Heirs: Women as Physicians in the U.S., 1880–1920." Unpublished paper, 2005.

Canavan, Margaret M., Walter J. Meyer, III, and Deborah C. Higgs. "The Female Experience of Sibling Incest." *Journal of Marital and Family Therapy, 18,* 2, 1992:129–142.

Canedy, Dana. "Critics of Graduation Exam Threaten Boycott in Florida." *New York Times,* May 13, 2003.

Cannon, Lou. *Official Negligence: How Rodney King and the Riots Changed Los Angeles and the LAPD.* New York: Times Books, 1998.

Cantril, Hadley. *The Psychology of Social Movements.* New York: Wiley, 1941.

Caproni, Paula J. "Work/Life Balance: You Can't Get There from Here." *Journal of Applied Behavioral Science, 40,* 2, June 2004:208–218.

Carey, Benedict. "In the Hospital, a Degrading Shift From Person to Patient." *New York Times,* August 16, 2005.

Carlson, Bonnie E., Katherine Maciol, and Joanne Schneider. "Sibling Incest: Reports from Forty-One Survivors." *Journal of Child Sexual Abuse, 15,* 4, 2006:19–34.

Carlson, Lewis H., and George A. Colburn. *In Their Place: White America Defines Her Minorities, 1850–1950.* New York: Wiley, 1972.

Carnevale, Anthony P., and Stephen J. Rose. "Socioeconomic Status, Race/Ethnicity, and Selective College Admissions." New York: The Century Foundation, March 2003.

Carpenito, Lynda Juall. "The Myths of Acquaintance Rape." *Nursing Forum, 34,* 4, October-December 1999:3.

Carpenter, Betsy. "Redwood Radicals." *U.S. News & World Report, 109,* 11, September 17, 1990:50–51.

Carper, James C. "Pluralism to Establishment to Dissent: The Religious and Educational Context of Home Schooling." *Peabody Journal of Education, 75,* 1–2, 2000:8–19.

Carr, Deborah, Carol D. Ryff, Burton Singer, and William J. Magee. "Bringing the 'Life' Back into Life Course Research: A 'Person-Centered' Approach to Studying the Life Course." Paper presented at the 1995 meetings of the American Sociological Association.

Carrington, Tim. "Developed Nations Want Poor Countries to Succeed on Trade, But Not Too Much." *Wall Street Journal,* September 20, 1993:A10.

Carroll, William K., and Colin Carson. "The Network of Global Corporations and Elite Policy Groups: A Structure for Transnational Capitalist Class Formation?" *Global Networks, 3,* 1, February 21, 2003:29–57.

Cartwright, Dorwin, and Alvin Zander, eds. *Group Dynamics,* 3rd ed. Evanston, Ill.: Peterson, 1968.

Casper, Monica J. *The Making of the Unborn Patient: A Social Anatomy of Fetal Surgery.* New Brunswick, N.J.: Rutgers University Press, 1998.

Cassel, Russell N. "Examining the Basic Principles for Effective Leadership." *College Student Journal, 33,* 2, June 1999:288–301.

Casselman, Anne. "Identical Twins' Genes Are Not Identical." *Scientific American,* April 3, 2008.

Catan, Thomas. "Spain's Showy Debt Collectors Wear a Tux, Collect the Bucks." *Wall Street Journal,* October 11, 2008.

Cauce, Ana Mari, and Melanie Domenech-Rodriguez. "Latino Families: Myths and Realities." In *Latino Children and Families in the United States: Current Research and Future Directions,* Josefina M. Contreras, Kathryn A. Kerns, and Angela M. Neal-Barnett, eds. Westport, Conn.: Praeger, 2002:3–25.

Cava, Marco R. della. "Working Out of a 'Third Place.'" *USA Today,* October 5, 2006.

Center for American Women and Politics. "Record Numbers of Women to Serve in Senate and House." 2008a, December 8.

Center for American Women and Politics. "Women Achieve Record Numbers in State Legislatures," 2008b, November 11.

Center for American Women and Politics. "Women in Elective Office 2007." April 2007.

Centers for Disease Control and Prevention. "WISQARS Injury Mortality Reports, 1999–2005." Atlanta, GA: National Center for Injury Prevention and Control, 2007.

Centers for Disease Control and Prevention. "A Glance at the HIV/AIDS Epidemic." January 2007a.

Centers for Disease Control and Prevention. "Native American Suicides per 100,000, Ages 0–19, IHS Areas, 1989–1998." June 13, 2007c.

Centers for Disease Control and Prevention. "Overweight and Obesity." January 7, 2009a.

Centers for Disease Control and Prevention. "State-Specific Smoking—Attributable Mortality and Years of Potential Life Lost—United States, 2000–2004." *MMWR Weekly,* January 23, 2009b.

Centers for Disease Control and Prevention. "Fact Sheet: Tobacco Industry Marketing," April 2007b.

Centers for Disease Control and Prevention. *National Nursing Home Survey,* 2008d.

Centers for Disease Control and Prevention. "Cases of HIV Infection and AIDS in the United States and Dependent Areas, 2006." 2008a.

Centers for Disease Control and Prevention. "HIV and AIDS in the United States: A Picture of Today's Epidemic." 2008b.

Centers for Disease Control and Prevention. "New HIV Incidence Estimates: CDC Responds." 2008c.

Centers for Disease Control. 2001 Surveillance Report. Divisions of HIV/AIDS Prevention, 2003.

Centers for Disease Control. *HIV/AIDS Surveillance Report,* 1997.

Cerulo, Karen A., and Janet M. Ruane. "Death Comes Alive: Technology and the Re-Conception of Death." In *Science as Culture,* 1996.

Chafetz, Janet Saltzman. *Gender Equity: An Integrated Theory of Stability and Change.* Newbury Park, Calif.: Sage, 1990.

Chafetz, Janet Saltzman, and Anthony Gary Dworkin. *Female Revolt: Women's Movements in World and Historical Perspective.* Totowa, N.J.: Rowman & Allanheld, 1986.

Chagnon, Napoleon A. *Yanomamo: The Fierce People,* 2nd ed. New York: Holt, Rinehart and Winston, 1977.

Chaker, Anne Marie. "A Backdoor Route to a College Dream." *Wall Street Journal,* June 26, 2003b.

Chaker, Anne Marie. "For Antidepressant Makers, Shopaholics Are New Market." *Wall Street Journal,* January 2, 2003a.

Chaker, Anne Marie, and Hilary Stout. "After Years off, Women Struggle to Revive Careers." *Wall Street Journal,* May 6, 2004.

Chalfant, H. Paul. "Stepping to Redemption: Twelve-Step Groups as Implicit Religion." *Free Inquiry in Creative Sociology, 20,* 2, November 1992:115–120.

Chalkley, Kate. "Female Genital Mutilation: New Laws, Programs Try to End Practice." *Population Today, 25,* 10, October 1997:4–5.

Chambliss, William J. *Power, Politics, and Crime.* Boulder: Westview Press, 2000.

Chambliss, William J. "The Saints and the Roughnecks." In *Down to Earth Sociology: Introductory Readings,* 14th ed., James M. Henslin, ed. New York: The Free Press, 2007. First published in 1973.

Chan, Sewell. "New York's Annual Estimate of Homeless Is Challenged." *New York Times,* May 22, 2007.

Chandler, Tertius, and Gerald Fox. *3000 Years of Urban Growth.* New York: Academic Press, 1974.

Chandra, Vibha P. "Fragmented Identities: The Social Construction of Ethnicity, 1885–1947." Unpublished paper, 1993a.

Chandra, Vibha P. "The Present Moment of the Past: The Metamorphosis." Unpublished paper, 1993b.

Chase, Marilyn. "Scientists Extend Life Span of Worms by Altering Genes." *Wall Street Journal,* October 24, 2003.

Chawkins, Steve. "Medical Community Eyes Case." *Los Angeles Times,* February 28, 2008.

Chen, Edwin. "Twins Reared Apart: A Living Lab." *New York Times Magazine.* December 9, 1979:112.

Chen, Kathy. "China's Growth Places Strains on a Family's Ties." *Wall Street Journal,* April 13, 2005.

Cherlin, J. Andrew. "Remarriage as an Incomplete Institution." In *Marriage and Family in a Changing Society,* 3rd ed., James M. Henslin, ed. New York: Free Press, 1989:492–501.

Chernow, Ron. Titan: *The Life of John D. Rockefeller, Sr.* New York: Random House, 1998.

"Child Day Care Services." U.S. Department of Labor, Bureau of Labor Statistics, Online Career Guide to Industries, January 3, 2009.

Chin, Nancy P., Alicia Monroe, and Kevin Fiscella. "Social Determinants of (Un)Healthy Behaviors." *Education for Health: Change in Learning and Practice, 13,* 3, November 2000:317–328.

Chivers, C. J. "Officer Resigns Before Hearing in D. W. I. Case." *New York Times,* August 29, 2001.

Chivers, C. J. "Putin Urges Plan to Reverse Slide in the Birth Rate." *New York Times,* May 10, 2006.

Chodorow, Nancy J. "What Is the Relation Between Psychoanalytic Feminism and the Psychoanalytic Psychology of Women?" In *Theoretical Perspectives on Sexual Difference,* Deborah L. Rhode, ed. New Haven, Conn.: Yale University Press, 1990:114–130.

Chung, He Len, and Laurence Steinberg. "Relations Between Neighborhood Factors, Parenting Behaviors, Peer Deviance, and Delinquency Among Serious Juvenile Offenders." *Developmental Psychology, 42,* 2, 2006:319–331.

Churchill, Ward. *A Little Matter of Genocide: Holocaust and Denial in the Americas, 1492 to the Present.* San Francisco: City Lights Books, 1997.

CIA World Factbook. Washington, D.C: U.S. Government Printing Office, 2008. Published annually.

Clair, Jeffrey Michael., David A. Karp, and William C. Yoels. *Experiencing the Life Cycle: A Social Psychology of Aging,* 2nd ed. Springfield, Ill.: Thomas, 1993.

Clark, Candace. *Misery and Company: Sympathy in Everyday Life.* Chicago: University of Chicago Press, 1997.

Clarke, Lee. "Panic: Myth or Reality?" *Contexts,* Fall 2002:21–26.

Claxton, Amy, and Maureen Perry-Jenkins. "No Fun Anymore: Leisure and Marital Quality Across the Transition to Parenthood." *Journal of Marriage and Family, 70,* February 2008:28–43.

Clay, Jason W. "What's a Nation?" *Mother Jones,* November-December 1990:28, 30.

Clearfield, Melissa W., and Naree M. Nelson. "Sex Differences in Mothers' Speech and Play Behavior with 6-, 9-, and 14-Month-Old Infants." *Sex Roles, 54,* 1–2, January 2006:127–137.

Cleeland, Nancy. "Slowdown's Silent Victims." *Los Angeles Times,* October 21, 2001.

Clifford, Stephanie. "Billboards That Look Back." *New York Times,* May 31, 2008.

Cloud, John. "For Better or Worse." *Time,* October 26, 1998:43–44.

Cloward, Richard A., and Lloyd E. Ohlin. *Delinquency and Opportunity: A Theory of Delinquent Gangs.* New York: Free Press, 1960.

CNN. "Election Poll." 2008.

Cockerham, William C. "Health Lifestyles and the Absence of the Russian Middle Class." *Sociology of Health and Illness, 29,* 3, 2007:457–473.

Cohen, Margot. "India's New Beauty Ideal Is a Wisp of Its Former Self." *New York Times,* September 28, 2007.

Cohen, Patricia. "Forget Lonely. Life Is Healthy at the Top." *New York Times,* May 15, 2004.

Cohen, Roger. "The Magic Mountain." *New York Times,* February 15, 2009.

"Coke Adds Life, But It Cannot Always Explain It." *Lancet, 354,* 9174, July 17, 1999:173.

Colapinto, John. *As Nature Made Him: The Boy Who Was Raised as a Girl.* New York: HarperCollins, 2001.

Cole, Elizabeth R., and Safiya R. Omari. "Race, Class and the Dilemmas of Upward Mobility for African Americans." *Journal of Social Issues, 59,* 4, 2003:785–802.

Coleman, James S., and Thomas Hoffer. *Public and Private Schools: The Impact of Communities.* New York: Basic Books, 1987.

Coleman, James William. "Politics and the Abuse of Power." In *Down to Earth Sociology: Introductory Readings,* 8th ed., James M. Henslin, ed. New York: Free Press, 1995:442–450.

Coleman, Marilyn, Lawrence Ganong, and Mark Fine. "Reinvestigating Remarriage: Another Decade of Progress." *Journal of Marriage and the Family, 62,* 4, November 2000:1288–1307.

Collins, Randall. *The Credential Society: An Historical Sociology of Education.* New York: Academic Press, 1979.

Collins, Randall. "Socially Unrecognized Cumulation." *American Sociologist, 30,* 2, Summer 1999:41–61.

Collins, Randall. *Theoretical Sociology.* San Diego, Calif.: Harcourt, Brace Jovanovich, 1988.

Collins, Randall, Janet Saltzman Chafetz, Rae Lesser Blumberg, Scott Coltrane, and Jonathan H. Turner. "Toward an Integrated Theory of Gender Stratification." *Sociological Perspectives, 36,* 3, 1993:185–216.

Collymore, Yvette. "Conveying Concerns: Women Report on Gender-Based Violence." Washington, D.C.: Population Reference Bureau, 2000.

Committee on Non-Heart-Beating Transplantation II. Non-Heart-Beating Organ. Bethesda, MD.

Conahan, Frank C. "Human Experimentation: An Overview on Cold War Era Programs." Washington, D.C.: U.S. General Accounting Office, September 28, 1994:1–11.

Conklin, John E. *Why Crime Rates Fell.* Boston: Allyn and Bacon, 2003.

Conley, Dalton. "Reading Class Between the Lines (of This Volume): A Reflection on Why We Should Stick to Folk Concepts of Social Class." In *Social Class: How Does It Work?* Annette Lareau and Dalton Conley, eds. New York: Russell Sage, 2008:366–373.

Conlin, Michelle. "Get Healthy—Or Else." *Business Week,* February 26, 2007.

Connolly, Ceci. "Surgery Checklist Lowers Death Rate." *Washington Post,* January 15, 2009.

Connors, L. "Gender of Infant Differences in Attachment: Associations with Temperament and Caregiving Experiences." Paper presented at the Annual Conference of the British Psychological Society, Oxford, England, 1996.

Conrad, Peter. "Public Eyes and Private Genes: Historical Frames, New Constructions, and Social Problems." *Social Problems, 44,* 2, May 1997:139–154.

Cook, Bradley J. "Islam and Egyptian Higher Education: Student Attitudes." *Comparative Education Review, 45,* 3, August 2001:379–403.

Cookson, Peter W., Jr., and Caroline Hodges Persell. "Preparing for Power: Cultural Capital and Elite Boarding Schools." In *Life in Society: Readings to Accompany Sociology A Down-to-Earth Approach, Seventh Edition,* James M. Henslin, ed. Boston: Allyn and Bacon, 2005:175–185.

Cooley, Charles Horton. *Human Nature and the Social Order.* New York: Scribner's, 1902.

Cooley, Charles Horton. *Social Organization.* New York: Schocken Books, 1962. First published by Scribner's, 1909.

Coontz, Stephanie. *The Way We Never Were: American Families and the Nostalgia Trap.* New York: Basic Books, 2000.

Cooper, Bruce S., and John Sureau. "The Politics of Homeschooling: New Developments, New Challenges." *Educational Policy, 21,* 2007:110–131.

Corbett, Sara. "A Cutting Tradition." *New York Times,* January 20, 2008.

Corbett, Sara. "Portrait of an Artist as Avatar." *New York Times,* March 5, 2009.

Corcoran, Mary. "Mobility, Persistence, and Consequences of Poverty for Children: Child and Adult Outcomes." In *Understanding Poverty,* Sheldon H. Danziger and Robert H. Haveman, eds. New York: Russell Sage, 2001:127–161.

Cose, Ellis. "Black Versus Brown." *Newsweek,* July 3, 2006:44–45.

Cose, Ellis. "The Good News About Black America." *Newsweek,* June 7, 1999:29–40.

Cose, Ellis. "What's White Anyway?" *Newsweek,* September 18, 2000:64–65.

Coser, Lewis A. *Masters of Sociological Thought: Ideas in Historical and Social Context,* 2nd ed. New York: Harcourt Brace Jovanovich, 1977.

Costello, Daniel. "Online House Calls Click with Doctors." *Los Angeles Times,* February 4, 2008.

Cottin, Lou. *Elders in Rebellion: A Guide to Senior Activism.* Garden City, N. Y.: Anchor Doubleday, 1979.

Council of Economic Advisers. "Immigration's Economic Impact." Washington, D.C.: June 20, 2007.

"Country Statistics at a Glance." World and News, Fact Monster, online, 2005.

Cousins, Albert N., and Hans Nagpaul. *Urban Man and Society: A Reader in Urban Sociology.* New York: McGraw-Hill, 1970.

Cowell, Alan. "4 Suspects in '94 Massacres of Rwanda Tutsi Are Held in London to Face Extradition." *New York Times,* November 30, 2006.

Cowen, Emory L., Judah Landes, and Donald E. Schaet. "The Effects of Mild Frustration on the Expression of Prejudiced Attitudes." *Journal of Abnormal and Social Psychology.* January 1959:33–38.

Cowgill, Donald. "The Aging of Populations and Societies." *Annals of the American Academy of Political and Social Science, 415,* 1974:1–18.

Cowley, Geoffrey. "Attention: Aging Men." *Newsweek,* November 16, 1996:66–75.

Cowley, Joyce. *Pioneers of Women's Liberation.* New York: Merit, 1969.

Crary, David. "Forces on Abortion See Power Shift." Associated Press, January 22, 2009.

Crawford, Bridget J. "Toward a Third-Wave Feminist Legal Theory: Young Women, Pornography and the Praxis of Pleasure." Pace Law Faculty Publications, 2007.

Crime Situation in South Africa: Trends, Spatial Distribution and Interpretation. South African Police Service: Crime Information Management, June 2008.

"Crop Prospects and Food Situation." The Global Information and Early Warning System on Food and Agriculture, February 2009.

Crosnoe, Robert. "Gender, Obesity, and Education." *Sociology of Education, 80,* July 2007:241–260.

Crosnoe, Robert, and Glen H. Elder, Jr. "Successful Adaptation in the Later Years: A Life Course Approach to Aging. "*Social Psychology Quarterly, 65,* 4, 2002:309–328.

Crosnoe, Robert, Catherine Riegle-Crumb, Sam Field, Kenneth Frank, and Chandra Muller. "Peer Group Contexts of Girls' and Boys' Academic Experiences." *Child Development, 79,* 1, February 2008:139–155.

Crossen, Cynthia. "Before Social Security, Most Americans Faced Very Bleak Retirement." *Wall Street Journal,* September 15, 2004.

Crossen, Cynthia. "Deja Vu." *Wall Street Journal,* March 5, 2003.

Crossen, Cynthia. "How Pygmy Ota Benga Ended Up in Bronx Zoo as Darwinism Dawned." *Wall Street Journal,* February 6, 2006.

Crossen, Cynthia. "Margin of Error: Studies Galore Support Products and Positions, But Are They Reliable?" *Wall Street Journal,* Nov 14, 1991:A1.

Crossen, Cynthia. "When Worse Than a Woman Who Voted Was One Who Smoked." *Wall Street Journal,* January 7, 2008.

Crossette, Barbara. "Caste May Be India's Moral Achilles' Heel." *New York Times,* October 20, 1996.

Crossland, David. "Gas Dispute Has Europe Trembling." *Spiegel Online,* January 2, 2006.

Crowder, Kyle, and Scott J. South. "Spatial Dynamics of White Flight: The Effects of Local and Extralocal Racial Conditions on Neighborhood Out-Migration." *American Sociological Review, 73,* 5, October 2008:792–812.

Cumming, Elaine. "Further Thoughts on the Theory of Disengagement." In *Aging in America: Readings in Social Gerontology,* Cary S. Kart and Barbara B. Manard, eds. Sherman Oaks, Calif.: Alfred Publishing, 1976:19–41.

Cumming, Elaine, and William E. Henry. *Growing Old: The Process of Disengagement.* New York: Basic Books, 1961.

Dabbs, James M., Jr., Marian F. Hargrove, and Colleen Heusel. "Testosterone Differences Among College Fraternities: Well-Behaved vs. Rambunctious." *Personality and Individual Differences, 20,* 1996:157–161.

Dabbs, James M., Jr., and Robin Morris. "Testosterone, Social Class, and Antisocial Behavior in a Sample of 4,462 Men." *Psychological Science, 1,* 3, May 1990:209–211.

Dabbs, James M., Jr., Timothy S. Carr, Robert L. Frady, and Jasmin K. Riad. "Testosterone, Crime, and Misbehavior Among 692 Male Prison Inmates." *Personality and Individual Differences, 18,* 1995:627–633.

Dahl, Gordon B., and Enrico Moretti. "The Demand for Sons." *Review of Economic Studies, 75,* 2008:1085–1120.

Dahl, Robert A. *Dilemmas of Pluralist Democracy: Autonomy vs. Control.* New Haven, Conn.: Yale University Press, 1982.

Dahl, Robert A. *Who Governs?* New Haven, Conn.: Yale University Press, 1961.

Dao, James. "Instant Millions Can't Halt Winners' Grim Side." *New York Times,* December 5, 2005.

Darley, John M., and Bibb Latané. "Bystander Intervention in Emergencies: Diffusion of Responsibility." *Journal of Personality and Social Psychology, 8,* 4, 1968:377–383.

Darwin, Charles. *The Origin of Species.* Chicago: Conley, 1859.

Dasgupta, Nilanjana, Debbie E. McGhee, Anthony G. Greenwald, and Mahzarin R. Banaji. "Automatic Preference for White Americans: Eliminating the Familiarity Explanation." *Journal of Experimental Social Psychology, 36,* 3, May 2000:316–328.

Davis, Ann, Joseph Pereira, and William M. Bulkeley. "Security Concerns Bring Focus on Translating Body Language." *Wall Street Journal,* August 15, 2002.

Davis, Donald R., and David E. Weinstein. "Technological Superiority and the Losses From Migration." Working Paper. National Bureau of Economic Research. June 2002.

Davis, Kingsley. "Extreme Isolation." In *Down to Earth Sociology: Introductory Readings,* 14th ed., James M. Henslin, ed. New York: The Free Press, 2007. Originally published as "Extreme Social Isolation of a Child." *American Journal of Sociology, 45,* 4 Jan. 1940:554–565.

Davis, Kingsley, and Wilbert E. Moore. "Reply to Tumin." *American Sociological Review, 18,* 1953:394–396.

Davis, Kingsley, and Wilbert E. Moore. "Some Principles of Stratification." *American Sociological Review, 10,* 1945:242–249.

Davis, Nancy J., and Robert V. Robinson. "Class Identification of Men and Women in the 1970s and 1980s." *American Sociological Review, 53,* February 1988:103–112.

Davis, Stan. *Lessons From the Future: Making Sense of a Blurred World.* New York: Capstone Publishers, 2001.

De May, J. "A Picture History of Kew Gardens, N.Y.—Kitty Genovese." Online. April 15, 2005.

De Moor, Marleen H. M., Tim D. Spector, Lynn F. Cherkas, Mario Falchi, Jouke Jan Hottenga, Dorret I. Boomsma', and Eco J. C. De Geus. "Genome-Wide Linkage for Athlete Status in 700 British Female DZ Twin Pairs." *Twin Research and Human Genetics, 10,* 6, December 2007:812–820.

"Death Squads Roam Davao—UN Monitors." *Manila Times,* February 13, 2008.

Deaver, Michael V. "Democratizing Russian Higher Education." *Demokratizatsiya, 9,* 3, Summer 2001:350–366.

DeCrow, Karen. Foreword to *Why Men Earn More* by Warren Farrell. New York: AMACOM, 2005:xi-xii.

Deegan, Mary Jo. "W. E. B. Du Bois and the Women of Hull-House, 1895–1899." *American Sociologist,* Winter 1988:301–311.

Deflem, Mathieu, ed. *Sociological Theory and Criminological Research: Views from Europe and the United States.* San Diego: JAI Press, 2006.

DeFrancis, Marc. "U.S. Elder Care Is in a Fragile State." *Population Today, 30,* 1, January 2002:1–3.

Deliege, Robert. *The Untouchables of India.* New York: Berg Publishers, 2001.

DeMartini, Joseph R. "Basic and Applied Sociological Work: Divergence, Convergence, or Peaceful Co-existence?" *The Journal of Applied Behavioral Science, 18,* 2, 1982:203–215.

DeMause, Lloyd. "Our Forebears Made Childhood a Nightmare." *Psychology Today 8,* 11, April 1975:85–88.

Demidov, Vadim. "Ten Years of Rolling the Minicircles: RCA Assays in DNA Diagnostics." *Expert Review of Molecular Diagnostics, 5,* 4, July 2005:477–478. <http://www.future-drugs.com/loi/erm;jsessionid=o_3C1_i2Jnr- mGoATO>

Denham, Bryan E. "Folk Devils, New Icons and the Construction of Moral Panics." *Journalism Studies, 9,* 6, December 2008:945–961.

Denzin, Norman K. "The Suicide Machine." *Society,* July–August, 1992:7–10.

Denzin, Norman K. *Symbolic Interactionism and Cultural Studies: The Politics of Interpretation.* Cambridge, Mass.: Blackwell 2007.

Deutscher, Irwin. *Accommodating Diversity: National Policies that Prevent Ethnic Conflict.* Lanham, Md.: Lexington Books, 2002.

Dhillon, Navtej, Amina Fahmy, and Djavad Salehi-Isfahani. "Egypt's Education System: Parents and Students Emerge as a New Force for Reform." Brookings, December 4, 2008.

Diamond, Edwin, and Robert A. Silverman. *White House to Your House: Media and Politics in Virtual America.* Cambridge, Mass.: MIT Press, 1995.

Diamond, Milton, and Keith Sigmundson. "Sex Reassignment at Birth: Long-term Review and Clinical Implications." *Archives of Pediatric and Adolescent Medicine, 151,* March 1997:298–304.

Dickey, Christopher, and John Barry. "Iran: A Rummy Guide." *Newsweek,* May 8, 2006.

Dietz, Tracy L. "An Examination of Violence and Gender Role Portrayals in Video Games." *Women and Language, 23,* 2, Fall 2000:64–77.

DiFonzo, Nicholas. *The Watercooler Effect: A Psychologist Explores the Extraordinary Power of Rumors.* New York: Avery, 2008

Digest of Education Statistics. Washington, D.C.: National Center for Education Statistics, 2007.

Dillon, Sam. "Public Schools Begin to Offer Classes Online." *New York Times,* August 2, 2005a.

Dillon, Sam. "States' Data Obscure How Few Finish High School." *New York Times,* March 20, 2008.

Dillon, Sam. "Students Ace State Tests, But Earn D's From U.S." *New York Times,* November 25, 2005b.

DiSilvestro, Roger L. *In the Shadow of Wounded Knee: The Untold Final Chapter of the Indian Wars.* New York: Walker & Co., 2006.

Doane, Ashley W., Jr. "Dominant Group Ethnic Identity in the United States: The Role of 'Hidden' Ethnicity in Intergroup Relations." *The Sociological Quarterly, 38,* 3, Summer 1997:375–397.

Dobash, Russell P., R. Emerson Dobash, Margo Wilson, and Martin Daly. "Marital Violence Is Not Symmetrical: A Response to Campbell." *SSSP Newsletter, 24,* 3, Fall 1993:26–30.

Dobash, Russell P., R. Emerson Dobash, Margo Wilson, and Martin Daly. "The Myth of Sexual Symmetry in Marital Violence." *Social Problems, 39,* 1, February 1992:71–91.

Dobriner, William M. "The Football Team as Social Structure and Social System." In *Social Structures and Systems: A Sociological Overview.* Pacific Palisades, Calif.: Goodyear, 1969a:116–120.

Dobriner, William M. *Social Structures and Systems.* Pacific Palisades, California: Goodyear, 1969b.

Dobyns, Henry F. *Their Numbers Became Thinned: Native American Population Dynamics in Eastern North America.* Knoxville: University of Tennessee Press, 1983.

Dodds, Peter Sheridan, Roby Muhamad, and Duncan J. Watts. "An Experimental Study of Search in Global Social Networks." *Science, 301,* August 8, 2003:827–830.

Dollard, John, et al. *Frustration and Aggression.* New Haven, Conn.: Yale University Press, 1939.

Domhoff, G. William. "The Bohemian Grove and Other Retreats." In *Down to Earth Sociology: Introductory Readings,* 10th ed., James M. Henslin, ed. New York: Free Press, 1999a:391–403.

Domhoff, G. William. "C. Wright Mills, Power Structure Research, and the Failures of Mainstream Political Science." *New Political Science, 29,* 2007:97–114.

Domhoff, G. William. *The Power Elite and the State: How Policy Is Made in America.* Hawthorne, N. Y.: Aldine de Gruyter, 1990.

Domhoff, G. William. "State and Ruling Class in Corporate America (1974): Reflections, Corrections, and New Directions." *Critical Sociology, 25,* 2–3, July 1999b:260–265.

Domhoff, G. William. *Who Rules America? Power and Politics in the Year 2000,* 3rd ed. Mountain View, Calif: Mayfield Publishing, 1998.

Domhoff, G. William. *Who Rules America? Power, Politics, and Social Change,* 5th ed. New York: McGraw-Hill, 2006.

Donlon, Margie M., Ori Ash, and Becca R. Levy. "Re-Vision of Older Television Characters: A Stereotype-Awareness Intervention." *Journal of Social Issues, 61,* 2, June 2005.

Dougherty, Conor. "The End of White Flight." *Wall Street Journal,* July 19, 2008a.

Dougherty, Conor. "The New American Gentry." *Wall Street Journal,* January 19, 2008b.

Douglas, Carol Anne, et al. "Kenya: FGM Increasingly Occurring in Hospitals." *Off Our Backs, 35,* January-February 2005:5.

Douthat, Ross. "Abortion Politics Didn't Doom the G.O.P." *New York Times,* December 7, 2008.

Douthat, Ross. "The Truth About Harvard." *Atlantic Monthly,* March 2005.

Dove, Adrian. "Soul Folk 'Chitling' Test or the Dove Counterbalance Intelligence Test." no date. (Mimeo)

Dowd, Maureen. "The Knife Under the Tree." *New York Times,* December 5, 2002.

Drape, Joe. "Growing Cheers for the Home-Schooled Team." *New York Times,* March 16, 2008.

Dreazen, Yochi J. "Rate of Sexual Assault in Army Prompts an Effort at Prevention." *Wall Street Journal,* October 3, 2008.

Drivonikou, G. V., P. Kay, T. Regier, R. B. Ivry, A. L. Gilbert, A. Franklin, and I. R. L. Davies. "Further Evidence That Whorfian Effects Are Stronger in the Right Visual Field Than in the Left." *PNAS, 104,* 3, January 16, 2007: 1097–1102.

Drucker, Peter F. "There's More Than One Kind of Team." *Wall Street Journal,* February 11, 1992:A16.

Du Bois, W. E. B. *Black Reconstruction in America: An Essay Toward a History of the Part Which Black Folk Played in the Attempt to Reconstruct Democracy in America, 1860–1880.* New York: Atheneum, 1992. First published in 1935.

Du Bois, W. E. B. *The Autobiography of W. E. B. Du Bois: A Soliloquy on Viewing My Life from the Last Decade of Its First Century.* New York: International, 1968.

Du Bois, W. E. B. *The Philadelphia Negro: A Social Study.* New York: Schocken Books, 1967. First published in 1899.

Du Bois, W. E. B. *The Souls of Black Folk: Essays and Sketches.* Chicago: McClurg, 1903.

Duff, Christina. "Superrich's Share of After-Tax Income Stopped Rising in Early '90s, Data Show." *Wall Street Journal,* November 22, 1995:A2.

Duffy, Michael. "Can This Machine Be Trusted?" *Time,* October 29, 2006.

Dugger, Celia W. "Abortion in India Is Tipping Scales Sharply Against Girls." *New York Times,* April 22, 2001.

Dugger, Celia W. "In South Africa, TB Patients Behind Barbed Wire." *International Herald Tribune,* March 24, 2008.

Dugger, Celia W. "Wedding Vows Bind Old World and New." *New York Times,* July 20, 1998.

Duneier, Mitchell. *Sidewalk.* New York: Farrar, Straus and Giroux, 2001.

Dunlap, Riley E., and William R. Catton, Jr. "Environmental Sociology." *Annual Review of Sociology, 5,* 1979:243–273.

Dunlap, Riley E., and William R. Catton, Jr. "What Environmental Sociologists Have in Common Whether Concerned with 'Built' or 'Natural' Environments." *Sociological Inquiry, 53,* 2–3, 1983:113–135.

Durkheim, Emile. *The Division of Labor in Society.* George Simpson, trans. New York: Free Press, 1933. First published in 1893.

Durkheim, Emile. *The Elementary Forms of the Religious Life.* New York: Free Press, 1965. First published in 1912.

Durkheim, Emile. *The Rules of Sociological Method.* Sarah A. Solovay and John H. Mueller, trans. New York: Free Press, 1938, 1958, 1964. First published in 1895.

Durkheim, Emile. *Suicide: A Study in Sociology.* John A. Spaulding and George Simpson, trans. New York: Free Press, 1966. First published in 1897.

Durning, Alan. "Cradles of Life." In *Social Problems 90/91,* LeRoy W. Barnes, ed. Guilford, Conn.: Dushkin, 1990:231–241.

Dush, Claire M. Kamp, Catherine L. Cohan, and Paul R. Amato. "The Relationship Between Cohabitation and Marital Quality and Stability: Change Across Cohorts?" *Journal of Marriage and Family, 65,* 3, August 2003: 539–549.

Dye, Jane Lawler. "Fertility of American Women, June 2004." U.S. Bureau of the Census. *Current Population Reports,* December 2005.

Dye, Jane Lawler. "Fertility of American Women: 2006." Washington, D.C. U.S. Bureau of the Census, August 2008.

Dyer, Gwynne. "Anybody's Son Will Do." In *Down to Earth Sociology: Introductory Readings,* 14th ed., James M. Henslin, ed. New York: The Free Press, 2007.

Easley, Hema. "Indian Families Continue to Have Arranged Marriages." *The Journal News,* June 9, 2003.

Ebaugh, Helen Rose Fuchs. *Becoming an Ex: The Process of Role Exit.* Chicago: University of Chicago Press, 1988.

Eberstadt, Nicholas. "China's One-Child Mistake." *New York Times,* September 17, 2007.

Eckholm, Erik. "Desire for Sons Drives Use of Prenatal Scans in China." *New York Times,* June 21, 2002.

Eder, Donna. "On Becoming Female: Lessons Learned in School." In *Down to Earth Sociology: Introductory Readings,* 14th ed., James M. Henslin, ed. New York: The Free Press, 2007.

Eder, Donna. *School Talk: Gender and Adolescent Culture.* New Brunswick, N.J.: Rutgers University Press, 1995.

Eder, Klaus. "The Rise of Counter-Culture Movements Against Modernity: Nature as a New Field of Class Struggle." *Theory, Culture & Society, 7,* 1990:21–47.

Edgerton, Robert B. *Deviance: A Cross-Cultural Perspective.* Menlo Park, Calif.: Benjamin/Cummings, 1976.

Edgerton, Robert B. *Sick Societies: Challenging the Myth of Primitive Harmony.* New York: Free Press, 1992.

Egan, Timothy. "Many Seek Security in Private Communities." *New York Times,* September 3, 1995:1, 22.

Ehrenreich, Barbara, and Deidre English. *Witches, Midwives, and Nurses: A History of Women Healers.* Old Westbury, N. Y.: Feminist Press, 1973.

Ehrlich, Paul R., and Anne H. Ehrlich. "Humanity at the Crossroads." *Stanford Magazine,* Spring-Summer 1978:20–23.

Ehrlich, Paul R., and Anne H. Ehrlich. *Population, Resources, and Environment: Issues in Human Ecology,* 2nd ed. San Francisco: Freeman, 1972.

Eibl-Eibesfeldt, Irrenäus. *Ethology: The Biology of Behavior.* New York: Holt, Rinehart, and Winston, 1970.

Eisenhart, R. Wayne. "You Can't Hack It, Little Girl: A Discussion of the Covert Psychological Agenda of Modern Combat Training." *Journal of Social Issues, 31,* Fall 1975:13–23.

Ekman, Paul. *Faces of Man: Universal Expression in a New Guinea Village.* New York: Garland Press, 1980.

Ekman, Paul, Wallace V. Friesen, and John Bear. "The International Language of Gestures." *Psychology Today,* May 1984:64.

Elder, Glen H., Jr. "Age Differentiation and Life Course." *Annual Review of Sociology, 1,* 1975:165–190.

Elder, Glen H., Jr. *Children of the Great Depression: Social Change in Life Experience.* Boulder: Westview Press, 1999.

Elias, Paul. "'Molecular Pharmers' Hope to Raise Human Proteins in Crop Plants." *St. Louis Post-Dispatch,* October 28, 2001:F7.

Elinson, Elaine. "Lifting the Veil on Government Surveillance." *ACLU News.* Spring 2004.

Elkins, Stanley M. *Slavery: A Problem in American Institutional and Intellectual Life,* 2nd ed. Chicago: University of Chicago Press, 1968.

Elliott, Joel. "Birth Control Allowed for Maine Middle Schoolers." *New York Times,* October 18, 2007.

Elsworth, Catherine. "Doctor 'Hastened Death of Patient for Organs.'" *London Telegraph,* February 29, 2008.

Elwert, Felix, and Nicholas A. Christakis. "The Effect of Widowhood on Mortality by the Causes of Death of Both Spouses." *American Journal of Public Health, 98,* 11, November 2008:2092–2098.

England, Paula. "The Impact of Feminist Thought on Sociology." *Contemporary Sociology: A Journal of Reviews,* 2000:263–267.

Epstein, Cynthia Fuchs. *Deceptive Distinctions: Sex, Gender, and the Social Order.* New Haven, Conn.: Yale University Press, 1988.

Epstein, Cynthia Fuchs. "Great Divides: The Cultural, Cognitive, and Social Bases of the Global Subordination of Women." *American Sociological Review, 72,* February 2007:1–22.

Epstein, Cynthia Fuchs. Letter to the author, January 26, 1989.

Epstein, Cynthia. "Similarity and Difference: The Sociology of Gender Distinction." In *Handbook of the Sociology of Gender,* Janet Saltzman Chafetz, ed.. New York: Kluwer Academic/Plenum Publishers, 1999.

Erikson, Kai T. *Everything In Its Path: Destruction of Community in the Buffalo Creek Flood.* New York: Simon and Schuster, 1978.

Ernst, Eldon G. "The Baptists." In *Encyclopedia of the American Religious Experience: Studies of Traditions and Movements,* Vol. 1, Charles H. Lippy and Peter W. Williams, eds. New York: Scribners, 1988:555–577.

Ertel, Karen A., M. Maria Glymour, and Lisa F. Berkman. "Effects of Social Integration on Preserving Memory Function in a Nationally Representative US Elderly Population." *American Journal of Public Health, 98,* 7, July 2008:1215–1220.

Eshleman, J. Ross. *The Family,* 9th ed. Boston: Allyn and Bacon, 2000.

Espinosa, Linda M., and James M. Laffey. "Urban Primary Teacher Perceptions of Children with Challenging Behaviors." *Journal of Children and Poverty, 9,* 2, 2003:135–156.

Evans, Peter, and James E. Rauch. "Bureaucracy and Growth: A Cross-National Analysis of the Effects of 'Weberian' State Structures on Economic Growth." *American Sociological Review, 64,* October 1999:748–765.

Evenson, Ranae J., and Robin W. Simon. "Clarifying the Relationship Between Parenting and Depression." *Journal of Health and Social Behavior, 46,* December 2005:341–358.

Ezekiel, Raphael S. *The Racist Mind: Portraits of American Neo-Nazis and Klansmen.* New York: Viking, 1995.

Fabrikant, Geraldine. "Old Nantucket Warily Meets the New." *New York Times,* June 5, 2005.

Fadiman, Anne. *The Spirit Catches You and You Fall Down.* Farrar, Straus and Giroux, 1997.

Fagot, Beverly I., Richard Hagan, Mary Driver Leinbach, and Sandra Kronsberg. "Differential Reactions to Assertive and Communicative Acts of Toddler Boys and Girls." *Child Development, 56,* 1985:1499–1505.

Falkenberg, Katie. "Pakistani Women Victims of 'Honor.'" *Washington Times,* July 23, 2008.

Fan, Maureen. "After Quake, China's Elderly Long for Family." *Washington Post,* June 3, 2008.

Faris, Robert E. L., and Warren Dunham. *Mental Disorders in Urban Areas.* Chicago: University of Chicago Press, 1939.

Farkas, George, Daniel Sheehan, and Robert P. Grobe. "Coursework Mastery and School Success: Gender, Ethnicity, and Poverty Groups Within an Urban School District." *American Educational Research Journal, 27,* 4, Winter 1990b:807–827.

Farkas, George, Robert P. Grobe, Daniel Sheehan, and Yuan Shuan. "Cultural Resources and School Success: Gender, Ethnicity, and Poverty Groups Within an Urban School District." *American Sociological Review, 55,* February 1990a:127–142.

Farkas, George. *Human Capital or Cultural Capital?: Ethnicity and Poverty Groups in an Urban School District.* New York: Walter DeGruyter, 1996.

Farley, John E., and Gregory D. Squires. "Fences and Neighbors: Segregation in twenty first Century America." *Contexts,* Winter 2005:33–39.

Fathi, Nazila. "Starting at Home, Iran's Women Fight for Rights." *New York Times,* February 12, 2009.

Fattah, Hassan M. "After First Steps, Saudi Reformers See Efforts Stall." *New York Times,* April 26, 2007.

Fattig, Paul. "Good Intentions Gone Bad." *Mail Tribune,* June 6, 2007.

Faunce, William A. *Problems of an Industrial Society,* 2nd ed. New York: McGraw-Hill, 1981.

FBI Uniform Crime Reports. Washington, D.C.: U.S. Government Printing Office, published annually.

Featherman, David L. "Opportunities Are Expanding." *Society, 13,* 1979:4–11.

Feder, Barnaby J. "Services at the First Church of Cyberspace." *New York Times,* May 15, 2004.

Feder, Barnaby. "Billboards That Know You by Name." *New York Times,* January 29, 2007.

Feldman, Saul D. "The Presentation of Shortness in Everyday Life—Height and Heightism in American Society: Toward a Sociology of Stature." Paper presented at the 1972 meetings of the American Sociological Association.

Felsenthal, Edward. "Justices' Ruling Further Defines Sex Harassment." *Wall Street Journal,* March 5, 1998:B1, B2.

Felton, Lee Ann, Andrea Gumm, and David J. Pittenger. "The Recipients of Unwanted Sexual Encounters Among College Students." *College Student Journal, 35,* 1, March 2001:135–143.

Ferraro, Kathleen J. "Intimate Partner Violence." In *Social Problems,* 7th ed., by James M. Henslin. Upper Saddle River, N. J.: Prentice Hall, 2006:373.

Ferraro, Susan. "Future Fighters: How Military Technology is Advancing Medical Science." *Daily News,* July 11, 2001.

Feshbach, Murray. "Russia's Farms, Too Poisoned for the Plow." *Wall Street Journal,* May 14, 1992:A14.

Feuer, Alan. "Accommodations for the Discreetly Superrich." *New York Times,* October 6, 2008.

Fialka, John J. "A Dirty Discovery Over Indian Ocean Sets Off a Fight." *Wall Street Journal,* May 6, 2003:A1, A6.

Findlater, Jamie. "Electronic Warfare Offers New Jobs for Tech-Savvy Professionals." American Forces Press Services, February 12, 2009.

Finke, Roger, and Rodney Stark. *The Churching of America, 1776–1990: Winners and Losers in Our Religious Economy.* New Brunswick, N.J.: Rutgers University Press, 1992.

Finkelhor, David, and Kersti Yllo. *License to Rape: Sexual Abuse of Wives.* New York: Henry Holt, 1985.

Finkelhor, David, and Kersti Yllo. "Marital Rape: The Myth Versus the Reality." In *Marriage and Family in a Changing Society,* 3rd ed., James M. Henslin, ed. New York: Free Press, 1989:382–391.

Fischer, Claude S. *The Urban Experience.* New York: Harcourt, 1976.

Fischer, Tamar F. C., Paul M. De Graaf, and Matthijs Kalmijn. "Friendly and Antagonistic Contact Between Former Spouses After Divorce." *Journal of Family Issues, 26,* 8, November 2005:1131–1163.

Fish, Jefferson M. "Mixed Blood." *Psychology Today, 28,* 6, November-December 1995:55–58, 60, 61, 76, 80.

Fisher, Bonnie S., Francis T. Cullen, and Michael G. Turner. *The Sexual Victimization of College Women.* Washington, D.C.: U.S. Department of Justice, 2000.

Fisher, Bonnie S., Leah E. Daigle, Francis T. Cullen, and Michael G. Turner. "Reporting Sexual Victimization to the Police and Others: Results from a National-Level Study of College Women." *Criminal Justice and Behavior, 30,* 1, February 2003:6–38.

Fisher, Ian, and Elisabetta Provoledo. "Surprising Few, Italy's Government Collapses." *New York Times,* January 25, 2008.

Fisher, Sue. *In the Patient's Best Interest: Women and the Politics of Medical Decisions.* New Brunswick, N.J.: Rutgers University Press, 1986.

Flanagan, William G. *Urban Sociology: Images and Structure.* Boston: Allyn and Bacon, 1990.

Flavel, John H., et al. *The Development of Role-Taking and Communication Skills in Children.* New York: Wiley, 1968.

Flavel, John, Patricia H. Miller, and Scott A. Miller. *Cognitive Development,* 4th ed. Upper Saddle River, N.J.: Prentice Hall, 2002.

Flegal, Katherine M., Barry I. Graubard, David F. Williamson, and Mitchell H. Gail. "Cause-Specific Excess Deaths Associated With Underweight, Overweight, and Obesity." *Journal of the American Medical Association, 298,* 17, November 7, 2007.

Fleming, Kevin C., Jonathan M. Evans, and Darryl S. Chutka. "A Cultural and Economic History of Old Age in America." *Mayo Clinic Proceedings, 78,* July 2003:914–921.

Flexner, Abraham. *Medical Education in the United States and Canada: A Report to the Carnegie Foundation for the Advancement of Teaching.* Bulletin No. 4. Boston: Merrymount Press, 1910.

Flexner, E. *Century of Struggle.* Cambridge, Mass.: Belknap, 1971. In Claire M. Renzetti and Daniel J. Curran, *Women, Men, and Society,* 4th ed. Boston: Allyn and Bacon, 1999.

Flink, James J., *The Automobile Age.* Cambridge, Mass.: MIT Press, 1990.

Flippen, Annette R. "Understanding Groupthink From a Self-Regulatory Perspective." *Small Group Research, 30,* 2, April 1999:139–165.

Foley, Douglas E. "The Great American Football Ritual." In *Society: Readings to Accompany Sociology: A Down-to-Earth Approach, Core Concepts,* James M. Henslin, ed. Boston: Allyn and Bacon, 2006: 64–76. First published in 1990.

Foley, Meraiah. "Australia to Test Web Filter to Block Banned Content." *New York Times,* December 14, 2008.

Fonseca, Felicia. "Navajo Nation Seeks Control of National Monument." Associated Press, September 11, 2008.

Food and Agriculture Organization of the United Nations. "World and Regional Review: Facts and Figures." 2006.

"Food Outlook: Global Market Analysis." The Global Information and Early Warning System on Food and Agriculture, November 2008.

Foote, Jennifer. "Trying to Take Back the Planet." *Newsweek, 115,* 6, February 5, 1990:24–25.

Forelle, Charles. "Ivy League Schools Begin to Offer Online Courses." *Wall Street Journal,* January 15, 2003.

Form, William. "Comparative Industrial Sociology and the Convergence Hypothesis." In *Annual Review of Sociology, 5,* 1, 1979, Alex Inkeles, James Coleman, and Ralph H. Turner, eds.

Fountain, Henry. "Archaeological Site in Peru Is Called Oldest City in Americas." *New York Times,* April 27, 2001.

Fowler, Geoffrey A., and Amy Chozick. "Cartoon Characters Get Big Makeover for Overseas Fans." *Wall Street Journal,* October 16, 2007.

Fox, Elaine, and George E. Arquitt. "The VFW and the 'Iron Law of Oligarchy.'" In *Down to Earth Sociology,* 4th ed., James M. Henslin, ed. New York: Free Press, 1985:147–155.

Frank, Reanne. "What to Make of It? The (Re)emergence of a Biological Conceptualization of Race in Health Disparities Research." *Social Science & Medicine, 64,* 2007:1977–1983.

Franklin, John Hope, and John Whittington Franklin. *My Life and an Era: The Autobiography of Buck Colbert Franklin.* Baton Rouge: Louisiana State University, 1997.

Fraser, Graham. "Fox Denies Free Trade Exploiting the Poor in Mexico." *Toronto Star,* April 20, 2001.

Freedman, Jane. *Feminism.* Philadelphia: Open University Press, 2001.

Freidson, Eliot. *Professionalism: The Third Logic.* Chicago: University of Chicago Press, 2001.

Fremson, Ruth. "Dead Bachelors in Remote China Still Find Wives." *New York Times,* October 5, 2006.

French, Howard W. "As Girls 'Vanish,' Chinese City Battles Tide of Abortions." *New York Times,* April 14, 2004.

Freund, Charles Paul. "A Riot of Our Own." *Reason, 32,* 10, March 2001:10.

Frey, William H. "Diversity Spreads Out: Metropolitan Shifts in Hispanic, Asian, and Black Populations Since 2000." Washington: Brookings Institution, March 2006.

Frey, William H. "The New Great Migration: Black Americans' Return to the South, 1965–2000." Washington: Brookings Institution, May 2004.

Friedl, Ernestine. "Society and Sex Roles." In *Conformity and Conflict: Readings in Cultural Anthropology,* James P. Spradley and David W. McCurdy, eds. Glenview, Ill.: Scott, Foresman, 1990:229–238.

Frommer, Arthur. *Peru.* New York: Wiley, 2007.

Frosch, Dan. "Its Native Tongue Facing Extinction, Arapaho Tribe Teaches the Young." *New York Times,* October 17, 2008.

Frumkin, Robert M. "Early English and American Sex Customs." In *Encyclopedia of Sexual Behavior,* Vol. 1. New York: Hawthorne Books, 1967.

Fuller, Rex, and Richard Schoenberger. "The Gender Salary Gap: Do Academic Achievement, Internship Experience, and College Major Make a Difference?" *Social Science Quarterly, 72,* 4, December 1991:715–726.

Fund, John. "English-Only Showdown." *Wall Street Journal,* November 28, 2007.

Furstenberg, Frank F., Jr., and Kathleen Mullan Harris. "The Disappearing American Father? Divorce and the Waning Significance of Biological Fatherhood." In *The Changing American Family: Sociological and Demographic Perspectives,* Scott J. South and Stewart E. Tolnay, eds. Boulder, Colo.: Westview Press, 1992:197–223.

Furstenberg, Frank F., Jr., Sheela Kennedy, Vonnie C. McLoyd, Ruben G. Rumbaut, and Richard A. Settersten, Jr. "Growing Up Is Harder to Do." *Contexts, 3,* 3, Summer 2004:33–41.

Galbraith, John Kenneth. *The Nature of Mass Poverty.* Cambridge Mass.: Harvard University Press, 1979.

Galliher, John F. *Deviant Behavior and Human Rights.* Englewood Cliffs, N.J.: Prentice Hall, 1991.

Gallmeier, Charles P. "Methodological Issues in Qualitative Sport Research: Participant Observation among Hockey Players." *Sociological Spectrum, 8,* 1988:213–235.

Gallup Poll. "Americans More Likely to Believe in God Than the Devil, Heaven More Than Hell." June 13, 2007.

Gallup Poll. "Americans: 2.5 Children Is 'Ideal' Family Size." Princeton, N.J.: Gallup Organization, June 26, 2007.

Gallup Poll. "Election Polls—Vote by Groups, 2008." Princeton, N.J.: Gallup Organization, 2008a.

Gallup Poll. "No Evidence Bad Times Are Boosting Church Attendance." Princeton, N.J.: The Gallup Organization, 2008b.

Gallup Poll. "Questions and Answers About Americans' Religion." Princeton, N.J.: The Gallup Organization, December 24, 2007.

Gallup Poll. "Religion and Social Trends." Princeton, N.J.: The Gallup Organization, 2005.

Gallup, George, Jr. *The Gallup Poll: Public Opinion 1989.* Wilmington, Dela.: Scholarly Resources, 1990.

Gamerman, Ellen. "The New Pranksters." *Wall Street Journal,* September 12, 2008.

Gampbell, Jennifer. "In Northeast Thailand, an Cuisine Based on Bugs." *New York Times,* June 22, 2006.

Gans, Herbert J. *People and Plans: Essays on Urban Problems and Solutions.* New York: Basic Books, 1968.

Gans, Herbert J. *People, Plans, and Policies: Essays on Poverty, Racism, and Other National Urban Problems.* New York: Columbia University Press, 1991.

Gans, Herbert. J., "Public Sociologies: Reply to Hausknecht." *Footnotes,* January 2003:8.

Gans, Herbert J. *The Urban Villagers.* New York: Free Press, 1962.

Gantz, Walter, Nancy Schwartz, James R. Angelini, and Victoria Rideout. *Food for Thought: Television Food Advertising to Children in the United States.* Kaiser Family Foundation, March 2007.

Garfinkel, Harold. "Conditions of Successful Degradation Ceremonies." *American Journal of Sociology, 61,* 2, March 1956:420–424.

Garfinkel, Harold. *Ethnomethodology's Program: Working Out Durkheim's Aphorism.* Lanham, MD: Rowman & Littlefield, 2002.

Garfinkel, Harold. *Studies in Ethnomethodology.* Englewood Cliffs, N.J.: Prentice Hall, 1967.

Gates, Eddie Faye. "The Oklahoma Commission to Study the Tulsa Race Riot of 1921." *Harvard Black Letter Law Journal, 20,* 2004:83–89.

Gatewood, Willard B. *Aristocrats of Color: The Black Elite, 1880–1920.* Bloomington, Ind.: Indiana University Press, 1990.

Gauch, Sarah. "In Egyptian Schools, A Push for Critical Thinking." *Christian Science Monitor,* February 9, 2006.

Gautham S. "Coming Next: The Monsoon Divorce." *New Statesman, 131,* 4574, February 18, 2002:32–33.

Geis, Gilbert, Robert F. Meier, and Lawrence M. Salinger. *White-Collar Crime: Classic and Contemporary Views,* 3rd ed. New York: Free Press, 1995.

Genetski, Robert. "Privatize Social Security." *Wall Street Journal,* May 21, 1993.

Gerhard, Jane. "Revisiting 'The Myth of the Vaginal Orgasm': The Female Orgasm in American Sexual Thought and Second Wave Feminism." *Feminist Studies, 26,* 2, Fall 2000:449–477.

Gerth, H. H., and C. Wright Mills. *From Max Weber: Essays in Sociology.* New York: Galaxy, 1958.

Gerth, Jeff. "Two Companies Pay Penalties for Improving China Rockets." *New York Times,* March 3, 2003.

Gettleman, Jeffrey. "Starvation and Strife Menace Torn Kenya." *New York Times,* February 28, 2009.

Gibbs, Nancy. "Affirmative Action for Boys." *Time,* April 3, 2008.

Gilbert, Dennis L. *The American Class Structure in an Age of Growing Inequality,* 6th ed. Belmont, Calif.: Wadsworth Publishing, 2003.

Gilbert, Dennis, and Joseph A. Kahl. *The American Class Structure: A New Synthesis.* 4th ed. Belmont, Calif.: Wadsworth Publishing, 1998.

Gilligan, Carol. *In a Different Voice: Psychological Theory and Women's Development.* Cambridge, Mass.: Harvard University Press, 1982.

Gilligan, Carol. *Making Connections: The Relational World of Adolescent Girls at Emma Willard School.* Cambridge, Mass.: Harvard University Press, 1990.

Gillum, R. F. "Frequency of Attendance at Religious Services and Smoking: The Third National Health and Nutrition Examination Survey." *Preventive Medicine, 41,* 2005:607–613.

Gilman, Charlotte Perkins. *The Man-Made World or, Our Androcentric Culture.* New York: 1971. First published 1911.

Girshick, Lori B. *Woman-To-Woman Sexual Violence: Does She Call It Rape?* Boston: Northeastern University Press, 2002.

Gitlin, Todd. *The Twilight of Common Dreams: Why America Is Wracked by Culture Wars.* New York: Metropolitan Books, 1997.

Gitomer, Drew H. "Teacher Quality in a Changing Policy Landscape: Improvements in the Teacher Pool." Princeton, New Jersey: Educational Testing Service, 2007.

Glascock, Jack. "Gender Roles on Prime-Time Network Television: Demographics and Behaviors." *Journal of Broadcasting and Electronic Media, 45,* Fall 2001:656–669.

Glaze, Lauren E. and Laura M, Maruschak. "Parents in Prison and Their Minor Children." Bureau of Justice Statistics Special Report, August 2008:1–25.

Gleason, Carmen L. "Officials Emphasize Zero Tolerance of Sexual Assault." Army News Service, April 5, 2007.

Glenn, Evelyn Nakano. "Chinese American Families." In *Minority Families in the United States: A Multicultural Perspective,* Ronald L. Taylor, ed. Englewood Cliffs, N.J.: Prentice Hall, 1994:115–145.

Glick, Paul C., and S. Lin. "More Young Adults Are Living with Their Parents: Who Are They?" *Journal of Marriage and Family, 48,* 1986:107–112.

"Global 2000." *Forbes,* April 8, 2009.

Goetting, Ann. *Getting Out: Life Stories of Women Who Left Abusive Men.* New York: Columbia University Press, 2001.

Goffman, Erving. *Asylums: Essays on the Social Situation of Mental Patients and Other Inmates.* Chicago: Aldine, 1961.

Goffman, Erving. *Stigma: Notes on the Management of Spoiled Identity.* Englewood Cliffs, N.J.: Prentice Hall, 1963.

Gold, Ray. "Janitors Versus Tenants: A Status-Income Dilemma." *American Journal of Sociology, 58,* 1952:486–493.

Goldberg, Steven. *Fads and Fallacies in the Social Sciences.* Amherst, N. Y.: Humanity/Prometheus, 2003.

Goldberg, Steven. *The Inevitability of Patriarchy,* rev. ed. New York: Morrow, 1974.

Goldberg, Steven. "Reaffirming the Obvious." *Society,* September–October 1986:4–7.

Goldberg, Steven. *Why Men Rule: A Theory of Male Dominance.* Chicago: Open Court, 1993.

Goldberg, Susan, and Michael Lewis. "Play Behavior in the Year-Old Infant: Early Sex Differences." *Child Development, 40,* March 1969:21–31.

Goldman, Kevin. "Seniors Get Little Respect on Madison Avenue." *Wall Street Journal,* September 20, 1993:B6.

Goldstein, Jacob. "In Plain Sight, A Woman Dies Unassisted on Hospital Floor." *Wall Street Journal,* July 1, 2008.

Goldstein, Jacob. "A Simple Surgical Checklist Saves Lives." *Wall Street Journal,* January 15, 2009.

Goleman, Daniel. "Pollsters Enlist Psychologists in Quest for Unbiased Results." *New York Times,* September 7, 1993:C1, C11.

Gonzales, Alberto R. "Memorandum for Albert R. Gonzales, Counsel to the President: Re: Standards of Conduct for Interrogation Under *18 U.S.C. 2340–2340A.*" August 2, 2002.

Goode, William J. "Encroachment, Charlatanism, and the Emerging Profession: Psychology, Sociology, and Medicine." *American Sociological Review, 25,* 6, December 1960:902–914.

Goozen, Stephanie H. M. van, Graeme Fairchild, Heddeke Snoek, and Gordon T. Harold. "The Evidence for a Neurobiological Model of Childhood Antisocial Behavior." *Psychological Bulletin, 133,* 1, 2007:149–182.

Gorman, Christine. "The Disease Detective." *Time,* January 6, 1997: 56–65.

Gorman, James. "High-Tech Daydreamers Investing in Immortality." *Wall Street Journal,* November 1, 2003.

Gorman, Peter. "A People at Risk: Vanishing Tribes of South America." *The World & I.* December 1991:678–689.

Gornick, Janet C., and Alexandra Heron. "The Regulation of Working Time as Work-Family Reconciliation Policy: Comparing Europe, Japan, and the United States." *Journal of Comparative Policy Analysis, 8,* 2, June 2006:149–166.

Gorsky, Paul. "The Myth of the 'Culture of Poverty.'" *Educational Leadership, 65,* 7, April 2008.

Gottfredson, Michael R., and Travis Hirschi. *A General Theory of Crime.* Stanford, Calif.: Stanford University Press, 1990.

Gottschalk, Peter, Sara McLanahan, and Gary Sandefur, "The Dynamics and Intergenerational Transmission of Poverty and Welfare Participation." In *Confronting Poverty: Prescriptions for Change,* Sheldon H. Danziger, Gary D. Sandefur, and Daniel H. Weinberg, eds. Cambridge, Mass.: Harvard University Press, 1994.

Grabe, Shelly, L. Monique Ward, and Janet Shibley Hyde. "The Role of the Media in Body Image Concerns Among Women: A Meta-Analysis of Experimental and Correlational Studies." *Psychological Bulletin, 134,* 3: 2008:460–476.

Gracey, Harry L. "Kindergarten as Academic Boot Camp." In *Down to Earth Sociology: Introductory Readings,* fourteenth ed., James M. Henslin, ed. New York: The Free Press, 2007. Also appeared in the 6th edition of this book, 1991:377–390.

Grant, Peter. "Looking for Love (Or a Date) on Cable TV." *Wall Street Journal,* December 15, 2005.

Gray Panthers. "Age and Youth in Action." No date.

Greeley, Andrew M. "The Protestant Ethic: Time for a Moratorium." *Sociological Analysis, 25,* Spring 1964:20–33.

Green, Alexander R., Dana R. Carney, Daniel J. Pallin, Long H.Ngo, Kristal L. Raymond, Lisa I. Iezzoni, and Mahzarin R. Banaji. "Implicit Bias among Physicians and Its Prediction of Thrombolysis Decisions for Black and White Patients." *Journal of General Internal Medicine,* June 27, 2007.

Greene, Jay P., and Marcus A. Winters. "Public High School Graduation and College-Readiness Rates, 1991–2002." Center for Civic Innovation at the Manhattan Institute. *Education Working Paper, 8*, 2005.

Greenhouse, Linda. "Justices Decline Case on 200-Year Sentence for Man Who Possessed Child Pornography." *New York Times,* February 27, 2007.

Greenhouse, Steven. "Young and Old Are Facing Off for Jobs." *New York Times,* March 20, 2009.

Greenwald, Anthony G., and Linda Hamilton Krieger. "Implicit Bias: Scientific Foundations." *California Law Review,* July 2006.

Grimmett, Richard F. "Conventional Arms Transfers to Developing Nations, 1997–2004." Washington, D.C.: Congressional Research Service, August 29, 2005.

Gross, Jan T. *Neighbors.* New Haven: Yale University Press, 2001.

Gross, Jane. "A Grass-Roots Effort to Grow Old at Home." *New York Times,* August 14, 2007.

Gross, Jane. "In the Quest for the Perfect Look, More Girls Choose the Scalpel." *New York Times,* November 29, 1998.

Grossman, Lev. "Tag, You're It." *Time,* October 18, 2007.

Gu, Dongfeng, Tanika N. Kelly, Xigui Wu, Jing Chen, et al. "Mortality Attributable to Smoking in China." *New England Journal of Medicine, 360,* January 8, 2009:150–159.

Guensburg, Carol. "Bully Factories." *American Journalism Review, 23,* 6, 2001:51–59.

Guessous, Fouad, Thorsten Juchem, and Norbert A. Hampp. In *Optical Security and Counterfeit Deterrence Techniques,* Rudolf L. van Renesse, ed. *Proceedings of the SPIE, 5310,* 2004.

Guice, Jon. "Sociologists Go to Work in High Technology." *Footnotes,* November 1999:8.

"Guilds." *Columbia Encyclopedia,* 6th ed. New York: Columbia University Press, 2008.

Gunther, Marc. "The Mosquito in the Tent." *Fortune, 149,* 11, May 31, 2004:158.

Gupta, Giri Raj. "Love, Arranged Marriage, and the Indian Social Structure." In *Cross-Cultural Perspectives of Mate Selection and Marriage,* George Kurian, ed. Westport, Conn.: Greenwood Press, 1979.

Guru, Gopal, and Shiraz Sidhva. "India's 'Hidden Apartheid.'" *UNESCO Courier,* September 2001:27.

Guthrie, Doug. "The Great Helmsman's Cultural Death." *Contexts, 7,* 3, Summer 2008:26–31.

Haas, Jack. "Binging: Educational Control Among High-Steel Iron Workers." *American Behavioral Scientist, 16,* 1972:27–34.

Hacker, Helen Mayer. "Women as a Minority Group." *Social Forces, 30,* October 1951:60–69.

Hafner, Katie. "Welding Kitchen Knives and Honing Office Skills." *New York Times,* January 13, 2007.

Hage, Dave. *Reforming Welfare by Rewarding Work.* Minneapolis: University of Minnesota Press, 2004.

Hall, Edward T. *The Hidden Dimension.* Garden City, N. Y.: Anchor Books, 1969.

Hall, Edward T. *The Silent Language.* New York: Doubleday, 1959.

Hall, Edward T., and Mildred R. Hall. "The Sounds of Silence." In *Down to Earth Sociology: Introductory Readings,* 14th ed., James M. Henslin, ed. New York: The Free Press, 2007.

Hall, G. Stanley. *Adolescence: Its Psychology and Its Relations to Physiology, Anthropology, Sociology, Sex, Crime, Religion, and Education.* New York: Appleton, 1904.

Hall, J. Camille. "The Impact of Kin and Fictive Kin Relationships on the Mental Health of Black Adult Children of Alcoholics." *Health and Social Work, 33,* 4, November 2008:259–266.

Hall, Richard H. "The Concept of Bureaucracy: An Empirical Assessment." *American Journal of Sociology, 69,* July 1963:32–40.

Hall, Ronald E. "The Tiger Woods Phenomenon: A Note on Biracial Identity." *The Social Science Journal, 38,* 2, April 2001:333–337.

Hamermesh, Daniel S., and Jeff E. Biddle. "Beauty and the Labor Market." *American Economic Review, 84,* 5, December 1994:1174–1195.

Hamid, Shadi. "Between Orientalism and Postmodernism: The Changing Nature of Western Feminist Thought Towards the Middle East." *HAWWA, 4,* 1, 2006:76–92.

Hampson, Rick. "Studies: Gentrification a Boost for Everyone." *USA Today,* April 19, 2005.

Hardy, Dorcas. *Social Insecurity: The Crisis in America's Social Security and How to Plan Now for Your Own Financial Survival.* New York: Villard Books, 1991.

Harford, Tim. "Why Divorce is Good for Women." The Undercover Economist, *Slate,* January 16, 2008.

Harlow, Harry F., and Margaret K. Harlow. "The Affectional Systems." In *Behavior of Nonhuman Primates: Modern Research Trends,* Vol. 2, Allan M. Schrier, Harry F. Harlow, and Fred Stollnitz, eds. New York: Academic Press, 1965:287–334.

Harlow, Harry F., and Margaret K. Harlow. "Social Deprivation in Monkeys." *Scientific American, 207,* 1962:137–147.

Harper, Charles L., and Kevin T. Leicht. *Exploring Social Change: America and the World.* Upper Saddle River, N.J.: Prentice Hall, 2002.

Harrington, Michael. *The Vast Majority: A Journey to the World's Poor.* New York: Simon & Schuster, 1977.

Harris, Chauncey D. "The Nature of Cities and Urban Geography in the Last Half Century." *Urban Geography, 18,* 1997.

Harris, Chauncey D., and Edward Ullman. "The Nature of Cities." *Annals of the American Academy of Political and Social Science, 242,* 1945:7–17.

Harris, Craig. "Fallout from Ariz. Employer Sanctions Law." *Arizona Republic,* September 15, 2008.

Harris, Gardiner. "Drug Makers Told Studies Would Aid It, Papers Say." *New York Times,* March 19, 2009.

Harris, Gardiner. "F.D.A. Says Bayer Failed to Reveal Drug Risk Study." *New York Times,* September 30, 2006.

Harris, Kim, Dwight R. Sanders, Shaun Gress, and Nick Kuhns. "Starting Salaries for Agribusiness Graduates From an AASCARR Institution: The Case of Southern Illinois University." *Agribusiness, 21,* 1, 2005:65–80.

Harris, Marvin. "Why Men Dominate Women." *New York Times Magazine,* November 13, 1977:46, 115, 117–123.

Harrison, Paul. *Inside the Third World: The Anatomy of Poverty,* 3rd ed. London: Penguin Books, 1993.

Hart, Charles W. M., and Arnold R. Pilling. *The Tiwi of North Australia,* Fieldwork Edition. New York: Holt, Rinehart and Winston, 1979.

Hart, Hornell. "Acceleration in Social Change." In *Technology and Social Change,* Francis R. Allen, Hornell Hart, Delbert C. Miller, William F. Ogburn, and Meyer F. Nimkoff. New York: Appleton, 1957:27–55.

Hart, Paul. "Groupthink, Risk-Taking and Recklessness: Quality of Process and Outcome in Policy Decision Making." *Politics and the Individual, 1,* 1, 1991:67–90.

Hartley, Eugene. *Problems in Prejudice.* New York: King's Crown Press, 1946.

Hartocollis, Anemona. "Harvard Faculty Votes to Put the Excellence Back in the A." *New York Times,* May 22, 2002.

Hatch, Laurie Russell. *Beyond Gender Differences: Adaptation to Aging in Life Course Perspective.* Amityville, N. Y.: Baywood Publishing Company, 2000.

Haub, Carl, and Mary Mederlos Kent. "World Population Data Sheet." Washington, D.C.: Population Reference Bureau, 2008.

Haub, Carl, and Nancy Yinger. "The U. N. Long-Range Population Projections: What They Tell Us." Washington, D.C.: Population Reference Bureau, 1994.

Haub, Carl. "World Population Data Sheet." Washington, D.C.: Population Reference Bureau, 2004.

Haughney, Christine. "Harlem's Real Estate Boom Becomes a Bust." *New York Times,* July 8, 2009.

Haughney, Christine, and Eric Konigsberg. "Despite Tough Times, Ultrarich Keep Spending." *New York Times,* April 14, 2008.

Hauser, Philip, and Leo Schnore, eds. *The Study of Urbanization.* New York: Wiley, 1965.

Hawkes, Nigel. "Asbestos-Related Diseases Will Rise for 20 Years." *The Times,* September 25, 2001.

Hawley, Amos H. *Urban Society: An Ecological Approach.* New York: Wiley, 1981.

Hay, Carter, and Walter Forrest. "The Development of Self-Control: Examining Self-Control Theory's Stability Thesis." *Criminology, 44,* 4, 2006:739–774.

Hayashi, Gina M., and Bonnie R. Strickland. "Long-Term Effects of Parental Divorce on Love Relationships: Divorce as Attachment Disruption." *Journal of Social and Personal Relationships, 15,* 1, February 1998:23–38.

Heames, Joyce Thompson, Michael G. Harvey, and Darren Treadway. "Status Inconsistency: An Antecedent to Bullying Behavior in Groups." *International Journal of Human Resource Management, 17,* 2, February 2006:348–361.

Hechinger, John. "Class of '08 Fails to Lift SAT Scores." *Wall Street Journal,* August 27, 2008.

Hechter, Michael. *Containing Nationalism.* New York: Oxford University Press, 2000.

Helliker, Kevin. "Body and Spirit: Why Attending Religious Services May Benefit Health." *Wall Street Journal,* May 3, 2005.

Hellinger, Daniel, and Dennis R. Judd. *The Democratic Facade.* Pacific Grove, Calif.: Brooks/Cole, 1991.

Hemmings, Annette. "The 'Hidden' Corridor Curriculum." *High School Journal, 83,* December 1999:1–12.

Hendin, Herbert. "Euthanasia and Physician-Assisted Suicide in the Netherlands." *New England Journal of Medicine, 336,* 19, May 8, 1997:1385–1387.

Hendin, Herbert. "Suicide, Assisted Suicide, and Medical Illness." *Harvard Mental Health Letter, 16,* 7:January 2000:4–7.

Hendrix, Lewellyn. "What Is Sexual Inequality? On the Definition and Range of Variation." *Gender and Society, 28,* 3, August 1994:287–307.

Henley, Nancy, Mykol Hamilton, and Barrie Thorne. "Womanspeak and Manspeak." In *Beyond Sex Roles,* Alice G. Sargent, ed. St Paul, MN: West, 1985.

Henslin, James M. "On Becoming Male: Reflections of a Sociologist on Childhood and Early Socialization." In *Down to Earth Sociology: Introductory Readings,* 14th ed., James M. Henslin, ed. New York: The Free Press, 2007.

Henslin, James M. *Social Problems: A Down-to-Earth Approach,* 8th ed. Boston: Allyn & Bacon, 2008.

Henslin, James M., and Mae A. Biggs. "Behavior in Pubic Places: The Sociology of the Vaginal Examination." In *Down to Earth Sociology: Introductory Readings,* 14th ed., James M. Henslin, ed. New York: The Free Press, 2007. Originally published 1971.

Herring, Cedric. "Is Job Discrimination Dead?" *Contexts,* Summer 2002: 13–18.

Hetherington, Mavis, and John Kelly. *For Better or For Worse: Divorce Reconsidered.* New York: W. W. Norton, 2003.

Hewitt Associates. *Worklife Benefits Provided by Major U.S. Employers, 2003–2004.* Lincolnshire, Ill.: Hewitt Associates, 2004.

Higginbotham, Elizabeth, and Lynn Weber. "Moving with Kin and Community: Upward Social Mobility for Black and White Women." *Gender and Society, 6,* 3, September 1992:416–440.

Hill, Andrew J. "Motivation for Eating Behaviour in Adolescent Girls: The Body Beautiful." *Proceedings of the Nutrition Society, 65,* 2006:376–384.

Hill, Mark E. "Skin Color and the Perception of Attractiveness Among African Americans: Does Gender Make a Difference?" *Social Psychology Quarterly, 65,* 1, 2002:77–91.

Hilliard, Asa, III. "Do We Have the *Will* to Educate All Children?" *Educational Leadership, 49,* September 1991:31–36.

Hiltz, Starr Roxanne. "Widowhood." In *Marriage and Family in a Changing Society,* 3rd ed., James M. Henslin, ed. New York: Free Press, 1989:521–531.

Hippler, Fritz. Interview in a television documentary with Bill Moyers in *Propaganda,* in the series "Walk Through the 20th Century," 1987.

Hirschi, Travis. *Causes of Delinquency.* Berkeley: University of California Press, 1969.

Historical Statistics of the United States: From Colonial Times to the Present. New York: Basic Books, 1976.

Hitt, Jack. "The Next Battlefield May Be in Outer Space." *New York Times,* August 5, 2001.

Hochschild, Arlie. "Feelings around the World." *Contexts, 7,* 2, Spring 2008:80.

Hofferth, Sandra. "Did Welfare Reform Work? Implications for 2002 and Beyond." *Contexts,* Spring 2002:45–51.

Holder, Kelly. "Voting and Registration in the Election of November 2004." *Current Population Reports,* March 2006.

Holmwood, John. "Sociology as Public Discourse and Professional Practice: A Critique of Michael Burawoy." *Sociological Theory, 25,* 1, March 2007:46–66.

Holtzman, Abraham. *The Townsend Movement: A Political Study.* New York: Bookman, 1963.

Homblin, Dora Jane. *The First Cities.* Boston: Little, Brown, Time-Life Books, 1973.

Honeycutt, Karen. "Disgusting, Pathetic, Bizarrely Beautiful: Representations of Weight in Popular Culture." Paper presented at the 1995 meetings of the American Sociological Association.

Hong, Lawrence. "Marriage in China." In *Til Death Do Us Part: A Multicultural Anthology on Marriage,* Sandra Lee Browning and R. Robin Miller, eds. Stamford, Conn.: JAI Press, 1999.

hooks, bell. *Where We Stand: Class Matters.* New York: Routledge, 2000.

Hookway, James. "In Thailand, Insulting the King Can Mean 15 Years in Jail." *Wall Street Journal,* October 16, 2008.

Horn, James P. *Land As God Made It: Jamestown and the Birth of America.* New York: Basic Books, 2006.

Horowitz, Donald L. *The Deadly Ethnic Riot.* Berkeley: University of California Press, 2001.

Horowitz, Ruth. *Honor and the American Dream: Culture and Identity in a Chicano Community.* New Brunswick, N.J.: Rutgers University Press, 1983.

Horowitz, Ruth. "Studying Violence Among the 'Lions.' " In James M. Henslin, *Social Problems.* Upper Saddle River, New Jersey: Prentice Hall, 2005:135.

Horwitz, Allan V., and Jerome C. Wakefield. *The Loss of Sadness: How Psychiatry Transformed Normal Sorrow into Depressive Disorder.* New York: Oxford University Press, 2007.

Hostetler, John A. *Amish Society,* 3rd ed. Baltimore: Johns Hopkins University Press, 1980.

Hotz, Robert Lee. "Most Science Studies Appear to Be Tainted by Sloppy Analysis." *Wall Street Journal,* September 14, 2007.

Hougham, Victoria. "Sociological Skills Used in the Capture of Saddam Hussein." *Footnotes,* July–August 2005.

"House Divided." *People Weekly,* May 24, 1999:126.

Hout, Michael. "How Class Works: Objective and Subjective Aspects of Class Since the 1970s." In *Social Class: How Does It Work?* Annette Lareau and Dalton Conley, eds. New York: Russell Sage, 2008:52–64.

Houtman, Dick. "What Exactly Is a 'Social Class'?: On the Economic Liberalism and Cultural Conservatism of the 'Working Class'." Paper presented at the 1995 meetings of the American Sociological Association.

Howe, Henry, John Lyne, Alan Gross, Harro VanLente, Aire Rip, Richard Lewontin, Daniel McShea, Greg Myers, Ullica Segerstrale, Herbert W. Simons, and V. B. Smocovitis. "Gene Talk in Sociobiology." *Social Epistemology, 6,* 2, April-June 1992:109–163.

Howells, Lloyd T., and Selwyn W. Becker. "Seating Arrangement and Leadership Emergence." *Journal of Abnormal and Social Psychology, 64,* February 1962:148–150.

Hoyt, Homer. "Recent Distortions of the Classical Models of Urban Structure." In *Internal Structure of the City: Readings on Space and Environment,* Larry S. Bourne, ed. New York: Oxford University Press, 1971:84–96.

Hoyt, Homer. *The Structure and Growth of Residential Neighborhoods in American Cities.* Washington, D.C.: Federal Housing Administration, 1939.

Hsu, Francis L. K. *The Challenge of the American Dream: The Chinese in the United States.* Belmont, Calif.: Wadsworth, 1971.

Huber, Joan. "Micro-Macro Links in Gender Stratification." *American Sociological Review, 55,* February 1990:1–10.

Huddle, Donald. "The Net National Cost of Immigration." Washington, D.C.: Carrying Capacity Network, 1993.

Hudson, Valerie M., and Andrea M. den Boer. *Bare Branches: The Security Implications of Asia's Surplus Male Population.* Cambridge, Mass.: MIT Press, 2004.

Huffstutter, P. J. "God Is Everywhere on the Net." *Los Angeles Times,* December 14, 1998.

Huggins, Martha K. "Moral Universes of Brazilian Torturers." Lecture, April 11, 2004.

Huggins, Martha K., and Sandra Rodrigues. "Kids Working on Paulista Avenue." *Childhood, 11,* 2004:495–514.

Huggins, Martha K., Mika Haritos-Fatouros, and Philip G. Zimbardo. *Violence Workers: Police Torturers and Murderers Reconstruct Brazilian Atrocities.* Berkeley: University of California Press, 2002.

Hughes, Everett C. "Good People and Dirty Work." In *Life in Society: Readings to Accompany Sociology: A Down-to-Earth Approach, Seventh Edition,* James M. Henslin, ed. Boston: Allyn and Bacon, 2005: 125–134. Article originally published in 1962.

Hughes, Everett C. "Good People and Dirty Work." *Social Problems, 10,* 1, Summer 1962:3–11. Reprinted in *Society: Readings to Accompany Sociology: A Down-to-Earth Approach, Core Concepts,* James M. Henslin, ed. Boston: Allyn and Bacon, 2006:154–163.

Hughes, H. Stuart. *Oswald Spengler: A Critical Estimate,* rev. ed. New York: Scribner's, 1962.

Hughes, Kathleen A. "Even Tiki Torches Don't Guarantee a Perfect Wedding." *Wall Street Journal,* February 20, 1990:A1, A16.

Hummer, Robert A., Christopher G. Ellison, Richard G. Rogers, Benjamin E. Moulton, and Ron R. Romero. "Religious Involvement and Adult Mortality in the United States: Review and Perspective." *Southern Medical Journal, 97,* 2004:1223–1230.

Hummer, Robert A., Richard G. Rogers, Charles B. Nam, and Christopher G. Ellison. "Religious Involvement and U.S. Adult Mortality." *Demography, 36,* 1999:273–285.

Humphreys, Laud. "Impersonal Sex and Perceived Satisfaction." In *Studies in the Sociology of Sex,* James M. Henslin, ed. New York: Appleton-Century-Crofts, 1971:351–374.

Humphreys, Laud. *Tearoom Trade: Impersonal Sex in Public Places,* enlarged ed. Chicago: Aldine, 1975. Originally published 1970.

Hundley, Greg. "Why Women Earn Less Than Men in Self-Employment." *Journal of Labor Research, 22,* 4, Fall 2001:817–827.

Hunt, Stephen. *The Life Course: A Sociological Introduction.* London: Palgrave Macmillan, 2005.

Hurtado, Aída, David E. Hayes-Bautista, R. Burciaga Valdez, and Anthony C. R. Hernández. *Redefining California: Latino Social Engagement in a Multicultural Society.* Los Angeles: UCLA Chicano Studies Research Center, 1992.

Hutchinson, Earl Ofari. "The Latino Challenge to Black America." *Washington Post,* January 11, 2008.

Huttenbach, Henry R. "The Roman *Porajmos:* The Nazi Genocide of Europe's Gypsies." *Nationalities Papers, 19,* 3, Winter 1991:373–394.

Hutton, Will. *The Writing on the Wall: Why We Must Embrace China as a Partner or Face It as an Enemy.* New York: The Free Press, 2007.

Hutzler, Charles. "Yuppies in China Protest Via the Web—And Get Away With It." *Wall Street Journal,* March 19, 2004.

Hylton, Hillary. "Turning Up the Heat on Polygamists." *Time,* July 24, 2008.

Hymowitz, Carol. "Managers Find Ways to Get Generations to Close Culture Gaps." *Wall Street Journal,* July 9, 2007.

Hymowitz, Carol. "Raising Women to Be Leaders." *Wall Street Journal,* February 12, 2007.

Hymowitz, Carol. "Through the Glass Ceiling." *Wall Street Journal,* November 8, 2004.

Hyra, Derek S. "Racial Uplift? Intra-Racial Class Conflict and the Economic Revitalization of Harlem and Bronzeville." *City and Community, 5,* 1, March 2006:71–92.

"In Perspective: America's Conflicts." *New York Times,* April 20, 2003:B16.

Iori, Ron. "The Good, the Bad and the Useless." *Wall Street Journal,* June 10, 1988:18R.

Ismail, M. Asif. "The Clinton Top 100: Where Are They Now?" Washington, D.C.: The Center for Public Integrity, 2003.

"It's So Much Nicer on K Street." The *New York Times,* June 8, 2008.

Itard, Jean Marc Gospard. *The Wild Boy of Aveyron.* Translated by George and Muriel Humphrey. New York: Appleton-Century-Crofts, 1962.

Jacobs, Andrew. "One-Child Policy Lifted for Quake Victims' Parents." *New York Times,* May 27, 2008.

Jacobs, David, Zhenchao Qian, Jason T. Carmichael, and Stephanie L. Kent. "Who Survives on Death Row? An Individual and Contextual Analysis." *American Sociological Review, 72,* August 2007:610–632.

Jacobs, Janet. "Abuse in New Religious Movements: Challenges for the Sociology of Religion." In *Teaching New Religious Movements,* David G. Bromley, ed. New York: Oxford University Press, 2007:231–244.

Jacobs, Jerry A. "Detours on the Road to Equality: Women, Work and Higher Education." *Contexts,* Winter 2003:32–41.

Jaffee, Sara, and Janet Shibley Hyde. "Gender Differences in Moral Orientation: A Meta-Analysis." *Psychological Bulletin, 126,* 5, 2000:703–726.

Jaffrelot, Christophe. "The Impact of Affirmative Action in India: More Political than Socioeconomic." *India Review, 5,* 2, April 2006:173–189.

Jaggar, Alison M. "Sexual Difference and Sexual Equality." In *Theoretical Perspectives on Sexual Difference,* Deborah L. Rhode, ed. New Haven, Conn.: Yale University Press, 1990:239–254.

James, Randy. "Chinese Internet Censorship." *Time,* March 18, 2009.

Janis, Irving L. *Victims of Groupthink.* Boston, Mass.: Houghton Mifflin, 1972.

Janis, Irving. L. *Groupthink: Psychological Studies of Policy Decisions and Fiascoes.* Boston: Houghton Mifflin, 1982.

Jankowiak, William R., and Edward F. Fischer. "A Cross-Cultural Perspective on Romantic Love." *Journal of Ethnology, 31,* 2, April 1992:149–155.

Jansz, Jeroen, and Raynel G. Martis. "The Lara Phenomenon: Powerful Female Characters in Video Games." *Sex Roles, 56,* 2007:141–148.

Jashik, Scott. "The SAT's Growing Gaps." *Inside Higher Ed,* August 27, 2008.

Jasper, James M. "Moral Dimensions of Social Movements." Paper presented at the annual meetings of the American Sociological Association, 1991.

Jasper, James M. "Social Movements." In *Blackwell Encyclopedia of Sociology,* George Ritzer, ed. Malden, MA: Blackwell, January 2007:4443–4451.

Jenkins, Philip. "The Next Christianity." *Atlantic Monthly,* October 2002:53–68.

Jeong, Yu-Jin, and Hyun-Kyung You. "Different Historical Trajectories and Family Diversity Among Chinese, Japanese, and Koreans in the United States." *Journal of Family History, 33,* 3, July 2008:346–356.

Jerrome, Dorothy. *Good Company: An Anthropological Study of Old People in Groups.* Edinburgh, England: Edinburgh University Press, 1992.

Jneid, Hani, Gregg C. Fonarow, Christopher P. Cannon, et al. "Sex Differences in Medical Care and Early Death After Acute Myocardial Infarction." *Circulation,* December 8, 2008.

Johansson, Perry. "Consuming the Other: The Fetish of the Western Woman in Chinese Advertising and Popular Culture." *Postcolonial Studies, 2,* 3, November 1999.

Johnson, Benton, "On Church and Sect." *American Sociological Review, 28,* 1963:539–549.

Johnson, Carrie. "Medical Fraud a Growing Problem." *Washington Post,* June 13, 2008.

Johnson, Gail. "Time to Broaden Diversity." *Training, 41,* 19, September 2004, 16.

Johnson, Johna Till. "The Costs and Benefits of Remote Workers." *Network World,* December 20, 2004:24.

Johnson, Norris R. "Panic at 'The Who Concert Stampede': An Empirical Assessment." In *Collective Behavior and Social Movements,* Russell L. Curtis, Jr., and Benigno E. Aguirre, eds. Boston: Allyn and Bacon, 1993:113–122.

Johnson-Weiner, Karen. *Train Up a Child: Old Order Amish and Mennonite Schools.* Baltimore: Johns Hopkins University Press, 2007.

Johnston, David Cay. "Is Live Sex On-Demand Coming to Hotel TVs?" *New York Times,* January 17, 2007.

Johnston, David, and Scott Shane. "Memo Sheds New Light on Torture Issue." *New York Times,* April 3, 2008

Johnston, Drue M., and Norris R. Johnson. "Role Extension in Disaster: Employee Behavior at the Beverly Hills Supper Club Fire." *Sociological Focus, 22,* 1, February 1989:39–51.

Johnston, Lloyd D., Patrick M. O'Malley, Jerald G. Bachman, and John E. Schulenberg. *Monitoring the Future: National Survey results on drug use, 1975–2007:* Volume II, College students and adults ages 19–45. Bethesda, MD: National Institute on Drug Abuse, 2008b.

Johnston, Lloyd D., Patrick M. O'Malley, Jerald G. Bachman, and John E. Schulenberg. "Various stimulant drugs show continuing gradual declines among teens in 2008, most illicit drugs hold steady." University of Michigan News Service, 2008a.

Johnston, Lloyd. D., Patrick M. O'Malley, Jerald J. Bachman, and John E. Schulenberg. *Monitoring the Future, National Results on Adolescent Drug Use: Overview of Key Findings, 2006.* Bethesda, MD: National Institute on Drug Abuse, May 2007.

Johnston, Lloyd. D., Patrick M. O'Malley, Jerald J. Bachman, and John E. Schulenberg. *Monitoring the Future, National Survey Results on Drug Use, 1975–2005, Volume II, College Students and Adults, Ages 19–45.* Bethesda, MD: National Institute on Drug Abuse, 2006.

Jones, Allen. "Let Nonviolent Prisoners Out." *Los Angeles Times,* June 12, 2008.

Jones, Dale E., et al. "Religious Congregations and Membership in the United States 2000: An Enumeration by Region, State and County. Based on Data Reported by 149 Religious Bodies." Nashville, Tenn.: Glenmary Research Center, 2002.

Jones, James H. *Bad Blood: The Tuskegee Syphilis Experiment,* 2nd ed. New York: Free Press, 1993.

Jordan, Miriam. "Among Poor Villagers, Female Infanticide Still Flourishes in India." *Wall Street Journal,* May 9, 2000:A1, A12.

Josephson, Matthew. "The Robber Barons." In *John D. Rockefeller: Robber Baron or Industrial Statesman?,* Earl Latham, ed. Boston: Heath, 1949:34–48.

"Judge Rules Against Ford in Discrimination Lawsuit." *New York Times,* March 17, 2005.

Judge, Timothy A., and Daniel M. Cable. "The Effect of Physical Height on Workplace Success and Income: Preliminary Test of a Theoretical Model." *Journal of Applied Psychology, 89,* 3, 2004:428–441.

Juergensmeyer, Mark. *Terror in the Mind of God: The Global Rise of Religious Violence.* Berkeley: University of California Press, 2000.

Kaebnick, Gregory E. "On the Sanctity of Nature." *Hastings Center Report, 30,* 5, September-October 2000:16–23.

Kagan, Jerome. "The Idea of Emotions in Human Development." In *Emotions, Cognition, and Behavior,* Carroll E. Izard, Jerome Kagan, and Robert B. Zajonc, eds. New York: Cambridge University Press, 1984:38–72.

Kageyama, Yuri. "Mazda Profit Up on Sold Vehicle Sales Growth." Associated Press, July 31, 2008.

Kahn, Joseph. "China Shows Assertiveness in Weapons Test." *New York Times,* January 20, 2007a.

Kahn, Joseph. "China's Elite Learn to Flaunt It While the New Landless Weep." *New York Times,* December 25, 2004.

Kahn, Joseph. "In China, a Lake's Champion Imperils Himself." *New York Times,* October 14, 2007c.

Kahn, Joseph. "Thousands Reportedly Riot in China." *International Herald-Tribune,* March 13, 2007b.

Kahn, Waheed. "Rescued Gulf Camel Jockeys Become Misfits in Pakistan." Reuters, February 19, 2007.

Kalb, Claudia. "Faith and Healing." *Newsweek,* November 10, 2003:44–56.

Kalberg, Stephen. *Introduction to Max Weber, The Protestant Ethic and the Spirit of Capitalism,* 3rd ed. Los Angeles: Roxbury Publishing, 2002.

Kanazawa, Satoshi, and Jody L. Kovar. "Why Beautiful People Are More Intelligent." *Intelligence, 32,* 2004:227–243.

Kane, Yukariitwatani, and Phred Dvorak. "Howard Stringer, Japanese CEO." *Wall Street Journal,* March 3, 2007.

Kanter, James, and Andrew C. Revkin. "Scientists Detail Climate Changes, Poles to Tropics." *New York Times,* April 7, 2007.

Kanter, Rosabeth Moss. *The Change Masters: Innovation and Entrepreneurship in the American Corporation.* New York: Simon & Schuster, 1983.

Kanter, Rosabeth Moss. *Men and Women of the Corporation.* New York: Basic Books, 1977.

Kantor, Jodi. "In First Family, a Nation's Many Faces." *New York Times,* January 16, 2009.

Kantor, Jodi. "On the Job, Nursing Mothers Find a 2-Class System." *New York Times,* September 1, 2006.

Kaplan, Robert D. "A Tale of Two Colonies." *Atlantic Monthly,* April 2003.

Karamouzis, Stamos T., and Dee Wood Harper. "An Artificial Intelligence System Suggests Arbitrariness of Death Penalty." *International Journal of Law and Information Technology, 16,* 1:2007.

Karp, David A., Gregory P. Stone, and William C. Yoels. *Being Urban: A Sociology of City Life,* 2nd ed. New York: Praeger, 1991.

Katz, Bruce, and Jennifer Bradley. "The Suburban Challenge." *Newsweek,* January 26, 2009.

Katz, Richard S. "Electoral Reform in Italy: Expectations and Results." *Acta Politica, 41,* 2006:285–299.

Katz, Sidney. "The Importance of Being Beautiful." In *Down to Earth Sociology: Introductory Readings,* 14th ed., James M. Henslin, ed. New York: The Free Press, 2007.

Kaufman, Joanne. "Married Maidens and Dilatory Domiciles." *Wall Street Journal,* May 7, 1996:A16.

Kaufman, Jonathan, and Carol Hymowitz. "At the Barricades in the Gender Wars." *Wall Street Journal,* March 29, 2008.

Kaufman, Jonathan, and Gary Fields. "Election of Obama Recasts National Conversation on Race." *Wall Street Journal,* November 10, 2008.

Kaufman, Leslie. "Bloomberg Seeks New Way to Decide Who Is Poor." *New York Times,* December 20, 2007.

Keates, Nancy. "Alternative Care Crops Up At 'Traditional' Hospitals." *Wall Street Journal,* March 28, 2003.

Kefalas, Maria. "Looking for the Lower Middle Class." *City and Community, 6,* 1, March 2007:63–68.

Keith, Jennie. *Old People, New Lives: Community Creation in a Retirement Residence,* 2nd ed. Chicago: University of Chicago Press, 1982.

Kelley, Tina. "In an Era of School Shootings, a New Drill." *New York Times,* March 25, 2008.

Kelly, Joan B. "How Adults React to Divorce." In *Marriage and Family in a Changing Society,* 4th ed., James M. Henslin, ed. New York: Free Press, 1992:410–423.

Kenchaiah, Satish, et. al. "Obesity and the Risk of Heart Failure." *New England Journal of Medicine, 347,* August 1, 2002:305–313.

Keniston, Kenneth. *Youth and Dissent: The Rise of a New Opposition.* New York: Harcourt, Brace, Jovanovich, 1971.

Kent, Mary, and Robert Lalasz. "In the News: Speaking English in the United States." Population Reference Bureau, January 18, 2007.

Kephart, William M., and William W. Zellner. *Extraordinary Groups: An Examination of Unconventional Life-Styles,* 7th ed. New York: Worth Publishing, 2001.

Kerr, Clark. *The Future of Industrialized Societies.* Cambridge, Mass.: Harvard University Press, 1983.

Kershaw, Sarah. "New York City Puts Hospital Error Data Online." *New York Times,* September 7, 2007.

Kerswill, Paul. "Socio-economic Class." In *The Routledge Companion to Sociolinguistics,* Carmen Llamas and Peter Stockwell, eds. London: Routledge, 2006.

Khattak, Mizuko Ito. "Anime's 'Transnational Geekdom.'" UCLA's Asia Institute, January 23, 2007.

Kibria, Nazli. *Family Tightrope: The Changing Lives of Vietnamese Americans.* Princeton, N.J.: Princeton University Press, 1993.

Kifner, John. "Building Modernity on Desert Mirages." *New York Times,* February 7, 1999.

Kilbourne, Jean. "Beauty and the Beast of Advertising." In *Down to Earth Sociology: Introductory Readings,* 12th ed., James M. Henslin, ed. New York: The Free Press, 2003:421–424.

Kim, Richard. "The L Word." *The Nation,* October 19, 2004.

Kingsbury, Alex, "Many Colleges Reject Women at Higher Rates Than for Men." *U.S. News & World Report,* June 17, 2007.

Kingsnorth, Rodney F., and Randall MacIntosh. "Intimate Partner Violence: The Role of Suspect Gender in Prosecutorial Decision-Making." *Justice Quarterly, 24,* 3, 2007:460–495.

Kingston, Maxine Hong. *The Woman Warrior.* New York: Vintage Books, 1975:108. Quoted in Frank J. Zulke and Jacqueline P. Kirley. *Through the Eyes of Social Science,* 6th ed. Prospect Heights, Ill.: Waveland Press, 2002.

Kinsella, Kevin, and David R. Phillips. "Global Aging: The Challenge of Success." Washington, D.C.: Population Reference Bureau, 2005.

Klahanie Association Web site. February 19, 2009, http://www.klahanie.com/

Klandermans, Bert. *The Social Psychology of Protest.* Cambridge, Mass.: Blackwell, 1997.

Kleinfeld, Judith S. "Gender and Myth: Data about Student Performance." In *Through the Eyes of Social Science,* 6th ed., Frank J. Zulke and Jacqueline P. Kirley, eds. Prospect Heights, Ill.: Waveland Press, 2002a:380–393.

Kleinfeld, Judith S. "The Small World Problem." *Society,* January–February, 2002b:61–66.

Kluegel, James R., and Eliot R. Smith. *Beliefs About Inequality: America's Views of What Is and What Ought to Be.* Hawthorne, N.Y.: Aldine de Gruyter, 1986.

Knapp, Daniel. "What Happened When I Took My Sociological Imagination to the Dump." *Footnotes,* May–June, 2005:4.

Knauth, Donna G. "Predictors of Parental Sense of Competence for the Couple During the Transition to Parenthood." *Research in Nursing and Health, 23,* 2000:496–509.

Knickerbocker, Brad. "Firebrands of 'Ecoterrorism' Set Sights on Urban Sprawl." *Christian Science Monitor,* August 6, 2003.

Kochbar, Rakesh, and Ana Gonzalez-Barrera. "Through Boom and Bust: Minorities, Immigrants and Homeownership." Washington, D.C.: Pew Hispanic Center, May 12, 2009.

Kohlberg, Lawrence. "A Current Statement on Some Theoretical Issues." In *Lawrence Kohlberg: Consensus and Controversy,* Sohan Modgil and Celia Modgil, eds. Philadelphia: Falmer Press, 1986:485–546.

Kohlberg, Lawrence. "Moral Education for a Society in Moral Transition." *Educational Leadership, 33,* 1975:46–54.

Kohlberg, Lawrence. *The Psychology of Moral Development: Moral Stages and the Life Cycle.* San Francisco: Harper and Row, 1984.

Kohlberg, Lawrence, and Carol Gilligan. "The Adolescent as a Philosopher: The Discovery of the Self in a Postconventional World." *Daedalus, 100,* 1971:1051–1086.

Kohn, Alfie. "Make Love, Not War." *Psychology Today,* June 1988:35–38.

Kohn, Melvin L. *Class and Conformity: A Study in Values,* 2nd ed. Homewood, Ill.: Dorsey Press, 1977.

Kohn, Melvin L. "Occupational Structure and Alienation." *American Journal of Sociology, 82,* 1976:111–130.

Kohn, Melvin L. "Social Class and Parental Values." *American Journal of Sociology, 64,* 1959:337–351.

Kohn, Melvin L. "Social Class and Parent-Child Relationships: An Interpretation." *American Journal of Sociology, 68,* 1963:471–480.

Kohn, Melvin L., and Carmi Schooler. "Class, Occupation, and Orientation." *American Sociological Review, 34,* 1969:659–678.

Kohn, Melvin L., Kazimierz M. Slomczynski, and Carrie Schoenbach. "Social Stratification and the Transmission of Values in the Family: A Cross-National Assessment." *Sociological Forum, 1,* 1, 1986:73–102.

Kolata, Gina. "The Genesis of an Epidemic: Humans, Chimps and a Virus." *New York Times,* September 4, 2001.

Kontos, Louis, David Brotherton, and Luis Barrios, eds. *Gangs and Society: Alternative Perspectives.* New York: Columbia University Press, 2003.

Kornhauser, William. *The Politics of Mass Society.* New York: Free Press, 1959.

Koropeckyj-Cox, Tanya. "Attitudes About Childlessness in the United States." *Journal of Family Issues, 28,* 8, August 2007:1054–1082.

Kraft, Dina. "African AIDS Fight Uses Israeli Circumcision Skills." *The Jewish Journal,* November 26, 2008.

Kramer, Andrew E. "Putin's Grasp of Energy Drives Russian Agenda." *New York Times,* January 29, 2009.

Krane, Vikki, Julie A. Stiles-Shipley, Jennifer Waldron, and Jennifer Michalenok. "Relationships Among Body Satisfaction, Social Physique Anxiety, and Eating Behaviors in Female Athletes and Exercisers." *Journal of Sport Behavior, 24,* 3, September 2001:247–264.

Krause, Neal, and Christopher G. Ellison. "Forgiveness by God, Forgiveness of Others, and Psychological Well-Being in Late Life." *Journal for the Scientific Study of Religion, 42,* 1, 2003:77–93.

Kraybill, Donald B. *The Riddle of Amish Culture.* Revised edition. Baltimore, Md.: Johns Hopkins University Press, 2002.

Kristensen, Peer Hull, and Glenn Morgan. "Multinationals: Institutionalizing Agents and Institutionalized Agency." Copenhagen: International Center for Business and Politics, Working Paper 30, 2006.

Kristoff, Nicholas D. "Interview With a Humanoid." *New York Times,* July 23, 2002.

Kroeger, Brooke. "When a Dissertation Makes a Difference." *New York Times,* March 20, 2004.

Krueger, Alan B. "The Apple Falls Close to the Tree, Even in the Land of Opportunity." *New York Times,* November 14, 2002.

Krugman, Paul. "White Man's Burden." *New York Times,* September 24, 2002.

Kübler-Ross, Elisabeth. *Living with Death and Dying.* New York: Macmillan, 1981.

Kübler-Ross, Elisabeth. *On Death and Dying.* New York: Macmillan, 1969. 40th anniversary edition published by Routledge in 2008.

Kubrin, Charis E., and Ronald Weitzer. "Retaliatory Homicide: Concentrated Disadvantage and Neighborhood Culture." *Social Problems, 50,* 2, May 2003:157–180.

Kuhn, Margaret E. "The Gray Panthers." In *Social Problems,* 2nd ed., James M. Henslin, Englewood Cliffs, N.J.: Prentice Hall, 1990:56–57.

Kurian, George Thomas. *Encyclopedia of the First World,* Vols. 1, 2. New York: Facts on File, 1990.

Kurian, George Thomas. *Encyclopedia of the Second World.* New York: Facts on File, 1991.

Kurian, George Thomas. *Encyclopedia of the Third World,* Vols. 1, 2, 3. New York: Facts on File, 1992.

Kurlantzick, Josh. "China's Future: A Nation of Single Men?" *Los Angeles Times,* October 21, 2007.

La Barre, Weston. *The Human Animal.* Chicago: University of Chicago Press, 1954.

Lacey, Marc. "Tijuana Journal: Cities Mesh Across Blurry Border, Despite Physical Barrier. *New York Times,* March 5, 2007.

Lacy, Karyn R. *Blue-Chip Black: Class and Status in the New Black Middle Class.* Berkeley, Calif.: University of California Press, 2007.

Lacy, Karyn R., and Angel L. Harris. "Breaking the Class Monolith: Understanding Class Differences in Black Adolescents' Attachment to Racial Identity." In *Social Class: How Does It Work?* Annette Lareau and Dalton Conley, eds. New York: Russell Sage, 2008:152–178.

LaFraniere, Sharon. "Africa's World of Forced Labor, in a 6-Year-Old's Eyes." *New York Times,* October 29, 2006.

LaFraniere, Sharon. "African Crucible: Cast as Witches, Then Cast Out." *New York Times,* November 15, 2007.

LaFraniere, Sharon. "Health Workers Race to Block Deadly Virus in Angolan Town." *New York Times,* April 11, 2005.

Lagnado, Lucette. "Home Remedy." *Wall Street Journal,* June 24, 2008.

Lagnado, Lucette. "'Grandfamilies' Come Under Pressure." *Wall Street Journal,* April 4, 2009.

LaHart, Justin, Patrick Barta, and Andrew Batson. "New Limits to Growth Revive Malthusian Fears." *Wall Street Journal,* March 24, 2008.

Lambert, Bruce. "Manufacturer in $2 Million Accord With U.S. on Deficient Kevlar in Military Helmets." *Wall Street Journal,* February 6, 2008.

Lamptey, Peter R., Jami L. Johnson, and Marya Khan. "The Global Challenge of HIV and AIDS." *Population Bulletin, 61,* 1, March 2006:1–24.

Landry, Brett J. L., Sathi Mahesh, and Sandra Hartman. "The Changing Nature of Work in the Age of E-Business." *Journal of Organizational Change Management, 18,* 2, 2005:132–144.

Landtman, Gunnar. *The Origin of the Inequality of the Social Classes.* New York: Greenwood Press, 1968. First published in 1938.

Lang, Kurt, and Gladys E. Lang. *Collective Dynamics.* New York: Crowell, 1961.

Lareau, Annette. "Invisible Inequality: Social Class and Childrearing in Black Families and White Families." *American Sociological Review, 67,* October 2002:747–776.

Lareau, Annette, and Dalton Conley, eds. *Social Class: How Does It Work?* New York: Russell Sage, 2008.

Lareau, Annette, and Elliot B. Weininger. "Class and the Transition to Adulthood." In *Social Class: How Does It Work?* Annette Lareau and Dalton Conley, eds. New York: Russell Sage, 2008:118–151.

Larson, Mary Strom. "Interactions, Activities and Gender in Children's Television Commercials: A Content Analysis." *Journal of Broadcasting and Electronic Media, 45,* Winter 2001:41–51.

Laszewski, Chuck. "The Sociologists' Take on the Environment." *Contexts, 7,* 2, Spring 2008:20–24.

Lauer, Jeanette, and Robert Lauer. "Marriages Made to Last." In *Marriage and Family in a Changing Society,* 4th ed., James M. Henslin, ed. New York: Free Press, 1992:481–486.

Laumann, E. O., S. A. Leitsch, and L. J. Waite. "Elder Mistreatment in the United States: Prevalence Estimates from a Nationally Representative Study." *The Journals of Gerontology, 63,* 4, July 2008:S248–S254.

Lawler, Steph. " 'Getting Out and Getting Away': Women's Narratives of Class Mobility." *Feminist Review,* 63, Autumn 1999:3–24.

Lazarsfeld, Paul F., and Jeffrey G. Reitz. "History of Applied Sociology." *Sociological Practice, 7,* 1989:43–52.

Leacock, Eleanor. *Myths of Male Dominance.* New York: Monthly Review Press, 1981.

LeBon, Gustave. *Psychologie des Foules (The Psychology of the Crowd).* Paris: Alcan, 1895. Various editions in English.

LeDuff, Charlie. "Handling the Meltdowns of the Nuclear Family." *New York Times,* May 28, 2003.

Lee, Alfred McClung, and Elizabeth Briant Lee. *The Fine Art of Propaganda: A Study of Father Coughlin's Speeches.* New York: Harcourt Brace, 1939.

Lee, Raymond M. *Unobtrusive Methods in Social Research.* Philadelphia: Open University Press, 2000.

Lee, Sharon M. "Asian Americans: Diverse and Growing." *Population Bulletin, 53,* 2, June 1998:1–39.

Leeson, Peter T. "Cooperation and Conflict: Evidence on Self-enforcing Arrangements and Heterogeneous Groups." *American Journal of Economics and Sociology,* October 2006.

Leland, John. "A New Harlem Gentry in Search of Its Latte." *New York Times,* August 7, 2003.

Leland, John, and Gregory Beals. "In Living Colors." *Newsweek,* May 5, 1997:58–60.

Lemann, Nicholas, "The Myth of Community Development." *New York Times Magazine,* January 9, 1994, p. 27.

Lengermann, Madoo, and Gillian Niebrugge. *The Women Founders: Sociology and Social Theory, 1830–1930.* Prospect Heights, Illinois: Waveland Press, 2007.

Lenski, Gerhard. *Power and Privilege: A Theory of Social Stratification.* New York: McGraw-Hill, 1966.

Lenski, Gerhard. "Status Crystallization: A Nonvertical Dimension of Social Status." *American Sociological Review, 19,* 1954:405–413.

Lenski, Gerhard, and Jean Lenski. *Human Societies: An Introduction to Macrosociology,* 5th ed. New York: McGraw-Hill, 1987.

Leo, Jen. "Google's Space Explorer Sergey Brin." *Los Angeles Times,* June 12, 2008.

Lerner, Gerda. *Black Women in White America: A Documentary History.* New York: Pantheon Books, 1972.

Lerner, Gerda. *The Creation of Patriarchy.* New York: Oxford, 1986.

"Lesbian and Gay Parenting." Washington, D.C.: American Psychological Association, 2005.

"Less Rote, More Variety: Reforming Japan's Schools." *The Economist,* December 16, 2000:8.

Lesser, Alexander. "War and the State." In *War: The Anthropology of Armed Conflict and Aggression,* Morton Fried, Marvin Harris, and Robert Murphy, eds. Garden City, N. Y.: Natural History, 1968:92–96.

Letherby, Gayle. "Childless and Bereft? Stereotypes and Realities in Relation to 'Voluntary' and 'Involuntary' Childlessness and Womanhood." *Sociological Inquiry, 72,* 1, Winter 2002:7–20.

Letiecq, Bethany, Sandra J. Bailey, and Marcia A. Kurtz. "Depression Among Rural Native American and European American Grandparents Rearing Their Grandchildren." *Journal of Family Issues, 29,* 3, March 2008:334–356.

Levi, Ken. "Becoming a Hit Man." In *Exploring Social Life: Readings to Accompany Essentials of Sociology, A Down-to-Earth Approach,* 8th ed., 4th ed, James M. Henslin, ed. Boston: Allyn and Bacon, 2009. Originally published 1981.

Levine, Robert. "Planned Gun N' Roses Deal Underscores Power of Video to Sell Songs" *Wall Street Journal,* July 14, 2008.

Levinson, D. J. *The Seasons of a Man's Life.* New York: Knopf, 1978.

Levy, Clifford J. "Doctor Admits He Did Needless Surgery on the Mentally Ill." *New York Times,* May 20, 2003.

Levy, Clifford J., and Michael Luo. "New York Medicaid Fraud May Reach into Billions." *New York Times,* July 18, 2005.

Lewin, Tamar. "Colleges Regroup After Voters Ban Race Preferences." *New York Times,* January 26, 2007.

Lewis, Neil A. "Justice Dept. Toughens Rules on Torture." *New York Times,* January 1, 2005.

Lewis, Oscar. "The Culture of Poverty." *Scientific American, 115,* October 1966a:19–25.

Lewis, Oscar. *La Vida.* New York: Random House, 1966b.

Li, Zheng. "China Faces Elderly Dilemma." *China Daily,* August 21, 2004.

Lichter, Daniel T., and Martha L. Crowley. "Poverty in America: Beyond Welfare Reform." *Population Bulletin, 57,* 2, June 2002:1–36.

Lichter, Daniel T., and Zhenchao Qian. "Serial Cohabitation and the Marital Life Course." *Journal of Marriage and Family, 70,* November 2008:861–878.

Lieberson, Stanley. *A Matter of Taste: How Names, Fashions, and Culture Change.* New Haven: Yale University Press, 2000.

Liebow, Elliott. *Tally's Corner: A Study of Negro Streetcorner Men.* Boston: Little, Brown, 1999. Originally published in 1967.

Liedtke, Michael. "Twitter: Fad or Lasting Business?" Associated Press, February 23, 2009.

Lightfoot-Klein, A. "Rites of Purification and Their Effects: Some Psychological Aspects of Female Genital Circumcision and Infibulation (Pharaonic Circumcision) in an Afro-Arab Society (Sudan)." *Journal of Psychological Human Sexuality, 2,* 1989:61–78.

Lind, Michael. *The Next American Nation: The New Nationalism and the Fourth American Revolution.* New York: Free Press, 1995.

Lindau, Stacy Tessler, L. Philip Schumm, Edward O. Laumann, Wendy Levinson, Colm A. O'Muircheartaigh, and Linda J. Waite. "A Study of Sexuality and Health among Older Adults in the United States." *New England Journal of Medicine, 357,* 8, August 23, 2007:762–774.

Linden, Eugene. "Lost Tribes, Lost Knowledge." *Time,* September 23, 1991:46, 48, 50, 52, 54, 56.

Lines, Patricia M. "Homeschooling Comes of Age." *Public Interest,* Summer 2000:74–85.

Linton, Ralph. *The Study of Man.* New York: Appleton-Century-Crofts, 1936.

Linz, Daniel, Paul Bryant, et al. "An Examination of the Assumption that Adult Businesses Are Associated with Crime in Surrounding Areas: A Secondary Effects Study in Charlotte, North Carolina." *Law & Society, 38,* 1, March 2004:69–104.

Lippitt, Ronald, and Ralph K. White. "An Experimental Study of Leadership and Group Life." In *Readings in Social Psychology,* 3rd ed., Eleanor E. Maccoby, Theodore M. Newcomb, and Eugene L. Hartley, eds. New York: Holt, Rinehart and Winston, 1958:340–365. (As summarized in Olmsted and Hare 1978:28–31.)

Lipset, Seymour Martin. "The Social Requisites of Democracy Revisited." Presidential address to the American Sociological Association, Boston, Massachusetts, 1993.

Liptak, Adam. "Prosecution of Midwife Casts Light on Home Births." *New York Times,* April 3, 2006.

Littleton, Heather, Carmen Radecki Breitkopf and Abbey Berenson. "Women Beyond the Campus: Unacknowledged Rape among Low-Income Women." *Violence Against Women, 14,* 3, March 2008:269–286.

Liu, Haiyong. "Growing Up Poor and Childhood Weight Problems." Institute for Research on Poverty, Discussion Paper. DP 1324-07, April 2007.

Lleras-Muney, Adriana. "The Relationship Between Education and Adult Mortality in the United States." *Review of Economic Studies, 72,* 2005:189–221.

Lofland, John F. *Protest: Studies of Collective Behavior and Social Movements.* New Brunswick, New Jersey: Transaction Books, 1985.

Logue, John, and Jacquelyn Yates. "Modeling an Employee Ownership Sector." *Peace Review, 12,* 2, June 2000:243–249.

Lombroso, Cesare. *Crime: Its Causes and Remedies,* H. P. Horton, trans. Boston: Little, Brown, 1911.

Lopez, Mark Hugo, and Paul Taylor. "Dissecting the 2008 Electorate: Most Diverse in U.S. History." Washington, D.C.: Pew Research Center, April 30, 2009.

Lorber, Judith. *Paradoxes of Gender.* New Haven, Conn.: Yale University Press, 1994.

Lublin, Joann S. "Living Well." *Wall Street Journal,* April 8, 1999.

Lublin, Joann S. "Trying to Increase Worker Productivity, More Employers Alter Management Style." *Wall Street Journal,* February 13, 1991:B1, B7.

Lucas, Samuel Roundfield. *Tracking Inequality: Stratification and Mobility in American High Schools.* New York: Teachers College Press, 1999.

Luke, Timothy W. *Ideology and Soviet Industrialization.* Westport, Conn.: Greenwood Press, 1985.

Lumpkin, James R. "Grandparents in a Parental or Near-Parental Role." *Journal of Family Issues, 29,* 3, March 2008:357–372.

Lurie, Nicole, Jonathan Slater, Paul McGovern, Jacqueline Ekstrum, Lois Quam, and Karen Margolis. "Preventive Care for Women: Does the Sex of the Physician Matter?" *New England Journal of Medicine, 329,* August 12, 1993:478–482.

Lynn, Michael, Michael Sturman, Christie Ganley, Elizabeth Adams, Mathew Douglas, and Jessica McNeil. "Consumer Racial Discrimination in Tipping: A Replication and Extension." *Journal of Applied Social Psychology, 38,* 4, 2008:1045–1060.

Macartney, Jane. "China's Men Lack Millions of Brides." *The Australian,* January 15, 2007.

Macartney, Jane. "A Nation in Search of 30 Million Brides for 30 Million Bachelors." *The Times,* January 13, 2007.

MacDonald, William L., and Alfred DeMaris. "Remarriage, Stepchildren, and Marital Conflict: Challenges to the Incomplete Institutionalization Hypothesis." *Journal of Marriage and the Family, 57,* May 1995:387–398.

MacFarquhar, Neil. "Many Muslims Turn to Home Schooling" *New York Times,* March 26, 2008.

Mack, Raymond W., and Calvin P. Bradford. *Transforming America: Patterns of Social Change,* 2nd ed. New York: Random House, 1979.

Mackay, Charles. *Memories of Extraordinary Popular Delusions and the Madness of Crowds.* London: Office of the National Illustrated Library, 1852.

Madigan, Nick. "Judge Questions Long Sentence in Drug Case." *New York Times,* November 17, 2004.

Mahoney, John S., Jr., and Paul G. Kooistra. "Policing the Races: Structural Factors Enforcing Racial Purity in Virginia (1630–1930)." Paper presented at the 1995 meetings of the American Sociological Association.

Mahoney, Patricia. "High Rape Chronicity and Low Rates of Help-Seeking Among Wife Rape Survivors in a Nonclinical Sample: Implications for Research and Practice." *Violence Against Women, 5,* 9, September 1999:993–1016.

Maier, Mark. "Teaching from Tragedy: An Interdisciplinary Module on the Space Shuttle *Challenger.*" *T. H. E. Journal,* September 1993:91–94.

Main, Jackson Turner. *The Social Structure of Revolutionary America.* Princeton, N.J.: Princeton University Press, 1965.

Maldin, Michael. "A First Look at Money in the House and Senate Elections." Washington, D.C.: The Campaign Finance Institute, November 6, 2008.

Malinowski, Bronislaw. *Sex and Repression in Savage Society.* Cleveland, Ohio: World, 1927.

Malthus, Thomas Robert. *First Essay on Population 1798.* London: Macmillan, 1926. Originally published in 1798.

Mamdani, Mahmood. "The Myth of Population Control: Family, Caste, and Class in an Urban Village." New York: Monthly Review Press, 1973.

Mander, Jerry. *In the Absence of the Sacred: The Failure of Technology and the Survival of the Indian Nations.* San Francisco, Calif.: Sierra Club Books, 1992.

Manheimer, Ronald J. "The Older Learner's Journey to an Ageless Society." *Journal of Transformative Education, 3,* 3, 2005.

Manpower Report to the President. Washington, D.C.: U.S. Department of Labor, Manpower Administration, April 1971.

Manzo, Kathleen Kennedy. "History in the Making." *Community College Week, 13,* 15, March 5, 2001:6–8.

Marcus, Amy Dockser. "Mideast Minorities: Kurds Aren't Alone." *Wall Street Journal,* September 5, 1996:A12.

Mardell, Mark. "Europe in Khaki." *BBC News,* June 14, 2007.

Marino, David. "Border Watch Group 'Techno Patriots' Still Growing." Tucson, Arizona: KVOA News 4, February 14, 2008.

"Marital History for People 15 Years Old and Over by Age, Sex, Race and Ethnicity: 2001." Annual Demographic Survey, Bureau of Labor Statistics and the Bureau of the Census. 2004.

Marolla, Joseph, and Diana Scully. "Attitudes Toward Women, Violence, and Rape: A Comparison of Convicted Rapists and Other Felons." *Deviant Behavior, 7,* 4, 1986:337–355.

Marquardt, Elizabeth. *Between Two Worlds: The Inner Lives of Children of Divorce.* New York: Crown Publishers, 2005.

Marshall, Samantha. "It's So Simple: Just Lather Up, Watch the Fat Go Down the Drain." *Wall Street Journal,* November 2, 1995:B1.

Marshall, Samantha. "Vietnamese Women Are Kidnapped and Later Sold in China as Brides." *Wall Street Journal,* August 3, 1999.

Martin, Joyce A., Brady E. Hamilton, Paul D. Sutton, et al. "Births: Final Data for 2005." *National Vital Statistics Reports, 56,* 6, December 5, 2007.

Martineau, Harriet. *Society in America.* Garden City, N. Y.: Doubleday 1962. First published in 1837.

Martinez, Barbara. "Cash Before Chemo: Hospitals Get Tough." *Wall Street Journal,* April 28, 2008.

Marx, Gary T. "The Road to the Future." In *Triumph of Discovery: A Chronicle of Great Adventures in Science.* New York: Holt, 1995:63–65.

Marx, Gary T. "Thoughts On a Neglected Category of Social Movement Participant: The Agent Provocateur and the Informant." In *Collective Behavior and Social Movements,* Russell L. Curtis, Jr., and Benigno E. Aguirre, eds. Boston: Allyn and Bacon, 1993:242–258.

Marx, Karl, and Friedrich Engels. *Communist Manifesto.* New York: Pantheon, 1967. First published in 1848.

Marx, Karl. "Contribution to the Critique of Hegel's Philosophy of Right." In *Karl Marx: Early Writings,* T. B. Bottomore, ed. New York: McGraw-Hill, 1964:45. First published in 1844.

Masheter, Carol. "Postdivorce Relationships Between Ex-spouses: The Role of Attachment and Interpersonal Conflict." *Journal of Marriage and the Family, 53,* February 1991:103–110.

Massey, Douglas S., and Garvey Lundy. "Use of Black English and Racial Discrimination in Urban Housing Markets: New Methods and Findings." *Urban Affairs Review, 36,* 2001:451–468.

Mathews, Anna Wilde. "Fraud, Errors Taint Key Study of Widely Used Sanofi Drug." *Wall Street Journal,* May 1, 2006.

Mathews, T. J., and Brady E. Hamilton. "Mean Age of Mother, 1970–2000." *National Vital Statistics Report, 51,* 1, December 11, 2002.

Mattioli, Dana. "Ways Women Can Hold Their Own in a Male World." *Wall Street Journal,* November 25, 2008.

Mauss, Armand. *Social Problems as Social Movements.* Philadelphia, Penn.: Lippincott, 1975.

Mayer, Anita P., Julia A. Files, Marcia G. Ko, and Janis E. Blair. "Academic Advancement of Women in Medicine: Do Socialized Gender Differences Have a Role in Mentoring?" *Mayo Clinic Proceedings, 83,* 2, February 2008:204–207.

Mayer, John D. *Personality: A Systems Approach.* Boston: Allyn and Bacon, 2007.

Mayo, Elton. *Human Problems of an Industrial Civilization.* New York: Viking, 1966.

McAdam, Doug, John D. McCarthy, and Mayer N. Zald. "Social Movements." In *Handbook of Sociology,* Neil J. Smelser, ed. Newbury Park, Calif.: Sage, 1988:695–737.

McCabe, J. Terrence, and James E. Ellis. "Pastoralism: Beating the Odds in Arid Africa." In *Conformity and Conflict: Readings in Cultural Anthropology,* James P. Spradley and David W. McCurdy, eds. Glenview, Ill.: Scott, Foresman, 1990:150–156.

McCall, Leslie. "What Does Class Inequality Among Women Look Like? A Comparison with Men and Families, 1970 to 2000." In *Social Class: How Does It Work?* Annette Lareau and Dalton Conley, eds. New York: Russell Sage, 2008:293–325.

McCarthy, John D., and Mayer N. Zald. "Resource Mobilization and Social Movements: A Partial Theory." *American Journal of Sociology, 82,* 6, 1977:1212–1241.

McCarthy, Michael J. "Granbury, Texas, Isn't a Rural Town: It's a 'Micropolis.'" *Wall Street Journal,* June 3, 2004.

McCarthy, Michael J. "James Bond Hits the Supermarket: Stores Snoop on Shoppers' Habits to Boost Sales." *Wall Street Journal,* August 25, 1993:B1, B8.

McCormick, John. "Change Has Taken Place." *Newsweek,* June 7, 1999b:34.

McCormick, John. "The Sorry Side of Sears." *Newsweek,* February 22, 1999:36–39.

McDonald, Michael P. "2008 Current Population Survey Voting and Registration Supplement." George Mason University, Fairfax, Virginia: United States Elections Project, April 6, 2009.

McDowell, Bart. "Mexico City: An Alarming Giant." *National Geographic, 166,* 1984:139–174.

McElroy, Damien. "Russian General Says Poland a Nuclear 'Target.'" *Telegraph,* August 15, 2008.

McFalls, Joseph A., Jr. "Population: A Lively Introduction, 5th ed." *Population Bulletin, 62,* 1, March 2007:1–30.

McGee, Glenn. "Cloning, Sex, and New Kinds of Families." *Journal of Sex Research, 37,* 3, August 2000:266–272.

McGinn, Daniel, and Jason McLure. "Home School: The Ring." *Newsweek,* November 10, 2003:12.

McIntosh, Peggy. "White Privilege and Male Privilege: A Personal Account of Coming to See Correspondences through Work in Women's Studies." Working Paper #189. Wellesley College Center for Research on Women, 1988.

McIntyre, Jamie. "Army Rape Case Renews Debate on Coed Training." April 30, 1997: CNN Internet article.

McKenna, George. "On Abortion: A Lincolnian Position." *Atlantic Monthly,* September 1995:51–67.

McKeown, Thomas. *The Modern Rise of Population.* New York: Academic Press, 1977.

McKinley, Jesse. "Surgeon Accused of Speeding a Death to Get Organs." *New York Times,* February 27, 2008.

McKinley, Jesse, and Laurie Goodstein. "Bans in 3 States on Gay Marriage." *New York Times,* November 5, 2008.

McKinnish, Terra G. "Sexually Integrated Workplaces and Divorce: Another Form of On-the-Job Search." *Journal of Human Resources, 42,* 2, 2007:331–352.

McKinnish, Terra, Randall Walsh, and Kirk White. "Who Gentrifies Low-Income Neighborhoods?" National Bureau of Economic Research, Working Paper 14036, May 2008.

McKown, Clark, and Rhona S. Weinstein. "Modeling the Role of Child Ethnicity and Gender in Children's Differential Response to Teacher Expectations." *Journal of Applied Social Psychology, 32,* 1, 2002:159–184.

McKown, Clark, and Rhona S. Weinstein. "Teacher Expectations, Classroom Context, and the Achievement Gap." *Journal of School Psychology, 46,* 2008:235–261.

McLanahan, Sara, and Dona Schwartz. "Life Without Father: What Happens to the Children?" *Contexts, 1,* 1, Spring 2002:35–44.

McLanahan, Sara, and Gary Sandefur. *Growing Up with a Single Parent: What Hurts, What Helps.* Cambridge, Mass.: Harvard University Press, 1994.

McLemore, S. Dale. *Racial and Ethnic Relations in America.* Boston: Allyn and Bacon, 1994.

McNeil, Donald G., Jr. "Circumcision Halves H.I.V. Risk, U.S. Agency Finds." *New York Times,* December 14, 2006.

McNeill, David. "Facing Enrollment Crisis, Japanese Universities Fight to Attract Students." *Chronicle of Higher Education,* July 11, 2008.

McNeill, William H. "How the Potato Changed the World's History." *Social Research, 66,* 1, Spring 1999:67–83.

McPhail, Clark. "Blumer's Theory of Collective Behavior: The Development of a Non-Symbolic Interaction Explanation." *Sociological Quarterly, 30,* 3, 1989:401–423.

McPhail, Clark. *The Myth of the Madding Crowd.* Hawthorne, N. Y.: Aldine de Gruyter, 1991.

McShane, Marilyn, and Frank P. Williams, III., eds. *Criminological Theory.* Upper Saddle River, N.J.: Prentice Hall, 2007.

Mead, George Herbert. *Mind, Self and Society.* Chicago: University of Chicago Press, 1934.

Mead, Margaret. *Sex and Temperament in Three Primitive Societies.* New York: New American Library, 1950. First published in 1935.

Meara, Ellen R., Seth Richards, and David M. Cutler. "The Gap Gets Bigger: Changes In Mortality And Life Expectancy, By Education, 1981–2000." *Health Affairs, 27,* 2, March/April 2008:350–360.

Medlin, Richard G. "Home Schooling and the Question of Socialization." *Peabody Journal of Education, 75,* 1–2, 2000:107–123.

Meese, Ruth Lyn. "A Few New Children: Postinstitutionalized Children of Intercountry Adoption." *Journal of Special Education, 39,* 3, 2005:157–167.

Meier, Barry. "Defective Heart Devices Force Some Scary Medical Decisions." *New York Times,* June 20, 2005

Meier, Barry. "Guidant Debated Device Peril." *New York Times,* January 20, 2006.

Meier, Barry. "Health Studies Suggest Asbestos Substitutes Also Pose Cancer Risk." *Wall Street Journal,* May 12, 1987:1, 21.

Meier, Barry. "New Rules on Doctors and Medical Firms Amid Ethics Concerns." *New York Times,* January 23, 2009.

"Melee Breaks Out at Retirement Home." *The Daily News,* March 5, 2004.

Meltzer, Scott A. "Gender, Work, and Intimate Violence: Men's Occupational Spillover and Compensatory Violence." *Journal of Marriage and the Family, 64,* 2, November 2002:820–832.

Melucci, Alberto. *Nomads of the Present: Social Movements and Individual Needs in Contemporary Society.* Philadelphia: Temple University Press, 1989.

Menaghan, Elizabeth G., Lori Kowaleski-Jones, and Frank L. Mott. "The Intergenerational Costs of Parental Social Stressors: Academic and Social Difficulties in Early Adolescence for Children of Young Mothers." *Journal of Health and Social Behavior, 38,* March 1997:72–86.

Mende, Nazer, and Damien Lewis. *Slave: My True Story.* New York: Public Affairs, 2005.

Menzel, Peter. *Material World: A Global Family Portrait.* San Francisco: Sierra Club, 1994.

Mero, Jenny. "Fortune 500 Women CEOs." *CNN Money,* April 20, 2007.

Merton, Robert K. "The Social-Cultural Environment and *Anomie.*" In *New Perspectives for Research on Juvenile Delinquency,* Helen L. Witmer and Ruth Kotinsky, eds. Washington, D.C.: U.S. Department of Health, Education, and Welfare, 1956:24–50.

Merton, Robert K. *Social Theory and Social Structure.* Glencoe, Ill.: Free Press, 1949, Enlarged ed., 1968.

Merwine, Maynard H. "How Africa Understands Female Circumcision." *New York Times,* November 24, 1993.

Messner, Michael A., Margaret Carlisle Duncan, and Cheryl Cooky. "Silence, Sports Bras, and Wrestling Porn." *Journal of Sport and Social Issues, 27,* 1, February 2003:38–51.

Mesure, Susie. "Newspaper Owner 'Kidnapped by Russian Mafia.'" *New Zealand Herald,* March 23, 2008.

Meyers, Laurie. "Asian-American Mental Health." *APA Online,* February 2006.

Michels, Robert. *Political Parties.* Glencoe, Ill.: Free Press, 1949. First published in 1911.

Milbank, Dana. "Guarded by Greenbelts, Europe's Town Centers Thrive." *Wall Street Journal,* May 3, 1995:B1, B4.

Milgram, Stanley. "Behavioral Study of Obedience." *Journal of Abnormal and Social Psychology, 67,* 4, 1963:371–378.

Milgram, Stanley. "Some Conditions of Obedience and Disobedience to Authority." *Human Relations, 18,* February 1965:57–76.

Milgram, Stanley. "The Small World Problem." *Psychology Today, 1,* 1967:61–67.

Milkie, Melissa A. "Social World Approach to Cultural Studies." *Journal of Contemporary Ethnography, 23,* 3, October 1994:354–380.

Miller, Claire Cain. "Doctors Will Make Web Calls in Hawaii." *New York Times,* January 5, 2009.

Miller, Laura L. "Women in the Military." In *Down to Earth Sociology: Introductory Readings,* 14th ed., James M. Henslin, ed. New York: The Free Press, 2007. First published in 1997.

Miller, Walter B. "Lower Class Culture as a Generating Milieu of Gang Delinquency." *Journal of Social Issues, 14,* 3, 1958:5–19.

Miller-Loessi, Karen. "Toward Gender Integration in the Workplace: Issues at Multiple Levels." *Sociological Perspectives, 35,* 1, 1992:1–15.

Mills, C. Wright. *The Power Elite.* New York: Oxford University Press, 1956.

Mills, C. Wright. *The Sociological Imagination.* New York: Oxford University Press, 1959.

Mills, Karen M., and Thomas J. Palumbo. *A Statistical Portrait of Women in the United States: 1978.* U.S. Bureau of the Census, *Current Population Reports,* Series P-23, no. 100, 1980.

Miner, Horace. "Body Ritual Among the Nacirema." In *Down to Earth Sociology: Introductory Readings,* 14th ed., James M. Henslin, ed. New York: The Free Press, 2007. First published in 1956.

Minkler, Meredith, and Ann Robertson. "The Ideology of 'Age/Race Wars': Deconstructing a Social Problem." *Ageing and Society, 11,* 1, March 1991:1–22.

Mintz, Beth A., and Michael Schwartz. *The Power Structure of American Business.* Chicago: University of Chicago Press, 1985.

Mirola, William A. "Asking for Bread, Receiving a Stone: The Rise and Fall of Religious Ideologies in Chicago's Eight-Hour Movement." *Social Problems, 50,* 2, May 2003:273–293.

Mishin, Stanislav. "American Capitalism Gone with a Whimper." *Pravda,* April 27, 2009.

Mizruchi, Mark S., and Thomas Koenig. "Size, Concentration, and Corporate Networks: Determinants of Business Collective Action." *Social Science Quarterly, 72,* 2, June 1991:299–313.

Mohal, Paul, and Robin Saha. "Racial Inequalities in the Distribution of Hazardous Waste: A National-Level Reassessment." *Social Problems, 54,* 3, 2007:343–370.

Mohawk, John C. "Indian Economic Development: An Evolving Concept of Sovereignty." *Buffalo Law Review, 39,* 2, Spring 1991:495–503.

Mol, Arthur P. *Globalization and Environmental Reform: The Ecological Modernization of the Global Economy.* Cambridge, Mass.: MIT Press, 2001.

Monahan, Brian A., Joseph A. Marolla, and David G. Bromley. "Constructing Coercion: The Organization of Sexual Assault." *Journal of Contemporary Ethnography, 34,* 3, June 2005:284–316.

Money, John, and Anke A. Ehrhardt. *Man and Woman, Boy and Girl.* Baltimore: Johns Hopkins University Press, 1972.

"'Monkey' Gives Delhi Claws for Alarm." *The Australian,* May 17, 2001.

Montagu, M. F. Ashley. *The Concept of Race.* New York: Free Press, 1964.

Montagu, M. F. Ashley. *Introduction to Physical Anthropology,* 3rd ed. Springfield, Ill.: Thomas, 1960.

Montagu, M. F. Ashley, ed. *Race and IQ: Expanded Edition.* New York: Oxford University Press, 1999.

Morgan, Lewis Henry. *Ancient Society.* New York: Holt, 1877.

Morin, Monte. "$1.7 Million Awarded in Retirement Home Death." *Los Angeles Times,* October 17, 2001.

Morin, Rich, and D'Vera Cohn. "Women Call the Shots at Home; Public Mixed on Gender Roles in Jobs." Pew Research Center Publications: September 25, 2008.

Morris, Aldon. "Black Southern Student Sit-In Movement: An Analysis of Internal Organization." In *Collective Behavior and Social Movements,* Russell L. Curtis, Jr., and Benigno E. Aguirre, eds. Boston: Allyn and Bacon, 1993:361–380.

Morris, Joan M., and Michael D. Grimes. "Moving Up from the Working Class." In *Down to Earth Sociology: Introductory Readings,* 13th ed., James M. Henslin, ed. New York: The Free Press, 2005:365–376.

Morrow, Betty Hearn. "Urban Families as Support after Disaster: The Case of Hurricane Andrew." Paper presented at the 1995 meetings of the American Sociological Association.

Mosca, Gaetano. *The Ruling Class.* New York: McGraw-Hill, 1939. First published in 1896.

Moscos, Charles, C., and Sydney Butler. *All That We Can Be: Black Leadership and Racial Integration the Army Way.* New York: Basic Books, 1997.

Mosher, Steven W. "China's One-Child Policy: Twenty-Five Years Later." *Human Life Review,* Winter 2006:76–101.

Mosher, Steven W. "Too Many People? Not by a Long Shot." *Wall Street Journal,* February 10, 1997:A18.

Mosher, Steven W. "Why Are Baby Girls Being Killed in China?" *Wall Street Journal,* July 25, 1983:9.

Mosher, William D., Anjani Chandra, and Jo Jones, "Sexual Behavior and Selected Health Measures." *Advance Data from Vital and Health Statistics, 362,* September 15, 2005:1–56.

Mouawad, Jad. "Saudi Officials Seek to Temper the Price of Oil." *Bloomberg News,* January 27, 2007.

Mouawad, Jad. "Shell to Pay $15.5 Million to Settle Nigerian Case." *New York Times,* June 8, 2009.

Mount, Ferdinand. *The Subversive Family: An Alternative History of Love and Marriage.* New York: Free Press, 1992.

"Mujer 'resucite blye' en España." *BBC Mundo,* February 17, 2006.

"Mujer Con Cabeza Humana Alega Religion en Defensa." AOL Online News, February 14, 2006.

Mukherjee, Krittivas. "Rent-a-womb in India Fuels Surrogate Motherhood Debate." Reuters. February 5, 2007.

Murdock, George Peter. "The Common Denominator of Cultures." In *The Science of Man and the World Crisis,* Ralph Linton, ed. New York: Columbia University Press, 1945.

Murdock, George Peter. "Comparative Data on the Division of Labor by Sex." *Social Forces, 15,* 4, May 1937:551–553.

Murdock, George Peter. *Social Structure.* New York: Macmillan, 1949.

Murphy, John, and Miho Inada. "Japan's Recession Hits 'Temps.'" *Wall Street Journal,* December 5, 2008.

Murray, Christopher J. L., Sandeep C. Kulkarni, Catherine Michard, Niels Tomijima, Maria T. Bulzaccheili, Terrell J. Landiorio, and Majid Ezzati. "Eight Americas: Investigating Mortality Disparities across Races, Counties, and Race-Counties in the United States." *PLoS Medicine, 3,* 9, September 2006:1513–1524.

Murray, G. W. *Sons of Ishmael.* London: Routledge, 1935.

Muslim Americans: Middle Class and Mostly Mainstream. Washington, D.C.: Pew Research Center, May 22, 2007.

Mydans, Seth. "A Fervor of Capitalism Sweeps Vietnam." *International Herald Tribune,* April 26, 2006.

Mydans, Seth. "Inflation Delivers a Blow to Vietnam's Spirits." *New York Times,* August 24, 2008.

Nabhan, Gary Paul. *Cultures in Habitat: On Nature, Culture, and Story.* New York: Counterpoint, 1998.

Naik, Gautam. "Doing Hard Time in Greenland Isn't Really That Hard." *Wall Street Journal,* January 13, 2004.

Nakamura, Akemi. "Abe to Play Hardball with Soft Education System." *The Japan Times,* October 27, 2006.

Nakao, Keiko, and Judith Treas. "Occupational Prestige in the United States Revisited: Twenty-Five Years of Stability and Change." Paper presented at the annual meetings of the American Sociological Association, 1990. (As referenced in Kerbo, Harold R. *Social Stratification and Inequality: Class Conflict in Historical and Comparative Perspective,* 2nd ed. New York: McGraw-Hill, 1991:181.)

Nakao, Keiko, and Judith Treas. "Updating Occupational Prestige and Socioeconomic Scores: How the New Measures Measure Up." *Sociological Methodology, 24,* 1994:1–72.

Nash, Gary B. *Red, White, and Black.* Englewood Cliffs, N.J.: Prentice Hall, 1974.

Nathan, John. *Sony: The Private Life.* New York: Houghton Mifflin, 1999.

National Center for Health Statistics. *Advance Data No. 351,* December 15, 2004.

National Coalition for the Homeless. NCH Fact Sheet #2, June 2008.

National Hospice and Palliative Care Organization. "NHPCO Facts and Figures: Hospice Care in America." October 2008.

National Institute of Child Health and Human Development. "Child Care and Mother-Child Interaction in the First 3 Years of Life." *Developmental Psychology, 35,* 6, November 1999:1399–1413.

National Ombudsman Reporting System Data Tables. Washington, D.C.: U.S. Administration on Aging, 2003.

National School Safety Center. "School Associated Violent Deaths." Westlake Village, California, 2009.

Nauta, André. "That They All May Be One: Can Denominationalism Die?" Paper presented at the annual meetings of the American Sociological Association, 1993.

Navarro, Mireya. "For New York's Black Latinos, a Growing Racial Awareness." *New York Times,* April 28, 2003.

Navarro, Vicente, ed. *The Political Economy of Social Inequalities: Consequences for Health and Quality of Life.* Amityville, N. Y.: Baywood Publishing, 2002.

Needham, Sarah E. "Grooming Women for the Top: Tips from Executive Coaches." *Wall Street Journal,* October 31, 2006.

Neil, Martha. "New 'Big Brother' Software Will Monitor Workers' Facial Expressions." *ABA Journal,* January 16, 2008.

Nemtsova, Anna. "In Russia, Corruption Plagues the Higher-Education System." *Chronicle of Higher Education,* February 22, 2008.

Neugarten, Bernice L. "Middle Age and Aging." In *Growing Old in America,* Beth B. Hess, ed. New Brunswick, N.J.: Transaction, 1976:180–197.

Neuman, W. Lawrence. *Social Research Methods: Qualitative and Quantitative Approaches,* 6th ed. Boston: Allyn and Bacon, 2006.

Newman, Michael. "Class, State and Democracy: Laski, Miliband and the Search for a Synthesis." *Political Studies, 54,* 2006:328–348.

Nicol, Adelheid A. M., "Social Dominance Orientation, Right-wing Authoritarianism, and Their Relation with Alienation and Spheres of Control." *Personality and Individual Differences, 43,* 2007:891–899.

Niebuhr, H. Richard. *The Social Sources of Denominationalism.* New York: Holt, 1929.

Noah, Timothy. "White House Forms Panel to Investigate Cold War Radiation Tests on Humans." *Wall Street Journal,* January 4, 1994:A12.

"Nonfamily Abducted Children: National Estimates and Characteristics." National Incidence Studies of Missing, Abducted, Runaway, and Thrownaway Children. October 2002.

Nordland, Rod. "That Joke Is a Killer." *Newsweek,* May 19, 2003:10.

Nuland, Sherwin B. "The Debate Over Dying." *USA Weekend,* February 3–5, 1995:4–6.

Nusbaum, Marci Alboher. "New Kind of Snooping Arrives at the Office." *New York Times,* July 13, 2003.

Nussenbaum, Evelyn. "Video Game Makers Go Hollywood. Uh-Oh." *New York Times,* August 22, 2004.

O'Brien, John E. "Violence in Divorce-Prone Families." In *Violence in the Family,* Suzanne K. Steinmetz and Murray A. Straus, eds. New York: Dodd, Mead, 1975:65–75.

O'Brien, Timothy L. "Fed Assesses Citigroup Unit $70 Million in Loan Abuse." *New York Times,* May 28, 2004.

O'Hare, William P. "A New Look at Poverty in America." *Population Bulletin, 51,* 2, September 1996a:1–47.

O'Hare, William P. "U.S. Poverty Myths Explored: Many Poor Work Year-Round, Few Still Poor After Five Years." *Population Today: News, Numbers, and Analysis, 24,* 10, October 1996b:1–2.

Oberschall, Anthony. *Social Conflict and Social Movements.* Englewood Cliffs, N.J.: Prentice Hall, 1973.

Offen, Karen. "Feminism and Sexual Difference in Historical Perspective." In *Theoretical Perspectives on Sexual Difference,* Deborah L. Rhode, ed. New Haven, Conn.: Yale University Press, 1990:13–20.

Office of Immigration Statistics. "Annual Report: Immigration Enforcement Actions: 2007." Washington, D.C.: U.S. Department of Homeland Security, December 2008.

Ogburn, William F. "The Hypothesis of Cultural Lag." In *Theories of Society: Foundations of Modern Sociological Theory,* Vol. 2, Talcott Parsons, Edward Shils, Kaspar D. Naegele, and Jesse R. Pitts, eds. New York: Free Press, 1961:1270–1273.

Ogburn, William F. *On Culture and Social Change: Selected Papers,* Otis Dudley Duncan, ed. Chicago: University of Chicago Press, 1964.

Ogburn, William F. *Social Change with Respect to Culture and Human Nature.* New York: W. B. Huebsch, 1922. (Other editions by Viking in 1927, 1938, and 1950.)

Ohmae, Kenichi. *The End of the Nation State: The Rise of Regional Economies.* New York: Free Press, 1995.

Olmsted, Michael S., and A. Paul Hare. *The Small Group,* 2nd ed. New York: Random House, 1978.

Olneck, Michael R., and David B. Bills. "What Makes Sammy Run? An Empirical Assessment of the Bowles-Gintis Correspondence Theory." *American Journal of Education, 89,* 1980:27–61.

Olshansky, S. Jay, Bruce Carnes, Richard G. Rogers, and Len Smith. "Infectious Diseases—New and Ancient Threats to World Health." *Population Bulletin, 52,* 2, July 1997:1–51.

"On History and Heritage: John K. Castle." *Penn Law Journal,* Fall 1999.

Orme, Nicholas. *Medieval Children.* New Haven: Yale University Press, 2002.

Orwell, George. *1984.* New York: Harcourt Brace, 1949.

Osborne, Cynthia, Wendy D. Manning, and Pamela J. Smock. "Married and Cohabiting Parents' Relationship Stability: A Focus on Race and Ethnicity." *Journal of Marriage and Family, 69,* December 2007:1345–1366.

Osborne, Lawrence. "Got Silk." *New York Times Magazine,* June 15, 2002.

Ouchi, William. "Decision-Making in Japanese Organizations." In *Down to Earth Sociology: Introductory Readings,* 7th ed., James M. Henslin, ed. New York: Free Press, 1993:503–507.

Padgett, Tim. "An Ivy Stepladder." *Time,* April 4, 2005.

Pagelow, Mildred Daley. "Adult Victims of Domestic Violence: Battered Women." *Journal of Interpersonal Violence, 7,* 1, March 1992:87–120.

Pager, Devah. "Blacks and Ex-Cons Need Not Apply." *Context, 2,* 3, Fall 2003:58–59.

Pager, Devah. "The Mark of a Criminal Record." *American Journal of Sociology, 108,* 5, March 2003:937–975.

Pager, Devah. *Marked: Race, Crime, and Finding Work in an Era of Mass Incarceration.* Chicago: University of Chicago Press, 2007.

Palen, J. John. *The Urban World.* Boulder: Paradigm, 2008.

Palen, J. John. *The Urban World,* 7th ed. Boston: McGraw Hill, 2005.

Panzarella, Jamie. "Achieving the Dream: Helping Community Colleges Focus on Student Success." *Footnotes, 36,* 1, January 2008:6.

Parfit, Michael, "Earth First!ers Wield a Mean Monkey Wrench." *Smithsonian, 21,* 1, April 1990:184–204.

Parilla, Leslie. "Transplant Surgeon Hootan Roozrokh Acquitted in Sierra Vista Organ Harvest Case." *San Luis Obispo Tribune,* December 18, 2008.

Park, Robert. *Masse und Publikum.* Berlin: Lack and Grunau, 1904.

Park, Robert Ezra. "Human Ecology." *American Journal of Sociology, 42,* 1, July 1936:1–15.

Park, Robert Ezra, and Ernest W. Burgess. *Human Ecology.* Chicago: University of Chicago Press, 1921.

Parsons, Talcott. "An Analytic Approach to the Theory of Social Stratification." *American Journal of Sociology, 45,* 1940:841–862.

Partington, Donald H. "The Incidence of the Death Penalty for Rape in Virginia." *Washington and Lee Law Review, 22,* 1965:43–75.

Passel, Jeffrey S. and D'Vera Cohn. "A Portrait of Unauthorized Immigrants in the United States." Washington, D.C.: Pew Hispanic Center, April 14, 2009.

Patterson, Orlando. "The Root of the Problem." *Time,* April 26, 2007.

Paulson, Tom. "Bellevue Billionaire Charles Simonyi Heads for Space Again." *Seattle Post-Intelligencer,* October 6, 2008.

Pear, Robert. "9 of 10 Nursing Homes Lack Adequate Staff, Study Finds." *New York Times,* February 18, 2002.

Pear, Robert. "Violations Reported at 94% of Nursing Homes." *New York Times,* September 28, 2008.

Pearlin, L. I., and Melvin L. Kohn. "Social Class, Occupation, and Parental Values: A Cross-National Study." *American Sociological Review, 31,* 1966:466–479.

Peck, Grant "Australian Convicted of Insulting Thai Monarchy." Associated Press, January 19, 2009.

Pedersen, R. P. "How We Got Here: It's Not How You Think." *Community College Week, 13,* 15, March 15, 2001:4–5.

Pennar, Karen, and Christopher Farrell. "Notes from the Underground Economy." *Business Week,* February 15, 1993:98–101.

Perrin, Ellin C. "Technical Report: Coparent or Second-Parent Adoption by Same-Sex Parents." *Pediatrics, 109,* 2, February 2002:341–344.

Perrow, Charles. "A Society of Organizations." *Theory and Society, 20,* 6, December 1991:725–762.

Perry, Barbara. "Nobody Trusts Them! Under- and Over-Policing Native American Communities." *Critical Criminology, 14,* 2006:411–444.

Perry, William J., Ashton B. Carter, and Michael M. May. "After the Bomb." *New York Times,* June 12, 2007.

Peter, Laurence J., and Raymond Hull. *The Peter Principle: Why Things Always Go Wrong.* New York: Morrow, 1969.

Petersen, Melody. "Court Papers Suggest Scale of Drug's Use." *New York Times,* May 30, 2003.

Petersen, Melody. "Suit Says Company Promoted Drug in Exam Rooms." *New York Times,* May 15, 2002.

Peterson, Iver. "1993 Deal for Indian Casino Is Called a Model to Avoid." *New York Times,* June 30, 2003.

Peterson, Janice. "Welfare Reform and Inequality: The TANF and UI Programs." *Journal of Economic Issues, 34,* 2, June 2000:517–526.

Petty, Gregory C., Doo Hun Lim, Seung Won Yoon, and Johnny Fontan. "The Effect of Self-Directed Work Teams on Work Ethic." *Performance Improvement Quarterly, 21,* 2, 2008:49–63.

Pfann, Gerard A., et al. "Business Success and Businesses' Beauty Capital." *Economics Letters, 67,* 2, May 2000:201–207.

Pflanz, Mike. "Rwanda's Women Lead the Miraculous Recovery." *Telegraph,* October 17, 2008.

Phillips, Barbara D. "America's Forgotten Plague." *Wall Street Journal,* February 9, 1998:A15.

Phillips, Mary. "Midwives Versus Medics: A 17th-Century Professional Turf War." *Management and Organizational History, 2,* 1, 2007:27–44.

Piaget, Jean. *The Construction of Reality in the Child.* New York: Basic Books, 1954.

Piaget, Jean. *The Psychology of Intelligence.* London: Routledge & Kegan Paul, 1950.

"Piden en Holanda aplicar la eutanasia infantil." BBC Mundo. December 15, 2004.

Pillemer, Karl, and Beth Hudson. "A Model Abuse Prevention Program for Nursing Assistants." *Gerontologist, 33,* 1, 1993:128–131.

Pillemer, Karl, and J. Jill Suitor. "Violence and Violent Feelings: What Causes Them Among Family Caregivers?" *Journal of Gerontology, 47,* 4, 1992:165–172.

Pillemer, Karl, and Rosalie S. Wolf. *Elder Abuse: Conflict in the Family.* Dover, Mass.: Auburn House, 1987.

Pilling, D., and M. Kellmer Pringle. *Controversial Issues in Child Development.* London: Paul Elek, 1978.

Pines, Maya. "The Civilizing of Genie." *Psychology Today, 15,* September 1981:28–34.

Piotrow, Phylis Tilson. *World Population Crisis: The United States' Response.* New York: Praeger, 1973.

Piven, Frances Fox. "Can Power from Below Change the World?" *American Sociological Review, 73,* 1, February 2008:1–14.

Piven, Frances Fox. "The Neoliberal Challenge." *Contexts, 6,* 3, 2007:13–15.

Polgreen, Lydia. "Court Rules Niger Failed by Allowing Girl's Slavery." *New York Times,* October 27, 2008.

Polgreen, Lydia, and Marlise Simons. "Global Sludge Ends in Tragedy for Ivory Coast." *New York Times,* October 2, 2006.

Polsby, Nelson W. "Three Problems in the Analysis of Community Power." *American Sociological Review, 24,* 6, December 1959:796–803.

Pope, Liston. *Millhands and Preachers: A Study of Gastonia.* New Haven, Conn.: Yale University Press, 1942.

Popenoe, David. "Cohabitation, Marriage and Child Wellbeing: A Cross-National Sample." Rutgers: The National Marriage Project, 2008.

Popescu, Ioana, Mary S. Vaughan-Sarrazin, and Gary E. Rosenthal. *Journal of the American Medical Association, 297,* 22, 2007:2489–2495.

"Population Today." Washington, D.C.: Population Reference Bureau, 4, 5, September 1998.

Portés, Alejandro, and Ruben G. Rumbaut. *Immigrant America.* Berkeley: University of California Press, 1990.

Powell, Lynda H., Leila Shahabi, and Carl E. Thoresen. "Religion and Spirituality: Linkages to Physical Health." *American Psychologist, 58,* 1, January 2003:36–52.

Powell, Michael, and Janet Roberts. "Minorities Hit Hardest by Foreclosures in New York." *New York Times,* May 15, 2009.

Pratt, Laura A., Achintya N. Dey, and Alan J. Cohen. "Characteristics of Adults with Serious Psychological Distress as Measured by the K6 Scale: United States, 2001–04." *Vital and Health Statistics, 382,* March 30 2007:1–18.

Presser, Stanley, and Linda Stinson. "Data Collection Mode and Social Desirability Bias in Self-Reported Religious Attendance." *American Sociological Review, 63,* February 1998:137–145.

Preston, Howard L. *Automobile Age Atlanta: the Making of a Southern Metropolis, 1900–1935.* Athens: University of Georgia Press, 1979.

Preston, Steven C. The Third Annual Homeless Assessment Report to Congress. Washington, D.C.: U.S. Department of Housing and Urban Development, July 2008.

Proctor, Robert N. *The Nazi War on Cancer.* Princeton, N.J.: Princeton University Press, 1999.

"Prosecutorial Decision-Making." *Justice Quarterly, 24,* 3, 2007:460–495.

Qian, Zhenchao, and Daniel T. Lichter. "Social Boundaries and Marital Assimilation: Interpreting Trends in Racial and Ethnic Intermarriage." *American Sociological Review, 72,* February 2007:68–94.

Quadagno, Jill. *Aging and the Life Course: An Introduction to Gerontology,* 4th ed. New York: McGraw-Hill, 2007.

Rafalovich, Adam. "Exploring Clinician Uncertainty in the Diagnosis and Treatment of Attention Deficit Hyperactivity Disorder." *Sociology of Health and Illness, 27,* 3, April 2005:305–323.

Raghunathan, V. K. "Millions of Baby Girls Killed in India." *The Straits Times,* February 8, 2003.

Rainwater, Lee, and Timothy M. Smeeding. *Poor Kids in a Rich Country: America's Children in Comparative Perspective.* New York: Russell Sage, 2003.

Raisfeld, Robin, and Rob Patronite. "Shirako Season." *New York Magazine,* December 25, 2006.

Ramos, Jorge. "Project Minuteman Is Meaningless." *Oakland Tribune.* April 10, 2005.

Ramsey-Klawsnik, H., P. B. Teaster, M. S. Mendiondo, J. L. Marcum, and E. L. Abner. "Sexual Predators Who Target Elders: Findings from the First National Study of Sexual Abuse in Care Facilities." *Journal of Elder Abuse and Neglect, 20,* 4, 2008:353–376.

Rand, Michael, and Shannan Catalano. "Criminal Victimization, 2006." *Bureau of Justice Statistics Bulletin,* December 2007.

Ray, J. J. "Authoritarianism Is a Dodo: Comment on Scheepers, Felling and Peters." *European Sociological Review, 7,* 1, May 1991:73–75.

Read, Madlen. "Citi Pays $18M for Questioned Credit Card Practice." Associated Press, August 26, 2008.

Reat, Noble Ross. *Buddhism: A History.* Berkeley, Calif: Asian Humanities Press, 1994.

Reay, Diane, Gill Crozier, David James, Sumi Hollingworth, Katya Williams, Fiona Jamieson, and Phoebe Beedell. "Re-Invigorating Democracy?: White Middle Class Identities and Comprehensive Schooling." *The Sociological Review, 56,* 2, 2008:238–255.

Reckless, Walter C. *The Crime Problem,* 5th ed. New York: Appleton, 1973.

Reed, Don Collins. "A Model of Moral Stages." *Journal of Moral Education, 37,* 3, September 2008:357–376.

Reed, Susan, and Lorenzo Benet. "Ecowarrior Dave Foreman Will Do Whatever It Takes in His Fight to Save Mother Earth." *People Weekly, 33,* 15, April 16, 1990:113–116.

Regalado, Antonio. "Seoul Team Creates Custom Stem Cells from Cloned Embryos." *Wall Street Journal,* May 20, 2005.

Reibstein, Larry. "Managing Diversity." *Newsweek,* January 25, 1996:50.

Reiman, Jeffrey. *The Rich Get Richer and the Poor Get Prison: Ideology, Class, and Criminal Justice,* 7th ed. Boston: Allyn and Bacon, 2004.

Reiser, Christa. *Reflections on Anger: Women and Men in a Changing Society.* Westport, Conn.: Praeger Publishers, 1999.

Reisman, Lonny. "Hospital Errors: The Tip of the Medical-Error Iceberg." *Managed Care Quarterly,* Spring 2003:36–38.

Rennison, Callie Marie. "Intimate Partner Violence, 1993–2001." Washington, D.C.: Bureau of Justice Statistics, February 2003.

Reskin, Barbara F. *The Realities of Affirmative Action in Employment.* Washington, D.C.: American Sociological Association, 1998.

Resnik, David B. "Financial Interests and Research Bias." *Perspectives on Science, 8,* 3, Fall 2000:255–283.

Reuters. "Fake Tiger Woods Gets 200-Years-To-Life in Prison." April 28, 2001.

Reuters. "HSBC Joins Race to Cash in on China's New Millionaires." *International Herald Tribune,* March 31, 2008.

Revkin, Andrew C., and Matthew L. Wald. "Material Shows Weakening of Climate Reports." *New York Times,* March 20, 2007.

Rhoads, Christopher. "Web Site to Holy Site: Israeli Firm Broadcasts Prayers for a Fee." *Wall Street Journal,* January 25, 2007.

Rhone, Nedra. "Widespread Violations Found at Care Homes." *Los Angeles Times,* April 18, 2001.

Richardson, Stacey, and Marita P. McCabe. "Parental Divorce During Adolescence and Adjustment in Early Adulthood." *Adolescence, 36,* Fall 2001:467–489.

Richman, Joe. "From the Belgian Congo to the Bronx Zoo." National Public Radio, September 8, 2006.

Richtel, Matt. "For Liars and Loafers, Cellphones Offer an Alibi." *New York Times,* June 26, 2004.

Richtel, Matt. "A Thaw in Investment Prospects for Sex-Related Businesses? Maybe." *New York Times,* July 27, 2007.

Ricks, Thomas E. "'New' Marines Illustrate Growing Gap Between Military and Society." *Wall Street Journal,* July 27, 1995:A1, A4.

Rieker, Patricia P., Chloe E. Bird, Susan Bell, Jenny Ruducha, Rima E. Rudd, and S. M. Miller, "Violence and Women's Health: Toward a Society and Health Perspective." Unpublished paper, 1997.

Riessman, Catherine Kohler. "Women and Medicalization: A New Perspective." In *Dominant Issues in Medical Sociology,* 3rd ed., Howard D. Schwartz, ed. New York: McGraw-Hill, 1994:190–211.

Rifkin, Glenn. "The Amish Flock from Farms to Small Businesses." *New York Times,* January 7, 2009.

Riley, Nancy E. "China's Population: New Trends and Challenges." *Population Bulletin, 59,* 2, June 2004:3–36.

Rist, Ray C. "Student Social Class and Teacher Expectations: The Self-Fulfilling Prophecy in Ghetto Education." *Harvard Educational Review, 40,* 3, August 1970:411–451.

Ritzer, George. "The McDonaldization of Society." In *Down to Earth Sociology: Introductory Readings,* 11th ed., James M. Henslin, ed. New York: The Free Press, 2001:459–471.

Ritzer, George. *The McDonaldization of Society: An Investigation into the Changing Character of Contemporary Life.* Thousand Oaks, Calif.: Pine Forge Press, 1993.

Ritzer, George. *The McDonaldization Thesis: Explorations and Extensions.* Thousand Oaks, Calif.: Sage Publications, 1998.

Rivlin, Gary. "Beyond the Reservation." *New York Times,* September 22, 2007.

Robb, John. "The Coming Urban Terror." *City Journal,* Summer 2007. Online.

Robbins, John. *Healthy at 100.* New York: Random House, 2006.

Robertson, Ian. *Sociology,* 3rd ed. New York: Worth, 1987.

Rodash, Mary Flannery. "The College of Midwifery: A Sociological Study of the Decline of a Profession." Unpublished doctoral dissertation, Southern Illinois University at Carbondale, 1982.

"Rodney King." *Time,* April 25, 2007.

Rodriguez, Richard. "The Education of Richard Rodriguez." *Saturday Review,* February 8, 1975:147–149.

Rodriguez, Richard. *Hunger of Memory: The Education of Richard Rodriguez.* Boston: Godine, 1982.

Rodriguez, Richard. "The Late Victorians: San Francisco, AIDS, and the Homosexual Stereotype." *Harper's Magazine,* October 1990:57–66.

Rodriguez, Richard. "Mixed Blood." *Harper's Magazine, 283,* November 1991:47–56.

Rodriguez, Richard. "Searching for Roots in a Changing Society." In *Down to Earth Sociology: Introductory Readings,* 8th ed., James M. Henslin, ed. New York: Free Press, 1995:486–491.

Rodríguez, Victor M. "Los Angeles, U.S. A. 1992: 'A House Divided Against Itself . . . ' ?" *SSSP Newsletter,* Spring 1994:5–12.

Roediger, David R. *Colored White: Transcending the Racial Past.* Berkeley: University of California Press, 2002.

Rohter, Larry. "For Chilean Coup, Kissinger Is Numbered Among the Hunted." *New York Times,* March 28, 2002.

Rohter, Larry. "Tracking the Sale of a Kidney on a Path of Poverty and Hope." *New York Times,* May 23, 2004.

Rohwedder, Cecilie. "London Parents Scramble for Edge in Preschool Wars." *Wall Street Journal,* February 12, 2007.

Rosaldo, Michelle Zimbalist. "Women, Culture and Society: A Theoretical Overview." In *Women, Culture, and Society,* Michelle Zimbalist Rosaldo, and Louise Lamphere, eds. Stanford: Stanford University Press, 1974.

Rose, Frederick. "Los Angeles Tallies Losses; Curfew Is Lifted." *Wall Street Journal,* May 5, 1992:A3, A18.

Rosenbaum, David E. "U.S. Breaks a Ring That Smuggled in Thousands of Workers." *New York Times,* November 21, 1998.

Rosenberg, Charles E. *The Care of Strangers: The Rise of America's Hospital System.* New York: Basic Books, 1987.

Rosenfeld, Richard. "Crime Decline in Context." *Contexts, 1,* 1, Spring 2002:25–34.

Rosenthal, Elisabeth. "Cat Lovers Lining Up for No-Sneeze Kitties." *New York Times,* October 6, 2006.

Rosenthal, Elisabeth. "China Increases Lead as Biggest Carbon Dioxide Emitter." *New York Times,* June 14, 2008.

Rosenthal, Elisabeth. "Harsh Chinese Reality Feeds a Black Market in Women." *New York Times,* June 25, 2001.

Rosenthal, Elisabeth, and Andrew C. Revkin. "Science Panel Calls Global Warming 'Unequivocal.'" *New York Times,* February 2, 2007.

Rosenthal, Robert, and Lenore Jacobson. *Pygmalion in the Classroom: Teacher Expectation and Pupils' Intellectual Development.* New York: Holt, Rinehart, and Winston, 1968.

Ross, Joseph S., Kevin P. Hill, David S. Egilman, and Harlan M. Krumholz. "Guest Authorship and Ghostwriting in Publications Related to Rofecoxib." *Journal of the American Medical Association, 290,* 15, April 15, 2008:1800–1812.

Rossi, Alice S. "A Biosocial Perspective on Parenting." *Daedalus, 106,* 1977:1–31.

Rossi, Alice S. "Gender and Parenthood." *American Sociological Review, 49,* 1984:1–18.

Rossi, Peter H. *Down and Out in America: The Origins of Homelessness.* Chicago: University of Chicago Press, 1989.

Rossi, Peter H. "Going Along or Getting It Right?" *Journal of Applied Sociology, 8,* 1991:77–81.

Rossi, Peter H. "Half Truths with Real Consequences: Journalism, Research, and Public Policy." *Contemporary Sociology,* 1999:1–5.

Rossi, Peter H., Gene A. Fisher, and Georgianna Willis. *The Condition of the Homeless of Chicago.* Amherst: University of Massachusetts, September 1986.

Rossi, Peter H., James D. Wright, Gene A. Fisher, and Georgianna Willis. "The Urban Homeless: Estimating Composition and Size." *Science, 235,* March 13, 1987:1136–1140.

Roth, Louise Marie. "Selling Women Short: A Research Note on Gender Differences in Compensation on Wall Street." *Social Forces, 82,* 2, December 2003:783–802.

Rothkopf, David. *Superclass: The Global Power Elite and the World They Are Making.* New York: Farrar, Straus and Giroux, 2008.

Rothman, Barbara Katz. "Midwives in Transition: The Structure of a Clinical Revolution." In *Dominant Issues in Medical Sociology,* 3rd ed. Howard D. Schwartz, ed. New York: McGraw-Hill, 1994:104–112.

Rothschild, Joyce, and J. Allen Whitt. *The Cooperative Workplace: Potentials and Dilemmas of Organizational Democracy and Participation.* Cambridge, England: Cambridge University Press, 1986.

Rubin, Zick. "The Love Research." In *Marriage and Family in a Changing Society,* 2nd ed., James M. Henslin, ed. New York: Free Press, 1985.

Rudner, Lawrence M. "The Scholastic Achievement of Home School Students." *ERIC/AE Digest,* September 1, 1999.

Ruggles, Patricia. "Short and Long Term Poverty in the United States: Measuring the American 'Underclass.'" Washington, D.C.: Urban Institute, June 1989.

Russell, Diana E. H. "Preliminary Report on Some Findings Relating to the Trauma and Long-Term Effects of Intrafamily Childhood Sexual Abuse." Unpublished paper.

Russell, Diana E. H. *Rape in Marriage.* Bloomington: Indiana University Press, 1990.

"Russia Sets Out to Fight Corruption in Education With a New Standardized Test." Associated Press, February 2, 2007.

Sabol, William J., and Heather Couture. "Prison Inmates at Midyear 2007." *Bureau of Justice Statistics Bulletin,* June 2007:1-24.

Sadler, Anne G., Brenda M. Booth, Brian L. Cook, and Bradley N. Doebbeling. "Factors Associated With Women's Risk of Rape in the Military Environment." *American Journal of Industrial Medicine, 43,* 2003:252–273.

Saenz, Rogelio. "Latinos and the Changing Face of America." Washington, D.C.: Population Reference Bureau, 2004:1–28.

Sageman, Marc. "Explaining Terror Networks in the 21st Century." *Footnotes,* May–June 2008a:7.

Sageman, Marc. *Leaderless Jihad: Terror Networks in the Twenty-First Century.* Philadelphia: University of Pennsylvania Press, 2008b.

Sahlins, Marshall D. *Stone Age Economics.* Chicago: Aldine, 1972.

Sahlins, Marshall D., and Elman R. Service. *Evolution and Culture.* Ann Arbor: University of Michigan Press, 1960.

Salomon, Gisela, "In Miami, Spanish Is Becoming the Primary Language." Associated Press, May 29, 2008.

Salopek, Paul. "Shattered Sudan: Drilling for Oil, Hoping for Peace." *National Geographic, 203,* 2, February 2003:30–66.

Samor, Geraldo, Cecilie Rohwedder, and Ann Zimmerman. "Innocents Abroad?" *Wall Street Journal,* May 5, 2006.

Sampson, Robert J., Gregory D. Squires, and Min Zhou. *How Neighborhoods Matter: The Value of Investing at the Local Level.* Washington, D.C.: American Sociological Association, 2001.

Sampson, Robert J., Jeffrey D. Morenoff, and Felton Earls. "Beyond Social Capital: Spatial Dynamics of Collective Efficacy for Children." *American Sociological Review, 64,* October 1999:633–660.

Samuelson, Paul Anthony, and William D. Nordhaus. *Economics,* 18th ed. New York: McGraw Hill, 2005.

Sanchez, Juan I., and Nohora Medkik. "The Effects of Diversity Awareness Training on Differential Treatment." *Group and Organization Management, 29,* 4, August 2004:517–536.

Sanchez-Jankowski, Martin. "Gangs and Social Change." *Theoretical Criminology, 7,* 2, 2003:191–216.

Sánchez-Jankowski, Martín. *Islands in the Street: Gangs and American Urban Society.* Berkeley: University of California Press, 1991.

Sanders, Peter. "Casinos Bet on Radio-ID Gambling Chips." *Wall Street Journal,* May 13, 2005.

Sanderson, Warren, and Sergei Scherbov. "Rethinking Age and Aging." *Population Bulletin, 63,* 4, December 2008.

Sang-Hun, Choe. "Where Boys Were Kings, a Shift Toward Baby Girls." *New York Times,* December 23, 2007.

Santos, Fernanda. "Are New Yorkers Satisfied? That Depends." *New York Times,* March 7, 2009.

Sapir, Edward. *Selected Writings of Edward Sapir in Language, Culture, and Personality.* David G. Mandelbaum, ed. Berkeley, Calif.: University of California Press, 1949.

Saranow, Jennifer. "The Snoop Next Door." *Wall Street Journal,* January 12, 2007.

Sayres, William. "What Is a Family Anyway?" In *Marriage and Family in a Changing Society,* 4th ed., James M. Henslin, ed. New York: Free Press, 1992:23–30.

Schaefer, Richard T. *Race and Ethnicity in the United States,* 5th ed. Upper Saddle River, New Jersey: Prentice Hall, 2008.

Schaefer, Richard T. *Racial and Ethnic Groups,* 9th ed. Upper Saddle River, N.J.: Prentice Hall, 2004.

Schaefer, Richard T. *Sociology,* 3rd ed. New York: McGraw-Hill, 1989.

Scheff, Thomas J. *Being Mentally Ill: A Sociological Theory,* 3rd ed. New York: Aldine de Gruyter, 1999.

Schellenberg, James A. *Conflict Resolution: Theory, Research, and Practice.* Albany: New York University Press, 1996.

Schemo, Diana Jean. "Education Dept. Says States Have Lax Standard for Teachers." *New York Times,* June 13, 2002.

Schemo, Diana Jean. "Rate of Rape at Academy Is Put at 12% in Survey." *New York Times,* August 29, 2003b.

Schemo, Diana Jean. "When Students' Gains Help Teachers' Bottom Line." *New York Times,* May 9, 2004.

Schemo, Diana Jean. "Women at West Point Face Tough Choices on Assaults." *New York Times,* May 22, 2003a.

Schmiege, Cynthia J., Leslie N. Richards, and Anisa M. Zvonkovic. "Remarriage: For Love or Money?" *Journal of Divorce and Remarriage,* May-June 2001:123–141.

Schmitt, Eric. "How Army Sleuths Stalked the Adviser Who Led to Hussein." *New York Times,* December 20, 2003.

Schmitt, Eric. "Rapes Reported by Servicewomen in the Persian Gulf and Elsewhere." *New York Times,* February 26, 2004.

Schoenborn, Charlotte A. "Marital Status and Health: United States, 1999–2002." *Vital and Health Statistics, 351,* December 15, 2004:1–32.

Schottland, Charles I. *The Social Security Plan in the U.S.* New York: Appleton, 1963.

Schulz, William F. "The Torturer's Apprentice: Civil Liberties in a Turbulent Age." *The Nation,* May 13, 2002.

"Schwab Study Finds Four Generations of American Adults Fundamentally Rethinking Planning for Retirement." Reuters, July 15, 2008.

Schwartz, Mildred A. *A Sociological Perspective on Politics.* Englewood Cliffs, N.J.: Prentice Hall, 1990.

Scolforo, Mark. "Amish Population Nearly Doubles in 16 Years." *Chicago Tribune,* August 20, 2008.

Scommegna, Paola. "Increased Cohabitation Changing Children's Family Settings." *Population Today, 30,* 7, October 2002:3, 6.

Scott, Monster Cody. *Monster: The Autobiography of an L. A. Gang Member.* New York: Penguin Books, 1994.

Scott, Susie. "The Medicalization of Shyness: From Social Misfits to Social Fitness." *Sociology of Health and Illness, 28,* 2, 2006:133–153.

Scully, Diana. "Negotiating to Do Surgery." In *Dominant Issues in Medical Sociology,* 3rd ed., Howard D. Schwartz, ed. New York: McGraw-Hill, 1994:146–152.

Scully, Diana. *Understanding Sexual Violence: A Study of Convicted Rapists.* Boston: Unwin Hyman, 1990.

Scully, Diana, and Joseph Marolla. "Convicted Rapists' Vocabulary of Motive: Excuses and Justifications." *Social Problems, 31,* 5, June 1984:530–544.

Scully, Diana, and Joseph Marolla. "'Riding the Bull at Gilley's': Convicted Rapists Describe the Rewards of Rape." In *Down to Earth Sociology: Introductory Readings,* 14th ed., James M. Henslin, ed. New York: The Free Press, 2007.

"Second Life Affair Ends in Divorce." CNN Online. November 15, 2008.

Segal, Nancy L., and Scott L. Hershberger. "Virtual Twins and Intelligence." *Personality and Individual Differences, 39,* 6, 2005:1061–1073.

Seib, Gerald F., and John Harwood. "America's Race to the Middle." *Wall Street Journal,* May 10, 2008.

Seiden, Samuel C., and Paul Barach. "Wrong-Side/Wrong-Site, Wrong Procedure, and Wrong-Patient Adverse Events." *Archives of Surgery, 141:*2006:931–939.

Seltzer, Judith A. "Consequences of Marital Dissolution for Children." *Annual Review of Sociology, 20,* 1994:235–266.

Semple, Kirk. "Idea of Afghan Women's Rights Starts Taking Hold." *New York Times,* March 2, 2009.

Senders, John W., and Regine Kanzki. "The Egocentric Surgeon or the Roots of Wrong Side Surgery." *Quality and Safety in Health Care 17,* 2008:396–400.

Sengupta, Somini. "In the Ancient Streets of Najaf, Pledges of Martyrdom for Cleric." *New York Times,* July 10, 2004.

Sennett, Richard, and Jonathan Cobb. "Some Hidden Injuries of Class." In *Down to Earth Sociology: Introductory Readings,* 5th ed., James M. Henslin ed. New York: Free Press, 1988:278–288. Excerpts from Richard Sennett and Jonathan Cobb. *The Hidden Injuries of Class.* New York: Knopf, 1972.

Shane, Scott. "Documents Laid Out Interrogation Procedures." *Wall Street Journal,* July 25, 2008.

Shane, Scott. "Through the Revolving Door, a Pot of Gold Still Awaits." *New York Times,* December 28, 2004.

Shanker, Thom. "U.S. Troops Were Subjected to a Wider Toxic Testing." *New York Times,* October 8, 2002.

Shapiro, Joseph P. "Euthanasia's Home." *U.S. News and World Report, 122,* 1, January 13, 1997:24–27.

Sharp, Deborah. "Miami's Language Gap Widens." *USA Today,* April 3, 1992:A1, A3.

Sharp, Lauriston. "Steel Axes for Stone-Age Australians." In *Down to Earth Sociology: Introductory Readings,* 8th ed., James M. Henslin, ed. New York: Free Press, 1995:453–462.

Shefner, Jon. "The New Left in Latin America and the Opportunity for a New U.S. Foreign Policy." In *Agenda for Social Justice: Solutions 2008,* Robert Perrucci, Kathleen Ferraro, JoAnn Miller and Glenn Muschert, eds. Society for the Study of Social Problems, 2008:16–22.

Shellenbarger, Sue. "Some Companies Rethink the Telecommuting Trend." *Wall Street Journal,* February 28, 2008.

Shellenbarger, Sue. "When Caring for Aging Relatives Stirs Up Unwelcome Emotions." *New York Times,* July 17, 2003.

Shenon, Philip. "Arguments Conclude in Army Sex Hearing." *New York Times,* August 26, 1997.

Shenon, Philip. "Mukasey Offers View on Waterboarding." *New York Times,* January 30, 2008.

Sherif, Muzafer, and Carolyn Sherif. *Groups in Harmony and Tension.* New York: Harper & Row, 1953.

Shields, Stephanie A. *Speaking from the Heart: Gender and the Social Meaning of Emotion.* New York: Cambridge University Press, 2002.

Shively, JoEllen. "Cowboys and Indians: Perceptions of Western Films Among American Indians and Anglos." *American Sociological Review, 57,* December 1992:725–734.

Shively, JoEllen. "Cultural Compensation: The Popularity of Westerns Among American Indians," Paper presented at the annual meetings of the American Sociological Association, 1991.

Sills, David L. "Voluntary Associations: Sociological Aspects." In *International Encyclopedia of the Social Sciences, 16,* David L. Sills, ed. New York: Macmillan, 1968:362–379.

Sills, David L. *The Volunteers.* Glencoe, Ill.: Free Press, 1957.

Silverman, Eric K. "Anthropology and Circumcision." *Annual Review of Anthropology, 33,* 2004:419–445.

Simmel, Georg. *The Sociology of Georg Simmel,* Kurt H. Wolff, ed. and trans. Glencoe, Ill.: Free Press, 1950. First published between 1902 and 1917.

Simon, Julian L. *The Ultimate Resource.* Princeton, N.J.: PrincetonR University Press, 1981.

Simon, Robin W. "The Joys of Parenthood, Reconsidered." *Contexts, 7,* 2, May 5, 2008:40–45.

Simons, Andre B., and Jeannine Willie. "Runaway or Abduction. Assessment Tools for the First Responder." *FBI Law Enforcement Bulletin,* November 2000:1–7.

Simons, Marlise. "Social Change and Amazon Indians." In *Exploring Social Life: Readings to Accompany Essentials of Sociology: A Down-to-Earth Approach, Sixth Edition,* 2nd edition, James M. Henslin, ed. Boston: Allyn and Bacon, 2006:157–165.

Simpson, George Eaton, and J. Milton Yinger. *Racial and Cultural Minorities: An Analysis of Prejudice and Discrimination,* 4th ed. New York: Harper & Row, 1972.

Sindayen, Nelly. "I Once Was Lost. But Now I'm Wired." *Time, 157,* 22, June 4, 2001:80–83.

Skeels, H. M. *Adult Status of Children with Contrasting Early Life Experiences: A Follow-up Study.* Monograph of the Society for Research in Child Development, *31,* 3, 1966.

Skeels, H. M., and H. B. Dye. "A Study of the Effects of Differential Stimulation on Mentally Retarded Children." *Proceedings and Addresses of the American Association on Mental Deficiency, 44,* 1939:114–136.

Skinner, Jonathan, James N. Weinstein, Scott M. Sporer, and John E. Wennberg. "Racial, Ethnic, and Geographic Disparities in Rates of Knee Arthroplasty Among Medicare Patients." *New England Journal of Medicine, 349,* 14, October 2, 2003:1350–1359.

Sklair, Leslie. *Globalization: Capitalism and Its Alternatives,* 3rd ed. New York: Oxford: University Press, 2001.

Slackman, Michael. "Voices Rise in Egypt to Shield Girls from an Old Tradition." *New York Times,* September 20, 2007.

Sledzik, Paul S., and Nicholas Bellantoni. "Bioarcheological and Biocultural Evidence for the New England Vampire Folk Belief." *American Journal of Physical Anthropology, 94,* 1994.

Sloan, Allan. "A Lot of Trust, But No Funds." *Newsweek,* July 30, 2001:34.

Smart, Barry. "On the Disorder of Things: Sociology, Postmodernity and the 'End of the Social.'" *Sociology, 24,* 3, August 1990:397–416.

Smedley, Audrey, and Brian D. Smedley. "Race as Biology Is Fiction, Racism as a Social Problem Is Real: Anthropological and Historical Perspectives on the Social Construction of Race." *American Psychologist, 60,* 1, January 2005:16–26.

Smith, Beverly A. "An Incest Case in an Early 20th-Century Rural Community." *Deviant Behavior, 13,* 1992:127–153.

Smith, Christian, and Robert Faris. "Socioeconomic Inequality in the American Religious System: An Update and Assessment." *Journal for the Scientific Study of Religion, 44,* 1, 2005:95–104.

Smith, Clark. "Oral History as 'Therapy': Combatants' Account of The Vietnam War." In *Strangers at Home: Vietnam Veterans Since the War,* Charles R. Figley and Seymore Leventman, eds. New York: Praeger, 1980:9–34.

Smith, Craig S. "China Becomes Industrial Nations' Most Favored Dump." *Wall Street Journal,* October 9, 1995:B1.

Smith, Harold. "A Colossal Cover-Up." *Christianity Today,* December 12, 1986:16–17.

Smith, Jackie, Charles Chatfield, and Ron Pagnucco. *Transnational Social Movements and Global Policy: Solidarity Beyond the State.* Syracuse, N. Y.: Syracuse University Press, 1997.

Smith, Nicola. "'Sworn Virgins' Dying Out as Albanian Girls Reject Manly Role." *Sunday Times,* January 8, 2008.

Smith, Simon C. "The Making of a Neo-Colony? Anglo-Kuwaiti Relations in the Era of Decolonization." *Middle Eastern Studies, 37,* 1, January 2001:159–173.

Smith, Wesley J. "Dependency or Death? Oregonians Make a Chilling Choice." *Wall Street Journal,* February 25, 1999.

Smith-Lovin, Lynn, and Charles Brody. "Interruptions in Group Discussions: The Effects of Gender and Group Composition." *American Sociological Review, 54,* 1989:424–435.

Snow, David A., Louis A. Zurcher, Jr., and Sheldon Ekland-Olson. "Social Networks and Social Movements: A Microstructural Approach to Differential Recruitment." In *Collective Behavior and Social Movements,* Russell L. Curtis, Jr., and Benigno E. Aguirre, eds. Boston: Allyn and Bacon, 1993a:323–334.

Snyder, Karrie Ann, and Adam Isaiah Green. "Revisiting the Glass Escalator: The Case of Gender Segregation in a Female Dominated Occupation." *Social Problems, 55,* 2, May 2008:271–299.

Snyder, Mark. "Self-Fulfilling Stereotypes." In *Down to Earth Sociology: Introductory Readings,* 7th ed., James M. Henslin, ed. New York: Free Press, 1993:153–160.

Solomon, Jolie. "Companies Try Measuring Cost Savings from New Types of Corporate Benefits." *Wall Street Journal,* December 29, 1988:B1.

Song, Jaymes. "In Hawaii, the Doctor Is Always In—Online." Associated Press, January 15, 2009.

Sorokin, Pitirim A. *Social and Cultural Dynamics.* 4 vols. New York: American Book Company, 1937–1941.

Soss, Joe. "Lessons of Welfare: Policy Design, Political Learning, and Political Action." *American Political Science Review, 93,* 1999:363–380.

Sourcebook of Criminal Justice Statistics. Washington, D.C.: U.S. Government Printing Office, published annually.

Spector, Malcolm, and John Kitsuse. *Constructing Social Problems.* Menlo Park, Calif.: Cummings, 1977.

Spector, Tim. "Ageing Linked to Social Status." *BBC News,* March 29, 2007.

Spencer, Jane. "Shirk Ethic: How to Face a Hard Day at the Office." *Wall Street Journal,* May 15, 2003:D1, D3.

Spengler, Oswald. *The Decline of the West,* 2 vols. Charles F. Atkinson, trans. New York: Knopf, 1926–1928. First published in 1919–1922.

Spickard, P. R. S. *Mixed Blood: Intermarriage and Ethnic Identity in Twentieth Century America.* Madison: University of Wisconsin Press, 1989.

Spitzer, Steven. "Toward a Marxian Theory of Deviance." *Social Problems, 22,* June 1975:608–619.

Spivak, Gayatri Chakravorty. "Feminism 2000: One Step Beyond." *Feminist Review, 64,* Spring 2000:113.

Spragins, Ellyn E. "To Sue or Not to Sue?" *Newsweek,* December 9, 1996:50.

Sprecher, Susan, and Rachita Chandak. "Attitudes About Arranged Marriages and Dating Among Men and Women from India." *Free Inquiry in Creative Sociology, 20,* 1, May 1992:59–69.

Spring, Silvia. "The Trade in Fertility." *Newsweek,* April 12, 2006.

Srole, Leo, et al. *Mental Health in the Metropolis: The Midtown Manhattan Study.* Albany, N. Y.: New York University Press, 1978.

Stack, Carol B. *All Our Kin: Strategies for Survival in a Black Community.* New York: Harper, 1974.

Stampp, Kenneth M. *The Peculiar Institution: Slavery in the Ante-Bellum South.* New York: Vintage Books, 1956.

Stanley, Alessandra. "What Are You Doing? Media Twitterers Can't Stop Typing." *New York Times,* February 28, 2009.

Staples, Brent. "Loving v. Virginia and the Secret History of Race." *New York Times,* May 14, 2008.

Stark, Rodney. *Sociology,* 3rd ed. Belmont, Calif.: Wadsworth, 1989.

Starr, Paul. *The Social Transformation of American Medicine.* New York: Basic Books, 1982.

"State of the World's Children 2001." *Reading Today, 18,* 4, February–March 2001:24.

Statham, Anne, Eleanor M. Miller, and Hans O. Mauksch. "The Integration of Work: Second-Order Analysis of Qualitative Research." In *The Worth of Women's Work: A Qualitative Synthesis.* Statham, Anne, Eleanor M. Miller, and Hans O. Mauksch, eds. Albany, N. Y.: State University of New York Press, 1988:11–35.

Statistical Abstract of the United States. Washington D.C.: Bureau of the Census, published annually.

Stein, Rob. "FDA Approves Implantable Identity Chip." *Washington Post,* October 14, 2004.

Steinhauer, Jennifer and Ford Fessenden. "Medical Retreads: Doctor Punished by State But Prized at the Hospitals." *New York Times,* March 27, 2001.

Stevens, Amy, and Sarah Lubman. "Deciding Moment of the Trial May Have Been Five Months Ago." *Wall Street Journal,* May 1, 1992:A6.

Stevens, Mitchell L. *Kingdom of Children: Culture and Controversy in the Home-schooling Movement.* Princeton: Princeton University Press, 2001.

Stevenson, Betsey, and Justin Wolfers. "Marriage and Divorce: Changes and Their Driving Forces." Federal Reserve Bank of San Francisco, Working Paper No. 2007–03:February 2007.

Stevenson, Richard W. "U.S. Debates Investing in Stock for Social Security." *New York Times,* July 27, 1998.

Stewart, Susan D. "Nonresident Parenting and Adolescent Adjustment: The Quality of Nonresident Father-Child Interaction." *Journal of Family Issues, 24,* March 2003:217–244.

"Sticky Ticket: A New Jersey Mother Sues Her Son Over a Lottery Jackpot She Claims Belongs to Them Both." *People Weekly,* February 9, 1998:68.

Stiglitz, Joseph E. "War at Any Cost? The Total Economic Costs of the War Beyond the Federal Budget." Testimony before the Joint Economic Committee of the U.S. Senate, February 28, 2008.

Stiles, Daniel. "The Hunters Are the Hunted." *Geographical, 75,* June 2003:28–32.

Stinnett, Nicholas. "Strong Families." In *Marriage and Family in a Changing Society,* 4th ed., James M. Henslin, ed. New York: Free Press, 1992:496–507.

Stipp, David. "Himalayan Tree Could Serve as Source of Anti-cancer Drug Taxol, Team Says." *Wall Street Journal,* April 20, 1992:B4.

Stockard, Jean, and Miriam M. Johnson. *Sex Roles: Sex Inequality and Sex Role Development.* Englewood Cliffs, N.J.: Prentice Hall, 1980.

Stockwell, John. "The Dark Side of U.S. Foreign Policy." *Zeta Magazine,* February 1989:36–48.

Stodgill, Ralph M. *Handbook of Leadership: A Survey of Theory and Research.* New York: Free Press, 1974.

Stolberg, Sheryl Gay. "Blacks Found on Short End of Heart Attack Procedure." *New York Times,* May 10, 2001.

Stolberg, Sheryl Gay. "Richest Nations Pledge to Halve Greenhouse Gas." *New York Times,* July 9, 2008.

Stouffer, Samuel A., Arthur A. Lumsdaine, Marion Harper Lumsdaine, Robin M. Williams, Jr., M. Brewster Smith, Irving L. Janis, Shirley A. Star, and Leonard S. Cottrell, Jr. *The American Soldier: Combat and Its Aftermath,* Vol. 2. New York: Wiley, 1949.

Stout, David. "Pentagon Toughens Policy on Sexual Assault." *New York Times,* January 5, 2005.

Strang, David, and Michael W. Macy. "In Search of Excellence: Fads, Success Stories, and Adaptive Emulation." *American Journal of Sociology, 197,* 1, July 2001:147–182.

Strategic Energy Policy: Challenges for the 21st Century. New York: Council on Foreign Relations, 2001.

Straus, Murray A. "Explaining Family Violence." In *Marriage and Family in a Changing Society,* 4th ed., James M. Henslin, ed. New York: Free Press, 1992:344–356.

Straus, Murray A., and Richard J. Gelles. "Violence in American Families: How Much Is There and Why Does It Occur?" In *Troubled Relationships,* Elam W. Nunnally, Catherine S. Chilman, and Fred M. Cox, eds. Newbury Park, Calif.: Sage, 1988:141–162.

Stross, Randall. "How to Lose Your Job on Your Own Time." *New York Times,* December 30, 2007.

Suizzo, Marie-Anne. "The Social-Emotional and Cultural Contexts of Cognitive Development: Neo-Piagetian Perspectives." *Child Development, 71,* 4, August 2000:846–849.

Sullivan, Andrew. "What We Look Up to Now." *New York Times,* November 15, 1998.

Sullivan, Andrew. "What's So Bad about Hate?" *New York Times Magazine,* September 26, 1999.

Sullivan, Kevin. "India Embraces Online Worship." *Washington Post,* March 15, 2007.

Sullivan, Leila Gonzalez. "Preparing Latinos/as for a Flat World: The Community College Role." *Journal of Hispanic Higher Education, 6,* 4, October 2007:397–422.

Sulloway, Frank J. *Born to Rebel: Birth Order, Family Dynamics, and Creative Lives.* New York: Vintage Books, 1997.

Sumner, William Graham. *Folkways: A Study in the Sociological Importance of Usages, Manners, Customs, Mores, and Morals.* New York: Ginn, 1906.

Sun, Lena H. "China Seeks Ways to Protect Elderly." *Washington Post,* October 23, 1990:A1.

Sunstein, Cass R., and Reid Hastie. "Four Failures of Deliberating Groups." The Law School, University of Chicago, John M. Olin Program in Law and Economics Working Paper Series, April 2008.

Surgeon General of the United States. *The Health Consequences of Involuntary Exposure to Tobacco Smoke.* Washington, D.C.: Centers for Disease Control and Prevention, 2006.

Surgeon General of the United States. *The Surgeon General's Annual Report: Health Consequences of Smoking.* Washington, D.C.: Centers for Disease Control, 2005.

Surowiecki, James. *The Wisdom of Crowds.* New York: Anchor Books, 2005.

Sutherland, Edwin H. *Criminology.* Philadelphia: Lippincott, 1924.

Sutherland, Edwin H. *Principles of Criminology,* 4th ed. Philadelphia: Lippincott, 1947.

Sutherland, Edwin H. *White Collar Crime.* New York: Dryden Press, 1949.

Sutherland, Edwin H., Donald R. Cressey, and David F. Luckenbill. *Principles of Criminology,* 11th ed. Dix Hills, N. Y.: General Hall, 1992.

Suzuki, Bob H. "Asian-American Families." In *Marriage and Family in a Changing Society,* 2nd ed., James M. Henslin, ed. New York: Free Press, 1985:104–119.

Swanson, Christopher B. *Cities in Crisis: A Special Analytic Report on High School Graduation.* Bethesda, MD: Editorial Projects in Education, 2008.

Swati, P and Ey. "Do You Take This Stranger?" *Los Angeles Times,* June 26, 2008.

"Swedish Health Care in the 1990s." Stockholm: Federation of Swedish County Councils, July 2002.

Sweeney, Megan M. "Remarriage and the Nature of Divorce: Does It Matter Which Spouse Chose to Leave?" *Journal of Family Issues, 23,* 3, April 2002:410–440.

Sykes, Gresham M., and David Matza. "Techniques of Neutralization." In *Down to Earth Sociology: Introductory Readings,* 5th ed., James M. Henslin, ed. New York: Free Press, 1988:225–231. First published in 1957.

Szasz, Thomas S. *Cruel Compassion: Psychiatric Control of Society's Unwanted.* Syracuse: Syracuse University Press, 1998.

Szasz, Thomas S. *The Myth of Mental Illness,* rev. ed. New York: Harper & Row, 1986.

Szasz, Thomas S. "Mental Illness Is Still a Myth." In *Deviant Behavior 96/97,* Lawrence M. Salinger, ed. Guilford, Conn.: Dushkin, 1996:200–205.

Tach, Laura, and George Farkas. "Ability Grouping and Educational Stratification in the Early School Years." Unpublished paper, 2003.

Tafoya, Sonya M., Hans Johnson, and Laura E. Hill. "Who Chooses to Choose Two?" Washington, D.C.: Population Reference Bureau, 2005.

Taneja, V., S. Sriram, R. S. Beri, V. Sreenivas, R. Aggarwal, R. Kaur, and J. M. Puliyel. " 'Not by Bread Alone': Impact of a Structured 90-Minute Play Session on Development of Children in an Orphanage." *Child Care, Health & Development, 28,* 1, 2002:95–100.

Tapia, Andres. "Churches Wary of Inner-City Islamic Inroads." *Christianity Today, 38,* 1, January 10, 1994:36–38.

Tappan, Mark B. "Moral Function as Mediated Action." *Journal of Moral Education, 35,* 1, March 2006:1–18.

Taubes, Gary. *Good Calories, Bad Calories.* New York, Knopf, 2007.

Taylor, Monique M. *Harlem: Between Heaven and Hell.* Minneapolis: University of Minnesota Press, 2002.

Terhune, Chad. "Pepsi, Vowing Diversity Isn't Just Image Polish, Seeks Inclusive Culture." *Wall Street Journal,* April 19, 2005.

Thau, Richard. "Are We Heading for Intergenerational War?" *Across the Board, 38,* 4, July/August, 2001:70–74.

"The Boss's Pay." *Wall Street Journal,* April 7, 2007.

The Statistical History of the United States: From Colonial Times to the Present. New York: Basic Books, 1976.

"The Wall Street Journal Survey of CEO Compensation." *Wall Street Journal,* April 2, 2009.

Thomas, Paulette. "Boston Fed Finds Racial Discrimination in Mortgage Lending Is Still Widespread." *Wall Street Journal,* October 9, 1992:A3.

Thomas, Paulette. "U.S. Examiners Will Scrutinize Banks with Poor Minority-Lending Histories." *Wall Street Journal,* October 22, 1991:A2.

Thomas, W. I., and Dorothy Swaine Thomas. *The Child in America: Behavior Problems and Programs.* New York: Alfred A. Knopf, 1928.

Thompson, Clive. "Brave New World of Digital Intimacy." *New York Times,* September 7, 2008.

Thompson, Ginger. "Chasing Mexico's Dream into Squalor." *New York Times,* February 11, 2001.

Thompson, Ginger. "Where Education and Assimilation Collide." *New York Times,* March 14, 2009.

Thomson, Irene Tavis. "The Theory That Won't Die: From Mass Society to the Decline of Social Capital." *Sociological Forum, 20,* 3, September 2005:421–448.

Thornton, Russell. *American Indian Holocaust and Survival: A Population History Since 1492.* Norman: University of Oklahoma Press, 1987.

Thurow, Roger. "Farms Destroyed, Stricken Sudan Faces Food Crisis." *Wall Street Journal,* February 7, 2005.

Tierney, John. "Diet and Fat: A Severe Case of Mistaken Consensus." *New York Times,* October 9, 2007.

Tilly, Charles. *Social Movements, 1768–2004.* Boulder Colo.: Paradigm Publishers, 2004.

Timasheff, Nicholas S. *War and Revolution.* Joseph F. Scheuer, ed. New York: Sheed & Ward, 1965.

Tobias, Andrew. "The 'Don't Be Ridiculous' Law." *Wall Street Journal,* May 31, 1995:A14.

Tocqueville, Alexis de. *Democracy in America,* J. P. Mayer and Max Lerner, eds. New York: Harper & Row, 1966. First published in 1835.

Todosijevic, Jelica, Esther D. Rothblum, and Sondra E. Solomon. "Relationship Satisfaction, Affectivity, and Specific Stressors in Same-Sex Couples Joined in Civil Unions." *Psychology of Women Quarterly, 29,* 2005:158–166.

Tokoro, Masabumi. "The Shift Towards American-style Human Resource Management Systems and the Transformation of Workers' Attitudes at Japanese Firms." *Asian Business and Management, 4,* 2005:23–44.

Tolchin, Martin. "Surgeon General Asserts Smoking Is an Addiction." *New York Times,* May 17, 1988:A1, C4.

Tomsho, Robert, and Daniel Golden. "Educating Eric." *Wall Street Journal,* May 12, 2007.

Tönnies, Ferdinand. *Community and Society (Gemeinschaft und Gesellschaft),* with a new introduction by John Samples. New Brunswick, N.J.: Transaction, 1988. First published in 1887.

Torres, Jose B., V. Scott H. Solberg, and Aaron H. Carlstrom. "The Myth of Sameness Among Latino Men and Their Machismo." *American Journal of Orthopsychiatry, 72,* 2, 2002:163–181.

Toynbee, Arnold. *A Study of History,* D. C. Somervell, abridger and ed. New York: Oxford University Press, 1946.

Tracy, Jon. "Sometimes in War, You Can Put a Price on Life." *New York Times,* May 16, 2007.

Trafficking in Persons Report. Washington, D.C.: U.S. Department of State, June 4, 2008.

Transplantation: Practice and Protocols. Washington, DC: The National Academies Press, 2000.

Treiman, Donald J. *Occupational Prestige in Comparative Perspective.* New York: Academic Press, 1977.

Tresniowski, Alex. "Payday Or Mayday?" *People Weekly,* May 17, 1999:128–131.

Trice, Harrison M., and Janice M. Beyer. "Cultural Leadership in Organization." *Organization Science, 2,* 2, May 1991:149–169.

Troeltsch, Ernst. *The Social Teachings of the Christian Churches.* New York: Macmillan, 1931.

Trofimov, Yaroslav. "Brutal Attack in India Shows How Caste System Lives On." *New York Times,* December 27, 2007.

Troiano, R. P. "Physical Activity Among Young People." *New England Journal of Medicine, 347,* September 5, 2002:706–707.

"Tsunami Deaths Over 283,000." *News 24.com,* January 27, 2005.

Tuhus-Dubrow, Rebecca. "Rites and Wrongs." *Boston Globe,* February 11, 2007.

Tumin, Melvin M. "Some Principles of Social Stratification: A Critical Analysis." *American Sociological Review 18,* August 1953:394.

Turner, Jonathan H. *The Structure of Sociological Theory.* Homewood, Ill.: Dorsey, 1978.

Turner, Ralph H. "Collective Behavior." In *Handbook of Modern Sociology,* Robert E. L. Faris, ed. Chicago: Rand McNally, 1964:382–425.

Turner, Ralph H., and Lewis M. Killian. *Collective Behavior,* 2nd ed. Englewood Cliffs, N.J.: Prentice Hall, 1987.

Twenge, Jean M., W. Keith Campbell, and Craig A. Foster. "Parenthood and Marital Satisfaction: A Meta-Analytical Review." *Journal of Marriage and Family, 65,* August 2003:574–583.

Tyler, Patrick E. "A New Life for NATO? But It's Sidelined for Now." *New York Times,* November 20, 2002.

Tyre, Peg. "Professor in Your Pocket." *Newsweek,* November 28, 2005:46–47.

U.S. Census Bureau. *Historical Statistics of the United States, Colonial Times to 1970, Bicentennial Edition.* Washington, D.C.: U.S. Government Printing Office, 1975.

U.S. Census Bureau. *Statistical Abstract of the United States: The National Data Book.* Washington, D.C.: U.S. Government Printing Office. Published annually.

U.S. Census Bureau, Current Population Survey, March and Annual Social and Economic Supplements, Fertility and Family Statistics Branch, July 2008.

U.S. Census Bureau. "50 Million Children Lived with Married Parents in 2007." Washington, D.C.: U.S. Government Printing Office, 2007b.

U.S. Census Bureau. "Annual Social and Economic Supplement to Current Population Survey." Washington, D.C.: U.S. Government Printing Office, 2007a.

U.S. Department of Education, Institute of Education Sciences, National Center for Education Statistics. *The Condition of Education, 2007.*

U.S. Department of Education, National Center for Education Statistics. "Projections of Education Statistics to 2017," September 2008:Table 10.

U.S. Department of Energy, Advisory Committee on Human Radiation Experiments. Final Report, 1995. Washington, D.C.: U.S. Government Printing Office, 1995.

U.S. Religious Landscape Survey. "Religious Affiliation: Diverse and Dynamic." Washington, D.C.: PEW Foundation, February 2008.

Uchitelle, Louis. "How to Define Poverty? Let Us Count the Ways." *New York Times,* May 28, 2001.

Udry, J. Richard. "Biological Limits of Gender Construction." *American Sociological Review, 65,* June 2000:443–457.

Udy, Stanley H., Jr. "Bureaucracy and Rationality in Weber's Organizational Theory: An Empirical Study." *American Sociological Review, 24,* December 1959:791–795.

Ullman, Edward, and Chauncey Harris. "The Nature of Cities." In *Urban Man and Society: A Reader in Urban Ecology,* Albert N. Cousins and Hans Nagpaul, eds. New York: Knopf, 1970:91–100.

UNAIDS. "Report on the Global AIDS Epidemic." Joint United Nations Programme on HIV/AIDS, July 2008.

UNAIDS. *Aids Epidemic Update,* December 2006.

UNESCO. "Global Action Plan: Improving Support to Countries in Achieving the EFA Goals." 2007.

UNESCO. *Education for All Global Monitoring Report,* 2006.

UNESCO Institute for Statistics. "Gender Parity in Education: Not There Yet." March 2008.

UNESCO Institute for Statistics. "World Illiteracy Rates." 2005.

UNIFEM. *Progress of the World's Women 2008/2009.* United Nations Development Fund for Women, 2008.

Uniform Crime Reports. Washington D.C.: FBI, published annually.

United Nations. "Agriculture: Towards 2015/30." Technical Interim Report, Food and Agriculture Organization (FAO) of the United Nations, Economic and Social Department. April 2000.

United Nations. "An Overview of Urbanization, Internal Migration, Population Distribution and Development in the World." United Nations Population Division, January 14, 2008.

Urban Institute. "A Decade of Welfare Reform: Facts and Figures." June 2006.

Usdansky, Margaret L. "English a Problem for Half of Miami." *USA Today,* April 3, 1992:A1, A3, A30.

Useem, Michael. *The Inner Circle: Large Corporations and the Rise of Business Political Activity in the U.S. and U. K.* New York: Oxford University Press, 1984.

"VA Testing Drugs on War Veterans." *Washington Post,* June 17, 2008.

Van Noy, Michelle, James Jacobs, Suzanne Korey, Thomas Bailey, and Katherine L. Hughes. "Noncredit Enrollment in Workforce Education: State Policies and Community College Practices." Washington, D.C.: American Association of Community Colleges, 2008.

Vanderburg, David. "The Story of Semco: The Company that Humanized Work." *Bulletin of Science, Technology & Society, 24,* 5, October 2004:430–434.

Varese, Federico. *The Russian Mafia: Private Protection in a New Market Economy.* Oxford: Oxford University Press, 2005.

Vartabedian, Ralph, and Scott Gold. "New Questions on Shuttle Tile Safety Raised." *Los Angeles Times,* February 27, 2003.

Vaughan, Diane. "Uncoupling: The Social Construction of Divorce." In *Marriage and Family in a Changing Society,* 2nd ed., James M. Henslin, ed. New York: Free Press, 1985:429–439.

Veblen, Thorstein. *The Theory of the Leisure Class.* New York: Macmillan, 1912.

Vega, William A. "Hispanic Families in the 1980s: A Decade of Research." *Journal of Marriage and the Family, 52,* November 1990:1015–1024.

Venkatesh, Sudhir. *Off the Books: The Underground Economy of the Urban Poor.* Cambridge: Harvard University Press, 2006.

Venkatesh, Sudhir. *Gang Leader for a Day: A Rogue Sociologist Takes to the Streets.* New York: Penguin, 2008.

Vergakis, Brock. "Bill Would Limit Future Utah Nuclear Power Plants." Associated Press, February 12, 2009.

Vincent, John A. "Ageing Contested: Anti-ageing Science and the Cultural Construction of Old Age" *Sociology, 40,* 2006.

Volti, Rudi. *Society and Technological Change,* 3rd ed. New York: St. Martin's Press, 1995.

Von Hoffman, Nicholas. "Sociological Snoopers." *Transaction 7,* May 1970:4, 6.

Wade, Nicholas. "In Dusty Archives, a Theory of Affluence." *New York Times,* August 7, 2007.

Wadensten, Barbro. "The Theory of Gerotranscendence as Applied to Gerontological Nursing: Part 1." *International Journal of Older People Nursing, 2,* 2007:289–294.

Wagley, Charles, and Marvin Harris. *Minorities in the New World.* New York: Columbia University Press, 1958.

Wald, Matthew L., and John Schwartz. "Alerts Were Lacking, NASA Shuttle Manager Says." *New York Times,* July 23, 2003.

Waldholz, Michael. "Major Hospitals Use Trances for Fractures, Cancer, Burns; Speeding Surgery Recoveries." *Wall Street Journal,* October 7, 2003.

Waldrop, Deborah P., and Joseph A. Weber. "From Grandparent to Caregiver: The Stress and Satisfaction of Raising Grandchildren." *Families in Society: The Journal of Contemporary Human Services,* 2001:461–472.

Walker, Alice, and Pratibha Parmar. *Warrior Marks: Female Genital Mutilation and the Sexual Blinding of Women.* New York: Harcourt Brace, 1993.

Walker, Marcus, and Andrew Higgins. "Zimbabwe Can't Paper Over Its Million Percent Inflation Anymore." *Wall Street Journal,* July 2, 2008.

Wallace, Anthony F. C. *Religion: An Anthropological View.* New York: Random House, 1966.

Wallace, John M., Ryoko Yamaguchi, Jerald G. Bachman, Patrick M. O'Malley, John E. Schulenberg, and Lloyd D. Johnston. "Religiosity and Adolescent Substance Use: The Role of Individual and Contextual Influences." *Social Problems, 54,* 2, 2007:308–327.

Wallerstein, Immanuel. *The Capitalist World-Economy.* New York: Cambridge University Press, 1979.

Wallerstein, Immanuel. "Culture as the Ideological Battleground of the Modern World-System." In *Global Culture: Nationalism, Globalization, and Modernity,* Mike Featherstone, ed. London: Sage, 1990:31–55.

Wallerstein, Immanuel. *The Modern World System: Capitalist Agriculture and the Origins of the European World-Economy in the Sixteenth Century.* New York: Academic Press, 1974.

Wallerstein, Judith S., Sandra Blakeslee, and Julia M. Lewis. *The Unexpected Legacy of Divorce: A 25-Year Landmark Study.* Concord, N. H.: Hyperion Press, 2001.

Walter, Lynn. *Women's Rights: A Global View.* Westport, Conn.: Greenwood Press, 2001.

Walters, Alan. "Let More Earnings Go to Shareholders." *Wall Street Journal,* October 31, 1995:A23.

Wang, Hongyu, and Paul R. Amato. "Predictors of Divorce Adjustment: Stressors, Resources, and Definitions." *Journal of Marriage and the Family, 62,* 3, August 2000:655–668.

Wanzer, Sidney. "'Dr. Death' Served Us All With Time in Prison." *USA Today,* June 6, 2007.

Wark, Gillian R., and Dennis L. Krebs. "Gender and Dilemma Differences in Real-Life Moral Judgment." *Developmental Psychology, 32,* 1996:220–230.

Warren, Jennifer, Adam Gelb, Jake Horowitz, and Jessica Riordan. "One in 100: Behind Bars in America 2008." Washington, D.C.: Pew Charitable Trust, February 2008.

Watson, J. Mark. "Outlaw Motorcyclists." In *Society: Readings to Accompany Sociology: A Down-to-Earth Approach, Core Concepts,* James M. Henslin ed. Boston: Allyn and Bacon, 2006:105–114. First published in 1980 in *Deviant Behavior, 2,* 1.

Wayne, Julie Holliday, Christine M. Riordan, and Kecia M. Thomas. "Is All Sexual Harassment Viewed the Same? Mock Juror Decisions in Same-and Cross-Gender Cases." *Journal of Applied Psychology, 86,* 2, April 2001:179–187.

Weber, Max. *Economy and Society,* G. Roth and C. Wittich, eds. Berkeley: University of California Press, 1978. First published in 1922.

Weber, Max. *From Max Weber: Essays in Sociology.* Hans Gerth and C. Wright Mills, trans. and ed. New York: Oxford University Press, 1946.

Weber, Max. *The Protestant Ethic and the Spirit of Capitalism.* New York: Scribner's, 1958. First published in 1904–1905.

Weber, Max. *The Theory of Social and Economic Organization,* A. M. Henderson and Talcott Parsons, trans., Talcott Parsons, ed. Glencoe, Ill.: Free Press, 1947. First published in 1913.

Weiner, Tim. "Air Force Seeks Bush's Approval for Space Weapons Programs." *New York Times,* May 18, 2005.

Weiner, Tim. "A New Model Army Soldier Rolls Closer to Battle." *New York Times,* February 16, 2005.

Weiner, Tim. "Pentagon Envisioning a Costly Internet for War." *New York Times,* November 13, 2004.

Weiss, Rick. "Mature Human Embryos Cloned." *Washington Post,* February 12, 2004:A1.

Weitoft, Gunilla Ringback, Anders Hjern, Bengt Haglund, and Mans Rosen. "Mortality, Severe Morbidity, and Injury in Children Living with Single Parents in Sweden: A Population-Based Study." *Lancet, 361,* January 25, 2003:289–295.

Wen, Ming. "Family Structure and Children's Health and Behavior." *Journal of Family Issues, 29,* 11, November 2008:1492–1519.

Werner, Erica. "Indian Casinos Gross $25 Billion in 2006." Associated Press, June 5, 2007.

Wertz, Richard W., and Dorothy C. Wertz. "Notes on the Decline of Midwives and the Rise of Medical Obstetricians." In *The Sociology of Health and Illness: Critical Perspectives,* Peter Conrad and Rochelle Kern, eds. New York: St. Martin's Press, 1981:165–183.

"What Scares Doctors? Being the Patient." *Time,* May 1, 2006.

Wheaton, Blair, and Philippa Clarke. "Space Meets Time: Integrating Temporal and Contextual Influences on Mental Health in Early Adulthood." *American Sociological Review, 68,* 2003:680–706.

White, Emily. "School Away from School." *New York Times,* December 7, 2003.

White, Jack E. "Forgive Us Our Sins." *Time,* July 3, 1995:29.

White, James A. "When Employees Own Big Stake, It's a Buy Signal for Investors." *Wall Street Journal,* February 13, 1991:C1, C19.

White, Joseph B., Stephen Power, and Timothy Aeppel. "Death Count Linked to Failures of Firestone Tires Rises to 203." *Wall Street Journal,* June 19, 2001:A4.

White, Richard D., Jr. "Are Women More Ethical? Recent Findings on the Effects of Gender Upon Moral Development." *Journal of Public Administration Research and Theory, 9,* 3, July 1999:459–471.

Whitehead, Barbara Dafoe, and David Popenoe. "The Marrying Kind: Which Men Marry and Why." Rutgers University: The State of Our Unions: The Social Health of Marriage in America, 2004.

Whiteman, Maura K., Susan D. Hillis, Denise J. Jamieson, Brian Morrow, Michelle N. Podgornik, Kate M. Brett, and Polly A. Marchbanks. "Inpatient Hysterectomy Surveillance in the United States, 2000–2004." *American Journal of Obstetrics and Gynecology,* January 2008:34e1–34e7.

Whorf, Benjamin. *Language, Thought, and Reality,* J. B. Carroll, ed. Cambridge, MA: MIT Press, 1956.

Whyte, William Foote. "Street Corner Society." In *Down to Earth Sociology: Introductory Readings,* 11th ed., James M. Henslin, ed. New York: The Free Press, 2001:61–69.

Whyte, William H. *The City: Rediscovering the Center.* New York: Doubleday, 1989.

Wilford, John Noble. "In Maya Ruins, Scholars See Evidence of Urban Sprawl." *New York Times,* December 19, 2000.

Williams, Jasmin K. "Utah—The Beehive State." *New York Post,* June 12, 2007.

Williams, Rhys H. "Constructing the Public Good: Social Movements and Cultural Resources." *Social Problems, 42,* 1, February 1995:124–144.

Williams, Robin M., Jr. *American Society: A Sociological Interpretation,* 2nd ed. New York: Knopf, 1965.

Williams, Thomas D. "The Year of Tolerance." Rome: Anteneo Pontificio, 2003.

Williams, Timothy. "Old Sound in Harlem Draws New Neighbors' Ire." *New York Times,* July 6, 2008.

Willie, Charles Vert. "Caste, Class, and Family Life Experiences." *Research in Race and Ethnic Relations, 6,* 1991:65–84.

Willie, Charles Vert, and Richard J. Reddick. *A New Look at Black Families,* 5th ed. Walnut Creek, Calif.: AltaMira Press, 2003.

Wilson, Duff. "Harvard Medical School in Ethics Quandary." *New York Times,* March 2, 2009.

Wilson, Edward O. *Sociobiology: The New Synthesis.* Cambridge, Mass.: Harvard University Press, 1975.

Wilson, James Q., and Richard J. Herrnstein. *Crime and Human Nature.* New York: Simon & Schuster, 1985.

Wilson, William Julius. *The Bridge over the Racial Divide: Rising Inequality and Coalition Politics.* Berkeley: University of California Press, 2000.

Wilson, William Julius. *The Declining Significance of Race: Blacks and Changing American Institutions.* Chicago: University of Chicago Press, 1978.

Wilson, William Julius. "Jobless Poverty: A New Form of Social Dislocation in the Inner-City Ghetto." In *The Inequality Reader: Contemporary and Founda-*

tional Readings in Race, Class and Gender, David B. Grusky and Szonja Szelenyi, eds. Boulder: Westview Press, 2007:142–152.

Wilson, William Julius. *The Truly Disadvantaged: The Inner City, the Underclass, and Public Policy.* Chicago: University of Chicago Press, 1987.

Wilson, William Julius. *When Work Disappears: The World of the New Urban Poor.* Chicago: University of Chicago Press, 1996.

Wilson, William Julius, and Richard P. Taub. *There Goes the Neighborhood: Racial, Ethnic, and Class Tensions in Four Chicago Neighborhoods and Their Meaning for America.* New York: Knopf, 2006.

Wines, Michael. "Africa Adds to Miserable Ranks of Child Workers." *New York Times,* August 24, 2006a.

Wines, Michael. "How Bad Is Inflation in Zimbabwe?" *Wall Street Journal,* May 2, 2006b.

Wines, Michael. "Virulent TB in South Africa May Imperil Millions." *Wall Street Journal,* January 28, 2007.

Winfield, Nicole. "Vatican Launches Pope YouTube Channel." Associated Press, January 23, 2009.

"Winner, Dumbest Moment, Marketing." CNN, February 1, 2006.

Wirth, Louis. "The Problem of Minority Groups." In *The Science of Man in the World Crisis,* Ralph Linton, ed. New York: Columbia University Press, 1945.

Wirth, Louis. "Urbanism as a Way of Life." *American Journal of Sociology, 44,* July 1938:1–24.

Wise, Raul Delgado, and James M. Cypher. "The Strategic Role of Mexican Labor Under NAFTA: Critical Perspectives on Current Economic Integration." *Annals of the American Academy of Political and Social Science, 610,* March 2007:120–142.

Wolfensohn, James D., and Kathryn S. Fuller. "Making Common Cause: Seeing the Forest for the Trees." *International Herald Tribune,* May 27, 1998:11.

Wolfinger, Nicholas H. "Family Structure Homogamy: The Effects of Parental Divorce on Partner Selection and Marital Stability." *Social Science Research, 32,* 2003:80–97.

Wolinsky, Frederic D., Timothy E. Stump, and Christopher M. Callahan. "Does Being Placed in a Nursing Home Make You Sicker and More Likely to Die?" In *Societal Mechanisms for Maintaining Competence in Old Age,* Sherry L. Willis, K. Warner Schaie, and Mark Hayward, eds. New York: Springer Publishing Company, 1997:94–130.

Womack, James P., Daniel T. Jones, and Daniel Roos. *The Machine That Changed the World: The Story of Lean Production.* New York: Harper Perrenial, 1991.

"Women of Our World." Washington, D.C.: Population Reference Bureau, 2002.

Wonacott, Peter. "India's Skewed Sex Ratio Puts GE Sales in Spotlight." *Wall Street Journal,* April 18, 2007.

Wood, Daniel B., "Latinos Redefine What It Means to Be Manly." *Christian Science Monitor, 93,* 161, July 16, 2001.

Woodward, Kenneth L. "Heaven." *Newsweek, 113,* 13, March 27, 1989:52–55.

World Bank. "Cost of Pollution in China: Economic Estimates of Physical Damages." Washington, D.C: World Bank, February 2007.

World Health Organization. *Constitution of the World Health Organization.* New York: World Health Organization. Washington, D.C.: Interim Commission, 1946.

World Health Organization. *Eliminating Female Genital Mutilation: An Interagency Statement.* United Nations, 2008.

Worsley, Peter. *The Trumpet Shall Sound.* London: MacGibbon and Kee, 1957.

Wright, Erik Olin. *Class.* London: Verso, 1985.

Wright, Lawrence. "Double Mystery." *New Yorker,* August 7, 1995:45–62.

Wright, Lawrence. "One Drop of Blood." *New Yorker,* July 25, 1994:46–50, 52–55.

Wyatt, Edward. "City Plans to Let Company Run Some Public Schools in a First." *New York Times,* December 21, 2000.

Xie, Yu, and Kimberly A. Goyette. "A Demographic Portrait of Asian Americans." Washington, D.C.: Population Reference Bureau, 2004:1–32.

Yamaguchi, Kazuo. "Subjective Rationality of Initiators and of Threshold-Theoretical Behavior of Followers in Collective Action." *Rationality and Society, 12,* 2, May 2000:185–225.

Yan, Yunxiang. *Private Life Under Socialism: Love, Intimacy, and Family Change in a Chinese Village, 1949–1999.* Stanford, Calif.: Stanford University Press, 2003.

Yao, Ping. "Until Death Do Us Unite: Afterlife Marriages in Tang China, 618–906." *Journal of Family History, 27,* 3, 2002:207–226.

Yardley, Jim. "Faces of Abortion in China: A Young, Single Woman." *New York Times,* May 13, 2007.

Yardley, Jim. "Married for the Afterlife in China." *International Herald Tribune,* October 4, 2006.

Yardley, Jim, and Keith Bradsher. "China, an Engine of Growth, Faces a Global Slump." *New York Times,* October 22, 2008.

Ying, Yu-Wen, and Meekyung Han. "Parental Contributions to Southeast Asian American Adolescents' Well-Being." *Youth and Society, 40,* 2, December 2008:289–306.

Yinger, J. Milton. *The Scientific Study of Religion.* New York: Macmillan, 1970.

Yinger, J. Milton. *Toward a Field Theory of Behavior: Personality and Social Structure.* New York: McGraw-Hill, 1965.

Yonas, Michael A., Patricia O'Campo, Jessica G. Burke, and Andrea C. Gielen. "Neighborhood-Level Factors and Youth Violence: Giving Voice to the Perception of Prominent Neighborhood Individuals." *Health, Education, and Behavior OnlineFirst,* July 21, 2006.

Zachary, G. Pascal. "Behind Stocks' Surge Is an Economy in Which Big U.S. Firms Thrive." *Wall Street Journal,* November 22, 1995:A1, A5.

Zakaria, Fareed. *The Post-American World.* New York: W. W. Norton, 2008.

Zald, Mayer N. "Looking Backward to Look Forward: Reflections on the Past and the Future of the Resource Mobilization Research Program." In *Frontiers in Social Movement Theory,* Aldon D. Morris and Carol McClurg Mueller, eds. New Haven, Conn.: Yale University Press, 1992:326–348.

Zald, Mayer N., and John D. McCarthy, eds. *Social Movements in an Organizational Society.* New Brunswick, N.J.: Transaction, 1987.

Zamiska, Nicholas. "Pressed to Do Well on Admissions Tests, Students Take Drugs." *Wall Street Journal,* November 8, 2004.

Zamiska, Nicholas. "Videos Teach China's Rural Doctors." *Wall Street Journal,* July 10, 2007.

Zaslow, Jeffrey. "Will You Still Need Me When I'm . . . 84? More Couples Divorce After Decades." *Wall Street Journal,* June 17, 2003:D1.

Zellner, William W. *Countercultures: A Sociological Analysis.* New York: St. Martin's, 1995.

Zeng, Douglas Zhihua, and Shuilin Wang. "China and the Knowledge Economy: Challenges and Opportunity." World Bank Policy Research Working Paper 4223, May 2007.

Zernike, Kate. "The Harvard Guide to Happiness." *New York Times,* April 8, 2001.

Zerubavel, Eviatar. *The Fine Line: Making Distinctions in Everyday Life.* New York: Free Press, 1991.

Zhang, Yuanting, and Franklin W. Goza. "Who Will Care for the Elderly in China?" Center for Family and Demographic Research, Bowling Green, OH: May 2007.

Zoepf, Katherine. "A Dishonorable Affair." *New York Times,* September 23, 2007.

Zola, Irving K. *Socio-Medical Inquiries.* Philadelphia: Temple University Press, 1983.

Zuboff. Shoshanna. "New Worlds of Computer-Mediated Work." In *Down to Earth Sociology: Introductory Readings,* 6th edition, James M. Henslin, ed. New York: The Free Press, 1991:476–485.

Zuckerman, Laurence. "Management Employee-Ownership Experiment Unravels at United." *New York Times,* March 14, 2001.

Zumbrun, Joshua. "The Sacrifices of Albania's 'Sworn Virgins.'" *Washington Post,* August 11, 2007.

Zweigenhaft, R. L., and G. William Domhoff. *Diversity in the Power Elite: How It Happened, Why It Matters.* New York: Rowman and Littlefield, 2006.

Jim Henslin's Down-to-Earth Approach to Sociology

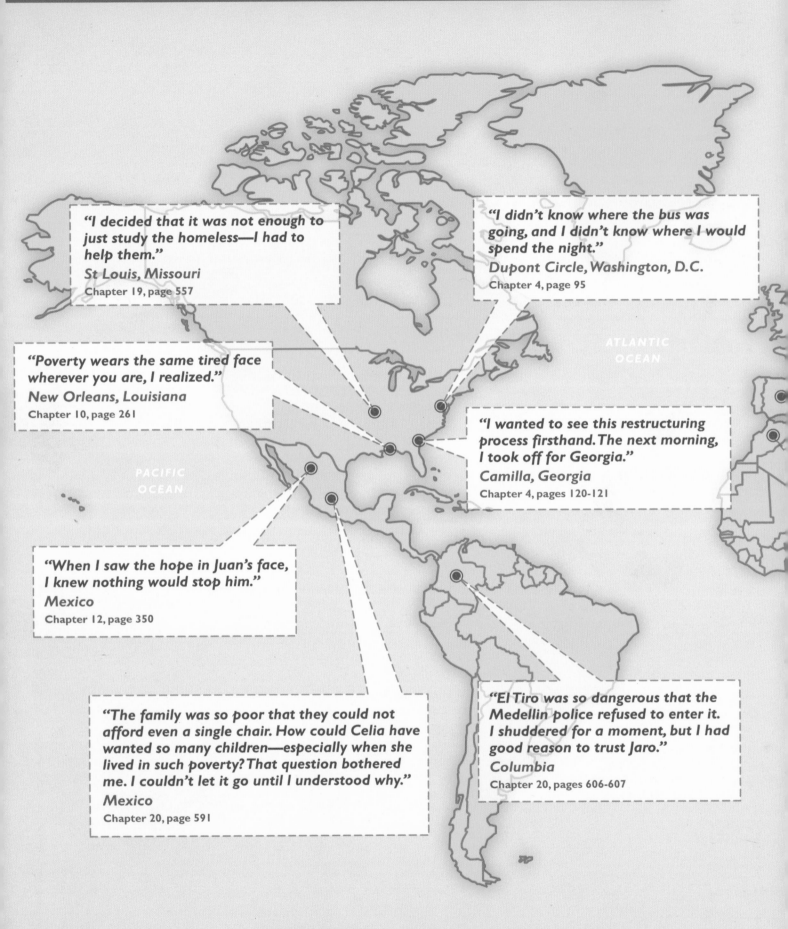

"I decided that it was not enough to just study the homeless—I had to help them."
St Louis, Missouri
Chapter 19, page 557

"I didn't know where the bus was going, and I didn't know where I would spend the night."
Dupont Circle, Washington, D.C.
Chapter 4, page 95

"Poverty wears the same tired face wherever you are, I realized."
New Orleans, Louisiana
Chapter 10, page 261

"I wanted to see this restructuring process firsthand. The next morning, I took off for Georgia."
Camilla, Georgia
Chapter 4, pages 120-121

"When I saw the hope in Juan's face, I knew nothing would stop him."
Mexico
Chapter 12, page 350

"The family was so poor that they could not afford even a single chair. How could Celia have wanted so many children—especially when she lived in such poverty? That question bothered me. I couldn't let it go until I understood why."
Mexico
Chapter 20, page 591

"El Tiro was so dangerous that the Medellin police refused to enter it. I shuddered for a moment, but I had good reason to trust Jaro."
Columbia
Chapter 20, pages 606-607

ATLANTIC OCEAN

PACIFIC OCEAN